# AMERICA

*brief eleventh high school edition*

# AMERICA

## A Narrative History

David Emory Shi

W. W. NORTON & COMPANY, INC.

New York · London

W. W. Norton & Company has been independent since its founding in 1923, when William Warder Norton and Mary D. Herter Norton first published lectures delivered at the People's Institute, the adult education division of New York City's Cooper Union. The firm soon expanded its program beyond the Institute, publishing books by celebrated academics from America and abroad. By midcentury, the two major pillars of Norton's publishing program—trade books and college texts—were firmly established. In the 1950s, the Norton family transferred control of the company to its employees, and today—with a staff of four hundred and a comparable number of trade, college, and professional titles published each year—W. W. Norton & Company stands as the largest and oldest publishing house owned wholly by its employees.

Editor: Jon Durbin
High School Group Director: Jenna Bookin Barry
Associate Managing Editor: Melissa Atkin
Editorial Assistant: Lily Gellman
Managing Editor, College: Marian Johnson
Managing Editor, College Digital Media: Kim Yi
Production Managers: Ashley Horna and Benjamin Reynolds
Media Editor: Carson Russell
Media Project Editor: Rachel Mayer
Media Associate Editor: Sarah Rose Aquilina
Media Editorial Assistant: Alexandra Malakhoff
Marketing Manager, History: Sarah England Bartley
High School Marketing and Market Development Manager: Christina Magoulis
Design Director: Hope Goodell Miller
Photo Editor: Travis Carr
Composition: SixRedMarbles / Jouve – Brattleboro, VT
Manufacturing: Transcontinental Interglobe

The Library of Congress has cataloged the Full, One-Volume, Edition as follows:

Names: Shi, David Emory, author.
Title: America : a narrative history / David Emory Shi.
Description: Eleventh edition. | New York : W. W. Norton & Company, 2019. |
  Includes bibliographical references and index.
Identifiers: LCCN 2018046039 | ISBN 9780393689693 (hardcover : alk. paper)
Subjects: LCSH: United States—History—Textbooks.
Classification: LCC E178.1 .T55 2019 | DDC 973—dc23 LC record available at
  https://lccn.loc.gov/2018046039

ISBN this edition: 978-0-393-66899-5

W. W. Norton & Company, Inc., 500 Fifth Avenue, New York, NY 10110-0017
wwnorton.com

W. W. Norton & Company Ltd., 15 Carlisle Street, London W1D 3BS
1 2 3 4 5 6 7 8 9 0

FOR
GEORGE B. TINDALL (1921–2006)
HISTORIAN, COLLEAGUE, FRIEND

DAVID EMORY SHI is a professor of history and the president emeritus of Furman University. He also taught for seventeen years at Davidson College, where he chaired the history department, served as the Frontis Johnson Professor of History, and won the Distinguished Teaching Award. He is the author of several books on American cultural history, including the award-winning *The Simple Life: Plain Living and High Thinking in American Culture*, *Facing Facts: Realism in American Thought and Culture, 1850–1920*, and *The Bell Tower and Beyond: Reflections on Learning and Living*.

# CONTENTS

List of Maps • xvii
Preface • xxi
Acknowledgments • xxxi


# PART ONE   A NOT-SO-"NEW" WORLD   1

## 1   The Collision of Cultures   4

Early Cultures in America 6 • European Visions of America 15 • Religious Conflict in Europe 21 • The Spanish Empire 27 • The Columbian Exchange 31 • The Spanish in North America 32 • Challenges to the Spanish Empire 40 • English Exploration of America 42


## 2   England's Colonies   46

The English Background 48 • Religious Conflict and War 48 • American Colonies 50 • The English Civil War in America 69 • The Restoration in the Colonies 70 • The Middle Colonies and Georgia 73 • Native Peoples and English Settlers 83 • Slavery in the Colonies 87 • Thriving Colonies 90


## 3   Colonial Ways of Life   94

The Shape of Early America 96 • Society and Economy in the Southern Colonies 102 • Society and Economy in New England 103 • Society and Economy in the Middle Colonies 109 • Race-Based Slavery 112 • First Stirrings of a Common Colonial Culture 116 • Colonial Cities 117 • The Enlightenment in America 120 • The Great Awakening 123

# 4 From Colonies to States 132

Competing Neighbors 134 • An Emerging Colonial System 139 • Warfare in the Colonies 140 • Regulating the Colonies 150 • The Crisis Grows 156 • The Spreading Conflict 165 • Independence 168


# PART TWO BUILDING A NATION 179

# 5 The American Revolution, 1776–1783 182

Mobilizing for War 184 • American Society at War 192 • Setbacks for the British (1777) 194 • 1778: Both Sides Regroup 197 • A War of Endurance 206 • War as an Engine of Change 209 • The Social Revolution 212 • Slaves and the Revolution 214 • The Emergence of an American Nationalism 218


# 6 Strengthening the New Nation 222

Power to the People 223 • The Confederation Government 225 • The "Gathering Crisis" 230 • Creating the Constitution 232 • The Fight for Ratification 241 • The Federalist Era 245 • Hamilton's Vision of a Prosperous America 250 • Foreign and Domestic Crises 257 • Western Settlement 263 • Transfer of Power 264 • The Adams Administration 265


# 7 The Early Republic, 1800–1815 274

Jeffersonian Republicanism 276 • War in Europe 290 • The War of 1812 294 • The Aftermath of the War 307


# PART THREE AN EXPANDING NATION 315

# 8 The Emergence of a Market Economy, 1815–1850 318

The Market Revolution 320 • Industrial Development 330 • Popular Culture 339 • Immigration 341 • Organized Labor and New Professions 345

**9** Nationalism and Sectionalism, 1815–1828  352

A New Nationalism  354  •  Debates over the American System  358  •  "An Era of Good Feelings"  359  •  Nationalist Diplomacy  363  •  The Rise of Andrew Jackson  367

**10** The Jacksonian Era, 1828–1840  378

Jacksonian Democracy  380  •  Jackson as President  382  •  Nullification  393  • War over the B.U.S.  401  •  Jackson's Legacy  410

**11** The South, Slavery, and King Cotton, 1800–1860  414

The Distinctiveness of the Old South  416  •  The Cotton Kingdom  419  • Whites in the Old South  425  •  Black Society in the South  429  •  Forging a Slave Community  439

**12** Religion, Romanticism, and Reform, 1800–1860  450

A More Democratic Religion  452  •  Romanticism in America  463  • The Reform Impulse  473  •  The Anti-Slavery Movement  485

**PART FOUR  A HOUSE DIVIDED AND REBUILT**  499

**13** Western Expansion, 1830–1848  502

Moving West  504  •  The Mexican-American War  529

**14** The Gathering Storm, 1848–1860  540

Slavery in the Territories  541  •  California Statehood  546  •  The Emergence of the Republican Party  556  •  The Response in the South  569

**15**  The War of the Union, 1861–1865   578

Choosing Sides  580  •  Fighting in the West  591  •  Fighting in the
East  596  •  Emancipation  598  •  The War behind the Lines  608  •  The Faltering
Confederacy  614  •  A Transformational War  632


**16**  The Era of Reconstruction, 1865–1877   638

The War's Aftermath in the South  640  •  Debates over Political
Reconstruction  642  •  Black Society under Reconstruction  655  •  The Grant
Administration  664  •  Reconstruction's Significance  678


# PART FIVE  GROWING PAINS  683


**17**  Business and Labor in the Industrial Era,
       1860–1900   686

Industrial and Agricultural Growth  688  •  The Rise of Big Business  699  •
The Alliance of Business and Politics  706  •  An Industrial Society  708


**18**  The New South and the New West,
       1865–1900   730

The Myth of the New South  732  •  The Failings of the New South  734  •  Race
Relations during the 1890s  737  •  The Settling of the New West  746  •  Life in
the New West  752  •  The Fate of Western Indians  758  •  The End of the
Frontier  767


**19**  Political Stalemate and Rural Revolt,
       1865–1900   772

Urban America  773  •  The New Immigration  776  •  Cultural Life  780  •  Gilded
Age Politics  787  •  Hayes and Civil Service Reform  791  •  Farmers and the
"Money Problem"  800

# PART SIX  MODERN AMERICA  815

## 20  Seizing an American Empire, 1865–1913  818

Toward the New Imperialism  820  •  Expansion in the Pacific  821  •
The Spanish-American War (The War of 1898)  824  •  Consequences of
Victory  830  •  Roosevelt's "Big-Stick" Diplomacy  838

## 21  The Progressive Era, 1890–1920  850

The Progressive Impulse  852  •  The Sources of Progressivism  853  •
Progressives' Aims and Achievements  861  •  Progressivism under Roosevelt and
Taft  868  •  Woodrow Wilson: A Progressive Southerner  879

## 22  America and the Great War, 1914–1920  894

An Uneasy Neutrality  896  •  Mobilizing a Nation  907  •  The American Role in
the War  914  •  The Politics of Peace  922  •  Stumbling from War to Peace  931

## 23  A Clash of Cultures, 1920–1929  940

The Nation in 1920  943  •  The "Jazz Age"  951  •  The Modernist Revolt  963

## 24  The Reactionary Twenties  972

Reactionary Conservatism and Immigration Restriction  974  •  A Republican
Resurgence  985  •  The Rise of Herbert Hoover  998  •  1929—A Turning
Point  1002  •  The Onset of the Great Depression  1002  •  The Human Toll
of the Depression  1006  •  From Hooverism to the New Deal  1011

## 25  The New Deal, 1933–1939  1018

Roosevelt's New Deal  1020  •  The New Deal under Fire  1031  •
The Second New Deal  1043

**26** The Second World War, 1933–1945  1054

The Rise of Fascism in Europe 1056 • From Isolationism to Intervention 1059 • Arsenal of Democracy 1073 • The Allied Drive toward Berlin 1082 • The Pacific War 1095 • A New Age Is Born 1101

# PART SEVEN THE AMERICAN AGE 1107

**27** The Cold War and the Fair Deal, 1945–1952  1110

Truman and the Cold War 1112 • The Containment Policy 1115 • Expanding the New Deal 1122 • The Cold War Heats Up 1133 • Another Red Scare 1140

**28** America in the Fifties  1148

Moderate Republicanism 1150 • A People of Plenty 1155 • Cracks in the Picture Window 1165 • The Civil Rights Movement 1169 • Foreign Policy in the Fifties 1177

**29** A New Frontier and a Great Society, 1960–1968  1190

The New Frontier 1192 • Civil Rights Triumphant 1204 • The Great Society 1217 • The Tragedy of Vietnam 1227 • The Turmoil of the Sixties 1233

**30** Rebellion and Reaction, 1960s and 1970s  1240

"Forever Young": The Youth Revolt 1242 • Social Activism Spreads 1251 • Nixon and the Revival of Conservatism 1262 • "Peace with Honor": Ending the Vietnam War 1270 • The Nixon Doctrine and a Thawing Cold War 1277 • Watergate 1281

**31** Conservative Revival, 1977–1990  1292

The Carter Presidency  1294  •  The Rise of Ronald Reagan  1300  •  The Reagan Revolution  1304  •  An Anti-Soviet Foreign Policy  1310  •  The Changing Economic and Social Landscape  1316  •  The Presidency of George H. W. Bush  1320

**32** Twenty-First-Century America, 1993–Present  1332

America's Changing Population  1334  •  The Clinton Presidency (1993–2001)  1335  •  A Chaotic Start to a New Century  1345  •  Second-Term Blues  1355  •  A Historic New Presidency  1358  •  A Populist President  1385  •  The 100-Day Mark  1392

**Glossary**  A1

**Appendix**  A69

**Further Readings**  A133

**Credits**  A171

**Index**  A177

# MAPS

Columbus's Voyages — 18

Spanish Explorations of the Mainland — 29

English, French, and Dutch Explorations — 41

Early Maryland and Virginia — 60

Early New England Settlements — 63

Early Settlements in the South — 71

The Middle Colonies — 74

European Settlements and Indian Societies in Early North America — 80–81

The African Slave Trade, 1500–1800 — 88

Atlantic Trade Routes — 106

Major Immigrant Groups in Colonial America — 110

North America, 1713 — 146

North America, 1763 — 147

Major Campaigns in New York and New Jersey, 1776–1777 — 191

Major Campaigns in New York and Pennsylvania, 1777 — 196

Western Campaigns, 1776–1779 — 200

Major Campaigns in the South, 1778–1781 — 205

Yorktown, 1781 — 206

North America, 1783 — 210

The Old Northwest, 1785 — 229

The Growth of Railroads, 1860 — 327

Population Density, 1820 — 336

Population Density, 1860 — 337

The Growth of Industry in the 1840s — 338

The Missouri Compromise, 1820 — 362

The Election of 1828 — 372

Indian Removal, 1820–1840 — 386

The Election of 1840 — 409

Cotton Production, 1821 — 422

Population Growth and Cotton Production, 1821–1859 — 423
The Slave Population, 1820 — 434
The Slave Population, 1860 — 435
Mormon Trek, 1830–1851 — 462
Wagon Trails West — 505
Major Campaigns of the Mexican-American War — 532
The Kansas-Nebraska Act — 555
The Election of 1856 — 560
The Election of 1860 — 570
Secession, 1860–1861 — 581
Campaigns in the West, February–April 1862 — 593
The Peninsular Campaign, 1862 — 596
Campaigns in Virginia and Maryland, 1862 — 605
Campaigns in the East, 1863 — 619
Grant in Virginia, 1864–1865 — 625
Sherman's Campaigns, 1864–1865 — 628
Reconstruction, 1865–1877 — 661
Transcontinental Railroad Lines, 1880s — 698
Sharecropping and Tenancy, 1880–1900 — 736
The New West — 748–749
Indian Wars — 765
The Emergence of Large Cities, 1880 — 775
The Emergence of Large Cities, 1920 — 776
The Election of 1896 — 811
U.S. Interests in the Pacific — 835
U.S. Interests in the Caribbean — 841
Women's Suffrage, 1869–1914 — 860
The Election of 1912 — 882
The Great War in Europe, 1914 — 899
The Great War, the Western Front, 1918 — 919
Europe after the Treaty of Versailles, 1918 — 928
Aggression in Europe, 1935–1939 — 1064
Japanese Expansion before the Attack on Pearl Harbor — 1071
World War II in Europe and Africa, 1942–1945 — 1088
World War II in the Pacific, 1942–1945 — 1098
The Occupation of Germany and Austria — 1120
The Election of 1948 — 1132
The Korean War, 1950 and 1950–1953 — 1138

The Election of 1952                                                            1152

Postwar Alliances: The Far East                                                1181

Postwar Alliances: Europe, North Africa, the Middle East                       1184

The Election of 1960                                                           1195

Vietnam, 1966                                                                  1230

The Election of 1968                                                           1236

The Election of 1980                                                           1305

The Election of 1988                                                           1321

The Election of 2000                                                           1346

The Election of 2004                                                           1355

The Election of 2008                                                           1360

The Election of 2016                                                           1385

# PREFACE

This Eleventh Edition of *America: A Narrative History* Brief High School Edition improves upon a textbook celebrated for its compelling narrative history of the American experience. Over the past thirty years, I have sought to write an engaging book centered on political and economic developments animated by colorful characters, informed by balanced analysis and social texture, and guided by the unfolding of key events. Those classic principles, combined with a handy size and low price, have helped make *America: A Narrative History* one of the most popular and well-respected textbooks in the field.

This Eleventh Brief High School Edition of *America* features important changes designed to make the text more teachable and classroom-friendly. The Eleventh Brief Edition is fifteen percent shorter than the Full Edition, and is a more affordable option for students. The overarching theme of the new edition is the importance of immigration to the American experience. Since 1776, the United States has taken in more people from more nations than any other country in the world. By welcoming newcomers, America has enriched its economy, diversified its people and culture, and testified to the appeal of a democracy committed to equal opportunity and equal treatment. Writer Vivian Gornick, the daughter of Russian Jewish immigrants, cherished the ethnic mosaic of her childhood New York City neighborhood: "The 'otherness' of the Italians or the Irish or the Jews among us lent spice and interest, a sense of definition, an exciting edge to things that was openly feared but secretly welcomed." At times, however, the nation's Open Door policy has also generated tension, criticism, prejudice, and even violence. Those concerned about immigration, past and present, have complained about open borders and called into question the nation's ability to serve as the world's "melting pot." The shifting attitudes and policies regarding immigration have testified to the continuing debate over the merits of newcomers. Immigration remains one of the nation's most cherished yet contested values, and as such it deserves fresh emphasis in textbooks and classrooms. While an introductory textbook must necessarily focus on major political, constitutional, diplomatic, economic, and social changes, it is also essential to convey how ordinary people managed everyday concerns—housing, jobs, food, recreation, religion, and entertainment—and surmounted exceptional challenges—depressions, wars, and racial injustice.

I have continued to enrich the political narrative by incorporating more social and cultural history into this new edition. The text has been updated to include the following key new discussions:

- **Chapter 1** "The Collision of Cultures" highlights President John F. Kennedy's emphasis on the United States as "a nation of immigrants," and revised assessments of Christopher Columbus's roles as colonial governor, ship captain, and slave trader.
- **Chapter 2** "England's Colonies" includes expanded coverage of the various factors that led Europeans to relocate to the American colonies, new discussion of the varied fates of British convicts and others who were sent involuntarily to America, the experience of indentured servants, and expanded focus on Chief Powhatan and his response to English colonists who were determined to "invade my people."
- **Chapter 3** "Colonial Ways of Life" features fresh insights into nativism and xenophobic sentiment toward German immigrants in the American colonies, including anti-immigrant comments from Benjamin Franklin in Pennsylvania; and discussion of the plight of immigrant women who worked in Virginia's textile factories.
- **Chapter 4** "From Colonies to States" includes new assessment of the small, but distinctive French immigration to North America before 1750; new focus on the massive surge in immigration and slave imports after the French and Indian War; and, new treatments of the first Revolutionary battles.
- **Chapter 5** "The American Revolution" features new discussion of the system of enslaved labor during the War of Independence, the discriminatory legal status of African Americans, and British characterizations of American colonies as the "land of the free and the land of the slave." There is also a profile of Thomas Jeremiah, a South Carolina "boatman" whom colonial authorities executed after he alerted enslaved blacks that British soldiers were coming to "help the poor Negroes." The chapter also includes a new photo depicting free black soldiers fighting in the Revolution.
- **Chapter 6** "Strengthening the New Nation" expands discussion of the delegates to the Constitutional Convention and their involvement with slavery, features debates over immigration in the new nation, offers new perspective on Alexander Hamilton's development as an

immigrant to the United States, and includes new photos of naturalization in 1790.

- **Chapter 7** "The Early Republic" includes expanded treatment of the Lewis and Clark expedition, of the strategic significance of the Louisiana Purchase, and the legacy of the War of 1812.
- **Chapter 8** "The Emergence of a Market Economy" includes new discussions on anti-Catholic and anti-Irish sentiments during the first half of the nineteenth century, the changing dynamics among immigrants of different nationalities, and the challenges immigrant workers faced in forming unions. New photos that depict symbols of organized labor have been added.
- **Chapter 9** "Nationalism and Sectionalism" features a revised profile of John Quincy Adams and fresh coverage of Henry Clay.
- **Chapter 10** "The Jacksonian Era" includes expanded coverage of Andrew Jackson's Indian Removal policy, the Deposit and Distribution Act, the Specie Circular, and the Eaton Affair.
- **Chapter 11** "The South, Slavery, and King Cotton" highlights the changing dynamics between slave labor and immigrant labor in the Old South and new coverage of sexual violence upon female slaves in the New Orleans slave trade and other regions.
- **Chapter 12** "Religion, Romanticism, and Reform" includes revised discussions of religious awakenings, Mormonism, and transcendentalism, with expanded focus on transcendentalist Henry David Thoreau and Christian revivalist Peter Cartwright. The chapter also features social developments in women's rights and the transition from gradualism to abolitionism among those opposed to slavery.
- **Chapter 13** "Western Expansion" includes a new biographical sketch of John A. Sutter, the Swiss settler who founded a colony of European emigrants in California and created a wilderness empire centered on the gold rush. There is also expanded content on Irish and German immigrants in the Saint Patrick's Battalion in the Mexican army. The chapter also reveals the development of John C. Calhoun's race-based ideology following the Texas Revolution and includes a new photograph of the Donner party.
- **Chapter 14** "The Gathering Storm" features new discussion of the California gold rush's impact on the Native American population, new biographical material on Presidents James Buchanan and Abraham Lincoln, and expanded coverage of the Lincoln-Douglas debates.
- **Chapter 15** "The War of the Union" discusses the substantial immigrant participation in the Civil War, features a new biographical sketch and

photo of Private Lyons Wakeman—a young woman who disguised herself as a man in order to fight in the Union army.

- **Chapter 16** "The Era of Reconstruction" explains changing immigration policy in the context of the Naturalization Act of 1870 and offers new treatments of Indian policies, Congressional Reconstruction, and the legacies of Reconstruction.

- **Chapter 17** "Business and Labor in the Industrial Era" includes broader discussion of immigrant women, the contributions of inventors like Croatian immigrant Nikola Tesla, the relationship between immigration—especially Chinese immigration—and the railroad boom beginning in the 1860s. There is fuller coverage of immigrants and the settlement house movement, union organizers such as Eugene Debs, and textile mill and factory strikers.

- **Chapter 18** "The New South and the New West" expands explanation of the spread of institutional racial segregation and the emergence of the southern tobacco industry after the Civil War.

- **Chapter 19** "Political Stalemate and Rural Revolt" includes new coverage of the unemployed protesters who marched in Coxey's Army protesting the recession of the late nineteenth century.

- **Chapter 20** "Seizing an American Empire" includes expanded content and a new photo regarding Japanese immigration to the United States.

- **Chapter 21** "The Progressive Era" features increased discussion of the social gospel movement and the women's suffrage movement, new biographical material on Presidents Taft, Roosevelt, and Wilson, and expanded focus on the racial biases of the Wilson administration.

- **Chapter 22** "America and the Great War" includes expanded coverage of immigrants, including Italian American Tony Monanco, who fought in World War I; new coverage of Woodrow Wilson's prosecution of immigrants who spread the poison of disloyalty during the war; nativism's ties to racism and eugenics; and increased discussion of the Palmer raids.

- **Chapter 23** "A Clash of Cultures" includes new discussion of flappers, the sexual revolution, and the new woman; revised treatments of Albert Einstein, scientific developments, and the impact of the radio; and, fresh insights into Ernest Hemingway and the "Lost Generation."

- **Chapter 24** "The Reactionary Twenties" expands discussion of reactionary conservatism and restrictive immigration policies; extends content on the revival of the Ku Klux Klan, prohibition, racial progressivism, and President Herbert Hoover's financial and social policies; and adds new coverage of the Johnson-Reed Act.

- **Chapter 25** "The New Deal" features expanded coverage of the New Deal's impact on women and Native Americans; there is new material on President Franklin Delano Roosevelt's relationship with his wife Eleanor Roosevelt.
- **Chapter 26** "The Second World War" includes expanded coverage of social and racial prejudice against African Americans and Japanese Americans; features a new discussion of army enlistment after the attack on Pearl Harbor; and a new set piece on the Battle of the Bulge.
- **Chapter 27** "The Cold War and the Fair Deal" includes discussion of the Immigration and Nationality (McCarran-Walter) Act of 1952 within the contexts of the Red Scare and McCarthyism.
- **Chapter 28** "America in the Fifties" highlights the emergence of a "car culture," expanded discussion of the communist politics of Cuba, and bolstered coverage regarding Elizabeth Eckford, the student who attempted to enter Little Rock High School in Arkansas after the desegregation of public schools.
- **Chapter 29** "A New Frontier and a Great Society" includes fresh coverage of the Immigration and Nationality Services Act of 1965, of the Logan Act regarding communication with foreign governments, and of U.S. Attorney General Robert Kennedy. It also features new set pieces highlighting the work of organizers Audre Lorde and Angela Davis, both of whom were involved with the Black Panther party.
- **Chapter 30** "Rebellion and Reaction" features new discussions on the founding of the United Farm Workers and the organizing efforts of Dolores Huerta and Cesar Chavez, including Chavez's twenty-five-day hunger strike in 1968 and the pathbreaking worker's rights negotiations with grape growers in the 1970s. It also includes a new set piece spotlighting feminist pioneer and *Ms.* magazine founder Gloria Steinem, and another covering clinical psychology professor Timothy Leary's crusade on behalf of psychedelic drugs.
- **Chapter 31** "Conservative Revival" includes expanded discussion of the Carter administration, new coverage of the Immigration Act of 1990, and revised treatment of George H. W. Bush's presidency.
- **Chapter 32** "Twenty-First-Century America" includes new coverage and photos of the Black Lives Matter movement, the 2016 election, and the Me Too movement. New Trump administration coverage includes the efforts to restrict immigration and movement (travel ban, family separation, and increased border security); the proposed ban of transgender service members; and Supreme Court appointments.

In addition, I have incorporated throughout this edition fresh insights from important new books and articles covering many significant topics. Whether you consider yourself a political, social, cultural, or economic historian, you'll find new material to consider and share with your students.

As part of making the new editions even more teachable and classroom friendly, the new Eleventh Brief High School Edition of *America: A Narrative History* also makes history an immersive experience through its innovative pedagogy and digital resources. Norton InQuizitive for History—W. W. Norton's groundbreaking, formative, and adaptive new learning program—enables both students and instructors to assess learning progress at the individual and classroom level. The Norton Coursepack provides an array of support materials—free to instructors—who adopt the text for integration into their local learning-management system. The Norton Coursepack includes valuable assessment and skill-building activities like new primary source exercises, review quizzes, and interactive map resources. In addition, we've created new Chapter Overview videos that give students a visual introduction to the key themes and historical developments they will encounter in each chapter (see pages xxvi–xxx for information about student and instructor resources).

## MEDIA RESOURCES FOR INSTRUCTORS AND STUDENTS

*America*'s new student resources are designed to develop more-discriminating readers, guiding students through the narrative while simultaneously developing their critical thinking and history skills.

The comprehensive ancillary package features a groundbreaking new formative and adaptive learning system, as well as innovative interactive resources, including maps and primary sources, all designed to help students master the Focus Questions in each chapter and continue to nurture their work as historians. W. W. Norton is unique in partnering to develop these resources exclusively with subject-matter experts who teach the course. As a result, instructors have all the course materials needed to manage their U.S. history class.

## NEW! HISTORY SKILLS TUTORIALS

With the Eleventh Brief High School Edition we've expanded our digital resources to include a new series of tutorials to build students' critical analysis skills. The History Skills Tutorials combine video and interactive assessments to teach students how to analyze documents, images, and maps. By utilizing a three-step process, students learn a framework for analysis through videos featuring David Shi, and then are challenged to apply what they have learned through a series of interactive assessments. The History Skills Tutorials can be assigned at the beginning of the semester to prepare students for analysis of the sources in the textbook and beyond, or they can be integrated as remediation tools throughout the course.

## NEW! CHAPTER OVERVIEW VIDEOS

New Chapter Overview Videos, featuring author David Shi, combine images and primary sources to provide visual introduction to the key themes and historical developments students will encounter in each chapter. These are in addition to the Author Videos in which David Shi explains essential developments and difficult concepts, with available closed captioning.

## NORTON InQUIZITIVE FOR HISTORY

This groundbreaking formative, adaptive learning tool improves student understanding of the Focus Questions in each chapter. Students receive personalized quiz questions on the topics with which they need the most help. Questions range from vocabulary and concepts to interactive maps and primary sources that challenge students to begin developing the skills necessary to do the work of a historian. Engaging game-like elements motivate students as they learn. As a result, students come to class better prepared to participate in discussions and activities.

## STUDENT SITE

Free and open to all students, the Student Site includes additional resources and tools.

- **Author Videos:** These segments include the NEW! Chapter Overview Videos and feature David Shi discussing essential developments and difficult concepts from the book.
- **Online Reader:** This resource offers a collection of primary source documents and images for use in assignments and activities.
- **iMaps:** Interactive maps allow students to view layers of information on each map with accompanying printable **Map Worksheets** for offline labeling.

## NORTON EBOOKS

Norton Ebooks give students and instructors an enhanced reading experience at a fraction of the cost of a print textbook. Students are able to have an active reading experience and can take notes, bookmark, search, highlight, and even read offline. As an instructor, you can add your own notes for students to see as they read the text. Norton ebooks can be viewed on—and synced between—all computers and mobile devices. The ebook for the Eleventh Brief High School Edition includes imbedded Author Videos, including the new Chapter Overview Videos; pop-up key term definitions; and enlargeable images and maps.

## NORTON LMS RESOURCES

Easily add high quality Norton digital media to your course—all at no cost. Norton Coursepacks work within your existing learning-management system; there's no new system to learn, and access is free and easy. Content is customizable and includes:

- **Author Videos:** These segments include the NEW! Chapter Overview Videos and illuminate key events, developments, and concepts in each chapter by bringing the narrative to life with additional context and anecdotes.
- **Primary Source Exercises:** These activities feature primary sources with multiple-choice and short-response questions to encourage close reading and analysis.
- **iMaps:** These interactive tools challenge students to better understand the nature of change over time by allowing them to explore the different layers of maps from the book. Follow-up map worksheets help build geography skills by allowing students to test their knowledge by labeling.
- **Review Quizzes:** Multiple-choice and true/false questions allow students to test their knowledge of the chapter content and then identify where they need to focus their attention to better understand difficult concepts.
- **Online Reader:** This resource includes about 1,000 additional primary sources (textual and visual). These are also available grouped by **Research Topic** for further investigation and writing assignments.
- **Flashcards:** This tool aligns key terms and events with brief descriptions and definitions.
- **Forum Prompts:** Three to five suggested topics per chapter offer additional opportunities for class discussion.

# INSTRUCTOR'S MANUAL

The Instructor's Manual for *America: A Narrative History*, Eleventh Brief High School Edition, is designed to help instructors prepare lessons. It contains chapter summaries; chapter outlines; lecture ideas; in-class activities; discussion questions; a NEW! Quality Matters correlation guide.

# TEST BANK

This Test Bank features over 2,000 questions, including traditional multiple-choice questions that assess concept recall; prompt-based multiple-choice questions that test concept application, quantitative analysis, visual analysis, and more; true/false; matching; and long essay questions that focus on concept application, qualitative analysis, and argument. For AP® instructors, this Test Bank features all of the question types on the redesigned AP® exam, including eight full-length DBQs. The Test Bank questions are available with the ExamView Test Generator software, allowing instructors to effortlessly create, administer, and manage assessments.

# CLASSROOM PRESENTATION TOOLS

- **Lecture PowerPoint Slides:** These ready-made presentations feature images and maps from the book as well as bullet points to encourage student comprehension and engagement.
- **Image Files:** All images and maps from the book are available separately in JPEG and PowerPoint format for instructor use.
- **Norton American History Digital Archive:** The archive includes over 1,700 images, audio and video files that are arranged chronologically and by theme.

# PRIMARY SOURCE READERS TO ACCOMPANY *AMERICA: A NARRATIVE HISTORY*

- **NEW!** Seventh Edition of *For the Record: A Documentary History of America*, by David E. Shi and Holly A. Mayer (Duquesne University), is the perfect companion reader for *America: A Narrative History*. *For the Record* now features 268 primary-source readings from diaries, journals, newspaper articles, speeches, government documents, and novels, including several readings that highlight the substantially updated theme of immigration history in this new edition of *America*. If you haven't scanned *For the Record* in a while, now would be a good time to take a look.

- **Norton Mix: American History** enables instructors to build their own custom reader from a database of nearly 300 primary- and secondary-source selections. The custom readings can be packaged as a standalone reader or integrated with chapters from *America* into a custom textbook.

# ACKNOWLEDGMENTS

As always, my colleagues at W. W. Norton shared with me their dedicated expertise and their poise amid tight deadlines, especially Jon Durbin, Melissa Atkin, Lily Gellman, Carson Russell, Sarah Rose Aquilina, Ben Reynolds, Sarah England Bartley, Hope Goodell Miller, Travis Carr, and Marne Evans. In addition, Jim Stewart, a patient friend and consummate editor, helped winnow my wordiness.

Finally, I have dedicated this Eleventh Edition of *America* to George B. Tindall, my friend and co-author who until his death in 2006 shared his wisdom, knowledge, wit, and humor with me. Although few of his words remain in this book, his spirit continues to animate its pages.

# AMERICA

# part one

# A NOT-SO- "NEW" WORLD

History is filled with ironies. Luck and accidents—the unexpected happenings of life—often shape events more than intentions do. Long before Christopher Columbus happened upon the Caribbean Sea in search of a westward passage to the Indies (east Asia), the native peoples he mislabeled "Indians" had occupied and transformed the lands of the Western Hemisphere (also called the Americas—North, Central, and South) for thousands of years. The "New World" was thus *new* only to the Europeans who began exploring, conquering, and exploiting the region at the end of the fifteenth century.

Over time, indigenous peoples had developed hundreds of strikingly different societies. Some were rooted in agriculture; others focused on trade or conquest. Many Native Americans (also called Amerindians) were healthier, better fed, and lived longer than Europeans, but when the two societies—European and Native American—collided, Amerindians were often exploited, infected, enslaved, displaced, and exterminated.

Yet the conventional story of invasion and occupation oversimplifies the process by which Indians, Europeans, and Africans interacted in the sixteenth and seventeenth centuries. Native Americans were more than passive victims of European power; they were also trading partners and military allies of the transatlantic newcomers. They became neighbors and advisers, religious converts and loving spouses. As such, they participated actively in the creation of the new society known as America.

The European colonists who risked their lives to settle in the Western Hemisphere were a diverse lot. They came from Spain, Portugal, France, the British Isles, the Netherlands (Holland), Scandinavia, Italy, and the German states. (Germany would not become a united nation until the mid–nineteenth century.) What they shared was a presumption that Christianity was superior to all religions and that all other peoples were inferior to them and their culture.

A variety of motives inspired Europeans to undertake the harrowing transatlantic voyage. Some were fortune seekers lusting for gold, silver, and spices. Others were eager to create kingdoms of God in the New World. Still others were adventurers, convicts, debtors, servants, landless peasants, and political or religious exiles. Most were simply seeking opportunities for a better life. A settler in Pennsylvania noted that workers "here get three times the wages for their labor than they can in England."

Yet such wages never attracted enough workers to keep up with the rapidly expanding colonial economies, so Europeans eventually turned to Africa for their labor needs in the New World. Beginning in 1503, European nations—especially Portugal and Spain—transported captive Africans to the Western Hemisphere. Throughout the sixteenth century, slaves were delivered to ports as far south as Chile to as far north as Canada. Thereafter, the English and Dutch joined the effort to exploit enslaved Africans. Few Europeans saw the contradiction between the promise of freedom in America for themselves and the institution of race-based slavery.

The intermingling of people, cultures, plants, animals, microbes, and diseases from the continents of Africa, Europe, and the Western Hemisphere gave colonial American society its distinctive vitality and variety. The shared quest for a better life gave America much of its drama—and conflict.

The Europeans unwittingly brought to the Americas a range of infectious diseases that would prove disastrous for the indigenous peoples—who had no natural immunities to them—and no knowledge of how to cope with them. As many as 90 percent of Native Americans would eventually die from European-borne diseases. Proportionally, it would be the worst human death toll in history.

At the same time, bitter rivalries among the Spanish, French, English, and Dutch triggered costly wars in Europe and around the world. Amid such conflicts, the monarchs of Europe struggled to manage often-unruly colonies, which, as it turned out, played crucial roles in their frequent wars.

Many of the colonists displayed a feisty independence, which led them to resent government interference in their affairs. A British official in North Carolina reported that the colonists were "without any Law or Order. Impudence is so very high, as to be past bearing."

The colonists and their British rulers maintained an uneasy partnership throughout the seventeenth century. As the royal authorities tightened their control during the mid–eighteenth century, however, they met resistance, which exploded into revolution.

# 1

# The Collision
# of Cultures

**De Soto and the Incas** This 1596 color engraving shows Spanish conquistador
Hernando de Soto's first encounter with King Atahualpa of the Inca Empire. Although
artist Theodor de Bry never set foot in North America, his engravings helped shape
European perceptions of Native Americans in the sixteenth century.

America was born in melting ice. Tens of thousands of years ago, during a period known as the Ice Age, immense glaciers some two miles thick inched southward from the Arctic Circle at the top of the globe. The advancing ice crushed hills, rerouted rivers, gouged out lakebeds and waterways, and scraped bare all the land in its path.

The glacial ice sheets covered much of North America—Canada, Alaska, the Upper Midwest, New England, Montana, and Washington. Then, as the continent's climate began to warm, the ice slowly started to melt, year after year, century after century. As the ice sheets receded, they opened pathways for the first immigrants to roam the continent.

Debate still rages about when and how humans first arrived in North America. Yet one thing is certain: the ancestors of *every* person living in the United States originally came from somewhere else. America is indeed "a nation of immigrants," a society of striving people attracted by a mythic new world promising new beginnings and a better life in a new place of unlimited space. Geography may be destiny, as the saying goes, but without pioneering people of determination and imagination, geography would have destroyed rather than sustained the first Americans.

Until recently, archaeologists had assumed that ancient peoples from northeast Asia began following herds of large game animals across the Bering Strait, a waterway that now connects the Arctic and Pacific Oceans. During the Ice Age, however, the Bering Strait was dry—a treeless, windswept, frigid tundra that connected eastern Siberia with Alaska.

The place with the oldest traces of human activity in the Bering region is Broken Mammoth, a 14,400-year-old site in central Alaska where the first

## focus questions

**1.** Why were there so many diverse societies in the Americas before Europeans arrived?

**2.** What major developments in Europe enabled the Age of Exploration?

**3.** How did the Spanish conquer and colonize the Americas?

**4.** How did the Columbian Exchange between the "Old" and "New" Worlds affect both societies?

**5.** In what ways did the Spanish form of colonization shape North American history?

aboriginal peoples, called Paleo-Indians (Ancient Indians), arrived in North America. More recently, archaeologists in central Texas unearthed evidence of people dating back almost 16,000 years.

Over thousands of years, as the climate kept warming and the glaciers and ice sheets continued to melt, small nomadic groups fanned out from Alaska on foot or in boats and eventually spread across the Western Hemisphere, from the Arctic Circle to the southern tip of South America. The Paleo-Indians lived in transportable huts with wooden frames covered by animal skins or grasses ("thatch").

Paleo-Indians were skilled hunters and gatherers in search of game animals, whales, seals, fish, and wild plants, berries, nuts, roots, and seeds. As they moved southward, they trekked across prairies and plains, working in groups to track and kill massive animals unlike any found there today: mammoths, mastodons, giant sloths, camels, lions, saber-toothed tigers, cheetahs, and giant wolves, beavers, and bears.

Recent archaeological discoveries in North and South America, however, suggest that prehistoric humans may have arrived thousands of years earlier from various parts of Asia. Some may even have crossed the Pacific and Atlantic Oceans in boats from Polynesian islands in the southern Pacific or from southwestern Europe.

Regardless of when, where, or how humans first set foot in North America, the continent eventually became a dynamic crossroads for adventurous peoples from around the world, all bringing with them distinctive backgrounds, cultures, technologies, religions, and motivations that helped form the multicultural society known as America.

## EARLY CULTURES IN AMERICA

Archaeologists have labeled the earliest humans in North America the *Clovis* peoples, named after a site in New Mexico where ancient hunters killed tusked woolly mammoths using "Clovis" stone spearheads. Over the centuries, as the climate warmed, days grew hotter and many of the largest mammals—mammoths, mastodons, and camels—grew extinct. Hunters then began stalking more-abundant mammals: deer, antelope, elk, moose, and caribou.

Over time, the Ancient Indians adapted to their diverse environments—coastal forests, grassy plains, southwestern deserts, eastern woodlands. Some continued to hunt with spears and, later, bows and arrows; others fished or trapped small game. Some gathered wild plants and herbs and collected acorns and seeds, while others farmed using stone hoes. Most did some of each.

By about 7000 B.C.E. (before the Common Era), Native American societies began transforming into farming cultures, supplemented by seasonal hunting and gathering. Agriculture provided reliable, nutritious food, which accelerated population growth and enabled once nomadic people to settle in villages. Indigenous peoples became expert at growing plants that would become the primary food crops of the hemisphere, chiefly **maize** (corn), beans, and squash, but also chili peppers, avocados, and pumpkins.

Maize-based societies viewed corn as the "gift of the gods" because it provided many essential needs. They made hominy by soaking dried kernels in a mixture of water and ashes and then cooking it. They used corn cobs for fuel and the husks to fashion mats, masks, and dolls. They also ground the kernels into cornmeal, which could be mixed with beans to make protein-rich succotash.

**Mayan society** A fresco depicting the social divisions of Mayan society. A Mayan high priest, at the center, is ceremonially dressed.

## The Mayans, Incas, and Mexica

Around 1500 B.C.E., farming towns appeared in what is now Mexico. Agriculture supported the development of sophisticated communities complete with gigantic temple-topped pyramids, palaces, and bridges in Middle America (*Mesoamerica*, what is now Mexico and Central America). The Mayans, who dominated Central America for more than 600 years, developed a written language and elaborate works of art. Mayan civilization featured sprawling cities, hierarchical government, terraced farms, and spectacular pyramids.

Yet in about A.D. 900, the Mayan culture collapsed. Why it disappeared remains a mystery, but a major factor was ecological. The Mayans destroyed much of the rain forest, upon whose fragile ecosystem they depended. As an archaeologist has explained, "Too many farmers grew too many crops on too much of the landscape." Widespread deforestation led to hillside erosion and a catastrophic loss of nutrient-rich farmland.

Overpopulation added to the strain on Mayan society, prompting civil wars. The Mayans eventually succumbed to the Toltecs, a warlike people who conquered most of the region in the tenth century. Around A.D. 1200, however, the Toltecs mysteriously withdrew after a series of droughts, fires, and invasions.

**THE INCAS** Much farther south, many diverse people speaking at least twenty different languages made up the sprawling Inca Empire. By the fifteenth century, the Incas' vast realm stretched 2,500 miles along the Andes Mountains in the western part of South America. It featured irrigated farms, stone buildings, and interconnected networks of roads made of stone.

**THE MEXICA (AZTECS)** During the twelfth century, the **Mexica** (Me-SHEE-ka)—whom Europeans later called Aztecs ("People from Aztlán," the place they claimed as their original homeland)—began drifting southward from northwest Mexico. Disciplined, determined, and aggressive, they eventually took control of central Mexico, where in 1325 they built the city of Tenochtitlán ("place of the stone cactus") on an island in Lake Tetzcoco, at the site of present-day Mexico City.

Tenochtitlán would become one of the grandest cities in the world. It served as the capital of a sophisticated **Aztec Empire** ruled by a powerful emperor and divided into two social classes: noble warriors and priests (about 5 percent of the population) and the free commoners—merchants, craftsmen, and farmers.

When the Spanish invaded Mexico in 1519, they found a vast Aztec Empire connected by a network of roads serving 371 city-states organized into

38 provinces. Towering stone temples, broad paved avenues, thriving market-places, and some 70,000 *adobe* (sunbaked mud) huts dominated Tenochtitlán. As the empire expanded across central and southern Mexico, the Aztecs developed elaborate societies supported by detailed legal systems and a complicated political structure. They advanced efficient new farming techniques, including terracing of fields, crop rotation, large-scale irrigation, and other engineering marvels. Their arts flourished, their architecture was magnificent. Their rulers were invested with godlike qualities, and nobles, priests, and warrior-heroes dominated the social order. The emperor's palace had 100 rooms and 100 baths replete with amazing statues, gardens, and a zoo; the aristocracy lived in large stone dwellings, practiced polygamy (multiple wives), and were exempt from manual labor.

Like most agricultural peoples, the Mexica were intensely spiritual and worshipped multiple gods. Their religious beliefs focused on the inter-connection between nature and human life and the sacredness of natural elements—the sun, moon, stars, rain, mountains, rivers, and animals. They believed that the gods had sacrificed themselves to create the sun, moon, people, and maize. They were therefore obliged to feed the gods, especially Huitzilopochtli, the Lord of the Sun and War, with the vital energy provided by human hearts and blood. So the Mexica, like most Mesoamerican societies, regularly offered live human sacrifices.

Warfare was a sacred ritual for the Mexica, but it involved a peculiar sort of combat. Warriors fought with wooden swords—to wound rather than kill; they wanted live captives to sacrifice to the gods and to work as slaves. Gradually, the Mexica conquered many neighboring societies, forcing them to make payment of goods and labor as tribute to the empire.

In elaborate weekly rituals, captured warriors or virgin girls would be daubed with paint, given a hallucinatory drug, and marched up many steps to the temple platform, where priests cut out the victims' beating hearts and offered them to the sun god. The constant need for human sacrifices fed the Mexica's relentless warfare against other indigenous groups. A Mexica song celebrated their warrior code: "Proud of itself is the city of Mexico-Tenochtitlán. Here no one fears to die in war. This is our glory."

## NORTH AMERICAN CIVILIZATIONS

North of Mexico, in the present-day United States, many indigenous societies blossomed in the early 1500s. Over the centuries, small kinship groups (*clans*) had joined together: first to form larger *bands* involving hundreds of people, which then evolved into much larger regional groups, or *tribes*, whose members spoke the same language. Although few had an alphabet or written language, the different societies developed rich oral traditions that passed on spiritual myths and social beliefs, especially those concerning the sacredness of nature, the necessity of communal living, and a deep respect for elders.

Like the Mexica, most indigenous peoples believed in many "spirits." To the Sioux, God was Wakan Tanka, the Great Spirit, who ruled over all spirits. The Navajo believed in the Holy People: Sky, Earth, Moon, Sun, Thunders, Winds, and Changing Woman. Many Native Americans believed in ghosts, who acted as their bodyguards in battle.

The importance of hunting to many Indian societies helped nurture a warrior ethic in which courage in combat was the highest virtue. War dances the night before a hunt or battle invited the spirits to unleash magical powers. Yet, Native American warfare mostly consisted of small-scale raids intended to enable individual warriors to demonstrate their courage rather than to seize territory or destroy villages. Casualties were minimal. Taking a few captives often signaled victory.

## DIVERSE SOCIETIES

For all their similarities, the indigenous peoples of North America developed markedly different ways of life. In North America alone in 1492, when the first Europeans arrived, there were perhaps several million native peoples organized into 240 different societies speaking many different languages.

These Native Americans practiced diverse customs and religions, passed on distinctive cultural myths, and developed varied economies. Some wore clothes they had woven or made using animal skins, and still others wore nothing but colorful paint, tattoos, or jewelry. Some lived in stone houses, others in circular timber wigwams or bark-roofed longhouses. Still others lived in sod-covered or reed-thatched lodges, or in portable tipis made from animal skins. Some cultures built stone pyramids graced by ceremonial plazas, and others constructed huge burial or ritual mounds topped by temples.

Few North American Indians permitted absolute rulers. Tribes had chiefs, but the "power of the chiefs," reported an eighteenth-century British trader, "is an empty sound. They can only persuade or dissuade the people by the force of good-nature and clear reasoning." Likewise, Henry Timberlake, a British soldier, explained that the Cherokee government, "if I may call it a government, which has neither laws nor power to support it, is a mixed aristocracy and democracy, the chiefs being chosen according to their merit in war."

For Native Americans, exile from the group was the most feared punishment. They owned land in common rather than individually as private property, and they had well-defined social roles. Men were hunters, warriors, and leaders. Women tended children; made clothes, blankets, jewelry, and pottery; cured and dried animal skins; wove baskets; built and packed tipis; and grew, harvested, and cooked food. When the men were away hunting or fighting, women took charge of village life. Some Indian nations, like the Cherokee and Iroquois, gave women political power.

**THE SOUTHWEST** The arid (dry) Southwest (present-day Arizona, New Mexico, Nevada, and Utah) featured a landscape of high mesas, deep canyons, vast deserts, long rivers, and snow-covered mountains that hosted corn-growing societies. The Hopis, Zunis, and others still live in the multistory adobe cliff-side villages (called *pueblos* by the Spanish), which were erected by their ancient ancestors.

About 500 C.E. (Common Era), the Hohokam ("those who have vanished") people migrated from Mexico northward to southern and central Arizona, where they built extensive canals to irrigate crops. They also crafted decorative pottery and turquoise jewelry, and constructed *temple mounds* (earthen pyramids used for sacred ceremonies).

The most widespread and best known of the Southwest pueblo cultures were the Anasazi (Ancient Ones), or Basketmakers. Unlike the Aztecs and Incas, however, Anasazi society did *not* have a rigid class structure. The Anasazi engaged in warfare only as a means of self-defense, and the religious leaders and warriors worked much as the rest of the people did.

**THE NORTHWEST** Along the narrow coastal strip running up the heavily forested northwest Pacific coast, shellfish, salmon, seals, whales, deer, and edible wild plants were abundant. Here, there was little need to rely on farming. In fact, many of the Pacific Northwest peoples, such as the Haida, Kwakiutl, and Nootka, needed to work only two days to provide enough food for a week.

Such population density enabled the Pacific coast cultures to develop intricate religious rituals and sophisticated woodworking skills. They carved towering totem poles featuring decorative figures of animals and other symbolic characters. For shelter, they built large, earthen-floored, cedar-plank houses up to 500 feet long, where groups of families lived together. They also created sturdy, oceangoing canoes made of hollowed-out red cedar tree trunks—some large enough to carry fifty people. Socially, they were divided into slaves, commoners, and chiefs. Warfare was usually a means to acquire slaves.

**THE GREAT PLAINS** The many tribal nations living on the Great Plains, a vast, flat land of cold winters and hot summers west of the Mississippi River, included the Arapaho, Blackfeet, Cheyenne, Comanche, Crow,

Apache, and Sioux. As nomadic hunter-gatherers, they tracked herds of buffaloes (technically called bison) across a sea of grassland, collecting seeds, nuts, roots, and berries as they roamed.

At the center of most hunter-gatherer religions is the idea that the hunted animal is a willing sacrifice provided by the gods (spirits). To ensure a successful hunt, these nomadic peoples performed sacred rites of gratitude beforehand. Once a buffalo herd was spotted, the hunters would set fires to drive the stampeding animals over cliffs, often killing far more than they could harvest and consume.

**THE MISSISSIPPIANS**   East of the Great Plains, in the vast woodlands reaching from the Mississippi River to the Atlantic Ocean, several "mound-building" cultures prospered. Between 700 B.C.E. and 200 C.E., the Adena and later the Hopewell societies developed communities along rivers in the Ohio Valley. The Adena-Hopewell cultures grew corn, squash, beans, and sunflowers, as well as tobacco for smoking. They left behind enormous earthworks and elaborate **burial mounds** shaped like snakes, birds, and other animals, several of which were nearly a quarter mile long.

Like the Adena, the Hopewell developed an extensive trading network with other Indian societies from the Gulf of Mexico to Canada, exchanging

**Great Serpent Mound**  More than 1,300 feet in length and three feet high, this snake-shaped burial mound in Adams County, Ohio, is the largest of its kind in the world.

exquisite carvings, metalwork, pearls, seashells, copper ornaments, bear claws, and jewelry. By the sixth century, however, the Hopewell culture disappeared, giving way to a new phase of development east of the Mississippi River, the *Mississippian* culture.

The Mississippians were corn-growing peoples who built substantial agricultural towns around central plazas and temples. They developed a far-flung trading network that extended to the Rocky Mountains, and their ability to grow large amounts of corn in the fertile flood plains spurred rapid population growth around regional centers.

**CAHOKIA** The largest of these advanced regional centers, called *chiefdoms*, was **Cahokia** (600–1300 c.e.), in southwest Illinois, near the confluence of the Mississippi and Missouri Rivers (across from what is now St. Louis). The Cahokians constructed an enormous farming settlement with monumental public buildings, spacious ceremonial plazas, and more than eighty flat-topped earthen mounds with thatch-roofed temples on top. The largest of the mounds, called Monks Mound, was ten stories tall, encompassed fourteen acres, and required 22 million cubic feet of soil. At the height of its influence, Cahokia hosted 15,000 people on some 3,200 acres, making it the largest city north of Mexico.

Cahokia, however, vanished around 1300 c.e., and its people dispersed. Its collapse remains a mystery, but the overcutting of trees to make fortress walls may have set in motion ecological changes that doomed the community when a massive earthquake struck. The loss of trees led to widespread flooding and the erosion of topsoil, which finally forced people to seek better lands. As Cahokia disappeared, its former residents took its advanced ways of life to other areas across the Midwest and into what is now the American South.

## EASTERN WOODLANDS PEOPLES

After the collapse of Cahokia, the **Eastern Woodlands peoples** spread along the Atlantic Seaboard from Maine to Florida and along the Gulf coast to Louisiana. They included three regional groups distinguished by their different languages: the Algonquian, the Iroquoian, and the Muskogean. These were the indigenous societies that Europeans would first encounter when they arrived in North America.

**THE ALGONQUIANS** The Algonquian-speaking peoples stretched westward from the New England Seaboard to lands along the Great Lakes and into the Upper Midwest and south to New Jersey, Virginia, and the Carolinas.

*The manner of their attire and painting them selues when they goe to their generall huntings, or at theire Solemne feasts.*

**Algonquian in war paint** From the notebook of English settler John White, this sketch depicts a Native American chieftain.

They lived in small, round *wigwams* or in multifamily longhouses surrounded by a tall *palisade*, a timber fence to defend against attackers. Their villages typically ranged in size from 500 to 2,000 people.

The Algonquians along the Atlantic coast were skilled at fishing and gathering shellfish; the inland Algonquians excelled at hunting. They often traveled the region's waterways using canoes made of hollowed-out tree trunks (dugouts) or birch bark.

All Algonquians foraged for wild food (nuts, berries, and fruits) and practiced agriculture to some extent, regularly burning dense forests to improve soil fertility and provide grazing room for deer. To prepare their vegetable gardens, women broke up the ground with hoes tipped with sharp clamshells or the shoulder blades from deer. In the spring, they cultivated corn, beans, and squash.

**THE IROQUOIANS** West and south of the Algonquians were the powerful Iroquoian-speaking peoples (including the Seneca, Onondaga, Mohawk, Oneida, and Cayuga nations, as well as the Cherokee and Tuscarora), whose lands spread from upstate New York southward through Pennsylvania and into the upland regions of the Carolinas and Georgia. The Iroquois were farmer/hunters who lived in extended family groups (clans), sharing bark-covered longhouses in towns of 3,000 or more people. The oldest woman in each longhouse served as the "clan mother."

Unlike the Algonquian culture, in which men were dominant, women held the key leadership roles in the Iroquoian culture. As an Iroquois elder explained, "In our society, women are the center of all things. Nature, we believe, has given women the ability to create; therefore it is only natural that women be in positions of power to protect this function." A French priest who lived among the Iroquois for five years marveled that "nothing is more real than women's superiority. . . . It is they who really maintain the tribe."

Iroquois men and women operated in separate social domains. No woman could be a chief; no man could head a clan. Women selected the chiefs, controlled the distribution of property, supervised the slaves, and planted and harvested the crops. They also arranged marriages. After a wedding ceremony, the man moved in with the wife's family. In part, the Iroquoian matriarchy reflected the frequent absence of Iroquois men, who as skilled hunters and traders traveled extensively for long periods, requiring women to take charge of domestic life.

**EASTERN WOODLANDS INDIANS**  The third major Native American group in the Eastern Woodlands included the peoples along the coast of the Gulf of Mexico who farmed and hunted and spoke the Muskogean language: the Creek, Choctaw, Chickasaw, Seminole, Natchez, Apalachee, and Timucua. Like the Iroquois, they were often matrilineal societies, meaning that ancestry flowed through the mother's line, but they had a more rigid class structure. The Muskogeans lived in towns arranged around a central plaza. Along the Gulf coast, many of their thatch-roofed houses had no walls because of the mild winters and hot, humid summers.

Over thousands of years, the native North Americans had displayed remarkable resilience, adapting to the uncertainties of frequent warfare, changing climate, and varying environments. They would display similar resilience against the challenges created by the arrival of Europeans.

# European Visions of America

The European exploration of the Western Hemisphere resulted from several key developments during the fifteenth century. Dramatic intellectual changes and scientific discoveries, along with sustained population growth, transformed religion, warfare, family life, and national economies. In addition, the resurgence of old vices—greed, conquest, exploitation, oppression, racism, and slavery—helped fuel European expansion abroad.

By the end of the fifteenth century, medieval feudalism's agrarian social system, in which peasant serfs worked for local nobles in exchange for living on and farming the land, began to disintegrate. People were no longer forced to remain in the same area and keep the same social status in which they were born. A new "middle class" of profit-hungry bankers, merchants, and investors emerged. They were committed to a more dynamic commercial economy fueled by innovations in banking, currency, accounting, and insurance.

The growing trade-based economy in Europe freed kings from their dependence on feudal nobles, enabling the monarchs to unify the scattered cities ruled by princes (principalities) into large kingdoms with stronger, more-centralized governments. The rise of towns, cities, and a merchant class provided new tax revenues. Over time, the new class of monarchs, merchants, and bankers displaced the landed nobility.

This process of centralizing political power was justified in part by claims that European kings ruled by divine right rather than by popular mandate: since God appointed them, only God, not the people, could hold them responsible for their actions.

**THE RENAISSANCE**    At the same time, the rediscovery of ancient Greek and Roman writings about representative government (republics) spurred the *Renaissance* (rebirth), an intellectual revolution that transformed the arts as well as traditional attitudes toward religion and science. The Renaissance began in Italy and spread across western Europe, bringing with it a more *secular* outlook that took greater interest in humanity than in religion. Rather than emphasizing God's omnipotence, Renaissance *humanism* highlighted the power of inventive people to exert their command over nature.

The Renaissance was an essential force in the transition from medievalism to early modernism. From the fifteenth century on, educated people throughout Europe began to challenge prevailing beliefs as well as the absolute authority of rulers and churchmen. They discussed controversial new ideas, engaged in scientific research, and unleashed their artistic creativity. In the process, they fastened on a new phrase—"to discover"—which first appeared in 1553. Voyages of exploration became voyages of discovery.

The Renaissance also sparked the Age of Exploration. New knowledge and new technologies made possible the construction of larger sailing ships capable of oceanic voyages. The development of more accurate magnetic compasses, maps, and navigational instruments such as *astrolabes* and *quadrants* helped sailors determine their ship's location. The fifteenth and sixteenth centuries also brought the invention of gunpowder, cannons, and firearms—and the printing press.

**THE RISE OF GLOBAL TRADE**    By 1500, trade between western European nations and the Middle East, Africa, and Asia was booming. The Portuguese took the lead, bolstered by crews of expert sailors and fast, three-masted ships called *caravels*. Portuguese ships roamed along the west coast of

Africa collecting grains, gold, ivory, spices, and slaves. Eventually, these mariners continued around Africa to the Indian Ocean in search of the fabled *Indies* (India and Southeast Asia). They ventured on to China and Japan, where they found spices (cinnamon, cloves, ginger, nutmeg, black pepper) to enliven bland European food, sugar made from cane to sweeten food and drink, silk cloth, herbal medicines, and other exotic goods.

Global trade was enabled by the emergence of four powerful nations in western Europe: England, France, Portugal, and, especially, Spain. The arranged marriage of King Ferdinand II of Aragon and Queen Isabella I of Castile in 1469 unified their two kingdoms into one formidable new nation, Spain. However, for years thereafter, it remained a loose confederation of separate kingdoms and jurisdictions, each with different cultural and linguistic traditions.

The new king and queen were eager to spread the Catholic faith. On January 1, 1492, after nearly eight centuries of warfare between Spanish Christians and Moorish Muslims on the Iberian Peninsula, Ferdinand and Isabella declared victory for Catholicism at Granada, the last Muslim stronghold in southern Spain. The monarchs then set about instituting a fifteenth-century version of ethnic cleansing. They gave practicing Muslims and Jews living in Spain and Portugal one choice: convert to Catholicism or leave.

The forced exile of Muslims and Jews was one of many factors that enabled Europe's global explorations at the end of the fifteenth century. Other factors—urbanization, world trade, the rise of centralized nations, advances in knowledge, technology, and firepower—all combined with natural human curiosity, greed, and religious zeal to spur efforts to find alternative routes to the Indies. More immediately, the decision of Chinese rulers to shut off the land routes to Asia in 1453 forced merchants to focus on seaborne options. For these reasons, Europeans set in motion the events that, as one historian has observed, would bind together "four continents, three races, and a great diversity of regional parts."

## The Voyages of Columbus

Born in the Italian seaport of Genoa in 1451, the son of a woolen weaver, Christopher Columbus took to the sea at an early age, teaching himself geography, navigation, and Latin. By the 1480s, he was eager to spread Christianity across the globe and win glory and riches for himself.

The tall, red-haired Columbus spent a decade trying to convince European rulers to finance a western voyage across the Atlantic. England, France, Portugal, and Spain turned him down. Yet he persevered and eventually persuaded Ferdinand and Isabella to fund his voyage. The monarchs agreed to award him a one-tenth share of any riches he gathered; they would keep the rest.

## COLUMBUS'S VOYAGES

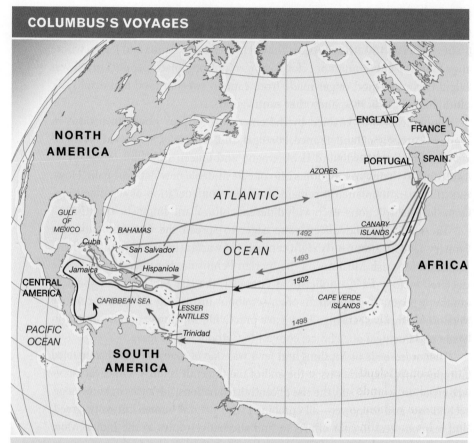

- How many voyages did Columbus make to the Americas?
- What is the origin of the name for the Caribbean Sea?
- What happened to the colony that Columbus left on Hispaniola in 1493?

**CROSSING THE ATLANTIC** On August 3, 1492, Columbus and a crew of ninety men and boys, mostly from Spain but from seven other nations as well, set sail on three tiny ships, the *Santa María*, the *Pinta*, and the *Niña*. They traveled first to Lisbon, Portugal, and then headed west to the Canary Islands, where they spent a month loading supplies and making repairs. On September 6, they headed west across the open sea, hoping desperately to sight the shore of east Asia. By early October, worried sailors rebelled at the "madness" of sailing blindly and forced Columbus to promise that they would turn back if land were not sighted within three days.

Then, on October 12, a sailor on watch atop the masthead yelled, "Tierra! Tierra!" ("Land! Land!"). He had spotted a small island in the Bahamas east of Florida that Columbus named San Salvador (Blessed Savior). Columbus mistakenly assumed that they must be near the Indies, so he called the native people "Indios" and named the surrounding islands the West Indies. At every encounter with the peaceful native people, known as Tainos, his first question, using sign language, was whether they had gold. If they did, the Spaniards seized it; if they did not, the Europeans forced them to search for it.

The Tainos, unable to understand or repel the strange visitors, offered gifts of food, water, spears, and parrots. Columbus described them as "well-built, with good bodies, and handsome features"—brown-skinned, with straight black hair. He marveled that they could "easily be made Christians" and "would make fine servants," boasting that "with fifty men we could subjugate them all and make them do whatever we want." He promised to bring six "natives" back to Spain for "his highnesses." Thus began the typical European bias toward the Indians: the belief that they were inferior peoples worthy of being exploited and enslaved.

**EXPLORING THE CARIBBEAN**  After leaving San Salvador, Columbus, excited by native stories of "rivers of gold" to the west, landed on the north shore of Cuba. He exclaimed that it was the "most beautiful land human eyes have ever beheld."

After a few weeks, Columbus sailed to the island he named Hispaniola ("the Spanish island"), present-day Haiti and the Dominican Republic. He described the island's indigenous people as the "best people in the world," full "of love and without greed." They had no weapons, wore no clothes, and led a simple life, cultivating cassava plants to make bread but spending most of their time relaxing, "seemingly without a care in the world."

Columbus decided that the Indians were "fitted to be ruled and be set to work" generating riches for Spain. He decreed that all Indians over age 14 must bring him at least a thimbleful of gold dust every three months. As it turned out, the quota was often unattainable—there was not as much gold in the Caribbean as Columbus imagined. Nevertheless, those who failed to supply enough gold had their hands cut off, causing many of them to bleed to death. If they fled, they were hunted down by dogs. Huge numbers died from overwork or disease. Others committed suicide. During fifty years of Spanish control, the Indians on Hispaniola virtually disappeared. In their place, the Spanish began importing enslaved Africans.

At the end of 1492, Columbus, still convinced he had reached an outer island of Japan, sailed back to Spain, taking a dozen Tainos as gifts for the king and queen. After receiving a hero's welcome, he promised Ferdinand and Isabella that his discoveries would provide them "as much gold as they need . . . and as many slaves as they ask."

Thanks to the newly invented printing press, news of Columbus's path-breaking voyage spread rapidly across Europe and helped spur a restless desire to explore the world. The Spanish monarchs told Columbus to prepare for a second voyage, instructing him to "treat the Indians very well and lovingly and abstain from doing them any injury." Columbus and his men would repeatedly defy this order.

Spain worked quickly to secure its legal claim to the Western Hemisphere. With the help of the Spanish-born pope, Alexander VI, Spain and Portugal signed the Treaty of Tordesillas (1494). It divided the non-Christian world, giving most of the Western Hemisphere to Spain, with Africa and what would become Brazil granted to Portugal. In practice, this meant that while Spain developed its American empire in the sixteenth century, Portugal provided it with most of its enslaved African laborers.

In 1493, Columbus returned to the New World, crossing the Atlantic with seventeen ships and 1,400 sailors, soldiers, and settlers—all men. Also on board were Catholic priests eager to convert the native peoples to Christianity. Upon his arrival back in Hispaniola, Columbus discovered that the forty men he had left behind had lost their senses, raping women, robbing villages, and, as his son later added, "committing a thousand excesses for which they were mortally hated by the Indians."

**NAMING AMERICA**    Columbus proved to be a much better ship captain than a colonizer and governor. His first business venture in the New World was as a slave trader. When he returned to Spain from his second voyage with hundreds of captive Indians, Queen Isabella, who detested slavery, was horrified. "Who is this Columbus who dares to give out my vassals [Indians] as slaves?"

This incident set in motion a series of investigations into Columbus's behavior. The queen sent a Spanish royal commissioner, Francis Bobadilla, to Hispaniola. The first things he saw were the corpses of six Spanish settlers hanging from a gallows; more colonists were to be hanged the next day. Bobadilla was so shocked that he canceled the executions and announced that he was supplanting Columbus as governor. When Columbus objected, Bobadilla had him jailed for two months before shipping the explorer, now nearly blind and crippled by arthritis, back to Spain in chains in 1500.

To the end of his life, in 1506, Columbus insisted that he had discovered the outlying parts of Asia. By one of history's greatest ironies, this led Europeans to name the New World not for Columbus but for another Italian sailor-explorer, Amerigo Vespucci.

In 1499, with the support of Portugal's monarchy, Vespucci sailed across the Atlantic, landing first at Brazil and then sailing along 3,000 miles of the South American coastline in search of a passage to Asia. In the end, Vespucci decided that South America was so large and so densely populated that it must be a *new* continent. In 1507, a German mapmaker paid tribute to Vespucci's navigational skills by labeling the New World using the feminine Latin variant of the explorer's first name: America.

**PROFESSIONAL EXPLORERS** News of the remarkable voyages of Columbus and Vespucci stimulated more expeditions. The first explorer to sight the North American continent was John Cabot, an Italian sponsored by King Henry VII of England. Cabot's landfall in 1497 at what the king called "the new founde lande," in present-day Canada, gave England the basis for a later claim to *all* of North America. On a return voyage, however, Cabot and his four ships disappeared.

The English were actually unaware that Norsemen ("Vikings") from Scandinavia (Denmark, Norway, Sweden) had been the first Europeans to "discover" and colonize areas of North America. As early as the tenth century, Norsemen had landed on the rocky, fogbound shore of Greenland, a large island off the northeast coast of North America, and established farming settlements that had lasted hundreds of years before disappearing after prolonged cold weather forced them back to Scandinavia.

## RELIGIOUS CONFLICT IN EUROPE

While explorers were crossing the Atlantic, powerful religious conflicts were tearing Europe apart in ways that would shape developments in the Western Hemisphere. When Columbus sailed west in 1492, all of Europe acknowledged the thousand-year-old supremacy of the Roman Catholic Church and its pope in Rome. The pope led a huge religious empire, and the Catholics were eager to spread their faith around the world.

The often brutal efforts of the Spanish to convert native peoples in the Western Hemisphere to **Roman Catholicism** illustrated the murderous intensity with which European Christians embraced religious life in the sixteenth century. Spiritual concerns inspired, comforted, and united them. People fervently believed in heaven and hell, demons and angels, magic and miracles. And they were willing to kill and die for their religious beliefs.

## MARTIN LUTHER

**Martin Luther** A theologian and critic of the Catholic Church, Luther is best remembered for his ninety-five "theses," an incendiary document that served as a catalyst for the Protestant revolution.

The enforced unity of Catholic Europe began to crack on October 31, 1517, when an obscure, thirty-three-year-old German monk who taught at the University of Wittenberg in the German state of Saxony, sent his ninety-five "theses" on the "corrupt" Catholic Church to church officials. Little did Martin Luther (1483–1546) know that his defiant stance and explosive charges would ignite history's fiercest spiritual drama, the **Protestant Reformation**, or that his controversial ideas would forever change the Christian world and plunge Europe into decades of religious strife.

Luther was a spiritual revolutionary who fractured Christianity by undermining the authority of the Catholic Church. He called the pope "the greatest thief and robber that has appeared or can appear on earth" who had subjected the Christian family to levels of "satanic" abuse. Luther especially criticized the widespread sale of *indulgences,* whereby priests would forgive sins in exchange for money. The Catholic Church had made a profitable business out of forgiving sins, using the revenue from indulgences to raise huge armies and build lavish cathedrals. Luther condemned indulgences as a crass form of thievery. He insisted that God alone, through the grace and mercy of Christ, offered salvation; people could not purchase it from church officials. As Luther exclaimed, "By faith alone are you saved!" To him, the Bible was the sole source of Christian truth; believers had no need for the "den of murderers"—Catholic priests, bishops, and popes.

Through this simple but revolutionary doctrine of "Protestantism," Luther sought to revitalize Christianity's original faith and spirituality. The common people, he declared, represented a "priesthood of all believers." Individuals could seek their own salvation. "All Christians are priests," he said; they "have the power to test and judge what is correct or incorrect in matters of faith" by themselves. Luther went on to produce the first Bible in a German translation so that everyone—male or female, rich or poor—could read it.

Luther's rebellion spread quickly across Europe thanks to the circulation of thousands of inexpensive pamphlets, which served as the social media of the time. Without the new printing presses, there may not have been a Protestant Reformation.

Lutheranism began as an intense religious movement, but it soon developed profound social and political implications. By proclaiming that "all" are equal before God, Protestants disrupted traditional notions of wealth, class, and monarchical supremacy. Their desire to practice a faith independent of papal or government interference contributed to the ideal of limited government. By the end of the sixteenth century, King James VI of Scotland grew nervous that his Protestant subjects were plotting to install a "democratic form of government."

**THE CATHOLIC REACTION** What came to be called Lutheranism quickly found enthusiastic followers, especially in the German-speaking states. In Rome, however, Pope Leo X lashed out at Luther's "dangerous doctrines," calling him "a leper with a brain of brass and a nose of iron."

Luther, aware that his life was at stake, fought back, declaring that he was "born to war" and refusing to abide by any papal decrees: "I will recant nothing!" The "die is cast, and I will have no reconciliation with the Pope for all eternity." When the pope expelled Luther from the Catholic Church in 1521 and the Holy Roman emperor sentenced him to death, civil war erupted throughout the German principalities. A powerful prince protected Luther from the church's wrath by hiding him in his castle.

Luther's conflict with the pope plunged Europe into decades of religious warfare during which both sides sought to eliminate dissent by torturing and burning at the stake those called "heretics." A settlement between Lutherans and Catholics did not come until 1555, when the Treaty of Augsburg allowed each German prince to determine the religion of his subjects. For a while, they got away with such dictatorial policies, for most people still deferred to ruling princes. Most of the northern German states, along with Scandinavia, became Lutheran.

# JOHN CALVIN

If Martin Luther was the lightning that sparked the Reformation, John Calvin provided the thunder. Soon after Luther began his revolt against Catholicism, Swiss Protestants also challenged papal authority. In Geneva, a city of 16,000 people, the movement looked to John Calvin (1509–1564), a brilliant French theologian and preacher who had fled from Catholic France to Geneva at age twenty-seven and quickly brought it under the sway of his powerful beliefs.

Calvin deepened and broadened the Reformation that Luther initiated by developing a strict way of life for Protestants to follow. His chief contribution was his emphasis upon humanity's inherent sinfulness and utter helplessness before an awesome and all-powerful God who had predetermined who would be saved and who would be left to eternal damnation, regardless of their behavior.

Calvin and Luther were the twin pillars of early Protestantism, but whereas Luther was a volatile personality who loved controversy and debate, Calvin was a cool, calculating, analytical theorist who sought to create a Protestant absolutism rigidly devoid of all remnants of Catholicism. Under his leadership, Geneva became a theocracy in which believers sought to convince themselves and others that God had chosen them for salvation.

Calvin came to rule Geneva with uncompromising conviction. He summoned the citizenry to swear allegiance to a twenty-one-article confession of religious faith. No citizen could be outside the authority of the church, and Calvin viewed himself as God's appointed judge and jury. No aspect of life in Geneva escaped his strict control. Dancing, card-playing, and theatergoing were outlawed. Censorship was enforced, and informers were recruited to report wrongdoing. Visitors staying at inns had to say a prayer before dining. Everyone was required to attend church and to be in bed by nine o'clock. Even joking was outlawed.

Calvin urged that some thirty "witches" in Geneva be burned, drowned, or hanged for supposedly causing an epidemic. Overall, he had fifty-eight people put to death. Calvin also banished scores of people who fell short of his demanding standards, including members of his extended family. He exiled his sister-in-law for adultery and ordered his stepdaughter jailed for fornication. "I have found it to be true," observed a witty Genevan, "that men who know what is best for society are unable to cope with their families."

**CALVINISM**  For all of its harshness, Calvinism as embodied in Geneva spread like wildfire across France, Scotland, and the Netherlands. It even penetrated Lutheran Germany. Calvinism formed the basis for the German Reformed Church, the Dutch Reformed Church, the Presbyterians in Scotland, and the Huguenots in France, and it prepared the way for many forms of American Protestantism. Like Luther, Calvin argued that Christians did not need popes or kings, archbishops, and bishops to dictate their search for salvation; each congregation should elect its own elders and ministers to guide their worship and nurture their faith.

Over time, Calvin exerted a greater effect upon religious belief and practice in the English colonies than did any other leader of the Reformation. His
emphasis on humankind's essential depravity, his concept of predestination,
his support for the primacy and autonomy of each congregation, and his belief
in the necessity of theocratic government formed the ideological foundation
for Puritan New England.

**THE COUNTER-REFORMATION** The Catholic Church furiously
resisted the emergence of new "protestant" faiths by launching a "Counter-
Reformation" that reaffirmed basic Catholic beliefs while addressing some of
the concerns about priestly abuses raised by Luther, Calvin, and others. In
Spain, the monarchy established an "Inquisition" to root out Protestants and
heretics. In 1534, a Spanish soldier, Ignatius de Loyola, organized the Society
of Jesus, a militant monastic order created to revitalize Catholicism. Its members, the black-robed Jesuits, fanned out across Europe and the Americas as
missionaries and teachers.

Throughout the sixteenth and seventeenth centuries, Catholics and Protestants persecuted, imprisoned, tortured, and killed each other. Every major
international conflict in early modern Europe became, to some extent, a religious holy war between Catholic and Protestant nations.

**THE REFORMATION IN ENGLAND** In England, the Reforma-
tion followed a unique course. The Church of England (the Anglican Church)
emerged through a gradual process of integrating Calvinism with English
Catholicism. In early modern England, the Catholic church and the national
government were united and mutually supportive. The monarchy required
people to attend religious services and to pay taxes to support the church. The
English rulers also supervised the church officials: two archbishops, twenty-six
bishops, and thousands of parish clergy, who were often instructed to preach
sermons in support of government policies. As one English king explained,
"People are governed by the pulpit more than the sword in time of peace."

**KING HENRY VIII** The English Reformation originated because
of purely political reasons. King Henry VIII, who ruled between 1509 and
1547, had won from the pope the title Defender of the Faith for initially refut-
ing Martin Luther's rebellious ideas. But Henry turned against the Catholic
Church over the issue of divorce. His marriage to Catherine of Aragon, his
elder brother's widow and the youngest daughter of the Spanish monarchs Ferdinand and Isabella, had produced a girl, Mary, but no boy. Henry's obsession
for a male heir convinced him that he needed a new wife, and he had grown

smitten with another woman, sharp-witted Anne Boleyn. But first he had to convince the pope to annul, or cancel, his twenty-four-year marriage to Catherine, who rebelled against her husband's plan. She had a powerful ally in her nephew, Charles V, king of Spain and ruler of the Holy Roman Empire, whose armies were in control of the church in Rome.

The pope refused to grant an annulment—in part because Charles V had placed him under arrest to encourage him to make the right decision. In 1533, Henry VIII responded by severing England's nearly 900-year connection with the Catholic Church. The archbishop of Canterbury then granted the annulment, thus freeing Henry to marry his mistress, the pregnant Anne Boleyn. The pope then excommunicated Henry from the Catholic Church, whereupon Parliament passed an Act of Supremacy declaring that the king, not the pope, was head of the Church of England. Henry quickly banned all Catholic "idols," required Bibles to be published in English rather than Latin, and confiscated the vast land holdings of the Catholic Church across England.

In one of history's greatest ironies, Anne Boleyn gave birth not to a male heir but to a daughter named Elizabeth. The disappointed king refused to attend the baby's christening. Instead, he accused Anne of adultery and had her beheaded, and he declared the infant Elizabeth a bastard. (He would marry four more times.) Elizabeth, however, would grow up to be a nimble, cunning, and courageous queen.

**THE REIGN OF ELIZABETH**   In 1547, Henry VIII died and was succeeded by nine-year-old Edward VI, his son by his third wife, Jane Seymour. Edward approved efforts to further "reform" the Church of England. Priests were allowed to marry, church services were conducted in English rather than Latin, and new articles of faith were drafted and published.

When Edward grew gravely ill in 1553, he declared that his cousin, Lady Jane Grey, should succeed him, but nine days after his death, his Catholic half-sister, Mary, led an army that deposed Lady Jane and later ordered her beheaded. The following year, Queen Mary shocked many by marrying Philip, the Holy Roman emperor and king of Spain. With his blessing, she restored Catholic supremacy in England, ordering hundreds of Protestants burned at the stake and others exiled.

"Bloody Mary" died in 1558, and her Protestant half-sister, Henry VIII's daughter Elizabeth, ascended the throne at the age of twenty-five. Over the next forty-five years, despite political turmoil, religious strife, economic crises, and foreign wars, Elizabeth proved to be one of the greatest rulers in history. During her long reign, the Church of England again became Protestant, while retaining much of the tone and texture of Catholicism.

# THE SPANISH EMPIRE

Throughout the sixteenth century, Spain struggled to manage its colonial empire while trying to repress the Protestant Reformation. Between 1500 and 1650, some 450,000 Spaniards, 75 percent of them poor, single, unskilled men, made their way to the Western Hemisphere. During that time, Spain's colonies in the Western Hemisphere shipped some 200 tons of gold and 16,000 tons of silver to Spain. By plundering, conquering, and colonizing the Americas and converting and enslaving its inhabitants, the Spanish planted Christianity in the Western Hemisphere and gained the financial resources to rule the world.

**SPAIN IN THE CARIBBEAN** The Caribbean Sea served as the gateway through which Spain entered the Americas. After establishing a trading post on Hispaniola, the Spanish proceeded to colonize Puerto Rico (1508), Jamaica (1509), and Cuba (1511–1514). Their motives, as one soldier explained, were simple: "To serve God and the king, and also to get rich." As their New World colonies grew more numerous, the monarchy created an administrative structure to govern them and a name to encompass them: New Spain.

## A CLASH OF CULTURES

The often-violent encounters between Spaniards and Native Americans involved more than a clash of cultures. They involved contrasting forms of technological development. The Indians of Mexico used wooden canoes for water transportation, while the Europeans traveled in much larger, heavily armed sailing vessels. The Spanish ships also carried warhorses and fighting dogs, long steel swords, crossbows, firearms, gunpowder, and armor. "The most essential thing in new lands is horses," reported one Spanish soldier. "They instill the greatest fear in the enemy and make the Indians respect the leaders of the army."

**CORTÉS'S CONQUEST** The most dramatic European conquest of a major Indian civilization occurred in Mexico. On February 18, 1519, Hernán Cortés, a Spanish soldier of fortune who went to the New World "to get rich, not to till the soil like a peasant," sold his Cuban lands to buy ships and supplies, then set sail for Mexico.

Cortés's fleet of eleven ships carried nearly 600 soldiers and sailors. Also on board were 200 indigenous Cuban laborers, sixteen warhorses, greyhound fighting dogs, and cannons. The Spanish first stopped on the Yucatan Peninsula, where they defeated a group of Mayans. The vanquished chieftain gave Cortés twenty young women. Cortés distributed them to his captains but kept one of the girls ("La Malinche") for himself and gave her the name of Doña

**Cortés in Mexico** Page from the *Lienzo de Tlaxcala*, a historical narrative from the sixteenth century. The scene, in which Cortés is shown seated on a throne, depicts the arrival of the Spanish in Mexico.

Marina. Malinche spoke Mayan as well as Nahuatl, the language of the Aztecs, with whom she had previously lived. She became Cortés's interpreter—and his mistress; she would later bear the married Cortés a son.

After leaving Yucatan, Cortés and his ships sailed west and landed at a place he named Veracruz ("True Cross"), where they convinced the local Totomacs to join his assault against their hated rivals, the Mexica (Aztecs). To prevent his soldiers, called *conquistadores* (conquerors), from deserting, Cortés had the ships scuttled, sparing only one vessel to carry the expected gold back to Spain.

With his small army and Indian allies, Cortés brashly set out to conquer the extensive Mexica Empire, which extended from central Mexico to what is today Guatemala. The army's nearly 200-mile march through the mountains to the Mexica capital of Tenochtitlán (modern Mexico City) took almost three months.

**SPANISH INVADERS**  As Cortés and his army marched across Mexico, they heard fabulous stories about Tenochtitlán. With some 200,000 inhabitants scattered among twenty neighborhoods, it was one of the largest cities in the world. Laid out in a grid pattern on an island in a shallow lake, divided by long cobblestone avenues, crisscrossed by canals, connected to the mainland by wide causeways, and graced by formidable stone pyramids, the city and its massive buildings seemed impregnable.

Through a combination of threats and deceptions, the Spanish entered Tenochtitlán peacefully. The emperor, Montezuma II, a renowned warrior who had ruled since 1502, mistook Cortés for the exiled god of the wind and sky, Quetzalcoatl, come to reclaim his lands. Montezuma gave the Spaniards a lavish welcome, housing them close to the palace and exchanging gifts of gold and women.

Within a week, however, Cortés executed a palace coup, taking Montezuma hostage while outwardly permitting him to continue to rule. Cortés ordered many religious statues destroyed and coerced Montezuma to end the ritual sacrifices of slaves.

In the spring of 1520, disgruntled Mexica priests orchestrated a rebellion after deciding that Montezuma was a traitor. According to Spanish accounts, the Mexica stoned the emperor to death; more recently, scholars argue that the Spanish did the deed. One account says that they poured molten gold down Montezuma's throat. Whatever the cause of the emperor's death, the Spaniards were forced to retreat from the capital city.

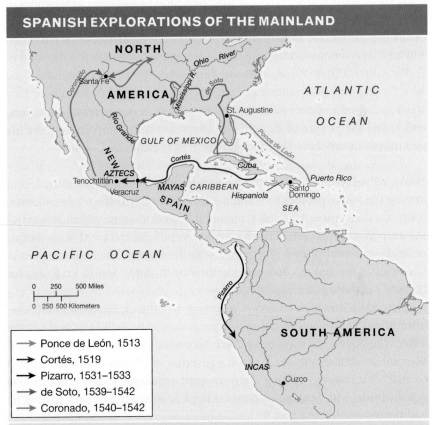

**SPANISH EXPLORATIONS OF THE MAINLAND**

→ Ponce de León, 1513
→ Cortés, 1519
→ Pizarro, 1531–1533
→ de Soto, 1539–1542
→ Coronado, 1540–1542

- What were the Spanish conquistadores' goals for exploring the Americas?
- How did Cortés conquer the Mexica?
- Why did the Spanish first explore North America, and why did they establish St. Augustine, the first European settlement in what would become the United States?

Cortés, however, was undaunted. His many Indian allies remained loyal, and the Spaniards gained reinforcements from Cuba. They then laid siege to Tenochtitlán for eighty-five days, cutting off its access to water and food, and allowing a smallpox epidemic to devastate the inhabitants.

After three months, the siege came to a bloody end in August 1521. The ravages of smallpox and the support of thousands of anti-Mexica Indians help explain how such a small force of Spaniards vanquished a proud nation with millions of people. A conquistador remembered that as he entered the capital city after its surrender, the streets "were so filled with sick and dead people that our men walked over nothing but bodies.

Cortés became the first Governor General of "New Spain" and quickly began replacing the Mexica leaders with Spanish bureaucrats and church officials. He ordered that a grand Catholic cathedral be built from the stones of Montezuma's destroyed palace.

In 1531, Francisco Pizarro mimicked the conquest of Mexico when he led a band of 168 conquistadores and sixty-seven horses down the Pacific coast of South America from Panama toward Peru, where they brutally subdued the Inca Empire and its 5 million people. The Spanish killed thousands of Inca warriors, seized imperial palaces, took royal women as mistresses and wives, and looted the empire of its gold and silver. From Peru, Spain extended its control southward through Chile and north to present-day Colombia.

**NEW SPAIN**  As the sixteenth century unfolded, the Spanish shifted from looting the native peoples to enslaving them. To reward the conquistadores, Spain transferred to America a medieval socioeconomic system known as the *encomienda*, whereby favored soldiers or officials received huge parcels of land—and control over the people who lived there. The Spanish were to Christianize the Indians and provide them with protection in exchange for "tribute"—a share of their goods and labor.

New Spain became a society of extremes: wealthy *encomenderos* and powerful priests at one end of the spectrum, and Indians held in poverty at the other. The Spaniards used brute force to ensure that the Indians accepted their role as serfs. Nuño de Guzman, a governor of a Mexican province, loved to watch his massive fighting dog tear apart rebellious Indians. But he was equally brutal with Spanish colonists. After a Spaniard talked back to him, he had the man nailed to a post by his tongue.

**A CATHOLIC EMPIRE**  The Spanish launched a massive effort to convert the Indians into Catholic servants. During the sixteenth century, hundreds of priests fanned out across New Spain.

Most of the missionaries decided that the Indians could be converted only by force. "Though they seem to be a simple people," a priest declared in 1562, "they are up to all sorts of mischief, and without compulsion, they will never speak the [religious] truth." By the end of the sixteenth century, there were more than 300 monasteries or missions in New Spain, and Catholicism had become a major instrument of Spanish imperialism.

Some officials criticized the forced conversion of Indians and the *encomienda* system. A Catholic priest, Bartolomé de Las Casas, observed with horror the treatment of Indians by Spanish settlers in Hispaniola and Cuba. To ensure obedience, they tortured, burned, and cut off the hands and noses of the native peoples. Las Casas resolved in 1514 to spend the rest of his life aiding the Indians, and he began urging the Spanish to change their approach.

Las Casas spent the next fifty years advocating better treatment for indigenous people, earning the title "Protector of the Indians." He urged that the Indians be converted to Catholicism only through "peaceful and reasonable" means, and he eventually convinced the monarchy and the Catholic Church to issue new rules calling for better treatment of the Indians. Still, the use of "fire and the sword" continued, and angry colonists on Hispaniola banished Las Casas from the island. In 1564, two years before his death, he bleakly predicted that "God will wreak his fury and anger against Spain some day for the unjust wars waged against the Indians."

## THE COLUMBIAN EXCHANGE

The first European contacts with the Western Hemisphere began the **Columbian Exchange**, a worldwide transfer of plants, animals, and diseases, which ultimately worked in favor of the Europeans at the expense of the indigenous peoples.

The plants and animals of the two worlds differed more than the peoples and their ways of life. Europeans had never encountered iguanas, buffaloes, cougars, armadillos, opossums, sloths, tapirs, anacondas, rattlesnakes, catfish, condors, or hummingbirds. Nor had the Native Americans seen the horses, cattle, pigs, sheep, goats, chickens, and rats that soon flooded the Americas.

**THE EXCHANGE OF PLANTS AND FOODS** The exchange of plant life between the Western Hemisphere and Europe/Africa transformed the diets of both regions. Before Columbus's voyage, Europeans had no knowledge of maize (corn), potatoes (sweet and white), or many kinds of beans (snap, kidney, lima). Other Western Hemisphere food plants included peanuts, squash, peppers, tomatoes, pumpkins, pineapples, avocados, cacao (the source of chocolate), and chicle (for chewing gum). Europeans in turn introduced rice, wheat, barley, oats, grapevines, and sugarcane to the Americas. The new crops changed diets and spurred a dramatic increase in the European population, which in turn helped provide the restless, adventurous young people who would colonize the New World.

AN EXCHANGE OF DISEASES The most significant aspect of the Columbian Exchange was, by far, the transmission of **infectious diseases**. During the three centuries after Columbus's first voyage, Europeans and enslaved Africans brought deadly diseases that Native Americans had never encountered: smallpox, typhus, malaria, mumps, chickenpox, and measles. The results were catastrophic. By 1568, just seventy-five years after Columbus's first voyage, infectious diseases had killed 80 to 90 percent of the Indian population—the greatest loss of human life in history.

Smallpox was an especially ghastly killer. In central Mexico alone, some 8 million people, perhaps a third of the entire Indian population, died of smallpox within a decade of the arrival of the Spanish. Unable to explain or cure the diseases, Native American chieftains and religious leaders often lost their stature—and their lives—as they were usually the first to meet the Spanish and thus were the first infected. As a consequence of losing their leaders, the indigenous peoples were less capable of resisting the European invaders. Many Europeans, however, interpreted such epidemics as diseases sent by God to punish those who resisted conversion to Christianity.

# THE SPANISH IN NORTH AMERICA

Throughout the sixteenth century, no European power other than Spain held more than a brief foothold in the Americas. Spanish explorers had not only arrived first but had stumbled onto those regions that would produce the quickest profits. While France and England were preoccupied with political disputes and religious conflict at home, Catholic Spain had forged an authoritarian national and religious unity that enabled it to dominate Europe as well as the New World.

HISPANIC AMERICA For most of the colonial period, much of what is now the United States was governed by Spain. Spanish culture etched a lasting imprint upon America's future ways of life. Hispanic place-names—San Francisco, Santa Barbara, Los Angeles, San Diego, Santa Fe, San Antonio,

Pensacola, St. Augustine—survive to this day, as do Hispanic influences in art, architecture, literature, music, law, and food.

## St. Augustine

In 1513, Juan Ponce de León, then governor of Puerto Rico, made the earliest known European exploration of Florida. Meanwhile, Spanish explorers sailed along the Gulf coast from Florida to Mexico, scouted the Atlantic coast all the way to Canada, and established a short-lived colony on the Carolina coast.

In 1539, Hernando de Soto and 600 conquistadores landed on the western shore of La Florida (Land of Flowers) and soon set out on horseback to search for riches. Instead of gold, they found "great fields of corn, beans and squash . . . as far as the eye could see." De Soto, who a companion said was "fond of the sport of killing Indians," led the expedition north as far as western North Carolina, and then moved westward across Tennessee, Georgia, and Alabama before happening upon the Mississippi River near what today is Memphis. After crossing the Mississippi, the conquistadores went up the Arkansas River, looting and destroying Indian villages along the way. In the spring of 1542, de Soto died near Natchez, Mississippi; the next year, the survivors among his party floated down the Mississippi River, and 311 of the original adventurers made their way to Spanish Mexico.

In 1565, in response to French efforts to colonize north Florida, the Spanish king dispatched Pedro Menendez de Aviles with a ragtag group of 1,500 soldiers and colonists to found an outpost on the Florida coast. St. Augustine became the first permanent European settlement in the present-day United States. The Spanish settled St. Augustine in response to French efforts to colonize north Florida. In the 1560s, French Protestant refugees (called Huguenots) established France's first American colonies, one on the coast of what became South Carolina and the other in Florida. The settlements did not last long.

At dawn on September 20, 1565, some 500 Spanish soldiers from St. Augustine assaulted Fort Caroline, the French Huguenot colony in northeastern Florida, and hanged all the men over age fifteen. Only women, girls, and young boys were spared. The Spanish commander notified his Catholic king that he had killed all the French he "had found [in Fort Caroline] because . . . they were scattering the odious Lutheran doctrine in these Provinces." Later, when survivors from a shipwrecked French fleet washed ashore on Florida beaches after a hurricane, the Spanish commander told them they must abandon Protestantism and swear their allegiance to Catholicism. When they refused, his soldiers killed 245 of them.

**THE SPANISH SOUTHWEST** The Spanish eventually established other permanent settlements in what are now New Mexico, Texas, and California. From the outset, however, the settlements were sparsely populated, inadequately supplied, dreadfully poor, and consistently neglected by Spanish colonial officials.

In New Spain, civil liberties and notions of equal treatment were nonexistent; people were expected to follow orders. There was no freedom of speech, religion, or movement; no local elections; no real self-government. The military officers, bureaucrats, wealthy landowners, and priests appointed by the king regulated every detail of colonial life. Settlers could not travel within the colonies without official permission.

New Mexico  The land that would later be called **New Mexico** was the first center of Catholic missionary activity in the American Southwest. In 1595, Juan de Oñate, the rich son of a Spanish family in Mexico, received a land grant for *El Norte*, the mostly desert territory north of Mexico above the Rio Grande—Texas, New Mexico, Arizona, California, and parts of Colorado. Over the next three years, he recruited colonists willing to move north with him: soldier-settlers and Mexican Indians and *mestizos* (the offspring of Spanish and indigenous parents).

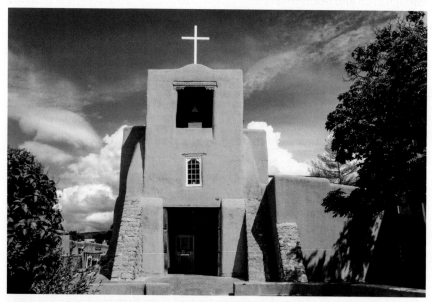

**Missionaries in the New World** A Spanish mission in New Mexico, established to spread the Catholic faith among the indigenous peoples.

In 1598, the caravan of 250 colonists, including women, children, horses, goats, sheep, and 7,000 cattle, began moving north from the mountains above Mexico City across the harsh desert landscape. "O God! What a lonely land!" one traveler wrote to relatives in Mexico City.

After walking more than 800 miles in seven months, they established the colony of New Mexico, the farthest outpost of New Spain. It took wagon trains eighteen months to travel to Mexico City and back. The Spanish labeled the local Indians "Pueblos" (a Spanish word meaning village) for the city-like aspect of their terraced, multistoried buildings, sometimes chiseled into the steep walls of cliffs.

Hopis, Zunis, and other Pueblo peoples sought peace rather than war, yet they were often raided by Apaches (from a Pueblo word meaning "enemy"). "Their government," Oñate noted, "is one of complete freedom, for although they have chieftains, they obey them badly and in few matters."

The goals of Spanish colonialism were to find gold, silver, and other valuable commodities while forcing the Native Americans to adopt the Spanish religion and way of life. Oñate, New Mexico's first governor, told the Pueblos that if they embraced Catholicism and followed his orders, they would receive "an eternal life of great bliss" instead of "cruel and everlasting torment."

There was, however, little gold or silver in New Mexico. Nor was there enough corn and beans to feed the Spanish invaders, who had to be resupplied by caravans traveling for months from Mexico City. Eventually Oñate forced the Indians to pay tributes (taxes) to the Spanish authorities in the form of a yard of cloth and a bushel of corn each year.

**CATHOLIC MISSIONS**  Once it became evident that New Mexico had little gold, the Spanish focused on religious conversion. Priests forced Indians to build and support Catholic missions and to work in the fields they had once owned. They also performed personal tasks for the priests and soldiers— cooking, cleaning, even sexual favors. Whips were used to herd the Indians to church services and to punish them for not working hard enough. A French visitor reported that it "reminded us of a . . . West Indian [slave] colony."

Some Indians welcomed the Spanish as "powerful witches" capable of easing their burdens. Others tried to use the European invaders as allies against rival Indian groups. Still others rebelled. Before the end of New Mexico's first year of Spanish rule, in December 1598, the Acoma Pueblo revolted, killing eleven soldiers and two servants.

Oñate's response was even more brutal. Over three days, Spanish soldiers destroyed the entire pueblo, demolishing buildings and killing 500 Pueblo men and 300 women and children. Survivors were enslaved, and children were separated from their parents and moved into a Catholic mission, where, Oñate remarked, "they may attain the knowledge of God and the salvation of their souls."

**THE MESTIZO FACTOR**   Few Spanish women journeyed to New Spain in the sixteenth century. Those who did had to be married and accompanied by a husband. As a result, there were so few Spanish women in North America that the government encouraged soldiers and settlers to marry Native Americans and did not discriminate against the children (*mestizos*) of the mixed marriages. By the eighteenth century, mestizos were a majority in Mexico and New Mexico. Such widespread interbreeding and intermarriage led the Spanish to adopt a more inclusive social outlook toward the Indians than the English later did in their colonies along the Atlantic coast. Since most colonial officials were mestizo themselves, they were less likely to belittle or abuse the Indians. At the same time, many Native Americans falsely claimed to be mestizo as a means of improving their legal status and avoiding having to pay annual tribute.

**Smallpox**   Mexica victims of the 1538 smallpox epidemic are covered in shrouds (center) as two others lie dying (at right).

**THE PUEBLO REVOLT** In 1608, the Spanish government decided to turn New Mexico into a royal province and moved its capital to Santa Fe ("Holy Faith" in Spanish). It became the first permanent seat of government in the present-day United States. By 1630, there were fifty Catholic churches and monasteries in New Mexico as well as some 3,000 Spaniards. Roman Catholic missionaries in New Mexico claimed that 86,000 Pueblos had embraced Christianity during the seventeenth century.

In fact, however, resentment among the Indians increased as the Spanish stripped them of their ancestral ways of life. "The heathen," reported a Spanish soldier, "have conceived a mortal hatred for our holy faith and enmity [hatred] for the Spanish nation."

In 1680, a charismatic Indian spiritual leader named Popé (meaning "Ripe Plantings") organized a massive rebellion of warriors from nineteen villages. The Indians burned Catholic churches; tortured, mutilated, and executed 21 priests and 400 Spanish settlers; destroyed all relics of Christianity; and forced the 2,400 survivors to flee. The entire province of New Mexico was again in Indian hands, and the Spanish governor reported that the Pueblos "are very happy without religion or Spaniards."

The Pueblo Revolt was the greatest defeat Indians ever inflicted on European efforts to conquer the New World. It took twelve years and four military assaults for the Spanish to reestablish control over New Mexico.

## Horses and the Great Plains

Another major consequence of the Pueblo Revolt was the opportunity it gave Indian rebels to acquire Spanish horses. (Spanish authorities had made it illegal for Indians to ride or own horses.) The Pueblos established a thriving horse trade with other tribes. By 1690, horses were in Texas, and soon they spread across the Great Plains.

Before the arrival of horses, Indians had hunted on foot and used dogs as their beasts of burden. Dogs are carnivores, however, and it was difficult to find enough meat to feed them. The vast grasslands of the Great Plains were the perfect environment for horses, since the prairies offered plenty of forage.

With horses, the Indians in the Great Plains gained a new source of mobility and power. Horses could haul up to seven times as much weight as dogs; their speed and endurance made the Indians much more effective hunters and warriors. Horses grew so valuable that they became a form of Indian currency and a sign of wealth and prestige. On the Great Plains, a warrior's status reflected the number of trained horses he owned. The more horses, the more wives he could support and the more buffalo robes he could exchange for more horses.

**Plains Indians** The horse-stealing raid depicted in this hide painting demonstrates the essential role horses played in plains life.

Horses gave the Indians on the Great Plains a new source of mobility and power. Horses could haul up to seven times as much weight as dogs; their speed and endurance made the Indians much more effective hunters and warriors. Horses grew so valuable that they became a form of Indian currency and a sign of wealth and prestige. On the Great Plains, a warrior's status reflected the number of horses he owned. The more horses, the more wives he could support and the more buffalo robes he could exchange for more horses.

By the late seventeenth century, the Indians were fighting the Spaniards on more equal terms. This helps explain why the Indians of the Southwest and Texas, unlike the Indians in Mexico, were able to sustain their cultures for the next 300 years. On horseback, they were among the most fearsome fighters in the world.

**BUFFALO HUNTING** The Arapaho, Cheyenne, Comanche, Kiowa, and Sioux reinvented themselves as horse-centered cultures. They left their traditional woodland villages and became nomadic buffalo hunters.

A bull buffalo could weigh more than a ton and stand five feet tall at the shoulder. Indians used virtually every part of the buffalo: meat for food; hides for clothing, shoes, bedding, and shelter; muscles and tendons for thread and bowstrings; intestines for containers; bones for tools; horns for eating utensils; hair for headdresses; and dung for fuel. They used tongues for hair brushes and tails for fly swatters. One scholar has referred to the buffalo as the "tribal department store."

Women and girls butchered and dried the buffalo meat and tanned the hides. As the value of the hides grew, Indian hunters began practicing polygamy, because more wives could process more buffalo carcasses. The rising value of wives eventually led Plains Indians to raid other tribes in search of brides.

The introduction of horses on the Great Plains was a mixed blessing; they brought prosperity and mobility but also triggered more conflicts among the Plains Indians. Over time, the Indians on horseback eventually killed more buffaloes than the herds could replace. Further, horses competed with the buffaloes for food, often depleting the prairie grass. As horse-centered culture enabled Indians to travel greater distances and encounter more people, infectious diseases spread more widely. Yet horses overall brought a better quality of life. By 1800, a white trader in Texas would observe that "this is a delightful country, and were it not for perpetual wars, the natives might be the happiest people on earth."

## THE SPANISH EMPIRE IN DECLINE

During the one and a half centuries after 1492, the Spanish developed the most extensive empire the world had ever known. It spanned southern Europe and the Netherlands, much of the Western Hemisphere, and parts of Asia.

Yet the Spanish rulers overreached. The religious wars of the sixteenth and seventeenth centuries killed millions, created intense anti-Spanish feelings among the English and Dutch, and eventually helped bankrupt the Spanish government. At the same time, the Spanish Empire grew so vast that its size and complexity overtaxed the government's resources.

Spain's colonial system was mostly disastrous for the peoples of Africa and the Americas. Spanish explorers, conquistadores, and priests imposed Catholicism on the native peoples, as well as a cruel system of economic exploitation and dependence. As Bartolomé de Las Casas concluded, "The Spaniards have shown not the slightest consideration for these people, treating them (and I speak from first-hand experience, having been there from the outset) . . . as piles of dung in the middle of the road. They have had as little concern for their souls as for their bodies." In the end, the lust for empire ("God, Glory, and Gold") brought decadence and decline to Spain and much of Europe.

# Challenges to the Spanish Empire

Catholic Spain's conquests in the Western Hemisphere spurred Portugal, France, England, and the Netherlands (Holland) to begin their own explorations and exploitations of the New World.

The French were the first to pose a serious threat. Spanish treasure ships sailing home from Mexico, Peru, and the Caribbean offered tempting targets for French pirates. At the same time, the French began explorations in North America. In 1524, the French king sent Italian Giovanni da Verrazano across the Atlantic. Upon sighting land (probably at Cape Fear, North Carolina), Verrazano ranged along the coast as far north as Maine. On a second voyage, in 1528, he was killed by Caribbean Indians.

**NEW FRANCE**  Unlike the Verrazano voyages, those of Jacques Cartier, beginning in the next decade, led to the first French effort at colonization in North America. During three voyages, Cartier ventured up the St. Lawrence River, which today is the boundary between Canada and New York. Twice he got as far as present-day Montreal, and twice he wintered at Quebec, near which a short-lived French colony appeared in 1541–1542.

France after midcentury, however, plunged into religious civil wars, and the colonization of Canada had to await the arrival of Samuel de Champlain, "the Father of New France," after 1600. Over thirty-seven years, Champlain would lead twenty-seven expeditions from France to Canada—and never lose a ship.

**THE DUTCH REVOLT**  From the mid-1500s, greater threats to Spanish power in the New World arose from the Dutch and the English. In 1566, the Netherlands included seventeen provinces. The fragmented nation had passed by inheritance to the Spanish king in 1555, but the Dutch soon began a series of rebellions against Spanish Catholic rule.

A long, bloody struggle ensued in which Queen Elizabeth aided the Dutch, sending some 8,000 English soldiers to support their efforts. The Dutch revolt, as much a civil war as a war for national independence, was a series of different uprisings in different provinces at different times. Each province had its own institutions, laws, and rights. Although seven provinces joined together to form the Dutch Republic, the Spanish did not officially recognize the independence of the entire Netherlands until 1648.

**THE DEFEAT OF THE ARMADA**  Almost from the beginning of the Protestant revolt in the Netherlands, the Dutch captured Spanish treasure ships in the Atlantic and carried on illegal trade with Spain's colonies. While

## ENGLISH, FRENCH, AND DUTCH EXPLORATIONS

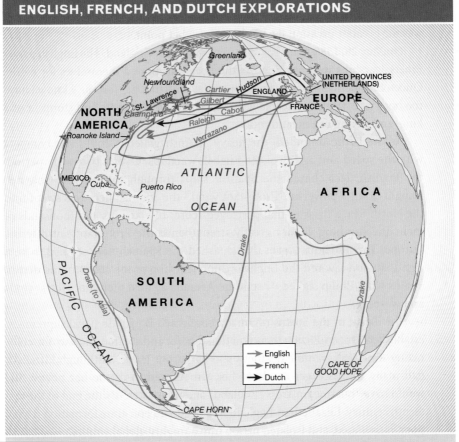

- Who were the first European explorers to rival Spanish dominance in the New World, and why did they cross the Atlantic?
- Why was the defeat of the Spanish Armada important to the history of English exploration?
- What was the significance of the voyages of Gilbert and Raleigh?

England's Queen Elizabeth steered a tortuous course to avoid open war with Spain, she desperately sought additional resources to defend her island nation. She encouraged English privateers such as Sir Francis Drake to attack Spanish ships and their coastal colonies in America, leading the Spanish to call her the "pirate queen."

English raids on Spanish ships and settlements continued for some twenty years before open war erupted between the two nations. Philip II, the king of Spain who was Elizabeth's brother-in-law and fiercest opponent, finally had enough and began plotting an invasion of England. To do so, he assembled the massive **Spanish Armada**: 132 warships, 8,000 sailors, and 18,000 soldiers. It was the greatest invasion fleet in history to that point.

On May 28, 1588, the Armada began sailing for England. The English navy's ninety warships were waiting. As the fleets positioned themselves for battle, Queen Elizabeth donned a silver breastplate and told her forces, "I know I have the body of a weak and feeble woman, but I have the heart and stomach of a king, and a King of England too."

As the battle unfolded, the heavy Spanish galleons could not compete with the speed and agility of the English warships. Over a two-week period, the English fleet chased the Spanish ships through the English Channel. Caught up in a powerful "Protestant wind," the Spanish fleet was swept into the North Sea, a disaster that destroyed scores of warships and thousands of men. The stunning victory greatly strengthened the Protestant cause across Europe. The ferocious storm that smashed the Spanish fleet seemed to be a sign that God favored the English. Upon learning of the catastrophic defeat, Spain's King Philip sighed, "I sent the Armada against men, not God's winds and waves."

The defeat of the Spanish Armada confirmed England's naval supremacy, established Queen Elizabeth as a national hero, and cleared the way for colonizing America's "remote heathens and barbarous lands." Although Elizabeth had many suitors eager to marry her, she refused to divide her power. She would have "but one mistress [England] and no master." By the end of the sixteenth century, Elizabethan England had begun an epic transformation from a poor, humiliated, and isolated nation into a mighty global empire.

## ENGLISH EXPLORATION OF AMERICA

English efforts to colonize America began a few years before the battle with the Spanish Armada. In 1584, Queen Elizabeth asked Sir Walter Raleigh to organize a colonizing mission on the North American coast. His expedition discovered the Outer Banks of North Carolina and landed at Roanoke Island. Raleigh named the area Virginia, in honor of Elizabeth, the "Virgin Queen."

After several false starts, Raleigh in 1587 sponsored another expedition of about 100 colonists, including 26 women and children, led by Governor John White. White spent a month helping launch the settlement on Roanoke Island and then returned to England for supplies, leaving behind his daughter Elinor and his granddaughter Virginia Dare, the first English child born in the Americas.

**The English in Virginia**  The arrival of English explorers on the Outer Banks, with Roanoke Island at left.

White's journey back to Virginia was delayed because of the naval war with Spain. When he finally returned, in 1590, the Roanoke colony had been abandoned and pillaged. On a post at the entrance to the village, someone had carved the word "CROATOAN," leading White to conclude that the settlers had set out for the island of that name some fifty miles south, where friendly Indians lived.

The English never found the "lost colonists." They may have been killed by Indians or Spaniards. The most recent evidence indicates that the "Lost Colony" suffered from a horrible drought that prevented the settlers from growing enough food to survive. While some may have gone south, most went north, to the southern shores of Chesapeake Bay, where they lived for years until Indians killed them.

Whatever the fate of the lost colonists, there were no English settlements in North America when Queen Elizabeth died in 1603. The Spanish controlled the only colonial outposts on the continent. This was about to change, however. Inspired by the success of the Spanish in exploiting the New World, the English—as well as the French and Dutch—would soon develop colonial empires of their own.

# CHAPTER REVIEW

## SUMMARY

- **Native American Societies**   Hunter-gatherers came across the Bering Strait by foot and settled the length and breadth of the Americas, forming groups with diverse cultures, languages, and lifestyles. Global warming enabled an agricultural revolution that allowed the hunter-gatherers to settle and build empires, such as that of the *Mexica*, whose *Aztec Empire* included subjugated peoples and a vast system of trade and tribute. Some North American peoples developed an elaborate continental trading network and impressive cities like *Cahokia*; their *burial mounds* reveal a complex and stratified social organization. The *Eastern Woodlands peoples* that the Europeans would first encounter included both patriarchal and matriarchal societies as well as extensive language-based alliances. Warfare was an important cultural component, leading to shifting rivalries and alliances among tribes and with European settlers.

- **Age of Exploration**   By the 1490s, Europeans were experiencing a renewed curiosity about the larger world. Warfare, plagues, and famine undermined the agricultural feudal system in Europe, and in its place arose a middle class that monarchs could tax. Powerful new nations replaced the estates and cities ruled by princes. Scientific and technological advances led to the creation of better maps and navigation techniques, as well as new weapons and ships. Navies became the critical component of global trade and world power. Two motives drove the Spanish efforts to colonize the New World: the conversion of Indians to *Roman Catholicism* and a lust for gold and silver. The rivalries of the *Protestant Reformation* in Europe shaped the course of conquest in the Americas.

- **Conquering and Colonizing the Americas**   Spanish *conquistadores,* such as Hernán Cortés, exploited their advantages in military technology, including steel, gunpowder, and domesticated animals, such as the horse, to conquer the powerful Aztec and Inca Empires. European diseases, first introduced to the New World by Columbus, did even more to ensure Spanish victories. The Spanish *encomienda* system demanded goods and labor from their new subjects. As the Indian population declined, the Portuguese and Spanish began to import enslaved Africans into the Americas.

- **Columbian Exchange**   Contact between the Old World and the New resulted in the *Columbian Exchange*, sometimes called the great biological exchange. Crops native to the New World such as *maize*, beans, and potatoes became staples in Europe, and native peoples incorporated into their culture such Eurasian animals as the horse and pig. But the invaders also carried *infectious diseases* that set off pandemics of smallpox, plague, and other illnesses to which Indians had no immunity. The Americas were depopulated and cultures destroyed.

- **Spanish Legacy**    Spain left a lasting legacy from California to Florida. Spanish horses eventually transformed Indian life on the plains, and Catholic missionaries contributed to the destruction of the old ways of life by exterminating "heathen" beliefs in the Southwest, a practice that led to open rebellion in *New Mexico* in 1598 and 1680. Spain's rival European nation-states began competing for gold and glory in the New World. England's defeat of the *Spanish Armada* cleared the path for English dominance in North America.

## CHRONOLOGY

| | |
|---|---|
| **by 22,000 B.C.E.** | Humans have migrated to the Americas |
| **5000 B.C.E.** | The agricultural revolution begins in Mexico |
| **600–1300 C.E.** | The city of Cahokia flourishes in North America |
| **1325** | The Mexica (Aztec) Empire is founded in Central Mexico |
| **1492** | Columbus makes his first voyage of discovery to the Americas |
| **1503** | Spaniards bring the first African slaves to the Americas |
| **1517** | Martin Luther launches the Protestant Reformation |
| **1519** | Cortés begins the Spanish conquest of Mexico |
| **1531** | Pizarro subdues the Inca Empire in South America for Spain |
| **1565** | Spaniards build settlement at St. Augustine, the first permanent European outpost in the present-day United States |
| **1584–1587** | Raleigh's Roanoke Island venture |
| **1588** | The English navy defeats the Spanish Armada |
| **1680** | Pueblo Revolt |

## KEY TERMS

maize p. 7

Mexica p. 8

Aztec Empire p. 8

burial mounds p. 12

Cahokia p. 13

Eastern Woodlands peoples p. 13

Roman Catholicism p. 21

Protestant Reformation p. 22

conquistadores p. 28

*encomienda* p. 30

Columbian Exchange p. 31

infectious diseases p. 32

New Mexico p. 34

Spanish Armada p. 42

 INQUIZITIVE

Go to InQuizitive to see what you've learned—and learn what you've missed—with personalized feedback along the way.

# 2 England's Colonies

**"Ould Virginia"** As one of the earliest explorers and settlers of the Jamestown colony, John Smith put his intimate knowledge of the region to use by creating this seventeenth-century map of Virginia. In the upper right-hand corner is a Susquehannock warrior, whom Smith called a "G[i]ant-like people."

For thousands of seekers and adventurers, America in the seventeenth century was a vast unknown land of new beginnings and new opportunities. The English settlers who poured into coastal America and the Caribbean islands found not a "virgin land" of uninhabited wilderness but a developed region populated by Native Americans. As was true in New Spain and New France, European diseases such as smallpox overwhelmed the Indians and wiped out whole societies. William Bradford of the Plymouth colony in Massachusetts reported that the Indians "fell sick of the smallpox, and died most miserably . . . like rotten sheep."

Native Americans dealt with Europeans in different ways. Many resisted, others retreated, and still others developed thriving trade relationships with the newcomers. In some areas, land-hungry colonists quickly displaced or decimated the Indians. In others, Indians found ways to live in cooperation with English settlers—if they were willing to adopt the English way of life.

After creating the Virginia, Maryland, and New England colonies, the English would go on to conquer Dutch-controlled New Netherland, settle Carolina, and eventually establish the rest of the thirteen original American mainland colonies. The diverse English colonies had one thing in common: To one extent or another, they all took part in the enslavement of other peoples, either Native Americans or Africans or both. Slavery, common throughout the world in the seventeenth and eighteenth centuries, enriched a few, corrupted many, and compromised the American dream of equal opportunity for all.

## focus questions

**1.** What motivated English monarchs and investors to establish American colonies?

**2.** What were the characteristics of the English colonies in the Chesapeake region, the Carolinas, the middle colonies—Pennsylvania, New York, New Jersey, and Delaware—and New England prior to 1700?

**3.** In what ways did the English colonists and Native Americans adapt to each other's presence?

**4.** What role did indentured servants and the development of slavery play in colonial America?

**5.** How did the English colonies become the most populous and powerful region in North America by 1700?

# THE ENGLISH BACKGROUND

Over the centuries, the island nation of England had developed political practices and governing principles similar to those on the continent of Europe—but with key differences. European societies were tightly controlled hierarchies. From birth, people learned their place in the social order. Commoners bowed to priests, priests bowed to bishops, peasants pledged their loyalty to landowners, and nobles knelt before the monarchs, who claimed God had given them absolute power to rule over their domain.

Since the thirteenth century, however, English monarchs had *shared* power with the nobility and with a lesser aristocracy, the *gentry*. England's tradition of parliamentary monarchy began with the Magna Carta (Great Charter) of 1215, a statement of fundamental rights and liberties that nobles forced the king to approve. The Magna Carta established that England would be a nation ruled by laws. Everyone was equal before the law, and no one was above it.

The people's representatives formed the national legislature known as Parliament, which comprised the hereditary and appointed members of the House of Lords and the elected members of the House of Commons. The most important power allocated to Parliament was the authority to impose taxes. By controlling tax revenue, the legislature exercised leverage over the monarchy.

# RELIGIOUS CONFLICT AND WAR

When Queen Elizabeth, who never married, died in 1603, her cousin, James VI of Scotland, became King James I of England. He called his joint kingdom Great Britain. While Elizabeth had ruled through constitutional authority, James claimed to govern by "divine right," which meant he answered only to God.

James I confronted a divided Church of England, with the reform-minded **Puritans** in one camp and the Anglican establishment, headed by the archbishop and bishops, in the other. In seventeenth-century England, those who criticized the Anglican Church were called *Dissenters*.

The Puritans believed that the Church of England needed further "purifying." All "papist" (Roman Catholic) rituals must be eliminated. No use of holy water, candles, or incense. No "Devil's bagpipes" (pipe organs). No priestly robes (then called vestments). No lavish cathedrals, stained glass windows, or statues of Jesus. They even sought to ban the use of the term *priest*.

The Puritans wanted to simplify religion to its most basic elements: people worshipping God in plain, self-governing congregations without the formal trappings of Catholic and Anglican ceremonies. They had hoped the new king would support their efforts, but James I, who had been baptized in the Catholic faith, embraced the Anglican Church to avoid a civil war and sought to banish the Puritans from England.

Some Puritans decided that the Church of England was so corrupt and corrupting that it could not be reformed, so they created their own separate congregations, thus earning the name *Separatists*, derived in part from Paul's biblical command to "come out from among them, and be ye separate." Such rebelliousness infuriated the leaders of the Church of England, who required people by law to attend Anglican church services.

During the late sixteenth century, the Separatists (also called *Nonconformists*) were "hunted and persecuted on every side." Many left England, and some, who would eventually be known as Pilgrims, decided to sail for America. James's son, Charles I, succeeded

**The Execution of Charles I** Flemish artist John Weesop witnessed the king's execution and painted this gruesome scene from memory. He was so disgusted by "a country where they cut off their king's head" that he refused to visit England again.

his father in 1625 and proved to be an even more stubborn defender of absolute royal power. He raised taxes without consulting Parliament, harassed the Puritans, and actually disbanded Parliament from 1629 to 1640.

The monarchy went too far, however, when it forced Anglican forms of worship on Presbyterian Scots. In 1638, Scotland rose in revolt, and in 1640, Charles, desperate to save his skin, revived Parliament, ordering its members to raise taxes for the defense of his kingdom. Parliament, led by militant Puritans, refused.

In 1642, when the king tried to arrest five members of Parliament, a civil war erupted in England between Royalists and Parliamentarians, leading many New England Puritans to return home to fight against the Royalist army. In 1646, parliamentary forces led by Puritan Oliver Cromwell captured Charles and, in a public trial, convicted him of high treason and contempt of Parliament, labeling him a "tyrant, traitor, murderer, and public enemy." He was beheaded in 1649. As it turned out, however, the Puritans had killed a king but not slain the monarchy.

Cromwell ruled like a military dictator, calling himself Lord Protector. He outlawed Roman Catholics and Anglicans. Many Anglican Royalists, called *Cavaliers*, escaped by sailing to Virginia. After Cromwell's death in 1658, the army allowed new elections for Parliament and in 1660 supported the Restoration of the monarchy under Charles II, eldest son of the executed king.

Unlike his father, King Charles II agreed to rule jointly with Parliament. His younger brother, the Duke of York (who became King James II in 1685), was more rigid. James openly embraced Catholicism, murdered or imprisoned political opponents, and defied Parliament.

The English tolerated James II's rule so long as they expected one of his Protestant daughters, Mary or Anne, to succeed him. In 1688, however, the birth of a royal son who would be raised Roman Catholic stirred a revolt. Political, religious, and military leaders urged the king's daughter Mary and her Protestant husband, William III of Orange (the ruling Dutch prince), to oust her father and assume the English throne as joint monarchs. A month after William landed in England with a huge army, King James II fled to France.

Amid this dramatic transfer of power, which became known as the Glorious Revolution, Parliament reasserted its right to counterbalance the authority of the monarchy. Kings and queens could no longer suspend Parliament, create armies, or impose taxes without Parliament's consent. The monarchy would henceforth derive its power not from God ("divine right") but from the people through their representatives in Parliament.

## AMERICAN COLONIES

**PEOPLE AND PROFITS** During these eventful years of the seventeenth century, all but one of England's North American colonies—Georgia—were founded. From the outset, English colonization differed in important ways from the Spanish pattern, in which the government regulated all aspects of colonial life.

The monarchy treated its original American colonies much like it dealt with neighboring Ireland. The English had brutally conquered the Irish during the reign of Queen Elizabeth and thereafter extended their control over Catholic Ireland through the "planting" of Protestant settlements in Ireland called *plantations*. By confiscating Irish lands and repopulating them with 120,000 Protestants, the government sought to reduce the influence of Roman Catholicism and smother any rebellious Irish nationalism.

English soldiers and colonizers inflicted a variety of cruelties on the Irish, whom they regarded as every bit as "savage" and "barbarous" as the Indians of North America. In time, the English would impose their rule and religion upon the Native Americans.

England envied the riches taken from the New World by Spain, especially the enormous amounts of gold and silver. Much of the wealth and lands the Spanish accumulated in the Americas, however, became the property of the monarchs who funded the conquistadores. In contrast, English colonization in the Americas was led by churches and companies: those seeking freedom from religious persecution, both Protestants and Catholics, and those seeking land and wealth.

Planting colonies in America was an expensive undertaking. Investors banded together to buy shares in what were called **joint-stock companies**. That way, large amounts of money could be raised and, if a colony failed, no single investor would suffer the entire loss. If a colony succeeded, the investors would share the profits based on the amount of stock (shares) they owned. The joint-stock companies represented the most important organizational innovation of the Age of Exploration and provided the first instruments of English colonization in America.

**SELF-SUSTAINING COLONIES**   The English settlements in America were much more compact than those in New Spain, and the native peoples along the Atlantic coast were less numerous and less wealthy than the Mexica and the Incas.

England's colonies were also much more populous than the Spanish, French, and Dutch colonies. In 1660, for example, there were 58,000 colonists in New England, Virginia, and Maryland, compared with 3,000 in New France and 5,000 in Dutch New Netherland. By 1750, English colonists (male and female) still outnumbered the French (mostly male) nearly twenty to one, while in the northernmost areas of New Spain—the lands that became Texas, New Mexico, Arizona, Florida, and California—there were only 20,000 Spaniards.

The English government and individual investors had two primary goals for their colonies: (1) to provide valuable raw materials, such as timber for shipbuilding, tobacco for smoking, and fur pelts for hats and coats; and (2) to develop a thriving market for English manufactured goods. To populate the colonies, the English encouraged social rebels, religious dissenters, and the homeless and landless to migrate to America, thereby reducing social and economic tensions at home.

In some cases, immigrants had no choice. Some 50,000 British convicts were shipped to America as servants for hire, as were several thousand Royalist prisoners, mostly Scots. Many of them did very well. In 1665, a Scottish minister in Virginia reported that several exiled Royalist soldiers were "living better than ever their forefathers" after being "sold as slaves here."

The most powerful enticement to colonists was to offer them land and the promise of a better way of life—what came to be called the American dream. Land, plentiful and cheap, was English America's treasure—once it was taken from the Native Americans.

What virtually all immigrants shared was an impulse to escape the constraints and corruptions of the old and the courage to risk everything for a life of freedom and adventure in the new. In the process of discovering a New World of opportunities and dangers, they also re-created themselves as Americans.

**THE LANDLESS ENGLISH**   During the late sixteenth century, England experienced a population explosion that created a surplus of landless workers. Many of the jobless laborers found their way to America. An additional social strain for the English poor was the *enclosure* of farmlands on which peasants had lived and worked for generations. As trade in woolen products grew, landlords decided to "enclose" farmlands and evict the farmworkers in favor of grazing sheep.

The enclosure movement, coupled with the rising population, generated the great number of beggars and vagrants who wandered across England during the late sixteenth century. The problems created by this uprooted peasant population provided a compelling reason to send many of them to colonies in America and the Caribbean. As the Reverend Richard Hakluyt explained, "Valiant youths rusting [from] lack of employment" would flourish in America and generate trade that would enrich England.

**VIRGINIA**   In 1606, King James I chartered a joint-stock enterprise named the Virginia Company. It was owned by investors, called "adventurers," who sought to profit from the gold and silver they hoped to find in America. King James also gave the Virginia Company a spiritual mission by ordering the settlers to take the "Christian religion" to the Indians, who "live in darkness and miserable ignorance of the true knowledge and worship of God."

In December 1606, the Virginia Company sent to America three ships carrying 104 colonists, all men and boys. In May 1607, after five storm-tossed months at sea, they reached the broad expanse of Chesapeake Bay, which extends 200 miles along the coast of Virginia and Maryland. To avoid Spanish raiders, the colonists chose to settle about forty miles inland along a large river. They called it the James, in honor of the king, and named their settlement Jamestown.

The ill-prepared settlers had expected to find gold, friendly Indians, and easy living. Instead they found disease, drought, starvation, violence, and death. Virtually every colonist fell ill within a year. "Our men were destroyed with cruel diseases," a survivor wrote, "but for the most part they died of mere famine."

In the colony's desperate early weeks and months, the settlers struggled to find enough to eat, for many of them were either poor townsmen unfamiliar with farming or "gentlemen" who despised manual labor. All most of them did, according to one colonist, was "complain, curse, and despair." For fifteen years, the Jamestown settlers blundered their way from one mishap to another. Unwilling to invest the time and labor in growing their own food, they stole or traded for Indian corn.

The 14,000 Indians living along the Virginia coast were dominated by the **Powhatan Confederacy,** which had conquered or intimidated the other Indian peoples in the region. Powhatan, as the English called the imperial chieftain, lorded over several hundred villages (of about 100 people each) orga-

**Chief Powhatan** In this 1624 line engraving from John Smith's "Generall Historie of Virginia," Cheif Powhatan holds court from a dominant, seated position.

nized into thirty chiefdoms in eastern Virginia. When the colonists arrived, Powhatan was preoccupied with destroying the Chesapeakes, who lived along the Virginia coast.

At the time, the Powhatan Confederacy may have been the most powerful group of native peoples along the Atlantic coast. Focused on raising corn and conquering their neighbors, they lived in oval-shaped houses framed with bent saplings and covered with bark or mats. Their walled villages included forts, buildings for storing corn, and temples.

Chief Powhatan lived in an imposing lodge on the York River not far from Jamestown, where he was protected by forty bodyguards and supported by 100 wives. Colonist John Smith reported that Powhatan "sat covered with a great robe, made of raccoon skins, and all the tails hanging by," flanked by "two rows of men, and behind them as many women, with all their heads and shoulders painted red."

The Powhatans, Smith observed, were "generally tall and straight," "very ingenious," and handsome. Some attached feathers and chains to their pierced ears, and many painted their bodies. During the winter, they wore fur skins; in the summer, they were mostly naked.

The Powhatans lived in family clusters. Some villages had 20 huts; others had 200. The Powhatan men, Smith stressed, avoided "woman's work." When they were not hunting, fishing, or fighting, they sat watching the "women and children do the rest of the work": gardening, making baskets and pottery, cooking, and "all the rest."

Powhatan was as much an imperialist as the English or Spanish. He forced the peoples he had conquered to give him corn. Upon learning of the English settlement at Jamestown, he planned to impose his will on the "Strangers." When Powhatans discovered seventeen Englishmen stealing their corn, they killed them, stuffing their mouths with ears of corn. Only too late did Powhatan realize that the English had not come to Virginia to trade but "to invade my people, and possess my country."

The colonists found a match for Powhatan in twenty-seven-year-old John Smith, a canny, iron-willed international mercenary (soldier for hire). At five feet three inches, he was a stocky runt of a man full of tenacity, courage, and overflowing confidence.

The Virginia Company, impressed by Smith's exploits, had appointed him to help manage the new colony. Smith imagined "abounding America" as a land of freedom and opportunity. "Here every man may be master of his own labor and land," he wrote, "so long as settlers were willing to work patiently at humble tasks such as farming and fishing."

Smith confronted a colony on the verge of collapse. Of the original 105 settlers, only 38 survived the first nine months. At one point, said Smith, all their food was gone, "all help abandoned, each hour expecting the fury of the savages." He imposed strict military discipline and forced everyone to work long days in the fields. He also bargained effectively with the Indians. Through his efforts, Jamestown survived—but only barely.

The influx of new settlers nearly overwhelmed the struggling colony. During the winter of 1609–1610, the food supply again ran out, and most of the colonists died. Desperate settlers consumed their horses, cats, and dogs, then rats, mice, and snakes. A few even ate their leather shoes and boots and the starch in their shirt collars. Some summoned the effort to "dig up dead corpses out of graves and to eat them." One hungry man killed, salted, and ate his pregnant wife. Horrified by such cannibalism, his fellow colonists tried, convicted, tortured and executed him. Still, the cannibalism continued as the starvation worsened. "So great was our famine," Smith wrote, "that a savage we slew and buried, the poorer sort [of colonists] took him up again and ate him."

In late May 1610, Sir Thomas Gates brought some 150 new colonists to Jamestown. They found the settlement in shambles. The fort's walls had been torn down, the church was in ruins, and cabins had been "rent up and burnt." Only sixty or so skeletal colonists remained, and most were bedridden from disease and malnourishment. They greeted the newcomers by shouting, "We are starved! We are starved!"

Gates loaded the surviving colonists on his ships and they made their way downriver, headed for the Chesapeake Bay and the Atlantic. But no sooner had they started than they spied three relief ships headed upriver. The ships carried a new governor, Thomas West, known as Lord De La Warr (Delaware would be named for him), several hundred men, and plentiful supplies. De La Warr ordered Gates to turn around; Jamestown would not be abandoned.

That chance encounter was a turning point for the struggling colony. After De La Warr returned to England in 1611, Gates rebuilt the settlements and imposed a strict system of laws. The penalties for running away included shooting, hanging, and burning. Gates also ordered the colonists to attend church services on Thursdays and Sundays. Religious uniformity became an essential instrument of public policy and civil duty in colonial Virginia.

Over the next several years, the Jamestown colony limped along until at last the settlers found a profitable crop: **tobacco**. The plant had been grown on Caribbean islands for years, and smoking had become a popular habit in Europe. In 1612, settlers in Virginia began growing tobacco for export to England. By 1620, the colony was shipping 50,000 pounds of tobacco each year; by 1670, Virginia and Maryland were exporting 15 million pounds annually.

Large-scale tobacco farming required additional cleared lands for planting and more laborers to work the fields. A Jamestown planter said he needed lots of "lusty laboring men . . . capable of hard labor, and that can bear and undergo heat and cold."

**INDENTURED SERVANTS** To support their investment in tobacco lands, planters employed **indentured servants**. The colonists who signed a contract ("indenture") exchanged several years of labor for the cost of passage to America and, they hoped, an eventual grant of land. Indentured servitude increased the flow of immigrant workers and became the primary source of laborers in English America during the colonial period. Of the 500,000 English immigrants to America from 1610 to 1775, some 350,000 came as indentured servants, most of them penniless young men and boys. In the 1630s, the gender ratio in Virginia was 6 men to every woman; by the 1650s, it had dropped to three men to every one woman.

Not all indentured servants came voluntarily. Many homeless children in London were "kid-napped" and sold into servitude in America. In addition, Parliament in 1717 declared that convicts could avoid prison or the hangman by relocating to the colonies, and some 50,000 were banished to the New World.

Once in America, servants were provided food and a bed, but life was harsh and their rights were limited. They could be sold, loaned, or rented to others, and masters could whip them or chain them in iron collars and extend their length of service as penalty for bad behavior. Marriages required the master's permission.

Being indentured was almost like being a slave, but servants, unlike slaves, could file a complaint with the local court. Elizabeth Sprigs, a servant in Maryland, told of "toiling day and night, and then [being] tied up and whipped to that degree you would not beat an animal, scarce [fed] anything but Indian corn and salt."

The most important difference between servanthood and slavery was that it did not last a lifetime. When the indenture ended, usually after four to seven years, the servant could claim the "freedom dues" set by custom and law: tools, clothing, food, and, on occasion, small tracts of land.

Some former servants did well. By 1629, seven members of the Virginia legislature had arrived as indentured servants, and by 1637, fifteen were serving in the Maryland Assembly. Such opportunities were much less common in England or Europe, giving people even more reason to travel to America.

**POCAHONTAS**    One of the most remarkable Powhatans was Pocahontas, the favorite daughter of Chief Powhatan. In 1607, then only eleven years old, she figured in perhaps the best-known story of the settlement, her plea for the life of John Smith. After Indians attacked Smith and a group of Englishmen trespassing on their land, killing two of them and capturing the rest, Chief Powhatan asked Smith why they were on his territory. Smith lied, claiming they had been chased there by wicked Spaniards. Powhatan saw through the ruse and ordered his warriors to kill Smith. They told him to kneel and place his head on a stone altar. As they prepared to smash his skull with war clubs, according to the unreliable Smith, young Pocahontas made a dramatic appeal for his life, convincing her father to release him in exchange for muskets, hatchets, beads, and trinkets.

Schoolchildren still learn the story of Pocahontas and John Smith, but through the years the story's facts have become distorted or even falsified. Pocahontas and John Smith were friends, not Disney World lovers. Moreover, the Indian princess saved Smith on more than one occasion, before she herself was kidnapped by English settlers in an effort to blackmail Powhatan.

Pocahontas, however, surprised her English captors by choosing to join them. She embraced Christianity, was baptized and renamed Rebecca, and fell in love with John Rolfe, a twenty-eight-year-old widower who introduced tobacco to Jamestown. After their marriage, they moved in 1616 with their infant son, Thomas, to London. There the young princess drew excited attention from the royal family and curious Londoners. Just months after arriving, however, Rebecca, only twenty years old, contracted a lung disease and died.

**THE VIRGINIA COMPANY PROSPERS** Jamestown remained fragile until 1618, when Sir Edwin Sandys, a prominent member of Parliament, became head of the Virginia Company. He created a **headright** (land grant) program to attract more colonists. Any Englishman who bought a share in the company and could pay for passage to Virginia could have fifty acres upon arrival, and fifty more for each servant he brought along.

The Virginia Company also promised the settlers all the "rights of Englishmen," including an elected legislature, arguing that "every man will more willingly obey laws to which he has yielded his consent." Such a commitment to representative democracy was a crucial development, for the English had long enjoyed the broadest civil liberties and the least-intrusive government in Europe. Now the colonists in Virginia were to have the same rights.

They were also to have the benefits of marriage. In 1619, a ship carrying ninety young women arrived at Jamestown. Men rushed to claim them as wives by providing 125 pounds of tobacco to cover the cost of their transatlantic passage. Also in 1619, a Dutch ship, the *White Lion,* stopped near Jamestown and unloaded "20 Negars," the first enslaved Africans known to have reached English America. These captives from the Portuguese colony of Angola in West Africa were sold into slavery, the first of some 450,000 people who would be shipped from Africa to America as slaves. Thus began an inhumane system that would spur dramatic economic growth, sow moral corruption, and generate horrific suffering for African Americans.

By 1624, some 8,000 English men, women, and children had migrated to Jamestown, although only 1,132 had survived or stayed, and many of them were in "a sickly and desperate state." In 1622 alone, 1,000 colonists had died of disease or were victims of an Indian massacre. In 1624, the Virginia Company declared bankruptcy, and Virginia became a royal colony.

The settlers were now free to own property and start businesses. The king, however, would thereafter appoint their governors. Sir William Berkeley, who arrived in 1642, presided over the colony's rapid growth for most of the next thirty-five years. Tobacco prices surged, and wealthy planters began to dominate social and political life.

The Jamestown experience did not invent America, but the colony's gritty will to survive, its mixture of greed and piety, and its exploitation of both Indians and Africans formed the model for many of the struggles, achievements, and ironies that would come to define the American spirit.

**BACON'S REBELLION** The relentless stream of new settlers into Virginia exerted constant pressure on Indian lands and created growing tensions among whites. The largest planters sought to live like the wealthy "English gentlemen" who owned huge estates in the countryside. In Virginia, these men acquired the most fertile land along the coast and rivers, compelling freed servants to become farmworkers or forcing them inland to gain their own farms. In either case, the poorest Virginians found themselves at a disadvantage. By 1676, one-fourth of the free white men were landless. They roamed the countryside, squatting on private property, working odd jobs, poaching game, and struggling to survive.

STRANGE NEWS

FROM

# VIRGINIA;

Being a full and true

# ACCOUNT

OF THE

# LIFE and DEATH

OF

*Nathanael Bacon* Esquire,

Who was the only Cause and Original of all the late Troubles in that COUNTRY.

With a full Relation of all the Accidents which have happened in the late War there between the Chriftians and Indians.

*LONDON,*
Printed for *William Harris,* next door to the Turn-Stile without *Moor-gate.* 1677.

**News of the rebellion** A pamphlet printed in London provided details about Bacon's Rebellion.

The simmering tensions among the landless colonists contributed to what came to be called **Bacon's Rebellion**. The discontent erupted when a squabble between a white planter and Native Americans on the Potomac River led to the murder of the planter's herdsman and, in turn, to retaliation by frontier vigilantes, who killed some two dozen Indians. When five native chieftains were later murdered, enraged Indians took revenge on frontier settlements.

When Governor Berkeley refused to take action against the Indians, Nathaniel Bacon, a young planter, led more than 1,000 men determined to terrorize the "protected and darling Indians." Bacon said he would kill all the Indians in Virginia and promised to free any servants and slaves who joined him.

Bacon's Rebellion quickly became a battle of landless servants, small farmers, and even some slaves against Virginia's wealthiest planters and political leaders. Bacon's ruthless assaults against Indians and his lust for power and land (rather than any commitment to democratic principles) sparked his conflict with the governing authorities and the planter elite.

For his part, Berkeley opposed Bacon's efforts because he didn't want to disrupt the profitable deerskin trade the colonists enjoyed with the Native Americans. Bacon issued a "Declaration of the People of Virginia" accusing Berkeley of corruption and attempted to take the governor into custody. Berkeley's forces resisted—feebly—and Bacon's men burned Jamestown in frustration.

Bacon, however, fell ill and died a month later, after which the rebellion disintegrated. Berkeley had twenty-three of the rebels hanged. For such severity, the king denounced Berkeley as a "fool" and recalled him to England, where he died within a year.

**MARYLAND**  In 1634, ten years after Virginia became a royal colony, a neighboring settlement appeared on the northern shore of Chesapeake Bay. Named Maryland in honor of English queen Henrietta Maria, its 12 million acres were granted to Sir George Calvert, Lord Baltimore, by King Charles I. It became the first *proprietary* colony—that is, an individual owned it, not a joint-stock company.

Calvert had long been one of the king's favorites. In 1619, he became one of two royal secretaries of state for the nation. Forced to resign after a squabble with the king's powerful advisers, Calvert announced that he had converted from Anglicanism to Catholicism. Thereafter, he asked the new king, James II, to grant him a charter for an American colony north of Virginia. However, Calvert died before the king could act, so the charter went to his devoted son Cecilius, the second Lord Baltimore, who actually founded the colony and spent the rest of his life making it sustainable.

Cecilius Calvert wanted Maryland to be a refuge for English Catholics. Yet he also wanted the colony to be profitable and to avoid antagonizing Protestants. To that aim, he instructed his brother, Leonard, the colony's first proprietary governor, to ensure that Catholic colonists worshipped in private and remained "silent upon all occasions of discourse concerning matters of religion."

In 1634, the Calverts planted the first settlement in coastal Maryland at St. Marys, near the mouth of the Potomac River, about eighty miles up the Chesapeake Bay from Jamestown. Cecilius sought to avoid the mistakes made

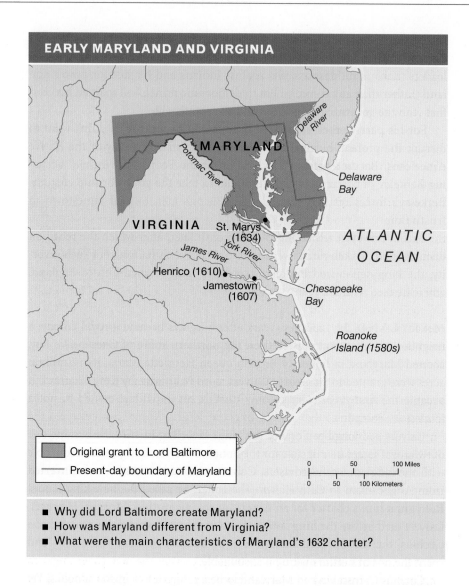

## EARLY MARYLAND AND VIRGINIA

Delaware River

MARYLAND

Potomac River

Delaware Bay

VIRGINIA St. Marys (1634)

James River

York River

Henrico (1610)

Jamestown (1607)

ATLANTIC OCEAN

Chesapeake Bay

Roanoke Island (1580s)

■ Original grant to Lord Baltimore
— Present-day boundary of Maryland

0   50   100 Miles
0   50   100 Kilometers

■ Why did Lord Baltimore create Maryland?
■ How was Maryland different from Virginia?
■ What were the main characteristics of Maryland's 1632 charter?

at Jamestown, so he recruited a more committed group of colonists—made up of families intending to stay rather than just single men seeking quick profits.

In addition, the Calverts did not want a colony of scattered farms and settlements vulnerable to Indian attack, like Virginia, or to be dependent solely on tobacco. They sought to create a more diversified agriculture and to build fortified towns designed to promote social interaction. The Calverts also wanted to avoid the extremes of economic wealth and poverty that had developed in Virginia. In that vein, they provided 100 acres to each adult and 50 more for each child. Maryland also had an explicit religious objective: the "conversion and civilizing of those barbarous heathens that live like beasts without the light of faith." Jesuit priests served as missionaries to the Indians. To avoid the chronic Indian wars suffered in Virginia, the Calverts resolved to purchase land from the Native Americans rather than take it by force.

Still, the early years in Maryland were as difficult as in Virginia. Nearly 30 percent of infants born in the colony died in their first year, and nearly half of the colonists died before reaching age twenty-one. Some 34,000 colonists would arrive between 1634 and 1680, but in 1680 the colony's white population was only 20,000.

The charter from the king gave the Calverts the power to make laws with the consent of the *freemen* (all property holders). Yet they could not attract enough Roman Catholics to develop a self-sustaining economy. The majority of the servants who came to the colony were Protestants, both Anglicans and Puritans. To recruit servants and settlers, the Calverts offered "a quiet life sweetened with ease and plenty" on small farms. In the end, Maryland succeeded more quickly than Virginia because of its focus on growing tobacco from the start. Its long coastline along the Chesapeake Bay gave planters easy access to shipping.

Despite the Calverts' caution "concerning matters of religion," sectarian squabbles impeded the colony's early development. Catholics and Protestants feuded as violently as they had in England. When Oliver Cromwell and the Puritans took control in England and executed King Charles I in 1649, Cecilius Calvert feared he might lose his colony.

To avoid such a catastrophe, Calvert appointed Protestants to the colony's ruling council and wrote the Toleration Act (1649), a revolutionary document that acknowledged the Puritan victory and welcomed all Christians, regardless of their denomination or beliefs. (It also promised to execute anyone who denied the divinity of Jesus.)

Still, Calvert's efforts were not enough to prevent the new government in England from installing Puritans in positions of control in Maryland. They rescinded the Toleration Act in 1654, stripped Catholic colonists of voting rights, and denied them the right to worship.

The once-persecuted Puritans had become persecutors themselves, at one point driving Calvert out of his own colony. Were it not for its success in growing tobacco, Maryland may well have disintegrated. In 1692, following the Glorious Revolution in England, Catholicism was effectively banned in Maryland. Only after the American Revolution would Marylanders again be guaranteed religious freedom.

## SETTLING NEW ENGLAND

Very different English settlements were emerging north of the Chesapeake Bay colonies. Unlike Maryland and Virginia, the New England colonies were intended to be self-governing religious utopias based on the teachings of John Calvin. The New England settlers were not indentured servants as in the Chesapeake colonies; they were mostly middle-class families that could pay their own way across the Atlantic. Most male settlers were small farmers, merchants, seamen, or fishermen. New England also attracted more women than did the southern colonies.

Although its soil was not as fertile as that of the Chesapeake region and its growing season was much shorter, New England was a healthier place to live. Because of its colder climate, settlers avoided the infectious diseases like malaria that ravaged the southern colonies. Still, only 21,000 colonists arrived in New England, compared to the 120,000 who went to the Chesapeake Bay colonies. By 1700, however, New England's thriving white population exceeded that of Maryland and Virginia.

The land-hungry Pilgrims and Puritans who arrived in Massachusetts were willing to sacrifice everything to create a model Christian society. These self-described "visible saints" intended to purify their churches of *all* Catholic and Anglican rituals and enact a code of laws and a government structure based upon biblical principles. Unlike the Anglican Church, which allowed anyone, including sinners, to join, the Puritans limited membership in their churches only to saints—those who had been chosen by God for salvation. They also sought to stamp out gambling, swearing, and Sabbath breaking. Their blameless lives and holy communities, they hoped, would provide a beacon of righteousness for a wicked England to emulate.

**PLYMOUTH**   The first permanent English settlement in New England was established by the Plymouth Company, a group of seventy British investors. Eager to make money by exporting the colony's abundant natural resources, the joint-stock company agreed to finance settlements in exchange for the furs, timber, and fish they would ship back to England for sale.

Among the first to accept the company's offer were Puritan Separatists, or Pilgrims, who were forced to leave England because of their refusal to worship in Anglican churches. The Separatist "saints" demanded that each congregation govern itself rather than be ruled by a bureaucracy of bishops and archbishops.

The Separatists, mostly simple farm folk, sought to live in "peace, love, and holiness." Tired of being "clapped up in prison," they made the heartbreaking

## EARLY NEW ENGLAND SETTLEMENTS

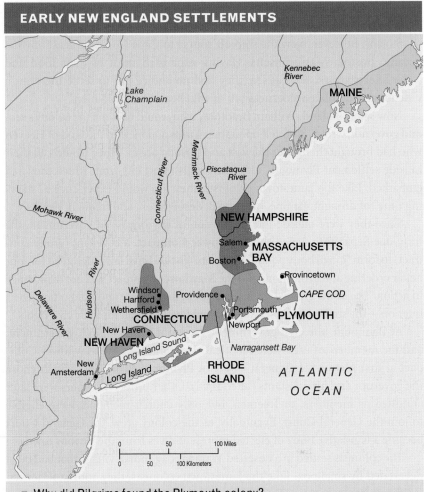

Kennebec River

Lake Champlain

MAINE

Merrimack River

Connecticut River

Piscataqua River

Mohawk River

NEW HAMPSHIRE

Salem · **MASSACHUSETTS BAY**
Boston ·

· Provincetown

Hudson River

Windsor ·
Hartford ·    Providence ·
Wethersfield ·

**CONNECTICUT**

New Haven ·

**NEW HAVEN**

Long Island Sound

New Amsterdam

Long Island

*CAPE COD*

Portsmouth ·
Newport ·    **PLYMOUTH**

*Narragansett Bay*

**RHODE ISLAND**

Delaware River

*ATLANTIC OCEAN*

| 0 | | 50 | 100 Miles |
|---|---|---|---|

| 0 | 50 | 100 Kilometers |
|---|---|---|

- Why did Pilgrims found the Plymouth colony?
- How were the settlers of the Massachusetts Bay Colony different from those of Plymouth?
- What was the origin of the Rhode Island colony?

choice to leave England for Holland, where, over time, they worried that their children were becoming Dutch. Such concerns led them to leave Europe and create a holy community in America.

In September 1620, about 100 women, men, and children, some of whom were called "strangers" rather than saints because they were *not* part of the religious group, crammed aboard the tiny *Mayflower*, a leaky, three-masted vessel only 100 feet long, and headed across the Atlantic bound for the Virginia colony, where they had obtained permission to settle. Each colonist received one share in the enterprise in exchange for working seven years in America.

Storms, however, blew the ship off course to Cape Cod, southeast of what became Boston, Massachusetts. Having exhausted most of their food and water after sixty-six days at sea, they had no choice but to settle there in "a hideous and desolate wilderness full of wild beasts and wild men."

Now safely on land, William Bradford, who would become the colony's second governor, wrote, "they fell upon their knees and blessed the God of Heaven who had brought them over the vast and furious ocean." They would call their hillside settlement Plymouth, after the English port city from which they had embarked. Like the Jamestown colonists, they too would experience a "starving time" of drought, famine, bitter cold, desperation, and frequent deaths.

Since they were outside the jurisdiction of any organized government, the forty-one Separatists signed the **Mayflower Compact**, a covenant (group contract) to form "a civil body politic" based on "just and civil laws" designed for "our better ordering and protection." But the Mayflower Compact was not democracy in action. The saints granted themselves the rights to vote and hold office. Their inferiors—the strangers and servants—would have to wait for their civil rights.

At Plymouth, the civil government grew out of the church government, and the members of each were identical. The signers of the Mayflower Compact at first met as the General Court of Plymouth Plantation, which chose the governor and his assistants (or council). Other property owners were later admitted as members, or freemen, but only church members were eligible to join the General Court. Eventually, as the colony grew, the General Court became a legislative body of elected representatives from the various towns.

The colonists settled in a deserted Wampanoag Indian village that had been devastated by smallpox. Like the Jamestown colonists, they, too, experienced a difficult "starving time." During the first winter, half of them died, including thirteen of the eighteen married women. Only the discovery of stored Indian corn buried underground enabled the survivors to persist.

Eventually, a local Indian named Squanto taught the colonists how to grow corn, catch fish, gather nuts and berries, and negotiate with the Wampanoags. Still, when a shipload of colonists arrived in 1623, they "fell a-weeping" as they found the original colonists in such a "low and poor condition." By the 1630s, Governor Bradford was lamenting the failure of Plymouth to become the thriving holy community he and others had envisioned.

**MASSACHUSETTS BAY** The Plymouth colony's population never rose above 7,000, and after ten years it was overshadowed by its much larger neighbor, the Massachusetts Bay Colony. Like Plymouth, the new colony was also intended to be a holy commonwealth for Puritans, but the Massachusetts Bay Puritans were different from the Pilgrims. They remained Anglicans—they wanted to purify the Church of England from within. They were called nonseparating *Congregationalists* because their churches were governed by their congregations rather than by an Anglican bishop in England. Like the Pilgrims, the Puritans limited church membership to "visible saints"—those who could demonstrate that they had received the gift of God's grace.

In 1629, King Charles I gave a royal charter to the Massachusetts Bay Company, a group of Calvinist Puritans led by John Winthrop, a lawyer with intense religious convictions and mounting debts. Winthrop wanted the colony to be a haven for Puritans and a model Christian community where Jesus Christ would be exalted and faith would flourish. They would create "a City upon a Hill," as he declared, borrowing the phrase from Jesus's Sermon on the Mount. "The eyes of all people are on us," Winthrop said, so they must live up to their sacred destiny.

Winthrop shrewdly took advantage of an oversight in the company charter: It did not require that the joint-stock company maintain its home office in England. The Puritans took the royal charter with them, thereby transferring government authority from London to Massachusetts, where they hoped to govern themselves.

In 1630, Winthrop, his wife, three of his sons, and eight servants joined some 700 Puritan settlers on eleven ships loaded with cows, horses, supplies, and tons of beer, which remained safely drinkable much longer than did water. Unlike the first colonists in Virginia, most of the Puritans in Massachusetts arrived as family groups.

On June 12, Winthrop's ships landed at Salem. The Puritans then moved to the mouth of the Charles River, where they built a village and called it Boston, after the English town of that name. Winthrop was delighted to discover that the local Indians had been "swept away by the small-pox . . . so God hath hereby cleared

**John Winthrop** The first governor of the Massachusetts Bay Colony, he envisioned the colony as "a City upon a Hill."

our title to this place." Yet disease knew no boundaries. Within eight months, some 200 Puritans had died, and many others had returned to England.

Planting colonies was not for the faint-hearted. Anne Bradstreet, who became one of the first colonial poets, spoke for many when she lamented the difficult living conditions: "After I was convinced it was the way of God, I submitted to it." Such submissiveness to divine will sustained the Puritans through many trials. What allowed the Massachusetts Bay Colony eventually to thrive was a flood of additional colonists who brought money, skills, and needed supplies.

Winthrop was a commanding figure determined to enforce religious devotion and ensure social stability. He and other Puritan leaders prized law and order and hated the idea of democracy—the people ruling themselves. As the Reverend John Cotton explained, "If the people be governors, who shall be governed?" Cotton, Winthrop, and others spent much of their time trying to convince or force the growing population to conform to their beliefs.

New England villages were fractious places; people loved to argue and judge their neighbors' conduct. John Winthrop never embraced religious toleration, political freedom, social equality, or cultural diversity. The only freedom he tolerated was the freedom to do what was "good, just, and honest." He and the Puritans worked to suppress other religious views in New England. Catholics, Anglicans, Quakers, and Baptists were punished, imprisoned, banished, and sometimes executed.

**Anne Hutchinson** Puritans who spoke out against religious or political policies were quickly condemned. For example, Anne Hutchinson, the strong-willed wife of a prominent merchant, raised thirteen children, served as a midwife helping deliver neighbors' babies, and hosted meetings in her home to discuss sermons.

Soon, however, the discussions turned into large twice-weekly gatherings at which Hutchinson shared her passionate convictions about religious matters. According to one participant, she "preaches better Gospel than any of your black coats [male ministers]." Blessed with vast biblical knowledge and a quick wit, Hutchinson criticized mandatory church attendance and the absolute power of ministers and magistrates. Most controversial of all, she claimed to know which of her neighbors had been saved and which were damned, including ministers. Puritan leaders saw her as a "dangerous" woman who threatened their authority.

A pregnant Hutchinson was hauled before the all-male General Court in 1637. For two days she sparred with the Puritan leaders, at one point reminding them of the biblical injunction that "elder women should instruct the younger." She steadfastly refused to acknowledge any wrongdoing. Her ability to cite chapter-and-verse biblical defenses of her actions led an exasperated Governor Winthrop to explode: "We are your judges, and not you ours. . . . We do not mean to discourse [debate] with those of your sex." As the trial continued, Hutchinson was eventually lured into convicting herself by claiming direct revelations from God—blasphemy in the eyes of mainstream Puritans. In 1638, Winthrop and the General Court banished Hutchinson as a "leper" not fit for "our society."

Hutchinson initially resettled with her family and about sixty followers on an island south of Providence, Rhode Island. The hard journey took its toll, however. Hutchinson grew sick, and her baby was stillborn, leading her critics to claim that the "monstrous birth" was God's way of punishing her.

**The trial of Anne Hutchinson** In this nineteenth-century wood engraving, Anne Hutchinson stands her ground against charges of heresy from the all-male leaders of Puritan Boston.

Her spirits never recovered. After her husband's death in 1642, she and her followers resettled along a river in the Bronx, near New Amsterdam (New York City), which was then under Dutch control. The following year, Indians massacred Hutchinson, six of her children, and nine others. Her murder, wrote John Winthrop, was "a special manifestation of divine justice." Recent research suggests that Winthrop may have encouraged the Indian raid.

**REPRESENTATIVE GOVERNMENT** The transfer of the Massachusetts Bay Colony's royal charter, whereby an English trading company evolved into a provincial government, was a unique venture in colonization. Unlike "Old" England, New England had no lords or bishops, kings or queens. The Massachusetts General Court, wherein power rested under the royal charter, consisted of all shareholders, or property owners, called freemen. At first, the freemen had no power except to choose "assistants," who in turn elected the governor and deputy governor. In 1634, however, the freemen turned themselves into the General Court, with two or three deputies to represent each town.

The Puritans, having fled religious persecution, ensured that their liberties in America were spelled out and protected. Over time, membership in a Puritan church replaced the purchase of stock as the means of becoming a freeman (and thus a voter) in Massachusetts Bay. In sum, the vital godliness and zeal of the New England Puritans shaped their society and governed their lives.

**RHODE ISLAND**  More by accident than design, the Massachusetts Bay Colony became the staging area for other New England colonies created by people dissatisfied with Puritan ways. Roger Williams (1603–1683), who had arrived from England in 1631, was among the first to cause problems, precisely because he was the purest of Puritans—a Separatist who criticized "impure" Puritans for not abandoning the "whorish" Church of England.

Where John Winthrop cherished strict governmental and clerical authority, Williams championed individual liberty. The Puritan leaders were mistaken, he claimed, in requiring everyone, including nonmembers, to attend church. To Williams, true *puritanism* required complete separation of church and state and freedom from all coercion in matters of faith. "Forced worship," he declared, "stinks in God's nostrils."

Williams held a brief pastorate in Salem, north of Boston, and then moved south to Separatist Plymouth, where he took the time to learn Indian languages and continued to question the right of English settlers to confiscate Native American lands. He then returned to Salem, where he came to love and support the Indians.

Williams posed a radical question: If one's salvation depends solely upon God's grace, as John Calvin had argued, why bother to have churches at all? Why not give individuals the right to worship God directly, in their own way? His belief that a true church must include only those who had received God's gift of grace eventually convinced him that no true church was possible, unless perhaps it consisted of his wife and himself.

Such "dangerous opinions" threatened the foundations of New England Puritanism and led Governor Winthrop and the General Court to banish Williams to England. Before authorities could ship him back, however, he and his wife slipped away and found shelter among the Narragansett Indians. He studied their language, defended their rights as human beings, and in 1636 he bought land from them to establish a town he named Providence, at the head of Narragansett Bay. It was the first permanent settlement in Rhode Island and the first in America to allow complete freedom of religion and to give voting rights to all "free inhabitants," meaning those property owners who were not enslaved or indentured servants.

From the beginning, Rhode Island was the most democratic of the colonies, governed by the heads of households rather than by church members. The colony welcomed all who fled religious persecution. For their part, Puritans in Boston came to view Rhode Island as "Rogue Island," a refuge for rebels and radicals. A Dutch visitor reported that the colony was "the sewer of New England." Yet by the 1670s, an English official would describe Rhode Island as the "most profitable part of New England."

**CONNECTICUT, NEW HAMPSHIRE, AND MAINE** Other New England colonies had more conventional beginnings. In 1636, the Reverend Thomas Hooker led three church congregations from the Boston area to Connecticut, where they organized a self-governing colony and founded the town of Hartford. Hooker resented John Winthrop's iron grip on politics in the Bay Colony and believed that all men, not just church members, should be able to vote.

In 1639, the Connecticut General Court adopted the Fundamental Orders, a series of laws that provided for a "Christian Commonwealth" like that of Massachusetts, except that all freemen could vote. The Connecticut constitution specified that the Congregational Church would be the colony's official religion, and it commanded each governor to rule according to "the word of God."

In 1622, territory north of Hartford was granted to Sir Ferdinando Gorges and Captain John Mason. In 1629, Mason took the southern part, which he named the Province of New Hampshire, and Gorges took the northern part, which became the Province of Maine.

During the early 1640s, Massachusetts took over New Hampshire, and in the 1650s it extended its authority to the scattered settlements in Maine. This led to lawsuits, and in 1678 English judges decided against Massachusetts in both cases. In 1679, New Hampshire became a royal colony, but Massachusetts continued to control Maine. A new Massachusetts charter in 1691 finally incorporated Maine into Massachusetts.

## THE ENGLISH CIVIL WAR IN AMERICA

By 1640, English settlers in New England and around Chesapeake Bay had established two great beachheads on the Atlantic coast, with the Dutch colony of New Netherland in between. After 1640, however, the struggle between king and Parliament in England diverted attention from colonization, and migration to America dwindled. During the English Civil War (1642–1651) and Oliver Cromwell's Puritan dictatorship (1653–1658), the mother country pretty much left its American colonies alone.

# THE RESTORATION IN THE COLONIES

The restoration of Charles II to the English throne in 1660 revived interest in colonial expansion. Within twelve years, the English would conquer New Netherland and settle Carolina. In the middle region, formerly claimed by the Dutch, four new colonies would emerge: New York, New Jersey, Pennsylvania, and Delaware. The king awarded them to men (proprietors) who had remained loyal to the monarchy during the civil war. In 1663, Charles II granted a vast parcel of land south of Virginia to eight prominent supporters who became lords proprietor (owners) of the region they called Carolina, from the Latin spelling of Charles.

**THE CAROLINAS**  From the start, the southernmost mainland colony in the seventeenth century consisted of two widely separated areas that eventually became the colonies of North Carolina and South Carolina. The northernmost, initially called Albemarle, had been settled in the 1650s by colonists from Virginia. For half a century, Albemarle was an isolated cluster of farms along the shores of Albemarle Sound. Not until 1712 would Carolina be separated into northern and southern colonies.

The eight lords proprietor focused on more-promising sites in southern Carolina. To speed their efforts to generate profits from sugarcane, they recruited English planters from the Caribbean island of Barbados, the oldest, richest, and most heavily populated colony in English America.

**BARBADOS**  The mostly male English in Barbados had developed a hugely profitable sugar plantation system based on the hard labor of enslaved Africans. The "king sugar" colony, the easternmost island in the Caribbean, was dominated by a few extraordinarily wealthy planters who exercised powerful political influence in the mother country. In a reference to Barbados and the other "sugar colonies," an Englishman pointed out in 1666 that "these Settlements have been made and upheld by Negroes and without constant supplies of them cannot subsist."

By 1670, Barbados hosted some 25,000 whites and more than 35,000 enslaved Africans. All available land on Barbados had been claimed, and the sons and grandsons of the planter elite were forced to look elsewhere to find estates of their own. Many seized the chance to settle Carolina and bring the Barbadian plantation system to the new American colony.

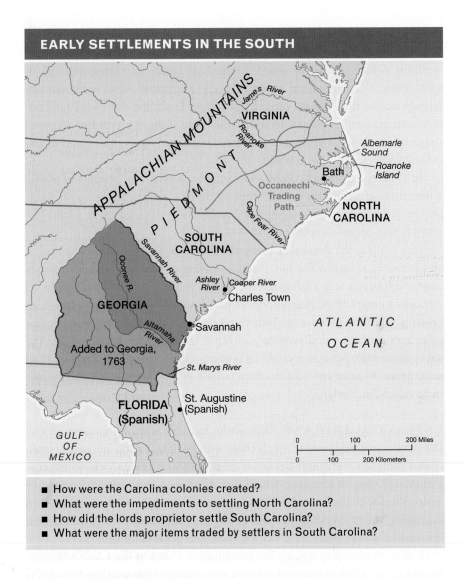

**EARLY SETTLEMENTS IN THE SOUTH**

- How were the Carolina colonies created?
- What were the impediments to settling North Carolina?
- How did the lords proprietor settle South Carolina?
- What were the major items traded by settlers in South Carolina?

**CAROLINA**  The first English colonists in South Carolina arrived in 1669 at Charles Town (later Charleston). Over the next twenty years, half the colonists came from Barbados and other island colonies in the Caribbean, such as Nevis, St. Kitts, and Jamaica.

From the start, South Carolina was a slave-based colony. Planters from the Caribbean brought enormous numbers of enslaved Africans to Carolina to clear land, plant crops, and herd cattle. Carolina, a Swiss immigrant said, "looks more like a negro country than like a country settled by white people."

The government of Carolina grew out of a unique document, the Fundamental Constitutions of Carolina, drafted by one of the eight proprietors, Lord Anthony Ashley Cooper. It awarded large land grants to prominent Englishmen. From the beginning, however, every immigrant who could pay for passage across the Atlantic received headright land. The Fundamental Constitutions granted religious toleration, which gave Carolina a greater degree of religious freedom (extending to Jews and "heathens") than in England or any other colony except Rhode Island.

In 1712, the Carolina colony was formally divided into North and South. After rebelling against the lords proprietor, South Carolina became a royal colony in 1719. North Carolina remained under the proprietors' rule until 1729, when it, too, became a royal colony.

Rice became the dominant commercial crop in South Carolina because it was perfectly suited to the hot, humid growing conditions. Rice, like sugarcane and tobacco, was a labor-intensive crop, and planters preferred enslaved Africans to work their plantations, in part because West Africans had been growing rice for generations. Both Carolinas also had huge forests of yellow pine trees that provided lumber and other materials for shipbuilding. The sticky resin from pine trees could be boiled to make tar, which was needed to waterproof the seams of wooden ships (which is why North Carolinians came to be called Tar Heels).

**ENSLAVING INDIANS** One of the quickest ways to make money in Carolina's early years was through trade with Indians. In the late seventeenth century, English merchants began traveling southward from Virginia into the Piedmont region of Carolina, where they developed a prosperous commerce in deerskins with the Catawbas. Between 1699 and 1715, Carolina exported an average of 54,000 deerskins per year to England, where they were transformed into leather gloves, belts, hats, work aprons, and book bindings.

English traders also quickly became interested in buying enslaved Indians. To do so, the traders at times fomented war between Indian tribes; they knew that the best Indian slave catchers were other Indians. That Native Americans had for centuries captured and enslaved other indigenous peoples helped the Europeans justify and expand the sordid practice.

In Carolina, as many as 50,000 Indians were sold as slaves in Charles Town between 1670 and 1715, with many being shipped to faraway lands—Barbados, Antigua, New York. More enslaved Indians were exported during that period than Africans were imported, and thousands of others were sold to "slavers" who took them to islands in the Caribbean.

The growing commerce in people, however, triggered bitter struggles between rival Indian nations and helped ignite unprecedented violence. In 1712, the Tuscaroras of North Carolina attacked German and English colonists who had encroached upon their land. North Carolina authorities appealed to South Carolina for aid, and the colony, eager for more slaves, dispatched two expeditions made up mostly of Indian allies of the English—Yamasees, Cherokees, Creeks, and Catawbas. They destroyed a Tuscarora town, executed 162 male warriors, and took 392 women and children captive for sale in Charles Town. The surviving Tuscaroras fled north, where they joined the Iroquois.

The Tuscarora War sparked more conflict in South Carolina. The Yamasees felt betrayed when white traders paid them less for their Tuscarora captives than they wanted. In April 1715, Yamasees attacked coastal plantations and killed more than 100 whites.

The governor mobilized all white and black men to defend the colony; other colonies supplied weapons. But it wasn't until the governor bribed the Cherokees to join them that the Yamasee War ended—in 1717. The defeated Yamasees fled to Spanish-controlled Florida. By then, hundreds of whites had been killed and dozens of plantations destroyed and abandoned. To prevent another conflict, the colonial government outlawed all private trading with Indians.

## THE MIDDLE COLONIES AND GEORGIA

The area between New England and the Chesapeake—Maryland and Virginia—included the "middle colonies" of New York, New Jersey, Delaware, and Pennsylvania, which were initially controlled by the Netherlands, a newly independent republic of 2 million people. By 1670, the mostly Protestant Dutch had the largest merchant fleet in the world and controlled northern European commerce. They had become one of the most diverse and tolerant societies in Europe—and England's fiercest competitor in international commerce.

**NEW NETHERLAND BECOMES NEW YORK** In London, King Charles II decided to pluck out that old Dutch thorn in the side of the English colonies in America: New Netherland, which was older than New England. The Dutch East India Company (organized in 1602) had hired English sea captain Henry Hudson to explore America in hopes of finding a northwest passage to the Indies. Sailing along the coast of North America in 1609, Hudson crossed Delaware Bay and then sailed ninety miles up the "wide and deep" river that eventually would be named for him in New York State.

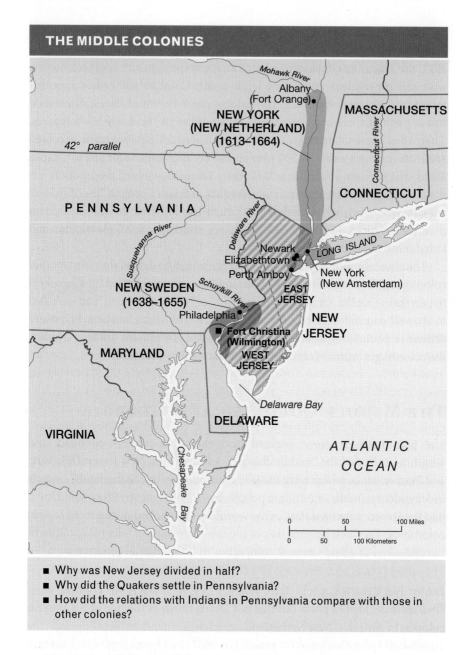

## THE MIDDLE COLONIES

- Why was New Jersey divided in half?
- Why did the Quakers settle in Pennsylvania?
- How did the relations with Indians in Pennsylvania compare with those in other colonies?

The Hudson River would become one of the most strategically important waterways in America; it was wide and deep enough for oceangoing vessels to travel far north into the interior, where the Dutch traded various goods for the fur pelts harvested by Indian trappers. In 1625, Dutch traders acquired 5,295 beaver pelts and 463 otter skins, which they shipped to the Netherlands.

Like Virginia and Massachusetts, New Netherland was created as a profit-making enterprise. "Everyone here is a trader," explained one resident. And like the French, the Dutch were interested mainly in the fur trade, as the European demand for beaver hats created huge profits. In 1610, the Dutch established fur-trading posts on Manhattan Island and upriver at Fort Orange (later called Albany).

In 1626, the Dutch governor purchased Manhattan (an Indian word meaning "island of many hills") from the Indians for 60 guilders, or about $1,000 in current values. The Dutch then built a fort and a fur-trading post at the lower end of the island. The village of New Amsterdam (eventually New York City), which grew up around the fort, became the capital of New Netherland.

New Netherland was a corporate colony governed by the newly organized Dutch West India Company. It controlled political life, appointing the colony's governor and advisory council and forbid any form of elected legislature. All commerce with the Netherlands had to be carried in the company's ships, and the company controlled the beaver trade with the Indians.

In 1629, the Dutch West India Company decided that it needed more settlers outside Manhattan to help protect the colony from Indian attacks. To encourage settlers to move into the surrounding countryside, it awarded wealthy individuals a large estate called a *patroonship* in exchange for peopling it with fifty adult settlers within four years. Like a feudal lord, the *patroon* (from the Latin word for father) provided cattle, tools, and buildings. His tenants paid him rent, used his gristmill for grinding flour, gave him first option to purchase surplus crops, and submitted to a court he established.

These arrangements, which amounted to transplanting the feudal manor to America, met with little success. Most settlers took advantage of the company's provision that they could have as farms (*bouweries*) all the lands they could improve.

Unlike most of the other European colonies in the Americas, the Dutch embraced ethnic and religious diversity, since their passion for profits outweighed their social prejudices. In 1579, the treaty creating the Dutch Republic declared that "everyone shall remain free in religion and . . . no one may be persecuted or investigated because of religion."

Both the Dutch Republic and New Netherland welcomed exiles from Europe: Spanish and German Jews, French Protestants (Huguenots), English Puritans, and Catholics. There were even Muslims in New Amsterdam, where in the 1640s the 500 residents communicated in eighteen different languages. So from its inception, New York City was America's first multiethnic community, and immigrant minorities dominated its population.

But the Dutch did not show the same tolerance for Native Americans. Soldiers regularly massacred Indians in the region around New Amsterdam. At Pound Ridge, Anglo-Dutch soldiers surrounded an Indian village, set it ablaze, and killed all who tried to escape. Such horrific acts led the Indians to respond in kind.

Dutch tolerance had other limitations. In September 1654, a French ship arrived in New Amsterdam harbor carrying twenty-three *Sephardim*, Jews of Spanish-Portuguese descent. They had come seeking refuge from Portuguese-controlled Brazil and were the first Jewish settlers to arrive in North America.

The colonial governor, Peter Stuyvesant, refused to accept them, however. A short-tempered leader who had lost a leg to a Spanish cannonball, Stuyvesant dismissed Jews as a "deceitful race" and "hateful enemies." Dutch officials in Amsterdam overruled him, however, pointing out that it would be "unreasonable and unfair" to refuse to provide the Jews a safe haven. They wanted to "allow everyone to have his own belief, as long as he behaves quietly and legally, gives no offense to his neighbor, and does not oppose the government."

It would not be until the late seventeenth century that Jews could worship in public, however. Such restrictions help explain why the American Jewish community grew so slowly. In 1773, more than 100 years after the first Jewish refugees arrived, Jews represented only one tenth of 1 percent of the entire colonial population. Not until the nineteenth century would the American Jewish community experience dramatic growth.

In 1626, the Dutch West India Company began importing enslaved Africans to meet its labor shortage. By the 1650s, New Amsterdam had one of the largest slave markets in America.

The extraordinary success of the Dutch economy also proved to be its downfall, however. Like imperial Spain, the Dutch Empire expanded too rapidly. They dominated the European trade with China, India, Africa, Brazil, and the Caribbean, but they could not control their far-flung possessions. It did not take long for European rivals to exploit the sprawling empire's weak points.

The New Netherland governors were mostly corrupt or inept autocrats who were especially clumsy at Indian relations. They depended upon a small army for defense, and the residents of Manhattan, many of whom were not Dutch, were often contemptuous of the government. In 1664, the colonists showed almost total indifference when Governor Stuyvesant called on them to defend the colony against an English flotilla carrying 2,000 soldiers. Stuyvesant finally surrendered without firing a shot.

The English conquest of New Netherland had been led by James Stuart, Duke of York, who would later become King James II. Upon the capture of

New Amsterdam, his brother, King Charles II, granted the entire region to him. The Dutch, however, negotiated an unusual surrender agreement that allowed New Netherlanders to retain their property, churches, language, and local officials. The English renamed the harbor city of New Amsterdam as New York, in honor of the duke.

**NEW JERSEY** Shortly after the conquest of New Netherland, the Duke of York granted the lands between the Hudson and Delaware Rivers to Sir George Carteret and Lord John Berkeley and named the territory for Carteret's native Jersey, an island in the English Channel. In 1676, by mutual agreement, the new royal colony was divided into East and West Jersey, with Carteret taking the east and Berkeley the west. Finally, in 1682, Carteret sold out to a group of investors.

New settlements gradually arose in East Jersey. Disaffected Puritans from New Haven founded Newark, Carteret's brother brought a group to found Elizabethtown, and a group of Scots founded Perth Amboy. In the west, a scattering of Swedes, Finns, and Dutch remained, but they were soon overwhelmed by swarms of English and Welsh Quakers, as well as German and Scots-Irish settlers (mostly Presbyterian Scots who had been encouraged by the English government to migrate to Ireland and thereby dilute the appeal of Catholicism). In 1702, East and West Jersey were united as the single royal colony of New Jersey.

**PENNSYLVANIA** The Quakers, as the Society of Friends was called (because they believed that no one could know Christ without "quaking and trembling"), became the most uncompromising and controversial of the radical religious groups that emerged from the English Civil War. Founded in England in 1647 by George Fox, the Friends rebelled against *all* forms of political and religious authority, including salaried ministers, military service, and paying taxes. They insisted that everyone could experience a personal revelation from God, what they called the "Inner Light" of the Holy Spirit.

Quakers believed that people were essentially good rather than depraved and could achieve salvation through a personal communion with God. They demanded complete religious freedom for everyone, promoted equality of the sexes, and discarded all formal religious creeds and rituals, including an ordained priesthood. When gathered for worship, they kept silent, knowing that the "Inner Light" would move them to say what was fitting at the right moment.

The Quakers were also pacifists who stressed the need to lead lives of service to society. Some early Quakers went barefoot; others wore rags, and a

**Quaker meeting** The presence of women speaking at this Friends meeting is evidence of progressive Quaker views on gender equality.

few went naked and smeared themselves with excrement to demonstrate their "primitive" commitment to Christ.

The Quakers suffered often violent abuse for their odd behavior because their beliefs were so threatening to the social and religious order. Authorities accused them of disrupting "peace and order" and undermining "religion, Church order, and the state." Quakers were especially hated because they refused to acknowledge the supremacy of Puritanism. New England Puritans first banned Quakers, then lopped off their ears, pierced their tongues with a red-hot rod, and finally executed them. Still, the Quakers kept coming. In fact, they often sought out abuse and martyrdom as proof of their intense Christian commitment. As the French philosopher Voltaire (François-Marie Arouet) said, "Getting persecuted is a great way of making converts" to one's religious views.

The settling of English Quakers in West Jersey encouraged other Friends to migrate, especially to the Delaware River side of the colony, where William Penn's Quaker commonwealth, the colony of Pennsylvania, soon arose. Penn, the son of wealthy Admiral Sir William Penn, had attended Oxford University, from which he was expelled for criticizing the university's requirement that students attend daily chapel services. His furious father banished his son from their home.

The younger Penn lived in France for two years, then studied law before moving to Ireland to manage the family's estates. There he was arrested in 1666 for attending a Quaker meeting. Much to the chagrin of his parents, he became a Quaker and was arrested several more times for his religious convictions.

Upon his father's death, Penn inherited a fortune, including a huge tract of land in America, which the king urged him to settle as a means of ridding England of Quakers. The land was named, at the king's insistence, for Penn's father—Pennsylvania (literally, "Penn's Woods")—and it was larger than England itself. Penn encouraged people of different religions from different countries to settle in the new colony, which he considered a "holy experiment" for people of all faiths and nations to live together in harmony. By the end of 1681, thousands of immigrants had responded, and a bustling town emerged at the junction of the Schuylkill and Delaware Rivers. Penn called it Philadelphia (meaning "City of Brotherly Love").

The relations between the Native Americans and the Pennsylvania Quakers were unusually good because of the Quakers' friendliness and Penn's policy of purchasing land titles from the Native Americans. For some fifty years, the settlers and Native Americans lived in peace.

The colony's government, which rested on three Frames of Government drafted by Penn, resembled that of other proprietary colonies except that the freemen (owners of at least fifty acres) who professed their belief in Jesus Christ elected the council members as well as the assembly. The governor had no veto, although Penn, as proprietor, did. Penn hoped to show that a colonial government could operate in accordance with Quaker principles, that it could maintain peace and order, and that religion could flourish without government support and with absolute freedom of conscience.

Over time, however, the Quakers struggled to forge a harmonious colony. In Pennsylvania's first ten years, it went through six governors. A disappointed Penn wrote from London: "Pray stop those scurvy quarrels that break out to the disgrace of the province."

**DELAWARE**  In 1682, the Duke of York granted Penn the area of Delaware, another part of the former Dutch territory. At first, Delaware—named for the Delaware River—became part of Pennsylvania, but after 1704 it was granted the right to choose its own assembly. From then until the American Revolution, Delaware had a separate assembly but shared Pennsylvania's governor.

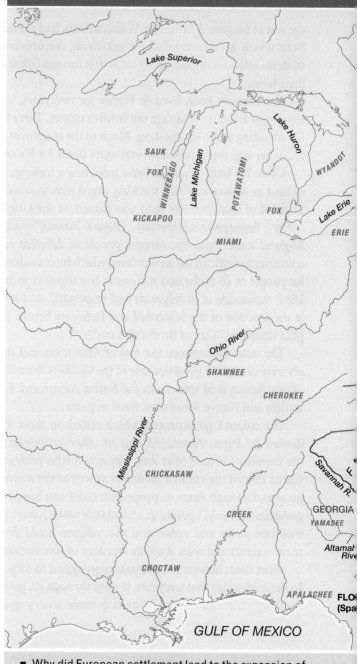

# EUROPEAN SETTLEMENTS AND INDIAN

Lake Superior

Lake Huron

Lake Michigan

Lake Erie

SAUK

FOX

WINNEBAGO

POTAWATOMI

WYANDOT

KICKAPOO

FOX

ERIE

MIAMI

Ohio River

SHAWNEE

CHEROKEE

Mississippi River

Savannah R.

CHICKASAW

CREEK

GEORGIA

YAMASEE

CHOCTAW

Altamal
Rive

APALACHEE

FLO
(Spa

GULF OF MEXICO

- Why did European settlement lead to the expansion of hostilities among the Indians?
- What were the consequences of trade and commerce between the English settlers and the southern indigenous peoples?
- How were the relationships between the settlers and the members of the Iroquois League different from those between settlers and tribes in other regions?

Quebec •

**NEW FRANCE**

MAINE

Montreal •

*ABENAKI*

*MAHICAN*

HURON

Lake Ontario

MOHAWK

*MASSACHUSETT*

Hudson R.

MA • Boston

*ONEIDA*
*ONONDAGA*
*CAYUGA*
*SENECA*

Albany •

*WAMPANOAG*

*NAUSET*

*IROQUOIS*

Hartford •

• Providence

RI

*NARRAGANSETT*

CONNECTICUT

Delaware R.

New York •

PA

NJ

Philadelphia •

*DELAWARE*

MD

DE

Potomac R.

*NANTICOKE*

• St. Marys

*POWHATAN*

VIRGINIA

James R.

• Jamestown

Occaneechi
Trading
Path

ATLANTIC

*TUSCARORA*

FALL LINE

NORTH
CAROLINA

OCEAN

*CATAWBA*

SOUTH
CAROLINA

• Charleston

• Savannah

*TIMUCUA*

DA
ish)

| 0 | 100 | 200 Miles |
| 0 | 100 | 200 Kilometers |

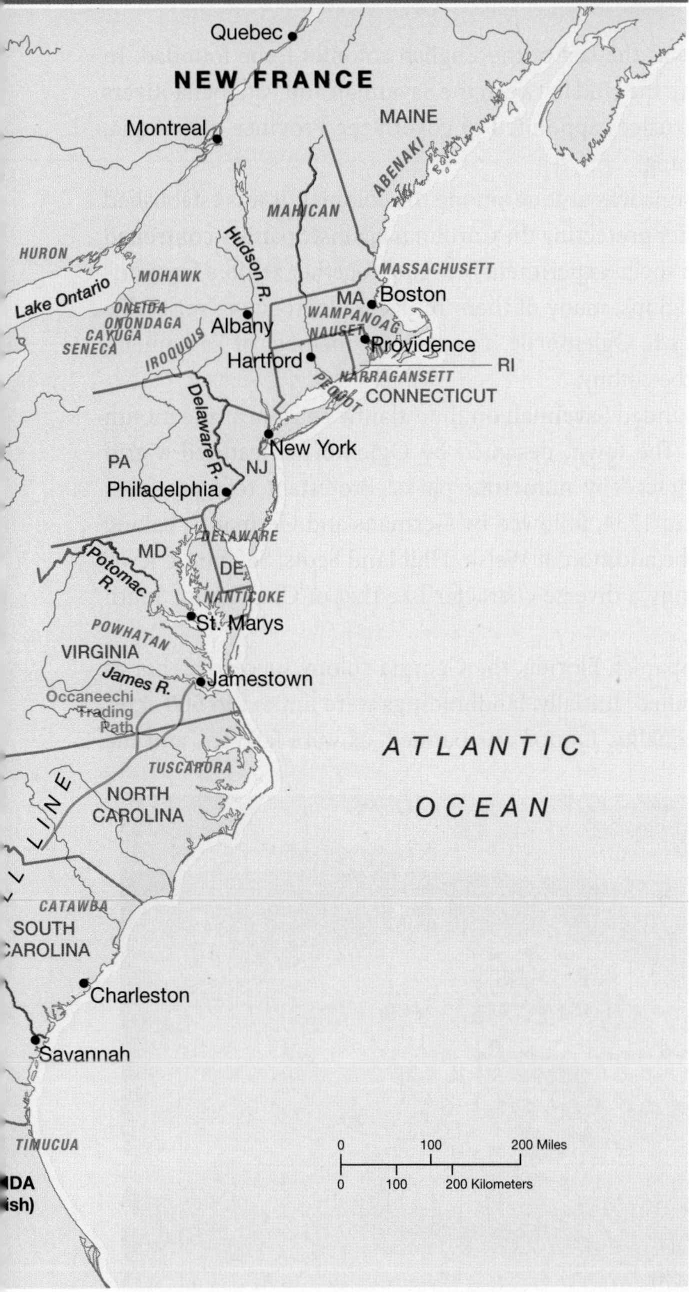

**GEORGIA**  Georgia was the last of the English colonies to be founded. In 1732, King George II gave the land between the Savannah and Altamaha Rivers to twenty-one English trustees appointed to govern the Province of Georgia, named in honor of the king.

In two respects, Georgia was unique among the colonies. It was established to provide a military buffer protecting the Carolinas against Spanish-controlled Florida and to serve as a social experiment bringing together settlers from different countries and religions, many of them refugees, debtors, or "miserable wretches." General James E. Oglethorpe, a prominent member of Parliament, was appointed to head the colony.

In 1733, colonists founded Savannah on the Atlantic coast near the mouth of the Savannah River. The town, designed by Oglethorpe, featured a grid of crisscrossing roads graced by numerous parks. Protestant refugees from Austria began to arrive in 1734, followed by Germans and German-speaking Moravians and Swiss. The addition of Welsh, Highland Scots, Sephardic Jews, and others gave the colony a diverse character like that of Charleston, South Carolina.

As a buffer against Spanish Florida, the Georgia colony succeeded, but as a social experiment, it failed. Initially, landholdings were limited to 500 acres to promote economic equality. Liquor was banned, as were lawyers, and the

**Savannah, Georgia**  The earliest known view of Savannah, Georgia (1734). The town's layout was carefully planned.

importation of slaves was forbidden. The idealistic rules soon collapsed, however, as the colony struggled to become self-sufficient. The regulations against rum and slavery were widely disregarded and finally abandoned.

In 1754, Georgia became a royal colony, and it began to grow rapidly after 1763. Georgians exported rice, lumber, beef, and pork, and they carried on a profitable trade with Caribbean islands. Almost unintentionally, the colony became an economic success and a slave-centered society.

# NATIVE PEOPLES AND ENGLISH SETTLERS

Most English colonists adopted a strategy for dealing with the Indians quite different from that of the French and the Dutch, who focused on exploiting the fur trade. The thriving commerce in animal skins helped spur exploration of the vast American continent. It also enriched and devastated the lives of Indians.

To protect a steady supply of fur pelts, the French and Dutch built outposts in upper New York and along the Great Lakes, where they established friendly relations with the Hurons and Algonquians who sought French support in their wars with the Iroquois nations. In contrast to the French experience in Canada, the English colonists were more interested in pursuing their "God-given" right to hunt and farm on Indian lands and to fish in Indian waters.

**NATIVE AMERICANS AND CHRISTIANITY** The New England Puritans aggressively tried to convert Native Americans to Christianity and "civilized" living. They insisted that Indian converts abandon their religion, language, clothes, names, and villages, and forced them to move to what were called "praying towns" to separate them from their "heathen" brethren.

**THE PEQUOT WAR** Indians in the English colonies who fought to keep their lands were forced out or killed. In 1636, settlers in Massachusetts accused a Pequot of murdering two white traders. The English took revenge by burning a Pequot village. As the Indians fled, the Puritans killed them. The militia commander declared that God had guided his actions "to smite our Enemies . . . and give us their land for an Inheritance."

Sassacus, the Pequot chief, organized the survivors and counterattacked. During the ensuing Pequot War of 1637, the colonists and their Mohegan and Narragansett allies set fire to a Pequot village and killed hundreds, including women and children. William Bradford, the governor of Plymouth, admitted that it was "a fearful sight" to see the Indians "frying in the fire and the streams

**King Philip's War**  A 1772 engraving by Paul Revere depicts Metacom (King Philip), leader of the Wampanoags.

of blood quenching" the flames, but "the victory seemed a sweet sacrifice" delivered by God.

The scattered remnants of the Pequot Nation were then hunted down. Under the terms of the Treaty of Hartford (1638), the Pequot Nation was dissolved. Captured warriors and boys were sold as slaves to plantations on Barbados and Jamaica in exchange for African slaves. Pequot women were enslaved in New England as house servants.

**KING PHILIP'S WAR**  For almost forty years after the Pequot War, relations between colonists and Indians improved somewhat, but the continuing influx of English settlers and the decline of the beaver population eventually reduced the Native Americans to poverty. In the process, the Indians and English settlers came to fear each other deeply.

The era of peaceful coexistence ended in 1675. Native American leaders, especially the chief of the Wampanoags, Metacom (known to the colonists as King Philip), resented the efforts of Europeans to take their lands and convert Indians to Christianity. In the fall of 1674, John Sassamon, a Christian Indian who had graduated from Harvard College, warned the Plymouth governor that the Wampanoags were preparing for war.

A few months later, Sassamon was found dead in a frozen pond. With little evidence to go on, colonial authorities nevertheless convicted three Wampanoags of murder and hanged them. Enraged Wampanoag warriors then burned Puritan farms on June 20, 1675. Three days later, an Englishman shot a Wampanoag; the Wampanoags retaliated by ambushing a group of Puritans, "beheading, dismembering, and mangling" the bodies in a "most inhumane" manner.

The shocking violence soon spun out of control in what came to be called **King Philip's War**, or Metacom's War. Over fourteen months, the fighting resulted in more deaths and destruction in New England in proportion to the population than any conflict since. Rival Indian nations fought on opposite sides. The colonists launched a surprise attack that killed 300 Narragansett warriors and 400 women and children. The Narragansetts retaliated by destroying Providence, Rhode Island, and threatening Boston itself, prompting a minister to call it "the saddest time with New England that was ever known." A Boston merchant lamented that unless the tide was reversed, "these colonies will soon be ruined." The situation grew so desperate that the colonies passed America's first conscription laws, drafting into the militia all males between the ages of sixteen and sixty.

In the end, 600 colonists, 5 percent of the white male population, died during the war. Some 1,200 homes were burned and 8,000 cattle killed. The Wampanoags and their allies suffered even higher casualties, perhaps as many as 4,000 dead. The colonists destroyed numerous villages and shipped off hundreds of Indians as slaves to the Caribbean islands.

The war and its aftermath slashed New England's Indian population in half, to fewer than 9,000. Those who remained were forced into villages supervised by English officials. Metacom initially escaped, only to be hunted down and killed. The victorious New Englanders marched Metacom's severed head to Plymouth, where it stayed atop a pole for twenty years, a grisly reminder of the English determination to ensure their dominance over Native Americans.

**THE IROQUOIS LEAGUE**  The same combination of forces that wiped out the Indian populations of New England and the Carolinas affected the native peoples around New York City and the lower Hudson Valley. The inability of Indian groups to unite effectively, as well as their vulnerability to infectious diseases, doomed them to conquest and exploitation. Yet indigenous peoples throughout the colonies, drawing upon their spiritual traditions in the face of barbarous suffering, came together to reconstruct their devastated communities.

In the interior of New York, for example, the Iroquois nations—Seneca, Cayuga, Onondaga, Oneida, and Mohawk—were convinced by Hiawatha, a Mohawk, to forge an alliance. The **Iroquois League**, known to its members as the *Haudenosaunee*, or Great Peace, became so strong that the Dutch and, later, English traders were forced to work with them. By the early seventeenth century, a council of some fifty sachems (chieftains) oversaw the 12,000 members of the Iroquois League.

The League benefited from a remarkable constitution, called the Great Law of Peace, which had three main principles: peace, equity, and justice. Each person was to be a shareholder in the wealth of the nation. The constitution established a Great Council of fifty male *royaneh* (religious and political leaders), each representing one of the female-led clans of the Iroquois nations. The Great Law of Peace insisted that every time the royaneh dealt with "an especially important matter or a great emergency," they had to "submit the matter to the decision of their people," both men and women, for their consent.

The search for furs and captives led Iroquois war parties to range widely across what is today eastern North America. They gained control over a huge area from the St. Lawrence River to Tennessee and from Maine to Michigan. For more than twenty years, warfare raged across the Great Lakes region between the Iroquois (supported by Dutch and English fur traders) and the Algonquians and Hurons (and their French allies).

In the 1690s, the French and their Indian allies destroyed Iroquois crops and villages, infected them with smallpox, and reduced the male Iroquois population by more than a third. Facing extermination, the Iroquois made peace in 1701. During the first half of the eighteenth century, they stayed out of the almost constant wars between the English and French, which enabled them to play the two European powers off against each other while creating a thriving fur trade for themselves.

**Algonquian ceremony celebrating harvest** As with most Native Americans, the Algonquians' dependence on nature for survival shaped their religious beliefs.

# SLAVERY IN THE COLONIES

**SLAVERY IN NORTH AMERICA**  By 1700, enslaved Africans made up 11 percent of the total American population. (Slaves would comprise more than 20 percent by 1770.) But slavery differed greatly from region to region. Africans were a tiny minority in New England (about 2 percent). Because there were no large plantations there and fewer slaves were owned, "family slavery" prevailed, with masters and slaves usually living under the same roof.

Slavery was much more common in the Chesapeake colonies and the Carolinas. By 1730, the black slave population in Virginia and Maryland had achieved a self-sustaining rate of growth, enabling the population to replenish itself naturally, thereby removing the need for slaves imported from Africa.

**SLAVERY'S AFRICAN ROOTS**  The transport of African captives to the Americas was the largest forced migration in world history. More than 10 million people eventually made the journey to the Western Hemisphere, the vast majority of them going to Portuguese Brazil or Caribbean sugar islands such as Barbados and Jamaica.

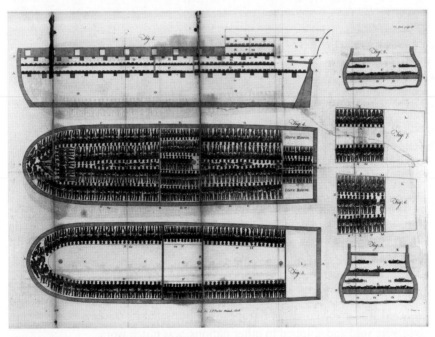

**Slave ship**  One in six Africans died while crossing the Atlantic in ships like this one, from an American diagram ca. 1808.

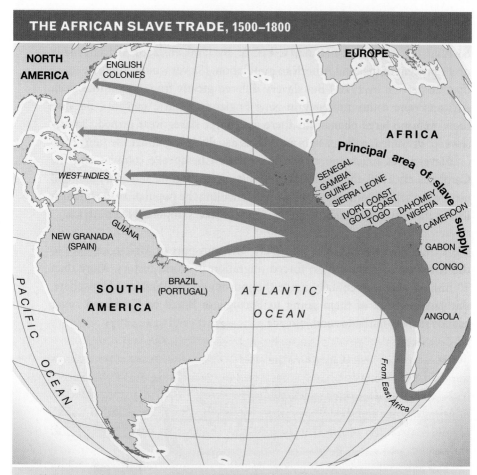

THE AFRICAN SLAVE TRADE, 1500–1800

- How were Africans captured and enslaved?
- Describe how captive Africans were treated during the Middle Passage.
- How did enslaved African Americans create a new culture in the colonies?

Enslaved Africans spoke as many as fifty different languages and worshipped many different gods. In their homelands, Africans had preyed upon other Africans. Warfare was almost constant, as rival tribes conquered, kidnapped, enslaved, and sold one another.

Slavery in Africa, however, was less brutal than in the Americas. In Africa, slaves lived with their captors, and their children were not automatically enslaved. The involvement of Europeans in transatlantic slavery, whereby captives were sold and shipped to other nations, was much worse.

During the seventeenth and eighteenth centuries, African slave traders brought captives to dozens of "slave forts" along the West African coast. After languishing for weeks or months, the captured Africans would be led to waiting ships owned by Europeans. As one of them remembered, "it was a most horrible scene; there was nothing to be heard but rattling of chains, smacking of whips, and groans and cries of our fellow men."

Once purchased, the captives were branded on the back or buttocks with a company mark, put in chains, and loaded onto slave ships. They were packed below deck and subjected to a transatlantic voyage that could last up to six months. It was known as the **Middle Passage** because it served as the middle leg of the so-called *triangular trade* in which British ships traveled on the first leg to West Africa, where they exchanged rum, clothing, and guns for slaves. The slaves then were taken on the second leg to American ports, where they were sold. The ships were then loaded with commodities and timber before returning to Britain and Europe on the final leg of the triangular trade. By the mid–eighteenth century, Britain was the largest slaving nation in the world.

The rapid growth of slavery was driven by high profits and justified by a widespread racism that viewed Africans as beasts of burden rather than human beings. Once in America, Africans were treated as property (chattel), herded in chains to public slave auctions, and sold to the highest bidder.

On large southern plantations that grew tobacco, sugarcane, or rice, slaves were organized into work gangs supervised by black "drivers" and white overseers. The slaves were often quartered in barracks, fed like livestock, and issued ill-fitting clothes and shoes. They were whipped, branded, shackled, castrated, or sold away, often to the Caribbean islands, where few survived the harsh working conditions.

The enslaved Africans, however, found ingenious ways to cope. Some rebelled by resisting work orders, sabotaging crops and stealing tools, faking illness or injury, or running away. If caught, runaways faced terrible punishment. If successful, however, they faced uncertain freedom. Where would they run *to* in a society ruled by whites and governed by racism?

**SLAVE CULTURE** While being forced into lives of bondage, Africans forged a new identity as African Americans. At the same time, they wove into American culture many strands of their heritage, including new words such as *tabby, tote, goober, yam,* and *banana*. More significant were African influences upon American music, folklore, and religious practices. Slaves often used songs, stories, and religious preachings to circulate coded messages expressing their distaste for masters or overseers. The fundamental theme of slave religion, adapted from the Christianity that was forced upon them, was deliverance: God would free them and open the gates to heaven's promised land.

**African cultural heritage in the South**  The survival of African culture among enslaved Americans is evident in this late eighteenth-century painting of a South Carolina plantation. The musical instruments and pottery are of African origin (probably Yoruban).

## THRIVING COLONIES

By the early eighteenth century, the English colonies in the New World had outstripped those of both the French and the Spanish. English America had become the most populous, prosperous, and powerful of the European empires. Yet many settlers found hard labor, desperation, and an early death in the New World. Others flourished only because they were able to exploit Indians, indentured servants, or Africans.

The English colonists did enjoy crucial advantages over their European rivals. While the tightly controlled colonial empires of Spain and France stifled innovation, the English colonies were organized as profit-making enterprises with a minimum of royal control. Where New Spain was dominated by wealthy men who often intended to return to Spain, many English colonists ventured to America because, for them, life in England had grown intolerable. The leaders of the Dutch and non-Puritan English colonies, unlike the Spanish and French, welcomed people from a variety of nationalities and religions. Perhaps most important, the English colonies enjoyed a greater degree of self-government, which made them more dynamic and creative than their French and Spanish counterparts.

Throughout the seventeenth century, geography reinforced England's emphasis on the concentrated settlements of its American colonies. The farthest western expansion of English settlement stopped at the eastern slopes of the Appalachian Mountains. To the east lay the wide expanse of ocean, which served as a highway from Europe to America. But the ocean also served as a barrier that separated old ideas from new, allowing the English colonies to evolve from a fragile stability to a flourishing prosperity in a "new world"— while developing new ideas about economic freedom and political liberties that would emerge in the eighteenth century.

# CHAPTER REVIEW

## Summary

- **English Background**  England's colonization of North America differed from
  that of its European rivals. While chartered by the Crown, English colonization
  was funded by *joint-stock companies*, groups of investors eager for profits. Colonial
  governments reflected the English model of a two-house Parliament and civil liberties. The colonization of the Eastern Seaboard occurred at a time of religious and
  political turmoil in England, strongly affecting colonial culture and development.

- **English Settlers and Colonization**  The early years of Jamestown and Plymouth were grim. In time, *tobacco* flourished, and its success paved the way for a
  slave-based economy in the South. To entice colonists, the Virginia and Plymouth
  companies granted *headrights*, or land grants. Sugar and rice plantations developed
  in the proprietary Carolina colonies, which operated with minimal royal intrusion.
  Family farms and a mixed economy characterized the middle and New England
  colonies. Religion was the primary motivation for the founding of several colonies.
  *Puritans* drafted the *Mayflower Compact* and founded Massachusetts Bay Colony
  as a Christian commonwealth. Rhode Island was established by Roger Williams,
  a religious dissenter from Massachusetts. Maryland was founded as a refuge for
  English Catholics. William Penn, a Quaker, founded Pennsylvania and invited
  Europe's persecuted sects to his colony. The Dutch allowed members of all faiths to
  settle in New Netherland.

- **Indian Relations**  Trade with the *Powhatan Confederacy* in Virginia helped
  Jamestown survive its early years, but brutal armed conflicts such as *Bacon's Rebellion* occurred as settlers invaded Indian lands. Puritans retaliated in the Pequot
  War of 1637 and in *King Philip's War* from 1675 to 1676. Among the principal
  colonial leaders, only Roger Williams and William Penn treated Indians as equals.
  The powerful *Iroquois League* played the European powers against one another to
  control territories.

- **Indentured Servants and Slaves**  The colonies increasingly relied on *indentured
  servants*, immigrants who signed contracts (indentures) that required them to
  work for several years upon arriving in America. By the end of the seventeenth
  century, enslaved Africans had become the primary form of labor in the Chesapeake. The demand for slaves in the sugar plantations of the West Indies drove
  European slave traders to organize the transport of Africans via the dreaded
  *Middle Passage* across the Atlantic. African cultures fused with others in the
  Americas to create a native-born African American culture.

- **Thriving English Colonies**  By 1700, England had become a great trading
  empire, and English America was the most populous and prosperous region of
  North America. Minimal royal interference in the proprietary for-profit colonies

and widespread landownership encouraged settlers to put down roots. Religious diversity attracted a variety of investors and settlers.

## CHRONOLOGY

| | |
|---|---|
| 1603 | James I takes the throne of England |
| 1607 | The Virginia Company establishes Jamestown |
| 1619 | First Africans arrive in English America |
| 1620 | The Plymouth colony founded by Pilgrims; Mayflower Compact |
| 1626 | The Dutch purchase Manhattan from Indians |
| 1630 | Massachusetts Bay Colony is founded by Puritans |
| 1634 | Settlement of Maryland begins |
| 1637 | The Pequot War in New England |
| 1642–1651 | The English Civil War (Puritans versus Royalists) |
| 1649 | The Toleration Act in Maryland |
| 1660 | Restoration of English Monarchy |
| 1664 | English take control of New Amsterdam (New York City) |
| 1669 | Charles Town is founded in the Carolina colony |
| 1675–1676 | King Philip's War in New England |
| 1676 | Bacon's Rebellion in Virginia |
| 1681 | Pennsylvania is established |
| 1733 | Georgia is founded |

## KEY TERMS

Puritans p. 48

joint-stock companies p. 51

Powhatan Confederacy p. 53

tobacco p. 55

indentured servants p. 55

headright p. 57

Bacon's Rebellion (1676) p. 58

Mayflower Compact (1620) p. 64

King Philip's War (1675–1676) p. 84

Iroquois League p. 85

Middle Passage p. 89

 INQUIZITIVE

Go to InQuizitive to see what you've learned—and learn what you've missed—with personalized feedback along the way.

# 3 Colonial Ways of Life

**The artisans of Boston (1766)** While fishing, shipbuilding, and maritime trade dominated New England economies, many young men entered apprenticeships, learning a trade from a master craftsman in the hopes of becoming blacksmiths, carpenters, gunsmiths, printers, candlemakers, leather tanners, and more.

The daring people who colonized America during the seventeenth and eighteenth centuries were part of a massive social migration occurring throughout Europe and Africa. Everywhere, it seemed, people were in motion—moving from farms to villages, from villages to cities, and from homelands to colonies. Rapid population growth and the rise of commercial agriculture squeezed poor farmworkers off the land and into cities, where they struggled to survive. That most Europeans in the seventeenth and eighteenth centuries were desperately poor helps explain why so many were willing to migrate to the American colonies. Others sought political security or religious freedom. A tragic exception was the Africans, who were captured and transported to new lands against their will.

Whatever their origins or social status, by the late eighteenth century a French immigrant living in New York named J. Hector St. John de Crevecoeur could announce that the diverse peoples in America were being "melted into a new race of men, whose labors and posterity [children and grandchildren] will one day cause great changes in the world."

Those who initially settled in colonial America were mostly young (more than half were under twenty-five), male, single, and poor, and almost half were indentured servants or slaves. A young servant girl in Maryland wrote her father that she was "toiling almost day and night," had "scarce anything but Indian corn and salt to eat," and had "no shoes nor stockings to wear."

Once in America, many of the newcomers kept moving within and across colonies in search of better lands or business opportunities. This extraordinary

## focus questions

1. What were the major factors that contributed to the demographic changes in the English colonies during the eighteenth century?

2. What roles did women play in the English colonies?

3. What were the differences and similarities between the societies and economies of the southern, New England, and middle colonies?

4. How did race-based slavery develop during the seventeenth century, and in what ways did it impact the social and economic development of colonial America?

5. In what ways did the Enlightenment and Great Awakening shape American thought?

mosaic of adventurous, resilient, and often ingenious people created America's enduring institutions and values, as well as its distinctive spirit and restless energy.

## THE SHAPE OF EARLY AMERICA

Life in early America was hard and often short. Many of the first colonists died of disease or starvation; others were killed by Native Americans. The average **death rate** in the early years of settlement was 50 percent. Once colonial life became more settled, however, the colonies grew rapidly. On average, the population doubled every twenty-five years during the colonial period. By 1750, the number of colonists had passed 1 million; by 1775, it approached 2.5 million. By comparison, the combined population of England, Scotland, and Ireland in 1750 was 6.5 million. An English visitor reported in 1766 that America would surely become "the most prosperous empire the world had ever seen." But that meant trouble for Britain: "How are we to rule them?"

**POPULATION GROWTH**  Benjamin Franklin, a keen observer of life in British America, said that the extraordinary growth in the colonial population came about because land was plentiful and cheap, and laborers were scarce and expensive. In contrast, Europe suffered from overpopulation and expensive farmland. From this reversal of conditions flowed many of the changes that European culture underwent during the colonization of America—not the least being that more land and good fortune lured enterprising immigrants and led the colonists to have large families, in part because farm children could help in the fields.

**Colonial farm**  This plan of a newly cleared farm shows how trees were cut and the stumps left to rot.

Colonists, men and women, tended to marry and start families at an earlier age than was common in Europe. In England, the average age at marriage for women was twenty-five or twenty-six; in America, it was twenty. The

**birth rate** rose accordingly, since women who married earlier had time for about two additional pregnancies during their childbearing years. On average, a married woman had a child every two to three years before menopause. Some women had as many as twenty pregnancies over their lifetimes.

Birthing children, however, was also dangerous, since most babies were delivered at home in unsanitary conditions. Miscarriages were common. Between 25 and 50 percent of women died during birthing or soon thereafter, and almost a quarter of all babies did not survive infancy, especially during the early stages of a colonial settlement. More deaths occurred among young children than any other age group.

Disease and epidemics were rampant in colonial America. Half of the children born in Virginia and Maryland died before reaching age twenty. In 1713, Boston minister Cotton Mather lost three of his children and his wife to a measles epidemic. (Mather lost eight of fifteen children in their first year of life.) Martha Custis, the Virginia widow who married George Washington, had four children during her first marriage. They all died young, at ages two, three, sixteen, and seventeen. Overall, however, mortality rates in the colonies were lower than in Europe. Between 1670 and 1700, the white population of the English colonies doubled, while the black population increased fivefold.

During the eighteenth century, the average age in the colonies was about sixteen; because the colonial population was younger, Americans were less susceptible to disease than were those living in Europe. The majority of colonists lived in sparsely populated settlements and were less likely to be exposed to infectious diseases. That began to change, however, as colonial cities grew larger and more congested, and trade and travel increased. By the mid–eighteenth century, the colonies were beginning to see levels of contagion much like those in the cities of Europe.

**ANTI-IMMIGRANT PREJUDICES**  Nativism began to emerge in the colonies during the eighteenth century. Although Pennsylvania was founded as a haven for people from all countries and religions, by the mid-eighteenth century, concerns arose about the influx of Germans. Benjamin Franklin described the German arrivals as "the most ignorant" group in Pennsylvania. Many of them refused to learn English, and they "herded together" in their own communities. He feared that they would "soon outnumber us" and be a source of constant tension. Why, Franklin asked, "should Pennsylvania, founded by the English, become a Colony of Aliens?" He was "not against the admission of Germans in general, for they have their Virtues," but he urged that they be spread across the colonies so as not to allow them to become a majority anywhere.

## WOMEN IN THE COLONIES

In contrast to New Spain and New France, English America had far more women, which largely explains the difference in population growth rates among the European empires in the Americas. More women did not mean more equality, however. As a New England minister stressed, "The woman is a weak creature not endowed with [the] strength and constancy of mind [of men]."

Women, as had been true for centuries, were expected to focus on what was called "housewifery," or the "domestic sphere." They were to obey and serve their husbands, nurture their children, and maintain their households. Governor John Winthrop insisted that a "true wife" would find contentment only "in subjection to her husband's authority." The wife's role, said another Puritan, was "to guide the house etc. and not guide the husband."

Not surprisingly, the lopsided power relationship in colonial households at times generated tensions. One long-suffering wife used the occasion of her husband's death to commission the following inscription on his tombstone: "Stranger, call this not a place of fear and gloom \ To me it is a pleasant spot— It is my husband's tomb." Another woman focused on her own tombstone. It read: "She lived with her husband fifty years / And died in confident hope of a better life."

Women in most colonies could not vote, hold office, attend schools or colleges, bring lawsuits, sign contracts, or become ministers. Divorces were allowed only for desertion or "cruel and barbarous treatment," and no matter who was named the "guilty party," the father received custody of the children. A Pennsylvania court did see fit to send a man to prison for throwing a loaf of hard bread at his wife, "which occasioned her Death in a short Time."

"WOMEN'S WORK" Virtually every member of a household worked, and no one was expected to work harder than women. As John Cotton, a Boston minister, admitted in 1699, "Women are creatures without which there is no Comfortable living for a man." Women who failed to perform the work expected of them were punished as if they were servants or slaves.

In 1643, Margaret Page of Salem, Massachusetts, was jailed "for being a lazy, idle, loitering person." In Virginia, two seamstresses were whipped for fashioning shirts that were too short, and a female indentured servant was forced to

***The First, Second, and Last Scene of Mortality*** Prudence Punderson's needlework (ca. 1776) shows the domestic path, from cradle to coffin, followed by most affluent colonial women.

work in the tobacco fields even though she was sick. She died in a furrow, with a hoe still in her hands. Such harsh conditions prompted a song popular with women and aimed at those back in England: "The Axe and Hoe have wrought my overthrow. If you do come here, you will be weary, weary, weary."

During the eighteenth century, **women's work** typically involved activities in the house, garden, and fields. Many unmarried women moved into other households to help with children or to make clothes. Others took in children or spun thread into yarn to exchange for cloth. Still others hired themselves out as apprentices to learn a skilled trade or craft, or operated laundries or bakeries. Technically, any money earned by a married woman was the property of her husband.

Farm women usually rose and prepared breakfast by sunrise and went to bed soon after dark. They were responsible for building the fire and hauling water. They fed and watered the livestock, cared for the children throughout the day, tended the garden, prepared lunch (the main meal) and dinner, milked the cows, and cleaned the kitchen before retiring. Women also combed, spun, spooled, wove, and bleached wool for clothing; knitted linen and cotton, hemmed sheets, and pieced quilts; made candles and soap;

chopped wood, mopped floors, and washed clothes. Female indentured servants in the southern colonies commonly worked as field hands.

One of the most lucrative trades among colonial women was the oldest: prostitution. Many servants took up prostitution after their indenture was fulfilled, and port cities had thriving brothels. They catered to sailors and soldiers, but men from all walks of life frequented what were called "bawdy houses," or, in Puritan Boston, "disorderly houses." Local authorities frowned on such activities. In Massachusetts, convicted prostitutes were stripped to the waist, tied to the back of a cart, and whipped as it moved through the town. In South Carolina, several elected public officials were dismissed because they were caught "lying with wenches." Some enslaved women whose owners expected sexual favors turned the tables by demanding compensation.

**Elizabeth Lucas Pinckney's dress** This rare sack-back gown made of eighteenth-century silk has been restored and displayed at the Charleston Museum in South Carolina.

**ELIZABETH LUCAS PINCKNEY** On occasion, circumstances forced women to exercise leadership outside the domestic sphere. Such was the case with South Carolinian Elizabeth Lucas Pinckney (1722–1793). Born in the West Indies, raised on the island of Antigua, and educated in England, "Eliza" moved to Charleston, South Carolina, at age fifteen, when her father, George Lucas, inherited three plantations. The following year, however, Lucas, a British army officer and colonial administrator, was called back to Antigua, leaving Eliza to care for her ailing mother and younger sister—and to manage three plantations worked by slaves. She wrote a friend, "I have the business of three plantations to transact, which requires much writing and more business and fatigue . . . [but] by rising early I find I can go through much business."

Eliza loved the "vegetable world" and experimented with several crops before focusing on *indigo*, a West Indian plant that produced a coveted blue dye for coloring fabric, especially military uniforms. Indigo made Eliza's family a fortune, as it did for many other plantation owners. In 1744, she married Charles Pinckney, a wealthy widower twice her age, who was speaker of the South Carolina Assembly. She made him promise that she could continue to manage her plantations.

In 1758, Pinckney died of malaria. Now a thirty-six-year-old widow, Eliza responded by adding her husband's plantations to her already substantial managerial responsibilities. Self-confident and fearless, Eliza signaled the possibility of women breaking out of the confining tradition of housewifery and assuming roles of social prominence and economic leadership.

**WOMEN AND RELIGION**  During the colonial era, no denomination allowed women to be ordained as ministers. Only the Quakers let women hold church offices and preach (exhort) in public. Puritans cited biblical passages claiming that God required "virtuous" women to submit to male authority and remain "silent" in congregational matters.

Women who challenged ministerial authority were usually prosecuted and punished. Yet by the eighteenth century, as is true today, women made up the overwhelming majority of church members. Their disproportionate attendance at services and revivals worried many ministers, since a feminized church was presumed to be a church in decline.

In 1692, the influential Boston minister Cotton Mather observed that there "are far more Godly Women in the world than there are Godly Men." In explaining this phenomenon, Mather argued that the pain associated with childbirth, which had long been interpreted as the penalty women paid for Eve's sinfulness, was in part what drove women "more frequently, & the more fervently" to commit their lives to Christ.

In colonial America, the religious roles of black women were different from those of their white counterparts. In most West African tribes, women frequently served as priests and cult leaders. Although some enslaved Africans had been exposed to Christianity or Islam, most tried to sustain their traditional African religion once they arrived in the colonies.

The acute shortage of women in the early settlement years made them more highly valued in the colonies than they were in Europe; thus over time, women's status improved slightly. The Puritan emphasis on a well-ordered family life led to laws protecting wives from physical abuse and allowing for divorce. In addition, colonial laws gave wives greater control over the property that they had brought into a marriage or that was left after a husband's death. But the age-old notion of female subordination and domesticity remained firmly entrenched in colonial America.

# SOCIETY AND ECONOMY IN THE SOUTHERN COLONIES

As the southern colonies matured, inequalities of wealth became more visible, and social life grew more divided. The use of enslaved Indians and Africans to grow and process crops generated enormous wealth for a few landowners and their families. Socially, the planters and merchants increasingly became a class apart from the "common folk." They dominated the legislatures, bought luxury goods from London and Paris, and built brick mansions with formal gardens—all the while looking down upon their "inferiors," both white and black.

Warm weather and plentiful rainfall helped the southern colonies grow the profitable **staple crops** (also called cash crops) valued by the mother country: tobacco, rice, sugarcane, and indigo. Tobacco production soared during the seventeenth century. "In Virginia and Maryland," wrote a royal official in 1629, "tobacco . . . is our All, and indeed leaves no room for anything else."

The same was true for rice in South Carolina and Georgia. Using only hand tools, slaves transformed the coastal landscapes, removing trees from swamps and wetlands infested with snakes, alligators, and mosquitos. They then created a system of floodgates to allow workers to drain or flood the fields as needed. Over time, rice planters became the wealthiest group in the British colonies. As plantations grew, the demand for enslaved laborers rose dramatically.

The first English immigrants to Virginia and Maryland built primitive one-room huts that provided limited protection and rotted quickly. Eventually, colonists built cabins on stone or brick foundations, roofed with thatched straw. The spaces between the log timbers were "chinked" with "wattle and daub"—a mix of mud, sand, straw, and wooden stakes that when dried formed a sturdy wall or seam. Most colonial homes had few furnishings;

INDIGOFERA TINCTORIA

**Indigo plant** A sketch of an indigo plant reveals the bright appearance of this important cash crop on Southern colonial plantations.

residents slept on the floor. Rarely did they have glass to fill windows. Instead, they used wooden shutters to cover the openings.

# SOCIETY AND ECONOMY IN NEW ENGLAND

Environmental, social, and economic factors contributed to the remarkable diversity among the early American colonies. New England was quite different from the southern and middle Atlantic regions: it was more governed by religious concerns, less focused on commercial agriculture, more engaged in trade, more centered on village and town life, and much less involved with slavery.

**TOWNSHIPS** Whenever New England towns were founded, the first public structure built was usually a church. By law, every town had to collect taxes to support a church, and every resident—church member or not—was required to attend midweek and Sunday religious services. The average New Englander heard more than 7,000 sermons in a lifetime.

The Puritans believed that God had created a *covenant*, or contract, in which people formed a congregation for common worship. This led to the idea of people joining to form governments, but the principles of democracy and equality were not part of Puritan political thought. Puritan leaders sought to do the will of God, and the ultimate source of authority was not majority rule but the Bible as interpreted by the ministers and magistrates (political leaders).

Unlike the settlers in the southern colonies or in Dutch New York, few New Englanders received huge tracts of land. *Township grants* were usually awarded to organized groups of settlers, often already gathered into a church congregation. They would request a "town" (what elsewhere was commonly called a township), then would divide the land according to a rough principle of equity. Those who invested more or had larger families or greater status might receive more land. The town retained some pasture and woodland in common and held other tracts for future arrivals.

**DWELLINGS AND DAILY LIFE** The first colonists in New England initially lived in caves, tents, or cabins, but they eventually built simple wood-frame houses with steeply pitched roofs to reduce the buildup of snow. By the end of the seventeenth century, most New England homes were plain but sturdy dwellings. Interior walls were often plastered and whitewashed, but it was not until the eighteenth century that the exteriors of most houses were painted, usually a deep "Indian" red, as the colonists called it. The interiors were dark, illuminated by candles or oil lamps, both of which were expensive; most people usually went to sleep soon after sunset.

There were no bathrooms ("privies"). Most families relieved themselves outside, often beside the walls of the house, indifferent to the stench. Family life revolved around the main room on the ground floor, called the hall, where meals were cooked in a fireplace and where the family lived most of the time. Hence, they came to be called *living* rooms.

Food was served at a table of rough-hewn planks, called the board, and the only eating utensils were spoons and fingers. The father was sometimes referred to as the "chair man" because he sat in the only chair (the origin of the term *chairman of the board*). The rest of the family usually stood or sat on stools or benches. A typical meal consisted of corn, boiled meat, and vegetables washed down with beer, cider, rum, or milk. Cornbread was a daily favorite, as was cornmeal mush, known as hasty pudding.

**THE NEW ENGLAND ECONOMY** As John Winthrop and the Puritans prepared to embark for New England in 1630, he stressed that God had made some people powerful and rich and others helpless and poor—so that the elite would show mercy and the masses would offer obedience. He reminded the Puritans that all were given a noble "calling" by God to work hard and ensure that material pursuits never diminished the importance of spiritual devotion.

Once in New England, the Puritans implanted their Protestant work ethic and the primacy of religion as bedrock American values. They also celebrated the idea that newness was the prime creator of culture, and they lived in the expectation of something new and dramatic: Christ's second coming and his reign on earth, the Millennium. Newness was to Americans what antiquity was to Europeans—a sign of integrity, the mark of a special relationship to history and to God. It affirmed the idea of American exceptionalism. Puritanism, in this sense, underwrote the American Revolution with its promise of political renewal.

Early New England farmers and their families led hard lives. Clearing rocks might require sixty days of hard labor per acre. The growing season was short, and no staple crops grew in the harsh climate. The crops and livestock were those familiar to the English countryside: wheat, barley, oats, some cattle, pigs, and sheep.

Many New Englanders turned to the sea for their livelihood. Codfish had been a regular element of the European diet for centuries, and the waters off the New England coast had the heaviest concentrations of cod in the world. Whales supplied ambergris, a waxy substance used in the manufacture of perfumes, as well as oil for lighting and lubrication.

New Englanders exported dried fish to Europe, with lesser grades going to the West Indies as food for slaves. The thriving fishing industry encouraged the development of shipbuilding and spurred transatlantic commerce. Rising incomes and a booming trade with Britain and Europe soon brought a taste for luxury goods in New England that clashed with the Puritan ideal of plain living and high thinking.

**SHIPBUILDING**  The forests of New England represented a source of enormous wealth. Old-growth trees were prized for use as ships' masts and spars (on which sails were attached). Early on, the British government claimed the tallest and straightest trees, mostly white pines and oaks, for use by the Royal Navy. At the same time, British officials encouraged the colonists to develop their own shipbuilding industry, and American-built ships quickly became known for their quality and price. It was much less expensive to purchase ships built in America than to transport timber to Britain for ship construction, especially since a large ship might require as many as 2,000 trees. Nearly a third of all British ships were made in the colonies during the eighteenth century.

**TRADE**  By the end of the seventeenth century, the New England colonies had become part of a complex North Atlantic commercial network, trading not only with the British Isles and the British West Indies but also—often illegally—with Spain, France, Portugal, the Netherlands, and their colonies.

Trade in New England and the middle colonies differed from that in the South in two respects. The lack of staple crops to exchange for English goods was a relative disadvantage, but the success of shipping and commercial enterprises worked in their favor. After 1660, to protect its agriculture and fisheries, the English government placed prohibitive duties (taxes) on fish, flour, wheat, and meat, while leaving the door open to high-demand products such as timber, furs, and whale oil. Between 1698 and 1717, New England and New York bought more from England than they exported to it, creating an unfavorable trade balance.

These circumstances gave rise to the **triangular trade**. New England merchants shipped rum to the west coast of Africa, where it was exchanged for slaves. Ships then took the enslaved Africans to Caribbean islands to sell. The

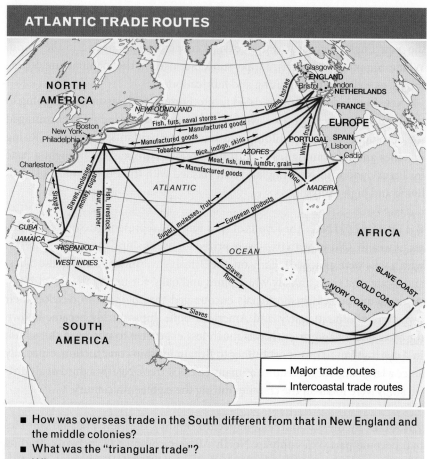

**ATLANTIC TRADE ROUTES**

- Major trade routes
- Intercoastal trade routes

■ How was overseas trade in the South different from that in New England and the middle colonies?

■ What was the "triangular trade"?

■ What were North America's most important exports?

ships returned home with various commodities, including molasses, from which New Englanders manufactured rum. In another version, they shipped provisions to the Caribbean, carried sugar and molasses to England, and returned with goods manufactured in Europe.

**PURITANICAL PURITANS?** The Puritans were religious fundamentalists who looked to the Bible for authority and inspiration. For most, the Christian faith was a living source of daily inspiration and obligation.

Although the Puritans sailed to America to create pious, prosperous communities, the traditional caricature of the dour, black-clothed Puritan, hostile to anything that gave pleasure, is false. Yes, they banned card playing, dancing in taverns, swearing, and bowling. They even fined people for celebrating

Christmas, for in their view only pagans marked the birth date of their rulers with merrymaking. Puritans also frowned on hurling insults, disobeying parents, and disrespecting civil and religious officials. In 1631, a servant named Phillip Ratcliffe had both of his ears cut off for making scandalous comments about the governor and the church in Salem.

Yet Puritans also wore colorful clothing, enjoyed secular music, and imbibed prodigious quantities of beer and rum. "Drink is in itself a good creature of God," said the Reverend Increase Mather, "but the abuse of drink is from Satan." Drunks were arrested, and repeat offenders were forced to wear the letter *D* in public.

Moderation in all things except piety was the Puritan guideline, and it applied to sexual life as well. Although sexual activity outside of marriage was strictly forbidden, New England courts overflowed with cases of adultery and illicit sex. A man found guilty of coitus with an unwed woman could be jailed, whipped, fined, and forced to marry the woman. Female offenders were also jailed and whipped, and in some cases adulterers were forced to wear the letter *A* in public.

**WITCHES IN SALEM** At times, the religious zeal of Puritan communities boiled over. The strains of Massachusetts's transition from Puritan utopia to royal colony reached a tragic climax in 1692–1693 amid the witchcraft hysteria at Salem Village (now called Danvers), a community on the northern edge of Salem Town, a flourishing port some fifteen miles north of Boston.

Belief in witchcraft was widespread in the seventeenth century. Prior to the dramatic episode in Salem Village, almost 300 New Englanders (mostly middle-aged women) had been accused of practicing witchcraft, and more than 30 had been hanged.

The Salem episode was unique in its scope and intensity, however. During

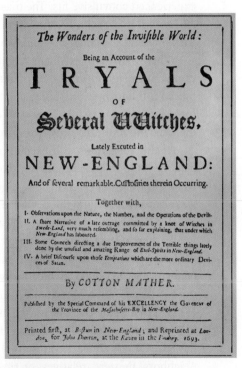

***The Wonders of the Invisible World*** Title page of the 1693 London edition of Cotton Mather's account of the Salem witchcraft trials. Mather, a prominent Boston minister, warned his congregation that the devil's legions were assaulting New England.

the brutally cold winter of 1692, several preteen girls became fascinated with a fortune teller named Tituba, an Indian slave from Barbados. Two of the girls, nine-year-old Betty Parris and eleven-year-old Abigail Williams, the daughter and niece of the village minister, Samuel Parris, began to behave oddly. They writhed, shouted, barked, sobbed hysterically, and flapped their arms as if to fly. When asked who was tormenting them, they replied that three women—Tituba, Sarah Good, and Sarah Osborne—were Satan's servants.

Parris beat Tituba, his slave, until she confessed to doing Satan's bidding. (Under the rules of the era, those who confessed were jailed; those who denied the charges were hanged.) Tituba described one of the devil's companions as "a thing all over hairy, all the face hairy and a long nose."

Authorities arrested Tituba and the other accused women. Two of them were hanged, but not before they named other supposed witches and more young girls experienced convulsive fits. The mass hysteria extended to surrounding towns, and within a few months, the Salem Village jail was filled with more than 150 men, women, and children—and two dogs—all accused of practicing witchcraft.

When a prominent farmer, Giles Corey, was accused of supernatural crimes, his neighbors stripped off his clothes, lowered him into an open grave, placed a board over his body, and began loading it with heavy boulders to force a confession. After three days of such abuse, the defiant old man finally died, having muttered only two words: "More weight!"

As the allegations and executions multiplied and spread beyond Salem, leaders of the Massachusetts Bay Colony began to worry that the witch hunts were spinning out of control. The governor finally intervened when his wife was accused of serving the devil. He disbanded the special court in Salem and ordered the remaining suspects released.

By then, nineteen people (fourteen women and five men, including a former minister) had been hanged—all justified by the biblical verse that tells believers not to "suffer a witch to live." A little over a year after it had begun, the witchcraft frenzy was finally over.

What explains Salem's mass hysteria? It may have represented nothing more than theatrical adolescents trying to enliven the dreary routine of everyday life. Others suggest community tensions may have led people to accuse neighbors, masters, relatives, or rivals as an act of spite or vengeance. Some historians have stressed that most of the accused witches were women, many of whom had in some way defied the traditional roles assigned to females.

Still another interpretation suggests that the accusations may have reflected the psychological strains caused by frequent Indian attacks just north of Salem, along New England's northern frontier. Some of the convulsing girls had seen their families killed or mutilated by Indians and suffered from what today is called post-traumatic stress disorder.

# SOCIETY AND ECONOMY IN THE MIDDLE COLONIES

Both geographically and culturally, the middle colonies (New York, New Jersey, Pennsylvania, Delaware, and Maryland) stood between New England and the South. They reflected the diversity of colonial life and foreshadowed the pluralism of the future nation.

**AN ECONOMIC MIX**   The middle colonies produced surpluses of foodstuffs for export to the slave-based plantations of the South and the West Indies: wheat, barley, oats and other grains, flour, and livestock. Three great rivers—the Hudson, Delaware, and Susquehanna—and their tributaries provided access to the backcountry of Pennsylvania and New York, and to a rich fur trade with Native Americans. The region's bustling commerce thus rivaled that of New England.

Land policies followed the *headright* system prevalent in the Chesapeake colonies. In New York, the early royal governors continued the Dutch practice of the patroonship, granting vast estates to influential men (called patroons). The patroons controlled large domains farmed by tenants (renters) who paid fees to use the landlords' mills, warehouses, smokehouses, and docks. With free land available elsewhere, however, New York's population languished, and new waves of immigrants sought the promised land of Pennsylvania.

**AN ETHNIC MIX**   In the makeup of their population, the middle colonies differed from New England's Puritan settlements and the biracial plantation colonies to the south. In New York and New Jersey, Dutch culture and language lingered. Along the Delaware River near Philadelphia, the first settlers—Swedes and Finns—were overwhelmed by an influx of Europeans. By the mid–eighteenth century, the middle colonies were the fastest-growing region in North America.

The Germans came to America (primarily Pennsylvania) mainly from the Rhineland region of Europe, where brutal religious wars had pitted Protestants against Catholics. William Penn's recruiting brochures circulated throughout central Europe, and his promise of religious freedom appealed to many persecuted sects, especially the Mennonites, German Baptists whose beliefs resembled those of the Quakers.

In 1683, a group of Mennonites founded Germantown, near Philadelphia. They represented the first wave of German migrants, most of whom were indentured servants. The large numbers of German immigrants during the eighteenth century alarmed many English colonists.

Throughout the eighteenth century, the Scots-Irish moved still farther out into the Pennsylvania backcountry. ("Scotch-Irish" is the more common but

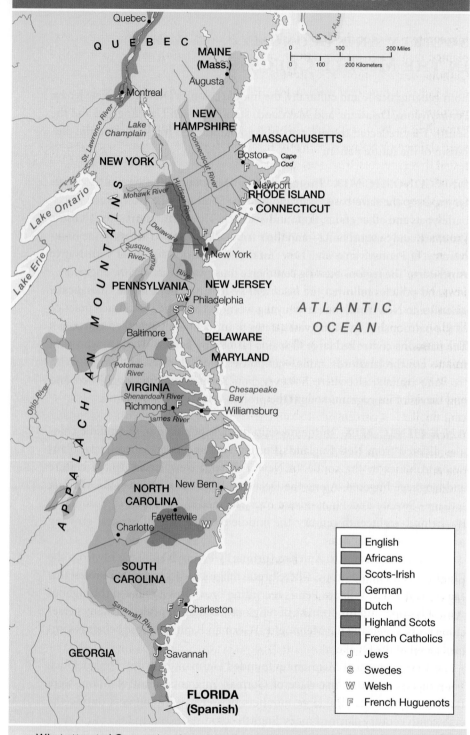

# MAJOR IMMIGRANT GROUPS IN COLONIAL AMERICA

Quebec

QUEBEC

MAINE
(Mass.)

Augusta

Montreal

Lake
Champlain

NEW
HAMPSHIRE

MASSACHUSETTS

St. Lawrence River

Boston
F

Cape
Cod

Lake Ontario

NEW YORK

Connecticut River

Newport
J RHODE ISLAND
CONNECTICUT

Mohawk River

Hudson River

F

Lake Erie

APPALACHIAN MOUNTAINS

Delaware River

F

Susquehanna
River

F J New York

ATLANTIC
OCEAN

PENNSYLVANIA

NEW JERSEY

Ohio River

W J Philadelphia
S S

Baltimore

DELAWARE

MARYLAND

Potomac
River

VIRGINIA

Shenandoah River
Richmond F

Chesapeake
Bay

Williamsburg

James River

NORTH
CAROLINA

New Bern
F

Fayetteville
W

Charlotte

SOUTH
CAROLINA

F F Charleston
J

Savannah River

GEORGIA

J Savannah

FLORIDA
(Spanish)

0        100        200 Miles
0     100     200 Kilometers

| Legend | |
|---|---|
| | English |
| | Africans |
| | Scots-Irish |
| | German |
| | Dutch |
| | Highland Scots |
| | French Catholics |
| J | Jews |
| S | Swedes |
| W | Welsh |
| F | French Huguenots |

- What attracted German immigrants to the middle colonies?
- Why did the Scots-Irish spread across the Appalachian backcountry?
- Where did the first Jews settle in America? How were they received?

inaccurate name for the Scots-Irish, a mostly Presbyterian population transplanted from Scotland to northern Ireland by the English government to give Catholic Ireland a more Protestant tone.)

Land was the great magnet for the poor Scots-Irish. They were, said a recruiting agent, "full of expectation to have land for nothing" and were "unwilling to be disappointed." In most cases, the lands they "squatted on" were claimed by Native Americans. In 1741, a group of Delaware Indians protested that the Scots-Irish were taking "our land" without giving "us anything for it." If the colonial government did not stop the flow of whites, the Delawares threatened, they would "drive them off."

The Scots-Irish and Germans became the largest non-English ethnic groups in the colonies. Other ethnic minorities also enriched the population: Huguenots (French Protestants whose religious freedom had been revoked in 1685, forcing many to leave France), Irish, Welsh, Swiss, and Jews. New York had inherited from the Dutch a tradition of ethnic and religious tolerance, which had given the colony a diverse population before the English conquest: French-speaking Walloons (a Celtic people of southern Belgium), French, Germans, Danes, Portuguese, Spaniards, Italians, Bohemians, Poles, and others, including some New England Puritans.

In the eighteenth century, the population in British North America soared, and the colonies grew more diverse. In 1790, the white population was 61 percent English; 14 percent Scottish and Scots-Irish; 9 percent German; 5 percent Dutch, French, and Swedish; 4 percent Irish; and 7 percent "unidentifiable," a category that included people of mixed origins as well as "free blacks." If one adds to the 3,172,444 whites in the 1790 census the 756,770 nonwhites, without even considering the almost 100,000 Native Americans who went uncounted, only about half the nation's inhabitants, and perhaps fewer, could trace their origins to England.

**THE BACKCOUNTRY** Pennsylvania became the great distribution point for the ethnic groups of European origin, just as the Chesapeake Bay region and Charleston, South Carolina, became the distribution points for African peoples. Before the mid–eighteenth century, settlers in the Pennsylvania backcountry had reached the Appalachian mountain range. Rather than crossing the steep ridges, the Scots-Irish and Germans filtered southward. Germans were the first white settlers in the Upper Shenandoah Valley in southern Pennsylvania, western Maryland, and northern Virginia, and the Scots-Irish filled the lower valley in western Virginia and North Carolina. The German and Scots-Irish settlers built cabins and tended farms on Indian lands, built churches, and established isolated communities along the frontier.

# Race-Based Slavery

During the late seventeenth century, slavery was legalized in all colonies but was most prevalent in the South. In 1642, Leonard Calvert paid a ship captain 24,000 pounds of tobacco for fourteen "negro men-slaves, of between 16 & 26 years old, able & sound of body and limbs." His son acknowledged that "we are naturally inclin'd to love negros [as workers] if our purses would endure it."

White colonists viewed **race-based slavery** as a normal aspect of everyday life; few considered it a moral issue. They believed that God determined one's "station in life." Slavery was therefore not a social evil but a "personal misfortune." Not until the late eighteenth century did meaningful numbers of white Europeans and Americans begin to raise ethical questions about slavery.

The first Africans in America were treated much like indentured servants, with a limited term of service, after which they gained their freedom (but not equality). Until the mid–seventeenth century, no laws in the colonies specified the meaning and scope of the word *slavery*. Gradually, however, *lifelong* slavery for blacks became the custom—and the law—of the land. By the 1660s, colonial legislatures formalized the institution of race-based slavery, with detailed **slave codes** regulating most aspects of slaves' lives. The South Carolina code, for example, defined all "Negroes, Mulattoes, and Indians" sold into bondage as slaves *for life*, as were the children born of enslaved mothers.

In 1667, the Virginia legislature declared that slaves could not serve on juries, travel without permission, or gather in groups of more than two or three. Some colonies even prohibited owners from freeing their slaves (manumission). The codes allowed owners to punish slaves by whipping them, slitting their noses, cutting their ankle cords, castrating men, or killing them. A 1669 Virginia law declared that accidentally killing a slave who was being whipped or beaten was not a serious crime. William Byrd II, a wealthy Virginia planter, confessed that the "unhappy effect of owning many Negroes is the necessity of being severe." In 1713, a South Carolina planter punished a slave by closing him up in a tiny coffin to die, only to have the trapped man's son slip in a knife so that he could kill himself rather than suffocate.

**COLOR PREJUDICE** More than a century before the English arrived in America, the Portuguese and Spanish had established a global trade in enslaved Africans. While English settlers often enslaved Indian captives, as had the Spanish and Portuguese before them, the Europeans did not enslave other Europeans who were captured in warfare. Color was the crucial difference, or at least the rationalization used to justify slavery and its hellish brutalities.

The English associated the color black with darkness and evil. To them, the different appearance, behavior, and customs of Africans and Native Americans represented savagery and heathenism. Colonial Virginians convinced themselves that blacks (and Indians) were naturally lazy, treacherous, and stupid.

**SLAVES REPLACE SERVANTS** During the seventeenth and eighteenth centuries, the profitable sugar-based economies of the French and British West Indies and Portuguese Brazil sparked greater demand for enslaved Africans, as sugar became valued almost as much as gold or silver. By 1675, the island colonies in the Caribbean had more than 100,000 slaves, while the American colonies had about 5,000.

As tobacco, rice, and indigo crops became more established in Maryland, Virginia, and the Carolinas, however, the number of African slaves in those colonies grew substantially, while the flow of white indentured servants from Britain and Europe to America slowed. Until the eighteenth century, English immigrants made up 90 percent of American colonists. After 1700, the largest number of new arrivals were enslaved Africans, who totaled more than all European immigrants combined.

Slavery was rooted in the ancient Mediterranean societies, both Christian and Muslim. By the sixteenth century, European slave traders, with the encouragement of their monarchs, had established a network of relationships with various African rulers, who provided slaves in exchange for European goods—cloth, metal objects, muskets, and rum. Over some 400 years, more than 11 million Africans were transported to the Americas.

During the late seventeenth century, the profitability of African slavery led to the emergence of dozens of new slave-trading companies both in Europe and America, thus expanding the availability of enslaved Africans and lowering the price. American colonists preferred slaves because they were officially viewed as property with no civil rights, and they (and their offspring) were servants for life. The colonists preferred Africans over enslaved Indians because they could not escape easily in a land where they stood out because of their dark skin. In short, African slaves offered a better investment.

**THE MARKET IN SLAVES** Once a slave ship arrived at an American port, Africans in chains would be auctioned to the highest bidder and taken away to begin lifelong work for a complete stranger. They were usually forbidden to use their native languages, practice African religions, or sustain their native cultures. With only rare exceptions, slaves were prohibited from owning anything unrelated to their work.

The vast majority of enslaved Africans worked on farms or plantations from dawn to dusk, in oppressive heat and humidity. As Jedidiah Morse, a prominent Charleston minister, admitted in the late eighteenth century, "No white man, to speak generally, ever thinks of settling a farm, and improving it for himself, without negroes."

During the eighteenth century, the demand for slaves soared in the southern colonies. By 1750, there were almost 250,000 slaves in British America. The vast majority, about 150,000, resided in Virginia and Maryland, with 60,000 in South Carolina and Georgia.

As the number of slaves grew, so, too, did their talents and expertise. Over time, slaves became skilled blacksmiths, carpenters, and bricklayers. Many enslaved women worked as household servants and midwives.

**SLAVE RESISTANCE** Despite the overwhelming power and authority of slave owners, slaves found ways to resist and rebel—and escape.

In a newspaper, a Georgia slave owner asked readers to be on the lookout for "a negro fellow named Mingo, about 40 years old, and his wife Quante, a sensible wench about 20 with her child, a boy about 3 years old, all this country born."

In a few cases, slaves organized rebellions in which they stole weapons, burned and looted plantations, and killed their captors. On Sunday morning, September 9, 1739, while white families were attending church, some twenty African-born slaves attacked a store in Stono, South Carolina, twenty miles southwest of Charleston. Led by a slave named Jemmy, they killed and decapitated two shopkeepers, seized weapons, and headed south toward freedom in Spanish Florida, gathering more recruits along the way. Within a few days, the slaves had burned six plantations and killed about two dozen whites, sparing one white innkeeper because he was "kind to his slaves."

The growing army of rebel slaves marched in military formation, waving a banner proclaiming "Liberty" and freeing more slaves as they moved southward. Then the well-armed and mounted militiamen caught up with them. Most of the rebels were killed, and sixty were eventually captured and decapitated by enraged planters. In the end, forty-four blacks were killed in the largest slave uprising of the colonial period.

The **Stono Rebellion** so frightened white planters that they convinced the colonial assembly to ban the importation of African slaves for ten years and pass the so-called Negro Act of 1740, which called for more oversight of slave activities and harsher punishments for rebellious behavior. Slaves could no longer grow their own food, gather in groups, learn to read or write, or earn money on the side. The new law also reduced the penalty for a white killing a slave to a minor offense and banned slaves from testifying in courts.

**Slavery in New Amsterdam (1642)** The significance of African slaves to the colonial economy is the focus of this engraving of the Dutch colony New Amsterdam, later known as New York City.

**SLAVERY IN NEW YORK CITY**  In contrast to their experience in the southern colonies, most slaves in the northern colonies lived in towns or cities, which gave them more opportunities to move about. New York City had more slaves than any American city, and by 1740 was second only to Charleston in the percentage of slaves in its population.

As the number of slaves increased in the city, fears and tensions mounted—and occasionally exploded. In 1712, several dozen slaves revolted; they started fires and used swords, axes, and guns to kill whites who attempted to fight the fires. Called out to restore order, the militia captured twenty-seven slaves, six of whom committed suicide. The rest were executed; some were burned alive. (Authorities postponed the execution of two pregnant African women at the request of their owners so that they could enslave the babies and thereby recover their investment.) New York officials thereafter passed a citywide *black code* that strictly regulated slave behavior.

The harsh regulations did not prevent another major racial incident. In the bitterly cold March of 1741, city dwellers worried that slaves were setting a series of suspicious fires, including one at the governor's house. "The Negroes are rising!" shouted terrified whites.

The frantic city council launched an investigation. Mary Burton, a sixteen-year-old white indentured servant, told authorities that slaves and poor whites were plotting to "burn the whole town" and kill the white men. The plotters were supposedly led by John Hughson, a white trafficker in stolen goods. His wife, two slaves, and a prostitute were charged as coconspirators. Despite their denials, all were convicted and hanged. Within weeks, more than half of the adult male slaves in the city were in jail. What came to be called the Conspiracy of 1741 finally ended after seventeen slaves and four whites were hanged. Thirteen more blacks were burned at the stake, while many others were deported.

At its most basic level, slavery is a system in which the powerless are brutalized by the powerful. Many slaves who ran away in colonial America faced ghastly punishments when caught. Antonio, a West African man shipped as a slave to New Amsterdam and then to Maryland, worked in the tobacco fields. He tried to escape several times. After his last attempt, in 1656, his owner, a young Dutch planter named Syman Overzee, tortured and killed him. Authorities charged Overzee with murder—and an all-white jury acquitted him.

Slavery in the Western Hemisphere was a rapidly growing phenomenon by the time of the American Revolution. White Europeans believed they were justified in dehumanizing an entire class of human beings because of the supposed "backwardness" of Africans and Indians. Not even the American Revolution's ideals of freedom and equality (for whites) would change that attitude.

# FIRST STIRRINGS OF A COMMON COLONIAL CULTURE

By the middle of the eighteenth century, the thirteen colonies were growing and maturing. Schools and colleges were springing up, and the standard of living was rising. More and more colonists were able to read about the latest ideas circulating in London and Paris while purchasing the latest consumer goods from Europe.

The rage for luxury goods, especially jewelry, fine clothing, and beaver hats, heightened the recognition of social inequality, particularly in the cities. Many ministers complained that wealthy Americans were ignoring their commitment to Christian ideals. In 1714, a Bostonian regretted the "great extravagance that people are fallen into, far beyond their circumstances, in their purchases, buildings, families, expenses, apparel—generally in their whole way of living."

English merchants required Americans to buy their goods only with *specie* (gold or silver coins). This left little "hard money" in the colonies. American merchants tried various ways to get around the shortage of specie. Some engaged in *barter*, using commodities such as tobacco or rice as currency in exchange for manufactured goods and luxury items. The issue of money—what kind and how much—would become one of the major areas of dispute between the colonies and Britain.

# COLONIAL CITIES

Throughout the seventeenth and eighteenth centuries, the colonies were mostly populated by farmers or farmworkers. But a handful of cities blossomed into dynamic centers of political and social life. Economic opportunity drove most city dwellers.

Colonial cities hugged the coastline or, like Philadelphia, sprang up on rivers large enough to handle oceangoing vessels. Never comprising more than 10 percent of the colonial population, the large coastal cities had a disproportionate influence on commerce, politics, society, and culture. By the end of the colonial period, Philadelphia, with some 30,000 people, was the largest city in the colonies, and New York City, with about 25,000, ranked second. Boston numbered 16,000; Charleston, South Carolina, 12,000; and Newport, Rhode Island, 11,000.

**THE SOCIAL AND POLITICAL ORDER** The urban social elite was dominated by wealthy merchants and property owners served by a middle class of shop owners, innkeepers, and skilled craftsmen. Almost two thirds of urban male workers were artisans—carpenters and coopers (barrel makers), shoemakers and tailors, silversmiths and blacksmiths, sailmakers, stonemasons, weavers, and potters. At the bottom of the social order were sailors, manual laborers, servants, and slaves.

Colonial cities were busy, crowded, and dangerous. Epidemics such as cholera, malaria, and yellow fever were common. The use of open fireplaces caused frequent fires, which in turn led to the development of fire companies. Rising crime and violence required increased policing by sheriffs and local militias.

Colonists also were concerned about the poor and homeless. The number of Boston's poor receiving aid rose from 500 in 1700 to 4,000 in 1736; in

New York City, it rose from 250 in 1698 to 5,000 in the 1770s. Those designated "helpless" were often provided money, food, clothing, and fuel. In some towns, "poorhouses" were built to house the homeless and provide them with jobs.

**THE URBAN WEB** The first American roads were Indian trails that were widened with frequent travel. Overland travel was initially by horse or by foot. Inns and taverns (also called public houses, or pubs) were essential social institutions, since travel at night was treacherous—and Americans loved to drink. (It was said that when the Spanish settled an area, they would first build a church; the Dutch would first erect a fort; and the English would first construct a tavern.)

Taverns and inns were places to eat, relax, read a newspaper, play cards, gossip and conduct business, and enjoy alcoholic beverages: beer, hard cider, and rum. But ministers and magistrates began to worry that the pubs were promoting drunkenness and social rebelliousness. Not only were poor whites drinking heavily but also Indians, which, one governor told the assembly, would have "fatal consequences to the Government."

Early in the eighteenth century, ministers succeeded in passing an anti-tavern law in Massachusetts Bay Colony. The Act Against Intemperance, Immorality, and Profaneness targeted taverns that had become "nurseries of intemperance." It tightened the process of issuing licenses for the sale of liquor,

**Taverns** A tobacconist's business card from 1770 captures men talking in a Philadelphia tavern while they drink ale and smoke pipes.

eliminated fiddle-playing in pubs, called for public posting of the names of "common drunkards," and banned the sale of rum and brandy, the most potent beverages.

After a few years, however, the law was rarely enforced, but the concerns remained. In 1726, a Bostonian declared that "the abuse of strong Drink is becoming Epidemical among us, and it is very justly Supposed . . . that the Multiplication of Taverns has contributed not a little to this Excess of Riot and Debauchery." The failed law was the last legislative effort to restrict alcohol consumption before the Revolution.

By the end of the seventeenth century, there were more taverns in America than any other business. They were the most important social institutions in the colonies—and the most democratic. They were places where rich and poor intermingled, and by the mid–eighteenth century, they would become gathering spots for protests against British rule.

Long-distance communication was a more complicated matter. Postal service was almost nonexistent—people gave letters to travelers or sea captains in hopes that they would be delivered. Under a parliamentary law of 1710, the postmaster of London named a deputy in charge of the colonies. A postal system eventually emerged along the Atlantic Seaboard, providing the colonies with an effective means of communication that would prove crucial in the growing controversy with Great Britain. More reliable mail delivery also spurred the growing popularity of newspapers.

**CITIZENSHIP IN THE EMPIRE**  Prior to the eighteenth century, the individual colonies, except New Hampshire, competed for immigrants from around the world. They needed settlers to generate economic growth and to conquer Native Americans. One way to entice colonists was to give them the opportunity to acquire the same civil rights as those born in the colonies ("birthright citizenship"). To that end, the colonies developed "naturalization" policies outlining the path to citizenship. Each colony had slightly different rules, but the rights of naturalization typically included acquiring property, voting and holding office, and receiving royal grants of land.

From the start, therefore, British America was an immigrant-welcoming society. The preamble to Virginia's naturalization acts of 1680 and 1705 urged "persons of different nations to transport themselves hither with their families and stocks, to settle, plant or reside, by investing them with all the rights and privileges of his majesty's natural free born subjects within the said colony."

But why were the colonies so welcoming? Because, as South Carolina's law explained, immigrants, "by their industry, diligence and trade, have very much enriched and advanced this colony and settlement thereof."

By contrast, England sought to restrict immigration to the home country, fearing that Protestant sects such as Presbyterians, Baptists, and Methodists would undermine the authority of the Church of England. Others feared that naturalized immigrants, if given the right to vote and hold office, "might endanger our ancient polity and government, and by frequent intermarriages go a great way to blot out and extinguish the English race."

To sustain high levels of immigration to British America, Parliament in 1740 passed the Naturalization Act. It announced that immigrants ("aliens") living in America for seven years would become subjects in the British Empire after swearing a loyalty oath and providing proof that they were Protestants. While excluding "papists" (Roman Catholics), the new law did make exceptions for Jews.

# THE ENLIGHTENMENT IN AMERICA

The most significant of the new European ideas circulating in eighteenth-century America grew out of a burst of intellectual activity known as the **Enlightenment**. The Enlightenment celebrated rational inquiry, scientific research, and individual freedom. Enlightened people sought the truth, wherever it might lead, rather than remain content with believing ideas and dogmas passed down through the ages or taken from the Bible.

Immanuel Kant, the eighteenth-century German philosopher, summed up the Enlightenment point of view: "Dare to know! Have the courage to use your own understanding." He and others used the power of reason to analyze the workings of nature, and they employed new tools like microscopes and telescopes to engage in close observation, scientific experimentation, and precise mathematical calculation.

**THE AGE OF REASON**  The Enlightenment, often called the Age of Reason, was triggered by a scientific revolution in the sixteenth century that transformed the way educated people observed and understood the world. Just as early explorers alerted Europeans to the excitement of new geographical discoveries, early modern scientists began to realize that social "progress" could occur through a series of intellectual and technological discoveries enabled by the adaptation of mathematical techniques for observing the natural world. The engines of curiosity and inventiveness drove a scientific revolution whose findings over the course of 150 years would prove astonishing.

The ancient Christian view that the God-created earth was at the center of the universe, with the sun revolving around it, was overthrown by the controversial solar system described by Nicolaus Copernicus, a Polish astronomer and Catholic priest. In 1533, Copernicus asserted that the earth and other planets orbit the sun. Catholic officials scorned his theory until it was later confirmed by other scientists using telescopes.

In 1687, Englishman Isaac Newton announced his transformational theory of the earth's gravitational pull. Using both astronomy and mathematical physics, especially calculus, Newton challenged biblical notions of the world's workings by depicting a changing, dynamic universe moving in accordance with natural laws that could be grasped by human reason and explained by mathematics. He implied that natural laws (rather than God) govern all things, from the orbits of the planets to the effects of gravity to the science of human relations: politics, economics, and society.

Some enlightened people, called **Deists**, carried Newton's scientific outlook to its logical conclusion, claiming that God created the world and designed its "natural laws," which governed the operation of the universe. In other words, Deism maintained that God planned the universe and set it in motion, but no longer interacted directly with the earth and its people. Their rational God was nothing like the intervening God of the Christian tradition, to whom believers prayed for daily guidance and direct support.

Evil, according to the Deists, resulted not from humanity's inherent *sinfulness* as outlined in the Bible but from human *ignorance* of the rational laws of nature. Therefore, the best way to improve society and human nature, according to Deists such as Thomas Jefferson and Benjamin Franklin, was by cultivating Reason, which was the highest Virtue. (Followers of the Enlightenment thinkers often capitalized both words.)

By using education, reason, and scientific analysis, societies were bound to improve their knowledge as well as their quality of life. In this sense, the word *enlightenment* meant that people were learning to think for themselves rather than blindly accept what tradition, the Bible, and political and religious elites directed them to believe. In sum, the perspectives of the Enlightenment helped people to stop fearing nature and to begin controlling and manipulating it to improve the quality of life—for all.

Enlightened "freethinkers" refused to allow church and state to limit what they could study and investigate. In this sense, the Enlightenment was a disruptive and even dangerous force in European thought. It spawned not just revolutionary ideas but revolutionary movements.

Faith in the possibility of human progress was one of the most important beliefs of the Enlightenment. Equally important was the notion of political freedom. Both Thomas Jefferson and Benjamin Franklin, among many other eighteenth-century British Americans, were intrigued by English political philosopher John Locke, who maintained that "natural law" called for a

**Benjamin Franklin** A champion of rational thinking and common sense behavior, Franklin was an inventor, philosopher, entrepreneur, and statesman.

government that rested on the consent of the governed and respected the "natural rights" of all. Those "rights" included the basic civic principles of the Enlightenment—human rights, political liberty, religious toleration— that would later influence colonial leaders' efforts to justify a revolution.

**THE AMERICAN ENLIGHTEN-MENT** Benjamin Franklin epitomized the American version of the Enlightenment. Born in Boston in 1706, he left home at the age of seventeen, bound for Philadelphia. Six years later, he bought a print shop and began editing and publishing the *Pennsylvania Gazette* newspaper. When he was twenty-six, he published *Poor Richard's Almanack*, a collection of seasonal weather forecasts, puzzles, household tips, and witty sayings.

Franklin was a pragmatist who focused on getting things done and relished helping people learn to work together and embrace the necessity of compromise. Most of all, he celebrated the virtue and benefit of public service. Before he retired from business at the age of forty-two, Franklin had founded a public library, started a fire company, helped create what became the University of Pennsylvania, and organized a debating club that grew into the American Philosophical Society.

Franklin became a highly regarded diplomat, politician, and educator. Above all, he was an inventive genius devoted to scientific investigation. His wide-ranging experiments extended to the fields of medicine, meteorology, geology, astronomy, and physics. He developed the Franklin stove, the lightning rod, bifocal spectacles, and a glass harmonica.

Although raised as a Presbyterian, Franklin was no churchgoer. A Deist who prized science, reason, and a robust social life, he did not believe in the sacredness of the Bible or the divinity of Jesus. Like the European Deists, Franklin came to believe that God had created a universe directed by natural laws, but thereafter the Creator was not a daily force in human life.

For Franklin and others, to be *enlightened* meant exercising an all-encompassing curiosity about life that in turn nurtured the confidence and capacity to think critically. For them, it was intolerable to accept what tradition dictated as truth without first testing its legitimacy.

**EDUCATION IN THE COLONIES** White colonial Americans were among the most literate people in the world. Almost 90 percent of men (more than in England) could read. The colonists were concerned about educating their young, and education in the traditional ideas and manners of society—even literacy itself—was primarily the responsibility of family and church. (The modern concept of free public education would not be fully embraced until the nineteenth century.)

The Puritan emphasis on reading Scripture, which all Protestants shared to some degree, led to the strong focus on literacy. In 1647, the Massachusetts Bay Colony required every town to support a grammar school (a "Latin school" that could prepare a student for college).

| | |
|---|---|
| A | In *Adam's* Fall We Sinned all. |
| B | Thy Life to Mend This *Book* Attend. |
| C | The *Cat* doth play And after flay. |
| D | A *Dog* will bite A Thief at night. |
| E | An *Eagles* flight Is out of fight. |
| F | The Idle *Fool* Is whipt at School. |

**Colonial education** A page from the rhymed alphabet of *The New England Primer*, a popular American textbook first published in the 1680s.

The Dutch in New Netherland were as interested in education as the New England Puritans. In Pennsylvania, the Quakers established private schools. In the southern colonies, however, schools were rare. The wealthiest southern planters and merchants hired tutors or sent their children to England for schooling.

# THE GREAT AWAKENING

The growing popularity of Enlightenment rationalism posed a direct threat to traditional religious life in Europe and America. But Christianity has always shown remarkable resilience. This was certainly true in the early eighteenth century, when the American colonies experienced a revival of spiritual zeal designed to restore the primacy of emotion in the religious realm.

Between 1700 and 1750, when the controversial ideas of the Enlightenment were circulating among the best-educated colonists, hundreds of new Christian congregations were founded. Most Americans (85 percent) lived in colonies with an "established" church, meaning that the colonial government endorsed—and collected taxes to support—a single official denomination.

The Church of England, also known as Anglicanism, was the established church in Virginia, Maryland, Delaware, and the Carolinas. Puritan Congregationalism was the official faith in most of New England. In New York, Anglicanism vied with the Dutch Reformed Church for control. Pennsylvania had no state-supported church, but Quakers dominated the legislative assembly. New Jersey and Rhode Island had no official denomination and hosted numerous Christian splinter groups.

Most colonies organized religious life around local parishes, which defined their theological boundaries and defended them against people who did not hold to the same faith. In colonies with official tax-supported religions, people of other faiths could not preach without the permission of the parish. In the 1730s and 1740s, the parish system was thrown into turmoil by the arrival of traveling evangelists, called *itinerants,* who claimed that most of the local parish ministers were incompetent. In their emotionally charged sermons, the itinerants, several of whom were white women and African Americans, insisted that Christians must be "reborn" in their convictions and behavior.

**REVIVALISM**  During the early 1730s, worries about the erosion of religious fervor helped spark a series of emotional revivals known as the **Great Awakening**. The revivals spread up and down the Atlantic coast, divided congregations, towns, and families, and fueled popular new denominations, especially the Baptists and Methodists, who accounted for most of the growth. A skeptical Benjamin Franklin admitted that the Awakening was having a profound effect on social life: "Never did the people show so great a willingness to attend sermons. Religion is become the subject of most conversation."

**JONATHAN EDWARDS**  In 1734–1735, a remarkable spiritual transformation occurred in the congregation of Jonathan Edwards, a prominent Congregationalist minister in the Massachusetts town of Northampton. One of America's most brilliant philosophers and theologians, Edwards had entered Yale College in 1716, at age thirteen, and graduated at the top of his class four years later.

When Edwards arrived in Northampton in 1727, he was shocked by the town's lack of religious conviction. He claimed that the young people were preoccupied with sinful pleasures and indulged in "lewd practices" that "corrupted others." He warned that Christians had become obsessed with making and spending money, and that the ideas associated with the Enlightenment were eroding the importance of religious life.

Edwards rushed to restore the emotional side of religion. "Our people," he said, "do not so much need to have their heads stored [with new scientific knowledge] as to have their hearts touched [with spiritual intensity]."

Edwards was fiery and charismatic, and his vivid descriptions of the torments of hell and the delights of heaven helped rekindle spiritual intensity among his congregants. By 1735, he reported that "the town seemed to be full of the presence of God; it never was so full of love, nor of joy."

In 1741, Edwards delivered his most famous sermon, "Sinners in the Hands of an Angry God," in which he

**Jonathan Edwards** One of the foremost preachers of the Great Awakening, Edwards dramatically described the torments that awaited sinners in the afterlife.

reminded the congregation that hell is real and that God "holds you over the pit of hell, much as one holds a spider, or some loathsome insect, over the fire, abhors you, and is dreadfully provoked. . . . He looks upon you as worthy of nothing else, but to be cast into the fire." When he finished, he had to wait several minutes for the congregants to quiet down before he could lead them in a closing hymn.

**GEORGE WHITEFIELD** The most celebrated promoter of the Great Awakening was a young English minister, George Whitefield, whose reputation as a spellbinding evangelist preceded him to the colonies.

Whitefield set out to restore the fires of religious intensity in America. In the autumn of 1739, the twenty-five-year-old evangelist began a fourteen-month tour, preaching to huge crowds in every colony. His critics were as fervent as his admirers. A disgusted Bostonian described a revival meeting's theatrics: "The meeting was carried on with . . . some screaming out in Distress and Anguish . . . some again jumping up and down . . . some lying along on

**George Whitefield** The English minister's dramatic eloquence roused Americans, inspiring many to experience a religious rebirth.

the floor. . . . The whole with a very great Noise, to be heard at a Mile's Distance, and continued almost the whole night."

Whitefield enthralled audiences with his golden voice, flamboyant style, and unparalleled eloquence. Even Benjamin Franklin, a confirmed rationalist who saw Whitefield preach in Philadelphia, was so excited by the sermon that he emptied his pockets into the collection plate.

Whitefield urged his listeners to experience a "new birth"—a sudden, emotional moment of conversion and salvation. By the end of his sermon, one listener reported, the entire congregation was "in utmost Confusion, some crying out, some laughing, and Bliss still roaring to them to come to Christ, as they answered, I will, I will, I'm coming, I'm coming."

**RADICAL EVANGELISTS** Edwards and Whitefield inspired many imitators, the most radical of whom carried emotional evangelism to extremes, stirring up women as well as those at the bottom of society—laborers, seamen, servants, slaves, and landless farm folk—and ordaining their own ministers.

William Tennent, an Irish-born Presbyterian, charged that local ministers were "cold and sapless," afraid to "thrust the nail of terror into sleeping souls." Tennent's oldest son, Gilbert, also an evangelist, defended his tactics by explaining that he and other traveling preachers invaded parishes only when the local minister showed no interest in the "Getting of Grace and Growing in it."

The Tennents urged people to renounce their ministers and pursue salvation on their own. They also attacked the excesses of the wealthy and powerful. Worried members of the colonial elite charged that the radical revivalists were spreading "anarchy, levelling, and dissolution."

Equally unsettling to the elite was the Reverend James Davenport, who urged Christians to renounce "rationalist" ministers influenced by the Enlightenment and become the agents of their own salvation through a purely emotional conversion experience. A Connecticut minister warned that Davenport and other extremists were "frightening people out of their senses."

## WOMEN AND REVIVALS

The Great Awakening's most controversial element was the emergence of women who defied convention by speaking in religious services. Among them was Sarah Haggar Osborne, a Rhode Island schoolteacher who organized prayer meetings that eventually included men and women, black and white. When concerned ministers told her to stop, she refused to "shut my mouth and doors and creep into obscurity."

Similarly, in western Massachusetts, Bathsheba Kingsley spread the gospel among her neighbors because she had received "immediate revelations from heaven." When her husband tried to intervene, she pummeled him with "hard words and blows," praying loudly that he "go quick to hell."

For all the turbulence created by the revivals, however, churches remained male bastions of political authority.

**A CHANGING RELIGIOUS LANDSCAPE** The Great Awakening made religion intensely personal by creating both a deep sense of spiritual guilt and an intense yearning for redemption. Yet it also undermined many of the established churches by emphasizing that all individuals, regardless of wealth or social status, could receive God's grace without the guidance of ministers. Denominations became bitterly divided as "Old Light" conservatives criticized democratic revivalism and sparred with "New Light" evangelicals who delighted in provoking emotional outbursts and celebrating individual freedom in matters of faith.

New England religious life would never be the same, as the Great Awakening shattered the Puritan ideal of religious uniformity. Isaac Stiles, a crusty Connecticut minister, denounced the "intrusion of choice into spiritual matters" and charged that the "multitudes were seriously, soberly, and solemnly out of their wits" in their embrace of ultra-emotional religion. John Henry Goetschius, a Dutch Reformed evangelist, shot back that Stiles and other Old Lights were determined to "impose on many people, against their will, their old, rotten, and stinking routine religion."

In the more sedate churches of Boston, a focus on rational or enlightened religion gained the upper hand; ministers found Puritan theology too cold and forbidding, and they considered irrational the Calvinist concept that people could be forever damned by predestination. They embraced Enlightenment rationalism, arguing that God created laws of nature that people could discover and exploit.

**RELIGIOUS COLLEGES** In reaction to taunts that "born-again" revivalist ministers lacked learning, the Awakening gave rise to denominational colleges that became a distinctive characteristic of American higher education. The three colleges already in existence had religious origins: Harvard College in Massachusetts, founded in 1636 because the Puritans dreaded "to leave an illiterate ministry to the church when our present ministers shall lie in the dust"; the College of William and Mary in Virginia, created in 1693 to strengthen the Anglican ministry; and Yale College, set up in 1701 to educate the Puritans of Connecticut, who believed that Harvard was drifting from the strictest orthodoxy. The College of New Jersey, later Princeton University, was founded by Presbyterians in 1746.

In close succession came King's College (1754) in New York, later renamed Columbia University, an Anglican institution; the College of Rhode Island (1764), later called Brown University, which was Baptist; New Jersey's Queens College (1766), later known as Rutgers, which was Dutch Reformed; and Dartmouth College (1769) in New Hampshire, which was Congregationalist.

**THE HEART VERSUS THE HEAD** Like a ferocious fire that burned intensely before dying out, the Great Awakening subsided by 1750. Like the Enlightenment, however, it influenced the forces leading to the revolution against Great Britain and set in motion powerful currents that still flow in American life.

The Awakening implanted in American culture the evangelical impulse and the emotional appeal of revivalism, weakened the status of the old-fashioned clergy and state-supported churches, and encouraged believers to exercise their own individual judgment. By encouraging the proliferation of denominations, it heightened the need for toleration of dissent.

In some respects, however, the Awakening and the Enlightenment, one stressing the urgings of the spirit and the other celebrating the cold logic of reason, led by different roads to similar ends. Both movements spread across the mainland colonies and thereby helped bind the regions together. Both emphasized the power and right of individual decision-making, and both aroused hopes that America would become the promised land in which people might attain the perfection of piety or reason, if not both.

By urging believers to exercise their own spiritual judgment, revivals weakened the authority of the established churches and their ministers, just as resentment of British economic regulations would later weaken colonial loyalty to the king. As such, the Great Awakening and the Enlightenment helped nurture a growing commitment to individual freedom and resistance to authority that would play a key role in the rebellion against British "tyranny" in 1776.

# CHAPTER REVIEW

## SUMMARY

- **Colonial Demographics**  Cheap land lured poor immigrants to America. The initial shortage of women eventually gave way to a more equal gender ratio and a tendency to earlier marriage than in Europe, leading to higher *birth rates* and larger families. *Death rates* were lower in the colonies than in Europe, which led to rapid population growth.

- **Women in the Colonies**  English colonists brought their beliefs and prejudices with them to America, including convictions about the inferiority of women. Colonial women remained largely confined to *women's work* in the house, yard, and field. Over time, though, necessity created opportunities for women outside their traditional roles.

- **Colonial Differences**  A thriving colonial trading economy sent raw materials such as fish, timber, and furs to England in return for manufactured goods. The expanding economy created new wealth and a rise in the consumption of European goods, and it fostered the expansion of slavery. Tobacco was the *staple crop* in Virginia, rice in the Carolinas. Plantation agriculture based on slavery became entrenched in the South. New England's shipping industry created a profitable *triangular trade* among Africa, America, and England. By 1790, German, Scots-Irish, Welsh, and Irish immigrants, as well as other European ethnic groups, had settled in the middle colonies, along with Quakers, Jews, Huguenots, and Mennonites.

- **Race-Based Slavery**  Deep-rooted prejudice led to *race-based slavery*. Africans were considered "heathens" whose supposed inferiority entitled white Americans to use them as slaves. Africans brought diverse skills to help build America's economy. The use of African slaves was concentrated in the South, where landowners used them to produce lucrative staple crops, such as tobacco, rice, and indigo. But slaves lived in cities, too, especially New York. As the slave population increased, race relations grew tense, and *slave codes* were created to regulate the movement of enslaved people. Sporadic slave uprisings, such as the *Stono Rebellion*, occurred in both the North and South.

- **The Enlightenment and the Great Awakening**  Printing presses, education, and city life created a flow of new ideas that circulated via long-distance travel, tavern life, the postal service, and newspapers. The attitudes of the *Enlightenment* were transported along international trade routes. Sir Isaac Newton's scientific discoveries culminated in the belief that reason could improve society. Benjamin Franklin, who believed that people could shape their own destinies, became the face of the Enlightenment in America. *Deism* expressed the religious views of the Age of Reason. By the 1730s, a revival of faith, the *Great Awakening*, swept through the colonies. New congregations formed as evangelists insisted that Christians be "reborn." Individualism, not orthodoxy, was stressed in this first popular religious movement in America's history.

## CHRONOLOGY

| | |
|---|---|
| **1619** | First Africans arrive at Jamestown |
| **1636** | Harvard College is established |
| **1667** | Virginia enacts slave code declaring that enslaved children who were baptized as Christians remained slaves |
| **1692–1693** | Salem witchcraft trials |
| **1730s–1740s** | Great Awakening |
| **1739** | Stono Rebellion |
| | George Whitefield preaches his first sermon in America, in Philadelphia |
| **1741** | Jonathan Edwards preaches "Sinners in the Hands of an Angry God" |

## KEY TERMS

**death rate** p. 96

**birth rate** p. 97

**women's work** p. 99

**staple crops** p. 102

**triangular trade** p. 105

**race-based slavery** p. 112

**slave codes** p. 112

**Stono Rebellion (1739)** p. 114

**Enlightenment** p. 120

**Deists** p. 121

**Great Awakening** p. 124

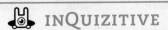 **INQUIZITIVE**

Go to InQuizitive to see what you've learned—and learn what you've missed—with personalized feedback along the way.

# 4 From Colonies to States

**Boston Tea Party** Disguised as Native Americans, a swarm of Patriots boarded three British ships and dumped more than 300 chests of East India Company tea into Boston Harbor.

Four great European naval powers—Spain, France, England, and the Netherlands (Holland)—created colonies in North America during the sixteenth and seventeenth centuries as part of their larger fight for global supremacy. Throughout the eighteenth century, wars raged across Europe, mostly pitting the Catholic nations of France and Spain against Protestant Great Britain and the Netherlands. The conflicts spread to the Americas, and by the middle of the eighteenth century, North America had become a primary battleground, involving both colonists and Native Americans allied with different European powers.

Spain's sparsely populated settlements in the borderlands north of Mexico were small and weak compared to those in the British colonies. Spain had failed to create substantial colonies with robust economies. Instead, it emphasized the conversion of native peoples to Catholicism, prohibited manufacturing within its colonies, strictly limited trade with Native Americans, and searched—in vain—for gold.

The French and British colonies developed a thriving trade with Native Americans at the same time that the fierce rivalry between Great Britain and France gradually shifted the balance of power in Europe. By the end of the eighteenth century, Spain and the Netherlands were in decline, leaving France and Great Britain to fight for dominance. Their nearly constant warfare led Great Britain to tighten its control over the American colonies to raise the funds needed to combat Catholic France and Spain. Tensions over these British efforts to preserve their empire at the expense of American freedoms would lead to rebellion and eventually to revolution.

## focus questions

**1.** What were the similarities and differences in the way that the British and French Empires administered their colonies before 1763?

**2.** Analyze how the French and Indian War changed relations among the European powers in North America.

**3.** Describe how after the French and Indian War the British tightened their control over the colonies, and then summarize the colonial responses.

**4.** What were the underlying factors in the events of the 1770s that led the colonies to declare their independence from Britain?

## COMPETING NEIGHBORS

The bitter rivalry between Great Britain and France fed France's desire to challenge the English presence in the Americas by establishing Catholic settlements in the Caribbean, Canada, and the region west of the Appalachian Mountains. Yet the French never invested enough people or resources in North America. During the 1660s, the population of New France was less than that of the tiny English colony of Rhode Island. By the mid–eighteenth century, the residents of New France numbered less than 5 percent of British Americans.

## NEW FRANCE

The actual settlement of New France began in 1605, when soldier-explorer Samuel de Champlain founded Port-Royal in Acadia, along the Atlantic coast of Canada. Three years later, Champlain established Quebec, to the west, along the St. Lawrence River. Until his death in 1635, Champlain governed New France on behalf of trading companies looking to create a prosperous commercial colony tied to fur trade with the Indians and fishing opportunities off the Atlantic coast.

In 1627, however, the French government ordered that only Catholics could live in New France. This restriction stunted the settlement's growth—as did the harsh winter climate. As a consequence, the number of French who colonized Canada was *much* smaller than the number of British, Dutch, and Spanish colonists in other North American colonies, and they were almost all men. From the start, France spent far more to maintain its North American colony than it gained from the furs and fish exported to France for sale.

Champlain knew that the French could survive only by befriending the native peoples. To that end, he dispatched trappers and traders to live with the indigenous nations, learn their languages and customs, and marry their women. Many of these hardy woodsmen pushed into the forested regions around the Great Lakes and developed a flourishing fur trade.

In 1663, French King Louis XIV converted New France into a royal colony led by a governor-general who modeled his rule after that of the absolute monarchy. New France was fully subject to the French king; colonists had no political rights or elected legislature.

To solidify New France, Louis XIV dispatched soldiers and settlers, including shiploads of young women to be wives for the mostly male colonists. He also awarded large grants of land, called *seigneuries*, to lure aristocratic settlers. The poorest farmers usually rented land from the *seigneur*.

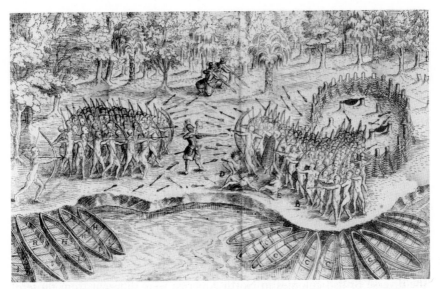

**Champlain in New France** Samuel de Champlain firing at a group of Iroquois, killing two chieftains (1609).

Still, only about 40,000 French immigrants came to the Western Hemisphere during the seventeenth and eighteenth centuries. By 1750, when the British colonists in North America numbered about 1.5 million, the total French population was only 70,000.

From their Canadian outposts along the Great Lakes, French explorers in the early 1670s moved down the Mississippi River to the Gulf of Mexico. Louis Jolliet, a fur trader born in Quebec, teamed with Father Jacques Marquette, a Jesuit priest fluent in Indian languages, to explore the Wisconsin River south to the Mississippi. Traveling in canoes, they paddled to within 400 miles of the Gulf of Mexico, where they turned back for fear of encountering Spanish soldiers.

Other French explorers followed. In 1682, René-Robert Cavelier, sieur de La Salle, organized an expedition that started in Montreal, crossed the Great Lakes, and went down the Mississippi to the Gulf of Mexico, the first European to do so. Near what is today Venice, Mississippi, La Salle erected a cross, claiming for France the vast Ohio and Mississippi Valleys—all the way to the Rocky Mountains. He named the region Louisiana, after Louis XIV. New France had one important advantage over the British: access to the great inland rivers that led to the heartland of the continent and thus to the pelts of such fur-bearing animals as beaver, otter, and mink.

Settlement of the Louisiana Territory finally began in 1699, when the French established a colony near Biloxi, Mississippi. The main settlement then moved to Mobile Bay and, in 1710, to the present site of Mobile, Alabama.

For nearly fifty years, the driving force in Louisiana was Jean-Baptiste Le Moyne, sieur de Bienville. In 1718, he founded New Orleans, which soon became the capital of the sprawling Louisiana colony encompassing much of the interior of the North American continent.

That same year, the Spanish, concerned about the French presence in Louisiana, founded San Antonio in the Texas province of New Spain. They built a Catholic mission (later called the "Alamo") and a fort (*presidio*) to convert the indigenous people and to fend off efforts by the French to expand into Texas.

## THE BRITISH COLONIAL SYSTEM

The diverse British colonies in North America were different from those of New France. Colonial governments were typically headed by a royal governor or proprietor who could appoint and remove officials, command the militia, and grant pardons to people convicted of crimes.

Yet the British colonists enjoyed rights and powers absent in Britain—as well as in New France. In particular, they had *elected* legislatures. Representatives in the "lower" houses were chosen by popular vote, but only adult males owning a specified amount of property could vote. Because property holding was so widespread in America, however, a greater proportion of the male population could vote in the colonies than could anywhere else in the world.

The most important political trend in eighteenth-century America was the growing power of the colonial legislatures. Like Parliament, the colonial assemblies controlled the budget and could pass laws and regulations. Most assemblies exercised influence over the royal governors by paying their salaries. Throughout the eighteenth century, the assemblies expanded their power and influence. Self-government in British America became first a habit, then a cherished "right."

MERCANTILISM The English Civil War during the 1640s sharply reduced the flow of money and people to America and forced English Americans to take sides in the conflict between Royalists and Puritans.

Oliver Cromwell's victory over the monarchy in 1651 had direct effects in the colonies. As England's new ruler, Cromwell embraced a more rigidly enforced **mercantilism**, a political and economic policy adopted by most European monarchs during the seventeenth century in which the government controlled all economic activities. Key industries were regulated, taxed, or "subsidized" (supported by payments from the government), and people with specialized skills or knowledge of new technologies, such as textile machinery, were not allowed to leave the country.

Mercantilism also supported the creation of global empires. Colonies, it was assumed, enriched the mother country in several ways: (1) by providing silver and gold as well as crucial raw materials [furs, fish, grains, timber, sugar, tobacco, indigo, tar, etc.]; (2) by creating a captive market of colonial consumers who were forced to buy goods created in the home country; (3) by relieving social tensions and political unrest in the home country, because colonies could become a haven for the poor, unemployed, and imprisoned; and (4) by not producing goods that would compete with those produced in the home country.

**NAVIGATION ACTS** Such mercantilist assumptions prompted Oliver Cromwell to adopt the first in a series of **Navigation Acts** intended to increase control over the colonial economies. The Navigation Act of 1651 required that all goods going to and from the colonies be carried *only* in English-owned ships. The law was intended to hurt the Dutch, who had developed a flourishing shipping business between America and Europe. Dutch shippers charged much less to transport goods than did the English, and they actively encouraged smuggling in the American colonies as a means of defying the Navigation Acts. By 1652, England and the Netherlands were at war—the first of three naval conflicts between 1652 and 1674 involving the two Protestant rivals.

After the monarchy was restored to power in England in 1660, the Royalist Parliament passed the Navigation Act of 1660, which specified that certain colonial products (such as tobacco) were to be shipped *only* to England or other colonies. The Navigation Act of 1663, called the Staples Act, required that *all* shipments from Europe to America first stop in Britain to be offloaded and taxed before being sent to the colonies.

In 1664, English warships conquered New Netherland, removing the Dutch from North America. By 1700, the English had surpassed the Dutch as the world's leading maritime power, and most products sent to and from America via Europe and Africa were carried in English ships. What the English government did not expect was that the mercantile system would arouse intense resentment in the colonies.

**COLONIAL RESENTMENT** Colonial merchants and shippers complained about the Navigation Acts, but the English government refused to

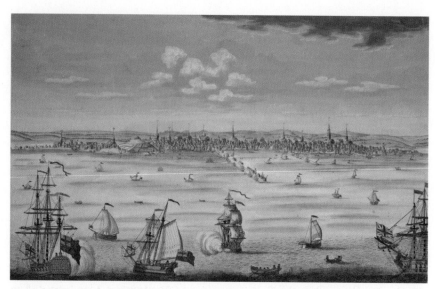

**Boston from the southeast** This view of eighteenth-century Boston shows the importance of shipping and its regulation in the colonies.

lift the restrictions. New England was particularly hard hit. In 1678, a defiant Massachusetts legislature declared that the Navigation Acts had no legal standing. In 1684, King Charles II tried to teach the rebellious colonists a lesson by revoking the royal charter for Massachusetts.

The following year, Charles died and his brother, King James II, succeeded him, becoming the first Catholic monarch in more than 100 years. To demonstrate his power, the new king reorganized the New England colonies into a single supercolony called the Dominion of New England.

In 1686, a new royal governor, the authoritarian Sir Edmund Andros, arrived in Boston. Andros stripped New Englanders of their civil rights, imposed new taxes, ignored town governments, strictly enforced the Navigation Acts, and punished smugglers.

## THE GLORIOUS REVOLUTION

In 1688, the Dominion of New England added the former Dutch provinces of New York, East Jersey, and West Jersey to its control, just a few months before the **Glorious Revolution** erupted in England. People called the revolution "glorious" because it took place with little bloodshed. Catholic James II, fearing imprisonment in the Tower of London, fled to France and was replaced by the king's daughter Mary and her husband William III, the ruling Dutch Prince. Both were Protestants.

William III and Mary II would govern England as constitutional monarchs, their powers limited by Parliament. They soon issued a religious Toleration Act and a Bill of Rights to ensure that there never again would be an absolute monarchy in England.

In 1689, Americans in Boston staged their own revolution. A group of merchants, ministers, and militiamen (citizen-soldiers) arrested Governor Andros and his aides and removed Massachusetts Bay Colony from the new Dominion of New England. Within a few weeks, the other colonies that had been absorbed into the Dominion also restored their independence.

William and Mary, however, were determined to crack down on smuggling and rebelliousness. They appointed new royal governors in Massachusetts, New York, and Maryland. In Massachusetts, the governor was given authority to veto acts of the colonial assembly, and he removed the requirement that only church members could vote in elections.

**JOHN LOCKE ON REVOLUTION** The removal of King James II in the Glorious Revolution showed that a monarch could be deposed according to constitutional principles. In addition, the long-standing geographical designation "Great Britain" for the united kingdoms of England, Scotland, and Wales would soon be revived as the nation's official name.

A powerful justification for revolution appeared in 1690 when English philosopher John Locke published *Two Treatises on Government*, which had an enormous impact on political thought in the colonies. Locke rejected the traditional "divine" right of monarchs to govern with absolute power and insisted that people are endowed with **natural rights** to life, liberty, and property. He noted that it was the need to protect those natural rights that led people to establish governments in the first place. When rulers failed to protect the property and lives of their subjects, Locke argued, the people had the right—in extreme cases—to overthrow the monarch and change the government.

## AN EMERGING COLONIAL SYSTEM

In early 1689, New Yorkers sent a message to King William thanking him for delivering England from "tyranny, popery, and slavery." Many colonists were disappointed, however, when the king cracked down on American smugglers. The Act to Prevent Frauds and Abuses of 1696 required royal governors to enforce the Navigation Acts, allowed customs officials in America to use "writs of assistance" (general search warrants that did not have to specify the place to be searched), and ordered that accused smugglers be tried in royal *admiralty* courts (because juries in colonial courts rarely convicted their peers).

Soon, however, British efforts to enforce the Navigation Acts waned. King George I and George II, German princes who were descendants of James I, showed much less interest in enforcing colonial trade laws. Robert Walpole, the long-serving prime minister (1721–1742) and lord of the treasury, decided that the American colonies should be left alone to export needed raw materials (timber, tobacco, rice, indigo) and to buy manufactured goods from the mother country.

Under Walpole's leadership, Britain followed a policy of "salutary neglect" of the Navigation Acts, allowing the colonies greater freedom to pursue their economic interests, in part because the British did not want to pay the huge expense of enforcing the imperial regulations. What Walpole did not realize was that **salutary neglect** would create among many colonists an independent attitude that would eventually blossom into revolution.

**THE HABIT OF SELF-GOVERNMENT** Government within the American colonies evolved during the eighteenth century as the colonial assemblies acquired powers, particularly with respect to government appointments, which Parliament had yet to exercise itself.

The English colonies in America benefited from elected legislative assemblies. Whether called the House of Burgesses (Virginia), Delegates (Maryland), Representatives (Massachusetts), or simply the assembly, the "lower" houses were chosen by popular vote. Only male property owners could vote. Because property holding was much more widespread in America than in Europe, a greater proportion of the male population could vote and hold office. Members of the colonial assemblies tended to be wealthy, but there were exceptions. One unsympathetic colonist observed in 1744 that the New Jersey Assembly "was chiefly composed of mechanicks and ignorant wretches; obstinate to the last degree."

The most profound political trend during the eighteenth century was the growing power and influence of the colonial assemblies. They controlled the budget through their vote on taxes and expenditures, and they held the power to initiate legislation. Most of the assemblies also exerted leverage on the royal governors by controlling their salaries. By midcentury, the colonies had become largely self-governing.

## WARFARE IN THE COLONIES

The Glorious Revolution of 1688 transformed relations among the great powers of Europe. Protestants William and Mary, for example, were passionate foes of Catholic France's Louis XIV. They organized an alliance of European nations against the French in a transatlantic war known in the American colonies as King William's War (1689–1697).

It would be the first of four major wars fought in Europe and the colonies over the next seventy-four years pitting Britain and its European allies against France or Spain and their allies. By the end of the eighteenth century, the struggle between the British and French would shift the balance of power in Europe.

The prolonged warfare had a devastating effect on New England, especially Massachusetts, which was closest to the battlefields of French Canada. It also reshaped the relationship between America and Great Britain, which emerged from the wars as the most powerful nation in the world. Thereafter, international commerce became increasingly essential to the expanding British Empire, thus making the American colonies even more strategically significant.

**THE FRENCH AND INDIAN WAR** The most important conflict between Britain and France (and its Catholic ally Spain) in North America was the **French and Indian War** (1756–1763), globally known as the **Seven Years' War**. Unlike the three earlier wars, the French and Indian War started in America and ended with a decisive victory. It was sparked by French and British competition for the ancestral Indian lands in the vast Ohio Valley; whichever nation or colony (both Pennsylvania and Virginia claimed jurisdiction over it) controlled the "Ohio Country" would control the entire continent because of the strategic importance of the Ohio and Mississippi Rivers.

To defend their interests, the French pushed south from Canada and built forts in the Ohio Country. When Virginia's governor learned of the forts, he sent a twenty-two-year-old militia officer, Major George Washington, to warn the French to leave. But Washington was rudely rebuffed by the French.

A few months later, in the spring of 1754, Washington, now a lieutenant colonel, went back to the Ohio Country with 150 volunteer soldiers and Indian allies. They planned to build a fort where the Allegheny, Monongahela, and Ohio Rivers converged (where the city of Pittsburgh later developed). The so-called Forks of the Ohio was the key strategic gateway to the vast territory west of the Appalachian Mountains, and both sides were determined to control it.

After two months of travel through densely forested, hilly terrain, Washington learned that French soldiers had beaten him to the site and built Fort Duquesne in western Pennsylvania. Washington decided to camp about forty miles away. The next day, the Virginians ambushed a French scouting party, killing ten soldiers, including the commander—the first fatalities in what would become the French and Indian War.

Washington and his troops, reinforced by more Virginians and British soldiers dispatched from South Carolina, hastily constructed a tiny circular stockade. They called it Fort Necessity. Washington remarked that the valley provided "a charming field for an encounter," but there was nothing charming about the battle that erupted when a large French force surrounded and attacked on July 3, 1756.

After the day-long, lopsided Battle of Great Meadows, Washington surrendered, having seen a third of his 300 men killed or wounded. The French and their Indian allies lost only three men. The French commander then forced Washington to surrender his French prisoners and admit that he had "assassinated" the group of French soldiers at the earlier encounter. On July 4, 1754, Washington and the defeated Virginians began trudging home.

France was now in undisputed control of the Ohio Country. Yet Washington's bungled expedition wound up triggering what would become a massive world war. As a British politician exclaimed, "the volley fired by a young Virginian in the backwoods of America set the world on fire."

**THE ALBANY PLAN** British officials in America, worried about war with the French and their Indian allies, urgently called a meeting of the northern colonies. Twenty-one representatives from seven colonies gathered in Albany, New York. It was the first time that a large group of colonial delegates had met to take joint action.

At the urging of Pennsylvania's Benjamin Franklin, the Albany Congress (June 19–July 11, 1754) approved the **Albany Plan of Union**. It called for eleven colonies to band together, headed by a president appointed by the king. Each colonial assembly would send two to seven delegates to a "grand council," which would have legislative powers. The Union would have jurisdiction over Indian affairs.

The Albany Plan of Union was too radical for the time, however. British officials and the colonial legislatures, eager to maintain their powers, wanted simply a military alliance against Indian attacks, so they rejected the Albany Plan. Franklin later maintained that the Plan of Union, had it been approved, might have postponed or eliminated the eventual need for a full-scale colonial revolution. His proposal, however, would become the model for the form of governance (Articles of Confederation) created by the new American nation in 1777.

**WAR IN NORTH AMERICA** With the failure of the Albany Plan, the British decided to force a showdown with the "presumptuous" French. In June 1755, a British fleet captured the French forts protecting Acadia, along the Atlantic coast of Canada. The British then expelled 11,500 Acadians, the Catholic French residents. Hundreds of them eventually found their way to French Louisiana, where they became known as Cajuns.

In 1755, the British government sent 1,000 soldiers to dislodge the French from the Ohio Country. The arrival of unprecedented numbers of "redcoat" soldiers on American soil would change the dynamics of British North America. Although the colonists endorsed the use of force against the

French, they later would oppose the use of British soldiers to enforce colonial regulations.

**BRADDOCK'S DEFEAT** The British commander in chief in America, General Edward Braddock, was a stubborn, overconfident officer who refused to recruit large numbers of Indian allies. Braddock viewed Indians with contempt, telling those willing to fight with him that he would not reward them with land: "No savage should inherit the land." His dismissal of the Indians and his ignorance of unconventional warfare would prove fatal.

With the addition of some American militiamen, including George Washington as a volunteer officer, Braddock's force left northern Virginia to confront the French, hacking a 125-mile-long road west through the Allegheny Mountains toward Fort Duquesne.

On July 9, 1755, as the British neared the fort, they were ambushed by French soldiers, Canadian militiamen, and Indians; they suffered shocking losses. Braddock was shot; he died three days later. Washington, his coat riddled by four bullets, helped lead a hasty retreat.

What came to be called the Battle of Monongahela was one of the worst British defeats in history. The French and Indians captured the British cannons and supplies and killed 63 of 86 British officers and 914 of 1,373 soldiers. The

**The first American political cartoon** Benjamin Franklin's plea to the colonies to unite against the French in 1754 would become popular again twenty years later, when the colonies faced a different threat.

Indians burned alive twelve wounded British soldiers left behind on the battlefield. A devastated Washington wrote his brother that the vaunted British redcoats had "been scandalously beaten by a trifling body of men" and had "broke & run as sheep pursued by hounds." The Virginians, he noted, "behaved like Men and died like Soldiers."

**A WORLD WAR** While Braddock's defeat sent shock waves through the colonies, Indians allied with the French began attacking American farms throughout western Pennsylvania, Maryland, and Virginia, killing, scalping, or capturing hundreds of men, women, and children. Desperate to respond,

**From La Roque's Encyclopedie des Voyages** An Iroquois warrior in an eighteenth-century French engraving.

the Pennsylvania provincial government offered 130 Spanish dollars for each male Indian scalp and 50 dollars for female scalps.

Indians and colonists killed each other mercilessly throughout 1755 and 1756. It was not until May 1756, however, that Protestant Britain and Catholic France formally declared war in Europe. The first true "world war," the Seven Years' War in Europe (the French and Indian War in North America) would eventually be fought on four continents and three oceans. In the end, it would redraw the political map of North America.

France, governed by the inept Louis XV, entered the war without excitement, fought with little distinction, and emerged battered, humiliated, and bankrupt. When the war began, the British had the smaller army but three times as many warships. By the end, the French had lost nearly 100 ships, and the British had captured more than 64,000 French sailors.

The onset of war brought into office a new British government, with William Pitt as prime minister. Pitt determined that defeating the French required a different military policy. Realizing that the colonial legislatures had largely resisted British efforts to coerce American colonists into embracing the war as their own, he decided to treat the colonies as allies rather than inferiors. Instead of forcing them to help finance the war, he provided funds that convinced the legislatures to become full partners in the quest to oust the French from Canada.

Pitt's shrewd approach enabled British commanders to assemble a force of 45,000 British troops and American militiamen, and in August 1759, they captured French forts near the Canadian border at Ticonderoga, Crown Point, and Niagara.

**THE BATTLE OF QUEBEC** In 1759, the French and Indian War reached its climax with a series of British triumphs. The most decisive victory was at Quebec, the hilltop fortress city and the capital of French Canada. During the dark of night, some 4,500 British troops scaled the cliffs above the St. Lawrence River and at dawn surprised the French defenders in a battle that lasted only ten minutes. The French surrendered four days later.

The Battle of Quebec marked the turning point in the war. Thereafter, the conflict in North America ebbed, although the fighting dragged on until 1763. In the South, fighting flared between the Carolina settlers and the Cherokee Nation. A force of British regulars and colonial militia broke Cherokee resistance in 1761.

**A NEW BRITISH KING** On October 25, 1760, the ailing British King George II arose at 6 A.M., drank his chocolate milk, and adjourned to his toilet closet. A few minutes later, a servant heard a strange noise, opened the door, and found the king dead, the result of a ruptured artery. His death shocked the nation and brought an untested new king—George II's twenty-two-year-old grandson—to the throne.

Although initially shy and insecure, King George III would surprise his

**George III** The young king of a victorious empire.

family by becoming a strong-willed leader who oversaw the military defeat of France and Spain in the Seven Years' War.

**THE TREATY OF PARIS (1763)** The **Treaty of Paris**, signed in February 1763, gave Britain control of important French colonies around the world, including many in India, several highly profitable "sugar island" colonies in the Caribbean, and all of France's North American possessions east

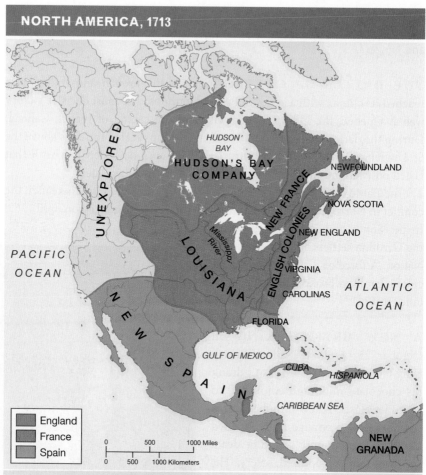

**NORTH AMERICA, 1713**

HUDSON'
BAY

HUDSON'S BAY
COMPANY

NEWFOUNDLAND

NEW FRANCE

NOVA SCOTIA

UNEXPLORED

NEW ENGLAND

Mississippi
River

ENGLISH COLONIES

VIRGINIA

PACIFIC
OCEAN

LOUISIANA

CAROLINAS

ATLANTIC
OCEAN

FLORIDA

NEW

SPAIN

GULF OF MEXICO

CUBA

HISPANIOLA

CARIBBEAN SEA

England
France
Spain

0      500      1000 Miles
0    500    1000 Kilometers

NEW
GRANADA

- What events led to the first clashes between the French and the British in the late seventeenth century?
- Why did New England suffer more than other regions of North America during the wars of the eighteenth century?
- What were the long-term financial, military, and political consequences of the wars between France and Britain?

of the Mississippi River. This encompassed all of Canada and what was then called Spanish Florida, including much of present-day Alabama and Mississippi. As compensation, the treaty gave Spain control over the vast Louisiana Territory, including New Orleans and all French land west of the Mississippi. France was left with no territory on the North American continent.

British Americans were delighted with the outcome of the war. As a New England minister declared, Great Britain had reached the "summit of earthly grandeur and glory." The French menace had been removed, and British

**NORTH AMERICA, 1763**

UNEXPLORED

RUSSIANS

HUDSON BAY

HUDSON'S BAY COMPANY

NEWFOUNDLAND

ST.-PIERRE ET MIQUELON (FRANCE)

QUEBEC

NOVA SCOTIA

NEW ENGLAND

OREGON (Disputed by Russia and Spain)

PACIFIC OCEAN

LOUISIANA

Mississippi River

INDIAN RESERVE

THE THIRTEEN COLONIES

VIRGINIA

CAROLINAS

ATLANTIC OCEAN

N E W

S P A I N

EAST FLORIDA

WEST FLORIDA

GULF OF MEXICO

HAITI (FRANCE)

GUADELOUPE (FRANCE)

CUBA

HISPANIOLA

MARTINIQUE (FRANCE)

BRITISH HONDURAS

CARIBBEAN SEA

MOSQUITO COAST

NEW GRANADA

| 0 | 500 | 1000 Miles |
| 0 | 500 | 1000 Kilometers |

- England
- Spain
— Proclamation line of 1763

- How did the map of North America change between 1713 and 1763?
- How did Spain win the Louisiana Territory?
- What were the consequences of the British gaining all the land east of the Mississippi River?

Americans could now enjoy the highest quality of life of any people in the Western Hemisphere.

Yet Britain's spectacular military success on land and sea created massive challenges. The national debt had doubled during the war, and the new cost of maintaining the sprawling North American empire, including the permanent stationing of thousands of British soldiers in the colonies, was staggering. Moreover, British leaders developed what one historian has called an "arrogant triumphalism," which led them to tighten—and ultimately lose—their control over the Indians and colonists in North America. In managing a vastly larger empire, the British would soon find themselves at war with their own colonies.

**MANAGING A NEW EMPIRE** No sooner was the Treaty of Paris signed than George III and his cabinet, working through Parliament, began regulating the colonies in new ways. With Britain no longer burdened by overpopulation, royal officials now rejected efforts by the colonies to encourage more immigrants, such as paying for their Atlantic crossing.

The king also encouraged his ministers to enforce economic regulations on the American colonies to help reduce the crushing national debt caused by the war. In 1763, the average British citizen paid twenty-six times as much in annual taxes as did the average American colonist. With that in mind, British leaders thought it only fair that the Americans should pay more of the expenses for administering and defending the colonies.

Many Americans disagreed, however, arguing that the various Navigation Acts restricting their economic activity were already a form of taxation. The resulting tension set in motion a chain of events that would lead to revolution and independence. "It is truly a miserable thing," said a Connecticut minister in December 1763, "that we no sooner leave fighting our neighbors, the French, but we must fall to quarreling among ourselves."

**PONTIAC'S REBELLION** After the war, colonists began squabbling over Indian-owned land west of the Appalachian Mountains that had been ceded to the British in the Treaty of Paris. Native American leaders, none of whom attended the meetings leading to the treaty, were shocked to learn that the French had "given" their ancestral lands to the British, who were intent upon imposing a harsh settlement on those Indians who had been allies of the French. The new British commander, General Jeffrey Amherst, announced that the British would no longer provide "gifts" to the Indians, as the French had done. Ohio Indians complained to British army officers that "as soon as you conquered the French, you did not care how you treated us."

The frustrated Indians fought back in the spring of 1763, capturing most of the British forts around the Great Lakes and in the Ohio Valley. "Never was panic more general," reported the *Pennsylvania Gazette*, "than that of the Back[woods] Inhabitants, whose terrors at this time exceed that followed on the defeat of General Braddock."

Native Americans also raided colonial settlements in Pennsylvania, Maryland, and Virginia, destroying farms and killing thousands. "Every day, for some time past," reported a Marylander, "has offered the melancholy scene of poor distressed families . . . who have deserted their plantations, for fear of falling into the cruel hands of our savage enemies."

The widespread Indian attacks came to be called **Pontiac's Rebellion** because of the prominent role played by the Ottawa chieftain in trying to unify several tribes in the effort to stop British expansion. Pontiac told a British official that the "French never conquered us, neither did they purchase a foot of our Country, nor have they a right to give it to you."

In December 1763, frontier ruffians in Pennsylvania took the law into their own hands. Outraged at the unwillingness of pacifist Quakers in the Pennsylvania assembly to protect white settlers on the frontier from marauding Indians, a group called the Paxton Boys, Scots-Irish farmers from Paxton, near Harrisburg, took revenge by massacring and scalping peaceful Conestogas— men, women, and children. Then they threatened to kill the so-called Moravian Indians, a group of Christian converts living near Bethlehem. When the Indians took refuge in Philadelphia, some 1,500 Paxton Boys marched on the capital, where Benjamin Franklin helped persuade them to return home.

**THE PROCLAMATION LINE**   To help keep peace with the Indians and to abide by the terms of an earlier agreement with the Delawares and Shawnees, King George III issued the **Royal Proclamation of 1763**, which drew an imaginary line along the crest of the Appalachian Mountains from Canada to Georgia. Americans ("our loving subjects") were forbidden to go west of the line to ensure that the Indians would not be "molested or disturbed" on their ancestral lands.

For the first time, royal officials were curtailing territorial expansion, and Americans did not like it. Virginia planter George Washington was among those who objected. Like thousands of other British Americans, he wanted "to secure some of the most valuable lands in the King's part" even if it meant defying "the Proclamation that restrains it at present." He interpreted the Proclamation Line as a short-term way to appease Indian concerns about colonial expansion into their ancestral lands.

In practice, the Proclamation Line ended the activities of speculators buying huge tracts of Indian lands but did not keep land-hungry settlers from pushing across the Appalachian ridges into the Indian lands in the Ohio Valley. By 1767, an Indian chief was complaining that whites were "making more encroachments on their Country than ever they had before."

**IMMIGRATION SOARS** One unexpected result of the war's end was a surge in European immigration to the American colonies. With the French no longer a threat, colonists were more comfortable in testing the American wilderness. Between 1763 and 1775, more than 30,000 English, 55,000 Protestant Irish, and 40,000 Scots left the British Isles for the colonies. In addition, 12,000 German and Swiss settlers came in search of a better life. At the same time, some 85,000 enslaved Africans were brought to America's southern colonies, especially the Carolinas and Virginia. It was the greatest mass migration in history to that point, and it provided the foundation for much of America's development thereafter.

Most of the new arrivals were young males who had served as apprentices to learn a craft or trade. Many others were poor farm families who emigrated as a group. Half of them could not afford to pay the cost of crossing the Atlantic and therefore arrived as indentured servants.

The settlers were entering an exotic new civilization that had no rigid aristocracy. America was a fluid environment in which people could make their way on their abilities alone. A young English farmer wrote to say that he missed his friends but valued more his chance to become "independent" in ways unavailable at home.

# REGULATING THE COLONIES

As Britain tightened its hold over the colonies—and the Indians—after 1763, Americans reminded Parliament that their original charters guaranteed that they should be treated as if they were English citizens, with all the rights and liberties protected by the nation's constitutional traditions. Why should they be governed by a distant legislature in which they had no elected representatives? Such arguments, however, fell on deaf ears in Parliament. As one member explained, the British were determined "to make North America pay [for] its own army."

**GRENVILLE'S COLONIAL POLICY** Just as the Proclamation of 1763 was being drafted, a new British government, led by prime minister George Grenville, began to grapple with the huge debts the government had accumulated during the Seven Years' War, along with the added expenses of maintaining troops in America. Grenville insisted that the Americans must pay for the soldiers defending them. He also resented the large number of American merchants who engaged in smuggling to avoid paying British taxes on imported goods. Grenville ordered colonial officials to tighten enforcement of the Navigation Acts and sent warships to capture smugglers.

**THE SUGAR ACT** Grenville's effort to enforce the Navigation Acts posed a serious threat to New England's prosperity. Distilling rum out of molasses, a sweet syrup made from sugarcane, had become quite profitable, especially if the molasses could be smuggled in from Caribbean islands still controlled by the French.

To generate more money from the colonies, Grenville put through the American Revenue Act of 1764, commonly known as the Sugar Act, which cut the tax on molasses in half. Doing so, he believed, would reduce the temptation to smuggle French molasses or to bribe royal customs officers. The Sugar Act, however, also added new *duties* (taxes) on other goods (sugar, wines, coffee, spices) imported into America. The new revenues, Grenville believed, would help pay for "the necessary expenses of defending, protecting, and securing, the said colonies."

With the Sugar Act, Parliament, for the first time, adopted a policy designed to raise *revenues* from the colonies and not merely to *regulate* trade with other nations. Colonists claimed that the Sugar Act taxed them without their consent, since they had no elected representatives in Parliament. British officials argued, however, that Parliament's power over the colonies was absolute and indivisible. If the Americans accepted parliamentary authority in *any* area, they had to accept it in *every* area. In the end, however, the cost of enforcing the new sugar tax proved to be four times greater than the revenue it generated.

**THE CURRENCY ACT** The colonies had long faced a chronic shortage of "hard" money (gold and silver coins, called *specie*), which kept flowing overseas to pay debts in England. To address the lack of specie, many colonies issued their own paper money, which could not be used in other colonies. British creditors feared payment in a currency of such fluctuating value, so Grenville implemented the Currency Act of 1764, a set of regulatory measures that prohibited the colonies from coining or printing money, while requiring that all payments for imported British goods be in gold or silver coins or in a commodity like tobacco. By banning paper money, the value of existing paper money plummeted. As a Philadelphia newspaper complained, "The Times are Dreadful, Dismal, Doleful, Dolorous, and dollar-less."

**THE STAMP ACT** Grenville excelled at repeatedly doing the wrong thing. In 1765, for example, he persuaded Parliament to pass the Quartering Act, which required Americans to feed and house British troops. Most Americans saw no need for so many British soldiers. If the British were there to defend against Indians, why were they positioned in cities far from the frontier?

Some colonists decided that the Quartering Act was actually an effort to bully them. William Knox, a British colonial official, admitted as much in 1763 when he said that the "main purpose" of keeping an army in America was "to secure the dependence of the colonies on Great Britain."

In February 1765, Grenville aggravated colonial concerns by pushing through an even more controversial measure. The **Stamp Act** required colonists to purchase paper with an official government stamp for virtually every possible use: newspapers, pamphlets, bonds, leases, deeds, licenses, insurance policies, college diplomas, even playing cards. The requirement was to go into effect November 1.

The Stamp Act was the first effort by Parliament to place a tax directly on American goods and services rather than levying an "external" tax on imports and exports, and it offended just about everyone. Benjamin Franklin's daughter Sarah ("Sally") wrote to her father in London, where he was representing the colonies. She reported that the only subject of conversation in America was the Stamp Act, "and nothing else is talked of. . . . everybody has something to say" about the hated tax, in part because, when combined with the Sugar and Currency Acts, it promised to bring economic activity to a halt.

**THE WHIG POINT OF VIEW** Grenville's colonial policies especially outraged Americans living in the large port cities: Boston, New York, Philadelphia, and Charleston. Unwittingly, the prime minister had stirred up protests and set in motion a violent debate about the proper relationship between Great Britain and her colonies. In the late eighteenth century, the Americans who opposed British policies began to call themselves Patriots, or *Whigs*, a name earlier applied to British critics of royal power. In turn, Whigs labeled the king and his "corrupt" government ministers and Parliamentary supporters as *Tories*, a term of abuse meaning friends of the king.

In 1764 and 1765, American Whigs felt that Grenville was violating their rights in several ways. A professional army was usually a weapon used by tyrants, and with the French defeated and Canada solidly under British control, thousands of British soldiers remained in America. Were the troops there to protect the colonists or scare them into obedience?

The Whigs also argued that although British citizens had the right to be taxed only by their elected representatives in Parliament, Americans had no such representatives. British leaders countered that the colonists enjoyed **virtual representation**, but William Pitt, a staunch supporter of American rights in Parliament, dismissed virtual representation as "the most contemptible idea that ever entered into the head of a man." Many others, in both Britain and America, agreed. Sir Francis Bernard, the royal governor of Massachusetts, correctly predicted that the new stamp tax "would cause a great Alarm & meet much Opposition" in the colonies.

**PROTESTS IN THE COLONIES** The Stamp Act did arouse fierce resentment and resistance. In a flood of pamphlets, speeches, resolutions, and street protests, critics repeated a slogan familiar to Americans: "No taxation without representation [in Parliament]."

Protesters, calling themselves **Sons of Liberty**, emerged in every colony, often meeting beneath "liberty trees"—in Boston a great elm, in Charleston a live oak. In Virginia, Patrick Henry convinced the assembly to pass the "Stamp Act Resolutions," which asserted that the colonists could not be taxed without being first consulted by the British government or represented in Parliament by their own elected members.

**THE NONIMPORTATION MOVEMENT** Since the mid–seventeenth century, colonial consumers could not get enough imported British manufactured goods—textiles, ceramics, glassware, and printed products. Now, however, militants saw such consumerism as a bold new weapon of political protest. To put economic pressure on the British government and show that they had not become "dependent" on Britain's "empire of goods," patriots by the thousands signed nonimportation agreements pledging not to buy or consume British goods.

The nonimportation movement of the 1760s and 1770s united Whigs from different communities and different colonies. It also enabled women to play a role in the resistance. Calling themselves **Daughters of Liberty**, many colonial women stopped buying imported British clothes and quit drinking British tea to "save this abused Country from Ruin and Slavery." Using herbs and flowers, they made "Liberty Tea" instead.

The Daughters of Liberty also participated in public "spinning bees," whereby they would gather in the town square to spin yarn and wool into fabric, known as "homespun." In 1769, the *Boston Evening Post* reported that the "industry and frugality of American ladies" were enabling "the political salvation of a whole continent."

**COLONIAL UNITY** The boycotts worked; imports of British goods fell by 40 percent. At the same time, the Virginia House of Burgesses struck the first official blow against the Stamp Act with the Virginia Resolves, a series of resolutions inspired by the fiery Patrick Henry. Virginians, Henry declared, were entitled to all the rights of Englishmen, and Englishmen could be taxed only by their elected representatives. Because Virginians had no elected representatives in Parliament, they could only be taxed by the Virginia legislature, for example. Newspapers spread the Virginia Resolves throughout the colonies, and other assemblies hastened to follow Virginia's example.

In 1765, the Massachusetts House of Representatives invited the other colonial assemblies to send delegates to New York City to discuss opposition to the Stamp Act. Nine responded, and from October 7 to October 25, the Stamp Act Congress formulated a Declaration of the Rights and Grievances of the Colonies. The delegates insisted that they would accept no taxes being "imposed on them" without "their own consent, given personally, or by their representatives."

**REPEAL OF THE STAMP ACT** The storm over the Stamp Act had scarcely erupted before Grenville, having lost the confidence of King George III, was replaced by Lord Rockingham in July 1765. The growing violence in America and the success of the nonimportation movement convinced Rockingham that the Stamp Act was a mistake, and a humiliated Parliament repealed it in February 1766. To save face, Parliament passed the Declaratory Act, in which it asserted its power to govern the colonies "in all cases whatsoever." The repeal of the Stamp Act set off excited demonstrations throughout the colonies.

A British newspaper reported that the debate over the Stamp Tax had led some Americans to express a desire for "independence." The editor predicted that eventually the colonies would "shake off all subjection. If we yield to them . . . by repealing the Stamp Act, it is all over."

**THE TOWNSHEND ACTS** In July 1766, George III replaced Lord Rockingham with William Pitt, the former prime minister who had exercised heroic leadership during the Seven Years' War. For a time, the guiding force in the Pitt ministry was Charles Townshend, the treasury chief whose "abilities were superior to those of all men," said a colleague, "and his judgment [common sense] below that of any man."

In 1767, Townshend pushed through Parliament an ill-fated plan to generate more colonial revenue. A few months later, he died at age forty-two, leaving behind a bitter legacy: the **Townshend Acts**. The Revenue Act of 1767, which

ON THE FUNERAL OF MISS AMERIC-STAMP

***The Repeal, or The Funeral Procession of Miss Americ-Stamp*** This 1766 cartoon
shows Grenville carrying the dead Stamp Act in its coffin. In the background, trade with
America starts up again.

taxed colonial imports of glass, lead, paint, paper, and tea, was the most hated.
It posed an even more severe threat than Grenville's taxes had, for Townshend
planned to use the new tax revenues to pay the salaries of the royal governors in the colonies. Until that point, the colonial assemblies paid the salaries, thus giving them leverage over the governors. John Adams observed that
Townshend's plan would make the royal governor "independent of the people"
and disrupt "that balance of power which is essential to all free governments."
Writing in the *Boston Gazette*, Adams insisted that such "an INDEPENDENT
ruler, [is] a MONSTER in a free state."

## DISCONTENT ON THE FRONTIER

While the disputes over British regulatory policy raged along the seaboard,
parts of the backcountry stirred with quarrels that had nothing to do with
the Stamp and Townshend Acts. Rival claims to lands east of Lake Champlain
pitted New York against New Hampshire. Eventually, the residents of the disputed area would form their own state of Vermont, which would be recognized as a member of the Union in 1791.

In South Carolina, frontiersmen issued a chorus of complaints about the lack of military protection from horse thieves, cattle rustlers, and Indians. They organized societies, called Regulators, to administer vigilante justice in the region, and refused to pay taxes until they gained effective government. The assembly finally set up six circuit courts in the region but did not respond to demands for representation.

In North Carolina, the protests were less over the lack of government than over abuses and extortion by appointees from the eastern part of the colony. Western farmers felt especially oppressed by the government's refusal to issue paper money or accept produce in payment of taxes, and in 1766 they organized to resist. The efforts of these Regulators to stop seizures of property and other court proceedings led to more disorders and the enactment of a bill that made the rioters guilty of treason. That the Regulators tended to be Baptists, Methodists, and Presbyterians who preached plain living, while the coastal elite tended to be wealthy Anglicans, injected a religious and social element into the squabbles.

In the spring of 1771, William Tryon, the royal governor of North Carolina, led 1,200 militiamen to victory over some 2,000 ill-organized Regulators in the Battle of Alamance. Tryon's men then ranged through the backcountry, forcing some 6,500 Piedmont settlers to sign an oath of allegiance to the king.

These disputes and revolts illustrated the diversity of opinion and outlook among Americans on the eve of the Revolution. Colonists were of many minds about many things, including British rule, but they also differed with one another about how best to protest against their particular grievances.

## THE CRISIS GROWS

The Townshend Acts surprised and angered many colonists. As American rage bubbled over, Samuel ("Sam") Adams of Boston, a failed beer brewer who had become one of the most radical rebels, decided that a small group of determined Whigs could generate a mass movement. "It does not take a majority to prevail," Adams insisted, "but rather an irate, tireless minority, keen on setting brushfires of freedom in the minds of men."

Early in 1768, Adams and Boston attorney James Otis Jr. convinced the Massachusetts Assembly to circulate a letter that restated the illegality of taxation without representation and invited the support of the other colonies. British officials ordered the Massachusetts Assembly to withdraw the letter. They refused, and the king ordered the assembly dissolved.

In October 1768, in response to an appeal by the royal governor concerned about keeping order, 4,000 British troops arrived in Boston, the hotbed of colonial resistance. **Loyalists**, as the Americans who supported the king and Parliament were often called, welcomed the soldiers; **Patriots**, those rebelling against British authority, viewed the troops as an occupation force. Meanwhile, in London, the king appointed still another new chief minister, Frederick, Lord North.

**THE FIRST BLOODSHED** In 1765, Benjamin Franklin had predicted that although British soldiers sent to America would "not find a rebellion; they may indeed make one." The growing tensions triggered several violent incidents. The first, called the Battle at Golden Hill, occurred in New York City, where "Liberty Boys" kept erecting "liberty poles," only to see British soldiers knock them down. The soldiers, cursed as "lobsterbacks" or "redcoats," also began posting signs declaring that the Sons of Liberty were "the real enemies of society."

On January, 18, 1770, a group of Patriots captured two British soldiers. Soon an angry crowd formed around the twenty British soldiers sent to rescue their comrades, and the outnumbered soldiers retreated. When they reached Golden Hill, more soldiers arrived. At that point, the redcoats turned on the crowd. They attacked, and in the confusion, several on both sides were seriously hurt. The first blood had been shed over American liberties, and it was soon followed by more violence.

**THE BOSTON MASSACRE (1770)** In Boston, the presence of thousands of British soldiers had become a constant source of irritation. Crowds frequently heckled the soldiers, many of whom had earned the abuse by harassing Americans.

On the evening of March 5, 1770, two dozen "saucy" Boston rowdies—teens, Irishmen, blacks, and sailors—began throwing icicles and oyster shells at Hugh White, a British soldier guarding the Customs House. Someone rang the town fire bell, drawing a larger crowd to the scene, as the taunting continued: "Kill him, kill him, knock him down. Fire, damn you, fire, you dare not fire!"

A squad of soldiers arrived to help White, but the surly crowd surrounded them. When someone knocked a soldier down, he arose and fired his musket. Others joined in. After the smoke had cleared, five people lay dead or dying on the cobblestone street, and eight more were wounded. The first one killed, or so the story goes, was Crispus Attucks, a former slave who worked at the docks. The *Boston Gazette* called it a "horrid massacre."

***The Bloody Massacre*** Paul Revere's engraving of the Boston Massacre (1770).

The next day, nine British soldiers were arrested and jailed. Never before in Massachusetts had a trial generated such passion and excitement. Samuel Adams and other firebrands demanded quick justice. Months passed, however, before the trial convened. Finally, in late October, two of the British soldiers, convicted of manslaughter, were branded on the thumb.

The so-called **Boston Massacre** sent shock waves throughout the colonies and all the way to London. Virtually the entire city of Boston attended the funerals for the deceased. Only the decision to postpone the trial for six months allowed tensions to subside. At the same time, the impact of the colonial boycott of British products persuaded prime minister Lord North to modify the Townshend Acts.

Late in April 1770, Parliament repealed all the Townshend duties except for the tea tax, which the king wanted to keep as a symbol of Parliament's authority. Colonial discontent subsided for two years. The redcoats left Boston but remained in Canada, and the British navy still patrolled the New England coast looking for smugglers.

**THE GASPÉE INCIDENT** In June 1772, a naval incident further eroded the colonies' fragile relationship with the mother country. Near Warwick, Rhode Island, the HMS *Gaspée*, a British warship, ran aground while chasing smugglers. Its hungry crew seized local sheep, hogs, and chickens. An enraged crowd, some poorly disguised as Mohawk Indians, then boarded the *Gaspée*, shot the captain, removed the crew, and looted and burned the ship.

The *Gaspée* incident symbolized the intensity of growing anti-British feelings among Americans. When the British tried to take the suspects to London for trial, Patriots organized in protest. Thomas Jefferson said it was the threat of transporting Americans for trials in Britain that reignited anti-British activities in Virginia.

In response to the *Gaspée* incident, Samuel Adams organized the **Committee of Correspondence**, which issued a statement of American rights and grievances and invited other towns to do the same. Similar committees sprang up across the colonies, forming a unified network of resistance. "The flame is kindled and like lightning it catches from soul to soul," reported Abigail Adams, the high-spirited wife of future president John Adams. By 1772, Thomas Hutchinson, the royal governor of Massachusetts, could tell the colonial assembly that the choice facing Americans was stark: They must choose between obeying "the supreme authority of Parliament" and "total independence."

**THE BOSTON TEA PARTY** The British prime minister, Lord North, soon provided the spark to transform resentment into rebellion. In 1773, he tried to bail out the struggling East India Company, which had in its warehouses some 17 million pounds of tea that it desperately needed to sell before it rotted. Parliament passed the Tea Act of 1773 to allow the company to send its tea directly to America without paying any taxes. British tea merchants could thereby undercut the prices charged by their American competitors, most of whom were smugglers who bought tea from the Dutch. At the same time, King George III told Lord North to "compel obedience" in the colonies.

In Massachusetts, the Committees of Correspondence alerted colonists that the British government was trying to purchase colonial submission with cheap tea. ("Tea stands for Tyranny!") The reduction in the price of tea was a clever trick to make colonists accept taxation without consent. In Boston, furious citizens decided that their passion for liberty outweighed their love for tea. On December 16, 1773, scores of Patriots dressed as Indians boarded three

British ships in Boston Harbor and dumped overboard 342 chests filled with forty-six tons of East India Company tea.

The **Boston Tea Party** pushed British officials in London to the breaking point. The destruction of so much valuable tea convinced the king and his advisers that a forceful response was required. "The colonists must either submit or triumph," George III wrote to Lord North, who decided to make Boston an example to the rest of the colonies.

**THE COERCIVE ACTS**    In 1774, Lord North convinced Parliament to punish Boston and the province of Massachusetts by passing a cluster of harsh laws, called the **Coercive Acts**. (Americans renamed them the "Intolerable" Acts.) The Port Act closed Boston harbor until the city paid for the lost tea. (It never did.) Many people lost their jobs, and the cost of consumer goods skyrocketed as trade ceased. A new Quartering Act ordered colonists to provide lodging for British soldiers. The Impartial Administration of Justice Act said that any royal official accused of a major crime would be tried in London rather than in the colony.

Finally, the Massachusetts Government Act stripped Americans of their representative governments, effectively disenfranchising them. It gave the royal governor the authority to appoint the colony's legislative council, which until then had been elected by the people, as well as local judges and sheriffs. It also banned town meetings. In May, Lieutenant General Thomas Gage, commander in chief of British forces in North America, became governor of Massachusetts and assumed command of the British soldiers who had returned to Boston.

The Intolerable Acts shocked colonists. No one had expected such a severe reaction to the Boston Tea Party. Many towns held meetings in violation of the new laws, and voters elected their own unauthorized provincial legislative assemblies—which ordered town governments to quit paying taxes to the royal governor. By August 1774, Patriots across Massachusetts had essentially taken control of local governments. They also began stockpiling weapons and gunpowder in anticipation of an eventual clash with British troops.

Elsewhere, colonists across America rallied to help Boston by raising money, sending supplies, and boycotting, burning, or dumping British tea. In Virginia, George Washington found himself in a debate with Bryan Fairfax, an old friend and self-described Royalist. Fairfax blamed the Boston rebels for the tensions with London. Washington disagreed, defending the "quiet and steady conduct of the people of the Massachusetts Bay." It was time, he added, for Americans to stand up for their rights or "submit" to being treated like "abject slaves."

In Williamsburg, when the Virginia assembly (House of Burgesses) met in May, a member of the Committee of Correspondence, Thomas Jefferson, suggested that June 1, the effective date of the Boston Port Act, become an official day of fasting and prayer.

The royal governor responded by dissolving the assembly, whose members then retired to the Raleigh Tavern and decided to form a Continental Congress to represent all the colonies. As Samuel Savage, a Connecticut colonist, wrote in May 1774, the conflict had come down to a single question: "Whether we shall or shall not be governed by a British Parliament." Each step the colonists might take next was fraught with risk, but the opposition to "tyranny" was growing.

**THE FIRST CONTINENTAL CONGRESS** On September 5, 1774, the fifty-five delegates from twelve colonies (Georgia was absent) making up the First Continental Congress assembled in Philadelphia, the largest American city. Never before had representatives from all the colonies met to coordinate resistance to British policies. Now the Continental Congress was serving as a provisional national government. Over seven weeks, the Congress endorsed the Suffolk Resolves, which urged Massachusetts to resist British tyranny with force. The Congress then adopted a Declaration of American Rights, which proclaimed once again the rights of Americans as British citizens and denied Parliament's authority to regulate internal colonial affairs. "We demand no new rights," said the Congress. "We ask only for peace, liberty, and security."

Finally, the Congress adopted the Continental Association of 1774, which recommended that every colony organize committees to enforce a complete boycott of all imported British goods, a dramatic step that would be followed by a refusal to export American goods to Britain. The Association was designed to show that Americans could deny themselves the "baubles of Britain" and demonstrate their commitment to colonial liberties and constitutional rights.

The county and city committees forming the Continental Association became the organizational network for the resistance movement. Seven thousand men across the colonies served on the local committees, and many more women helped put the boycotts into practice. The committees required colonists to sign an oath refusing to purchase British goods. In East Haddam, Connecticut, Patriots tarred, feathered, and rubbed pig dung on a Loyalist, who refused to join the boycott. Such violent incidents led Loyalists to claim that it was better to be a slave to the king than to be enslaved by a Patriot mob.

Thousands of men and women participated in the boycott of British goods, and their sacrifices provided the momentum leading to revolution. It was common people who enforced the boycott, volunteered in Patriot militia units, attended town meetings, and ousted royal officials. As Pittsfield, Massachusetts, affirmed in a petition, "We have always believed that the people are the fountain of power."

Royal officials marveled at the colonists' ability to thwart British authority. "The ingenuity of these people," declared an army officer, "is singular in their modes of mischief." Loyalist Thomas Hutchinson, however, assured the king that the Americans could not remain united. "A union of the Colonies was utterly impracticable," he wrote, because "the people were greatly divided among themselves in every colony." Hutchinson had no doubt "that all America would *submit*, and that they *must*, and moreover would, *soon*."

Hutchinson could not have been more wrong. The rebellion now extended well beyond simple grievances over taxation. Patriots decided that there was a *conspiracy* against their liberties among Parliament, the king, and his ministers. By the end of 1774, more and more colonists came to reject the authority of Parliament. Across the colonies, Patriots ousted royal governors, forcing them to take refuge on British ships, and replaced them with provisional "committees of safety" committed to independence. Many committees began secretly purchasing weapons and gunpowder from European nations.

The colonies were mobilizing, and growing numbers of people came to expect an explosion. "Government has now devolved upon the people," wrote an irritated Tory in 1774, "and they seem to be for using it." In Boston, an increasingly nervous General Thomas Gage requested more British troops to suppress the growing "flames of sedition." He reported that "civil government is near its end, the Courts of Justice expiring one after another."

**LAST-MINUTE COMPROMISE** In London, King George fumed. He wrote Lord North that "blows must decide" whether the Americans "are to be subject to this country or independent." In early 1775, Parliament declared that Massachusetts was officially "in rebellion" and prohibited the New England colonies from trading with any nation outside the British Empire. A few Whigs stood in Parliament to defend the Americans. Edmund Burke, a prominent Irish statesman, stressed that the "fierce spirit of liberty is stronger in the English Colonies probably than in any other people on earth."

London officials hired Samuel Johnson, a distinguished poet, essayist, and ardent Tory, to write a pamphlet called *Taxation No Tyranny* (1775), expressing the government's perspective on the colonists and their slogan, "No taxation without representation." The people who settled America, Johnson wrote, had left Britain, where they had the vote but little property, for a colonial life where they had no vote but lots of property. However much Americans might complain about taxes, they remained British subjects who should obey government actions. If the Americans wanted to participate in Parliament, Johnson suggested, they could move to England and purchase an estate. Whatever the case, Johnson expressed confidence that the dispute between England and America would be resolved through "English superiority and American obedience."

**BOLD TALK OF WAR** While most Patriots believed that Britain would back down, Patrick Henry of Virginia dramatically declared that war was unavoidable. The twenty-nine-year-old Henry, a full-throated farmer and storekeeper turned lawyer, claimed that the colonies had "done everything that could be done to avert the storm which is now coming on," but had been met only by "violence and insult." Freedom, Henry shouted, could be bought only with blood: "We must fight!" If forced to choose, he supposedly shouted, "Give me liberty"—he then paused dramatically, clenched his fist as if it held a dagger, and plunged it into his chest—"Or give me death."

As Henry predicted, events quickly moved toward armed conflict. By mid-1775, the king and Parliament had effectively lost control; they could neither persuade nor force the Patriots to accept new regulations and revenue measures. In Boston, General Gage warned that armed conflict would unleash the "horrors of civil war." But Lord Sandwich, head of the British navy, dismissed the rebels as "raw, undisciplined, cowardly men" without an army or navy. Major John Pitcairn, a British army officer, agreed, writing from Boston that "one active campaign, a smart action, and burning two or three of their towns, will set everything to rights."

**LEXINGTON AND CONCORD** Major Pitcairn soon had his chance to quash the resistance. On April 14, 1775, the British army received secret orders to stop the "open rebellion" in Massachusetts. General Gage had decided to arrest rebel leaders such as Samuel Adams and seize the militia's gunpowder stored at Concord, sixteen miles northwest of Boston.

After dark on April 18, some 800 British soldiers secretly boarded boats and crossed the Charles River to Cambridge, then set out on foot to Lexington, about eleven miles away. When Patriots got wind of the plan, Paul Revere and William Dawes mounted their horses for their famous "midnight ride" to warn rebel leaders that the British were coming.

In the gray dawn of April 19, an advance unit of 238 redcoats found American Captain John Parker and about 70 "Minutemen" (Patriot militia who could

***The Battle of Lexington***  Amos Doolittle's impression of the Battle of Lexington as shooting begins between the Royal Marines and the Minutemen.

assemble at a "minute's" notice) lined up on the Lexington town square, while dozens of villagers watched. "Stand your ground," shouted Parker. "Don't fire unless fired upon; but if they mean to have a war, let it begin here!"

Parker and his men intended only a silent protest, but Major Pitcairn rode onto the Lexington Green, swinging his sword and yelling, "Disperse, you damned rebels! You dogs, run!" The outnumbered militiamen were backing away when someone fired. (Both sides blamed the other for shooting first.) The British then shot at the Minutemen and charged them with bayonets amid a "continual roar of musketry," leaving eight dead and ten wounded.

The British officers brought their men under control and led them west to Concord, where they destroyed hidden military supplies. While marching out of the town, they encountered American riflemen. Shots were fired, and a dozen or so British soldiers were killed or wounded. More important, the short skirmish and ringing church bells alerted nearby rebel farmers, ministers, craftsmen, and merchants to grab their muskets. They were, as one of them said, determined to "be free or die."

By noon, the exhausted redcoats began a ragged retreat back to Lexington. It soon turned into a disaster. Less than a mile out of Concord, they suffered the first of many ambushes. The narrow road turned into a gauntlet of death as rebel marksmen fired from behind stone walls, trees, barns, and houses. "It was a day full of horror," one of the soldiers recalled.

By nightfall, the redcoat survivors were safely back in Boston, having marched some forty miles and suffered three times as many dead and wounded as the Americans. A British general reported that the colonists had earned his respect: "Whoever looks upon them as an irregular mob will find himself much mistaken." The Salem newspaper reported that now "we are involved in the horrors of a civil war." Others found the news exhilarating. When Samuel Adams heard the firing at Lexington, he shouted: "O what a glorious morning is this!"

Warfare may be glorious when heard from long distance, but its deadly results bring home its tragic reality. Hannah Davis, a mother of four living in Acton, was awakened on April 19 by the alarm bells calling the militiamen to assemble. She dutifully helped her thirty-year-old husband Isaac get his musket and powder horn. "He said but little that morning. He seemed serious and thoughtful; but never seemed to hesitate." His only words were: "Take care of the children." That afternoon, she recalled, "he was brought home a corpse."

Until the Battles of Lexington and Concord, both sides had mistakenly assumed that the other would back down. Instead, the clash turned a resistance movement into a war of rebellion. Masses of ordinary people were determined to fight for their freedoms against a British Parliament and king bent on denying them their civil and legal rights. In Virginia, Thomas Jefferson reported that the news from Concord and Lexington had unleashed "a frenzy of revenge" among "all ranks of people." In Georgia, the royal governor noted that "a general rebellion throughout America is coming on suddenly and swiftly."

Joseph Warren, a Bostonian, warned: "Our all is at stake. Death and devastation are the instant consequences of delay. Every moment is infinitely precious. An hour lost may deluge our country in blood, and entail perpetual slavery."

## THE SPREADING CONFLICT

On June 15, 1775, the Second Continental Congress unanimously selected forty-three-year-old George Washington to lead the new Continental Army. His service in the French and Indian War had made him one of the few experienced American officers. He was also admired for his success as a planter, surveyor, and land speculator, as well as for his service in the Virginia legislature and the Continental Congress. Perhaps more important, he *looked* like a leader. Standing more than six feet tall and weighing 200 pounds, Washington was a fearless fighter accustomed to command. His courage in battle, perseverance after defeat, and integrity in judgment would earn him the respect of his troops and the nation.

**Attack on Bunker Hill** The Battle of Bunker Hill and the burning of Charlestown Peninsula.

Washington humbly accepted the responsibility of leading the American war effort and refused to be paid. Poet Mercy Otis Warren wrote a friend in London that Washington was "a man whose military abilities & public & private virtue place him in the first class of the Good & the Brave." Washington's first act was to draft a will and write his wife, Martha, explaining that he had done his best to avoid being considered for the position, but that in the end it seemed his "destiny" to lead the revolution.

**THE BATTLE OF BUNKER HILL** On Saturday, June 17, the day that George Washington was named commander in chief, Patriot militiamen engaged British forces in their first major clash, the Battle of Bunker Hill (Breed's Hill was the battle's actual location).

In an effort to strengthen their control over the area around Boston, some 2,400 British troops based in the city boarded boats and crossed over the Charles River to the Charlestown Peninsula, where they formed lines and advanced up Breed's Hill in tight formation through waist-high grass and across pasture fences, as the American defenders watched from behind their earthworks.

"Don't fire until you see the whites of their eyes," yelled Israel Putnam as he rode along the American lines. "Fire low because you are shooting downhill— and focus your fire on the officers." The militiamen, mostly farmers, waited until the redcoats had come within thirty paces, then loosed a volley that sent the attackers retreating in disarray. An American said the British fell like "grass when mowed."

The British re-formed their lines and attacked again, but the Patriot riflemen forced them back a second time. General William Howe could not believe his eyes. All his aides had been killed or wounded, and his professional soldiers were being stymied by a "rabble" of untrained farmers. It was, he said, "a moment that I never felt before."

During the third British assault, the colonists ran out of gunpowder and retreated in panic and confusion, but the British were too tired to follow. They had suffered 1,054 casualties, more than twice the American losses. "A dearly bought victory," said British general Henry Clinton. A British officer reported to London that "we have lost a thousand of our best men and officers" because of "an absurd and destructive confidence, carelessness, or ignorance."

There followed a nine-month stalemate around Boston, with each side hoping for a negotiated settlement of the dispute. Abigail Adams wrote that the Patriots still living in Boston, where the British army governed by martial law, were being treated "like abject slaves under the most cruel and despotic of tyrants."

Thirty-eight days later, word of the Battle of Bunker Hill reached London. The king and Lord North agreed that this meant all-out war. George III issued a Proclamation of Rebellion that said all his subjects ("unhappy people") were "bound by law . . . to disclose all traitorous conspiracies . . . against us, our Crown and Dignity." If the American colonies were lost, the king believed, Britain's other colonies in the West Indies and around the world would fall like dominoes.

"**OPEN AND AVOWED ENEMIES**" Three weeks after the Battle of Bunker Hill, in July 1775, the Continental Congress sent King George the Olive Branch Petition, urging him to negotiate. When the petition reached London, however, he arrogantly dismissed it and denounced the Americans as "open and avowed enemies."

**OUTRIGHT REBELLION** Resistance had grown into outright rebellion, but few Patriots were ready to call for independence. They still considered themselves British subjects. When the Second Continental Congress convened at Philadelphia on May 10, 1775, most delegates still wanted Parliament to restore their rights so that they could resume being loyal British colonists.

Meanwhile, the British army in Boston was under siege by American militia units and small groups of musket-toting men who had arrived from across

New England to surround the city. They were still farmers and shopkeepers, not trained soldiers, and the uprising still had no organized command structure or effective support system. The Patriots also lacked training, discipline, ammunition, and blankets. What they did have was a growing sense of confidence and resolve. As a Massachusetts Patriot said, "Our all is at stake. Death and devastation are the instant consequences of delay. Every moment is infinitely precious."

With each passing day, war fever infected more and more colonists. "Oh that I were a soldier!" John Adams wrote home to his wife, Abigail, from Philadelphia. "I will be. I am reading military books. Everybody must, and will, and shall be a soldier."

The fever of war excited men of faith as well as militiamen. In early 1776, the Reverend Peter Muhlenberg told his congregation in Woodstock, Virginia: "The Bible tells us 'there is a time for all things.' And there is a time to preach and a time to pray. But the time for me to preach has passed away; and there is a time to fight, and that time has now come." He then stepped down from the pulpit and took off his robe to reveal a Continental army uniform. Drums then sounded outside the church as husbands kissed their wives goodbye and walked down the aisle to enlist. Within an hour, 162 men had followed their minister's call to arms.

## INDEPENDENCE

The Revolutionary War was well under way in January 1776 when Thomas Paine, a thirty-nine-year-old English immigrant who had found work as a radical journalist in Philadelphia, published a stirring pamphlet titled **Common Sense**. Until it appeared, most Patriots had directed their grievances at Parliament. Paine, however, directly attacked the king.

The "common sense" of the matter, Paine stressed, was that King George III, "the royal brute unfit to be the ruler of a free people," had caused the rebellion and had ordered the denial of American rights. "Even brutes do not devour their young," he wrote, "nor savages make war upon their families." Paine urged Americans to abandon the monarchy: "The blood of the slain, the weeping voice of nature cries, 'TIS TIME TO PART.'" It was time for those who "oppose not only the tyranny but the tyrant [King George] to stand forth! . . . Time hath found us!" The "cause of America," he proclaimed, "is the cause of all mankind." It was America that had long "been the asylum for the persecuted lovers of civil and religious liberty from every part of Europe," and

**The coming revolution**  The Continental Congress votes for independence, July 2, 1776.

Paine urged Revolutionaries to ensure that America would always be a haven for the oppressed peoples of the world.

Paine's fiery pamphlet changed the course of history by convincing American rebels that independence was inevitable. Only by declaring independence, he predicted, could the colonists gain the crucial support of France and Spain: "The cause of America is in great measure the cause of all mankind." The rest of the world, he said, would welcome and embrace an independent America; it would be the "glory of the earth." Paine concluded that the "sun had never shined on a cause of greater worth."

Within three months, more than 150,000 copies of *Common Sense* were circulating throughout the colonies and around the world, an enormous number for the time. "*Common Sense* is working a powerful change in the minds of men," George Washington reported.

**BREAKING THE BONDS OF EMPIRE** *Common Sense* inspired the colonial population from Massachusetts to Georgia and helped convince British subjects still loyal to the king to embrace the radical notion of independence. "Without the pen of Paine," remembered John Adams, "the sword of Washington would have been wielded in vain." During the spring and summer of 1776, some ninety local governments, towns, and colonial legislatures issued declarations of independence.

Momentum for independence was building in the Continental Congress, too, but John Dickinson of Pennsylvania urged delay. On June 1, he warned that independence was a dangerous step since America had no national government or European allies. But his was a lone voice of caution.

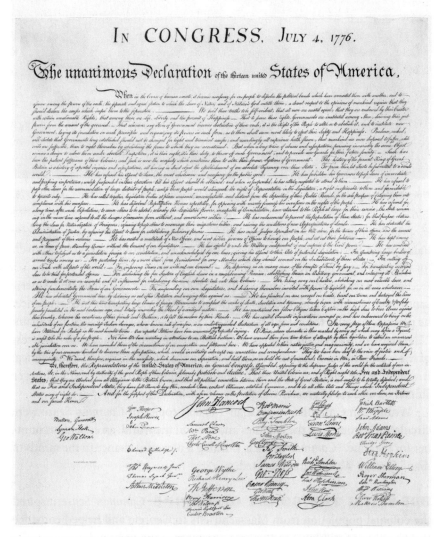

**The Declaration of Independence**   The Declaration in its most frequently reproduced form, an 1823 engraving by William J. Stone.

In June 1776, one by one, the colonies authorized their delegates in the Continental Congress to take the final step. On June 7, Richard Henry Lee of Virginia moved "that these United Colonies are, and of right ought to be, free and independent states." At first, six colonies were not ready, but Lee's resolution finally passed on July 2, a date that John Adams predicted would "be the most memorable" in the history of America.

The more memorable date, however, became July 4, 1776, when the Congress formally adopted the **Declaration of Independence** creating the "United States of America." A few delegates refused to sign the document; others, said Adams, "signed with regret . . . and with many doubts." Most, however, signed wholeheartedly, knowing full well that by doing so they were likely to be hanged if captured by British troops. Benjamin Franklin acknowledged how high the stakes were: "Well, Gentlemen," he told the Congress, "we must now hang together, or we shall most assuredly hang separately." Portly Benjamin Harrison injected needed wit at that point, noting that when it was his turn to try on a British noose, his plentiful weight would bring him a mercifully swift death.

**JEFFERSON'S DECLARATION** In Philadelphia, thirty-three-year-old Thomas Jefferson, a brilliant Virginia planter and attorney serving in the Continental Congress, had drafted a statement of independence that John Adams and Benjamin Franklin then edited.

The Declaration of Independence was crucially important not simply because it marked the creation of a new nation but because of the ideals it expressed and the grievances it listed. Over the previous ten years, colonists had deplored acts of Parliament that impinged on their freedoms. Now, Jefferson directed colonial resentment at King George III himself, arguing that the monarch should have reined in Parliament's efforts to "tyrannize" the colonies.

In addition to highlighting the efforts to tax the colonists and restrict their liberties, Jefferson also noted the king's 1773 decree that sought to restrict population growth in the colonies by "obstructing the laws for the naturalization of foreigners." British authorities had grown worried that the mass migration to America threatened to "de-populate" the home country. So, beginning in 1767, the government began banning "bounties" offered to immigrants by many colonies and ended the practice of providing large land grants in America to encourage settlement.

After listing the objections to British actions, Jefferson asserted that certain truths were self-evident: that "all men are created equal and independent" and have the right to create governments of their own choosing. Governments, he explained, derive "their just powers from the consent of the people," who are entitled to "alter or abolish" those governments when denied their "unalienable rights" to "life, liberty, and the pursuit of happiness." Because King George III was trying to impose "an absolute tyranny over these states," the "Representatives of the United States of America" declared the thirteen "United Colonies" of British America to be "Free and Independent States."

**THE CONTRADICTIONS OF FREEDOM** Once the Continental Congress chose independence, its members revised Jefferson's draft declaration before sending it to London. Southern representatives insisted on deleting Jefferson's section criticizing George III for perpetuating the African slave trade. In doing so, they revealed the major contradiction at work in the movement for independence. The rhetoric of freedom that animated the Revolution did not apply to the widespread system of slavery that fueled the southern economy. Slavery was the absence of liberty, yet few Americans confronted the inconsistency of their protests in defense of freedom—for whites.

In 1764, a group of slaves in Charleston watching a demonstration against British tyranny by white Sons of Liberty got caught up in the moment and began chanting, "Freedom, freedom, freedom." But that was not what southern planters wanted for African Americans. In 1774, when a group of slaves killed four whites in a desperate attempt to gain their freedom, Georgia planters captured the rebels and burned them alive.

James Otis, a Harvard-educated lawyer, was one of the few Whigs who demanded freedom for blacks and women. In 1764, he had argued that "the colonists, black and white, born here, are free British subjects, and entitled to all the essential civil rights of such." He went so far as to suggest that slavery itself should be ended, since "all men . . . white or black" were "by the law of nature freeborn."

Otis also asked, "Are not women born as free as men? Would it not be infamous to assert that the ladies are all slaves by nature?" His sister, Mercy Otis Warren, became a tireless advocate of

*I am very affectionately your Friend*
*Phillis Wheatley*
*Boston March 21. 1774.*

**Phillis Wheatley** An autographed portrait of America's first African American poet.

American resistance to British "tyranny" through her poems, pamphlets, and plays. In a letter to a friend, she noted that British officials needed to realize that America's "daughters are politicians and patriots and will aid the good work [of resistance] with their female efforts."

Slaves insisted on independence too. In 1773, a group of enslaved African Americans in Boston appealed to the royal governor of Massachusetts to free them just as white Americans were defending their freedoms against British tyranny. In many respects, the slaves argued, they had a more compelling case for liberty: "We have no property, We have no wives! No children! No city! No country!"

A few months later, a group of four Boston slaves addressed a public letter to the town government in which they referred to the hypocrisy of slave-holders who protested against British regulations and taxes. "We expect great things from men who have made such a noble stand against the designs of their fellow-men to enslave them," they noted. But freedom in 1776 was a celebration to which slaves were not invited.

George Washington himself acknowledged the contradictory aspects of the Revolutionary movement when he warned that the alternative to declaring independence was to become "tame and abject slaves, as the blacks we rule over with such arbitrary sway [absolute power]." Washington and other slaveholders at the head of the Revolutionary movement, such as Thomas Jefferson, were in part so resistant to "British tyranny" because they witnessed every day what actual slavery was like—for the blacks under their control.

Jefferson admitted the hypocrisy of slave-owning Revolutionaries. "Southerners," he wrote to a French friend, are "jealous of their own liberties but trampling on those of others." Phillis Wheatley, the first African American writer to publish her poetry in America, highlighted the "absurdity" of white colonists claiming their freedom while continuing to exercise "oppressive power" over enslaved Africans.

"WE ALWAYS HAD GOVERNED OURSELVES" Historians still debate the causes of the American Revolution. Americans in 1775–1776 were not desperately poor; overall, they probably enjoyed a higher standard of living than most other societies and lived under the freest institutions in the world. Their diet was better than that of Europeans, as was their average life span. In addition, the percentage of free property owners in the thirteen colonies was higher than in Britain or Europe. At the same time, the new taxes forced on Americans after 1763 were not as great as those imposed on the British people. And many American colonists, perhaps as many as half, were indifferent, hesitant, or actively opposed to rebellion.

So why did the Americans revolt? Historians have highlighted many factors: the clumsy British efforts to tighten their regulation of colonial trade, the restrictions on colonists eager to acquire western lands, the growing tax burden, the mounting debts to British merchants, the lack of American representation in Parliament, and the role of radicals such as Samuel Adams and Patrick Henry in stirring up anti-British feelings.

Yet other reasons were not so selfless or noble. Many wealthy New Englanders and New Yorkers most critical of tighter British regulations, such as Boston merchant John Hancock, were smugglers; paying more British taxes would have cost them a fortune. Likewise, South Carolina's Henry Laurens and Virginia's Landon Carter, both prosperous planters, worried that the British might abolish slavery.

Overall, however, what Americans most resented were the British efforts to constrict colonists' civil liberties, thereby denying their rights as British citizens. As Hugh Williamson, a Pennsylvania physician, explained, the Revolution resulted not from "trifling or imaginary" injustices but from "gross and palpable" violations of American rights that had thrown "the miserable colonists" into the "pit of despotism."

Yet how did the diverse colonies develop such a unified resistance? Although most Patriots were of English heritage, many other peoples were represented: Scots, Irish, Scots-Irish, Welsh, Germans, Dutch, Swedes, Finns, Swiss, French, and Jews, as well as growing numbers of Africans and diminishing numbers of Native Americans.

What most Americans—regardless of their backgrounds—had come to share by 1775 was a defiant attachment to the civil rights and legal processes guaranteed by the English constitutional tradition. This outlook, rooted in the defense of sacred constitutional principles, made the Revolution conceivable. Armed resistance made it possible, and independence, ultimately, made it achievable.

The Revolution reflected the shared political notion that all citizens were equal and independent, and that all governmental authority had to be based on longstanding constitutional principles and the consent of the governed. This "republican ideal" was the crucial force that transformed a prolonged effort to preserve rights and liberties enjoyed by British citizens into a movement to create an independent nation. With their declaration of independence, the Revolutionaries—men and women, farmers, artisans, mechanics, sailors, merchants, tavern owners, and shopkeepers—had become determined to develop their own society. Americans wanted to trade freely with the world and to expand what Jefferson called their "empire of liberty" westward, across the Appalachian Mountains.

The Revolutionaries knew the significance of what they were attempting. They were committing themselves, stressed John Adams, to "a Revolution, the most complete, unexpected, and remarkable of any in the history of nations."

Perhaps the last word should belong to Levi Preston, a Minuteman from Danvers, Massachusetts. Asked late in life about the British efforts to impose new taxes and regulations on the colonists, Preston responded, "What were they? Oppressions? I didn't feel them." He was then asked, "What, were you not oppressed by the Stamp Act?" Preston replied that he "never saw one of those stamps . . . I am certain I never paid a penny for one of them." What about the tax on tea? "Tea-tax! I never drank a drop of the stuff; the boys threw it all overboard." His interviewer finally asked why he decided to fight for independence. "Young man," Preston explained, "what we meant in going for those redcoats was this: we always had governed ourselves, and we always meant to. They didn't mean we should."

# CHAPTER REVIEW

## SUMMARY

- **British and French Colonies**   New France followed the Spanish model of absolute power in governing its far-flung trading outposts. On the other hand, Great Britain's policy of *salutary neglect* allowed the colonies a large degree of self-government, until its decision to enforce more rigidly its policy of *mercantilism*, as seen in such measures as the *Navigation Acts*, became a means to enrich its global empire. The *Glorious Revolution* in Great Britain inspired new political philosophies that challenged the divine right of kings with the *natural rights* of free men.

- **The French and Indian War**   Four European wars between the British and French and their allies affected America between 1689 and 1763. The *Seven Years' War*, known as the *French and Indian War* (1756–1763) in the colonies, eventually was won by the British. Early in the war, the colonies created the *Albany Plan of Union*, which formed an early blueprint for an independent American government. In the *Treaty of Paris* (1763), France lost all its North American possessions, Britain gained Canada and Florida, and Spain acquired the vast Louisiana Territory. The Indians fought to regain control of their ancestral lands in *Pontiac's Rebellion*, and Great Britain, weary of war, negotiated the *Royal Proclamation of 1763* to keep colonists out of Indian lands.

- **British Colonial Policy**   After the French and Indian War, the British government was saddled with enormous debt. To reduce that burden, prime minister George Grenville implemented various taxes to compel colonists to pay for their own defense. The colonists resisted, claiming that they could not be taxed because they were not represented in Parliament. British officials countered that the colonists had *virtual representation* in Parliament, since each member was supposed to represent his district as well as the empire as a whole. Colonial reaction to the *Stamp Act* of 1765 was the first intimation of real trouble for British authorities. Conflicts between Whigs and Tories intensified when the *Townshend Acts* imposed additional taxes. The *Sons of Liberty* and the *Daughters of Liberty* mobilized resistance, particularly through boycotts of British goods.

- **Road to the American Revolution**   But the crisis worsened. Spontaneous resistance led to the *Boston Massacre*; organized protesters later staged the *Boston Tea Party*. The British response, called the *Coercive Acts*, sparked further violence between *Patriots* and *Loyalists*. The First Continental Congress formed *Committees of Correspondence* to organize and spread resistance. Thomas Paine's pamphlet *Common Sense* helped kindle revolutionary fervor and plant the seed of independence, and the Continental Congress delivered its *Declaration of Independence*.

# CHRONOLOGY

| | |
|---|---|
| **1651** | First Navigation Act passed by Parliament |
| **1688–1689** | Glorious Revolution |
| **1756–1763** | French and Indian War |
| **1763** | Pontiac's Rebellion begins |
| | Treaty of Paris ends French and Indian War |
| | Royal Proclamation |
| **1765** | Stamp Act; Stamp Act Congress |
| **1766** | Repeal of the Stamp Act |
| **1767** | Townshend Acts |
| **1770** | Boston Massacre |
| **1773** | Tea Act; Boston Tea Party |
| **1774** | Coercive Acts |
| **1775** | Military conflict at Lexington and Concord |
| **1776** | Thomas Paine publishes *Common Sense* |
| | Continental Congress declares independence |

# KEY TERMS

**mercantilism** p. 136

**Navigation Acts (1650–1775)** p. 137

**Glorious Revolution (1688)** p. 138

**natural rights** p. 139

**salutary neglect** p. 140

**French and Indian War (Seven Years' War)(1756–1763)** p. 141

**Albany Plan of Union (1754)** p. 142

**Treaty of Paris (1763)** p. 146

**Pontiac's Rebellion (1763)** pp. 149

**Royal Proclamation of 1763** p. 149

**Stamp Act (1765)** p. 152

**virtual representation** p. 153

**Sons of Liberty** p. 153

**Daughters of Liberty** p. 153

**Townshend Acts (1767)** p. 154

**Loyalists** p. 157

**Patriots** p. 157

**Boston Massacre (1770)** p. 158

**Committee of Correspondence** p. 159

**Boston Tea Party (1773)** p. 160

**Coercive Acts (1774)** p. 160

*Common Sense* **(1776)** p. 168

**Declaration of Independence (1776)** p. 171

 INQUIZITIVE

**Go to InQuizitive to see what you've learned—and learn what you've missed—with personalized feedback along the way.**

# part two

# BUILDING A NATION

In August 1776, Benjamin Rush, a Philadelphia physician and dedicated Revolutionary, recognized that the thirteen diverse colonies somehow had to behave like a united nation. "We are now a new Nation ... dependent on each other—not totally independent states."

Yet it was one thing for Patriot leaders to declare independence and quite another to win it on the battlefield. The odds greatly favored the British; fewer than half of the 2.5 million colonists were Patriots who *actively* supported the Revolution, and many others—the

Loyalists—fought against it. Still others sought just to stay alive, often by changing sides "with the circumstances of every day," as Thomas Paine groaned. Many Americans were initially worried and confused by the course of events, suspicious of both sides, and hesitant to embrace an uncertain cause.

The thirteen independent states had new, untested governments; the Continental Congress struggled to serve as a national government with few powers; and General George Washington found himself in charge of an inexperienced and poorly equipped army of amateurs facing the world's greatest military power.

Yet the Revolutionaries would persevere and prevail. As a military leader, Washington proved to be more dogged than brilliant. He did have extensive knowledge of the nation's geography and used it to his advantage. He chose excellent advisers and generals, inspired loyalty among his troops, and quickly perceived that politics was as crucial to victory as gunpowder.

Equally important to the Revolutionary cause was the decision by the French (and later the Spanish and Dutch) to join the fight against Britain. The Franco-American alliance, negotiated in 1778, was the turning point in the war. In 1783, after eight years of sporadic fighting and heavy human and financial losses, the British gave up their American colonies.

While fighting the British, the Patriots also had to create new governments for themselves. The deeply ingrained resentment of British imperial rule led Americans to give more power to the individual states than to the weak new national government, called the Confederation. As Thomas Jefferson declared, "Virginia is my country."

Such powerful local ties help explain why the Articles of Confederation, the original constitution organizing the thirteen states, provided only minimal national authority when it was finally ratified in 1781. After the Revolutionary War, the flimsy political bonds authorized by the Articles of Confederation could not meet the needs of the new nation. This realization led to the calling of the Constitutional Convention in 1787. The process of drafting and approving the new constitution generated heated debate about the respective powers granted to the states and the national government, a debate that became the central theme of American political thought.

The Revolution also helped reshape American society. What would be the role of women, African Americans, and Native Americans? How would the diverse regions of the new United States develop different economies? Who would control access to the vast Native American ancestral lands to the west? How would the United States relate to the world?

These questions gave birth to the first national political parties. During the 1790s, the Federalist party, led by George Washington, John Adams, and Alexander Hamilton, and the Democratic-Republican party, led by Thomas Jefferson and James Madison, furiously debated the political and economic future of the new nation.

With Jefferson's election as president in 1800, the Democratic-Republicans gained the upper hand in national politics and would remain dominant for the next quarter century. In the process, they presided over a maturing republic that expanded westward at the expense of Native Americans, embraced industrial development, engaged in a second war with Great Britain, and witnessed growing tensions between North and South over slavery.

# 5

# The American Revolution

## 1776–1783

**The Death of General Mercer at the Battle of Princeton (ca. 1789–1831)** After the American victory at Trenton, New Jersey, George Washington (center, on horseback) launched a surprise attack on the British at the Battle of Princeton. The Americans won the battle, but one of the casualties was Washington's close friend, General Hugh Mercer (bottom), whose death created a rallying symbol for the Revolution.

ew Europeans thought the untested Americans could win a war against the world's most powerful empire. Although the British did win most of the major battles in the Revolutionary War, the Patriots outlasted them and eventually forced them to grant independence to the upstart United States of America.

This stunning result reflected the tenacity of the Patriots as well as the difficulties the British faced in fighting a prolonged war 3,000 miles from home and in adjusting to the often unorthodox American ways of warfare.

What began as a war for independence became both a *civil war* between Americans (Patriots/Whigs versus Loyalists/Tories), joined by their Indian allies, and a *world war* involving numerous "allied" European nations. The crucial development in the war was the ability of the United States to forge military alliances with France, Spain, and the Netherlands, all of which were eager to humble Great Britain. As Britain's adversaries, they provided the Revolutionaries with money, supplies, weapons, soldiers, and warships. The French and Spanish also sent warships to the English Channel, which forced much of the Royal Navy to remain at home and thus weakened the British effort to blockade American ports.

The war for independence unleashed unexpected social and political changes, as it required "common people" to take a more active role in governments at all levels—local, state, and national. Ordinary folk readily took advantage of their new opportunities. In Virginia, voters in 1776 elected a new state legislature that, an observer noted, "was composed of men not quite so well dressed, nor so politely educated, nor so highly born" as had been the case in the past.

## focus questions

**1.** What challenges did the British and American military leaders face in the Revolutionary War?

**2.** What were some of the key turning points in the Revolutionary War? How did they change its direction?

**3.** In what ways did the American Revolution function as a civil war?

**4.** How was the Revolutionary War an "engine" for political and social change?

**5.** How did the Revolutionary War impact African Americans, women, and Native Americans?

# Mobilizing for War

The British Empire sent some 35,000 soldiers and half its huge navy across the Atlantic to put down the American rebellion. The British also hired foreign soldiers (mercenaries), as some 30,000 professional German soldiers served in the British armies. Most were from the German state of Hesse-Cassel. Americans called them *Hessians*.

The British also recruited Loyalists, Native Americans, and African Americans to fight on their behalf, but there were never as many enlisting as they had hoped. Further, the British initially assumed that there would be enough food for their troops and forage for their horses in America. As the war ground on, however, most of their supplies had to come from Britain. The war's increasing costs—in human lives and war debt—demoralized the British.

The British government under Lord North also never had a consistent war strategy. At first, the British tried to use their naval superiority to blockade New England's seaports and strangle American commerce. When that failed, they sought to destroy George Washington's troops in New York. Despite early success, the British commanders failed to pursue and eliminate the retreating Continental army. They next tried to drive a wedge between New England and New York, splitting the colonies in two. That too would fail, leading to the final British strategy: moving the main army into the southern colonies in hopes of rallying Loyalists in the region.

**THE CONTINENTAL ARMY**  While the Patriots had the advantage of fighting on their home ground, they also had to create an army and navy from scratch, and with little money. Before the war, **citizen-soldiers** (militiamen) were primarily civilians summoned from their farms and shops. Once the immediate danger passed, they quickly dispersed and returned to their homes. Many militiamen were unreliable and ungovernable. They were, reported General Washington, "nasty, dirty, and disobedient." They "come in, you cannot tell how, go, you cannot tell when, and act, you cannot tell where, consume your provisions, exhaust your stores [supplies], and leave you at last at a critical moment."

Washington knew that militiamen alone could not win against the veteran British and German soldiers. He therefore convinced the Continental Congress to create a professional *Continental army* with full-time, well-trained soldiers. About half of the 200,000 Americans who served in the war were militiamen ("Minutemen") and half were in the Continental army. They were relatively poor farmers, laborers, indentured servants, or recently arrived immigrants, and most were young and single. Some 5,000 African Americans also served.

What the Continental army needed most at the start of the war were capable officers, intensive training, modern weapons, reliable supplies, and multiyear enlistment contracts. Its soldiers also needed strict discipline, for they had no room for error against the British. As Washington and his officers began whipping the army into shape, those who violated the rules were jailed, flogged, sent packing, or even hanged as an example to others.

Many Patriots found army life unbearable and combat horrifying. As General Nathanael Greene, a Rhode Island Quaker who abandoned pacifism for the war effort and became Washington's ablest commander, pointed out, few Patriots had engaged in mortal combat, and they were hard-pressed to "stand the shocking scenes of war, to march over dead men, to hear without concern the groans of the wounded."

Desertions grew as the war dragged on. The Continental army became an ever-shifting group, "part turnstile and part accordion." At times, Washington could put only a few thousand men in the field. Eventually, Congress provided more generous enticements, such as land grants and cash bonuses, to encourage recruits to serve in the army for the duration of the war.

**PROBLEMS OF FINANCE AND SUPPLY** Financing the Revolution was much harder for the Americans than it was for Great Britain. Lacking the power to impose taxes, the Confederation Congress could only *ask* the states to provide funds for the national government. Yet the states rarely provided their expected share of the war's expenses, and the Congress reluctantly had to allow Patriot armies to take supplies directly from farmers in return for written promises of future payment.

In a predominantly agricultural society like America, turning farmers into soldiers hurt the national economy. William Hooper, a North Carolinian who signed the Declaration of Independence, grumbled that "a soldier made is a farmer lost." Many states found a ready source of revenue in the sale of abandoned Loyalist homes, farms, and plantations. Nevertheless, Congress and the states still fell short of funding the war's cost and were forced to print more and more paper money, which eroded its value.

**NATIVE AMERICANS AND THE REVOLUTION** Both the British and Americans recruited Indians to fight with them, but the British were far more successful at it, largely because they had longstanding relationships with chieftains and promised to protect Indian lands. The tribes making up the Iroquois League split their allegiances, with most Mohawks, Onondagas,

Cayugas, and Senecas joining the British, and most Oneidas and Tuscaroras supporting the Patriots. In the Carolinas, the Cherokees joined the British in hopes of driving out American settlers who had taken their lands. Most Indians in New England tried to remain neutral or sided with the Patriots.

**DISASTER IN CANADA** In July 1775, the Continental Congress authorized a military expedition in Canada against Quebec in the vain hope of convincing the French Canadians to become allies.

The Americans, having spent six weeks struggling through dense forests, crossing roaring rapids, and wading through frost-covered marshes, arrived outside Quebec in September, tired, exhausted, freezing, and hungry. A silent killer then ambushed them: smallpox. As the virus raced through the American camp, General Richard Montgomery faced a brutal dilemma. Most of his soldiers had signed up for short tours of duty, and many were scheduled for discharge at the end of the year. Because of the impending departure of his men, Montgomery could not afford to wait until spring for the smallpox to subside. Seeing little choice but to fight, he ordered an attack on the British forces defending Quebec on December 31, 1775.

The assault was a disaster. More than 400 Americans were taken prisoner; the rest of the Patriot force retreated to their camp outside the walled city and appealed to the Continental Congress for reinforcements. The British, sensing weakness, attacked and sent the Patriots on a frantic retreat up the St. Lawrence River to the American-held city of Montreal, and eventually back to New York and New England.

By the summer of 1776, the Patriots had come to realize that their quest for independence would be neither short nor easy. George Washington confessed to his brother that his efforts to form an effective army out of "the great mixture of troops" were filled with "difficulties and distresses."

**WASHINGTON'S NARROW ESCAPE** During the summer of 1776, the British decided to invade New York City, hoping to capture the new nation's leading commercial seaport. By the end of summer, two-thirds of the British army, veterans of many campaigns around the world, were camped on Staten Island, just a mile off the coast of Manhattan.

The British commanders, General William Howe and his brother, Admiral Richard Howe, sympathized with American grievances but felt strongly that the rebellion must be crushed. They met with Patriot leaders in an attempt to negotiate a settlement. After the negotiations failed, a British fleet of 427 ships carrying 32,000 troops, including 8,000 hired German soldiers, began landing on Long Island near New York City. It was the largest seaborne military expedition in history to that point.

After ousting the British from Boston earlier in the year, George Washington had moved his forces to defensive positions around New York City in February 1776. Although it was too small an army to protect New York, the Continental Congress insisted that the city be defended at all costs. As John Adams explained, New York was the "key to the whole continent."

Washington had never commanded a large force. He confessed to the Continental Congress that he had no "experience to move [armies] on a large scale" and had only "limited . . . knowledge . . . in military matters." He was still learning the art of generalship. The British invasion of New York taught him some painful lessons.

In late August 1776, the Americans entrenched on Long Island waited for the British to attack. Washington walked back and forth behind his outnumbered men with two loaded pistols, warning them that he would shoot anyone who turned tail and ran. He assured them that he would "fight as long as I have a leg or an arm."

Many Americans lost arms and legs as the Battle of Long Island and White Plains unfolded. A Marylander reported that a British cannonball careened through the American lines. It "first took the head off . . . a stout heavy man; then took off Chilson's arm, which was amputated . . . It then struck Sergeant Garret . . . on the hip. . . . What a sight that was to see . . . men with legs and arms and packs all in a heap."

The inexperienced American army suffered a humiliating defeat. In the face of steadily advancing ranks of British soldiers with bayonet-tipped muskets, many American defenders and their officers had panicked. Washington had urged his soldiers to fight "like men, like soldiers," but the more numerous redcoats overwhelmed the Patriots.

The smoke and chaos of battle, the "confusion and horror," disoriented the untested Americans. The disorganized, undisciplined, and indecisive Americans steadily gave ground, leading British commanders to assume that the Revolution was about to end. On August 28, while fighting continued in Brooklyn Heights, Admiral Lord Richard Howe hosted two captured American generals aboard his flagship. Over dinner, he shared his ideas for ending the war and restoring British authority over the wayward colonies.

At the same time Admiral Howe was discussing the end of the war, General Washington had decided there would be no surrender as the redcoats continued to maul his Patriots. On August 29, Washington realized the only hope for his battered army was to organize a hasty retreat that night. Thanks to a timely rainstorm and the heroic efforts of experienced New England boatmen, the 9,500 Americans and their horses and equipment were rowed across the East River to Manhattan through the night. An early morning fog cloaked the final stages of the risky retreat. The British did not realize what was happening until it was too late. Admiral Howe's hopes for a quick end to the Revolution were dashed.

Had General William Howe's army moved more quickly in pursuit of the retreating Patriots, it could have trapped Washington's entire force. Rather than sustaining their momentum, however, the British rested as the main American army made a miraculous escape over the next several weeks, crossing the Hudson River and retreating into New Jersey, and then over the Delaware River into Pennsylvania.

Washington was "wearied almost to death" as the ragged remnants of his army outraced their British pursuers over 170 miles in two months. "In one thing only" did the British fail, reported an observer; "they could not run as fast as their Foe."

New York City became the headquarters of both the Royal Navy and the British army. Local Loyalists, or "Tories" as the Patriots mockingly called them, excitedly welcomed the British occupation. "Hundreds in this colony are against us," a New York City Patriot wrote to John Adams. "Tories openly express their sentiments in favor of the enemy."

**Thomas Paine** Thomas Paine originally published his inspiring pamphlet *Common Sense* anonymously because the British viewed it as treasonous.

By December 1776, the American Revolution was near collapse. A British officer reported that many "rebels" were "without shoes or stockings, and several were observed to have only linen drawers . . . without any proper shirt. They must suffer extremely" in the winter weather. Indeed, the Continental army was shrinking before Washington's eyes. He had only 3,000 men left. Unless a new army could be raised quickly, he warned, "I think the game is pretty near up."

Then, almost miraculously, help emerged from an unexpected source: the English-born war correspondent, Thomas Paine. Having opened the eventful year of 1776 with his inspiring pamphlet *Common Sense*, Paine now composed *The American Crisis*, in which he wrote these stirring lines:

> These are the times that try men's souls: The summer soldier and the sunshine patriot will, in this crisis, shrink from the service of his country; but he that stands it NOW deserves the love and thanks of man and woman. Tyranny, like Hell, is not easily conquered. Yet we have this consolation with us, that the harder the conflict, the more glorious the triumph.

Paine's rousing pamphlet boosted the Patriots' flagging spirits. Washington had *The American Crisis* read aloud to his dwindling army. Members of the Continental Congress were also emboldened, and on December 27, 1776, Congress gave Washington "large powers" to strengthen the war effort, including the ability to offer recruits cash, land, clothing, and blankets.

Washington had learned some hard lessons. The feisty frontier militiamen he had relied upon to bolster the Continental army came and went as they pleased, in part because they resisted traditional forms of military discipline. Washington acknowledged that "a people unused to restraint must be led; they will not be driven."

His genius was to learn from his mistakes and to use resilience and flexibility as weapons. With soldiers deserting every day, Washington modified his conventional top-down approach in favor of allowing soldiers to tell him their concerns and offer suggestions. What he heard led him to change his strategy. The British would not be defeated in large battles. He needed to use his limited forces in surprise attacks, hit-and-run campaigns that would confuse the British and preserve his struggling army. Unknowingly, the British fell into his trap.

In December 1776, General William Howe, commander of the British forces in North America, decided to wait out the winter in New York City. (Eighteenth-century armies rarely fought during the winter months.) By not pursuing the Americans into Pennsylvania, Howe had lost a great opportunity to end the Revolution. He instead settled down with his "flashing blonde" Loyalist mistress (twenty-five-year-old Elizabeth Loring, the wife of a New England Tory). One American general quipped that Howe "shut his eyes, fought his battles, drank his bottle and had his little whore."

**A DESPERATE GAMBLE**    George Washington, however, was not ready to hibernate. He decided that the Revolutionary cause desperately needed "some stroke" of good news. So he hatched a plan to surprise the British forces before more of his soldiers decided to return home.

On a fearfully cold Christmas night in 1776, Washington secretly led some 2,400 men, packed into forty-foot-long boats, across the ice-clogged Delaware

**George Washington at Princeton**
Commissioned for Independence Hall in Philadelphia, this 1779 painting by Charles Willson Peale portrays Washington as the hero of the Battle of Princeton.

River into New Jersey. It was a risky endeavor, made even riskier by the weather and the rough river currents. Twice the Americans had to turn back, but on the third try they made it across the river. It had taken nine hours, and the howling winds, sleet, and blinding snow continued to slow their progress as they marched inland.

Near sunrise at Trenton, the Americans surprised 1,500 sleeping Hessians. The **Battle of Trenton** was a total rout. Just two of Washington's men were killed, and only four wounded. After the battle, Washington hurried his men and their German captives back across the river, urging his troops to treat the prisoners "with humanity, and let them have no reason to complain of our copying the brutal example of the British army."

Four days later, the Americans again crossed the Delaware River, won another battle at Trenton, and then headed north to attack British forces around Princeton before taking shelter in winter quarters at Morristown, New Jersey. A British officer grumbled that the Americans had "become a formidable enemy."

The American victories at Princeton and Trenton saved the cause of independence and shifted the war's momentum. A fresh wave of Patriots signed up to serve in the army, and Washington regained the confidence of his men.

A British officer recognized that the victories at Trenton and Princeton would "revive the dropping spirits of the rebels and increase their force." British war correspondents claimed that Washington was more talented than any of their commanders. Yet although the "dark days" of late 1776 were over, unexpected challenges quickly chilled the Patriots' excitement.

**WINTER IN MORRISTOWN** During the record-cold winter in early 1777, George Washington's ragged army was again much diminished, as six-month enlistment contracts expired and deserters fled the hardships caused by the brutal weather, inadequate food, and widespread disease. One soldier

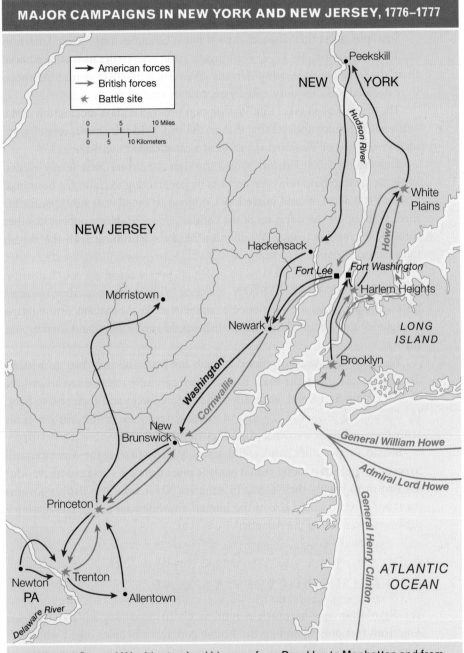

## MAJOR CAMPAIGNS IN NEW YORK AND NEW JERSEY, 1776–1777

- Why did General Washington lead his army from Brooklyn to Manhattan and from there to New Jersey?
- How could the British army commander, General William Howe, have ended the rebellion in New York?
- What was the significance of the Battle of Trenton?

recalled that "we were absolutely, literally starved. . . . I saw several of the men roast their old shoes and eat them."

Smallpox and other diseases caused more casualties among the American armies than combat. By 1777, Washington had come to dread smallpox more than "the Sword of the Enemy." On any given day, a fourth of American troops were deemed unfit for duty, usually because of smallpox.

The threat was so great that Washington ordered a mass inoculation of the entire army, a risky undertaking that, in the end, paid off. The successful inoculation was one of Washington's greatest strategic accomplishments.

Only about 1,000 Patriots stayed through the brutal New Jersey winter. With the spring thaw, however, recruits began arriving to claim the bounty of $20 and 100 acres of land offered by Congress to those who would enlist for three years or for the duration of the conflict, if less. Having cobbled together some 9,000 regular troops, Washington began skirmishing with the British forces in northern New Jersey.

**A STRATEGY OF EVASION**   General William Howe had been making his own plans, however. He hoped to maneuver the Americans into fighting a single "decisive action" that the British would surely win—and thereby end the war.

Washington, however, refused to take the bait. The only way to win, he decided, was to evade the main British army, carefully select when and where to attack, and, in the end, wear down the enemy forces and their will to fight. He was willing to concede control of major cities to the British, for it was his army, "not defenseless towns, [that] they have to subdue."

Britain, on the other hand, could win only by destroying the American will to resist. With each passing year, it became more difficult—and expensive—for the British to supply their forces in America. Over time, the British government and people would tire of the human and financial toll of conducting a prolonged war across the Atlantic.

# AMERICAN SOCIETY AT WAR

The Revolution was as much a ruthless civil war among bitterly opposed American factions (including the Native American peoples allied with both sides) as it was a prolonged struggle against Great Britain. The necessity of choosing sides divided families and friends, towns and cities.

Benjamin Franklin's illegitimate son, William, for example, was the royal governor of New Jersey. An ardent Loyalist, he sided with Great Britain. His

Patriot father later removed him from his will. Similarly, eighteen-year-old Bostonian Lucy Flucker defied her Loyalist father's wishes and married bookseller Henry Knox in 1774. (Knox would become an American general.) Lucy's estranged family fled with the British army when it left Boston in 1776, and she never saw them again. "I have lost my father, mother, brother, and sister, entirely lost them," she wrote.

Overall, the colonists were generally divided into three groups: (1) Patriots, who formed the Continental army and fought in state militias; (2) Loyalists, or Tories, siding with Britain and the king; and, (3) a less committed middle group that sought to remain neutral but were eventually swayed by the better organized and more energetic Patriots. Loyalists may have represented 20 percent of the American population, but Patriots were the largest of the three groups.

Some Americans (like Benedict Arnold) switched sides during the war, some as many as four or five times. Both the Patriots and the British, once they took control of a city or community, would often require the residents to swear an oath of loyalty to their cause. In Pennsylvania, Patriots tied a rope around the neck of John Stevens, a Loyalist, and dragged him behind a canoe in the Susquehanna River because he refused to sign a loyalty oath to the American cause.

The Loyalists, whom George Washington called "abominable pests of society," viewed the Revolution as an act of treason. The British Empire, they felt, was much more likely than an independent America to protect them from foreign foes and enable them to prosper. As the Reverend Mather Byles explained, "They call me a brainless Tory, but tell me . . . which is better—to be ruled by one tyrant 3,000 miles away or by 3,000 tyrants [Patriots] one mile away?"

Loyalists were most numerous in the seaport cities, especially New York and Philadelphia, as well as the Carolinas, and they came from all walks of life. Governors, judges, and other royal officials were almost all Loyalists; most Anglican ministers also preferred the mother country. Many small farmers who had largely been unaffected by the controversies over British efforts to tighten colonial regulations rallied to the British side. More New York men joined Loyalist regiments than enlisted in the Continental army. In few places, however, were there enough Loyalists to assume control without the support of British troops.

The Loyalists did not want to "dissolve the political bands" with Britain, as the Declaration of Independence demanded. Instead, as some 700 of them in New York City said in a petition to British officials, they "steadily and uniformly opposed" this "most unnatural, unprovoked Rebellion."

***Four Soldiers*** (ca. 1781)  This illustration drawn by a French lieutenant captures the varied uniforms worn by Patriot forces in the war (left to right): a black soldier (freed for joining the 1st Rhode Island Regiment), a New England militiaman, a frontiersman, and a French soldier.

The British, however, were repeatedly frustrated by both the failure of Loyalists to materialize in strength and the collapse of Loyalist militia units once British troops departed. Because Patriot militias quickly returned whenever the British left an area, Loyalists faced a difficult choice: either accompany the British and leave behind their property, or stay and face the wrath of the Patriots. Even more disheartening was what one British officer called "the licentiousness of the [Loyalist] troops, who committed every species of rapine and plunder" and thereby converted potential friends to enemies.

The Patriots, both moderates and radicals, supported the war because they realized that the only way to protect their liberty was to separate themselves from British control. They also wanted to establish an American republic that would convert them from being *subjects* of a king to being *citizens* with the power to elect their own government and pursue their own economic interests.

## SETBACKS FOR THE BRITISH (1777)

In 1777, the British launched a three-pronged assault on the state of New York. The complicated plan called for an army, based in Canada and led by General John Burgoyne, to advance southward from Quebec via Lake Champlain to the Hudson River. At the same time, another British force would move eastward from Oswego, in western New York. General William Howe would lead a third army up the Hudson River from New York City. All three armies would eventually converge in central New York and wipe out any remaining Patriot resistance.

The British armies, however, failed in their execution—and in their communications with one another. At the last minute, Howe changed his mind and decided to move south from New York City to attack the Patriot capital, Philadelphia. General Washington withdrew most of his men from New Jersey to meet the threat in Pennsylvania, while other American units banded together in upstate New York to deal with the British there.

On September 11, 1777, at Brandywine Creek, southwest of Philadelphia, the British overpowered Washington's army and occupied Philadelphia, then the largest and wealthiest American city. Caught up in the fighting, the members of the Continental Congress fled. Battered but still intact, Washington and his army withdrew to winter quarters twenty miles away at Valley Forge, while Howe and his men remained in Philadelphia.

**THE CAMPAIGN OF 1777** Meanwhile, an overconfident General Burgoyne (nicknamed "General Swagger") led his army southward from Canada, eventually reaching Lake Champlain in June 1777. The British then pushed south toward the Hudson River. Eventually, they ran short of food and provisions, leaving them no choice but to make a desperate attempt to reach Albany. Growing numbers of Patriot soldiers slowed their advance, however.

The American army commander in New York was General Horatio Gates. Thirty-two years earlier, in 1745, he and Burgoyne had served as officers in the same British regiment. Now they were commanding opposing armies.

As Patriot militiamen converged from across central New York, Burgoyne pulled his forces back to the village of Saratoga (now called Schuylerville), where the reinforced American army surrounded the British. In the ensuing three-week-long **Battles of Saratoga**, the British, desperate for food and ammunition, twice tried—and failed—to break through the encircling Americans. On October 17, 1777, Burgoyne surrendered his outnumbered army. "The fortunes of war," he told Gates, "have made me your prisoner." Burgoyne also turned over 5,800 troops, 7,000 muskets, and 42 cannons to the Americans.

The news from New York unhinged King George. He fell "into agonies on hearing the account." The Saratoga campaign was the greatest loss that the British had ever suffered, and they would never recover. William Pitt, the former British

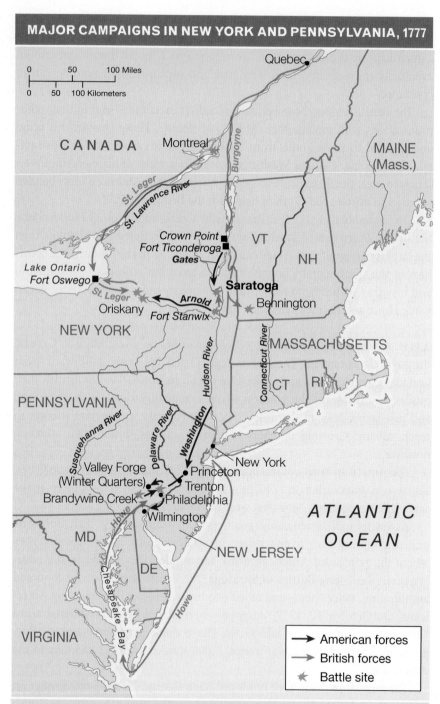

MAJOR CAMPAIGNS IN NEW YORK AND PENNSYLVANIA, 1777

American forces
British forces
Battle site

- What were the consequences of Burgoyne's strategy of dividing the colonies by invading upstate New York from Canada?
- How did life in the American winter camp at Valley Forge transform the army?
- Why were the Battles of Saratoga a turning point in the American Revolution?

prime minister, made a shocking prediction to Parliament after the defeat: *"You cannot conquer America."*

**ALLIANCE WITH FRANCE** The surprising victory at Saratoga was a strategic turning point for the new nation because it brought about an **alliance with France**, which had lost four wars to the British in the previous eighty years.

Under the Treaty of Alliance, on February 6, 1778, the parties agreed, first, that if France entered the war, both countries would fight until American independence was won; second, that neither would conclude a "truce or peace" with Great Britain without "the formal consent of the other"; and, third, that each would guarantee the other's possessions in America "from the present time and forever against all other powers." France further agreed not to seek Canada or other British possessions on the mainland of North America.

**General John Burgoyne** Burgoyne was commander of Britain's northern forces. He and most of his troops surrendered to the Americans at Saratoga on October 17, 1777.

In the end, the French intervention determined the outcome of the war. The Americans would also form important alliances with the Spanish (1779) and the Dutch (1781), but neither provided as much direct support as the French.

After the British defeat at Saratoga and the news of the French alliance with the United States, Parliament tried to end the war by granting all the demands the Americans had made before they had declared independence. The Continental Congress, however, would not negotiate until Britain officially recognized American independence and withdrew its forces. King George refused.

## 1778: BOTH SIDES REGROUP

**VALLEY FORGE AND STALEMATE** For George Washington's army at **Valley Forge**, near Philadelphia, the winter of 1777–1778 was a time of intense suffering. The 12,000 Patriots, including some twelve-year-old soldiers accompanied by their mothers, lacked shoes and blankets. All were miserably hungry, and their makeshift log-and-mud huts offered little protection from the harsh weather. Bare feet froze, turned black, and were amputated. "Why are we sent here to starve and freeze?" wrote a Connecticut Patriot. "Poor food . . . hard logging . . . cold weather . . . it snows . . . I'm sick . . . I can't endure it. . . . Lord, Lord, Lord."

By February 1778, some 7,000 troops were too ill for duty. More than 2,500 soldiers died at Valley Forge; another 1,000 deserted, and several hundred officers resigned or left before winter's end. Washington sent urgent messages to Congress, warning that if fresh food and supplies were not provided, the army would be forced "to starve, dissolve, or disperse."

Fortunately for the Revolutionaries, the plodding General Howe again remained content to ride out the winter in the company of his charming companion, Mrs. Loring, this time amid the comforts of Philadelphia. Their cozy relationship prompted a Patriot to pen a bawdy song:

> Sir William, he, snug as a flea
> Lay all this while a snoring;
> Nor dream'd of harm as he lay warm
> In bed with Mrs. Loring.

Yet there was little singing among the Americans. Desperate to find relief for his long-suffering soldiers, Washington sent troops across New Jersey, Delaware, and the Eastern Shore of Maryland to confiscate horses, cattle, and hogs in exchange for "receipts" promising future payment.

In the early spring of 1778, Washington sought to boost morale and distract the soldiers from their challenges by organizing a rigorous training program. To do so, he turned to an energetic, heavy-set Prussian soldier of fortune, Friedrich Wilhelm, Baron von Steuben, who volunteered without rank or pay.

Soon after his arrival at Valley Forge on February 23, 1778, Steuben reported being shocked by the "horrible conditions" he found. Knowing no more English than "Goddamn," Steuben used an interpreter as he issued instructions to the haggard Americans, teaching them how to march, shoot, and attack in formation. Once, when Steuben had grown frustrated at the soldiers' lack of attentiveness, he screamed for his translator: "These fellows won't do what I tell them. Come swear for me!" In Europe, he complained, soldiers blindly followed orders; in America, they demanded to know *why* they should listen to officers.

Steuben was one of several foreign volunteers who joined the American army at Valley Forge. Another was a nineteen-year-old, red-haired French orphan named Gilbert du Motier, Marquis de Lafayette. A wealthy idealist excited by the American cause, Lafayette offered to serve in the Continental army for no pay in exchange for being named a major general. He then gave $200,000 to the war effort, outfitted a ship, recruited other French volunteers, and left behind his pregnant wife and year-old daughter to join the "grand adventure."

Washington was initially skeptical of the young French aristocrat, but Lafayette soon became the commander in chief's most trusted aide. Washington noted that Lafayette possessed "a large share of bravery and military ardor." The young French general also proved to be an able diplomat in forging the military alliance with France.

Patriot morale had risen when the Continental Congress promised extra pay and bonuses after the war, and again with the news of the military alliance with France. In the spring of 1778, British

**Lafayette** Marquis de Lafayette, portrayed in this colored mezzotint by Charles Willson Peale, was a key figure in the Revolutionary War. The French statesman and soldier lived from 1757 to 1834.

forces withdrew from Pennsylvania to New York City, with the American army in hot pursuit. From that time on, the combat in the north settled into a long stalemate.

**WAR IN THE WEST**  The Revolution had created two wars. In addition to the main conflict in the east, a frontier guerrilla war of terror and vengeance pitted Indians and Loyalists against isolated Patriot settlers living along the northern and western frontiers. In the Ohio Valley, as well as western New York and Pennsylvania, the British urged frontier Loyalists and their Indian allies to raid settlements and offered to pay bounties for American scalps.

To end the English-led attacks, early in 1778 George Rogers Clark took 175 Patriot frontiersmen on flatboats down the Ohio River. On the evening of July 4, the Americans captured English-controlled Kaskaskia, in present-day Illinois. Then, without bloodshed, Clark took Cahokia (in Illinois across the Mississippi River from St. Louis) and Vincennes (in present-day Indiana).

After the British retook Vincennes, Clark led his men across icy rivers and flooded prairies to attack the British garrison. Clark's rugged frontiersmen, called Rangers, captured five Indians carrying American scalps. He ordered

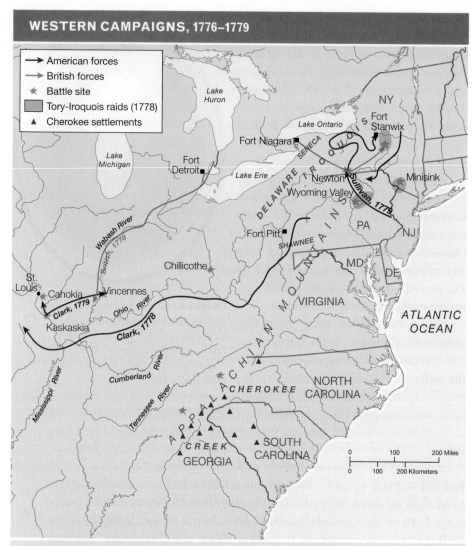

## WESTERN CAMPAIGNS, 1776–1779

- → American forces
- → British forces
- ✳ Battle site
- ▨ Tory-Iroquois raids (1778)
- ▲ Cherokee settlements

- How did George Rogers Clark secure Cahokia and Vincennes?
- Why did the American army destroy Iroquois villages in 1779?
- Why were the skirmishes between settlers and Indian tribes significant for the future of the trans-Appalachian frontier?

them to kill the Indians in sight of the fort. After watching the executions, the British surrendered.

While Clark's Rangers were in Indiana, a much larger U.S. force moved against Iroquois strongholds in western New York, where Loyalists (Tories) and their Indian allies had been terrorizing frontier settlements. The Iroquois attacks had killed hundreds of Patriot militiamen.

In response, George Washington sent 4,000 men under General John Sullivan to crush "the hostile tribes" and "the most mischievous of the Tories." At Newtown, New York, on August 29, 1779, Sullivan's soldiers did as ordered: they destroyed about forty Seneca and Cayuga villages, which broke the power of the Iroquois Confederacy.

The Patriots also desecrated Indian graves, raped native women, and mutilated warriors they had killed. An Indian chieftain reported that the Americans "put to death all the women and children, excepting some of the young women, whom they carried away for the use of the soldiers and were afterwards put to death in a more shameful manner."

In the Kentucky Territory, legendary frontiersman Daniel Boone and his small band of settlers repeatedly clashed with the Shawnees and their British and Loyalist allies. In 1778, Boone and some thirty men, aided by their wives and children, held off an assault by more than 400 Indians at Boonesborough. In early 1776, a delegation of northern Indians—Shawnees, Delawares, and Mohawks—had talked the Cherokees into attacking frontier settlements in Virginia and the Carolinas. Swift retaliation had followed as Carolina militiamen, led by Andrew Pickens, burned dozens of Cherokee villages. By weakening the major Indian tribes along the frontier, the American Revolution cleared the way for white settlers to seize Indian lands after the war.

## THE WAR MOVES SOUTH

In late 1778, the British launched their southern strategy, built on the assumption that large numbers of Loyalists in the Carolinas, Virginia, and Georgia would join their cause. Once the British gained control of the southern colonies, they would have the shrinking United States pinched between Canada and the South.

In December 1778, General Sir Henry Clinton, the new commander in chief of British forces, sent 3,000 redcoats, Hessians, and Loyalists to take the port city of Savannah, on the southeast Georgia coast, and roll northeast from there. He enlisted support from local Loyalists and the Cherokees, led by Chief Dragging Canoe, who promised to leave the ground "dark and bloody."

**BRITISH MOMENTUM** Initially, Clinton's southern strategy worked beautifully. Within twenty months, the British and their allies had defeated three American armies; seized the strategic cities of Savannah and Charleston; occupied Georgia and much of South Carolina; and killed, wounded, or captured some 7,000 American soldiers. This success led Lord George Germain, the British official in London overseeing the war, to predict a "speedy and happy termination of the American war."

Germain's optimistic prediction, however, fell victim to three developments: first, the Loyalist strength in the South was weaker than estimated; second, the British effort to unleash Indian attacks convinced many undecided backcountry settlers to join the Patriot side; and, third, some British and Loyalist soldiers behaved so harshly that they drove Loyalists to switch sides.

**WAR IN THE CAROLINAS**  The Carolina campaign took a major turn when British forces, led by generals Clinton and Charles Cornwallis, bottled up an entire American army on the Charleston Peninsula for six weeks. Benjamin Lincoln, the inexperienced U.S. commander, begged local planters to arm their slaves and let them join the defense of the city, but the slaveholders refused. Prominent South Carolina leaders then used their control of local militia units to prevent Lincoln and his army from escaping.

On May 12, 1780, Lincoln surrendered Charleston and its 5,500 defenders. It was the greatest Patriot loss of the war. Soon thereafter, General Cornwallis, in charge of the British troops in the South, defeated a much larger American force led by General Horatio Gates at Camden, South Carolina. The British leader sought to intimidate other Revolutionaries by hanging captured Patriots.

Cornwallis had Georgia and most of South Carolina under British control by 1780. Then he made a tactical blunder by sending lieutenants into the countryside to organize Loyalist fighters to assault Patriots. In doing so, they mercilessly burned homes and murdered surrendering rebels. Their behavior alienated many poor rural folk who had been neutral. Francis Kinlock, a Loyalist, warned a British official that "the lower sort of people, who were in many parts . . . originally attached to the British government, have suffered so severely and been so frequently deceived, that Great Britain now has a hundred enemies where it had one before."

In mid-1780, small bands of Patriots based in the swamps and forests of South Carolina launched a successful series of hit-and-run raids. Led by colorful fighters such as Francis Marion, "the Swamp Fox," and Thomas Sumter, "the Carolina Gamecock," the Patriot guerrillas gradually wore down British confidence and morale. By August 1780, the British commanders were forced to admit that South Carolina was "in an absolute state of rebellion."

Warfare in the Carolinas was especially brutal. Neighbors fought neighbors, and families were split. Fathers fought sons, and brothers killed brothers. Both sides looted farms and plantations and tortured, scalped, and executed prisoners. Edward Lacey, a young South Carolina Patriot who commanded a militia unit, had to tie his Tory father to a bedstead to prevent him from informing the British of his whereabouts. In Virginia, planter Charles Lynch set up vigilante courts to punish Loyalists by "lynching" them—which in this case meant whipping them. Others were covered with bubbling-hot tar and feathers.

In the "backcountry" of the Carolinas and Georgia, British commanders encouraged their poorly disciplined Loyalist allies to wage a scorched-earth war of terror, arson, and intimidation. British general Charles Cornwallis urged his commanders to use the "most *vigorous* measures to *extinguish the rebellion.*"

Tory militiamen took civilian hostages, assaulted women and children, plundered and burned houses and churches, stole property, bayoneted wounded Patriots, and tortured and executed unarmed prisoners. Vengeful Patriots responded in kind.

**THE BATTLE OF KINGS MOUNTAIN** Cornwallis's most cold-blooded cavalry officers, Sir Banastre Tarleton and Major Patrick Ferguson, were in charge of training Loyalist militiamen. The British officers often let their men burn Patriot farms, liberate slaves, and destroy livestock.

Yet they eventually overreached. Ferguson sealed his doom when he threatened to march over the Blue Ridge Mountains, hang the mostly Scots-Irish Presbyterian Patriot leaders ("backwater barbarians"), and destroy their farms "with fire and sword." Instead, the feisty "over the mountain men" from southwestern Virginia and western North and South Carolina, all experienced hunters and riflemen who had often fought Cherokees, went hunting for Ferguson and his army of Loyalists in late September 1780.

On October 7, the two sides clashed near Kings Mountain, a heavily wooded ridge along the border between North and South Carolina. In a ferocious hour-long battle, Patriot sharpshooters devastated the Loyalist troops.

Major Ferguson, resplendent in a black and red checkered coat, had boasted beforehand that "all the rebels in hell could not push him off" Kings Mountain. By the end of the battle, his lifeless body was pocked with seven bullets, and both his arms were broken. Seven hundred Loyalists were captured, and nine of them were later hanged. "The division among the people is much greater than I imagined," an American officer wrote to one of General Washington's aides. The Patriots and Loyalists, he said, "persecute each other with . . . savage fury."

As with so many confrontations in the South, the Battle of Kings Mountain resembled an extended family feud. Seventy-four sets of brothers fought on opposite sides, and twenty-nine sets of fathers and sons.

Five brothers in the Goforth family from Rutherford County, North Carolina, fought at Kings Mountain; three were Loyalists, and two were Patriots.

Only one of them survived. Two of the brothers, Preston and John Preston, fighting on opposite sides, recognized each other during the battle, took deadly aim as if in a duel, and fired simultaneously, killing each other.

The American victory at Kings Mountain undermined the British strategy in the South. Afterward, Cornwallis's forces retreated to South Carolina—and found it virtually impossible to recruit more Loyalists.

**SOUTHERN RETREAT**   In late 1780, the Continental Congress chose a new commander for the American army in the South: General Nathanael Greene, "the fighting Quaker" of Rhode Island. A former blacksmith blessed with unflagging persistence, he was bold and daring, and well-suited to a drawn-out war.

Greene arrived in Charlotte, North Carolina, to find himself in charge of a "shadow army." The 2,200 troops lacked everything "necessary either for the Comfort or Convenience of Soldiers." Greene wrote General Washington that the situation was "dismal, and truly distressing." Yet he also knew that if his army were not victorious, the South would be "re-annexed" to Britain.

Like Washington, Greene adopted a hit-and-run strategy. From Charlotte, he moved his army eastward while sending General Daniel Morgan and about 700 riflemen on a sweep to the west of Cornwallis's headquarters at Winnsboro, South Carolina.

On January 17, 1781, Morgan's force took up positions near Cowpens in northern South Carolina, about twenty-five miles from Kings Mountain. There he lured Sir Banastre Tarleton's army into an elaborate trap. Tarleton rushed his men forward, only to be ambushed by Morgan's cavalry. Tarleton escaped, but 110 British soldiers died and more than 700 were taken prisoner. Cowpens was the most complete victory for the Americans in the Revolution and was one of the few times that the Patriots won a battle in which the two sides were evenly matched.

Morgan's army then moved into North Carolina and linked up with Greene's troops. Greene lured the starving British army north, then attacked the redcoats at Guilford Courthouse (near what became Greensboro, North Carolina) on March 15, 1781.

The Americans lost the Battle of Guilford Courthouse but inflicted such heavy losses that Cornwallis left behind his wounded and marched his weary men toward Wilmington, on the North Carolina coast, to lick their wounds and take on supplies from British ships. The British commander reported that the Americans had "fought like demons."

Greene then resolved to go back into South Carolina, hoping to draw Cornwallis after him or force the British to give up the state. Greene connected with local guerrilla bands led by Francis Marion, Andrew Pickens, and

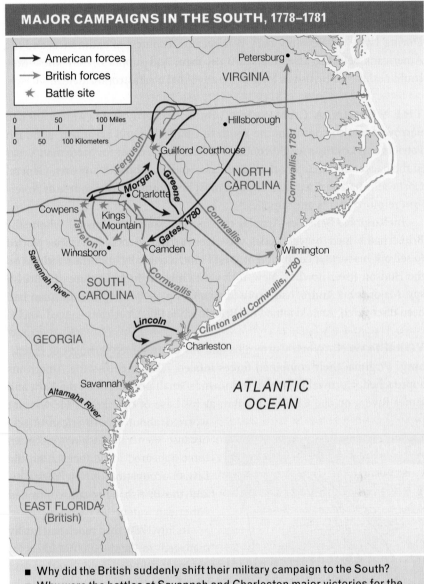

## MAJOR CAMPAIGNS IN THE SOUTH, 1778–1781

→ American forces
→ British forces
✳ Battle site

0    50    100 Miles
0    50    100 Kilometers

Petersburg
VIRGINIA
Hillsborough
Ferguson
Guilford Courthouse
NORTH CAROLINA
Morgan
Greene
Charlotte
Cowpens
Kings Mountain
Tarleton
Cornwallis
Cornwallis, 1781
Gates, 1780
Cornwallis
Winnsboro
Camden
Wilmington
Savannah River
SOUTH CAROLINA
Cornwallis
Clinton and Cornwallis, 1780
Lincoln
GEORGIA
Charleston
Savannah
Altamaha River
ATLANTIC OCEAN
EAST FLORIDA (British)

- Why did the British suddenly shift their military campaign to the South?
- Why were the battles at Savannah and Charleston major victories for the British?
- How did General Greene undermine British control of the Lower South?

Thomas Sumter. By targeting outlying British units and picking them off one by one, the guerrillas eventually forced the British back into Charleston and Savannah. George Washington praised Greene for having done "great things with little means."

# A War of Endurance

During 1780, the Revolutionary War became a contest of endurance, and the Americans held the advantage in time, men, and supplies. They knew they could outlast the British as long as they avoided a catastrophic defeat.

**THE VIRGINIA CAMPAIGN** By September 1781, the Americans had narrowed British control in the South to Charleston and Savannah, although Patriots and Loyalists would continue to battle each other for more than a year in the backcountry. Before the Carolinas could be subdued, however, General Cornwallis had decided that Virginia must be eliminated as a source of American reinforcements and supplies.

In Virginia, Benedict Arnold, the former American general whom the British had bribed to switch sides, was eager to strike. Arnold had earlier plotted to sell out his former command of West Point, a critically important fortress on the Hudson River north of New York City. Only the lucky capture of a British spy, Major John André, had exposed Arnold's plot. Warned that his plan had been discovered, Arnold joined the British, while the Americans hanged André.

**YORKTOWN** When Cornwallis and his army joined Arnold's at Petersburg, Virginia, their combined forces totaled 7,200 men. As the Americans approached, Cornwallis picked Yorktown, a small port between the York and James Rivers on the Chesapeake Bay, as his base of operations. He was not worried about an American attack, because General Washington's main force appeared to be focused on the British occupation of New York City, and the British navy still controlled American waters.

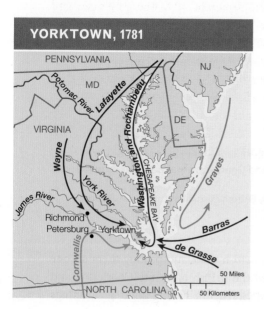

**YORKTOWN, 1781**

In July 1780, the French had finally managed to land 6,000 soldiers at Newport, Rhode Island, but they had been bottled up there for a year, blockaded by the British fleet. As long as the British navy maintained supremacy along the coast, the Americans could not hope to win the war.

In May 1781, however, the elements for a combined French-American action suddenly fell into place. As Cornwallis's army moved into Virginia, Washington persuaded the commander of the French army in Rhode Island to join an attack on the British in New York City. Before they could strike, however, word came from the Caribbean that Admiral François-Joseph-Paul de Grasse was headed for the Chesapeake Bay with his fleet of French warships and some 3,000 soldiers.

This unexpected news led Washington to change his plans. He immediately begin moving his army south toward Yorktown. At the same time, French ships slipped out of the British blockade at Newport and also headed south. Somehow, in an age when communications were difficult, the French and Americans coordinated a secret plan to combine naval and army forces and destroy the main British army. Success depended on the French fleet getting to the Chesapeake Bay before the British navy did.

On August 30, Admiral de Grasse's twenty-four warships won the race to Yorktown, and French troops joined the Americans. The allies were about to spring their trap. Once Cornwallis realized what was happening, it was too late. The British commander sent an urgent plea for reinforcements: "If you cannot relieve me very soon, you must be prepared to hear the worst."

On September 6, the day after a British fleet appeared, de Grasse attacked and forced the British navy to abandon Cornwallis's surrounded army, leaving him with no access to fresh food and supplies. De Grasse then sent ships up the Chesapeake to ferry down the soldiers who had marched south from New York, bringing the combined American and French armies to 19,000 men—more than double the size of Cornwallis's army.

The **Battle of Yorktown** began on September 28. The American and French troops soon closed off Cornwallis's last escape route and began bombarding the British with cannons, sending some 3,600 shells raining down on the French lines. The British held out for three grim weeks, but on October 17, 1781—the anniversary of the American victory at Saratoga—Cornwallis surrendered. Two days later, the 7,000 British soldiers laid down their weapons as the band played "The World Turned Upside Down."

Claiming to be ill but sick only with humiliation, Cornwallis sent a painfully brief report to the British commander in chief in New York: "I have the mortification to inform your Excellency that I have been forced to surrender the troops under my command."

## The Treaty of Paris (1783)

Although Cornwallis had surrendered, the war was not yet over. The British still had more than 20,000 troops in America. They controlled New York City, Charleston, and Savannah, and their warships still blockaded other American ports. Yet any lingering British hopes of a military victory vanished at Yorktown. In London, prime minister Lord North exclaimed, "Oh God, it is all over."

In December 1781, King George decided against sending more troops to America. Early in 1782, the British contacted Benjamin Franklin in Paris to ask if the Americans would be willing to sign a peace treaty without involving the French. Franklin replied that the United States had no intention of deserting its "noble" French ally to sign a treaty with "an unjust and cruel Enemy."

On February 27, 1782, Parliament voted to begin negotiations to end the war, and on March 20, Lord North resigned. In part, the British leaders chose peace in America so that they could concentrate on their continuing global war with France and Spain. At the same time, France let Franklin know that it was willing to let the United States negotiate its own treaty with Great Britain.

**A NEGOTIATED PEACE**  Upon learning of the British decision to negotiate, the Continental Congress named a group of prominent Americans to go to Paris to discuss terms. They included John Adams, who was then representing the United States in the Netherlands; John Jay, minister (ambassador) to Spain; and Benjamin Franklin, already in France. The cranky Adams was an odd choice since, as Thomas Jefferson said, "He hates [Benjamin] Franklin, he hates John Jay, he hates the French, he hates the English." In the end, Franklin and, especially, Jay did most of the work.

The negotiations dragged on for months until, on September 3, 1783, the warring nations signed the Treaty of Paris. Its provisions were surprisingly favorable to the United States. Great Britain recognized the independence of the thirteen former colonies and agreed that the Mississippi River was America's western boundary, thereby more than doubling the territory of the new nation. Native Americans had no role in the negotiations, and they were by far the biggest losers.

The treaty's unclear references to America's northern and southern borders would be a source of dispute for years. Florida, as it turned out, passed back to Spain. As for the prewar debts owed by Americans to British merchants, the U.S. negotiators promised that British merchants should "meet with no legal impediment" in seeking to collect money owed them.

However imperfect the peace treaty was, the upstart Americans had humbled the British Empire. "A great revolution has happened," acknowledged Edmund Burke, a prominent British politician. "A revolution made, not by chopping and changing of power in any one of the existing states, but by the appearance of a new state, of a new species, in a new part of the globe."

In winning the war, the Americans had acquired a robust sense of their own power and an awareness of the limitations of British power. Most important, the Americans had earned their legitimate right to decide their own future.

Whatever the failings and hypocrisies of the Revolution, it severed America's connection with monarchical rule and provided the catalyst for the creation of a representative democracy.

In late November 1783, the remaining British troops left New York City for home. On December 23, George Washington appeared before the Continental Congress in Annapolis, Maryland. With trembling hands and a rasping voice, he asked the members to accept his retirement. "Having now finished the work assigned to me, I retire from the great theater of Action . . . and take my leave of all employments of public life."

# WAR AS AN ENGINE OF CHANGE

Like all major wars, the American war for independence had unexpected effects on political, economic, and social life. It upset traditional social relationships and affected the lives of people who had long been discriminated against—African Americans, women, and Indians. In important ways, then, the Revolution was an engine for political experimentation and social change, and it ignited a prolonged debate about what new forms of government would best serve the new American republic.

**REPUBLICAN IDEOLOGY** American Revolutionaries embraced a **republican ideology** instead of the aristocratic or monarchical outlook that had long dominated Europe. The new republic was not a democracy in the purest sense of the word. In ancient Greece, the Athenians had practiced *direct democracy*, which meant that citizens voted on all major decisions affecting them. The new United States, however, was technically a *representative democracy*, in which property-holding white men governed themselves through the concept of republicanism—they elected representatives, or legislators, to make decisions on their behalf. As Thomas Paine observed, representative democracy had many advantages over monarchies, one of which was greater transparency: "Whatever are its excellencies and defects, they are visible to all."

To preserve the delicate balance between liberty and power, Revolutionary leaders believed that they must protect the rights of individuals and states from being violated by the national government. The war for independence thus sparked a wave of new **state constitutions**. Not only was a nation coming into being as a result of the Revolutionary War, but new state-level governments were being created, all of which were designed to reflect the principles of the republican ideology limiting the powers of government so as to protect the rights of the people.

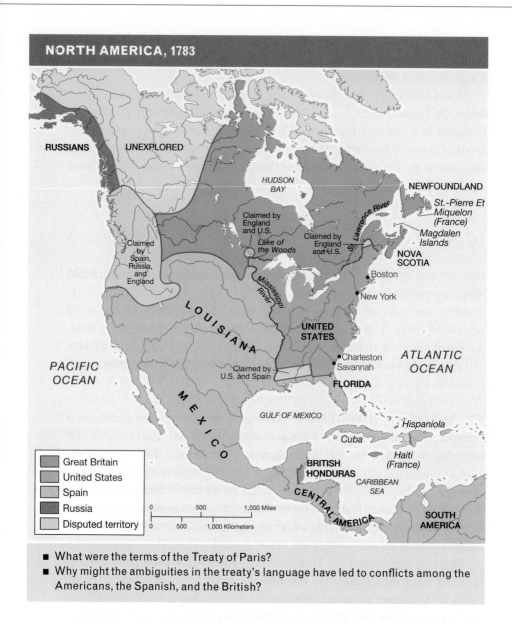

## NORTH AMERICA, 1783

RUSSIANS   UNEXPLORED

HUDSON BAY

NEWFOUNDLAND

St.-Pierre Et Miquelon (France)

Magdalen Islands

NOVA SCOTIA

Claimed by England and U.S.

Lake of the Woods

Claimed by England and U.S.

St. Lawrence River

Claimed by Spain, Russia, and England

Mississippi River

Boston

New York

LOUISIANA

UNITED STATES

PACIFIC OCEAN

Claimed by U.S. and Spain

Charleston
Savannah

ATLANTIC OCEAN

FLORIDA

MEXICO

GULF OF MEXICO

Hispaniola

Cuba

Haiti (France)

BRITISH HONDURAS

CARIBBEAN SEA

CENTRAL AMERICA

SOUTH AMERICA

- Great Britain
- United States
- Spain
- Russia
- Disputed territory

0      500      1,000 Miles
0   500   1,000 Kilometers

- What were the terms of the Treaty of Paris?
- Why might the ambiguities in the treaty's language have led to conflicts among the Americans, the Spanish, and the British?

**STATE GOVERNMENTS**   Most of the political experimentation between 1776 and 1787 occurred at the state level in the form of written constitutions in which the people granted limited authority to their governments. The first state constitutions created governments during the War of Independence much like the colonial governments, but with *elected* governors and senates instead of royally *appointed* governors and councils. Most of the constitutions also included a bill of rights that protected freedom of speech, trial by jury, and freedom from self-incrimination, while limiting the powers of governors and strengthening the powers of the legislatures.

**THE ARTICLES OF CONFEDERATION**   Once the colonies had declared their independence in 1776, the Patriots needed to form a *national* government. Before March 1781, the Continental Congress had exercised emergency powers without any legal or official authority.

Plans for a permanent form of government emerged quickly. As early as July 1776, a committee appointed by the Continental Congress had produced a draft constitution called the *Articles of Confederation and Perpetual Union.* When the **Articles of Confederation** were finally ratified in March 1781, they essentially legalized the way things had been operating since independence had been declared, although the Continental Congress became the Confederation Congress.

The Confederation reflected the long-standing fears of monarchy by not allowing for a president or chief executive. In the Confederation government, Congress had full power over foreign affairs and disputes between the states. Yet the Confederation had no national courts and no power to enforce its resolutions and ordinances. It could not levy taxes, and its budgetary needs depended on requisitions from the states, which state legislatures often ignored.

The states were in no mood to create a strong central government. The Confederation Congress, in fact, was granted less power than the colonists had once accepted in the British Parliament, since it could not regulate interstate and foreign commerce. For certain important acts, moreover, a "special majority" in the Confederation Congress was required. Nine states had to approve measures dealing with war, treaties, coinage, finances, and the military. Unanimous approval from the states was needed to impose tariffs (often called "duties," or taxes) on imports and to amend the Articles.

For all its weaknesses, however, the Confederation government represented the most practical structure for the new nation. After all, the Revolution had yet to be won, and an America besieged by British armies and warships could not risk divisive debates over the distribution of power.

**EXPANSION OF POLITICAL PARTICIPATION**   The new political opportunities afforded by the creation of state governments led more citizens to participate than ever before. Property qualifications for voting, which already allowed an overwhelming majority of white men to vote, were lowered after 1776. As a group of farmers explained, "No man can be free and independent" unless he possesses "a voice . . . in the most important offices in the legislature." In Pennsylvania, Delaware, North Carolina, and Georgia, any male taxpayer could vote, regardless of how much, if any, property he owned. Farmers, tradesmen, and shopkeepers were soon elected to state legislatures. In general, a higher percentage of American males could vote in the late eighteenth and early nineteenth century than could their counterparts in Great Britain.

# THE SOCIAL REVOLUTION

The American Revolution was fought in the name of liberty, a virtuous ideal that proved elusive—even in victory. What did the Revolution mean to the workers, servants, farmers, and freed slaves who participated? Many hoped that it would remove the elite's traditional political and social advantages. Wealthy Patriots, on the other hand, would have been content to replace royal officials with the rich, the wellborn, and the able—and let it go at that.

In the end, the new republic's social fabric and political culture were visibly different after the war. The energy created by the concepts of liberty, equality, and democracy changed the dynamics of social and political life in ways that people could not have imagined in 1776.

**THE EXODUS OF LOYALISTS**   The Loyalists suffered for their stubborn support of King George III and their refusal to pledge allegiance to the new United States. During and after the Revolution, their property was confiscated or destroyed, and many were assaulted, brutalized, and executed by Patriots (and vice versa).

After the American victory at Yorktown, tens of thousands of panicked Loyalists made their way to seaports to board British ships and flee the United States. Thousands of African Americans, mostly runaway slaves, also flocked to New York City, Charleston, and Savannah, with many of their owners in hot pursuit. Boston King, a runaway, said he saw white slave owners grabbing their escaped slaves "in the streets of New York, or even dragging them out of their beds."

General Guy Carleton, commander in chief of British forces in North America, organized the mass evacuation. He intentionally violated the provisions of the Treaty of Paris by refusing to return slaves to their owners, defiantly telling a furious George Washington that his slaves from Mount Vernon had already escaped and boarded British ships bound for Canada.

Some 80,000 desperate refugees—white Loyalists, free blacks, freed slaves, and Native Americans who had allied with the British—dispersed throughout the British Empire. Among those who resettled in Canada were 3,500 former slaves who had been freed in exchange for joining the British army. Some 2,000 freed blacks chose to go to Sierra Leone, where British abolitionists helped them create an experimental colony called Freetown.

About 12,000 Georgia and South Carolina Loyalists, including thousands of their slaves (the British granted freedom only to the slaves of Patriots), went to British-controlled East Florida, only to see their new home handed over to Spain in 1783. Spanish authorities gave them a hard choice: swear allegiance to the Spanish king and convert to Catholicism, or leave. Most of them left.

Some of the doubly displaced Loyalists sneaked back into the United States, but most went to British islands in the Caribbean. "We are all cast off," complained one Loyalist. "I shall ever tho' remember with satisfaction that it was not I deserted my King [George III], but my King that deserted me." The largest number of exiles landed in Canada.

The departure of so many Loyalists from America was one of the most important social consequences of the Revolution. Their confiscated homes, lands, and vacated jobs created new social, economic, and political opportunities for Patriots.

**Religious development** The Congregational Church developed a national presence in the early nineteenth century. Lemuel Haynes, depicted here, was its first African American minister.

**FREEDOM OF RELIGION** The Revolution also tested traditional religious loyalties and set in motion important changes in the relationship between church and government. Before the Revolution, Americans *tolerated* religious dissent; after the Revolution, they insisted on complete *freedom* of religion as embodied in the principle of separation of church and state.

The Anglican Church, established as the official religion in five colonies and parts of two others, was especially vulnerable to changes prompted by the war. Anglicans tended to be pro-British, and non-Anglicans, notably Baptists and Methodists, outnumbered Anglicans in all states except Virginia. All but Virginia eliminated tax support for the church before the fighting was over, and Virginia did so soon afterward. Although Anglicanism survived in the form of the new Episcopal Church, it never regained its pre-Revolutionary stature.

In 1776, the Virginia Declaration of Rights had guaranteed the free exercise of religion. Ten years later, the **Virginia Statute of Religious Freedom** (written by Thomas Jefferson) declared that "no man shall be compelled to frequent or support any religious worship, place or ministry whatsoever" and "that all men shall be free to profess, and by argument to maintain, their opinions in matters of religion." These statutes, and the Revolutionary ideology that justified them, helped shape the course that religious life would take in the United States: diverse and voluntary rather than monolithic and enforced by the government.

## SLAVES AND THE REVOLUTION

The sharpest irony of the American Revolution was that Great Britain offered enslaved blacks more opportunities for freedom than did the United States. In November 1775, the British royal governor of Virginia, John Murray (Lord Dunmore), himself a slave owner, announced that all slaves and indentured servants would gain their freedom if they joined the Loyalist cause. Within a month, the British had attracted more than 300 former servants and slaves to what came to be called the "Ethiopian Regiment." The number soon grew to almost 1,000 males and twice as many women and children.

The British recruitment of slaves outraged George Washington, Thomas Jefferson, and other white plantation owners in Virginia, where 40 percent of the population was black. Washington predicted that if Dunmore's efforts were "not crushed" soon, the number of slaves joining the British army would "increase as a Snow ball by Rolling."

Jefferson expressed the same concerns after twenty-three slaves escaped from his plantation outside Charlottesville. He eventually reclaimed six of them, only to sell them for their "disloyalty."

In 1775, authorities in Charleston, South Carolina executed Thomas Jeremiah, a free man of color who was the wealthiest black man in North America. A harbor pilot, Jeremiah owned slaves himself. His crime? He supposedly incited a rebellion by telling slaves that British troops were coming "to help the poor Negroes."

At Jeremiah's "trial" in a "slave court," which had no judge, jury, or attorneys, Henry Laurens, a planter and former slave trader who would be elected president of the Continental Congress, charged that Jeremiah "was a forward fellow, puffed up by prosperity, ruined by Luxury & debauchery" and prone to "vanity & ambition." Lau-

***The Death of Major Peirson*, 1783**
In this detail of the John Singleton Copley painting, a free Black soldier is depicted fighting on the side of the British in the Revolutionary War.

rens demanded that "nothing less than Death Should be the Sentence." On August 18, 1775, authorities hanged Jeremiah and burned his body to ashes.

Such brutalities led a British abolitionist to remark that America during its Revolution was "the land of the brave and the land of the slave." Many southern revolutionaries were fighting less for independence from "British tyranny" than to retain their slave-labor system.

**SOUTHERN BACKLASH**  In the end, the British policy of recruiting slaves backfired. The "terrifying" prospect of British troops arming slaves persuaded many fence-straddling southerners to join the Patriot cause. Edward Rutledge of South Carolina said that the British decision to arm slaves did more to create "an eternal separation between Great Britain and the colonies than any other expedient."

For Rutledge and many other southern whites, the Revolution became primarily a war to defend slavery. Racial prejudice thus helped fuel revolutionary rebellion. What South Carolinians wanted from the Revolutionary War, explained Pierce Butler, "is that their slaves not be taken from them."

In response to the British recruitment of enslaved African Americans, at the end of 1775 a desperate General Washington authorized the enlistment of free blacks—but not slaves—into the American army. In February 1776, however, southern representatives convinced the Continental Congress to instruct Washington to enlist no more African Americans, free or enslaved. Two states, South Carolina and Georgia, refused to allow any blacks to serve. As the American war effort struggled, however, Massachusetts organized two all-black army units, and Rhode Island organized one, which also included Native Americans. About 5,000 African Americans fought on the Patriot side, most of them free blacks from northern states.

While thousands of free blacks and runaway slaves fought in the war, the vast majority of African Americans did not choose sides so much as they chose freedom. Several hundred thousand enslaved blacks, mostly in the southern states, took advantage of the disruptions caused by the war to seize their freedom. Others used the impetus of the Revolution to promote freedom for all.

As early as the summer of 1776, Lemuel Haynes, a free black who served in the Massachusetts militia, borrowed the language of the Declaration of Independence for an abolitionist sermon. He highlighted the "self-evident truth" that all men had the "unalienable right" to liberty, which was "as precious to a black man, as it is to a white one, and bondage as equally as intolerable to the one as it is to the other."

In the North, which had far fewer slaves than the South, the ideals of liberty and freedom led most states to end slavery, either during the war or shortly afterward. But those same ideals had little to no impact in the southern states. These contrasting attitudes toward slavery would continue to shape the political disputes of the young nation.

**THE STATUS OF WOMEN**   The ideal of liberty spawned by the Revolution applied to the status of women as much as to that of African Americans. The legal status of women was governed by British common law, which essentially treated them like children, limiting their roles to child rearing and maintaining the household. Women could not vote or hold office. Few had access to formal education. Boys were taught to read and write; girls were taught to read and sew. Until married, women were subject to the dictates of their fathers.

Once a woman married, she essentially became the possession of her husband, and all property she brought to the marriage became his. A married woman had no right to buy, sell, or manage property. Technically, any wages a wife earned belonged to the husband. Women could not sign contracts, file lawsuits, or testify in court. A husband could beat and even rape his wife without fearing legal action. Divorces were extremely difficult to obtain.

Yet the Revolution offered women opportunities to broaden their social roles and to support the armies in various ways. They handled supplies, served as messengers or spies, and worked as "camp followers," cooking, washing, sewing, and nursing in exchange for daily rations. Some officers paid women to be their personal servants.

Often women had no choice but to follow their husbands into war because they had no place to live or food to eat. Some camp followers tended cattle, sheep, or hogs, and guarded supplies. Others sold various items. A few of the single women were prostitutes. In 1777, George Washington ordered that commanders take measures to "prevent an inundation of bad women [prostitutes] from Philadelphia." He also urged that soldiers fraternize only with "clean" women to prevent the spread of venereal diseases.

Wives who were camp followers sometimes brought along their children, again because they had no choice. Washington would have preferred to ban women and children, but he was forced to accept them because he was afraid to lose "a number of men, who very probably would have followed their wives" home.

Women risked their lives in battle, tending the wounded or bringing water to the soldiers. On occasion, wives took the place of their soldier-husbands. In 1777, some 400 armed women mobilized to defend Pittsfield, Vermont. The men of the town had gone off to fight when a band of Loyalists and Indians approached the village. The women held off the attackers until help arrived.

Several women disguised themselves and fought as ordinary soldiers. Deborah Sampson joined a Massachusetts regiment as "Robert Shurtleff" and served from 1781 to 1783 thanks to the "artful concealment" of her gender. Ann Bailey did the same. In 1777, eager to get the enlistment bonus payment, she cut her hair, dressed like a man, and used a husky voice to join the Patriot army in New York as "Samuel Gay." Bailey performed so well that she was promoted to corporal, only to be discovered as a woman, dismissed, jailed, and fined.

**WOMEN AND LIBERTY** America's war against Great Britain led some women to demand their own independence. Early in the struggle, Abigail Adams, one of the most learned and spirited women of the time, wrote to her husband John: "In the new Code of Laws which I suppose it will be necessary for you to make, I desire you would remember the Ladies. . . . Do not put such unlimited power into the hands of the Husbands." Since men were "Naturally

Tyrannical," she wrote, "why then, not put it out of the power of the vicious and the Lawless to use us with cruelty and indignity with impunity." Otherwise, "if particular care and attention is not paid to the Ladies we are determined to foment a Rebellion, and will not hold ourselves bound by any Laws in which we have no voice, or Representation."

John Adams could not help but "laugh" at his wife's radical proposals. He insisted on retaining the traditional privileges enjoyed by males: "Depend upon it, we know better than to repeal our Masculine systems." If women were to be granted equality, he warned, then "children and apprentices" and "Indians and Negroes" would also demand equal rights and freedoms.

Thomas Jefferson shared Adams's outlook. In his view, women should not "wrinkle their foreheads with politics" but instead "soothe and calm the minds of their husbands." Improvements in the status of women would have to wait.

**NATIVE AMERICANS AND THE REVOLUTION** Most Native Americans sought to remain neutral in the war, but both British and American agents urged the chiefs to fight on their side. The result was chaos. Indians on both sides attacked villages, burned crops, and killed civilians.

During and after the war, the new government assured its Indian allies that it would respect their lands and their rights. But many white Americans used the disruptions of war to destroy and displace Native Americans. Once the war ended and independence was secured, there was no peace for the Indians. By the end of the eighteenth century, land-hungry Americans were again pushing into Indian territories on the western frontier.

# THE EMERGENCE OF AN AMERICAN NATIONALISM

On July 2, 1776, when the Second Continental Congress had resolved "that these United Colonies are, and of right ought to be, free and independent states," John Adams had written Abigail that future generations would remember that date as their "day of deliverance." Adams got everything right but the date. As luck would have it, July 4, the date the Declaration of Independence was approved, became Independence Day rather than July 2, when independence was formally declared.

The celebration of Independence Day quickly became the most important public ritual in the United States. People suspended their normal routines to devote a day to parades, patriotic speeches, and fireworks displays. In the process, the infant republic began to create its own myth of national identity.

The new nation was not rooted in antiquity. Its people, except for the Native Americans, had not inhabited it over many centuries, nor was there any notion of a common ethnic descent. "The American national consciousness," one observer wrote, "is not a voice crying out of the depth of the dark past, but is proudly a product of the enlightened present, setting its face resolutely toward the future."

Many people, at least since the time of the Pilgrims, had thought of the New World as singled out by God for a special mission. John Adams proclaimed the opening of America "a grand scheme and design in Providence for the illumination and the emancipation of the slavish part of mankind all over the earth."

This sense of providential mission provided much of the energy for America's development as a new republic. From the democratic rhetoric of Thomas Jefferson to the pragmatism of George Washington to heady toasts bellowed in South Carolina taverns, patriots everywhere claimed a special role for American leadership. People believed that God was guiding the United States to lead the world toward greater liberty and equality. Benjamin Rush, a Philadelphia doctor and scientist, issued a prophetic statement in 1787: "The American war is over: but this is far from being the case with the American Revolution. On the contrary, but the first act of the great drama is closed."

George Washington acknowledged that important work remained. While retiring from military service, he penned a letter to the thirteen colonies in which he told the American people it would be "their choice . . . and conduct" that would determine whether the United States would become "respectable and prosperous, or contemptible and miserable as a Nation." Yet he remained hopeful, for Americans had already done the impossible: winning their independence on the battlefield. So he urged the citizenry to rejoice and be grateful as they set about demonstrating to a skeptical world that a large and unruly republic could survive and flourish.

# CHAPTER REVIEW

## SUMMARY

- **Military Challenges**   In 1776, the British had the mightiest army and navy in the world, and they supplemented their might by hiring professional German soldiers called *Hessians* to help put down the American Revolution. The Americans had to create an army—the Continental army—from scratch. George Washington realized that the Americans had to turn unreliable *citizen-soldiers* into a disciplined fighting force and try to wage a long, costly war that would force the British army, fighting thousands of miles from its home base, to cut its losses and eventually give up.

- **Turning Points**   After forcing the British to evacuate Boston, the American army suffered a string of defeats before George Washington surprised the Hessians at the *Battle of Trenton* at the end of 1776. The victory bolstered American morale and prompted more enlistments in the Continental army. The French were likely allies for the colonies from the beginning because they resented their losses to Britain in the Seven Years' War. After the British defeat at the *Battles of Saratoga (1777)*, the colonies brokered an *alliance with France*. Washington's ability to hold his ragged forces together, despite daily desertions and especially difficult winters in Morristown and *Valley Forge (1777–1778)*, provided another turning point. The British lost support on the frontier and in the southern colonies when terrorist tactics backfired. The Battle of Kings Mountain drove the British into retreat, and French supplies and the French fleet helped tip the balance and ensure the American victory at the *Battle of Yorktown (1781)*.

- **Civil War**   The American Revolution was also a civil war, dividing families and communities. There were at least 100,000 Loyalists in the colonies. They included royal officials, Anglican ministers, wealthy southern planters, and the elite in large seaport cities; they also included many humble people, especially recent immigrants. After the hostilities ended, many Loyalists, including slaves who had fled plantations to support the British cause, left for Canada, the West Indies, or England.

- **A Political and Social Revolution**   The American Revolution disrupted and transformed traditional class and social relationships. Revolutionaries embraced a *republican ideology*, and more white men gained the right to vote as property requirements were removed. But fears of a monarchy being reestablished led colonists to vest power in the states rather than in a national government under the *Articles of Confederation*. New *state constitutions* instituted more elected positions, and most included bills of rights that protected individual liberties. The *Virginia Statute of Religious Freedom (1786)* led the way in guaranteeing the separation of church and state, and religious toleration was transformed into religious freedom.

- **African Americans, Women, and Native Americans**  Northern states began to free slaves, but southern states were reluctant. Although many women had undertaken nontraditional roles during the war, afterward they remained largely confined to the domestic sphere, with no changes to their legal or political status. The Revolution had catastrophic effects on Native Americans, regardless of which side they had allied with during the war. American settlers seized Native American land, often in violation of existing treaties.

## CHRONOLOGY

| | |
|---|---|
| 1776 | British forces seize New York City |
| | General Washington's troops defeat British forces at the Battle of Trenton |
| | States begin writing new constitutions |
| 1777 | American forces defeat British in a series of battles at Saratoga |
| 1778 | Americans and French form a military alliance |
| | George Rogers Clark's militia defeats British troops in Mississippi Valley |
| 1779 | American forces defeat the Iroquois Confederacy at Newtown, New York |
| 1780 | Patriots defeat Loyalists at the Battle of Kings Mountain |
| 1781 | British invasion of southern colonies turned back at the Battles of Cowpens and Guilford Courthouse |
| | American and French forces defeat British at Yorktown, Virginia |
| | Articles of Confederation are ratified |
| | Continental Congress becomes Confederation Congress |
| 1783 | Treaty of Paris is signed, formally ending the Revolutionary War |
| 1786 | Virginia adopts the Statute of Religious Freedom |

## KEY TERMS

Hessians p. 184

citizen-soldiers p. 184

Battle of Trenton (1776) p. 190

Battles of Saratoga (1777) p. 195

alliance with France p. 197

Valley Forge (1777–1778) p. 197

Battle of Yorktown (1781) p. 207

republican ideology p. 209

state constitutions p. 209

Articles of Confederation p. 211

Virginia Statute of Religious Freedom (1786) p. 214

 INQUIZITIVE

**Go to InQuizitive to see what you've learned—and learn what you've missed—with personalized feedback along the way.**

# 6 Strengthening the New Nation

**Washington as a Statesman at the Constitutional Convention (1856)** This painting by Junius Brutus Stearns is one of the earliest depictions of the drafting of the Constitution, capturing the moment after the convention members, including George Washington (right), completed the final draft.

D uring the 1780s, the United States of America was rapidly emerging as the lone large republic in an unstable world dominated by monarchies. The new nation was distinctive in that it was born out of a conflict over ideas, principles, and ideals rather than from centuries-old racial or ancestral bonds, as in Europe and elsewhere.

America was a democratic republic "brought forth" by certain self-evident political ideals—that people should govern themselves through their elected representatives, that everyone should have an equal opportunity to prosper ("the pursuit of happiness"), and that governments exist to protect liberty and promote the public good. Those ideals were captured in lasting phrases: All men are created equal. Liberty and justice for all. *E pluribus unum* ("Out of many, one"—the phrase on the official seal of the United States). How Americans understood, applied, and violated these ideals shaped the nation's development after 1783.

## POWER TO THE PEOPLE

The American Revolution created not only an independent republic but also a different conception of politics than prevailed in Europe. What Americans most feared was governmental abuse of power. Memories of the "tyranny" of Parliament, King George III, his prime ministers, and royal colonial governors were still raw. Freedom from such arbitrary power had been the ideal guiding

## *focus questions*

1. What were the strengths and weaknesses of the Articles of Confederation? How did they prompt the creation of a new U.S. constitution in 1787?

2. What political innovations did the 1787 Constitutional Convention develop for the new nation?

3. What were the debates surrounding the ratification of the Constitution? Explain how they were resolved.

4. In what ways did the Federalists' vision for the United States differ from that of their Republican opponents during the 1790s?

5. Assess how the attitudes toward Great Britain and France shaped American politics in the late eighteenth century.

the American Revolution, while the freedom to "pursue happiness" became the ideal driving the new nation.

To ensure their new freedoms, the Revolutionaries wrestled with a fundamental question: What is the proper role and scope of government? In answering that question, they eventually developed new ways to divide power among the various branches of government so as to manage the tensions between ensuring liberty and maintaining order.

But America after the war was a nation in name only. The Confederation was less a national government of "united states" than a league of thirteen independent, squabbling states. After all, the Articles of Confederation had promised that "Each state retains its sovereignty, freedom, and independence." The quest for true nationhood after the Revolution was the most significant political transformation in modern history, for Americans would insist that sovereignty (ultimate power) resided not with a king or aristocracy but with "the people," the mass of ordinary citizens.

**FORGING A NEW NATION**   Americans had little time to celebrate victory in the Revolutionary War. As Alexander Hamilton, a brilliant army officer turned congressman, noted in 1783, "We have now happily concluded the great work of independence, but much remains to be done to reach the fruits of it."

The transition from war to peace was neither simple nor easy. America was independent but not yet a self-sustaining nation. In fact, the Declaration of Independence never mentioned the word *nation*. Its official title was "the unanimous Declaration of the thirteen united States of America."

Forging a new *nation* out of a *confederation* of thirteen rebellious colonies-turned-"free-and-independent"-states posed huge challenges, not the least of which was managing what George Washington called a "deranged" economy suffocating in war-related debts. The accumulated debt was $160 million, a huge amount at the time.

The period from the drafting of the Declaration of Independence in 1776, through the creation of the new federal constitution in 1787, and ending with the election of Thomas Jefferson as president in 1800, was fraught with instability and tension. From the start, the new nation experienced political divisions, economic distress, and foreign troubles.

Three fundamental questions shaped political debate during the last quarter of the eighteenth century. Where would sovereignty reside in the new nation? What was the proper relationship of the states to each other and to the national government? And what was required for the new republic to flourish as an independent nation? The efforts to answer those questions created powerful tensions that continue to complicate American life.

# THE CONFEDERATION GOVERNMENT

John Quincy Adams, a future president, called the years between 1783 and 1787 the "Critical Period" when American leaders developed sharp differences about economic policies, international relations, and the proper relationship of the states to the national government. Debates over those issues unexpectedly gave birth to the nation's first political parties and, to this day, continue to influence the American experiment in **federalism** (the sharing of power among national, state, and local governments).

After the war, many Patriots who had feared government power and criticized British officials for abusing it now directed their attacks at the new state and national governments. At the same time, state legislatures desperate for funds to pay off their war debts sparked unrest and riots by raising taxes.

The clashes between the working poor and state governments were a great disappointment to Washington, John Adams, and other Revolutionary leaders. For them and others disillusioned by the surge of "democratic" rebelliousness, the Critical Period was a time of hopes frustrated, a story shaded by regret at the absence of national loyalty and international respect. The weaknesses of the Articles of Confederation in dealing with the postwar turmoil led political leaders to design an entirely new national constitution and federal government.

**A LOOSE ALLIANCE OF STATES**  The **Articles of Confederation**, formally approved in 1781, had created a loose alliance (confederation) of thirteen independent states that were united only in theory. In practice, each state government acted on its own. The first major provision of the Articles insisted that "each state retains its sovereignty, freedom, and independence."

The weak national government under the Articles had only one component, a one-house legislature. There was no president, no executive branch, no national judiciary (court system). State legislatures, not voters, appointed the members of the Confederation Congress, in which each state, regardless of size or population, had one vote. This meant that Rhode Island, with 68,000 people, had the same power in the Congress as Virginia, with more than 747,000 inhabitants.

George Washington called the Confederation "a half-starved, limping government." It could neither regulate trade nor create taxes to pay off the country's war debts. It could approve treaties but had no power to enforce their terms. It could call for raising an army but could not force men to serve.

The Congress, in short, could not enforce its own laws, and its budget relied on "voluntary" contributions from the states. In 1782, for example, the Confederation asked the states to provide $8 million for the national government; they sent $420,000. The lack of state support forced the Congress to print paper money, called Continentals, whose value plummeted to 2 cents on the dollar as more and more were printed, leading to the joking phrase, "Not worth a Continental." Virtually no gold and silver coins remained in circulation; they had all gone abroad to purchase items for the war.

It was hard to find people to serve in such a weak Congress, and people openly doubted the stability of the new republic. As John Adams wrote to Thomas Jefferson, "The Union is still to me an Object of as much Anxiety as ever independence was."

**ROBERT MORRIS** The closest thing to an executive leader of the Confederation was Robert Morris, who as superintendent of finance in the final years of the war became the most influential figure in the government. Morris wanted to make both himself and the Confederation government more powerful. He envisioned a program of taxation and debt management to make the national government financially stable. "A public debt supported by public revenue will prove the strongest cement to keep our confederacy together," he confided to a friend.

The powerful financiers who had lent the new government funds to buy supplies and pay its bills, Morris believed, would give stronger support to a government committed to paying its debts. He therefore welcomed the chance to enlarge the national debt by issuing new government bonds that would help pay off wartime debts. With a sounder federal Treasury—one with the power to raise taxes—the bonds could be expected to rise in value, creating new capital with which to finance banks and economic development.

To anchor his plan, Morris in 1781 secured a congressional charter for the Bank of North America, which would hold government cash, lend money to the government, and issue currency. Though a national bank, it was in part privately owned and was expected to turn a profit for Morris and other shareholders, in addition to performing a crucial public service. Morris's program, however, depended upon the government having a secure income, and it foundered on the requirement of unanimous state approval for amendments to the Articles of Confederation.

**LAND POLICY**  In ending the Revolutionary War, the Treaty of Paris doubled the size of the United States, extending the nation's western boundary to the Mississippi River. Under the Articles of Confederation, land outside the boundaries of the thirteen original states became *public domain*, owned and administered by the national government.

Between 1784 and 1787, the Confederation Congress created three major ordinances (policies) detailing how the lands in the West would be surveyed, sold, and developed. These ordinances rank among the Confederation's greatest achievements, for they provided the framework for western settlement that would shape much of the nation's development during the nineteenth century.

Thomas Jefferson drafted the Land Ordinance Act of 1784, which urged states to drop their competing claims to Indian-held territory west of the Appalachian Mountains so that the vast, unmapped area could be divided into as many as fourteen self-governing *territories* of equal size. In the new territories, all adult white males would be eligible to vote, hold office, and write constitutions for their territorial governments. When a territory's population equaled that of the smallest existing state (Rhode Island), it would be eligible for statehood. In other words, the western territories would not be treated as American colonies but as future states governed by republican principles.

Jefferson assumed that individual pioneers should be allowed to settle the western territories. George Washington and others, however, predicted chaos if migration were unregulated. Clashes with Indians would generate constant warfare, and disputes over land and boundaries would foster incessant bickering.

So before Jefferson's plan could take effect, the Confederation Congress created the Land Ordinance of 1785. It called for organizing the Northwest Territory on America's immediate western border (what would become the states of Ohio, Michigan, Indiana, Illinois, and Wisconsin) into townships of thirty-six square miles that would be surveyed, sold for less than a dollar an acre, and settled. Then the surveyors would keep moving westward, laying out more townships for settlement.

Wherever Indian lands were purchased—or taken—they were surveyed and divided into six-mile-square townships laid out along a grid running east–west and north–south. Each township was in turn divided into thirty-six sections one mile square (640 acres), with each section divided into four farms. The 640-acre sections of "public lands" were to be sold at auctions, the proceeds of which would go to the national Treasury.

**THE NORTHWEST ORDINANCE** Two years after passage of the Land Ordinance of 1785, the Confederation Congress passed the **Northwest Ordinance** of 1787. It set forth two key principles to better manage western expansion: the new western territories would eventually become coequal states, as Jefferson had originally proposed, and slavery would be banned from the region north of the Ohio River. (Slaves already living there would remain slaves.) The Northwest Ordinance also included a promise, which would be repeatedly broken, that Indian lands "shall never be taken from them without their consent."

For a new territory to become a state, the Northwest Ordinance specified a three-stage process. First, Congress would appoint a territorial governor and other officials to create a legal code and administer justice. Second, when the population of adult males reached 5,000, they could elect a territorial legislature. Third, when a territory's population reached 60,000 "free inhabitants," the adult males could draft a constitution and apply to Congress for statehood.

**DIPLOMACY** After the Revolutionary War, relations with Great Britain and Spain remained tense because both nations retained trading posts, forts, and soldiers on American soil, and both encouraged Indians to resist American efforts to settle on tribal lands. The British refused to remove their troops stationed south of the Canadian border in protest of the failure of Americans to pay their prewar debts. Another major irritant was the American seizure of Loyalist property during the war.

With Spain, the chief issues pertained to disputes about the location of the southern boundary of the United States and the right for Americans to send boats or barges down the Mississippi River, which Spain then controlled. After the Seven Years' War in 1763, Spain had acquired the Louisiana Territory, which included the port of New Orleans, the Mississippi River, and all the area west to the Rocky Mountains. After the Revolution, Spain closed the Mississippi to American use, infuriating settlers in Kentucky and Tennessee. Spain had also regained ownership of Florida, which then included southern Alabama. Thereafter, the Spanish governor in Florida provided firearms to Creek Indians, who resisted American encroachment on their lands in south Georgia.

**TRADE AND THE ECONOMY** More troublesome than the behavior of the British and the Spanish was the fragile state of the American economy. Seven years of warfare had nearly bankrupted the new nation. At the same time, many who had served in the army had never been paid. Nor had civilians who had loaned money, supplies, crops, and livestock to the war effort been reimbursed.

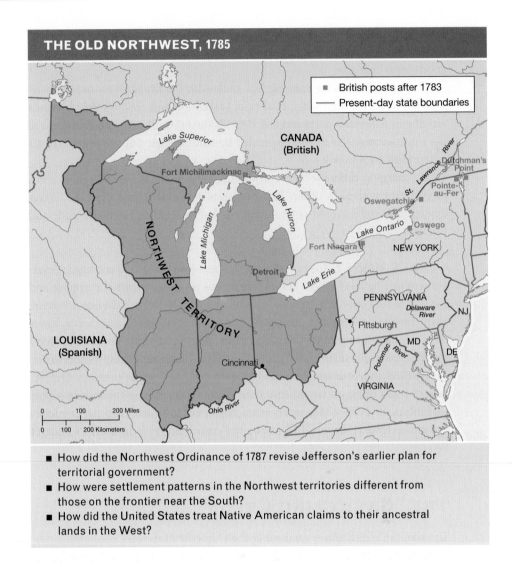

## THE OLD NORTHWEST, 1785

British posts after 1783

Present-day state boundaries

Lake Superior

CANADA
(British)

Fort Michilimackinac

Lake Michigan

Lake Huron

St. Lawrence River

Dutchman's Point

Pointe-au-Fer

Oswegatchie

Lake Ontario

Oswego

Fort Niagara

NEW YORK

NORTHWEST TERRITORY

Detroit

Lake Erie

PENNSYLVANIA

Delaware River

NJ

Pittsburgh

LOUISIANA
(Spanish)

Cincinnati

Potomac River

MD

DE

VIRGINIA

Ohio River

| 0 | 100 | 200 Miles |
| 0 | 100 | 200 Kilometers |

- How did the Northwest Ordinance of 1787 revise Jefferson's earlier plan for territorial government?
- How were settlement patterns in the Northwest territories different from those on the frontier near the South?
- How did the United States treat Native American claims to their ancestral lands in the West?

After the war, the British treated the United States as an enemy nation, insisting that all Americans who had been born in England were still bound by allegiance to King George III. British warships began stopping and boarding American ships in the Atlantic, kidnapping English-born American sailors, and "impressing" them into service in the Royal Navy.

The British also closed their profitable Caribbean island colonies to American commerce. New England shipowners and southern planters were especially hard-hit, as exports of tobacco, rice, rum, and other commodities remained far below what they had been before the war. After 1783, merchant ships were allowed to deliver American products to England and return to the United States with English goods. But U.S. vessels could not carry British goods anywhere else.

To punish Britain for banning U.S. trade with the British West Indies, many state governments imposed special taxes (called tonnage fees) on British vessels arriving in American ports and levied tariffs (taxes) on British goods brought to the United States. The British responded by sending their ships to ports in states whose tariff rates were lower.

By charging different tariffs on the same products, the states waged commercial war with each other. The result was economic chaos. By 1787, it was evident that the national government needed to regulate interstate trade and foreign relations.

**SCARCE MONEY** Complex financial issues also hampered economic development during the Critical Period. There was no stable national currency, and the nation had only three banks—in Philadelphia, New York City, and Boston. Farmers who had profited during the war found themselves squeezed by lower crop prices and mounting debts and taxes. The widespread shortage of "hard money" (gold and silver coins) caused people to postpone paying their bills.

By 1785, indebted citizens urged states to print new paper currency. Debtors believed that doing so would ease their plight by increasing the money supply (inflation). In 1785–1786, seven states began issuing their own paper money to help indebted farmers and to pay the cash bonuses promised to military veterans.

## THE "GATHERING CRISIS"

The economic difficulties weakening the Confederation were compounded by growing fears among wealthy "gentlemen" leaders ("natural aristocrats") that the democratic energies unleashed by the Revolution were undermining the authority of the social and economic elite. Class distinctions were disappearing as many among the working poor and "middling classes" stopped deferring to their "betters."

The so-called better sort of people were appalled at the "leveling" behavior of the "antifederal peasants," "little folks," and "demagogues." A Virginia aristocrat grumbled that the "spirit of independency" that inspired the Revolution was being "converted into equality."

The political culture was also changing. More men could vote and hold office as property-owning qualifications were reduced or eliminated in several states. The nation, said wealthy New Yorker John Jay, was headed toward "Evils and Calamities" because the masses were gaining power and often taking the law into their own hands. At the same time, Jay declared the federal government "incompetent." Achieving nationhood had become more challenging than gaining independence. The Confederation was less a government than an association of independent states.

No sooner was the war over than Americans with large debts again began to protest taxes. To pay their war debts, most state legislatures had sharply increased taxes. In fact, during the 1780s, most Americans paid three times as much in taxes as they had under British "tyranny." Earlier, they had objected to taxation *without* representation; now, they objected to taxation *with* representation.

In New Hampshire, in what was called the Exeter Riot, hard-pressed farmers surrounded the legislative building, demanding that the representatives print paper money to ease their plight. Similar appeals occurred in other states. The economic and political elites were horrified that the "new men" were endangering the real value of property by encouraging the printing of more money, for doing so would inflate the money supply and thereby reduce the purchasing power of currency.

**SHAYS'S REBELLION** Fears of a taxpayer "revolt from below" became all too real in western Massachusetts, when struggling farmers, many of them former Revolutionary soldiers, demanded that the state issue more paper money and give them additional time to pay "unjust" taxes. Farmers also resented the new state constitution because it *raised* the property qualifications for voting and holding elected office, thus stripping poorer men of political power.

When the merchant-dominated Massachusetts legislature refused to provide tax relief, three rural counties erupted in a disorganized revolt in 1786. Armed groups of angry farmers, called Regulators, banded together to force judges and sheriffs to stop seizing the cattle and farms of those who could not pay their taxes. "Close down the courts," they shouted.

**Shays's Rebellion** Shays and his followers demanded that states issue paper currency to help ease the payment of debts and the right to postpone paying taxes until the postwar agricultural depression lifted.

The situation worsened when a ragtag "army" of unruly farmers that included thirty-nine-year-old Daniel Shays, a distinguished war veteran, marched on the federal arsenal at Springfield in the winter of 1787. The state government responded by sending 4,400 militiamen, who scattered the debtor army with a single cannon blast that left four farmers dead and many wounded. Shays fled to Vermont. Several rebels were arrested, and two were hanged. The rebels nevertheless earned a victory of sorts, as the legislature agreed to eliminate some of the taxes and fees.

News of **Shays's Rebellion** sent shock waves across the nation. In Massachusetts, Abigail Adams, the wife of future president John Adams, dismissed Shays and his followers as "ignorant, restless desperadoes, without conscience or principles." George Washington was equally concerned. America, he said, needed a "government by which our lives, liberty, and properties will be secured." Unless an alternative could be found to the weak Confederation government, "anarchy and confusion will inevitably ensue."

## CREATING THE CONSTITUTION

In the wake of Shays's Rebellion, a collective shiver passed through what John Jay called "the better kind of people." Many among the "rich and well-born" agreed with George Washington that the nation was "tottering." The time had come to empower the national government to bring social order and economic stability.

THE "CRISIS IS ARRIVED"  During the 1780s, newspapers warned that the nation's situation had grown "critical and dangerous. The states were behaving like thirteen ungovernable nations, pursuing their own trade regulations and foreign policies. "Our present federal government," said Henry Knox, a Boston bookseller and much-celebrated Revolutionary War general, "is a name, a shadow, without power, or effect."

Such concerns led political leaders to revise their assessment of the republic. It was time, said James Madison, to create a new federal constitution that would repair the "vices of the political system" and "decide forever the fate of republican government." Alexander Hamilton urged that a national gathering of delegates be given "full powers" to revise the Articles of Confederation.

THE CONSTITUTIONAL CONVENTION  In 1787, the Confederation Congress responded by calling for a special "federal" convention to gather in the East Room of Philadelphia's State House (now known as Independence

Hall) for the "purpose of revising the Articles of Confederation." Only Rhode Island refused to participate. That the delegates would be meeting in the same room where the Declaration of Independence had been debated and signed gave the convention added significance.

The delegates began work on May 25, 1787, meeting five hours a day, six days a week. Although the states appointed fifty-five delegates, there were never that many in attendance. Some quit in disgust; others were distracted by other priorities. Yet after fifteen weeks of deliberations, thirty-nine delegates signed the new federal constitution on September 17. Only three refused to sign.

The durability of the Constitution reflects the thoughtful and talented men who created it. They were all white; their average age was forty-two, with the youngest being twenty-six. Most were members of the political and economic elite. Twenty-

**James Madison**  This 1783 miniature shows Madison at thirty-two years old, just four years before he would assume a major role in drafting the Constitution.

six were college graduates, two were college presidents, and thirty-four were lawyers. Others were planters, merchants, bankers, and clergymen.

About twenty-five delegates owned slaves, including George Washington and James Madison. In fact, Washington arrived in Philadelphia with three of his slaves, one of whom, Billy Lee, stood behind his chair at every session, tending to his owner's personal needs.

Yet the "Founding Fathers" were also practical men of experience. Of the twenty-two who had fought in the Revolutionary War, five had been captured and imprisoned. Seven had been state governors, and eight had helped write their state constitutions. Most had been members of the Continental or Confederation Congresses, and eight had signed the Declaration of Independence.

**DRAFTING THE CONSTITUTION**  George Washington was unanimously elected as the presiding officer at the Federal Convention (later renamed the Constitutional Convention). He participated little in the debates, however, for fear that people would take his opinions too seriously. The governor of Pennsylvania, eighty-one-year-old Benjamin Franklin, the oldest delegate, was in such poor health that he had to be carried to the meetings in a special chair, borne aloft by four husky inmates from the Walnut Street jail. Like Washington, Franklin said little from the floor but provided a wealth of experience, patience, wit, and wisdom behind the scenes.

Most active at the Convention was James Madison of Virginia, the ablest political theorist in the group. A thirty-six-year-old attorney who owned a huge tobacco plantation called Montpelier, not far from Thomas Jefferson's Monticello, Madison had arrived in Philadelphia with trunks of books about government—and a head full of ideas.

Barely five feet tall and weighing only 130 pounds (a colleague said he was "no bigger than half a piece of soap"), Madison was too frail and sickly to serve in the Revolutionary army. Madison "speaks low, his person [body] is little and ordinary," and he was "too timid in his politics," remarked Fisher Ames of Massachusetts.

Although shy and soft-spoken, Madison had an agile mind, a huge appetite for learning, and a commitment to public service. He had served in the Continental Congress, where he had become a full-blooded nationalist. Now he resolved to ensure the "supremacy of national authority." The logic of his arguments—and his willingness to compromise—proved decisive in shaping the new constitution. "Every person seems to acknowledge his greatness," said a Georgia delegate.

Most delegates agreed with Madison that the republic needed a stronger national government, weaker state legislatures, and the power to restrain the "excessive" democratic impulses unleashed by the Revolution. "The evils we experience," said Elbridge Gerry of Massachusetts, "flow from the excess of democracy."

Two interrelated assumptions guided the Constitutional Convention: that the national government must have direct authority over the citizenry rather than governing through the state governments, and that the national government must derive its legitimacy from the "genius of the people" rather than from the state legislatures. Thus, the final draft of the Constitution begins: "We the people of the United States, in Order to form a more perfect Union, . . . do ordain and establish this Constitution for the United States of America."

The insistence that the voters were "the legitimate source of all authority," as James Wilson of Pennsylvania stressed, was the most important political innovation since the Declaration of Independence. No other nation endowed "the people" with such authority. By declaring the Constitution to be the voice of the people, the founders authorized the federal government to limit the powers of the states.

The delegates realized, too, that an effective national government needed authority to collect taxes, borrow and issue money, regulate commerce, fund an army and navy, and make laws. This meant that the states must be stripped of the power to print paper money, make treaties, wage war, and levy taxes and tariffs on imported goods. This concept of dividing authority between the national government and the states came to be called federalism.

**THE VIRGINIA AND NEW JERSEY PLANS** James Madison drafted the framework for the initial discussions at the Constitutional Convention. His proposals, called the Virginia Plan, started with a radical suggestion: that the delegates scrap their original instructions to *revise* the Articles of Confederation and instead create a *new* constitution.

Madison's Virginia Plan called for a "*national* government [with] a *supreme* legislative, executive, and judiciary." It proposed a Congress divided into two houses (bicameral): a lower House of Representatives chosen by the "people of the several states" and an upper house of senators elected by the state legislatures. The more populous states would have more representatives in Congress than the smaller states. Madison also wanted to give Congress the power to veto state laws.

The Virginia Plan sparked furious disagreements. When asked why the small states were so suspicious of the plan, Gunning Bedford of Delaware replied: "I do not, gentlemen, trust you."

On June 15, Bedford and other delegates submitted an alternative called the New Jersey Plan, developed by William Paterson of New Jersey. It sought to keep the existing equal representation of the states in a unicameral (one-house) national legislature. It also gave Congress the power to collect taxes and regulate commerce and the authority to name a chief executive as well as a supreme court, but not the right to veto state laws.

## THE THREE BRANCHES OF GOVERNMENT

The intense debate over congressional representation was resolved in mid-July by the so-called Great Compromise, which used elements of both plans. Roger Sherman of Connecticut suggested that one chamber of the proposed Congress have its seats allotted according to population, with the other preserving the principle of one vote for each state. And that is what happened. The more populous states won apportionment (the allocation of delegates to each state) by population in the proposed House of Representatives, while the delegates who sought to protect state power won equality of representation in the Senate, where each state would have two members elected by the legislatures.

**THE LEGISLATURE** The Great Compromise embedded the innovative concept of **separation of powers** in the new Congress. While Madison believed that in "a republican government, the legislative authority necessarily predominates," he and others also sought to keep the Congress from becoming too powerful. To do so, they divided it into two separate houses, with the House of Representatives representing voters at large and the Senate representing state legislatures.

The House of Representatives would be, in George Mason's words, "the grand repository of the democratic principle of the Government." Its members would be elected by voters every *two* years. (Under the Articles of Confederation, members of Congress had been chosen by state legislatures.) Madison argued that allowing individual citizens to elect the people's House was "essential to every plan of free government." Indeed, such representative democracy centered on majority rule was the essence of a republican form of government.

Several delegates did not share such faith in representative democracy. The problems arising since the end of the war, according to Elbridge Gerry, "flow from an excess of democracy." Yet, as Benjamin Franklin countered, if the "common people" and "lower classes" were noble enough to fight for independence, then they were capable of exercising good citizenship. Madison agreed. The citizens of the American republic should be the "People of the United States"—"not the rich, more than the poor; not the learned more than the ignorant; not the haughty heirs of distinguished names, more than the humble sons of obscure fortune."

The Framers viewed the upper house, or Senate, as a check on the excesses of democracy. It would be a more elite group of substantial property holders, its members elected by state legislatures for *six*-year terms. The Senate could use its power to overrule the House or the president. Madison explained that the Senate would help "protect the minority of the opulent against the majority."

**THE PRESIDENCY** The Constitutional Convention struggled over issues related to the executive branch. Some delegates wanted a powerful president who could veto acts of Congress. Others felt that the president should simply "execute" the laws as passed by Congress. Still others, like Benjamin Franklin, wanted a "plural executive" rather than a single man governing the nation.

The eventual decision to have a single chief executive, a "natural born Citizen" at least thirty-five years old of any or no religion, caused many delegates "considerable pause," according to Madison. George Mason of Virginia feared that a single president might start behaving like a king.

In the end, several compromises ensured that the president would be powerful enough to counterbalance the Congress. The president, to be elected for four-year terms, could veto acts of Congress, which would then be subject to being overridden by a two-thirds vote in each house. The president became the nation's chief diplomat and commander in chief of the armed forces, and was responsible for implementing the laws made by Congress.

Yet the president's powers were also limited in key areas. The chief executive could neither declare war nor make peace; only Congress could. Moreover, the president could be removed from office. The House of Representatives could impeach (bring to trial) the chief executive—and other civil officers—on charges of treason, bribery, or "other high crimes and misdemeanors." An impeached president must leave office if two-thirds of the Senate voted for conviction.

To preserve the separation of the three branches of government, the president would be elected every four years by a group of highly qualified "electors" chosen by "the people" in local elections. Each state's number of electors would depend upon the combined number of its congressional representatives and senators. This "electoral college" was a compromise between those wanting the president elected by Congress and those preferring a direct vote of qualified citizens.

**THE JUDICIARY** The third proposed branch of government, the judiciary, sparked little debate. The Constitution called for a supreme national court headed by a chief justice. The court's role was not to make laws (a power reserved to Congress) or to execute and enforce the laws (reserved to the presidency), but to *interpret* the laws and to ensure that every citizen received *equal justice* under the law.

The U.S. Supreme Court had final authority in interpreting the Constitution and in settling constitutional disputes between states. Furthermore, Article VI of the Constitution declared that the federal Constitution, federal laws, and treaties were "the supreme Law of the Land."

## THE LIMITS OF THE CONSTITUTION

The men who drafted the new constitution claimed to be representing all Americans. In fact, however, as Senator Stephen Douglas of Illinois would note seventy years later, the Constitution was "made by white men, for the benefit of white men and their posterity [descendants] forever."

Important groups were left out of the Constitution's protections. Native Americans, for example, could not be citizens unless they paid taxes, which

***Signing the Constitution, September 17, 1787*** Thomas Pritchard Rossiter's painting shows George Washington presiding over what Thomas Jefferson called "an assembly of demi-gods" in Philadelphia.

few did. The Constitution declared that Native American "tribes" were not part of the United States but instead were separate "nations."

**SLAVERY** Of all the issues that emerged during the Constitutional Convention of 1787, none was more explosive than slavery. As James Madison stressed, "the great division of interest" among the delegates "did not lie between the large & small states: it lay between the Northern & Southern," primarily from "their having or not having slaves."

When the Patriots declared independence in 1776, slavery existed in every state. By 1787, however, Massachusetts, Pennsylvania, Connecticut, and Rhode Island had abolished the dreadful system.

Many of the framers viewed slavery as an embarrassing contradiction to the principles of liberty and equality embodied in the Declaration of Independence and the new Constitution. A New Jersey delegate declared that owning human beings was "utterly inconsistent with the principles of Christianity and humanity."

By contrast, most southern delegates stoutly defended slavery. "Religion and humanity [have] nothing to do with this [slavery] question," argued John Rutledge of South Carolina. "Interest alone is the governing principle of nations." His fellow South Carolinian, Charles Pinckney, stressed the practical reality in the southern states: "South Carolina and Georgia cannot do without slaves."

Most southern delegates would have walked out of the convention had there been an attempt to abolish slavery. So in drafting the new constitution, the framers decided not to include any plan for limiting or ending slavery, nor did they view the enslaved as human beings with civil rights.

If the slaves were not to be freed or their rights to be acknowledged, however, how were they to be counted? Since the size of state delegations in the proposed House of Representatives would be based on population, southern delegates argued that slaves should be counted to help determine how many representatives their state would have. Northerners countered that it made no sense to count slaves for purposes of congressional representation when they were treated as property.

The delegates finally agreed to a compromise in which three-fifths of "all other persons" (the enslaved) would be included in population counts as a basis for apportioning a state's congressional representatives. In a constitution intended to "secure the blessings of liberty to ourselves and our posterity," the three-fifths clause was a glaring example of compromise being divorced from principle.

The corrupt bargain over slavery would bedevil the nation for the next seventy-five years, for the more slaves southern states imported from Africa, the more seats in Congress they would gain. Gouverneur Morris of New York, who would draft the final version of the Constitution, asked the delegates to imagine a Georgian or Carolinian going to Africa, where, "in defiance of the most sacred laws of humanity, [he] tears away his fellow creatures from their dearest connections & damns them to the most cruel bondages." By doing so, the southern slaveholder "shall have more votes in a Govt. instituted for the protection of the rights of mankind than the citizen of Pennsylvania or New Jersey who views with a laudable horror so nefarious a practice."

***Charles Calvert and His Slave*** **(1761)** In military regalia, the five-year-old descendant of Lord Baltimore, founder of Maryland, towers over his slave, who is dressed as a drummer boy.

In another concession to southerners, the original Constitution never mentions the word *slavery*. As slaveholder James Madison explained, it would be "wrong to admit in the Constitution the idea that there could be property in men." Instead, the document speaks of "free persons" and "all other persons" and of persons "held to service of labor." The word *slavery* would not appear in the Constitution until the Thirteenth Amendment (1865) abolished it.

Delaware's John Dickinson protested that "omitting of the WORD will be regarded [by the world] as an Endeavor to conceal a principle of which we are ashamed." As it was. The Constitution openly violated Thomas Jefferson's idealistic assertion in the Declaration of Independence that "all men are created equal."

**THE ABSENCE OF WOMEN** The delegates at the Constitutional Convention dismissed any discussion of political rights for women. Yet not all women were willing to maintain their subordinate role. Just as the Revolutionary War enabled many African Americans to seize their freedom, it also inspired some brave women to demand political equality.

Eliza Yonge Wilkinson, born in 1757 to a wealthy plantation family near Charleston, South Carolina, lost her husband early in the war. In June 1780, after Wilkinson was assaulted and robbed by "inhuman" British soldiers, she became a fiery Patriot who "hated Tyranny in every shape." She assured a friend, "We may be *led*, but we never will be *driven*!"

Likewise, Wilkinson expected greater freedom for women after the war. "The men say we have no business [with politics]," she wrote to a friend. "I won't have it thought that because we are the weaker sex as to bodily strength, my dear, we are capable of nothing more than minding the dairy, visiting the poultry-house, and all such domestic concerns." Wilkinson demanded more. "They won't even allow us the liberty of thought, and that is all I want."

Judith Sargent Murray, a Massachusetts writer, argued that the rights and liberties fought for by Patriots belonged not just to men but to women, too. In her essay "On the Equality of the Sexes," published in 1790, she challenged the prevailing view that men had greater intellectual capacities than women. She insisted that any differences resulted from prejudice and discrimination that prevented women from having access to formal education and worldly experience.

The arguments for gender equality, however, fell mostly on deaf ears. The Constitution does not even include the word *women*. Writing from Paris,

Thomas Jefferson expressed the hope that American "ladies" would be "contented to soothe and calm the minds of their husbands returning ruffled from political debate."

**IMMIGRATION** Although America was a nation of immigrants, leaders of the new nation had differing views about whether the United States should remain a nation open to foreigners of all sorts. Thomas Jefferson, for example, worried that many immigrants would not understand or embrace the new republic's democratic premises. Would not the new nation, he asked, be "more homogeneous, more peaceful, more durable" without large-scale immigration?

The Constitution said little about immigration and naturalization (the process of gaining citizenship), and most of what it said was negative. In Article II, Section 1, it prohibits any future immigrant from becoming president, limiting the office to a "born Citizen." On defining citizenship, the Constitution gives Congress the authority "to establish a uniform Rule of Naturalization" but offers no further guidance. As a result, naturalization policy has changed repeatedly over the years in response to fluctuating social attitudes, economic needs, and political moods.

## THE FIGHT FOR RATIFICATION

On September 17, 1787, the Federal Convention reported that it had completed the new constitution. George Washington was the first to sign. "Gentlemen," announced Benjamin Franklin, "you have a republic, if you can keep it."

Then, for the first time in world history, the people were invited to discuss, debate, and vote on the national constitution. The Confederation Congress sent the final draft of the Constitution to thirteen special state conventions for approval (ratification). Over the next ten months, people from all walks of life debated the new constitution's merits. As Alexander Hamilton noted, the debate would reveal whether the people could establish good government "by reflection and choice" or by "accident and force."

**CHOOSING SIDES** Advocates for the Constitution assumed the name *Federalists*; opponents became **anti-Federalists**. The two sides formed the seeds for America's first two-party political system.

The Federalists, led by James Madison and Alexander Hamilton, had several advantages. First, they had a concrete proposal, the draft constitution itself; their opponents had nothing to offer but criticism. Second, their leaders were, on average, ten to twelve years younger and more energetic than the anti-Federalists; many of them had been members of the Constitutional Convention and were familiar with the disputed issues in the document. Third, the Federalists were more unified and better organized.

The anti-Federalist leaders—Virginians Patrick Henry, George Mason, Richard Henry Lee, and future president James Monroe; George Clinton of New York; Samuel Adams, Elbridge Gerry, and Mercy Otis Warren of Massachusetts; Luther Martin and Samuel Chase of Maryland—were a diverse group. Some wanted to retain the Confederation. Others wanted to start over. Still others wanted to revise the proposed constitution. Patrick Henry wanted the preamble to read "We the states" rather than "We the people," and he worried about a new constitution that "squints toward monarchy" by creating a powerful presidency.

Most anti-Federalists feared that the new government would eventually grow corrupt and tyrannical. A Philadelphia writer denounced those who drafted the Constitution as representing "the Aristocratic Party" intent upon creating a "monarchical" national government.

The anti-Federalists especially criticized the absence of a "bill of rights" to protect individuals and states from the growing power of the national government. Other than the bill of rights, however, the anti-Federalists had no comprehensive alternative to the Constitution.

*THE FEDERALIST* Among the supreme legacies of the debate over the Constitution is what came to be called *The Federalist Papers*, a collection of eighty-five essays published in New York newspapers between 1787 and 1788. Written by James Madison, Alexander Hamilton, and John Jay, the essays defended the concept of a strong national government and outlined the major principles and assumptions embodied in the Constitution. Thomas Jefferson called *The Federalist Papers* the "best commentary on the principles of government which ever was written."

In the most famous of the *Federalist* essays, No. 10, Madison warned that democracies "have in general been as short in their lives as they have been violent in their deaths." Their inherent flaw was the tendency of majorities to tyrannize minorities. As Benjamin Franklin explained, a "democracy is two wolves and a lamb voting on what to have for lunch."

Madison stressed that the greatest threat to rule by the people was the rise of "factions," special interest groups whose goals conflict with the interests and welfare of the greater community. Yet any effort to eliminate factions would require tyrannical controls. The goal instead should be to minimize the negative effects of factions.

To that end, Madison turned the conventional wisdom about republics on its head. From ancient times, it had been assumed that self-governing republics survived only if they were small and homogeneous. Madison, however, argued that small republics usually fell victim to warring factions. In the United States, he explained, the size and diversity of the expanding nation would make it impossible for any single faction to form a majority that could corrupt the federal government—or society at large. The contending factions would, in essence, cancel each other out. In addition, he argued that it was the responsibility of the Congress to regulate "these various and interfering interests." Madison and the other framers created a legal and political system designed to protect minorities from a tyranny of the majority.

Given a federal government in which power was shared among the three federal branches, a large republic could work better than a small one to balance "clashing interests" and keep them in check. "Extend the [geographic] sphere," Madison wrote, "and you take in a greater variety of parties and interests; you make it less probable that a majority of the whole will have a common motive to invade the rights of other citizens."

If men were angels, Madison noted in *Federalist* No. 51, all forms of government would be unnecessary. In framing a national government "which is to be administered by men over men," however, "the great difficulty lies in this: you must first enable the government to control the governed; and in the next place oblige it to control itself."

**THE STATES DECIDE** Delaware, New Jersey, and Georgia were among the first states to ratify the Constitution. Massachusetts, still sharply divided in the aftermath of Shays's Rebellion, was the first state in which the outcome was close, approving the Constitution by 187 to 168 on February 6, 1788.

On June 21, 1788, New Hampshire became the ninth state to ratify the Constitution, thereby reaching the minimum number of states needed for approval. The Constitution, however, could hardly succeed without the approval of Virginia, the largest, wealthiest, and most populous state, or New York, which had the third-highest population and occupied a key position geographically. Both states included strong opposition groups who were eventually won over by an agreement to add a bill of rights.

Upon notification of New Hampshire's decision to ratify the Constitution, the Confederation Congress chose New York City as the national

**New beginnings** An engraving from the title page of *The Universal Asylum and Columbian Magazine* (published in Philadelphia in 1790). America is represented as a woman laying down her shield to engage in education, art, commerce, and agriculture.

capital and called for the new government to assume power in 1789. The Constitution was adopted, but the resistance to it convinced the new Congress to propose the first ten constitutional amendments, now known as the Bill of Rights.

"Our Constitution is in actual operation," Benjamin Franklin wrote a friend in 1789. "Everything appears to promise that it will last; but in this world nothing is certain but death and taxes." George Washington was even more uncertain, predicting that the Constitution would not "last for more than twenty years."

The Constitution has lasted much longer, of course, and its complexity and adaptability have provided a model of resilient republican government in which, as Jefferson noted, power was "created and constrained at the same time." The Constitution was by no means perfect (after all, it has been amended twenty-seven times); it was a bundle of messy compromises and concessions that left many issues, notably slavery, undecided or ignored. But most of its supporters believed that it was the best frame of government obtainable and that it would continue to evolve and improve. It laid the groundwork and

## RATIFICATION OF THE CONSTITUTION

| ORDER OF RATIFICATION | STATE | DATE OF RATIFICATION |
|:---:|:---:|:---:|
| 1 | Delaware | December 7, 1787 |
| 2 | Pennsylvania | December 12, 1787 |
| 3 | New Jersey | December 18, 1787 |
| 4 | Georgia | January 2, 1788 |
| 5 | Connecticut | January 9, 1788 |
| 6 | Massachusetts | February 6, 1788 |
| 7 | Maryland | April 28, 1788 |
| 8 | South Carolina | May 23, 1788 |
| 9 | New Hampshire | June 21, 1788 |
| 10 | Virginia | June 25, 1788 |
| 11 | New York | July 26, 1788 |
| 12 | North Carolina | November 21, 1789 |
| 13 | Rhode Island | May 29, 1790 |

provided the ideals for later generations to build upon, and it remains the oldest national constitution in the world.

The Constitution confirmed that the United States would be the first *democratic republic* in history. The founders believed that they were creating a unique political system based on a "new science of politics" combining the best aspects of democracies and republics. In a democracy, the people rule; in a republic, officials elected by the people rule. At the Constitutional Convention, the delegates combined elements of both approaches so that they balanced and regulated each other, and ensured that personal freedoms and the public welfare were protected.

# THE FEDERALIST ERA

The Constitution was ratified because it promised to create a more powerful national government better capable of managing a rapidly growing republic. Yet it was one thing to ratify a new constitution and quite another to make the new government run smoothly.

With each passing year, the United States debated how to interpret and apply the provisions of the new constitution. During the 1790s, the federal government would confront rebellions, states threatening to secede, international tensions, and foreign wars, as well as the formation of competing political parties—Federalists and Democratic Republicans, more commonly known as **Jeffersonian Republicans**, or simply as Republicans.

The two parties came to represent different visions for America. The Democratic Republicans were mostly southerners, like Virginians Thomas Jefferson and James Madison, who wanted the country to remain a rural nation of small farmers dedicated to republican values. They distrusted the national government, defended states' rights, preferred a "strict" interpretation of the Constitution, and placed their trust in the masses. "The will of the majority, the natural law of every society," Jefferson insisted, "is the only sure guardian of the rights of men."

The Federalists, led by Alexander Hamilton and John Adams, were clustered in New York and New England. They embraced urban culture, industrial development, and commercial growth. Federalists feared the "passions" of the common people and advocated a strong national government and a flexible interpretation of the Constitution. As Hamilton stressed, "the people are turbulent and changing; they seldom judge or determine right."

**THE FIRST PRESIDENT** On March 4, 1789, the new Congress convened in New York City. A few weeks later, the presiding officer of the Senate certified that George Washington, with 69 electoral college votes, was the nation's first president. John Adams of Massachusetts, with 34 votes, the second-highest number, became vice president. (At this time, no candidates ran specifically for the vice presidency; the presidential candidate who came in second, regardless of party affiliation, became vice president.)

Washington greeted the news of his unanimous election with a "heart filled with distress," likening himself to "a culprit who is going to the place of his execution." He would have preferred to stay in "retirement" at Mount Vernon, his "peaceful" Virginia plantation, but agreed to serve because he had been "summoned by [his] country."

Some complained that Washington's personality was too cold and aloof, and that he lacked sophistication. Adams groused that Washington was "too illiterate, unlearned, [and] unread" to be president. As a French diplomat observed, however, Washington had "the soul, look, and figure of a hero in action."

Born in Virginia in 1732, Washington was a largely self-educated former surveyor, land speculator, and soldier whose father had died when he was eleven. In 1759 he married Martha Dandridge Custis, a young widow with two small children and one of the largest fortunes in Virginia. In the years that followed, he became a prosperous tobacco planter and land speculator. Although reserved and dignified in public, Washington loved riding horses, hunting foxes, playing cards or billiards, fishing, hosting oyster roasts, and drinking wine.

The fifty-seven-year-old Washington brought to the presidency both a detached reserve and a remarkable capacity for leadership. Although capable of angry outbursts, he was honest, honorable, and disciplined; he had extraordinary stamina and patience, integrity and resolve, courage and resilience. And he exercised sound judgment and remarkable self-control. Most of all, he was fearless. Few doubted that he was the best person to lead the new nation. People already were calling him the "father of his country."

In his inaugural address, Washington appealed for unity, pleading with the Congress to abandon "local prejudices" and "party animosities" to create the "national" outlook necessary for the fledgling republic to thrive. Within a few months, he would see his hopes dashed. Personal rivalries, sectional tensions, and political infighting would dominate life in the 1790s.

**WASHINGTON'S CABINET** President Washington faced massive challenges, and he knew full well that every decision he made would be invested with special significance. "The eyes of America—perhaps of the world—are turned to this Government," he said. He was entering "untrodden ground" and therefore must ensure that his actions were based on "true principles."

During the summer of 1789, Congress created executive departments corresponding to those formed under the Confederation. To head the Department of State, Washington named Thomas Jefferson. To lead the Department of the Treasury, he appointed Alexander Hamilton, who was widely read in matters of government finance. Henry Knox was secretary of war and John Jay became the first chief justice of the Supreme Court.

Washington routinely called his chief staff members together to discuss matters of policy. This was the origin of the president's *cabinet*, an advisory body for which the Constitution made no formal provision. The office of vice president also took on what would become its typical character. "The Vice-Presidency," John Adams wrote his wife Abigail, is the most "insignificant office . . . ever . . . contrived."

**THE BILL OF RIGHTS** To address concerns raised by opponents of the new federal government, James Madison, now a congressman from Virginia, presented to Congress in May 1789 a set of constitutional amendments intended to protect individual rights. As Thomas Jefferson explained, such a "bill of rights is what the people are entitled to against every government on earth, general or particular, and what no just government should refuse." After considerable debate, Congress approved twelve amendments in September 1789. By the end of 1791, the necessary three-fourths of the states had approved *ten* of the twelve proposed amendments, now known as the **Bill of Rights**.

The Bill of Rights provided safeguards for individual rights of speech, assembly, religion, and the press; the right to own firearms; the right to refuse to house soldiers; protection against unreasonable searches and seizures; the right to refuse to testify against oneself; the right to a speedy public trial, with an attorney present, before an impartial jury; and protection against "cruel and unusual" punishments. The Tenth Amendment addressed the widespread demand that powers not delegated to the national government "are reserved to the States respectively, or to the people."

The amendments were written in broad language that seemed to exclude no one. In fact, however, they technically applied only to property-owning white males. Native Americans were entirely outside the constitutional system, an "alien people" in their own land. And, like the Constitution itself, the Bill of Rights gave no protections to enslaved Americans. Similar restrictions applied to women, who could not vote in most state and national elections. Equally important, the Bill of Rights had a built-in flaw: it did not protect citizens from states violating their civil rights.

Still, the United States was the first nation to put such safeguards into its government charter. While the Constitution had designed a vigorous federal government binding together the thirteen states, the Bill of Rights provided something just as necessary: codifying the individual rights and freedoms without which the government or a tyrannical majority might abuse "the people."

**RELIGIOUS FREEDOM** The debates over the Constitution and the Bill of Rights generated a religious revolution as well as a political revolution. Unlike the New England Puritans, whose colonial governments enforced their particular religious beliefs, the Christian men who drafted and amended the Constitution made no direct mention of God. They were determined to protect religious life from government interference and coercion.

In contrast to the monarchies of Europe, the United States would keep the institutions of church and government separate and allow people to choose their own religions ("freedom of conscience"). To that end, the First Amendment declared that "Congress shall make no law respecting an establishment of religion or prohibiting the free exercise thereof." This statement has since become one of the most important—and controversial—principles of American government.

The First Amendment created a framework within which people of all religious persuasions could flourish and prohibited the federal government from endorsing or supporting any denomination or interfering with the religious choices that people make. As Thomas Jefferson later explained, the First Amendment erected a "wall of separation between church and State."

**IMMIGRATION AND NATURALIZATION** In the list of grievances against King George in the Declaration of Independence, Thomas Jefferson had charged that the monarch had "endeavored to prevent the population of these States" by "obstructing the laws for naturalization of foreigners, [and] refusing to pass others to encourage their migration hither."

To ensure that America continued to share its "blessings of liberty" with immigrants, the Constitution called upon Congress to create policies to accommodate the continuing stream of immigrants from around the world. George Washington had strong feelings on the matter. He viewed America's open embrace of refugees and immigrants as one of the nation's most important values.

In 1783, amid the excitement of the end of the Revolutionary War, General Washington had assured a group of recent Irish immigrants that "the bosom of America is open to receive not only the opulent & respectable Stranger, but the oppressed & persecuted of all Nations & Religions." Five years later, he reiterated his desire for America to continue to be "a safe and agreeable asylum to the virtuous and persecuted part of mankind, to whatever nation they might belong." He and many other founders viewed a growing population as a national blessing.

President Washington, in his first address to Congress in 1790, urged the legislators to craft a "liberal" naturalization law to attract immigrants. Congress responded with the Naturalization Act of 1790, which specified that any "free white person" could gain citizenship ("naturalization") after living at least two years

A BILL to eſtabliſh an uniform Rule of Naturalization, and to enable Aliens to hold Lands under certain Reſtrictions.

**Naturalization in 1790** A detail of the bill that established "an uniform Rule of Naturalization" that made it possible for immigrants to hold lands.

in the United States. (In 1795, Congress increased the residency requirement to five years.) This law established an important principle: immigrants were free to renounce their original citizenship to become American citizens.

During the 1790s, some 100,000 European immigrants arrived in the United States, beginning a process that would grow with time. Because of its liberal naturalization policy, the United States has admitted more people from more places than any other nation in the world.

## HAMILTON'S VISION OF A PROSPEROUS AMERICA

In 1776, the same year that Americans were declaring their independence, Adam Smith, a Scottish philosopher, published a revolutionary book titled *An Inquiry into the Nature and Causes of the Wealth of Nations*. It provided the first full description of what would come to be called a modern *capitalist* economy and its social benefits. (The term *capitalism* would not appear until 1850.)

*The Wealth of Nations* was a declaration of independence from Great Britain's mercantilist system. Under *mercantilism*, national governments had exercised tight control over economic life. Smith argued that instead of controlling economic activity, governments should allow individuals and businesses to compete freely for profits in the marketplace. By liberating individual self-interest and entrepreneurial innovation from the constraints of government authority, he theorized, the welfare of society would be enhanced. The poverty that had entrapped the masses of Europe for centuries would end to the extent that governments allowed for "free enterprise," by which individuals, through their hard work and ingenuity, could at last gain earthly happiness and prosperity.

**Alexander Hamilton** The powerful Secretary of the Treasury from 1789 to 1795.

Smith also explained that the strongest national economies would be those in which *all* the major sectors were flourishing—agriculture, trade, banking, finance, and manufacturing. By allowing investors to funnel cash into productive enterprises, jobs would increase, profits would soar, and economic growth would ensue.

Alexander Hamilton greatly admired *The Wealth of Nations*, and as secretary of the Treasury he took charge of managing the nation's complicated financial affairs. He grasped the complex issues of government finance and envisioned what America would become: the world's most prosperous capitalist nation. He believed that the federal government should encourage the creative spirit that distinguished Americans from other peoples.

Hamilton was a self-made and self-educated aristocrat—and he was also an immigrant. Born out of wedlock in the West Indies in 1755, he was deserted at age ten by his Scottish father and left an orphan at thirteen by the death of his mother. With the help of friends and relatives, he found his way to New Jersey in late 1772 before moving a year later to New York City. There he entered King's College (now Columbia University).

When the war with Britain erupted, Hamilton joined the Continental army as a captain at the age of nineteen. He distinguished himself in the battles of Trenton and Princeton and became one of General Washington's favorite aides. After the war, he established a thriving legal practice in New York City, married into a prominent family, and served as a member of the Confederation Congress.

Hamilton became the foremost advocate for an "energetic government" promoting vibrant economic development. In contrast to Jefferson, the southern planter, Hamilton, the urban financier, believed that the United States was too dependent on agriculture. He championed trade, banking, finance, investment, and manufacturing, as well as bustling commercial cities, as the most essential elements of America's future.

**HAMILTON'S ECONOMIC REFORMS** The United States was born in debt. To fight the war for independence, it had borrowed heavily from the Dutch and the French. After the war, it had to find a way to pay off the debts. Yet there was no national bank, no national currency, and few mills and factories. In essence, the American republic was bankrupt. It fell to Alexander Hamilton to determine how the debts should be repaid and how the new national government could balance its budget.

Governments have four basic ways to pay their bills: (1) impose taxes or fees on individuals and businesses; (2) levy tariffs (taxes on imported goods); (3) borrow money by selling interest-paying government bonds to investors; and, (4) print money.

Under Hamilton's leadership, the United States did all these things—and more. To raise funds, Congress, with Hamilton's support, enacted tariffs of 5 to 10 percent on a variety of imported items. Tariffs were hotly debated because they were the source of most of the federal government's annual revenue, and they "protected" American manufacturers by taxing their foreign competitors, especially those in Britain.

By discriminating against imported goods, tariffs enabled American manufacturers to charge higher prices for their products sold in the United States. This penalized consumers, particularly those in the southern states that were most dependent upon imported goods. In essence, tariffs benefited the nation's young manufacturing sector, most of which was in New England, at the expense of the agricultural sector, since farm produce was rarely imported. Tariff policy soon became an explosive political issue.

**DEALING WITH DEBTS**  The levying of tariffs marked but one element in Alexander Hamilton's plan to put the new republic on sound financial footing. In a series of "Reports on Public Credit" submitted to Congress between January 1790 and December 1791, Hamilton outlined his visionary program for the economic development of the United States.

The first report dealt with how the federal government should refinance the massive debt the states and the Confederation government had accumulated. Hamilton insisted that the debts be repaid. After all, he explained, a robust economy depended upon its integrity and reliability: debts being paid, contracts being enforced, and private property being protected.

Selling government bonds to pay the interest due on the war-related debts, Hamilton argued, would provide investors ("the monied interest") a direct stake in the success of the new government. He also insisted that the federal government pay ("assume") the state debts from the Revolutionary War because they were a *national* responsibility; all Americans had benefited from the war for independence. "The debt of the United States," he stressed, "was the price of liberty." A well-managed federal debt that absorbed the state debts, he claimed, would be a "national blessing," provide a "mechanism for national unity," and promote long-term prosperity.

**SECTIONAL DIFFERENCES**  Hamilton's far-sighted proposals created a storm of controversy, in part because many people, then and since, did not understand their complexities. James Madison, Hamilton's close ally in the fight for the new constitution, broke with him over the federal government "assuming" the states' debts.

Madison was troubled that northern states owed far more than southern states. Four states (Virginia, North Carolina, Georgia, and Maryland) had already paid off most of their war debts. The other states had not been as conscientious. Why should the southern states, Madison asked, subsidize the debts of the northern states?

Madison's fierce opposition to Hamilton's debt-assumption plan ignited a vigorous debate in Congress. In April 1790, the House of Representatives voted down the "assumption" plan, 32–29. Hamilton did not give up, however. After failing to get members of Congress to switch their votes, he asked Jefferson, the new secretary of state, to help break the impasse. In June 1790, Jefferson invited Hamilton and Madison to join him for dinner at his lodgings in New York City.

By the end of the evening, they had reached a famous compromise. First, they agreed that the national capital should move from New York City to Philadelphia for the next ten years, and then move to a new city to be built in a ten-mile-square "federal district" astride the Potomac River, sandwiched between the slave states of Maryland and Virginia. Hamilton agreed to find the votes in Congress to approve the move in exchange for Madison pledging to find the two votes needed to pass the debt-assumption plan.

The Compromise of 1790 went as planned. Congress voted as hoped, and the federal government moved in late 1790 to Philadelphia. Ten years later, the nation's capital moved again, this time to the new city of Washington, in the federal District of Columbia.

Hamilton's debt-funding scheme proved a success. The bonds issued by the federal government in 1790 were quickly snatched up by investors, providing money to begin paying off the war debts. In addition, Hamilton obtained new loans from European governments.

To raise additional revenue, Hamilton convinced Congress to create *excise* taxes on particular products, such as carriages, sugar, and salt. By 1794, the nation had a higher financial credit rating than all the nations of Europe. By making the new nation financially solvent, Hamilton set in motion the greatest economic success story in world history.

**A NATIONAL BANK**  Part of the opposition to Hamilton's debt-financing scheme grew out of opposition to Hamilton himself. The young Treasury secretary, arrogant and headstrong, viewed himself as President Washington's prime minister. That his Department of Treasury had *forty* staff members while Thomas Jefferson's State Department had *five* demonstrated the priority that Washington gave to the nation's financial situation.

Hamilton was on a mission to develop an urban-centered economy anchored in finance and manufacturing. After securing congressional approval of his debt-funding scheme, he called for a national bank modeled after the Bank of England. Such a bank, Hamilton believed, would enable much greater "commerce among individuals" and provide a safe place for the federal government's cash.

By their nature, Hamilton explained, banks were essential. They would increase the nation's money supply by issuing currency in amounts greater than the actual "reserve"—gold and silver coins and government bonds—in their vaults. By issuing loans and thereby increasing the amount of money in circulation, banks served as the engines of prosperity: "industry is increased, commodities are multiplied, agriculture and manufactures flourish, and herein consist the true wealth and prosperity" of a "genuine nation."

Once again, Madison and Jefferson led the opposition, arguing that, since the Constitution said nothing about creating a national bank, the government could not start one. Jefferson also believed that Hamilton's proposed bank would not help most Americans. Instead, a small inner circle of self-serving financiers and investors would, over time, exercise corrupt control over Congress.

Hamilton, however, had the better of the argument. Representatives from the northern states voted 33–1 in favor of the national bank; southern congressmen opposed it 19–6. The lopsided vote illustrated the growing political division between the North and South.

Before signing the bill, President Washington sought the advice of his cabinet, where he found an equal division of opinion. The result was the first great debate on constitutional interpretation. Were the powers of Congress only those *explicitly* stated in the Constitution, or were other powers *implied*? The argument turned chiefly on Article I, Section 8, which authorized Congress to "make all Laws which shall be necessary and proper for carrying into Execution the foregoing Powers."

Such language left lots of room for disagreement and led to a savage confrontation between Jefferson and Hamilton. The Treasury secretary had come to view Jefferson as a man of "profound ambition & violent passions," a "contemptible hypocrite" who was guided by an "unsound & dangerous" agrarian economic philosophy.

**Thomas Jefferson** A 1791 portrait by Charles Willson Peale.

Jefferson hated commerce, speculators, factories, banks, and bankers—almost as much as he hated the "monarchist" Hamilton. To thwart the proposed national bank, Jefferson pointed to the Tenth Amendment of the Constitution, which reserves to the states and the people powers not explicitly delegated to Congress. Jefferson argued that a bank might be a convenient aid to Congress in collecting taxes and regulating the currency, but it was not *necessary*, as Article I, Section 8 specified.

In a 16,000-word report to the president, Hamilton countered that the power to charter corporations was an "implied" power of any government. As he pointed out, the three banks already in existence had been chartered by states, none of whose constitutions specifically mentioned the authority to incorporate banks.

Hamilton convinced Washington to sign the bank bill. In doing so, the president had, in Jefferson's words, opened up "a boundless field of power," which in coming years would lead to a further broadening of the president's implied powers, with the approval of the Supreme Court.

The new **Bank of the United States** (B.U.S.), based in Philadelphia, had three primary responsibilities: (1) to hold the government's funds and pay its bills; (2) to provide loans to the federal government and to other banks to promote economic development; and (3) to manage the nation's money supply by regulating the power of state-chartered banks to issue paper currency or banknotes. The B.U.S. could issue national banknotes as needed to address the chronic shortage of gold and silver coins. By 1800, the B.U.S. had branches in four cities, and four more were soon added.

**ENCOURAGING MANUFACTURING** Hamilton's bold economic vision was not yet complete. In the last of his recommendations to Congress, the "Report on Manufactures," distributed in December 1791, he set in place the capstone of his design for a modern capitalist economy: the active governmental promotion of new manufacturing and industrial enterprises (mills, mines, and factories). Industrialization, Hamilton believed, would bring diversification to an American economy dominated by agriculture and dangerously dependent on imported British goods; improve productivity through greater use of machinery; provide work for those not ordinarily employed outside the home, such as women and children; and encourage immigration of skilled industrial workers from other nations.

To foster industrial development, Hamilton recommended that the federal government increase tariffs on imports, three quarters of which came from Britain, while providing financial incentives (called bounties) to key industries making especially needed products such as wool, cotton cloth, and window glass. Such government support, he claimed, would enable new industries to compete "on equal terms" with long-standing European enterprises. Finally, Hamilton asked Congress to fund major transportation improvements, including the development of roads, canals, and harbors.

Few of Hamilton's pro-industry ideas were enacted because of strong opposition from Jefferson, Madison, and other southerners. Hamilton's proposals, however, provided arguments for future advocates of manufacturing and federally funded transportation projects (called "internal improvements").

**HAMILTON'S VISIONARY ACHIEVEMENTS** Hamilton's leadership was monumental. During the 1790s, as the Treasury department began to pay off the Revolutionary War debts, foreign capitalists and banks invested heavily in the American economy, and European nations as well as China began a growing trade with the United States. Economic growth, so elusive in the 1780s, blossomed as the number of new businesses soared. A Bostonian reported that the nation had never "had a brighter sunshine of prosperity. . . . Our agricultural interest smiles, our commerce is blessed, our manufactures flourish."

All was not well, however. By championing the values and institutions of a bustling capitalist system and the big cities and industries that went with it, Hamilton upset many people, especially in the agricultural South and along the western frontier. Thomas Jefferson and James Madison had grown increasingly concerned that Hamilton's urban-industrial economic program and his political deal making threatened American liberties. Hamilton recognized that his successes had led Jefferson and Madison to form a party "hostile to me," one intent on making Jefferson the next president.

The political competition between Jefferson and Hamilton boiled over into a feud of pathological intensity. Both were visionaries, but where Hamilton envisioned a developing American economy and society modeled on that of Britain, Jefferson preferred to follow the example of France. The two men also had markedly different hopes for the nation's economic development and contrasting views of how the Constitution should be interpreted.

Jefferson told President Washington that Hamilton's efforts to create a capitalist economy would "undermine and demolish the republic" and lead to "the most corrupt government on earth." Hamilton, he added, was "really a colossus [giant] to the anti-republican party." In turn, Hamilton called Jefferson an "intriguing incendiary" who had circulated "unkind whispers" about him. He accused Jefferson of being an agrarian romantic who failed to see that manufacturing, industry, and banking would drive the nation's economic future.

Jefferson's intensifying opposition to Hamilton's politics and policies fractured Washington's cabinet. Jefferson wrote that he and Hamilton "daily pitted in the cabinet like two cocks [roosters]." Washington urged them to rise above their toxic "dissensions," but it was too late. They had become mortal enemies, as well as the leaders of the first loosely organized political parties, the Federalists and the Democratic Republicans.

## FEDERALISTS AND DEMOCRATIC REPUBLICANS

The Federalists were centered in New York and New England, and were also powerful among the planter elite in South Carolina. Generally, they feared the excesses of democracy, distrusted the "common people," and wanted a strong central government led by the wisest leaders who would be committed to economic growth, social stability, and national defense. What most worried the Federalists, as Alexander Hamilton said, was the "poison" of "DEMOCRACY." The people, he stressed, were "turbulent and changing; they seldom judge or determine right [wisely]."

By contrast, the Democratic Republicans, led by Thomas Jefferson and James Madison, were most concerned about threats to individual freedoms and states' rights posed by a strong national government. They trusted the people. As Madison said, "Public Opinion sets bounds to every government and is the real sovereign in every free one." The Democratic Republicans were strongest in the southern states—Virginia, North Carolina, and Georgia. Most Democratic Republicans promoted an agricultural economy.

Unexpected events in Europe influenced the two parties. In July 1789, violence erupted in France when masses of the working poor, enraged over soaring prices for bread and in part inspired by the American Revolution, revolted against the absolute monarchy of Louis XVI.

The **French Revolution** captured the imagination of many Americans, especially Jefferson and the Democratic Republicans, as royal tyranny was displaced by a democratic republic that gave voting rights to all adult men regardless of how much property they owned. Americans formed forty-two Democratic-Republican clubs that hosted rallies on behalf of the French Revolution and in support of local Republican candidates.

## FOREIGN AND DOMESTIC CRISES

During the nation's fragile infancy, George Washington was the only man able to rise above party differences. In 1792, he was unanimously reelected to a second term—and quickly found himself embroiled in the cascading consequences of the French Revolution.

In 1791, the monarchies of Prussia and Austria had invaded France to stop the revolutionary movement from infecting their absolutist societies. The invaders, however, only inspired the French revolutionaries to greater efforts to spread their ideal of democracy.

By early 1793, the most radical of the French revolutionaries, called *Jacobins*, had executed the king and queen, as well as hundreds of aristocrats and priests. The Jacobins not only promoted democracy, religious toleration, and human rights, but social, racial, and sexual equality. Then, on February 1, 1793, the French revolutionary government declared war on Great Britain, Spain, and the Netherlands, thus beginning a European-wide conflict that would last twenty-two years.

As the French republic plunged into warfare, the Revolution entered its worst phase, the so-called Reign of Terror. In 1793–1794, Jacobins executed thousands of "counterrevolutionary" political prisoners and Catholic priests, along with many revolutionary leaders. Barbarism ruled the streets.

Secretary of State Thomas Jefferson, who loved French culture and democratic ideals, wholeheartedly endorsed the Revolution. He even justified the Reign of Terror by asserting that the "tree of liberty must be refreshed from time to time with the blood of patriots and tyrants." By contrast, Alexander Hamilton and John Adams saw the French Revolution as vicious and godless, and they sided with Great Britain and its allies. Such conflicting attitudes transformed the first decade of American politics into one of the most fractious periods in the nation's history—an "age of passion."

The European war tested the ability of the United States to remain neutral in world affairs. Both France and Britain purchased goods from America, and each sought to stop the other from trading with the United States, even if it meant attacking U.S. merchant ships.

As President Washington began his second term in 1793, he faced an awkward decision. By the 1778 Treaty of Alliance, the United States was a *perpetual* ally of France. Americans, however, wanted no part of the war.

Hamilton and Jefferson agreed that entering the conflict would be foolish. Where they differed was in how best to stay out. Hamilton wanted to declare the military alliance formed with the French during the American Revolution invalid because it had been made with a monarchy that no longer existed. Jefferson preferred to use the alliance with France as a bargaining point with the British.

In the end, Washington took a wise middle course. On April 22, 1793, he issued a neutrality proclamation that declared the United States "friendly and impartial toward the belligerent powers" and warned U.S. citizens that they might be prosecuted for "aiding or abetting hostilities" or taking part in other unneutral acts. Instead of settling matters in his cabinet, however, the neutrality proclamation brought to a boil the ugly feud between Jefferson and Hamilton.

**CITIZEN GENÊT** At the same time that President Washington issued the neutrality proclamation, he accepted Thomas Jefferson's argument that the United States should officially recognize the French revolutionary government and welcome its ambassador to the United States, the cocky, twenty-nine-year-old Edmond-Charles Genêt.

In April 1793, Citizen Genêt, as he became known, landed at Charleston, South Carolina, to a hero's welcome. He then openly violated U.S. neutrality by recruiting four American privateers (privately owned warships) to capture English and Spanish merchant vessels.

After five weeks in South Carolina, Genêt traveled to the American capital, Philadelphia, where his efforts to draw America into the war on France's side embarrassed his friends in the Republican party. When Genêt threatened to go around President Washington and appeal directly to the American people, even Thomas Jefferson disavowed "the French monkey." In August 1793, Washington, at Hamilton's urging, demanded that the French government replace Genêt.

The growing excesses of the radicals in France were quickly cooling U.S. support for the Revolution. Jefferson, however, was so disgusted by his feud with Hamilton and by Washington's refusal to support the French that he resigned as secretary of state at the end of 1793 and returned to his Virginia home, eager to be rid of the "hated occupation of politics."

Vice President Adams greeted Jefferson's departure by saying "good riddance." President Washington felt the same way. He never forgave Jefferson and Madison for organizing Democratic-Republican clubs to oppose his policies. After accepting Jefferson's resignation, Washington never spoke to him again.

**JAY'S TREATY** During 1794, tensions between the United States and Great Britain threatened to renew warfare between the old enemies. The Treaty of Paris (1783) that ended the Revolutionary War had left the western and southern boundaries of the United States in dispute. In addition, in late 1793, British warships violated international law by seizing U.S. merchant ships that carried French goods or were sailing for a French port. By early 1794, several hundred American ships had been confiscated, and their crews were given the terrible choice of joining the British navy, a process called "impressment," or being imprisoned. At the same time, British troops in the Ohio Valley gave weapons to Indians, who in turn attacked American settlers.

On April 16, 1794, President Washington sent Chief Justice John Jay to London to settle the major issues between the two nations. Jay agreed to the British demand that America not sell products to France for the construction of warships. The British refused, however, to stop intercepting American merchant ships and "impressing" their sailors. Finally, Jay conceded that the British need not compensate U.S. citizens for the enslaved African Americans who had escaped to the safety of British forces during the Revolutionary War.

In return, Jay won three important promises from the British: They would (1) evacuate their six forts in northwest America by 1796; (2) reimburse Americans for the seizures of ships and cargo in 1793–1794; and, (3) grant U.S. merchants the right to trade again with the island economies of the British West Indies.

When the terms of **Jay's Treaty** were disclosed, many Americans, especially Republicans, were outraged. The wildly unpopular treaty deepened the division between Federalists and Republicans. Jefferson dismissed the treaty as an "infamous act" intended to "undermine the Constitution." The uproar created the most serious crisis of Washington's presidency. Some called for his impeachment. Yet the president decided that the proposed agreement was the only way to avoid a war with Britain that the United States was bound to lose.

In 1795, with Washington's support, Jay's Treaty barely won the necessary two-thirds majority in the Senate. Some 80 percent of the votes *for* the treaty came from New England or the middle Atlantic states; 74 percent of those opposed were southerners, most of them Jeffersonian Republicans.

Washington sighed that he had ridden out "the Storm," but he could never forget the "pernicious" figures "disseminating the acidic poison" against him. Weary of partisan squabbles, he longed to return home to Virginia. But Washington had given the young nation a precious gift—peace. No other leader could have pushed the controversial treaty through Congress.

FRONTIER TENSIONS Meanwhile, new conflicts erupted in the Ohio Valley between American settlers and Native Americans. In the fall of 1793, General "Mad" Anthony Wayne led a military expedition into the Northwest Territory's "Indian Country." His troops marched north from Cincinnati, built Fort Greenville in western Ohio, and soon went on the offensive in what became known as the Northwest Indian War, a conflict that arose after the British transferred the Ohio Country to the United States. The Native Americans living in the region insisted that the British had no right to give away their ancestral lands. As pioneers moved into the Northwest Territory, the various Indian nations formed the Western Confederacy to resist American settlement.

In August 1794, the Western Confederacy of some 2,000 Shawnee, Ottawa, Chippewa, Delaware, and Potawatomi warriors, supported by the British and reinforced by Canadian militiamen, attacked General Wayne's troops and Indian allies in the Battle of Fallen Timbers, along the Michigan-Ohio border. The Americans decisively defeated the Indians, destroyed their crops and villages, and built a line of forts in northern Ohio and Indiana. The Indians finally agreed to the Treaty of Greenville, signed in August 1795, by which the United States bought most of the territory that would form the state of Ohio and the cities of Detroit and Chicago. The treaty also established clear boundaries between Indian and American territories.

**THE WHISKEY REBELLION** Soon after the Battle of Fallen Timbers, the Washington administration displayed another show of strength in the backcountry, this time against the so-called **Whiskey Rebellion**.

Alexander Hamilton's 1791 tax on "distilled spirits" had ignited resistance among cash-poor farmers throughout the western frontier. Liquor made from grain or fruit was the region's most valuable product; it even was used as a form of currency. When efforts to repeal the tax failed, many turned to violence and intimidation. Beginning in September 1791, angry groups of farmers, militiamen, and laborers attacked federal tax collectors and marshals.

In the summer of 1794, the discontent exploded into rebellion in western Pennsylvania, home to a fourth of the nation's whiskey stills. A mob of angry farmers threatened to assault nearby Pittsburgh, loot the homes of the rich, and set the town ablaze. After negotiations failed, a U.S. Supreme Court justice declared on August 4, 1794, that western Pennsylvania was in a "state of rebellion." It was the first great domestic challenge to the federal government, and George Washington responded decisively.

At Hamilton's urging, Washington ordered the whiskey rebels ("enemies of order") to disperse by September 1 or he would send in the militia. When the rebels failed to respond, some 12,500 militiamen from several states began marching to western Pennsylvania. Washington donned his military uniform and rode on horseback to greet the soldiers. It was the first and last time that a sitting president would lead troops in the field.

The huge army, commanded by Virginia's governor, Henry "Lighthorse Harry" Lee, panicked the whiskey rebels, who vanished into the hills. Two dozen were charged with high treason; two were sentenced to hang, only to be pardoned by Washington.

**Whiskey Rebellion** George Washington as commander in chief reviews the troops mobilized to quell the Whiskey Rebellion in Pennsylvania in 1794.

The government had made its point, and the show of force led the rebels and their sympathizers to change their tactics. Rather than openly defying federal laws, they voted for Republicans, who won heavily in the next Pennsylvania elections.

**PINCKNEY'S TREATY** While events were unfolding in Pennsylvania, the Spanish began negotiations over control of the Mississippi River and the disputed northern boundary of their Florida colony, which they had acquired at the end of the Revolutionary War. U.S. negotiator Thomas Pinckney pulled off a diplomatic triumph in 1795 when he convinced the Spanish to accept a southern American boundary at the 31st parallel in west Florida, along the northern coast of the Gulf of Mexico (the current boundary between Florida and Georgia). The Spanish also agreed to allow Americans to ship goods, grains, and livestock down the Mississippi River to Spanish-controlled New Orleans. Senate ratification of Pinckney's Treaty (also called the Treaty of San

Lorenzo) came quickly, for westerners were eager to transport their crops and livestock to New Orleans.

# WESTERN SETTLEMENT

The treaties signed by John Jay and Thomas Pinckney spurred a new wave of settlers into the western territories. Their lust for land aroused a raging debate in Congress over what the federal government should do with the vast areas it had acquired or taken from the British, the Spanish, and the Native Americans.

**LAND POLICY** Federalists wanted the government to charge high prices for western lands to keep the East from losing both political influence and a labor force important to the growth of manufacture. They also preferred that government-owned lands be sold in large parcels to speculators, rather than in small plots to settlers. Thomas Jefferson and James Madison were reluctantly prepared to go along with these policies for the sake of reducing the national debt, but Jefferson preferred that government-owned land be sold to farmers rather than speculators.

For the time being, the Federalists prevailed. With the Land Act of 1796, Congress doubled the price of federal land (public domain) to $2 per acre. Half the townships would be sold in 640-acre sections, making the minimum cost $1,280, a price well beyond the means of ordinary settlers. By 1800, federal land offices had sold fewer than 50,000 acres. Criticism of the policies led to the Land Act of 1800, which reduced the minimum parcel to 320 acres and spread payments over four years. Thus, with a down payment of $160, one could buy a farm.

**THE WILDERNESS ROAD** The lure of western lands led thousands of settlers to follow pathfinder Daniel Boone into the territory known as Kentucky, or Kaintuck, from the Cherokee KEN-TA-KE (Great Meadow). In the late eighteenth century, the Indian-held lands in Kentucky were a farmer's dream and a hunter's paradise, with their fertile soil, bluegrass meadows, abundant forests, and countless buffalo, deer, and wild turkeys.

Born on a small farm in 1734 in central Pennsylvania, Boone became one of America's first folk heroes, a larger-than-life figure known as the "Columbus of the Woods." He was a deadeye marksman, experienced farmer, and accomplished woodsman.

**Daniel Boone Escorting Settlers through the Cumberland Gap**
Painting by George Caleb Bingham.

After hearing numerous reports about the lands over the Appalachian Mountains, he set out in 1769 to find a trail into Kentucky. He discovered what was called the Warriors' Path, a narrow foot trail that buffalo, deer, and Native Americans had worn along the steep ridges over the centuries.

In 1773, Boone led a group of white settlers into Kentucky. Two years later, he and thirty woodsmen used axes to widen the 208-mile-long Warriors' Path into what became known as the Wilderness Road, a passageway that more than 300,000 settlers would use over the next twenty-five years.

At a point where a branch of the Wilderness Road intersected with the Kentucky River, near what is now Lexington, Boone built the settlement of Boonesborough.

## TRANSFER OF POWER

In 1796, President Washington decided that serving two terms in office was enough. Weary of the criticism directed at him, he was eager to retire to Mount Vernon. He would leave behind a formidable record of achievement, including the organization of a new national government, a prosperous economy, the recovery of territory from Britain and Spain, a stable northwestern frontier, and the admission of three new states: Vermont (1791), Kentucky (1792), and Tennessee (1796). Of the nine presidents who were slave owners, he alone would grant his slaves their freedom upon his death.

WASHINGTON'S FAREWELL On September 17, 1796, Washington delivered a farewell address in which he criticized the rising spirit of political partisanship and the emergence of political parties. They endangered the republic, he felt, because they pursued the narrow interests of minorities rather than the good of the nation. In foreign relations, Washington advised, the United States should stay away from Europe's quarrels by avoiding "permanent alliances with any portion of the foreign world." His warning would serve as a fundamental principle in U.S. foreign policy until the early twentieth century.

**THE ELECTION OF 1796** With Washington out of the race, the United States had its first contested election for president. The Federalist "caucus," a group of leading congressmen, chose high-spirited Vice President John Adams as their candidate. As expected, the Republicans chose Thomas Jefferson. Aaron Burr, a young New York attorney and senator, also ran as a Republican.

The campaign was nasty. The Federalists were attacked for unpopular taxes, excessive spending, and abuses of power. Republicans called the pudgy John Adams "His Rotundity" and labeled him a monarchist because he loved symbols of power and despised "the people." Federalists countered that Jefferson was a French-loving atheist eager for another war with Great Britain and charged that he was not decisive enough to be president.

Adams won the election with 71 electoral votes, but in an odd twist, Jefferson, who received 68 electoral votes, became vice president. The Federalists won control of both houses of Congress.

## THE ADAMS ADMINISTRATION

Vain and prickly, opinionated and stubborn, John Adams had long lusted for the presidency, but he was a much better political theorist than he was a political leader. An independent thinker with a combative spirit and volcanic temper, he fought as often with his fellow Federalists, especially Alexander Hamilton, as with his Republican opponents. Benjamin Franklin said Adams was "always an honest man, often a wise one, but sometimes . . . absolutely out of his senses."

Widely recognized as the hardest-working member of the Continental Congress, Adams had authored the Massachusetts state constitution. During the Revolution, he had served as an exceptional diplomat in France, Holland, and Great Britain, and he had been George Washington's vice president.

In contrast to the tall, lanky Jefferson, the short, stocky Adams feared democracy and despised equality. He once referred to ordinary Americans as the "common herd of mankind." He also felt that he was never properly appreciated—and he may have been right. Yet on the essential issue of his presidency, war and peace, he kept his head when others about him were losing theirs—probably at the cost of his reelection.

**John Adams** Political philosopher and politician, Adams was the first president to take up residence in the Executive Mansion, in the new national capital of Washington, D.C., in 1801.

**THE WAR WITH FRANCE** As America's second president, John Adams inherited a "Quasi War" with France, a by-product of the angry French reaction to Jay's Treaty between the United States and Great Britain. The navies of both nations were capturing U.S. ships headed for the other's ports. By the time of Adams's inauguration, in 1797, the French had plundered some 300 American vessels and broken diplomatic relations with the United States.

Adams sought to ease tensions by sending three Americans to Paris to negotiate an end to the attacks on U.S. ships. When the Americans arrived, however, they were accosted by three French officials (labeled X, Y, and Z by Adams in his report to Congress) who announced that negotiations could begin only if the United States paid a bribe of $250,000 and loaned France $12 million.

Such bribes were common in the eighteenth century, but the answer from the American side was "no, no, not a sixpence." When the so-called XYZ Affair became public, American hostility toward France soared. Many Republicans—with the exception of Vice President Jefferson—joined with Federalists in calling for war.

Federalists in Congress voted to construct warships and triple the size of the army. Adams asked George Washington to command the army again. Washington reluctantly agreed on the condition that his favorite lieutenant, Alexander Hamilton, be appointed a major general. By the end of 1798, French and American ships were engaged in an undeclared naval war in the Caribbean Sea.

**THE WAR AT HOME** The conflict with France sparked an intense debate between Federalists eager for a formal declaration of war and Republicans sympathetic to France. Amid the superheated emotions, Vice President Jefferson observed that a "wall of separation" divided the nation's leaders.

For his part, Adams had tried to take the high ground. Soon after his election, he had invited Jefferson to join him in creating a bipartisan administration.

**Conflict with France**  A cartoon indicating the anti-French sentiment generated by the XYZ Affair. The three American negotiators (at left) reject the Paris Monster's demand for bribery money before discussions could begin.

Jefferson refused, saying that he would not be a part of the cabinet and would only preside over the Senate as vice president, as the Constitution specified. Within a year, he and Adams were at each other's throats. Adams regretted losing Jefferson as a friend but "felt obliged to look upon him as a man whose mind is warped by prejudice." Jefferson, he claimed, had become "a child and the dupe" of the Republicans in Congress.

Jefferson and other Republicans were convinced that the real purpose of the French crisis was to give Federalists an excuse to quiet their American critics. Perhaps no issue was more divisive in the 1790s than that posed by the immigrants coming from the war-torn European nations. Federalists worried that in the shadow of the French Revolution, the newcomers would bring social and political radicalism with them.

The **Alien and Sedition Acts of 1798** confirmed Republican suspicions that the Federalists were willing to go to any lengths to suppress freedom of speech. These partisan laws, passed amid a wave of patriotic war fervor, gave the president extraordinary powers to violate civil liberties protected by the Bill of Rights, all in a clumsy effort to stamp out criticism of the administration. They limited freedom of speech and of the press, as well as the liberty of "aliens" (immigrants who had not yet gained citizenship).

Adams's support of the Alien and Sedition Acts ("war measures") would prove to be the greatest mistake of his presidency. Timothy Pickering, his secretary of state, claimed that Adams agreed to the acts without consulting "any member of the government and for a reason truly remarkable—because he knew we should all be opposed to the measure."

Three of the four Alien and Sedition Acts reflected hostility toward French and Irish immigrants, many of whom had supported the French Revolution or the Irish Rebellion against British authority and had become militant Democratic Republicans in America. The Naturalization Act lengthened from five to fourteen years the residency requirement for immigrants ("aliens") to gain U.S. citizenship. It also required all immigrants to register with the federal government. The Alien Friends Act empowered the president to jail and deport "dangerous" aliens, and the Alien Enemies Act authorized the president in wartime to expel or imprison aliens from enemy nations. Finally, the Sedition Act outlawed writing, publishing, or speaking anything of "a false, scandalous and malicious" nature against the government or any of its officers.

Of the ten people convicted under the Sedition Act, all were Republicans. The case of Matthew Lyon, a Democratic-Republican congressman from Vermont, reveals how the prosecutions not only failed to silence those critical of the Adams administration, but created martyrs of the dissidents.

Lyon, who had come to America from Ireland in 1764, had accused Adams of "an unbounded thirst for ridiculous pomp, foolish adulation, and selfish avarice." Charged with defaming the president, Lyon was so bold as to ask the Federalist trial judge if he had "dined with the President and observed his ridiculous pomp and parade." The judge replied that he never saw the president engage in "pomp and display" but instead found Adams remarkable in his "plainness and simplicity."

The jury convicted Lyon, and the judge sentenced him to four months in prison. The defiant Lyon, who was up for reelection, centered his campaign on his prosecution, claiming that the Sedition Act was unconstitutional. His strategy worked, as he became the first congressman to win reelection while in prison. Democratic-Republican supporters paid his fines, for he had become a hero in the cause of free speech and civil liberties.

To counter what Jefferson called the "reign of witches" unleashed by the Alien and Sedition Acts, he and James Madison drafted the Kentucky and Virginia Resolutions, which were passed by the legislatures of those two states in late 1798. The resolutions were as troubling as the acts they denounced. While Jefferson appropriately described the Alien and Sedition Acts as "alarming infractions" of constitutional rights, he threatened disunion in claiming that state legislatures should "nullify" (reject and ignore) acts of Congress that violated the constitutional guarantee of free speech.

Meanwhile, Adams was seeking peace with France. In 1799, he dispatched another team of diplomats to negotiate with a new French government under First Consul Napoléon Bonaparte, whose army had overthrown the republic. In a treaty called the Convention of 1800, the Americans won the best terms they could. They dropped their demands to be repaid for the ships taken by the French, and the French agreed to end the military alliance with the United States dating to the Revolutionary War. The Senate quickly ratified the agreement, which became effective on December 21, 1801.

**REPUBLICAN VICTORY IN 1800** The furor over the Alien and Sedition Acts influenced the pivotal presidential election of 1800. The Federalists nominated Adams, although Alexander Hamilton publicly questioned Adams's fitness to be president, citing his "disgusting egotism." Adams reciprocated by telling a friend that Hamilton was "devoid of every moral principle."

Thomas Jefferson and Aaron Burr, the Republican candidates, once again represented the alliance of the two most powerful states, Virginia and New York. The Federalists claimed that Jefferson's election would bring civil war and anarchy. A Federalist newspaper predicted that if the "godless" Jefferson were elected, "murder, robbery, rape, adultery, and incest will be openly taught and practiced."

Not to be outdone, a Republican newspaper dismissed Adams as a "hideous hermaphroditical character with neither the force nor firmness of a man nor the gentleness and sensibility of a woman," adding that he was a "blind, bald, crippled, toothless man who wants to start a war with France."

In the raucous **election of 1800**, Jefferson and Burr, the two Republicans, emerged with 73 electoral votes each. Adams received 65. When Burr shockingly refused to withdraw in favor of Jefferson, the tie vote in the electoral college sent the election into the House of Representatives (a constitutional defect corrected in 1804 by the Twelfth Amendment).

The tie vote created an explosive political crisis. Federalist Fisher Ames predicted that Burr "might impart vigor to the country," while Jefferson "was absurd enough to believe his own nonsense."

The three months between the House vote for president in December 1800 and Jefferson's inauguration in March 1801 were so tense that people talked openly of civil war. There were even wild rumors of plots to assassinate Jefferson. In the end, it took thirty-six ballots for the House to choose Jefferson over Burr.

## THE ELECTION OF 1800

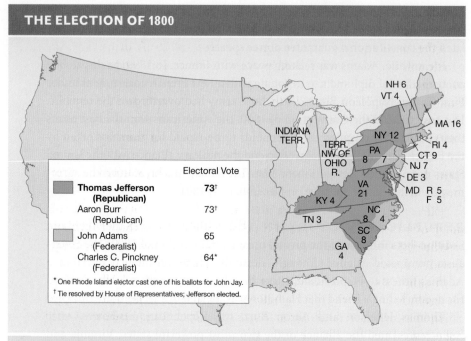

| | Electoral Vote |
|---|---|
| **Thomas Jefferson** **(Republican)** | **73†** |
| Aaron Burr (Republican) | 73† |
| John Adams (Federalist) | 65 |
| Charles C. Pinckney (Federalist) | 64* |

\* One Rhode Island elector cast one of his ballots for John Jay.
† Tie resolved by House of Representatives; Jefferson elected.

NH 6
VT 4
MA 16
INDIANA TERR.
TERR. NW OF OHIO R.
NY 12
PA 8    7
RI 4
CT 9
NJ 7
DE 3
VA 21
MD    R 5
F 5
KY 4
NC 8    4
TN 3
SC 8
GA 4

- Why was the election of 1800 a key event in American history?
- What voting patterns emerged in the election of 1800?
- How did Congress break the tie between Thomas Jefferson and Aaron Burr?

Before the Federalists turned over power on March 4, 1801, President Adams and Congress passed the Judiciary Act of 1801. Adams intended it to ensure Federalist control of the judicial system by creating sixteen federal circuit courts, with a new judge for each. It also reduced the number of Supreme Court justices from six to five in an effort to deprive the next president of appointing a new member. Before he left office, Adams appointed Federalists to all the new positions. The Federalists, quipped Jefferson, had "retired into the judiciary as a stronghold." They never again would exercise significant political power.

**A NEW ERA** The election of 1800 did not resolve the fundamental political tensions that had emerged between ardent nationalists like Adams and Hamilton and those like Jefferson and Madison who clung to ideals of states' rights and an agriculture-based economy. In fact, the election further divided the young republic into warring political factions and marked a major turning point in the nation's history. It was the first time one party had relinquished presidential power to the opposition party, and it was the only election that pitted a sitting president (Adams) against his own vice president (Jefferson).

Jefferson's hard-fought victory signaled the emergence of a new, more democratic political culture dominated by bitterly divided parties and wider public participation. Before and immediately after independence, socially prominent families—the "rich, the able, and the wellborn"—still dominated political life. However, the political battles of the late 1790s, culminating with Jefferson's election, established the right of "common" men to play a more active role in governing the young republic. With the gradual elimination of the requirement that citizens must own property to vote, the electorate expanded enormously in the early nineteenth century.

Jefferson called his election the "Revolution of 1800," for it marked the triumph of the Republican party and the slaveholding South. Three Republican slaveholders from Virginia—Jefferson, James Madison, and James Monroe—would hold the presidency for the next twenty-four years.

A bitter John Adams was so upset by his defeat (as well as by the death of his alcoholic son Charles) that he refused to participate in Jefferson's inauguration in the new federal capital in Washington, D.C. He and Jefferson would not communicate for the next twelve years.

As Adams returned to work on his Massachusetts farm with his wife, Abigail, he told his eldest son, John Quincy, who would become the nation's sixth president, that anyone governing the United States "has a hard, laborious, and unhappy life." Jefferson would soon feel the same way.

# CHAPTER REVIEW

## Summary

- **Confederation Government**   Despite its many weaknesses, the national government created by the *Articles of Confederation* managed to construct important alliances during the Revolutionary War, help win the War of Independence, and negotiate the Treaty of Paris (1783). It created executive departments and established, through the *Northwest Ordinance (1787)*, the process by which new western territories would be organized and governments formed before they applied for statehood. Yet the Articles of Confederation did not allow the national government to raise taxes to fund its debts. *Shays's Rebellion (1786–1787)* made many Americans fear that such uprisings would eventually destroy the new republic unless the United States formed a stronger national government.

- **Constitutional Convention**   Delegates gathered at the convention in Philadelphia in 1787 to revise the existing government, but almost immediately they decided to scrap the Articles of Confederation and start over. An entirely new document emerged, creating a system called *federalism* in which a strong national government with *separation of powers* among executive, legislative, and judicial branches functioned alongside state governments with clearly designated responsibilities. Arguments about how best to ensure that the rights of individual states were protected and that "the people" were represented in the new Congress were resolved by establishing a Senate, with equal representation for each state, and a House of Representatives, the number of whose delegates was determined by population counts.

- **Ratification of the Constitution**   Ratification of the Constitution was hotly contested. *Anti-Federalists,* such as Virginia's Patrick Henry, opposed the new structure of government because the absence of a bill of rights would lead to a loss of individual and states' rights. To sway New York State toward ratification, Alexander Hamilton, James Madison, and John Jay wrote *The Federalist Papers*. Ratification became possible only when the Federalists promised to add a *Bill of Rights (1791)*.

- **Federalists versus Republicans**   Alexander Hamilton and the Federalists wanted to create a diverse economy in which agriculture was balanced by trade, finance, and manufacturing. As secretary of the Treasury, Hamilton crafted a federal budget that funded the national debt through tariff and tax revenues, and he created a national bank, the first *Bank of the United States (1791)*. Thomas Jefferson and others, known as *Jeffersonian Republicans,* worried that Hamilton's plans violated the Constitution and made the federal government too powerful. They envisioned a nation dominated by farmers and planters where the rights of states would be protected against federal power.

- **Trouble Abroad**   During the *French Revolution*, George Washington's policy of neutrality violated the terms of the 1778 treaty with France. At the same time, Americans sharply criticized *Jay's Treaty (1794)* with the British for giving too much away. French warships began seizing British and American ships, and an undeclared war was under way. Federalists supported Washington's approach, while Republicans were more supportive of France.

## CHRONOLOGY

| | |
|---|---|
| **1781** | Articles of Confederation take effect |
| **1783** | Treaty of Paris ends the War of Independence |
| **1786–1787** | Shays's Rebellion |
| **1787** | Northwest Ordinance |
| | The Constitutional Convention is held in Philadelphia |
| **1787–1788** | *The Federalist Papers* are published |
| **1789** | President George Washington is inaugurated |
| **1791** | Bill of Rights is ratified |
| | Bank of the United States is created |
| **1793** | Washington issues a proclamation of neutrality |
| **1794** | Jay's Treaty is negotiated with England |
| | Whiskey Rebellion in Pennsylvania |
| | U.S. Army defeats Western Confederacy of Indian nations in the Battle of Fallen Timbers |
| **1796** | John Adams is elected president |
| **1798** | Alien and Sedition Acts are passed |
| **1800** | Thomas Jefferson is elected president |

## KEY TERMS

federalism p. 225

Articles of Confederation p. 225

Northwest Ordinance (1787) p. 228

Shays's Rebellion (1786–1787) p. 232

separation of powers p. 236

anti-Federalists p. 241

*The Federalist Papers* p. 242

Jeffersonian Republicans p. 246

Bill of Rights (1791) p. 248

Bank of the United States (1791) p. 255

French Revolution p. 257

Jay's Treaty (1794) p. 260

Whiskey Rebellion (1794) p. 261

Alien and Sedition Acts of 1798 p. 267

election of 1800 p. 269

 INQUIZITIVE

**Go to InQuizitive to see what you've learned—and learn what you've missed—with personalized feedback along the way.**

# 7 The Early Republic

## 1800–1815

***We Owe Allegiance to No Crown* (ca. 1814)** The War of 1812 generated a renewed spirit of nationalism, inspiring Philadelphia sign painter John Archibald Woodside to create this patriotic painting.

W hen President Thomas Jefferson took office in 1801, the United States and its western territories reached from the Atlantic Ocean to the Mississippi River. Nine of ten Americans lived on farms, but entrepreneurs were rapidly developing a worldwide commercial economy. Everywhere people were on the make and on the move, leading one newspaper to claim that what made America different from other nations was "the almost universal ambition to get forward." The desire for profits was, according to Congressman Henry Clay, "a passion as unconquerable as any with which nature has endowed us. You may attempt to regulate [it]—[but] you cannot destroy it."

Intoxicated by their freedom, Americans were a people of possibilities in a land of dreams. They excelled at westward expansion, economic development, rapid population growth, and intense political activity because they believed in a brighter future. Former president John Adams observed that "there is no people on earth so ambitious as the people of America . . . because the lowest can aspire as freely as the highest."

Thomas Jefferson described the United States in the early nineteenth century as an "empire of liberty" spreading westward. In 1800, people eager to own their own farms bought 67,000 acres of government-owned land; the next year, they bought 498,000 acres. Native Americans resisted the invasion of their ancestral lands but ultimately succumbed to a federal government (and army) determined to relocate them.

Most whites, however, were more concerned with seizing their own economic opportunities than the plight of Native Americans. Isaac Weld, a British visitor, remarked that Americans were "always on the lookout for something

## focus questions

**1.** What were the major domestic political developments during Thomas Jefferson's administration?

**2.** Describe how foreign events affected the United States during the Jefferson and Madison administrations.

**3.** What were the primary causes of the American decision to declare war on Great Britain in 1812?

**4.** What were the significant outcomes of the War of 1812 on the United States?

better or more profitable." Restless mobility and impatient striving soon came to define the American way of life.

## JEFFERSONIAN REPUBLICANISM

The 1800 presidential campaign between Federalists and Jeffersonian Republicans had been so fiercely contested that some predicted civil war as the House of Representatives decided the outcome of the election. On March 4, 1801, however, fifty-seven-year-old Thomas Jefferson was inaugurated without incident. It was the first democratic election in modern history that resulted in the orderly transfer of power from one political party to another.

Jefferson's installation marked the emerging dominance of the nation's political life by Republicans—and Virginians. The nation's most populous state, Virginia supplied a quarter of the Republican congressmen in the House of Representatives that convened in early 1801.

Politics in the young republic was becoming increasingly sectional. Another Federalist, former secretary of state Timothy Pickering of Massachusetts, acknowledged that the northeastern states, where Federalism was centered, could no longer "reconcile their habits, views, and interests with those of the South and West," two fast-growing regions that were beginning to rule the nation with "a rod of iron."

Jefferson was the first president inaugurated in the new national capital of Washington, District of Columbia. The unfinished city of barely 3,000 people was crisscrossed with muddy avenues connecting a few buildings clustered around two unfinished centers, Capitol Hill and the "Executive Mansion." (It would not be called the White House until 1901.) Cows grazed along the Mall while pigs prowled the unpaved streets. Workers, many of them enslaved, had barely completed building the Capitol and the Executive Mansion before Jefferson was sworn in.

**THE "PEOPLE'S PRESIDENT"**   During his inauguration, Jefferson emphasized his connection to the "plain and simple" ways of the "common" people. Instead of wearing a ceremonial sword and riding in a horse-drawn carriage, as George Washington and John Adams had done, Jefferson left his boardinghouse on New Jersey Avenue and walked to the Capitol building, escorted by members of Congress and Virginia militiamen. He read his inaugural address in a "femininely soft," high-pitched voice, then took the presidential oath administered by Chief Justice John Marshall, his cousin, with whom he shared a cordial hatred.

Jefferson's deliberate display of **republican simplicity** set the tone for his administration. He wanted Americans to notice the difference between the monarchical style of the Federalists and the simplicity and frugality of the Republicans.

In his eloquent inaugural address, Jefferson imagined America as "a rising nation, spread over a wide and fruitful land, traversing all the seas with the productions of their industry, engaged in commerce" across the globe. Although determined to overturn many Federalist policies and programs, he urged Americans to work together. "We are all Republicans—we are all Federalists," Jefferson stressed, noting that "every difference of opinion is not a difference of principle."

It was a splendid message, but Jefferson's appeal for unity proved illusory, in part because of his fierce partisanship and bitter anti-Federalist prejudices. In a letter to a British friend, Jefferson said he feared that Federalists, a "herd of traitors," wanted to destroy "the liberties of the people" and convert the republic into a monarchy.

**A MORE DEMOCRATIC AMERICA**  Jefferson's inauguration ushered in a more democratic political culture in which common people played a much larger role. During and after the Revolutionary War, an increasing proportion of white males, especially small farmers, wage laborers, artisans, mechanics, and apprentices, gained the right to vote or hold office as states reduced or eliminated requirements that voters and candidates own a specified amount of property.

Many among the founding generation of leaders in both political parties worried that men of humble origins, some of whom were uneducated and illiterate, were replacing the social and political elite ("natural aristocracy") in the state legislatures. "Since the war," a Massachusetts Federalist complained, "blustering ignorant men . . . have been attempting to push themselves into office." A Virginian noted the rising evidence of the "turbulence and follies of democracy."

As the nineteenth century unfolded, voters were not content to be governed solely by "their betters"; they wanted to do the governing themselves. And indeed, more than half of the members of the Republican-controlled Congress elected in 1800 were first-time legislators. Federalist John Adams so detested the democratic forces transforming politics and social life that he despaired for the nation's future: "Oh my Country," he moaned, "how I mourn over . . . thy contempt of Wisdom and Virtue and overweening admiration of fools and knaves! the never failing effects of *democracy!*"

**A CONTRADICTORY GENIUS** Thomas Jefferson, who owned hundreds of slaves, was a unique bundle of contradictions. He was progressive and enlightened in some areas, self-serving and hypocritical in others. He loathed political skullduggery, yet was a master at it. He championed government frugality, yet nearly went bankrupt buying expensive wines, paintings, silverware, and furniture. Jefferson, who had written in the Declaration of Independence that "all men are created equal," also bought, bred, flogged, and sold slaves while calling slavery "an abominable crime" and a "hideous blot" on civilization.

Jefferson wrote about the evils of racial mixing because of the "inferior" attributes of African Americans, yet after his wife Martha died, he used her half-sister, a beautiful mulatto slave named Sarah "Sally" Hemings, as his concubine; she gave birth to six of his children. For Jefferson, Hemings became what a friend called his "substitute for a wife" in a plantation world where complicated power relationships were hidden behind a veil of silence. Political foes used Jefferson's relationship with Sally against him, but he never responded.

Like George Washington, Jefferson was a wealthy planter with expensive tastes. He was also an inventive genius of staggering learning and exceptional abilities. As a self-trained architect, he designed the state capitol in Richmond, Virginia, as well as his thirty-three-room mountaintop mansion near Charlottesville called *Monticello* (Little Mountain). He was an expert in constitutional law, civil liberties, and political philosophy; religion and ethics; classical history; progressive education; natural science, paleontology, and mathematics; music and linguistics; and farming, gardening, cooking, and wine.

Yet while Jefferson lived the luxurious life, he championed the "honest heart" of the common people. His faith in expanding the number of eligible voters and his determination to reduce the power of the national government opened a more democratic era in American life.

**JEFFERSON IN OFFICE** For all his natural shyness and admitted weakness as a public speaker, Thomas Jefferson was the first president to pursue the role of party leader, and he openly cultivated congressional support at frequent social gatherings.

In his cabinet, the leading figures were Secretary of State James Madison, his best friend and political ally, and Secretary of the Treasury Albert Gallatin, a Pennsylvania Republican whose financial skills had won him the respect of Federalists and Republicans alike.

In filling lesser offices, however, Jefferson often succumbed to pressure from Republicans to remove Federalists, only to discover that there were few qualified candidates to replace some of them. When Gallatin asked if he might appoint women to some posts, Jefferson revealed the limits of his

**The Capitol building** This 1806 watercolor was painted by the building's architect, Benjamin Henry Latrobe, and inscribed to Thomas Jefferson. A prominent dome would be added later, after the building was damaged in the War of 1812.

liberalism: "The appointment of a woman to office is an innovation for which the public is not prepared, nor am I."

*MARBURY V. MADISON* In one area—the federal judiciary—the new president decided to remove most of the offices altogether, in part because the court system was the only branch of the government still controlled by Federalists. In 1802, at Jefferson's urging, the Republican-controlled Congress repealed the Judiciary Act of 1801, which the Federalists had passed just before the transfer of power to the Jeffersonian Republicans. The Judiciary Act had ensured Federalist control of the judicial system by creating sixteen federal circuit courts and appointing—for life—a Federalist judge for each. The controversial effort to repeal the judgeships sparked the landmark case of *Marbury v. Madison* **(1803).**

The case went to the Supreme Court, presided over by Chief Justice John Marshall, a Virginia Federalist who had served in the army during the Revolutionary War, attended law school at the College of William and Mary, and become a respected Richmond attorney. In 1788, Marshall helped Madison convince Virginians to ratify the U.S. Constitution. He later served in Congress and became secretary of state under President Adams, who appointed him chief justice early in 1801.

Blessed with a keen intellect and an analytical mind, Marshall was a fierce critic and lifelong enemy of Jefferson, whom he considered a war-shirking aristocrat who prized the states over the national government.

In 1801, John Jay, the first chief justice, admitted that the Supreme Court did not have "the energy, weight, and dignity" necessary to serve its role in balancing the powers of Congress and the presidency. Jefferson and the Republicans liked it that way. Marshall, however, set out to strengthen the judiciary. By the time he completed thirty-five years of service on the Supreme Court (1801–1835), he had made it the most powerful court in the world, distinctive for its emphasis on protecting individual rights while insisting upon the supremacy of the national government over the states, a principle that put him at odds with Jefferson.

The Marbury case involved the appointment of Maryland Federalist William Marbury as justice of the peace in the District of Columbia. Marbury's letter of appointment (called a commission), signed by President Adams two days before he left office, was still undelivered when James Madison took office as secretary of state, and Jefferson directed Madison to withhold it. Marbury then sued for a court order directing Madison to deliver his commission.

In the unanimous *Marbury v. Madison* ruling, Marshall and the Court held that Marbury deserved his judgeship. Marshall, however, denied that the Court had jurisdiction in the case. The Federal Judiciary Act of 1789, which gave the Court authority in such proceedings, was unconstitutional, Marshall ruled, because the Constitution specified that the Court should have original jurisdiction only in cases involving foreign ambassadors or nations. The Court, therefore, could issue no order in the case.

With one bold stroke, Marshall had elevated the stature of the Court by reprimanding Jefferson while avoiding an awkward confrontation with an administration that might have defied his order. More important, the ruling subtly struck down a federal law, the Judiciary Act of 1789, because it violated provisions of the Constitution, the "fundamental and paramount law of the nation." Marshall stressed that the Supreme Court was "emphatically" empowered "to say what the law is," even if it meant overruling both Congress and the president.

The *Marbury* decision granted the Supreme Court a power not mentioned in the Constitution: the right of what came to be called *judicial review*, whereby the Court determines whether acts of Congress (and the presidency) are constitutional. Marshall established that the Supreme Court was the final authority in all constitutional interpretations.

Jefferson fumed over the "irregular" ruling. Giving judges "the right to decide which laws are constitutional, and what not," he wrote Abigail Adams, "would make the judiciary a despotic branch."

Jefferson, however, would lose that argument. Although the Court did not declare another federal law unconstitutional for fifty-four years, it has since struck down more than 150 acts of Congress and more than 1,100 "unconstitutional" acts of state legislatures, all in an effort to protect individual liberties and civil rights. Marshall essentially created American constitutional law, making the unelected, life-tenured justices of the Supreme Court more-effective allies of a strong national government than even the framers had imagined.

**JEFFERSON'S ECONOMIC POLICIES** President Jefferson's first term did include some triumphs. Surprisingly, he did not dismantle Alexander Hamilton's Federalist economic program. Instead, following the advice of Treasury Secretary Albert Gallatin, Jefferson, who like many other southern planters never understood the function of banks, learned to accept the national bank as essential to economic growth.

Jefferson, however, rejected Hamilton's argument that a federal debt was a national "blessing" because it gave bankers and investors who bought government bonds a financial stake in the success of the new republic. If the debt were not eliminated, Jefferson told Gallatin, "we shall be committed to the English career of debt, corruption, and rottenness, closing with revolution."

To pay down the debt, Jefferson slashed the federal budget. He fired all federal tax collectors and cut the military budget in half, saying that state militias and small navy gunboats provided adequate protection against foreign enemies. Jefferson's was the first national government in history to *reduce* its own scope and power.

Jefferson also repealed the whiskey tax that Hamilton and George Washington had implemented in 1791. In doing so, he admitted that he had a peculiar affection for the "men from the Western side of the mountains"—grain farmers and backwoods distillers for whom whiskey was often the primary source of income.

The nation's prosperous economy helped the federal budget absorb the loss of the whiskey taxes. In addition, revenues from federal tariffs on imports rose with the growing European trade, and the sale of government-owned western lands soared as Americans streamed westward.

**THE BARBARY PIRATES** Upon assuming the presidency, Jefferson promised "peace, commerce, and honest friendship with all nations," but some nations preferred war. On the Barbary Coast of North Africa, the Islamic rulers of Morocco, Algiers, Tunis, and Tripoli had for centuries preyed upon unarmed European and American merchant ships. The U.S. government made numerous blackmail payments to the **Barbary pirates** in exchange for captured American merchant ships and crews.

***Burning of the Frigate* Philadelphia**  Lieutenant Stephen Decatur set fire to the captured *Philadelphia* during the United States' standoff with Tripoli over the enslavement of American sailors in North Africa.

In 1801, however, the ruler of Tripoli upped his blackmail demands and declared war on the United States. Jefferson sent warships to blockade Tripoli, and a sporadic naval war dragged on until 1805, punctuated in 1804 by the notable exploits of Lieutenant Stephen Decatur, who slipped into Tripoli Harbor by night and set fire to the frigate *Philadelphia,* which had been captured after it ran aground. A force of U.S. Marines marched 500 miles across the desert to assault Derna, Tripoli's second largest town, a feat highlighted in the Marine Corps hymn ("to the shores of Tripoli"). The Tripoli ruler finally agreed to a $60,000 ransom and released the *Philadelphia*'s crew. It was still blackmail (called "tribute" in the nineteenth century), but less than the $300,000 the pirates had demanded and much less than the cost of an outright war.

## WESTERN EXPANSION

Where Alexander Hamilton always faced east, looking to Great Britain for his model of national greatness, Thomas Jefferson looked to the west for his inspiration, across the mountains and even across the Mississippi River. Only by expanding westward, he believed, could America avoid the social turmoil and misery common in the cities of Europe—and remain a nation primarily of self-sufficient farmers.

To ensure continuing westward settlement, Jefferson and the Republicans strove to reduce the cost of federal lands. Ohio's admission to the Union in 1803 increased the number of states to seventeen. Government land sales west of the Appalachian Mountains skyrocketed as settlers shoved Indians aside and established homesteads. Jefferson, however, wanted more western land, and in 1803 a stroke of good fortune allowed him to double the new nation's size.

**THE LOUISIANA PURCHASE** In 1801, American diplomats in Europe heard rumors that Spain had been forced to transfer its huge Louisiana province back to France, now led by Napoléon Bonaparte. The French First Consul had a massive ego, remarkable self-confidence, and a single-minded hunger for victory and power. Short of stature but a giant on the battlefield, Napoléon had gone from penniless immigrant to army general by the age of twenty-six. He was a military genius, the most feared ruler in the world, conqueror of Egypt and Italy. After taking control of the French government in 1799, Napoléon set out to restore his country's North American empire (Canada and Louisiana) that had been lost to Great Britain in 1763.

President Jefferson referred to Napoléon as both a "scoundrel" and "a gigantic force" threatening the future of the United States. A weak Spain controlling the territory west of the Mississippi River could have been tolerated, Jefferson explained, but Napoleonic France in control of the Mississippi Valley would lead to "eternal friction" and eventually war.

To prevent France from seizing the Mississippi River, Jefferson sent New Yorker Robert R. Livingston to Paris in 1801 as ambassador to France. Livingston's primary objective was to acquire the strategic port city of New Orleans, situated at the mouth of the Mississippi River. Jefferson told Livingston that purchasing New Orleans and West Florida (the territory along the Gulf coast from Pensacola, Florida, to New Orleans) was of absolute importance, for "the day that France takes possession of New Orleans, . . . we must marry ourselves to the British fleet and nation" for protection.

Over the years, New Orleans had become a dynamic crossroads where some 50,000 people of different nationalities readily intermingled, garnering huge profits from the vast amount of goods floating down the Mississippi. For years, Americans living in Tennessee and Kentucky had threatened to secede if the federal government did not ensure that they could send their crops and goods downriver to New Orleans.

In early 1803, Jefferson grew so concerned about the stalled negotiations in Paris that he sent James Monroe, his trusted friend and Virginia neighbor, to assist the sixty-six-year-old Livingston. "All eyes, all hopes, are now fixed on you," Jefferson told Monroe.

No sooner had Monroe arrived than Napoléon surprisingly offered to sell not just New Orleans but *all* of the immense, unmapped Louisiana Territory, from the Mississippi River west to the Rocky Mountains and from the Canadian border south to the Gulf of Mexico.

The unpredictable Napoléon had reversed himself because his large army on the Caribbean island of Saint-Domingue (Haiti) had been decimated by epidemics of malaria and yellow fever and by a massive slave revolt led by Touissaint L'Ouverture, who had proclaimed the Republic of Haiti. It was the first successful slave rebellion in history, and it panicked slaveholders in the southern states who feared that news of the revolt would spread to America.

Napoléon had tried to regain control of Saint-Domingue because it was a profitable source of coffee and sugar. He also had hoped to connect New Orleans and Haiti as a first step in expanding France's North American trading empire. But after losing more than 24,000 soldiers to disease and warfare, Napoléon decided to cut his losses by selling the Louisiana Territory to the United States and using the proceeds to finance his "inevitable" next war with Great Britain.

By the Treaty of Cession, dated May 2, 1803, the United States agreed to pay the modest sum of $15 million (3¢ an acre) for the entire Louisiana Territory. When Livingston and Monroe asked Charles-Maurice de Talleyrand, Napoléon's negotiator, about the precise extent of the territory they were buying, the Frenchman replied: "I can give you no direction. You have made a noble bargain for yourselves. I suppose you will make the most of it." A delighted Livingston said that "from this day the United States take their place among the powers of the first rank." He called the land transfer the "noblest work of our whole lives."

The arrival of the signed treaty in Washington, D.C., presented Jefferson, who for years had criticized the Federalists for stretching the meaning of the Constitution, with a political dilemma. Nowhere did the Constitution mention the purchase of territory. Was such an action legal?

In the end, Jefferson's desire to double the size of the republic trumped his concerns about an unconstitutional exercise of executive power. Acquiring the Louisiana Territory, the president explained, would serve "the immediate interests of our Western citizens" and promote "the peace and security of the nation in general" by removing the French threat and creating a protective buffer separating the United States from the rest of the world. Jefferson also imagined that the region might be a place to relocate Indian nations or freed slaves, since he feared a multiracial society.

New England Federalists strongly opposed the purchase. Fisher Ames of Massachusetts argued that the Louisiana Territory was a waste of money, a "wilderness unpeopled with any beings except wolves and wandering Indians." Ames and others feared that adding the vast territory would weaken New England and the Federalist party, since the new western states were likely to be settled by wage laborers from New England seeking cheap land and by southern slaveholders, all of whom were Jeffersonian Republicans. As a newspaper editorialized, "Will [Jefferson and the] Republicans, who glory in their sacred regard to the rights of human nature, purchase an *immense wilderness* for the purpose of cultivating it with the labor of slaves?"

In a reversal of traditional stances, Federalists found themselves arguing for strict construction of the Constitution in opposing the Louisiana Purchase. "We are to give money of which we have too little for land of which we already have too much," argued a Bostonian in the *Columbian Centinel*. Eager to close the deal, Jefferson called a special session of Congress on October 17, 1803, at which the Senate ratified the treaty by a vote of 26–6. On December 20, 1803, U.S. officials took formal possession of the Louisiana Territory. The purchase included 875,000 square miles of land (529,402,880 acres). Six states in their entirety, and most or part of nine more, would be carved out of the Louisiana Purchase, from Louisiana north to Minnesota and west to Montana.

The **Louisiana Purchase** was the most significant event of Jefferson's presidency and one of the most important developments in American history. It spurred western exploration and expansion, and it enticed cotton growers to settle in the Old Southwest—Alabama, Mississippi, and Louisiana.

**THE LEWIS AND CLARK EXPEDITION (1804–1806)** To learn more about the Louisiana Territory's geography, plants, and animals, as well as its prospects for trade and agriculture, Jefferson asked Congress to fund an expedition to find the most "practicable water communication across this continent." The president then appointed two friends, army captains Meriwether Lewis and William Clark, to lead what came to be known as the **Lewis and Clark expedition**. The twenty-nine-year-old Lewis was Jefferson's private secretary. Jefferson admired his "boldness, enterprise, and discretion." Thirty-three-year-old Clark, from Louisville, Kentucky, was an accomplished frontiersman and "as brave as Caesar."

On a rainy May morning in 1804, Lewis and Clark's "Corps of Discovery," numbering about thirty "stout" men, set out from Wood River, a village near the former French town of St. Louis. They traveled in two large dugout canoes (called *pirogues*) and one large, flat-bottomed, single-masted keelboat filled with food, weapons, medicine, and gifts for the Indians. They traveled up the

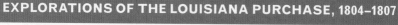

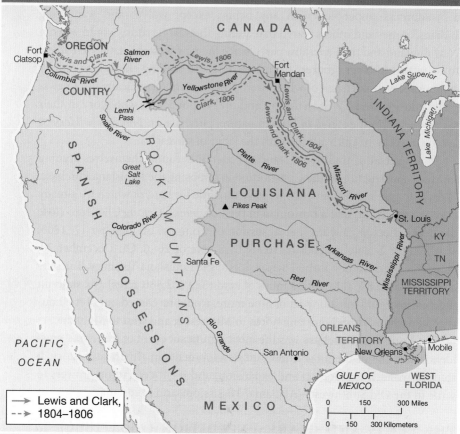

EXPLORATIONS OF THE LOUISIANA PURCHASE, 1804–1807

- How did the United States acquire the Louisiana Purchase?
- What was the mission of Lewis and Clark's expedition?
- What were the consequences of Lewis and Clark's widely circulated reports about the western territory?

Mississippi to the mouth of the treacherous Missouri River, where they added a dozen more men before proceeding through some of the most rugged territory in North America. Unsure of where they were going and what or whom they might encounter, they were eager to discover if the Missouri made its way to the Pacific Ocean.

Six months later, near the Mandan Sioux villages in what would become Bismarck, North Dakota, the Corps of Discovery built Fort Mandan and wintered in relative comfort, sending downriver a barge loaded with maps, soil samples, the skins and skeletons of weasels, wolves, and antelope, and live specimens of prairie dogs and magpies, previously unknown in America.

In the spring of 1805, the Corps of Discovery added two guides: a French fur trader and his remarkable wife, a Shoshone woman named Sacagawea ("Bird Woman"). In appreciation for Lewis and Clark's help in delivering her baby boy, Baptiste, Sacagawea provided crucial assistance as a guide, translator, and negotiator as they explored the Upper Missouri and encountered various Native Americans, most of whom were "hospitable, honest, and sincere people."

From Fort Mandan, the adventurers headed out, crossing the Rocky Mountains and descending the Snake and Columbia Rivers to the Pacific Ocean, where they arrived in November. "Ocean in view! O! the joy!" Clark wrote in his journal. Near the future site of Astoria, Oregon, at the mouth of the Columbia River, they built Fort Clatsop, where they spent a cold, rainy winter.

**Sacagawea** Of the many memorials devoted to Sacagawea, this statue by artist Alice Cooper was unveiled at the 1905 Lewis and Clark Centennial Exposition.

In the spring of 1806 they headed back to St. Louis, having been forced to eat their dogs and horses. Tough characters all, they had weathered blizzards, broiling sun, fierce rapids, pelting hail, grizzly bears, injuries, illnesses, and swarms of mosquitoes. "I have been wet and as cold in every part as I ever was in my life," Clark noted. "Indeed I was at one time fearful my feet would freeze in the thin moccasins which I wore." Only one member of the group died, and that was because of a ruptured appendix.

The expedition, which lasted twenty-eight months and covered some 8,000 miles, returned with remarkably extensive journals that described their experiences and observations while detailing some 180 plants and 125 animals. Their splendid maps attracted traders and trappers to the region and led the United States to claim the Oregon Country (the entire Pacific Northwest) by right of discovery and exploration.

POLITICAL SCHEMES The Lewis and Clark expedition and the Louisiana Purchase strengthened Thomas Jefferson's already solid support in the South and West. In New England, however, Federalists panicked because they assumed that new states carved out of the Louisiana Territory would be dominated by Jeffersonian Republicans. To protect their interests, Federalists hatched a scheme to link New York politically to New England by trying to elect Vice President Aaron Burr, Jefferson's ambitious Republican rival, as governor of New York. Burr chose to drop his Republican affiliation and run as an independent candidate.

Several leading Federalists opposed the scheme, however. Alexander Hamilton urged Federalists not to vote for Burr, calling him "a dangerous man, and one who ought not to be trusted with the reins of government." Burr ended up losing the election to the Republican candidate, who had been endorsed by Jefferson.

A furious Burr blamed Hamilton's "base slanders" for his defeat and challenged him to a duel "on the field of honor." At dawn on July 11, 1804, the two men met near Weehawken, New Jersey, on the Hudson River above New York City. Hamilton, whose son had been killed in a duel at the same location, fired first but intentionally missed as a demonstration of his religious and moral principles, knowing full well that it might cost him his life. Burr showed no such scruples. He shot Hamilton in the hip; the bullet ripped through his liver and lodged in his spine. He died the next day. Burr, who was still the nation's vice president, was charged with murder. He fled to South Carolina, where his daughter lived.

JEFFERSON REELECTED In the meantime, the presidential campaign of 1804 began. A congressional caucus of Republicans renominated Jefferson and chose George Clinton of New York as the vice presidential candidate. To avoid the problems associated with parties running multiple candidates for the presidency, in 1803, Congress had ratified the Twelfth Amendment to the Constitution, stipulating that the members of the electoral college must use separate ballots to vote for the president and vice president.

Given Jefferson's first-term achievements, the Federalist candidates, South Carolinian Charles C. Pinckney and New Yorker Rufus King, never had a chance. Jefferson had accomplished much: the Louisiana Purchase, a prosperous economy, and a reduced federal government budget and national debt.

A Massachusetts Republican claimed that the United States was "never more respected abroad. The people were never more happy at home." Jefferson and Clinton won 162 of 176 electoral votes.

**DIVISIONS IN THE REPUBLICAN PARTY** Jefferson's land-slide victory, however, created problems within his own party. Freed from strong opposition—Federalists made up only a quarter of the new Congress in 1805—the Republican majority began to divide into warring factions, one calling itself the Jeffersonian or Nationalist Republicans, and the other, the anti-Jeffersonian Old Republicans.

Fiery Virginian John Randolph was initially a loyal Jeffersonian, but over time he emerged as the most colorful of the radically conservative "Old Republicans"—a group mostly of southern agrarian political purists for whom protecting states' rights was more important than the need for a strong national government. Randolph, for example, broke with Jefferson over the Louisiana Purchase.

The imperious Randolph, another of the president's cousins, was the Senate's most flamboyant character. He often entered the chamber wearing a long white coat and white boots with spurs, trailed by a hunting hound that would sleep under his desk. He lubricated his speeches with gulps of whiskey and described himself as an old-fashioned "aristocrat. I love liberty. I hate equality."

Randolph and other Old Republicans were best known for what they opposed: any compromise with the Federalists, any expansion of federal authority at the expense of states' rights, any new taxes or tariffs, and any change in the South's agrarian way of life rooted in slavery.

The Jeffersonian Republicans, on the other hand, were more moderate, pragmatic, and nationalistic. They were willing to compromise their states' rights principles to maintain national tariffs on imports, preserve a national bank, and stretch the "implied powers" of the Constitution to accommodate the Louisiana Purchase. Such compromises, said Randolph, were catastrophic. "The old Republican party," he claimed, "is already ruined, past redemption."

**THE BURR CONSPIRACY** Meanwhile, Aaron Burr continued to connive and scheme. After the controversy over his duel with Alexander Hamilton subsided, he tried to carve out his own personal empire in the West. What came to be known as the Burr Conspiracy was hatched when Burr and General James Wilkinson, an old friend then serving as senior general of the U.S. Army, plotted to use a well-armed force of volunteers to separate part of the Louisiana Territory from the Union. The plan was then to declare it an independent republic, with New Orleans as its capital and Burr as its ruler. Burr claimed that "the people of the western country were ready for revolt."

In late 1806, Burr floated down the Ohio and Mississippi Rivers toward New Orleans with 100 volunteers, only to have Wilkinson turn on him and alert Jefferson to the scheme. The president ordered that Burr be arrested. Militiamen captured Burr in February 1807 and took him to Richmond, Virginia, where, in August, he was tried for treason before Chief Justice John Marshall.

Jefferson was hellbent on seeing Burr hanged, claiming that he had tried to separate "the western states from us, of adding Mexico to them, and of placing himself at their head." In the end, however, Burr was acquitted because of a lack of evidence. Marshall had instructed the jury that a verdict of treason required an "act of war" against the United States confirmed by at least two witnesses.

Jefferson was disgusted. "It now appears we have no law but the will of the judge," he wrote a friend. The president considered proposing a constitutional amendment to limit the power of the judiciary and even thought about asking Congress to impeach Marshall. In the end, however, he did nothing. With further charges pending, the slippery Burr skipped bail and took refuge first in England, then in France. He returned to America in 1812 and resumed practicing law in New York.

**ENDING THE SLAVE TRADE** While shrinking the federal budget and reducing the national debt, Jefferson signed a landmark bill that outlawed the importation of enslaved Africans into the United States, in part because southerners had come to believe that African-born slaves were prone to revolt. The new law took effect on January 1, 1808. At the time, South Carolina was the only state that still permitted the purchase of enslaved Africans. For years to come, however, illegal global trafficking in African slaves would continue; as many as 300,000 were smuggled into the United States between 1808 and 1861.

# War in Europe

In the spring of 1803, soon after completing the sale of Louisiana to America, Napoléon Bonaparte declared war on Great Britain. The conflict would last eleven years and eventually involve all of Europe. Most Americans wanted to remain neutral, but the British and French were determined to keep that from happening.

**NAVAL HARASSMENT** During 1805, the spreading war reached a stalemate: the French army controlled most of Europe, and the British navy dominated the seas. In May 1806, Britain issued a series of declarations called

Orders in Council that imposed a naval blockade of the European coast to prevent merchant ships from other nations, including the United States, from making port in France. Although British leaders recognized America's independence in principle, they were eager to humble and humiliate the upstart republic by asserting their dominance over Atlantic trade.

Soon British warships began seizing American merchant ships bound for France. An angry Congress responded by passing the Non-Importation Act, which banned the importation of British goods. In early 1807, Napoléon announced that French warships would blockade the ports of Great Britain. The British responded that they would no longer allow foreign ships to trade with the French-controlled islands in the Caribbean. Soon thereafter, British warships appeared along the American coast and began stopping and searching U.S. merchant vessels as they headed for the Caribbean or Europe.

The tense situation posed a dilemma for American shippers. If they agreed to British demands to stop trading with the French, the French would retaliate by seizing U.S. vessels headed to and from Great Britain. If they agreed to French demands that they stop trading with the British, the British would seize American ships headed to and from France. Some American merchants decided to risk becoming victims of the Anglo-French war—and many paid a high price for their pursuit of overseas profits. During 1807, British and French warships captured hundreds of American ships.

**IMPRESSMENT** For American sailors, the danger on the high seas was heightened by the practice of *impressment*, whereby British warships stopped U.S. vessels, boarded them, and kidnapped sailors they claimed were British citizens. American merchant ships attracted British deserters because they paid more than twice as much as did the Royal Navy. Fully half the sailors on American ships, about 9,000 men, had been born in Britain.

The British often did not bother to determine the citizenship of those they "impressed" into service. As a British

**Preparation for War to Defend Commerce** Shipbuilders, like those pictured here constructing the *Philadelphia*, played an important role in America's early wars.

officer explained, "It is my duty to keep my ship manned, & I will do so wherever I find men that speak the same language with me." Between 1803 and 1811, some 6,200 American sailors were "impressed" into the British navy.

**THE *CHESAPEAKE* INCIDENT (1807)**  The crisis boiled over on June 22, 1807, when the British warship HMS *Leopard* stopped a smaller U.S. vessel, the *Chesapeake*, eight miles off the Virginia coast. After the *Chesapeake's* captain refused to allow the British to search his ship for English deserters, the *Leopard* opened fire without warning, killing three Americans and wounding eighteen. A search party then boarded the *Chesapeake* and seized four men, one of whom, an English deserter, was hanged.

The attack on the *Chesapeake* was both an act of war and a national insult. Public anger was so great that President Jefferson could have declared war on the spot. "We have never, on any occasion, witnessed . . . such a thirst for revenge," the *Washington Federalist* reported.

In early July, Jefferson met with his cabinet before issuing a proclamation banning all British warships from American waters. He also called on state governors to mobilize their militias. Like John Adams before him, however, Jefferson resisted war fever, in part because the undersized U.S. Army and Navy were not prepared to fight. Jefferson's caution outraged his critics.

**THE EMBARGO**  President Jefferson decided on a strategy of "peaceable coercion" to force Britain and France to stop violating American rights. Late in 1807, he somehow convinced enough Republicans in Congress to cut off *all* American foreign trade. As Jefferson said, his choices were "war, embargo, or nothing."

The unprecedented **Embargo Act** (December 1807) stopped all American exports by prohibiting U.S. ships from sailing to foreign ports to "keep our ships and seamen out of harm's way." Jefferson and his secretary of state, James Madison, mistakenly assumed that the embargo would force the warring European nations to quit violating American rights. They were wrong.

With each passing month, the embargo devastated the Republicans and the economy while reviving the political appeal of the Federalists, especially in New England, where merchants howled because the embargo cut off their primary industry: oceangoing commerce. The value of U.S. exports plummeted from $48 million in 1807 to $9 million a year later, and federal revenue from tariffs plunged from $18 million to $8 million. Shipbuilding declined by two-thirds, and farmers and planters in the South and West suffered as prices for exported farm crops were cut in half. New England's once-thriving port cities became ghost towns; thousands of ships and sailors were out of work. Meanwhile, smuggling soared, especially along the border with British Canada.

Americans raged at what critics called "Jefferson's embargo." One letter writer told the president that he had paid four friends "to shoot you if you don't take off the embargo," while another addressed the president as "you red-headed son of a bitch."

The embargo turned American politics upside down. To enforce it, Jefferson, once the leading advocate for *reducing* the power of the federal government, now found himself *expanding* federal power into every aspect of the nation's economic life. In effect, the United States used its own warships to blockade its own ports. Jefferson even activated the New York state militia in an effort to stop smuggling across the Canadian border.

Congress finally voted 70–0 to end the embargo effective March 4, 1809, the day the "splendid misery" of Jefferson's second presidential term ended. The dejected Jefferson left the presidency feeling like a freed prisoner. No one, he said, could be more relieved "on shaking off the shackles of power." His stern critic, Congressman John Randolph, declared that never had a president "left the nation in a state so deplorable and calamitous."

Jefferson learned a hard lesson that many of his successors would also discover: a second presidential term is rarely as successful as the first. As he admitted, "No man will ever carry out of that office the reputation which carried him into it."

In the election of 1808, the presidency passed to another prominent Virginian, Secretary of State James Madison. The Federalists, again backing Charles C. Pinckney of South Carolina and Rufus King of New York, won only 47 electoral votes to Madison's 122.

**JAMES MADISON AND THE DRIFT TO WAR**  In his inaugural address, President Madison acknowledged that he inherited a situation "full of difficulties." He soon made things worse. Although Madison had been a talented legislator and the "Father of the Constitution," he proved to be a weak, indecisive chief executive. He was a persuader, not a commander.

Madison's sparkling wife, Dolley, was the only truly excellent member of the president's inner circle. Seventeen years younger than her husband, she was a superb First Lady who excelled at entertaining political leaders and foreign dignitaries. Journalists called her the "Queen of Washington City."

From the beginning, Madison's presidency was entangled in foreign affairs and crippled by his lack of executive experience. Like Jefferson, Madison and his advisers repeatedly overestimated the young republic's diplomatic leverage and military strength. The result was international humiliation.

Madison insisted on upholding the principle of freedom of the seas for the United States and other neutral nations, but he was unwilling to create a navy strong enough to enforce it. He continued the policy of "peaceable coercion" against the European nations, which was as ineffective for him as it had been for Jefferson.

In place of the disastrous embargo, Congress passed the Non-Intercourse Act (1809), which reopened trade with all countries *except* France and Great Britain and their colonies. It also authorized the president to reopen trade with France or Great Britain if either should stop violating American rights on the high seas.

In December 1810, France issued a vague promise to restore America's neutral rights, whereupon Madison gave Great Britain three months to do the same. The British refused, and the Royal Navy continued to seize American vessels, their cargoes, and crews.

A reluctant Madison asked Congress to declare war against the United Kingdom of Great Britain and Ireland on June 1, 1812. If the United States did not defend its maritime rights, he explained, then Americans were "not independent people, but colonists and vassals."

The congressional vote to declare war was the closest in America's history of warfare. On June 5, the House of Representatives voted for war 79–49. Two weeks later, the Senate followed suit, 19–13. Every Federalist in Congress opposed "Mr. Madison's War," while 80 percent of Republicans supported it. The southern and western states wanted war; the New England states opposed it.

By declaring war, Madison and the Republicans hoped to unite the nation and discredit the Federalists. They also planned to end British-led Indian attacks along the Great Lakes and in the Ohio Valley by invading British Canada. To generate popular support, Jefferson advised Madison that he needed, above all, "to stop Indian barbarities. The conquest of Canada will do this." Jefferson presumed that the French Canadians were eager to rise up against their British rulers. With their help, the Republicans predicted, American armies would conquer Britain's vast northern colony. It did not work out that way.

## THE WAR OF 1812

**The War of 1812** marked the first time that Congress declared war. Great Britain was preoccupied with defeating Napoléon in Europe, and in fact, on June 16, 1812, it had promised to quit interfering with American shipping. President Madison and the Republicans, however, believed that only war would end the practice of impressment and stop British-inspired Indian attacks along the western frontier.

**SHIPPING RIGHTS AND NATIONAL HONOR** Why the United States chose to start the war is still debated by historians. Its main cause—the repeated British violations of American maritime rights and the practice of "impressing" sailors—dominated President Madison's war message. Most of the votes in Congress for war came from legislators representing rural regions, from Pennsylvania southward and westward, where the economic interests of farmers and planters were being hurt by the raids on American merchant ships. However, the representatives from the New England states, which bore the brunt of British attacks on U.S. shipping, voted 20–12 *against* the declaration of war.

One explanation for this seeming inconsistency is that many Americans in the South and West, especially Tennessee, Kentucky, and South Carolina, voted for war because they believed America's national *honor* was at stake. Andrew Jackson, a proud anti-British Tennessean who was the state's first congressman, announced that he was eager to fight "for the re-establishment of our national character."

**NATIVE AMERICAN CONFLICTS** Another factor leading to war was the growing number of Indian attacks, supported by the British, in the Ohio Valley. The story took a new turn with the rise of two Shawnee leaders, Tecumseh and his half brother, Tenskwatawa, who lived in a large village called Prophetstown on the Tippecanoe River in northern Indiana.

Tecumseh ("Shooting Star") knew that the fate of the Indians depended on their being unified. He hoped to create a single nation powerful enough, with British assistance, to fend off further American expansion. Tenskwatawa (the

**Tecumseh** The Shawnee leader, who tried to unite Native American peoples across the United States in defense of their lands, was killed in 1813 at the Battle of the Thames.

"Open Door"), who was known as "the Prophet," gained a large following among Native Americans for his predictions that white Americans ("children of the devil") were on the verge of collapse. He demanded that the indigenous peoples abandon all things European: clothing, customs, Christianity, and especially liquor. If they did so, the Great Spirit would reward them by turning the whites' gunpowder to sand.

A "TRAIL OF BLOOD"   Inspired by his brother's spiritual message, Tecumseh attempted to form alliances with other Native American nations in 1811. In Alabama, he told a gathering of 5,000 Indians that they should "let the white race perish" because "they seize your land; they corrupt your women; they trample on the ashes of your dead!" The whites "have driven us from the sea to the lakes," he noted. "We can go no further."

William Henry Harrison, governor of the Indiana Territory, met with Tecumseh twice and described him as "one of those uncommon geniuses who spring up occasionally to produce revolutions and overturn the established order of things."

Yet in the fall of 1811, Harrison gathered 1,000 troops and advanced on Prophetstown. What became the Battle of Tippecanoe was a disastrous defeat for the Native Americans, as Harrison's troops burned the village and destroyed its supplies. **Tecumseh's Indian Confederacy** went up in smoke, and he fled to Canada.

THE LUST FOR CANADA AND FLORIDA   Some Americans wanted war with Great Britain because they sought to seize control of Canada. That there were nearly 8 million Americans and only 300,000 Canadians led many to believe that doing so would be quick and easy. Thomas Jefferson, for instance, wrote President Madison that the "acquisition of Canada" was simply a "matter of marching" north with a military force.

The British were also vulnerable far to the south. East Florida, which had returned to Spain's control in 1783, posed a threat because Spain was too weak, or too unwilling, to prevent Indian attacks across the border with Georgia. In the absence of a strong Spanish presence, British agents and traders remained in East Florida, smuggling goods and conspiring with Indians against Americans.

Spanish Florida had also long been a haven for runaway slaves from Georgia and South Carolina. Many Americans living along the Florida-Georgia border hoped that the war would enable them to oust the British and the Spanish from Florida.

**WAR HAWKS**  In the Congress that assembled in late 1811, new anti-British representatives from southern and western districts shouted for war to defend "national honor" and rid the Northwest of the "Indian problem" by invading Canada. Among the most vocal "war hawks" were Henry Clay of Kentucky and John C. Calhoun of South Carolina.

Clay, the brash young Speaker of the House, was "for resistance by the *sword*." He boasted that the Kentucky militia alone could conquer Canada. His bravado inspired others. "I don't like Henry Clay," Calhoun said. "He is a bad man, an imposter, a creator of wicked schemes. I wouldn't speak to him, but, by God, I love him" for wanting war against Britain. When Calhoun learned that President Madison had finally decided on war, he threw his arms around Clay's neck and led his colleagues in a mock Indian war dance.

In New England and much of New York, however, there was little enthusiasm for war. Great Britain remained those states' largest trading partner; the sentiment was that military conflict could cripple the shipping industry. Both Massachusetts and Connecticut refused to send soldiers to fight, and merchants openly sold supplies to British troops in Canada.

**WAR PREPARATIONS**  One thing was certain: the United States was woefully unprepared for war, both financially and militarily, and James Madison lacked the leadership ability and physical stature to inspire public confidence and military resolve.

The national economy was weak, too. In 1811, Republicans had let the charter of the Bank of the United States expire. Many Republican congressmen owned shares in state banks and wanted the B.U.S. dissolved because it both competed with and regulated the local banks. Once the B.U.S. shut down, however, the number of unregulated state banks mushroomed, all with their own forms of currency, creating commercial chaos.

Once war began, it did not go well. The mighty British navy blockaded American ports, which caused federal tariff revenues to tumble. In March 1813, Treasury Secretary Gallatin warned Madison that the United States had "hardly enough money to last till the end of the month." Furthermore, Republicans in Congress were so afraid of public criticism that they delayed approving tax increases needed to finance the war.

The military situation was almost as bad. In 1812, the British had 250,000 professional soldiers and the most powerful navy in the world. By contrast, the U.S. Army numbered only 3,287 ill-trained and poorly equipped men, led by mostly incompetent officers with little combat experience. In January 1812, Congress authorized an army of 35,000 men, but a year later, just

18,500 had been recruited—many of them Irish American immigrants who hated the English and were enticed to enlist by congressional promises of cash and land.

President Madison, who refused to allow free blacks or slaves to serve in the army, had to plead with state governors to provide militiamen, only to have the Federalist governors in anti-war New England decline. The British, on the other hand, had thousands of soldiers stationed in Canada and the West Indies. And, as was true during the Revolutionary War, the British recruited more Native American allies than did the Americans.

The U.S. Navy was in better shape than the army, with able officers and well-trained seamen, but it had only 16 warships compared to Britain's 600. The lopsided military strength of the British led Madison to mutter that the United States was in "an embarrassing situation."

**A CONTINENTAL WAR**  For these reasons and more, the War of 1812 was one of the strangest wars in history. In fact, it was three wars fought on three fronts. One theater of conflict was the Chesapeake Bay along the coast of Maryland and Virginia, including Washington, D.C. The second was in the South—Alabama, Mississippi, and West and East Florida—where American forces led by Andrew Jackson invaded lands owned by the Creeks and the Spanish. The third front might be more accurately called the Canadian-American War. It began in what is now northern Indiana and Ohio, southeastern Michigan, and the contested border regions around the Great Lakes. The fighting raged back and forth across the border as the United States repeatedly invaded British Canada, only to be repulsed.

**THE WAR IN THE NORTH**  Like the American Revolution, the War of 1812, often called America's second war for independence, was very much a civil war. The Canadians, thousands of whom were former American Loyalists who had fled north after the Revolutionary War, remained loyal to the British Empire, while the Americans and a few French Canadians and Irish Canadians sought to push Britain out of North America and annex Canada.

In some cases, Americans fought former Americans, including families that were divided in their allegiances. Siblings even shot each other. Once, after killing an American militiaman, a Canadian soldier began taking the clothes off the corpse, only to realize that it was his brother. He grumbled that it served him right to have died for a bad cause.

Indians armed by the British dominated the wooded borderlands around the Great Lakes. Michigan's governor recognized that "The British cannot hold Upper Canada [Ontario] without the assistance of the Indians," but the "Indians

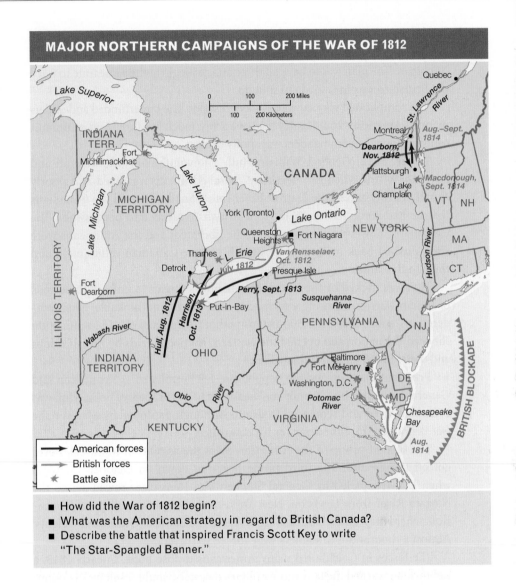

## MAJOR NORTHERN CAMPAIGNS OF THE WAR OF 1812

Legend:
- ➔ American forces
- ➔ British forces
- ✳ Battle site

- How did the War of 1812 begin?
- What was the American strategy in regard to British Canada?
- Describe the battle that inspired Francis Scott Key to write "The Star-Spangled Banner."

cannot conduct a war without the assistance of a civilized nation [Great Britain]." So the American assault on Canada involved attacking Indians, Canadians, and British soldiers.

**INVADING CANADA** President Madison approved a three-pronged plan for the invasion of British Canada. It called for one army to move north through upstate New York, along Lake Champlain, to take Montreal, while another was to advance into Upper Canada by crossing the Niagara River between Lakes Ontario and Erie. The third attack would come from the west, with an American force moving east into Upper Canada from Detroit, Michigan. The plan was to have all three attacks begin at the same time to force the British troops in Canada to split up.

The complicated plan, however, was a disaster. The underfunded and undermanned Americans could barely field one army, much less three, and communication among the commanders was spotty at best.

In July 1812, General William Hull, a Revolutionary War veteran and governor of the Michigan Territory, marched his disorganized and poorly supplied army across the Detroit River into Canada. He told the Canadians that he had come to free them from British "tyranny and oppression." The Canadians, however, did not want to be liberated, and the Americans were soon pushed back to Detroit by British troops, Canadian militiamen, and their Indian allies.

Hull was tricked by the British commander's threats to unleash thousands of Indian warriors. Fearing a massacre, Hull did the unthinkable: he surrendered his entire force of 2,500 troops without firing a shot. His capitulation shocked the nation and opened the western frontier to raids by British troops and their Canadian and Indian allies.

President Madison and the Republicans felt humiliated. A Republican said General Hull must be a "traitor" or "nearly an idiot" or "part of both." Hull was eventually tried and sentenced to death. Although pardoned by Madison, he was dismissed from the army for his cowardice.

The second prong of the American plan, the assault on Montreal, never got off the ground. The third prong began at dawn on October 13, 1812, when U.S. troops led by General Stephen Van Rensselaer rowed across the Niagara River from Lewiston, New York, to the Canadian village of Queenston, where they suffered a crushing defeat in the Battle of Queenston Heights. Almost a thousand U.S. soldiers were forced to surrender.

The losses in Canada led many Americans to lose hope. In early 1813, a Kentuckian warned that any more military disasters would result in "disunion" and that the "cause of Republicanism will be lost."

Then there was a glimmer of good news. In April 1813, Americans led by General Zebulon Pike attacked York (later renamed Toronto), the provincial capital of Upper Canada. The British and Canadian militiamen surrendered, and over the next several days, in part because Pike had been killed, the U.S. soldiers rampaged out of control, plundering the city and burning government buildings.

After the burning of York, the Americans sought to gain naval control of the Great Lakes and other inland waterways along the Canadian border. If they could break the British naval supply line and secure Lake Erie, they could divide the British from their Indian allies.

In 1813, at Presque Isle, Pennsylvania, near Erie, twenty-eight-year-old Oliver Hazard Perry supervised the construction of warships from timber cut in nearby forests. By the end of the summer, Commodore Perry's new warships set out in search of the British, finally finding them at Lake Erie's Put-in-Bay on September 10.

Two British warships pounded the *Lawrence*, Perry's flagship. After four hours, none of the *Lawrence*'s guns was working, and most crew members were dead or wounded. Perry refused to quit, however. He switched to another vessel, kept fighting, and, miraculously, ended up accepting the surrender of the entire British squadron. Hatless and bloodied, Perry famously reported, "We have met the enemy and they are ours."

American control of Lake Erie forced the British to evacuate Upper Canada. They gave up Detroit and were defeated at the Battle of the Thames in southern Canada on October 5, 1813. During the battle, the British fled, leaving the great chief Tecumseh and 500 warriors to face the wrath of the Americans. When Tecumseh was killed, the remaining Indians retreated.

Perry's victory and the defeat of Tecumseh enabled the Americans to recover control of most of Michigan and seize the Western District of Upper Canada. Thereafter, the war in the north lapsed into a military stalemate, with neither side able to dislodge the other.

**THE CREEK WAR** War also flared in the South in 1813. The Creek Indians in western Georgia and Alabama had split into two factions: the Upper Creeks (called Red Sticks because of their bright-red war clubs), who opposed American expansion and sided with the British, and the Lower Creeks, who wanted to remain on good terms with the Americans. On August 30, Red Sticks attacked Fort Mims on the Alabama River and massacred hundreds of white and African American men, women, and children.

Americans were incensed. Thirsting for revenge, Andrew Jackson, commanding general of the Army of West Tennessee, recruited about 2,500 volunteer militiamen and headed south. With him were David Crockett, a famous sharpshooter, and Sam Houston, a nineteen-year-old Virginia frontiersman who would later lead the Texas War for Independence against Mexico.

Jackson was a natural warrior and gifted commander. His soldiers nicknamed him "Old Hickory" in recognition of his toughness. From a young age, he had embraced violence, gloried in it, and prospered by it. He told all "brave Tennesseans" that their "frontier [was] threatened with invasion by the savage

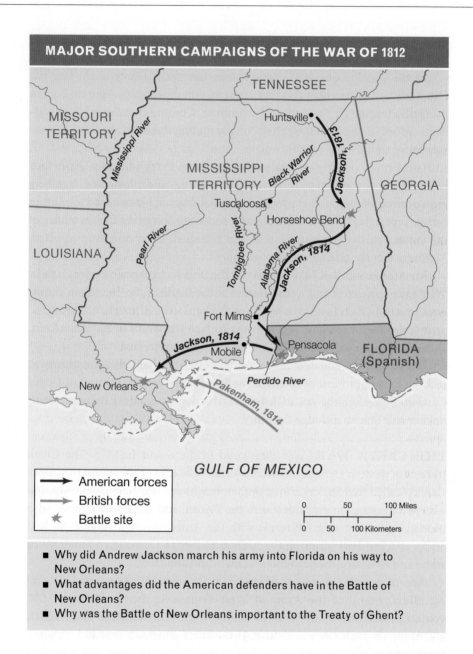

MAJOR SOUTHERN CAMPAIGNS OF THE WAR OF 1812

- Why did Andrew Jackson march his army into Florida on his way to New Orleans?
- What advantages did the American defenders have in the Battle of New Orleans?
- Why was the Battle of New Orleans important to the Treaty of Ghent?

foe" and that the Indians were advancing "with scalping knives unsheathed, to butcher your wives, your children, and your helpless babes. Time is not to be lost."

Jackson's expedition across Alabama was not easy. It was difficult to keep his men fed and supplied. Some of the men went home once their enlistment period ended. A few deserted or rebelled. When a seventeen-year-old soldier threatened an officer, he was tried and sentenced to death. Jackson had the young man shot in front of the rest of the army to demonstrate his steely determination to win the war.

Jackson's grizzled volunteers crushed the Red Sticks in a series of bloodbaths in Alabama. The decisive battle occurred on March 27, 1814, on a peninsula formed by the Horseshoe Bend on the Tallapoosa River. Jackson's soldiers, with crucial help from Cherokee and Creek allies, surrounded a Red Stick fort, set fire to it, and shot the Indians as they tried to escape. Nine hundred were killed, including 300 who drowned in a desperate effort to cross the river. Jackson reported that the "*carnage was dreadful.*" Fewer than fifty of his soldiers were killed.

The Battle of Horseshoe Bend was the worst defeat ever inflicted upon Native Americans, and it effectively ended the Creeks' ability to wage war. With the Treaty of Fort Jackson, signed in August 1814, the Red Stick Creeks gave up two-thirds of their land—some 23 million acres—including southwest Georgia and much of Alabama. Red Eagle, chief of the Red Sticks, told Jackson: "I am in your power. . . . My people are all gone. I can do no more but weep over the misfortunes of my nation." President Madison rewarded Jackson by naming him a major general in the regular U.S. Army.

Events in Europe soon took a dramatic turn when the British, Spanish, and Portuguese armies repelled French emperor Napoléon's attempt to conquer Spain and Portugal. Now free to focus on the American war, the British sent 16,000 soldiers to try yet again to invade America from Canada. The British navy also received reinforcement, enabling it to extend its blockade to New England ports and to bombard coastal towns from Delaware to Florida. The final piece of the British plan was to seize New Orleans and sever American access to the Mississippi River.

**FIGHTING ALONG THE CHESAPEAKE BAY**  In February 1813, the British had more warships in the Chesapeake Bay than were in the entire American navy, and they frequently captured and burned American merchant vessels. The British also launched numerous raids along the Virginia and Maryland shore, in effect mocking the Madison administration's ability to defend the nation.

The presence of British ships on the coast and inland rivers led many slaves to escape or revolt. As had happened during the Revolutionary War, British naval commanders promised freedom to slaves who aided or fought with them. More than 3,000 slaves in Maryland and Virginia escaped to the safety of British ships.

In September 1813, the British organized some 400 former slaves into an all-black military unit called the Colonial Marines. The recruits were provided uniforms, meals, and $6 a month in wages. News of the Colonial Marines panicked whites along the Chesapeake Bay; they feared that the former slaves would "have no mercy on them." Virginia's John Randolph spoke for many when he insisted that the "question of slavery, as it is called, is to us a question of life and death."

**THE BURNING OF WASHINGTON** During the late summer of 1814, U.S. forces suffered their most humiliating experience of the war when British troops captured and burned Washington, D.C.

In August, 4,000 British soldiers landed at Benedict, Maryland, routed the American militia at Bladensburg, and headed for the nation's capital a few miles away. Thousands fled the city. President Madison frantically called out the poorly led and untrained militia, then left Washington, D.C. to help rally the troops. His efforts failed, however, as the American defense disintegrated.

On August 24, British redcoats marched unopposed into the American capital. Madison and his wife, Dolley, fled just in time after first saving a portrait of George Washington and a copy of the Declaration of Independence. The vengeful British, aware that American troops had burned York, the Canadian capital, torched the Executive Mansion, the Capitol, the Library of Congress, and other government buildings before heading north to assault Baltimore. A tornado the next day compounded the damage.

The destruction of Washington, D.C., shocked, embarrassed, and infuriated Americans. Even worse, people had lost confidence in the government and the military. David Campbell, a Virginia congressman, told his brother that America was "ruled by fools and the administration opposed by knaves."

John Armstrong, the secretary of war, resigned. Madison replaced him with James Monroe, who was also secretary of state. A desperate Monroe soon proposed enlisting free blacks into the army. But many worried that such changes were too few and too late. A Virginia official noted that without a miracle, "*This union is inevitably dissolved.*"

President Madison called an emergency session of Congress and appealed to Americans to "expel the invaders." A Baltimore newspaper reported that the "spirit of the nation is roused." That determination showed itself when fifty British warships sailed into Baltimore Harbor on September 13, while 4,200 British soldiers, including the all-black Colonial Marines, assaulted

***Washington Burning*, 1814**  In this illustration by Joseph Boggs Beale, Washington residents evacuate the city as the White House and the Capitol blaze with flames in the background.

the city by land. About 1,000 Americans held Fort McHenry on an island in the harbor.

Throughout the night of September 13, the British bombarded Fort McHenry. "The portals of hell appeared to have been thrown open," an observer reported. Yet the Americans refused to surrender. At daybreak, the soldiers in the battered fort stood defiant, guns at the ready. The frustrated British sailed away.

Francis Scott Key, a slaveholding lawyer from an old Maryland plantation family who later would become district attorney for Washington, D.C., watched the assault from a British warship, having been sent to negotiate the release of a captured American. The sight of the massive U.S. flag still flying over Fort McHenry at dawn inspired Key to scribble the verses of what came to be called "The Star-Spangled Banner," which began, "Oh, say can you see, by the dawn's early light?"

Later revised and set to the tune of an English drinking song, it became America's national anthem in 1931. Less well known is that Key was a rabid white supremacist who declared that Africans in America were "a distinct and inferior race of people, which all experience proves to be the greatest evil that afflicts a community."

The lesser-known third stanza of the "Star-Spangled Banner" refers to the slaughtering of those slaves who had joined the British army in exchange for their freedom:

> No refuge could save the hireling and the slave
> From the terror of night or the gloom of the grave
> And the star-spangled banner in triumph doth wave
> O'er the land of the free and the home of the brave.

Just weeks before, Key had served as a volunteer aide to a U.S. Army general during the Battle of Bladensburg near Washington, D.C. The Colonial Marines, composed of runaway slaves, had played a crucial role in the rout of American troops that day.

**THE BATTLE OF LAKE CHAMPLAIN** The failure to conquer Baltimore nixed British hopes of a quick victory while giving the Americans a desperately needed morale boost. More good news soon arrived from upstate New York, where the outnumbered Americans at Plattsburgh, along Lake Champlain, were saved by the ability of Commodore Thomas Macdonough, commander of the U.S. naval squadron.

On September 11, 1814, just days after the burning of Washington, D.C., British soldiers attacked at Plattsburgh while their navy engaged Macdonough's warships in a battle that ended with the entire British fleet either destroyed or captured. The Battle of Lake Champlain (also called the Battle of Plattsburgh) forced the British to abandon the northern campaign—their main military push in the war—and retreat into Canada.

In November, an army led by Andrew Jackson in Florida seized Spanish-controlled Pensacola, on the Gulf coast, preventing another British army from landing and pushing northward into the southern states. The American victories in New York and Florida convinced Congress not to abandon Washington, D.C. Instead, the members voted to rebuild the Capitol and the Executive Mansion.

# THE AFTERMATH OF THE WAR

While the fighting raged, U.S. diplomats, including Henry Clay and John Quincy Adams, son of the former president, had begun meeting with British officials in Ghent, near Brussels in present-day Belgium, to discuss ending the war. Negotiations dragged on for weeks, but on Christmas Eve 1814, the diplomats finally reached an agreement.

**THE TREATY OF GHENT**  The weary British decided to end the war in part because of military setbacks but also because London merchants were eager to renew trade with America.

By the **Treaty of Ghent (1814)**, the two countries agreed to return each side's prisoners and restore the previous boundaries. This was a godsend for the Americans, since British forces at the time still controlled eastern Maine, northern Michigan, a portion of western New York, and several islands off the coast of Georgia. The British also pledged to stop supporting Indian attacks along the Great Lakes.

What had begun as an American effort to protect its honor, end British impressment, and conquer Canada had turned into a second war of independence. At the end of the negotiations, John Quincy Adams wrote to his wife that he had had the honor of "redeeming our union." Although the Americans lost the war for Canada and saw their national capital destroyed, they won the southern war, defeating the Indians and taking their lands. More important, the Treaty of Ghent saved the splintered republic from possible civil war and financial ruin.

**THE BATTLE OF NEW ORLEANS**  Because it took six weeks for news of the Treaty of Ghent to reach the United States, fighting continued at the end of 1814. On December 1, Andrew Jackson arrived in New Orleans to prepare for a British invasion of the strategic city. He announced that he "would drive the British into the sea, or perish in the effort." Jackson declared martial law and transformed New Orleans into an armed camp.

On December 12, a British fleet with sixty ships and thousands of soldiers took up positions on the coast of Louisiana, hoping to capture New Orleans and gain control of the Mississippi River. But British general Sir Edward Pakenham's painfully careful preparation for an assault gave Jackson time to organize hundreds of slaves "loaned" by planters. They dug trenches, built ramparts bristling with cannons, stacked cotton bales and barrels of sugar, and dug a ten-foot-wide moat for protection.

The 4,500 Americans—including militiamen, Choctaws, African Americans, Tennessee and Kentucky sharpshooters, and Creole pirates—built an almost-invulnerable position at Chalmette Plantation seven miles south of New Orleans. Sporadic fighting occurred for more than three weeks before Pakenham rashly ordered a frontal assault at dawn on Sunday, January 8, 1815. His 5,300 soldiers marched in two columns, each eighty men abreast, into a murderous hail of artillery shells and rifle fire. When the smoke cleared, a Kentucky militiaman said that the battlefield looked first like "a sea of blood. It was not blood itself, but the red coats in which the British soldiers were dressed. The field was entirely covered in prostrate bodies."

In just 25 minutes, the British had lost some 2,100 men, including Pakenham. The Americans suffered only seventy-one killed or wounded. A British naval officer wrote that there "never was a more complete failure."

Although the **Battle of New Orleans** occurred after the Treaty of Ghent had been signed, it was vitally important psychologically. Had the British won, they might have tried to revise the treaty in their favor. Jackson's victory ensured that both governments would act quickly to approve the treaty. The unexpected American triumph also generated a wave of patriotism. As a Washington, D.C., newspaper crowed, "ALMOST INCREDIBLE VICTORY!"

Such pride in the Battle of New Orleans would later help transform Jackson into a dynamic presidential candidate eager to move the nation into an even more democratic era in which the "common man" would be celebrated and empowered. Jackson, wrote a southerner in April 1815, "is everywhere hailed as the savior of the country. . . . He has been feasted, caressed, & I may say idolized."

**THE HARTFORD CONVENTION**  A few weeks before the Battle of New Orleans, many New England Federalists, frustrated by the rising expense of "Mr. Madison's War," which they had opposed, tried to take matters into their own hands at the **Hartford Convention** in Hartford, Connecticut.

On December 15, 1814, the convention assembled with delegates from Massachusetts, Rhode Island, Connecticut, Vermont, and New Hampshire. Over the next three weeks, they proposed seven constitutional amendments designed to limit Republican (and southern) influence. The amendments included abolishing the counting of slaves in determining a state's representation in Congress, requiring a two-thirds supermajority rather than a simple majority vote to declare war or admit new states, prohibiting trade embargoes lasting more than sixty days, excluding immigrants from holding federal office, limiting the president to one term, and barring successive presidents from the same state (a provision clearly directed at Virginia).

The delegates also discussed the possibility that some New England states might "secede" from the United States if their demands were dismissed. Yet the threat quickly evaporated. In February 1815, when messengers from the convention reached Washington, D.C., they found the capital celebrating the good news from New Orleans. Ignored by Congress and the president, the delegates turned tail for home. The sorry episode proved fatal to the Federalist party, which never recovered from the shame of disloyalty stamped on it by the Hartford Convention.

The victory at New Orleans and the arrival of the peace treaty from Europe transformed the national mood. Almost overnight, President Madison went from being denounced and possibly impeached to being hailed a national hero.

**THE WAR'S LEGACIES**   There was no clear military victor in the War of 1812, nor much clarification about the issues that had ignited the war.

For all the clumsiness with which the war was managed, however, it generated an intense patriotism across much of the nation and reaffirmed American independence. The young republic was at last secure from British or European threats. As James Monroe said, "we have acquired a character and a rank among the other nations, which we did not enjoy before."

Americans soon decided that the war was a glorious triumph. The people, observed Treasury Secretary Albert Gallatin, "are more American; they feel and act more as a nation; and I hope that the permanency of the Union is thereby better secured." Yet the war also revealed the limitations of relying on militiamen and the need for a larger professional army.

Soon after the official copy of the Treaty of Ghent arrived in Washington, D.C., in February 1815, Virginian William H. Cabell wrote his brother that the "glorious peace for America . . . has come exactly when we least expected but when we most wanted it." Another Virginian, Colonel John Taylor, recognized the happy outcome as largely resulting from "a succession of lucky accidents" that "enabled the administration to get the nation out of the war."

The war also propelled the United States toward economic independence, as the interruption of trade with Europe forced America to expand its own manufacturing sector and become more self-sufficient. The British blockade of the coast created a shortage of cotton cloth in the United States, leading to the creation of the nation's first cotton-manufacturing industry, in Waltham, Massachusetts.

By the end of the war, there were more than 100 cotton mills in New England and 64 more in Pennsylvania. Even Thomas Jefferson admitted in 1815 that his beloved agricultural republic had been transformed: "We must now place the manufacturer by the agriculturalist." The new American republic was emerging as an agricultural, commercial, and industrial world power.

Perhaps the strangest result of the War of 1812 was the reversal of attitudes among Republicans and Federalists. For James Madison, the British invasion of Washington, D.C., convinced him of the necessity of a strong army and navy. In addition, the lack of a national bank had hurt the federal government's efforts to finance the war; state banks were so unstable that it was difficult to raise the funds needed to pay military expenses. In 1816, Madison created the Second Bank of the United States. The rise of new industries prompted manufacturers to call for increased tariffs on imports to protect American companies from unfair foreign competition. Madison went along, despite his criticism of tariffs in the 1790s.

While Madison reversed himself by embracing nationalism and a broader interpretation of the Constitution, the Federalists similarly reversed themselves and took up Madison's and Jefferson's original emphasis on states' rights and strict construction of the Constitution to defend the special interests of their regional stronghold, New England. It was the first great reversal of partisan political roles in constitutional interpretation. It would not be the last.

The War of 1812 proved devastating to the eastern Indian nations, most of which had fought with the British. The war accelerated westward settlement, and Native American resistance was greatly diminished after the death of Tecumseh and his Indian Confederacy. The British essentially abandoned their Indian allies, and none of their former lands were returned to them.

Lakota chief Little Crow expressed the betrayal felt by Native Americans when he rejected the consolation gifts from the local British commander: "After we have fought for you, endured many hardships, lost some of our people, and awakened the vengeance of our powerful neighbors, you make peace for yourselves. . . . You no longer need our service; you offer us these goods to pay us for [your] having deserted us. But no, we will not take them; we hold them and yourselves in equal contempt."

As the Indians were pushed out, tens of thousands of Americans moved into the Great Lakes region and into Georgia, Alabama, and Mississippi, occupying more territory in a single generation than had been settled in the 150 years of colonial history. The federal government hastened western migration by providing war veterans with 160 acres of land between the Illinois and Mississippi Rivers.

The trans-Appalachian population soared from 300,000 to 2 million between 1800 and 1820. By 1840, more than 40 percent of Americans lived west of the Appalachians in eight new states. At the same time, the growing dispute over slavery and its expansion into new western territories set in motion an explosive debate that would once again test the grand experiment in republican government.

# CHAPTER REVIEW

## SUMMARY

- **Jefferson's Administration**  The Jeffersonian Republicans did not dismantle much of Hamilton's economic program, but they did repeal the whiskey tax, cut government expenditures, and usher in a *republican simplicity* that championed the virtues of smaller government and plain living. While Republicans idealized the agricultural world that had existed prior to 1800, the first decades of the nineteenth century were a period of transformational economic and population growth in the United States. Commercial agriculture and exports to Europe flourished; Americans moved to the West in huge numbers. The *Louisiana Purchase (1803)* dramatically expanded the boundaries of the United States. Thomas Jefferson's *Lewis and Clark expedition (1804–1805)* explored the new region and spurred interest in the Far West. In *Marbury v. Madison (1803)*, the Federalist chief justice of the Supreme Court, John Marshall, declared a federal act unconstitutional for the first time. With that decision, the Court assumed the right of judicial review over acts of Congress and established the constitutional supremacy of the federal government over state governments.

- **War in Europe**  Jefferson sent warships to subdue the *Barbary pirates* in North Africa and negotiated with the Spanish and French to ensure that the Mississippi River remained open to American commerce. Renewal of war between Britain and France in 1803 complicated matters for American commerce. Neither country wanted its enemy to purchase U.S. goods, so both blockaded each other's ports. In retaliation, Jefferson convinced Congress to pass the *Embargo Act (1897)*, which prohibited all foreign trade.

- **War of 1812**  President James Madison ultimately declared war against Great Britain over the issue of neutral shipping rights and the fear that the British were inciting Native Americans to attack frontier settlements. Indian nations took sides in the war. Earlier, at the Battle of Tippecanoe (1811), U.S. troops had defeated elements of *Tecumseh's Indian Confederacy*, an alliance of Indian nations determined to protect their ancestral lands. At the Battle of the Thames (1813), Tecumseh was killed. The Confederacy disintegrated soon thereafter.

- **Aftermath of the War of 1812**  The *Treaty of Ghent (1814)* ended the war by essentially declaring it a draw. A smashing American victory in January 1815 at the *Battle of New Orleans* helped to ensure that the treaty would be ratified and enforced. The conflict established the economic independence of the United States, as many goods previously purchased from Britain were now manufactured at home. During and after the war, Federalists and Republicans seemed to exchange roles. Delegates from the waning Federalist party met at the *Hartford Convention (1814)* to defend states' rights and threaten secession, while Republicans promoted nationalism and a broad interpretation of the Constitution.

# CHRONOLOGY

| | |
|---|---|
| **1800** | U.S. population surpasses 5 million |
| **1801** | Thomas Jefferson inaugurated as president in Washington, D.C. |
| | Barbary pirates harass U.S. shipping |
| | The pasha of Tripoli declares war on the United States |
| **1803** | Supreme Court issues *Marbury v. Madison* decision |
| | Louisiana Purchase |
| **1804–1806** | Lewis and Clark expedition |
| **1804** | Jefferson overwhelmingly reelected |
| **1807** | British interference with U.S. shipping increases |
| **1808** | International slave trade ended in the United States |
| **1811** | Defeat of Tecumseh Indian Confederacy at the Battle of Tippecanoe |
| **1812** | Congress declares war on Britain |
| | U.S. invasion of Canada |
| **1813–1814** | "Creek War" |
| **1814** | British capture and burn Washington, D.C. |
| | Hartford Convention assembles |
| **1815** | Battle of New Orleans |
| | News of the Treaty of Ghent reaches the United States |

# KEY TERMS

republican simplicity p. 277

*Marbury v. Madison* (1803) p. 279

Barbary pirates p. 281

Louisiana Purchase (1803) p. 285

Lewis and Clark expedition (1804–1806) p. 285

Embargo Act (1807) p. 292

War of 1812 (1812–1815) p. 294

Tecumseh's Indian Confederacy p. 296

Treaty of Ghent (1814) p. 307

Battle of New Orleans (1815) p. 308

Hartford Convention (1814) p. 308

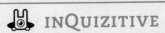 INQUIZITIVE

Go to InQuizitive to see what you've learned—and learn what you've missed—with personalized feedback along the way.

# part three

# AN EXPANDING NATION

During the nineteenth century, the United States experienced wrenching changes. With each passing decade, its predominantly agrarian society gave way to a more diverse economy and urban society, with factories and cities emerging alongside farms and towns. The pace of life quickened with industrialization. Between 1790 and 1820, the nation's boundaries expanded, and its population—both white and black—soared, while the number of Native Americans continued to decline. Immigrants from Ireland, Germany, Scandinavia, and China poured

315

into the United States seeking land, jobs, and freedom. By the early 1820s, the number of enslaved Americans was more than two and a half times greater than in 1790, and the number of free blacks had doubled. The white population grew just as rapidly.

Accompanying the emergence of an industrial economy in the Northeast was relentless westward expansion. Until the nineteenth century, most of the American population was clustered near the seacoast and along rivers flowing into the Atlantic Ocean or the Gulf of Mexico. After 1800, the great theme of American development was the migration of millions across the Allegheny and Appalachian Mountains into the Ohio Valley and the Middle West. Waves of adventurous Americans then crossed the Mississippi River and spread out across the Great Plains. By the 1840s, American settlers had reached the Pacific Ocean.

These developments—the emergence of a market-based economy, the impact of industrial development, and dramatic territorial expansion—made the second quarter of the nineteenth century a time of optimism and rapid change. As a German visitor noted, "Ten years in America are like a century elsewhere."

Americans were nothing if not brash and self-assured. In 1845, an editorial in the *United States Journal* claimed that "we, the American people, are the most independent, intelligent, moral, and happy people on the face of the earth." Many observers commented on the "rise of the common man" in politics and culture as the republic governed by "natural aristocrats" such as Thomas Jefferson, James Madison, James Monroe, and John Quincy Adams gave way to the frontier democracy promoted by Andrew Jackson and Henry Clay.

During the first half of the nineteenth century, two very different societies—North and South—grew more competitive with one another. The North, the more dynamic and faster-growing region, embraced industrial growth, large cities, foreign immigrants, and the ideal of "free labor" as opposed to the system of slavery in the southern states. The South remained rural, agricultural, and increasingly committed to enslaved labor as the backbone of its cotton-centered economy. Two underlying fears worried southerners: the threat of mass slave uprisings and the possibility that a northern-controlled Congress might abolish slavery. The planter elite's determination to preserve and expand slavery stifled change and reform in the South and ignited a prolonged political controversy that would eventually lead to civil war.

# 8

# The Emergence of a Market Economy

## 1815–1850

***Lackawanna Valley* (1855)** Often hailed as the father of American landscape painting, George Inness was commissioned by a railroad company to capture its trains coursing through the lush Lackawanna Valley in northeastern Pennsylvania. New inventions and industrial development would continue to invade and transform the rural landscape.

N o sooner had the celebrations marking the end of the war of 1812 subsided than Americans busily set about transforming their young nation. Prosperity returned as British and European markets again welcomed American ships and commerce. During the war, the loss of trade with Britain and Europe had forced the United States to develop more factories and mills of its own, spurring the growth of the diverse economy that Alexander Hamilton had envisioned in the 1790s.

Between 1815 and 1850, the United States also became a transcontinental power, expanding all the way to the Pacific coast. Hundreds of thousands of land-hungry people streamed westward. Between 1815 and 1821, six new states joined the Union: Alabama, Illinois, Indiana, Mississippi, Missouri, and Maine.

Nineteenth-century Americans were a restless, ambitious people, and the country's energy and mobility were dizzying. A Boston newspaper commented that the entire American "population is in motion." Everywhere, it seemed, people were moving to the next town, the next farm, the next opportunity. In many cities, half the population moved every ten years. In 1826, the newspaper editor in Rochester, New York, reported that 120 people left the city every day while 130 moved in. Frances Trollope, an English traveler, said that Americans were "a busy, bustling, industrious population, hacking and hewing their way" westward.

The lure of cheap land and plentiful jobs, as well as the promise of political and religious freedom, attracted millions of hardworking immigrants. This great wave of humanity was not always welcomed, however. Ethnic prejudices, anti-Catholicism, and language barriers made it difficult for many immigrants,

## focus questions

**1.** How did changes in transportation and communication alter the economic landscape during the first half of the nineteenth century?

**2.** How did industrial development impact the way people worked and lived?

**3.** In what ways did immigration alter the nation's population and shape its politics?

**4.** How did the expanding "market-based economy" impact the lives of workers, professionals, and women?

especially the Irish, Germans, and Chinese, to assimilate themselves into American society and culture.

In the Midwest, large-scale commercial agriculture emerged as big farms raised corn, wheat, pigs, and cattle to be sold in distant markets and across the Atlantic. In the South, cotton became so profitable that it increasingly dominated the region's economy, luring farmers and planters (wealthy farmers with hundreds or even thousands of acres worked by large numbers of slaves) into the new states of Alabama, Mississippi, Louisiana, and Arkansas.

Cotton from the American South provided most of the clothing for people around the world. As the cotton economy expanded, it required more enslaved workers, many of whom were sold by professional slave traders and relocated from Virginia and the Carolinas to the Old Southwest—western Georgia and the Florida Panhandle, Alabama, Mississippi, Louisiana, and Arkansas.

Meanwhile, the Northeast experienced a surge of industrial development. Labor-saving machines and water- and steam-powered industries reshaped the region's economic and social life. Mills and factories began to transform the way people labored, dressed, ate, and lived. With the rise of the factory system, more and more economic activity occurred outside the home and off the farm. "The transition from mother-daughter power [in the home] to water and steam power" in the mills and factories, said a farmer, was producing a "complete revolution in social life and domestic manners." An urban middle class began to emerge as Americans, including young women, moved to towns and cities, lured by jobs in new mills, factories, stores, and banks.

By 1850, the United States boasted the world's fastest-growing economy. The industrial economy changed politics, the legal system, family dynamics, and social values. These developments in turn helped expand prosperity and freedom for whites and free blacks.

They also sparked vigorous debates over economic policies, transportation improvements, and the extension of slavery into the new territories. In the process, the nation began to divide into three regions—North, South, and West—whose shifting alliances and disputes would shape political life until the Civil War.

# THE MARKET REVOLUTION

A market revolution that had begun before the war for independence accelerated the transformation of the American economy into a global powerhouse. In the eighteenth century, most Americans were isolated farmers who produced just enough food, livestock, and clothing for their own family's needs and perhaps a little more to barter (exchange) with their neighbors. Their lives revolved around a regular farmstead routine.

As the nineteenth century unfolded, however, more and more farm families began engaging in *commercial* rather than *subsistence* agriculture, producing surplus crops and livestock to sell for cash in regional and even international markets. In 1851, the president of the New York Agricultural Society noted that until the nineteenth century, "'production for consumption' was the leading purpose" of the farm economy. Now, however, "no farmer could find it profitable to do everything for himself. He now sells for money." With the cash they earned, farm families were able to buy more land, better equipment, and the latest manufactured household goods.

Such farming for sale rather than for consumption, the first stage of a **"market-based economy,"** produced boom-and-bust cycles and was often built upon the backs of slave laborers, immigrant workers, and displaced Mexicans. Overall, however, the standard of living rose, and Americans enjoyed unprecedented opportunities for economic gain and geographic mobility. What the market economy most needed were "internal improvements"—deeper harbors, lighthouses, and a national network of canals, bridges, roads, and railroads—to improve the flow of goods. In 1817, for example, South Carolina congressman John C. Calhoun expressed his desire to "bind the Republic together with a perfect system of roads and canals." As the world's largest republic, the United States desperately needed a national transportation system.

Calhoun's idea sparked a fierce debate over how to fund such infrastructure improvements: Should it be the responsibility of the federal government, the individual states, or private corporations? Since the Constitution said nothing about the federal government's role in funding transportation improvements, many argued that such projects must be initiated by state and local governments. Others insisted that the Constitution gave the federal government broad powers to promote the "general welfare," which included enhancing transportation and communication. The debate over internal improvements would continue throughout the nineteenth century.

**BETTER ROADS** Until the nineteenth century, travel had been slow, tedious, uncomfortable, and expensive. It took a horse-drawn coach, for example, four days to go from New York City to Boston. Because of long travel times, many farm products could be sold only locally before they spoiled. That soon changed, as an array of innovations—larger horse-drawn wagons (called *Conestogas*), new roads, canals, steamboats, and railroads—knit together the expanding national market for goods and services and greatly accelerated the pace of life.

**TRANSPORTATION WEST, ABOUT 1840**

- Why were river towns important commercial centers?
- What was the economic impact of the steamboat and the flatboat in the West?
- How did the Erie Canal transform the economy of New York and the Great Lakes region?

Better roads led to faster travel. In 1803, when Ohio became a state, Congress ordered that 5 percent of the money from land sales in the state should go toward building a National Road from the Atlantic coast across Ohio and westward. Construction finally began in 1811. Originally called the Cumberland Road, it was the first interstate roadway financed by the federal government. By 1818, the road was open from Cumberland, Maryland, to

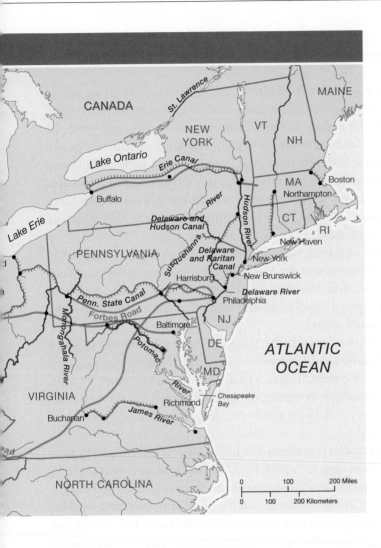

Wheeling, Virginia (now West Virginia), where it crossed the Ohio River. By 1838, the National Road extended 600 miles farther westward to Vandalia, Illinois.

The National Road quickened the settlement of the West and the emergence of a truly national market economy by reducing transportation costs, opening up new markets, and stimulating the growth of towns. Farmers increasingly took their produce and livestock to sell in distant markets.

To the northeast, a movement for paved roads gathered momentum after the Philadelphia-Lancaster Turnpike opened in 1794. (The term *turnpike* derived from a pole, or pike, at the tollgate, which was turned to admit the traffic in exchange for a small fee, or toll.) By 1821, some 4,000 miles of turnpikes had been built, and stagecoach and freight companies emerged to move more people and cargo at lower rates.

**WATERWAYS**  By the early 1820s, the turnpike boom was giving way to advances in water transportation. Steamboats, flatboats (barges driven by men using long poles and mules), and canal barges carried people and goods far more cheaply than did horse-drawn wagons. Hundreds of flatboats floated goods, farm produce, livestock, and people from Tennessee, Kentucky, Indiana, Ohio, western Pennsylvania, and other states down the Ohio and Mississippi Rivers. Flatboats, however, went in only one direction: downstream. Once unloaded in Natchez, Mississippi, or New Orleans, Louisiana, they were sold and dismantled to provide lumber for construction.

The difficulties of getting back upriver were solved when Robert Fulton and Robert R. Livingston sent the *Clermont*, the first commercial steamboat, up the Hudson River from New York City in 1807. Thereafter, the use of wood-fired **steamboats** spread rapidly, opening nearly half the continent to water traffic along the major rivers.

By bringing two-way travel to the Mississippi Valley, steamboats created a transcontinental market and a commercial agricultural empire that produced much of the nation's cotton, timber, wheat, corn, cattle, and hogs. By 1836, there were 750 steamboats operating on American rivers. As steamboat use increased, the price for shipping goods plunged, thus increasing profits and stimulating demand.

The use of steamboats transformed St. Louis, Missouri, from a sleepy frontier village into a booming river port. New Orleans developed even faster. By 1840, it was perhaps the wealthiest American city, having developed a thriving trade with the Caribbean islands and the new Latin American republics that had overthrown Spanish rule. A thousand steamboats a year visited New Orleans. The annual amount of trade shipped through the river city doubled that of New York City by 1843, in large part because of the explosion in cotton production.

Wood-burning steamboats were a risky form of transportation. Accidents, explosions, and fires were common, and sanitation was poor. Passengers crowded on board along with pigs and cattle. There were no toilets on steamboats until the 1850s; passengers shared the same two washbasins and towels. Despite the inconveniences, however, steamboats were the fastest and most convenient form of transportation in the first half of the nineteenth century.

Canals also sped the market revolution. The historic **Erie Canal** in central New York connected the Great Lakes and the Midwest to the Hudson River and New York City. New York Governor DeWitt Clinton took the lead in promoting the risky project, which Thomas Jefferson dismissed as "little short of madness." Clinton, however, boasted that New York had the opportunity to "create a new era in history, and to erect a work more stupendous, more magnificent, and more beneficial, than has hitherto been achieved by the human race."

It was not an idle boast. After the Erie Canal opened in 1825, having taken eight years to build, it drew eastward much of the midwestern trade (furs, lumber, textiles) that earlier had been forced to go to Canada or make the long journey down the Ohio and Mississippi Rivers to New Orleans and the Gulf of Mexico. Thanks to the Erie Canal, the backwoods village of Chicago developed into a bustling city because of its commercial connection via the Great Lakes to New York City, and eventually to Europe.

The Erie Canal was a triumph of engineering audacity. Forty feet wide and four feet deep, it was the longest canal in the world, extending 363 miles across New York from Albany in the east to Buffalo and Lake Erie in the west, and rising some 675 feet in elevation.

The canal was built by thousands of laborers, mostly German and Irish immigrants who were paid less than a dollar a day to drain swamps, clear forests, build stone bridges and aqueducts, and blast through solid rock. It brought a "river of gold" to New York City in the form of an unending stream

**The Erie Canal** *Junction of the Erie and Northern Canals* (1830–1832), by John Hill.

of lumber, grain, flour, and other goods, and it unlocked the floodgates of western settlement. The canal also reduced the cost of moving a ton of freight from $100 to $5. It was so profitable that it paid off its construction costs in just seven years.

The Erie Canal also had enormous economic and political consequences, as it tied together the regional economies of the Midwest and the East while further isolating the Deep South. The Genesee Valley in western New York became one of the most productive grain-growing regions in the world; Rochester became a boom town, processing wheat and corn into flour and meal. Syracuse, Albany, and Buffalo experienced similarly dramatic growth.

The business of moving goods and people along the canal involved some 4,000 boats and more than 25,000 workers. Canal boats, usually eleven feet wide and seventy feet long, were pulled by teams of horses or mules walking along a towpath adjacent to the canal. The success of the Erie Canal and the entire New York canal system inspired other states to build some 3,000 miles of waterways by 1837. Canals spurred the economy by enabling speedier and less expensive transport of goods and people. They also boosted real estate prices for the lands bordering them and transformed sleepy villages into booming cities.

**RAILROADS** The canal era was short-lived, however. During the second quarter of the nineteenth century, a much less expensive but much more efficient and versatile form of transportation emerged: the railroad.

In 1825, the year the Erie Canal was completed, the world's first steam-powered railway began operating in England. Soon thereafter, a railroad-building "epidemic" infected the United States. In 1830, the nation had only twenty-three miles of railroad track. Over the next twenty years, railroad coverage grew to 30,626 miles.

The railroad quickly surpassed other forms of transportation because trains could move people and freight faster, farther, and cheaper than could wagons or boats. The early **railroads** averaged ten miles per hour, more than twice the speed of stagecoaches and four times that of boats and barges. That locomotives were able to operate year-round gave rail travel a huge advantage over canals that froze in winter and dirt roads that became rivers of mud during rainstorms.

Railroads also provided indirect benefits by encouraging western settlement and the expansion of commercial agriculture. A westerner reported that the opening of a new rail line resulted in the emergence of three new villages along the line. The depot or rail station became the central building in every town, a public place where people from all walks of life converged.

# THE GROWTH OF RAILROADS, 1860

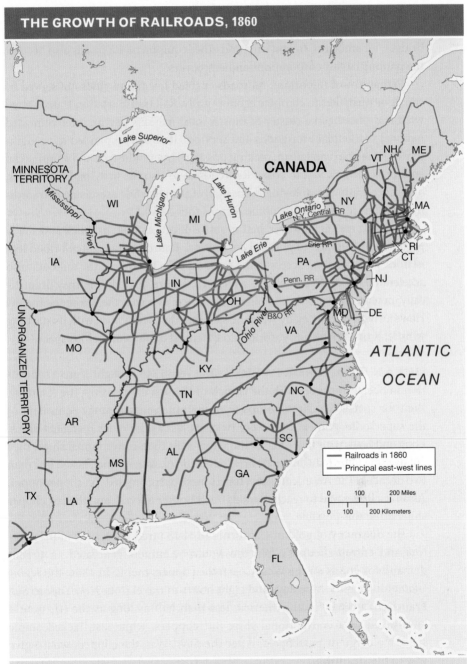

- Why did the number of railroads expand rapidly from 1850 to 1860?
- What were the principal east–west lines?

Building railroads stimulated the national economy not only by improving transportation but by creating a huge demand for iron, wooden crossties, bridges, locomotives, freight cars, and other equipment. Railroads also became the nation's largest corporations and employers.

Perhaps most important, railroads enabled towns and cities not served by canals or turnpikes to compete economically. Rail transportation transformed what had once been a cluster of mostly local markets into an interconnected national marketplace for goods and services. Railroads expanded the geography of American capitalism, making possible larger industrial and commercial enterprises from coast to coast. Railroads were also the first "big" businesses, huge corporations employing thousands of people while exercising extraordinary influence over the life of the regions they served.

Railroad mania, however, had negative effects as well. Its quick and shady profits frequently led to political corruption. Railroad titans often bribed legislators. By facilitating access to the trans-Appalachian West, the railroads also accelerated the decline of Native American culture. In addition, they dramatically increased the tempo, mobility, and noise of everyday life. Writer Nathaniel Hawthorne spoke for many when he said that the locomotive, with its startling whistle, brought "the noisy world into the midst of our slumberous space."

**OCEAN TRANSPORTATION**  The year 1845 brought a great innovation in ocean transport with the launch of the first clipper ship, the *Rainbow*. Built for speed, the **clipper ships** were the nineteenth-century equivalent of the supersonic jetliner. They were twice as fast as the older merchant ships. Long and lean, with taller masts and larger sails than conventional ships, they cut dashing figures during their brief but colorful career, which lasted less than two decades. The American thirst for Chinese tea prompted the clipper boom. Asian tea leaves had to reach markets quickly after harvest, and the fast clipper ships made this possible.

The discovery of gold in California in 1848 lured thousands of prospectors and entrepreneurs. When the would-be miners generated an urgent demand for goods on the West Coast, the clippers met it. In 1854, the *Flying Cloud* took eighty-nine days and eight hours to travel from New York to San Francisco, around South America, less than half as long as the trip would have taken in a conventional ship. But clippers, while fast, lacked ample space for cargo or passengers. After the Civil War, the clippers would give way to the steamship.

**COMMUNICATIONS**  Innovations in transportation also helped spark improvements in communications, which knit the nation even closer together.

**Building a clipper ship** This 1833 oil painting captures the Messrs. Smith & Co. Ship Yard in Manhattan, where shipbuilders are busy shaping timbers to construct a clipper ship.

At the beginning of the nineteenth century, traveling was slow and difficult. It often took days or weeks for news to travel along the Atlantic Seaboard. For example, after George Washington died in 1798 in Virginia, word of his death did not appear in New York City newspapers until a week later. By 1829, however, it was possible to deliver Andrew Jackson's inaugural address from Washington, D.C., to New York City by relay horse riders in less than twenty hours.

Mail deliveries also improved. The number of post offices soared from 75 in 1790 to 28,498 in 1860. In addition, new steam-powered printing presses enabled the mass production of newspapers, reducing their cost from 6¢ to a penny each.

But the most important advance in communications was the national electromagnetic **telegraph system**, invented by Samuel F. B. Morse. In May 1844, Morse sent the first intercity telegraph message from Washington, D.C., to Baltimore, Maryland. It read: "What Hath God Wrought?"

By the end of the decade, most major cities benefited from telegraph lines. By allowing people to communicate faster and more easily across long distances, the telegraph system triggered many changes, not the least of which was helping railroad operators schedule trains more precisely and thus avoid collisions. A New Orleans newspaper claimed that, with the invention of the telegraph, "scarcely anything now will appear to be impossible."

**THE ROLE OF GOVERNMENT** Steamboats, canals, and railroads connected the western areas of the country with the East, boosted trade, helped open the Far West for settlement, and spurred dramatic growth in cities. Between 1800 and 1860, an undeveloped nation of scattered farms, primitive roads, and modest local markets became an engine of capitalist expansion, urban energy, and global reach.

The national government bought stock in turnpike and canal companies and, after the success of the Erie Canal, awarded land grants to several western states to support canal and railroad projects. In 1850, Stephen A. Douglas, a powerful Democratic senator from Illinois, convinced Congress to provide a major land grant to support a north–south rail line connecting Chicago and Mobile, Alabama. The 1850 congressional land grant set a precedent for other bounties that totaled about 20 million acres by 1860. However, this would prove to be a small amount when compared to the land grants that Congress would award transcontinental railroads during the 1860s and after.

## INDUSTRIAL DEVELOPMENT

The concentration of huge numbers of people in commercial and factory cities, coupled with the transportation and communication revolutions, greatly increased the number of potential customers for given products. Such expanding market demand in turn gave rise to a system of *mass production*, whereby companies used new technologies (labor-saving machines) to produce greater quantities of products that could be sold at lower prices to more people, thus generating higher profits.

The introduction of steam engines, as well as the application of new technologies to make manufacturing more efficient, sparked a wave of unrelenting **industrialization** in Europe and America from the mid–eighteenth century to the late nineteenth century. "It is an extraordinary era in which we live," reported Daniel Webster in 1847. "It is altogether new. The world has seen nothing like it before."

New machines and improvements in agricultural and industrial efficiency led to a remarkable increase in productivity. By 1860, one farmer, miner, or mill worker could produce twice as much wheat, twice as much iron, and more than four times as much cotton cloth as in 1800.

**AMERICAN TECHNOLOGY** Improvements in productivity were enabled by the inventiveness of Americans. Between 1790 and 1811, the U.S. Patent Office approved an annual average of 77 patents certifying new inventions;

by the 1850s, the Patent Office was approving more than 28,000 new inventions each year.

Many inventions generated dramatic changes. In 1844, for example, Charles Goodyear patented a process for "vulcanizing" rubber, making it stronger, more elastic, waterproof, and winter-proof. Vulcanized rubber was soon being used for everything from shoes and boots to seals, gaskets, hoses and, eventually, tires.

In 1846, Elias Howe patented his design of the sewing machine. It was soon improved upon by Isaac Merritt Singer, who founded the Singer Sewing Machine Company, which initially produced only industrial sewing machines for use in textile mills but eventually offered machines for home use. The availability of sewing machines helped revolutionize "women's work" by dramatically reducing the time needed to make clothes at home, thus freeing up more leisure time for many women.

Technological advances improved living conditions; houses could be larger, better heated, and better illuminated. The first sewer systems helped rid city streets of human and animal waste. Mechanization of factories meant that more goods could be produced faster and with less labor, and machines helped industries produce "standardized parts" that could be assembled by unskilled wage workers. Machine-made clothes using standardized forms fit better and were less expensive than those sewn by hand; machine-made newspapers and magazines were more abundant and affordable, as were clocks, watches, guns, and plows.

**THE IMPACT OF THE COTTON GIN** In 1792, New Englander Eli Whitney visited Mulberry Grove plantation on the Georgia coast, where he "heard much said of the difficulty of ginning cotton"—that is, separating the fibers from the seeds. Cotton had been used for clothing and bedding from ancient times, but until the nineteenth century, cotton cloth was rare and expensive because it took so long to separate the lint (fibers) from the sticky seeds. One person working all day could separate barely one pound by hand.

At Mulberry Grove, Whitney learned that the person who could invent a "machine" to gin cotton would become wealthy overnight. Within a few days, he had devised what he called "an absurdly simple contrivance" using nails attached to a roller, to remove the seeds from cotton bolls. Over time, Whitney continued to refine his gin until it was patented in 1794. The **cotton gin** (short for *engine*) proved to be fifty times more productive than a hand laborer. Almost overnight, it made cotton America's most profitable crop. In the process, it transformed southern agriculture, northern industry, race-based slavery, national politics, and international trade.

**KING COTTON** Southern-grown **cotton** became the dominant force driving both the national economy and the controversial efforts to expand slavery into the western territories. Cotton, or "white gold," brought enormous wealth to southern planters and merchants, New England mill owners, and New York shipowners.

Because of the widespread use of cotton gins, by 1812 the cost of producing cotton yarn had plunged by 90 percent, and the spread of textile mills overseas had created a growing global market for southern cotton. By the mid–nineteenth century, people worldwide were wearing more-comfortable and easier-to-clean cotton clothing. When British textile manufacturers chose the less brittle American cotton over the varieties grown in the Caribbean, Brazil, and India, the demand for southern cotton skyrocketed, as did its price.

Cotton became America's largest export product and the primary driver of the nation's extraordinary economic growth. By 1860, British textile mills were processing a billion pounds a year, 92 percent of which came from the American South.

**Whitney's cotton gin** Eli Whitney's drawing, which accompanied his 1794 federal patent application, shows the side and top of the machine as well as the sawteeth that separated the seeds from the fiber.

Cotton growing first emerged in the Piedmont region of the Carolinas and Georgia. After the War of 1812, it migrated into the contested Indian lands to the west—Tennessee, Alabama, Florida, Mississippi, Louisiana, Arkansas, and Texas. New Orleans became a bustling port—and active slave market—because of the cotton grown throughout the region and shipped down the Mississippi River. From the mid-1830s to 1860, cotton accounted for more than half of American exports. Planter capitalists in the South harvested raw cotton, and northern buyers and shipowners carried it to New England, Great Britain, and France, where textile mills spun the fiber into thread and fabric. Bankers in New York City and London financed the growth of global cotton capitalism.

**THE EXPANSION OF SLAVERY**  Because cotton was a labor-intensive crop, growers were convinced that only slaves could make their farms and plantations profitable. As a result, the price of slaves soared. When farmland in Maryland and Virginia lost its fertility after years of relentless tobacco planting, many whites shifted to growing corn and wheat, since the climate was too cold for cotton, and they sold their surplus slaves to work in the new cotton-growing areas in Georgia, Alabama, Mississippi, and Louisiana. In 1790, planters in Virginia and Maryland had owned 56 percent of all the slaves in the United States; by 1860, they owned only 15 percent.

Cotton created boom times. A cotton farmer in Mississippi urged a friend in Kentucky to sell his farm and join him: "If you could reconcile it to yourself to bring your negroes to the Mississippi Territory, they would certainly make you a handsome fortune in ten years by the cultivation of Cotton." Slaves became so valuable that stealing them became a common problem in the southern states.

**FARMING THE MIDWEST**  By 1860, more than half the nation's population lived west of the Appalachian Mountains. The flat, fertile farmlands in the Midwest—Ohio, Michigan, Indiana, Illinois, and Iowa—drew farmers from the rocky hillsides of New England and the exhausted soils of Virginia. By 1860, an estimated 30 to 40 percent of Americans born in New England had moved west, looking to start fresh on their *own* land made available by the government.

After land was cleared, corn was typically the first crop grown. Women and children often planted the seeds in small mounds about three feet apart. Once the corn sprouted, pumpkin, squash, or bean seeds would be planted around the seedlings. Corn kernels could be boiled to make porridge or ground up to make flour and cornmeal that was baked into a bread called johnnycake, and corn stalks were stored to provide winter feed for the cattle and hogs.

Over time, technological advances led to greater agricultural productivity. The development of durable iron plows (replacing wooden ones) eased the backbreaking job of tilling the soil. In 1819, Jethro Wood of New York introduced an iron plow with separate parts that were easily replaced when needed. Further improvements would follow, including Vermonter John Deere's steel plow (1837), whose sharp edges could cut through the tough prairie grass in the Midwest and Great Plains.

Other technological improvements quickened the growth of commercial agriculture. By the 1840s, new mechanical seeders had replaced the process of sowing seed by hand. Even more important, in 1831 twenty-two-year-old Virginian Cyrus Hall McCormick invented a mechanical reaper to harvest wheat, a development as significant to the agricultural economy of the Midwest, Old Northwest, and Great Plains as the cotton gin was to the South.

In 1847, **McCormick reapers** began selling so fast that McCormick moved to Chicago and built a manufacturing plant. Within a few years, he had sold thousands of his machines, in the process transforming the scale of commercial agriculture. Using a handheld sickle, a farmer could harvest a half acre of wheat a day; with a McCormick reaper, two people could work twelve acres a day.

**EARLY TEXTILE MANUFACTURERS**   While technological breakthroughs quickened agricultural development and created a national and international marketplace, other advances altered the economic landscape even more profoundly. Industrial capitalists who financed and built the first factories were the revolutionaries of the nineteenth century.

Mills and factories were initially powered by water wheels, then coal-fired steam engines. The shift from water to coal as a source of energy initiated a worldwide industrial era destined to end Britain's long domination of the global economy.

The foundations of Britain's advantage were the invention of the steam engine in 1705, its improvement by James Watt in 1765, and a series of additional inventions that mechanized the production of textiles (including thread, fabric, bedding, and clothing). Britain carefully guarded its industrial secrets, forbidding the export of machines or the publication of descriptions of them, and even restricting the emigration of skilled mechanics.

In 1800, the output of America's mills and factories amounted to only one sixth of Great Britain's production, and the growth rate remained slow until Thomas Jefferson's embargo in 1807 stimulated the domestic production of cloth. By 1815, hundreds of textile mills in New England, New York, and Pennsylvania were producing thread, cloth, and clothing.

After the War of 1812, however, British textile companies blunted America's industrial growth by flooding the United States with cheap cotton cloth in an effort to regain their customers who had been shut off by the war. Such postwar "dumping" nearly killed the American textile industry. A delegation of New England mill owners traveled to Washington, D.C., to demand a federal tariff (tax) on imported British cloth to make American textile mills more competitive. Their efforts created a culture of industrial lobbying for congressional tariff protection against imported products that continues to this day.

What the mill owners neglected to admit was that import tariffs hurt consumers by forcing them to pay higher prices. Over time, as Scotsman Adam Smith explained in *The Wealth of Nations* (1776), consumers not only pay higher prices for foreign goods as a result of tariffs, but higher prices for domestic goods, since businesses invariably seize opportunities to raise the prices charged for their products.

Tariffs helped protect American industries from foreign competition, but competition is the engine of innovation and efficiency in a capitalist economy. New England shipping companies opposed higher tariffs because they would reduce the amount of goods carried in their vessels across the Atlantic from Britain and Europe. Many southern planters opposed tariffs because of fears that Britain and France would retaliate by imposing tariffs on American cotton and tobacco shipped to their ports.

In the end, Congress passed the Tariff Bill of 1816, which placed a tax of 25¢ on every yard of imported cloth. By impeding foreign competition, the tariffs enabled American manufacturers to dominate the national marketplace.

**THE LOWELL SYSTEM** The factory system, centered on wage-earning workers, emerged at Waltham, Massachusetts, in 1813, when a group known as the Boston Associates constructed the first textile mill in which the mechanized processes of spinning yarn and weaving cloth were brought together under one roof.

In 1822, the Boston Associates, led by Francis Cabot Lowell, developed another cotton mill at a village along the Merrimack River twenty-eight miles north of Boston. Renamed Lowell, it soon became the model for textile mill towns throughout New England.

The founders of the **Lowell system** sought not just to improve efficiency but to develop model industrial communities. They located their four- and five-story brick-built mills along rivers in the countryside.

The mill owners hired mostly young women ages fifteen to thirty from farm families. The owners preferred women laborers because of their skill in operating textile machines. Also valued was their general ability to endure the mind-numbing boredom of operating

**Mill girls** Massachusetts mill workers of the mid–nineteenth century, photographed holding shuttles used in spinning thread and yarn.

spinning machines and looms for a wage of $2.50 per week—a wage lower than that paid to men for the same work. At the time, these jobs offered the highest wages, for women, of any in the world.

Moreover, by the 1820s, New England had a surplus of women because so many men had migrated westward. In the early 1820s, a steady stream of single women began flocking to Lowell. To reassure worried parents, mill owners promised to provide the "Lowell girls" with tolerable work, prepared meals, comfortable boardinghouses (four girls to a room), moral discipline, and educational and cultural opportunities.

Initially the "Lowell idea" worked. The Lowell girls lived in dormitories staffed by housemothers who enforced church attendance and evening curfews. Despite thirteen-hour work days and five-and-a-half day work weeks (longer hours than those imposed upon prison inmates), some of the women found time to form study groups, publish a literary magazine, and attend lectures. By 1840, there were thirty-two mills and factories in Lowell.

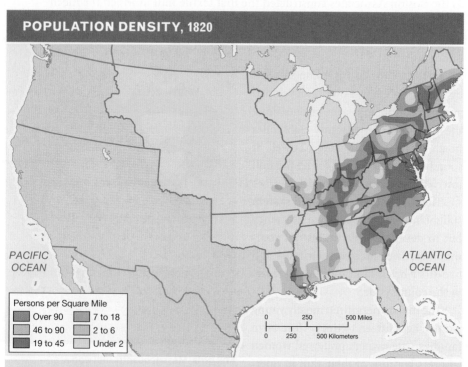

**POPULATION DENSITY, 1820**

PACIFIC
OCEAN

ATLANTIC
OCEAN

Persons per Square Mile

| | |
|---|---|
| Over 90 | 7 to 18 |
| 46 to 90 | 2 to 6 |
| 19 to 45 | Under 2 |

0    250    500 Miles

0    250    500 Kilometers

- In 1820, which regions had the greatest population density? Why?
- How did the changes in the 1820 land law encourage western expansion?
- What events caused the price of land to decrease between 1800 and 1841?

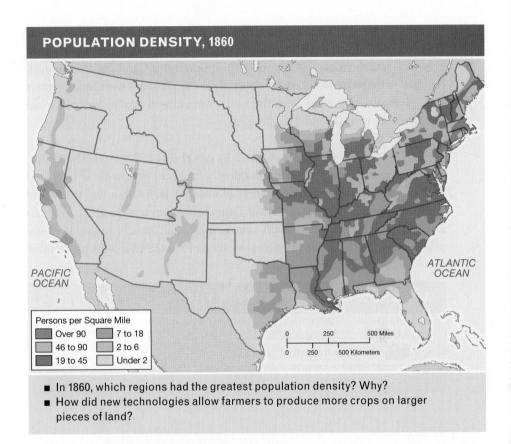

## POPULATION DENSITY, 1860

PACIFIC
OCEAN

ATLANTIC
OCEAN

Persons per Square Mile

- Over 90
- 46 to 90
- 19 to 45
- 7 to 18
- 2 to 6
- Under 2

0    250    500 Miles
0    250    500 Kilometers

- In 1860, which regions had the greatest population density? Why?
- How did new technologies allow farmers to produce more crops on larger pieces of land?

As Lowell grew, however, the once rural village became a grimy industrial city. Mill owners produced too much cloth, which depressed prices. To maintain their profits, they cut wages and quickened the pace of work. As a worker said, "We go in at five o'clock [in the morning]; at seven we come out to breakfast; at half-past seven we return to our work, and stay until half past twelve. At one . . . we return to our work, and stay until seven at night."

In 1834, about a sixth of the native-born Lowell women mill workers went on strike to protest their working and living conditions. The mill owners labeled the 1,500 striking women "ungrateful" and "unfeminine"—and tried to get rid of the strike's leaders.

Two years later, the Lowell workers again walked out, this time in protest of the owners raising rents in the company-owned boarding houses. Although the owners backed down, they soon began hiring Irish immigrants who were so desperate for jobs that they rarely complained about the working conditions. By 1850, some 40 percent of the mill workers were Irish.

The economic success of the New England textile mills raises an obvious question: Why didn't the South build its own mills close to the cotton fields to keep profits in the region? A few mills did appear in the Carolinas and Georgia, but they struggled because whites generally resisted factory work, and planters refused to allow slaves to leave the fields. Agricultural slavery had made the planters rich. Why should they change?

## INDUSTRIALIZATION, CITIES, AND THE ENVIRONMENT

The rapid growth of commerce and industry drove the expansion of cities and mill villages. Lowell's population in 1820 was 200. By 1830, it was 6,500, and ten years later it had soared to 21,000. Other factory centers sprouted up across New England, filling the air with smoke, noise, and stench. In addition, the profusion of dams—built to harness water to turn the mill wheels—flooded

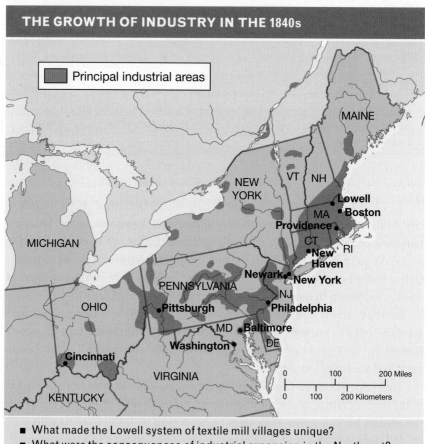

**THE GROWTH OF INDUSTRY IN THE 1840s**

Principal industrial areas

MAINE

NEW YORK

VT  NH

Lowell

MA  Boston

Providence

MICHIGAN

CT

New Haven  RI

Newark  New York

PENNSYLVANIA

NJ

OHIO  Pittsburgh  Philadelphia

MD  Baltimore

Washington  DE

Cincinnati

VIRGINIA

0    100    200 Miles

KENTUCKY

0    100    200 Kilometers

■ What made the Lowell system of textile mill villages unique?
■ What were the consequences of industrial expansion in the Northeast?

pastures, decimated fish populations, and spawned rapid urban growth that polluted rivers.

Between 1820 and 1840, the number of Americans engaged in manufacturing increased 800 percent, and the number of city dwellers more than doubled. As Thomas Jefferson and other agrarians had feared, the United States was rapidly becoming a global industrial power.

Between 1790 and 1860, the proportion of urban to rural populations grew from 3 percent to 16 percent. New Orleans became the nation's fifth-largest city because of its location and role in shipping goods floated down the Mississippi River for distribution to the East Coast and to Europe. By 1860, New York had become the first city to surpass 1 million in population, largely because of its superior harbor and its unique access to commerce along the Erie Canal and the Atlantic Ocean.

## POPULAR CULTURE

During the colonial era, working-class Americans had little time for amusement. Most adults worked from dawn to dusk six days a week. In rural areas, free time was often spent in communal activities, such as barn raisings, shooting matches, and footraces, while coastal residents sailed and fished. In cities, people attended dances, went on sleigh rides and picnics, and played "parlor games" such as billiards, cards, and chess.

By the early nineteenth century, however, an increasingly urban society enjoyed more diverse forms of recreation. A distinctive urban culture emerged, and laborers and shopkeepers sought new forms of leisure and entertainment.

**URBAN RECREATION**   Social drinking was pervasive during the first half of the nineteenth century. In 1829, the secretary of war estimated that three quarters of the nation's laborers drank at least four ounces of "hard liquor" daily. Taverns and social or sporting clubs served as centers of recreation and leisure.

So-called blood sports were also popular, especially among the working poor. Cockfighting and dogfighting attracted frenzied betting, but prizefighting (boxing) eventually displaced the animal contests and proved popular with all social classes. The early contestants tended to be Irish or English immigrants who fought with bare knuckles, and the results were brutal. A match ended only when a contestant could not continue. One bout in 1842 lasted 119 rounds and ended when a fighter died in his corner. Such deaths prompted several cities to outlaw boxing, only to see it reappear as an underground activity.

**Bare Knuckles** Blood sports emerged as popular urban entertainment for men of all social classes, but especially among the working poor.

**THE POPULAR ARTS** Theaters became the most popular form of indoor entertainment. People from all walks of life flocked to opera houses, playhouses, and music halls to watch a wide spectrum of performances: Shakespeare's tragedies, "blood and thunder" melodramas, comedies, minstrel shows, operas, and local pageants. Audiences were predominantly men. "Respectable" women rarely attended, as the prevailing "cult of domesticity" kept them at home.

The 1830s brought the first uniquely American form of mass entertainment: blackface minstrel shows, featuring white performers made up as blacks. "Minstrelsy," which drew upon African American folklore and reinforced racial stereotypes, featured banjo and fiddle music, "shuffle" dances, and lowbrow humor. Between the 1830s and the 1870s, minstrel shows were immensely popular, especially among northern working-class ethnic groups and southern whites.

The most popular minstrel songs were written by a white composer named Stephen Foster. In 1846, he composed "Oh! Susanna," which immediately became a national favorite. Its popularity catapulted Foster into the limelight, and he responded with equally well-received tunes such as "Old Folks at Home" (popularly known as "Way Down upon the Swanee River"), "Massa's in de Cold, Cold Ground," "My Old Kentucky Home," and "Old Black Joe," all of which perpetuated the sentimental myth of contented slaves.

**The Crow Quadrilles**  This sheet-music cover, printed in 1837, shows vignettes caricaturing African Americans. Minstrel shows enjoyed nationwide popularity while reinforcing racial stereotypes.

# IMMIGRATION

More than ever, the United States continued to be a nation of immigrants. Warfare in Europe at the start of the nineteenth century restricted travel to America. After 1815, however, when Napoléon was defeated and forced into exile, new U.S. territories and states in the West actively recruited immigrants from Europe, often offering special incentives such as voting rights after only six-months' residency.

Why did people risk their lives and abandon their homelands to come to the United States? America offered jobs, higher wages, lower taxes, cheap and fertile land, no entrenched aristocracy, religious freedom, and voting rights.

After 1837, a worldwide economic slump accelerated the pace of immigration. American employers recruited foreigners, in large part because they were often willing to work for lower wages than native-born Americans. The *Chicago Daily Tribune* observed that the tide of German immigrants was perfect for the "cheap and ingenious labor of the country." A German laborer was willing "to live as cheaply and work infinitely more intelligently than the negro."

The years from 1845 to 1854 marked the greatest proportional influx of immigrants in U.S. history, 2.4 million, or about 14.5 percent of the total population in 1845. By far the largest number of immigrants between 1840 and 1860 came from Ireland and Germany.

**THE IRISH**  No nation proportionately sent more of its people to America than Ireland. A prolonged agricultural crisis caused many Irish to flee their homeland in the mid–nineteenth century. Irish farmers primarily grew potatoes; a third of them were dependent on the potato harvest for survival.

In 1845, a fungus destroyed the potato crop and triggered what came to be called the Irish Potato Famine. More than a million people died, and almost 2 million more left Ireland, whose total population was only 8 million. Most traveled to Canada and the United States. By the 1850s, the Irish made up more than half the population of Boston and New York City and were almost as dominant in Philadelphia. Most of them were crowded into filthy, poorly ventilated tenement apartments, and Irish neighborhoods were plagued by crime, diseases, prostitution, and alcoholism. The archbishop of New York described the Irish as "the poorest and most wretched population that can be found in the world."

The Irish often took on the hardest and most dangerous jobs. A visiting Irish journalist wrote that there were "several sorts of power working at the fabric of the Republic: water-power, steam-power, horse-power, and Irish power. The last works hardest of them all." It was mostly Irish men who built the canals and railroads, and mostly Irish women who worked in the textile mills and cleaned the houses of upper-middle-class Americans. One Irishman groaned that he worked like "a slave for the Americans."

Irish immigrants were stereotyped as filthy, bad-tempered, and heavy drinkers. They also encountered anti-Catholic prejudice among native-born Protestants. Many employers posted signs reading "No Irish Need Apply."

Irish Americans, however, could be equally mean-spirited toward other groups, such as free African Americans, who competed with them for low-wage, mostly unskilled jobs. In 1850, the *New York Tribune* expressed concern that the Irish, having escaped from "a galling, degrading bondage" in their homeland, opposed equal rights for blacks and frequently arrived at the polls shouting, "Down with the Nagurs! Let them go back to Africa, where they belong."

Many African Americans viewed the Irish with equal contempt. In 1850, a slave noted that his "master" "treats me badly as if I were a common Irishman." Irish immigrants often worked as waiters, dockworkers, and deliverymen— jobs that had long been held by African Americans. One frustrated free black said that the Irish were "crowding themselves into every place of business and labor, and driving the poor colored American citizen out."

Some enterprising Irish immigrants did forge remarkable careers in America, however. Twenty years after arriving in New York, Alexander T. Stewart became the owner of the nation's largest department store and vast real estate holdings. Michael Cudahy, who began working at age fourteen in a Milwaukee meatpacking business, became head of the Cudahy Packing Company and developed a process for the curing of meats under refrigeration. Dublin-born Victor Herbert emerged as one of America's most revered composers, and Irish dancers and playwrights came to dominate the stage.

By the start of the Civil War, Irish immigrants had energized American trade unions, become the most important ethnic group supporting the Democratic party, and made the Roman Catholic Church the nation's largest denomination. Years of persecution had instilled a fierce loyalty to the Catholic Church as "the supreme authority over all the affairs of the world." Such passion for Catholicism generated unity among Irish Americans—and fear among Protestants.

**THE GERMANS** German immigrants were almost as numerous as the Irish. Unlike the Irish, however, the Germans included skilled craftsmen and well-educated professional people—doctors, lawyers, teachers, engineers— some of whom were refugees from the failed German revolution of 1848.

The Germans brought with them a variety of religious preferences. Most were Protestants (usually Lutherans), a third were Roman Catholics, and a significant number were Jews. Among the Germans who prospered in the New World were Heinrich Steinweg, a piano maker who in America changed his name to Steinway and became famous for the quality of his instruments, and Levi Strauss, a Jewish tailor who followed the gold rush to California and began making work pants, later dubbed "Levi's."

Germans settled more often in rural areas. Many were independent farmers, skilled workers, and shopkeepers who were able to establish themselves immediately. More so than the Irish, they migrated in families and groups. This clannish quality helped them better sustain elements of their language and culture. More of them also returned to Germany. About 14 percent eventually went back to their homeland, compared with 9 percent of the Irish.

**THE BRITISH, SCANDINAVIANS, AND CHINESE** Immigrants from Great Britain and Canada continued to arrive in large numbers during the first half of the nineteenth century. They included professionals, independent farmers, and skilled workers. Two other large groups of immigrants were from Scandinavia and China. Norwegians and Swedes, mostly farmworkers, gravitated to Illinois, Wisconsin, and the Minnesota Territory, where the cold climate and dense forests reminded them of home. By the 1850s, the rapid development of California was attracting a growing number of Chinese, who, like the Irish in the East, did the heavy work of construction, especially on railroad tracks and bridges.

**NATIVISM** Not all Americans welcomed the flood of immigrants. A growing number of "nativists," people born in the United States who resented the newcomers, sought to restrict or stop immigration altogether. The flood of Irish and German Catholics especially angered Protestants. A Boston minister described Catholicism as "the ally of tyranny, the opponent of material prosperity, the foe of thrift, the enemy of the railroad, the caucus, and the school."

**Nativists** eventually organized to stop the tide of immigrants. The Order of the Star-Spangled Banner, founded as an oath-bound secret society in New York City in 1849, soon spread to most other large cities. In the early 1850s, it had grown into a powerful political group known in some cities as the American party. In 1855, the American party became a national organization. Members pledged never to vote for foreign-born or Catholic candidates. When asked about their secretive organization, they were told to say, "I know nothing," a phrase which gave rise to the informal name for the party: the **Know-Nothings**.

For a while, the Know-Nothings appeared to be on the brink of major-party status, especially during the 1850s, when the number of immigrants was five times as large as it had been during the 1840s. In the state and local campaigns of 1854, they swept the Massachusetts legislature, winning all but two seats in the lower house, and that fall they elected more than forty congressmen.

**A Know-Nothing cartoon** This cartoon shows the Catholic Church supposedly attempting to control American religious and political life through Irish immigration.

The Know-Nothings demanded that immigrants and Roman Catholics be excluded from public office and that the waiting period for naturalization (earning citizenship) be extended from five to twenty-one years. The party, however, was never strong enough to enact such legislation. For a while, the Know-Nothings threatened to control New England, New York, and Maryland, but the anti-Catholic movement subsided when slavery became the focal issue of the 1850s, and after 1856 members opted either for the Republican or Democratic parties.

## ORGANIZED LABOR AND NEW PROFESSIONS

While most Americans continued to work as farmers, a growing number found employment in textile mills, shoe factories, banks, railroads, publishing, retail stores, teaching, preaching, medicine, law, construction, and engineering. Technological innovations (steam power, mechanized tools, and new modes of transportation) and their social applications (mass communication, turnpikes, the postal service, banks, and corporations) fostered an array of new industries and businesses that transformed the nature of work for both men and women.

**The shoe factory**  When Philadelphia shoemakers went on strike in 1806, a court found them guilty of a "conspiracy to raise wages." Here, shoemakers work at a Massachusetts factory.

EARLY UNIONS   In 1800, only 12 percent of Americans worked for wages; by 1860, that number had grown to 40 percent. The rapid growth of wage workers often came at the expense of skilled, self-employed artisans and craftsmen who owned small shops where they made or repaired carriages, shoes, hats, saddles, silverware, jewelry, glass, ropes, furniture, boats, and a broad array of other products. Other skilled craftsmen were blacksmiths, printers, or barrel makers.

Throughout the first half of the nineteenth century, the number of self-employed craftsmen steadily declined as the number of factories and mills increased. Those who emphasized quality and craftsmanship in their custom-made products found it increasingly hard to compete with the low prices for similar products made in much larger numbers in factories and mass-production workshops.

The production of shoes, for example, was transformed by the shift to mass manufacturing. Until the nineteenth century, boots and shoes were made by hand for local customers. Working in their own home or small shop, shoemakers might also employ one or two journeymen (assistants) as well as an apprentice, a young man learning the skilled trade.

That changed during the early nineteenth century, as the number and size of shoe shops increased in New England, largely driven by the demand for inexpensive shoes, many of which were shipped south for the rapidly growing slave population. Shoe shops were displaced by factories, and the master shoemaker became a manager rather than an artisan. Instead of creating a shoe from start to finish, workers were given specific tasks, such as cutting the leather or stitching the "uppers" onto the soles.

Skilled workers forced to make the transition to mass production and a strict division of labor often resented the change. A Massachusetts worker complained that the factory owners were "little stuck up, self-conceited individuals" who forced workers to follow their orders or be fired. In 1850, the Board of Health in Lynn, Massachusetts, reported that the life expectancy of a shoe worker was almost twenty years shorter than a farmer.

A growing fear that they were losing status led artisans in the major cities to become involved in politics and unions. At first, these workers organized into interest groups representing their individ-

**Symbols of organized labor**
A pocket watch with an International Typographical Union insignia.

ual skills or trades. Philadelphia furniture craftsmen, for example, called for their peers to form a "union" to protect "their mutual independence."

Such "trade associations" were the first type of labor unions. They pressured politicians for tariffs to protect their industries from foreign imports, provided insurance benefits, and drafted regulations to improve working conditions. In addition, they sought to control the number of tradesmen in their profession so as to maintain wage levels.

Early labor unions faced major legal obstacles—in fact, they were prosecuted as unlawful conspiracies. In 1842, though, the Massachusetts Supreme Judicial Court issued a landmark ruling in *Commonwealth v. Hunt* declaring that forming a trade union was not in itself illegal, nor was a demand that employers hire only members of the union. The court also said that union workers could strike if an employer hired laborers who refused to join the union.

Until the 1820s, labor organizations took the form of local trade unions, each confined to one city and one craft or skill. From 1827 to 1837, however, organization on a larger scale began to take hold. In 1834, the **National Trades' Union** was formed to organize local trade unions into a stronger national association. At the same time, shoemakers, printers, carpenters, and weavers established their own national craft unions.

Women also formed trade unions. Sarah Monroe, who helped organize the New York Tailoresses' Society, said that if it was "unfashionable for men to bear [workplace] oppression in silence, why should it not also become unfashionable

**Tailoresses at work in New York** A line engraving of a workroom inside Douglas & Sherwood's skirt factory in New York. Many tailoresses doing work such as this would go on to join labor unions to combat the poor working conditions and paltry wages in the textile industry.

with the women?" In 1831, the women tailors went out on strike demanding a "just price for labor."

Skilled workers also formed political organizations to represent their interests. A New York newspaper reported that people were organizing Workingmen's political parties to protect "those principles of liberty and equality unfolded in the Declaration of our Independence." Workingmen's parties called for laws to regulate banks and abolish the practice of imprisoning people who could not pay their debts.

## THE RISE OF THE PROFESSIONS

The dramatic changes in everyday life opened up an array of new **professions**. Bustling new towns required new services—retail stores, printing shops, post offices, newspapers, schools, banks, law firms, medical practices. In 1849, Henry Day delivered a lecture titled "The Professions" at the Western Reserve School of Medicine. He declared that the most important social functions in modern life were the professional skills and claimed that society had become utterly dependent upon "professional services."

**TEACHING**   Teaching was one of the fastest-growing professions in the first half of the nineteenth century. Horace Mann of Massachusetts was instrumental in promoting the idea of free public education as the best way to transform children into disciplined, judicious citizens. Many states, especially in the North, agreed, and the number of schools exploded. New schools required teachers, and Mann helped create "normal schools" to train future teachers. Public schools initially preferred men as teachers, usually hiring them at age seventeen or eighteen. The pay was so low that few stayed in the profession their entire career, but for many educated young adults, teaching offered independence and social status, as well as an alternative to the rural isolation of farming. Church groups and civic leaders started private academies, or seminaries, for girls.

**LAW, MEDICINE, AND ENGINEERING**   Teaching was a common stepping-stone for men who became lawyers. In the decades after the American Revolution, young men would teach for a year or two before joining an experienced attorney as an apprentice (what today would be called an *intern*). They would learn the practice of law in exchange for their labors. (There were no law schools yet.)

Like attorneys, physicians often had little formal academic training. Healers of every stripe assumed the title of *doctor* and established medical practices. Most were self-taught or had assisted a physician for several years, while occasionally taking classes at the handful of medical schools. By 1860, there were 60,000 self-styled physicians, many of whom were "quacks" or frauds. As a result, the medical profession lost the public's confidence until the emergence of formal medical schools.

The industrial expansion of the United States also spurred the profession of engineering, a field that would eventually become the nation's largest professional occupation for men. Specialized expertise was required to build canals and railroads, develop machine tools and steam engines, and construct roads, bridges, and factories.

"WOMEN'S WORK"  Most women still worked primarily in the home or on a farm. The only professions readily available to them were nursing (often midwifery, the delivery of babies) and teaching. Many middle-class women did religious and social-service work. Then as now, women were the backbone of most churches.

A few women, however, courageously pursued careers in male-dominated professions. Elizabeth Blackwell of Ohio managed to gain admission to Geneva Medical College (now Hobart and William Smith College) in western New York despite the disapproval of the faculty. When she arrived at her first class, a hush fell upon the students "as if each member had been struck with paralysis." Blackwell had the last laugh when she finished first in her class in 1849, but thereafter the medical school refused to admit more women. The first American woman to earn a medical degree, Blackwell went on to start the New York Infirmary for Women and Children and later had a long career as a professor of gynecology at the London School of Medicine for Women.

## EQUAL OPPORTUNITIES

The market-based economy that emerged during the first half of the nineteenth century helped spread the idea that individuals should have equal opportunities to better themselves through their abilities and hard work. Equality of opportunity, however, did not assume equal outcomes. Americans wanted an equal chance to earn unequal amounts of wealth.

The same ideals that prompted so many white immigrants to come to the United States were equally appealing to African Americans and women. By the 1830s, they, too, began to demand their right to "life, liberty, and the pursuit of happiness." Such desires for equality of opportunity would quickly spill over into the political arena. Still, progress in those arenas was achingly slow. The prevailing theme of American political life in the first half of the nineteenth century would be the continuing democratization of opportunities for white men, regardless of income or background, to vote and hold office.

# CHAPTER REVIEW

## SUMMARY

- **Transportation and Communication Revolutions**  Canals and other improvements in transportation, such as the *steamboat*, allowed goods to reach markets more quickly and cheaply and transformed the more isolated "household economy" of the eighteenth century into a *market-based economy* in which people bought and sold goods for profit. *Clipper ships* shortened the amount of time it took to transport goods across the oceans. The *railroads* (which expanded rapidly during the 1850s) and the *telegraph system* diminished the isolation of the West and united the country economically and socially. The *Erie Canal (1825)* contributed to New York City's emerging status as the nation's economic center even as it boosted the growth of Chicago and other midwestern cities. Improvements in transportation and communication linked rural communities to a worldwide marketplace.

- **Industrialization**  New machine tools and technology as well as innovations in business organization spurred a wave of *industrialization* during the nineteenth century. The *cotton gin* dramatically increased cotton production, and a rapidly spreading *cotton* culture boomed in the South, with a resultant increase in slavery. Other inventions, such as John Deere's steel plow and the mechanized *McCormick reaper*, helped Americans, especially westerners, farm more efficiently and more profitably. In the North, mills and factories, powered first by water and eventually by coal-fired steam engines, spread rapidly. Mills produced textiles for clothing and bedding from southern cotton, as well as iron, shoes, and other products. The federal government's tariff policy encouraged the growth of domestic manufacturing, especially cotton textiles, by reducing imports of British cloth. Between 1820 and 1840, the number of Americans engaged in manufacturing increased 800 percent. Many mill workers, such as the women in the *Lowell system* of New England textile factory communities, worked long hours for low wages in unhealthy conditions. Industrialization, along with increased commerce, helped spur the growth of cities. By 1860, urban areas held 16 percent of the country's population.

- **Immigration**  The promise of cheap land and good wages drew millions of immigrants to America. By 1844, about 14.5 percent of the population was foreign born. The devastating potato famine led to an influx of destitute Irish Catholic families. By the 1850s, they represented a significant portion of the urban population in the United States, constituting a majority in New York and Boston. German migrants, many of them Catholics and Jews, migrated during this same time. Not all native-born Americans welcomed the immigrants. *Nativists* became a powerful political force in the 1850s, with the *Know-Nothings* nearly achieving major-party status with their message of excluding immigrants and Catholics from the nation's political community.

- **Workers, Professionals, and Women**  Skilled workers (artisans) formed trade associations to protect their members and lobby for their interests. As industrialization spread, some workers expanded these organizations nationally, forming the *National Trades' Union*. The growth of the market economy also expanded opportunities for those with formal education to serve in new or emerging *professions*. The number of physicians, teachers, engineers, and lawyers grew rapidly. By the mid–nineteenth century, women, African Americans, and immigrants began to agitate for equal social, economic, and political opportunities.

## CHRONOLOGY

| | |
|---|---|
| **1794** | Eli Whitney patents the cotton gin |
| | Philadelphia-Lancaster Turnpike is completed |
| **1807** | Robert Fulton and Robert Livingston launch steamship transportation on the Hudson River near New York City |
| **1825** | Erie Canal opens in upstate New York |
| **1831** | Cyrus McCormick invents a mechanical reaper |
| **1834** | National Trades' Union is organized |
| **1837** | John Deere invents the steel plow |
| **1842** | Massachusetts Supreme Judicial Court issues *Commonwealth v. Hunt* decision |
| **1845** | The *Rainbow*, the first clipper ship, is launched |
| | Irish Potato Famine |
| **1846** | Elias Howe invents the sewing machine |
| **1855** | Know-Nothing party (American party) formed |

## KEY TERMS

market-based economy p. 321

steamboats p. 324

Erie Canal (1825) p. 324

railroads p. 326

clipper ships p. 328

telegraph system p. 329

industrialization p. 330

cotton gin p. 331

cotton p. 332

McCormick reapers p. 334

Lowell system p. 335

nativists p. 344

Know-Nothings p. 344

National Trades' Union p. 347

professions p. 348

 INQUIZITIVE

**Go to InQuizitive to see what you've learned—and learn what you've missed—with personalized feedback along the way.**

# 9 Nationalism and Sectionalism
## 1815–1828

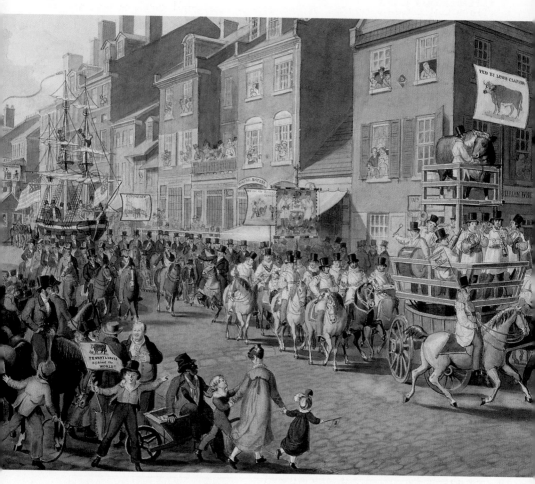

***Parade of the Victuallers*** **(1821)** On a beautiful day in March 1821, Philadelphia butcher William White organized a parade celebrating America's high-quality meats. This watercolor by John Lewis Krimmel captures the new, vibrant nationalism that emerged in America after the War of 1812.

After the War of 1812, the British stopped interfering with American shipping. The United States could now develop new industries and exploit new markets around the globe. Yet it was not simply Alexander Hamilton's financial initiatives and the capitalistic energies of wealthy investors and entrepreneurs that sparked America's dramatic economic growth. Prosperity also resulted from the willingness of ordinary men and women to take risks, uproot families, use unstable paper money issued by unregulated local banks, and tinker with new machines, tools, and inventions.

By 1828, the young agrarian republic was poised to become a sprawling commercial nation connected by networks of roads and canals as well as regional economic relationships—all enlivened by a restless spirit of enterprise, experimentation, and expansion.

For all the energy and optimism exhibited by Americans after the war, however, the fundamental tension between *nationalism* and *sectionalism* remained: how to balance the economic and social needs of the nation's three growing regions—Northeast, South, and West?

Nationalists promoted the interests of the country as a whole, an outlook that required each region to recognize that no single section could get all it wanted without threatening the survival of the nation. Many sectionalists, however, were single-mindedly focused on their region's priorities: shipping, manufacturing, and commerce in the Northeast; slave-based agriculture in the South; low land prices and transportation improvements in the West. Of all the issues dividing the young republic, the passions aroused by the expansion of slavery proved to be the most difficult to resolve.

## focus questions

1. How did the new spirit of nationalism that emerged after the War of 1812 affect economic and judicial policies?

2. What issues and ideas promoted sectional conflict?

3. How did the "Era of Good Feelings" emerge? What factors led to its demise?

4. What were the federal government's diplomatic accomplishments during this era? What was their impact?

5. What developments enabled Andrew Jackson to become president? How did he influence national politics in the 1820s?

# A New Nationalism

After the War of 1812, Americans experienced a wave of patriotic excitement. They had won their independence from Britain for a second time, and a postwar surge of prosperity fed a widespread sense of optimism.

**POSTWAR NATIONALISM** In a message to Congress in late 1815, President James Madison revealed how much the challenges of the war, especially the weaknesses of the armed forces and federal financing, had changed his attitudes about the role of the federal government.

Now, Madison and other leading southern Republicans acted like nationalists rather than states' rights sectionalists. They abandoned many of Thomas Jefferson's presidential initiatives (for example, his efforts to reduce the armed forces and his opposition to the national bank) in favor of the *economic nationalism* advanced by Federalists Alexander Hamilton and George Washington. Madison now supported a larger army and navy, a new national bank, and tariffs to protect American manufacturers from foreign competition. "The Republicans have out-Federalized Federalism," one New Englander commented after Madison's speech.

**THE BANK OF THE UNITED STATES** After President Madison and congressional Republicans allowed the charter for the First Bank of the United States to expire in 1811, the nation's finances fell into a muddle. States began chartering local banks with little or no regulation, and their banknotes (paper money) flooded the economy with different currencies of uncertain value.

In response to the growing financial turmoil, Madison in 1816 urged Congress to establish the **Second Bank of the United States** (B.U.S.), and with the help of powerful congressmen Henry Clay of Kentucky and John C. Calhoun of South Carolina, Congress followed through. The B.U.S. was intended primarily to support a stable national currency that would promote economic growth. In return for issuing paper money and opening branches in every state, it was to handle all federal government funds without charge, lend the government up to $5 million upon demand, and pay the government $1.5 million.

The bitter debate over the B.U.S., then and later, helped set the pattern of regional alignment for most other economic issues. Generally speaking, westerners opposed the national bank because it catered to eastern customers.

The controversy over the B.U.S. was also noteworthy because of the leading roles played by the era's greatest statesmen: Calhoun, Clay, and Daniel Webster of New Hampshire (and later Massachusetts). Calhoun introduced the banking bill and pushed it through, justifying its constitutionality by citing the congressional power to regulate the currency.

Clay, who had long opposed a national bank, now argued that new economic circumstances had made it indispensable. Webster led the opposition among New England Federalists, who feared the growing financial power of Philadelphia. Later, Webster would return to Congress as the champion of a much stronger national government—at the same time that unexpected events would steer Calhoun away from economic nationalism and toward a defiant embrace of states' rights, slavery, and even secession.

**A PROTECTIVE TARIFF**  The long controversy with Great Britain over shipping rights convinced most Americans of the need to develop their own manufacturing sector to end their dependence on imported British goods. Efforts to develop iron and textile industries, begun in New York and New England during the embargo of 1807, had accelerated during the War of 1812 when America lost access to European goods.

After the war ended, however, British companies flooded U.S. markets with less-expensive products, which undercut their American competitors. In response, northern manufacturers lobbied Congress for federal tariffs to protect their infant industries from what they called "unfair" British competition.

Congress responded by passing the **Tariff of 1816**, which placed a 20 to 25 percent tax on a long list of imported goods. Tariffs benefited some regions (the Northeast) more than others (the South), thus aggravating sectional grievances. Debates over tariffs would dominate national politics throughout the nineteenth century, in part because tariffs provided much of the annual federal revenue and in part because they benefited manufacturers rather than consumers.

The few southerners who voted for the tariff, led by John C. Calhoun, did so because they hoped that the South might also become a manufacturing center. Within a few years, however, New England's manufacturing sector would roar ahead of the South, leading Calhoun to do an about-face and begin opposing tariffs.

**INTERNAL IMPROVEMENTS**  The third major element of economic nationalism involved federal financing of "**internal improvements**," what is today called *infrastructure*—the construction of roads, bridges, canals, and harbors. Most American rivers flowed from north to south, so the nation needed a network of roads running east to west, including what became known as the National Road connecting the Midwest with the East Coast.

In 1817, John C. Calhoun urged the House to fund internal improvements. He believed that a federally financed network of roads and canals in the West would help the South by opening up trade between the two regions. Support for Calhoun's proposal came largely from the West, which badly needed transportation infrastructure. Opposition centered in New England, which expected to gain the least from such projects.

**POSTWAR NATIONALISM AND THE SUPREME COURT** The postwar emphasis on economic nationalism also surfaced in the Supreme Court, where Chief Justice John Marshall strengthened the constitutional powers of the federal government at the expense of states' rights. In the path-breaking case of *Marbury v. Madison* (1803), the Court had, for the first time, declared a federal law unconstitutional. In *Martin v. Hunter's Lessee* (1816) and *Cohens v. Virginia* (1821), the Court ruled that the Constitution could remain the supreme law of the land only if the Court could review and at times overturn the decisions of state courts.

**PROTECTING CONTRACT RIGHTS** The Supreme Court made two major decisions in 1819 that strengthened the power of the federal government. One, **Dartmouth College v. Woodward**, involved the New Hampshire legislature's effort to change the Dartmouth College charter to stop the college's trustees from electing their own successors. In 1816, the state's legislature created a new board of trustees. The original trustees sued to block the move. They lost in the state courts but won on appeal to the Supreme Court.

The college's original charter, wrote John Marshall in drafting the Court's opinion, was a valid contract that the state legislature had impaired, an act forbidden by the Constitution. This decision implied an enlarged definition of *contract* that seemed to put corporations beyond the reach of the states that chartered them. Thereafter, states commonly wrote into the charters incorporating businesses and other organizations provisions making charters subject to modification. Such provisions were then part of the "contract."

**PROTECTING A NATIONAL CURRENCY** The second major Supreme Court case of 1819 was Chief Justice Marshall's most significant interpretation of the constitutional system: **McCulloch v. Maryland**. James McCulloch, a B.U.S. clerk in Baltimore, had refused to pay state taxes on B.U.S. currency as required by a Maryland law. The state indicted McCulloch. He appealed to the Supreme Court, which ruled unanimously that Congress had the authority to charter the B.U.S. and that states had no right to tax the national bank.

Speaking for the Court, Marshall ruled that given the "implied powers" granted it, Congress had the right to take any action not forbidden by the Constitution as long as the purpose was within the "scope of the Constitution." One great principle that "entirely pervades the Constitution," Marshall wrote, is "that the Constitution and the laws made in pursuance thereof are supreme: . . . They control the Constitution and laws of the respective states, and cannot be controlled by them." The effort by a state to tax a federal bank therefore was unconstitutional, for the "power to tax involves the power to destroy."

**REGULATING INTERSTATE COMMERCE** John Marshall's last major decision, *Gibbons v. Ogden* (1824), affirmed the federal government's supremacy in regulating *interstate* commerce.

In 1808, the New York legislature granted Robert Fulton and Robert R. Livingston the sole right to operate steamboats on the state's rivers and lakes. Fulton and Livingston then gave Aaron Ogden the exclusive right to ferry people and goods up the Hudson River between New York and New Jersey. Thomas Gibbons, however, operated ships under a federal license that

***Steamboat Travel on the Hudson River* (1811)** This watercolor of an early steamboat was painted by a Russian diplomat, Pavel Petrovich Svinin, who was fascinated by early technological innovations and the unique culture of America.

competed with Ogden. On behalf of a unanimous Court, Marshall ruled that the monopoly granted by the state to Ogden conflicted with the federal license issued to Gibbons.

Thomas Jefferson detested John Marshall's judicial nationalism. The Court's ruling in the *Gibbons* case, said the eighty-two-year-old former president, revealed how "the Federal branch of our Government is advancing towards the usurpation of all the rights reserved to the States, and the consolidation in itself of all powers, foreign and domestic."

# DEBATES OVER THE AMERICAN SYSTEM

The major economic initiatives debated by Congress after the War of 1812—the national bank, federal tariffs, and federally financed roads, bridges, ports, and canals—were interrelated pieces of a comprehensive economic plan called the **American System**.

The term was coined by Henry Clay, the powerful young Kentucky congressman who would serve three terms as Speaker of the House before becoming a U.S. senator. Clay wanted to free America's economy from its dependence on Great Britain while tying together the diverse regions of the nation politically. He said, "I know of no South, no North, no East, no West to which I owe my allegiance. The Union is my country."

In promoting his American System, Clay sought to give each section of the country its top economic priority. He argued that high tariffs on imports were needed to block the sale of British products in the United States and protect new industries in New England and New York from unfair foreign competition.

To convince the western states to support the tariffs, Clay first called for the federal government to use tariff revenues to build much-needed infrastructure—roads, bridges, canals, and other internal improvements—in the frontier West to enable speedier travel and faster shipment of goods to markets.

Second, his American System would raise prices for federal lands sold to the public and distribute the revenue from the land sales to the states to help finance more roads, bridges, and canals. Third, Clay endorsed a strong national bank to create a national currency and to regulate the often unstable state and local banks.

Clay's program depended on each section's willingness to compromise. For a while, it worked. Critics, however, argued that higher prices for federal lands would discourage western migration and that tariffs benefited the northern manufacturing sector at the expense of southern and western farmers and the "common" people, who had to pay more for the goods produced by tariff-protected industries. Many westerners and southerners also feared that the Second Bank of the United States would become so powerful and corrupt that it could dictate the nation's economic future at the expense of states' rights and the needs of particular regions. Missouri senator Thomas Hart Benton predicted that cash-strapped western towns would be at the mercy of the national bank in Philadelphia. Westerners, Benton worried, "are in the jaws of the monster! A lump of butter in the mouth of a dog! One gulp, one swallow, and all is gone!"

## "An Era of Good Feelings"

Near the end of his presidency, James Madison turned to James Monroe, a fellow Virginian, to be his successor. In the 1816 election, Monroe overwhelmed his Federalist opponent, Rufus King of New York, by a 183–34 margin in the electoral college. The "Virginia dynasty" of presidents continued.

Soon after his inauguration, Monroe embarked on a goodwill tour of New England, the stronghold of the Federalist party. In Boston, a Federalist newspaper complimented the Republican president for striving to "harmonize feelings, annihilate dissentions, and make us one people." Those words of praise were printed under the heading "Era of Good Feelings," which became a popular label for Monroe's administration.

**JAMES MONROE** Like George Washington, Thomas Jefferson, and James Madison, James Monroe was a slaveholding planter from Virginia. At the outbreak of the Revolutionary War, he dropped out of the College of William and Mary to join the army. He served under Washington, who called him a "brave, active, and sensible army officer."

After studying law under Jefferson, Monroe served as a representative

**James Monroe** Portrayed as he began his presidency in 1817.

in the Virginia Assembly, as governor, as a representative in the Confederation Congress, as a U.S. senator, and as U.S. minister (ambassador) to Paris, London, and Madrid. Under President Madison, he was secretary of state and doubled as secretary of war during the War of 1812. John C. Calhoun said that Monroe was "among the wisest and most cautious men I have ever known." Jefferson described him as "a man whose soul might be turned wrong side outwards without discovering a blemish to the world."

Although Monroe's presidency began peacefully enough, two major events signaled the end of the Era of Good Feelings and warned of stormy times ahead: the financial Panic of 1819 and the political conflict over statehood for Missouri.

**THE PANIC OF 1819** The young republic experienced its first economic depression when the **Panic of 1819** led to a prolonged financial slowdown. Like so many other economic collapses, it resulted from greed: too many people trying to get rich too quickly.

After the War of 1812, European demand for American products, especially cotton, tobacco, and flour, soared, leading farmers and planters to increase production. To fuel the roaring postwar economy, unsound local and state banks made it easy—too easy—for people and businesses to get loans. The B.U.S. aggravated the problem by issuing risky loans, too.

At the same time, the federal government sold vast tracts of public land, which spurred reckless real estate speculation by people buying large parcels with the intention of reselling them. On top of all that, good weather in Europe led to a spike in crop production there, thus reducing the need to buy American commodities. Prices for American farm products plunged.

The Panic of 1819 was ignited by the sudden collapse of cotton prices after British textile mills quit buying high-priced American cotton—the nation's leading export—in favor of cheaper cotton from other parts of the world. As the price of cotton fell and the flow of commerce slowed, banks began to fail, and unemployment soared. The collapse of cotton prices was especially devastating for southern planters, but it also reduced the world demand for other American goods. Owners of new factories and mills, most of them in New England, New York, and Pennsylvania, struggled to find markets for their goods and to fend off more-experienced foreign competitors.

As the financial panic deepened, a widespread distrust of banks and bankers emerged. Tennessee congressman David Crockett dismissed the "whole Banking system" as nothing more than "swindling on a large scale." Thomas Jefferson told John Adams that "the paper [money] bubble is then burst. This is what you and I, and every reasoning man . . . have long foreseen."

Other factors caused the financial panic to become a depression. Business owners, farmers, and land speculators had recklessly borrowed money to expand their ventures or to purchase more land. With the collapse of crop prices and the decline of land values, both speculators and settlers saw their income plummet.

The equally reckless lending practices of the numerous new state banks compounded the problems. To generate more loans, the banks issued more paper money. Even the Second Bank of the United States, which was supposed to provide financial stability, got caught up in the easy-credit mania.

In 1819, newspapers uncovered extensive fraud and embezzlement in the Baltimore branch of the B.U.S. The scandal prompted the appointment of Langdon Cheves, a former South Carolina congressman, as the bank's new president. Cheves restored confidence in the national bank by forcing state banks to keep more gold coins in their vaults to back up the loans they were making. State banks in turn put pressure on their debtors, who found it harder to renew old loans or to get new ones.

The depression lasted about three years, and many blamed the B.U.S. After the panic subsided, many Americans, especially in the South and the West, remained critical of the national bank.

### THE MISSOURI COMPROMISE

In the midst of the financial panic, another dark cloud appeared on the horizon: the onset of a fierce sectional controversy over expanding slavery into the western territories. The possibility of western territories becoming "slave states" created the greatest political debate of the nineteenth century. By 1819, the country had an equal number of slave and free states—eleven of each. The Northwest Ordinance (1787) had banned slavery north of the Ohio River, and the Southwest Ordinance (1790) had authorized slavery south of the Ohio.

West of the Mississippi River, however, slavery had existed since France and Spain first colonized the area. St. Louis became the crossroads through which southerners brought slaves into the Missouri Territory.

In 1819, Missouri Territory residents asked the House of Representatives to let them draft a constitution and apply for statehood, as the region's population had passed the minimum of 60,000 white settlers. (There were also some 10,000 slaves.) It would be the first state west of the Mississippi River.

At that point, Representative James Tallmadge Jr., a New York Republican, proposed a resolution to ban the transport of any more slaves into Missouri. Tallmadge's resolution enraged southern slaveholders, many of whom had developed a profitable business selling slaves to traders, who resold them in the western territories. Any effort to restrict slavery in the western territories, they believed, could lead to "disunion" and civil war.

## THE MISSOURI COMPROMISE, 1820

BRITISH POSSESSIONS

OREGON COUNTRY
Joint occupation by Britain and U.S.

UNORGANIZED TERRITORY

SPANISH POSSESSIONS

PACIFIC OCEAN

MICHIGAN TERRITORY

Mississippi River

MAINE 1820
VT
NH
NY
MA
PA
CT
RI
NJ
OH
IL
IN
Ohio River
DE
MD
MISSOURI 1821
VA
KY
ARKANSAS TERRITORY
TN
NC
SC
MS
AL
GA
LA

ATLANTIC OCEAN

FLORIDA TERRITORY

GULF OF MEXICO

BRITISH
SPANISH

Free states
Slave states
States and territories covered by the compromise

0    250    500 Miles
0    250    500 Kilometers

■ What caused the sectional controversy over slavery in 1819?
■ What were the terms of the Missouri Compromise?
■ What was Henry Clay's solution to the Missouri constitution's ban on free blacks in that state?

Southerners also worried that the addition of Missouri as a free state would tip the balance of power in the Senate against the slave states. Their fears were heightened when Congressman Timothy Fuller, an anti-slavery Republican from Massachusetts, declared that it was both "the right and duty of Congress" to stop the spread "of the intolerable evil and the crying enormity of slavery." After fiery debates, the House, with its northern majority, passed the Tallmadge Amendment on an almost strictly sectional vote. The Senate, however, rejected it—also along sectional lines.

At about the same time, Maine, which had been part of Massachusetts, applied for statehood. The Senate decided to link Maine's request for statehood with Missouri's, voting in 1820 to admit a year later Maine as a free state and Missouri as a slave state, thus maintaining the political balance between free and slave states.

Illinois senator Jesse Thomas revised the so-called **Missouri Compromise** (1820) by introducing an amendment to exclude slavery in the rest of the Louisiana Purchase north of latitude 36°30', Missouri's southern border. Slavery thus would continue in the Arkansas Territory and in Missouri but would be excluded from the remainder of the area west of the Mississippi River. By a narrow margin, the Thomas Amendment passed.

Then another issue arose. The pro-slavery faction in Missouri's constitutional convention inserted in the proposed state constitution a provision excluding free blacks and mulattoes (mixed-race people) from residing in the state. This threatened to unravel the deal to admit Maine and Missouri as states until Henry Clay fashioned a "second" Missouri Compromise in which Missouri would be admitted only if its legislature pledged never to deny free blacks their constitutional rights. On August 10, 1821, Missouri became the twenty-fourth state, and the twelfth where slavery was allowed.

Nationalists praised the Missouri Compromise, but it actually settled little. Instead, it hardened positions on both sides and revealed a widening divide in the country among the Northeast, dominated by shipping, commerce, and manufacturing; the Midwest, centered on small farms; and the South, more and more dependent on cotton and slavery.

## NATIONALIST DIPLOMACY

Henry Clay's support of economic nationalism and John Marshall's decisions affirming *judicial* nationalism were reinforced by efforts to practice *diplomatic* nationalism. President Monroe's secretary of state, John Quincy Adams, son of former president John Adams, worked to clarify and expand the nation's boundaries. He also wanted Europeans to recognize America's dominance in the Western Hemisphere.

**RELATIONS WITH BRITAIN** The Treaty of Ghent (1814) had ended the War of 1812, but it left unsettled several disputes between the United States and Great Britain. Adams oversaw the negotiations of two important treaties, the Rush-Bagot Treaty of 1817 (named after the diplomats who arranged it) and the Convention of 1818.

In the Rush-Bagot Treaty, the two nations limited the number of warships on the Great Lakes. The Convention of 1818 was even more important. It settled the disputed northern boundary of the Louisiana Purchase by extending it along the 49th parallel westward, from what would become Minnesota to the Rocky Mountains. West of the Rockies, the Oregon Country would be jointly occupied by the British and the Americans.

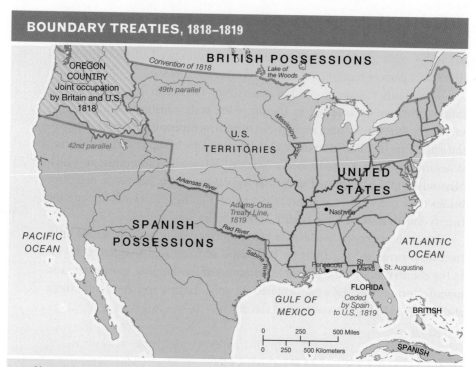

**BOUNDARY TREATIES, 1818–1819**

- How did the Convention of 1818 settle boundary disputes between Spain and the United States?
- How did Andrew Jackson's aggressive military actions in Florida help John Quincy Adams claim territory from Spain?

**FLORIDA** Still another disputed boundary involved western Florida. Spanish control over Florida during the early nineteenth century was more a technicality than an actuality. Spain was now a declining power, unable to enforce its obligations under Pinckney's Treaty of 1795 to keep Indians in the region from making raids into south Georgia.

In 1816, U.S. soldiers clashed with runaway slaves in West Florida, in the present-day Florida Panhandle. At the same time, Seminole warriors fought white settlers in the area. In 1817, Americans burned a Seminole village on the border, killing five Indians.

At that point, Secretary of War John C. Calhoun ordered General Andrew Jackson to lead an army from Tennessee into Florida, igniting what became known as the First Seminole War. Calhoun told Jackson to pursue marauding Indians into Spanish Florida but not to attack Spanish forts. Jackson, frustrated by the restrictions, wrote President Monroe that if the United States wanted Spanish Florida, he could conquer it in sixty days.

***Massacre of the Whites by Indians and Blacks in Florida*** (1836) Published in a southerner's account of the Seminole War, this is one of the earliest known depictions of African Americans and Native Americans fighting as allies.

In early 1818, Jackson's force of 2,000 federal soldiers, volunteer Tennessee militiamen, and Indian allies moved into Spanish Florida. In April, they assaulted a Spanish fort at St. Marks and destroyed several Seminole villages along the Suwannee River.

Jackson's soldiers also captured and court-martialed two British traders accused of provoking Indian attacks. When told that a military trial of the British citizens was illegal, Jackson replied that the laws of war did not "apply to conflicts with savages."

Jackson ordered the immediate execution of the British troublemakers, which outraged the British government and alarmed Monroe's cabinet. But the impulsive Jackson kept moving. In May, he captured Pensacola, the Spanish capital of West Florida, where he established a provisional American government.

While Jackson's conquests excited expansionists, Spain demanded the return of its territory and that Jackson be punished for violating international law. Monroe's cabinet was at first prepared to disavow Jackson's illegal acts. Privately, Calhoun criticized Jackson for disobeying orders—a stand that would later cause bad blood between them.

Jackson, however, remained a hero to most Americans. He also had an important friend in the cabinet—Secretary of State John Quincy Adams, who realized that Jackson's unauthorized conquest of Florida had strengthened his own hand in negotiating with the Spanish to purchase the territory.

In 1819, Adams convinced the Spanish to sign the **Transcontinental Treaty** (also called the Adams-Onís Treaty), in which the United States acquired all of Florida for $5 million in exchange for abandoning any claims to Texas. In 1821, Florida became a U.S. territory; in 1845, it would become a state.

**John Quincy Adams** A brilliant man but an ineffective leader, he appears here in his study in 1843. He was the first U.S. president to be photographed.

The treaty also clarified the contested western boundary separating the Louisiana Territory from New Spain. The boundary would run from the Gulf of Mexico north to the 42nd parallel and then west to the Pacific coast. The United States finally spanned the continent.

Adams also reaffirmed George Washington's belief that the United States should avoid "entangling" itself in European affairs. It would sympathize with democratic movements abroad, but it would not become embroiled in wars supporting such causes. In 1821, Adams declared that America "goes not abroad in search of monsters to destroy. She is the well-wisher to the freedom and independence of all. She is the champion and vindicator only of her own."

**THE MONROE DOCTRINE** The most important diplomatic policy crafted by President Monroe and Secretary of State Adams involved a determined effort to prevent any future European colonialism in the Western Hemisphere. The Spanish, British, French, Portuguese, Dutch, and Russians still controlled one or more colonies in the Americas.

One consequence of the Napoleonic Wars in Europe was the French occupation of Spain and Portugal. The turmoil in those two nations helped trigger independence movements among their colonies in the Americas. Within little more than a decade after the flag of rebellion was raised in 1809 in Ecuador, Spain had lost almost its entire empire in the Americas: La Plata (later Argentina), Bolivia, Chile, Ecuador, Peru, Colombia, Mexico, Paraguay, Uruguay, and Venezuela had all proclaimed their independence, as had Portuguese Brazil. The only areas still under Spanish control were the islands of Cuba and Puerto Rico and the colony of Santo Domingo on the island of Hispaniola.

In 1823, rumors reached America that the monarchs of Europe were planning to help Spain recover its Latin American colonies. The British foreign minister, George Canning, told the United States that the two countries should jointly oppose any new incursions by European nations in the Western Hemisphere. Monroe initially agreed—if the London government would recognize the independence of the new nations of Latin America. The British refused.

Adams, however, advised Monroe to go it alone in prohibiting further European involvement in the hemisphere, stressing that "it would be more candid as well as more dignified" for America to ban further European intervention than to tag along with a British statement.

Monroe agreed. In his annual message to Congress in December 1823, he outlined the four major points of what became known as the **Monroe Doctrine**: (1) That "the American continents . . . are henceforth not to be considered as subjects for future colonization by any European powers"; (2) that the United States would consider any attempt by a European nation to intervene "in this hemisphere as dangerous to our peace and safety"; (3) that the United States would not interfere with existing European-controlled colonies in the Americas; and (4) that the United States would keep out of the internal affairs of European nations.

Reaction to the Monroe Doctrine was mixed. In France, Marquis de Lafayette, the freedom-loving volunteer in the American Revolution, hailed the policy "as the best little bit of paper that God had ever permitted any man to give to the world." Others were not as impressed. No European nation recognized the validity of the Monroe Doctrine.

To this day, the Monroe Doctrine has no official standing in international law. Symbolically, however, it has been an important statement of American intentions to prevent European involvement in the Western Hemisphere and an example of the young nation's determination to take its place among the world's powers. Since it was announced, not a single Latin American nation has lost its independence to an outside invader.

## THE RISE OF ANDREW JACKSON

After the War of 1812, the United States had become a one-party political system. The refusal of the Federalists to support the war had virtually killed the party. In 1820, President Monroe was reelected without opposition.

While the Democratic Republican party was dominant for the moment, however, it was about to follow the Federalists into oblivion. If Monroe's first term was the Era of Good Feelings, his second became an Era of Bad Feelings, as sectional controversies erupted into violent disputes that gave birth to a new political party, the Democrats, led by Andrew Jackson.

ANDREW JACKSON Born in 1767 along the border between the Carolinas, Jackson grew up in a struggling single-parent household. His father was killed in a farm accident three weeks before Andrew was born, forcing his widowed mother, Elizabeth, to scratch out a living as a housekeeper while raising three sons.

During the Revolution, the Jackson boys fought against the British. One of them, sixteen-year-old Hugh, died of heat exhaustion during a battle; another, Robert, died while trudging home from a prisoner-of-war camp.

In 1781, fourteen-year-old Andrew was captured. When a British officer demanded that the boy shine his boots, Jackson refused, explaining that he was a prisoner of war and expected "to be treated as such." The angry officer slashed him with his sword, leaving ugly scars on Andrew's head and hand. Soon after he was released, Elizabeth Jackson, who had helped nurse injured American soldiers, died of cholera. Her orphaned son thereafter despised the British.

After the Revolution, Jackson went to Charleston, South Carolina, where he learned to love racehorses, gambling, and fine clothes. He returned home and tried saddle-making and teaching before moving to Salisbury, North Carolina, where he earned a license to practice law. He also enjoyed life. A friend recalled that Jackson was "the most roaring, rollicking, game-cocking, card-playing, mischievous fellow that ever lived in Salisbury."

In 1788, at age twenty-one, Jackson moved to Nashville and became a frontier attorney.

In 1796, when Tennessee became a state, voters elected Jackson to the U.S. House and later to the Senate, where he served only a year before returning to Tennessee and becoming a judge. Jackson also made a lot of money, first as an attorney, then as a buyer and seller of horses, land, and slaves. He eventually owned 100 slaves on his cotton plantation, called the Hermitage. He had no moral reservations about slavery and could be a cruel master.

Many American political leaders cringed at the thought of the combative, short-tempered Jackson, who had run roughshod over international law in his war against the British and Seminoles in Florida, presiding over the nation. "His passions are terrible," said Thomas Jefferson. John Quincy Adams scorned Jackson "as a barbarian and savage who could scarcely spell his name." Jackson dismissed such criticism as an example of the "Eastern elite" trying to maintain control of American politics. He responded to Adams's criticism by commenting that he never trusted a man who could think of only one way to spell a word.

PRESIDENTIAL POLITICS No sooner had James Monroe started his second presidential term, in 1821, than leading Republicans began positioning themselves to be the next president, including three members of the cabinet: secretary of war, John C. Calhoun; secretary of the Treasury, William H. Crawford; and secretary of state, John Quincy Adams. The Speaker of the House, Henry Clay, also hungered for the presidency. And there was Andrew Jackson, who was elected to the Senate in 1823. The emergence of so many viable candidates revealed how fractured the Republican party had become.

In 1822, the Tennessee legislature named Jackson its long-shot choice to succeed Monroe. Two years later, Pennsylvania Republicans endorsed Jackson for president and chose Calhoun for vice president. Meanwhile, the Kentucky legislature had nominated its favorite son, Clay, in 1822. The Massachusetts legislature nominated Adams in 1824. That same year, a group of Republican congressmen nominated Crawford, a cotton planter from Georgia.

Crawford's friends emphasized his devotion to states' rights. Clay continued to promote the economic nationalism of his American System. Adams, the only non-slaveholder in the race, shared Clay's belief that the national government should finance internal improvements to stimulate economic development, but he was less strongly committed to tariffs.

Jackson declared himself the champion of the common people and the foe of the entrenched social and political elite. He claimed to represent the "old republicanism" of Thomas Jefferson. But Jefferson believed Jackson lacked the education, polish, and prudence to be president. "He is," Jefferson told a friend, "one of the most unfit men I know." Jefferson supported Crawford.

As a self-made military hero, Jackson was an attractive candidate, especially to voters of Irish background. The son of poor Scots-Irish colonists, he was beloved for having defeated the hated English in the Battle of New Orleans. In addition, his commitment to those he called the "common men" resonated with many Irish immigrants who associated aristocracy with centuries of English rule over Ireland.

**THE "CORRUPT BARGAIN"** The initial results of the 1824 presidential election were inconclusive. Jackson won the popular vote and the electoral college, where he had 99 votes, Adams 84, Crawford 41, and Clay 37. But Jackson did not have the necessary majority of electoral votes. In such a circumstance, as in the 1800 election, the Constitution specified that the House of Representatives would make the final decision from among the top three vote-getters. By the time the House could convene, however, Crawford had suffered a stroke and was ruled out. So the election came down to Adams and Jackson.

Henry Clay's influence as Speaker of the House would be decisive. While Adams and Jackson courted Clay's support, he scorned them both, claiming they provided only a "choice of evils." But he regarded Jackson as a "military chieftain," a frontier Napoléon unfit for the presidency. Jackson's election, Clay predicted, would "be the greatest misfortune that could befall the country."

**Henry Clay of Kentucky** Clay entered the Senate at twenty-eight, despite the requirement that senators be at least thirty years old. Here, Clay is pictured in an oil painting by Charles Willson Peale.

Although Clay and Adams disliked each other, the nationalist Adams supported most of the policies that Clay wanted, particularly high tariffs, transportation improvements, and a strong national bank. Clay also expected Adams to name him secretary of state, the office that usually led to the White House. In the end, they made a deal on January 9, 1825. Clay convinced the House of Representatives to elect Adams.

The controversial victory proved costly for Adams, however, as it united his foes and crippled his administration before it began. A furious Jackson dismissed Clay as the "Judas of the West" who had entered into a **"corrupt bargain"** with Adams. Their "corruptions and intrigues," he charged, had "defeated the will of the People." American politics had now entered an Era of Bad Feelings.

Almost immediately, Jackson's supporters launched a campaign to undermine the Adams administration and elect their hero in 1828. Crawford's supporters soon joined the Jackson camp, as did the new vice president, John C. Calhoun, who quickly found himself at odds with President Adams.

**JOHN QUINCY ADAMS** Adams was one of the ablest men, hardest workers, and finest intellects ever to enter the White House. Groomed for greatness by his parents, John and Abigail Adams, he had been ambassador to four European nations, a U.S. senator, a Harvard professor, and an outstanding secretary of state. He had helped negotiate the end to the War of 1812 and had drafted the Monroe Doctrine.

Yet for all his accomplishments, Adams proved to be an ineffective president, undercut from the start by the controversy surrounding his deal with Henry Clay. Strong-willed and intelligent, but socially awkward and a stubborn moralist, Adams lacked the common touch and the politician's gift for compromise. He was easy to admire but hard to like and impossible to love.

His sour personality was shaped in part by family tragedies: He saw two brothers and two sons die from alcoholism. He also suffered from bouts of depression that reinforced his grim self-righteousness and tendency toward self-pity, qualities that did not endear him to others. Poet Ralph Waldo Emerson said Adams was so stern and irritable that he must be taking sulfuric acid with his tea. Even Adams's son Charles Francis admitted that his father "makes enemies by perpetually wearing the iron mask."

Adams detested the democratic politicking that Andrew Jackson represented. He worried, as had his father, that republicanism was rapidly turning into democracy, and that government *of* the people was degenerating into government *by* the people, many of whom, in his view, were uneducated and incompetent. He wanted politics to be a "sacred" arena for the "best men," a profession limited to the "most able and worthy" leaders motivated by a sense of civic duty rather than a selfish quest for power and stature. Poet Walt Whitman wrote that although Adams was "a virtuous man—a learned man . . . he was not a man of the People."

Adams was determined to create an activist federal government with expansive goals. His first State of the Union message, in December 1825, included a grand blueprint for national development, but it was set forth so bluntly that it became a political disaster.

The federal government, Adams stressed, should finance a national transportation network (internal improvements—new roads, canals, harbors, and bridges), create a great national university in Washington, D.C., support scientific explorations of the Far West, build an astronomical observatory ("lighthouse of the skies"), and establish a Department of the Interior to manage the extensive government-owned lands. He challenged Congress to approve his proposals and not be paralyzed "by the will of our constituents."

Reaction was overwhelmingly negative. Newspapers charged that Adams was behaving like an aristocratic tyrant, and Congress quickly revealed that it would approve none of his proposals. The disastrous start shattered Adams's confidence. He wrote in his diary that he was in a "protracted agony of character and reputation."

Adams's effort to expand the powers of the federal government was so divisive that the Democratic-Republican party split, creating a new party system. Those who agreed with the economic nationalism of Adams and Clay began calling themselves National Republicans. The opposition—made up of those who supported Andrew Jackson and states' rights—began calling themselves Democrats. They were strongest in the South and West, as well as among the working class in large eastern cities.

The Democrats were the first party in America to recruit professional state organizers, such as Martin Van Buren of New York, who developed sophisticated strategies for mobilizing voters and orchestrating grassroots campaigns featuring massive rallies, barbecues, and parades.

Perhaps most important, the Democrats convinced voters that their primary allegiance should be to their party rather than to any particular candidate. Party loyalty became the most powerful weapon the Democrats could muster against the "privileged aristocracy" running the state and federal governments.

Adams's opponents sought to use the always controversial tariff issue against him. In 1828, anti-Adams congressmen introduced a new tariff bill designed to help elect Jackson. The bill placed duties (taxes) on imported raw materials such as wool, hemp, and iron that were also produced in key states where Jackson needed support: Pennsylvania, New York, Ohio, Kentucky, and Missouri.

## THE ELECTION OF 1828

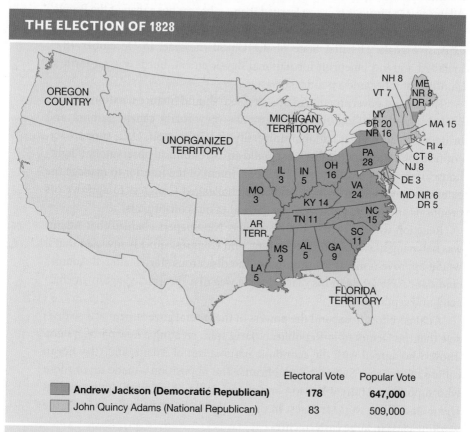

| | Electoral Vote | Popular Vote |
|---|---|---|
| Andrew Jackson (Democratic Republican) | 178 | 647,000 |
| John Quincy Adams (National Republican) | 83 | 509,000 |

- How did the two presidential candidates, John Quincy Adams and Andrew Jackson, portray each other?
- Why did Jackson seem to have the advantage in the election of 1828?
- How did the broadening of voting rights affect the presidential campaign?

The measure passed, only to be condemned as the "Tariff of Abominations" by the cotton states of the Lower South. John C. Calhoun wrote the *South Carolina Exposition and Protest* (1828), in which he ominously declared that a state could nullify an act of Congress that it found unconstitutional, such as the new tariff.

**JACKSON'S ELECTION**  These maneuverings launched the savage **election campaign of 1828** between John Quincy Adams and Andrew Jackson, the National Republicans versus the Jacksonian Democrats.

Both sides launched vicious personal attacks. Adams's supporters denounced Jackson as a hot-tempered, ignorant barbarian, a gambler and slave trader who thrived on confrontation and violence and whose fame rested upon his reputation as a cold-blooded killer.

Their most scurrilous charge was that Jackson had lived in adultery with his wife, Rachel Donelson Robards. In fact, they had lived together as husband and wife for two years in the mistaken belief that her divorce from her first husband was final. As soon as the divorce was official, Andrew and Rachel had remarried to end all doubts about their status. A furious Jackson blamed Henry Clay for spreading the slurs, calling the Kentuckian "the basest, meanest scoundrel that ever disgraced the image of his god."

**Andrew Jackson** The controversial general was painted by Anna Claypoole Peale in 1819, the year of his military exploits in Florida. She captured Jackson's confident demeanor that made him so popular.

The Jacksonians, for their part, condemned Adams as "a lordly, purse-proud" aristocrat, a career politician who had never had a real job and had been corrupted in the courts of Europe. Adams's opponents even claimed that during his time as ambassador to Russia, he had allegedly acted as a pimp, delivering young girls to serve the lust of Czar Alexander I. Adams was left to gripe about the many "forgeries now swarming in the newspapers against me."

As a fabled Indian fighter, Jackson was beloved as the "people's champion" by farmers and working men, and as a planter, lawyer, and slaveholder, he had the trust of the southern political elite. He supported a small federal government, individual liberty, an expanded military, and white supremacy. Above all, he was a nationalist committed to preserving the Union.

Jackson benefited from a growing spirit of democracy in which many viewed Adams as an elitist. Jackson insisted that the election came down to one question: "Shall the government or the people rule?" As president, he promised, he would fight against the entrenched power of the wealthy and powerful.

When Adams's supporters began referring to Jackson as a "jackass," Jackson embraced the name, using the animal as a symbol for his "tough" campaign. The jackass eventually became the enduring symbol of the Democratic party.

**THE "COMMON MAN" IN POLITICS** Andrew Jackson's campaign explicitly appealed to the common voters, many of whom were able to vote in a presidential election for the first time. By 1824, twenty-one of the twenty-four states had dropped property-owning requirements for voting. Only Virginia and the Carolinas, still dominated by the planter elite, continued to resist the democratizing trend. This "democratization" of politics also affected many free black males in northern states, half of which allowed blacks to vote.

The extension of voting rights to common men led to the election of politicians sprung from "the people" rather than from the social elite. Jackson, a frontiersman of humble origin and limited education who had scrambled up the political ladder by sheer tenacity, symbolized this emerging democratic ideal.

**LABOR POLITICS** With the widespread removal of property qualifications for voting, the working class (laborers paid hourly wages) became an important political force in the form of the Working Men's parties. They were first organized in 1828 in Philadelphia, the nation's largest manufacturing center.

The Working Men's parties promoted the interests of laborers, such as shorter working hours and allowing all males to vote regardless of the amount of property they owned. But their overarching concern was the widening inequality of wealth in America.

The Working Men's parties faded quickly, however. The inexperience of labor politicians left them vulnerable to manipulation by political professionals. In addition, major national parties, especially the Jacksonian Democrats, co-opted many of their issues.

Yet the working-class parties succeeded in drawing attention to their demands. They promoted free public education for all children, called for an end to imprisoning people for indebtedness, and supported a ten-hour workday to prevent employers from abusing workers. Union members loved Andrew Jackson, and the new Democratic party proved adept at building a national coalition of working-class supporters.

**PRESIDENT JACKSON** When the 1828 election returns came in, Jackson had won handily, taking every state west and south of Pennsylvania. Equally important was the surge in voter turnout; more than twice as many men voted as in the 1824 election.

As Andrew Jackson prepared to enter the White House, he was determined to be the "people's president." He would launch a new "democratic" era that would silence his critics, restore government to "the people," and take power away from the "Eastern elite." In doing so, he would transform the nation's political landscape—for good and for ill, as it turned out.

# CHAPTER REVIEW

## SUMMARY

- **Nationalism**  After the War of 1812, the federal government pursued many policies to strengthen the *national* economy. The *Tariff of 1816* protected American manufacturing, and the *Second Bank of the United States* provided a stronger currency. Led by John Marshall, the Supreme Court strengthened the power of the federal government in *Dartmouth College v. Woodward (1819)* and *McCulloch v. Maryland (1819)*. The Marshall court interpreted the Constitution as giving Congress the right to take any action not forbidden by the Constitution as long as the purpose of such laws was within the "scope of the Constitution." In *Gibbons v. Ogden (1824)*, the Court established the federal government's supremacy over interstate commerce, thereby promoting growth of the national economy.

- **Sectionalism**  Henry Clay's *American System* supported economic nationalism by endorsing a national bank, a protective tariff, and federally funded *internal improvements* such as roads and canals. Many Americans, however, were more tied to the needs of their particular sections of the country. People in the different regions—Northeast, South, and Midwest—disagreed about which economic policies best served their interests. As settlers streamed west, the extension of slavery into the new territories became the predominant political concern, eventually requiring both sides to compromise repeatedly to avoid civil war.

- **Era of Good Feelings**  James Monroe's term in office began with peace and prosperity. Two major events, however, ended the Era of Good Feelings: the financial *Panic of 1819* and the Missouri Compromise (1820). The explosive growth of the cotton culture transformed life in the South, in part by encouraging the expansion of slavery, which moved west with migrating southern planters. In 1819, however, the sudden collapse of world cotton prices devastated the southern economy. The *Missouri Compromise (1820)*, a short-term solution to the issue of allowing slavery in the western territories, exposed the emotions and turmoil that the expansion of slavery generated.

- **National Diplomacy**  The main diplomatic achievements after the War of 1812 extended America's boundaries and enabled the resumption of trade with Great Britain. To the north, U.S. diplomatic achievements established borders with Canada. To the south, the *Transcontinental Treaty (1819)* with Spain extended the boundaries of the United States. The *Monroe Doctrine (1823)* declared that the Americas were no longer open to European colonization.

- **The Election of 1828**  The demise of the Federalists left the Republicans as the only national political party. The Republicans' seeming unity was shattered by the election of 1824, which Andrew Jackson lost as a result of what he believed was a *corrupt bargain* between John Quincy Adams and Henry Clay. Jackson won the presidency in the *election campaign of 1828* by rallying southern and western voters with his promise to serve the interests of the common people.

## CHRONOLOGY

| | |
|---|---|
| 1816 | Second Bank of the United States is established |
| | First protective tariff goes into effect |
| 1817 | Rush-Bagot Treaty between the United States and Great Britain |
| 1818 | The Convention of 1818 establishes the northern border of the Louisiana Purchase at the 49th parallel |
| 1819 | Panic of 1819 |
| | Supreme Court issues *McCulloch v. Maryland* decision |
| | United States and Spain agree to the Transcontinental (Adams-Onís) Treaty |
| 1820 | Congress accepts the Missouri Compromise |
| 1821 | Maine and Missouri become states |
| | Florida becomes a territory |
| 1823 | President Monroe announces the Monroe Doctrine |
| 1824 | Supreme Court issues *Gibbons v. Ogden* decision |
| | John Quincy Adams wins the presidential election by what some claim is a "corrupt bargain" with Henry Clay |
| 1828 | Andrew Jackson wins presidency |

## KEY TERMS

Second Bank of the United States (B.U.S.) p. 354

Tariff of 1816 p. 355

internal improvements p. 355

*Dartmouth College v. Woodward* (1819) p. 356

*McCulloch v. Maryland* (1819) p. 356

*Gibbons v. Ogden* (1824) p. 357

American System p. 358

Panic of 1819 p. 360

Missouri Compromise (1820) p. 362

Transcontinental Treaty (Adams-Onís Treaty) (1819) p. 365

Monroe Doctrine (1823) p. 367

corrupt bargain p. 370

election campaign of 1828 p. 373

 INQUIZITIVE

Go to InQuizitive to see what you've learned—and learn what you've missed—with personalized feedback along the way.

# 10 The Jacksonian Era

## 1828–1840

**Hard times in the Jacksonian era** Although Andrew Jackson championed the "poor and humble," his economic policies contributed to the Panic of 1837, a financial crisis that hit the working poor the hardest. This cartoon illustrates New York City during the seven-year depression: A frantic mob storms a bank, while in the foreground a widow begs on the street with her child, surrounded by a banker or landlord and a barefoot sailor. At left are a drunken member of the Bowery Toughs gang and a down-on-his-luck militiaman. The cartoonist places the blame on Jackson, whose hat, glasses, and pipe overlook the scene. The white flag at left wryly states: "July 4, 1837, 61st Anniversary of Our Independence."

Andrew Jackson was a unique personality and a transformational leader. He was the first president from a western state (Tennessee), the first to have been born in a log cabin, the first *not* from a prominent colonial family, the last to have participated in the Revolutionary War, and the first to carry two bullets lodged in his lung and arm from a duel and a barroom brawl. Most important, Jackson was the polarizing emblem of a new democratic era.

Jackson was short-tempered and thin-skinned, proud and insecure. If his prickly sense of honor were challenged or his authority questioned, he never hesitated to fight or get even. For Jackson, politics was personal and combative.

Jackson believed in simple pleasures. He smoked a corncob pipe and chewed—and spit—tobacco. (He installed twenty spittoons in the White House.) Tall and lean, Jackson weighed only 140 pounds but was an intimidating figure with his penetrating blue eyes, long nose, jutting chin, silver-gray hair, and intense, iron-willed personality. "Old Hickory," however, was not in good health when he assumed the presidency. He suffered from blinding headaches and other ailments that led rival Henry Clay to describe him as "feeble in body and mind."

Despite his physical challenges, Jackson remained sharply focused and keenly sure of himself. More than previous presidents, he loved the rough-and-tumble combat of the raucous new democratic political culture. "I was born for a storm," he once boasted. "A calm [life] does not suit me."

Jackson took the nation by storm. No political figure was so widely loved or more deeply despised. As a self-made soldier, lawyer, planter, and politician, he helped create and shape the Democratic party, and he ushered in new

## focus questions

**1.** What were Andrew Jackson's major beliefs regarding democracy, the presidency, and the proper role of government in the nation's economy?

**2.** What was Jackson's legacy regarding the status of Indians in American society?

**3.** How did Jackson respond to the nullification crisis?

**4.** What brought about the economic depression of the late 1830s and the emergence of the Whig party?

**5.** What were the strengths and weaknesses of Jackson's transformational presidency?

elements of modern presidential campaigning into electoral politics. Jackson continued to champion the emergence of the "common man" in politics (by which he meant white men only), and he stamped his name and, more important, his ideas, personality, and values on an entire era of American history.

# JACKSONIAN DEMOCRACY

Andrew Jackson's election marked the culmination of thirty years of democratic innovations in politics. During the 1820s and 1830s, as America grew in population and people continued to move westward, most white men, whether they owned property or not, were allowed to vote and hold office. "The principle of universal suffrage," announced the *U.S. Magazine and Democratic Review*, "meant that white males of age constituted the political nation." Jackson promised to protect "the poor and humble" from the "tyranny of wealth and power." His populist goal was to elevate the "laboring classes" of white men who "love liberty and desire nothing but equal rights and equal laws."

Such democratization gave previously excluded white men equal status as citizens, regardless of wealth or background. No longer was politics an exclusive arena for only the most prominent and wealthiest white Americans.

**POLITICAL DEMOCRACY**   Campaigning was also democratized. Politics became the most popular form of mass entertainment, as people from all walks of life were remarkably well informed about public policy issues. Politics was "the only pleasure an American knows," observed visiting Frenchman Alexis de Tocqueville. "Even the women frequently attend public meetings and listen to political harangues as a recreation from their household labors."

Jackson was the most openly partisan and politically involved president in history to that point. Unlike previous presidents, who viewed campaigning as unseemly, he actively sought votes among the people, lobbied congressmen, and formed "Hickory Clubs" to campaign for him. Jackson also benefited from a powerful Democratic party "machine" run by his trusted secretary of state (later his vice president), Martin Van Buren, a shrewd New York lawyer.

Democracy, of course, is a slippery and elastic concept, and Jacksonians rarely defined what they meant by the "rule of the people." Noah Webster, the Connecticut Federalist who produced the nation's first reliable dictionary of homegrown American English, complained that "the men who have preached these doctrines [of democracy] have never defined what they mean by the *people*, or what they mean by *democracy*, nor how the *people* are to govern themselves." Jacksonian Democrats also showed little concern for the *undemocratic* constraints on African Americans, Native Americans, and women of every race, all of whom were denied basic political and civil rights.

**ANTI-DEMOCRATIC FORCES** Many southern slaveholders worried that the surge of democratic activism would eventually threaten the slave system. Virginian Muscoe Garnett, a planter and attorney, declared that "democracy is indeed incompatible with slavery, and the whole system of Southern society." His fellow Virginian, George Fitzhugh, was more explicit in his disdain for democratic ideals. In every society, he asserted, "some were born with saddles on their backs, and others booted and spurred to ride them."

**DEMOCRACY UNLEASHED** The inauguration of President Jackson symbolized the democratization of political life. Dressed in a black mourning suit in honor of his recently deceased wife, America's seventh president stepped out of the Capitol Building at noon on March 4, 1829. Waiting for him in the cold were 15,000 people who collectively roared and waved their hats when he emerged. "I never saw anything like it before," marveled Daniel Webster, the distinguished senator from Massachusetts.

Once the wild cheering subsided, Jackson bowed with great dignity, acknowledging the crowd's excitement and urging them to settle down. He then delivered a typically brief speech in which he committed his administration to "the task of reform" in the federal government, taking jobs out of "unfaithful or incompetent hands" and balancing states' rights with the exercise of national power. He also pledged to pursue the will of the people.

After being sworn in by Chief Justice John Marshall, Jackson mounted his white horse and rode down Pennsylvania Avenue to the White House, then called the Executive Mansion, where a wild celebration ensued. The huge crowd of jubilant western Democrats turned into a drunken mob. Dishes, glasses, and furniture were smashed, and muddy-booted revelers broke windows, ripped down draperies, and trampled on rugs. A Washington lady marveled at the arrival of frontier democracy in the nation's capital: "What a scene we did witness! The majesty of the people had disappeared, and a rabble, a mob, of boys, negroes, women, children, scrambling, fighting, romping. What a pity, what a pity!"

Those already skeptical of Jackson's qualifications for office saw the boisterous inaugural party as a symbol of all that was wrong with the "democratic" movement. Supreme Court Justice Joseph Story said he had never seen such "a mixture" of rowdy people, from the "highest and most polished down to the most vulgar and gross in the nation."

To his supporters, Jackson was a military hero and gifted leader. To his opponents, he was a self-serving tyrant. One critic dismissed as "humbug" the "mischievous popularity of this illiterate, violent, vain, and iron-willed soldier."

***All Creation Going to the White House*** In this depiction of Andrew Jackson's inauguration party, satirist Robert Cruikshank draws a visual parallel to Noah's Ark, suggesting that people from all walks of life were now welcome in the White House.

## JACKSON AS PRESIDENT

Andrew Jackson sought to increase the powers of the presidency at the expense of the legislative and judicial branches. One of his opponents noted that previous presidents had assumed that Congress was the primary branch of government. Jackson, however, believed that the presidency was "superior." The ruling political and economic elite must be removed, he said, for "the people" are the government, and too many government officials had grown corrupt and self-serving at the expense of the public interest.

To dislodge the "corrupt" eastern political elite, Jackson launched a policy he called "rotation in office," whereby he replaced many federal officials with his supporters. Government jobs—district attorneys, federal marshals, customs collectors—belonged to the people, not to career bureaucrats. Democracy, he believed, was best served when "newly elected officials" appointed new government officials. Such partisan behavior came to be called "the spoils system," since, as a prominent New York Democrat declared, "to the victor belong the spoils."

Jackson also sought to cut federal spending, to help pay off the federal debt. He supported internal improvements that were national in scope, promoted a "judicious tariff," hoped to destroy the Second Bank of the United States

(B.U.S.), and called for the relocation of the "ill-fated race" of Indians still living in the East to western lands across the Mississippi River. He claimed that displacing the Indians was for their own protection, but his primary motive was to enable whites to exploit Indian ancestral lands.

**THE EATON AFFAIR** Yet Jackson soon found himself preoccupied with squabbles within his cabinet. From the outset, his administration was divided between supporters of Secretary of State Martin Van Buren of New York and those allied with Vice President John C. Calhoun of South Carolina, both of whom wanted to succeed Jackson as president. Jackson did not trust Calhoun, a Yale graduate of towering intellect and fiery self-interest, who in many ways was a loner distrusted by members of both parties. Although once a Republican nationalist, Calhoun now focused on defending southern interests, especially the preservation of the slave-based cotton economy that had made him a wealthy planter.

In his rivalry with Calhoun, Van Buren would eventually take full advantage of a juicy scandal known as the Peggy Eaton affair. Widower John Eaton, a former U.S. senator from Tennessee and one of Jackson's closest friends, had long been associated with Margaret "Peggy" O'Neale Timberlake, a devastatingly attractive Washington temptress married to John Timberlake, a naval officer frequently at sea. While her husband was away, the flirtatious Mrs. Timberlake enjoyed "the attentions of men, young and old." She took special delight in Senator John Eaton.

In April 1828, John Timberlake died at sea. Although the official cause of death was respiratory failure, rumors swirled that he had committed suicide after learning of his wife's affair with Eaton.

Soon after the 1828 presidential election, John Eaton had written President-elect Jackson about the spiteful gossip aimed at himself and Peggy Timberlake. Jackson responded quickly and firmly: "Marry her and you will be in a position to defend her." Eaton did so on January 1, 1829.

Eaton's enemies quickly criticized the "unseemly haste" of the marriage and continued to savage Peggy Eaton as a whore. Louis McLane, a U.S. senator from Delaware who would later serve in Jackson's cabinet, sneered that John Eaton, soon to be named Jackson's secretary of war, "has just married his mistress, and the mistress of eleven dozen others." Floride Calhoun, the vice president's imperious wife, especially objected to Peggy Eaton's unsavory past. At Jackson's inaugural ball, she openly ignored her, as did the other cabinet members' wives.

The constant gossip led Jackson to explode: "I did not come here [to Washington] to make a Cabinet for the Ladies of this place, but for the Nation." Peggy Eaton's plight reminded him of the mean-spirited gossip that had plagued

BORN TO COMMAND.

OF VETO MEMORY.

HAD I BEEN CONSULTED.

KING ANDREW THE FIRST.

**King Andrew the First** Opponents considered Jackson's veto of the Maysville Road Bill an abuse of power. This cartoon shows "King Andrew" trampling on the Constitution, internal improvements, and the Bank of the United States.

his own wife, Rachel. Intensely loyal to John Eaton, the president defended Peggy, insisting that she was as pure "as a virgin." His cabinet members, however, were unable to cure their wives of what Martin Van Buren dubbed "the Eaton Malaria." The rumoring and sniping became a time-consuming distraction for the president.

Jackson blamed the Eaton scandal, also known as the "Petticoat Affair," on Henry Clay and John C. Calhoun. The president assumed that Calhoun and his wife had targeted John Eaton because Eaton did not support Calhoun's desire to be president. One of Calhoun's friends wrote in April 1829 that the United States was "governed by the President—the President by the Secretary of War—and the latter by his Wife." Jackson concluded that Calhoun "would sacrifice his friend, his country, and forsake his god, for selfish personal ambition." For his part, Calhoun dismissed Jackson as a "self-infatuated man . . . blinded by ambition [and] intoxicated by flattery and vanity!"

**THE MAYSVILLE ROAD VETO** When President Jackson was not dealing with the Petticoat Affair, he used his executive authority to limit the role of the federal government—while delivering additional blows to John C. Calhoun and Henry Clay.

In 1830, Congress passed a bill pushed by Calhoun and Clay that authorized the use of federal monies to build a sixty-mile-long road across the state of Kentucky from the city of Maysville to Lexington, Clay's hometown. Jackson, urged on by Martin Van Buren, who wanted to preserve the Erie Canal's monopoly over western trade, vetoed the bill on the grounds that the proposed road was a "purely local matter," being solely in the state of Kentucky and thus outside the domain of Congress, which had authority only over *interstate* commerce. Federal funding for such local projects would thus require a constitutional amendment.

Clay was stunned. "We are all shocked and mortified by the rejection of the Maysville road," he wrote a friend. But he had no luck convincing Congress to override the veto.

## The Eastern Indians

President Jackson's forcible removal of Indians from their ancestral lands was his highest priority and one of his lowest moments. Like most white frontiersmen, he saw Indians as barbarians who were to be treated as "subjects," not "nations." He claimed that Indians and land-hungry white settlers could never live in harmony, so the Indians had to go if they were to survive. Henry Clay felt the same way, arguing that the Indians were "destined to extinction" and not "worth preserving."

After Jackson's election in 1828, he urged that the remaining eastern Indians (east of the Mississippi River) be moved to reservations west of the Mississippi, in what became Oklahoma. Jackson believed that moving the Indians would serve their best interests as well as the national interest, for the states in the Lower South, especially the Carolinas, Georgia, and Alabama, were aggressively restricting the rights of Indian nations and taking their land. Jackson often told Indian leaders that he was their "Great Father" trying to protect them from greedy state governments. He claimed that relocating the eastern Indians was a "wise and humane policy" that would save them from "utter annihilation" if they tried to hold on to their lands in the face of state actions.

**INDIAN REMOVAL**  In 1830, Jackson submitted to Congress the **Indian Removal Act**, which authorized him to ignore commitments made by previous presidents and to convince the Indians remaining in the East and South to move to federal lands west of the Mississippi River. The federal government, the new program promised, would pay for the Indian exodus and give them initial support in their new lands ("Indian Territory") in Oklahoma.

Indian leaders were skeptical. As a federal agent reported, "They see that our professions are insincere, that our promises are broken, that the happiness of the Indian is a cheap sacrifice to the acquisition of new lands."

Jackson's proposal also provoked heated opposition among reformers who distrusted his motives and doubted the promised support from the federal government. Critics flooded Congress with petitions that criticized the policy and warned that Jackson's plan would bring "enduring shame" on the nation.

But to no avail. In late May 1830, the Senate passed the Indian Removal Act by a single vote, and Jackson eagerly signed it. The Cherokees responded by announcing that "we see nothing but ruin before us."

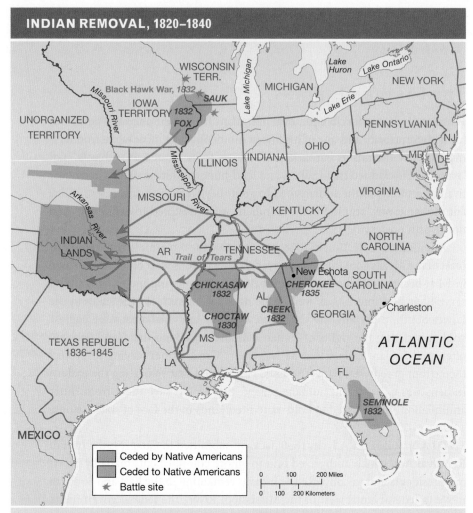

**INDIAN REMOVAL, 1820–1840**

- Why did Congress relocate the Choctaws, Chickasaws, Creeks, Seminoles, and Cherokees to territory west of Arkansas and Missouri?
- How far did the exiled Indians have to travel, and what were the conditions on the journey?
- Why were they not forced to move before the 1830s?

**RESISTANCE** Most northern Indians were relocated. In Illinois and the Wisconsin Territory, however, Sauk and Fox Indians fought to regain their ancestral lands. The Black Hawk War erupted in April 1832, when Chief Black Hawk led 1,000 Sauks—men, women, and children who had been relocated to the Iowa Territory—back across the Mississippi River to their homeland in Illinois, land shared with the Fox Nation. After several skirmishes, Indiana and Illinois militia chased the Sauk and Fox into the Wisconsin Territory and caught them on the eastern bank of the Mississippi, a few miles downstream from the mouth of the Bad Axe River.

The soldiers misinterpreted the Indians' effort to surrender, and fighting erupted. In what became known as the Bad Axe Massacre, the militiamen murdered hundreds of women and children as they tried to escape. The soldiers then scalped the dead Indians and cut long strips of flesh from several of them for use as strops to sharpen razors. Six weeks later, Black Hawk was captured and imprisoned.

In Florida, the Seminoles, led by Osceola (called by U.S. soldiers "the still unconquered red man"), ferociously resisted the federal removal policy. For eight years, the Seminoles would fight a guerrilla war in the swamps of the Everglades—the longest, most costly, and deadliest war ever fought by Native Americans. Some 1,500 were killed on both sides. At times, Seminole women killed their children rather than see them captured.

But Seminole resistance waned after 1837, when Osceola was treacherously captured under a white flag of truce, imprisoned, and left to die of malaria at Fort

**Hiding in a Mangrove Swamp** An armed group of Seminoles crouch under a mangrove in the Florida Everglades during the Second Seminole War, out of sight of the American sailors passing by.

Moultrie near Charleston, South Carolina. After 1842, only a few hundred Seminoles remained. It was not until 1934 that the surviving Seminoles in Florida became the last Native American tribe to end its war with the United States.

**THE CHEROKEES** The Cherokee Nation also tried to defy the federal removal policy. Cherokees had long occupied northwest Georgia and the mountainous areas of northern Alabama, eastern Tennessee, and western North Carolina. In 1827, relying upon their established treaty rights, they adopted a constitution as an independent nation in which they declared that they were not subject to the laws or control of any state or federal government. Georgia officials had other ideas.

In 1828, shortly after Andrew Jackson's election, the Georgia government announced that after June 1, 1830, the authority of state law would extend to the Cherokees. The "barbarous and savage tribes" must give way to the march of white civilization. Under the new state laws, they would not be allowed to vote, own property, or testify against whites in court.

The discovery of gold in north Georgia in 1829 had increased whites' lust for Cherokee land, attracted trespassing prospectors, and led to the new law. It prohibited the Cherokees from digging for gold on their own lands. The Cherokees sought relief in the Supreme Court, arguing that "we wish to remain on the land of our fathers. We have a perfect and original right to remain without interruption or molestation."

In *Cherokee Nation v. Georgia* (1831), Chief Justice John Marshall ruled that the Cherokees had "an unquestionable right" to maintain control of their ancestral lands, but the Court could not render a verdict because of a technicality: the Cherokees had filed suit as a "foreign nation," but in Marshall's view they were "domestic dependent nations." If it were true that "wrongs have been inflicted," Marshall explained, "this is not the tribunal which can redress the past or prevent the future."

The following year, the Supreme Court *did* rule in favor of the Cherokees in *Worcester v. Georgia* (1832). The case arose when Georgia officials arrested a group of white Christian missionaries who were living among the Cherokees in violation of a state law forbidding such interaction. Two of the missionaries, Samuel Worcester and Elihu Butler, were sentenced to four years at hard labor. They appealed to the Supreme Court.

In the *Worcester* case, John Marshall said the missionaries must be released. The anti-Cherokee laws passed by the Georgia legislature, he declared, had violated "the Constitution, laws, and treaties of the United States." He added that the Cherokee Nation was "a distinct political community" within which Georgia law had no force.

President Jackson, however, refused to enforce the Court's "wicked" decisions, claiming that he had no constitutional authority to intervene in Georgia. A New York newspaper editor reported that Jackson said, "John Marshall has made his decision, now let him enforce it."

Thereafter, Jackson gave the Cherokees and other Indian nations a terrible choice: either abide by discriminatory new state laws or relocate to federal lands west of the Mississippi River, which would be theirs "forever." Jackson told the Creeks that they and whites could not live "in harmony and peace" if they remained on their ancestral lands and that "a speedy removal" to the West was their only option. Soon, Georgia officials began selling Cherokee lands.

The irony of the new Georgia policy was that of all the southern tribes, the Cherokees had come closest to adopting the customs of white America. They had abandoned traditional hunting practices to develop farms, build roads, schools, and churches, and create trading posts and newspapers. Many Cherokees had married whites, adopted their clothing and food, and converted to Christianity. And the Cherokees owned some 2,000 enslaved African Americans.

**THE TRAIL OF TEARS** The federal officials responsible for implementing the Indian Removal Act developed a strategy of divide and conquer with the Cherokees. In 1835, for example, a minority faction of the Cherokees signed the fraudulent Treaty of New Echota, in which they agreed to move to the Indian Territory in Oklahoma. The treaty was rejected by 90 percent of the Cherokee people but readily accepted by the U.S. Senate and enforced by the U.S. Army.

In 1838, after President Jackson had left office and Martin Van Buren was president, 17,000 Cherokees were evicted and moved West under military guard on the **Trail of Tears,** an 800-mile forced journey marked by the harshness of soldiers and the neglect of irresponsible private contractors assigned to manage the process. Some 4,000 refugees died along the way. For his part, Van Buren told Congress in December 1838 that he took "sincere pleasure" in reporting that the entire Cherokee Nation had been relocated.

The Trail of Tears was, according to a white Georgian, "the cruelest work I ever knew." A few Cherokees held out in the mountains of North Carolina; they became known as the "Eastern Band" of Cherokees. The Creeks and Chickasaws followed the Trail of Tears a few years later, after Alabama and Mississippi took control of their tribal lands.

Some 100,000 eastern Indians were relocated to the West during the 1820s and 1830s, and the government sold some 100 million acres of Indian land,

**Trail of Tears** Thousands of Cherokees died on a nightmarish march from Georgia to Oklahoma after being forced from their native lands.

most of it in the prime cotton-growing areas of Georgia, Alabama, and Mississippi, known as the Old Southwest.

## THE BANK WAR

Andrew Jackson showed the same principled stubbornness in dealing with the national bank as he did in removing the Indians. The charter for the First Bank of the United States (B.U.S.) had expired in 1811 but was renewed in 1816 as the Second Bank of the United States. It soon became the largest corporation in the nation and the only truly national business enterprise.

The second B.U.S. (the federal government owned only 20 percent of the bank's capital) was a private corporation with extensive public responsibilities— and powers. To benefit the government, the B.U.S. held all federal funds, including tax collections (mostly from land sales and tariff revenues), and disbursed federal payments for its obligations, all in exchange for an annual $1.5 million fee. The B.U.S., however, conducted other business like a commercial bank and was free to use the government deposits in its vaults as collateral for loans to businesses. Headquartered in Philadelphia and supported by twenty-nine branches around the nation, the B.U.S. competed with state-chartered banks for local business.

The B.U.S. helped accelerate business expansion by making loans to individuals, businesses, and state banks. It also helped promote a stable money supply and deter excessive lending by requiring the 464 state banks to keep enough gold and silver coins (called specie) in their vaults to back their own paper currency, which they in turn loaned to individuals and businesses. The primary benefit of the B.U.S. was its ability to monitor and regulate many of the state banks.

With federal revenues soaring from land sales during the early 1830s, the B.U.S., led by Nicholas Biddle, had accumulated massive amounts of money—and economic clout. Even though the B.U.S. benefited the national economy, state banks, especially in the South and West, feared its growing "monopolistic" power. Critics claimed that Biddle and the B.U.S. were restricting lending by state banks and impeding businesses from borrowing as much as they wanted.

Andrew Jackson, like many westerners, had always hated banks and bankers, whom he called "vipers and thieves." His prejudice grew out of his experiences in the 1790s, when he had suffered huge financial losses. Now, he claimed to speak for ordinary Americans who felt that banks favored the "rich and powerful" in the East.

Jackson distrusted banks because they printed too much paper money, causing prices to rise (inflation). He wanted only gold and silver coins to be used for economic transactions. Jackson also disliked Biddle because he was everything that Jackson was not: an Easterner born to wealth, highly educated, financially sophisticated, and a world traveler. Ironically, Biddle had voted for Jackson.

The **Bank War** between Jackson and Biddle revealed that the president never truly understood the national bank's role or policies, and he let personal animosity drive many of his policy decisions. The B.U.S. had provided a stable monetary system for the expanding economy, as well as a mechanism for controlling the pace and integrity of economic growth by regulating the ability of branch banks and state banks to issue paper currency.

**THE RECHARTER EFFORT** Although the Second Bank's charter ran through 1836, leaders of the newly named National Republican party, especially Senators Henry Clay and Daniel Webster (who was a paid legal counsel to the B.U.S.), told Nicholas Biddle that the charter needed to be renewed before the 1836 presidential election. They assured him that Congress would renew the charter, leading Biddle to grow overconfident about the bank's future. Jackson, he said, "thinks because he has scalped Indians . . . he is to have his way with the Bank."

**Rechartering the Bank** Jackson's effort to defeat the recharter of the B.U.S. is likened to fighting a hydra, a many-headed serpent from Greek mythology. Just as the hydra would sprout two heads when one was severed, for each B.U.S. supporter that Jackson subdued, even more would emerge to take his place.

Biddle and his allies, however, failed to appreciate Jackson's tenacity or the depth of his hatred for the B.U.S. And most voters were on Jackson's side. In the end, Biddle, Clay, and the National Republicans unintentionally handed Jackson a popular issue on the eve of the 1832 election. At their nominating convention in December 1831, the National Republican party, also called the Anti-Jackson party, endorsed Clay as their presidential candidate and approved the renewal of the B.U.S.

Early in the summer of 1832, both houses of Congress passed the bank recharter bill, in part because Biddle used bribes to win votes. Upon learning of such shenanigans, Jackson's chief of staff concluded that the B.U.S. was "becoming desperate: *caught in its own net.*"

Biddle, Webster, and Clay assumed that Jackson would not veto the recharter bill because doing so might cost him reelection. On July 10, 1832, however, Jackson nixed the bill, sending it back to Congress and harshly criticizing the bank for making the "rich richer and the potent more powerful" while discriminating against "the humble members of society—the farmers, mechanics, and laborers."

Webster accused Jackson of using the bank issue "to stir up the poor against the rich." To Clay, Jackson's veto represented another example of the president's desire to concentrate "all power in the hands of one man." Clay and Webster, however, could not convince the Senate to override the veto, thus setting the stage for a nationwide debate and a dramatic presidential campaign.

The overriding issue in the election was the future of the Bank of the United States. Let the people decide, Jackson argued. "I have now done my duty to the citizens of this country," he said in explaining his veto. "If sustained by my fellow-citizens [in the upcoming election], I shall be grateful and happy; if not, I shall find in the motives which impel me ample grounds for contentment and peace."

## NULLIFICATION

Andrew Jackson eventually would veto twelve congressional bills, more than all previous presidents combined. Critics claimed that his behavior was "monarchical." Jackson, however, believed that the president represented *all* the people, unlike congressmen who were elected locally. His commitment to nationalism over sectionalism was nowhere more evident than in his handling of the nullification crisis in South Carolina.

**CALHOUN AND THE TARIFF** Vice President John C. Calhoun became President Jackson's fiercest critic—and vice versa. In part because of his feud with the president, Calhoun had become the leading states' rights advocate for the South.

Changing economic conditions in his home state frustrated Calhoun. The financial panic of 1819 had sparked a nationwide depression, and through the 1820s, South Carolina continued to suffer from falling cotton prices. The state lost almost 70,000 people during the decade as residents moved West in search of cheaper and more-fertile land for growing cotton. Twice as many would leave during the 1830s.

Most South Carolinians blamed their woes on the Tariff of 1828, which was labeled the **Tariff of Abominations**. By taxing British cloth coming into U.S. markets, the tariff hurt southern cotton growers by reducing British demand for raw cotton from America. It also hurt southerners by raising prices for imported products.

In a pamphlet called the *South Carolina Exposition and Protest* (1828), Calhoun claimed that the Tariff of 1828 favored the interests of New England textile manufacturing over southern agriculture. Under such circumstances, he argued, a state could "nullify," or veto, a federal law it deemed unconstitutional.

***Webster Replying to Senator Hayne*** **(1848)** The eloquent Massachusetts senator challenges the argument for nullification in the Webster–Hayne debate.

**Nullification** was the ultimate weapon for those determined to protect states' rights against federal authority. As Jackson and others pointed out, however, allowing states to pick and choose which federal laws they would follow would create national chaos.

**CLASH OF TITANS–WEBSTER VERSUS HAYNE** The controversy over the Tariff of 1828 simmered until 1830, when the Webster–Hayne debate in Congress sharpened the lines between states' rights and national authority. In a fiery speech, Senator Robert Y. Hayne of South Carolina argued that the anti-slavery Yankees were invading the South, "making war upon her citizens, and endeavoring to overthrow her principles and institutions." In Hayne's view, the Union was created by the states, and the states therefore had the right to nullify, or ignore, federal laws they disliked. The independence of the states was to him more important than the preservation of the Union.

Massachusetts senator Daniel Webster challenged Hayne's arguments. Blessed with a thunderous voice and a theatrical flair, Webster pointed out that the U.S. Constitution was created not by the states but by the American people. If states were allowed to nullify a federal law, the Union would be nothing but a "rope of sand." South Carolina's defiance of federal authority, he charged, "is nothing more than resistance by *force*—it is disunion by *force*—it is secession by *force*—it is civil war."

Webster's powerful closing statement—"Liberty and Union, now and forever, one and inseparable"—was printed in virtually every newspaper in the nation. Abraham Lincoln later called it "the very best speech ever delivered." Even Hayne was awestruck. He told Webster that "a man who can make such speeches as that ought never to die." In the end, Webster had the better argument.

**CALHOUN VERSUS JACKSON** That Jackson, like Calhoun, was a cotton-planting slaveholder led many southerners to assume that the president would support their resistance to the federal tariff. Jackson was sympathetic—until Calhoun and others in South Carolina threatened to nullify federal laws.

On April 13, 1830, the Democratic party hosted scores of congressmen and political leaders at the first annual Jefferson Day dinner. When it was Jackson's turn to salute Thomas Jefferson's memory, he rose to his feet, raised his glass, and, glaring at Calhoun, growled: "Our Union—it must be preserved!"

People gasped, knowing that the vice president must reply to Jackson's threat to nullification. Calhoun, trembling with emotion, countered with a defiant toast to "the Union, next to our liberty the most dear!" In that dramatic exchange, Jackson and Calhoun laid bare the fundamental tension between federal authority and states' rights that has remained an animating theme of the American republic.

Soon thereafter, another incident deepened the animosity between the two men. On May 12, 1830, the president saw for the first time a letter from 1818 in which Calhoun, then secretary of war under James Monroe, had wanted to discipline Jackson for his unauthorized invasion of Spanish-held Florida. After exchanging heated letters about the incident with Calhoun, Jackson told a friend that he was finally through with the "double dealing of J.C.C."

The rift prompted Jackson to take a dramatic step suggested by Secretary of State Martin Van Buren, his closest adviser. During one of their daily horseback rides together, Van Buren offered himself up as a sacrifice as a way to remove all Calhoun supporters from the cabinet and thereby end the ongoing Eaton affair that had fractured the administration.

As the first step in the cabinet coup, Van Buren convinced John Eaton to resign as secretary of war on April 4, 1831. Four days later, Van Buren resigned as secretary of state. "The long agony is over," crowed Samuel Ingham, the secretary of the Treasury, in a letter to Attorney General John Berrien. "Mr. V. B. and Major Eaton have resigned." What Ingham and Berrien did not realize was that a few days later, Jackson would force them—both Calhoun supporters—to resign as well. Jackson now had a clean slate on which to create another cabinet.

Critics saw through the secretary of state's scheme: "Mr. Van Buren may be called the 'Great Magician,'" wrote the *New York Courier*, "for he *raises his wand, and the whole Cabinet disappears.*" Others claimed that the cabinet purge showed that Jackson did not have the political skill to lead the nation. One newspaper announced that the ship of state "is sinking and the rats are flying! The hull is too leaky to mend, and the hero of two wars and a half has not the skill to keep it afloat."

The next act in the running political drama occurred when John Eaton challenged Ingham to a duel. The ousted Treasury secretary chose instead to retreat to his home in Pennsylvania. After the Eatons left Washington, D.C., a gloating Henry Clay retrieved William Shakespeare's characterization of Egyptian queen Cleopatra to mark Peggy's departure: "Age cannot wither nor time stale her infinite virginity."

**NEW CABINET** By the end of August 1831, President Jackson had appointed a new cabinet. At the same time, he increasingly relied upon the advice of Martin Van Buren and others making up his so-called "kitchen cabinet," an informal group of close friends and supporters, many of them Democratic newspaper editors.

The kitchen cabinet soon convinced Jackson to drop his pledge to serve only one term. They explained that it would be hard for Van Buren, the president's chosen successor, to win the 1832 Democratic nomination because Calhoun would do everything in his power to stop him—and might win the nomination himself.

**THE ANTI-MASONIC PARTY** In 1832, for the first time in a presidential election, a third political party entered the field. The Anti-Masonic party grew out of popular hostility toward the Masonic fraternal order, a large, all-male social organization that had originated in Great Britain. The Freemasons often claimed to be the natural leaders of their communities, the "best men." By 1830, more than 2,000 Masonic "lodges" were scattered across the United States with about 100,000 Freemason members, including Andrew Jackson and Henry Clay.

The new Anti-Masonic party owed its origins to William Morgan, a fifty-two-year-old unemployed bricklayer in Batavia, New York. Morgan had been thrown out of the Masons because of his joblessness. Seeking revenge, he convinced a local printer to publish a widely circulated pamphlet revealing the secret rituals of the Masonic order. Masons then burned the print shop where the pamphlet had been published. They also had Morgan arrested on a trumped-up charge of indebtedness.

Soon thereafter, on September 12, 1826, someone paid for Morgan's release from jail and spirited him away. A year later, a man's decomposed body washed up in Oak Orchard Creek, near Lake Ontario. Morgan's grieving wife confirmed that it was her husband. Governor Dewitt Clinton, himself a Mason, offered a reward for anyone who would identify the kidnappers.

The Morgan mystery became a major political issue. New York launched more than twenty investigations into Morgan's disappearance (and presumed murder) and conducted a dozen trials of several Masons but never gained a conviction. Each legal effort aroused more public indignation because most of the judges, lawyers, and jurors were Masons.

People began to fear that the Masons had become a self-appointed aristocracy lacking the education and character necessary for self-denying civic leadership. John Quincy Adams said that disbanding the "Masonic institution" was the most important issue facing "us and our posterity."

Suspicion of the Masonic order gave rise to the Anti-Masonic party, whose purpose was to protect republican values from corruption by self-serving, power-hungry Masonic insiders. The Anti-Masons claimed that they were determined to "hand down to posterity unimpaired the republic we inherited from our forefathers."

***The Verdict of the People*** George Caleb Bingham's painting depicts a socially diverse electorate, suggesting the increasingly democratic politics of the Jacksonian era.

The new party drew most of its support from New Englanders and New Yorkers alienated by both the Democratic and National Republican parties. Anti-Masonic adherents tended to be rural evangelical Protestants, many of whom also opposed slavery.

Although opposition to a fraternal organization was hardly the foundation upon which to build a lasting political coalition, the Anti-Masonic party had three important "firsts" to its credit: In addition to being the first third party with a national base of support, it was the first political party to hold a national convention to nominate a presidential candidate, and the first to announce a formal platform of specific policy goals.

**THE 1832 ELECTION**  In preparing for the 1832 election, the Democrats and National Republicans followed the example of the Anti-Masonic party by holding nominating conventions of their own. In December 1831, the National Republicans nominated Henry Clay.

The Democratic convention first adopted the two-thirds rule for nomination (which prevailed until 1936, when the requirement became a simple majority), and then named Martin Van Buren as Andrew Jackson's running mate. The Democrats, unlike the other two parties, adopted no formal platform and relied to a substantial degree upon the popularity of the president to carry their cause.

Nicholas Biddle invested the vast resources of the Bank of the United States into the campaign against Jackson and paid for thousands of pamphlets promoting Clay. By the summer of 1832, Clay declared that "the campaign is over, and I think we have won the victory." But his blinding ego prevented him from seeing the sources of Jackson's popularity. Where he dismissed Jackson as a power-hungry military chief, most Americans saw the president as someone fighting for them.

Clay also failed to understand Jackson's effectiveness as a political candidate. The *National Intelligencer*, a newspaper that supported Clay, acknowledged that Jackson's eager participation in campaign events was "certainly a new mode of electioneering. We do not recollect before to have heard of a President of the United States descending in person into the political arena." Jackson gave stump speeches, dived into crowds to shake hands, and walked in parades or ate barbecue with supporters who cheered and mobbed him.

In the end, Jackson earned 219 electoral votes to Clay's 49 and enjoyed a solid victory in the popular vote, 688,000 to 530,000. William Wirt, the Anti-Masonic candidate, carried only Vermont, winning 7 electoral votes. Dazzled by the president's strong showing, Wirt observed that Jackson could "be President for life if he chooses."

## THE NULLIFICATION CRISIS

In the fall of 1831, President Jackson tried to defuse the confrontation with South Carolina by calling on Congress to reduce tariff rates. Congress responded with the Tariff of 1832, which lowered rates on some products but kept them high on British cotton fabric and clothing.

The new tariff disappointed John C. Calhoun and others eager for the British to buy more southern cotton. South Carolinians seethed with resentment toward the federal government. Living in the only state where enslaved Africans were a majority of the population, they feared that if the northern representatives in Congress were powerful enough to create tariffs that proved so harmful to the South, they might eventually vote to end slavery itself. Calhoun declared that the "peculiar domestic institutions of the southern states" (slavery) were at stake.

**SOUTH CAROLINA NULLIFIERS** In November 1832, just weeks after Andrew Jackson was reelected, a special convention in South Carolina passed an Ordinance of Nullification that disavowed the "unconstitutional" federal tariffs of 1828 and 1832, declaring them "null, void, and no law." If federal authorities tried to use force to collect the tariffs on foreign goods unloaded in Charleston Harbor, South Carolina would secede from the Union, they vowed. The state legislature then selected Senator Robert Hayne as governor and named Calhoun to replace him as U.S. senator. Calhoun resigned as vice president so that he could defend his nullification theory in Congress and oppose Jackson's "tyrannical" actions.

**JACKSON SAYS NO TO NULLIFICATION** President Jackson's public response was measured yet forthright. He promised to use "firmness and forbearance" with South Carolina but stressed that nullification "means insurrection and war; and the other states have a right to put it down."

In private, however, Jackson was furious. He asked the secretary of war how many soldiers it would take to go to South Carolina and "crush the monster [nullification] in its cradle." He also threatened to hang Calhoun and other "nullifiers" if there were any bloodshed.

During the fall of 1832, most northern state legislatures passed resolutions condemning the nullificationists. Southern states expressed sympathy for South Carolina, but none endorsed nullification. "We detest the tariff," explained a Mississippian, "but we will hold to the Union." South Carolina was left standing alone.

On December 10, 1832, the unyielding Jackson issued his official response to the people of South Carolina. In his blistering proclamation, he dismissed nullification as "an absurdity," a "mad project of disunion" that was "*incompatible with the existence of the Union, contradicted expressly by the letter of the Constitution, unauthorized by its spirit, inconsistent with every principle on which It was founded, and destructive of the great object for which it was formed.*" He warned that nullification would lead to secession (formal withdrawal of a state from the United States), and secession meant civil war. "Be not deceived by names. Disunion by armed force is TREASON. Are you really ready to incur its guilt?"

**CLAY STEPS IN**  President Jackson then sent federal soldiers and a warship to Charleston to protect the federal customs house where tariffs were applied to products imported from Europe. Governor Hayne responded by mobilizing the state militia. A South Carolina Unionist reported to Jackson that many "reckless and dangerous men" were "looking for civil war and scenes of bloodshed." While taking forceful actions, Jackson still wanted "peaceably to nullify the nullifiers."

In early 1833, the president requested from Congress the authority to use the U.S. Army to "force" compliance with federal law in South Carolina. Calhoun exploded on the Senate floor, exclaiming that he and the others defending his state's constitutional rights were being threatened by what they called the **Force Bill** "to have our throats cut, and those of our wives and children." The greatest threat facing the nation, he argued, was not nullification but presidential despotism.

Calhoun and the nullifiers, however, soon backed down, and the South Carolina legislature postponed implementation of the nullification ordinances in hopes that Congress would pass a more palatable tariff bill.

Passage of a compromise bill, however, depended upon the support of Senator Henry Clay, himself a slaveholding planter, who finally yielded to those urging him to step in and save the day. A senator told Clay that these "South Carolinians are good fellows, and it would be a pity to see Jackson hang them."

Clay agreed. On February 12, 1833, he circulated a plan suggested by Jackson to gradually reduce the federal tariff on key imported items. Clay urged Congress to treat South Carolina with respect and display "that great principle of compromise and concession which lies at the bottom of our institutions." The tariff reductions were less than South Carolina preferred, but Clay's compromise helped the nullifiers out of the dilemma they had created. Calhoun supported the compromise: "He who loves the Union must desire to see this agitating question [the tariff] brought to a termination."

On March 1, 1833, Jackson signed into law the compromise tariff and the Force Bill, the latter being a symbolic statement of the primacy of the Union. Calhoun rushed home to convince the rebels to back down. The South Carolina convention then met and rescinded its nullification of the tariff acts. In a face-saving gesture, the delegates nullified the Force Bill, which Jackson no longer needed.

Both sides felt they had won. Jackson had defended the supremacy of the Union without firing a shot, and South Carolina's persistence had brought tariff reductions. Joel Poinsett, a South Carolina Unionist, was overjoyed with the resolution but added that the next crisis would force a choice between "union and disunion."

Despite the compromise, southern slaveholders felt increasingly threatened by anti-slavery sentiment in the North. "There is no liberty—no security for the South," groused South Carolina radical Robert Barnwell Rhett. Jackson concluded that the "tariff was only the pretext [for the nullification crisis], and disunion and southern confederacy the real object. The next pretext will be the negro, or slavery question." Two days after the nullification crisis was resolved, Jackson was sworn in for a second term as president.

## WAR OVER THE B.U.S.

Jackson interpreted his lopsided reelection as a "decision of the people against the bank." Having vetoed the renewal of the Bank of the United States charter, Jackson ordered the Department of the Treasury to transfer federal monies from the national bank to twenty-three mostly western state banks—called "pet banks" by Jackson's critics because many were run by the president's allies. When the Treasury secretary balked, Jackson fired him.

**BIDDLE'S RESPONSE** B.U.S. head Nicholas Biddle responded by ordering the bank to quit making loans and demanded that state banks exchange their paper currency for gold or silver coins. Through such deflationary policies, Biddle was trying to bring the economy to a halt, create a depression, and thus reveal the importance of maintaining the national bank. An enraged Jackson said the B.U.S. under Biddle was "trying to kill me, *but I will kill it!*"

Biddle's plan worked. Northern Democrats worried that the president's "lawless and reckless" Bank War would ruin the party. But Jackson refused to flinch. When state bankers visited the White House to plead for relief, Jackson said, "We have no money here, gentlemen. Biddle has all the money."

In the Senate, Calhoun and Clay argued that Jackson's transfer of government cash from the B.U.S. to the pet banks was illegal. On March 28, 1834,

Clay convinced a majority in the Senate to *censure* Jackson for his actions. Jackson was so angry that he wanted to challenge Clay to a duel so that he could "bring the rascal to a dear account."

**THE NEW WHIG PARTY** The president's war on the bank led his opponents to create a new political party. They claimed that he was ruling like a monarch, dubbed him "King Andrew the First," and called his Democratic supporters *Tories*. The new anti-Jackson coalition called themselves **Whigs**, a name that had also been used by the Patriots of the American Revolution (as well as by the parliamentary opponents of the Tories in Britain).

The Whig party grew directly out of the National Republican party led by John Quincy Adams, Henry Clay, and Daniel Webster. The Whigs also found support among Anti-Masons and even some Democrats who resented Jackson's war on the national bank. Of the forty-one Democrats in Congress who had voted against Jackson on rechartering the national bank, twenty-eight had joined the Whigs by 1836.

The Whigs, like the National Republicans they replaced, were economic nationalists who wanted the federal government to promote manufacturing, support a national bank, and finance a national road network. In the South, the Whigs tended to be bankers and merchants. In the West, they were mostly farmers who valued government-funded internal improvements. Unlike the Democrats, who attracted Catholic voters from Germany and Ireland, northern Whigs tended to be native-born Protestants—Congregationalists, Presbyterians, Methodists, and Baptists—who advocated the abolition of slavery and efforts to restrict alcoholic beverages. For the next twenty years, the Whigs and the Democrats would be the two major political parties.

**KILLING THE B.U.S.** In the end, a relentless President Jackson won his battle with Nicholas Biddle's bank. The B.U.S. would shut down completely by 1841, and the United States would not have a central banking system until 1914. Jackson exulted in his "glorious triumph," but his controversial efforts to destroy the B.U.S. aroused so much opposition that some in Congress talked of impeaching him. He received so many death threats that he decided his political opponents were trying to kill him.

In January 1835, the threat became real. After attending a funeral for a member of Congress, Jackson was leaving the Capitol when an unemployed housepainter named Richard Lawrence emerged from the shadows and, from point-blank range, aimed a pistol at the president's heart. When Lawrence pulled the trigger, however, the gun misfired. Jackson lifted his walking stick and charged at the man, who pulled out another pistol, but it, too, miraculously misfired, enabling police to arrest him.

Jackson assumed that his political foes had planned the attack. A jury, however, decided that Lawrence, the first person to attempt to assassinate a U.S. president, was insane and ordered him confined in an asylum.

The destruction of the B.U.S. illustrated Jackson's strengths and weaknesses. He was a cunning and ferocious fighter. Yet his determination to destroy the B.U.S. ended up hurting the national economy. Without the B.U.S., there was nothing to regulate the nation's money supply or its banks. The number of state banks more than doubled between 1829 and 1837. Of even greater concern, however, was that the dollar amount of loans made by these unregulated banks quadrupled, preparing the way for a financial panic and a terrible depression.

Jackson and the Democrats grew increasingly committed to the expansion of slavery westward into the Gulf coast states, driven by an unstable banking system. "People here are run mad with [land] speculation," wrote a traveler through northern Mississippi. "They do business in a kind of frenzy." Gold was scarce but paper money was plentiful, and people rushed to buy lands freed up by the removal of Indians. With the restraining effects of Biddle's national bank removed, scores of new state banks sprouted like mushrooms in the cotton belt, each irresponsibly printing its own paper currency that was often lent recklessly to land speculators and new businesses, especially in cotton-growing states like Mississippi and Louisiana.

The result was chaos. Too many banks had inadequate capital and expertise. As Senator Thomas Hart Benton, one of Jackson's most loyal supporters, said in 1837, he had not helped the president kill the B.U.S. to create a "wilderness of local banks. I did not join in putting down the paper currency of a national bank to put up a national paper currency of a thousand local banks."

But that is what happened. After 1837, anyone who could raise a certain minimum amount of money ("capital") could open a bank. And many did. With no central bank to regulate and oversee the "wildcat" banks, many of them went bankrupt after only a few months or years, leaving their depositors empty handed.

**THE MONEY QUESTION** During the 1830s, the federal government acquired huge amounts of money from the sale of government-owned lands. Initially, the Treasury department used the annual surpluses from land sales to pay down the accumulated federal debt, which it eliminated completely in 1835—the first time any nation had done so. By 1836, the federal budget was generating an annual surplus, which led to intense discussions about what to do with the increasingly worthless paper money flowing into Treasury's vaults.

The surge of unstable paper money peaked in 1836, when two key initiatives endorsed by the Jackson administration devastated the nation's financial system and threw the economy into a sudden tailspin.

First, in June 1836, Congress approved the **Distribution Act**, initially proposed by Henry Clay and Daniel Webster. It required the federal government to "distribute" to the states surplus federal revenue from land sales. The surpluses would be "deposited" into eighty-one state banks in proportion to each state's representation in Congress. The state governments would then draw upon those deposits to fund roads, bridges, and other internal (infrastructure) improvements.

A month later, Jackson issued the Specie Circular, which announced that the federal government would accept only specie (gold or silver coins) in payment for land purchased by speculators. (Farmers could still pay with paper money.) The Specie Circular upset westerners because most of the government land sales were occurring in their states. They helped convince Congress to pass an act overturning Jackson's policy. The president, however, vetoed it.

Once enacted, the Deposit and Distribution Act and the Specie Circular put added strains on the nation's already tight supplies of gold and silver. Eastern banks had to transfer much of their gold and silver reserves to western banks. In doing so, they had to reduce their lending. Soon, the once-bustling economy began to slow as the money supply contracted, and it became much more difficult for individuals and businesses to get loans. Nervous depositors rushed to their local banks to withdraw their money, only to learn that there was not enough specie to redeem their deposits. In killing the B.U.S., Jackson had unwittingly thrown the economy into chaos.

**CENSORING THE MAIL** While concerns about the strength of the economy grew, slavery emerged again as a flashpoint issue. In 1835, northern organizations began mailing anti-slavery publications to prominent white southerners, hoping to convince them to end the "peculiar institution." They found little support. Angry pro-slavery South Carolinians in Charleston broke into the federal post office, stole bags of the abolitionist mailings, and ceremoniously burned them; southern state legislatures passed laws banning such "dangerous" publications. Jackson asked Congress to pass a federal censorship law that would prohibit "incendiary" materials intended to incite "the slaves to insurrection."

Congress took action in 1836, but instead of banning abolitionist materials, a bipartisan group of Democrats and Whigs reaffirmed the sanctity of the federal mail. Southern post offices began censoring the mail anyway, arguing that federal authority ended when the mail arrived at the post office door. Jackson decided not to enforce the congressional action, creating what would become a growing split in the Democratic party over the future of slavery.

***New Method of Assorting the Mail, As Practised by Southern–Slave Holders, Or Attack on the Post Office, Charleston S.C.*** **(1835)** On the wall of the post office a sign reads "$20,000 Reward for Tappan," referring to the bounty placed on the head of Arthur Tappan, founder and president of the American Anti-Slavery Society.

The controversy over the mails proved to be a victory for the growing abolitionist movement. One anti-slavery publisher said that instead of stifling their efforts, Jackson and the southern radicals "put us and our principles up before the world—just where we wanted to be." Abolitionist groups started mailing their pamphlets and petitions to members of Congress. James Hammond, a pro-slavery South Carolinian, called for Congress to ban such petitions. When his proposal failed, Congress in 1836 adopted an informal solution suggested by Martin Van Buren: Whenever a petition calling for the end of slavery was introduced, someone would immediately move that it be tabled. The plan, Van Buren claimed, would preserve the "harmony of our happy Union."

The supporters of this "gag rule" soon encountered a formidable obstacle in John Quincy Adams, the former president who now was a congressman from Massachusetts. He devised an array of procedures to get around the rule. Henry Wise of Virginia called Adams "the acutest, the astutest, the archest enemy of southern slavery that ever existed." In the 1838–1839 session of Congress, thanks to Adams, some 1,500 anti-slavery petitions were filed with 163,845

**Martin Van Buren** Van Buren earned the nickname the "Great Magician" for his "magical" ability to exploit his political and social connections.

signatures. Andrew Jackson dismissed Adams, his old rival, as "the most reckless and depraved man living."

**THE ELECTION OF 1836** In 1835, eighteen months before the presidential election, the Democrats nominated Jackson's handpicked successor, Vice President Martin Van Buren. The Whig coalition, united chiefly by its opposition to Jackson, adopted a strategy of nominating multiple candidates, hoping to throw the election into the House of Representatives.

The Whigs put up three regional candidates: New Englander Daniel Webster, Hugh Lawson White of Tennessee, and William Henry Harrison of Indiana. But the strategy failed. In the popular vote of 1836, Van Buren defeated the entire Whig field, winning 170 electoral votes while the others combined to collect only 113.

**THE EIGHTH PRESIDENT** Martin Van Buren was a skillful politician. Elected governor of New York in 1828, he had resigned to join Andrew Jackson's cabinet, first as secretary of state, and then as vice president in 1833. He was the first New Yorker to be elected president.

Van Buren had been Jackson's closest political adviser and most trusted ally, but many considered him too self-centered to do the work of the people. John Quincy Adams wrote that Van Buren was "by far the ablest" of the Jacksonians, but that he had wasted "most of his ability upon mere personal intrigues. His principles are all subordinate to his ambition." Van Buren's rival, John C. Calhoun, was even more cutting. "He is not of the race of the lion or the tiger." Rather, he "belongs to a lower order—the fox."

At his inauguration, Van Buren promised to follow "in the footsteps" of the enormously popular Jackson. Before he could do so, however, the nation's financial sector began collapsing. On May 10, 1837, several large state banks in New York, running out of gold and silver, suddenly refused to convert customers' paper money into coins. Other banks quickly did the same, creating a panic among depositors across the nation. More than a third of the banks went under. This financial crisis would become known as the **Panic of 1837** and would soon mushroom into the country's worst depression, lasting some seven years.

**THE PANIC OF 1837** The causes of the financial crisis went back to the Jackson administration, but Van Buren got the blame. The problem actually started in Europe. During the mid-1830s, Great Britain, America's largest trading partner, experienced an acute financial crisis when the Bank of England, worried about a run on the gold and silver in its vaults, curtailed its loans. This forced most British companies to reduce their trade with America. As British demand for American cotton plummeted, so did the price paid for cotton. On top of everything else, in 1836 there had been a disastrous U.S. wheat crop.

As creditors hastened to foreclose on businesses and farms unable to make their debt payments, government spending plunged. Many canals under construction were shut down, and many state governments could not repay their debts. In April 1837, some 250 businesses failed in New York City alone. By early fall, 90 percent of the nation's factories had closed down.

Not surprisingly, the economic crisis frightened people. As a newspaper editorial complained in December 1836, the economy "has been put into confusion and dismay by a well-meant, but *extremely mistaken*" pair of decisions by Congress and President Jackson: the Specie Circular and the elimination of the B.U.S.

In April 1836, *Niles' Weekly Register*, the nation's leading business journal, reported that the economy was "approaching a momentous crisis." The federal government was lucky to sell land for $3 an acre that had been going for $10 an acre. More and more people could not pay their debts. Many fled their creditors altogether by moving to Texas, then a province of Mexico. Forty percent of the state banks shut their doors. The federal government itself, having put most of its gold and silver in state banks, was verging on bankruptcy. The *National Intelligencer* newspaper reported in May that the federal Treasury "has not a dollar of gold or silver in the world!"

The poor, as always, were particularly hard hit. By the fall of 1837, one third of the nation's workers were jobless, and those still fortunate enough to be employed had their wages cut by 30 to 50 percent within two years. At the same time, prices for food and clothing soared. As the winter of 1837 approached, a New York City journalist reported that 200,000 people were "in utter and hopeless distress with no means of surviving the winter but those provided by charity." The nation had a "poverty-struck feeling."

**POLITICS AMID THE DEPRESSION** The unprecedented economic calamity sent shock waves through the political system. Critics among the Whigs called the president "Martin Van Ruin" because he did not believe that he or the federal government had any responsibility to rescue farmers, bankers, or businessmen, or to provide relief for the jobless and homeless. Van Buren insisted that any efforts to help people in distress must come from the states.

How best to deal with the unprecedented depression clearly divided Democrats from Whigs. Unlike Van Buren, Whig Henry Clay insisted that suffering people were "entitled to the protecting care of a parental Government." To him, an enlarged role for the federal government was the price of a maturing, expanding republic in which elected officials had an obligation to promote the "safety, convenience, and prosperity" of the people. Van Buren and the Democrats believed that the government had no such obligations. Clay and others savaged the president for his "cold and heartless" attitude.

**AN INDEPENDENT TREASURY**   Martin Van Buren believed that the federal government should stop risking its cash deposits in the insecure "pet" state banks that Jackson had selected. Instead, Van Buren wanted to establish an Independent Treasury system whereby the government would keep its funds in its own vaults and do business entirely in gold or silver. He wanted the federal government to regulate the nation's supply of gold and silver and let the marketplace regulate the supply of paper currency.

It took him more than three years to convince Congress to pass the **Independent Treasury Act**. Although it lasted little more than a year (the Whigs repealed it in 1841), it would be restored in 1846. But it was a political disaster. The state banks that lost control of the federal funds howled in protest. Moreover, it did nothing to end the widespread suffering caused by the deepening depression.

**THE 1840 CAMPAIGN**   By 1840, an election year, President Van Buren and the Democrats were in deep trouble. Aside from the growing financial crisis, the hot potato of Texas was also an issue. In 1837, Van Buren had decided *not* to annex the Republic of Texas, claiming that there was no provision in the Constitution for absorbing another nation and that doing so would trigger a war with Mexico. The decision outraged his political mentor, Andrew Jackson, and aroused strong criticism among southern Democrats.

The Whigs now sensed that they could win the presidency. At their nominating convention, they passed over Henry Clay, Jackson's longtime foe, in favor of William Henry Harrison, whose credentials were impressive: victor at the Battle of Tippecanoe against Tecumseh's Shawnees in 1811, former governor of the Indiana Territory, and former congressman and senator from Ohio.

To balance the ticket geographically, the Whigs nominated John Tyler of Virginia as their vice president. Clay was bitterly disappointed, complaining that "my friends are not worth the powder and shot it would take to kill them. I am the most unfortunate man in the history of parties."

## THE ELECTION OF 1840

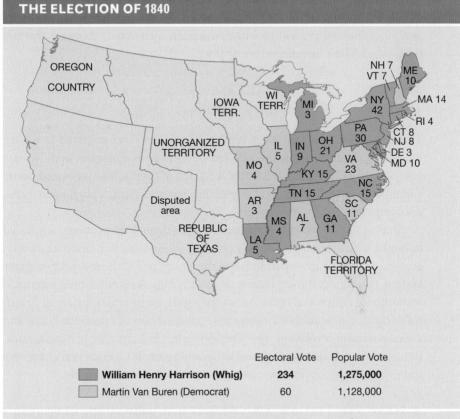

| | Electoral Vote | Popular Vote |
|---|---|---|
| **William Henry Harrison (Whig)** | **234** | **1,275,000** |
| Martin Van Buren (Democrat) | 60 | 1,128,000 |

- Why did Van Buren carry several western states but few others?
- How did the Whigs achieve a decisive electoral victory over the Democrats?
- How was the Whig strategy in 1840 different from their campaign in 1836?

The Whigs refused to take a stand on major issues. They did, however, seize upon a catchy campaign slogan: "Tippecanoe and Tyler Too." When a Democratic newspaper declared that Harrison was the kind of man who would spend his retirement "in a log cabin [sipping apple cider] on the banks of the Ohio [River]," the Whigs chose the cider and log cabin symbols to depict Harrison as a humble man sprung from the working poor, in contrast to Van Buren's aristocratic lifestyle. (Harrison was actually from one of Virginia's wealthiest families.)

Harrison defeated Van Buren easily, winning 234 electoral votes to 60. The Whigs had promised a return to prosperity without explaining how it would happen. It was simply time for a change.

What was most remarkable about the election of 1840 was the turnout. By this time almost every state had dropped property qualifications for voting, and more than 80 percent of white American men voted, many for the first time—the highest turnout before or since.

## JACKSON'S LEGACY

The nation that President-elect William Henry Harrison prepared to govern was vastly different from the one led by George Washington and Thomas Jefferson. In 1828, the United States consisted of twenty-four states and nearly 13 million people. The national population was growing at a phenomenal rate, doubling every twenty-three years.

During the so-called Jacksonian era, the unregulated economy witnessed booming industrialization; rapidly growing cities; rising tensions over slavery; accelerating westward expansion; and the emergence of the **second two-party system**, this time featuring Democrats and Whigs. A surge in foreign demand for southern cotton and other American goods, along with substantial British investment in new American enterprises, helped fuel an economic boom and a transportation revolution. That President-elect Jackson rode to his inauguration in a horse-drawn carriage and left Washington, D.C., eight years later on a train symbolized the dramatic changes occurring in American life.

**A NEW POLITICAL LANDSCAPE** A transformational figure in a transformational era, Andrew Jackson helped reshape the American political landscape. Even his ferocious opponent, Henry Clay, acknowledged that Jackson had "swept over the Government . . . like a tropical tornado."

In his 1837 farewell address, Jackson stressed his crusade on behalf of "the farmer, the mechanic, and the laboring classes of society—the bone and sinew of the country—men who love liberty and desire nothing but equal rights and equal laws."

Jackson championed opportunities for the "common man" to play a greater role in the political arena at the same time that working men were forming labor unions to increase their economic power and political clout. He helped establish the modern Democratic party and attracted to it the working poor and immigrants from eastern cities, as well as farmers from the South and East. Through a nimble combination of force and compromise, he saved the Union by suppressing the nullification crisis.

And, with great fanfare on January 1, 1835, Jackson announced that the government had paid off the national debt accumulated since the Revolutionary

War, which he called a "national curse." The *Washington Globe* noted that the elimination of the debt coincided with the twentieth anniversary of the Battle of New Orleans, writing that "New Orleans and the National Debt—the first of which paid off our scores to *our enemies*, whilst the latter paid off the last cent to *our friends.*"

Jackson's concept of "the people," however, was limited to a "white men's democracy," as it had been for all previous presidents. The phenomenon of Andrew Jackson, the heroic symbol of the common man and the democratic ideal, continues to spark historical debate, as it did during his lifetime.

In 1828, William P. Anderson, who had been one of Jackson's horse-racing friends and political supporters but turned into an outspoken opponent, wrote an open letter to the presidential candidate that was published in several newspapers. He brutally outlined Jackson's faults: "Your besetting sins are ambition and the love of money. . . . You are naturally and constitutionally irritable, overbearing and tyrannical. . . . When you become the enemy of any man, you will put him down if you can, no matter by what means, fair or foul. . . . You are miserably deficient in principle, and have seldom or never had power without abusing it."

Although the criticism was too harsh, it contained more than a grain of truth. Jackson was so convinced of the rightness and righteousness of his ideals that he was willing to defy constitutional limits on his authority when it suited his interests and satisfied his rage. He was both the instrument of democracy and its enemy, protecting "the humble people" and the Union by expanding presidential authority in ways that the founders had never envisioned, including removing federal money from the national bank, replacing government officials with party loyalists, censoring the mails, and ending nullification in South Carolina.

Jackson often declared that the only justification for using governmental power was to ensure equal treatment for everyone. Yet his own use of government force was at times contradictory and even hypocritical. While he threatened to "kill" the B.U.S. and hang John Calhoun and other South Carolina nullifiers, he refused to intervene when Georgia officials violated the legal rights of Cherokees. His inconsistent approach to executive power both symbolized and aggravated the perennial tension in the American republic between a commitment to democratic ideals and the exercise of presidential authority.

# CHAPTER REVIEW

## SUMMARY

- **Jackson's Views and Policies** The Jacksonians sought to democratize the political process and expand economic opportunity for the "common man" (that is, "poor and humble" white men). As the representative of "the people," Andrew Jackson expanded the role of the president in economic matters, reducing federal spending and eliminating the powerful Second Bank of the United States. His *Bank War* was hugely popular, but Jackson did not understand its long-term consequences. In addition, his views on limited government were not always reflected in his policies. He left the high taxes from the *Tariff of Abominations (1828)* in place until opposition in the South created a national crisis.

- **Indian Removal Act (1830)** The *Indian Removal Act* authorized the relocation of eastern Indians to federal lands west of the Mississippi River. The Cherokees used the federal court system to block this relocation. Despite the Supreme Court's decisions in their favor, President Jackson forced them to move; the event and the route they took came to be called the *Trail of Tears (1832–1840)*. By 1840, only a few Seminoles and Cherokees remained in remote areas of the Southeast.

- **Nullification Controversy** The concept of *nullification*, developed by South Carolina's John C. Calhoun, enabled a state to disavow a federal law. When a South Carolina convention nullified the Tariffs of 1828 and 1832, Jackson requested that Congress pass a *Force Bill (1833)* authorizing the U.S. Army to compel compliance with the tariffs. After South Carolina, under the threat of federal military force, accepted a compromise tariff put forth by Henry Clay, the state convention nullified the Force Bill. The immediate crisis was over, with both sides claiming victory.

- **Democrats and Whigs** Jackson's arrogant behavior, especially his use of the veto, led many to regard him as "King Andrew the First." Groups who opposed him coalesced into a new party, the *Whigs*, thus producing the country's *second two-party system*. Two acts—the *Distribution Act (1836)* and the Specie Circular—ultimately destabilized the nation's economy. Jackson's ally and vice president, Martin Van Buren, succeeded him as president, but Jacksonian bank policies led to the financial *Panic of 1837* and an economic depression. Congress and Van Buren responded by passing the *Independent Treasury Act (1840)* to safeguard the nation's economy but offered no help for individuals in distress. The economic calamity ensured a Whig victory in the election of 1840.

- **The Jackson Years** Andrew Jackson's America was very different from the America of 1776. Most white men had gained the vote, but political equality did not mean economic equality. Jacksonian Democrats wanted every American to have an equal chance to compete in the marketplace and in the political arena, but they never promoted equality of results. Inequality between rich and poor widened during the Jacksonian era.

## CHRONOLOGY

| | |
|---|---|
| **1828** | Tariff of Abominations goes into effect |
| **1830** | Congress passes the Indian Removal Act |
| | Andrew Jackson vetoes the Maysville Road Bill |
| **1831** | Supreme Court issues *Cherokee Nation v. Georgia* decision |
| **1832** | Supreme Court issues *Worcester v. Georgia* decision |
| | South Carolina passes Ordinance of Nullification |
| | Andrew Jackson vetoes the Bank Recharter Bill |
| **1833** | Congress passes the Force Bill, authorizing military force in South Carolina |
| | Congress passes Henry Clay's compromise tariff with Jackson's support |
| **1836** | Democratic candidate Martin Van Buren is elected president |
| **1837** | Financial panic deflates the economy |
| **1832–1840** | Eastern Indians are forced West on the Trail of Tears |
| **1840** | Independent Treasury established |
| | Whig candidate William Henry Harrison is elected president |

## KEY TERMS

**Indian Removal Act (1830)** p. 385

**Trail of Tears (1832–1840)** p. 389

**Bank War** p. 391

**Tariff of Abominations (1828)** p. 393

**nullification** p. 394

**Force Bill (1833)** p. 400

**Whigs** p. 402

**Distribution Act (1836)** p. 404

**Panic of 1837** p. 406

**Independent Treasury Act (1840)** p. 408

**second two-party system** p. 410

 INQUIZITIVE

**Go to InQuizitive to see what you've learned—and learn what you've missed—with personalized feedback along the way.**

# 11 The South, Slavery, and King Cotton

## 1800–1860

**The Old South** One of the enduring myths of the Old South is captured in this late-nineteenth-century painting of a plantation on the Mississippi River: muscular slaves tending the lush cotton fields, a steamboat easing down the wide river, and the planter's family relaxing in the cool shade of their white-columned mansion. Novels and films like *Gone with the Wind* (1939) would perpetuate the notion of the Old South as a stable, paternalistic agrarian society led by white planters who were the "natural" aristocracy of virtue and talent within their communities.

Of all the regions of the United States during the first half of the nineteenth century, the pre–Civil War Old South was the most distinctive. What had once been a narrow band of settlements along the Atlantic coast dramatically expanded westward and southward to form a subcontinental empire rooted in cotton.

The southern states remained rural and agricultural long after the rest of the nation had embraced cities, immigrants, and factories. Yet the Old South was also instrumental in the nation's capitalist development and its growing economic stature. After the War of 1812, southern-grown cotton became the key raw material driving industrial growth and feeding the textile mills of Great Britain and New England, where wage workers toiling over newly invented machines fashioned it into thread, yarn, and clothing.

The price of raw cotton doubled in the first year after the war, and the profits made by cotton producers flowed into the hands of northern and British bankers, merchants, and textile-mill owners, many of whom made loans to Southerners to buy more land and more slaves. Northerners also provided the cotton industry with insurance, financing, and shipping.

The story of how southern cotton clothed the world, spurred the expansion of global capitalism, and transformed history was woven with the threads of tragedy, however. The revolution spawned by the mass production of cotton accelerated the spread of slavery across the South and into Texas. A group of slaves in Virginia recognized the essential role they played when they asked, "Didn't we clear the land, and raise the crops of corn, of tobacco, rice, of sugar,

## *focus questions*

**1.** What factors made the South distinct from the rest of the United States during the early nineteenth century?

**2.** What role did cotton production and slavery play in the South's economic and social development?

**3.** What were the major social groups within southern white society? Why did each group support the expansion of slavery?

**4.** What was the impact of slavery on African Americans, both free and enslaved, throughout the South?

**5.** How did enslaved peoples respond to the inhumanity of their situation?

of everything? And then didn't the large cities in the North grow up on the cotton and the sugars and the rice that we made?"

# THE DISTINCTIVENESS OF THE OLD SOUTH

People have long debated what set the Old South apart from the rest of the nation. Most arguments focus on the region's climate and geography. Its warm, humid climate was ideal for cultivating profitable crops such as tobacco, cotton, rice, indigo, and sugarcane, which led to the plantation system of large commercial agriculture and its dependence upon enslaved labor.

Unlike the North, the South had few large cities or banks, and few railroads, factories, or schools. Most southern commerce was related to the storage, distribution, and sale of agricultural products, especially cotton. With the cotton economy booming, investors focused on buying land and slaves; there was little reason to create a robust industrial sector. "We want no manufactures; we desire no trading, no mechanical, or manufacturing classes," an Alabama politician told an English visitor.

Profitable farming thus remained the South's ideal pursuit of happiness. Education was valued by the planter elite for their sons, but there was little interest in public schooling for the masses. The illiteracy rate in the South was three times higher than in the North.

**A BIRACIAL CULTURE** What made the Old South most distinctive was not its climate or soil but its system of race-based slavery. The majority of southern whites did not own slaves, but they supported what John C. Calhoun called the South's "**peculiar institution**" because it was so central to their way of life. Calhoun's carefully crafted phrase allowed Southerners to avoid using the charged word *slavery*, while the adjective *peculiar* implied that slavery was *unique* to the South, as it essentially was.

The profitability and convenience of owning slaves created a sense of social unity among whites that bridged class differences. Poor whites who owned no slaves and resented the planters ("cotton snobs") could still claim racial superiority over enslaved blacks ("niggers"). Because of race-based slavery, explained Georgia attorney Thomas Reade Cobb, every white "feels that he belongs to an elevated class. It matters not that he is no slaveholder; he is not of the inferior race; he is a free-born citizen."

The Old South also differed from other sections of the country in its high proportion of native-born Americans. The region attracted few European immigrants after the Revolution in part because the main shipping routes from Britain and Europe took immigrants to northern port cities. Because most immigrants were penniless, they could not afford to travel to the South. Moreover, European immigrants, most of whom were manual laborers, could not compete with slave labor.

**CONFLICTING MYTHS** Southerners, a North Carolina editor wrote, are "a mythological people, created half out of dream and half out of slander, who live in a still legendary land." Myths are beliefs made up partly of truths and partly of lies. During the nineteenth century, a powerful myth emerged among white Southerners—that the South was both different from *and* better than the North. This blended notion of distinctiveness and superiority became central to Southerners' self-image. Even today, many Southerners tenaciously cultivate a separate identity from the rest of the nation.

In defending their way of life, Southerners claimed that their region was morally superior. Kind planters, according to the prevailing myth, provided happy slaves with food, clothing, shelter, and security—in contrast to a North

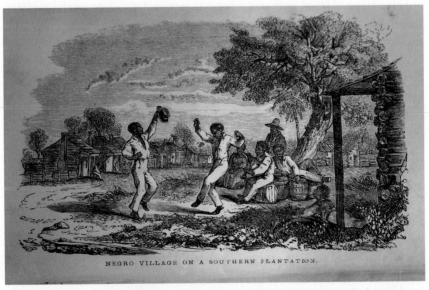

NEGRO VILLAGE ON A SOUTHERN PLANTATION.

*Negro Village on a Southern Plantation* This line drawing of slaves dancing after a day of work in the cotton fields is an example of the "happy slave" myth, wherein white Southerners glossed slavery as somehow cheerful and harmonious rather than oppressive. The drawing is from Mrs. Mary H. Eastman's *Aunt Phillis's Cabin; or, Southern Life as It Is*—a pro-slavery novel published in 1853 in response to Harriet Beecher Stowe's anti-slavery novel *Uncle Tom's Cabin*.

populated with greedy bankers and heartless factory owners who treated their wage laborers worse than slaves. John C. Calhoun insisted that in northern states the quality of life for free people of color had "become worse" since slavery there had been banned, whereas in the South the standard of living among enslaved African Americans had "improved greatly in every respect."

In this mythic version of the Old South, slavery benefited both slaves and owners. In *Aunt Phillis's Cabin; or, Southern Life as It Is* (1852), novelist Mary Henderson Eastman stressed "the necessity of the existence of slavery at present in our Southern States," and claimed "that, as a general thing, the slaves are comfortable and contented, and their owners humane and kind."

The agrarian ideal and the southern passion for guns, horsemanship, hunting, the military, and manly honor completed the self-gratifying image of the Old South. Its defenders viewed it as a region of honest small farmers, aristocratic gentlemen, young belles, and beautiful ladies who led leisurely lives of well-mannered graciousness, all the while sipping mint juleps in a carefree world of white-columned mansions.

The contrasting myth of the Old South was much darker. Northern abolitionists (those who wanted an immediate end to slavery) pictured the region as being trapped in an immoral economic system dependent on the exploitation of blacks and the displacement of Native Americans. In this version, the theme of violence—physical, mental, and emotional—ran deep.

Northern abolitionists such as Harriet Beecher Stowe portrayed southern planters as cunning capitalists who raped enslaved women, brutalized slaves, and lorded over their communities. They broke up their slaves' families and sold slaves "down the river" to toil in Louisiana sugar mills and on rice plantations. An English woman traveling in the South in 1830 noted that what slaves in Virginia and Maryland feared most was being "sent to *the south* and sold. . . . The sugar plantations [in Louisiana] and, more than all, the rice grounds of Georgia and the Carolinas, are the terror of the American negroes."

**MANY SOUTHS** The contradictory elements of these myths continue to fight for supremacy in the South, each pressing its claim to legitimacy, in part because both descriptions are built upon half-truths and fierce prejudices. The South has long been defined by two souls, two hearts, two minds competing for dominance. The paradoxes associated with southern mythmaking provided much of the region's variety, for the Old South, like the New South, was not a single culture but a diverse section with multiple interests and perspectives.

The Old South included three subsections with distinct patterns of economic development and diverging degrees of commitment to slavery. Throughout the first half of the nineteenth century, the seven states of the Lower South

(South Carolina, Georgia, Florida, Alabama, Mississippi, Louisiana, and parts of Texas) grew increasingly dependent upon commercial cotton production supported by slave labor. By 1860, slaves represented nearly half the population of the Lower South, largely because they were the most efficient producers of cotton in the world.

The states of the Upper South (Virginia, North Carolina, Tennessee, and Arkansas) had more-varied agricultural economies—a mixture of large commercial plantations and small family farms ("yeoman farms"), where crops were grown mostly for household use. Many states also had large areas without slavery, especially in the mountains of Virginia, the western Carolinas, eastern Tennessee, and northern Georgia, where the soil and climate were not suited to cotton or tobacco.

In the Border South (Delaware, Maryland, Kentucky, and Missouri), slavery was slowly disappearing because cotton could not thrive there. By 1860, approximately 90 percent of Delaware's black population and half of Maryland's were already free. Slave owners in the Lower South, however, had a much larger investment in slavery. They believed that only constant supervision, intimidation, and punishment would keep the fast-growing population of enslaved workers under control, in part because the working and living conditions were so brutal. "I'd rather be dead," said a white overseer in Louisiana, "than a nigger in one of those big [sugarcane] plantations."

## THE COTTON KINGDOM

After the Revolution, as the tobacco fields in Virginia and Maryland lost their fertility, tobacco farming spread into Kentucky and as far west as Missouri. Rice continued to be grown in the coastal areas ("low country") of the Carolinas and Georgia, where fields could easily be flooded and drained by tidal rivers flowing into the ocean. Sugarcane, like rice, was also an expensive crop to produce, requiring machinery to grind the cane to release the sugar syrup. During the early nineteenth century, only southern Louisiana focused on sugar production.

In addition to such "cash crops," the South led the nation in the production of livestock: hogs, horses, mules, and cattle. Southerners, both black and white, fed themselves largely on pork. John S. Wilson, a Georgia doctor, called the region the "Republic of Porkdom." Corn was on southern plates as often as pork. During the early summer, corn was boiled on the cob; by late summer and fall, it was ground into cornmeal, a coarse flour. Cornbread and hominy, as well as a "mush" or porridge made of whole-grain corn mixed with milk, were almost daily fare.

**Captaining the Cotton Kingdom** This photograph offers a glimpse of the staggering scale of cotton production. These 500-pound cotton bales are densely packed and plentiful on this steamboat photographed on the Mississippi River in Louisiana.

**KING COTTON** During the first half of the nineteenth century, cotton surpassed rice as the most profitable cash crop in the South, and its revenues spread far beyond the region. By the 1850s, New York City, where much of the cotton was bought, sold, and shipped abroad, garnered 40 percent of the revenue. Southern cotton (called "white gold") drove much of the national economy.

Cotton shaped the lives of the enslaved who cultivated it, the planters who grew rich by it, the mill girls who sewed it, the merchants who sold it, the people who wore it, and the politicians who warred over it. "Cotton is King," exclaimed the *Southern Cultivator* in 1859, "and wields an astonishing influence over the world's commerce." In 1832, more than eighty of America's largest companies were New England textile mills.

The Cotton Kingdom resulted largely from two crucial developments. Until the late eighteenth century, cotton fabric was a rarity produced by women in India using handlooms. Then British inventors developed machinery to convert raw cotton into thread and cloth. The mechanical production of cotton made Great Britain the world's first industrial nation, and the number of British textile mills grew so fast that owners could not get enough cotton fiber to meet their needs. American Eli Whitney solved the problem by constructing the first cotton gin, which mechanized the labor-intensive process of manually removing the sticky seeds from the bolls of what was called short-staple cotton.

Taken together, these breakthroughs helped create the world's largest industry—and transformed the South in the process. By 1815, just months after Andrew Jackson's victory over the British at New Orleans, some thirty British ships were docked at the city's wharves because, as an American merchant reported, "Europe must, and will have, cotton for her manufacturers." To be sure, other nations joined the cotton-producing revolution—India, Egypt, Brazil, and China—but the American South was the driving force of cotton capitalism.

**THE OLD SOUTHWEST** Because of its warm climate and plentiful rainfall, the Lower South became the global leader in cotton production. The region's cheap, fertile land, and the profits to be made in growing cotton, generated a frenzied mobility in which people constantly searched for more and better opportunities. Henry Watson, a New Englander who moved to Alabama, complained in 1836 that "nobody seems to consider himself settled [here]; they remain one, two, three or four years & must move on to some other spot."

The cotton belt moved south and west during the first half of the nineteenth century. As the oldest southern states—Virginia and the Carolinas—experienced soil exhaustion from the overplanting of tobacco and cotton, restless farmers moved to the **Old Southwest**—western Georgia, Alabama, Mississippi, Louisiana, Arkansas and, eventually, Texas.

In 1820, Virginia, the Carolinas, and Georgia had produced two thirds of the nation's cotton. By 1830, the Old Southwest states were the dominant cotton producers. An acre of land in South Carolina produced about 300 pounds of cotton, while an acre in Alabama or in the Mississippi Delta, a 200-mile-wide strip of fertile soil between the Yazoo and Mississippi Rivers, could generate 800 pounds. It was the most profitable farmland in the world.

Such profits, however, required backbreaking labor, most of it performed by enslaved blacks driven by the brutal efficiency of overseers. In marshy areas near the Gulf coast, slaves were put to work removing trees and stumps from the swampy muck. "None but men as hard as a Savage," said one worker, could survive such conditions.

The formula for growing rich was simple: cheap land, cotton seed, and slaves driven to exhaustion by profit-seeking planters who viewed them as property. Between 1810 and 1840, the combined population of Georgia, Alabama, and Mississippi increased from about 300,000 (252,000 of whom were

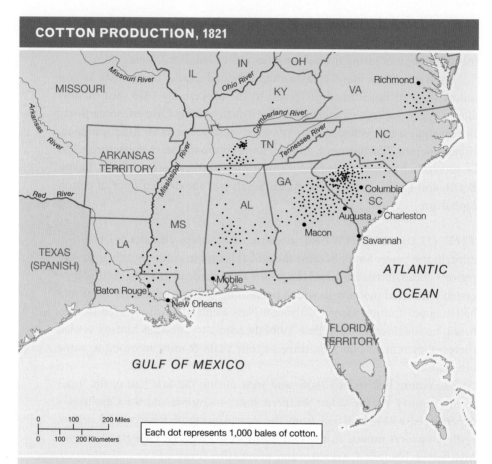

**COTTON PRODUCTION, 1821**

Each dot represents 1,000 bales of cotton.

- Why was cotton so profitable?
- What regions produced the most cotton in 1821?
- What innovations enabled farmers to move inland and produce cotton more efficiently?

in Georgia) to 1,657,799. Annual cotton production in the United States grew from 150,000 bales (a bundle of cotton weighing 500 pounds) in 1815 to 4 *million* bales in 1860.

**THE SOUTHERN FRONTIER** Farm families in the Old Southwest tended to be large. "There is not a cabin but has ten or twelve children in it," reported a traveling minister. "When the boys are eighteen and the girls are fourteen, they marry—so that in many cabins you will see . . . the mother looking as young as the daughter."

Women were a minority among migrants from Virginia and the Carolinas to the Old Southwest. Many resisted moving to what they had heard was

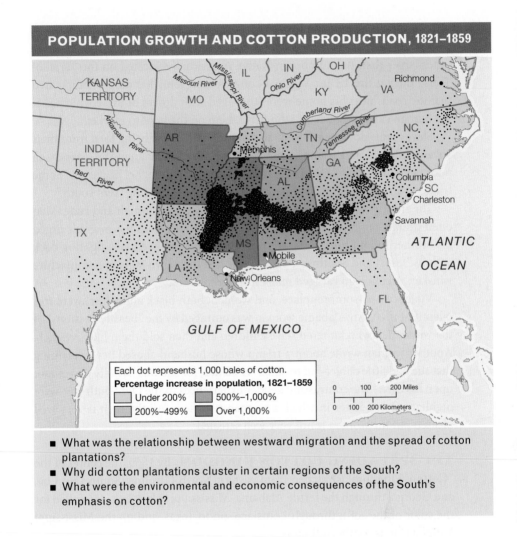

## POPULATION GROWTH AND COTTON PRODUCTION, 1821–1859

Each dot represents 1,000 bales of cotton.
**Percentage increase in population, 1821–1859**
Under 200%   500%–1,000%
200%–499%   Over 1,000%

- What was the relationship between westward migration and the spread of cotton plantations?
- Why did cotton plantations cluster in certain regions of the South?
- What were the environmental and economic consequences of the South's emphasis on cotton?

a disease-ridden, male-dominated, violent, and primitive territory. Others feared that life on the southern frontier would produce a "dissipation" of morals. They had heard wild stories of lawlessness, drunkenness, gambling, and whoring. A woman newly arrived in frontier Alabama wrote home that the farmers around her "live in a miserable manner. They think only of making money, and their houses are hardly fit to live in."

Enslaved blacks had many of the same reservations. Almost a million captive African Americans in Maryland, Virginia, and the Carolinas were forced to move to the Old Southwest during the first half of the nineteenth century. Herded onto steamboats or slave ships or forced to walk hundreds of miles handcuffed in pairs and manacled in iron collars and chains ("coffles"), they lived in "perpetual dread" of the Gulf states' harsh working conditions, heat, and humidity.

The forced resettlement of enslaved men, women, children, and babies along the "Slave Trail" from the tobacco South to the cotton South was twenty times larger than the number of Native Americans relocated on the "Trail of Tears" during the 1830s. Virginia congressman John Randolph complained that the roads near his home were "thronged with droves of these wretches & the human carcass-butchers, who drive them on the hoof to market."

Slaves sent "downriver" were also despondent about being torn from their wives, children, and friends. One song expressed their anguish: "Massa sell poor negro, ho, heave, O! / Leave poor wife and children, ho, heave, O!" Some tried to run away. Others maimed themselves to avoid being "sent south."

The frontier environment in the Old Southwest was rough and rude. Men often drank, gambled, and fought. In 1834, a South Carolina migrant urged his brother to join him in the west because "you can live like a fighting cock with us." Most Old Southwest plantations had their own stills to manufacture whiskey. Alcoholism ravaged many frontier families.

Violence was commonplace, and women, both black and white, were frequently abused. An Alabama woman was outraged by the "beastly passions" of the white men who fathered slave children and then sold them like livestock. Another woman wrote about a friend whose husband abused her, explaining that she had little choice but to suffer in silence, for she was "wholly dependent upon his care." The contrasting gender experiences in the Old Southwest were highlighted in a letter in which a woman reported: "All the men is very well pleased but the women is not very well satisfied."

**THE SPREADING COTTON KINGDOM**  By 1860, the center of the "**Cotton Kingdom**" stretched from eastern North Carolina, South Carolina, and Georgia through the fertile Alabama-Mississippi "black belt" (so called for the color of the soil), through Louisiana, on to Texas, and up the Mississippi Valley as far as southern Illinois.

Steamboats made the Mississippi River the cotton highway by transporting millions of bales to New Orleans, where sailing ships took the cotton to New York, New England, Great Britain, and France. King Cotton accounted for more than half of all U.S. exports.

By 1860, Alabama, Mississippi, and Louisiana were the top-producing cotton states, and two thirds of the richest Americans lived in the South. The rapid expansion of the cotton belt ensured that the South became more dependent on enslaved black workers.

Slavery was, as John Quincy Adams wrote in his diary, "the great and foul stain" upon the nation's commitment to liberty and equality. It persisted because it was a powerful engine of economic development—and a tangible sign of economic success. Enterprising young white men judged wealth and status by the number of slaves owned. By 1860, the dollar value of enslaved blacks outstripped the value of *all* American banks, railroads, and factories combined.

The soaring profitability of cotton also fostered a false sense of security—and bred cockiness. In 1860, a Mississippi newspaper boasted that the South, "safely entrenched behind her cotton bags . . . can defy the world—for the civilized world depends on the cotton of the South." In a speech to the U.S. Senate in 1858, South Carolina's former governor, James Henry Hammond, who owned a huge cotton plantation worked by more than 100 slaves, warned critics in the North: "You dare not make war on cotton. No power on earth dares make war upon it. Cotton is King."

What Hammond failed to acknowledge was that the southern economy had grown dangerously dependent on European demand for raw cotton. By 1860, Great Britain was importing more than 80 percent of its cotton from the American South. Southern leaders did not anticipate what they could least afford: a sudden collapse in demand for their cotton. In 1860, the expansion of the British textile industry peaked, and the price paid for southern cotton began a steady decline. By then, however, the Lower South was committed to large-scale cotton production for generations to come.

## WHITES IN THE OLD SOUTH

The culture of cotton and slavery shaped the South's social structure and provided much of its political power. Unlike in the North and Midwest, southern society was dominated by an elite group of planters and merchants.

**WHITE PLANTERS** Although there were only a few giant plantations in each southern state, their owners exercised overwhelming influence. As a Virginian observed in the mid-1830s, "the old slaveholding families exerted a great deal of control . . . and they affected the manner and prejudices of the slaveholding part of the state."

The richest planters and merchants were determined to control southern society, in part because of self-interest and in part because they assumed they were the region's natural leaders. "The planters here are essentially what the nobility are in other countries," claimed James Henry Hammond. "They stand at the head of society and politics. . . . Slavery does indeed create an aristocracy—an aristocracy of talents, of virtue, of generosity, and courage." Planters themselves rarely engaged in manual labor. They focused on managing the overseers and handling the marketing and sale of cotton, tobacco, rice, or sugar.

What distinguished a plantation from a farm, in addition to its size, was the use of a large number of slaves supervised by drivers and overseers. If, as historians have agreed, one had to own at least twenty slaves to be called a **planter**, only 1 out of 30 whites in 1860 qualified. Eleven planters, among the wealthiest people in the nation, owned 500 slaves each, and one planter, a South Carolina rice grower, owned 1,000. The 10,000 most powerful planters, making up less than 3 percent of white men in the South, held more than half the slaves. The total number of slaveholders was only 383,637 out of a white population of 8 million.

Over time, planters and their wives grew accustomed to being waited on by slaves day and night. A Virginia planter told a British visitor that a slave girl slept in the master bedroom with him and his wife. When his guest asked why, he replied: "Good heaven! If I wanted a glass of water during the night, what would become of me?"

The planter elite indulged expensive habits and tastes that they often could neither afford nor control. Living the storied life of a planter was the focus of their energies, their honor, and often their indebtedness. As a plantation slave recalled, his master on Sundays liked to "gamble, run horses, or fight game-cocks, discuss politics, and drink whisky, and brandy and water all day long."

Most planters began their careers as land traders, investors, cotton mer-chants (called "factors"), and farmers. Over time, they made enough money to acquire a plantation. Success required careful monitoring of the markets for cotton, land, and slaves, as well as careful management of the workers and production.

Most southern white men embraced an unwritten social code centered on a prickly sense of personal respectability in which they defended their repu-tations with words, fists, knives, or guns. Duels to the death (called "affairs of honor") were the ultimate expressions of manly honor.

Dueling was much more common in the South than in the rest of the nation, a fact that gave rise to the observation that Southerners were excessively polite until they grew angry enough to kill you. Many prominent southern leaders—congressmen, senators, governors, editors, and planters—engaged in duels with pistols, although dueling was technically illegal in many states. The roster of participants included President Andrew Jackson of Tennessee and Senator Henry Clay of Kentucky. But men of all classes were ready to fight at the first sign of disrespect.

**THE PLANTATION MISTRESS**  The South, like the North, was a male-dominated society, only more so because of the slave system. A prominent Geor-gian, Christopher Memminger, explained that slavery heightened the need for a hierarchical social and family structure. White wives and children needed to be as subservient and compliant as enslaved blacks. "Each planter," he declared, "is in fact a Patriarch—his position compels him to be a ruler in his household," and he requires "obedience and subordination."

The **plantation mistress** was no frail, helpless creature focused solely on planning parties and balls. Although she had slaves to attend to her needs, she supervised the household in the same way as the planter took care of the cotton business. Overseeing the supply and preparation of food and linens, she also managed the housecleaning and care of the sick, the birthing of babies, and the operations of the dairy.

A plantation slave remembered that her mistress "was with all the slave women every time a baby was born. Or, when a plague of misery hit the folks, she knew what to do and what kind of medicine to chase off the aches and pains." The son of a Tennessee slaveholder remembered that his mother and grandmother were "the busiest women I ever saw," in part because they themselves had babies every year or so.

Mary Boykin Chesnut, a plantation mistress in South Carolina, complained that "there is no slave, after all, like a wife." She admitted that she had few rights in the large household she managed, since her husband was the "master of the house."

A wife was expected to love, honor, obey, and serve her husband. Virginian George Fitzhugh, a Virginia attorney and writer, spoke for most southern men when he said that a "man loves his children because they are weak, helpless, and dependent. He loves his wife for similar reasons."

Planters had little interest in educated wives. When people tried to raise funds for a woman's college in Georgia, a planter angrily refused to contribute, explaining that "all that a woman needs to know is how to read the New Testament and to spin and weave clothing for her family. I would not have one of your graduates for a wife, and I will not give you a cent for any such project."

White southern women were expected to be examples of Christian

**Mary Boykin Chesnut** Her diary describing life in the Confederacy during the Civil War was republished in 1981 and won the Pulitzer Prize.

morality and sexual purity, even as their husbands, brothers, and sons often engaged in gambling, drinking, carousing, and sexually assaulting enslaved women. Such a double standard reinforced the arrogant authoritarianism of many white planters for whom the rape of slave women was common practice. In the secrecy of her famous diary, Mary Boykin Chesnut used sexual metaphors to express the limitations of most of the Carolina planters, writing that they "are nice fellows, but slow to move; impulsive but hard to keep moving. They are wonderful for a spurt, but that lets out all of their strength."

Yet for all their private complaints and daily burdens, few plantation mistresses spoke out. They largely accepted the role assigned them by men such as George Howe, a South Carolina religion professor. In 1850, he complimented southern women for understanding their subordinate place. "Born to lean upon others, rather than to stand independently by herself, and to confide in an arm stronger than hers," the southern woman had no desire for "power" outside the home, he said. The few women who were demanding equality were "unsexing" themselves and were "despised and detested" by their families and communities.

**OVERSEERS AND DRIVERS** On large plantations, *overseers* managed the slaves and were responsible for maintaining the buildings, fences, and grounds. They usually were white farmers or skilled workers, the sons of planters, or poor whites eager to rise in stature. Some were themselves slaveholders.

Overseers moved often in search of better wages and cheaper land. A Mississippi planter described white overseers as "a worthless set of vagabonds." Frederick Douglass, who escaped from slavery in Maryland, said his overseer was "a miserable drunkard, a profane swearer, and a savage monster" always armed with a blood-stained bullwhip and a club that he used so cruelly that he even "enraged" the plantation owner. The overseer tolerated no excuses or explanations. "To be accused was to be convicted, and to be convicted was to be punished," Douglass said.

Although there were a few black overseers, the highest managerial position a slave could usually hope for was that of *driver*, whose job was to supervise a small group ("gang") of slaves, getting them up and organized each morning by sunrise, and directing their work (and punishing them) until dark. Over the years, there were numerous examples of slaves murdering drivers for being too cruel.

**"PLAIN WHITE FOLK"** About half of white Southerners were small farmers (yeomen), **plain white folk** who were often illiterate and forced to scratch out lives of bare self-sufficiency. These yeomen typically lived with their families in simple two-room cabins on fifty acres or less. They raised a few pigs and chickens, grew enough corn and cotton to live on, and traded with neighbors more than they bought from stores.

Women on these farms worked in the fields during harvest time but spent most of their days doing household chores while raising lots of children. Farm children grew up fast. By age four they could carry a water bucket from the well to the house and collect eggs from the henhouse. Young boys could feed livestock, milk cows, and plant, weed, and harvest crops.

The average slaveholder was a small farmer working alongside five or six slaves. Such "middling" farmers usually lived in a log cabin rather than a columned mansion. In the backcountry and mountainous regions of the South, where slaves and plantations were scarce, small farmers dominated the social structure.

Southern farmers tended to be fiercely independent and suspicious of government authority, and they overwhelmingly identified with the Democratic party of Andrew Jackson. Although a minority of middle-class white farmers owned slaves, most of them supported the slave system. They feared that slaves, if freed, would compete with them for land and jobs, and they also enjoyed the privileged social status that race-based slavery afforded them. James Henry Hammond and other rich planters frequently reminded their white neighbors who owned no slaves that "in a slave country, every freeman is an aristocrat" because blacks were beneath them in the social order. Such racist sentiments pervaded the Lower South—and much of the nation—throughout the nineteenth century.

"**POOR WHITES**" Visitors to the Old South often had trouble telling small farmers apart from the "poor whites," the desperately poor people who were relegated to the least desirable land and lived on the fringes of society. The "poor whites," often derided as "crackers," "hillbillies," or "trash," were usually day laborers or squatters who owned neither land nor slaves. Some 40 percent of white Southerners worked as "tenants," renting land or, as farm laborers, toiling for others. They frequently took refuge in the pine barrens, mountain hollows, and swamps after having been pushed aside by the more enterprising and the more successful. They often made their own clothing and barely managed to keep their families warm, dry, and fed.

## BLACK SOCIETY IN THE SOUTH

Southern society was literally black and white. Whites had the power and often treated enslaved blacks as property rather than people. "We believe the negro to belong to an inferior race," one planter declared. Thomas Reade Cobb proclaimed that African Americans were better off "in a state of bondage."

Effective slave management therefore required teaching slaves to understand that they were supposed to be treated like animals. As Henry Garner, an escaped slave, explained, the aim of slaveholders was "to make you as much like brutes as possible." Some justified slavery as a form of benevolent paternalism. George Fitzhugh said that the enslaved black was "but a grown-up child, and must be governed as a child."

Such self-serving paternalism had one ultimate purpose: profits. Planters, explained a Southerner, "care for nothing but to buy Negroes to raise cotton & raise cotton to buy Negroes." In 1818, James Steer in Louisiana predicted that enslaved blacks would be the best investment that Southerners could make. Eleven years later, in 1829, the North Carolina Supreme Court declared that slavery existed to increase "the profit of the Master."

Those in the business of buying and selling slaves reaped huge profits. One of them reported in the 1850s that "a nigger that wouldn't bring over $300, seven years ago, will fetch $1000, cash, quick, this year." Thomas Clemson of South Carolina, the son-in-law of John C. Calhoun, candidly explained that "my object is to get the most I can for the property [slaves]. . . . I care but little to whom and how they are sold, whether together [as families] or separated."

Owning, working, and selling slaves was the quickest way to wealth and social status in the South. The wife of a Louisiana planter complained in 1829 that white people talked constantly about how the profits generated by growing cotton enabled them to buy "plantations & negroes." In 1790, the United States had fewer than 700,000 enslaved African Americans. By 1830, it had more than 2 million, and by 1860, there were 4 million, virtually all of them in the South and border states.

**THE SLAVE SYSTEM** Most southern whites viewed slaves as property rather than people. Babies became slaves at birth; slaves could be moved, sold, rented out, whipped, or raped, as their master saw fit. As the enslaved population grew, slaveholders developed an increasingly complex *system* of rules, regulations, and restrictions. Formal **slave codes** in each state regulated the treatment of slaves to deter runaways or rebellions. Slaves could not leave their owner's land or household without permission or stay out after dark without an identification pass. Some codes made it a crime for slaves to learn to read and write, for fear that they might pass notes to plan a revolt. Frederick Douglass said that slaveholders assumed that allowing slaves to learn to read and write "would spoil the best nigger in the world."

Slaves in most states could not testify in court, legally marry, own firearms, or hit a white man, even in self-defense. They could also be abused, tortured, and whipped. Despite such restrictions and brutalities, however, the enslaved managed to create their own communities and cultures, forging bonds of care, solidarity, recreation, and religion.

"**FREE PERSONS OF COLOR**" African Americans who were not enslaved were called free persons of color. They occupied an uncertain and often vulnerable social status between bondage and freedom. Many lived in constant fear of being kidnapped into slavery.

To be sure, free blacks had more rights than slaves. They could enter into contracts, marry, own property (including slaves of their own), and pass on their property to their children. They were not viewed or treated as equal to whites, however. In most states, they were treated as if they were enslaved: they could not vote, own weapons, attend white church services, or testify against whites in court. In South Carolina, free people of color had to pay an annual tax and were not allowed to leave the state. After 1823, they were required to have a white "guardian" and an identity card.

Some slaves were able to purchase their freedom, and others were freed ("manumitted") by their owners. By 1860, approximately 250,000 free blacks lived in the slave states, most of them in coastal cities such as Baltimore, Charleston, Savannah, Mobile, and New Orleans. Many were skilled workers. Some were tailors, shoemakers, or carpenters; others were painters, bricklayers, butchers, blacksmiths, or barbers. Still others worked on the docks or on steamships. Free black women usually worked as seamstresses, laundresses, or house servants.

Among the free black population were a large number of **mulattoes**, people of mixed racial ancestry. The census of 1860 reported 412,000 mulattoes in the United States, or about 10 percent of the black population— probably a drastic undercount. In cities such as Charleston and, especially, New Orleans, "colored" society occupied a shifting status somewhere between that of blacks and that of whites.

**Yarrow Mamout** As an enslaved African Muslim, Mamout purchased his freedom, acquired property, and settled in present-day Washington, D.C. Charles Willson Peale painted this portrait in 1819, when Mamout was over 100 years old.

**Free black persons** These badges, issued in 1860 in Charleston, South Carolina, were worn by free black persons so that they would not be mistaken for someone's "property."

Although most free people of color were poor, some mulattoes built substantial fortunes and even became slaveholders themselves. William Ellison was the richest freedman in the South. Liberated by his white father in 1816, he developed a thriving business in South Carolina making cotton gins while managing his own 900-acre plantation worked by more than sixty slaves. In Louisiana, a mulatto, Cyprien Ricard, paid $250,000 for an estate that had ninety-one slaves. In Natchez, Mississippi, William Johnson, son of a white father and a mulatto mother, operated three barbershops, owned 1,500 acres of land, and held several slaves.

Black or mulatto slaveholders were few in number, however. The 1830 census reported that 3,775 free blacks, about 2 percent of the total free black population, owned 12,760 slaves. Many of the African American slaveholders were men who bought or inherited their own family members.

**THE TRADE IN SLAVES** The rapid rise in the slave population during the early nineteenth century mainly occurred naturally, through slave births, especially after Congress and President Thomas Jefferson outlawed the purchase of slaves from Africa in 1808. By 1820, more than 80 percent of slaves had been born in America.

Once the African slave trade was outlawed, the slave-trading network *within* the United States became much more important—and profitable. Between 1800 and 1860, the average price of slaves *quadrupled*, in large part because of the dramatic expansion of the cotton culture in the Old Southwest.

In Virginia, slave breeding became the state's most profitable industry and primary cash crop. Over a twenty-year period, a Virginia plantation owned by John Tayloe III recorded 252 slave births and 142 slave deaths, thus providing Tayloe with 110 extra slaves to be deployed on the plantation, given to his sons, or sold to traders. Thomas Jefferson bragged to George Washington that the numerous births of black children were increasing Virginia's wealth by 4 percent per year.

To manage the growing slave trade, markets and auction houses sprang up in every southern city. New Orleans alone had twenty slave-trading businesses. Each year, thousands of slaves circulated through the city's "slave pens." There they were converted from people into products. They were bathed and groomed; "fattened up" with bacon, milk, and butter, like cattle; assigned categories such as Prime, No. 1, No. 2, and Second Rate; and "packaged" (dressed) for sale in identical blue suits or dresses. On auction day, they were paraded into the sale room. The tallest, strongest, and "blackest" young men brought the highest prices. As a slaver stressed, "I must have if possible the *jet black* Negroes, for they stand the climate best."

Buyers physically inspected each slave on the "auction block" as if they were horses or cattle. They squeezed their muscles, felt their joints, and pried open their mouths to examine their teeth and gums. They forced the slaves to strip and carefully inspected their naked bodies, looking for signs of disease or deformities. They particularly focused on any scars from whipping. As Solomon Northup noted, "scars on a slave's back were considered evidence of a rebellious or unruly spirit, and hurt [his chances for] sale."

Slave markets in New Orleans also featured the "fancy trade," which meant selling women as forced sexual partners. One reporter spied on the auction block "one of the most beautiful women I had ever saw. She was about sixteen, dressed in a cheap striped woolen gown, and bareheaded." Her name was Hermina, and she was "sold for $1250 [$35,000 today] to one of the most lecherous brutes I ever set eyes on." The same reporter noted that "a noble-looking woman" and her "bright-eyed seven-year-old" son were offered for sale as a pair. When no one bid on them, the auctioneer offered them separately. A man from Mississippi bought the boy, while the mother went to a Texan. As her son was dragged away, his mother "burst forth into the most frantic wails that ever despair gave utterance to."

**SLAVERY AS A WAY OF LIFE** The lives of slaves depended in part on the personality of their owner; in part on whether they cultivated rice, sugar, tobacco, or cotton, and in part on whether they were on farms or in cities. Although many slaves were artisans or craftsmen (carpenters, blacksmiths, furniture makers, butchers, boatmen, house servants, cooks, nurses, maids, weavers, basket makers, etc.), the vast majority were **field hands** who were often organized into work

## THE SLAVE POPULATION, 1820

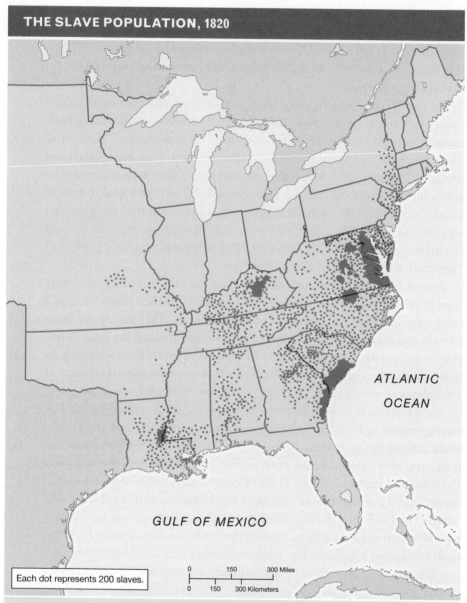

*ATLANTIC OCEAN*

*GULF OF MEXICO*

Each dot represents 200 slaves.

0    150    300 Miles

0    150    300 Kilometers

- Consider where the largest populations of slaves were clustered in the South in 1820. Why were most slaves living in these regions and not in others?
- How was the experience of plantation slavery different for men and women?

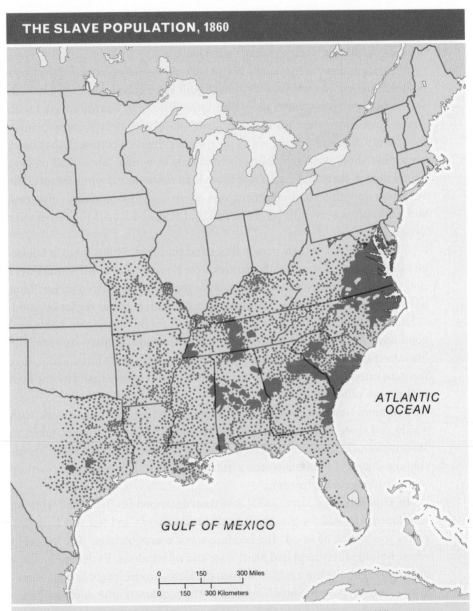

## THE SLAVE POPULATION, 1860

ATLANTIC OCEAN

GULF OF MEXICO

| 0 | 150 | 300 Miles |

| 0 | 150 | 300 Kilometers |

- Compare this map with the map of cotton production on page 423. What patterns do you see?
- Why did many slaves resist migrating West?

gangs supervised by a black driver or white overseer. Some slaves were hired out to other planters or to merchants, churches, or businesses. Others worked on Sundays or holidays to earn cash of their own.

Plantation slaves were usually housed in one- or two-room wooden shacks with dirt floors. The wealthiest planters built slave cabins out of brick. Beds were a luxury, even though they were little more than boards covered with straw. Most slaves slept on the cold, damp floor with only a cheap blanket for warmth. They received a set of inexpensive linen or cotton clothes twice a year, but shoes were generally provided only in winter. About half of slave babies died in their first year, a rate more than twice that of white infants. The weekly or monthly food allotment was cheap and monotonous: corn meal and pork, often served in bowls placed on the ground, as if the slaves were livestock.

Planters varied in their personalities and practices. Philip Jones, a Louisiana slave, observed that "many planters were humane and kind." Others were not. "Massa was purty good," one ex-slave recalled. "He treated us jus' 'bout like you would a good mule." Another said his owner "fed us reg'lar on good, substantial food, jus' like you'd tend to your hoss [horse], if you had a real good one." A slave born in 1850 had a life expectancy of thirty-six years; the life expectancy of whites was forty years. Some slaveholders hired white wage laborers, often Irish immigrants, for dangerous work rather than risk the lives of the more valuable slaves.

Solomon Northup, a freeborn African American from New York with a wife and three children, was kidnapped in 1845 by slave traders, taken to Washington, D.C., and then to New Orleans, and eventually sold to a "repulsive and coarse" Louisiana cotton planter. More than a decade later, Northup was able to regain his freedom.

In *Twelve Years a Slave* (1853), Northup described his living and working conditions. His bed "was a plank twelve inches wide and ten feet long. My pillow was a stick of wood. The bedding was a coarse blanket." The log cabin where he and others slept had a dirt floor and no windows. Each day, "an hour before daylight, the horn is blown. Then the slaves arouse, prepare their breakfast . . . and hurry to the field." If found in their "quarters after daybreak," they were flogged. "It was rarely that a day passed by without one or more whippings. . . . The crack of the lash, and the shrieking of the slaves, can be heard from dark till bed time."

Field hands worked from sunrise to sunset, six days a week. At times they worked at night as well, ginning cotton, milling sugarcane, grinding corn, or doing other indoor tasks. Women, remembered a slave, "had to work all day in de fields an' den come home an' do the housework at night." Sundays were precious days off. Slaves used the Sabbath to hunt, fish, dance, tell stories, or tend their own small gardens.

Beginning in August and lasting several months, the focus was on picking cotton. The productivity per slave increased dramatically during the first half of the nineteenth century, in large part because of the implementation of the "pushing system." During harvest season, each slave was assigned a daily quota of cotton to be picked, an amount that increased over the years.

Gangs of slaves, men and women, would sweep across a field, pull the bolls from the thorny pods, and stuff them in large sacks or baskets which they dragged behind them. All the while, an overseer, bullwhip in hand, would force them to keep up the pace. Solomon Northup remembered picking cotton until it was "too dark to

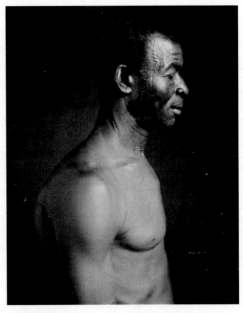

***Jack* (1850)** Daguerreotype of a slave identified only as Jack, on the plantation of B. F. Taylor in Columbia, South Carolina.

see, and when the moon is full, they oftentimes labor till the middle of the night." Each evening, the baskets would be weighed and the number of pounds recorded on a slate board by each picker's name. Those who fell short of their quota were scolded and whipped.

**THE VIOLENCE OF SLAVERY** Although some owners and slaves developed close and even affectionate relationships, slavery on the whole was a system rooted in brutality. The difference between a good owner and a bad one, according to one slave, was the difference between one "who did not whip you too much" and one who "whipped you till he'd bloodied you and blistered you."

Allen Sidney, a slave, recalled an incident on a Mississippi plantation that illustrated the ruthlessness of cotton production. A slave who fell behind in his work resisted when a black driver started to "whip him up." Upon seeing the fracas, the white overseer, mounted on horseback, galloped over and shot the resisting slave, killing him. "None of the other slaves," Sidney noted, "said a word or turned their heads. They kept on hoeing as if nothing had happened."

At times, whites turned the punishment of slaves into grisly spectacles to strike fear into anyone considering rebellion or escape. In Louisiana, whippings often followed a horrific procedure, as a visitor reported: "Three stakes is drove into the ground in a triangular manner, about six feet apart. The culprit [slave] is told to lie down . . . flat on his belly. The arms is extended out, sideways, and each hand tied to a stake hard and fast. The feet is both tied to the third stake, all stretched tight." The overseer would then step back "seven, eight or ten feet and with a rawhide whip about 7 feet long . . . lays on with great force and address across the Buttocks," cutting strips of flesh "7 or 8 inches long at every stroke."

**URBAN SLAVERY**  Slaves in cities such as Richmond, Memphis, Atlanta, New Orleans, or Charleston had a much different experience from those on isolated farms and plantations. "A city slave is almost a freeman," claimed a Maryland slave.

Slaves in urban households tended to be better fed and clothed and had more privileges. They interacted not only with their white owners but with the extended interracial community—shopkeepers and police, neighbors and strangers. Some were hired out to others and allowed to keep a portion of their wages.

**ENSLAVED WOMEN**  Although enslaved men and women often performed similar chores, especially on farms, they did not experience slavery in the same way. Once slaveholders realized how profitable a fertile female slave could be by giving birth to babies that could later be sold, they "encouraged" the women to have as many children as possible. Sometimes a woman would be locked in a cabin with a male slave, whose task was to impregnate her. Pregnant slaves were given less work and more food. Some plantation owners rewarded new mothers with dresses and silver dollars.

But if motherhood provided enslaved women with greater stature and benefits, it also was exhausting. Within days after childbirth, mothers were put back to work spinning, weaving, or sewing. A few weeks thereafter, they were sent back to the fields; breast-feeding mothers were often forced to take their babies with them, strapped to their backs. Enslaved women were expected to do "man's work": cut trees, haul logs, spread fertilizer, plow fields, dig ditches, slaughter animals, hoe corn, and pick cotton.

Once women passed their childbearing years, their workload increased. Slaveholders put middle-aged women to work full-time in the fields or performing other outdoor labor. On large plantations, elderly women, called *grannies*, tended the children during the day. Slave women also worked as cooks and seamstresses, midwives and nurses, healers and folk doctors.

Enslaved girls and women faced the constant threat of sexual abuse. Hundreds of thousands of mulattoes provided physical proof of interracial sexual assault. Mary Boykin Chesnut noted in her diary that "like the patriarchs of old, our men live all in one house with their wives & their concubines, & the Mulattoes one sees in every family exactly resemble the white children—& every lady tells you who is the father of all the Mulatto children in everybody's household, but those in her own, she seems to think drop from the clouds."

James Henry Hammond, the prominent South Carolina planter, confessed that he was a man of passion who nurtured a "system of roguery" among his female slaves. He had a long affair with young Sally Johnson, who bore several of his children. Later, to the horror of his long-suffering wife, Hammond began another affair with one of his and Sally's daughters, twelve-year-old Louisa, and fathered more children with her. (Hammond also forced himself upon four "lovely and luscious" teen-aged nieces and two daughters of his sister-in-law).

**CELIA** Slaves often could improve their circumstances only by making horrible choices that offered no guarantee of success. The tragic story of a slave girl named Celia reveals the moral complexity of slavery for African American women and the limited legal options available to them.

In 1850, fourteen-year-old Celia was purchased by Robert Newsom, a Missouri farmer who told his daughters that he had bought the girl to be their servant. In fact, however, the recently widowed Newsom wanted a sexual slave. After purchasing Celia, he raped her, and for the next five years, he treated her as his mistress, even building her a brick cabin fifty yards from his house. During that time, she gave birth to two children.

On June 23, 1855, the sixty-five-year-old Newsom entered Celia's cabin, ignored her frantic appeals, and kept assaulting her until she struck and killed him with a large stick and then burned his body in the fireplace. Celia was not allowed to testify at her murder trial because she was a slave. The judge and jury, all white men, pronounced her guilty, and on December 21, 1855, she was hanged.

Celia's grim story illustrates the lopsided power structure in southern society at the time. She bore a double burden, being both a slave and a woman living in a male-dominated society rife with racism and sexism.

## FORGING A SLAVE COMMUNITY

Despite being victims of terrible injustice and abuse, enslaved African Americans displayed endurance, resilience, and achievement. Wherever they could, they forged their own sense of community, asserted their individuality, and devised ingenious ways to resist. Many on the largest plantations would gather at secret "night meetings" where they would drink stolen alcohol, dance, sing, and tell stories of resistance. The stories often were derived from African tales, such as that of "Brer [Brother] Rabbit," who used his wits to elude the larger animals stalking him by hiding in a patch of prickly briars. Such stories impressed upon slaves the importance of deceiving those with power over them.

Many religious **spirituals** also contained double meanings, often expressing a longing to get to a "free country," what slaves called "Sweet Canaan" or the "promised land." The spiritual "Wade in the Water," for example, contained underlying instructions to runaways about how to evade capture by avoiding dry land and running in creek beds ("wading in the water"). Songs such as "The Gospel Train" and "Swing Low, Sweet Chariot" included disguised references to the Underground Railroad, the secret organization that helped slaves escape to the North.

Frederick Douglass recalled that the spirituals also were a form of protest. They "breathed the prayer and complaint of souls overflowing with the bitterest anguish. . . . The songs of the slave represent the sorrows of his heart, rather than his joys. Like tears, they were a relief to aching hearts."

**THE SLAVE FAMILY**    Although states did not recognize slave marriages, they did not prevent men and women from choosing life partners and forging families within the slave system. Many slaveholders considered unofficial marriages a stabilizing influence; a black man who supported a family, they assumed, would be more reliable and obedient. Sometimes slaveholders performed "weddings" in the slave quarters or had a minister conduct the service. Whatever the formalities, the norm for the slave community, as for the white, was the nuclear family, with the father as head of the household.

Enslaved African Americans often reached out to those who worked with them, with older slave women being addressed as "granny," or coworkers as "sis" or "brother." Such efforts to create a sense of extended family resembled kinship practices in Africa. One white teacher visiting a slave community observed that they "all belonged to one immense family."

## RELIGION IN THE OLD SOUTH

The Old South was made up of God-fearing people whose faith sustained them. Although there were pockets of Catholicism and Judaism in the large coastal cities—Baltimore, Richmond, Charleston, Savannah, and New Orleans—the vast majority of Southerners, white and black, embraced evangelical Protestant denominations such as Baptists and Methodists, both of which wanted to

**Slave family in a Georgia cotton field**  The invention of the cotton gin sent production soaring, deepening the South's dependence on slavery in the process.

create a Kingdom of God on earth before the millennium, when Jesus would return (the "second coming").

**SLAVERY AND RELIGION**  In the late eighteenth century, Baptists and Methodists had condemned slavery, welcomed blacks to their congregations, and given women important roles in their churches. Some slaveholders, led by George Washington and Thomas Jefferson, had agonized over the immorality of slavery.

By the 1830s, however, criticism of slavery in the southern states had virtually disappeared. Most preachers switched from attacking slavery to defending it as a divinely ordained, Bible-sanctioned social system. Alexander Glennie, a white minister, told slaves that their life of bondage was the "will of God." Most ministers who refused to promote slavery left the region.

**AFRICAN AMERICAN RELIGION**  Among the most important elements of African American culture was its dynamic religion, a mixture of

***Plantation Burial*** (1860)  The slaves of Mississippi governor Tilghman Tucker gather in the woods to bury and mourn one of their own. The painter of this scene, Englishman John Antrobus, would serve in the Confederate army during the Civil War.

African, Caribbean, and Christian elements. Religion provided slaves both relief for the soul and release for their emotions.

Most Africans brought with them to the Americas belief in a Creator, or Supreme God, whom they could recognize in the Christian God, and whom they might identify with Christ, the Holy Ghost, and the saints. But they also believed in spirits, magic, charms, and conjuring—the casting of spells. A conjurer, it was believed, was like a witch doctor or a voodoo priest who could suddenly make someone sick or heal the afflicted.

Whites usually tried to eliminate African religion and spirituality from the slave experience. Slaves responded by gathering secretly in what were called camp meetings, or bush meetings, to worship in their own way and share their joys, pains, and hopes.

By 1860, about 20 percent of adult slaves had joined Christian denominations. Many others practiced aspects of the Christian faith but were not considered Christians. As a white minister observed, some slaves had "heard of Jesus Christ, but who he is and what he has done for a ruined world, they cannot tell." Few whites, however, fully understood the dynamics or power of slave religion.

Slaves found the Bible inspiring in its support for the poor and oppressed, and they embraced its promise of salvation through the sacrifice of Jesus. Likewise, the lyrics of religious spirituals helped slaves endure the strain of field labor and express their dreams of gaining freedom in "the promised land." One popular spiritual, "Go Down, Moses," derived from the plight of the ancient Israelites held captive in Egypt, says: "We need not always weep and moan, / Let my people go. / And wear these slavery chains forlorn, / Let my people go."

Many white planters assumed that Christianized slaves would be more passive and obedient. A south Georgia planter declared that a Christian slave "is more profitable than an unfaithful one. He will do more and better work, be less troublesome, and [even] less liable to disease."

## SLAVE REBELLIONS

The greatest fear of whites in the Lower South was an organized slave revolt, as had occurred in 1791 in the French-controlled sugar colony of Saint-Domingue, which eventually became the independent Republic of Haiti. The slaves rose up and burned plantations, destroyed cane fields, and killed white planters and their families.

The unprecedented rebellion in Saint-Domingue, the world's richest colony and leading source of sugar and coffee, sent shock waves across the United States. Many terrified whites who fled Haiti arrived in Charleston, where they told of the horrors they had experienced. Despite repeated attempts by both French and British armies to reconquer Haiti, the former slaves, led by Touissaint L'Ouverture, defeated them all.

The revolt in Haiti was the southern slaveholder's greatest nightmare. As a prominent Virginian explained, a slave uprising would "deluge the southern country with blood." Any sign of resistance or rebellion among the enslaved therefore risked a brutal and even gruesome response.

In 1811, for example, two of Thomas Jefferson's nephews, Lilburn and Isham Lewis, tied a seventeen-year-old slave named George to the floor of their Kentucky cabin and killed him with an axe in front of seven other slaves, all because George had run away several times. They then handed the axe to one of the slaves and forced him to dismember the body and put the pieces in the fireplace. The Lewises, who had been drinking heavily, wanted "to set an example for any other uppity slaves."

**THE PROSSER CONSPIRACY**  The overwhelming authority and firepower of southern whites made organized resistance risky. The nineteenth-century South witnessed only four major slave insurrections. The first occurred in 1800, when a slave named Gabriel Prosser, a blacksmith on a plantation near Richmond, Virginia, hatched a revolt involving hundreds of slaves. They planned to seize key points in the city; capture the governor, James Monroe; and overthrow the white elite.

Gabriel expected the "poor white people" to join their effort. But it did not happen. Someone alerted whites to the scheme, and a ferocious rainstorm forced "Gabriel's army" to scatter. Gabriel and twenty-six of his "soldiers" were captured and hanged, while ten others were deported to the West Indies.

**REVOLT IN LOUISIANA** In early 1811, the largest slave revolt in American history occurred just north of New Orleans, where sugarcane planters had acquired a large population of slaves, many of whom were ripe for revolt because of the harshness of their working conditions.

Late on January 8, a group of slaves led by Charles Deslondes, a trusted black overseer, broke into their owner's plantation house along the east bank of the Mississippi River. The planter was able to escape, but his son was hacked to death. Deslondes and his fellow rebels seized weapons, horses, and militia uniforms. Reinforced by more slaves and emboldened by liquor, they headed toward New Orleans, some fifty miles away. Along the way, they burned houses, killed whites, and gathered more recruits. Over the next two days, their ranks swelled to more than 200.

Their victories were short-lived, however. The territorial governor mobilized a group of angry whites—as well as several free blacks who were later praised for their "tireless zeal and dauntless courage"—to suppress the insurrection. U.S. Army units and militia joined in. Dozens of slaves were killed or wounded, and most of those who fled were soon captured.

Deslondes had his hands chopped off and was shot in both thighs and his chest. As he was slowly bleeding to death, a bale of hay was scattered over him and ignited. As many as 100 slaves were tortured, killed, and beheaded, and the severed heads were placed on poles along the Mississippi River. A month after the rebellion, a white resident noted that "all the negro difficulties have subsided and gentle peace prevails."

**DENMARK VESEY** The Denmark Vesey plot in Charleston, South Carolina, involved a similar effort to assault the white population. Vesey was a Caribbean slave who, in 1785, was taken to Charleston, where, like many urban slaves, he was allowed to work for pay in his free time, at nights, and on Sundays. In 1799, he purchased a lottery ticket and won $1,500, which he used to buy his freedom and start his own carpentry shop. He learned to read and write and organized a Bible study class for other free blacks in the African Methodist Episcopal (AME) Church. Yet he retained a simmering hatred for whites and for the slave system.

In 1822, Vesey and several other blacks developed a plan for a massive slave revolt. They would first capture the city's arsenal and distribute hundreds of rifles to both free and enslaved blacks. All whites in the city would then be killed, along with any blacks who refused to join the rebellion. Vesey then planned to burn the city, seize ships, and head for the black republic of Haiti.

The plot never got off the ground, however. A slave told his owner about the planned rebellion, and soon Vesey and 135 others were captured, arrested, tried, and convicted. Vesey and thirty-four others were executed; three dozen more were transported to Spanish-controlled Cuba and sold into slavery. The Emanuel AME church in Charleston was closed and demolished. (The congregation continued to worship in secret and rebuilt the church following the Civil War.) When told that he would be hanged, Vesey replied that "the work of insurrection will go on."

Vesey's planned rebellion led South Carolina officials to place additional restrictions on the mobility of free blacks and black religious gatherings. It also influenced John C. Calhoun to abandon the nationalism of his early political career and become the South's most outspoken advocate for states' rights and slavery.

**NAT TURNER'S REBELLION** Nat Turner, a trusted black overseer in Southampton County, Virginia, where blacks were the majority, was also a preacher and healer who believed God had instructed him to "proclaim liberty to the captive" slaves and lead a rebellion that would enact "the day of vengeance of our God." He interpreted a solar eclipse in February 1831 as God's signal for him to act. Turner chose August 21 as the day to launch his insurrection in part because it was the fortieth anniversary of the Haitian slave rebellion.

The revolt began when Turner, in the middle of the night, unlocked the door of his master's house and let in a small group of slaves armed with axes. They methodically murdered the owner, Joseph Travis, and his wife Sally, their twelve-year-old son, a young apprentice, and a baby. The rebels, about forty in all, then repeated the process at other farmhouses, where more slaves and some free blacks joined them. Some slaves tried to protect or hide their owners. Before the two-day revolt ended, fifty-seven whites had been killed, most of them women and children, including ten students at a school.

Federal troops, Virginia militiamen, and volunteers crushed the revolt, indiscriminately killing nearly 200 slaves in the process. A newspaper described the behavior of the white vigilantes as comparable in "barbarity to the atrocities of the insurgents." Twenty African Americans were hanged, including three free blacks; several were decapitated, and their severed heads were placed on poles along the road. Turner, called the "blood-stained monster," was arrested, tried, and found guilty. While waiting to be hanged, he was asked if the revolt was worth it. "Was not Christ crucified?" he replied. His dead body was dismembered, with body parts given to the victims' families.

More than any other slave uprising, news of **Nat Turner's Rebellion** terrified whites across the South. The Virginia legislature debated whether slavery should be abolished. That proposal was defeated; instead, the delegates restricted the ability of slaves to learn to read, write, and gather for religious meetings. A state legislator claimed that people suspected "that a Nat Turner might be in every family, that the same bloody deed could be acted over at any time."

In response to Turner's rebellion, states created more armed patrols to track down runaways. A former slave highlighted the "thousand obstacles thrown in the way of the flying slave. Every white man's hand is raised against him—the patrollers are watching for him—the hounds are ready to follow on his track, and the nature of the country is such as renders it impossible to pass through it with any safety."

**THE LURE OF FREEDOM** Yet thousands of escaped slaves (called "fugitives") made it to freedom in spite of the obstacles facing them. The fugitive slaves were a powerful example of the enduring lure of freedom and the extraordinary courage of those who yearned for it. On average, some 50,000 enslaved people tried to escape each year. Others ran away for short periods of time, usually to avoid being beaten.

The odds were stacked against escape, however, in part because most slaves could not read, had no maps, and could not use public transportation such as stagecoaches, steamboats, and railroads. Whether free or enslaved, blacks had to have an identity pass or official emancipation papers to go anywhere on their own. Runaways, the vast majority of whom were young males, often were forced to return when they ran out of food or lost their way. Others were tracked down by bloodhounds or bounty hunters. Even in the 1850s—the height of efforts by many Northerners to help runaways—only 1,000 to 1,500 slaves each year made it to freedom.

Slaves who did not escape found other ways to resist. They often exasperated, enraged, and manipulated their owners. Some faked illness, stole or broke tools, destroyed crops, or secretly slaughtered and ate livestock. Others slacked off when unsupervised. As a slave song confessed, "You may think I'm working / But I ain't." Yet there were constraints on such rebellious behavior, for laborers would likely eat better on a prosperous plantation than on a struggling one. And the shrewdest slaveholders knew that offering rewards was more profitable than inflicting pain.

## THE SOUTH—A REGION APART

The rapid settlement of the western territories during the first half of the nineteenth century set in motion a ferocious competition between North and South for political influence in the West. Would the new western territories and states be "slave" or "free"? Congressmen from the newly admitted western states would tip the delicate political balance one way or the other.

Because of the rapidly growing profitability of slave-grown cotton, Southerners exercised immense political power, both to protect and expand the system of slavery and to embed the economy of cotton into national and world markets.

The aggressive efforts to expand slavery westward ignited a prolonged political controversy that would end in civil war. As the 1832 nullification controversy in South Carolina had revealed, Southerners despised being told what to do by outsiders, and they especially resented the growing demands to abolish slavery.

The recurring theme of southern politics and culture from the 1830s to the outbreak of civil war in 1861 was the region's determination to remain a society dominated by whites who lorded over people of color. A South Carolinian asserted that "slavery with us is no abstraction—but a great and vital fact. Without it, our every comfort would be taken from us."

Protecting their right to own, transport, and sell slaves in the new western territories became the overriding focus of southern political leaders during the 1830s and after. Race-based slavery provided the South's prosperity as well as its growing sense of separateness—and defensiveness—from the rest of the nation.

Throughout the 1830s, southern state legislatures were "one and indivisible" in their efforts to preserve and expand slavery. Virginia's General Assembly, for example, declared that only the southern states had the right to control slavery and that such control must be "maintained at all hazards." The Georgia legislature agreed, announcing that "upon this point there can be no discussion—no compromise—no doubt."

With each passing year, the leaders of the Old South equated the survival of their region with the preservation of slavery. The increasingly militant efforts of Northerners to restrict or abolish slavery helped reinforce southern unity while provoking an emotional defensiveness that would lead to secession and war—and the unexpected end of slavery and the Cotton Kingdom it enabled.

# CHAPTER REVIEW

## SUMMARY

- **Southern Distinctiveness**   The South remained rural and agricultural in the first half of the nineteenth century as the rest of the nation embraced urban industrial development. The region's climate favored the growth of cash crops such as tobacco, rice, indigo, and, increasingly, cotton. These crops led to the spread of the plantation system of large commercial agriculture dependent upon enslaved labor. The southern planter elite sought to preserve and expand slavery, despite growing criticism of the *peculiar institution*.

- **A Cotton Economy**   The Old South became increasingly committed to a cotton economy based on slave labor. Despite efforts to diversify the economic base, the wealth and status associated with cotton, as well as soil exhaustion and falling prices from Virginia to Georgia, prompted the westward expansion of the plantation culture to the *Old Southwest*. Slaves worked in harsh conditions as they prepared the terrain for cotton cultivation and experienced the breakup of their families. By 1860, the *Cotton Kingdom* stretched from the Carolinas and Georgia through eastern Texas and up the Mississippi River to Illinois. More than half of all slaves worked on cotton plantations. As long as cotton prices rose, southern planters searched for new land and invested in slaves.

- **Southern White Culture**   White society was divided between the planter elite—those who owned twenty slaves or more—and the rest. *Planters* represented only around 4 percent of the white population but exercised a disproportionately powerful political and social influence. Other whites owned a few slaves, but most owned none. A majority of whites were *plain white folk*—simple farmers who raised corn, cotton, hogs, and chickens. Southern farmers were highly mobile and willing to move West. Southern white women spent most of their time on household chores. The *plantation mistress* supervised her home and household slaves. Most whites were fiercely loyal to the institution of slavery. Even those who owned no slaves feared the competition they believed they would face if slaves were freed, and they enjoyed the privileged status that race-based slavery gave them.

- **Slave Culture**   As the southern economy became more dependent on slave labor, the enslaved faced more regulations and restrictions. The vast majority of southern blacks served as *field hands*. They could be bought and sold at any time; their movements were severely limited, and they had no ability to defend themselves. Any violations could result in severe punishments. Most southern blacks were slaves, but a small percentage were free. Many of the free blacks were *mulattoes*, having mixed-race parentage. Free blacks often worked for wages in towns and cities.

- **African American Resistance and Resilience**   During the colonial period, slaves were treated more as indentured servants and were eligible for freedom after a specified number of years. But *slave codes* eventually codified the practice of treating slaves as property rather than as people. Although many slaves attempted to escape, only a few openly rebelled because the consequences were so harsh. Organized revolts such as *Nat Turner's Rebellion (1831)* in Virginia were rare. Most slaves survived by relying on their own communities, family ties, and Christian faith, and by developing their own culture, such as the singing of *spirituals* to express frustration, sorrow, and hope for their eventual deliverance.

## CHRONOLOGY

| | |
|---|---|
| 1790 | The enslaved population of the United States is almost 700,000 |
| 1791 | Slave revolt in Saint-Domingue (Haiti) |
| 1800 | Gabriel Prosser conspiracy in Richmond, Virginia |
| 1808 | U.S. participation in the international slave trade is outlawed |
| 1811 | Charles Deslondes revolt in Louisiana |
| 1815 | Annual cotton production in the United States is 150,000 bales |
| 1822 | Denmark Vesey conspiracy is discovered in Charleston, South Carolina |
| 1830 | U.S. slave population exceeds 2 million |
| 1831 | Nat Turner leads slave insurrection in Virginia |
| 1840 | Population in the Old Southwest tops 1.5 million |
| 1860 | Annual cotton production in the United States reaches 4 million bales |
| | Slave population in the United States reaches 4 million |

## KEY TERMS

peculiar institution p. 416

Old Southwest p. 421

Cotton Kingdom p. 424

planters p. 426

plantation mistress p. 427

plain white folk p. 428

slave codes p. 430

mulattoes p. 431

field hands p. 433

spirituals p. 440

Nat Turner's Rebellion (1831) p. 446

 INQUIZITIVE

**Go to InQuizitive to see what you've learned—and learn what you've missed—with personalized feedback along the way.**

# 12 Religion, Romanticism, and Reform

## 1800–1860

***The Voyage of Life: Childhood* (1839–1840)** In his *Voyage of Life* series, Thomas Cole drew upon both the religious revivalism and Romantic ideals of the period to depict the four stages of a man's life: childhood (shown above), youth, manhood, and old age. In this painting, an infant drifts along the River of Life with his guardian angel into the fertile landscape from the dark cave, meant to be "emblematic of our earthly origin, and the mysterious Past."

During the first half of the nineteenth century, the United States was overflowing with restless energy and expansive optimism. Confidence was the American creed. "America is the country of the Future," Massachusetts philosopher-poet Ralph Waldo Emerson observed. "It is a country of beginnings, of projects, of designs, and expectations."

However, the dynamic young republic was also experiencing growing pains as the market revolution widened economic inequality. At the same time, sectional tensions over economic policies and increasingly heated debates over the morality and future of slavery created a combative political environment whose struggles overflowed into social and cultural life.

After the Revolution, Americans also became as interested in religious salvation as they were in exercising political rights. The country experienced a theological revolution whereby many people rejected Calvinist determinism. Salvation, they argued, was open to everyone, not just the "elect." By this logic, sin was voluntary rather than innate and inevitable. People were not helplessly depraved; they were free agents who could choose salvation and improve themselves and society.

Such notions democratized Christianity by giving everyone the path to salvation. So-called free-will ministers assured people that they could *choose* to be saved simply by embracing Jesus's promise of salvation, just as more men in Jacksonian America were allowed to vote and *choose* their elected officials.

Evangelicals assumed that America had a God-mandated mission to provide a shining example of representative government, much as Puritan New England had once stood as an example of an ideal Christian community. The concept of a God-given *mission* to create an ideal society (often called "manifest destiny") still carried strong spiritual overtones.

## focus questions

**1.** What major changes took place in the practice of religion in the early nineteenth century? What impact did they have on American society?

**2.** How did transcendentalism emerge in the early nineteenth century?

**3.** What were the origins of the major social-reform movements in the early nineteenth century? How did they influence American society and politics?

**4.** What were the impacts of the anti-slavery movement on society and politics?

It also contained an aspiration toward perfectionism: People could become more and more perfect by reforming themselves and society. Throughout the first half of the nineteenth century, reformers fanned out across the United States to root out injustice or suffering. The combination of religious energy and intense social activism brought major advances in human rights. It also triggered cynicism and disillusionment.

# A More Democratic Religion

The energies of the rational Enlightenment and the spiritual Great Awakening flowed from the colonial period into the nineteenth century. In different ways, these two powerful modes of thought, one scientific and rational and the other religious and optimistic, eroded the Calvinist view that people were innately sinful and that God had chosen only a select few (the elect) for salvation ("predestination").

During the nineteenth century, many Christians embraced the more democratic religious outlook that offered salvation to everyone. Just as Enlightenment rationalism stressed humanity's natural goodness and encouraged belief in progress through democratic reforms and individual improvement, Protestant churches stressed that all people were capable of perfection through the guiding light of Christ and their own activism.

**RATIONAL RELIGION** Enlightenment ideas, including the religious concept of *Deism*, inspired prominent leaders such as Thomas Jefferson and Benjamin Franklin. Deists believed in a rational God—the creator of the rational universe—and that all people were created as equals in the eyes of God. Deists prized science and reason over traditional religion and unquestioning faith.

Interest in Deism increased after the American Revolution. Through the use of reason and scientific research, Deists believed, people might grasp the natural laws governing the universe. Deists did not believe that every statement in the Bible was literally true, and they questioned the divinity of Jesus. They defended free speech and opposed religious coercion.

**UNITARIANISM AND UNIVERSALISM** The ideals of Enlightenment rationalism that excited Deists soon began to make deep inroads into American Protestantism. The old churches in and around Boston proved especially vulnerable to the appeal of anti-Puritan (anti-Calvinist) religious liberalism. By the end of the eighteenth century, well-educated New Englanders, most of them Congregationalists, were embracing Unitarianism, a "liberal" faith that emphasized the compassion of a loving God, the natural goodness of humankind, the superiority of calm reason over emotional forms of worship, the rejection of the Calvinist belief in predestination, and a general rather than literal reading of the Bible.

**Unitarians** abandoned the concept of the Trinity (God the Father, the Son, and the Holy Ghost) that had long been central to the Christian faith, believing instead that God and Jesus were separate. Jesus was a saintly man (but not divine) who set a shining example.

Unitarians also stressed that people were not inherently sinful. By following the teachings of Jesus and trusting their own consciences, *all* people were eligible for salvation from a God blessed with boundless love.

Boston became the center of the Unitarian movement. During the early nineteenth century, "liberal" churches adopted the name *Unitarian*, a spiritual outlook especially popular with the educated elite in major cities. A parallel anti-Calvinist religious movement, Universalism, attracted a different—and much larger—social group: the working poor. In 1779, John Murray, a British clergyman, founded the first Universalist church, in Gloucester, Massachusetts. Like the Unitarians, **Universalists** proclaimed the dignity and worth of all people. They stressed that believers must liberate themselves from the rule of priests and ministers and use their capacity to reason to explore the mysteries of existence.

To Universalists and Unitarians, hell did not exist. Salvation was "universal," available to everyone through the sacrifice of Jesus. In essence, Universalists thought God was too caring to damn people to hell, while Unitarians thought themselves too good to be damned. (The two denominations would combine in 1961, becoming the Unitarian Universalist faith.)

**THE SECOND GREAT AWAKENING** The rise of Universalism and Unitarianism did not mean that traditional religious beliefs were waning. In fact, evangelism remained widespread. During the first Great Awakening in the early 1700s, traveling revivalists had promoted a more intense and personal relationship with God. In addition, Anglicanism suffered from being aligned with the Church of England; it lost its status as the official religion in most states after the American Revolution. To help erase their pro-British image, Virginia Anglicans renamed themselves *Episcopalians*.

Yet the new name did not prevent the Episcopal Church from losing its leadership position in the South. Newer denominations, especially Baptists and Methodists, 20 percent of whom were African American, attracted excited followers. These Christian sects promoted more-democratic principles and allowed individual congregations to exercise more power than did the Anglican Church.

Around 1800, the United States experienced a massive wave of religious revivals called the Great Revival or the **Second Great Awakening**. Without religion, revivalists warned, the American republic would give way to "unbridled appetites and lust." By 1830, the percentage of churchgoers had doubled.

While all denominations grew as a result of the Second Great Awakening, the evangelical sects—Baptists, Methodists, and Presbyterians—experienced explosive popularity. In 1780, the nation had only 50 Methodist churches; by 1860, there were 20,000, far more than any other denomination. The percentage of Americans who joined Protestant churches increased sixfold between 1800 and 1860.

The Second Great Awakening involved two centers of activity. One developed among the New England colleges that were founded as religious centers of learning, then spread across western New York into Pennsylvania and Ohio, Indiana, and Illinois. The other emerged in the backwoods of Tennessee and Kentucky and spread across rural America. Both phases of Protestant revivalism shared a simple message: salvation is available not just to a select few, but to *anyone* who repents and embraces Christ.

**Religious revivalism** Frontier revivals and prayer meetings ignited religious fervor within both ministers and participants. In this 1830s camp meeting, the women are so intensely moved by the sermon that they shed their bonnets and fall to their knees.

**FRONTIER REVIVALS** In its frontier phase, the Second Great Awakening, like the first, generated tremendous excitement and emotional excesses. It gave birth to two religious phenomena—the traveling backwoods evangelist and the frontier camp meeting.

People in the early nineteenth century found the supernatural inside as well as outside of churches; they readily believed in magic, dreams, visions, miraculous healings, and speaking in tongues (a spontaneous babbling precipitated by the workings of the Holy Spirit). Evangelists and "exhorters" (spiritual speakers who were not formal ministers) with colorful nicknames such as Jumpin' Jesus, Crazy Dow, and Mad Isaac found ready audiences among lonely frontier folk hungry for spiritual intensity and a more authentic sense of community.

Mass revivals along the western frontier were family-oriented, community-building events that bridged social, economic, political, and even racial divisions. Women, especially, flocked to the revivals and served as the backbone of religious life on the frontier.

At the end of the eighteenth century, ministers visiting the western territories reported that there were few frontier churches and few people attending them. To remedy the situation, traveling evangelists emerged to organize "camp meetings."

The first large camp meeting occurred in August 1801 on a Kentucky hillside called Cane Ridge, east of Lexington. A Scots-Irish Presbyterian minister named James McGready invited Protestants in the region to attend, and as many as 20,000 camped in tents for nine days at what came to be called the Great Revival.

McGready sought to help his parishioners see heaven's "glories and long to be there" while reminding them of "hell and its horrors." To him, the purpose of Christianity was simple: to convince sinners to convert themselves to saints assured of eternal bliss. His sermons left his listeners "powerless, groaning, praying, and crying for mercy."

The **frontier revivals** generated intense emotions as people experienced on-the-spot conversions. As news of the unscrubbed energy of the Cane Ridge gathering spread, Protestant evangelists, especially Methodists, organized similar revivals in other states. One participant reported that the revivals created "such a gust of the power of God" that it seemed "the very gates of hell would give way."

Not all were swept up in the overwrought religious emotionalism, however. Frances Trollope, an English writer who toured the United States in 1827, attended a frontier revival and thought the participants behaved like raving lunatics. Similarly, a Catholic priest in Kentucky scoffed at the absurd "mob fanaticism" of the camp meetings.

The revivals, however, were quite popular with many Americans. "Hell is trembling, and Satan's kingdom falling," reported a South Carolinian in 1802. "The sacred flame" of religious revival is "extending far and wide." In 1776, about one in six Americans belonged to a church; by 1850, it was one in three.

**DENOMINATIONAL GROWTH** Among the established denominations, Presbyterianism was entrenched among those with Scots-Irish backgrounds, from Pennsylvania to Georgia. Presbyterians gained further from the Plan of Union with the Congregationalists. Since the Presbyterians and the Congregationalists agreed on theology, they were able to form unified congregations and "call" (recruit) a minister from either denomination. The result through much of the Old Northwest (Ohio, Michigan, Indiana, and Illinois) was that New Englanders became Presbyterians by way of the "Presbygational" churches.

Frontier revivals were dominated by Baptist and Methodist factions. There were Primitive Baptists, Hardshell Baptists, Freewill Baptists and Methodists, Particular Baptists, and many others.

The Baptist theology was grounded in biblical fundamentalism—a certainty that every word and story in the Bible were divinely inspired and literally true. Unlike the earlier Puritans, however, Baptists believed that *everyone* could gain salvation by choosing (via "free will") to receive God's grace and being baptized as adults. Baptists also stressed the social equality of all before God, regardless of wealth, status, or education.

Methodists, who also believed in free will, developed the most effective evangelical method: the "circuit rider," a traveling evangelist ("itinerant") on horseback who sought converts in remote frontier settlements. The itinerant system began with Francis Asbury, a British-born revivalist who traveled across fifteen states and preached thousands of sermons.

After Asbury, Peter Cartwright emerged as the most successful circuit rider. Cartwright grew up in one of the most violent and lawless regions of Kentucky. His brother was hanged as a murderer, and his sister was said to be a prostitute. Cartwright himself had been a hellion until, at age fifteen, he attended a frontier revival meeting:

> Divine light flashed all around me, unspeakable joy sprung up in my soul. I rose to my feet, opened my eyes, and it really seemed as if I was in heaven. . . . My mother raised the shout, my Christian friends crowded around me and joined me in praising God; and though I have been since then, in many instances, unfaithful, yet I have never for one moment, doubted that the Lord did, then and there, forgive my sins and give me religion.

The following year, Cartwright became a religious exhorter, preaching the faith even though he was not yet an ordained minister. At age eighteen, he began working as a Methodist circuit rider. For more than twenty years, he preached a sermon a day, three hours at a time. Crowds flocked to hear his message: Salvation is free for all to embrace.

Cartwright moved to Illinois in 1824 because of his opposition to slavery and a desire to live on "free soil." In Illinois, where clergymen were not prohibited from running for elective office, Cartwright was the first to inject evangelical preaching into politics. At one meeting, Cartwright, then running for Congress as an anti-slavery Jacksonian Democrat, asked those who thought they were going to heaven to stand. He then asked those who did not desire to go to hell to do the same.

The only person who did not stand for either choice was a thirty-seven-year-old Whig attorney named Abraham Lincoln—Cartwright's opponent in the election. "May I inquire of you, Mr. Lincoln," asked Cartwright, "where are you going?" Lincoln replied that he was "going to Congress." He wound up defeating Cartwright, who thereafter called Lincoln an "infidel."

**REVIVALISM AND AFRICAN AMERICANS** The revivals broke down conventional social barriers. Free African Americans were especially attracted to the emotional energies of the Methodist and Baptist churches, in part because many white circuit riders opposed slavery.

**Black Methodists Holding a Prayer Meeting (1811)** This caricature of an African American Methodist meeting in Philadelphia shows a preacher in the church doorway, while his congregation engages in exuberant prayer.

African American Richard Allen, a freed slave in Philadelphia, claimed in 1787 that "there was no religious sect or denomination that would suit the capacity of the colored people as well as the Methodist." He decided that the "plain and simple gospel suits best for any people; for the unlearned can understand [it]." Even more important, the Methodists actively recruited blacks. They were "the first people," Allen noted, "that brought glad tidings to the colored people." In 1816, Allen helped found the African Methodist Episcopal (AME) Church, the first black denomination in America.

Yet racial tensions increased as mostly-white Methodist congregations required blacks to sit in designated pews. Such discrimination led Allen and others to found the Bethel African Methodist Episcopal Church in 1793. In 1816, as the racial discrimination continued, Allen helped found a new denomination: the African Methodist Episcopal (AME) Church.

The denomination grew quickly. By 1846, it boasted 296 churches, almost 200 ministers, and 17,375 members. During the nineteenth century, AME extended its outreach, initiating the first civil rights movement and promoting economic and educational opportunities for people of color. (Allen University in South Carolina is named in honor of Richard Allen.)

**CAMP MEETINGS AND WOMEN**  The energies of the Second Great Awakening spread through the western states and into more-settled regions back East. The fastest growth was in rural areas, where camp meetings were an expression of the frontier's democratic spirit.

Baptist, Methodist, and Presbyterian ministers often worked as a team at revivals, and crowds would frequently number in the thousands. Infusions of the spirit sparked strange behavior. Some people went into trances; others contracted the "jerks," a spasmodic twitching. Still others babbled in unknown tongues or got down on all fours and barked like dogs to "tree the devil."

The camp meetings also offered a social outlet to isolated rural folk, especially women. Evangelical ministers repeatedly applauded the spiritual energies of women and affirmed their right to give public witness to their faith and to play a leading role in efforts at social reform.

At a time when women were banned from preaching, Jarena Lee, a free black who lived near Philadelphia, was the first African American woman to become a minister in the AME. As she wrote, "If the man may preach, because the Saviour died for him, why not the woman? Seeing [as] he died for her also." Lee became a tireless revivalist; according to her records, she "traveled 2,325 miles and preached 178 sermons."

The organizational needs of large revivals offered ample opportunities for women. Phoebe Worrall Palmer, for example, hosted prayer meetings in her

New York City home and eventually traveled across the country as a camp-meeting exhorter, assuring listeners that they could gain a life without sin.

Women found public roles within evangelical denominations because of their emphasis on individual religious experiences rather than conventional, male-dominated church structures. Palmer claimed a woman's right to preach by citing the biblical emphasis on obeying God rather than man. "It is always right to obey the Holy Spirit's command," she stressed, "and if that is laid upon a woman to preach the Gospel, then it is right for her to do so; it is a duty she cannot neglect without falling into condemnation." Such religious enthusiasm often inspired women to pursue social reforms for their benefit, including greater educational opportunities and the right to vote.

**RELIGION AND REFORM**  Regions roiled by revival fever were compared to forests devastated by fire. Western New York, in fact, experienced so much evangelical activity that people labeled it the *burned-over district*. One reason the area was such a hotbed was the Erie Canal, which opened in 1825. Both the construction of and traffic on the canal turned many towns into rollicking scenes of lawlessness: gambling, prostitution, public drunkenness, and crime. Such widespread sinfulness made the region ripe for revivalism.

**CHARLES G. FINNEY**  The most successful evangelist in the burned-over district was a former attorney turned Presbyterian minister named Charles Grandison Finney. In the winter of 1830–1831, he preached for six months in Rochester, at the time a canal boomtown in upstate New York. In the process, he became the most celebrated minister in the country and perfected religious revivals as orchestrated spectacles.

While rural camp-meeting revivals attracted farm families and other working-class groups, Finney's Northeast audiences attracted more-prosperous seekers. "The Lord," Finney declared, "was aiming at the conversion of the highest classes of society." In 1836, he built a huge church in New York City to accommodate his rapidly growing congregation.

Finney focused on one question: What role can the individual play in earning salvation? He and other free-will evangelists insisted that everyone, rich or poor, black or white, could *choose* to be "saved."

"The great business of the church," Finney asserted, is "to reform the world." By choosing Christ, a convert could thereafter be free of sin, but Christians also had an obligation to improve society by perfecting themselves. Christians should "aim to be holy and not rest satisfied until they are as perfect as God."

The revivals provided much of the energy behind the reform impulse that swept across America during the age of Jacksonian democracy. By the time the waves of reform crested at midcentury, the fabric of American society had been transformed. Catharine Beecher, a leading advocate for evangelical religion and social reform, stressed that the success of American democracy "depends upon the intellectual and moral character of the mass of people. If they are intelligent and virtuous, democracy is a blessing; but if they are ignorant and wicked, it is only a curse."

## JOSEPH SMITH AND THE MORMONS

The Second Great Awakening also spawned new religious groups. The burned-over district in New York gave rise to several movements, the most important of which was Mormonism. Its founder, Joseph Smith Jr., was the child of intensely religious Vermont farm folk who settled in the village of Palmyra, in western New York.

In 1823, the eighteen-year-old Smith reported that an angel named Moroni had appeared by his bedside and announced that God needed Smith's help. The angel had led him to a hillside near his father's farm, where he had unearthed a box containing golden plates on which was etched, in an ancient language, a lost "gospel" explaining the history of ancient America. It described a group of Israelites ("Nephites") who crossed the Atlantic and settled America 2,100 years before Columbus.

Smith set about laboriously translating the "reformed Egyptian" inscriptions on the plates, which no one else ever saw. Much of the language he transcribed was in fact drawn from the Bible. In 1830, he convinced a friend to pay for the publication of the first 5,000 copies of the 500-page text he called *The Book of Mormon: An Account Written by the Hand of Mormon upon Plates Taken from the Plates of Nephi.*

Smith began gathering thousands of converts ("saints"). Eventually, convinced that his authority came directly from God, he formed what he called the Church of Jesus Christ of Latter-day Saints, more popularly known as the **Mormons**. Smith maintained that God, angels, and people were all members of the same flesh-and-blood species.

In his self-appointed role as the Mormon Prophet, Smith dismissed as frauds all Christian denominations (Protestant and Catholic), criticized the sins of the rich; preached universal salvation; denied that there was a hell; urged his followers to avoid liquor, tobacco, and caffeine; and asserted that the Second Coming of Christ was looming. He promised followers "a nation, a new Israel, a people bound as much by heritage and identity as by belief." Within a few years, he had gathered thousands of converts, most of them poor farmers.

**YEARS OF PERSECUTION** From the outset, the Mormon "saints" upset both their "gentile" neighbors and the civil authorities. Mormons stood out with their secret rituals, their refusal to abide by local laws and conventions, and their clannishness. Smith denied the legitimacy of civil governments and the U.S. Constitution. As a result, no community wanted to host him and his "peculiar people," a term taken from the New Testament.

In their search for a refuge from persecution and for the "promised land," the ever-growing contingent of Mormons moved from western New York to Ohio, then to Missouri, where the governor called for them to be "exterminated or driven from the state." Forced out, Smith and the Mormons moved in 1839 to the half-built town of Commerce, Illinois, on the Mississippi River. They renamed the town Nauvoo, a crude translation of a Hebrew word meaning "beautiful land."

Within five years, Nauvoo had become the second largest city in the state, and Joseph Smith, "the Prophet," was Nauvoo's religious dictator. He owned the hotel and general store; published the newspaper; and served as mayor, chief justice, and commander of the city's 2,000-strong army.

Smith's lust for power and for women grew. He began excommunicating dissidents, and in 1844 he announced his intention to become president of the United States. He proclaimed that the nation should peacefully acquire not only Texas and Oregon but also Mexico and Canada, and that slavery should be ended.

Smith's remarkable sexual energy and extramarital adventures led him to announce that God wanted men to have multiple wives—"plural marriage" (polygamy). He practiced what he preached, accumulating more than two dozen wives, many of them already married to other men. He encouraged other Mormon leaders to do the same. In 1844, Mormon dissenters, including Smith's first wife, Emma, denounced his polygamy. The result was not only a split in the church but also an attack on Nauvoo by non-Mormons. (The Mormon Church would ban polygamy in 1889.)

**Brigham Young** Young headed the Mormons from 1847 to 1877.

When Smith ordered Mormons to destroy an opposition newspaper, he and his brother Hyrum were arrested and charged with treason. On June 27, 1844, a mob stormed the jail and killed the Smith brothers.

**BRIGHAM YOUNG** In the charismatic Brigham Young, however, the Mormons found a new and, in many ways, better leader. Young would not only preserve the Mormon Church but create a new theocratic empire.

Because Nauvoo continued to arouse the suspicions of non-Mormons, Young began to look for another home for his flock. It turned out to be 1,300 miles away, near the Great Salt Lake in Utah, a vast, sparsely populated area that was then part of Mexico. The first 149 "saints" to arrive in July 1847 found "a broad and barren plain hemmed in by the mountains, blistering in the

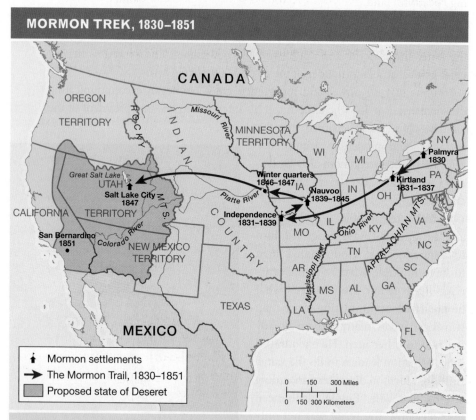

**MORMON TREK, 1830–1851**

Legend:
- ✝ Mormon settlements
- → The Mormon Trail, 1830–1851
- ▢ Proposed state of Deseret

- Where were Mormon settlements established between 1830 and 1851?
- Why did Joseph Smith initially lead his congregation west?
- Why was the Utah Territory an ideal place for the Mormons to settle, at least initially?

burning rays of the mid-summer sun. No waving fields, no swaying forests, no verdant meadows." Young, however, declared that "this is the place" to settle.

By the end of 1848, the Mormons had developed an irrigation system for their farms, and over the next decade they brought about a spectacular greening of the Utah desert. At first they organized their own state, named Deseret (meaning "Land of the Honeybee"), and elected Young governor.

But their independence was short-lived. In 1848, Mexico signed the Treaty of Guadalupe Hidalgo, transferring to the United States what is now California, Nevada, Utah, Texas, and parts of Arizona, New Mexico, Colorado, and Wyoming. Two years later, Congress incorporated the Utah Territory into the United States. Nevertheless, when Young was named the territorial governor, the new arrangement gave the Mormons virtual independence.

For more than twenty years, Young ruled with an iron hand, allowing no dissent and defying federal authority. Not until 1896, after the Mormons disavowed polygamy, was Utah admitted as a state. Out of its secret beginnings and early struggles, Mormonism today is the fourth largest religious denomination in the world.

## ROMANTICISM IN AMERICA

The revival of religious life during the early 1800s was one of many efforts to unleash the stirrings of the spirit throughout the United States and Europe. Another great cultural shift was the Romantic movement in thought, literature, and the arts.

The movement began in Europe as a rebellion against the well-ordered rational world promoted by scientific objectivity. Were there not, after all, more things in the world than reason, science, and logic could categorize and explain: spontaneous moods, impressions, and feelings; mysterious, unknown, and half-seen things?

In areas in which science could neither prove nor disprove concepts, the Romantics believed that people were justified in having faith. They preferred the stirrings of the heart over the calculations of the head, nonconformity over traditional behavior, and the mystical over the rational. Americans embraced this emphasis on individualism and the virtues of common people and civic democracy.

**TRANSCENDENTALISM** The most intense American advocates of Romantic ideals were the transcendentalists of New England. Transcendentalism was another of the diverse religious awakenings of the early nineteenth century, but it promoted a radical individualism and personal spirituality separate from organized religion. The word **transcendentalism** came from an emphasis on thoughts and behaviors that *transcend* (or rise above) the limits of reason and logic. To transcendentalists, the inner life of the spirit took priority over the hard facts of science and the rigidities of organized religion. Transcendentalism, said one of its champions, meant an interest in areas "a little beyond" the scope of reason.

Transcendentalism rejected both religious orthodoxy and the "corpse-cold" rationalism of Unitarianism. Reality was not simply what could be touched and seen and analyzed; it included the innate promptings of the mind and the spiritual world.

Above all, transcendentalists believed in "self-reliance" over conformity to social conventions and embraced a pure form of personal spirituality uncorrupted by theological dogma and denominational creeds. They wanted individuals to look *within* themselves for spiritual insights and to nurture a romantic spirituality in harmony with nature. Natural beauty, they assumed,

*The Indian's Vespers* **(1847)** Asher B. Durand's painting of a Native American saluting the sun captures the Romantic ideals of personal spirituality and the uncorrupted natural world that swept America during the early nineteenth century.

had the power to startle people into self-awareness, and they believed that all people had the capacity to tap the divine "spark" present throughout God's creations. Ralph Waldo Emerson, the movement's leader, viewed nature as the "symbol of spirit."

In short, transcendentalists wanted everyone to think their *own* thoughts and develop their *own* beliefs. Self-discovery was essential to fulfilling potential. By the 1830s, New England transcendentalism had become the most influential force in American culture.

**RALPH WALDO EMERSON**  More than anyone, Ralph Waldo Emerson embodied the transcendentalist gospel. To Emerson, self-knowledge opened the doors to self-improvement and self-realization.

Emerson became the nation's most popular speaker during the 1840s. "We have listened too long to the courtly muses of Europe," he said. "We will walk on our own feet; we will work with our own hands; we will speak with our own minds." He exhorted the young republic to shed its cultural inferiority complex and create its own distinctive literature, art, and thought.

The son of the minister of Boston's First Unitarian Church and the descendant of eight generations of clergymen, Emerson graduated from Harvard College in 1821 and became a Unitarian parson in 1829. But three years later, following the death of his wife after only eighteen months of marriage, he turned away from organized religions because they stifled free thinking. He sought instead to cultivate a personal spirituality in communion with nature. As he explained, "I am more of a Quaker than anything else. I believe in the 'still, small voice,' and that voice is Christ within us."

After traveling in Europe, where he met England's greatest Romantic writers, Emerson settled in Concord, Massachusetts, to take up the life of an essayist, poet, and lecturer ("preacher to the world"). He found God in nature and came to believe in human perfectibility. He celebrated the virtues of self-reliance and the individual's unlimited potential—if people would only learn to think for themselves and defy traditional assumptions and beliefs.

In 1836, Emerson published the pathbreaking book *Nature*, which helped launch the transcendental movement. In it, he stressed that people could "transcend" the material world and discover the "spirit" animating the universe. Individuals, in other words, could exercise godlike powers to counter the emotional starvation of New England intellectual life. Every human being, said Emerson, should enjoy an "original relation to the universe."

Emerson's lectures and writings provided the energetic core of the transcendentalist outlook. His essay "Self-Reliance" (1841) expressed the transcendentalist ideal of intellectual independence: "Whoso would be a man," he declared, "must be a nonconformist. . . . Nothing is at last sacred but the integrity of your own mind. . . . It is easy in the world to live after the world's opinion; it is easy in solitude to live after our own; but the great man is he who in the midst of a crowd keeps with perfect sweetness the independence of solitude."

Emerson championed a self-reforming individualism that reinforced the democratic energies inspiring Jacksonian America, and he inspired others to follow his notion of perfectionism in which individuals could tap their divine potential and express their spiritual humanism.

**THE TRANSCENDENTAL CLUB** In 1836, a diverse, informal discussion group that came to be called the Transcendental Club began to meet in Boston and nearby Concord to discuss philosophy, literature, and religion. In describing life in Concord, writer Nathaniel Hawthorne said there "never was a poor, little country village infested with such a variety of queer, strangely dressed, oddly behaved mortals."

The club included cultural rebels; social critics; liberal clergymen; utopian reformers; militant abolitionists; innovative writers; and women such as Elizabeth Peabody, her sister Sophia (who married Hawthorne), and Margaret Fuller, the author of *Woman in the Nineteenth Century* (1845).

A brilliant conversationalist, the dynamic Fuller organized a transcendentalist discussion group that met in Elizabeth Peabody's Boston bookstore. Their "Conversations" were designed to embolden the city's brightest women to think and act for themselves. Fuller helped launch and edit the *Dial* (1840–1844), an experimental transcendentalist magazine that introduced European Romanticism to American readers. "A much greater range of occupations," Fuller asserted, must be made available to women to enable them to express their full potential.

**HENRY DAVID THOREAU** Ralph Waldo Emerson's friend, Henry David Thoreau, fourteen years younger, practiced the thoughtful self-reliance and pursuit of perfection that Emerson preached. "I like people who can do things," Emerson said, and Thoreau could do many things: carpentry, masonry, painting, surveying, sailing, gardening, lecturing.

Thoreau was America's original wild child. From an early age, he displayed a headstrong sense of uncompromising integrity, prickly individuality, and proud rebelliousness. He loved to unearth forbidden questions and lay bare everyday hypocrisies. "If a man does not keep pace with his companions," he wrote, "perhaps it is because he hears a different drummer."

And Thoreau always marched to a different drummer. He described himself as "a mystic, a transcendentalist, and a natural philosopher" who questioned tradition and challenged authority. Emerson delighted in Thoreau because he displayed "as free & erect a mind as any I have ever met." Thoreau, he added, was "stubborn and implacable; always manly and wise, but rarely sweet." A neighbor was more blunt. "I love Henry," said Elizabeth Hoar, "but I do not like him."

Born in Concord in 1817, Thoreau attended Harvard. After a brief stint as a teacher, he worked with his father, a celebrated pencil maker. Like Emerson, however, Thoreau frequently escaped to the woods to absorb nature's spiritual energies. He viewed "the indescribable innocence" of nature as a living bible; the earth to him was a form

**Henry David Thoreau** Thoreau was a social rebel, environmentalist, and lifelong abolitionist.

of poetry, full of hidden meanings. Daily rambles across the hills, forests, and meadows inspired him more than attending church. Christianity, he believed, was a dying institution. His priorities were inward.

Thoreau showed little interest in social life and no interest in wealth, which he believed made people slaves to materialism. "The mass of men," he wrote, "lead lives of quiet desperation" because they were preoccupied with making money and exploiting nature. Thoreau yearned to escape the constraints of stuffy traditions, unjust laws, "good behavior," or the opinions of his elders. He committed himself to leading what Emerson called a simple life centered on "plain living and high thinking." Thoreau rented a room at the Emersons' home, where he tended the garden, worked as a handyman, and took long walks with his host. In 1844, when Emerson bought fourteen acres along Walden Pond, Thoreau decided to embark upon an unusual experiment in self-reliance.

On July 4, 1845, just shy of his twenty-eighth birthday, Thoreau took to the woods to live in a tiny, one-room cabin he had built at Walden Pond, a mile outside of Concord. His hut featured three chairs: "one for solitude, two for friendship, and three for society."

Living at Walden Pond was Thoreau's personal declaration of independence. His goal was to lead a simple life in which he could discover what nature "had to teach" about those things that money can't buy. "I went to the woods because I wished to live deliberately," he wrote in *Walden, or Life in the Woods* (1854), " . . . and not, when I came to die, discover that I had not lived."

Thoreau ate only one meal a day and disdained coffee, alcohol, jam, tobacco, and salt ("the grossest of groceries"). He regarded sex with disgust and suspicion. His minimalist ethic led Emerson to observe that he "was never affectionate, but superior, didactic," forever scorning his neighbors and claiming that he was "more favored by the gods."

*Walden* continues to attract readers because it contains some of the most evocative nature writing in America. A first-rate naturalist, Thoreau was blessed with superhuman powers of observation. He urged readers to open their eyes and hearts to the infinite spontaneity of everyday sensory experiences. "We can never have enough of nature," he wrote. "We need to witness our own limits transgressed, and some life pasturing freely where we never wander."

Loving the earth was Thoreau's true romance, for to him there was something sacred and liberating about nature's beauty and sensuality. His ecstatic descriptions of the natural world have made him the patron saint of the environmental movement. (Nearly a million people visit his cabin site at Walden Pond each year.) "In wildness is the preservation of the world," he wrote, and his scriptural statement later became the motto of the Sierra Club.

During Thoreau's two years, two months, and two days at Walden Pond, his conscience was pricked by the abolitionist movement. He harbored a runaway slave and considered President James K. Polk's declaration of war against Mexico an unjust action pushed by southern cotton planters eager to add more slave territory. His disgust for the war led him to refuse to pay taxes, for which he was put in jail (for only one night; an aunt paid his overdue bill).

This incident inspired Thoreau to write his classic essay, "Civil Disobedience" (1849), which would influence Martin Luther King Jr. in shaping the civil rights movement 100 years later. "If the law is of such a nature that it requires you to be an agent of injustice to another," Thoreau wrote, "then, I say, break the law."

Until his death in 1862, Thoreau kept a meticulous journal of "close observations" and philosophical reflections. He also attacked slavery and applauded those who worked to undermine it. The continuing influence of his creed of individual action against injustice shows the impact that a thoughtful person can have on an imperfect world.

**AN AMERICAN LITERATURE** Henry David Thoreau and Ralph Waldo Emerson portrayed the transcendentalist movement as an expression of moral idealism; critics dismissed it as outrageous self-centeredness. Although the transcendentalists attracted only a small following in their time, they inspired a generation of writers that produced the first great age of American literature.

The half decade of 1850 to 1855 brought an outpouring of extraordinary writing for a nation that had long suffered an inferiority complex about the quality of its arts. Among the works produced were *Representative Men* by Emerson; *Walden, or Life in the Woods* by Thoreau; *The Scarlet Letter* and *The House of the Seven Gables* by Nathaniel Hawthorne; *Moby-Dick* by Herman Melville; *Leaves of Grass* by Walt Whitman; and hundreds of unpublished poems by Emily Dickinson.

## Literary Giants

### NATHANIEL HAWTHORNE

Nathaniel Hawthorne, the supreme writer of the New England group, never shared the sunny optimism of his neighbors or their perfectionist belief in reform. A native of Salem, Massachusetts, he was haunted by the knowledge of evil bequeathed to him by his Puritan forebears, one of whom (John Hathorne) had been a judge at the Salem witchcraft trials. After college, Hawthorne worked in obscurity in Salem before earning a degree of fame with *Twice-Told Tales* (1837). His central themes examined sin and its consequences: pride and selfishness, secret guilt, and the impossibility of rooting sin out of the human soul.

**EMILY DICKINSON** Emily Dickinson, the most original of the New England poets, never married. From her birth in 1830 to her death in 1886,

**Emily Dickinson** Dickinson offered the world of New England literature a fresh female voice.

she lived with her parents and sister in Amherst, Massachusetts. There, in a spartan corner bedroom on the second floor of the family house, the slim, red-haired Dickinson found self-expression in poetry, ever grateful that "one is one's self & not somebody else."

Dickinson lived what her niece called a life of "exquisite self-containment." Fired by "the light of insight and the fire of emotion," she wrote verse remarkable for its simplicity and brevity. Only ten or so of her almost 1,800 poems were published before her death at age fifty-five. As she famously wrote, "Success is counted sweetest / By those who ne'er succeed."

Whether her solitary existence was the result of severe eye trouble, aching despair generated by her love for a married minister, or fear of her possessive father, Dickinson's isolation and lifelong religious doubts led her, in the "solitude of space . . . that polar privacy," to probe the "white heat" of her heartbreak and disappointment in ways unusual for the time. Her often-abstract themes were elemental: life, death, fear, loneliness, nature, and above all, the withdrawal of God, "a distant, stately lover" who no longer could be found.

**EDGAR ALLAN POE**   Edgar Allan Poe was fascinated by the menace of death. Born in Boston in 1809 and orphaned as a child, he was raised by foster parents in Richmond, Virginia.

Poe led a stormy life. Although a top student and popular storyteller at the University of Virginia, he left the school after ten months, having racked up excessive gambling debts. After a two-year stint in the army, he enrolled at the U.S. Military Academy at West Point, where in 1831 he was expelled for disobedience and missing classes.

After spending time in New York City and Baltimore, Poe relocated in 1835 to Richmond, where he became an assistant editor of the *Southern Literary Messenger*. He secretly married Virginia Clemm, his thirteen-year-old cousin, claiming that she was twenty-one. They moved to Philadelphia in 1837, where he edited magazines and wrote scathing reviews and terrifying mystery stories. As the creator of the detective story, his influence on literature has been enormous.

In 1844, Poe moved to New York City. The following year, he published "The Raven," a poem about a man who, "once upon a midnight dreary," having lost his lover, a "sainted maiden" named Lenore, responds to a rapping at his door, only to find "darkness there and nothing more." Scanning the darkness, "dreaming dreams no mortal ever dared to dream before," he confronts a silence punctuated only by his mumbled query, "Lenore?" The man closes the door, only to hear the strange knocking again. Both angered and perplexed, he flings open the door and, "with many a flirt and flutter," in flies a raven, that "grim, ungainly, ghastly, gaunt, and ominous bird of yore." The raven utters but one haunting word: "Nevermore."

"The Raven" made Poe a household name across America. In 1847, however, tragedy struck when his young wife died of tuberculosis. Thereafter, he was seduced as much by alcohol and drug abuse as by writing. He died at age forty of mysterious causes.

Poe left behind an extraordinary collection of "unworldly" tales and haunting poems. He used horror to explore the darkest corners of human psychology and satisfy his lifelong obsession with death. To him, fear was the most powerful emotion, so he focused on making the grotesque and supernatural seem disturbingly real. Anyone who has read "The Tell-Tale Heart" or "The Pit and the Pendulum" can testify to his success.

**HERMAN MELVILLE** Herman Melville, the author of *Moby-Dick*, was a New Yorker who went to sea as a youth. After eighteen months aboard a whaler, he arrived in the Marquesas Islands, in the South Seas, and jumped ship. He spent several weeks with natives in "the valley of the Typees" before signing on with an Australian whaler. He joined a mutiny in Tahiti and finally returned home as a seaman aboard a U.S. Navy frigate. An account of his adventures, *Typee* (1846), became an instant success, which he repeated in *Omoo* (1847).

In 1851, the thirty-two-year-old Melville published *Moby-Dick*, one of the world's greatest novels. In the story of Captain Ahab's obsessive quest for an "accursed" white whale that had devoured his leg, Melville explored the darker recesses of the soul.

On one level, the book is a ripping good yarn of adventure on the high seas. On another level, however, it explores the unfathomable depths and darkness of human complexity, as Ahab's crazed obsession with finding and killing the white whale turns him into a monster who sacrifices his ship and his crew.

**WALT WHITMAN** The most controversial writer during the nineteenth century was Walt Whitman, a New York journalist and poet. He was

**Walt Whitman** This engraving of a thirty-seven-year-old Walt Whitman appeared in his acclaimed poetry collection *Leaves of Grass*.

a self-promoting, robust personality. After meeting him, Henry David Thoreau wrote that Whitman "was not only eager to talk about himself but reluctant to have the conversation stray from the subject for long." Unlike Thoreau, Whitman wrote excitedly about industrial development, urban life, working men, sailors, and "simple humanity."

Born in 1819 on a farm in Long Island, New York, Whitman moved with his family to Brooklyn, where he worked as a carpenter, teacher, political activist, and editor of the *Brooklyn Eagle*. He frequently took the ferry across the East River to Manhattan, where the city's restless energy fascinated him.

By the time he met Ralph Waldo Emerson, Whitman had been "simmering, simmering." But Emerson "brought him to a boil" with his emphasis on defying tradition and celebrating the commonplaces of life, including sexuality and the body. These themes found their way into Whitman's controversial first book of unconventional, free verse poems, *Leaves of Grass* (1855). In its first year, it sold ten copies. One reviewer called it "an intensely vulgar, nay, absolutely *beastly* book." *Leaves of Grass*, however, became more influential with each passing year.

***Politics in an Oyster House*** **(1848)**
Commissioned by social activist John H. B. Latrobe, this painting captures the public debates that were fueled by newspapers and magazines.

Whitman introduced his book by declaring that "I celebrate myself, and sing myself." He was unapologetically "an American, one of the roughs . . . disorderly, fleshy, and sensual . . . eating, drinking, and breeding." Like Emerson, he was a self-proclaimed pioneer on behalf of "a new mightier world, a varied world," a bustling "world of labor" dignified by "common people." His poems, remarkable for their energy, exuberance, and intimacy, were seasoned with frank sexuality and homoerotic overtones. They expressed the color and texture of American democracy, "immense in passion, pulse, and power."

Although *Leaves of Grass* was banned in Boston because of its explicit sexuality, Emerson found it "the most extraordinary piece of wit and wisdom that America has yet contributed." More conventional literary critics, however, shuddered at the shocking "grossness" of Whitman's homosexual references ("manly love"; "the love of comrades"; "for the friend I love lay sleeping by my side"). Yet Whitman could never be truly honest about his sexuality (he identified as gay or bisexual in today's terms), for even discussing such perspectives was a felony in the nineteenth century.

**NEWSPAPERS** The flowering of American literature coincided with a massive expansion in newspaper readership sparked by rapid improvements in printing technology. The emerging availability of newspapers costing only a penny transformed daily reading into a form of popular entertainment. The "penny dailies," explained one editor, "are to be found in every street, lane, and alley; in every hotel, tavern, countinghouse, [and] shop."

By 1850, the United States had more newspapers than any other nation, and they forged a network of communications across the republic. As readership soared, the content of the papers expanded beyond political news and commentary to include society gossip, sports, and reports of sensational crimes and accidents. The proliferation of newspapers was largely a northern and western phenomenon, as literacy rates in the South lagged behind those of the rest of the country.

## THE REFORM IMPULSE

In 1842, the United States was awash in reform movements led by dreamers and activists who saw social injustice or immorality and fought to correct them. Lyman Beecher, a prominent preacher and champion of evangelical Christian revivalism (and the father of writer Harriet Beecher Stowe), stressed that the Second Great Awakening was not focused simply on promoting individual conversions; it was also intended to "reform human society." In 1840, Ralph Waldo Emerson told an English friend that "we are all a little wild with numberless projects of social reform."

While an impulse to "perfect" people and society helped excite the reform movements, social and economic changes, including the Panic of 1837 and the ensuing depression, invigorated many reformers, most of whom were women. The rise of an urban middle class enabled growing numbers of women to hire cooks and maids, thus freeing them to devote more time to societal concerns. Many joined churches and charitable organizations, most of which were led by men.

Both women and men belonging to evangelical societies fanned out across America to organize Sunday schools, spread the gospel, and distribute Bibles to the children of the working poor. Other reformers tackled issues such as living conditions in prisons and workplaces, care of the disabled, temperance (reducing the consumption of alcoholic beverages), women's rights, and the abolition of slavery. Transcendentalists sought to improve the lot of the poor, the disenfranchised, and the enslaved.

That these reformers often met resistance, persecution, violence, and even death testified to the sincerity of their convictions and the power of their example. As Emerson said, "Never mind the ridicule, never mind the defeat, up again, old heart!" For there is "victory yet for all justice."

**TEMPERANCE** The **temperance** crusade was among the most widespread of the reform movements. Many people argued that most social problems were rooted in alcohol abuse. William Cobbett, an English reformer who traveled in the United States, noted in 1819 that one could "go into hardly any man's house without being asked to drink wine or spirits, even *in the morning.*"

In 1826, a group of ministers in Boston organized the American Society for the Promotion of Temperance, which sponsored lectures, press campaigns, and the formation of local and state societies. A favorite tactic was to ask each person who took the pledge to put by his or her signature a letter *T* for "total abstinence." With that, a new word entered the English language: *teetotaler.*

In 1833, the society formed the American Temperance Union. Like nearly every reform movement of the day, temperance had a wing of absolutists. They passed a resolution that liquor ought to be prohibited by law. The Temperance Union, at its spring convention in 1836, called for abstinence from all alcoholic beverages—which caused moderates to abstain from the temperance movement.

For men and women who feared Jacksonian democracy, who worried about the surge of poor immigrants from Ireland and Germany, and dreaded change itself, reform was a means of restoring social control. They were afraid of anything that upset the social status quo. As Lyman Beecher warned, Americans were fast becoming "another people" as the result of massive immigration and Jacksonian democracy. Fears that Americans were turning away from the Protestant faith led Beecher and other evangelicals to found societies such as the American Bible Society, the American Sunday School Union, and the American Tract Society—all designed to shore up the centrality of religion and churches in community life. Evangelical reformers sought to restrict freedom: no more Sunday mail service or Sunday recreation, no more families without Bibles, no communities without ministers, no more liquor.

**PRISONS AND ASYLUMS** The Romantic impulse differed from the evangelical outlook in that it often included the belief that people are innately good and capable of perfection. Such an optimistic view brought about major changes in the treatment of prisoners, the disabled, and orphans. Public institutions (often called asylums) emerged for the treatment of social ills. If removed from society, the theory went, the needy and deviant could be made whole again. Unhappily, however, the underfunded and understaffed asylums often became breeding grounds for brutality and neglect.

The idea of the penitentiary—a place where the guilty paid for their crimes but also underwent rehabilitation—developed as a new approach to reforming criminals. An early model of the system was the Auburn Penitentiary, which opened in New York in 1816.

The prisoners at Auburn had separate cells and gathered only for meals and group labor. Discipline was severe. The men marched in lockstep and were never put face-to-face or allowed to talk. But they were reasonably secure from abuse by their fellow prisoners. The system, its advocates argued, had a beneficial effect on the prisoners and saved money, since the facility's workshops supplied prison needs and produced goods for sale at a profit. By 1840, the nation had twelve Auburn-type penitentiaries.

The Romantic reform impulse also found an outlet in the care of the insane. Before 1800, the insane were usually confined at home, with hired keepers, or in jails or almshouses, where homeless debtors were housed. After 1815, however, asylums that separated the disturbed from the criminal began to appear.

The most important figure in boosting awareness of the plight of the mentally ill was Dorothea Lynde Dix. A pious Boston schoolteacher, she was asked to instruct a Sunday-school class at the East Cambridge House of Correction in 1841. There she found a roomful of insane people who had been completely neglected.

The scene so disturbed her that she began a two-year investigation of jails and almshouses in Massachusetts. In a report to the state legislature in 1843, Dix revealed that insane people were confined "in *cages, closets, cellars, stalls, pens! Chained, naked, beaten with rods,* and *lashed* into obedience." She won the support of leading reformers and proceeded to carry her campaign on behalf of "the miserable, the desolate, and the outcast" throughout the country and abroad. In the process, she helped to transform social attitudes toward mental illness.

**WOMEN'S RIGHTS** While countless middle-class women devoted themselves to improving the quality of life in America, some argued that women should focus on enhancing home life. In 1841, Harriet Beecher Stowe's sister, Catharine Beecher, published *A Treatise on Domestic Economy*, which promoted the **cult of domesticity**, a powerful ideology that called upon women to accept and celebrate their role as manager of the household and nurturer of the children, separate from the man's sphere of work outside the home. Catharine Beecher and many others argued that young women should be trained not for the workplace but in the domestic arts. Thus, the prospects for women remained much as they had been in the colonial era. They were barred from the ministry and most other professions. They could not vote or serve on juries. College was rarely an option. A wife often had no control over her property or her children. She could not make a will, sign a contract, or bring suit in court without her husband's permission.

Julia Ward Howe, known mostly as the poet who would provide the lyrics to the "Battle Hymn of the Republic," the anthem of the Union army during the Civil War, was living testimony to the deadening aspects of the cult of domesticity. Like most nineteenth-century women, she spent her time at home with her children while pregnant more often than not. Yet she was anything but happy. "My books are all that keeps me alive," she sighed in private frustration.

Howe's much older husband, Samuel Gridley Howe, lorded over her like a tyrant. During their honeymoon, Julia composed poems with ominous lines: "Hope died as I was led / Unto my marriage bed." Her husband belittled her writings and refused to let her have any pain killers during childbirth, despite her tearful pleas. Women, he asserted, needed discipline: "The pains of childbirth are meant by a beneficent creator to be the means of leading them back to lives of temperance, exercise, and reason."

In 1847, Howe confessed to her sister that her life had become unbearable: "You cannot, cannot know the history, the inner history of the last four years." Nathaniel Hawthorne observed that Howe's poetry "let out a whole history of domestic unhappiness."

After her husband's death in 1876, Howe would become a leader of the women's suffrage movement. A few years before her death in 1910, she wrote in her journal: "I do not desire ecstatic, disembodied sainthood. . . . I would be human, and American, and a woman."

**SENECA FALLS** Gradually, however, women began to protest their subordinate status, and some men began to listen. An organized push for women's rights emerged in 1840, when the anti-slavery movement split over the question of women's involvement. In 1848, two prominent women's rights advocates, abolitionists Lucretia Mott, a Philadelphia Quaker, and Elizabeth Cady Stanton of New York, called a convention of men and women to gather in Stanton's hometown of Seneca Falls, in western New York, to discuss "the social, civil, and religious condition and rights of women."

On July 19, 1848, when the **Seneca Falls Convention** convened, revolution was in the air. In Italy, Germany, and other European states, militant nationalists, including many women, rebelled against monarchies and promoted unification. In France, the Society for the Emancipation for Women demanded that women receive equal political rights. In April, the French government abolished slavery in its Caribbean colonies, and in June, European feminists called for "the complete, radical abolition of all the privileges of sex, of birth, of race, of rank, and of fortune."

The activists at Seneca Falls did not go that far, but they did issue a clever paraphrase of the Declaration of Independence. The **Declaration of Rights and Sentiments** proclaimed that "all men and women are created equal." All laws that placed women "in a position inferior to that of men, are contrary to the great precept of nature, and therefore of no force or authority." Its most controversial demand was the right to vote.

Such ambitious goals and strong language were too radical for most of the 300 delegates, and only about a third of them signed the Declaration of Rights and Sentiments. The *Philadelphia Public Ledger* sneeringly asked why women would want to climb down from their domestic pedestal and get involved with politics: "A woman is nothing. A wife is everything. A pretty girl is equal to ten thousand men, and a mother is, next to God, all powerful." Despite such

**Elizabeth Cady Stanton and Susan B. Anthony** Stanton (left, in 1856) was a young mother who organized the Seneca Falls Convention, while Anthony (right, in 1848) started as an anti-slavery and temperance activist in her twenties. The two would meet in 1851 and form a lifelong partnership in the fight for women's suffrage.

opposition, the Seneca Falls gathering represented an important first step in the campaign for women's rights.

From 1850 until the outbreak of the Civil War in 1861, women's rights advocates held conventions, delivered lectures, and circulated petitions. But the movement struggled in the face of meager funds and widespread opposition. A mother and housewife criticized the women reformers, claiming that the typical activist "struts and strides, and thinks that she proves herself superior to the rest of her sex." The movement eventually succeeded because of a few undaunted women who refused to cower in facing the odds against them.

**SUSAN B. ANTHONY**  Susan B. Anthony, already active in temperance and anti-slavery groups, joined the women's crusade in the 1850s. Unlike Elizabeth Cady Stanton and Lucretia Mott, she was unmarried and therefore able to devote most of her attention to the movement. As one observer put it, Stanton "forged the thunderbolts and Miss Anthony hurled them." Both lived into the twentieth century, focusing after the Civil War on women's suffrage (the right to vote).

Women nationwide did not gain the vote in the nineteenth century, but they did make legal gains. In 1839, Mississippi became the first state to grant married women control over their property; by the 1860s, eleven more states had done so. Still, the only jobs open to educated women in any number were nursing and teaching, both of which brought relatively lower status and pay than "men's work."

**EARLY PUBLIC SCHOOLS**  Early America, like most rural societies, offered few educational opportunities. That changed in the first half of the nineteenth century as reformers lobbied for **public schools** to serve all children. The working poor wanted free schools to give their children an equal chance to pursue the American dream. Education, people argued, would improve manners while reducing crime and poverty.

A well-informed, well-trained citizenry was considered one of the basic premises of a republic. If political power resided with the people, as the Constitution asserted, then the citizenry needed to be well educated. By 1830, however, no state had a public school system.

Horace Mann of Massachusetts, a state legislator and attorney, led the early drive for statewide, tax-supported public school systems. He proposed that the schools be free to all children regardless of class, race, or ethnicity—including immigrant children. He sponsored the creation of a state board of education and served as its leader. Universal access to education, Mann argued, "was the great equalizer of the conditions of men—the balance-wheel of the social machinery."

**The George Barrell Emerson School, Boston (ca. 1850)** Although higher education for women initially met with some resistance, "seminaries" like this one were established in the 1820s and 1830s to teach women mathematics, physics, and history, as well as music, art, and social graces.

Mann went on to promote the first state-supported "normal school" for the training of teachers, a state association of teachers, and a minimum school year of six months. He saw the public school system as a way not only to ensure that everyone had a basic level of knowledge and skills but also to reinforce values such as hard work and clean living. "If we do not prepare children to become good citizens, if we do not enrich their minds with knowledge," Mann warned, "then our republic must go down to destruction."

By the 1840s, most states in the North and Midwest (but not the South) had joined the public school movement. The initial conditions, however, were seldom ideal. Funds for buildings, books, and equipment were limited; teachers were poorly paid and often poorly prepared. Most students going beyond the elementary grades attended private academies, often organized by churches. Such schools, begun in colonial days, multiplied until there were more than 6,000 by 1850.

In 1821, Boston English High School opened as the nation's first free public *secondary* school. Beginning in 1827, Massachusetts required every town of 500 or more residents to have a high school. Other states were not as progressive, however. Public high schools flourished only after the Civil War. In 1860, there were barely 300 in the nation.

Yet by 1850, half the nation's white children between ages five and nineteen were enrolled in primary schools. Few were Southerners, however. With only a few exceptions, southern states did not establish public schools until after the Civil War. In most states, enslaved children were prohibited from learning to read and write or attend school. The South had some 500,000 illiterate whites, more than half the total in the country. In the South, North Carolina led the way in state-supported education, enrolling more than two thirds of its white school-age population by 1860. But the school year was only four months long because of the state's need for children to do farmwork.

The prolonged disparities between North and South in the number and quality of educational opportunities helped explain the growing economic and cultural differences between the two regions. Then, as now, undereducated people were more likely to remain economically deprived, less healthy, and less engaged in political life.

**FOOD AND SEX**  The nation's widespread reform impulse excited causes and cranks of all sorts, including an array of health reformers, the most popular of whom was Sylvester Graham, a controversial preacher-turned-lecturer who blamed most of Americans' problems on bad eating and drinking habits.

Born in 1794 in West Suffield, Connecticut, Graham was the youngest of seventeen children. Soon after his minister father died, in 1796, his mother broke down, and Sylvester was sent to be raised by "strangers." As a young man he worked as a farmhand, clerk, and teacher before attending Amherst College in Massachusetts. He was expelled for his aggressive eccentricities, which did not prevent him from becoming a Presbyterian minister.

Religion inspired Graham less than nutrition did. He soon gave up preaching the Gospel of Christ to preach the gospel of bran and fiber. Although he had no medical training, Graham became the nation's leading health reformer after a massive cholera epidemic in 1832. Graham attributed cholera to people eating chicken pot pie and engaging in "excessive lewdness."

Thereafter, on the lecture circuit, in books, and in *Graham's Journal of Health and Longevity*, he preached convincingly against the dangers of alcohol and coffee, white flour, meat, gluttony, obesity, and body odor. Graham's "system" for a healthier America called for a diet of whole grains, fresh fruits, and nuts. The diet banned all meats and spices—including pepper and salt—as well as butter, cream, and soups. Alcohol and tobacco were also prohibited.

The centerpiece of Graham's celebrated vegetarian diet was the "Graham cracker," made of coarsely ground wheat bathed in molasses and baked. Graham stressed that daily meals of his crackers needed to be precisely six hours apart, with no snacking in between. The "Graham system" also prescribed fresh air, bathing in cold water, drinking only when thirsty (not with meals), and singing and dancing for exercise. He discouraged "excessive" sexual activity, meaning more than once a week for married couples, because it would cause indigestion, headache, feebleness of circulation, pulmonary consumption, spinal diseases, epilepsy, and insanity. He urged his followers to "avoid medicine and physicians—if you value your life."

Graham became one of the most famed and hated of the professional reformers. Butchers and bakers threatened to kill him, and many people laughed at his ideas. Yet others, called Grahamites, embraced his health system. There were Grahamite hotels in New York City, Boston, and Philadelphia, as well as stores, boarding houses, college dining halls, and a newspaper promoting his diet and ideas. One of Graham's followers called him an "eccentric and wayward genius."

## UTOPIAN COMMUNITIES

Amid the climate of reform, the quest for everyday utopias—ideal communities with innovative social and economic relationships—flourished. Plans for creating heaven on earth had long been an American passion, at least since the Puritans set out to build a holy colony in New England.

In the nineteenth century, more than 100 **utopian communities** were created. Religious motives animated many of the ideal societies while others reflected faith in the Enlightenment ideal that every social problem had a solution discoverable by scientific study.

Some utopias were *communitarian* experiments emphasizing the welfare of the entire community rather than individual freedom and private profits. Others experimented with "free love," socialism, and special diets. What they shared was a profound belief that mainstream society was fundamentally flawed and irredeemable.

**THE SHAKERS** Communities founded by the Shakers (the United Society of Believers in Christ's Second Appearing) proved to be long lasting. Ann Lee (known as Mother Ann Lee) arrived in New York from England with eight followers in 1774. The illiterate daughter of a blacksmith and the wife of an abusive husband, she grew up with seven siblings. Early on she came to believe in the "depravity of human nature and the odiousness of sin." No sooner did she marry than she was constantly pregnant, bearing four children, none of whom lived beyond six years of age. The trauma of childbirth and the loss of her children convinced Ann Lee that sexual activity was "indecent" and sinful.

She eventually took shelter among a group of renegade Shaking Quakers who nurtured in her the dream of a celibate, spotlessly clean utopia devoted to the Second Coming of Christ in which she would play the role of Jesus's female counterpart. She also believed that God and Jesus spoke directly to her ("direct revelation").

As Ann Lee recounted her visions of Christ, listeners decided that "the candle of the Lord was in her hand." That is, she was both a prophet and a seer who equated cleanliness, hard work, and chastity with saintliness. Under her leadership, the Shakers publicly attacked the Anglican Church, adopted lives of strict celibacy, and developed eccentric forms of worship featuring loud singing, "inspired" dancing, shrieking, stamping feet, speaking in unknown tongues, and shaking, hence their name.

In 1774, having suffered constant harassment by the authorities in England, Ann Lee and her followers immigrated to upstate New York. They settled on 200 acres that they named New Lebanon, built a log cabin that housed men on the first floor and women on the second, and pursued Christian perfection by molding a "body of believers" isolated from a corrupt world. Six years later, they began recruiting others to their austere paradise.

Mother Ann died in 1784, but the Shakers found new leaders who spread the movement from New York into New England, Ohio, and Kentucky. By 1830, an estimated 4,000 Shakers lived in about twenty settlements. In these earnest communities, rules ruled. No pets, no rugs (favorite hiding places of the devil, they believed), no mixing of garden plants, no more than one rocking chair in a room, no "scuffing along, but lift your feet squarely and properly." All property was held in common. Life and labor were communal, as in a monastery, and men and women were equal. People of color were welcome. Shaker farms became leading sources of garden seed and medicinal herbs, and many Shaker products, especially furniture, came to be prized worldwide for their clean lines and simple beauty.

The Shakers took great pride in their ability to create stable colonies outside the mainstream of American life. As Mother Ann observed, "We are the people who turned the world upside down." They displayed their utopian faith in the perfectibility of life on earth. What they did not perfect was an ability to convince the orphaned children under their care to follow their example. Of the nearly 200 orphans raised at New Lebanon in New York, only one decided to become a Shaker. The lure of a glittering outside world was too powerful.

**BROOK FARM** Brook Farm in Massachusetts was the most celebrated utopian community because it grew out of the transcendental movement. George Ripley, a Unitarian minister and transcendentalist, conceived of Brook Farm as a kind of early-day think tank, combining plain living, high thinking, individual expression, and manual labor. In trying to convince Ralph Waldo Emerson to join his effort, Ripley explained: "I have a passion for being independent of the world, and of every man in it." His planned utopia would "insure a more natural union between intellectual and manual labor" by creating a community "of liberal, intelligent, and cultivated persons" leading "a more simple and wholesome life." In 1841, Ripley and several dozen like-minded utopians moved to the 175-acre farm eight miles southwest of Boston.

Brook Farm became America's first secular utopian community. One of its members, novelist Nathaniel Hawthorne, called it "our beautiful scheme of a noble and unselfish life." (He would satirize the community in his novel *The Blithedale Romance*.) Its residents maintained the buildings, tended the fields, and prepared the meals. They also organized picnics, dances, lectures, and discussions. Emerson, Thoreau, and Margaret Fuller were among the visiting lecturers.

In 1846, however, Brook Farm's main building burned, and the community spirit died in the ashes. In the end, such utopian communities had little impact on the outside world.

**ONEIDA** John Humphrey Noyes, founder of the Oneida Community in upstate New York, took keen interest in Brook Farm but developed a much different vision of the ideal community. The son of a Vermont congressman, Noyes attended Dartmouth College and Yale Divinity School. But in 1834 he was expelled from Yale and his license to preach was revoked after he announced that he was "perfect" and free of all sin, and that God had singled him out to be his divine instrument on earth. He would shepherd people to perfection. In 1836, Noyes gathered a group of "Perfectionists" in Putney, Vermont.

Ten years later, Noyes announced a new doctrine, "complex marriage," which meant that every man in the community was married to every woman, and vice versa. "In a holy community," he claimed, "there is no more reason why sexual intercourse should be restrained by law than why eating and drinking should be." Authorities thought otherwise. They charged Noyes with adultery for practicing his theology of "free love."

He fled to New York and in 1848 established the Oneida Community, which had more than 200 members by 1851 and became famous for producing fine silverware. Oneida would outlive Brook Farm, Noyes claimed, because the Massachusetts commune had "left God out of their tale and they came to nothing." He also told his followers that they would not make the mistake of

**Oneida Community** Known for its practice of "complex marriage," Oneida was a utopian community that disavowed private property and emphasized "free love." In this photo from 1870, members of the Oneida Community relax on the front lawn of the Oneida Mansion.

the Shakers. True, the Shakers had realized that "the law of marriage 'worketh wrath'" by putting men and women into competition with one another and creating a corrosive "egotism for two." But the Shakers were mistaken to center their lives on sexual abstinence.

Oneida would survive by promoting free sex. Adults would have multiple sexual partners and access to surprisingly effective birth control methods. Noyes separated couples that grew too fond of each other ("sticky love") and conveniently announced that it was his duty as "first husband" to initiate virgin women into sexual activity. Equally repellent were his experiments in scientific breeding, where he paired couples based on their positive attributes. Over ten years, Oneida produced sixty-two children from these pairings, ten of whom were fathered by Noyes. It was Noyes that Emerson had in mind when he wrote that many reformers "have their high origin in an ideal justice, but they do not retain the purity of an idea."

Like the Shakers, the Oneida Community banned private property. The various types of work were shared and rotated among the entire community. Everyone labored for the common good; selfishness would be eliminated on the road to perfection.

What none of the hundred or so utopian experiments resolved was the fundamental tension inherent in all perfectionist schemes: how to maintain solidarity when residents develop and display conflicting notions of paradise and perfection. As Adin Ballou of the Massachusetts Hopedale commune said after it closed, "few people are near enough right in heart, head, and habits to live in close social intimacy."

Although only a few of the utopian communities survived, they provided inspiration and hope for seekers who had given up on life as it was. In the end, utopianism also provided a dose of everyday reality sufficient to send them back to mainstream society. Idealists desperate enough to build a heaven on earth are usually destined for an unexpected hell of their own making.

# THE ANTI-SLAVERY MOVEMENT

The collapse of perfectionist utopias created a vacuum in the reform movement that the anti-slavery crusade quickly filled. Many of those who participated in communitarian experiments ended up playing key roles in the abolitionist movement. Transcendentalist reformer Theodore Parker declared that slavery was "the blight of this nation, the curse of the North and the curse of the South."

The men who drafted the U.S. Constitution in 1787 hoped to keep the new nation from splitting apart over the question of slavery. To do so, they negotiated compromises to avoid dealing with the explosive issue. Still, most of the founders knew that eventually there would be a day of reckoning.

**EARLY OPPOSITION TO SLAVERY**  The first organized emancipation movement appeared in 1816 with the formation of the **American Colonization Society** (ACS) in Washington, D.C., whose mission was to raise funds to "repatriate" free blacks back to Africa. Its supporters included James Madison, James Monroe, Andrew Jackson, Henry Clay, John Marshall, and Daniel Webster.

Some supported the colonization movement because they opposed slavery; others saw it as a way to get rid of free blacks. "We must save the Negro," one missionary explained, "or the Negro will ruin us." White supremacy remained a powerful assumption.

Leaders of the free black community denounced the colonization idea. The United States, they stressed, was their native land, and they had as valid a claim on U.S. citizenship as anyone else. "America is more our country than it is the whites," argued David Walker, an African American living in Boston. "We have enriched it with our blood and tears."

Nevertheless, the ACS acquired land on the Ivory Coast of West Africa, and on February 6, 1820, the *Elizabeth* sailed from New York with eighty-eight emigrants who formed the nucleus of a new nation, the Republic of Liberia.

Thereafter, however, the African colonization movement waned. During the 1830s, only 2,638 African Americans migrated to Liberia. In all, only about 15,000 resettled in Africa.

**FROM GRADUALISM TO ABOLITIONISM** The fight against slavery started in Great Britain in the late eighteenth century, and the movement's success in ending British involvement in the African slave trade helped spur the anti-slavery cause in America. British abolitionists lectured across the northern United States and often bought freedom for runaway slaves. Most of the leading American abolitionists visited Great Britain and came away inspired by the breadth and depth of anti-slavery organizations there.

The British example helped convince leaders of the cause in America to adopt an aggressive new strategy in the early 1830s. Equally important was the realization that slavery in the cotton states of the South was not dying out; it was rapidly growing.

This hard reality led to a change in tactics among anti-slavery organizations, many of which were energized by evangelical religions and the emerging social activism of transcendentalism. Their initial efforts to promote a *gradual* end to slavery by prohibiting it in the western territories and using moral persuasion to convince owners to free their slaves steadily gave way to demands for *immediate* **abolition** everywhere.

The reason for the shift was largely religious: to a new generation of reformers who came of age amid the Second Great Awakening, slavery was not simply evil, it was a sin, and Christians had an obligation to purge all sins, personal and societal. The abolitionists found in the goal of immediate emancipation a perfectionist formula for casting off the guilt of slavery. Theirs would be a moral crusade rather than a political movement. As the preamble to the American Anti-Slavery Society promised: "We shall send forth agents to lift up the voice of remonstrance, of warning, of entreaty, and of rebuke" to slaveholders everywhere.

By the 1820s, every northern state had abolished slavery. As the anti-slavery movement grew, it came to encompass a wide spectrum of attitudes. Some, like Abraham Lincoln, were gradualists. They focused on preventing the extension of slavery into the new western territories in the hope that slavery would eventually die out in the South. Others, known as immediatists, called for the immediate abolition of slavery everywhere.

**WILLIAM LLOYD GARRISON** A zealous white activist named William Lloyd Garrison drove the movement. Born in 1805 in Newburyport, Massachusetts, Garrison learned the printing trade and moved to Boston.

There he embraced the reform spirit of the era, writing anonymous letters and essays decrying alcohol abuse, Sabbath-breaking, and war.

But it was slavery that most excited his indignation. In 1831, free blacks helped convince Garrison to launch an anti-slavery newspaper, *The Liberator*, which became the voice of the nation's first civil rights movement. Of the first 500 subscribers, 450 were free blacks, leading Garrison to explain that *The Liberator* did not belong to whites—"They do not sustain it." Rather, people of color kept the newspaper afloat—"It is their organ."

**William Lloyd Garrison** A militant abolitionist and a committed pacifist.

In the first issue, Garrison condemned "the popular but pernicious doctrine of gradual emancipation." He dreamed of immediate equality in all spheres of American life, including the status of women. In pursuing that dream, he vowed to be "as harsh as truth, and as uncompromising as justice. . . . I am in earnest—I will not equivocate—I will not excuse—I will *not retreat a* single inch—and I WILL BE HEARD."

Garrison's courage in denouncing slavery as "the one great, distinctive, all-conquering sin in America" outraged slaveholders in the South, as well as some whites in the North. In 1835, a mob of angry whites dragged him through the streets of Boston. The South Carolina and Georgia legislatures promised a $5,000 reward to anyone who kidnapped Garrison and brought him south for trial. The intensity of the southern reaction wrecked the assumption of "Garrisonians" that moral righteousness would trump evil and that their fellow Americans would listen to reason.

Garrison's unflagging efforts helped make the impossible—abolition—seem possible to more and more people. Two wealthy New York City silk merchants, Arthur and Lewis Tappan, provided financial support, and in 1833, they joined with Garrison and a group of Quaker reformers, free blacks, and evangelicals to organize the American Anti-Slavery Society (AASS).

That same year, Parliament freed some 800,000 enslaved colonial peoples throughout the British Empire by passing the Emancipation Act, which paid slaveholders to give up their "human property." In 1835, the Tappans hired revivalist Charles G. Finney to head the anti-slavery faculty at Oberlin, a new college in northern Ohio that would be the first to admit black students.

In 1835, the group began flooding the South with anti-slavery pamphlets and newspapers. The materials so enraged southern slaveholders that a Louisiana community offered a $50,000 reward for the capture of the "notorious abolitionist, Arthur Tappan, of New York." Post offices throughout the South began destroying "anti-slavery propaganda."

By 1840, some 160,000 people belonged to the American Anti-Slavery Society, which stressed that "slaveholding is a heinous crime in the sight of God, and that the duty, safety, and best interests of all concerned, require its *immediate abandonment*." The AASS even argued that blacks should have full social and civil rights.

**DAVID WALKER**  The most radical figure among the Garrisonians was David Walker, a free black who owned a used clothing store in Boston serving mostly seamen. In 1829, he published his *Appeal to the Colored Citizens of the World*, a pamphlet that denounced the hypocrisy of white Christians in the South for defending slavery, calling them "an unjust, jealous, unmerciful, avaricious, and bloodthirsty" people. Using religious imagery and spiritual fervor, he urged slaves to revolt. "The whites want slaves, and want us for their slaves," Walker warned, "but some of them will curse the day they ever saw us."

He challenged African Americans, slave and free, to use the "crushing arm of power" to gain their freedom. "Woe, woe will be to you," he threatened whites, "if we have to obtain our freedom by fighting."

Copies of Walker's *Appeal* were secretly carried to the South by black sailors who had frequented his shop, but whites in major cities seized the "vile" pamphlet. In 1830, the state of Mississippi outlawed efforts to "print, write, circulate, or put forth . . . any book, paper, magazine, pamphlet, handbill or circular" intended to arouse the "colored population" by "exciting riots and rebellion." By then, however, David Walker had been discovered dead near the doorway of his shop. His murderer was never found.

**A SPLIT IN THE MOVEMENT**  As the abolitionist movement spread, debates over tactics intensified. The Garrisonians, who felt that slavery had corrupted all aspects of American life, embraced every important reform movement of the day: abolition, temperance, pacifism, vegetarianism, and women's rights. Garrison's unconventional religious ideas and social ideals led him to break with the established Protestant churches, which, to his mind, were in league with slavery, as was the federal government. The U.S. Constitution, he charged, was "a covenant with death and an agreement with hell."

Garrison was such a moral purist that he even refused to vote and encouraged others to do the same, arguing that the nation could not continue to proclaim the ideal of liberty while tolerating the reality of slavery. He believed that the South could be shamed into ending slavery.

Other reformers saw American society as fundamentally sound and concentrated on purging it of slavery. Garrison struck them as an unrealistic fanatic whose radicalism hurt the cause. Even Harriet Beecher Stowe, who would write *Uncle Tom's Cabin* (1852), called Garrisonians "moral monomaniacs." The Tappan brothers eventually broke with Garrison over religion. They argued that the anti-slavery movement should be led only by men of "evangelical piety" and declared that the Unitarians and Universalists in New England failed to meet that standard.

**THE GRIMKÉ SISTERS** A showdown between the rival anti-slavery camps erupted in 1840 over the issue of women's rights, with the scandalous activities of the Grimké sisters serving as the catalyst.

Sarah and Angelina Grimké, born to a wealthy South Carolina family, grew up being served by slaves. In 1821, soon after her father's death, Sarah moved

**Sarah (left) and Angelina (right) Grimké** After moving away from their South Carolina slaveholding family, the Grimké sisters devoted themselves to abolitionism and feminism.

from Charleston to Philadelphia, joined the Society of Friends (Quakers), and renounced slavery. Angelina soon followed her, and in 1835, the sisters joined the abolitionist movement, speaking to northern women's groups. After they appealed to southern Christian women to end slavery, the mayor of Charleston told their mother that they would be jailed if they returned home.

The Grimké sisters traveled widely, speaking first to audiences of women and eventually to groups of both sexes. Their unconventional ("promiscuous") behavior in speaking to mixed-gender audiences prompted sharp criticism from ministers in the anti-slavery movement. Catharine Beecher reminded the sisters that women occupied "a subordinate relation in society to the other sex" and that they should limit their activities to the "domestic and social circle."

Angelina Grimké firmly rejected such arguments: "The investigation of the rights of the slave has led me to a better understanding of my own [rights]." For centuries, she noted, women had been raised to view themselves as "inferior creatures." Now, she insisted, "It is a woman's right to have a voice in all laws and regulations by which she is to be governed, whether in church or in state." Soon, she and her sister began linking their efforts to free the slaves with their desire to free women from male domination. "Men and women are CREATED EQUAL!" Sarah Grimké said. "Whatever is right for man to do is right for woman."

**THE ROLE OF WOMEN** The debate over the role of women in the anti-slavery movement exploded at the American Anti-Slavery Society's annual meeting in 1840, where the Garrisonians convinced a majority of delegates that women should participate equally in the organization. The Tappans and their supporters walked out and formed the American and Foreign Anti-Slavery Society.

A third faction of the American Anti-Slavery Society had grown skeptical that the nonviolent "moral suasion" promoted by Garrison would ever lead to abolition. They decided that political action was the most effective way to pursue their goal.

In 1840, activists formed the Liberty party in an effort to elect an American president who would restrict the spread of slavery. What had been a moral and religious crusade became a political movement. The Liberty party's presidential nominee, James Gillespie Birney, was a former Alabama slaveholder turned anti-slavery activist. His slogan was "vote as you pray, and pray as you vote." The platform called not for immediate abolition but for banning slavery in the western territories and the District of Columbia.

Yet the Liberty party found few supporters. In the 1840 election, Birney polled only 7,000 votes. In 1844, however, he would win 60,000. Thereafter, an anti-slavery party contested every national election until the Thirteenth Amendment officially ended slavery in 1865.

## BLACK ANTI-SLAVERY ACTIVITY

Although many whites worked to end slavery, most of them, unlike William Lloyd Garrison, still insisted that blacks were socially inferior, and many expected free blacks to take a backseat in the movement.

Yet free African Americans were crucial in transforming the struggle against slavery into a more ambitious fight against racial discrimination, which remained widespread in most states. Even free blacks were barred from public places—churches, schools, hotels, railroad stations, and cemeteries. As Garrison reported from Boston, "Hardly any doors but those of our state prisons were open to our colored brethren."

**WILLIAM WELLS BROWN** Much of the energy and appeal of the abolitionist movement derived from the compelling testimonies provided by former slaves. Henry Bibb and William Wells Brown, both runaways from Kentucky, and Frederick Douglass, who had escaped from Maryland, and Sojourner Truth, a runaway from New York, became the most effective critics of the South's "peculiar institution."

Brown was just twenty years old when he escaped from his owner, a steamboat pilot on the Ohio River. An Ohio Quaker named Wells Brown provided shelter to the runaway, and Brown adopted the man's name while forging a new identity as a free man. He settled in Cleveland, Ohio, where he was a dockworker. He married, had three children, and helped runaway slaves cross the border into Canada. By 1842, he had learned to read and write, begun to publish columns in abolitionist newspapers, and was in great demand as a speaker at anti-slavery meetings. In 1847, he moved to Boston, where the Massachusetts Anti-Slavery Society hired him as a traveling lecturer.

That same year, the organization published Brown's autobiography, *Narrative of William W. Brown, A Fugitive Slave, Written by Himself,* which became a best seller. Brown gave thousands of speeches calling for an end to slavery and equality for both blacks and women. He stressed that African Americans were "endowed with those intellectual and amiable qualities which adorn and dignify human nature."

**FREDERICK DOUGLASS** Frederick Douglass was an even more effective spokesman for abolitionism. After escaping from Maryland, he made his way to Massachusetts, where he began speaking at anti-slavery meetings

**Frederick Douglass and Sojourner Truth** Both former slaves, Douglass and Truth were leading African American abolitionists and captivating orators.

in black churches. The Massachusetts Anti-Slavery Society recruited him as a traveling speaker, sending him across New England and west to Ohio and Indiana. He recounted his painful encounters with "the whip, the chain, the gag, the thumbscrew, the bloodhound, the stocks, and all the other bloody paraphernalia of the slave system."

Through his writings and dazzling presentations, Douglass became the best-known man of color in America. "I appear before the immense assembly this evening as a thief and a robber," he told a Massachusetts group in 1842. "I stole this head, these limbs, this body from my master, and ran off with them."

After publishing his *Narrative of the Life of Frederick Douglass, An American Slave* (1845), Douglass, fearing that his prominence would make him accessible to fugitive slave catchers, left for an extended lecture tour of the British Isles. He returned two years later with enough money to purchase his freedom. He then started an abolitionist newspaper for blacks, the *North Star*, in Rochester, New York. He named the newspaper after the star that runaway slaves used to guide them toward freedom.

**SOJOURNER TRUTH** African American women were immensely influential in the abolitionist movement. Sojourner Truth was born to enslaved parents in upstate New York in 1797. She was given the name Isabella "Bell" Hardenbergh but renamed herself in 1843 after experiencing a conversation with God, who told her "to travel up and down the land" preaching "the truth" against slavery. A slave until she was freed in 1827, Truth spoke with conviction about the evils of the "peculiar institution" as well as the inequality of women.

She traveled throughout the North during the 1840s and 1850s. As she told the Ohio Women's Rights Convention in 1851, "I have plowed, and planted, and gathered into barns, and no man could head me—and ar'n't I a woman? I have borne thirteen children, and seen 'em mos' all sold off into slavery, and when I cried out with a mother's grief, none but Jesus heard—and ar'n't I a woman?"

Through such compelling testimony, Sojourner Truth tapped the distinctive energies that women brought to reformist causes. "If the first woman God ever made was strong enough to turn the world upside down all alone," she concluded in her address to the Ohio gathering, "these women together ought to be able to turn it back, and get it right side up again!"

**THE UNDERGROUND RAILROAD** Between 1810 and 1850, tens of thousands of southern slaves fled North. Runaways would make their way, usually at night, from one "station," or safe house, to the next. The organizations and the systems of safe houses and shelters in the border states such as Maryland and Kentucky (and farther north) were referred to as the **Underground Railroad**. The "conductors" helping the runaways included freeborn blacks, white abolitionists, former slaves, and Native Americans. Unitarians, Quakers, Presbyterians, Methodists, and Baptists participated in substantial ways.

In Philadelphia, William Still, a free black who was a clerk at the Pennsylvania Society for the Abolition of Slavery, sheltered runaway slaves as they made their way to Canada. In the fourteen years he worked as a conductor for the Underground Railroad, he helped almost 800 fugitive slaves make their way to freedom. He later published an account of his efforts, explaining that "It was my good fortune to lend a helping hand to the weary travelers flying from the land of bondage."

A few courageous runaway slaves returned to the South to organize more escapes. Harriet Tubman, the most celebrated member of the Underground Railroad, was born a slave on Maryland's Eastern Shore in 1820 but escaped to Philadelphia in 1849, traveling some 90 miles on foot across Delaware. "I was free," she recalled, "but there was no one to welcome me to the land of freedom. I was a stranger in a strange land." Dressed like a man, she would return to the South nineteen times to help some 300 fugitive slaves, including her parents and brothers. She "never lost a passenger" during her legendary acts of bravery. She carried a pistol with her, and when a fugitive slave would panic and have second thoughts about escaping, she would pull out her gun, point it at the ambivalent runaway, and say, "You'll be free or die a slave."

During the Civil War, Tubman worked as a northern spy and scout, leading Union gunboats in the Carolinas to liberate some 750 Confederate slaves. By then, slaveowners in Maryland were demanding her arrest, dead or alive, and placed a $40,000 bounty on her head. The fearless Tubman explained that "there was two things I had a right to, liberty or death: if I could not have one, I would have the other."

**ELIJAH P. LOVEJOY** Despite the growing efforts of anti-slavery organizations, racism remained widespread in the North, especially among the working poor. Abolitionist speakers confronted hostile white crowds who disliked blacks or found anti-slavery agitation bad for business. In 1837, a mob in Illinois killed Elijah P. Lovejoy, editor of an anti-slavery newspaper, giving the movement a martyr to the causes of both abolition and freedom of the press.

Lovejoy had begun his career as a Presbyterian minister in New England. After receiving a "sign by God" to focus his life on the "destruction of slavery," he moved to St. Louis, in slaveholding Missouri, where his newspaper denounced alcohol, Catholicism, and slavery. When a pro-slavery mob destroyed his printing office, he moved across the Mississippi River to a warehouse in Alton, Illinois, where he tried to start an anti-slavery society. There mobs twice more destroyed his printing press. When a new press arrived, Lovejoy and several supporters armed themselves and took up defensive positions.

On November 7, 1837, thugs began hurling stones and firing shots into the building. One of Lovejoy's allies fired back, killing a rioter. The mob then set fire to the warehouse. A shotgun blast killed Lovejoy, and his murder aroused a frenzy of indignation. John Quincy Adams said the murder "sent a shock as of any earthquake throughout this continent." In Illinois, young Abraham Lincoln felt those shockwaves. Lovejoy's murder, he noted, was an "ill omen," for the "mob violence" threatened America's core values: "liberty and equal rights."

**ABIGAIL KELLEY** The powerful appeal of abolitionism and the broader reform impulse is illustrated in the colorful life of Abigail "Abbie" Kelley. A teacher born in Pelham, Massachusetts, in 1811, she initially became a Grahamite, giving up coffee, alcohol, meat, and tea in favor of vegetables and Graham crackers. Soon thereafter, she attended a lecture by William Lloyd Garrison and embraced abolitionism, joining the Female Anti-Slavery Society. In 1837, she wrote her sister that she was supporting a variety of "moral enterprises—Grahamism, Abolition, and Peace."

Kelley was a compelling speaker. In 1840, she was the first woman to be elected an officer in the American Anti-Slavery Society. Many male abolitionists were furious. One of them described Kelley as being one of those "women of masculine minds and aggressive tendencies . . . who cannot be satisfied in domestic life." The prejudice she experienced among male officers revealed to her that she and other women "were manacled [chained] *ourselves*."

During the 1850s, Kelley, while still a passionate abolitionist, began to champion women's rights and temperance. She spoke at the fourth national woman's rights convention in Cleveland. Lucy Stone, one of the women's rights leaders, called Kelley a heroine who "stood in the thick of the fight for the slaves, and at the same time, she hewed out that path over which women are now walking toward their equal political rights."

## THE DEFENSE OF SLAVERY

The growing strength and visibility of the abolitionist movement, coupled with the profitability of cotton, prompted Southerners to launch an aggressive defense of slavery. During the 1830s and after, pro-slavery leaders worked out an elaborate rationale for what they considered the benefits of slavery. The Bible was their favorite weapon. Had not the patriarchs of the Hebrew Bible held people in bondage? Had not Saint Paul advised servants to obey their masters and told a runaway servant to return to his master? And had not Jesus remained silent on slavery?

Soon, bolder arguments emerged. In February 1837, South Carolina's John C. Calhoun told the Senate that slavery was "good—a great good," rooted in the Bible. He asserted that the "savage" Africans brought to America "had never existed in so comfortable, so respectable, or so civilized a condition, as that which is now enjoyed in the Southern states." If slavery were abolished, Calhoun warned, the principle of white racial supremacy would be compromised.

Calhoun and others also claimed that blacks were too shiftless, and if freed, they would be a danger to themselves and to others. White workers, on the other hand, feared the competition for jobs if slaves were freed.

The increasingly heated debate over slavery drove a deep wedge between North and South. In 1831, William Lloyd Garrison predicted that an eventual "separation between the free and slave States" was "unavoidable." By midcentury, a large number of Americans had decided that southern slavery was an abomination that should not be allowed to expand into the western territories. The militant reformers who were determined to prevent slavery from expanding outside the South came to be called "free soilers." Their crusade would reach a fiery climax in the Civil War.

# CHAPTER REVIEW

## SUMMARY

- **Religious Developments**  Starting in the late eighteenth century, *Unitarians* and *Universalists* in New England challenged the Christian notion of predestination by arguing that everyone (not just the select few) could receive salvation. The evangelical preachers of the *Second Great Awakening* generated widespread interest among Protestants in fiery *frontier revivals*. The more democratic sects, such as Baptists and Methodists, which promoted the idea of free-will salvation, gained huge numbers of converts, including women and people of color. Religion went hand in hand with reform in the "burned-over district" in western New York, which was also the birthplace of several religious movements, including the Church of Jesus Christ of Latter-day Saints (the *Mormons*).

- **Transcendentalists**  A group of New England poets, philosophers, writers, ministers, and reformers embraced a moral and spiritual idealism (Romanticism) in reaction to scientific rationalism and Christian orthodoxy. They sought to "transcend" reason and the material world and encourage more-independent thought and reflection. At the same time, *transcendentalism* influenced novelists, essayists, and poets, who created a uniquely "American" literature.

- **Social-Reform Movements**  The *cult of domesticity* celebrated a "woman's sphere" in the home and argued that young women should be trained not for the workplace but in the domestic arts—managing a kitchen, running a household, and nurturing children. However, the rise of an urban middle class offered growing numbers of women more time to devote to societal concerns. Social reformers—many of them women—sought to improve society and eradicate social evils. The most widespread reform movement focused on *temperance*—the elimination of excessive drinking. With the *Seneca Falls Convention* of 1848, social reformers launched the women's rights movement with the *Declaration of Rights and Sentiments*. In many parts of the country, reformers called for greater access to education through free *public schools*. Amid the pervasive climate of reform, more than 100 *utopian communities* were established, including the Shakers, Brook Farm, and the Oneida Community.

- **Anti-Slavery Movement**  Northern opponents of slavery promoted several solutions, including the *American Colonization Society's* call for gradual emancipation and the deportation of African Americans to colonies in Africa. *Abolitionism* emerged in the 1830s, demanding an immediate end to slavery. Some abolitionists went even further, calling for full social and political equality among the races, although they disagreed over tactics. Abolitionist efforts in the North provoked fear and resentment among southern whites. Yet many Northerners shared the belief in the racial inferiority of Africans and were hostile to the tactics and message of the abolitionists. African Americans in the North joined with abolitionists to create an *Underground Railroad*, a network of courageous people, both white and black, which helped runaway slaves escape.

## CHRONOLOGY

| | |
|---|---|
| 1826 | Ministers organize the American Society for the Promotion of Temperance |
| 1830 | Percentage of American churchgoers has doubled since 1800 |
| | Joseph Smith publishes the *Book of Mormon* |
| 1831 | Charles G. Finney begins preaching in upstate New York |
| | William Lloyd Garrison begins publishing *The Liberator* |
| 1833 | American Anti-Slavery Society is founded |
| 1836 | Transcendental Club holds its first meeting |
| 1837 | Abolitionist editor Elijah P. Lovejoy is murdered |
| 1840 | Abolitionists form the Liberty party |
| 1845 | *Narrative of the Life of Frederick Douglass* is published |
| 1846–1847 | Mormons, led by Brigham Young, make the difficult trek to Utah |
| 1848 | At the Seneca Falls Convention, feminists issue the Declaration of Rights and Sentiments |
| 1851 | Sojourner Truth delivers her famous "Ar'n't I a Woman?" speech |
| 1854 | Henry David Thoreau's *Walden, or Life in the Woods* is published |

## KEY TERMS

Unitarians p. 453

Universalists p. 453

Second Great Awakening p. 454

frontier revivals p. 455

Mormons p. 460

transcendentalism p. 464

temperance p. 474

cult of domesticity p. 475

Seneca Falls Convention (1848) p. 476

Declaration of Rights and Sentiments (1848) p. 477

public schools p. 478

utopian communities p. 481

American Colonization Society (ACS) p. 485

abolitionism p. 486

Underground Railroad p. 493

 INQUIZITIVE

Go to InQuizitive to see what you've learned—and learn what you've missed—with personalized feedback along the way.

# part four

# A HOUSE DIVIDED AND REBUILT

During the first half of the nineteenth century, Americans were optimistic about the future. The nation's population and its boundaries continued to grow rapidly; new roads, canals, and railroads overcame the barrier of distance; new inventions and labor-saving machinery increased dramatically; the economy grew; and tensions with Great Britain eased.

Above all, Americans continued to move westward in great numbers, where cheap land lured farmers, ranchers, miners,

and missionaries. By the end of the 1840s, the United States had again dramatically expanded its territory, from Texas west to California and the Pacific Northwest.

This extraordinary surge of territorial expansion was a mixed blessing, however. How to deal with slavery in the new western territories acquired from Mexico emerged as the nation's flashpoint issue.

A series of political compromises had glossed over the fundamental issue of slavery, but activists opposed efforts to extend slavery into the West, and an emerging generation of politicians proved less willing to compromise. The continuing debate led Abraham Lincoln and others to predict that the nation could not survive half-slave and half-free. Something had to give.

In a last-ditch effort to preserve the institution of slavery, eleven southern states seceded from the Union by 1861 and created a separate Confederate nation, igniting a civil war to restore the Union.

No one realized in 1861 how costly the war would be; some 750,000 soldiers and sailors would die in the struggle. Nor did anyone envision how sweeping the war's effects would be. The North's victory in 1865 restored the Union and helped accelerate America's transformation into a modern urban-industrial superpower. A national consciousness began to replace sectional divisions, and a Republican-led Congress passed legislation to promote industrial and commercial development and western expansion.

Although the Civil War ended slavery, the status of freed African Americans remained precarious during the Reconstruction era. Former slaves found themselves legally free, but few had property, homes, education, or training. Although the Fourteenth Amendment (1868) guaranteed the civil rights of African Americans and the Fifteenth Amendment (1870) declared that black men could vote, southern officials often ignored the new laws (as did some in northern states).

Bitterness and resistance grew among the defeated Southerners. Although Confederate leaders were stripped of voting rights, they continued to exercise considerable authority. In 1877, when the last federal troops were removed from the occupied South, former Confederates declared themselves "redeemed" from the supposed "stain" of northern military occupation and "black rule" during Reconstruction. By the end of the nineteenth century, most of the former Confederacy had developed a system of legal discrimination (the "Jim Crow" system) against blacks that re-created many aspects of slavery.

# 13 Western Expansion

## 1830–1848

**Emigrants Crossing the Plains, or the Oregon Trail (1869)** German American painter Albert Bierstadt captures the majestic sights of the frontier, though the transcontinental trek was also often grueling, bleak, and deadly.

I n the first half of the nineteenth century, most white Americans viewed the westward march of settlement as a renewable source of energy, hope, and yearning. Henry David Thoreau exclaimed that Americans "go westward as into the future, with a spirit of enterprise and adventure"—and the hope of freedom.

The West—whether imagined as the enticing lands over the Allegheny Mountains that became Ohio and Kentucky or, later, the farmlands of the Old Southwest, the fertile prairies watered by the Mississippi River, or the spectacular area along the Pacific coast that became the states of California, Oregon, and Washington—served as a powerful magnet for those who dreamed of freedom, self-fulfillment, and economic gain.

During the 1840s and after, waves of people moved westward. "If hell lay to the west," one pioneer declared, "Americans would cross heaven to get there." People endured unrelenting hardships to fulfill what many viewed as their "manifest destiny" to subdue the entire continent, even if it meant displacing Indians in the process. By 1860, some 4.3 million people had traversed the mile-wide Mississippi River and streamed across the Great Plains and Rocky Mountains to the Pacific coast.

Pioneers moved West largely for economic reasons. Enterprising trappers, farmers, miners, merchants, clerks, hunters, ranchers, teachers, household servants, and prostitutes, among others, headed West to seek their fortunes. "To make money was their chief object," said a Texas woman. Others sought religious freedom or converts to Christianity.

Of course, the West was not empty land. Others had been there long before the American migration. The Native American and Hispanic inhabitants of

## focus questions

**1.** Why did Americans move west of the Mississippi River during the 1830s and 1840s? How did they accomplish this, and where did they move to?

**2.** How did Texas become part of the United States? Why was the process so complicated, and how did it impact national politics?

**3.** What were the similarities and differences in how California and Texas were settled and how they became part of the United States?

**4.** How did opposition to the Mexican-American War complicate national politics?

the region, however, soon found themselves swept aside as U.S. presidents and congressmen encouraged the nation's continental expansion.

Westward expansion was especially important to Southerners, many of whom viewed the new territories as a source of cheap land on which to grow cotton using slave labor. Southerners wanted governments of new western states to ensure that Northerners in Congress could never abolish slavery. As a Mississippi senator said, "I would spread the blessings of slavery . . . to the uttermost ends of the earth." Such motives made the addition of western lands a flashpoint of sectional debate. Would the new western territories be slave or free?

Southerners had long enjoyed disproportionate political power because of the provision in the U.S. Constitution that counted slaves as part of the population in determining the number of congressional seats for each state. Most of the first sixteen presidents were from the South, and Southerners held most of the leadership positions in Congress. But as the industrializing Midwest and Northeast grew and increased their representation in Congress, southern influence began to wane. This raised the great fear in the South that they would soon be outnumbered in a Congress that could vote to eliminate slavery.

## Moving West

In 1845, New York newspaper editor John L. O'Sullivan gave a catchy name to the nation's aggressive expansion. "Our **manifest destiny**," he wrote, "is to overspread and to possess the whole of the continent which Providence has given us for the free development of our yearly multiplying millions . . . [and for the] great experiment of liberty." O'Sullivan spoke for many who wanted to take control of all of North America: "Yes, more, more, more . . . until our national destiny is fulfilled."

The idea of a "manifest destiny" assumed that the United States had a God-given mission to extend its Christian republic and capitalist civilization from the Atlantic to the Pacific—and beyond. It also took for granted the superiority of American ideals and institutions, including the opportunity to bring liberty and prosperity to native peoples. This notion of manifest ("self-evident") destiny offered a moral justification for territorial growth and the expansion of slavery. However idealized, though, manifest destiny was in essence a cluster of flimsy rationalizations and racist attitudes justifying the conquest of weaker peoples.

**THE WESTERN FRONTIER**    Most western pioneers were American-born whites from the Upper South and the Midwest. What spurred the massive migration was the population explosion in the United States and the

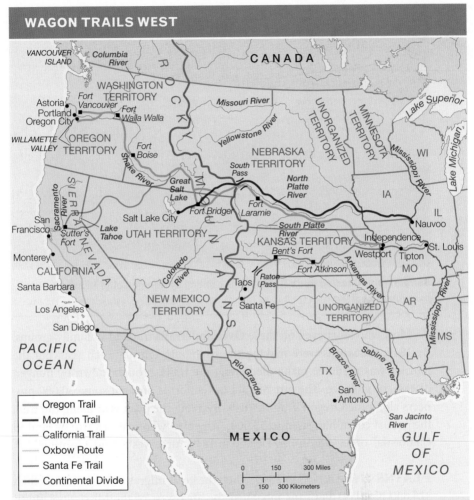

## WAGON TRAILS WEST

Legend:
— Oregon Trail
— Mormon Trail
— California Trail
— Oxbow Route
— Santa Fe Trail
— Continental Divide

- What did settlers migrating west of the Mississippi River hope to find?
- What were the perils of the Overland Trails?
- Describe the experience of a typical settler traveling on the Overland Trails.

widespread desire for land and wealth. California was an especially attractive destination, in part because gold was discovered there in 1848.

In the rush to the gold fields, some people traveled 13,000 miles by sea from Boston or New York City to reach California, sailing around the southern tip of South America and then up the Pacific coast. Most went overland, however. Between 1841 and 1867, some 350,000 men, women, and children made the difficult trek to California or Oregon, while many others settled in such areas as Colorado, Texas, and Arkansas.

***Buffalo Hunt, Chasing Back*** **(1860s)** This painting by George Catlin shows a hunter outrunning a buffalo.

Most who journeyed on these **Overland Trails** traveled in family groups. By 1845, thousands were making the six-month journey each year, but the journey was perilous: many died along the trails, brought down by hunger, disease, or violence. The lure of gold in California brought some 30,000 pioneers along the Oregon Trail in 1849. By 1850, the peak year along the trail, the annual count had risen to 55,000. "Any man who makes a trip by land to California," observed Alonzo Delano in 1849, "deserves to find a fortune."

**PLAINS INDIANS** In 1840, when the great migration began, more than 325,000 Native Americans inhabited the area west of the Mississippi River. They represented more than 200 nations, each with its own language, religion, cultural practices, and system of governance. Some were primarily farmers; others were nomadic hunters, following buffalo herds.

Native American life on the plains depended upon the abundance of buffalo, and the influx of white settlers and hunters posed a direct threat to the Indians' survival. When federal officials could not force Indian leaders to sell their lands, fighting ensued. After the discovery of gold in California, the wave of white expansion flowed all the way to the west coast, engulfing Native Americans and Mexicans in its wake.

**MEXICO AND THE SPANISH WEST** As American settlers trespassed across Indian lands, they also encountered Spanish-speaking peoples. Many whites were as prejudiced toward Hispanics as they were toward Indians and African Americans. Senator Lewis Cass from Michigan, who would be the Democratic candidate for president in 1848, expressed the common bias among white expansionists: "We do not want the people of Mexico, either as citizens or as subjects. All we want is their . . . territory."

The centuries-old Spanish efforts at colonization in the northernmost provinces of Mexico had been less successful in Arizona and Texas than in New Mexico and Florida. The Yuma and Apaches in Arizona and the Comanches and Apaches in Texas thwarted Spanish efforts to establish Catholic missions. By 1790, the Hispanic population in Texas numbered only 2,510, while in New Mexico it exceeded 20,000.

In 1807, French forces led by Napoléon had occupied Spain and imprisoned the king, creating confusion throughout Spain's colonial possessions in the Western Hemisphere, including Mexico. Miguel Hidalgo y Costilla, a creole priest (born in Mexico of European ancestry), took advantage of the fluid situation to convince Indians and Hispanics to revolt against Spanish rule in Mexico, but the poorly organized uprising failed.

In 1820, Mexican creoles again tried to liberate themselves. Facing a growing revolt, the last Spanish officials withdrew in 1821, and Mexico became an independent nation. However, it struggled to develop a stable government and an effective economy. Americans eagerly took advantage of Mexico's instability, especially in its northern provinces—areas that included present-day Texas, New Mexico, Arizona, Nevada, California, and portions of Colorado, Oklahoma, Kansas, and Wyoming.

Fur traders streamed into New Mexico and Arizona, developing a profitable commerce along the Santa Fe Trail to St. Louis. During the 1830s and 1840s, thousands of Americans made the journey in wagons on the Santa Fe Trail from Missouri to New Mexico. The trek was not for the fainthearted. In 1847 alone, marauding Indians, determined to stem the flow of the westward movement, killed forty-seven Americans, destroyed 330 wagons, and stole 6,500 horses, cattle, and oxen along the trail.

**THE OVERLAND TRAILS**  During the early nineteenth century, the Far Northwest consisted of the Nebraska, Washington, and Oregon Territories. The Oregon Country included what became the states of Oregon, Idaho, and Washington, parts of Montana and Wyoming, and the Canadian province of British Columbia. It was an unsettled region claimed by both Great Britain and the United States. By the Convention of 1818, the two nations agreed to "joint occupation" of the Oregon Country, each drawn there initially by the profitable trade in fur pelts.

During the 1820s and 1830s, the fur trade inspired a reckless breed of "mountain men" to embrace a rough-hewn, solitary existence in the wilderness.

***Fur Traders Descending the Missouri* (1845)** Originally titled "French-Trader, Half-Breed Son," this oil painting depicts a white settler sailing down the river with his half–Native American son—not an uncommon sight in western America.

Among the most rugged and adventurous of the fur trappers was Jedediah Smith, who in 1826 left the Great Salt Lake in Utah, crossed the Mojave Desert, and entered southern California, thereby becoming the first white American to enter California from the east.

**THE GREAT MIGRATION**    Word of Oregon's fertile soil, plentiful rainfall, and magnificent forests gradually spread eastward. By 1840, a trickle of farmers, missionaries, teachers, fur traders, and shopkeepers was flowing along the Oregon Trail, a 2,000-mile footpath that connected the Missouri River near St. Louis with the Columbia River valley in Oregon, slicing across the ancestral lands of Plains Indians.

Soon, "**Oregon fever**" swept the nation, especially after the federal government promised 160 acres of free land to any settler who worked the property for four years. Some pioneers desperately sought to escape debts, or dull lives, or bad marriages. "We had nothing to lose," wrote one woman, "and we might gain a fortune." Tens of thousands began moving their families West. Many never made it to Oregon.

In 1841 and 1842, the first sizable wagon trains made the long trip across half the continent, and in 1843 the movement became a mass migration. Most of the pioneers walked the 2,000 miles. All their food and worldly goods were packed in wagons called prairie schooners, or Conestogas, after the valley in Pennsylvania where they were first built. Teams of mules or oxen pulled the sturdy, canvas-covered wagons, whose ends were higher than the sides to keep cargo from falling out when traveling up mountain ridges. The wheels were especially wide to enable the wagons to traverse mud or sand, and they could be removed to float the wagons across streams and rivers.

One pioneer remembered that the wagon trains were like mobile communities. "Everybody was supposed to rise at daylight, and while the women were preparing breakfast, the men rounded up the cattle, took down the tents, yoked the oxen to the wagons, and made everything ready to start." They found Oregon in a "primitive state" requiring backbreaking work to create self-sustaining homesteads. Women worked as hard as men, day and night. "I am a very old woman," reported twenty-nine-year-old Sarah Everett. "My face is thin, sunken, and wrinkled, my hands bony, withered, and hard." One Oregon pioneer warned that a "woman that cannot endure almost as much as a horse has no business here."

The wagon trains followed the Oregon Trail west from Independence, Missouri, along the winding North Platte River into what is now Wyoming, through South Pass to Fort Bridger, then down the Snake River through what is now Idaho to the salmon-filled Columbia River. From there, they moved through the Cascade Mountains to Oregon.

As the numbers of migrants along the Oregon Trail grew, they tore through Native American lands and culture. Buffalo disappeared, and nations like the Cheyenne and the Arapaho were forced to split into northern and southern branches. In negotiating treaties with the Native Americans, the federal government insisted that they be relocated onto reservations far from the Oregon Trail, which eventually served as the route for the Union Pacific Railroad.

**LIFE ON THE TRAIL**   Traveling in prairie schooners, the sunburned settlers bumped and jostled their way across rugged trails, mountains, and plains blackened by vast herds of buffaloes.

Indians rarely attacked the wagon trains on the Oregon Trail; in fact, many served as guides, advisers, or traders. To be sure, as the number of pioneers grew during the 1850s, disputes with Indians over land and water increased, but never to the degree portrayed in novels, films, and television shows.

Still, the long journey west, usually five to six months, was an exodus of grinding hardship during broiling summers; fierce thunderstorms; and snowy, bitterly cold winters. Wagons broke down, oxen died, and diseases like cholera and dysentery took their toll. "The cowards never started," a popular saying went, "and the weak died on the way."

**WOMEN PIONEERS**   The diary of Amelia Knight, who set out for Oregon in 1853 with her husband and seven children, reveals the threats along the trail: "Chatfield quite sick with scarlet fever. A calf took sick and died before breakfast. Lost one of our oxen; he dropped dead in the yoke. I could hardly help shedding tears. Yesterday my eighth child was born."

Cholera claimed many lives because of tainted water and contaminated food. On average, there was one grave every eighty yards along the trail. Each step "of the slow, plodding cattle," wrote a woman emigrant, "carried us farther and farther from civilization into a desolate, barbarous country."

Initially, the pioneers adopted the same division of labor used back East. Women cooked, washed, sewed, and monitored the children, while men drove the wagons, tended the horses and cattle, and did the heavy labor. But the demands of the western trails soon dissolved such neat distinctions. Women found themselves gathering buffalo dung for fuel, driving wagons, working to dislodge wagons mired in mud, helping to construct makeshift bridges, pitching tents, or participating in other "unladylike" tasks.

Southerner Lavinia Porter described the trip along the California Trail as so difficult that it was still "a source of wonder to me how we [women] were able to endure it." She became convinced that the American woman was "endowed with the courage of her brave pioneer ancestors, and no matter what the environment she can adapt herself to all situations, even the perilous trip across the western half of this great continent."

The hard labor of the trail strained relationships and provoked social tensions. Divorces soared in the West. Many a tired pioneer could identify with the following comment in a girl's journal: "Poor Ma said only this morning, 'Oh, I wish we had never started.' She looks so sorrowful and dejected." Another woman wondered "what had possessed my husband, anyway, that he should have thought of bringing us away out through this God forsaken country."

Some of the emigrants turned back, but most continued on, and once in Oregon or California, they set about establishing stable communities. Noted one settler: "Friday, October 27. Arrived at Oregon City at the falls of the Willamette River. Saturday, October 28. Went to work."

The struggle to establish new lives devastated many migrants. The Malick family, for example, left Illinois in 1848 and started a farm in the Oregon Territory. George Malick, the father, died soon thereafter, as did three of the older children. "We are all well," widow Abigail Malick wrote in 1855 to relatives in Illinois. "All that are left of us."

**THE SETTLEMENT OF CALIFORNIA** California was also a powerful magnet. It had first felt the influence of European culture in 1769, when Spain, concerned about Russian seal traders moving south along the Pacific coast from Alaska, sent a naval expedition to settle the region. The Spanish discovered San Francisco Bay and constructed *presidios* (military garrisons)

**American pioneers** This 1850 photograph captures some of the many pioneers who headed west for brighter futures.

at San Diego and Monterey. Even more important, Franciscan friars, led by Junípero Serra, established a Catholic mission at San Diego. Over the next fifty years, Franciscans built twenty more missions, from San Diego northward to San Francisco.

The mission-centered culture in California was quite different from those in Texas and New Mexico, where the original missions were converted into secular communities and the property was divided among the Indians. In California, the missions were much larger, more influential, and longer lasting.

By the nineteenth century, Spanish Catholic missionaries, aided by Spanish soldiers, controlled most of the Indians living along the California coast. The friars (priests) enticed the Indians into missions by offering gifts or impressing them with "magical" religious rituals. Once inside the missions, the Indians were baptized as Catholics, taught Spanish, and stripped of their cultural heritage.

**CATHOLIC MISSIONS** The California Catholic missions served as churches, villages, fortresses, homes, schools, shops, farms, and outposts of Spanish rule. They quickly became agricultural enterprises, producing crops, livestock, clothing, and household goods, both for profit and to supply the neighboring presidios. Indians provided most of the labor.

A mission's daily routine began at dawn with the ringing of a bell, which summoned the community to prayer. Work began an hour later and did not end until an hour before sunset. Most Indian men worked in the fields. Women handled domestic chores, but during harvest season, everyone was expected to help in the fields. Instead of wages, the Indians received clothing, food, housing, and religious instruction.

Rebellious Native Americans were whipped or imprisoned, and mission Indians died at an alarming rate. One friar reported that "of every four Indian children born, three die in their first or second year, while those who survive do not reach the age of twenty-five." Infectious disease was the primary threat, but the grueling labor regimen took a high toll as well. The Native American population along the California coast declined from 72,000 in 1769 to 18,000 by 1821. Saving souls cost many lives.

With Mexican independence in 1821, the Spanish missions slowly fell into disuse. By the time the first Americans began to trickle into California, they found a vast, beautiful province with only a small, scattered population of 6,000 Mexicans ruled by a few dominant *caballeros* or *rancheros*—"gentlemen" who owned the largest ranches in the province, much like the planters who lorded over the Lower South.

Among the white immigrants to California was John A. Sutter, a Swiss settler who had founded a colony of European emigrants. He had left behind his debts and family in Europe to make his fortune in America. At the junction of the Sacramento and American Rivers (later the site of the city of Sacramento), Sutter hired local Indians and whites from America and Europe to build a fort with walls eighteen feet tall to protect the settlers and their workshops. Completed in 1843, Sutter's Fort stood at the end of the California Trail, which forked southward off the Oregon Trail and led through the Sierra Nevada.

Sutter set about creating a wilderness empire. In addition to trading furs, he put Indians to work making wool blankets and hats; cultivating vast acres of wheat and corn; and raising huge herds of cattle, sheep, hogs, and horses.

By 1846, there were perhaps 800 Americans in California, along with approximately 10,000 *Californios* and some 150,000 Native Americans. While Sutter paid his Indian workers, he also whipped, jailed, and even executed those who disobeyed his orders. The American migrants learned to speak Spanish, often embraced Catholicism, won Mexican citizenship, found Spanish or Native American spouses, and participated in local politics.

**THE DONNER PARTY**  The most tragic story of pioneers traveling to California involved the party headed by George Donner, a prosperous sixty-two-year-old farmer from Illinois.

In mid-April 1846, Donner led his family in a train of seventy-four other settlers and twenty-three wagons from Springfield, Illinois, to the Oregon Trail. Early on, Donner's wife's outlook was optimistic: "Indeed, if I do not experience something far worse than I have yet done, I shall say that the trouble all is in getting started."

But "the trouble" soon appeared, for the Donner party made several fatal mistakes: starting too late in the year, overloading their wagons, and taking a foolish shortcut to California southward across the Wasatch Mountains and toward the Great Salt Lake in the Utah Territory. The group had inadequate food, water, clothing, and experience. As their challenges mounted, discipline broke down. One settler was murdered for his gold; another was banished after killing a man in self-defense; and a third, unable to walk, was left behind to die.

In the Wasatch Range, the Donner party got lost and was forced to backtrack, losing three precious weeks in the process. An early September snow further slowed their progress. They eventually found their way into the desert leading to the Great Salt Lake, but crossing the parched desert exacted a terrible toll. They lost more than 100 oxen and had to abandon several wagons with their precious supplies. Yet their greatest loss was time as winter weather soon set in.

When the Donner party reached Truckee Pass in eastern California, the last barrier in the Sierra Nevada before they would reach the Sacramento Valley, a two-week-long blizzard trapped them in two separate camps. By December, the pioneers, half of them children, were marooned by twenty feet of snow, with only enough food to last through the end of the month. Seventeen of the strongest members, calling themselves the "Forlorn Hope," decided to cross the pass on their own, but they were trapped by more snow. Two turned back; eight more died of exposure and starvation.

**Donner party** This hand-colored engraving from the 1800s depicts these pioneers struggling in the snow on a trail leading over the Rocky Mountains.

Just before he died, Billy Graves urged his daughters to eat his corpse. The daughters were appalled at first, but soon saw no other choice. When two other members of the party died, they, too, were eaten. Only seven reached the Sacramento Valley.

Back at the main camps, the survivors had slaughtered and eaten the last of the livestock, then boiled hides and bones. They had also killed two Indian guides and eaten them. When a rescue party finally reached them two months later, they discovered that thirteen people had died, and cannibalism had become commonplace. One pioneer noted casually in his diary, "Mrs. Murphy said here yesterday that she thought she would commence on Milt and eat him." As the rescuers led the forty-seven survivors over the pass, George Donner, too weak and distressed to walk, stayed behind to die. His wife chose to remain with him.

**THE PATHFINDER: JOHN FRÉMONT**  Despite the dangers of the overland crossing, the Far West proved an irresistible attraction for hundreds of thousands of pioneers. The most enthusiastic champion of American settlement in Mexican California and the Far West was John Charles Frémont, an impetuous junior army officer who during the 1840s became America's most famous explorer.

Born and raised in the South, Frémont developed a robust love of the outdoors. In 1838, after attending the College of Charleston, he was commissioned a second lieutenant in the U.S. Topographical Corps, an organization whose mission was to explore and map new western territories. Frémont soon excelled at surveying, mapmaking, and woodcraft while becoming versed in geology, botany, ornithology, and zoology.

In 1841, Frémont courted and married seventeen-year-old Jessie Benton, the daughter of Thomas Hart Benton, the powerful Missouri senator. Once Benton's anger at his daughter subsided, he became Frémont's foremost booster and helped arrange the explorations that would bring his son-in-law fame.

In 1842, Frémont, who believed he was a man of God-determined destiny, set out from present-day Kansas City with two dozen soldiers to map the eastern half of the Oregon Trail. They spent five months collecting plant and animal specimens and drawing maps.

With his wife's considerable help, Frémont published in newspapers across the nation excerpts from a rip-roaring account of his explorations titled *A Report on an Exploration of the Country Lying between the Missouri River and the Rocky Mountains on the Line of the Kansas and Great Platte Rivers*. In describing the Great Plains, the Frémonts wrote that the "Indians and buffalo were the poetry and life of the prairie, and our camp was full of exhilaration."

The stories made Frémont an instant celebrity and earned him a nickname: "the Pathfinder." After reading about the expedition, Henry Wadsworth Longfellow, the nation's most popular poet, announced that "Frémont has touched my imagination. What a wild life, and what a fresh kind of existence! But ah, the discomforts!"

Frémont's success quickly led to another expedition, this one to map the more difficult half of the Oregon Trail from the South Pass, a twenty-mile gap in the Rocky Mountains in present-day Wyoming. The expedition would then go down the Snake River to the Columbia River and into Oregon, eventually making its way south through the Sierra Nevada to Sutter's Fort, near what would become Sacramento, California.

Frémont's group was the first to cross the snow- and ice-covered Sierra Nevada in the winter, a spectacular feat. His report of the expedition and the maps it generated spurred massive migrations to Utah, Oregon, and California throughout the 1840s, including the trek of the Mormons from Illinois to Salt Lake City, Utah.

Rarely one to follow orders, keep promises, or admit mistakes, Frémont surprised his superior officers when he launched a "military" expedition on his own. In August 1845, Frémont, now a captain, headed west from St. Louis on another mysterious expedition, this time leading sixty-two heavily armed soldiers, sailors, scientists, hunters, and frontiersmen.

In December, the adventurers swept down the western slopes of the Sierra Nevada and headed southward through the Central Valley of Mexican-controlled California. Frémont told Mexican authorities that his mission was strictly scientific and that his men were civilians. In Monterey, in January 1846, Frémont received secret instructions from President James Knox Polk indicating that the United States intended to take control of California from Mexico. Frémont was ordered to encourage a "spontaneous" uprising among the Americans living there.

Suspicious Mexican officials ordered Frémont to leave. He did, but soon devised a way to return. To cover his efforts to spark a revolution among the English-speaking Californians, most of whom were Americans, he officially resigned from the army so that he thereafter would be acting as a private citizen.

Then Frémont and his band of soldiers began stirring unrest. On June 14, 1846, American settlers captured Sonoma in northern California and proclaimed the Republic of California. They hoisted a flag featuring a grizzly bear and star, a version of which would later become the California state flag. On June 25, Frémont and his soldiers marched into Sonoma. All of California was in American control when news arrived of the outbreak of the Mexican-American War along the Texas border.

**AMERICAN SETTLEMENTS IN TEXAS** The American passion for new western land focused largely on Texas, an area of rich soil, lush prairie grass, plentiful timber, and abundant wildlife. During the 1820s, the United States had twice offered to buy Texas, but the Mexican government refused to sell. Mexicans were frightened and infuriated by the idea of Yankees taking their "sacred soil"—but that is what happened. By 1823, some 3,000 Americans or "*Texians*," called Anglos, were living in Texas illegally.

The leading promoter of American settlement in Mexican Texas was Stephen Fuller Austin, a visionary land developer (*empresario*) who convinced the Mexican government in 1824–1825 that he could recruit 300 American families to settle between the Colorado and Brazos Rivers along the Gulf coast of Texas and create a "buffer" on the northern frontier between the feared Comanche Indians and the Mexican settlements to the south. The Mexican government agreed to "legalize" American immigration as long as the settlers converted to Catholicism and did not bring slaves.

Americans who rushed to settle in Austin's Anglo "colony" each received 177 free acres and had access to thousands of acres of common pasture for ranching. Most of the Anglos were ranchers or farmers drawn to the fertile, inexpensive lands in the river valleys. A few were wealthy planters who brought slaves with them in spite of the law against it. The settlers marveled at the abundance of food sources. An American reported that eastern Texas was "literally alive with all kinds of game. We have only to go out a few miles into a swamp . . . to find as many wild cattle as one could wish." There were as many buffalo as cattle.

By 1830, coastal Texas had far more Americans than Tejanos (Spanish-speaking Texans) or Indians—about 20,000 white settlers and 1,000 enslaved blacks, brought to grow and harvest cotton. By 1835, there were 35,000 *Texians*, 3,000 African American slaves, and a booming cotton economy.

The flood of Americans into Texas led to numerous clashes with Indians as well as with Mexican officials, who began having second thoughts about their "tolerated guests." A Mexican congressman issued an accurate warning in 1830: "Mexicans! Watch closely, for you know all too well the Anglo-Saxon greed for territory. We have generously granted land to these Nordics; they have made their homes with us, but their hearts are with their native land. We are continually in civil wars and revolutions; we are weak, and know it—and they know it also. They may conspire with the United States to take Texas from us. From this time, be on your guard!"

**THE TEXAS WAR FOR INDEPENDENCE** Mexican officials were so worried about the intentions of the Texians that in April 1830 they outlawed further emigration from the United States. Americans, who viewed the

Mexicans with contempt, kept coming anyway—as illegal immigrants. By 1835, the *Texians* and their enslaved blacks outnumbered the Tejanos 10 to 1. In a letter to his cousin in 1835, Stephen F. Austin left no doubt about his plans: "It is very evident that Texas should be effectually, and fully, *Americanized*—that is—settled by a population that will harmonize with their neighbors on the *East*, in language, political principles, common origin, sympathy, and even interest. *Texas must be a slave country. It is no longer a matter of doubt.*"

A changing political situation aggravated the growing tensions between the Mexican government and the Texians. In 1834, General Antonio López de Santa Anna, the Mexican president, suspended the national congress and became a dictator, calling himself the "Napoleon of the West." Texans feared that Santa Anna planned to free "our slaves and to make slaves of us."

When Santa Anna imprisoned Austin in 1834 for inciting rebelliousness among the Texians, American settlers decided that the Mexican ruler had to go. Upon his release from jail eighteen months later, Austin called for Texans to revolt: "War is our only resource. There is no other remedy." He urged that Texas become a fully American territory promoting slavery, and then officially become a new state.

In the fall of 1835, Texans rebelled against Santa Anna's "despotism." The Mexican leader ordered all Americans expelled, all Texans disarmed, and all

**The Alamo** David Crockett, pictured fighting with his rifle over his head, joined the legendary effort to defend the Alamo against the Mexican army's repeated assaults.

rebels arrested and executed as "pirates." As sporadic fighting erupted, hundreds of armed volunteers from southern states rushed to assist the 30,000 *Texians* and Tejanos fighting against a Mexican nation of 7 million people. "The sword is drawn!" Austin proclaimed.

**THE ALAMO**    At San Antonio, the provincial capital in southern Texas, General Santa Anna's 3,000-man army assaulted a group of fewer than 200 *Texians*, Tejanos, and members of the Texas volunteer army holed up in an abandoned Catholic mission called the Alamo. The outnumbered and out-gunned Texas rebels were led by three colorful adventurers with checkered pasts: James "Jim" Bowie, William Barret Travis, and David Crockett.

Bowie, a ruthless slave trader and deceitful land speculator, was most famous for the "bowie knife" he used to wound and kill. He claimed he had never started a fight—nor lost one. In his most famous brawl, he was shot twice, stabbed, and impaled by a sword before he killed his opponent with his knife.

Bowie, who migrated from Louisiana to Texas in 1828, settled near San Antonio and came to own about a million acres of land. He married a prominent Mexican woman, became a Mexican citizen, and learned Spanish, but a cholera epidemic killed his wife and two children, as well as his in-laws.

Upon learning of the Texas Revolution, Bowie joined the volunteer army and commanded the Texas volunteers in the Alamo. William Travis, a hot-tempered, twenty-six-year-old lawyer and teacher, led the "regular army" soldiers.

Travis had come to Texas by way of Alabama, leaving a failed marriage; a pregnant wife; a two-year-old son; considerable debts; and, rumors claimed, a man he had killed. Travis pledged that he would redeem himself by doing something great and honorable in Texas—or die trying. His determination led him to refuse orders to retreat from the Alamo.

The most famous American at the Alamo was David Crockett, the Tennessee frontiersman, sharpshooter, bear hunter, and storyteller who had fought under Andrew Jackson and served in Congress as an anti-Jackson Whig. In his last speech before Congress after being defeated for reelection, Crockett, who was not called "Davy" until long after his death, told his colleagues that he "was done with politics for the present, and that they might go to hell, and I would go to Texas," where he planned to make "a fortune."

Soon after arriving with his trusty rifle, "Old Betsy," Crockett learned that he would receive 4,000 acres for his service as a fighter. He then was assigned to the garrison at the Alamo. Full of bounce and brag, the forty-nine-year-old Crockett was thoroughly expert at killing. As he once told his men, "Pierce the heart of the enemy as you would a feller that spit in your face, knocked down your wife, burnt up your houses, and called your dog a skunk!"

The defenders of the Alamo shared a commitment to liberty in the face of Santa Anna's growing despotism. In late February 1836, Santa Anna demanded that the Alamo surrender. By then, Bowie had fallen seriously ill and turned over command to Travis, who answered the Mexican ultimatum with cannon fire. He then sent appeals to Texian towns for supplies and more men, while promising that "*I shall never surrender or retreat* . . . VICTORY OR DEATH!"

Help did not come, however, and the Mexicans launched a series of assaults against the outnumbered defenders. For twelve days, however, the Mexicans suffered heavy losses.

The ferocious fighting at the Alamo turned the rebellion into a war for Texan independence. On March 2, 1836, delegates from all fifty-nine Texas towns met in the tiny village of Washington-on-the-Brazos, some 150 miles northeast of San Antonio. There they signed a declaration of independence and drafted a constitution for the new Republic of Texas. They then named Sam Houston commander-in-chief of their disorganized but growing "army."

Four days later, the defenders of the Alamo were awakened at four o'clock in the morning by the sound of Mexican bugles playing the dreaded "Degüello" ("Slashing of the Throat," symbolizing no mercy). Colonel Travis shouted: "The Mexicans are upon us—give 'em Hell!"

The climactic Battle of the Alamo was fought in the predawn dark. Santa Anna's men attacked from every direction. They were twice forced back, but on the third try they broke through the battered north wall. Travis was killed by a bullet between the eyes. In the end, virtually all of the Texans were killed or wounded.

Seven Alamo defenders, perhaps including Crockett, survived and were captured. Santa Anna ordered them hacked to death with swords. A Mexican officer wrote that the captives "died without complaining and without humiliating themselves before their torturers."

By dawn, the battle was over. The only survivors were a handful of women and children, and Joe, Travis's slave. It was a costly victory, however, as more than 600 Mexicans died. The Battle of the Alamo also provided a rallying cry for vengeful Texians. While Santa Anna proclaimed a "glorious victory," his aide wrote ominously in his diary, "One more such 'glorious victory' and we are finished."

**GOLIAD** Two weeks later, at the Battle of Coleto Creek, a Mexican force again defeated a smaller Texian army, then marched the 465 captured Texians to a fort in the nearby town of Goliad. Despite pleas from his men to show mercy, Santa Anna ordered the captives killed as "pirates and outlaws." On

Palm Sunday, March 27, 1836, more than 300 Texians were marched out and murdered. The massacres at the Alamo and Goliad fueled a burning desire for revenge among Texians.

**SAM HOUSTON** The fate of the **Texas Revolution** was now in the hands of the already legendary Sam Houston, a rowdy, larger-than-life frontier statesman born in Virginia to Scots-Irish immigrants. At age fourteen, after his father died, Houston had moved with his mother and siblings to eastern Tennessee. Two years later, he ran away from home and lived among the Cherokees, earning the nickname "The Raven." Like David Crockett, Houston had served under General Andrew Jackson during the War of 1812. Thereafter, he returned to Tennessee and became a federal Indian agent, an attorney, a U.S. congressman, commanding general of the Tennessee militia, and, in 1827, at the ripe age of thirty-four, governor.

Unlike Crockett, however, Houston adored Jackson and became his devoted disciple and surrogate son, leading many to speculate that he might become the next president. Like Jackson, however, Houston was at heart an oddball ruffian: he had an untamed yet gallant personality with a charming brashness that cloaked a violent temper. A friend called him a "magnificent barbarian."

Controversy dogged Houston. In 1829, he suddenly resigned the governorship of Tennessee because Eliza Allen, his beautiful, aristocratic, and much younger wife, had left him soon after their wedding and returned to her father's plantation near Nashville.

Houston never revealed the cause of the dispute, but Eliza's family accused him of "dishonoring" her. He, in turn, kept silent because, he explained to President Jackson, doing so reinforced his "notion of honor." If his character could not stand the "shock" of mean-spirited gossip, he said, then "let me lose it."

For years, wild rumors circulated about what had happened on Houston's wedding night. Some claimed that Eliza had discovered that Houston had sustained a "dreadful injury" (true, a wound in the groin from an Indian arrowhead) in the Creek War that had left him scarred and impotent (a falsehood). Others reported that his bride had confessed she was in love with someone else and had only married him to please her family. Whatever the cause, Houston later wrote that his ugly divorce threw him into an "agony of despair" over his "private afflictions" that had ruined his political career and exiled him from Nashville society.

The disconsolate Houston decided that suicide was his only option. As he was preparing to kill himself, however, an eagle suddenly swooped toward him and then soared upward into the sunset. Then and there, Houston later wrote, "I knew that a great destiny waited for me in the West."

In 1829, Houston boarded a steamboat and headed West, where he eventually joined the Cherokee; adopted their clothing, customs, and language; and changed his name. He married a Cherokee woman and was formally "adopted" by the Cherokee Nation.

Houston proved adept at helping rival Indian tribes—Cherokee, Creek, Osage, and Choctaws—negotiate among themselves and with the federal government. He also grew addicted to alcohol; the Cherokees called him "Big Drunk." In December 1832, he moved from the Arkansas Territory to Texas at Jackson's behest. Two months later, he sent a secret report to the president, indicating that Texas was ripe for revolt from Mexico, which was then embroiled in a civil war. Houston joined the rebellion.

**THE BATTLE OF SAN JACINTO** After learning of the Mexican victory at the Alamo, Sam Houston led his outnumbered troops on a long strategic retreat to buy time while hoping that Santa Anna's pursuing army would make a mistake. On April 21, 1836, the cocky Mexican general let his guard down. Houston's army of 900 fighters caught Santa Anna's 1,600 troops napping near the San Jacinto River, about twenty-five miles southeast of the modern city of Houston. The Texians and Tejanos charged, yelling "Remember the Alamo, Remember Goliad!" They overwhelmed the Mexicans. General

**Austin, Texas, in 1840** A view of the capital of the newly formed Republic of Texas—the town's population at the time numbered less than a thousand.

Santa Anna left his army leaderless that afternoon while he retreated to his tent, accompanied, some said, by his mistress.

The battle lasted only eighteen minutes, but Houston's troops spent the next two hours slaughtering fleeing Mexican soldiers. Some 650 Mexicans were killed and 300 captured. The Texians lost only eleven men. Santa Anna escaped but was captured the next day. He bought his freedom by signing a treaty recognizing the independence of the Republic of Texas, with the Rio Grande as its southern boundary with Mexico. The Texas Revolution had been accomplished in just seven weeks.

**THE LONE STAR REPUBLIC**  In 1836, the Lone Star Republic, as Texians called their new nation, legalized slavery, banned free blacks, elected Sam Houston as its first president, and voted overwhelmingly for annexation to the United States. But statehood for Texas soon became embroiled in the sectional dispute over slavery.

John C. Calhoun told the Senate that "there were powerful reasons why Texas should be part of this Union. The southern states, owning a slave population, were deeply interested in preventing that country from having the power to annoy them." Anti-slavery Northerners disagreed. In 1837, the Vermont legislature "solemnly protested" against the admission "of any state whose constitution tolerates domestic slavery."

President Andrew Jackson eagerly wanted Texas to join the Union. He knew, however, that adding Texas as a slave state would ignite an explosive quarrel between North and South that would fracture the Democratic party and endanger the election of New Yorker Martin Van Buren, his handpicked successor. Worse, any effort to add Texas to the Union would likely mean a war with Mexico, which refused to recognize Texan independence.

So, Jackson delayed official recognition of the Republic of Texas until his last day in office, early in 1837. Van Buren, Jackson's successor, did as predicted: he avoided all talk of Texas annexation during his single term as president.

**WHIGS AND DEMOCRATS**  When sixty-eight-year-old William Henry Harrison succeeded Martin Van Buren as president in 1841, he was the oldest man and the first Whig to win the office. The Whigs, who now controlled both houses of Congress, continued to promote federal government support for industrial development and economic growth, high tariffs to deter foreign imports, and federal funding for roads, bridges, and canals.

Yet Harrison won election primarily because of his prominence as a military hero. During the campaign he had avoided taking public stances on controversial issues. In the end, it mattered little, as he served the shortest term of any president. On April 4, 1841, exactly one month after his inauguration, he died of pneumonia. Vice President John Tyler became president.

Henry Clay, the formidable Kentucky senator, hoped to dominate the mild-mannered new president. Tyler "dares not resist," Clay threatened, or "I will drive him before me." Tyler, however, was not willing to be dominated.

**JOHN TYLER**  The tall, thin, slave-owning Virginian was a political maverick and, at fifty-one, the youngest president to date. But he had lots of political experience, having served as a state legislator, governor, congressman, and senator. Perhaps most important, he was a man of stubborn independence and considerable charm. An acquaintance said Tyler was "approachable, courteous, always willing to do a kindly action, or to speak a kindly word."

Originally a Democrat, Tyler had endorsed the Jeffersonian commitment to states' rights, strict construction of the Constitution, and opposition to national banks. He joined the Whigs after President Jackson's "condemnation" of South Carolina's attempt to nullify federal laws. Tyler believed that South Carolina had a constitutional right to secede from the nation. Yet he never truly embraced the Whigs. As president, he opposed everything associated with Henry Clay's celebrated program of economic nationalism (the American System), which called for high tariffs, a national bank, and internal improvements.

When Congress met in a special session in 1841, Clay introduced a series of controversial resolutions. He called for the repeal of the Independent Treasury Act and the creation of another Bank of the United States; he proposed to revive the distribution program whereby the money generated by federal land sales was given to the states, and urged that tariffs be raised on imported goods to hamper foreign competitors.

Clay might have avoided a nasty dispute with Tyler over financial issues, but for once, driven by his compulsive quest to be president, the Great Compromiser lost his instinct for compromise. Although Tyler agreed to the repeal of the Independent Treasury Act and signed a higher tariff bill, he vetoed Clay's pet project: the new national bank.

An incensed Clay responded by calling Tyler a traitor who had disgraced his party. He claimed that the president was left "solitary and alone, shivering by the pitiless storm" against his veto. Clay then convinced Tyler's entire cabinet to resign, with the exception of Secretary of State Daniel Webster. A three-year-long war between Clay and Tyler had begun.

Tyler replaced the defectors in his cabinet with anti-Jackson Democrats who, like him, had become Whigs. The Whigs then expelled Tyler from the party, calling him "His Accidency" and the "Executive Ass." By 1842, Tyler had become a president without a party, shunned by both Whigs and Democrats.

The political turmoil coincided with the economic depression that had begun in the late 1830s. Yet Tyler refused to let either the sputtering economy or an international crisis with Great Britain deter him from annexing more territory into the United States.

**TENSIONS WITH BRITAIN** In late 1841, slaves being transported from Virginia to Louisiana on the American ship *Creole* revolted and took charge of the ship. They sailed into Nassau, in the Bahamas, where British authorities set 128 of them free. (Great Britain had abolished slavery throughout its empire in 1834.)

It was the most successful slave revolt in American history. Southerners were infuriated, and the incident mushroomed into an international crisis. Secretary of State Daniel Webster demanded that the slaves be returned as American property, but the British refused.

Rather than risk a war that the United States might lose, Tyler and Webster acquiesced to the British. This enraged southern slaveholders. James Henry Hammond, the South Carolina planter, lashed out: "With such a stupid imbecile as Tyler at the head of affairs and such an unprincipled and cowardly Sec. of State as Webster, we should fare badly for a time. They are bent on peace."

At this point, the British government decided to send Alexander Baring, Lord Ashburton, to meet with Webster, who viewed good relations with Britain as essential for the American economy. The meetings produced the Webster-Ashburton Treaty (1842), which provided for joint naval patrols off Africa to police the outlawed slave trade. The treaty also resolved a long-standing dispute over the northeastern U.S. boundary with British Canada. But it did nothing about returning the freed slaves. The dispute was not settled until 1853, when England paid $110,000 to the slaves' former owners. In May 1843, Webster resigned as secretary of state.

**THE "EXTENSION OF OUR EMPIRE": TEXAS** From the moment he became president, John Tyler had his eyes on annexing the Republic of Texas. In his first address to Congress, he pledged to do so, explaining that there was nothing to fear from "the extension of our Empire."

Tyler's efforts to recruit senators to approve an annexation treaty exhilarated Texas leaders who were long frustrated that they had not been welcomed into the United States. Sam Houston threatened to expand the Republic of Texas to the Pacific coast. But with little money, a rising debt, and continuing tensions with Mexico, this was mostly talk.

The Lone Star Republic had no infrastructure—no banks, no schools, no industries. Houston decided that the rickety republic had two choices: annexation to the United States or closer economic ties to Great Britain, which had extended formal diplomatic recognition to the republic and then began buying cotton from Texas planters.

Meanwhile, thousands more Americans poured into Texas, enticed by its offer of 1,280 acres of land to each white family. The population more than tripled between 1836 and 1845, from 40,000 to 150,000; the enslaved black population grew even faster than the white population.

**A TRAGIC CRUISE** On February 28, 1844, President Tyler and a group of 300 dignitaries boarded the U.S.S. *Princeton*, a new warship, for an excursion on the Potomac River. As sailors fired the ship's fifteen-foot-long cannons, one of them, "the Peacemaker," exploded, killing eight people, including the secretary of state and secretary of the navy. More than a dozen others were seriously wounded. Tyler, who was below deck at the time of the accident, rushed to see what had happened: "A more heart-rending scene scarcely ever occurred," he wrote. "What a loss I have sustained . . . "

After the funerals, Tyler seized the opportunity created by the accident to reorganize his cabinet by naming southern Democrats to key positions. He appointed John C. Calhoun secretary of state, primarily because he wanted the South Carolinian to complete the annexation of Texas as a slave state. On April 12, 1844, Calhoun signed a treaty of annexation, and Tyler submitted it to the Senate for approval. Texas would become an American territory in exchange for the United States assuming all of its debts. Tyler explained that the addition of Texas would "add to national greatness and wealth" and "strengthen rather than weaken the Union."

Calhoun, however, unwittingly undermined the treaty by writing the British ambassador what he thought was a confidential letter in which he declared that blacks were inferior to whites and better off enslaved than free. Slavery, Calhoun insisted, was "essential to the peace, safety, and prosperity" of the South. Adding Texas, he concluded, was necessary to keep the South in the Union. On June 8, 1844, outraged Northerners in the Senate voted down Calhoun's annexation treaty 35 to 16.

**THE ELECTION OF 1844** Both political parties hoped to keep the divisive Texas issue out of the 1844 presidential campaign. Whig Henry Clay and Democrat Martin Van Buren, the leading candidates for each party's nomination, agreed that adding Texas to the Union would be a mistake, for it would aggravate tensions between North and South over slavery.

For his part, Tyler, having alienated both parties, initially announced that he would run for reelection as an independent, using the campaign slogan, "Tyler and Texas." Within a few weeks, however, he realized he had little support and dropped out of the race.

Van Buren's southern supporters, including former president Andrew Jackson, abandoned him because he opposed the annexation of Texas. They instead nominated James K. Polk, former Speaker of the House and former governor of Tennessee. Like Tyler, Polk was an enthusiastic expansionist. Unlike Tyler, he was a loyal Democrat who hated Whigs. On the ninth ballot, he became the first "dark horse" (unexpected) candidate to win a major-party nomination. The Democrats' platform called for the annexation of Texas and declared that the United States had a "clear and unquestionable claim" to all the Oregon Country.

The 1844 election proved to be one of the most significant in history. By promoting southern and western expansionism, the Democrats offered a winning strategy that forced Clay, the Whig candidate, to alter his position on Texas at the last minute. He now claimed that he had "no personal objection to the annexation" if it could be achieved "without dishonor, without war, with the common consent of the Union, and upon just and fair terms."

Clay's waffling shifted more anti-slavery votes to the new Liberty party (the anti-slavery party formed in 1840), which increased its count in the presidential election from about 7,000 in 1840 to more than 62,000 in 1844. In the western counties of New York, the Liberty party drew enough votes from Clay and the Whigs to give the crucial state to Polk.

Had Clay carried New York, he would have won the election by 7 electoral votes. Instead, Polk won a narrow national plurality of 38,000 popular votes—the first president since John Quincy Adams to win without a majority—but with a clear majority of the electoral college, 170 to 105. A devastated Clay had lost his third and last presidential election. He could not understand how he had lost to Polk, whom he considered a "third-rate" politician.

**JAMES K. POLK**     James K. Polk had been surprising people his whole career. Born near Charlotte, North Carolina, the oldest of ten children, he graduated first in his class at the University of North Carolina. Polk then moved to Tennessee, where he became a successful lawyer and planter. He then entered politics, serving fourteen years in Congress (four as Speaker of the House) and two years as governor.

At forty-nine, Polk was America's youngest president. Short, thin, and humorless, he was called "Young Hickory" because of his admiration for "Old

Hickory," Andrew Jackson. Like Jackson, he believed that any efforts by the federal government to promote economic growth necessarily helped some people and regions and hurt others. He thus opposed tariffs, a national bank, and federally funded roads.

Polk's greatest virtue was his work ethic. He often labored from dawn to midnight and rarely took a vacation. Such unrelenting intensity eventually wore him out, however. Polk would die in 1849, at fifty-three years old, just three months after leaving office.

**THE STATE OF TEXAS**   Texas joined the Union just *before* Polk was sworn in as president. In his final months in office, President John Tyler had asked Congress to annex Texas by joint resolution, which required only a simple majority in each house rather than the two-thirds Senate vote needed to ratify a *treaty* of annexation.

The resolution narrowly passed, with most Whigs opposed. In his final presidential action, Tyler admitted Texas as the twenty-eighth state, and fifteenth slave state, on December 29, 1845. On February 16, 1846, the Lone Star flag of the Republic of Texas was lowered, and the flag of the United States was raised over the largest state in the nation.

At the time, Texas had a population of 100,000 whites and 38,000 enslaved African Americans. By 1850, the population—both white and black—had soared by almost 50 percent. (The census then did not include Native Americans.) By 1860, Texas had 600,000 people, most of them from southern states focused on growing cotton.

**POLK'S GOALS**   Perhaps because he pledged to serve only one term, Polk was a president in a hurry. He focused on four major objectives, all of which he accomplished. He managed to (1) reduce tariffs on imports; (2) reestablish the Independent Treasury ("We need no national banks!"); (3) settle the Oregon boundary dispute with Britain; and (4) acquire California from Mexico.

Polk wanted lower tariffs to allow more foreign goods to compete in the American marketplace and thereby help drive consumer prices down. Congress agreed by approving the Walker Tariff of 1846, named after Robert J. Walker, the secretary of the Treasury.

The same year, Polk persuaded Congress to restore the Independent Treasury Act that Martin Van Buren had signed into law in 1840 and the Whig-dominated Congress had repealed the next year. The act established Independent Treasury deposit offices to receive all federal government funds. The system was intended to replace the Second Bank of the United States,

**Tariff of 1846** This political cartoon illustrates the public outcry—represented by a Quaker woman ready to whip Polk—against the Tariff of 1846, one of the lowest in the nation's history.

which Jackson had "killed," so as to offset the chaotic growth of unregulated state banks whose reckless lending practices had helped cause the depression of the late 1830s.

The new Independent Treasury entrusted the federal government, rather than state banks, with the exclusive management of government funds and required that all disbursements be made in gold or silver, or paper currency backed by gold or silver.

Polk also twice vetoed Whig-passed bills for federally funded infrastructure projects. His efforts to reverse Whig economic policies satisfied the slaveholding South but angered Northerners, who wanted higher tariffs to protect their industries from British competition, and westerners, who wanted federally financed roads and harbors.

**OREGON** Meanwhile, the dispute with Great Britain over the Oregon Country boundary heated up as expansionists insisted that Polk take the whole region rather than split it with the British. Polk was willing to go to the brink of war to achieve his goals. "If we do have war," the president blustered, "it will not be our fault."

Fortunately, the British were not willing to risk war. On June 15, 1846, James Buchanan, Polk's secretary of state, signed the Buchanan-Pakenham Treaty, which extended the border between the United States and British Canada westward to the Pacific coast along the 49th parallel. Once the treaty was approved by both nations, the *New York Herald* announced: "Now, we can thrash Mexico into decency at our leisure."

## THE MEXICAN-AMERICAN WAR

On March 6, 1845, two days after James Polk became president, the Mexican government broke off relations with the United States to protest the annexation of Texas. Polk was willing to wage war against Mexico to acquire California and New Mexico, but he did not want Americans to fire the first shot.

Nor did he want a war that might produce a military hero who would become a Whig candidate for the presidency. Senator Thomas Hart Benton of Missouri, a powerful Democrat, disclosed that Polk "wanted a small war, just large enough to require a treaty for peace, and not large enough to create military reputations" that might pose a political challenge after the war.

Polk ordered several thousand U.S. troops under General Zachary Taylor to take up positions around Corpus Christi, Texas, at the mouth of the Nueces River, which Mexico claimed as its border with the United States. In March, Polk ordered Taylor to move his force to the north bank of the Rio Grande, where they built Fort Brown opposite the Mexican town of Matamoros, a provocative move that the Mexican government viewed as an invasion.

On the evening of May 9, 1845, Polk learned that Mexican troops had attacked U.S. soldiers north of the Rio Grande. Eleven Americans were killed, five wounded, and the rest taken prisoner. Polk's scheme to provoke an attack had worked. On May 13, Congress declared war and authorized the recruitment of 50,000 soldiers.

Some congressmen, however, were skeptical of Polk's explanation. Whig Garret Davis of Kentucky asserted, "It is our own President who began this war." Even Democrats were concerned about the president's story. A New York senator, John Dix, said he would not be "surprised if the next accounts should show that there is no Mexican invasion of our soil." The war, he later added, "was begun in fraud . . . and I think will end in disgrace."

President Polk steadfastly denied that the war had anything to do with the expansion of slavery. He argued that his efforts to extend America's boundaries to the Pacific were intended to replace sectional tensions with national unity.

After all, he stressed, slavery could not flourish in places like New Mexico and California because cotton could not be grown there because of the climate.

Most Americans accepted the president's account and rushed to support the military. "LET US GO TO WAR," screamed a New York newspaper. Another headline blared: "MEXICO OR DEATH!" The South was especially excited because of the possibility of acquiring more territory. So many Southerners ("wild, reckless young fellows") rushed to volunteer that thousands had to be turned away.

Eventually, 112,000 whites served in the war. (Blacks were banned.) Among the warriors were young army officers who would later distinguish themselves as opposing leaders in the Civil War: Ulysses S. Grant, Joseph Hooker, Thomas Jackson, James Longstreet, Robert E. Lee, George McClellan, George Meade, and William T. Sherman.

**OPPOSITION TO THE WAR**    In New England and among northern abolitionists, there was much less enthusiasm for "Mr. Polk's War." Congressman John Quincy Adams, the former president who was now nearly eighty years old, called it "a most unrighteous war." He saw "Polk's War" as a southern scheme to extend slavery into new territories taken from Mexico.

William Lloyd Garrison, the fiery Boston abolitionist, charged that the war was one of "aggression, of invasion, of conquest." Henry David Thoreau spent a night in jail rather than pay taxes that might help fund the war. Thoreau's mentor, Ralph Waldo Emerson, predicted that the "United States will conquer Mexico, but it will be as the man who swallows arsenic, which brings him down in turn. Mexico will poison us."

Most northern Whigs, including a young Illinois congressman named Abraham Lincoln, opposed the war, arguing that Polk had maneuvered the Mexicans into attacking. The United States, many insisted, had no reason to place its army in the disputed border region between Texas and Mexico. In what came to be called "Spot Resolutions," Lincoln repeatedly asked the president to locate the precise "spot" where the American troops were fired upon, implying that they may have illegally crossed into Mexican territory.

Whig leader Henry Clay expressed concern that the nation was "becoming a warlike and conquering power," while Daniel Webster charged that the war's disputed origins were "unconstitutional." (Both Clay and Webster would lose sons in the war.)

**PREPARING FOR BATTLE**    The United States was again ill prepared for a major war. At the outset, the regular army numbered barely more than 7,000, in contrast to the Mexican force of 32,000. Before the war ended, however, the U.S. military had grown to almost 79,000 troops, many of whom were frontier toughs who lacked uniforms, equipment, and discipline. Repeatedly, some of these soldiers engaged in plunder, rape, and murder. Yet they outfought the larger Mexican forces.

The Mexican-American War would last from May 1846 to April 1848 and would be fought on four fronts: southern Texas/northern Mexico, central Mexico, New Mexico, and California. Early on, the U.S. Army scored victories north of the Rio Grande, at Palo Alto (May 8) and Resaca de la Palma (May 9).

On May 18, General Zachary Taylor's army crossed the Rio Grande and occupied Matamoros. Those quick victories brought Taylor, a Whig, instant popularity; Polk agreed to public demand that Taylor be made overall commander. It was an excellent choice, since Taylor, "Old Rough and Ready," had spent thirty-eight years in the army and had earned the respect and affection of his men.

**THE ANNEXATION OF CALIFORNIA**    President Polk's foremost objective was the acquisition of California. Not only did it have wonderful harbors (San Francisco, Monterey, and San Diego), but the president also feared that Great Britain or France would take control of California if the United States did not.

Polk had secretly instructed Commodore John D. Sloat, commander of the Pacific naval squadron, that if war erupted with Mexico, he was to use his warships to gain control "of the port of San Francisco, and blockade or occupy such other ports as your force may permit."

In May 1846, Sloat, having heard of the outbreak of hostilities along the Rio Grande, set sail for California. In early July, U.S. sailors and troops went ashore in San Francisco, took down the flag of the Republic of California, raised the American flag, and claimed California as part of the United States.

Soon thereafter, Sloat turned his command over to Commodore Robert F. Stockton, who sailed south to capture San Diego and Los Angeles. By mid-August, Mexican resistance had evaporated.

At the same time, another American military expedition headed for California. On August 18, General Stephen Kearny's army captured Santa Fe, the capital of New Mexico, then joined Stockton's forces in California. They took control of Los Angeles on January 10, 1847. The remaining Mexican forces surrendered three days later. Stockton and Kearny then quarreled over who was in command, since each carried orders to conquer and govern California.

In the meantime, the unpredictable John C. Frémont arrived from Sonoma with 400 newly recruited troops and claimed that Stockton was in charge.

Stockton responded by naming Frémont governor of California, and Frémont immediately set about giving orders, making proclamations, and appointing officials. This left Kearny in a bind; President Polk had ordered *him* to be the governor.

By June of 1847, Kearny had seen enough. He had Frémont arrested and transported him across the country for a court-martial. In the most celebrated

## MAJOR CAMPAIGNS OF THE MEXICAN-AMERICAN WAR

- Why did John C. Frémont and his troops initially march north, only to turn around and march south to San Francisco?
- How did Polk's fear of Zachary Taylor's popularity undermine the Americans' military strategy?

trial since that of Vice President Aaron Burr in 1807, Frémont was found guilty of mutiny and insubordination and dismissed from the army. President Polk, however, quickly reversed the sentence in light of Frémont's "meritorious and valuable services." He urged Frémont to remain in the army and "resume the sword," but "the Pathfinder" was so angry at his treatment that he resigned his commission and settled in California, where he would become the state's first U.S. senator.

**WAR IN NORTHERN MEXICO**  Both California and New Mexico had been taken before General Zachary Taylor fought his first major battle in northern Mexico. In September 1846, Taylor's army assaulted the fortified city of Monterrey, which surrendered after a five-day siege. Then, General Antonio López de Santa Anna, who had been forced out of power in 1845, sent word to Polk from his exile in Cuba that he would end the war if he were allowed to return to Mexico. Polk assured the exiled Mexican leader that the U.S. government would pay well for any territory taken from Mexico. In August 1846, on Polk's orders, Santa Anna was permitted to return to Mexico.

But Santa Anna had lied. Soon he was again president of Mexico and in command of the Mexican army. As it turned out, however, he was much more talented at raising armies than leading them in battle.

In October 1846, Santa Anna invited the outnumbered Americans to surrender. Taylor responded, "Tell him to go to hell." That launched the hard-fought Battle of Buena Vista (February 22–23, 1847), in northern Mexico. Both sides claimed victory, but the Mexicans suffered five times as many casualties as the Americans. Thereafter, the Mexicans continued to lose battles, but they refused to accept Polk's terms for surrender.

Frustrated by Taylor's inability to win a decisive victory, Polk authorized an assault on Mexico City, the nation's capital. On March 9, 1847, a large American force led by Winfield Scott, the general-in-chief of the U.S. Army, landed on the beaches south of Veracruz, the site of what was considered the strongest fortress in North America.

The American assault on Veracruz, the largest amphibious operation ever attempted by U.S. military forces, was carried out without loss. Veracruz surrendered on March 29, and the news made General Scott a national hero. The American troops then rested, accumulating supplies and awaiting reinforcements to replace the many volunteers whose enlistments had run out and who were eager to go home.

In August, Scott's formidable invasion force marched toward heavily defended Mexico City, 200 miles away. In England, the Duke of Wellington, who had defeated Napoléon at the Battle of Waterloo more than thirty years before, predicted that "Scott is lost—he cannot capture the city, and he cannot fall back upon his base."

Yet the Englishman was wrong. After four brilliantly orchestrated battles in which they overwhelmed the Mexican defenders, U.S. forces arrived at the gates of Mexico City in early September 1847. The Duke of Wellington now changed his tune, calling Scott the world's "greatest living soldier."

**THE SAINT PATRICK'S BATTALION**    General Winfield Scott's triumphant assault on Mexico City was not without problems, however. Since the start of the war, some 7,000 soldiers had deserted. Several hundred of them, mostly poor Irish and German Catholic immigrants, crossed over to form the Saint Patrick's Battalion in the Mexican army, which included many foreign fighters.

Why the American soldiers, called *San Patricios* in Spanish, chose to switch sides remains in dispute, but several factors were at work. Many of the Catholic defectors resented the abuse ("harsh and cruel handling") they received from native U.S. Protestant officers and the atrocities they saw committed against Catholic Mexicans. Some were also attracted by the higher wages, land grants, and

**St. Patrick's Battalion**  The men of St. Patrick's Battalion continue to be celebrated in Mexico as martyrs, with numerous cities, schools, and streets bearing the name *San Patricio.*

promises of citizenship by the Mexican government. The Mexican army circulated leaflets to American soldiers urging the foreign-born to switch sides and fight for their shared "sacred imperiled religion. If you are Catholic, the same as we, if you follow the doctrines of Our Savior, why are you murdering your brethren? Why are you antagonistic to those who defend their country and your own God?"

Whatever their motives, the *San Patricios* fought tenaciously. During one of the battles for Mexico City, the Americans captured seventy-two defectors. They were quickly tried, and most were sentenced to death. Although military law at the time called for traitors to be shot by a firing squad, General Scott ordered that about fifty of the deserters be hanged. The others were whipped and branded with a "D" on each cheek.

At dawn on September 13, 1847, twenty-nine of the captured *San Patricios*, their hands and feet bound, were made to stand in the hot sun under a gallows in sight of Chapultepec, the last Mexican fortress protecting Mexico City. There they were forced to watch the battle unfold over four hours. When the American troops finally scaled the walls of the fortress and raised the U.S. flag, the *San Patricios* were all hanged simultaneously.

Just before the mass execution, the army surgeon reported to Colonel William Harney, an officer infamous for his brutality, that one of the *San Patricios*, Francis O'Connor, had lost both legs in the fighting. The doctor asked what should be done with the man. Harney yelled: "Bring the damned son of a bitch out! My order was to hang thirty, and by God I'll do it." The Mexican government, which erected a monument to the *San Patricios,* described the executions as "improper in a civilized age, and [ironic] for a people who aspire to the title of illustrious and humane."

**THE TREATY OF GUADALUPE HIDALGO** After the fall of Mexico City, Santa Anna resigned and fled the country. The Mexican government was left in turmoil. Peace talks began on January 2, 1848, at the village of Guadalupe Hidalgo, just outside the capital, but dragged on for weeks, in part because different men claimed to have authority to speak for the Mexican government.

When the **Treaty of Guadalupe Hidalgo** was signed on February 2, a humiliated Mexico was forced to transfer the territories that would eventually become the states of Texas, California, Arizona, New Mexico—and significant parts of what would become Colorado, Utah, Wyoming and Nevada. This represented more than half the entire nation of Mexico.

With the addition of 30,000 square miles in southern Arizona and New Mexico through the Gadsden Purchase of 1853, these annexations rounded out the continental United States, doubled its size, and provided routes for eventual transcontinental rail lines. In return for what Polk called "an immense empire" that encompassed more than a half million square miles, the United States agreed to pay $15 million.

The Senate ratified the treaty ending the war on March 10, 1848. By the end of July, the last remaining U.S. soldiers had left Mexico. Ulysses S. Grant, who fought in the conflict, later called it "one of the most unjust wars ever waged by a stronger against a weaker nation."

**THE WAR'S LEGACIES** The Mexican-American War was America's first major military intervention outside the United States and the first time that U.S. military forces had conquered and occupied another country. More than 13,000 Americans died, 11,550 of them from disease, especially measles and dysentery. The war remains the deadliest in American history in terms of the percentage who died. Out of every 1,000 soldiers in Mexico, some 110 died.

The victory also helped end America's prolonged economic depression. As the years passed, however, the Mexican-American War was increasingly seen as a shameful war of conquest directed by a president bent on territorial expansion for the sake of slavery. Even General Zachary Taylor called it an "unnecessary and senseless" war.

News of the victory thrilled American expansionists, however. John O'Sullivan, who had coined the term *manifest destiny*, shouted, "More, More, More! Why not take all of Mexico?" Treasury Secretary Robert Walker was equally giddy about the addition of California and the Oregon Country. "Asia has suddenly become our neighbour . . . inviting our steamships upon the trade of a commerce greater than all of Europe combined."

John C. Calhoun spoke for many Southerners when he opposed the idea of taking more than the northernmost Mexican territories: "We have never dreamt of incorporating into our Union any but the Caucasian race—the free white race. To incorporate [all of] Mexico would be the very first instance of the kind of incorporating an Indian race . . . I protest against such a union as that! Ours, sir, is the government of the White race. The greatest misfortunes of Spanish America are to be traced to the fatal error of placing these colored races on equality with the white race."

Calhoun won the argument. The acquisition of the northern Mexican provinces made the United States a transcontinental nation and led to a dramatic expansion of the federal government. In 1849, Congress created the Department of the Interior to supervise the distribution of land, the creation of new territories and states, and the "protection" of the Indians and their reservations. Americans now had their long coveted western empire. But what were they to do with it?

President Polk had naively assumed that the expansion of American territory to the Pacific would strengthen "the bonds of Union." He was wrong. No sooner was Texas annexed and gold discovered in California than a violent debate erupted over the extension of slavery into the territories acquired from Mexico. That debate so enflamed sectional rivalries that it let to secession and civil war.

# CHAPTER REVIEW

## SUMMARY

- **Westward Migration** In the 1830s, Americans came to believe in *manifest destiny*—that the West was divinely ordained to be part of the United States. Although populated by Native Americans and Hispanics, the West was portrayed as an empty land. But a population explosion and the lure of cheap, fertile land prompted Americans to move along the *Overland Trails*, enduring great physical hardships, to settle in Oregon (*Oregon fever*) and California. Traders and trappers were the first Americans to move into California during the 1830s. The discovery of gold there in 1848 brought a flood of people from across the world. At the same time, many Southerners also moved to the Mexican province of Texas to grow cotton, taking their slaves with them. The Mexican government, however, outlawed slavery, and in 1830 forbade further immigration. *Texians* rebelled, winning their independence in the *Texas Revolution (1835–1836)*, but statehood would not come for another decade because political leaders were determined to avoid war with Mexico over the territory and the issue of adding another slave state to the Union.

- **Mexican-American War** When the United States finally annexed Texas in 1845, Mexico was furious. The newly elected U.S. president, James K. Polk, sought to acquire California and New Mexico as well, but negotiations soon failed. When Mexican troops crossed the Rio Grande, Polk urged Congress to declare war. American forces eventually won the war, despite high casualties. In 1848, in the *Treaty of Guadalupe Hidalgo*, Mexico ceded California and New Mexico to the United States and gave up claims to disputed land north of the Rio Grande. The vast acquisition did not strengthen the Union, however. Instead, it ignited a fierce dispute over the role of slavery in the new territories.

## CHRONOLOGY

| | |
|---|---|
| 1821 | Mexico gains independence from Spain |
| 1836 | Americans are defeated at the Alamo |
| 1841 | John Tyler becomes president |
| 1842 | Americans and British agree to the Webster-Ashburton Treaty |
| 1845 | United States annexes Texas |
| 1846 | Mexican-American War begins |
| 1848 | Treaty of Guadalupe Hidalgo ends the Mexican-American War |
| 1853 | With the Gadsden Purchase, the United States acquires an additional 30,000 square miles from Mexico needed for a transcontinental railroad route |

# KEY TERMS

manifest destiny p. 504

Overland Trails p. 506

Oregon fever p. 508

Texas Revolution (1835–1836) p. 520

Treaty of Guadalupe Hidalgo (1848) p. 535

 INQUIZITIVE

Go to InQuizitive to see what you've learned—and learn what you've missed—with personalized feedback along the way.

# 14 The Gathering Storm

## 1848–1860

**"Bleeding Kansas" (1856)** This engraving depicts the sack of Lawrence, Kansas, in May 1856 by pro-slavery "border ruffians." The violence sparked by these slave-holding Missourians proved to be a foreboding sign of the destruction that would engulf the nation in the coming decade.

A t midcentury, political storm clouds were forming over the fate of slavery. The United States, as Henry Clay said, was an "unhappy country" torn by the "uproar, confusion, and menace" caused by the deepening agony of slavery.

Without intending to, the United States had developed two different societies, one in the North and the other in the South. Those regions increasingly disagreed over the nation's future. In 1833, Andrew Jackson had predicted that pro-slavery militants ("fire-eaters") like John C. Calhoun "would do any act to destroy this union and form a southern confederacy bounded, north, by the Potomac River." By 1848, Jackson's prediction was coming true.

At midcentury, the sectional tensions over slavery generated constant political conflict. The tortuous Compromise of 1850 provided a short-term resolution, but new controversies such as the fate of slavery in the Kansas Territory, the creation of the anti-slavery Republican party, and the growing militancy of abolitionists led more and more people to decide that the United States, as Abraham Lincoln stressed, could not continue to be "half slave and half free." The result was first the secession of eleven southern states and then a bloody civil war to force them back into the Union. In the process, the "peculiar institution" of slavery ended.

## SLAVERY IN THE TERRITORIES

**THE WILMOT PROVISO** On August 8, 1846, soon after the Mexican-American War erupted, David Wilmot, a first-term Democratic congressman from Pennsylvania, rose in the House of Representatives to endorse the annexation of Texas as a slave state. Yet he added that if any *new* territory should be acquired as a result of war with Mexico, "God forbid" that slavery would be allowed there. He proposed a bill ("proviso") doing just that.

## *focus questions*

**1.** How did the federal government try to resolve the issue of slavery in the western territories during the 1850s?

**2.** Analyze the appeal of the Republican party to northern voters; how did it lead to Abraham Lincoln's victory in the 1860 presidential contest?

**3.** Why did seven southern states secede from the Union shortly after Lincoln's election in 1860?

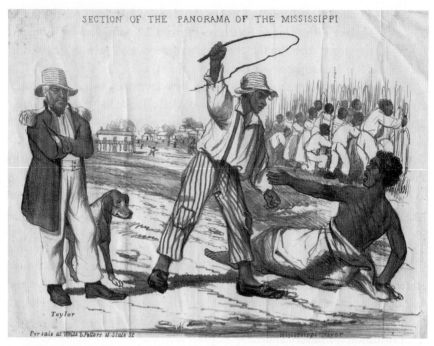

**The Wilmot Proviso** President Zachary Taylor would refuse to veto the proviso, even though he was a slave owner. This political cartoon, "Old Zack at Home," highlights his seeming hypocrisy.

President James K. Polk dismissed the **Wilmot Proviso** as a "mischievous and foolish amendment." The House approved it, but the Senate balked. When Congress reconvened in December 1846, Polk convinced Wilmot to withhold his amendment. By then, however, others were ready to take up the cause. In one form or another, Wilmot's idea would frame the debate over the westward expansion of slavery for the next fifteen years.

**POPULAR SOVEREIGNTY** Democrat Lewis Cass, the territorial governor of Michigan, tried to remove the controversy over slavery from national politics by proposing that voters in each *territory* be given the right to "regulate their own internal concerns in their own way," like the citizens of a state.

**Popular sovereignty**, as Cass's idea was called, appealed to many eager to protect states' rights because it seemed the most democratic solution to the debate over slavery. Its moral defects, however, were obvious. It did not allow African Americans to vote on their fate, and it allowed whites to strip blacks of the most basic human right: freedom.

When President Polk reaffirmed his pledge to serve only one term, Cass won the Democratic presidential nomination in 1848. But the party refused to endorse Cass's popular sovereignty plan. Instead, it claimed that Congress could not interfere with slavery in the states or territories.

The Whigs again passed over their leader, Henry Clay (three times a losing presidential nominee), and chose General Zachary Taylor, a hero of the Mexican-American War. Taylor owned a Louisiana plantation with 145 slaves, yet he opposed the extension of slavery into new western territories.

Taylor was a reluctant candidate. He had no political experience, claimed no party affiliation, and had never voted in a presidential election. No "sane person," he told his brother, would want to be president. In the end, however, he agreed to campaign "more from a sense of duty than from inclination."

**THE FREE-SOIL MOVEMENT**  Some Americans who worried about the evils of slavery but did not endorse abolition supported banning slavery from the western territories. As a result, "free soil" in the new territories became the rallying cry for the Free-Soil party, a new political organization focused solely on stopping the spread of slavery.

The **Free-Soil party** attracted northern Democrats, anti-slavery Whigs, and members of the abolitionist Liberty party. In 1848, Free-Soilers nominated former president Martin Van Buren as their candidate. Their campaign slogan shouted, "Free Soil, Free Speech, Free Labor, and Free Men."

In the election, the Free-Soilers split the Democratic vote enough to throw New York to Zachary Taylor; they split the Whig vote enough to give Ohio to Democrat Lewis Cass. Nationwide, however, Van Buren's 291,000 votes lagged well behind the 1,361,000 for Taylor and 1,222,000 for Cass. Taylor won the presidency with 163 to 127 electoral votes.

**THE CALIFORNIA GOLD RUSH**  Meanwhile, a new issue had emerged to complicate the debate over territorial expansion and slavery. On January 24, 1848, a group of workers building a sawmill discovered gold nuggets on the property of John A. Sutter, along the south fork of the American River in the Mexican province of California. Nine days later, California would be identified as the "great prize" transferred to the United States through the treaty ending the Mexican-American War.

News of the gold strike spread like wildfire, especially after President Polk told Congress that there was an "extraordinary abundance of gold." Within a year, nearly 100,000 Americans had set off for California. By 1854, the number would top 300,000, making it the greatest mass migration in American history to that point. The "forty-niners" included people from every social class and

**Gold miners** Chinese immigrants and white settlers mine for gold in the Auburn Ravine of California in 1856.

every state and territory, as well as local Indians and slaves brought by their owners. Thousands more came from Central and South America, Canada, Australia, Asia, and Europe. "Never was there such a gold-thirsty-race of men brought together," a Californian observed. "The principle is to get all of the wealth of the land possible in the shortest possible time, and then go *elsewhere to enjoy it.*"

Those infected with gold fever were fed by hope and fueled by greed. They quit jobs, left farms, sold businesses and belongings, borrowed money, and deserted families in the frantic pursuit of instant riches. So many men ("forty-niners") left New England as part of the **California gold rush** that it would be years before the region's gender ratio evened out again.

Between 1851 and 1855, California produced almost half the world's output of gold, and its infusion into the U.S. economy led to prolonged national prosperity. In addition, it shifted the nation's focus westward, spurred the construction of transcontinental railroads and telegraph lines, and excited dreams of an American commercial empire on the Pacific Coast linked to Asia.

At the same time, the influx of Americans into California proved disastrous for Native Americans and their ancestral lands. In 1850, the new California state legislature allowed whites to force "unemployed" Indians to work for them in exchange for food and clothing. Miners pushed them out of the gold diggings; those who resisted were killed. During the early 1850s, the Indian population in California plummeted by more than 80 percent. If infectious disease did not kill them, white settlers did.

The gold rush transformed the sleepy coastal village of San Francisco into the nation's largest city west of Chicago. In just two years, San Francisco grew from 800 residents to 20,000, its spacious harbor clogged by a forest of ship masts. Half the ships that arrived in the city never left, as their crews deserted and rushed to the mining towns in search of gold.

Fast-growing Sacramento became the staging area for the northern mines. New enterprises—saloons, taverns, restaurants, laundries, general stores— emerged to serve the burgeoning population of miners. The German-Jewish immigrant Levi Strauss supplied gold prospectors with trousers made of denim sailcloth. The rugged blue jeans, sewn to stand up to the physical labor of min-ing, included copper-rivet-reinforced pockets. "Levi's" are still sold today.

California quickly became a masculine society. At one point during the height of the gold rush, men outnumbered women in San Francisco 50 to 1, while across the state, it was 8 to 1. The few women who dared to live in the camps could demand a premium for their work as cooks, laundresses, enter-tainers, and prostitutes. One published a brutally candid ad for a husband in a local newspaper: "Her age is none of your business. She is neither handsome nor a fright, yet an *old* man need *not* apply, nor any who have not a little more education than she has, and a great deal more gold, for there must be $20,000 settled on her [paid] before she will" marry.

**MINING LIFE** California miners were mostly unmarried young men of varied ethnic and cultural backgrounds, including some 20,000 Chinese. Few were interested in staying in California; they wanted to strike it rich and return home. Mining camps sprang up like mushrooms and disappeared almost as rapidly. As soon as rumors of a new strike surfaced, miners converged on the area; when no more gold could be found, they moved on.

The mining camps and shantytowns were dirty, lawless, and dangerous places. In Calaveras County, there were fourteen murders in a single week. Vigilante justice prevailed; one newcomer reported that "in the short space of twenty-four days, we have had murders, fearful accidents, bloody deaths, a mob, whippings, a hanging, an attempt at suicide, and a fatal duel." Murderers who were caught were often lynched on the spot. Within six months of arriv-ing in California in 1849, one gold seeker in every five was dead. The gold-fields and mining towns were so dangerous that insurance companies refused to provide coverage. Suicides were common, and disease was rampant.

In the camps, whites often looked with disdain upon the Hawaiians, His-panics, African Americans, and Chinese, who were usually employed as wage laborers to help in the panning process, separating gold from sand and gravel. Whites, however, focused their contempt on the Indians; it was not a crime to kill Indians or to work them to death.

## California Statehood

California was important for reasons other than gold. New president Zachary Taylor decided in 1849 to use California's request for statehood to end the stalemate in Congress over slavery. Why not make California and New Mexico free states immediately, he argued, and bypass the volatile issue of slavery?

Californians, however, were ahead of him. By December 1849, without consulting Congress, they had put a free-state (no slavery) government into operation. New Mexico responded more slowly, but by 1850 Americans there had also adopted a free-state constitution.

**THE COMPROMISE OF 1850** On December 4, 1849, President Taylor endorsed immediate statehood for California and urged Congress to avoid injecting slavery into the issue. The new Congress, however, was in no mood for simple solutions.

Jefferson Davis, Taylor's son-in-law, dismissed the president's plan as being anti-southern, and irate Southerners threatened to leave the Union if Taylor brought California and New Mexico in as free states. "I avow before this House and country, and in the presence of the living God," shouted Robert Toombs, a Georgia congressman, "that if by your legislation you seek to drive us [slave-holders] from the territories of California and New Mexico . . . and to abolish slavery in this District [of Columbia] . . . *I am for disunion.*"

Americans began to worry for the fate of the republic. "Madness rules the hour," wrote Philip Hone, a New York Whig, in his diary. "Faction, personal recrimination, and denunciation prevail, and men for the first time in our history do not hesitate openly to threaten a dissolution of the Union."

As the controversy over the future of slavery unfolded, an all-star cast of outsized personalities with swollen egos resolved to find a way to preserve the Union. The "lions" of the Senate—Henry Clay, John C. Calhoun, and Daniel Webster (all of whom would die within two years)—took center stage, with William H. Seward, Stephen A. Douglas, and Jefferson Davis in supporting roles.

Together, they staged one of the great dramas of American politics: the **Compromise of 1850**, a ten-month-long debate over a series of resolutions intended to end the crisis between North and South.

**IN SEARCH OF COMPROMISE** With southern extremists threatening secession, congressional leaders again turned to an aging Henry Clay. As Abraham Lincoln acknowledged, Clay was "regarded by all, as *the* man for the crisis." No man had amassed a more distinguished political career. Clay had

**Clay's compromise (1850)**  Warning against an impending sectional conflict, Henry Clay outlines his plan for "compromise and harmony" on the Senate floor.

gained every position he had sought except the presidency: senator, congressman, Speaker of the House, secretary of state.

Now, as his career was winding down, the seventy-two-year-old Clay hoped to save the Union by presenting his own plan to end another sectional crisis. On December 3, 1849, as the Thirty-First Congress assembled, Clay strode into the Senate to waves of applause and kisses from female followers. He asked to be relieved of all committee responsibilities so that he could focus on the crisis. Unless some compromise could be found, the slaveholding Clay warned, a "furious" civil war would fracture the Union.

Southerners mobilized to oppose President Taylor's proposal to admit California as a free state, for doing so would tip the political balance against slavery, with sixteen free states to fifteen slave states. The slaveholding states would become a permanent minority. As Jefferson Davis argued, the South could not allow that to happen.

On January 29, 1850, having gained the wholehearted support of Daniel Webster, the senior senator from Massachusetts whom he had known for thirty-six years, Henry Clay presented his "amicable" plan for "compromise and harmony."

Using all his wit, charm, and passion, Clay pleaded with the Senate to pass eight resolutions, six of which were paired as compromises between North and South, and all of which were designed to settle the "controversy between the free and slave states, growing out of the subject of slavery." Clay proposed to (1) admit California as a free state; (2) let the residents of the territories of New Mexico and Utah decide whether to allow slavery; (3) deny Texas its claim to much of New Mexico; (4) compensate Texas by having the federal government pay the pre-annexation Texas debts; (5) retain slavery in the District of Columbia but abolish the sale of slaves there; (6) adopt a more effective federal law designed to recapture fugitive slaves; and (7) deny Congress the authority to interfere with the interstate slave trade. His complex cluster of proposals, called the Omnibus bill, became in substance the Compromise of 1850, but only after seven months of negotiations punctuated by the greatest debate in congressional history.

**THE GREAT DEBATE**  On March 4, a feeble Senator John C. Calhoun of South Carolina, desperately ill with tuberculosis, arrived in the Senate chamber. The uncompromising defender of slavery was so sick that a colleague had to read his defiant rejection of Clay's compromise.

The South, Calhoun explained, needed Congress to protect the rights of slave owners to take their "property" into the new territories. Otherwise, he warned, the "cords which bind" the Union would be severed. If California were admitted as a free state, the South could no longer "remain honorably and safely in the Union" because the free states would increasingly outnumber the slave states in Congress and in the Electoral College. Calhoun asserted that the only solution to the growing sectional divide was for the North to allow slavery in California and the other western territories. Otherwise, he threatened, the southern states would leave the Union (secede) and form their own national government.

Three days later, on March 7, Calhoun hobbled into the Senate to hear the "golden-throated" Daniel Webster speak. Widely recognized as the most eloquent orator in an age devoted to oratory, Webster, broad-shouldered and deep-chested, was resplendent in an indigo blue coat with shiny brass buttons.

"I wish to speak today," Webster began, "not as a Massachusetts man, not as a Northern man, but as an American . . . I speak today for the preservation of the Union." He blamed both Northerners and Southerners for the crisis but acknowledged that both regions had legitimate grievances: The South understandably objected to the excesses of "infernal fanatics and abolitionists" in the

North, and the North resented southern efforts to expand slavery into the new western territories.

With respect to escaped slaves, Webster reminded everyone that the Constitution of 1787 already required that every state cooperate in the recapture of runaways. He then shocked his fellow New Englanders and outraged abolitionists by declaring that "the South, in my judgment, is right, and the North is wrong." Fugitive slaves must be returned to their owners.

Webster, however, dismissed the notion of secession. Turning his withering gaze upon Calhoun, he said that he had no patience with men for whom "everything is absolute," who lack the capacity for compromise. Southern threats to leave the Union would bring civil war. "Secession! Peaceable secession! Sir, your eyes and mine are never destined to see that miracle." Instead of looking into such "caverns of darkness," let "men enjoy the fresh air of liberty and union. Let them look to a more hopeful future." For almost four hours, Webster, bathed in sweat, pleaded with his colleagues to rise above absolutism and become compromising statesmen.

Webster's evenhanded speech angered extremists on both sides. No sooner had he finished than someone in the overflowing gallery yelled, "Traitor!" Calhoun then stood to assert that the Union could indeed "be broken. Great moral causes will break it." Northern abolitionists savaged Webster for calling them fanatics and for his defense of the fugitive slave law.

On March 11, William Seward, the former New York governor who was now a first-year Whig senator, gave a provocative three-hour speech in which he declared that *any* compromise with slavery was "radically wrong and essentially vicious." There was, he insisted, "a *higher law* than the Constitution," and it demanded the abolition of slavery through acts of civil disobedience. Seward encouraged his fellow New Yorkers to defy the federal fugitive slave law by extending a "cordial welcome" to escaped slaves and defending them from efforts to return them south. The southern supporters of slavery, he concluded, must give way to the inevitable "progress of emancipation."

Seward's speech outraged Southerners, who repudiated his implication that the godly abolitionists were somehow above the law. Clay dismissed Seward's "wild, reckless, and abominable theories," and a Georgia newspaper said that Seward was a lunatic who should be ushered out of the Capitol in a straitjacket. The senator from New York, however, was unapologetic. He had sought to speak for the enslaved as well as all humankind.

**COMPROMISE EFFORTS**   For his part, Henry Clay confessed that he was "angry at everybody." The extremists were postponing a vote on his compromise proposal. He got little help from President Taylor, who continued to focus solely on the admission of California as a new state. In a letter to his son, Clay reported that the "Administration, the Abolitionists, the Ultra Southern men, and the timid Whigs of the North are all combined against" his plan. He had given his all for the Great Compromise, but despite his herculean efforts, the Omnibus Bill was dead in the water.

On July 4, 1850, Congress celebrated Independence Day by gathering beneath a broiling summer sun at the base of the unfinished Washington Monument. President Taylor suffered a mild sunstroke while listening to three hours of patriotic speeches. At the White House, he tried to recover by gorging himself on iced milk, cherries, and raw vegetables. That night, he developed a violent stomach disorder. Five days later, he prayed and asked for water. "I am about to die," he said. "I expect the summons soon. I have endeavored to discharge all of my duties faithfully." A few minutes later, he died.

Taylor's shocking death bolstered the chances of a compromise in Congress because his successor, Vice President Millard Fillmore, supported Clay's proposals. It was a striking reversal: Taylor, the Louisiana slaveholder, had been ready to make war on his native South to save the Union; Fillmore, whom Southerners thought opposed slavery, was ready to make peace. Fillmore asserted his control by asking the entire Taylor-appointed cabinet to resign. He then named Daniel Webster as secretary of state, signaling that he joined Webster in supporting compromise.

Fillmore benefited from the support of Illinois senator Stephen A. Douglas, a rising star in the Democratic party, the youngest man in the Senate, and a friend of the South. Pragmatic, brash, and brilliant, Douglas, the clever "Little Giant" (he stood just five feet four), suggested that the best way to salvage Clay's "comprehensive scheme" was to break it into separate proposals and vote on them one at a time. President Fillmore endorsed the idea.

The plan worked miraculously, in part because John C. Calhoun had died and was no longer in the Senate to obstruct efforts at conciliation. Each component of Clay's plan passed in the Senate and the House, several of them by the narrowest of margins. (Only five senators voted for all the items of the compromise.)

On September 7, 1850, when it became apparent that the Compromise of 1850 would become law, senators and congressmen burst into tears. That night, celebrants in the streets of Washington lit bonfires, rang church bells, chanted "the Union is saved," and applauded as soldiers fired cannons to salute the compromise. "The long agony is over," sighed President Fillmore.

In its final version, the Compromise of 1850 included the following elements: (1) California entered the Union as a free state, ending forever the old balance of free and slave states; (2) the Texas–New Mexico Act made New Mexico a separate territory and set the Texas state boundary at its present location. In return for relinquishing its claims to much of New Mexico, Texas received $10 million, which secured payment of the state's debt; (3) the Utah Act set up the Utah Territory and gave the territorial legislature authority over "all rightful subjects of legislation," including slavery; (4) a Fugitive Slave Act required the federal government and northern states to help capture and return runaway slaves to the South; and (5) as a gesture to anti-slavery groups, the public sale of slaves (but not slavery itself) was abolished in the District of Columbia.

As President Fillmore signed the last of the measures into law, he claimed that they represented a "final settlement" to the sectional tensions over slavery. Many Americans agreed. "Harmony is secured. Patriots rejoice!" trumpeted one newspaper. Henry Clay predicted that his solution would "pacify, tranquilize, and harmonize the country."

The Compromise of 1850, however, was not so much an example of warring people making concessions as it was a temporary and imperfect truce over the future of slavery. Extremists on both sides vowed to defy it. As Salmon P. Chase, an Ohio Free-Soiler, stressed, "the question of slavery in the territories has been avoided. It has not been settled." In the Lower South, pro-slavery zealots dismissed Clay's compromise as a surrender to the fanatical abolitionists. John Quitman of Mississippi announced that the only option for the South was secession, while northern abolitionists called the compromise an "enactment of hell" because of the fugitive slave provision.

In the end, the Compromise of 1850 only postponed secession and civil war for ten years. Soon, aspects of the compromise would reignite sectional tensions.

**THE FUGITIVE SLAVE ACT** Within two months of the passage of the Compromise of 1850, the squabbling between North and South resumed.

The **Fugitive Slave Act** was the most controversial element of the Compromise of 1850. It did more than strengthen the hand of slave catchers; it sought to recover slaves who had already escaped months or years before and considered themselves safe. It also inspired unscrupulous slave traders to kidnap free blacks in northern free states, claiming that they were runaway slaves. The law denied fugitives a jury trial and forced citizens to help locate and capture runaways.

Abolitionists fumed. "This filthy enactment was made in the nineteenth century, by people who could read and write," Ralph Waldo Emerson marveled in his diary. He urged people to break the new law "on the earliest occasion."

The mere existence of the Fugitive Slave Act was intolerable to many northern abolitionists, several of whom advocated violence. "The only way to make the Fugitive Slave Law a dead letter," Frederick Douglass threatened, "is to make half-a-dozen or more dead kidnappers." In Springfield, Massachusetts, fiery abolitionist John Brown formed an armed band of African Americans, called the League of Gileadites, to attack slave catchers. Such efforts led Horace Greeley, a prominent New York newspaper editor, to write that the Fugitive Slave Act was "a very bad investment for slaveholders" because it was creating such a backlash against slavery throughout the northern states.

*UNCLE TOM'S CABIN* During the 1850s, anti-slavery advocates gained a powerful new weapon in the form of Harriet Beecher Stowe's best-selling novel, *Uncle Tom's Cabin; or Life among the Lowly* (1852). Stowe, the daughter and sister of ministers, epitomized the deep religious underpinnings of the abolitionist movement. While raising six children in Cincinnati, Ohio, during the 1830s and 1840s, she helped runaway slaves who had crossed the Ohio River from Kentucky.

Like many anti-slavery activists, Stowe despised the Fugitive Slave Act. In the spring of 1850, having moved to Maine, she began writing *Uncle Tom's Cabin* "with her *heart's blood.*" She intended the book to energize the abolitionist movement. "The time has come," she said, "when even a woman or a child who can speak a word for freedom and humanity is bound to speak."

*Uncle Tom's Cabin* was a smashing success. Within two days, the first printing had sold out, and by the end of its first year, it had sold 300,000 copies in the United States and more than a million in Great Britain. Soon there was a children's version and a traveling theater production. By 1855, it was called "the most popular novel of our day."

*Uncle Tom's Cabin* depicts improbable saints and sinners, crude stereotypes, impossibly virtuous black victims, and melodramatic escapes involving fugitive slaves. The persecuted Uncle Tom, whose gentleness and generosity grow even as he is sold

135,000 SETS, 270,000 VOLUMES SOLD.

**UNCLE TOM'S CABIN**

**FOR SALE HERE.**

AN EDITION FOR THE MILLION, COMPLETE IN 1 Vol. PRICE 37 1-2 CENTS.
" " IN GERMAN. IN 1 Vol. PRICE 50 CENTS.
" " IN 2 Vols. CLOTH, 6 PLATES, PRICE $1.50.
SUPERB ILLUSTRATED EDITION. IN 1 Vol. WITH 153 ENGRAVINGS,
PRICES FROM $2.50 TO $5.00.

**The Greatest Book of the Age.**

**"The Greatest Book of the Age"** *Uncle Tom's Cabin*, as this advertisement indicated, was an influential best seller.

as a slave and taken south; the villainous white planter Simon Legree, who torments and tortures Tom before ordering his death; the angelic Little Eva, a white girl who dies after befriending Tom; and the beautiful but desperate Eliza, who escapes from slave catchers by carrying her baby to freedom across the icy Ohio River—all became stock characters in American folklore.

The novel reveals how the brutal realities of slavery harmed everyone associated with it. It ends with Stowe predicting that Almighty God's wrath would destroy America if slavery were not abolished.

Abolitionist leader Frederick Douglass said that *Uncle Tom's Cabin* was like "a flash" that lit "a million camp fires in front of the embattled host of slavery." The book incensed slaveholders, one of whom called Stowe that "wretch in petticoats." Another mailed her a parcel containing the severed ear of a disobedient slave.

**THE ELECTION OF 1852** In 1852, it took the Democrats forty-nine ballots before they chose Franklin Pierce of New Hampshire as their presidential candidate. When Pierce heard the results, he was stunned: "You are looking at the most surprised man who ever lived!" When his wife Jane learned of the nomination, she fainted. Their concerns were well-founded, for Pierce had few presidential qualities.

The Democrats' platform endorsed the Compromise of 1850, including enforcement of the Fugitive Slave Act. For their part, the Whigs repudiated Millard Fillmore, who had faithfully supported the Compromise of 1850, and chose General Winfield Scott, another hero of the Mexican-American War.

At six feet five and 300 pounds, Scott was a physically imposing leader and accomplished general. Yet he proved to be an inept campaigner—so conceited, short-tempered, and arrogant that he earned the nickname "Old Fuss and Feathers." He carried only the states of Tennessee, Kentucky, Massachusetts, and Vermont.

The Whigs, now without their greatest leaders, Henry Clay and Daniel Webster, had lost virtually all their support in the Lower South. Pierce overwhelmed Scott in the electoral college, 254 to 42, although the popular vote was close: 1.6 million to 1.4 million.

The forty-eight-year-old Pierce, a mediocre congressman and senator who had served as a general in the Mexican-American War, was, like James K. Polk, touted as another Andrew Jackson. Pierce promoted western expansion and the conversion of more territories into states, even if it meant adding more slave states to the Union. However, he also acknowledged that the Compromise of 1850 had defused a "perilous crisis." He urged North and South to avoid aggravating the other.

Pierce was burdened by the recent death of his eleven-year-old son, Benjamin. The president-elect and his wife had witnessed their son's death in a train accident just days before the inaugural ceremony. Benjamin was the third son that the Pierces had lost. Still in mourning, Jane Pierce refused to attend her husband's swearing in; she thereafter lived in seclusion, writing letters to her dead children, cursing politics, and blaming her husband for her troubles.

Pierce was an intelligent man capable of eloquent speechmaking, but he had tragic flaws and private demons. Blinded by a desire to be liked and cursed with raging ambition, he was a timid, indecisive leader who was often drunk. (He would die in 1869 of alcoholism.)

As president, Pierce sought—and failed—to acquire Cuba as a slave state and proved unable to unite the warring factions of his party. By the end of his first year in office, Democratic leaders had decided that he was a failure. James W. Forney, a political friend, confessed that the presidency "overshadows him [Pierce]. He is crushed by its great duties and seeks refuge in [alcohol]." Pierce was labeled a "doughface" by his opponents, meaning a Northern man with Southern principles who hated abolitionists for causing the tensions over slavery. His closest friend in the cabinet was Secretary of War Jefferson Davis, the future president of the Confederacy. Friendships such as this one led Harriet Beecher Stowe to call Pierce an "arch-traitor."

**Stephen A. Douglas, ca. 1852**
The Illinois Democratic senator authored the Kansas-Nebraska Act.

### KANSAS-NEBRASKA CRISIS

During the mid–nineteenth century, Americans discovered the vast markets of Asia. As trade with China and Japan grew, merchants and manufacturers called for a transcontinental railroad connecting the Eastern Seaboard with the Pacific coast to facilitate both the flow of commerce with Asia and the settlement of the western territories. Those promoting the railroad did not realize that the issue would renew sectional rivalries and reignite the debate over the westward extension of slavery.

In 1852 and 1853, Congress considered several proposals for a transcontinental rail line. Secretary of War Jefferson Davis of Mississippi favored a southern route across the territories acquired from Mexico. Senator Stephen A. Douglas of Illinois insisted that Chicago be the Midwest hub for the new rail line and urged Congress to pass the **Kansas-Nebraska Act** so that the territory west of Missouri and Iowa could be settled.

To win the support of southern legislators, Douglas championed popular sovereignty, whereby voters in each new territory would decide whether to allow slavery. It was a clever way to get around the 1820 Missouri Compromise, which banned slavery north of the 36th parallel, where Kansas and Nebraska were located.

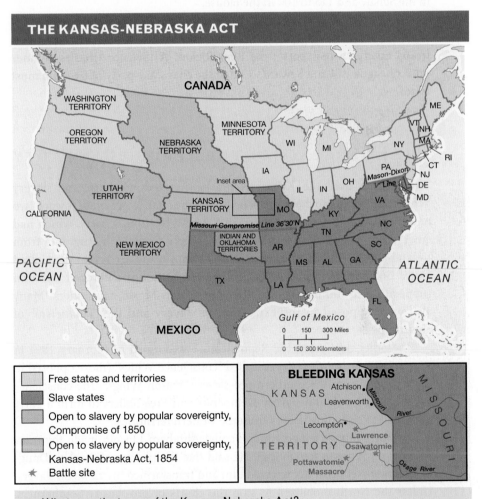

## THE KANSAS-NEBRASKA ACT

Free states and territories
Slave states
Open to slavery by popular sovereignty, Compromise of 1850
Open to slavery by popular sovereignty, Kansas-Nebraska Act, 1854
✳ Battle site

**BLEEDING KANSAS**

- What were the terms of the Kansas-Nebraska Act?
- How did it lead to the creation of the Republican party?
- What happened at Pottawatomie and Osawatomie?

Southerners demanded more, however, and Douglas complied, in part because he would make a fortune if the bill passed; he owned property needed by a transcontinental railroad. He supported the South in recommending the formal repeal of the Missouri Compromise and the creation of *two* territorial governments rather than one: Kansas, west of Missouri, and Nebraska, west of Iowa and Minnesota. This meant that millions of fertile acres would be opened to slaveholders.

In May 1854, Douglas convinced both Democrats and southern Whigs to pass the Kansas-Nebraska Act. The measure was approved by a vote of 37 to 14 in the Senate and 113 to 100 in the House.

The anti-slavery faction in Congress, mostly Whigs, had been crushed, and the national Whig party essentially died with them. Out of its ashes would emerge a new party: the Republicans. As Senator Charles Sumner told colleague William Seward, "Out of the chaos, the party of freedom must arise."

## THE EMERGENCE OF THE REPUBLICAN PARTY

The dispute over the Kansas-Nebraska Act led northern anti-slavery Whigs and some northern anti-slavery Democrats to gravitate toward two new parties. One was the American ("Know-Nothing") party, which had emerged in opposition to the surge of mostly Catholic immigrants from Ireland and Germany, nearly 3 million of whom had arrived in the United States between 1845 and 1854. The Know-Nothings embraced *nativism* (opposition to immigrants) by denying citizenship to newcomers. Many also were opposed to the expansion of slavery and the "fanaticism" of abolitionists.

The other new party, the Republicans, was formed in February 1854 in Ripon, Wisconsin, when the so-called "conscience Whigs" (those opposed to slavery) split from the southern pro-slavery "cotton Whigs." The conscience Whigs joined with anti-slavery Democrats and Free-Soilers to form a party dedicated to excluding slavery from the western territories.

A young Illinois congressman named Abraham Lincoln made the transition from Whig to Republican. He said that the passage of Stephen Douglas's Kansas-Nebraska Act angered him and transformed his views on slavery. Unless the North mobilized to stop the efforts of pro-slavery Southerners, Lincoln believed, the future of the Union was endangered. From that moment, he focused on reversing the Kansas-Nebraska Act and preventing the extension of slavery into new territories.

"**BLEEDING KANSAS**" The passage of the Kansas-Nebraska Act soon placed Kansas at the center of the increasingly violent debate over slavery. While Nebraska would become a free state, Kansas was up for grabs. According to the Kansas-Nebraska Act, the residents of the Kansas Territory were "perfectly free to form and regulate their domestic institutions [slavery] in their own way."

The law, however, said nothing about *when* Kansans could decide about slavery, so each side tried to gain political control of the vast territory. "Come on then, Gentlemen of the Slave States," New York senator William Seward taunted. "We will engage in competition for the virgin soil of Kansas, and God give the victory to the side which is stronger in numbers as it is in the right." South Carolina congressman Preston Brooks accepted the challenge, announcing that "the fate of the South is to be decided in Kansas."

Groups for and against slavery recruited armed emigrants to move to Kansas. When Kansas's first federal governor arrived in 1854, he reported to President Pierce that Southerners were arriving with a "dogged determination to force slavery into this Territory" in advance of the election of a territorial legislature in March 1855.

On Election Day, thousands of heavily armed border ruffians from Missouri traveled to Kansas, illegally elected pro-slavery legislators, and vowed to kill every "God-damned abolitionist in the Territory," as militia leader David Atchison urged. As soon as it convened, the territorial legislature expelled its few anti-slavery members and declared that the territory would be open to slavery. The governor then rushed to Washington, D.C., to plead with Pierce to intervene with federal troops. Pierce's spineless solution was to replace the governor with a man who would support the pro-slavery faction.

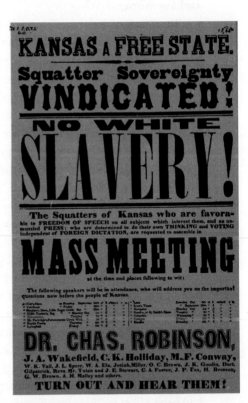

**Kansas a Free State** This broadside advertises a series of mass meetings in Kansas in support of the free-state cause, based on the principle of "squatter" or popular sovereignty, letting the residents decide the issue of slavery.

Outraged free-state advocates in Kansas, now a majority, spurned this "bogus" pro-slavery government and elected their own delegates to a constitutional convention that met in Topeka in 1855. There they applied for statehood and drafted a state constitution that excluded slavery. By 1856, a free-state "governor" and "legislature" were operating in Topeka. There were now two competing governments claiming to rule the Kansas Territory. Soon there was a territorial civil war, which journalists called "**Bleeding Kansas.**"

In May 1856, a pro-slavery force of more than 500 Missourians, Alabamans, and South Carolinians invaded the free-state town of Lawrence, Kansas, just twenty-five miles from the Missouri border. The mob rampaged through the town, destroying the newspaper printing presses, burning homes, and ransacking shops.

The "Sack of Lawrence" ignited the passions of abolitionist John Brown. The son of fervent Ohio Calvinists who taught their children that life was a crusade against sin, Brown believed that Christians must "break the jaws of the wicked" and that the wickedest Americans were those who owned and traded slaves. Upon meeting Brown, many declared him crazy; those who supported his efforts thought he was a saint. He was some of both.

By the mid-1850s, the fifty-five-year-old Brown had left his home in Springfield, Massachusetts, to become a holy warrior against slavery. In his view, blacks deserved liberty and full social equality. A newspaper reporter said that Brown was a "strange" and "iron-willed" old man with a "fiery nature and a cold temper, and a cool head—a volcano beneath a covering of snow."

Two days after the attack on Lawrence, Brown led four of his sons and a son-in-law to Pottawatomie, Kansas, a pro-slavery settlement near the Missouri border. On the night of May 24, the group dragged five men from their houses and hacked them to death with swords. "God is my judge," Brown told one of his sons. "We were justified under the circumstances." Without "the shedding of blood," he added, "there is no remission of sins."

The Pottawatomie Massacre launched a brutal guerrilla war in the Kansas Territory. On August 30, pro-slavery Missourians raided a free-state settlement at Osawatomie. They looted and burned houses and shot Frederick Brown, John's son, through the heart. By the end of 1856, about 200 settlers had been killed in "Bleeding Kansas."

**SENATE BLOODSHED** On May 22, 1856, an ugly incident in the U.S. Senate shocked the nation. Two days before, Republican senator Charles Sumner of Massachusetts, a passionate abolitionist, had delivered a scalding speech in which he showered slave owners with insults and charged them with unleashing vigilantes and assassins in Kansas. His most savage attack was directed at

Andrew Pickens Butler, an elderly senator from South Carolina. Butler, Sumner charged, was a fumbling old man who had "chosen a mistress . . . who . . . though polluted in the sight of the world, is chaste [pure] in his sight—I mean the harlot [prostitute], Slavery."

Sumner's speech enraged Butler's cousin, South Carolina congressman Preston S. Brooks. On May 22, Brooks confronted Sumner as he sat at his Senate desk, shouting that Sumner had slandered Butler and the state of South Carolina. He then began beating Sumner with a gold-knobbed cane. Sumner, his head gushing blood, nearly died; he would not return to the Senate for almost four years.

Southerners celebrated Brooks as a hero. The *Richmond Enquirer* described his attack as "good in conception, better in execution, and best of all in consequences." In satisfying his rage, though, Brooks had created a martyr—"Bloodied Sumner"—for the anti-slavery cause. Sumner's brutal beating also had an unintended political effect: it drove more Northerners into the Republican party.

**SECTIONAL SQUABBLES** The violence of "Bleeding Kansas" and "Bloodied Sumner" spilled over into the 1856 presidential election. At its first national convention, the Republicans fastened on the eccentric, shameless self-promoter, John C. Frémont, who had led the conquest of Mexican California.

The Republican platform borrowed heavily from the former Whigs. It endorsed federal funding for a transcontinental railroad and other transportation improvements. It denounced the repeal of the Missouri Compromise, the Democratic party's policy of territorial expansion, and the "barbarism" of slavery. For the first time, a major-party platform had taken a stand against slavery.

The southern-dominated Democrats dumped President Franklin Pierce, who remains the only elected president to be denied renomination by his party. Instead, they chose sixty-five-year-old James Buchanan of Pennsylvania, a mild-mannered former senator and secretary of state. Their platform endorsed the Kansas-Nebraska Act, called for vigorous enforcement of the Fugitive Slave Act, and stressed that Congress should not interfere with slavery in states or territories.

In the campaign of 1856, the Republicans had few southern supporters and only a handful in the border slave states of Delaware, Maryland, Kentucky, and Missouri. Frémont swept the northernmost states with 114 electoral votes, but Buchanan added five free states—Pennsylvania, New Jersey, Illinois, Indiana, and California—to his southern majority for a total of 174. The Democrats now would control the White House, the Congress, and the Supreme Court.

## THE ELECTION OF 1856

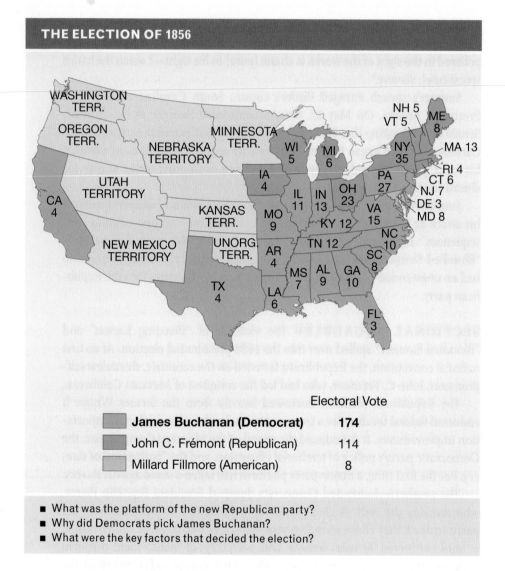

| | Electoral Vote |
|---|---|
| **James Buchanan (Democrat)** | **174** |
| John C. Frémont (Republican) | 114 |
| Millard Fillmore (American) | 8 |

- What was the platform of the new Republican party?
- Why did Democrats pick James Buchanan?
- What were the key factors that decided the election?

**PRESIDENT BUCHANAN** James Buchanan, America's first unmarried president, looked the part of a statesman. Blessed with a fine physique, he was handsome and had elegant manners. He had built an impressive political career on his commitment to states' rights and his aggressive promotion of territorial expansion. He believed that saving the Union depended upon ignoring abolitionists and making concessions to the South. Republicans charged that he lacked the backbone to stand up to the southern slaveholders who dominated the Democratic majorities in Congress.

Buchanan was one of the most experienced presidents of the nineteenth century. As it turned out, he had limited ability as a leader—and lots of bad luck. During his first six months in office, three major events caused his undoing: (1) a sharp downturn in the economy; (2) the Supreme Court decision in the *Dred Scott* case; and, (3) new troubles in strife-torn Kansas.

**THE PANIC OF 1857** By the summer of 1857, the economy was growing too fast. Too many railroads and factories were being built, and European demand for American corn and wheat was declining. The result was a financial panic triggered by the failure of the Ohio Life Insurance and Trust Company on August 24, 1857. If such a prestigious institution could close its doors, people worried, the entire economy might collapse.

Upon hearing the news, worried customers began withdrawing their money from banks. This forced the banks to call in loans, causing many businesses to go bankrupt. By the fall, tens of thousands had lost their jobs, and banks had started foreclosing on homes, farms, and businesses. Virtually every bank closed in New York City, where federal troops had to disperse angry mobs.

Buchanan and his administration refused to intervene in what came to be called the Panic of 1857. In his annual message in December 1857, he pledged that the government would do nothing to relieve the individual suffering caused by the financial panic. Most of those complaining the loudest, he maintained, were speculators who "deserved a gambler's fate."

Planters in the South, whose agricultural economy suffered the least during the panic, took great delight in the problems plaguing the northern economy. Senator James Henry Hammond of South Carolina gave a speech in early 1858 in which he told northern businessmen:

> Your slaves are white, of your own race; you are brothers of one blood. They are your equals in natural endowment of intellect, and they feel galled by your degradation. Our slaves do not vote. We give them no political power. Yours do vote, and being the majority, they are the depositories of all your political power.

Hammond suggested that the North adopt race-based slavery to prevent working-class whites from taking control of the social and political order. He added that southern slaves were happier, healthier, and better cared for than their "free" working-class counterparts in the North. Northern states needed to "enslave" their white workers so as to enjoy the social stability that slavery brought to the southern states.

**THE *DRED SCOTT* CASE**  In his inaugural address, President Buchanan asserted that the issue of slavery should be decided in the Supreme Court. Two days later, on March 6, 1857, the Court delivered a decision in the long-awaited case of ***Dred Scott v. Sandford,*** which had taken eleven years to work its way through the judicial process.

Scott, born a slave in Virginia, had been taken to St. Louis in 1830 and sold to an army surgeon, who took him to Illinois, then to the Wisconsin Territory (later Minnesota), and finally back to St. Louis in 1842. While in the Wisconsin Territory, Scott had married Harriet Robinson, and they eventually had two daughters.

In 1846, Scott, with the aid of abolitionist attorneys, filed suit in Missouri, claiming that his residence in Illinois and the Wisconsin Territory had made him free because slavery was outlawed in those areas. A Missouri jury decided in his favor, but the state Supreme Court ruled against him. When the case was appealed to the U.S. Supreme Court, the nation anxiously awaited its opinion.

Seven of the nine justices were Democrats, and five were Southerners. The vote was 7 to 2 against Scott, and five of the seven who voted against Scott were slaveholders. Seventy-nine-year-old Chief Justice Roger B. Taney

**Dred Scott**  The Supreme Court's refusal to give Scott and his family their freedom fanned the flames of the intense debate over slavery.

of Maryland, a supporter of the South and of slavery, ruled that Scott lacked legal standing because he was not a U.S. citizen and could never become one. When the Constitution was drafted in 1787, Taney claimed, African Americans were deemed "an inferior and subject race" and had been implicitly excluded from citizenship. On the issue of Scott's residency, Taney argued that the now-defunct Missouri Compromise of 1820 had deprived citizens of property by prohibiting slavery in selected states, an action "not warranted by the Constitution."

The notorious *Dred Scott* decision thus declared an act of Congress (the Missouri Compromise) unconstitutional for the first time since *Marbury v. Madison* (1803). Even more important, the decision challenged the concept of popular sovereignty. If Congress could not exclude slavery from a territory, as Taney argued, then neither could a territorial government created by an act of Congress. Suddenly, all of the West—and the North—was open to slavery.

Pro-slavery advocates loved the Court's decision. Even President Buchanan approved. Republicans and abolitionists, on the other hand, protested the *Dred Scott* decision because it nullified their anti-slavery program.

**THE LECOMPTON CONSTITUTION** Meanwhile, in the Kansas Territory, the fight over slavery continued, with both sides resorting to trickery and violence. Just before James Buchanan's inauguration, in early 1857, the pro-slavery territorial legislature scheduled a constitutional convention. The governor vetoed the measure, but the legislature overrode his veto. The governor resigned in protest, and Buchanan replaced him with Robert J. Walker.

With Buchanan's approval, Walker pledged to free-state Kansans (who made up an overwhelming majority of the residents) that the new constitution would be submitted to a fair vote. But when the pro-slavery constitutional convention, meeting at Lecompton, drafted a constitution under which Kansas would become a slave state and exclude free blacks, opponents of slavery boycotted the referendum on the constitution, enabling the pro-slavery constitution to be approved. It was then sent to Congress for endorsement.

At that point, Buchanan took a critical step. Influenced by southern advisers, he urged Congress to approve the Lecompton Constitution. A new wave of outrage swept across the northern states. Stephen A. Douglas, the most prominent midwestern Democrat, sided with anti-slavery Republicans because Buchanan's action would deny the majority of Kansas voters the right to decide the issue in a general election. Douglas told a newspaper reporter that "I made Mr. James Buchanan, and by God, sir, I will unmake him."

Meanwhile, in Kansas, a new acting governor scheduled another referendum on the proposed pro-slavery Lecompton constitution. On January 4, 1858, voters overwhelmingly rejected it, 10,226 to 138. In April 1858, Congress ordered that Kansans vote yet again. On August 2, 1858, they rejected the Lecompton constitution, 11,300 to 1,788. With that vote, Kansas cleared the way for its eventual admission as a free state.

**DOUGLAS VERSUS LINCOLN** The controversy over slavery in Kansas fractured the Democratic party. Stephen A. Douglas, one of the few remaining Democrats with support in both the North and the South, struggled to keep the party from fragmenting. First, however, he had to secure his home base in Illinois, where in 1858 he faced reelection to the Senate.

To challenge Douglas, Illinois Republicans selected a respected lawyer, Abraham Lincoln. Lincoln was born in Kentucky in 1809, the son of a farmer/carpenter so poor that he rented out his hardworking son to neighbors.

When Abraham was seven, the family moved to Indiana. Two years later, his "angel mother" Nancy died, and his father remarried. In March 1830, the Lincolns moved to Illinois. In Springfield, Lincoln worked as a farmer, rail-splitter, and surveyor. He later became an attorney and married Mary Todd, who was from a wealthy, slave-owning family in Lexington, Kentucky.

In 1834, Lincoln was elected to the Illinois legislature and served four terms as a Whig. He supported Henry Clay's leadership and Clay's promotion of the American System. "My politics are short and sweet," Lincoln said. "I am in favor of a national bank. I am in favor of the internal improvement system and a high protective tariff." He opposed the expansion of slavery, although he was no abolitionist. He did not believe that the nation should force the South to end what he referred to as "the monstrous injustice," but did insist that slavery not be expanded into new western territories.

In 1846, Lincoln won a seat in the U.S. Congress while pledging to serve only one term. After his single term, he returned to Springfield. In 1854, however, the Kansas-Nebraska Act drew him back into the political arena.

In 1856, Lincoln joined the Republican party, and two years later he emerged as the obvious choice to oppose Stephen A. Douglas. Lincoln sought to raise his profile by challenging Douglas to a series of debates across Illinois. The seven **Lincoln-Douglas debates** took place between August 21 and October 15, 1858. They attracted tens of thousands of spectators and transformed the Senate race into a battle for the future of the republic.

The two men differed as much physically as they did politically. Lincoln was tall and gangly, sinewy and craggy-featured, with a long neck, big ears, and deep-set, brooding gray eyes. Unassuming in manner and attire, he lightened his speeches with folksy humor and entertaining stories. To sympathetic observers, he conveyed an air of simplicity, sincerity, and common sense.

The short, stocky Douglas, on the other hand, was quite the dandy. He wore custom-tailored suits, traveled to the debate sites in a luxurious private railroad car, and strutted with the pugnacious air of a predestined champion. Yet he knew Lincoln was a formidable opponent, describing him as "the strong man of the party—full of wit, facts, dates, and the best stump speaker... in the West."

The basic dispute between the two candidates, Lincoln insisted, lay in Douglas's indifference to the immorality of slavery. Douglas, he said, was preoccupied with process (popular sovereignty); in contrast, Lincoln claimed to be focused on principle. "I have always hated slavery as much as any abolitionist," he stressed. The American government, he predicted, could not "endure, permanently half *slave* and half *free*. . . . It will become *all* one thing, or *all* the other."

Douglas disagreed, asking what was to keep the United States from tolerating both slavery for blacks and freedom for whites? Lincoln responded by displaying his own racism. "I am not nor ever have been," he maintained, "in favor of bringing about in any way the social and political equality of the white and black races." He did not endorse giving blacks the vote or allowing them to run for office, serve on juries, or marry whites. The white race, he concluded, must always remain in "the superior position."

At one point, Douglas accused his opponent of being "two-faced." Lincoln replied: "I leave it to my audience. If I had another face, do you think I would wear this one?"

Although Lincoln won the popular vote, Douglas was elected because he won the support of the Democratic-controlled state legislature. Lincoln's energetic campaign, however, had made him a national figure. And across the northern states, the Republicans won so many congressional seats in 1858 that they seized control of the House of Representatives.

**AN OUTNUMBERED SOUTH** In May 1858, the free state of Minnesota entered the Union; in February 1859, another nonslave territory, Oregon, gained statehood. The slave states of the South were quickly becoming a besieged minority, and their insecurity deepened.

At the same time, tensions over slavery were becoming more violent. In 1858, more than fifty members of Congress engaged in the largest brawl ever staged on the floor of the House of Representatives. The fracas ended when John "Bowie Knife" Potter of Wisconsin yanked off the hairpiece of a Mississippi congressman and shouted, "I've scalped him."

Like the scuffling congressmen, more and more Americans began to feel that compromise was impossible, and that slavery could be ended or defended only with violence. The editor of a pro-slavery Kansas newspaper wanted to kill abolitionists: "If I can't kill a man, I'll kill a woman; and if I can't kill a woman, I'll kill a child." Some Southerners were already talking of secession again. In 1858, former Alabama congressman William L. Yancey, the leader of the hot-tempered southern "fire-eaters," said that it would be easy "to precipitate the Cotton States into a revolution."

In the North, Frederick Douglass spoke for many when he claimed that the "pure slavery party" was determined to suppress abolitionists and increase its political power by launching a "murderous onslaught" against basic American rights. Yet Douglass saw in the pro-slavery party the irony of self-destruction.

"While crushing its millions [of enslaved blacks], it is also crushing itself" by leading more Northerners to embrace abolitionism.

**JOHN BROWN'S RAID** In October 1859, militant abolitionist John Brown surfaced again, this time in the East. Since the Pottawatomie Massacre in Kansas in 1856, he had kept a low profile while acquiring money and weapons from New England sympathizers, but his heartfelt commitment to abolishing slavery and promoting racial equality had intensified.

Brown was convinced that he was carrying out a divine mission. A moral absolutist who disdained compromise, he was one of the few whites willing to live among black people and die for them, and he was a brilliant propagandist for the abolitionist cause.

In 1859, Brown hatched a plan to steal federal weapons and give them to rebellious slaves in western Virginia and Maryland in the hope of triggering mass uprisings across the South. "I want to free all the negroes in this state," he said. "If the citizens interfere with me, I must burn the town and have blood."

On the cool, rainy night of October 16, 1859, Brown left a Maryland farm and crossed the Potomac River with about twenty men, including three of his sons and five African Americans. Under cover of darkness, they walked five miles to the federal rifle arsenal in Harpers Ferry, Virginia (now West Virginia), where they took the sleeping town by surprise, cut the telegraph lines, and occupied the arsenal with its 100,000 rifles. Brown then dispatched several men to kidnap prominent slave owners and sound the alarm for local slaves to join the rebellion.

Only a few heeded the call, however, and by dawn, armed townsmen had surrounded the raiders. Brown and a dozen of his men, along with eleven white hostages and two of their slaves, holed up in a firehouse. Meanwhile, hundreds of armed whites poured into Harpers, Ferry, and Lieutenant Colonel Robert E. Lee arrived with a force of U.S. Marines.

On the morning of October 18, the marines ordered the abolitionists to surrender. Brown replied that he preferred to die fighting, warning that he "would sell his life as dearly as possible." Twelve marines then broke open the barricaded doors. Lieutenant Israel Green reported that he found himself face to face with "an old man kneeling with a carbine in his hand, with a long gray beard falling away from his face." Green would have killed Brown had his sword not bent back double when he plunged it into the abolitionist's chest. He then beat Brown until he passed out.

Brown's men had killed four townspeople and one marine while wounding another dozen. Of their own force, ten were killed (including two of Brown's sons) and five were captured; another five escaped.

A week later, Brown and his accomplices were put on trial for treason, murder, and "conspiring with Negroes to produce insurrection." The jury found him guilty. At his sentencing, Brown delivered a powerful speech in which he expressed pride in his effort to "mingle my blood further with the blood of my children and with the blood of millions in this slave country whose rights are disregarded by wicked, cruel, and unjust enactments." Though Virginia may execute him, he said, the question of slavery "is still to be settled."

On December 2, 1859, some 1,500 Virginia militiamen, including a young actor named John Wilkes Booth, who would later assassinate Abraham Lincoln, assembled for Brown's execution. Just before being placed atop his coffin in a wagon to take him to the scaffold, Brown wrote a final message,

**John Brown** On his way to the gallows, Brown predicted that slavery would end only "after much bloodshed."

predicting that the "crimes of this *guilty* land will never be purged away, but with Blood."

Ralph Waldo Emerson called Brown a "saint" who had made "the gallows glorious like a cross." Frederick Douglass proclaimed him "our noblest American hero" whose commitment to ending slavery "was far greater than mine."

Caught up in a frenzy of fear after Brown's assault at Harper's Ferry, Southerners circulated wild rumors about slave rebellions. They "have declared war on us," warned Jefferson Davis. "Thank God there is no point left on which compromise can arise!"

Southern states strengthened their militia units and passed new restrictions on the movements of slaves. "We regard every man in our midst an enemy to the institutions of the South," said the *Atlanta Confederacy*, "who does not boldly declare that he believes African slavery to be a social, moral, and political blessing."

**THE DEMOCRATS DIVIDE** Amid such hysteria, the nation mobilized for another presidential election, destined to be the most fateful in its history.

In April 1860, the Democrats gathered for what would become a disastrous nominating convention in Charleston, South Carolina.

President Buchanan had chosen not to seek a second term, leaving Stephen A. Douglas as the frontrunner. Douglas's northern supporters tried to straddle the slavery issue by promising to defend the institution in the South while assuring Northerners that it would not spread to new states. Southern firebrands, however, demanded federal protection for slavery in the territories as well as the states.

When the pro-slavery advocates lost, delegates from eight southern states walked out of the convention. "We say, go your way," exclaimed a Mississippi delegate to Douglas's supporters, "and we will go ours." Alabama's William Yancey declared that "we shall go to the wall" in the effort to spread slavery into the western territories. Planter William Preston left no doubt about the reason for the split: "Slavery is our King; Slavery is our truth; Slavery is our divine right."

The Democratic Convention then disintegrated into warring factions. Douglas's supporters reassembled at the Front Street Theater in Baltimore on June 18 and nominated him for president. Southern Democrats met first in Richmond and then in Baltimore, where they adopted the pro-slavery platform that had been defeated in Charleston. They named John C. Breckinridge, vice president under Buchanan, as their candidate because he promised to ensure that Congress would protect the right of emigrants to take their slaves to the western territories. Thus, another cord binding the nation together had snapped. The fracturing of the Democratic party into northern and southern factions made a Republican victory in 1860 almost certain.

**LINCOLN'S ELECTION** The Republican convention was held in May in Chicago, where everything came together for Abraham Lincoln. When he won the nomination over New York senator William H. Seward, the resulting cheer, wrote one journalist, was "like the rush of a great wind." The party reaffirmed its opposition to the extension of slavery and, to gain broader support, endorsed a series of traditional Whig policies promoting national economic expansion: a higher protective tariff, free farms ("homesteads") on federal lands out West, and federally financed internal improvements, including a transcontinental railroad.

The presidential nominating conventions revealed that opinions tended to be more radical in the Northeast and the Lower South. Attitude followed latitude. In the border states of Maryland, Delaware, Kentucky, and Missouri, a sense of moderation aroused former Whigs to make one more try at reconciliation. Meeting in Baltimore a week before the Republicans met in Chicago, they reorganized as the Constitutional Union party and nominated John Bell of Tennessee for president. Their platform centered on a vague statement promoting "the Constitution of the Country, the Union of the States, and the Enforcement of the Laws."

The bitterly contested campaign became a choice between Lincoln and Douglas in the North, and Breckinridge and Bell in the South. (Lincoln was not even on the ballot in the South.) Douglas, the only candidate to mount a nationwide campaign, promised that he would "make war boldly against Northern abolitionists and Southern disunionists." His heroic effort did little good, however.

At midnight on November 6, Lincoln's victory was announced. He had won 39 percent of the popular vote, the smallest plurality ever, but garnered a clear majority (180 votes) in the electoral college. He carried all eighteen free states but none of the slave states.

**Abraham Lincoln** A lanky and rawboned small-town lawyer, Lincoln won the presidential election in 1860.

Douglas came in second, with 29 percent of the popular vote. (He would die seven months later.)

Lincoln's political experience was meager, his learning limited, and his popular support shallow. "Never did a President enter upon office with less means at his command," poet James Russell Lowell remarked.

Yet the unassuming prairie lawyer from Springfield, Illinois, would earn the respect of colleagues and opponents who had originally scorned him. He would become, as poet Walt Whitman wrote, "the grandest figure yet, on all the crowded canvas of the Nineteenth Century."

## THE RESPONSE IN THE SOUTH

Between November 8, 1860, when Lincoln was named president-elect, and March 4, 1861, when he was inaugurated, the United States of America disintegrated. Lincoln's election panicked Southerners who believed that the Republican party, as a Richmond newspaper asserted, was founded for one reason: "hatred of African slavery."

## THE ELECTION OF 1860

WASHINGTON TERR.

OR 3

UNORG. TERR.

NEBRASKA TERRITORY

MN 4

WI 5

MI 6

NH 5
VT 5

ME 8

NY 35

MA 13

UTAH TERRITORY

IA 4

PA 27

RI 4
CT 6

CA 4

KANSAS TERR.

IL 11

IN 13

OH 23

NJ 4
DE 3

MO 9

VA 15

MD 8

NEW MEXICO TERRITORY

UNORG. TERR.

AR 4

KY 12

TN 12

NC 10

SC 8

TX 4

LA 6

MS 7

AL 9

GA 10

FL 3

|  | | Electoral Vote | Popular Vote |
|---|---|---|---|
| ■ | **Abraham Lincoln (Republican)** | **180** | **1,866,000** |
| ■ | Stephen A. Douglas (Democrat—northern) | 12 | 1,383,000 |
| ■ | John C. Breckinridge (Democrat—southern) | 72 | 848,000 |
| ■ | John Bell (Constitutional Union) | 39 | 593,000 |

■ What caused the division within the Democratic party in 1860?
■ What were the major factors that led to Lincoln's electoral victory?

Southerners especially feared that Lincoln was determined to prevent the expansion of a cotton economy that in 1860 had produced four million 500-pound bales—a record crop that made up nearly 60 percent of *all* American exports. Former president John Tyler wrote that the nation "had fallen on evil times" and that the "day of doom for the great model Republic is at hand."

False rumors that Lincoln planned to free the slaves raced across the South. One newspaper editorial called the president-elect a "bigoted, unscrupulous, and cold-blooded enemy of peace and equality of the slaveholding states."

Lincoln responded that southern fears were misguided. He stressed in a letter to a Georgia congressman that he was not a radical abolitionist and that his administration would not interfere with slavery. Yet he refused to provide such assurances in public, in part because he misread the depth of southern anger and concern over his election.

**SOUTH CAROLINA SECEDES** Pro-slavery fire-eaters in South Carolina viewed Lincoln's election as the final signal to abandon the Union. After Lincoln's victory, the state's entire congressional delegation resigned and left Washington, D.C. The state legislature then appointed a convention to decide whether it should remain in the Union.

Meeting in Charleston on December 20, 1860, the special convention focused on a single question: "How shall we sustain African slavery in South Carolina from a series of annoying attacks?" The delegates responded by unanimously voting to secede from the Union.

David Jamison Rutledge, who presided over the convention, announced that "the Ordinance of Secession has been signed and ratified, and I proclaim the State of South Carolina an Independent Commonwealth." Judge James L. Petigru, one of the few South Carolina Unionists, quipped that his newly independent state was "too small to be a Republic but too large to be an insane asylum."

As the news of South Carolina's secession spread across the state, church bells rang and shops closed. "THE UNION IS DISSOLVED!" screamed the *Charleston Mercury*. One Unionist kept a copy of the newspaper, scribbling on the bottom of it: "You'll regret the day you ever done this. I preserve this to see how it ends." Georgian Alexander Stephens, who would become the Confederacy's vice president, warned that "revolutions are much easier started than controlled."

**PRESIDENT BUCHANAN BALKS** The imploding nation needed a bold, decisive president, but instead it suffered under James Buchanan, who blamed the crisis on the "agitation" of fanatical abolitionists. He declared secession illegal, then claimed that he lacked the constitutional authority to force a state to rejoin the Union. "I can do nothing," he sighed. In the face of the president's clueless inaction, Southerners seized federal forts in the seceded states.

Amid the crisis, a Louisville, Kentucky, newspaper asked: "Will James Buchanan, who occupies the chair of Andrew Jackson, emulate the energy of the great Tennessean, or will he like a craven, cower before . . . the mad antics of those overexcited fanatics [who engineered secession]?" It was a timely question. Buchanan's secretary of state, Lewis Cass, who had served as Jackson's

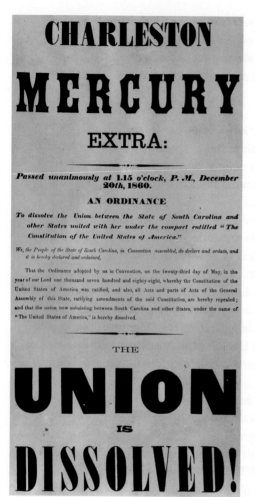

**CHARLESTON**

**MERCURY**

**EXTRA:**

*Passed unanimously at 1.15 o'clock, P. M., December 20th, 1860.*

**AN ORDINANCE**

*To dissolve the Union between the State of South Carolina and other States united with her under the compact entitled "The Constitution of the United States of America."*

We, the People of the State of South Carolina, in Convention assembled, do declare and ordain, and it is hereby declared and ordained,

That the Ordinance adopted by us in Convention, on the twenty-third day of May, in the year of our Lord one thousand seven hundred and eighty-eight, whereby the Constitution of the United States of America was ratified, and also, all Acts and parts of Acts of the General Assembly of this State, ratifying amendments of the said Constitution, are hereby repealed; and that the union now subsisting between South Carolina and other States, under the name of "The United States of America," is hereby dissolved.

THE

**UNION**

IS

**DISSOLVED!**

**"The Union Is Dissolved!"** An 1860 newspaper headline announcing South Carolina's secession from the Union.

secretary of war during the nullification crisis, urged the president to mimic Jackson and send federal troops and warships to the seceded states to show them that the Union would be preserved at all costs. Buchanan rejected the advice, prompting Cass to resign.

Among the federal facilities in the seceding states was Fort Sumter, nestled on a tiny man-made island at the mouth of Charleston Harbor. When South Carolina secessionists demanded that Major Robert Anderson, a Kentucky Unionist, surrender the fort, he refused. On January 5, 1861, Buchanan sent an unarmed ship, the *Star of the West*, to resupply Fort Sumter.

As the supply ship approached Charleston Harbor on January 9, Confederate cannons opened fire and drove it away. It was an act of war, but Buchanan chose to ignore the challenge, hoping that a compromise would be reached to avoid civil war. Many Southerners, however, were not in a compromising mood.

**SECESSION OF THE LOWER SOUTH** By February 1, 1861, the states of the Lower South—South Carolina, Mississippi, Florida, Alabama, Georgia, Louisiana, and Texas—had seceded. Although their secession ordinances mentioned various grievances against the federal government, they made it clear that their primary reason for leaving the Union was the preservation of slavery.

Texas's ordinance explained that the purpose of secession and the formation of the Confederacy was to "*secure the rights of the slave-holding States in their domestic institutions.*" The Texas convention displayed the racism underlying secession, calling Africans "an inferior and dependent race" for whom slavery was "beneficial."

In Mississippi, William Harris, the state's secession commissioner, argued that Republicans "now demand equality between the white and negro races, under our constitution; equality in representation, equality in the right of suffrage . . . equality in the social circle, equality in the rights of matrimony." Such a future could not be tolerated. The South, in his view, faced a stark choice: "Sink or swim, live or die, survive or perish." Mississippi, he vowed, "will never submit to the principles and policy of this black Republican administration."

On February 4, 1861, fifty representatives of the seceding states, all but one of them slave owners, met in Montgomery, Alabama, where they adopted a constitution for the Confederate States of America. It mandated that "the institution of negro slavery, as it now exists in the Confederate States, shall be recognized and protected."

The delegates elected as the Confederacy's first president Mississippi's Jefferson Davis, a West Point graduate who had served as a Democrat in the House of Representatives and the Senate and had been secretary of war under Franklin Pierce.

Alexander H. Stephens of Georgia was named vice president. The sickly, baby-faced Stephens, weighing no more than ninety pounds, declared, "Our new government is founded upon . . . the great truth that the negro is not equal to the white man; that slavery, subordination to the superior [white] race, is his natural and normal condition."

In mid-February, Davis, cheered by jubilant crowds, traveled from Mississippi to Montgomery, Alabama, the Confederate capital, for his installation. On February 18, Alabama fire-eater William Yancey introduced Davis to the crowd by announcing that the "man and the hour have met." In his remarks, Davis claimed that "the time for compromise is now passed."

**FINAL EFFORTS AT COMPROMISE** President-elect Lincoln still assumed that the southern states were bluffing. Members of Congress, however, desperately sought a compromise to avoid a civil war. On December 18, 1860, John J. Crittenden of Kentucky offered a series of resolutions that would allow the extension of slavery into the new western territories *south* of the Missouri Compromise line (36°30' parallel) and guarantee the preservation of slavery where it already existed. Lincoln, however, opposed any plan that would expand slavery westward, and the Senate defeated the Crittenden Compromise, 25–23.

Several weeks later, in February 1861, twenty-one states sent delegates to a peace conference in Washington, D.C. Former president John Tyler presided, but the conference's proposal, substantially the same as the Crittenden Compromise, won little support. (Tyler himself voted against it and urged Virginia to secede at once.) The only proposal that generated much interest was a constitutional amendment guaranteeing slavery where it existed. Many Republicans, including Lincoln, were prepared to go that far, but no further.

After passing the House, the slavery amendment passed the Senate 24 to 12 on the morning of March 4, 1861, Lincoln's inauguration day. It would have become the Thirteenth Amendment and would have been the first time the word *slavery* had appeared in the Constitution, but the states never ratified it. When the states eventually ratified the Thirteenth Amendment in 1865, it did not protect slavery—it ended it.

**LINCOLN'S INAUGURATION** In mid-February 1861, Abraham Lincoln boarded a train in Springfield, Illinois, headed to Washington, D.C., for his inauguration. Alerted to a plot to assassinate him when he changed trains in Baltimore, federal officials had Lincoln wear a disguise and board a secret train in Harrisburg, Pennsylvania. The train carrying Lincoln slipped through Baltimore unnoticed. On March 4, 1861—Inauguration Day—Lincoln and James Buchanan rode together in a carriage down Pennsylvania Avenue beneath the careful gaze of rooftop sharpshooters there to protect them.

In his inaugural address, the fifty-two-year-old Lincoln repeated his pledge not "to interfere with the institution of slavery in the states where it exists." Yet the immediate question had shifted from slavery to secession. Lincoln insisted that "the Union of these States is perpetual." No state, he stressed, "can lawfully get out of the Union." He pledged to defend "federal forts in the South," but beyond that "there [would] be no invasion, no using of force against or among the people anywhere." In closing, he appealed for the Union:

> We are not enemies, but friends. We must not be enemies. Though passion may have strained, it must not break our bonds of affection. The mystic chords of memory, stretching from every battlefield and patriot grave to every living heart and hearthstone all over this broad land, will yet swell the chorus of the Union, when again touched, as surely they will be, by the better angels of our nature.

Southerners were not impressed. A North Carolina newspaper warned that Lincoln's speech made civil war "inevitable." On both sides, however, people assumed that any war would be over quickly and that their lives would go on as usual.

**THE END OF THE WAITING GAME** On March 5, 1861, his first day in office, President Lincoln found a letter on his desk from Major Robert Anderson at Fort Sumter. Anderson reported that his men had enough food for only a few weeks, and that the Confederates were encircling the fort with a "ring of fire." It would take thousands of federal soldiers to rescue them.

On April 4, 1861, Lincoln ordered unarmed ships to take food and supplies to the sixty-nine soldiers at Fort Sumter. Jefferson Davis was equally determined to stop any effort to supply the fort, even if it meant using military force. The secretary of state for the Confederacy, Richard Lathers, warned Davis that if the South fired first, "There will be no compromise with Secession if war is forced upon the north." Davis ignored the warning.

On April 11, Confederate general Pierre G.T. Beauregard, who had studied under Anderson at West Point, urged his former professor to surrender and sent him cases of whiskey and boxes of cigars to help convince him. Anderson refused the gifts and the request. At four-thirty on the morning of April 12, Confederate cannons began firing on Fort Sumter.

The bright flashes and thundering booms awakened the city. Thousands rushed out to watch the shelling. Finally, the outgunned Anderson, his ammunition and food gone, lowered the "stars and stripes."

The attack on Fort Sumter "has made the North a unit," New York Democratic Congressman Daniel Sickles wrote Lincoln's secretary of war. "We are at war with a foreign power." A Kentucky man told a reporter that the assault on Fort Sumter changed everything: "I was a Kentuckian, but now I am an American." A civil war of unimagined horrors had begun. "War begins where reason ends," said Frederick Douglass, and the South's irrational fears confirmed the logic of his statement.

# CHAPTER REVIEW

## SUMMARY

- **Slavery in the Territories**   Representative David *Wilmot's Proviso*, although it never became law, declared that since Mexican territories acquired by the United States had been free, they should remain so. Like the Wilmot Proviso, the new *Free-Soil party* demanded that slavery not be expanded to the territories. But it was the discovery of gold in California and the ensuing *California gold rush (1849)* that escalated tensions. Californians wanted to enter the Union as a free state. Southerners feared that they would lose federal protection of their "peculiar institution" if there were more free states than slave states. It had been agreed that *popular sovereignty* would settle the status of the territories, but when the territories applied for statehood, the debate over slavery was renewed. Through the wildly celebrated *Compromise of 1850*, California entered the Union as a free state; the territories of Texas, New Mexico, and Utah were established without direct reference to slavery; the slave trade (but not slavery) was banned in Washington, D.C.; and a new *Fugitive Slave Act (1850)* was passed. Tensions turned violent with the passage of the *Kansas-Nebraska Act (1854)*, which overturned the Missouri Compromise by allowing slavery in the territories where the institution had been banned in 1821.

- **The Republican Party's Appeal**   The efforts of pro-slavery advocates in Kansas to force slavery on the territory enraged northern opinion, even though anti-slavery settlers such as John Brown were equally violent in the events known as *Bleeding Kansas (1856)*. The Supreme Court's *Dred Scott v. Sandford (1857)* decision, which ruled that Congress could not interfere with slavery in the territories, further fueled sectional conflict. Northern voters gravitated toward the Republican party as events unfolded. Republicans also advocated raising protective tariffs and funding the development of the nation's infrastructure, which appealed to northern manufacturers and commercial farmers. Abraham Lincoln's narrow failure to unseat Democrat Stephen A. Douglas in the 1858 Illinois Senate election, which included the famous *Lincoln-Douglas debates (1858)*, revealed the Republican party's growing appeal. In 1860, Lincoln carried every free state and won a clear electoral college victory.

- **The Secession of the Lower South and Civil War**   Following Lincoln's election, South Carolina seceded. Six other Lower South states quickly followed. Together they formed the Confederate States of America, citing their belief that secession was necessary for the preservation of slavery. In his inaugural address, Lincoln made it clear that secession was unconstitutional but that the North would not invade the South. However, the Confederate states stood by their declarations of secession, and war came when South Carolinians fired on the "stars and stripes" at Fort Sumter.

## CHRONOLOGY

| | |
|---|---|
| **1848** | Free-Soil party is organized |
| **1849** | California gold rush begins |
| **1854** | Congress passes the Kansas-Nebraska Act |
| | The Republican party is founded |
| **1856** | A pro-slavery mob sacks Lawrence, Kansas; John Brown stages the Pottawatomie Massacre in retaliation |
| | Charles Sumner of Massachusetts is caned and seriously injured by a pro-slavery congressman in the U.S. Senate |
| **1857** | U.S. Supreme Court issues the *Dred Scott* decision |
| | Lecompton Constitution declares that slavery will be allowed in Kansas |
| **1858** | Abraham Lincoln debates Stephen A. Douglas during the 1858 Illinois Senate race |
| **1859** | John Brown and his followers stage a failed raid at Harpers Ferry, Virginia, in an attempt to incite a slave insurrection |
| **1860–1861** | South Carolina and six other southern states secede from the Union |
| | Crittenden Compromise is proposed but fails |
| **March 4, 1861** | Abraham Lincoln is inaugurated president |
| **April 1861** | Fort Sumter falls to Confederate forces, triggers Civil War |

## KEY TERMS

Wilmot Proviso (1846) p. 542

popular sovereignty p. 542

Free-Soil party p. 543

California gold rush (1849) p. 544

Compromise of 1850 p. 546

Fugitive Slave Act (1850) p. 551

Kansas-Nebraska Act (1854) p. 555

Bleeding Kansas (1856) p. 558

*Dred Scott v. Sandford* (1857) p. 562

Lincoln-Douglas debates (1858) p. 564

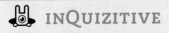 INQUIZITIVE

**Go to InQuizitive to see what you've learned—and learn what you've missed—with personalized feedback along the way.**

# 15 The War of the Union

## 1861–1865

**Lincoln's Drive through Richmond (1866)** Shortly after the Confederate capital of Richmond, Virginia, fell to Union forces in April 1865, President Abraham Lincoln visited the war-torn city. His carriage was swarmed by enslaved blacks who were freed by the war, as well as whites whose loyalties were with the Union.

The fall of Fort Sumter started the Civil War and triggered a wave of patriotic bluster on both sides. A southern woman prayed that God would "give us strength to conquer the Yankees, to exterminate *them*, to lay waste every Northern city, town and village, to destroy them utterly." Northern sentiment was not much different. Writer Nathaniel Hawthorne reported from Massachusetts that his transcendentalist friend Ralph Waldo Emerson was "breathing slaughter" as the Union army prepared for its first battle. Emerson, a pacifist, now said that "sometimes gunpowder smells good."

Many Southerners, then and since, argued that the Civil War was not about slavery but about the South's effort to defend states' rights. Confederate president Jefferson Davis, for example, claimed that the Rebels fought for the South's right to secede from the Union and its need to defend itself against a "tyrannical majority"—meaning those who had elected President Abraham Lincoln, the anti-slavery Republican.

For his part, Lincoln stressed repeatedly that the "paramount object in this struggle *is* to save the Union, and is *not* either to save or to destroy slavery. If I could save the Union without freeing *any* slave I would do it, and if I could save it by freeing *all* the slaves I would do it; and if I could save it by freeing some and leaving others alone I would also do that." If the southern states returned to the Union, he promised, they could retain their slaves. None of the Confederate states accepted Lincoln's offer, in large part because most white Southerners were convinced that he was lying. They believed the "Black Republican," as they called the president, was determined to end slavery.

## focus questions

**1.** What were the respective advantages of the North and South as the Civil War began? How did those advantages affect the military strategies of the Union and the Confederacy?

**2.** Why did Abraham Lincoln decide to issue the Emancipation Proclamation? How did it impact the war?

**3.** In what ways did the war affect social and economic life in the North and South?

**4.** What were the military turning points in 1863 and 1864 that ultimately led to the Confederacy's defeat?

**5.** How did the Civil War change the nation?

Southerners claimed their *right* to secede from the Union, but protecting slavery was the *reason* Confederate leaders repeatedly used to justify secession and war. The South Carolina Declaration on the Immediate Causes of Secession, for example, explained that the state left the Union because of the "increasing hostility on the part of the non-slaveholding states to the institution of slavery." Mississippi mentioned only one reason: preserving slavery. Georgian Alexander Stephens, vice president of the Confederate States of America, said that slavery was the "immediate cause" of secession and war and that white supremacy was the "cornerstone" of the Confederacy.

On April 15, three days after the Confederate attack on Fort Sumter, Lincoln directed the "loyal" states to supply 75,000 militiamen for ninety days to suppress the rebellion. The Civil War would force everyone—men and women, white and black, immigrants and Native Americans, free and enslaved—to choose sides. Neither the Union nor the Confederacy enjoyed unanimous support. Some 100,000 Southerners fought for the Union; thousands of Northerners fought for the Confederacy. Thousands of European volunteers fought on each side.

## CHOOSING SIDES

Of the slaveholding states along the border between North and South, Delaware remained firmly in the Union, but Maryland, Kentucky, and Missouri went through bitter struggles to decide which side to support. "I think to lose Kentucky is nearly the same as to lose the whole game," Lincoln told a friend. If Kentucky were to join the Confederacy, "we cannot hold Missouri, nor, as I think, Maryland." Lincoln was so determined to keep slaveholding Kentucky on the Union side that he muffled all talk of abolition.

If Maryland had seceded, Confederates would have surrounded Washington, D.C. To keep Maryland in the Union, Lincoln had pro-Confederate leaders there arrested, including Baltimore's mayor and chief of police. The fragile neutrality of Kentucky lasted until September 3, when Confederate and Union armies moved into the divided state. Kentucky voters elected a secessionist governor and a Unionist majority in the state legislature, as did Missouri, a state with many European immigrants, especially Germans.

When a pro-Confederate militia gathered in St. Louis, hoping to take control of the federal arsenal, it was surprised and disarmed by German immigrants "eager to teach the German-haters a never-to-be-forgotten lesson." The German militiamen then chased the pro-Confederate governor across the border to Arkansas. When news of the Civil War reached Missouri, 4,200 men volunteered to join the Union army; all but 100 were German Americans.

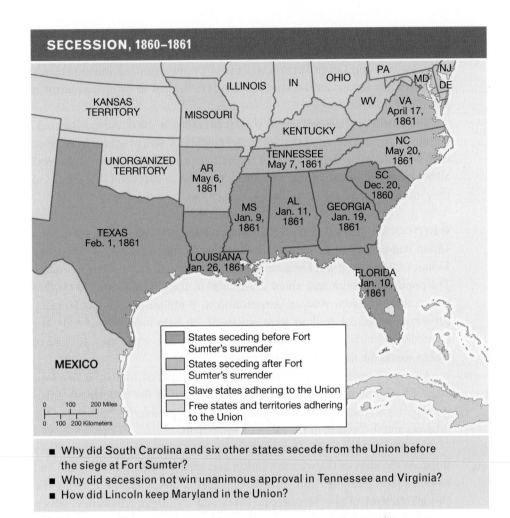

**SECESSION, 1860–1861**

Legend:
- States seceding before Fort Sumter's surrender
- States seceding after Fort Sumter's surrender
- Slave states adhering to the Union
- Free states and territories adhering to the Union

- Why did South Carolina and six other states secede from the Union before the siege at Fort Sumter?
- Why did secession not win unanimous approval in Tennessee and Virginia?
- How did Lincoln keep Maryland in the Union?

German immigrants overwhelmingly supported the Union. Having fled from German states where aristocratic elites and military officers suppressed democracy, they viewed the Confederacy as a similarly undemocratic society. New Yorker August Willich, a German immigrant who had been an army officer, wrote after the attack on Fort Sumter that German Americans needed to "protect their new republican homeland against the aristocracy of the South." Willich would become a Union army general.

In areas of the South where Union sentiment remained strong, the Civil War was brutally uncivil. In January 1863, a detachment of Confederate soldiers in Madison County, North Carolina, captured thirteen men and boys and began marching them to Knoxville, Tennessee, to be tried for desertion and treason. The prisoners never made it to Knoxville, however. Along the way, the detachment stopped, lined up the captives, and killed them. Thirteen-year-old David Shelton was the last to be executed, having already witnessed his father and brother's deaths. He begged to be spared but was killed like the rest.

The northern states witnessed similar brutality. In 1863, Anson Babcock, an Illinois farmer, reported that his "rebel neighbors" had poisoned his horses, destroyed his orchards, wrecked his fences, and "annoyed me in various ways," all because "'my politics don't suit'" them, for "I am 'a damned Lincolnite,' and they intend to drive me out of the neighborhood."

**REGIONAL ADVANTAGES**   Once battle lines were finally drawn, the Union had twenty-three states, including four border slave states—Missouri, Kentucky, Maryland, and Delaware—while the Confederacy had eleven states. The population count was about 22 million in the Union (some 400,000 of whom were enslaved African Americans) to 9 million in the Confederacy (of whom about 3.5 million were enslaved). To help balance the odds, the Confederacy mobilized 80 percent of its military-age white men, a third of whom would die during the four-year war.

An even greater asset for the North was its superior industrial development. The southern states produced just 7 percent of the nation's manufactured goods on the eve of the war. The Union states produced 97 percent of the firearms and 96 percent of the railroad equipment.

The North also had a huge advantage in transportation, particularly ships. At the start of the war, the Union had ninety warships; the South had none. Federal gunboats and transports played a direct role in securing the Union's control of the Mississippi River and its larger tributaries, which provided easy invasion routes into the center of the Confederacy. Early on, the Union navy's blockade of the major southern ports sharply reduced the amount of cotton that could be exported to Britain and France as well as the flow of goods (including military weapons) imported from Europe. In addition, the Union had more wagons and horses and an impressive edge in railroad locomotives.

The Confederates, however, had major geographic and emotional advantages: they could fight on their own territory in defense of their homeland. "For our people," Confederate general Stonewall Jackson said, "the war was a struggle for life and death." In warfare, it is usually easier to defend than to attack, since defending troops have the opportunity to dig protective trenches and fortifications. In the Civil War, armies that assaulted well-defended positions were mauled 90 percent of the time. Many Confederate leaders thought that if they could hold out long enough, disgruntled northern voters might convince Lincoln and Congress to end the war.

## THE WAR'S EARLY STRATEGIES

The two sides initially had different goals. The Confederacy sought to convince the Union and the world to recognize its independence. The United States, on the other hand, fought to restore the Union. The future of slavery was not yet an issue as the war started.

After the fall of Fort Sumter, excited newspaper editors and politicians on both sides pressured the generals to strike quickly. "Forward to Richmond!" screamed a New York newspaper headline. Most people thought the war would be, in President Lincoln's words, "a short and decisive one." They were sorely wrong.

In the summer of 1861, Jefferson Davis told General Pierre G. T. Beauregard to rush the main Confederate army to Manassas Junction, a railroad crossing in northern Virginia, about twenty-five miles west of Washington. Lincoln hoped that the Union army (often called *Federals*) would overrun the outnumbered Confederates (often called *Rebels*) and quickly push on to Richmond, only 107 miles to the south.

**FIRST BULL RUN** When word reached Washington, D.C., that the two armies were converging for battle, hundreds of civilians packed picnic lunches and rode out to watch, assuming that the first clash of arms would be short, glorious, and bloodless.

It was a hot, dry day on July 21, 1861, when 37,000 untested Union recruits marched to battle, some of them breaking ranks to eat blackberries or drink water from streams along the way. Many of them died with the berry juice still on their lips as they engaged the Confederates dug in behind a tree-choked branch of the Potomac River called Bull Run.

For most of the soldiers, the battle provided their first taste of the chaos and confusion of combat. Many were disoriented by the smoke from gunpowder and saltpeter, the roar of cannon fire, the screaming of fallen comrades, and the sound of bullets whizzing past. Because neither side yet wore standard-colored uniforms, the soldiers had trouble deciding friend from foe.

The Union troops almost won the battle early in the afternoon. "We fired a volley," wrote a Massachusetts private, "and saw the Rebels running. . . . The boys were saying constantly, in great glee, 'We've whipped them.' 'We'll hang Jeff Davis from a sour apple tree.' 'They're running.' 'The war is over.'"

But Confederate reinforcements poured in. Amid the furious fighting, a South Carolina officer rallied his troops by pointing to the courageous example of Thomas Jackson: "Look! There is General Jackson with his Virginians, standing like a stone wall!" Jackson ordered his men to charge, urging them to "yell like furies!" From that day forward, "Stonewall" became Jackson's popular nickname, and he would be the most celebrated—and feared—Confederate field commander.

The Union army panicked, and fleeing soldiers and terrified civilians clogged the road to Washington, D.C. The victorious Confederates, however, were so disorganized and exhausted that they failed to give chase.

Left behind was a battlefield strewn with the dead and dying—mangled men and bloated horses and mules scattered among discarded knapsacks, canteens, blankets, rifles, wagons, and cannons. Jackson wrote his wife that "we fought a great battle and gained a great victory, for which all the glory is due to God alone."

The news of the Confederate victory triggered sharp criticism of President Lincoln. Michigan senator Zachariah Chandler, a Republican, dismissed the president as "timid, vacillating & inefficient." An Ohio Republican was even more critical, denouncing Lincoln as "an admitted failure" who "has no will, no courage, no executive capacity."

The hallmark of Lincoln's presidency, however, was his ability to acknowledge mistakes and move forward. With each passing year, he would grow surer of himself as a wartime leader. As Stonewall Jackson later observed, the Confederacy emerged from the first major battle assuming that a quick and total victory was in its grasp. The North, while "mortified by defeat and stunned by ridicule, pulled itself together, raised armies, stirred up its people, and prepared for war in earnest."

**THE UNION'S "ANACONDA" PLAN**    The Battle of Bull Run demonstrated that the war would not be decided with one sudden stroke, as many had assumed. General Winfield Scott, the seventy-five-year-old commander of the Union war effort, devised a three-pronged strategy. First, the Army of the Potomac, the main Union army, would defend Washington, D.C., and exert constant pressure on the Confederate capital at Richmond.

Second, the Federal navy's blockade of southern ports would cut off the Confederacy's access to foreign goods and weapons. The third component of the plan called for other Union armies to divide the Confederacy by pushing south along the crucial inland water routes: the Mississippi, Tennessee, and Cumberland Rivers. This so-called **Anaconda Plan** was intended to slowly trap and crush the southern resistance, like an anaconda snake strangling its prey.

**CONFEDERATE STRATEGY** The Confederate plan was simpler. If the Union forces could be stalemated and the war prolonged, as Jefferson Davis and others hoped, then the British or French, desperate for southern cotton, might be persuaded to join the cause. Or perhaps a long war would change public sentiment in the North and force Lincoln to seek a negotiated settlement. So, while armies were forming in the South, Confederate diplomats were seeking military and financial assistance in London and Paris, and Confederate sympathizers in the North were urging an end to the Union's war effort.

The Confederate representatives in Paris won a promise from France to recognize the Confederacy as a new nation *if* Great Britain would do the same. But the British refused, partly in response to pressure from President Lincoln and partly out of their desire to maintain trade with the United States.

Confederate leaders had assumed that Britain would support the South in order to get its cotton. As it turned out, however, the British were able to import enough cotton from India to maintain production. In the end, Confederate diplomacy in Europe was more successful in purchasing military supplies than in gaining official recognition as an independent nation.

**FORMING ARMIES** Once fighting began, President Lincoln called for 500,000 more men, a staggering number and one that the Confederacy struggled to match.

In Illinois, Ulysses S. Grant, the Ohio-born West Point graduate who had distinguished himself in the Mexican-American War, rejoined the army in 1861. He had been ushered out of the peacetime military seven years earlier because of binge drinking. Thereafter, as a civilian, he pursued several business ventures in Missouri and Illinois, all of which were dismal failures. By 1861, he was virtually a pauper, forced to walk the streets of St. Louis hawking firewood out of a handcart.

The outbreak of war gave Grant renewed hope and purpose. Back in uniform and mobilizing an Illinois regiment, he explained that there "are but two parties now—traitors and patriots—and I want hereafter to be ranked with the latter."

Confederates were equally committed to their cause. Charleston, wrote Mary Chesnut, the literary wife of a prominent planter, was "crowded with soldiers" who feared "the war will be over before they get a sight of the fun." Sam Watkins of Tennessee reported that everyone "was eager for the war."

Although the average age of soldiers in the Civil War was twenty-six, the Union armies included more than 100,000 soldiers younger than fifteen. Almost a fifth of Union soldiers and sailors were immigrants—French, Germans, Poles, Italians, and other Europeans—and many could not speak

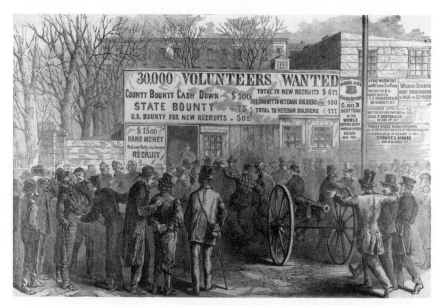

**The U.S. Army recruiting office in City Hall Park, New York City** The sign advertises the money offered to those willing to serve: $677 to new recruits, $777 to veteran soldiers, and $15 to anyone who brought in a recruit.

English. The Union army also included 50,000 Canadians and an equal number of Englishmen. Some 210,000 Irish-born men served in the war, 170,000 of them on the Union side.

Immigrants fought for many reasons: a strong belief in the Union cause, cash bonuses, extra food, regular pay, the need for a steady job. Whatever the reason, the high proportion of immigrants in the Union army gave it an ethnic diversity absent in the Confederate ranks.

Because the Confederacy had a smaller male population, Jefferson Davis was forced to enact a conscription law (mandatory military draft). On April 16, 1862, all white males between eighteen and thirty-five were required to serve in the army for three years. "From this time until the end of the war," a Tennessee soldier wrote, "a soldier was simply a machine, a conscript . . . All our pride and valor had gone, and we were sick of war and cursed the Southern Confederacy."

The conscription law included controversial loopholes. A draftee might avoid service either by paying a "substitute" who was not of draft age or by paying $500 to the government. Elected officials and key civilian workers, as well as planters with twenty or more slaves, were exempted from military service.

The Union waited nearly a year before forcing men into service. In 1863, with the war going badly, the U.S. government began to draft men. As in the South, Northerners found ways to avoid military service. A draftee might pay $300 to avoid service, and exemptions were granted to selected federal and state officeholders and to others on medical or compassionate grounds. Such exemptions led to bitter complaints on both sides about the conflict being "a rich man's war and a poor man's fight."

**WHY THEY FOUGHT** Most of those who fought on both sides were volunteers. Why did they risk their lives? The reasons varied, but many felt compelled by duty, honor, and patriotism. Their duties as *men* drove many combatants. As an Alabama planter who joined the Confederate army as a cavalryman explained to his wife, "My honor, my duty, your reputation & that of my darling little boy" forced him to don a uniform "when our bleeding country needs the services of every man." Likewise, an Illinois officer felt that Union soldiers were guided by "a high and noble sentiment, but after all a sentiment [preserving the Union and ending slavery]. They [Confederates] are fighting for independence and are animated by passion and hatred against invaders [Yankees]."

**A NEW YORK PRIVATE** Nineteen-year-old Lyons Wakeman, the eldest of nine children in an upstate New York farm family, enlisted in the Union army in 1862. In exchange for a $152 cash bonus, the five-foot-tall, blue-eyed Wakeman signed up for three years. The pay was $13 a month, some of which went home to help the family. Initially, at least, army life was tolerable, and the prospect of death in combat did not faze Wakeman: "I don't fear the rebel bullets, nor do I fear the cannon. If it is God's will for me to be killed here, it is my will to die." In letters home, first from Virginia and later from Louisiana,

**Private Wakeman** Sarah Rosetta Wakeman, alias Lyons Wakeman, served in the Union Army.

Private Wakeman asked about the family farm, how many hogs were slaughtered, what the new barn looked like, and how much it might cost to buy a farm on the Wisconsin prairie.

Yet Wakeman never became a farmer. In a fierce battle, the New Yorker faced "enemy bullets with my regiment. I was under fire about four hours and lay on the field of battle all night." Wakeman did not die from wounds but did succumb a few weeks later to dysentery (chronic diarrhea), after drinking from a stream contaminated with the carcasses of dead horses. The private was buried in a New Orleans cemetery, under a headstone that simply read: "Lyons Wakeman—N.Y."

What might have been added was that Lyons Wakeman was a woman. Born Sarah Rosetta Wakeman, she, like hundreds of women on both sides, had disguised her gender to serve in the war. Why she did so remains a mystery. Was it simply patriotism? Or did it also involve seizing the opportunity afforded by the war to explore alternative modes of gender identity?

**WHAT WAS AT STAKE** Many Confederates were convinced that defeat would enslave southern whites. "If we was to lose," a Mississippi private wrote his wife in 1862, "we would be slaves to the Yanks and our children would have a yoke of bondage thrown around their necks."

Most Confederates could not imagine life without black slavery. "This country without slave labor would be completely worthless," wrote a Mississippi lieutenant. "We can only live & exist by that species of labor: hence I am willing to fight to the last."

Many Union soldiers were fighting to preserve the Union rather than free the slaves, but a surprising number insisted that winning the war meant ending slavery. A private from Minnesota felt that the war "will never end until we end slavery."

Despite the patriotic fervor, people remained ambivalent about their loyalties. In Virginia, for example, Confederate Joseph Waddill admitted in his diary in 1863 that he actually regretted secession. "I never ceased to deplore the disruption [of the Union], and never could have loved my country and government as I loved the old United States."

**DIVIDED FAMILIES** The Civil War divided families. President Lincoln's wife, Mary Todd of Kentucky, for example, saw her youngest brother join the Confederate army, as did three of her half-brothers and a brother-in-law. At the same time, Varina Davis, the Confederate First Lady, had divided loyalties. While pro-slavery, she was privately pro-Union.

In June 1862, two brothers, Alexander and James Campbell, fought against each other at the Battle of Secessionville on James Island, South Carolina. Alexander joined the Union forces in assaulting a Confederate fort, where his brother served. Afterward, James wrote his brother, expressing astonishment that Alexander had been among the Union attackers. "I was . . . doing my best to Beat you, but I hope that you and I will never again meet face to face." If they should meet again in combat, he urged his brother to "do your duty to your cause, for I can assure you I will strive to discharge my duty to my country & my cause."

**THE LIFE OF A SOLDIER** The average Civil War soldier stood five feet eight inches tall and weighed 143 pounds. A third of the southern soldiers could neither read nor write. Half of the Union soldiers and two-thirds of the Confederates were farmers.

Army camps featured their own libraries, theatrical stages, churches, numerous "mascot" pets—and monotonous routine. Because most of the fighting occurred in the spring and summer, soldiers spent far more time preparing for war than actually fighting. A Pennsylvania private wrote home that "the first thing in the morning is drill. Then drill, then drill again. Then drill, drill, a little more drill, then drill, lastly drill."

When not training, soldiers spent time outdoors in makeshift shelters or small tents—talking, reading, playing cards or checkers, singing songs, smoking pipes, washing and mending clothes, and fighting swarms of lice, ticks, chiggers, and mosquitoes. Their diet was plain and dull: baked bread crackers (called hardtack), salted meat (pork or beef), and coffee.

Some soldiers on both sides were so overwhelmed by the rigors of combat and camp life or so concerned about their families and farms that they deserted, even though they risked execution if caught. Desertions soared with each passing year, as did incidents of drunkenness, thievery, and insubordination.

Punishments varied. Some deserters were shot or hanged. Others were tied to a ball and chain, forced to bury dead horses or tend to animals, or drummed out of the service. Most soldiers on both sides, however, came to view their military experience as beneficial.

**BECOMING WARRIORS** Sullivan Ballou, a thirty-two-year-old Rhode Island lawyer and legislator who enlisted in the Union army, wrote his wife that he would have loved nothing more than to have stayed and seen their sons grow to "honorable manhood," but his ultimate priority was serving his country. He felt a great debt to "those who went before us through the blood and sufferings of the Revolution." A week later, Ballou was killed in the first Battle of Bull Run. In his last letter to his wife, he had expressed a premonition of death: "do not mourn me dead . . . wait for me, for we shall meet again."

Southerners felt the same sense of patriotism and manly honor. As the months passed, however, enthusiasm faded for many combatants on both sides. Charles Biddlecom, a farmer from upstate New York, volunteered in May 1861 for the Union army. He was eager to whip the "Southern whelps." By 1863, however, Biddlecom had had enough. Sick with dysentery, overrun with lice, and miserably lonesome, he and three comrades were forced to live in a "little dog kennel" just four feet high. Although he hated slaveholders, he now felt it might have been "better in the end to have let the South go out peaceably and tried her hand at making a nation."

Like many other soldiers and sailors, Biddlecom's moods and motives fluctuated depending upon the course of the war. In 1864, he confessed that the Union army was "worn out, discouraged, [and] demoralized." He stuck it out, but "as for men fighting from pure love of country, I think them as few as white blackbirds." He declared that he was neither a "Union saver" nor a "freedom shrieker." At war's end, however, Biddlecom celebrated the defeat of the Confederacy, since it affirmed that "freedom shall extend over the whole nation." The "greatest nation of Earth" showed that it would not surrender to "traitors in arms."

**BLACKS IN THE SOUTH** As had happened during the Revolutionary War and the War of 1812, enslaved African Americans took advantage of the confusion created by the war to run away, engage in sabotage, join the fighting, or pursue their own interests.

Perhaps the most dramatic instance of slave rebelliousness occurred in Charleston Harbor. On May 13, 1862, twenty-three-year-old Robert Smalls, an enslaved black harbor pilot aboard the C.S.S. *Planter,* stole the ship and headed out to sea in a desperate quest for freedom. Sneaking past Confederate forts and cannons, he guided the *Planter* up the Cooper River and docked at a wharf where his wife, child, and the families of his crew were waiting.

Once they had boarded, the *Planter* and its seventeen passengers (nine men, five women, and three children) crept out of the harbor. As the sun rose, Smalls had a crew member hoist a white bed sheet to signal their intention to surrender, and they headed for the Union fleet blockading Charleston Harbor. A warship summoned Smalls onboard, whereupon he announced: "I am delivering this war material, including these cannons, and I think Uncle Abraham Lincoln can put them to good use."

**Union soldiers** Smoking their pipes, these soldiers share a moment of rest and a bottle of whiskey.

Smalls was hailed as a hero in the North. He met with President Lincoln at the White House, toured northern cities urging that blacks be allowed to serve in the Union army and navy, and became a ship pilot for the Union navy. After the war, he would become a South Carolina legislator and U.S. congressman.

## FIGHTING IN THE WEST

During the Civil War, fighting spilled across the Mississippi River into the Great Plains and all the way to California. In 1862, a small Confederate army tried to conquer the New Mexico territory but was repelled.

Amid the sporadic fighting, western settlement slowed but did not stop. New discoveries of gold and silver in eastern California and in Montana and Colorado lured more prospectors. Dakota, Colorado, and Nevada gained territorial status in 1861, Idaho and Arizona in 1863. Both Montana and silver-rich Nevada gained statehood in 1864.

**WAR IN THE WEST** The most intense fighting west of the Mississippi occurred along the Kansas-Missouri border, where the disputes that had developed between pro-slavery and anti-slavery settlers in the 1850s turned into brutal guerrilla warfare.

The most prominent pro-Confederate leader in the area was William Quantrill. He and his followers, mostly teenagers, fought under a black flag, meaning that they would kill anyone who surrendered. In destroying Lawrence, Kansas, in 1863, Quantrill ordered his men to "kill every male and burn every house." By the end of the day, they had massacred 182 men and boys. Their opponents, the Jayhawkers (originally slang for thieves), responded by torturing and hanging pro-Confederate prisoners, burning houses, and destroying livestock.

Many Indian nations were caught up in the war. Some 20,000 Native Americans allied with one side or the other. Several Indian tribes owned African American slaves and felt a bond with southern whites. Stand Watie, an Oklahoma Cherokee leader, chose the Confederacy in 1861 and raised a volunteer regiment called the Cherokee Mounted Rifles. By the end of the war, he had been promoted to brigadier general and was the principal chief of the Confederate Cherokees.

Oklahoma's proximity to Texas influenced the Choctaws and Chickasaws to support the Confederacy. The Cherokees, Creeks, and Seminoles were more divided in their loyalties. The Cherokees, for example, split in two, some supporting the Union and others the Confederacy. Caught in the crossfire of battle, one-third of Cherokee women ended up widows.

**KENTUCKY AND TENNESSEE** Little happened of military significance east of the Appalachian Mountains before May 1862. On the other hand, important battles occurred in the West (from the Appalachians to the Mississippi River).

Early in 1862, General Ulysses S. Grant made the first Union thrust against the Confederate army that was defending Kentucky and Tennessee. To combat his weakness for liquor, he looked to his chief of staff, John A. Rawlins, a teetotaler, to keep him sober. Rawlins took his role seriously, for when Grant was sober, he had only one equal as a military commander: Robert E. Lee.

Moving on boats out of Cairo, Illinois, and Paducah, Kentucky, the Union army captured two hastily built Confederate strongholds: Fort Henry on the east bank of the Tennessee River on February 6, 1862, and nearby Fort Donelson, perched on a hill overlooking the Cumberland River, where, on February 16, some 12,000 Confederates surrendered. Eight days later, Union forces took control of Nashville, then serving as Tennessee's capital.

These first major victories ignited wild celebrations throughout the North. They helped ensure that Kentucky would stay within the Union and gave the North access to the Cumberland and Tennessee Rivers. At the same time, the victory at Fort Donelson gave Grant a catchy nickname matching his initials:

"Unconditional Surrender" Grant. The *New York Times* reported that Grant's "prestige is second now to that of no general in the army." Admirers rushed him 10,000 cigars, and he soon began smoking twenty a day. (He would die in 1885 of throat cancer.)

President Lincoln's delight with the Union army's success, however, was tempered by the death of his eleven-year-old son Willie, of typhoid fever. The tragedy "overwhelmed" the president. A White House staff member said she had never seen "a man so bowed down in grief."

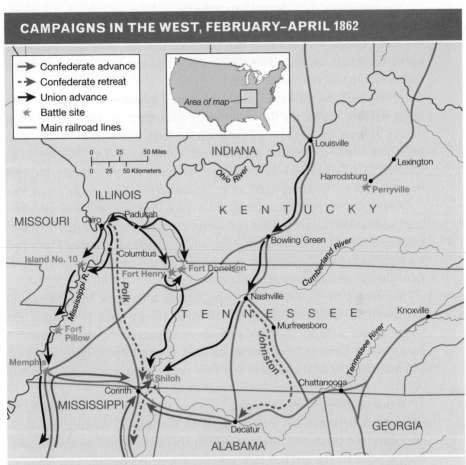

### CAMPAIGNS IN THE WEST, FEBRUARY–APRIL 1862

- Why was General Grant's campaign in Kentucky a significant victory for the Union army?
- Describe the events at Shiloh. What were the costs to the Union as a result of the battle?

**SHILOH** After the defeats in Kentucky and Tennessee, the Confederate forces fled southward before regrouping under General Albert Sydney Johnston at Corinth, in northern Mississippi, near the Tennessee border. Their goal was to protect the Memphis and Charleston Railroad linking the lower Mississippi Valley and the Atlantic coast.

While planning his attack on Corinth, General Grant made a costly mistake when he exposed his 42,000 troops on a rolling plateau between Lick and Snake Creeks flowing into the Tennessee River. He also failed to have his men dig defensive trenches. Johnston recognized Grant's blunder, and at dawn on Sunday, April 6, he launched a surprise attack.

The screaming Confederates struck the Union lines near Shiloh, a Methodist church in the center of the Union camp in southwestern Tennessee. Many of Grant's troops, half of whom had yet to see combat, were still sleeping or eating breakfast; some died in their tents. Panic-stricken soldiers dropped their weapons and ran for the river.

At one point on the battle's first day, General Johnston rode into the thick of the fighting, urging the Rebels forward: "Men, they are stubborn; we must use the bayonet. I will lead you!" Johnston led them well, only to be shot himself. His aide yelled, "General, are you hurt?" Johnston replied, "Yes, and I fear seriously." Soldiers helped the Confederate commander off his horse, his right boot full of blood from a severed artery. He died in the shade of a large oak tree.

After a day of confused fighting and terrible losses on both sides, the fleeing Union soldiers were pinned against the river. The new Confederate commander, Pierre G. T. Beauregard, telegraphed President Jefferson Davis that his army had scored "a complete victory, driving the enemy from every position." But his celebration was premature.

Reinforced by 25,000 fresh troops, Grant's army took the offensive at dawn, and the Confederates glumly withdrew twenty miles to Corinth. The Union troops were too battered and weary to pursue. Confederate private Sam Watkins observed that "those Yankees were whipped, fairly whipped, and according to all the rules of war they ought to have retreated. But they didn't."

Shiloh, a Hebrew word meaning "Place of Peace," was the costliest battle in which Americans had ever engaged to that point. Viewing the scene afterward, said General William Tecumseh Sherman, "would have cured anybody of war." Of the 100,000 men who participated, a quarter were killed or wounded, seven times the casualties at the Battle of Bull Run. And like Bull Run earlier and so many battles to come, Shiloh was a story of missed opportunities and lucky accidents. Throughout the war, winning armies would fail to pursue their retreating foes, allowing the wounded opponent to slip away, recover, and fight again.

After Shiloh, Union general Henry Halleck, a military bureaucrat jealous of Grant's success, spread a false rumor that Grant had been drinking during the battle. Grant stressed in a letter to his wife that he had been "sober as a deacon." Some urged Abraham Lincoln to fire the "unmilitary" Grant, but the president refused: "I can't spare this man; he fights." Halleck, however, took Grant's place as field commander, and soon thereafter the Union thrust in the Mississippi Valley ground to a halt. Lincoln quickly realized that Halleck was a paper-pusher who "shirked responsibility" and was a "moral coward."

**NEW ORLEANS** Just three weeks after the Battle of Shiloh, the Union won a great naval victory at New Orleans, as David G. Farragut's warships blasted their way past Confederate forts to take control of the largest city in the Confederacy. Union general Benjamin F. Butler thereafter served as the military governor of New Orleans.

When a Confederate sympathizer ripped down a Union flag, Butler had him hanged. After a Rebel woman leaned out her window and emptied her chamber pot on Farragut's head, Butler decreed that any woman who was disrespectful of Union soldiers would be treated as a "woman of the town plying her avocation"—that is, as a prostitute. Residents thereafter referred to Butler as "the Beast," but they quit harassing Union soldiers and sailors.

The loss of New Orleans was a devastating blow to the Confederate economy. The Union army gained control of 1,500 cotton plantations and liberated 50,000 slaves in the Mississippi Valley. As a result, the slave system in Louisiana was "forever destroyed and worthless," reported a northern journalist.

**PERRYVILLE** In the late summer of 1862, General Braxton Bragg's Army of Mississippi, 30,000 strong, used railroads to link up with General Edmund Kirby Smith's Army of East Tennessee. Their goal was to invade the North by taking control of the border state of Kentucky.

The Confederates met the Union Army of Ohio, led by General Don Carlos Buell, at the central Kentucky village of Perryville in October 1862. The outnumbered Confederates attacked the Union lines, pushing them back more than a mile. When Bragg learned that Union reinforcements were approaching, however, he ordered his army to withdraw south toward Tennessee. The Union retained control of Kentucky for the rest of the war.

## FIGHTING IN THE EAST

The fighting in the East remained fairly quiet for nine months after Bull Run. In the wake of the Union defeat there, Lincoln had appointed General George B. McClellan as head of the Army of the Potomac. The thirty-four-year-old McClellan, who encouraged journalists to call him "Little Napoleon," set about building the Union's most powerful, best-trained army.

Yet for all his boundless self-confidence and organizational ability, McClellan was afraid to attack. Months passed while he trained his massive army

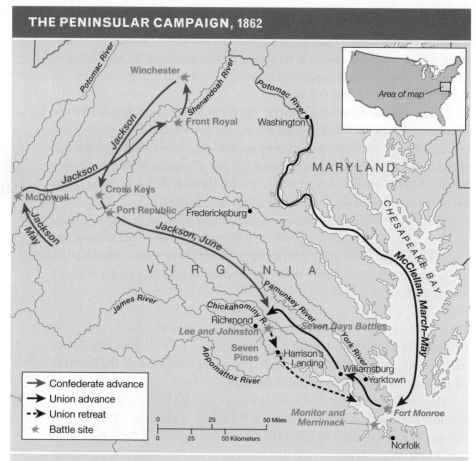

**THE PENINSULAR CAMPAIGN, 1862**

Legend:
- → Confederate advance
- → Union advance
- --→ Union retreat
- ✶ Battle site

- What was General McClellan's strategy for attacking Richmond?
- How did General Jackson divert the attention of the Union army?
- Why did President Lincoln demote McClellan after the Peninsular campaign?

to meet the superior numbers of Confederates he mistakenly believed were facing him. Lincoln finally lost his patience and ordered McClellan to attack.

**MCCLELLAN'S PENINSULAR CAMPAIGN**  In mid-March 1862, McClellan moved his army of 122,000 men on 400 ships and barges down the Potomac River and through the Chesapeake Bay to the mouth of the James River at the tip of the Yorktown peninsula, within sixty miles of the Confederate capital of Richmond, Virginia. Thousands of residents fled the city in panic, but McClellan waited too long to strike. A frustrated Lincoln told McClellan that the war could be won only by *engaging* the Rebel army. "Once more," Lincoln telegraphed, "it is indispensable that you strike a blow."

On May 31, 1862, Confederate general Joseph E. Johnston struck at McClellan's army along the Chickahominy River, six miles east of Richmond. In the Battle of Seven Pines (Fair Oaks), only the arrival of Federal reinforcements prevented a disastrous Union defeat. Both sides took heavy casualties, and Johnston was severely wounded.

At this point, Robert E. Lee assumed command of the main Confederate army, the Army of Northern Virginia, a development that changed the course of the war. Lee, a slave-owning planter whose father was a celebrated cavalry officer during the Revolutionary War, had graduated second in his class at West Point. During the Mexican-American War, he had impressed General Winfield Scott as the "very best soldier I ever saw in the field." Lee would prove to be a daring strategist who was as aggressive as McClellan was timid. "He is silent, inscrutable, strong, like a God," said a Confederate officer.

On July 9, when Lincoln visited McClellan's headquarters on the coast of Virginia, the general complained that the administration had failed to support him and lectured the president on military strategy. Such insubordination was ample reason to relieve McClellan of his overall command. After returning to Washington, Lincoln called Henry Halleck from the West to take charge.

**Robert E. Lee** Military adviser to President Jefferson Davis and later commander of the Army of Northern Virginia.

**SECOND BULL RUN** Lincoln and Halleck ordered McClellan to move his Army of the Potomac back to Washington, D.C., and join General John Pope, commander of the Union Army of Virginia, in a new assault on Richmond. In a letter to his wife, a jealous McClellan predicted—accurately—that "Pope will be thrashed and disposed of" by General Lee's army. He also dismissed Lincoln "as an idiot" and a "baboon."

Lee, aware that his only chance was to drive a wedge between the two larger Union armies so that he could deal with them one at a time, moved northward to strike Pope's army before McClellan's troops could arrive. Lee boldly divided his forces, sending Stonewall Jackson's "foot cavalry" around Pope's flank to attack the supply lines in the rear. At the Second Battle of Bull Run (or Manassas), fought on almost the same site as the earlier battle, a confused Pope assumed that he faced only Jackson, but Lee's main army by that time had joined in.

On August 30, 1862, a crushing Confederate attack drove the larger Union army from the field, giving the Confederates a sensational victory and leading a disheartened Union officer to confess from his deathbed that "General Pope had been outwitted . . . Our generals have defeated us." Pope was relieved of command on September 12. A Rebel soldier wrote home that "General Lee stands now above all generals in modern history. Our men will follow him to the end."

## EMANCIPATION

The Confederate victories in 1862 devastated morale in the North and convinced Lincoln that he had to take bolder steps. When fighting began in 1861, the need to keep the border slave states (Delaware, Kentucky, Maryland, and Missouri) in the Union dictated caution on the volatile issue of emancipation. In August 1862, Lincoln worried that "to arm the negroes would turn 50,000 bayonets from the loyal Border states *against* us that were *for* us." Beyond that, Lincoln had to contend with a deep-seated racial prejudice among most Northerners, who were willing to allow slavery to continue in the South as long as it was not allowed to expand into the West. Lincoln himself harbored doubts about his constitutional authority to end slavery, and he did not believe that blacks, if freed, could coexist with whites.

**SLAVES IN THE WAR** The expanding war forced the issue. As Federal forces pushed into the Confederacy, fugitive slaves began to arrive in Union army camps, and the commanders did not know what to do with them. One general designated them as "contraband of war," and thereafter the thousands of slaves who sought protection and freedom were known as **contrabands.** Some Union officers put the refugees to work digging trenches, building fortifications, tending livestock, and burying the dead; others simply set them free.

Lincoln, meanwhile, began to edge toward ending slavery. On April 16, 1862, he signed an act that abolished slavery in the District of Columbia; on June 19, he signed another bill that excluded slavery from the western territories. Still, he insisted that the war was about restoring the Union and ending secession, not freeing the slaves in the South.

Circumstances, however, changed Lincoln's outlook. In March 1862, he urged representatives of the four border states to begin gradually to emancipate their slaves. The next month, the Republican-controlled Congress passed the Second Confiscation Act, which declared that contrabands who had made it to Union army camps were "forever free." That summer, Lincoln decided that emancipation of all slaves in the Confederate states was necessary to win the war. In July 1862, he confided to his cabinet that "decisive and extreme measures must be adopted." Emancipation, he said, had become "a military necessity, absolutely necessary to the preservation of the Union. We must free the slaves or be ourselves subdued." Secretary of State William H. Seward agreed but advised Lincoln to delay the announcement until after a Union battlefield victory, to avoid being viewed as desperate.

**Contrabands** Former slaves on a farm in Cumberland Landing, Virginia, 1862.

**ANTIETAM: A TURNING POINT** Robert E. Lee made his own momentous decision in the summer of 1862: He would invade Maryland and force the "much weakened and demoralized" Army of the Potomac and its "timid" commander George McClellan to leave northern Virginia and thereby relieve the pressure on Richmond, the Confederate capital. "The idea of waiting for blows, instead of inflicting them, is altogether unsuited to the genius of our people," explained the *Richmond Examiner*.

Lee also hoped a northern invasion would influence the upcoming elections in the North. He also wanted to gain official British and French recognition of the Confederacy, which would bring his troops desperately needed supplies. In addition, Lee and Jefferson Davis planned to capture Maryland (with its many Confederate supporters), separate it from the Union, and gain control of its farms, crops, and livestock.

In September 1862, Lee and his 40,000 troops, many of them barefoot and underfed, pushed north across the Potomac River into western Maryland. "I have never seen such a mass of filthy, strong-smelling men," said a Marylander. "They are the roughest looking set of creatures I ever saw, their features, hair, and clothing matted with dirt and filth."

On September 17 the Union and Confederate armies clashed in the furious **Battle of Antietam** (Sharpsburg). Had not Union soldiers discovered Lee's detailed battle plans wrapped around three cigars that a Rebel soldier had carelessly dropped on the ground, the Confederates might have won.

And, had McClellan acted preemptively and moved his 100,000 men more quickly, he could have destroyed Lee's Army of Northern Virginia while it was scattered and still on the march. As always, however, McClellan mobilized slowly, enabling Lee and his troops to regroup at Sharpsburg, Maryland, between Antietam Creek and the Potomac River.

There, over the course of fourteen hours, the poorly coordinated Union army launched repeated attacks. The fighting was savage; a Union officer counted "hundreds of dead bodies lying in rows and in piles." The scene after "five hours of continuous slaughter" was "sickening, harrowing, horrible. O what a terrible sight!"

The next day, Lee braced for another Union attack that never came. That night, cloaked by fog and drizzling rain, the battered Confederates slipped back across the Potomac River to the safety of Virginia. "The 'barefoot boys' have done some terrible fighting," a Georgian wrote his parents. "We are a dirty, ragged set [of soldiers], mother, but courage & heroism find many a true disciple among us."

Although the battle was technically a draw, Lee's northern invasion had failed. One Rebel general called it the "hardest fought battle of the war."

McClellan, never known for his modesty, told his wife that he "had fought the battle splendidly" against great odds. To him, the Battle of Antietam was "the most terrible battle of the age." Indeed, it was the bloodiest day in American history. Some 6,400 soldiers on both sides were killed, twice as many as at Shiloh, and another 17,000 were wounded or listed as missing.

President Lincoln was pleased that Lee's army had been forced to retreat, but he was disgusted by McClellan's failure to pursue the Confederates and win the war. The exasperated president sent a sarcastic message to the general: "I have just read your dispatch about sore-tongued and fatigued horses. Will you pardon me for asking what the horses of your army have done . . . that fatigues anything?" Failing to receive a satisfactory answer, Lincoln sacked McClellan as commander of the Army of the Potomac and assigned him to recruiting duty in New Jersey. Never again would McClellan command troops, but he would challenge Lincoln for the presidency in 1864.

The Battle of Antietam revived sagging northern morale and dashed the Confederacy's hopes of forging alliances with Great Britain and France. It also convinced Lincoln to transform the war from an effort to restore the Union to a crusade to end slavery.

**Union view of the Emancipation Proclamation** A thoughtful Lincoln composes the proclamation with the Constitution and the Bible in his lap. The scales of justice hang on the wall behind him.

**EMANCIPATION PROCLAMATION**  On September 22, 1862, five days after the Battle of Antietam, President Lincoln issued the preliminary **Emancipation Proclamation**, which warned the Confederacy that if it did not stop fighting, all slaves still under its control were to be made "forever free" in exactly 100 days, on January 1, 1863.

The Emancipation Proclamation was not based on ideas of racial equality or abstract ideals of human dignity. It was, according to Lincoln, a "military necessity" and therefore an act of war. The proclamation would free only those slaves in areas still controlled by the Confederacy; it had no bearing on slaves in the four border states because they remained in the Union, and Lincoln had no constitutional authority to free them.

Lincoln believed that the Constitution allowed each state to decide the fate of slavery, so his only legal avenue was to act as commander in chief of the armed forces rather than as president. He would declare the end of slavery in Confederate-controlled areas as a "fit and necessary war measure" to save the Union.

When he signed the actual Emancipation Proclamation in January, however, Lincoln amended his original message, adding that the proclamation was "an act of justice" as well as a military necessity. His constitutional concerns

**Confederate view of the Emancipation Proclamation**  Surrounded by demonic faces hidden in his furnishings, Lincoln pens the proclamation with a foot trampling the Constitution. The devil holds the inkwell before him.

about abolishing slavery would lead him to promote the Thirteenth Amendment ending slavery across the nation. As Lincoln signed the Emancipation Proclamation, he said, "I never, in my life, felt more certain that I was doing the right thing than I do in signing this paper." Simply restoring the Union was no longer the purpose of the war; the transformation of the South and the slave system was now the goal.

**REACTIONS TO EMANCIPATION**    Abraham Lincoln's threat to free slaves under Confederate control triggered emotional reactions. The *Illinois State Register* savaged the president for violating the Constitution and causing "the permanent disruption of the republic." Democrats called his decision dictatorial, unconstitutional, and catastrophic. "We Won't Fight to Free the Nigger," proclaimed one popular banner. Many others felt likewise. In the months following the proclamation, thousands of Union troops deserted, explaining that they did not enlist to free slaves, much less to provide racial equality. In the November elections, Democrats, scolding Republicans as "Nigger Worshippers," took twenty-eight Republican seats.

Lincoln forcefully responded to his critics. "You say you will not fight to free negroes," he wrote. "Some of them seem willing to fight for you; but, no matter. Fight you, then, exclusively to save the Union. I issued the [emancipation] proclamation on purpose to aid you in saving the Union."

Although Lincoln's proclamation technically would free only the slaves where Confederates remained in control, many slaves in the northern border states and the South claimed their freedom anyway. As Lincoln had hoped, word spread rapidly among slave communities in the Confederacy, creating general confusion in the cities and encouraging hundreds of thousands to escape. A Union general said that emancipation "was like an earthquake. It shook and shattered the whole previously existing social system."

George Washington Albright, an enslaved teen in Mississippi, recalled that although white planters tried to prevent slaves from learning about the proclamation, word slipped through the "grapevine." His father was inspired to escape and join the Union army, and the younger Albright served as a "runner" for the 4Ls ("Lincoln's Legal Loyal League"), a secret group created to spread the news to slaves throughout the region.

Lincoln's proclamation incensed Confederate leaders, who predicted it would ignite a race war. By contrast, Frederick Douglass, the African American abolitionist leader, loved the "righteous decree"; he knew it would inspire abolitionists in the North and set in motion the eventual end of slavery everywhere.

As Lincoln had hoped, the Emancipation Proclamation boosted the Union war effort. It enabled African Americans to enlist in the Union army and navy, and it undermined support for the Confederacy in Europe. The conversion of the Civil War from a conflict to restore the Union into a crusade to end slavery gave the Federal war effort moral legitimacy in the eyes of Europeans.

As Union armies advanced deeper into the southern states, they became forces of liberation, freeing slaves and circulating thousands of copies of the Emancipation Proclamation. At Camp Saxton, a former plantation on the coast of South Carolina, the First South Carolina Volunteers, a Union regiment made up of former slaves, gathered on January 1, 1863, to celebrate Lincoln's signing of the Emancipation Proclamation.

After the proclamation was read aloud, it was "cheered to the skies." As Colonel Thomas W. Higginson, the unit's commander, unfurled an American flag, the black troops spontaneously began singing "My Country 'Tis of Thee / Sweet land of liberty / Of thee I sing!" "I never saw anything so electric," Higginson reported; "it made all other words cheap; it seemed the choked voice of a race at last unloosed."

**FREDERICKSBURG**   Meanwhile, the war was growing in scope and destruction. In Richmond, Mary Chesnut reported that everyone she encountered seemed shell-shocked: "They press your hand, tears stand in their eyes or roll down their cheeks . . . They have brothers, fathers, or sons—as the case may be—in the battle. And this thing now never seems to stop."

In his search for an effective commanding general, Lincoln turned in the fall of 1862 to Ambrose E. Burnside, whose greatest attribute was that he looked the part of a general: tall and imposing, with massive facial hair that gave rise to the term "sideburns." Twice before, Burnside had turned down the job, saying he was unfit for such responsibility. Now he accepted, although he remained full of self-doubts.

Burnside decided to try again to capture Richmond, the Confederate capital. To that end, in mid-November 1862, he positioned most of the 122,000 men in the Army of the Potomac east of the icy Rappahannock River overlooking the town of Fredericksburg, Virginia. Robert E. Lee rushed his Army of Northern Virginia to defend the town.

As the days passed, Lee's outnumbered forces established heavily fortified positions along a line of ridges and behind stone walls at the base of Marye's Heights, west of Fredericksburg. A Union soldier wrote home before the battle, predicting what was to happen: "It looks to me as if we are going over there to get murdered."

On December 13, the Union soldiers formed ranks south of town and began to assault Lee's entrenched positions. Confederate cannons and muskets chewed up the advancing Federals as they crossed a half mile of open

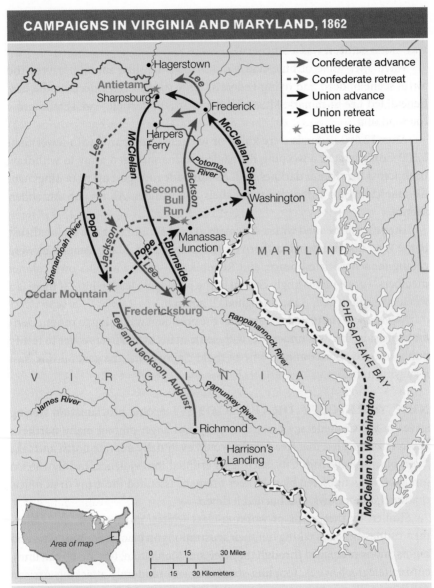

## CAMPAIGNS IN VIRGINIA AND MARYLAND, 1862

Legend:
- → Confederate advance
- --→ Confederate retreat
- → Union advance
- --→ Union retreat
- ✸ Battle site

Labels on map: Hagerstown, Lee, Antietam, Sharpsburg, Frederick, McClellan, Sept., Lee, McClellan, Harpers Ferry, Potomac River, Jackson, Second Bull Run, Jackson, Washington, Pope, Shenandoah River, Jackson, Pope, Lee, Burnside, Manassas Junction, MARYLAND, Cedar Mountain, Fredericksburg, Rappahannock River, CHESAPEAKE BAY, Lee and Jackson, August, V I R G I N I A, Pamunkey River, James River, Richmond, Harrison's Landing, McClellan to Washington

Inset: Area of map

Scale: 0 — 15 — 30 Miles / 0 — 15 — 30 Kilometers

- How did the Confederate army defeat General Pope at the Second Battle of Bull Run?
- Why was General Burnside's decision to attack at Fredericksburg a mistake?

land. The assault was, a Union general regretted, "a great slaughter-pen." The Pennsylvania governor, on hand to observe, later told President Lincoln that it was "not a battle, it was a butchery."

Wave after wave of blue-clad Union troops fell like autumn leaves. The awful scene of dead and dying Federals, some stacked three deep on the battlefield, led Lee to remark: "It is well that war is so terrible—we should grow too fond of it."

After 12,600 Federals were killed or wounded, compared with fewer than 5,300 Confederates, a weeping Burnside told his shattered army to withdraw back across the river as darkness fell. As Burnside rode past his retreating men, his aide called for three cheers for their commander. All he got was sullen silence.

The year 1862 ended with a stalemate in the East and with the Union thrust in the West mired down. Northern morale plummeted. Many Democrats were calling for a negotiated peace, and Republicans—even Lincoln's own cabinet members—grew increasingly critical of the president's leadership. "If there is a worse place than hell," Lincoln sighed, "I am in it."

Newspapers circulated rumors that the president was going to resign. General Burnside, too, was under fire, with some of his own officers eager to testify publicly to his shortcomings. One of them claimed that the general was "fast losing his mind."

**NEW YORK CITY DRAFT RIOTS** Lincoln's proclamation freeing slaves in the Confederacy created anxiety and anger among many northern laborers who feared that freed slaves would eventually migrate north and take their jobs. In New York City, such fears erupted into violence. In July 1863, a group of 500 whites, led by volunteer firemen, assaulted the army draft office, shattered its windows, and burned it down.

Swollen by thousands of working-class whites, mostly Irish, the rioters then ruthlessly began taking out their frustrations on blacks. For four days and nights, mobs rampaged through the streets of Manhattan, tearing up rail lines, cutting telegraph wires, toppling streetcars, and randomly attacking African Americans. The protesters also burned down more than fifty buildings, including the mayor's home, police stations, two Protestant churches, and the Colored Orphan Asylum, forcing 233 children to flee.

The violence killed 120 people and injured thousands. Only the arrival of Federal soldiers ended it.

**BLACK SOLDIERS AND SAILORS** In July 1862, in an effort to strengthen the Union war effort, the U.S. Congress had passed the **Militia Act**, which authorized the army to use freed slaves as laborers or soldiers. (They were

already eligible to serve in the navy.)
Lincoln, however, did not encourage
their use as soldiers because he feared
the reaction in the border states, where
slavery remained in place. Only after
the formal signing of the Emancipation
Proclamation in January 1863 did the
Union army recruit black soldiers in
large numbers.

On May 22, 1863, the U.S. War
Department created the Bureau of
Colored Troops to recruit free blacks
and freed slaves. More than 180,000
blacks enlisted. Some 80 percent of
them were from southern states, and
38,000 of them gave their lives. In the
navy, African Americans accounted
for about a fourth of all enlistments;
more than 2,800 of them died. Initially,
blacks were not allowed in combat, but
the need to win the war changed that.
A white Union army private reported
in the late spring of 1863 that the black
troops "fight like the Devil."

To be sure, racism in the North
influenced the status of African Americans in the military. Black soldiers
and sailors served in all-black units
led by white officers. They were paid
less than whites ($7 per month versus
$16 for white recruits) and were ineli-
gible for the enlistment bonus paid to

**Black Union army sergeant** Wearing
his uniform and sword, he poses with
a copy of J. T. Headley's *The Great
Rebellion* in his hand.

whites. Still, as Frederick Douglass declared, "this is no time for hesitation . . .
This is our chance, and woe betide us if we fail to embrace it."

Service in the Union army or navy provided former slaves a unique opportunity to grow in confidence, awareness, and maturity. A northern social
worker in the South Carolina Sea Islands was "astonished" at the positive
effects of "soldiering" on ex-slaves: "Some who left here a month ago to join
[the army were] cringing, dumpish, slow," but now they "are ready to look
you in the eye—are wide awake and active." Commenting on Union victories
at Port Hudson and Milliken's Bend, Louisiana, Lincoln reported that "some

of our commanders . . . believe that . . . the use of colored troops constitutes the heaviest blow yet dealt to the rebels." One African American soldier who recognized his former owner among a group of Confederate prisoners called out: "Hello master. Bottom rail on top this time!"

## THE WAR BEHIND THE LINES

Feeding, clothing, supplying, and nursing the vast armies required tremendous sacrifices. Farms and villages were transformed into battlefields, churches became makeshift hospitals, civilian life was disrupted, and families grieved for those who would not be coming home.

**CIVIL WAR MEDICINE** Medical knowledge lagged behind the development of military weapons during the war. Antibiotics had yet to be developed, and pain-killing medicines were in short supply. Amputation was the common treatment for gunshot wounds to the arm or leg, and stomach wounds were usually fatal because the resulting infection (peritonitis) could not be prevented. Of those killed by combat, some 60 percent died in battle, and 40 percent succumbed later to their wounds. Some 50,000 soldiers died in prisoner-of-war camps where infectious diseases—typhoid, typhus, malaria, pneumonia, smallpox, and measles—ran rampant.

**WOMEN AND THE WAR** While breaking the bonds of slavery, the Civil War also loosened traditional restraints on female activity. "No conflict in history," a journalist wrote, "was such a woman's war as the Civil War."

Women played prominent roles in both the North and South. They went to work in mills and factories, sewed uniforms, raised money and supplies, and volunteered as nurses. In Greenville, South Carolina, when T. G. Gower went off to fight, his wife Elizabeth took over the family business, converting production in their carriage factory to military wagons and ambulances. Three thousand northern women worked as nurses with the U.S. Sanitary Commission, a civilian agency that provided medical relief and other services for soldiers. Countless women, black and white, supported the freedmen's aid movement to help freed slaves.

In the North thousands of women served as nurses and health-related volunteers. The most famous were Clara Barton and Dorothea Lynde Dix. Barton explained that her place was "anywhere between the bullet and the battlefield." For her part, Dix, who was appointed superintendent of Union nurses in 1861, issued an appeal for "plain looking" women between the ages of thirty-five and fifty who wore no jewelry and could "bear the presence of suffering and exercise entire self-control."

Barton, who later founded the American Red Cross, decided to go to the killing fields on her own, delivering medical supplies and food to the sick and wounded. At Fredericksburg, she nursed some 1,200 wounded in a single building. "I wrung the blood from the bottom of my clothing before I could step," she reported, "for the weight about my feet" kept her from moving. "I am singularly free," she said, "—there are few to mourn for me, and I take my life in my hand and go where men fall and die, to see if perchance I can render some little comfort."

In many southern towns and counties, the home front became a world of white women and children and African American slaves. A resident of Lexing-

**Clara Barton** She oversaw the distribution of medicines to Union troops and would later help found the American Red Cross.

ton, Virginia, reported that there were "no men left" in town by mid-1862. Women suddenly found themselves full-time farmers or plantation managers, clerks, and schoolteachers.

Other women traveled with the armies as camp followers, cooking meals, writing letters, and assisting with amputations. Several dozen served as spies. New Yorker Mary Edwards Walker, a Union battlefield surgeon, was captured and imprisoned by the Confederates for spying, but later released in a prisoner exchange. She was the only woman in the war (and since) to be awarded the Congressional Medal of Honor, the nation's highest military award, which Lincoln had authorized in 1861. In 1864, President Lincoln told a soldier that all the praise of women over the centuries did not do justice "for their conduct during the war."

**WARTIME GOVERNMENT** While freeing the slaves in the Confederacy was a transformational development, a political revolution began as a result of the shift in congressional power from the South to the North after secession.

In 1862, the Republican-dominated Congress sought to promote the "prosperity and happiness of the whole people" by passing a more comprehensive

**Susie King Taylor** Born into slavery, she served as a nurse in Union-occupied Georgia and operated a school for freed slaves.

tariff bill (called the Morrill Tariff in honor of its sponsor, Vermont Republican congressman Justin Smith Morrill) to raise government revenue and "protect" America's manufacturing, agricultural, mining, and fishing industries from foreign competition.

Republicans in Congress, with Lincoln's support, enacted legislation reflecting their belief (and that of the old Whig party) that the federal government should actively promote economic development. To that end, Congress approved the Pacific Railway Act (1862), which provided funding and grants of land for construction of a 1,900-mile-long transcontinental railroad line from Omaha, Nebraska, to Sacramento, California. In addition, a **Homestead Act** (1862) granted 160 acres of public land to each settler who agreed to work that land for five years. To help farmers become more productive, Congress created a new federal agency, the Department of Agriculture.

Two other key pieces of legislation were the **Morrill Land Grant College Act** (1862), which provided states with 30,000 acres of federal land to finance the establishment of public universities that would teach "agriculture and mechanic arts," and the National Banking Act (1863), which created national banks that could issue paper money that would be accepted across the country. These wartime measures had long-term significance for the growth of the national economy—and the expansion of the federal government.

**UNION FINANCES** In December 1860, as southern states announced plans to secede, the federal Treasury was virtually empty. To meet the war's huge expenses, Congress needed money fast—and lots of it. It focused on three options: raising taxes, printing paper money, and selling government bonds to investors. The taxes came chiefly in the form of the Morrill Tariff on imports and a 3 percent tax on manufactures and most professions.

In 1862, Congress created the Internal Revenue Service to collect the first income tax on citizens and corporations. The tax rate was 3 percent on those with annual incomes of more than $800 and went up to 5 percent on incomes of more than $10,000. Yet only 250,000 people out of a population of 39 million had income high enough to pay taxes.

In the end, the tax revenues fell short of what was needed, meeting only 21 percent of wartime expenditures. In 1862, Congress approved the printing of paper money to help finance the war. With the Legal Tender Act of 1862, the Treasury issued $450 million in new paper currency, called *greenbacks* because of the color of the ink used to print the bills.

The federal government also relied upon the sale of bonds. A Philadelphia banker named Jay Cooke (the "Financier of the Civil War") mobilized a nation-wide campaign to sell $2 billion in government bonds to private investors.

**CONFEDERATE FINANCES**  In comparison to the Union, Confederate efforts to finance the war were a disaster. Jefferson Davis had to create a treasury and a revenue-collecting system from scratch. Moreover, the South's agrarian economy was land-rich but cash-poor. While the Confederacy owned 30 percent of America's assets (businesses, land, slaves) in 1861, its currency in circulation was only 12 percent of that in the North.

In its first year, the Confederacy created a property tax, which should have yielded a hefty amount of revenue. Collecting taxes was left to the states, however, and the result was chaos. In 1863, the desperate Confederate Congress began taxing nearly everything, but enforcement was poor and evasion easy. Altogether, taxes covered no more than 5 percent of Confederate war costs, and bond issues accounted for less than 33 percent. Treasury notes (paper money) accounted for more than 60 percent.

During the war, the Confederacy issued more than $1 billion in paper money, which, along with a shortage of consumer goods, caused prices to soar. By 1864, a turkey sold in the Richmond market for $100, and bacon was $10 a pound. Such rampant price increases caused great distress, and frustrations over the burdens of war erupted into rioting, looting, and mass protests.

By 1865, some 100,000 Confederate soldiers, hungry, weary and frustrated by delayed pay, were deserting the army and heading home. Some were upset that they were expected to risk their lives so that haughty planters could maintain their army of slaves. As one said, he and his comrades were "tired of fighting for this negro-owning aristockracy [sic]."

**UNION POLITICS**  The North also had its share of dissension and factionalism. But President Lincoln proved to be a remarkable conflict manager, in part because he refused to nurse grudges. He loved the jockeying of backroom politics, and he excelled at fending off uprisings and attempts to subvert his leadership.

Led by Thaddeus Stevens in the House and Charles Sumner in the Senate, the so-called Radical Republicans wanted more than the Confederacy's defeat; they wanted to "reconstruct" it by having Union armies seize southern plantations and give the land to the former slaves. The majority of Republicans, however, continued to back Lincoln's more cautious approach.

The Democratic party was devastated by the loss of its long-dominant southern wing and the death of its nationalist spokesman, Stephen A. Douglas. Peace Democrats favored restoring the Union "as it was [before 1860] and the Constitution as it is." They reluctantly supported Lincoln's war policies but opposed Republican economic legislation. Those referred to as the War Democrats, such as Tennessee senator Andrew Johnson and Secretary of War Edwin M. Stanton, backed Lincoln's policies.

A few Peace Democrats verged on treason. The **Copperhead Democrats** (named for copper coins they wore as lapel pins) were strongest in states such as Ohio, Indiana, and Illinois, where substantial numbers of former Southerners resided. The Copperheads openly sympathized with the Confederacy and called for an immediate end to the war.

**CIVIL LIBERTIES**  Such support for the enemy led President Lincoln to crack down hard. Like all wartime leaders, his challenge was to balance the urgent needs of winning a war with the protection of civil liberties. Using his authority as commander in chief, Lincoln exercised emergency powers, including suspending the writ of *habeas corpus*, which guarantees arrested citizens a speedy hearing before a judge. The Constitution states that the government may suspend habeas corpus only in cases of foreign invasion, but Supreme Court justice Roger Taney and several congressional leaders argued that Congress alone had the authority to take such action.

By the Habeas Corpus Act of 1863, Congress allowed the president to have people arrested on the "suspicion" of treason. Thereafter, Union soldiers and local sheriffs arrested thousands of Confederate sympathizers in the northern states without using a writ of habeas corpus. Union general Henry Halleck jailed a Missourian for saying, "[I] wouldn't wipe my ass with the stars and stripes."

**CONFEDERATE POLITICS AND STATES' RIGHTS**  As the war dragged on, discontented Confederates directed much of their frustration toward their leaders. A Richmond newspaper reported in 1862 that the Confederacy had "reached a very dark hour" because of Jefferson Davis's faulty leadership. It described the Rebel leader as "cold, haughty, peevish, narrow-minded, pig-headed, [and] malignant."

Poor white Southerners resented the planter elite while food grew scarce and prices skyrocketed. A food riot erupted in Richmond on April 2, 1863, when an angry mob, mostly women armed with pistols or knives, marched to the governor's mansion to demand that bread in Confederate warehouses be shared with civilians. When the governor announced that nothing could be done, the protesters shouted, "Bread or blood!" They broke into stores, stealing shoes and clothing as well as food. The riot ended only when President Davis arrived and threatened to shoot the protesters. Over several days, police arrested forty-four women and twenty-nine men. "We had forgotten Yankees and were fighting each other," Mary Chesnut confessed.

Davis's greatest challenge came from southern politicians who criticized the "tyrannical" powers of the Confederate government. As a general reported, "The state of feeling between the President [Davis] and Congress is bad—could not be worse." Critics asserted states' rights against the Confederate government, just as they had against the Union. Georgia governor Joseph Brown explained that he had joined the Confederacy to "sustain the rights of the states and prevent the consolidation of the Government, and I am still a *rebel* . . . *no* matter who may be in power."

While Lincoln was a shrewd pragmatist, Davis was a brittle ideologue with a waspish temper. Once he made a decision, nothing could change his mind, and he could never admit a mistake. One southern politician said that Davis was "as stubborn as a mule."

Such a dogmatic personality was ill-suited to the chief executive of an infant—and fractious—nation. Cabinet members resigned almost as soon as they were appointed. During its four years, the Confederacy had three secretaries of state and six secretaries of war. Vice President Alexander Stephens found Davis so "timid, petulant, peevish, and obstinate" that in 1862 he left Richmond, the Confederate capital, to sulk at his Georgia home.

**Jefferson Davis** President of the Confederacy.

# The Faltering Confederacy

Amid the political infighting, the war ground on. The Confederate strategy of fighting largely a defensive war was working well, and President Lincoln was still searching for a general-in-chief comparable to Robert E. Lee.

**CHANCELLORSVILLE**  After the Union disaster at Fredericksburg at the end of 1862, President Lincoln fired Ambrose Burnside and appointed General Joseph Hooker, a hard-drinking warrior known as "Fighting Joe," to lead the Army of the Potomac. With a force of 130,000 men, the largest Union army yet gathered, an overconfident Hooker attacked the Confederates at Chancellorsville, in eastern Virginia, during the first week of May 1863. "My plans are perfect," Hooker boasted. "May God have mercy on General Lee, for I will have none."

Hooker spoke too soon. Lee, with perhaps half as many troops, split his army in thirds and gave Hooker a painful lesson in the art of elusive mobility when Stonewall Jackson's 28,000 Confederates surprised the Union army by smashing into its exposed right flank. Jackson's surprise attack ultimately forced Hooker's army to retreat and resulted in a devastating defeat for the Union. "My God, my God," moaned Lincoln when he heard the news. "What will the country say?"

**Thomas "Stonewall" Jackson** The celebrated Confederate commander, Jackson would die of friendly fire in the Battle of Chancellorsville.

The Confederate victory was costly, however. As night fell during the second day of battle, Stonewall Jackson and several aides rode out beyond the skirmish line to locate the Union forces. Shooting erupted in the darkness, and nervous Confederates mistakenly opened fire on Jackson's group. Three bullets struck the celebrated commander, shattering his left arm and right hand. The next day, a surgeon amputated his arm. The indispensable Jackson seemed to be recovering, but he then contracted pneumonia and died. "I have lost my right arm," Lee lamented, and "I do not know how to replace him." The next day, Lee forced

Hooker's Union army to retreat. It was the peak of Lee's career, but Chancellorsville was his last significant victory.

**VICKSBURG** While General Lee frustrated the Federals in the East, General Grant had been inching his army down the Mississippi River toward the Confederate stronghold of Vicksburg, Mississippi, a busy commercial town situated on high bluffs overlooking a sharp, hairpin bend of the river. Capturing the Rebel stronghold, Grant stressed, "was of the first importance," because Vicksburg was the only rail and river junction between Memphis, Tennessee, and New Orleans. Yet he knew it would be difficult to conquer the "impregnable" Confederate defenses.

Meanwhile, Jefferson Davis stressed the importance of holding the Mississippi River open: "Vicksburg must not be lost!" If Union forces gained control of the river, they could split the Confederacy in two and prevent food and livestock from reaching Confederate armies in the East.

While Union warships sneaked past the Confederate cannons overlooking the river, Grant moved his army eastward across Mississippi on a campaign that President Lincoln later called "one of the most brilliant in the world." Grant's forces captured Jackson, Mississippi, the state capital, and won a half dozen battles before pinning 31,000 Rebel soldiers inside Vicksburg so tightly that "not a cat could have crept out . . . without being discovered." In late May and early June 1863, the Union forces dug twelve miles of interconnected trenches around the besieged city.

In the **Battle of Vicksburg**, Grant decided to use constant bombardment from gunboats and cannons to starve and gradually wear down the trapped Confederates. Many civilians were forced to live in cellars or caves dug as protection from the unending shelling. The Rebel soldiers and the city's residents could neither escape nor be reinforced nor resupplied with food and ammunition. As the weeks passed, they ate their horses and mules, then dogs and cats, and, finally, rats, which sold for a dollar each. One starving girl ate her pet bird.

General John C. Pemberton, the Confederate commander at Vicksburg, wrote Jefferson Davis that the situation was "hopeless." A group of ragged soldiers pleaded with their commander: "If you can't feed us, you had better surrender us, horrible as that idea is." Yet Pemberton, a Pennsylvanian whose Virginia-born wife convinced him to fight for the Confederacy, was determined to outlast Grant's troops.

**GETTYSBURG** Vicksburg's dilemma led Jefferson Davis to ask General Lee to send troops from Virginia to Mississippi to break the Union siege. Lee, however, thought he had a better plan. He would make another daring strike into the North in hopes of forcing the Union army surrounding Vicksburg to rush home to defend the northern heartland. He also wagered that a bold northern offensive would persuade peace-seeking Copperhead Democrats to try again to end the war on terms favorable to the Confederacy. The stakes were high. A Confederate general said the invasion across Maryland and into Pennsylvania would "either destroy the Yankees or bring them to terms." Or be a disaster for Lee.

In June 1863, the fabled Army of Northern Virginia, which Lee said was made up of "invincible troops" who would "go anywhere and do anything if properly led," moved northward, taking thousands of animals and wagons as well as throngs of slaves for support.

One reason Lee moved into the North was to find food for his men and horses. The Union armies had spent so much time in northern Virginia that there were not enough rations to go around. So as Lee's army moved north, his soldiers and slaves confiscated thousands of horses, cattle, and hogs, as well as tons of wheat and corn. They also captured free blacks in Maryland and Pennsylvania, returning them to slavery in Virginia.

Once the Union commander, General George Meade, realized the Confederates were again moving north, he gave chase, knowing that the next battle would "decide the fate of our country and our cause." As Lee's army moved into Pennsylvania, he lost track of the Federals following him because of the unexplained absence of General J. E. B. Stuart's 5,000 horse soldiers, who were Lee's "eyes and ears." Stuart, it turned out, had decided on his own to create a panic in the Union capital by threatening an attack on Washington, D.C. On June 28, an exasperated Lee exploded: "I cannot think what has become of Stuart. I ought to have heard from him long before now."

Neither side expected Gettysburg, a hilly farming town in southeastern Pennsylvania to be the site of the largest battle ever fought in North America. Unsuspecting Confederate troops entered the town at dawn on June 30 and collided with Union cavalry units that had been tracking their movements.

The main forces of both sides—65,000 Confederates and 85,000 Federals—then raced to the scene, and on July 1, the armies clashed in what came to be called the **Battle of Gettysburg**, the most dramatic contest of the war. While preparing to fight, a Union cavalryman yelled at soldiers from New York and Pennsylvania: "You stand alone, between the Rebel army and your homes. Fight like hell!"

Initially, the Confederates forced the Federals to retreat, but the Union troops regrouped to stronger positions on high ridges overlooking the town. General Meade rushed in reinforcements. That night he wrote his wife that both armies had been "shattered" by the first day's combat.

**"A Harvest of Death"** Timothy H. O'Sullivan's grim photograph of the dead at Gettysburg.

On July 2, wave after wave of screaming Confederates assaulted Meade's army, pushing the Federals back across blood-soaked wheat fields and through peach orchards, but never breaking through. A wounded Confederate officer scrawled a note before he died: "Tell my father I died with my face to the enemy." Some 16,000 were killed or wounded on both sides during the second day of fighting. Worse was to come.

The next day, July 3, against the objections of his senior general, Georgian James Longstreet, Robert E. Lee risked all on a gallant but doomed assault against the well-defended Union lines along Cemetery Ridge. For two hours, both sides bombarded the other, leading a Union soldier to write that it felt "as if the heavens and earth were crashing together."

Then, the cannons stopped. At about two o'clock on the broiling summer afternoon, three Confederate infantry divisions—about 12,500 men—emerged from the woods and prepared to attack in the 90-degree heat. General George Pickett, commander of the lead division, told his men to "Charge the enemy and remember Old Virginia!"

With drums pounding and bugles blaring, a gray wave of sweating Rebels began a mile-long dash up a grassy slope of newly mown hay crisscrossed with split-rail fences. Awaiting them behind a low stone wall at the top of Cemetery Ridge were 120 Union cannons and thousands of riflemen. It was as hopeless as the Union charge at Fredericksburg.

When the Federals opened fire, the Confederates were "enveloped in a dense cloud of dust. Arms, heads, blankets, guns, and knapsacks were tossed into the clear air." Only a few Rebels made it to the top, where they grappled in hand-to-hand combat. A Confederate general climbed atop the stone wall and shouted: "Come on, boys! Give them the cold steel! Who will follow me?" Two minutes later, he was dead—as was the Confederate attack—when Union soldiers held in reserve rushed to close the gap in their lines.

With stunning suddenness, the carnage was over. The surviving Confederates retreated to the woods, and the once roaring battlefield was now covered with the corpses of men and horses, a scene made ghastlier by the "moanings and groanings" of thousands of wounded. Each corpse told a poignant story. Scattered beside a dead Federal officer were papers granting him leave to go home and be married, and a letter from his soon-to-be bride expressing her "happiness at the approaching event." Five men from the Coffey family in North Carolina died on that battlefield, including twin brothers.

What General Lee had called the "grand charge" was, in the end, a grand failure. As he watched the survivors straggle back across the bloody field, he muttered, "All this has been my fault. It is I who have lost this fight." He ordered General Pickett to prepare his battered division for another attack, only to have Pickett reply: "General Lee, I have no division now." Half his men lay dead or wounded.

Lee sought to console Pickett by assuring him that he and his troops "have covered yourselves with glory." Pickett would have none of it. "Not all the glory in the world, General Lee, can atone for the widows and orphans this day has made."

Some 42,000 were dead, wounded, or missing after three days at Gettysburg. Thousands of horses were also killed and left to rot in the summer heat. A Union soldier wrote home: "Great God! When will this horrid war stop?"

Others asked the same question. John Futch, a Confederate private from North Carolina, had seen his brother Charley shot in the head. He wrote his wife that the slaughter had left him "half crazy." A few weeks after the battle, he quit his post and headed home, only to be captured, tried as a deserter, and executed.

**LEE'S RETREAT** Again, as after Antietam, Robert E. Lee's mangled army retreated to Virginia—and again, the Federals were slow to give chase. Had General Meade quickly pursued Lee's battered army, he might have ended the war. President Lincoln was outraged: "We had them within our grasp! Your golden opportunity is gone."

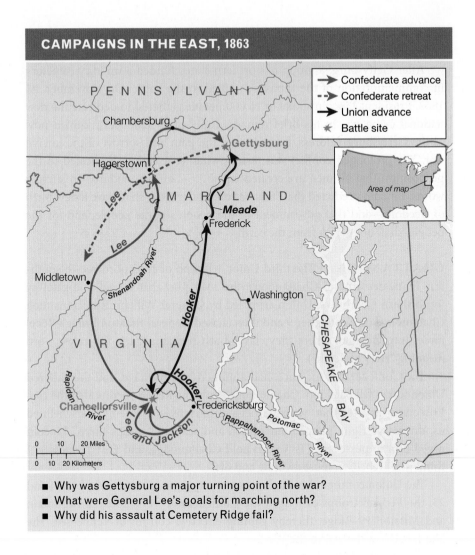

## CAMPAIGNS IN THE EAST, 1863

**Legend:**
→ Confederate advance
--→ Confederate retreat
→ Union advance
✷ Battle site

- Why was Gettysburg a major turning point of the war?
- What were General Lee's goals for marching north?
- Why did his assault at Cemetery Ridge fail?

The war would grind on for another twenty-one months. Still, Rebel morale plummeted. A barely literate Georgia soldier wrote his mother that "the Armey is broken harted" and "don't care which way the war closes, for we have suffered very much."

Lee's desperate gamble had failed in every way, not the least being its inability to relieve the pressure on Vicksburg, Mississippi. On July 4, as Lee's defeated army left Pennsylvania, General John Pemberton, the Confederate commander at Vicksburg, surrendered his starving 31,000-man army, ending the forty-seven-day siege. Union vessels now controlled the Mississippi River and the Confederacy was effectively split in two, with Louisiana, Texas, and

Arkansas cut off from the other Rebel states. Jefferson Davis said that it was the Confederacy's "period of disaster."

After Gettysburg, a group of northern states funded a military cemetery in commemoration of the thousands killed in the battle. On November 19, 1863, President Lincoln spoke to 15,000 people gathered to dedicate the new national cemetery. In his brief remarks (only nine sentences), known now as the Gettysburg Address, he expressed the pain and sorrow of the uncivil war. The prolonged conflict was testing whether a nation "dedicated to the proposition that all men are created equal . . . can long endure." In stirring words, Lincoln predicted that "this nation, under God, shall have a new birth of freedom—and that government of the people, by the people, and for the people, shall not perish from the earth."

**CHATTANOOGA**   The third Union triumph of 1863 occurred in southern Tennessee around Chattanooga, the river port that served as a gateway to northern Georgia. A Union army led by General William Rosecrans took Chattanooga on September 9 and then chased General Braxton Bragg's Rebel forces into Georgia, where they clashed at Chickamauga (a Cherokee word meaning "river of death").

The Confederates, for once, had a numerical advantage, and the battered Union forces fell back into Chattanooga while the Rebels surrounded the city. Rosecrans reported that "we have met a serious disaster. Enemy overwhelmed us, drove our right, pierced our center, and scattered troops there." Lincoln urged him to persevere: "If we can hold Chattanooga, and East Tennessee, I think [the] rebellion must dwindle and die."

The Union command rushed in reinforcements, and on November 24 and 25, the Federal troops dislodged the Confederates from Lookout Mountain and Missionary Ridge, thereby gaining effective control of Tennessee. The South had lost the war in the West.

**THE CONFEDERACY AT RISK**   The dramatic Union victories at Vicksburg, Gettysburg, and Chattanooga seemed to turn the tide against the Confederacy. During the summer and fall of 1863, however, Union generals in the East lost the momentum Gettysburg had provided, thereby allowing the Army of Northern Virginia to nurse its wounds and continue fighting.

By 1864, Robert E. Lee, whose offer to resign after Gettysburg was refused by Jefferson Davis, was ready to renew the war. His men were "in fine spirits and anxious for a fight." Still, the tone had changed. Confederate leaders had long assumed they could win the war. Now, they began to worry about defeat. A Confederate officer in Richmond noted in his diary after the defeat at Gettysburg that "today absolute ruin seems to be our fortune. The Confederacy totters to its destruction."

**A WARTIME ELECTION**  War or no war, 1864 was a presidential election year, and by autumn the contest would become a referendum on the war itself. No president since Andrew Jackson had won reelection, and Abraham Lincoln became convinced that he would lose without a dramatic change in the course of the war.

Radical Republicans, frustrated that the war had not been won, tried to prevent Lincoln's nomination for a second term, but he consistently outmaneuvered them. Once Lincoln was assured of the nomination, he selected Andrew Johnson, a War Democrat from Tennessee, as his running mate on the "National Union" ticket.

The War Democrats had indiscreetly asked General Grant to be their candidate. He firmly declined, explaining that "I am not a politician, never was, and hope never to be." Becoming president, he said, "is the last thing in the world I desire."

Spurned by Grant, the Democrats called for an immediate end to the fighting. They nominated General George B. McClellan, the former Union commander who had clashed with Lincoln. McClellan pledged to stop the war and, if the Rebels refused to return to the Union, he would allow the Confederacy to "go in peace."

Lincoln knew that the election would be decided on the battlefields. To save the Union, the president had brought Grant, his best commander, to Washington, D.C., in March 1864; promoted him to general in chief; and given him overall command of the war effort, promising all the troops and supplies he needed.

A New York newspaper reported that Lincoln's presidency was now "in the hands of General Grant, and the failure of the General will be the overthrow of the president." When a delegation visited the White House to complain about Grant's reputation as a heavy drinker, Lincoln told the visitors

**Ulysses S. Grant**  At his headquarters in City Point (now Hopewell), Virginia.

that if he could find the brand of whiskey Grant used, he would distribute it to the rest of his generals.

**GRANT'S STRATEGY**    General Grant was a hard-nosed warrior with unflagging energy and persistence. One soldier said that Grant always looked like he was "determined to drive his head through a brick wall and was about to do it." Yet the Union commander hated war. "I never went into battle willingly or with enthusiasm," he admitted. Nevertheless, he was a brilliant military strategist driven by a simple concept: "Find out where your enemy is, get to him as soon as you can, and strike him as hard as you can, and keep moving on"—regardless of the number of dead and wounded.

Grant's predecessors had focused on trying to capture Richmond; his purpose was to defeat Confederate armies. To do so, he would wage a relentless war of attrition, one in which victory would favor the side that could absorb the most punishment and keep fighting. He would pressure the shrinking Confederate armies wherever they were. Grant, as Abraham Lincoln noted, understood that winning the war was a matter of "awful arithmetic." The Union had the greater numbers, so victory was "only a matter of time."

To that end, Grant ordered the three largest Union armies, one in Virginia, one in Tennessee, and one in Louisiana, to launch offensives in the spring of 1864. No more short battles followed by long pauses. They would force the outnumbered Confederates to keep fighting, day after day, week after week, until they were worn out.

Grant assigned his trusted friend, General William Tecumseh Sherman, a rail-thin, red-haired Ohioan, to lead the Union army in Tennessee southward and apply a strategy of "complete conquest." Sherman, cool under pressure and obsessed with winning at all costs, owed much of his success to Grant's support. "He stood by me when I was crazy, and I stood by him when he was drunk," Sherman said.

**William Tecumseh Sherman** Sherman's campaign through Georgia hastened the end of the war.

Grant and Sherman would now wage total war, confiscating or destroying any civilian property that might be of use to the military. It was a ruthless and costly plan, but in the end, it would prove effective.

**FORT PILLOW MASSACRE**  As the war ground on, the fighting grew more brutal. On April 12, 1864, at Fort Pillow, perched on a bluff overlooking the Mississippi River forty miles north of Memphis, Tennessee, Confederate troops under General Nathan Bedford Forrest, who would help found the Ku Klux Klan after the war, murdered some 300 Union soldiers who had surrendered. Most of them were African Americans. A Confederate sergeant reported that "the poor, deluded negroes would run up to our men, fall upon their knees, and with uplifted hand scream for mercy, but were ordered to their feet and then shot down."

Word of the Fort Pillow Massacre spread across the nation. Violence begat violence. A few weeks later, a Union soldier from Wisconsin fighting in north Georgia wrote to his future wife about a recent battle. "Twenty-three of the Rebs surrendered but our boys asked if they remembered Fort Pillow and killed all of them. Where there is no officer with us, we take no prisoners . . . We want revenge for our brother soldiers and will have it."

**CHASING LEE**  In May 1864, General Grant's massive Army of the Potomac, numbering about 115,000 (nearly twice the size of General Lee's Army of Northern Virginia), moved south across the Rappahannock and Rapidan Rivers in eastern Virginia. In the nightmarish Battle of the Wilderness (May 5–6), the armies clashed in an impenetrable tangle of dense forest and thickets. Cannons set off brushfires that burned many wounded soldiers to death.

At one point in the intense battle, the Union forces threatened to overrun Lee's headquarters. Lee himself helped organize a counterattack, lining up soldiers from Texas to lead the effort. Spurred by a rush of adrenaline, he stood high in his stirrups, waved his hat, and yelled: "Texans always move them!" He then turned his horse toward the enemy to lead the charge. The soldiers shouted, "Go back, General Lee, go back!" But he kept moving forward. Finally, an officer pulled ahead of Lee, grabbed the reins of his horse, and prevented him from moving. "Can't I, too, die for my country?" the general muttered. His mood brightened as the Confederates swept the Federals from the field and broke the Union advance.

Grant's men suffered more casualties than the Confederates, but the Rebels struggled to find replacements. Always before, when bloodied by Lee's troops, Union armies had quit fighting to rest and nurse their wounds, but now Grant refused to halt. Instead, he continued to push southward, forcing the Rebels to keep fighting.

Lee knew what he was up against. As he told aides, the "great thing about Grant is his perfect coolness and persistency of purpose . . . he is not easily excited . . . and he has the grit of a bull-dog! Once let him get his 'teeth' in, and nothing can shake him off." When General John B. Gordon boasted after the Battle of the Wilderness that Grant was retreating, Lee corrected him: "You are mistaken, quite mistaken. Grant is not retreating; he is not a *retreating* man."

Lee predicted that Grant's army would head for Spotsylvania, which it did. There, it engaged Lee's men near Spotsylvania Court House, eleven miles southwest of Fredericksburg, on the road to Richmond. For twelve brutally hot days in May, the opposing armies were locked in some of the fiercest combat of the war. Grant's troops kept the pressure on.

In the first days of June, just as Republican leaders were gathering to renominate Abraham Lincoln as their presidential candidate, Grant foolishly ordered a poorly coordinated frontal assault on Lee's entrenched Rebels at Cold Harbor, near the Chickahominy River, just ten miles east of Richmond. In twenty minutes, almost 4,000 Federals, caught in a blistering cross fire, were killed or wounded. It was, according to a Union general, "one of the most disastrous days the Army of the Potomac has ever seen." A Confederate commander reported that "it was not war; it was murder."

The frightful losses nearly unhinged Grant, who later admitted that the botched attack was his greatest mistake as a commander. Critics, including Lincoln's wife Mary, called Grant "a butcher" who was "not fit to be at the head of an army." In just two months, Grant's massive offensive across Virginia, labeled the Overland Campaign, had cost some 65,000 killed, wounded, or missing Union soldiers and 33,000 Rebel casualties.

Criticism of Grant's campaign skyrocketed. Even Horace Greeley, the powerful Unionist publisher of the *New York Tribune*, urged Lincoln to negotiate with Confederate leaders to save the "bleeding, bankrupt, almost dying country." The Union war effort came close to ending.

Yet Grant, for all his mistakes, knew that his army could replace its dead and wounded; the Rebels could not. And, Grant reminded Lincoln, he was slowly pushing Lee's army toward Richmond, backing the Confederates into a corner from which they could not escape. Lincoln stood in awe of Grant's tenacity. So, too, did many of his soldiers. "Grant is striking out boldly in every possible direction," a Union officer wrote, "like a mad dog in a meat house."

In June 1864, Grant brilliantly maneuvered his battered forces around Lee's army and headed for Petersburg, a major supply center and railroad hub twenty-five miles south of Richmond. The opposing armies dug in above and

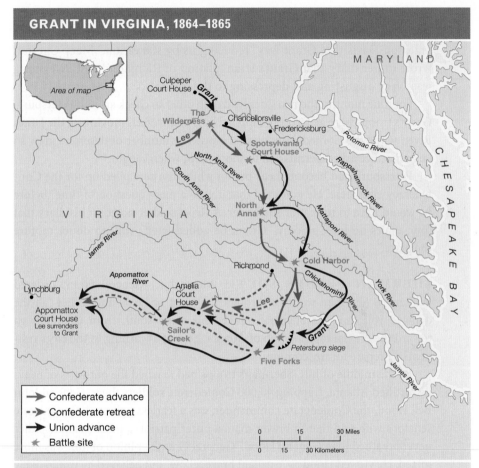

## GRANT IN VIRGINIA, 1864–1865

Confederate advance
Confederate retreat
Union advance
★ Battle site

0    15    30 Miles
0    15    30 Kilometers

■ How were General Grant's tactics in the Battle of the Wilderness different from the Union's previous encounters with General Lee's army?

■ Why did Grant have the advantage at Petersburg?

below Petersburg. Grant began a long siege of the trapped Confederate army, tightening the noose as he had done at Vicksburg.

To cut off supplies to the Rebel troops, Grant sent an army commanded by General Philip Sheridan to destroy the farms in the fertile Shenandoah Valley that kept Lee's army and its horses alive. Sheridan was pleased, for he believed that reducing Confederate farmers to poverty would shorten the war, which placed him "on the side of humanity."

Within weeks, residents of the Shenandoah Valley saw "columns of smoke . . . rising in every direction from burning houses and burning barns." Union troops burned stored grain and rounded up sheep, cattle, and horses to be sent to Grant's army. At the end of August, Lee reported to Jefferson Davis that Grant was "reducing us by starvation." Mary Chesnut wrote in her diary that Grant's strangulation of Richmond and Petersburg was "very disgusting and depressing to the spirits."

For nine months, the two sides held each other in check around Petersburg. Grant's troops were generously supplied by Union vessels moving up the James River, while the Confederates wasted away. The number of deserters grew so large that Lee asked permission to shoot them when caught.

Petersburg had become Lee's prison while disasters piled up for the Confederacy elsewhere. He admitted that it was "a mere question of time" before he would have to retreat or surrender. A Rebel soldier noted in his diary that "our affairs do look gloomy." Grant, he added later, "will no doubt capture the place."

**SHERMAN PUSHES SOUTH** Meanwhile, General Grant ordered William T. Sherman to drive through the heart of Dixie and inflict "all the damage you can." As Sherman moved his army south from Chattanooga toward the crucial railroad hub of Atlanta, he sent a warning to the city's residents: "Prepare for my coming."

By the middle of July, Sherman's troops had reached the outskirts of heavily fortified Atlanta, trapping 40,000 Confederate soldiers there. General John Bell Hood, the Confederate commander, was a fearless fighter. A Confederate senator's wife said that "a braver man, a purer patriot, a more gallant soldier never breathed than General Hood." General Grant's opinion of him was more mixed. He viewed Hood as "a gallant brave fellow" but believed he would likely "dash out and fight every time you raised a [Union] flag before him." And that is just what Grant and Sherman wanted him to do.

Hood's arm had been shattered at Gettysburg, and he had lost a leg at Chickamauga. Strapped to his saddle, he refused simply to "defend" Atlanta; instead, he attacked. Three times in eight days, the Confederates lashed out at the Union lines encircling the city. Each time they were repulsed, suffering *seven* times as many casualties as the Federals. The Battle of Atlanta left Hood's army wounded, surrounded, and outnumbered. "All lion," Robert E. Lee called Hood, "none of the fox."

Finally, on September 1, the Confederates evacuated the city. Sherman then moved in, gleefully telegraphing Lincoln in September 1864, "Atlanta is ours and fairly won."

Sherman's soldiers stayed in Atlanta until November, resting and resupplying themselves. The 20,000 residents were told to leave before he destroyed much of the city. When they protested, the Union commander replied: "War is cruelty." His men then set fire to the city's railroad station, iron foundries, shops, mills, hotels, and businesses. After Grant congratulated Sherman, he ordered him to commence another campaign, for "We want to keep the enemy constantly pressed to the end of the war."

**LINCOLN REELECTED** William Tecumseh Sherman's conquest of Atlanta turned the tide of the **election of 1864**. As a Republican senator said, the Union victory in Georgia "created the most extraordinary change in public opinion here [in the North] that ever was known." The capture of Mobile, Alabama, by Union naval forces in August, and Confederate defeats in Virginia's Shenandoah Valley in October, also spurred a dramatic revival of Abraham Lincoln's political support in the North. A Union newspaper editor reported that the fall of Atlanta "has secured a sudden unanimity for Mr. Lincoln." The South's hope that northern discontent would lead to a negotiated peace vanished.

In the 1864 election, the Democratic candidate, George McClellan, the former Union army commander, carried only New Jersey, Delaware, and Kentucky, winning just 21 electoral votes to Lincoln's 212 and 1.8 million popular votes (45 percent) to Lincoln's 2.2 million (55 percent). Union soldiers and sailors voted in large numbers, and almost 80 percent voted for Lincoln. The president's victory sealed the fate of the Confederacy, for it ensured that Union armies would keep the pressure on the Rebels.

**SHERMAN'S "MARCH TO THE SEA"** In November 1864, General Sherman led 60,000 soldiers out of Atlanta on their famous 300-mile **March to the Sea**. Sherman was eager to "make Georgia howl" by making every Rebel, soldier or civilian "feel the hard hand of war." Why? Because "we are not only fighting hostile armies, but a hostile people" who must be made "so sick of war" that they would never support a civil war again. Sherman pledged to break the will of Georgians.

John Bell Hood's Confederate Army of Tennessee, meanwhile, tried a desperate gamble by heading in the opposite direction from the Union forces, pushing northward into Alabama and then Tennessee. Hood hoped to trick Sherman into chasing him. Sherman refused to take the bait, however. He was determined to keep his main army moving southward to the Georgia coast and then into South Carolina, the seedbed of secession.

Sherman, however, did send General George Thomas and 30,000 soldiers to shadow Hood's Confederates. The two forces clashed in Tennessee. In the Battle of Franklin (November 30, 1864), near Nashville, Hood's 18,000 soldiers

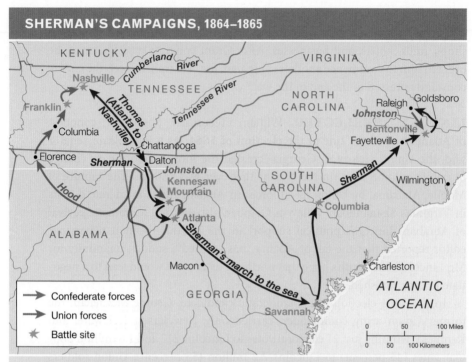

## SHERMAN'S CAMPAIGNS, 1864–1865

- What was General Sherman's goal as he marched across Georgia?
- How much damage did Sherman do in Georgia and South Carolina?
- How did it affect the Confederate war effort?

launched a hopeless frontal assault against well-fortified Union troops. In a few hours, Hood lost six generals and saw 6,252 of his men killed or wounded, a casualty figure higher than "Pickett's Charge" at Gettysburg. A Confederate captain wrote that the "wails and cries of the widows and orphans made at Franklin, Tennessee, will heat up the fires of the bottomless pit to burn the soul of General J. B. Hood for murdering their husbands and fathers." Two weeks later, in the Battle of Nashville, the Federals scattered what was left of Hood's bloodied army.

Meanwhile, Sherman's Union army raced southward across Georgia, living off the land while destroying plantations, barns, crops, warehouses, bridges, and rail lines. An Ohio sergeant said, "Every house, barn, fence, and cotton gin gets an application of the torch. That prospect is revolting, but war is an uncivil game, and can't be civilized."

Sherman's March through Georgia became infamous among Southerners as a supposed example of Union tyranny. After the war, however, a

Confederate officer acknowledged that the campaign was well-conceived and well-managed. "I don't think there was ever an army in the world that would have behaved better, in a similar expedition, in an enemy country. Our army certainly wouldn't have."

On December 24, 1864, Sherman sent a whimsical telegram to President Lincoln offering him the coastal city of Savannah as a Christmas present. By the time Union troops arrived in Savannah, they had freed more than 40,000 slaves, burned scores of plantations, and destroyed the railroads. "God bless you, Yanks!" shouted a freed slave. "Come at last! God knows how long I been waitin'."

**SOUTH CAROLINA** On February 1, 1865, Sherman's army headed north across the Savannah River into South Carolina, the "hell-hole of secession" in the eyes of Union troops. Sherman reported that his "whole army is burning with an insatiable desire to wreak vengeance upon South Carolina. I almost tremble at her fate, but feel she deserves all that seems in store for her."

South Carolina paid a high price for having led the southern states out of the Union. Sherman's men burned more than a dozen towns, including Barnwell, which they called "Burnwell." On February 17, 1865, they captured the state capital of Columbia. Soon thereafter, Charleston surrendered after Confederate soldiers torched to buildings containing material that would be valuable to the Yankees.

It was no accident that Sherman ordered two all-black regiments to lead the Union advance into the city that launched secession and war. On April 14, the Union general gave Major Robert Anderson the honor of raising the U.S. flag once again over Fort Sumter.

**A LOSING CAUSE** During late 1864 and early 1865, the Confederacy found itself besieged on all sides. Defeat was in the air. Some Rebel leaders, including Secretary of War John C. Breckinridge, wanted to negotiate a peace settlement. Breckinridge, who had been vice president under James Buchanan and had run for president in 1860, urged Robert E. Lee to pursue an honorable end to the war. "This has been a magnificent epic," he said. "In God's name, let it not terminate in a farce."

By December 1864, Grant had tightened the vice around Richmond, cutting off rail service "until the rebellion is crushed or strangled." His ruthless strategy slowly proved its worth.

Jefferson Davis stubbornly rejected any talk of surrender, however. If his armies should be defeated, he wanted soldiers to scatter and fight an unending guerrilla war. "The war came and now it must go on," he stubbornly insisted, "till the last man of this generation falls in his tracks, and his children seize his musket and fight our battle."

Davis, Lee, and others finally became so desperate that they did the unthinkable: On March 13, 1865, Davis signed a bill calling for the immediate recruitment of slaves into the army—with the permission of their owners. Most Confederates were not happy about this desperate step. Before African Americans could be enlisted and trained, however, the war came to an end.

**A SECOND TERM**  While Confederate forces made their last stands, Abraham Lincoln prepared for his second term as president. The weary commander in chief had weathered constant criticism during his first term, but he now garnered deserved praise. The *Chicago Tribune* observed that Lincoln "has slowly and steadily risen in the respect, confidence, and admiration of the people."

On March 4, 1865, amid rumors of a Confederate attempt to abduct or assassinate the president, some 30,000 people defied frigid weather to attend his second inauguration. Half of them were people of color. Lincoln, dressed in a black suit and stovepipe hat, delivered his address on the East Portico of the Capitol. Not 100 feet away, looking down from the Capitol porch, twenty-six-year-old John Wilkes Booth, who five weeks later would kill the president in a desperate attempt to do something "heroic" for his beloved South.

Lincoln's second inaugural address was more sermon than speech. Slavery, he said, had "somehow" caused the war, and everyone bore some guilt for the national shame of racial injustice and the awful war to end it. Both sides had known that war should be avoided at all costs, but "one of them would *make* war rather than let the nation survive; and the other would *accept* war rather than let it perish."

Lincoln longed for peace. "Fondly do we hope—fervently do we pray—that this mighty scourge of war may speedily pass away." He noted the paradoxical irony of both Unionists and Confederates reading the same Bible, praying to the same God, and appealing for divine support in their fight. Now the president urged the Union forces "to finish the work we are in," bolstered with "firmness in the right insofar as God gives us to see the right."

As Lincoln looked ahead to a "just and lasting peace," he stressed that vengeance must be avoided at all costs. Reconciliation must be pursued "with malice toward none; with charity for all." Those eight words captured his hopes for a restored Union. Redemption and reunion were his goals, not reprisals.

**APPOMATTOX**  During the spring of 1865, General Grant's army kept pounding the Rebels defending Petersburg, Virginia. Robert E. Lee had no way to replace the men he was losing, and his dwindling army couldn't kill enough Yankees to make Grant quit. On April 2, 1865, after General Philip Sheridan's horse soldiers cut off the last railroad serving the Confederate army in Petersburg, a desperate Lee made a desperate decision: the badly outnumbered Confederates abandoned Petersburg and headed west, with the Union army in hot pursuit. At the same time, the Confederate government fled Richmond, but not before burning anything of value.

The Confederacy was in chaos. "Women were weeping, children crying," noted a reporter in Richmond. "Men stood speechless, haggard, woebegone." Five days later, on April 7, Grant sent a note urging the trapped Lee to surrender. With the remnants of his army virtually surrounded and no food, Lee recognized that "there is nothing left for me to do but go and see General Grant, and I would rather die a thousand deaths."

On April 9 (Palm Sunday), four years to the day since the Confederate attack on Fort Sumter, the tall, dignified Lee, stiff and formal in his impeccable dress uniform, ceremonial sword, and shiny boots, met the short, mud-spattered Grant in a small brick house in the village of **Appomattox Court House**. Grant apologized for his "rough" appearance, explaining that he had left behind his dress uniform. Lee, in turn, stressed that he was in a new uniform because it was the only one he had left.

After some awkward exchanges about their service in the Mexican-American War, Lee asked Grant about the terms of surrender. In keeping with Lincoln's desire for a gracious peace with "malice toward none," Grant let the Confederates keep their pistols, horses, and mules, and he ensured that none of them would be tried for treason. Lee replied that "this would have a most happy effect" upon his men and accepted the terms as "more than he expected." He then confessed that his men were starving, and Grant ordered that they be provided food.

After drafting and signing the surrender documents, Lee mounted his horse. Grant and his men saluted him, raising their hats, and Lee responded in kind before returning to his defeated army. Grant ordered that there be no cheering or gloating. "The war is over," he said, adding that "the rebels are our countrymen again, and the best sign of rejoicing after the victory will be to abstain from all demonstrations in the field."

The next day, as the gaunt Confederates formed ranks for the last time, Joshua Chamberlain, the Union general in charge of the surrender ceremony, told his men to salute the Rebel soldiers as they paraded past to give up their muskets. His Confederate counterpart signaled his men to do likewise. Chamberlain remembered that there was not a sound, simply an "awed stillness . . . as if it were the passing of the dead." The remaining Confederate forces in Texas and North Carolina surrendered in May. Jefferson Davis, who had fled Richmond ahead of the advancing Federal troops, was captured in Georgia on May 10. He was eventually imprisoned in Virginia for two years.

The brutal war was at last over. Upon learning of the Union victory, John Wilkes Booth wrote in his diary that "something *decisive* and great must be done" to avenge the Confederate defeat. He began plotting to kill President Lincoln and members of his cabinet.

Two days after Lee surrendered, Lincoln gave a speech on the White House lawn in which he said he looked forward to "reconstructing" the Confederate states. He also hoped that literate freed blacks and those who had served in the Union military would be able to vote. Booth, who was in the audience, noted that Lincoln's pledge "meant nigger citizenship. Now, by God, I'll put him through [kill him]. That is the last speech he will ever make."

# A Transformational War

The Civil War was the most traumatic event in American history. "We have shared the incommunicable experience of war," reflected Oliver Wendell Holmes Jr., a twice-wounded Union officer who would become chief justice of the Supreme Court. "We have felt, we still feel, the passion of life to its top . . . In our youth, our hearts were touched by fire."

In Virginia, elderly Edmund Ruffin, the arch secessionist who had been given the honor of firing the first shots at Fort Sumter, was so devastated by the Confederate surrender that he put his musket barrel in his mouth and blew off the top of his head.

The nation had been transformed. A *New York Times* editorial reflected that the war had left "nothing as it found it . . . It leaves us a different people in everything." The war destroyed the South's economy, many of its railroads and factories, much of its livestock, and several of its cities. In 1860, the northern and southern economies had been essentially equal in size. By 1865, the southern economy's productivity had been halved.

**THE UNION PRESERVED**  The war ended the Confederacy and preserved the Union; shifted the political balance of power in Congress, the U.S. Supreme Court, and the presidency from South to North; strengthened the Republican party; and boosted the northern economy's industrial development, commercial agriculture, and western settlement. The Homestead Act (1862) made more than a billion acres in the West available to the landless. The power and scope of the federal government were expanded at the expense of states' rights. In 1860, the annual federal budget was $63 million; by 1865, it was more than $1 billion. In winning the war, the federal government had become the nation's largest employer.

By the end of the war, the Union was spending $2.5 million per day on the military effort, and whole new industries had been established to meet its needs for weapons, uniforms, food, equipment, and supplies. The massive amounts of preserved food required by the Union armies, for example, helped create the canning industry and transformed Chicago into the meatpacking capital of the world.

Federal contracts also provided money needed to accelerate the growth of new industries, such as the production of iron, steel, and petroleum, thus laying the groundwork for a postwar economic boom. Ohio senator John Sherman, in a letter to his brother, General William T. Sherman, said the war had dramatically expanded the vision "of leading capitalists" who now talked of earning "millions as confidently as formerly of thousands."

The war also influenced world events. Southern cotton had fed national prosperity during the first half of the nineteenth century, but the onset of war in 1861 changed that. In 1860, the South had sent nearly 4 million bales of cotton to Europe. By 1862, hardly any arrived in Europe. By cutting off the supply of southern cotton to Great Britain and Europe, the war fueled global colonialism, as European nations looked for other sources of cotton in India, Egypt, and West Africa.

**THE FIRST "MODERN" WAR**   In many respects, the Civil War was the first modern war. Its scope and scale were unprecedented, as it was fought across the entire continent. For the first time, armies used railroads and steamboats to move around.

One of every twelve men served in the war, and few families were unaffected. More than 750,000 soldiers and sailors (37,000 of whom were blacks fighting for the Union) died, 50 percent more than would die in the Second World War. The comparable number of deaths relative to today's population would be almost 7.5 million. Of the surviving combatants, 50,000 returned home with one or more limbs amputated. Disease, however, was the greatest threat to soldiers, killing twice as many as were lost in battle. Some 50,000 civilians died as well, and virtually every community had uncounted widows and orphans.

The Civil War also accelerated the American love affair with guns. Hundreds of thousands of men who had never owned or used a pistol or rifle now believed that the "right to own and use weapons" was an essential constitutional principle.

Unlike previous conflicts, much of the fighting in the Civil War was distant and impersonal, in part because of improvements in the effectiveness of muskets, rifles, and cannons. Men were killed at long distance, without knowing who had fired the shots that felled them. Among the array of new weapons and instruments were cannons with "rifled," or grooved, barrels for greater accuracy; repeating rifles; ironclad ships; railroad artillery; the first military telegraph; observation balloons; and wire entanglements. Civilians could also follow the war by reading the newspapers that sent reporters to the front lines, or by visiting exhibitions of photographs taken at the battlefields and camps.

**THIRTEENTH AMENDMENT** The most important result of the war was the liberation of almost 4 million slaves. The Emancipation Proclamation had technically freed only those slaves in areas still controlled by the Confederacy. As the war entered its final months, however, freedom for all slaves emerged as a legal reality, as President Lincoln moved from viewing emancipation as a military weapon to seeing it as the mainspring of the conflict itself.

Three major steps occurred in January 1865. Missouri and then Tennessee abolished slavery, and, at Lincoln's insistence, the U.S. House of Representatives passed an amendment to the Constitution that banned slavery everywhere. Upon ratification by three-fourths of the reunited states, the **Thirteenth Amendment** became law eight months after the war ended, on December 18, 1865. It removed any lingering doubts about the legality of emancipation. By then, slavery remained only in the border states of Kentucky and Delaware.

**THE DEBATE CONTINUES** Historians continue to debate the reasons for the Union victory. Some have focused on the weaknesses of the Confederacy: its lack of industry and railroads, the tensions between the states and the central government in Richmond, poor political leadership, faulty coordination and communication, the expense of preventing slave rebellions and runaways, and the advantages in population and resources enjoyed by the North. Still others have highlighted the erosion of Confederate morale in the face of terrible food shortages and unimaginable human losses.

The debate about why the North won and the South lost will probably never end, but Robert E. Lee's explanation remains accurate: "After four years of arduous service marked by unsurpassed courage and fortitude, the Army of Northern Virginia has been compelled to yield to overwhelming numbers and resources." General George Pickett had a similar view. When asked after the Battle of Gettysburg why the Confederates lost, he replied: "I've always thought the Yankees had something to do with it."

Whatever the reasons, the North's victory resolved a key issue: no state could divorce itself from the Union. The Union, as Lincoln had always maintained, was indissoluble. At the same time, the war led to the Constitution being permanently amended to eliminate slavery. The terrible war thus served to clarify the meaning of the ideals ("All men are created equal") on which the United States had been established. The largest slaveholding nation in the world had at last chosen liberty—for all.

In his first message to Congress in December 1861, Lincoln had recognized early on what was at stake: "The struggle of today is not altogether for today; it is for a vast future also." So it was. The "fiery trial" of a war both "fundamental and astounding" produced, as Lincoln said, not just a preserved Union but "a new birth of freedom."

# CHAPTER REVIEW

## SUMMARY

- **Civil War Strategies**   The Confederacy had a geographic advantage of fighting a defensive war on its own territory. The Union, however, had a larger population and greater industrial capability, particularly in the production of weapons, ships, and railroad equipment. After suffering a defeat at the First Battle of Bull Run, the Union adopted the "*Anaconda Plan*," imposing a naval blockade on southern ports and slowly crushing resistance on all fronts. As Union armies penetrated the Confederacy, runaway slaves, called *contrabands*, fled to their camps. *The Militia Act (1862)* allowed African Americans to serve as laborers and soldiers.

- **Emancipation Proclamation**   Initially, President Lincoln declared that the war's aim was to restore the Union and that slavery would be maintained where it existed. Gradually, however, he came to see that winning the war required ending slavery. He justified the *Emancipation Proclamation (1862)* as a military necessity because it would deprive the South of its captive labor force. After the *Battle of Antietam* in September 1862, he announced plans to free the slaves living in areas under Confederate control on January 1, 1863.

- **Wartime Home Fronts**   The federal government proved much more capable with finances than did the Confederacy. Through tariffs, income taxes, bond sales, and banking reforms, the Union was better able to absorb the war's soaring costs. In the absence of the southern delegation in Congress, Republicans approved a higher tariff, a transcontinental railroad, and a *Homestead Act (1862)*, all of which accelerated settlement of the West and the growth of a national economy.

- **The Winning Union Strategy**   Victories at the *Battles of Vicksburg and Gettysburg* in July 1863 turned the war in the Union's favor. With the capture of Vicksburg, the last Confederate-controlled city along the Mississippi River, Union forces cut the Confederacy in two, depriving armies in the East of supplies and manpower. In 1864, Lincoln placed General Ulysses S. Grant in charge of the Union's war efforts. For the next year, Grant's forces constantly attacked Robert E. Lee's forces in Virginia while, farther south, General William T. Sherman's *"March to the Sea"* destroyed plantations, railroads, and morale in Georgia and South Carolina. Their successes helped propel Lincoln to victory in the *election of 1864*. After that, southern resistance wilted. Lee surrendered to Grant at *Appomattox Court House* in April 1865.

- **The Significance of the Civil War**   The Civil War involved the largest number of casualties of any American war, and the Union's victory changed the course of the nation's development. Most important, the war ended slavery, embodied in the adoption of the *Thirteenth Amendment* to the U.S. Constitution in late 1865. Not only did the power of the federal government increase, but the center of political and economic power shifted away from the South and the planter class. The

Republican-controlled Congress enacted legislation during the war to raise tariffs, fund the first transcontinental railroad, and introduce many financial reforms that would drive the nation's economic development for the rest of the century.

## CHRONOLOGY

| | |
|---|---|
| **April 1861** | Virginia, North Carolina, Tennessee, and Arkansas join Confederacy; West Virginia splits from Virginia to stay with Union |
| **July 1861** | First Battle of Bull Run (Manassas) |
| **April–September 1862** | Battles of Shiloh, Second Bull Run, and Antietam |
| **September 1862** | Lincoln issues Emancipation Proclamation |
| **May–July 1863** | New York City draft riots; siege of Vicksburg; Battle of Gettysburg |
| **March 1864** | Lincoln places General Ulysses S. Grant in charge of Union military operations |
| **September 1864** | General William T. Sherman seizes and burns Atlanta |
| **November 1864** | Lincoln is reelected |
| **April 9, 1865** | General Robert E. Lee surrenders at Appomattox Court House |
| **December 1865** | Thirteenth Amendment is ratified |

## KEY TERMS

**Anaconda Plan** p. 584

**contrabands** p. 599

**Battle of Antietam (1862)** p. 600

**Emancipation Proclamation (1862)** p. 602

**Militia Act (1862)** p. 606

**Homestead Act (1862)** p. 610

**Morrill Land Grant College Act (1862)** p. 610

**Copperhead Democrats** p. 612

**Battle of Vicksburg (1863)** p. 615

**Battle of Gettysburg (1863)** p. 616

**election of 1864** p. 627

**Sherman's March to the Sea** p. 627

**Appomattox Court House** p. 631

**Thirteenth Amendment (1865)** p. 634

 INQUIZITIVE

**Go to InQuizitive to see what you've learned—and learn what you've missed—with personalized feedback along the way.**

# 16 The Era of Reconstruction

## 1865–1877

***A Visit from the Old Mistress* (1876)** This powerful painting by Winslow Homer depicts a plantation mistress visiting her former slaves in the postwar South. Although their living conditions are humble, these freedwomen stand firmly and eye-to-eye with the woman who had kept them in bondage.

In the spring of 1865, the terrible conflict was finally over. The war to restore the Union transformed American life. The United States was a "new nation," said an Illinois congressman, because it was now "wholly free." At a cost of some 750,000 lives and the destruction of the southern economy, the Union had won the war, and almost 4 million enslaved Americans had seized their freedom. But the end of slavery did not bring the end of racism, nor did it bring equality to people of color.

The defeated Confederates had seen their world turned upside down. The abolition of slavery, the disruptions to the southern economy, and the horrifying human losses had destroyed the plantation system and upended racial relations in the South. "Change, change, indelibly stamped upon everything I meet, even upon the faces of the people!" marveled Alexander Stephens, vice president of the Confederacy. His native region now had to come to terms with a new era and a new order as the U.S. government set about "reconstructing" the South and policing defiant ex-Confederates. Diarist Mary Chesnut expressed the anger and frustration felt by the southern white elite when she wished that "they were *all* dead—all Yankees!"

Freed slaves felt just the opposite. Yankees were their saviors. No longer would enslaved workers be sold and separated from their families or prevented from learning to read and write or attending church. "I felt like a bird out of a cage," said former slave Houston Holloway of Georgia, who had been sold to three different owners during his first twenty years. "Amen. Amen. Amen. I could hardly ask to feel any better than I did that day."

Few owners, however, willingly freed their slaves until forced to by the arrival of Union soldiers. A North Carolina planter pledged that he and other whites "will never get along with the free negroes" because they were an "inferior race."

## focus questions

1. What major challenges did the federal government face in reconstructing the South after the Civil War?

2. How and why did Reconstruction policies change over time?

3. In what ways did white and black Southerners react to Reconstruction?

4. What were the political and economic factors that helped end Reconstruction in 1877?

5. What was the significance of Reconstruction on the nation's future?

Similarly, a Mississippi planter predicted that "these niggers will all be slaves again in twelve months."

In South Carolina, violence against freedpeople was widespread. Union soldiers found "the bodies of murdered Negroes" strewn in the forest. When a South Carolina white man caught an enslaved mother and her children running toward freedom, he "drew his bowie-knife and cut her throat; also the throat of her boy, nine years old; also the throat of her girl, seven years of age; threw their bodies into the river, and the live baby after them."

Such brutal incidents illuminate the extraordinary challenges the nation faced in "reconstructing" a ravaged and resentful South while helping to transform ex-slaves into free workers and equal citizens. It would not be easy. The Rebels had been conquered, but they were far from being loyal Unionists.

Although the Reconstruction era lasted only twelve years, it was one of the most challenging and significant periods in U.S. history. At the center of the debate over how best to restore the Union were questions of continuing significance: Who is deserving of citizenship, and what does it entail? What rights should all Americans enjoy? What role should the federal government play in ensuring freedom and equality? Those questions are still shaping American life nearly 150 years later.

## THE WAR'S AFTERMATH IN THE SOUTH

In the spring of 1865, Southerners were emotionally exhausted; fully a fifth of southern white males had died in the war, and many others had been maimed for life. In 1866, Mississippi spent 20 percent of the state's budget on artificial limbs for Confederate veterans.

Property values had collapsed. In the year after the war ended, eighty-one plantations in Mississippi were sold for less than a tenth of what they had been worth in 1860. Confederate money was worthless; personal savings had vanished; tens of thousands of horses and mules had been killed in the fighting; and countless farm buildings and agricultural equipment had been destroyed.

Many of the largest southern cities—Richmond, Atlanta, Columbia—were devastated. Most railroads and many bridges were damaged or destroyed, and Southerners, white and black, were homeless and hungry. Along the path that General William Tecumseh Sherman's Union army had blazed across Georgia and the Carolinas, one observer reported in 1866, the countryside "looked for many miles like a broad black streak of ruin and desolation." Burned-out Columbia, South Carolina, said another witness, was "a wilderness of ruins"; Charleston, the birthplace of secession, had become a place of "vacant

**Richmond after the Civil War** Before evacuating Richmond, Virginia, the capital of the Confederacy, Rebels set fire to warehouses and factories to prevent them from falling into Union hands. Pictured here is one of Richmond's burned districts in April 1865. Women in mourning attire walk among the shambles.

houses, of widowed women, of rotting wharves, of deserted warehouses, of weed-wild gardens, of miles of grass-grown streets, of acres of pitiful and voiceless barrenness."

Between 1860 and 1870, northern wealth grew by 50 percent while southern wealth dropped 60 percent. Emancipation wiped out $4 billion invested in slavery, which had enabled the explosive growth of the cotton culture. Not until 1879 would the cotton crop again equal the record harvest of 1860. Tobacco production did not regain its prewar level until 1880, the sugar crop of Louisiana did not recover until 1893, and the rice economy along the coasts of South Carolina and Georgia never regained its prewar levels of production or profit.

In 1860, just before the Civil War, the South had generated 30 percent of the nation's wealth; in 1870, it produced but 12 percent. Amanda Worthington, a planter's wife from Mississippi, assessed the damage in the fall of 1865: "None of us can realize that we are no longer wealthy—yet thanks to the Yankees, the cause of all unhappiness, such is the case."

Resentment boiled over. Union soldiers were cursed and spat upon. A Virginia woman expressed a spirited defiance common among her Confederate friends: "Every day, every hour, that I live increases my hatred and detestation, and loathing of that race. They [Yankees] disgrace our common humanity. As a people I consider them vastly inferior to the better classes of our slaves." Fervent southern nationalists implanted in their children a similar hatred of Yankees and a defiance of northern rule.

Rebuilding the former Confederate states would not be easy, and the issues related to Reconstruction were complicated and controversial. For example, the process of forming new state governments required first determining the official status of the states that had seceded: Were they now conquered territories? If so, then the Constitution assigned Congress authority to re-create their state governments. But what if, as Abraham Lincoln argued, the Confederate states had never officially left the Union because the act of secession was itself illegal? In that circumstance, the president would be responsible for re-forming state governments.

Whichever branch of government—Congress or the presidency—directed the reconstruction of the South, it would have to address the most difficult issue: What would be the political, social, and economic status of the freedpeople? Were they citizens? If not, what was their status?

What former slaves most wanted was to become self-reliant, to be compensated for their labor, to reunite with their family members, to gain education for their children, to enjoy full participation in political life, and to create their own community organizations and social life. Most southern whites were determined to prevent that from happening.

## DEBATES OVER POLITICAL RECONSTRUCTION

Reconstruction of the former Confederate states actually began during the war and went through several phases, the first of which was called Presidential Reconstruction. In 1862, President Lincoln had named army generals to serve as temporary military governors for conquered Confederate areas. By the end of 1863, he had formulated a plan to reestablish governments in states liberated from Confederate rule.

**LINCOLN'S PLAN**  In late 1863, President Lincoln issued a Proclamation of Amnesty and Reconstruction, under which former Confederate states could re-create a Union government once a number equal to 10 percent of those who had voted in 1860 swore allegiance to the Constitution. They also received a presidential pardon acquitting them of treason. Certain groups, however, were denied pardons: Confederate government officials; senior officers of the Confederate army and navy; judges, congressmen, and military officers of the United States who had left their posts to join the rebellion; and those who had abused captured African American soldiers.

**CONGRESSIONAL PLANS** A few conservative and most moderate Republicans supported President Lincoln's "10 percent" program that immediately restored pro-Union southern governments. *Radical Republicans*, however, argued that Congress, not the president, should supervise Reconstruction.

The **Radical Republicans** favored a drastic transformation of southern society that would grant ex-slaves full citizenship. Many Radicals believed that all people, regardless of race, were equal in God's eyes. They wanted no compromise with the "sin" of racism.

They also hoped to replace the white, Democratic planter elite with a new generation of small farmers. "The middling classes who own the soil, and work it with their own hands," explained Radical leader Thaddeus Stevens, "are the main support of every free government."

**THE WADE-DAVIS BILL** In 1864, with war still raging, the Radicals tried to take charge of Reconstruction by passing the Wade-Davis Bill, named for two leading Republicans. In contrast to Lincoln's 10 percent Reconstruction plan, the Wade-Davis Bill required that a *majority* of white male citizens declare their allegiance to the Union before a Confederate state could be readmitted.

The bill never became law, however, because Lincoln vetoed it. In retaliation, Radicals issued the Wade-Davis Manifesto, which accused Lincoln of exceeding his constitutional authority. Unfazed by the criticism, Lincoln continued his efforts to restore the Confederate states to the Union. He also rushed assistance to the freedpeople in the South.

**THE FREEDMEN'S BUREAU** In early 1865, Congress approved the Thirteenth Amendment to the Constitution, officially abolishing slavery in the United States. It became law in December. Yet what did freedom mean for the former slaves, most of whom had no land, no home, no food, no jobs, and no education? The debate over what freedom should entail became the central issue of Reconstruction. "Liberty has been won," Senator Charles Sumner noted. "The battle for Equality is still pending."

To address the complex issues raised by emancipation, Congress on March 3, 1865, created the **Freedmen's Bureau** to assist "freedmen and their wives and children." It was the first federal effort to provide help directly to people rather than to states. And its task was daunting. When General William T. Sherman learned that his friend, General Oliver O. Howard, had been appointed to lead the Freedmen's Bureau, he warned: "It is not . . . in your power to fulfill one-tenth of the expectations of those who framed the Bureau."

Undeterred by such realities, in May 1865, Howard declared that freed slaves "must be free to choose their own employers, and be paid for their labor." He sent agents to the South to negotiate labor contracts between freed people and white landowners, many of whom resisted. The Bureau provided former slaves with medical care and food and clothing, and helped set up schools. Northern missionary societies also established schools for the former slaves. As a Mississippi freedman explained, education "was the next best thing to liberty."

By 1870, the Freedmen's Bureau was supervising nearly 4,000 new schools serving almost 250,000 students. The Freedmen's Bureau also helped former slaves reestablish connections with their family members and legalize marriages that had been banned prior to the war.

**SELF-SUSTAINING FREEDMEN** In July 1865, hundreds of freed slaves gathered on St. Helena Island off the South Carolina coast. There, Virginia-born freeman Martin Delaney, the highest-ranking officer in the U.S. Colored Troops, addressed them. Before the Civil War, he had been a prominent abolitionist in the North. Now, Major Delaney assured the gathering that slavery had indeed been "absolutely abolished." But abolition, he stressed, was less the result of Abraham Lincoln's leadership than it was the outcome of former slaves and free blacks like him undermining the Confederacy. Slavery was dead, and freedom was now in their hands. "Yes, yes, yes," his listeners shouted.

Delaney then noted that many of the white planters in the area claimed that former slaves were lazy and "have not the intelligence to get on for yourselves without being guided and driven to the work by [white] overseers." Delaney dismissed such assumptions as lies intended to restore a system of forced labor for blacks. He then told the freed slaves that their best hope was to become self-sustaining farmers: "Get a community and get all the lands you can—if you cannot get any singly." He added that if they could not become economically self-reliant, they would find themselves slaves again.

Several white planters attended Delaney's talk, and an army officer at the scene reported that they "listened with horror depicted in their faces." The planters predicted that such speeches would incite "open rebellion" among southern blacks.

**DEATH OF A PRESIDENT** The possibility of a lenient federal Reconstruction of the Confederacy would die with Abraham Lincoln. The president who had yearned for a peace "with malice toward none, with charity for all" offered his last view of Reconstruction in the final speech of his life.

On April 11, 1865, Lincoln rejected calls for a vengeful peace. He wanted "no persecution, no bloody work," no hangings of Confederate leaders, and no extreme efforts to restructure southern social and economic life. Three days later, on April 14, he and his wife Mary Todd attended a play at Ford's Theatre in Washington, D.C.

With his trusted bodyguard called away to Richmond, Lincoln was defenseless as twenty-six-year-old John Wilkes Booth, an actor and rabid Confederate, slipped into the unguarded presidential box and shot the president in the head. As Lincoln slumped forward, Booth pulled out a knife, stabbed the president's military aide, and jumped from the box to the stage, breaking his leg in the process. He then mounted a waiting horse and fled the city. Lincoln died nine hours later.

The nation was suddenly leaderless. Vice President Andrew Johnson was sworn in as the new president, but for a time chaos reigned. Secretary of War Edwin Stanton, not knowing if the assassination was a prelude to a Confederate invasion, summoned Ulysses S. Grant to defend the government in Washington, D.C. Eleven days later, Union troops found Booth hiding in a northern Virginia tobacco barn, where he was shot and killed. Booth whispered as he lay dying, "Tell my mother I died for my country."

The nation extracted a full measure of vengeance from the conspirators. Three of Booth's collaborators were convicted by a military court and hanged, as was Mary Surratt, who owned the Washington boardinghouse where the assassination had been planned.

The outpouring of grief after Lincoln's death was overwhelming. Planned victory celebrations were canceled. Even a Richmond, Virginia, newspaper called the assassination the "heaviest blow which has fallen on the people of the South."

**Andrew Johnson** A pro-Union Democrat from Tennessee, Johnson became president after Abraham Lincoln was assassinated during his vice presidency.

Lincoln's body lay in state for several days in Washington, D.C., before being transported 1,600 miles by train for burial in Springfield, Illinois. In Philadelphia, 300,000 mourners paid their last respects; in New York City, 500,000 people viewed the president's body. On May 4, Lincoln was laid to rest.

**JOHNSON'S PLAN** President Lincoln's shocking death propelled Andrew Johnson of Tennessee, a pro-Union Democrat, into the White House. Johnson had been added to Lincoln's National Union ticket in 1864 solely to help the president win reelection. Humorless, insecure, combative, and self-righteous, Johnson hated both the white southern elite and the idea of racial equality. He also had a weakness for liquor. At the inaugural ceremonies in 1865, he had delivered his vice-presidential address in a state of slurring drunkenness.

Like Lincoln, Johnson was a self-made man. Born in 1808 in a log cabin near Raleigh, North Carolina, he lost his father when he was three and never attended school. His illiterate mother apprenticed him to a tailor to learn a trade. He ran away from home at thirteen and eventually landed in Greeneville, in the mountains of East Tennessee, where he became a tailor. He taught himself to read, and his sixteen-year-old wife showed him how to write and do basic arithmetic.

Over time, Johnson prospered and acquired five slaves, which he sold in 1863. A natural leader, he eventually served as mayor, state legislator, governor, congressional representative, and U.S. senator. A friend described the trajectory of Johnson's life as "one intense, unceasing, desperate upward struggle" during which he identified with poor farmers and came to hate the "pampered, bloated, corrupted aristocracy" of wealthy planters.

During the Civil War, Johnson called himself a Jacksonian Democrat "in the strictest meaning of the term. I am for putting down the [Confederate] rebellion, because it is a war [of wealthy plantation owners] against democracy." Yet Johnson also shared the racist attitudes of most southern whites. "Damn the negroes," he exclaimed during the war. "I am fighting those traitorous aristocrats, their masters." Impoverished whites, Johnson maintained, were most hurt by the slave system, and he was an unapologetic white supremacist. "White men alone must manage the South," he declared.

As a states' rights Democrat, Johnson also insisted that the federal government be as small and inactive as possible. He strongly opposed Republican economic policies designed to spur industrial development.

In May 1865, Johnson issued a new Proclamation of Amnesty that excluded not only those ex-Confederates whom Lincoln had barred from a presidential pardon but also anyone with property worth more than $20,000. Johnson was determined to keep the wealthiest Southerners from regaining political power.

Surprisingly, however, by 1866 he had pardoned some 7,000 former Confederates, and he eventually pardoned most of the white "aristocrats" he claimed to despise. What brought about this change of heart? Johnson had decided that he could buy the political support of prominent Southerners by pardoning them, improving his chances of reelection.

**Johnson's Restoration Plan** mandated the appointment of a Unionist as provisional governor in each southern state. Each governor was given the authority to call a convention of men elected by "loyal" (not Confederate) voters. Johnson's plan required that each state convention ratify the Thirteenth Amendment. He also encouraged giving a few blacks voting rights, especially those who had some education or had served in the military, so as to "disarm" the "Radicals who are wild upon" giving *all* African Americans the right to vote. Except for Mississippi, each former Confederate state held a convention that met Johnson's requirements but ignored his suggestion about voting rights for blacks.

FREEDMEN'S CONVENTIONS Neither Abraham Lincoln nor Andrew Johnson saw fit to ask freedpeople in the South what they most needed. So the former slaves took matters into their own hands. They met and marched, demanding not just freedom but citizenship and full civil rights, land of their own, and voting rights. Especially in and around large cities such as New Orleans, Mobile, Norfolk, Wilmington, Nashville, Memphis, and Charleston, former slaves organized regular meetings, chose leaders, protested mistreatment, learned the workings of the federal bureaucracy, and sought economic opportunities.

During the summer and fall of 1865, liberated slaves and freepeople from the North ("missionaries") and South organized freedmen's conventions (sometimes called Equal Rights Associations). Often led by ministers, they met in state capitals "to impress upon the white men," as the Reverend James D. Lynch told the Tennessee freedmen's convention, "that we are part and parcel of the American republic." As such, they were eager to counter the whites-only state conventions organized under Johnson's Reconstruction plan.

The North Carolina freedmen's convention elected as its president James Walker Hood, a free black from Connecticut. In his acceptance speech, he emphasized their goals: "We and the white people have to live here together. Some people talk of emigration for the black race, some of expatriation, and some of colonization. I regard this as all nonsense. We have been living together for a hundred years and more, and we have got to live together still; and the best way is to harmonize our feelings as much as possible, and to treat all men respectfully." Hood then demanded three constitutional rights for

African Americans: the right to testify in courts, serve on juries, and "the right to carry [a] ballot to the ballot box."

In sum, the freedmen's conventions demanded that their voices be heard in Washington and southern state capitals. As the Virginia freedmen's convention asserted, "Any attempt to reconstruct the states . . . without giving to American citizens of African descent all the rights and immunities accorded to white citizens . . . is an act of gross injustice."

**THE RADICALS REBEL** President Johnson's initial assault on the southern planter elite pleased Radical Republicans, but not for long. The most extreme Radicals, led by Thaddeus Stevens of Pennsylvania and Charles Sumner of Massachusetts, wanted Reconstruction to provide social and political equality for blacks. They resented Johnson's efforts to bring the South back into the Union as quickly as possible.

Stevens argued that the Civil War had been fought to produce a "*radical revolution*" in southern life: The "whole fabric of southern society must be changed" to "revolutionize southern institutions, habits, and manners." The Confederate states were, in his view, "conquered provinces" to be readmitted to the Union by the U.S. Congress, not the president. Johnson, however, balked at such an expansion of federal authority. He was committed to the states' rights to control their affairs.

Former Confederates agreed with Johnson. After the war, most white Southerners resented and resisted the North's efforts to reconstruct their homeland. They wanted to rebuild the South as it had been before the war, and they were determined to do so in their own way and under their own leadership. As a white woman lamented, "Think of all our sacrifices—of broken hearts, and desolated homes—or our *noble, glorious* dead—and say for what? *Reconstruction!* How the very word galls."

So when the U.S. Congress met in December 1865 for the first time since the end of the war, the new southern state governments looked remarkably like the former Confederate governments. Southern voters had refused to extend voting rights to the newly freed slaves. Instead, they had elected former Confederate leaders as their new U.S. senators and congressmen. Georgia, for example, had elected Alexander Stephens, former vice president of the Confederacy.

Across the South, four Confederate generals, eight colonels, six Confederate cabinet members, and several Confederate legislators were also elected. Outraged Republicans denied seats to all such "Rebel" officials and appointed a Joint Committee on Reconstruction to develop a new plan to bring the former Confederate states back into the Union.

The Joint Committee discovered that white violence against blacks in the South was widespread. A former slave in Shreveport, Louisiana, testified that whites still bullwhipped blacks as if they were slaves. He estimated that 2,000 freedpeople had been killed in Shreveport in 1865.

In May and July of 1866, white mobs murdered African Americans in Memphis and New Orleans. General Grant reported that Memphis was "a scene of murder, arson, rape & robbery in which the victims were all help-less and unresisting negroes, stamping lasting disgrace upon the [white] civil authorities that permitted them." Memphis authorities arrested no one respon-sible for the mayhem.

The massacres, Radical Republicans argued, resulted from Andrew Johnson's lenient policy toward white supremacists. Senator Charles Sumner cried, "Who can doubt that the President is the author of these tragedies?" The race riots helped spur the Republican-controlled Congress to pass the Fourteenth Amendment (1868), extending federal civil rights protections to African Americans.

**BLACK CODES** The violence aga-inst southern blacks was triggered in part by black protests over restrictive laws passed by the new all-white south-ern state legislatures. These "**black codes**," as a white Southerner explained, would ensure "the ex-slave was not a free man; he was a free Negro." A North-erner visiting the South observed that the new black codes would guarantee that "the blacks at large belong to the whites at large."

Black codes varied from state to state. In South Carolina, African Americans were required to remain on their former plantations, forced to labor from dawn to dusk. Mississippi declared that blacks could not hunt or fish, making them even more depen-dent on their white employers.

Some black codes recognized black marriages but prohibited interra-cial marriage. The Mississippi codes

**"(?) Slavery Is Dead (?)" (1867)**
Thomas Nast's cartoon argues that southern blacks were still being treated as slaves despite the passage of the Fourteenth Amendment. This detail illustrates a case in Raleigh, North Carolina: a black man was whipped for a crime despite federal orders specifically prohibiting such forms of punishment.

stipulated that "no white person could intermarry with a freedman, free negro, or mulatto." Violators faced life imprisonment.

The codes also prohibited African Americans from voting, serving on juries, or testifying against whites. They could own property, but they could not own farmland in Mississippi or city property in South Carolina. In Mississippi, every black male over the age of eighteen had to be apprenticed to a white, preferably a former slave owner. Any blacks not apprenticed or employed by January 1866 would be jailed as "vagrants." If they could not pay the vagrancy fine—and most of them could not—they were jailed and forced to work for whites as convict laborers in "chain gangs."

In part, states employed this "convict lease" system as a means of increasing government revenue and cutting the expenses of housing prisoners. At its worst, however, convict leasing was one of the most exploitive labor systems in history, as people convicted of crimes, mostly African Americans often falsely accused, were hired out by county and state governments to work for individuals and businesses—coal mines, lumber camps, brickyards, railroads, quarries, mills, and plantations. Convict leasing, in other words, was a thinly disguised form of neo-slavery.

The black codes infuriated Republicans. "We [Republicans] must see to it," Senator William Stewart of Nevada resolved, "that the man made free by the Constitution of the United States is a freeman indeed." And that is what they set out to do.

**JOHNSON'S BATTLE WITH CONGRESS** Early in 1866, the Radical Republicans openly challenged Andrew Johnson over Reconstruction policies. Johnson started the fight when he vetoed a bill renewing funding for the Freedmen's Bureau. The Republicans could not overturn the veto. Then, on February 22, 1866, Johnson criticized the Radical Republicans for promoting black civil rights. Moderate Republicans thereafter deserted the president and supported the Radicals. Johnson had become "an alien enemy of a foreign state," Thaddeus Stevens declared.

In mid-March 1866, the Radical-led Congress passed the pathbreaking Civil Rights Act, which declared that "all persons born in the United States," including the children of immigrants, but excluding Native Americans, were citizens entitled to "full and equal benefit of all laws." The legislation infuriated Johnson. Congress, he fumed, could not grant citizenship to blacks, who did not deserve it. Claiming that the proposed Civil Rights Act discriminated against the "white race," Johnson vetoed it, but this time, on April 6, 1866, Republicans overrode the veto.

It was the first time in history that Congress had overturned a presidential veto of a major bill. From that point on, President Johnson steadily lost both public and political support. A New Yorker noted in his diary that "the feud between Johnson and the 'Radicals' grows more and more deadly every day." General Ulysses S. Grant told his wife that Johnson had become "a national disgrace."

## FOURTEENTH AMENDMENT

To remove all doubt about the legality of the new Civil Rights Act, Congress passed the **Fourteenth Amendment** to the U.S. Constitution in 1866 (it gained ratification in 1868). It guaranteed citizenship not just to freemen but also to immigrant children born in the United States. Taking direct aim at the black codes, it also prohibited any efforts to violate the civil rights of "citizens," black or white; to deprive any person "of life, liberty, or property, without due process of law"; or to "deny any person…the equal protection of the laws."

**A Man Knows A Man** A black soldier for the Union with an amputated leg clasps hands with a white amputee in this 1865 cartoon. The caption reads: "Give me your hand, comrade! We have each lost a leg for the good cause; but, thank God, we never lost heart."

With the Fourteenth Amendment, Congress gave the federal government responsibility for protecting (and enforcing) civil rights. Not a single Democrat in the House or Senate voted for it. All states in the former Confederacy were required to ratify the amendment before they could be readmitted to the Union and to Congress.

President Johnson urged the southern states to refuse to ratify the amendment. He predicted that the Democrats would win the congressional elections in November and then nix the new amendment. But Johnson was steadily losing support in the North. New York newspaper editor Horace Greeley called Johnson "an aching tooth in the national jaw, a screeching infant in a crowded lecture room."

**JOHNSON VERSUS RADICALS** To win votes for Democratic candidates in the 1866 congressional elections, Andrew Johnson went on a speaking tour of the Midwest during which he denounced Radical Republicans as traitors who should be hanged. His partisan speeches backfired, however.

In Cleveland, Ohio, Johnson described the Radical Republicans as "factious, domineering, tyrannical" men and exchanged hot-tempered insults with a heckler. At another stop, while the president was speaking from the back of a railway car, the engineer mistakenly pulled the train out of the station, making the president appear quite the fool. Republicans charged that such unseemly incidents confirmed Johnson's image as a "ludicrous boor" and a "drunken imbecile."

Voters agreed. The 1866 congressional elections brought a devastating defeat for Johnson and the Democrats; in each house, Radical Republican candidates won more than a two-thirds majority, the margin required to override presidential vetoes. Congressional Republicans would now take over the process of reconstructing the former Confederacy.

**CONGRESS TAKES CHARGE** On March 2, 1867, Congress passed, over President Johnson's vetoes, the First Reconstruction Act, which included three laws creating what came to be called **Congressional Reconstruction**: the Military Reconstruction Act, the Command of the Army Act, and the Tenure of Office Act.

The Military Reconstruction Act was the capstone of the Congressional Reconstruction plan. It abolished the new governments "in the Rebel States" established under Johnson's lenient Reconstruction policies. In their place, Congress established military control over ten of the eleven former Confederate states. (Tennessee was exempted because it had already ratified the Fourteenth Amendment.) The other ten states were divided into five military districts, each commanded by an army general who acted as governor.

Yet only 10,000 federal troops, mostly African Americans, were expected to police those sprawling "military districts." There were never enough soldiers to enforce Congressional Reconstruction. The entire state of Mississippi, for instance, had fewer than 400 soldiers assigned to ensure compliance.

The Military Reconstruction Act required each former Confederate state to create a new constitution that guaranteed all adult males the right to vote—black or white, rich or poor, landless or property owners. Women—black or white—were still not allowed to vote.

The act also stipulated that the new constitutions were to be drafted by conventions elected by male citizens "of whatever race, color, or previous condition." Once a majority of voters ratified the new constitutions, the state legislatures had to ratify the Fourteenth Amendment; once the amendment became part of the Constitution, the former Confederate states would be entitled to representation in Congress. Several hundred African American delegates participated in the constitutional conventions.

The Command of the Army Act required that the president issue all army orders through General-in-Chief Ulysses S. Grant. (The Radicals feared that President Johnson would appoint anti-black generals to head the military districts who would be too lenient toward defiant whites.)

The Tenure of Office Act stipulated that the Senate must approve any presidential effort to remove federal officials whose appointments the Senate had confirmed. Radicals intended this act to prevent Johnson from firing Secretary of War Edwin Stanton, the president's most outspoken critic in the cabinet.

Congressional Reconstruction embodied the most sweeping peacetime legislation in American history to that point. It sought to ensure that freed slaves could participate in the creation of new state governments in the former Confederacy. As Thaddeus Stevens explained, the Congressional Reconstruction plan would create a "perfect republic" based on the principle of *equal rights* for all citizens. "This is the promise of America," he insisted. "No More. No Less."

**IMPEACHING THE PRESIDENT** The first two years of Congressional Reconstruction produced dramatic changes in the South, as new state legislatures rewrote their constitutions and ratified the Fourteenth Amendment. Radical Republicans now seemed fully in control of Reconstruction, but one person still stood in their way—Andrew Johnson. During 1867 and early 1868, more and more Radicals decided that the president must be removed from office.

Johnson himself opened the door to impeachment (the formal process by which Congress charges the president with "high crimes and misdemeanors") when, in violation of the Tenure of Office Act, he fired Secretary of War Edwin Stanton, who had refused to resign from the cabinet despite his harsh criticism of the president's Reconstruction policy. Johnson, who considered the Tenure of Office Act an illegal restriction of presidential power, fired Stanton on August 12, 1867, and replaced him with Ulysses S. Grant.

The Radicals now saw their chance. By removing Stanton without congressional approval, Johnson had violated the Tenure of Office Act.

On February 24, 1868, the Republican-dominated House passed eleven articles of impeachment (that is, specific charges against the president), most of which dealt with Stanton's firing—and all of which were flimsy. In reality, the essential grievance against the president was that he had opposed the policies of the Radical Republicans. According to Secretary of the Navy Gideon Welles, Radicals were so angry at Johnson that they "would have tried to remove him had he been accused of stepping on a dog's tail."

The first Senate trial of a sitting president began on March 5, 1868. It was a dramatic spectacle before a packed gallery of journalists, foreign dignitaries, and political officials. As it began, Stevens warned the president: "Unfortunate, unhappy man, behold your doom!"

The five-week trial came to a stunning end when the Senate voted 35–19 for conviction, only *one* vote short of the two-thirds needed for removal.

Senator Edmund G. Ross, a young Radical from Kansas, cast the deciding vote in favor of acquittal, knowing that his vote would ruin his political career. He had decided that the evidence against Johnson was both insufficient for conviction and overtly partisan. "I almost literally looked down into my open grave," Ross explained afterward. "Friendships, position, fortune, everything that makes life desirable . . . were about to be swept away by the breath of my mouth." Angry Radicals thereafter shunned Ross. He lost his reelection campaign and died in near poverty.

In the end, the effort to remove Johnson was a grave political mistake, for it weakened public support for Congressional Reconstruction. The Richmond *Daily Dispatch* stressed that Johnson's acquittal was "a terrible rebuke on the Radical party, and diminished its physical force (it never had any other)." Nevertheless, the Radical cause did gain Johnson's private agreement to stop obstructing Congressional Reconstruction. (He would later break his pledge by turning a deaf ear to pleas for federal support in suppressing Klan violence.)

General Grant urged Johnson to let him exert more federal force in the South. To that end, he forwarded to the president a letter from a Tennessee legislator that documented gangs of whites "scouring the country by night—causing dismay & terror to all—Our civil authorities are powerless." Johnson declared that it was a local issue. Federal troops should stay out of it.

Grant refused to take no for an answer. He continued to barrage Johnson with fresh evidence of white efforts to terrorize blacks. "If Civil Government fails to protect the Citizen," Grant argued, "Military government should supply its place."

**REPUBLICAN RULE IN THE SOUTH**   In June 1868, congressional Republicans announced that eight southern states could again send delegates to Congress. The remaining former Confederate states—Virginia, Mississippi, and Texas—were readmitted in 1870, with the added requirement that they ratify the **Fifteenth Amendment**, which gave voting rights to African American men. As Frederick Douglass, himself a former slave, had declared in 1865, "slavery is not abolished until the black man has the ballot."

The Fifteenth Amendment prohibited states from denying a citizen's right to vote on grounds of "race, color, or previous condition of servitude." But Susan B. Anthony and Elizabeth Cady Stanton, leaders of the movement to secure voting rights for women, insisted that the amendment should have included women. As Anthony stressed in a famous speech, the U.S. Constitution refers to "We, the people; not we, the white male citizens; nor yet we, the male citizens; but we, the whole people, who formed the Union—women as well as men."

Most men, however, remained opposed to voting rights for women. Radical Republicans tried to deflect the issue by declaring that it was the "Negro's hour." Women seeking voting rights would have to wait—another fifty years, as it turned out.

# BLACK SOCIETY UNDER RECONSTRUCTION

When a federal official asked Garrison Frazier, a former Georgia slave, if he and others wanted to live among whites, Frazier said that they preferred "to live by ourselves, for there is a prejudice against us in the South that will take years to get over." In forging new lives, Frazier and many other former slaves set about creating their own social institutions.

**FREED BUT NOT EQUAL** African Americans were active agents in affecting the course of Reconstruction. It was not an easy process, however, because whites, both northern and southern, still practiced racism. A northern journalist traveling in the South after the war reported that the "whites seem wholly unable to comprehend that freedom for the negro means the same thing as freedom for them."

Once the excitement of freedom wore off, most southern blacks realized that their best chance to make a living was by working for pay for their former owners. In fact, the Freedmen's Bureau and federal soldiers urged and even ordered them to sign labor contracts with local whites. Many planters, however, conspired to control the amount of wages paid to freedmen. "It seems humiliating to be compelled to bargain and haggle with our own servants about wages," complained a white planter's daughter.

White Southerners were also determined to suppress black efforts to gain social and economic equality. In many respects, the war had not ended, as armed men organized to thwart federal efforts to reconstruct the South. In July 1866, a black woman in Clinch County, Georgia, was arrested and given sixty-five lashes for "using abusive language" during an encounter with a white woman. The Civil War brought freedom to enslaved African Americans, but it did not bring them protection against exploitation or abuse.

After emancipation, Union soldiers and northern observers often expressed surprise that freed slaves did not leave the South. But why would they leave what they knew so well? As a group of African Americans explained, they did not want to abandon "land they had laid their fathers' bones upon." A Union officer noted that southern blacks seemed "more attached to familiar places" than any other group in the nation.

Participation in the Union army or navy had given many freedmen training in leadership. Indeed, black military veterans would form the core of the first generation of African American political leaders in the postwar South. Military service also gave many former slaves their first opportunities to learn to read and write and alerted them to new possibilities for economic advancement, social respectability, and civic leadership.

**BLACK CHURCHES AND SCHOOLS** African American religious life in the South was transformed during and after the war. Many former slaves identified with the biblical Hebrews, who were led out of slavery into the "promised land." Emancipation demonstrated that God was on *their* side. Before the war, slaves who attended white churches were forced to sit in the back. After the war, with the help of many northern Christian missionaries, both black and white, ex-slaves established their own churches that became the crossroads for black community life.

Ministers emerged as social and political leaders. One could not be a real minister, one of them claimed, without looking "out for the political interests of his people." Many African Americans became Baptists or Methodists, in

**African American political figures of Reconstruction** Blanche K. Bruce (left) and Hiram Revels (right) served in the U.S. Senate. Frederick Douglass (center) was a major figure in the abolitionist movement.

part because these were already the largest denominations in the South and in part because they reached out to the working poor. In 1866 alone, the African Methodist Episcopal (AME) Church gained 50,000 members. By 1890, more than 1.3 million African Americans in the South had become Baptists, nearly three times as many as had joined any other denomination.

African American communities also rushed to establish schools. Starting schools, said a former slave, was the "first proof" of freedom. Before the Civil War, most plantation owners had denied an education to their slaves to keep them from reading abolitionist literature and organizing uprisings. After the war, the white elite worried that education would distract poor whites and blacks from their work in the fields or encourage them to leave the South in search of better social and economic opportunities.

**POLITICS AND AFRICAN AMERICANS** With many ex-Confederates denied voting rights, new African American voters helped elect some 600 blacks—most of them former slaves—as state legislators under Congressional Reconstruction. In Louisiana, Pinckney Pinchback, a northern free black and former Union soldier, was elected lieutenant governor. Several other African Americans were elected to high state offices. There were two black senators in Congress, Hiram Revels and Blanche K. Bruce, both Mississippi natives who had been educated in the North, while fourteen blacks served in the U.S. House of Representatives.

The election of black politicians appalled southern whites. Democrats claimed that Radicals were trying to "organize a hell in the South" by putting "the Caucasian race" under the rule of "their own negroes." Southern whites complained that freed slaves were illiterate and had no civic experience or appreciation of political issues and processes. In this regard, however, blacks were no different from millions of poor or immigrant white males who had been voting and serving in office for years.

**LAND, LABOR, AND DISAPPOINTMENT** Many ex-slaves argued that what they needed most was land. A New Englander traveling in the post-war South noted that the "sole ambition of the freedman" was "to become the owner of a little piece of land, there to erect a humble home, and to dwell in peace and security at his own free will and pleasure."

In several southern states, former slaves had been given land by Union armies after they had taken control of Confederate areas during the war. But Andrew Johnson reversed such transfers of white-owned property to former slaves. In South Carolina, the Union general responsible for evicting former slaves urged them to "lay aside their bitter feelings, and become reconciled

**Freedmen voting in New Orleans** The Fifteenth Amendment, ratified in 1870, guaranteed at the federal level the right of citizens to vote regardless of "race, color, or previous condition of servitude." But former slaves had been registering to vote—and voting in large numbers—in some state elections since 1867, as in this scene.

to their old masters." But the assembled freedmen shouted "No, never!" and "Can't do it!" They knew that ownership of land was the foundation of their freedom. They may have had no deeds or titles for the land they now worked, but it had been "earned by the sweat of *our* brows," said a group of Alabama freedmen. "Our wives, our children, our husbands, has been sold over and over again to purchase the lands we now locate on," a Virginia freedman noted. "Didn't we clear the land and raise de crops? We have a right to [that] land."

Thousands of former slaves were forced to return their farms to white owners. In addition, it was virtually impossible for former slaves to get loans to buy farmland because few banks were willing to lend to blacks. Their sense of betrayal was profound. An ex-slave in Mississippi said that he and others were left with nothing: "no *land*, no *house*, not so much as a place to lay our head."

As former slaves were stripped of their land, they had little choice but to become farmworkers under a new system: **sharecropping**. White landowners would provide land, seed, and tools to poor laborers in exchange for a *share* of the crop. This essentially re-enslaved the workers because, as a federal army officer said, no matter "how much they are abused, they cannot leave without permission of the owner." If they left, they would forfeit their portion of the crop. Workers who violated the terms of the contract could be evicted from the plantation, leaving them jobless and homeless—and subject to arrest as "vagrants." Across the former Confederacy, the growth of sharecropping revealed that most white plantation owners and small farmers were determined to control African Americans as if they were still enslaved. And if bad weather or insects or disease stunted the harvest, it pushed the sharecropper only deeper in debt.

Many freed blacks preferred sharecropping over working for wages, since it freed them from day-to-day supervision by white landowners. Over time, however, most sharecroppers, black and

**Sharecroppers** A family is shown outside their Virginia home in this 1899 photograph, taken by Frances Benjamin Johnston, one of the earliest American female photojournalists.

white, found themselves deep in debt to the landowner, with little choice but to remain tied to the same discouraging system of dependence that, over the years, felt much like slavery. As a former slave acknowledged, he and others had discovered that "freedom could make folks proud but it didn't make 'em rich."

**TENSIONS AMONG SOUTHERN BLACKS** African Americans in the postwar South were by no means a uniform community. They had their own differences and disputes, especially between the few who owned property and the many who did not. In North Carolina, for example, less than 7 percent of blacks owned land by 1870.

Affluent northern blacks and the southern free black elite, most of whom were city dwellers and "mulattos" (people of mixed racial parentage), often opposed efforts to redistribute land to the freedmen, and many insisted that political equality did not mean social equality. As an African American leader in Alabama stressed, "We do not ask that the ignorant and degraded shall be put on a social equality with the refined and intelligent." In general, however, unity prevailed, and African Americans focused on common concerns. "All we ask," said a black member of the state constitutional convention in Mississippi, "is justice, and to be treated like human beings."

**BLACKS IN POLITICS** Many African Americans served in state governments with distinction. Nonetheless, the scornful label "black Reconstruction," used by critics then and since, distorts African American political influence. Such criticism also overlooks the political clout of the large number of white Republicans, especially in the mountain areas of the Upper South, who favored the Radical plan for Reconstruction.

Only South Carolina's Republican state convention had a black majority. Louisiana's was evenly divided racially, and in only two other state conventions were more than 20 percent of the members black: Florida and Virginia. The Texas convention was only 10 percent black, and North Carolina's was 11 percent—which did not stop a white newspaper from calling it a group of "baboons, monkeys, mules . . . and other jackasses."

"CARPETBAGGERS" AND "SCALAWAGS" Unreconstructed white Southerners dismissed whites who served in the new Republican state governments as "carpetbaggers" or "scalawags." Carpetbaggers, critics argued, were the 30,000 scheming Northerners who rushed South with their belongings in cheap suitcases made of carpeting ("carpetbags") to grab political power or buy plantations.

Some of the Northerners who migrated south were corrupt opportunists. However, most were Union military veterans drawn to the South by the desire to rebuild the region's devastated economy. Many other so-called carpetbaggers were teachers, social workers, attorneys, physicians, editors, and ministers motivated by a genuine desire to help free blacks and poor whites improve their lives.

For example, Union general Adelbert Ames, who won the Medal of Honor, stayed in the South after the war because he felt a "sense of Mission with a large M" to help the former slaves develop healthy communities. He served as the military governor of Mississippi before being elected a Republican U.S. senator in 1870.

Southern Democrats especially hated the scalawags, or southern white Republicans, calling them traitors to their region. A Nashville newspaper editor described them as the "merest trash." Most scalawags had been Unionists opposed to secession. They were prominent in the mountain counties of Georgia and Alabama and especially in the hills of eastern Tennessee. What the scalawags had in common was a willingness to work with Republicans to rebuild the southern economy.

SOUTHERN RESISTANCE AND WHITE "REDEMPTION" Most southern whites viewed secession as a noble "lost cause." They used all means possible—legal and illegal—to "redeem" their beloved South from northern control, Republican rule, and black equality. An Alabama planter admitted that southern whites simply "can't learn to treat the freedmen like human beings."

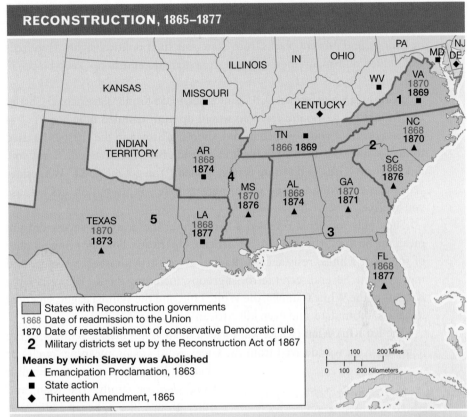

## RECONSTRUCTION, 1865–1877

States with Reconstruction governments
1868 Date of readmission to the Union
1870 Date of reestablishment of conservative Democratic rule
2 Military districts set up by the Reconstruction Act of 1867

**Means by which Slavery was Abolished**
▲ Emancipation Proclamation, 1863
■ State action
◆ Thirteenth Amendment, 1865

- How did the Military Reconstruction Act reorganize governments in the South in the late 1860s and 1870s?
- What did the former Confederate states have to do to be readmitted to the Union?
- Why did "Conservative" white parties gradually regain control of the South from the Republicans in the 1870s?

White southern ministers assured their congregations that God endorsed white supremacy. In an attempt to reunite the Protestant denominations of the North and South, many northern religionists became "apostles of forgiveness" for their southern white brethren. Even abolitionists such as the Reverend Henry Ward Beecher, whose sister Harriet Beecher Stowe had written *Uncle Tom's Cabin* (1857), called for southern whites—rather than federal officials or African Americans themselves—to govern the South after the war.

With each passing year during Reconstruction, African Americans suffered increasing exploitation and abuse. The black codes created by white state governments in 1865 and 1866 were the first of many efforts to deny equality.

Southern whites used terror, intimidation, and violence to disrupt black Republican meetings, target black and white Republican leaders for beatings or killings, and prevent blacks from exercising their political rights. Hundreds were killed and many more injured in systematic efforts to "keep blacks in their place."

In Texas, a white farmer, D. B. Whitesides, told a former slave named Charles Brown that his newfound freedom would do him "damned little good . . . as I intend to shoot you"—which he did, shooting Brown in the chest as he tried to flee. Whitesides then rode his horse beside Brown and asked, "I got you, did I Brown?" "Yes," a bleeding Brown replied. "You got me good." Whitesides yelled that the wound would teach "niggers [like you] to put on airs because you are free."

Such ugly incidents revealed a harsh truth: the death of slavery did not mean the birth of true freedom for African Americans. For a growing number of southern whites, resistance to Radical Reconstruction became more and more violent. Several secret terrorist groups, including the Ku Klux Klan, the Knights of the White Camelia, the White Line, and the White League, emerged to harass, intimidate, and even kill African Americans.

The **Ku Klux Klan** (KKK) was formed in 1866 in Pulaski, Tennessee. The name *Ku Klux* was derived from the Greek word *kuklos*, meaning "circle" or "band"; *Klan* came from the English word *clan*, or family. The Klan, and other groups like it, began initially as a social club, with spooky costumes and secret rituals. But its members, most of them former Confederate soldiers, soon began harassing blacks and white Republicans. General Philip Sheridan, who supervised the district that included Louisiana and Texas, reported that Klansmen were "terrorists" intent on suppressing black political participation.

**"Worse Than Slavery"** This Thomas Nast cartoon condemns the Ku Klux Klan for promoting conditions "worse than slavery" for southern blacks after the Civil War.

These groups' motives varied—anger over the Confederate defeat, resentment against federal soldiers occupying the South, complaints about having to pay black workers, and an almost paranoid fear that former slaves might seek revenge against whites. Klansmen marauded at night on horseback, spreading rumors, issuing threats, and burning schools and churches. "We are going to kill all the Negroes," a white supremacist declared during one massacre.

## THE LEGACY OF CONGRESSIONAL RECONSTRUCTION

One by one, the Republican state governments were gradually overturned. Yet they left behind an important accomplishment: The new constitutions they created remained in effect for years, and later constitutions incorporated many of their most progressive features.

Some of the significant innovations brought about by the Republican state governments protected black voting rights and restructured legislatures to reflect shifting populations. More state offices were changed from appointed to elective positions to weaken the "good old boy" tradition of rewarding political supporters with state government jobs. In South Carolina, former Confederate leaders opposed the Republican state legislature not simply because of its black members but because poor whites were also enjoying political clout for the first time, thereby threatening the dominance of wealthy white plantation owners and merchants.

Given the hostile circumstances under which Republican state governments operated in the South, their achievements were remarkable. They rebuilt an extensive railroad network and established public school systems funded by state governments and open to all children, although the buildings were segregated by race. Some 600,000 black pupils had enrolled in southern schools by 1877.

The Radicals also gave more attention to the poor and to orphanages, asylums, and institutions for the deaf and blind of both races. Much-needed infrastructure—roads, bridges, and buildings—was repaired or rebuilt. African Americans achieved rights and opportunities that would repeatedly be violated in coming decades but would never completely be taken away, at least in principle, such as equality before the law and the rights to own property, attend schools, learn to read and write, enter professions, and carry on business.

Yet government officials also engaged in corrupt practices. Bribes and kickbacks, whereby companies received government contracts in return for giving government officials cash or stock, were commonplace. In Louisiana, a twenty-six-year-old carpetbagger, Henry Clay Warmoth, somehow turned an annual salary of $8,000 into a million-dollar fortune during his four years as governor. (He was eventually impeached and removed from office.) "I don't pretend to be honest," he admitted. "I only pretend to be as honest as anybody in politics."

As was true in the North and the Midwest, southern state governments awarded money to corporations, notably railroads, under conditions that invited shady dealings and outright corruption. Some railroad corporations received state funds but never built railroads, and bribery was rampant. But the Radical Republican regimes did not invent such corruption, nor did it die with them. Governor Warmoth recognized as much: "Corruption is the fashion" in Louisiana, he explained.

## The Grant Administration

Andrew Johnson's crippled presidency created an opportunity for Republicans to elect one of their own in 1868. Both parties wooed Ulysses S. Grant, the "Lion of Vicksburg" credited by most with the Union victory in the Civil War. His falling-out with President Johnson, however, had pushed him toward the Republicans, who unanimously nominated him as their presidential candidate.

**THE ELECTION OF 1868** The Republican party platform endorsed Congressional Reconstruction. More important, however, were the public expectations driving the candidacy of Ulysses S. Grant, whose slogan was "Let us have peace." Grant promised that, if elected, he would enforce the laws and promote prosperity for all.

"This is a white man's country," the Democrats claimed, so "let white men rule." They charged that the Radical Republicans were subjecting the South "to military despotism and Negro supremacy." They nominated Horatio Seymour, the wartime governor of New York and a passionate critic of Congressional Reconstruction, who dismissed the Emancipation Proclamation as "a proposal for the butchery of women and children." His running mate, Francis P. Blair Jr., a former Union general from Missouri who had served in Congress, was an unapologetic racist who denounced Republicans for promoting equality for "a semi-barbarous race" who sought to "subject the white women to their unbridled lust." Blair attacked Grant for exercising military tyranny "over the eight millions of white people in the South, fixed to the earth with his bayonets."

A Democrat later said that Blair's "stupid and indefensible" remarks cost Seymour a close election. Grant won all but eight states and swept the electoral college, 214–80, but his popular majority was only 307,000 out of almost 6 million votes.

More than 500,000 African American voters, mostly in the South, accounted for Grant's margin of victory, and many risked their lives supporting him. Klan violence soared during the campaign, and hundreds of freedpeople paid with their lives. Still, the efforts of Radical Republicans to ensure voting rights for southern blacks had paid off. As Frederick Douglass explained, "the Republican party is the ship and all else is the sea" as far as black voters were concerned.

Grant, the youngest president (forty-six years old at the time of his inauguration), was a courageous defender of Congressional Reconstruction, but he was not a great president. He later admitted that he took office "without any previous experience either in civil or political life. I thought I could run the government of the United States as I did the staff of my army. It was my mistake, and it led me into other mistakes."

Grant passively followed the lead of Congress and was often blind to the political forces and self-serving influence peddlers around him. He showed poor judgment in his selection of cabinet members, often favoring friendship, family, loyalty, and military service over integrity and ability.

During his two terms in office, his seven cabinet positions changed twenty-four times. Some of the men betrayed his trust and engaged in criminal behavior. His former comrade in arms and close friend, General William T. Sherman, said he felt sorry for Grant because so many supposedly "loyal" Republicans used the president for their own selfish gains. Carl Schurz, a Union war hero who became a Republican senator from Missouri, expressed frustration that Grant was misled by cunning advisers who "prostituted" his administration.

Yet Grant excelled at bringing diversity to the federal government. During his two presidential terms, he appointed more African Americans, Native Americans, Jews, and women than any of his predecessors, and he fulfilled his campaign pledge to bring the nation "peace and prosperity."

**THE FIFTEENTH AMENDMENT** President Grant viewed Reconstruction of the South as the nation's top priority, and he doggedly insisted that freedpeople be allowed to exercise their civil rights without fear of violence. On March 30, 1870, Grant delivered a speech to Congress in which he celebrated the ratification of the Fifteenth Amendment, which gave voting rights to African American men nationwide. "It was," he declared, ". . . the most important event that has occurred since the nation came into life . . . the realization of the Declaration of Independence." Frederick Douglass appreciated Grant's efforts: "To Grant, more than any other man, the Negro owes his enfranchisement."

But the Fifteenth Amendment ignited a violent backlash in the South. The idea of the federal government guaranteeing the right of freedmen to vote deepened resentment of Reconstruction. In Georgia, white officials devised new ways to restrict black voting, such as poll taxes and onerous registration procedures. Other states followed suit.

Four months after the Fifteenth Amendment became the law of the land, Congress also passed the Naturalization Act of 1870. For the first time, it extended the process whereby immigrants had gained citizenship to include *"aliens of African nativity and to persons of African descent."* Efforts to include Asians and Native Americans in the new naturalization law were defeated, however.

**THE UNION LEAGUE** The Fifteenth Amendment had enormous political consequences. Southern whites feared nothing more than black voters, while Republicans were eager to recruit them. To do so, Republicans organized Union Leagues throughout the former Confederacy. Republicans had founded the Union League (also called Lincoln's Loyal League) in 1862 to rally voters behind Lincoln, the war, and the party. By late 1863, the leagues claimed more than 700,000 members in 4,554 councils across the nation.

In the South, the leagues operated like fraternities, with formal initiations and rituals and secret meetings to protect freedpeople from being persecuted by angry white Democrats. They met in churches, schools, homes, and fields, often hearing from northern speakers who traveled the South extolling the Republican party and encouraging blacks to register and vote. By the early 1870s, the Union League in the South had become one of the largest black social movements in history.

With the help of the Union Leagues, some 90 percent of southern freedmen registered to vote, almost all of them as Republicans, and they voted in record numbers (often as high as 80 to 90 percent). In Mississippi and South Carolina, black registered voters outnumbered whites.

Voting was not easy for freedmen, however, because most white Southerners were eager to deny them the vote. "All the blacks who vote against my ticket shall walk the plank," threatened former Georgia governor Howell Cobb, a Democrat who had been a Confederate general. Angry whites persecuted, evicted, or fired African American workers who "exercised their political rights," as a Union officer reported from Virginia.

Black Republicans were at times equally coercive. "The Negroes are as intolerant of opposition as the whites," a white South Carolina Democrat observed. They shunned, expelled, and even killed any "of their own" who "would turn democrats." He added that freedwomen were as partisan as men—and as intolerant of opposition: The "women are worse than the men, refusing to talk to or marry a renegade [black Democrat], and aiding [men] in mobbing him."

Yet the net result of the Union Leagues was the mobilization of African American voters, who enabled African American men to gain elected offices for the first time in the states of the former Confederacy. Francis Cardozo, a black minister who served as president of the South Carolina Council of Union Leagues, declared in 1870 that the state had "prospered in every respect" as a result of the enfranchisement of black voters enabled by the Union Leagues.

**INDIAN POLICY** President Grant was almost as progressive in his outlook toward Native Americans as he was toward African Americans. In 1869, he appointed General Ely Parker, a Seneca chief trained as an attorney and engineer, as the new Commissioner of Indian Affairs, the first Native American to hold the position. Parker had served as Grant's military secretary during the war. Now, as commissioner, Parker faced formidable challenges in creating policies for the 300,000 Indians across the nation, many of whom continued to be pressured by white settlers, miners, railroads, and telegraph companies to give up their ancestral lands.

Working with Parker, Grant created a new Peace Policy toward Native Americans. "The Indians," he observed, "require as much protection from the whites as the white does from the Indians." He did not want the army "shooting these poor savages; I want to conciliate them and make them peaceful citizens." His own experiences had shown that the "Indian problem" was in fact the result of "bad whites." Grant believed that lasting peace could only result from Indians abandoning their nomadic tradition and relocating to government reservations, where federal troops would provide them "absolute protection."

Grant also promised to end the chronic corruption whereby congressmen appointed cronies as licensed government traders with access to the Indian reservations. Many of the traders used their positions to swindle the Native Americans out of the federally supplied food, clothing, and other provisions intended solely for the reservations. One of the accused traders was the president's brother.

To clean up the so-called Indian Ring, Grant moved the Bureau of Indian Affairs out of the control of Congress and into the War Department. He also created a ten-man Board of Indian Commissioners, a new civilian agency whose mission was to oversee the operations of the Bureau of Indian Affairs to ensure that corruption was rooted out. Grant then appointed Quakers as reservation traders, assuming that their honesty, humility, and pacifism would improve the distribution of government resources. "If you can make Quakers out of the Indians," Grant told them, "it will take the fight out of them. Let us have peace." Yet Quakers proved no more able to manage Indian policy than government bureaucrats could.

Like other presidents, Grant discovered that there often emerged a gap between the policies he created and the implementation of them by others. Many of the officers and soldiers sent to the West to "pacify" Indian peoples in the Great Plains displayed an attitude toward Native Americans quite different from Grant's. For example, it was General Philip Sheridan who coined the infamous statement: "The only good Indians I know are dead." He also dismissed Indians as "the enemies of our race and of our civilization." Those "savages" who refused to move to government-mandated reservations should be killed, he argued. General William T. Sherman agreed. He stressed to Sheridan that "the more [Indians] we kill this year, the less we would have to kill next year."

Such attitudes led the abolitionist Wendell Phillips to ask why Indians were one of the only groups still denied citizenship. His answer was clear: "The great poison of the age is race hatred" directed at both African Americans and Native Americans. Most white Americans, however, did not care that racism was at work. "Wendell Phillips' new nigger," the editors of the *New York Herald* observed with disdain, "is the 'noble red man.'" Phillips responded, "We shall never be able to be just to other races . . . until we 'unlearn' contempt" for others different from us.

**SCANDALS** President Grant's naive trust in people led his administration to stumble into a cesspool of scandal. Perhaps because of his own disastrous efforts as a storekeeper and farmer before the Civil War, Grant was awestruck by men of wealth. As they lavished gifts and attention on him, he was lured into their webs of self-serving deception.

In the summer of 1869, two unprincipled financial schemers, Jay Gould and James Fisk Jr., both infamous for bribing politicians and judges, plotted with Abel Corbin, the president's brother-in-law, to "corner" (manipulate) the nation's gold market. They intended to create a public craze for gold by purchasing massive quantities of the precious metal to drive up its value.

The only danger to the complicated scheme lay in the possibility that the federal Treasury would burst the bubble by selling large amounts of its gold, which would deflate its market value. When Grant was seen in public with Gould and Fisk, people assumed that he supported their scheme. As the false rumor spread in New York City's financial district that the president endorsed the run-up in gold, its value soared.

On September 24, 1869—soon to be remembered mournfully as Black Friday—the Gould-Fisk scheme worked, at least for a while. Starting at $150 an ounce, the price of gold rose, first to $160, then $165, leading more and more investors to join the stampede.

Then, around noon, Grant and his Treasury secretary realized what was happening and began selling government gold. Within fifteen minutes, the price plummeted to $138. Schemers lost fortunes amid the chaotic trading. Some ruined traders wept. One fainted. Another committed suicide. Soon the turmoil spread to the entire stock market, claiming thousands of victims. As Fisk noted, each man was left to "drag out his own corpse."

For weeks after the gold bubble collapsed, financial markets were paralyzed and business confidence was shaken. Congressman James Garfield wrote privately to a friend that President Grant had compromised his office by his "indiscreet acceptance" of gifts from Fisk and Gould and that any investigation of Black Friday would lead "into the parlor of the President." One critic announced that U.S. Grant's initials actually stood for "uniquely stupid."

The plot to corner the gold market was only the first of several scandals that rocked the Grant administration. The secretary of war, it turned out, had accepted bribes from merchants who traded with Indians at army posts in the West. And in St. Louis, whiskey distillers bribed federal Treasury agents in an effort to avoid paying excise taxes on alcohol. Grant's personal secretary participated in the scheme, taking secret payments in exchange for confidential information. Grant, spotlessly honest himself, urged Congress to investigate. "Let no guilty man escape," he stressed. "No personal considerations should stand in the way of performing a public duty."

Various congressional committees uncovered no evidence that Grant was personally involved. His poor choice of associates, however, earned him widespread criticism. Democrats scolded Republicans for their "monstrous corruption and extravagance" and reinforced public suspicion that elected officials were less servants of the people than they were self-serving bandits.

**LIBERAL REPUBLICANS** Disputes over political corruption and the fate of Reconstruction helped divide Republicans into two factions: Liberals (or Conscience Republicans) and Stalwarts (or Grant Republicans).

Liberal Republicans, led by Senator Carl Schurz, embraced free enterprise capitalism and opposed government regulation of business and industry while championing gold coins as the only reliable currency. They wanted to oust the "tyrannical" Grant from the presidency and end Reconstruction. They also sought to lower the tariffs lining the pockets of big corporations, and promote "civil service reforms" to end the "partisan tyranny" of the "patronage system," whereby new presidents rewarded the "selfish greed" of political supporters with federal government jobs.

Liberal Republicans charged that Grant and his cronies were pursuing policies and making decisions solely to benefit themselves. They also opposed Grant's efforts to suppress racism and Ku Klux Klan terrorism. As the *Nation* magazine stressed, "Everybody is heartily tired of discussing [the Negro's] rights." They believed there was no more need for federal intervention in the South. "The removal of white prejudice against the negro depends almost entirely on the negro himself" rather than the presence of federal troops.

**THE 1872 ELECTION** In 1872, the Liberal Republicans, many of whom were elitist newspaper editors suspicious of the "working classes," held their own national convention in Cincinnati, during which they accused the Grant administration of corruption, incompetence, and "despotism." They then committed political suicide by nominating Horace Greeley, the editor of the *New York Tribune* and a longtime champion of causes ranging from abolitionism to socialism, vegetarianism, and spiritualism (communicating with the dead).

E. L. Godkin, editor of the *Nation* and a Liberal Republican sympathizer, could not imagine voting for Greeley, whom he dismissed as "a conceited, ignorant, half-cracked, obstinate old creature." Greeley's image as an eccentric who repeatedly reversed his political positions was matched by his record of hostility toward Democrats, whose support the Liberal Republicans needed if they were to win.

Southern Democrats, however, liked Greeley's criticism of Reconstruction policies. His newspaper, for example, claimed that "ignorant, superstitious, semi-barbarian" former slaves were "extremely indolent, and will make no exertion beyond what is necessary to obtain food enough to satisfy their hunger." Moreover, Radical Republicans had given the vote to "ignorant" former slaves whose "Nigger Government" exercised "absolute political supremacy" in several states and was transferring wealth from the "most intelligent" and "influential" southern whites to themselves.

Most Northerners, however, were appalled at Greeley's candidacy. By nominating Greeley, said the *New York Times*, the Liberal Republicans and Democrats had killed any chance of electoral victory.

In the 1872 balloting, Greeley carried only six southern states and none in the North. Grant won thirty-one states and tallied 3,598,235 votes to Greeley's 2,834,761. An exhausted Greeley confessed that he was "the worst beaten man who ever ran for high office." His wife died six days before the election, and he died three weeks later.

Grant was delighted that the "soreheads and thieves who had deserted the Republican party" were defeated, and he promised to avoid the "mistakes" he had made in his first term.

**THE MONEY SUPPLY** Complex financial issues—especially monetary policy—dominated Ulysses S. Grant's second term. Prior to the Civil War, the economy operated on a gold standard; state banks issued paper money that could be exchanged for an equal value of gold coins. So, both gold coins and state bank notes circulated as currency. **Greenbacks** (so called because of the dye used on the printed dollars) were issued by the federal Treasury during the Civil War to help pay for the war.

When a nation's supply of money grows faster than the economy itself, prices for goods and services increase (inflation). This happened when the greenbacks were issued. After the war, the U.S. Treasury assumed that the greenbacks would be recalled from circulation so that consumer prices would decline and the nation could return to a "hard-money" currency—gold, silver, and copper coins—which had always been viewed as more reliable in value than paper currency.

The most vocal supporters of a return to hard money were eastern creditors (mostly bankers and merchants) who did not want their debtors to pay them in paper currency. Critics of the gold standard tended to be farmers and other debtors. These so-called soft-money advocates opposed taking greenbacks out of circulation because shrinking the supply of money would bring lower prices (deflation) for their crops and livestock, thereby reducing their income and making it harder for them to pay their long-term debts. In 1868, congressional supporters of such a soft-money policy—mostly Democrats—forced the Treasury to stop withdrawing greenbacks.

President Grant sided with the hard-money camp. On March 18, 1869, he signed the Public Credit Act, which said that investors who purchased government bonds to help finance the war effort must be paid back in gold. The act led to a decline in consumer prices that hurt debtors and helped creditors. It also ignited a ferocious political debate over the merits of hard and soft money that would last throughout the nineteenth century—and beyond.

**FINANCIAL PANIC** President Grant's effort to withdraw greenbacks from circulation unintentionally helped cause a major economic collapse. During 1873, two dozen overextended railroads stopped paying their bills, forcing Jay Cooke and Company, the nation's leading business lender, to go bankrupt and close its doors on September 18, 1873.

The shocking news created a snowball effect, as other hard-pressed banks began shutting down. A Republican senator sent Grant an urgent telegram from New York City: "Results of today indicate imminent danger of general national bank panic."

The resulting **Panic of 1873** triggered a deep depression. Tens of thousands of businesses closed, 3 million workers lost jobs, and those with jobs saw their wages slashed. In major cities, the unemployed and homeless roamed the streets and formed long lines at soup kitchens.

The depression led the U.S. Treasury to reverse course and begin printing more greenbacks. For a time, the supporters of paper money celebrated, but in 1874, Grant overruled his cabinet and vetoed a bill to issue even more greenbacks. His decision pleased the financial community but ignited a barrage of criticism. A Tennessee Republican congressman called the veto "cold-blooded murder," and a group of merchants in Indiana charged that Grant had sold his soul to those "whose god is the dollar."

In the end, Grant's decision only prolonged what was then the worst depression in the nation's history. It also brought about a catastrophe for Republicans in the 1874 congressional elections, as Democrats blamed them for the economic hard times. In the House, Republicans went from a 70 percent majority to a 37 percent minority. They maintained control of the Senate but were placed on the defensive.

**WHITE TERROR** President Grant initially fought to enforce federal efforts to reconstruct the postwar South, but southern resistance to "Radical rule" increased and turned brutally violent. In Grayson County, Texas, a white man and two friends murdered three former slaves because they wanted to "thin the niggers out and drive them to their holes."

Klansmen focused their program of murder, violence, and intimidation on prominent Republicans, black and white—elected officials, teachers in black schools, state militias. In Mississippi, they killed a black Republican leader in front of his family. Three white scalawag Republicans were murdered in Georgia in 1870, and that same year an armed mob of whites assaulted a Republican political rally in Alabama, killing four blacks and wounding fifty-four. An Alabama Republican pleaded with President Grant to intervene. "Give us poor people some guarantee of our lives," G. T. F. Boulding wrote. "We are hunted and shot down as if we were wild beasts."

In South Carolina, white supremacists were especially violent. In 1871, some 500 masked men laid siege to the Union County jail and eventually lynched eight black prisoners. In March 1871, Klansmen killed thirty African Americans in Meridian, Mississippi.

At Grant's urging, Republicans in Congress responded with three Enforcement Acts (1870–1871). The first imposed penalties on anyone who interfered with a citizen's right to vote. The second dispatched federal supervisors to monitor elections in southern districts where political terrorism flourished. The third, called the Ku Klux Klan Act (1871), outlawed the main activities of the KKK—forming conspiracies, wearing disguises, resisting officers, and intimidating officials. It also allowed the president to send federal troops to any community where voting rights were being violated.

Once the legislation was approved, Grant sent Attorney General Amos Akerman, a Georgian, to recruit prosecutors and marshals to enforce it. The Klan, Akerman reported, "was the most atrocious organization that the civilized part of the world has ever known." Its violent acts "amount to war." In South Carolina alone, Akerman and federal troops and prosecutors convinced local juries to convict 1,143 Klansmen. By 1872, Grant's stern actions had effectively killed the Klan. In general, however, the Enforcement Acts were not consistently enforced. As a result, the violent efforts of southern whites to thwart Reconstruction escalated.

On Easter Sunday 1873 in the black Republican township of Colfax, Louisiana, a mob of 140 white vigilantes, most of them ex-Confederate soldiers led by Klansmen, used a cannon, rifles, and pistols to attack a group of black Republicans holed up in the courthouse, slaughtering eighty-one and burning the building.

When federal troops arrived, an officer reported that they found heaps of black bodies being picked over by dogs and buzzards. "We were unable to find the body of a single white man," he said. Many of the dead "were shot in the back of the head and neck." Most had "three to a dozen wounds."

President Grant told the Senate that the Colfax Massacre was unprecedented in its "barbarity." He declared parts of Louisiana to be in a state of insurrection and imposed military rule. Federal prosecutors used the Enforcement Acts to indict seventy whites, but only nine were put on trial and just three were convicted—but of "conspiracy," not murder.

**SOUTHERN "REDEEMERS"** The Klan's impact on southern politics varied from state to state. In the Upper South, it played only a modest role in helping Democrats win local elections. In the Lower South, however, Klan violence had more serious effects. In overwhelmingly black Yazoo County, Mississippi, vengeful whites used terrorism to reverse the political balance of power. In the 1873 elections, for example, the Republicans cast 2,449 votes and the Democrats 638; two years later, the Democrats polled 4,049 votes, the Republicans 7. Once Democrats regained power, they ousted black legislators, closed public schools for black children, and instituted poll taxes to restrict black voting.

The activities of white supremacists disheartened black and white Republicans alike. "We are helpless and unable to organize," wrote a Mississippi scalawag. We "dare not attempt to canvass [campaign for candidates], or make public speeches." At the same time, Northerners displayed a growing weariness with using federal troops to reconstruct the South. "The plain truth is," noted the *New York Herald*, "the North has got tired of the Negro."

President Grant, however, desperately wanted to use more federal force to preserve peace. He asked Congress to pass new legislation that would "leave my duties perfectly clear." Congress responded with the Civil Rights Act of 1875, which said that people of all races must be granted equal access to hotels and restaurants, railroads and stagecoaches, theaters, and other "places of public amusement."

Unfortunately for Grant, the new anti-segregation law provided little enforcement authority. Those who felt their rights were being violated had to file suit in court, and the penalties for violators were modest. In 1883, the U.S. Supreme Court, in an opinion arising from five similar cases, struck down the Civil Rights Act on the grounds that the Fourteenth Amendment focused only on the actions of state governments; it did not have authority over the policies of private businesses or individuals. Chief Justice Joseph Bradley added that it was time for blacks to assume "the rank of a mere citizen" and stop being the "special favorite of the laws." As a result, the *Civil Rights Cases* (1883) opened the door for a wave of racial segregation that washed over the South during the late nineteenth century.

Republican political control in the South and public interest in protecting civil rights gradually loosened during the 1870s as all-white "Conservative" parties mobilized the anti-Reconstruction vote. They called themselves Conservatives to distinguish themselves from northern Democrats. Conservatives—the so-called **redeemers** who supposedly "saved" the South from Republican control and "black rule"—used the race issue to excite the white electorate and threaten black voters. Where persuasion failed to work, Conservatives used trickery to rig the voting. As one boasted, "The white and black Republicans may outvote us, but we can outcount them."

Republican political control ended in Virginia and Tennessee as early as 1869 and collapsed a year later in Georgia and North Carolina, although North Carolina had a Republican governor until 1876. Reconstruction lasted longest in the Lower South, where whites abandoned Klan robes for barefaced intimidation in paramilitary groups such as the Mississippi Rifle Club and the South Carolina Red Shirts. The last Radical Republican regimes ended, however, after the elections of 1876, and the return of the old white political elite further undermined the country's commitment to Congressional Reconstruction.

**THE SUPREME COURT** Key rulings by the U.S. Supreme Court further eroded Congressional Reconstruction. The *Slaughterhouse Cases* (1873) limited the "privileges or immunities" of U.S. citizenship as outlined in the Fourteenth Amendment.

In 1869, the Louisiana legislature had granted the New Orleans livestock slaughtering business to a single company for twenty-five years as a means of protecting public health. Competing butchers sued the state, arguing that the monopoly violated their "privileges" as U.S. citizens under the Fourteenth Amendment and deprived them of property without due process of law.

In a 5–4 decision, the Court ruled that the monopoly did not violate the Fourteenth Amendment because its "privileges and immunities" clause applied only to U.S. citizenship, not state citizenship. States, in other words, retained legal jurisdiction over their citizens, and federal protection of civil rights did not extend to the property rights of businesses.

Dissenting Justice Stephen J. Field argued that the Court's ruling rendered the Fourteenth Amendment a "vain and idle enactment" with little scope or authority. By designating the rights of state citizens as being beyond the jurisdiction of federal law, the *Slaughterhouse Cases* unwittingly opened the door for states to discriminate against African Americans.

Three years later, in *United States v. Cruikshank* (1876), the Supreme Court further eroded the protections of individuals by overturning the convictions of William Cruikshank and two other white men who had led the Colfax Massacre. In doing so, the Court argued that the equal protection and due process clauses in the Fourteenth Amendment governed only state actions, not the behavior of individuals. Furthermore, the prosecution's failure to prove racial intent placed the convictions outside the reach of the Equal Protection Clause of the Fourteenth Amendment.

In Chief Justice Morrison Waite's view, the duty to protect the "equality of the rights of citizens" had been "originally assumed by the States; and it still remains there." He and the other justices thus struck down the Enforcement Acts, ruling that the states, not the federal government, were responsible for protecting citizens from attack by other private citizens.

Taken together, the *Slaughterhouse* and *Cruikshank* cases so gutted the Fourteenth Amendment that freedpeople were left even more vulnerable to violence and discrimination. The federal government was effectively abandoning its role in enforcing Reconstruction.

**THE CONTESTED ELECTION OF 1876** President Grant wanted to run for an unprecedented third term in 1876, but many Republicans had lost confidence in his leadership. In the summer of 1875, he acknowledged the inevitable and announced that he would retire. James Gillespie Blaine of Maine, former Speaker of the House, initially seemed the likeliest Republican to succeed Grant, but his candidacy crumbled when newspapers revealed that he had secretly promised political favors to railroad executives in exchange for shares of stock in the company.

The scandal led the Republican convention to select Ohio's favorite son, Rutherford B. Hayes. A former Union general who had been wounded five times during the Civil War, Hayes had served three terms as governor of Ohio. He was a civil service reformer eager to reduce the number of federal jobs subject to political appointment. But his chief virtue was that he offended neither Radicals nor reformers. As a journalist put it, he was "obnoxious to no one."

Hayes called for reforming the civil service to eliminate cronyism and corruption within his administration and promised to reject a second term for himself. The Republican platform criticized the "corrupt centralism" of the Grant administration that had infested the federal government with "incapacity, waste, and fraud."

The Democratic convention was uncharacteristically harmonious. On the second ballot, the nomination went to Samuel J. Tilden, a wealthy corporate lawyer and reform governor of New York.

The 1876 campaign avoided controversial issues. In the absence of strong ideological differences, Democrats highlighted the Republican scandals. Republicans responded by repeatedly waving "the bloody shirt," linking the Democrats to secession, civil war, and the violence committed against Republicans in the South. As Robert G. Ingersoll, the most celebrated Republican public speaker of the time, insisted: "The man that assassinated Abraham Lincoln was a Democrat . . . Soldiers, every scar you have on your heroic bodies was given you by a Democrat!"

Early election returns pointed to a victory for Tilden. Nationwide, he outpolled Hayes by almost 300,000 votes, and by midnight following Election Day, Tilden had won 184 electoral votes, just 1 short of the total needed for victory. Overnight, however, Republican activists realized that the election hinged on 19 disputed electoral votes from Florida, Louisiana, and South Carolina.

The Democrats needed only one of the challenged votes to claim victory; the Republicans needed all nineteen. Republicans in the three states had engaged in election fraud, while Democrats had used violence to keep black voters at home. All three states, however, were governed by Republicans who appointed the election boards, each of which reported narrow victories for Hayes. The Democrats immediately challenged the results.

In all three states, rival election boards submitted conflicting vote counts. Weeks passed with no solution. On January 29, 1877, Congress appointed an electoral commission to settle the dispute. Finally, on March 1, 1877, the commission voted 8–7 in favor of Hayes. The next day, the House of Representatives declared Hayes president by an electoral vote of 185–184.

Tilden decided not to protest the decision. His campaign manager explained that they preferred "four years of Hayes's administration to four years of civil war."

Hayes's victory hinged on the defection of key southern Democrats, who, it turned out, had made secret deals with the Republicans. On February 26, 1877, prominent Ohio Republicans and powerful southern Democrats had struck a private bargain—the **Compromise of 1877**—at Wormley's Hotel in Washington, D.C. The Republicans promised that if Hayes were named president, he would remove the last federal troops from the South.

For his part, President Grant was eager to leave the White House: "I never wanted to get out of a place as much as I did to get out of the Presidency." Others were sorry to see him leave. T. Jefferson Martin spoke for many African Americans when he wrote Grant upon his retirement: "As a colored man I feel in duty bound to return you my greatful [sic] and heartfelt thanks, for your firm, steadfast, and successful administrations of our country, both as military chieftain and civil ruler of this nation . . . My dear friend of humanity."

**THE END OF RECONSTRUCTION** In 1877, the Democrat-controlled House of Representatives refused to fund federal troops in the South after July, and President Hayes withdrew U.S. soldiers from Louisiana and South Carolina, whose Republican governments collapsed soon thereafter. In the Congressional elections of 1878, Hayes admitted that the balloting in southern states was corrupted by "violence of the most atrocious character," but he was not about to send federal troops again.

Over the next thirty years, federal protection of black civil rights in the South crumbled. As Henry Adams, a former Louisiana slave, observed in 1877, "The whole South—every state in the South—has got [back] into the hands of the very men that held us as slaves." New white state governments rewrote their constitutions, ousted the "carpetbaggers, scalawags, and blacks," and cut spending. "The Yankees helped free us, so they say," a former North Carolina slave named Thomas Hall remembered, "but [in 1877] they let us be put back in slavery again."

**THE "LOST CAUSE"** While white conservatives were reasserting control and reinforcing white supremacy, novelists, poets, and former Confederate leaders were fashioning what came to be called the Lost Cause narrative, a sanitized version of history in which a romanticized Confederacy could do no wrong during the "War of Northern Aggression."

Nostalgic apologists for secession glamorized the old plantation culture and insisted that the Civil War had little to do with slavery and everything to do with a noble defense of states' rights and the southern homeland against the aggressions of a tyrannical Republican party. As Jefferson Davis claimed in 1881, the loyal and faithful slaves in the South were "contented with their lot" in 1861. President Lincoln, however, hoodwinked them into believing they would be better off free and "sent them out to devastate their benefactors [owners]."

The Lost Cause myth also demonized abolitionists and idealized the leadership of Confederate generals Robert E. Lee ("the soldier who walked with God") and Stonewall Jackson, deifying them as chivalrous pillars of southern virtue who fought bravely and ethically against far larger Union armies led by ruthless outlaws such as Ulysses S. Grant and William T. Sherman.

To bolster this intentional reimagining of southern history, communities erected scores of monuments and memorials glorifying Confederate leaders. On Memorial Day 1890, for example, more than 100,000 people gathered in Richmond, Virginia, to celebrate the unveiling of a massive statue of General Lee seated on his celebrated warhorse, "Traveler." What the speakers at the event failed to mention was that Lee, before his death in 1871, had urged southerners *not* to create such memorials to a cause that was "lost" on the battlefields.

## RECONSTRUCTION'S SIGNIFICANCE

The collapse of Congressional Reconstruction in 1877 had tragic consequences, as the white South aggressively renewed traditional patterns of discrimination against African Americans. Black activist W. E. B. DuBois called the effort to make slaves into citizens a "splendid failure."

Yet for all its unfulfilled promises, Congressional Reconstruction did leave an enduring legacy—the Thirteenth, Fourteenth, and Fifteenth Amendments. If Reconstruction's experiment in interracial democracy failed to provide true social equality or substantial economic opportunities for African Americans, it did create the essential constitutional foundation for future advances in the quest for equality and civil rights—and not just for African Americans, but for women and other minority groups.

Until the pivotal Reconstruction era, the states were responsible for protecting citizens' rights. Thereafter, thanks to the Fourteenth and Fifteenth Amendments, blacks had gained equal rights (in theory), and the federal government had assumed responsibility for ensuring that states treated blacks equally. A hundred years later, the cause of civil rights would be embraced again by the federal government—this time permanently.

# CHAPTER REVIEW

## SUMMARY

- **Reconstruction Challenges**    With the defeat of the Confederacy, the federal government had to develop policies and procedures to address a number of vexing questions: What was the status of the defeated states, and how would they be reintegrated into the nation's political life? What would be the political status of the former slaves, and what would the federal government do to integrate them into the nation's social and economic fabric?

- **Reconstruction over Time**    Abraham Lincoln and his successor, Southerner Andrew Johnson, wanted a lenient plan for Reconstruction. *Johnson's Restoration Plan (1865),* like Lincoln's, said that when ten percent of a former Confederate state's voters swore a loyalty oath to the Union, that state could be readmitted. The *Freedmen's Bureau* helped to educate and aid freed slaves, negotiate labor contracts, and reunite families. Lincoln's assassination led many Northerners to favor the *Radical Republicans,* who wanted to end the grasp of the old plantation elite on the South's society and economy. Whites resisted and established *black codes* to restrict the freedom of former slaves. *Congressional Reconstruction* responded by stipulating that former Confederate states had to ratify the *Fourteenth (1868)* and *Fifteenth Amendments (1870)* to the U.S. Constitution to protect the rights of African Americans. Congress also passed the Military Reconstruction Act, which used federal troops to enforce the voting and civil rights of African Americans.

- **Views of Reconstruction**    After the war, land ownership reverted to the old white elite, reducing newly freed blacks to *sharecropping.* African Americans enthusiastically participated in politics, with many serving as elected officials. Along with white southern Republicans (scalawags) and northern carpetbaggers, they worked to rebuild the southern economy. Many white Southerners, however, supported the *Ku Klux Klan's* violent intimidation and conservative control of southern state governments.

- **Political and Economic Developments and the End of Reconstruction**    Scandals during the Grant administration involving an attempt to corner the gold market, plus the *Panic of 1873* and disagreement over whether to continue the use of *greenbacks* or return to the gold standard, eroded northern support for the status quo in government and weakened Reconstruction. Southern white *redeemers* were elected in 1874, successfully reversing the political progress of Republicans and blacks. In the *Compromise of 1877,* Democrats agreed to the election of Republican Rutherford B. Hayes, who put an end to the Radical Republican administrations in the southern states.

- **The Significance of Reconstruction**    Southern state governments quickly renewed long-standing patterns of discrimination against African Americans, but the Fourteenth and Fifteenth Amendments remained enshrined in the Constitution, creating the essential constitutional foundation for future advances in civil rights.

# Chronology

| | |
|---|---|
| **1865** | Congress sets up the Freedmen's Bureau |
| **April 14, 1865** | Lincoln assassinated |
| **1865** | Johnson issues Proclamation of Amnesty |
| | All-white southern state legislatures pass various black codes |
| **1866** | Ku Klux Klan organized |
| | Congress passes the Civil Rights Act |
| **1867** | Congress passes the Military Reconstruction Act |
| **1868** | Fourteenth Amendment is ratified |
| | The U.S. House of Representatives impeaches President Andrew Johnson; the Senate fails to convict him |
| | Grant elected president |
| | Eight former Confederate states readmitted to the Union |
| **1870** | Fifteenth Amendment ratified |
| | First Enforcement Acts passed in response to white terror in the South |
| **1872** | Grant wins reelection |
| **1873** | Panic of 1873 triggers depression |
| **1877** | Reconstruction ends; Hayes becomes president |

# Key Terms

**Radical Republicans** p. 643

**Freedmen's Bureau** p. 643

**Johnson's Restoration Plan** p. 647

**black codes** p. 649

**Fourteenth Amendment (1866)** p. 651

**Congressional Reconstruction** p. 652

**Fifteenth Amendment (1870)** p. 654

**sharecropping** p. 658

**Ku Klux Klan (KKK)** p. 662

**greenbacks** p. 671

**Panic of 1873** p. 672

**redeemers** p. 674

**Compromise of 1877** p. 677

 INQUIZITIVE

**Go to InQuizitive to see what you've learned—and learn what you've missed—with personalized feedback along the way.**

# part five

# GROWING PAINS

The defeat of the Confederacy in 1865 restored the Union and, in the process, helped accelerate America's transformation into an agricultural empire and an industrial powerhouse. A stronger sense of nationalism began to temper the regional conflicts of the prewar era.

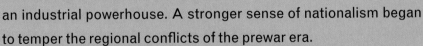

During and after the Civil War, the Republican-led Congress pushed through legislation to promote industrial and commercial development and western expansion at the same time that it was "reconstructing" the former Confederate states. The United States forged a dynamic new industrial economy serving an increasingly national and international market for American goods. Food production soared, as did exports. Railroads formed a web of economic development that created truly national markets. Yet the progress was tarnished by the relentless and ruthless relocation of Native Americans onto reservations and the reckless exploitation of the continent's natural resources.

Fueled by innovations in mass production and mass marketing and by advances in transportation and communication, such as transcontinental railroads and transatlantic telegraph systems, huge corporations began to dominate the economy. As social theorist William Graham Sumner remarked, the process of industrial development "controls us all because we are all in it. It creates the conditions of our own existence, sets the limits of our social activity, and regulates the bonds of our social relations."

Late nineteenth-century American life drew much of its energy from the mushrooming industrial cities. "This is the age of cities," declared midwestern writer Hamlin Garland. "We are now predominantly urban." Yet the transition from an economy made up of mostly small local and regional businesses to one dominated by large-scale national and international corporations affected rural life as well.

As early as 1869, novelist Harriet Beecher Stowe reported that the "simple, pastoral" America "is a thing forever gone. The hurry of railroads and the rush and roar of business" had displaced the Jeffersonian ideal of America as a nation of small farms.

She exaggerated, of course. Small farms and small towns survived the impact of the Industrial Revolution, but farm folk, as one New Englander stressed, now had to "understand farming as a business; if they do not it will go hard with them." The friction between the new forces of the national marketplace and the traditional folkways of small-scale family farming generated social unrest and political revolts during the last quarter of the nineteenth century.

The clash between tradition and modernity, sleepy farm villages and bustling cities, peaked during the 1890s, one of the most strife-ridden decades in American history. A deep economic depression, political activism by farmers, and violent conflicts between industrial workers and employers transformed the presidential campaign of 1896 into a clash between rival visions of America's future.

The Republican candidate, William McKinley, campaigned on modern urban and industrial values. William Jennings Bryan, the nominee of both the Democratic and Populist parties, was an eloquent defender of America's rural past. McKinley's victory proved to be a turning point in American political and social history. By 1900, the United States had emerged as one of the world's greatest industrial powers, and it would thereafter assume a new leadership role in world affairs—for good and for ill.

# 17 Business and Labor in the Industrial Era

## 1860–1900

**Carnegie Steel Company** Steelworkers operate the massive and dangerous Bessemer converters at Andrew Carnegie's steel mill in Pittsburgh, Pennsylvania.

Although the Civil War devastated the South, it provided a powerful stimulant to the northern economy. The wartime need to supply the Union armies with shoes, boots, uniforms, weapons, supplies, food, wagons, and railroads ushered in an era of unprecedented industrial development. The scope of the war favored large-scale businesses and hastened the maturation of a truly national economy. As an Indiana congressman told business leaders in 1864, the war had sparked the development of "resources and capabilities such as you never before dreamed you possessed."

During the war, the number of manufacturing companies in the United States almost doubled. In 1865, Ohio senator John Sherman wrote a letter to his brother, William T. Sherman, the celebrated Union general, in which he observed that the northern states had emerged from the war "unimpaired." The process of mass-producing mountains of goods for the war effort had given a widened "scope to the ideas of leading capitalists, far higher than anything undertaken in this country. They talk of millions as confidently as before [they talked] of thousands."

Between the end of the war and 1900, America experienced explosive growth. The nation's population tripled, agricultural production more than doubled, and manufacturing output grew *six* times over. When the Civil War ended, there was not a single industrial corporation listed on the New York Stock Exchange. By 1900, there were dozens of them employing hundreds of thousands of managers, clerks, and workers. In the thirty-five years after the Civil War, the United States achieved the highest rate of economic growth in

## *focus questions*

**1.** What factors stimulated the unprecedented industrial and agricultural growth in the late nineteenth century?

**2.** Who were the entrepreneurs who pioneered the growth of Big Business? What were their goals, and what strategies did they use to dominate their respective industries?

**3.** What role did the federal government play in the nation's economic development during this period?

**4.** Analyze the ways in which the class structure and lives of women changed in the late nineteenth century.

**5.** Assess the efforts of workers to organize unions to promote their interests during this era.

the world, and by 1900, American industries and corporate farms dominated global markets in steel, oil, wheat, and cotton.

Such phenomenal growth led to profound social changes, the most visible of which was the sudden prosperity of large industrial cities such as Pittsburgh, Chicago, and Cleveland. Millions of young adults left farms and villages to work in factories, mines, and mills and to revel in city life. In growing numbers, women left the "cult of domesticity" and entered the urban-industrial workplace as clerks, typists, secretaries, teachers, nurses, and seamstresses.

While a few made fortunes, most laborers remained in unskilled, low-wage jobs. The world of *Big Business*, a term commonly used to refer to the giant corporations that emerged after the Civil War, was as untamed and reckless as the cow towns and mining camps of the West were. New technologies and business practices outpaced the ability of the outdated legal system to craft new laws and fashion ethical norms to govern the rapidly changing economy. Business owners took advantage of this lawless environment to build fortunes, destroy reputations, exploit workers and the environment, and gouge consumers. Yet out of the scramble for profits emerged an undreamed-of prosperity and a rising standard of living that became the envy of the world.

Along with great wealth came great poverty, however. In a capitalist economy, people with different talents, opportunities, and resources receive unequal rewards from their labors. And, in a capitalist democracy like America, the tensions between equal political rights and unequal economic status generate social instability. In the decades after the Civil War, the overwhelming influence exercised by the business tycoons spurred the formation of labor unions and farm associations. Increasingly, tensions erupted into violent clashes that required government intervention and produced class conflict.

## Industrial and Agricultural Growth

Several factors converged during the second half of the nineteenth century to accelerate the nation's industrial development. Perhaps most important was the expansion of transportation systems—canals, steamboats, railroads, and the development of instantaneous communication networks enabled first by the telegraph, and later, the telephone. All together, these innovations combined to create a truly national marketplace for the sale and distribution of goods and services.

In addition, America enjoyed the benefits of its vast natural resources: land, forests, minerals, oil, coal, water, and iron ore. At the same time, a rising tide of immigrants created an army of low-wage, high-energy workers while expanding the pool of consumers eager to buy new products. Between 1865 and 1900, more than 15 million newcomers arrived in the United States.

A new generation of outsized business leaders drove the transition to an urban-industrial society. Admirers called them captains of industry, while critics called them robber barons because they controlled the flow of money and commerce.

Whatever the label, the post–Civil War tycoons were determined to create large enterprises never before imagined. They were proponents of free enterprise and self-reliance who were convinced that what was good for their businesses was good for the country. Hated, feared, envied, or admired, they were the catalysts for a new America of cities and factories, prosperity amid poverty, and growing social strife and political corruption.

Bigness was the driving goal of industrial capitalism. Daring entrepreneurs took advantage of new money-making opportunities, technologies, and political lobbying (including bribery) to build gigantic corporations that dominated industries such as oil refining, steel, sugar, and meatpacking.

Ingenuity became America's economic trademark. The promoters of Big Business ruthlessly improved efficiency and productivity, cut costs, bought politicians, and suppressed competition. These predatory men—Cornelius Vanderbilt, John D. Rockefeller, Andrew Carnegie, and J. P. Morgan, among others—wanted to *dominate* their industries. When Vanderbilt, a developer first of steamboats and then railroads, learned that some rivals had tried to steal one of his properties, he penned a brief message: "Gentlemen: You have undertaken to cheat me. I will not sue you, for law takes too long. I will ruin you." And he did.

## CORPORATE AGRICULTURE

At the same time that the manufacturing sector was experiencing rapid growth, the agricultural sector was shifting to a large-scale industrial model of operation. Giant corporate-owned "bonanza farms" spread across the West. They were run like factories by professional, college-educated managers, who would hire hundreds of migrant workers to harvest crops—usually wheat or corn destined for eastern or foreign markets.

The farm sector stimulated the industrial sector—and vice versa. In the West, bonanza farms using the latest machinery and scientific techniques became internationally famous for their productivity. By 1870, the United States had become the world's leading agricultural producer. With the growth of the commercial cattle industry, the process of slaughtering, packing, and shipping cattle, hogs, and sheep evolved into a major industry, especially in Chicago, the nation's fastest-growing city and the largest slaughterhouse in the world.

## TECHNOLOGICAL INNOVATIONS

America has always nurtured a culture of invention and innovation. Abraham Lincoln often praised the nation's peculiar talent for "discoveries and inventions," which became especially evident in the decades after the Civil War. Inventors, scientists, research laboratories, and business owners developed labor-saving machinery and mass-production techniques that spurred dramatic advances in efficiency, productivity, and the size of industrial enterprises.

Such innovations helped businesses turn out more products more cheaply, thus enabling more people to buy more of them. Technological advances created *economies of scale*, whereby larger business enterprises, including huge commercial farms, could afford expensive new machinery and large workforces that boosted their productivity.

After the Civil War, technological improvements spurred phenomenal increases in industrial productivity. The U.S. Patent Office, which had recorded only 276 inventions during the 1790s, registered almost 235,000 new patents in the 1890s. Women were inventive too. New Yorker Beulah Louisa Henry accounted for almost 50 of those patents, most of them improvements on household goods. The list of innovations produced in the late nineteenth century included barbed wire, mechanical harvesters, reapers and combines, refrigerated railcars, air brakes for trains, steam turbines, typewriters, sewing machines, vacuum cleaners, ice cream churns, and electric motors.

**BELL'S TELEPHONE** Few inventions could rival the importance of the telephone. In 1875, twenty-eight-year-old Alexander Graham Bell began experimenting with the concept of a "speaking telegraph," or talking through wires. The following year, he developed a primitive "electric speaking telephone" that enabled him to send a famous message to his assistant in another room: "Mr. Watson, come here, I want to see you." In 1876, Bell patented his device and started the American Telephone and Telegraph Company (AT&T), to begin manufacturing telephones. Five years later, he perfected the long-distance telephone lines that revolutionized communication. By 1895, more than 300,000 telephones were in use. Bell's patent became the most valuable one ever issued.

**TYPEWRITERS AND SEWING MACHINES** Other inventions changed the nature of work. Typewriters, for example, transformed the operations of business offices. Because managers assumed that women had greater dexterity in their fingers and because women could be paid less than men on

**Office typists** In new roles enabled by typewriters, women served as clerks or secretaries at many offices, such as the Remington Typewriter Company, pictured here.

the assumption that they were not supporting a household, owners hired them to operate typewriters. Clerical positions soon became the fastest-growing job category for women.

Likewise, the introduction of sewing machines for the mass production of clothing and linens opened new, though often exploitative, employment opportunities to women. So-called sweatshops emerged in the major cities, where large numbers of mostly young immigrant women worked long hours in cramped, stifling conditions.

**THOMAS EDISON** No American inventor was more influential or prolific than Thomas Alva Edison. As a boy in Michigan, he loved to "make things" and "do things." His mother homeschooled him and allowed him to explore the outdoors and perform what he called chemical "experiments." Edison later said his mother "let me follow my bent." His "bent" was toward telegraphy and electricity. He built his own telegraph set and dreamed of being a telegraph operator sending messages in Morse code.

When Edison was twelve, he began working for the local railroad, selling newspapers, food, and candy. "Being poor," he explained, "I already knew that money is a valuable thing." One day he was late for the train and ran after it.

A conductor reached down and lifted him into the train by his ears. Edison felt something snap in his head, and soon he was nearly deaf.

In 1862, early in the Civil War, the solitary Edison fastened on his real passion: being a telegraph operator, first in Cincinnati, then in Louisville and Boston. The clicking telegraph key enabled him to listen to others and tinker with the equipment.

Despite having no formal scientific education, Edison became a mechanical genius. In January 1869, at the age of twenty-one, he announced that he would "hereafter devote his full time to bringing out his inventions." He moved to New York City to be closer to the center of America's financial district; there he developed dozens of new machines, including a "stock market ticker" to report the transactions on Wall Street in real time. Soon, job offers and what he referred to as "real money" flooded his way. Edison, however, had a different goal: to become a full-time inventor.

In 1876, he moved into what he called his "science village" in Menlo Park, New Jersey, twenty-five miles southwest of New York City. There, in the nation's first industrial research laboratory, Edison and his assistants created the phonograph in 1877 and a long-lasting electric lightbulb in 1879. He also improved upon the telephone.

By the ripe age of thirty, Edison was the nation's foremost inventor. Altogether, he created or perfected hundreds of new devices and processes, including the storage battery, Dictaphone, mimeograph copier, electric motor, and motion picture camera and projector.

He soon became world famous. A magazine saluted him as the "Wizard of Menlo Park" and called him one of the "wonders of the world." President Rutherford B. Hayes invited him to the White House, and Congress honored him. Until Edison's inventions came along, the availability of daylight determined how people lived and worked. With the lightbulb, the distinction between night and day virtually disappeared.

**GEORGE WESTINGHOUSE AND ELECTRIC POWER** Before the 1880s, kerosene and gas lamps illuminated the nation after dark. All that changed in 1882, when the Edison Electric Illuminating Company launched the electric utility industry. Several companies that made lightbulbs merged into the Edison General Electric Company in 1888, later renamed General Electric.

The use of direct electrical current, however, limited Edison's lighting system to a radius of about two miles. To cover greater distances required an alternating current, which could be transmitted at high voltage and then stepped down by transformers. George Westinghouse, inventor of the railway air brake, developed the first alternating-current electric system in 1886, and he thereafter set up the Westinghouse Electric Company to manufacture the equipment.

Edison resisted the new method as too risky, but the Westinghouse system won the "battle of the currents," and the Edison companies had to switch over to AC (alternating current) from DC (direct current). In 1887, a twenty-eight-year-old Croatian immigrant named Nikola Tesla, who had briefly worked with Thomas Edison before the two parted ways, set up laboratories in New York where he invented the alternating-current (AC) motor, which he sold to George Westinghouse, who improved it, and the company began selling dynamos.

The invention of dynamos (electric motors) dramatically increased the power, speed, and efficiency of machinery. Electricity enabled factories to be located anywhere; factories and mills no longer had to cluster around waterfalls and coal deposits to have a ready supply of energy. Electricity also spurred urban growth by improving lighting, facilitating the development of trolley and subway systems, and stimulating the creation of elevators that enabled the construction of taller buildings.

## THE RAILROAD REVOLUTION

More than any other industry, railroads symbolized the impact of innovative technologies on industrial development and the maturation of a national economy. No other form of transportation played so large a role in the development of the interconnected national marketplace.

In 1888, William Cox, a Nebraska writer, reported that "a new railway has been commenced and completed" across the state, opening "up a great new artery of traffic, and bringing in its train joy and gladness for thousands of people." The rail line was "building up three new villages along the way, and infusing new life and activity into a fourth." The railroads, he concluded, were providing America a pathway to progress, profit, and modernity.

**TRAINS AND TIME** Railroads compressed time and distance. They moved masses of people and goods faster, farther, and cheaper than any other form of transportation. The railroad network prompted the creation of uniform national and international time zones and spurred the use of wristwatches, for the trains were scheduled to run on time. Towns that had rail depots thrived; those that did not died. The stations were the lifelines connecting small towns with the outside world. A town's connection to a railroad, observed Anthony Trollope, a British writer touring the United States, was "the first necessity of life, and gives the only hope of wealth."

Although the first great wave of railroad building occurred in the 1850s, the most spectacular growth took place after the Civil War. By 1997, the national rail network grew to nearly 200,000 miles, from a system of about 35,000 miles of track in 1865. Alongside each mile of track, a network of telegraph poles and wires were installed. Transportation and communication thus combined to forge a truly national economy.

**TRAINS AND THE INDUSTRIAL ERA** Railroads were America's first truly big business, the first beneficiaries of the great financial market known as Wall Street in New York City, the first industry to have operations in several states, and the first to develop a large-scale management bureaucracy.

The railroad boom was the catalyst for America's transition to an urban-industrial economy. From the 1860s to the 1960s, most people entered or left a city through its railroad stations. Trains opened the West to economic development, enabled federal troops to suppress Indian resistance, ferried millions of immigrants from New York City and other East Coast ports, helped transform commercial agriculture into a major international industry, and transported raw materials to factories and finished goods to retailers.

Railroads were expensive, however. Locomotives, railcars (called "rolling stock"), and the construction of track, trestles, and bridges required enormous investments. The railroad industry was the first to contract with "investment banks" to raise capital by selling shares of stock to investors. Railroads also stimulated other industries through their purchases of iron and steel, coal, timber, leather (for seats), and glass. In addition, railroad companies were the nation's largest employers.

**THE DOWNSIDE OF THE RAILROAD BOOM** Many railroad developers, however, cared more about making money than safety. Companies often overlooked working conditions that caused thousands of laborers to be killed or injured. Too many railroads were built; by the 1880s, there were twice as many as the economy could support.

Some railroads were poorly or even criminally managed and went bankrupt. Those that succeeded often broke the rules. Railroad lobbyists helped to corrupt state and federal legislators by "buying" the votes of politicians with cash or shares of stock in their companies. Charles Francis Adams Jr., head of the Union Pacific Railroad, admitted, "Our method of doing business is founded upon lying, cheating, and stealing—all bad things."

## BUILDING THE TRANSCONTINENTALS

For decades, visionaries had dreamed of the United States being the first nation to build a railroad spanning a continent. In the 1860s, the dream became reality as construction began on the first of four rail lines that would bridge the nation—and, as one promoter boasted, establish "our empire on the Pacific."

THE **"WORK OF GIANTS"** The transcontinental railroads were, in the words of General William T. Sherman, the "work of giants." Their construction required heroic feats by the surveyors, engineers, and laborers who laid the rails, built the bridges, and gouged out the tunnels through rugged mountains.

The first transcontinental railroads were much more expensive to build than the shorter "trunk" lines in the East. Because the western routes passed through vast stretches of unpopulated plains and deserts, construction materials as well as workers and supplies had to be hauled long distances. Locomotives, railcars, rails, ties, spikes, and much more were often transported by ships from the East Coast to San Francisco and then moved by train to the remote construction sites.

The construction process was like managing a moving army. Herds of cattle, horses, mules, and oxen had to be fed and tended. Huge mobile camps, called "Hell on Wheels," were built to house the crews and moved with them as the tracks progressed. The camps even included tents for dance halls, saloons, gambling, and prostitution. Nightlife was raucous. As a British reporter wrote,

**The Union Pacific meets the Central Pacific** On May 10, 1869, the celebration of the first transcontinental railroad's completion took place in Promontory Summit, Utah.

"Soldiers, herdsmen, teamsters, women, railroad men, are dancing, singing, or gambling. There are men here who would murder a fellow-creature for five dollars. . . . Not a day passes but a dead body is found somewhere in the vicinity with pockets rifled of their contents."

**THE PACIFIC RAILWAY ACT (1862)** Before the Civil War, construction of a transcontinental line had been delayed because northern and southern congressmen clashed over the choice of routes. Secession and the departure of southern congressmen for the Confederacy in 1861 finally permitted Republicans in Congress to pass the Pacific Railway Act in 1862. It authorized construction along a north-central route by two competing companies: the Union Pacific Railroad (UP) westward from Omaha, Nebraska, across the prairie, and the Central Pacific Railroad (CP) eastward from Sacramento, California, through the Sierra Nevada. Both companies began construction during the war, but most of the work was done after 1865.

Building a railroad across the continent entailed feats of daring, engineering, and construction. Laying rail around and through the mountains required extensive use of dynamite and required costly bridges and tunnels. Harsh weather led to frequent seasonal disruptions, and many workers were killed or injured over the course of construction. At times, some 15,000 people, mostly men, worked for each of the companies as they raced each other to complete their tasks. The company that laid the most track in the shortest time would be awarded more money by Congress.

The competition led both companies to cut corners. Collis Huntington, one of the CP owners, confessed that his goal was to build "the cheapest road that I could . . . so that it moves ahead fast." If bridges or trestles collapsed under the weight of freight trains, they could be fixed later. Mark Hopkins, one of Huntington's partners, agreed, noting that his goal was to build as "poor a road as we can."

**RAILROAD WORKERS** The UP crews were composed largely of young, unmarried former Civil War soldiers, both Union and Confederate, along with ex-slaves and Irish and German immigrants. The CP crews were mainly young Chinese workers lured to America by the California gold rush or by railroad jobs. Most of these "coolie" laborers were single men eager to earn money to take back to China. The term coolie derived from the Hindu word for manual laborer, but in the western United States it came to be a derogative term for workers willing to work for wages so low that they hurt all laborers. Their temporary status and dreams of a good life made them more willing than American laborers to endure the low pay, dangerous working conditions, and intense racial prejudice.

What distinguished Chinese from other laborers was their ability to work together in accomplishing daunting tasks. Mark Twain described them as "quiet, peaceable, tractable, free from drunkenness, and they are as industrious as the day is long. A disorderly Chinaman is rare, and a lazy one does not exist."

**LAYING TRACK** The process of building the rail lines involved a series of sequential tasks. First came the surveyors, who selected and mapped the routes and measured grade changes. Engineers then designed the bridges, trestles, tunnels, and snowsheds. Tree cutters and graders followed by preparing the rail beds. Wooden cross ties were then placed in the ground and leveled before thirty-foot-long iron rails weighing 560 pounds were laid atop them. Next came spikers, who used special hammers to wallop two-pound spikes attaching the rails to the ties. Finally, workers shoveled gravel between the ties to stabilize them against the weight of rolling trains.

This huge undertaking encountered constant interruptions: terrible weather, late deliveries of key items, accidents, epidemics, and Indian attacks. Arthur Ferguson, a supervisor who kept a journal, frequently noted the hazards of constructing the first transcontinental in 1868:

> May 17—Two more men drowned in the river yesterday.
>
> June 4—At about sunrise, were attacked by Indians and succeeded in shooting one.
>
> June 21—Indians killed two men. Both had been horribly mutilated about the face by cuts made by a knife or a tomahawk.
>
> June 30—Four men were killed and scalped today about two miles above camp.

It was not only Native American warriors doing the killing, however. Workers often fought and killed each other. On June 7, Ferguson recorded that "two men were shot this evening in a drunken row—one was instantly killed, and the other is not expected to live."

**THE RACE TO THE FINISH** The drama of constructing the first transcontinental railroad seized the nation's imagination. Every major newspaper carried stories about the progress of the competing companies. Finally, on May 10, 1869, former California governor Leland Stanford, one of the owners of the Central Pacific, drove a gold spike to complete the line at Promontory Summit in the Utah Territory north of the Great Salt Lake. The Union Pacific had built 1,086 miles of track compared with the Central Pacific's 689, much of it mountainous.

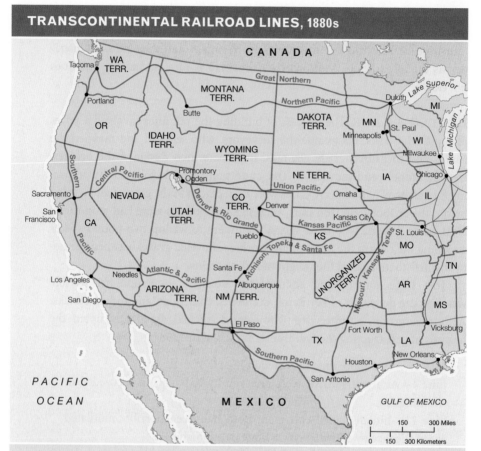

**TRANSCONTINENTAL RAILROAD LINES, 1880s**

- What was the route of the first transcontinental railroad, and why was it not in the South?
- Who built the railroads? How were they financed?

"In one sense," gushed the *Cincinnati Gazette*, the transcontinental railroad "is as great an achievement as the war, and as grand a triumph." The golden spike used to connect the final rails symbolized the uniting of East and West. Soon the process would be repeated, as other companies constructed more lines across the continent.

By connecting the nation from ocean to ocean, the railroads became the basis of a truly national market for goods and services, including tourism. In 1872, Congress established Yellowstone National Park. Within ten years, railroads had brought a burgeoning tourist business to the nation's first national park in remote northwest Wyoming, then a territory.

As they pushed into sparsely populated western states and territories, the railroad companies became the region's primary real estate developers. They transported millions of settlers from the East, many of them immigrants eager to buy land. In the end, the railroads changed the economic, political, and physical landscapes of the nation and enabled the United States to emerge as a world power.

# THE RISE OF BIG BUSINESS

The emergence of Big Business was one of the most significant developments in American history. Corporations grew much larger and more powerful, transacting business across the nation and abroad. Business leaders became more politically active as they worked to influence governors, legislators, Congress, and presidents.

The rapid expansion of Big Business had negative effects that did not go unnoticed. "The growing wealth and influence of our large corporations," warned the *New York Times*, "is one of the most alarming phenomena of our time. Our public companies already wield gigantic power, and they use it like unscrupulous giants."

## THE GROWTH OF CORPORATIONS

As businesses grew, they took one of several different forms. Some were owned by an individual; others were partnerships involving several owners. Increasingly, however, large companies that served national and international markets were converted into corporations—legal entities that separate the *ownership* of an enterprise from the *management* of its operations.

Once a corporation was registered ("chartered" or "incorporated") with a state government, it could raise money to operate ("capital") by selling shares of stock—representing partial ownership of the company—to people not otherwise involved with it. Shareholders elected a board of directors who appointed and evaluated the corporation's executives ("management"). One of the most important benefits of a corporation was "limited legal liability"; stockholders shared in its profits but could not be held liable for its debts if it fails.

## FIGHTING COMPETITION

Competition is supposed to be the great virtue of capitalism, since it forces businesses to produce better products at the lowest cost. As many businesses became giant corporations, however, some owners came to view competition as a burden. Financier J. P. Morgan, for example, claimed that "bitter, destructive competition" always led to "destruction and ruin."

To eliminate cutthroat competition and thereby stabilize production, wages, and prices, rival companies selling similar products often formed "pools" whereby they secretly agreed to keep production and prices at specified levels. Such pools rarely lasted long, however, because one or more participants usually violated the agreement. The more effective strategy for the most aggressive companies was to drive the weaker companies out of business—or buy them out.

Strategies like these, and the methods used to carry them out, led critics to call the corporate titans robber barons. When asked how people might react to the shady methods he used to build his network of railroads, William Henry Vanderbilt famously replied, "The public be damned!"

## THE BARONS OF BUSINESS

Most of the men who created large businesses in the late nineteenth century yearned to become rich and influential, and many religious leaders urged them on. "To secure wealth is an honorable ambition," stressed Russell Conwell, a prominent Baptist minister. "Money is power," he explained, and "every good man and woman ought to strive for power, to do good with it when obtained. I say, get rich! get rich!"

The industrial and financial giants personified the values that Conwell celebrated. They were men of grit and genius who found innovative—and at times unethical and illegal—ways to increase production and eliminate competition. They were also mercilessly adept at cutting costs and lowering prices.

Several business barons stood out for their extraordinary accomplishments: John D. Rockefeller and Andrew Carnegie for their innovations in organization, J. Pierpont Morgan for his development of investment banking, and Richard Sears and Alvah Roebuck for their creation of mail-order retailing.

**JOHN D. ROCKEFELLER** Born in New York in 1839, John D. Rockefeller moved as a child to Cleveland, Ohio. Raised by his mother, he developed a single-minded passion for systematic organization. As a young man, he decided to bring order and rationality to the new boom-and-bust oil industry. He was obsessed with precision, efficiency, tidiness—and money.

The railroad and shipping connections around Cleveland made it a strategic location for serving the booming oil fields of nearby western Pennsylvania. The first oil well in the United States began operating in 1859 in Titusville, Pennsylvania, and led to the Pennsylvania oil rush of the 1860s. Because oil could be refined into kerosene, which was widely used for lighting, heating, and cooking, the economic importance of the oil rush soon outstripped that of the California gold rush ten years earlier. Well before the end of the Civil War, oil refineries sprang up in Pittsburgh and Cleveland. Of the two cities, Cleveland had better rail service, so Rockefeller focused his energies there.

In 1870, Rockefeller teamed with his brother William and two other businessmen, Henry M. Flagler and Samuel Andrews, to establish the **Standard Oil Company** of Ohio. Although the company quickly became the largest oil refiner in the nation, John Rockefeller wanted to take control of the entire industry, in large part because he believed his competitors were inefficient and distracting.

During the 1870s, Rockefeller used various schemes to destroy his competitors. Early on, he pursued a strategy called **horizontal integration**, in which a dominant corporation buys or forces out most of its competitors. Rockefeller viewed competition as a form of warfare. In a few cases, he hired former competitors as executives, but only "the big ones," he said, "those who have already proved they can do a *big business*. As for the others, unfortunately they will have to *die*."

**John D. Rockefeller** The rags-to-riches capitalist who founded of the Standard Oil Company.

By 1879, Standard Oil controlled more than 90 percent of the nation's oil refining business. Still, Rockefeller's goal was a **monopoly**, a business so large that it controls an entire industry.

In pursuing a monopoly, Rockefeller methodically reduced expenses by improving productivity, squeezing suppliers, and eliminating any hint of waste. He was determined to avoid letting any of his suppliers earn "a profit" from him. Because Standard Oil shipped so much oil by rail, Rockefeller forced railroads to pay him secret rebates on the shipments, enabling him to spend less for shipping than his competitors did.

Most important, instead of depending upon the products or services of other firms, known as middlemen, Standard Oil eventually owned everything it needed to produce, refine, and deliver oil—from wells to the finished product. The company had its own pipelines, built factories to make its own wagons and storage barrels, did its own hauling, and owned its own storage tanks and tanker ships. In economic terms, this business strategy is called **vertical integration**.

During the 1870s, Standard Oil bought so many of its competitors that it developed a nearly complete monopoly over the industry. Many state legislatures responded by outlawing the practice of one corporation owning stock in competing ones. In 1882, Rockefeller tried to hide his monopoly by organizing the Standard Oil Trust.

A **trust** gives a corporation (the "trustee") the legal power to manage another company. Instead of owning other companies outright, the Standard Oil Trust controlled more than thirty companies by having their stockholders transfer their shares "in trust" to Rockefeller and eight other trustees. In return, the stockholders received *trust certificates*, which paid them annual dividends from the trust's earnings. During the Gilded Age, however, Americans began to call any huge corporation a trust.

The formation of corporate trusts generated intense criticism. In 1890, Congress passed the Sherman Anti-Trust Act, which declared that efforts to monopolize industries and thereby "restrain" competition were illegal. But the bill's language was so vague that its regulations were toothless.

State laws against monopolies were more effective than the Sherman Act. In 1892, Ohio's Supreme Court ordered the Standard Oil Trust dissolved. Rockefeller then developed another way to maintain control of his companies: a **holding company**, which is a huge corporation that controls other companies by "holding" most or all of their stock certificates. A holding company produces nothing itself; it simply owns a majority of the stock in other companies.

Rockefeller was convinced that ending competition was a good thing for the nation. Monopolies, he insisted, were the natural result of capitalism at work. "It is too late," he declared in 1899, "to argue about the advantages of [huge] industrial combinations. They are a necessity." That year, Rockefeller brought his empire under the direction of the Standard Oil Company of New Jersey, a gigantic holding company.

**ANDREW CARNEGIE** Like John D. Rockefeller, Andrew Carnegie, who created the largest steel company in the world, rose to wealth from boyhood poverty. Born in Scotland, the son of weavers, he migrated with his family in 1848 to western Pennsylvania. At age thirteen, he went to work twelve hours a day in a textile mill. In 1853, he became personal secretary to Thomas Scott, then district superintendent of the Pennsylvania Railroad and later its president. When Scott was promoted, Carnegie became superintendent. During the Civil War, when Scott became assistant secretary of war in charge of transportation, Carnegie went with him to Washington, D.C., and helped develop a military telegraph system.

Carnegie worked his way up—from telegraphy to railroading to bridge building, then to steelmaking and investments. In the early 1870s, he decided "to concentrate on the manufacture of iron and steel and be master in that." A tiny man (barely five feet tall), Carnegie wanted to tower over the steel industry, just as Rockefeller was doing with oil.

Until the mid–nineteenth century, steel, which is stronger and more flexible than iron, could be made only from wrought iron (expensive since it had to

**Andrew Carnegie** Scottish immigrant who established the Carnegie Steel Company and became the wealthiest man in the world.

be imported from Sweden) and could only be manufactured in small quantities. Bars of wrought iron were heated with charcoal over several days to add carbon and produce steel. It took three tons of coke, a high-burning fuel derived from coal, to produce one ton of steel.

That changed in the 1850s, when England's Sir Henry Bessemer invented the **Bessemer converter**, a process by which high-quality steel could be produced more quickly by blasting oxygen through the molten iron in a furnace. In the early 1870s, Carnegie decided to concentrate on the manufacture of steel because Bessemer's process had made it so inexpensive to produce—and the railroad industry required massive amounts of it.

As more steel was produced, its price dropped and its industrial uses soared. In 1860, the United States produced only 13,000 tons of steel. By 1880, production had reached 1.4 million tons annually. Between 1880 and 1900, Carnegie dominated the steel industry, acquiring competitors or driving them out of business by cutting prices and taking their customers. By 1900, the United States was producing more steel than Great Britain and Germany combined.

Carnegie insisted upon up-to-date machinery and equipment; he expanded production quickly and cheaply by purchasing struggling companies and preached a philosophy of continuous innovation to reduce operating costs. He also sought to expand his industry by vertical integration—gaining control of every phase of the business. He owned coal mines in West Virginia, bought huge deposits of iron ore in Michigan and Wisconsin, and transported the ore in his own ships across the Great Lakes and then by rail to his steel mills in Pittsburgh.

By 1900, the **Carnegie Steel Company**, with 20,000 employees, was the largest industrial company in the world. Carnegie's mills operated nonstop with two daily twelve-hour shifts, the only exception being the Fourth of July.

**J. PIERPONT MORGAN** Unlike John D. Rockefeller and Andrew Carnegie, J. Pierpont Morgan was born to wealth in Connecticut. His father was a partner in a large English bank. After attending school in Switzerland and college in Germany, Morgan was

sent in 1857 to work in New York City for a new enterprise started by his father, **J. Pierpont Morgan and Company**. The firm, under various names, invested European money with American businesses. It grew into a financial power by helping competing corporations merge and by purchasing massive amounts of stock in American companies and selling them at a profit.

Morgan, like Rockefeller and Carnegie, believed in capitalism but hated competition. In his view, high profits required order and stability, and stability required consolidating competitors into trusts that he could own and manipulate.

**J. Pierpont Morgan** Despite his privileged upbringing and financial success, he was self-conscious about his deformed nose, caused by chronic skin diseases.

Early on, Morgan recognized that railroads were essential to the nation's economy and growth, and by the 1890s, he controlled a sixth of the nation's railway system. But his crowning triumph was the consolidation of the steel industry. After a rapid series of mergers, he bought Carnegie's steel and iron holdings in 1901. Morgan added scores of related companies to form U.S. Steel Corporation, the world's first billion-dollar corporation, employing 168,000 people. It was the climactic event in the efforts of the great financial capitalists to dominate their industries.

**SEARS AND ROEBUCK** After the Civil War, American inventors helped manufacturers produce many new products. But the most important economic challenge was enabling the millions who lived on isolated farms and in small towns to buy the same goods available in cities.

A traveling salesman from Chicago named Aaron Montgomery Ward decided that he could reach more people by mail than on foot and thus eliminate the middlemen whose services increased the retail price of goods. Beginning in the early 1870s, Montgomery Ward and Company began selling goods at a 40 percent discount through mail-order catalogs.

By the end of the century, a new retailer had come to dominate the mail-order industry: Sears, Roebuck and Company, founded by two midwestern entrepreneurs, Richard Sears and Alvah Roebuck. The Sears, Roebuck catalog in 1897 was 786 pages long. It featured groceries, drugs, tools, furniture, household products, musical instruments, farm implements, shoes, clothes, books, and sporting goods. The company's ability to buy goods in high volume from wholesalers enabled it to sell items at prices below those offered in rural general stores. By 1907, Sears, Roebuck and Company, headquartered in Chicago, had become one of the largest businesses in the nation.

The Sears catalog helped transform the lives of millions of people. With the advent of free rural mail delivery in 1898, families on farms and in small towns could purchase by mail the products that had been either prohibitively expensive or available only to city dwellers. By the turn of the century, 6 million Sears catalogs were being distributed each year, and the catalog had become the most widely read book in the nation after the Bible.

**THE GOSPEL OF WEALTH** The aggressive captains of industry were convinced that they benefited the public by accelerating America's transformation into an industrial colossus. In their eyes, it was a law of societal evolution that those most talented at producing wealth should accumulate enormous fortunes.

Some of them, however, insisted that great wealth brought great responsibilities. In his essay "The Gospel of Wealth" (1889), Andrew Carnegie argued that "not evil, but good, has come to the [Anglo-Saxon] race from the accumulation of wealth by those who have the ability and energy that produces it."

Carnegie and John D. Rockefeller gave away much of their money, mostly to support education and medicine.

By 1900, Rockefeller had become the world's leading philanthropist. "I have always regarded it as a religious duty," he said late in life, "to get all I could honorably and to give all I could." He donated more than $500 million during his lifetime, including tens of millions to Baptist causes and $35 million to found the University of Chicago. His philanthropic influence continues today through the Rockefeller Foundation.

As for Carnegie, after retiring from business at age sixty-five, he declared that the "man who dies rich dies disgraced." He thereafter devoted himself to dispensing his $400 million fortune. Calling himself a "distributor" of wealth, he gave huge sums to numerous universities, built 2,500 public libraries, and helped fund churches, hospitals, parks, and halls for meetings and concerts, including New York City's Carnegie Hall.

## THE ALLIANCE OF BUSINESS AND POLITICS

Most of the businesses developed by Andrew Carnegie, John D. Rockefeller, and others had cozy relationships with local, state, and federal government officials, a process of buying influence ("lobbying") that continues to this day. Big Business has legitimate political interests, but at times it exercises a corrupt influence on government. Nowhere was this more evident than during the decades after the Civil War.

**REPUBLICANS AND BIG BUSINESS** During and after the Civil War, the Republican party and state and federal governments grew increasingly allied with Big Business. A key element of this alliance was tariff policy. Since 1789, the federal government had imposed **tariffs**—taxes on imported goods—to raise revenue and benefit American manufacturers by penalizing foreign competitors. In 1861, as the Civil War was starting, the Republican-dominated Congress enacted the Morrill Tariff, which doubled tax rates on hundreds of imported items, to raise money for the war and reward businesses that supported the Republican party.

After the war, President Ulysses S. Grant and other Republican presidents and Congresses continued the party's commitment to high tariffs despite complaints that the tariffs increased consumer prices at home by restricting foreign imports and thereby relieving American manufacturers of the need to keep prices down. Farmers in the South and Midwest especially resented tariffs because, while they had to sell their crops in an open world market, they had to buy manufactured goods whose prices were artificially high because of tariffs.

During the Civil War, Congress passed other key economic legislation. The Legal Tender Act of 1862 authorized the federal government to issue paper money ("greenbacks") to help pay for the war. Having a uniform paper currency across the nation was essential to a modern economy. To that end, the National Banking Act (1863) created national banks authorized to issue greenbacks, which discouraged state banks from continuing to print their own money.

Congress also took steps to tie the western states and territories into the national economy. The U.S. government owned vast amounts of western land, most of it acquired from the Louisiana Purchase of 1803, the Oregon Treaty with Britain in 1846, and the lands taken from Mexico in 1848 after the Mexican-American War. In the Homestead Act of 1862, Congress provided free 160-acre (or even larger) homesteads to settlers in the West. By encouraging western settlement, the Homestead Act created markets for goods and services and spurred railroad construction to connect scattered frontier communities with major cities. Still, half the homesteads failed within a few years.

**Homesteaders** An African American family poses outside their log and sod cabin.

The Morrill Land-Grant College Act of 1862 transferred to each state 30,000 acres of federal land for each member of Congress the state had. The sale of those lands provided funds for states to create colleges of "agriculture and mechanic arts," such as Iowa State University and Kansas State University. The land-grant universities were created specifically to support economic growth by providing technical training needed by farmers and rapidly growing industries such as mining, steel, petroleum, transportation, forestry, and construction (engineering).

**LAISSEZ-FAIRE** Equally important in propelling the postwar economic boom was what governments did *not* do. There were no sweeping investigations of business practices, no legislation to protect workers and consumers, and no effective regulatory laws or commissions. Elected officials deferred to business leaders.

In general, Congress and presidents opposed government regulation of business and accepted the traditional economic doctrine of **laissez-faire**, a French phrase meaning "let them do as they will." Business leaders spent time—and money—ensuring that government officials stayed out of their businesses. For their part, politicians were usually eager to help the titans of industry in exchange for campaign contributions—or bribes.

# AN INDUSTRIAL SOCIETY

Industrialization transformed not only the economy and the workplace, but also the nation's social life. Class divisions became more visible. The growing gap between rich and poor was like "social dynamite," said the Reverend Josiah Strong in 1885. Massachusetts reformer Lydia Maria Child reported that the rich "do not intermarry with the middle classes; the middle classes do not intermarry with the laboring class," nor did different classes "mix socially."

## THE WAYS OF THE WEALTHY

The financiers and industrialists who dominated social, economic, and political life in post–Civil War America amassed so much wealth and showed it off so publicly that the period is still called the Gilded Age. To "gild" something is to cover it with a thin layer of gold, giving it the appearance of having greater value than it warrants. The name derived from a popular novel by Mark Twain and Charles Dudley Warner, *The Gilded Age: A Tale of Today*, which mocked the crooked dealings of political leaders and the business elite.

In 1861, the United States had only a few dozen millionaires. By 1900, there were more than 4,000. Most of them were white Protestants who voted Republican. A few were women, including Madam C.J. Walker (born Sarah Breedlove, the daughter of former Louisiana slaves), who created specialized hair products for African Americans.

Many of the *nouveaux riches* (French for "newly rich") indulged in "conspicuous consumption," competing to host the fanciest parties and live in the largest and most extravagant houses. One tycoon gave a lavish dinner to honor his dog and presented it with a $15,000 diamond necklace. At a party at New York's Delmonico's restaurant, guests smoked cigarettes wrapped in $100 bills.

When not attending parties, the rich were relaxing in mansions overlooking the cliffs at Newport, Rhode Island, atop Nob Hill in San Francisco, along Chicago's Lake Shore Drive and New York City's Fifth Avenue, and down the "Main Line" in suburban Philadelphia. "Who knows how to be rich in America?" asked E. L. Godkin, a magazine editor. "Plenty of people know how to get money, but . . . to be rich properly is, indeed, a fine art. It requires culture, imagination, and character."

## A GROWING MIDDLE CLASS

It was left to the fast-growing middle class to practice traditional virtues such as self-discipline, restraint, simplicity, and frugality. The term *middle class* had first appeared in the 1830s and had become commonplace by the 1870s, as more and more Americans came to view themselves as members of a distinct social class between the ragged and the rich.

Most middle-class Americans working outside the home were salaried employees of large businesses who made up a new class of "white-collar" professionals: editors, engineers, accountants, supervisors, managers, marketers, and realtors. Others, mostly unmarried women, were clerks, secretaries, salespeople, teachers, and librarians.

During the 1870s, the number of office clerks quadrupled, and the number of accountants and bookkeepers doubled. At the same time, the number of attorneys, physicians, professors, journalists, nurses, and social workers also rose dramatically. The number of women working outside the home tripled between 1870 and 1900, when 5 million women (17 percent of all women) held full-time jobs. This development led one male editor to joke that he was being drowned "by the rising tide of femininity."

**MIDDLE-CLASS WOMEN** The growing presence of middle-class women in the workforce partly reflected the increasing number of women who were gaining access to higher education. Dozens of women's colleges were founded after the Civil War, and many formerly all-male colleges began admitting women. By 1900, a third of college students were women. "After a struggle of many years," a New York woman boasted, "it is now pretty generally admitted that women possess the capacity to swallow intellectual food that was formerly considered the diet of men exclusively."

To be sure, college women were often steered into "home economics" classes and "finishing" courses intended to perfect their housekeeping or social skills. Still, the doors of the professions—law, medicine, science, and the arts—were at least partially opened to women during the Gilded Age.

In this context, then, the "woman question" that created so much public discussion and controversy in the second half of the nineteenth century involved far more than the issue of voting rights; it concerned the liberation of at least some women from the home and from long-standing limits on their social roles. "If there is one thing that pervades and characterizes what is called the 'woman's movement,'" E. L. Youmans, a prominent science writer,

**College women** By the end of the century, women made up more than a third of college students. Here, an astronomy class at New York's Vassar College is under way in 1880.

remarked, "it is the spirit of revolt against the home, and the determination to escape from it into the outer spheres of activity."

**NEURASTHENIA** Women who tried to escape the cult of domesticity often paid a high price. Many contracted a peculiar and baffling affliction which male physicians called *neurasthenia*, an energy-draining psychological and physical disorder whose symptoms included insomnia, hysteria, headaches, depression, and a general state of fatigue. Although neurasthenia plagued both genders, it most often affected college-educated women.

Some doctors sought to use the prevalence of neurasthenia to force women back into the cult of domesticity. Neurologist George M. Beard concluded—incorrectly—that women were "more nervous, immeasurably, than men" and that female neurasthenics tended to be "overly active" outside the home. This explanation led one doctor to insist that neurasthenia provided the best "argument against higher education of women."

Many women objected to such arguments. Charlotte Perkins Gilman wrote her short story "The Yellow Wallpaper" to expose the horrors of the "rest cure" she was subjected to at age twenty-seven. A doctor had ordered her to "live as domestic a life as possible; have your child with you all the time; lie down an hour after each meal; have but two hours intellectual life a day; and *never touch pencil, brush, or pen as long as you live*." This excruciating regimen, Gilman explained, took her "as near lunacy as one can."

**JANE ADDAMS** Social worker Jane Addams also struggled with neurasthenia. After graduating in 1881 from Rockford College in Illinois, she found few opportunities to use her degree and lapsed into a state of depression during which she developed an intense "desire to live in a really *living* world."

Addams's desire to engage "real life" eventually led her to found Hull House in Chicago. There, she and other social workers helped immigrants adapt to American life and mentored young women to "learn of life from life itself." Addams and others helped convince many middle-class women to enter the "real" world. By 1890, *Arena* magazine would urge progressive-minded people to recognize the traditional view of "women as homebodies" for what it was: "hollow, false, and unreal."

**THE *LADIES' HOME JOURNAL*** Many women, however, identified with the domestic life that was the focus of numerous mass-circulation magazines, the most popular of which was *Ladies' Home Journal*. By 1910, it had almost 2 million subscribers, the largest circulation of any magazine in the world.

Edward Bok became editor of the *Ladies' Home Journal* in 1889 at age twenty-six. Under his direction, the magazine provided a "great clearing house of information" to the rapidly growing urban middle class, including sections on sewing, cooking, religion, politics, and fiction.

Bok was no activist for gender equality; "my idea," he stressed, "is to keep women in the home." There, he believed, they would maintain a high moral tone for society, for women were "better, purer, conscientious, and morally stronger than men." Bok saw the middle-class woman as the "steadying influence" between the "unrest among the lower classes and [the] rottenness among the upper classes."

Bok's view of the ideal life for a woman included "a healthful diet, simple, serviceable clothing, a clean, healthy dwelling-place, open-air exercise, and good reading." He preached contentment rather than conspicuous consumption, a message directed not just to middle-class readers but also to the working poor. In a Christmas editorial, though, Bok recognized that "it is a hard thing for those who have little to believe that the greatest happiness of life is with them: that it is not with those who have abundance."

## The Working Class

Railroads, factories, mills, mines, slaughterhouses, and sweatshops had growing needs for unskilled workers, which attracted new groups to the workforce, especially immigrants and women and children. In addition, millions of rural folk, especially young people, formed a migratory stream from the agricultural regions of the South and Midwest to cities and factories across the country.

Although wage levels rose during the Gilded Age, there was great disparity in the pay received by skilled and unskilled workers. During the economic recessions and depressions that occurred about every six years, unskilled workers were the first to be laid off or to have their wages slashed. In addition, working conditions were difficult and often dangerous for those at the bottom of the occupational scale. The average workweek was fifty-nine hours, or nearly six 10-hour days.

American industry had the highest rate of workplace accidents and deaths in the world, and there were virtually no safety regulations. Few machines had safety devices; few factories or mills had fire escapes. Respiratory diseases were common in mines, textile mills, and unventilated buildings. Between 1888 and 1894, some 16,000 railroad workers were killed and 170,000 maimed in on-the-job accidents. The United States was also the only industrial nation with no insurance program to cover medical expenses for on-the-job injuries.

**WORKING WOMEN** Mills, mines, factories, and large businesses needed far more unskilled workers than skilled ones. Employers often recruited women and children for the unskilled jobs because they were willing to work for lower wages than men. In addition to operating sewing machines or tending to textile machines spinning yarn or thread, women worked as maids, cooks, or nannies. In the manufacturing sector, women's wages averaged $7 a week, compared to $10 for unskilled men.

**CHILD LABOR** Young people had always worked in America; farms required everyone to pitch in. In the late nineteenth century, however, millions of children took up work outside the home, sorting coal, stitching clothes, shucking oysters, peeling shrimp, canning food, blowing glass, tending looms, and operating other kinds of machinery. **Child labor** increased as parents desperate for income put their children to work. By 1880, one of every six children under age fourteen was working full-time; by 1900, the United States had almost 2 million child laborers.

In Pennsylvania, West Virginia, and eastern Kentucky, soot-smeared boys worked in the coal mines. In New England and the South, children labored in dusty textile mills where, during the night shift, they had water thrown in their faces to keep them awake. In the southern mills, a fourth of the employees were below age fifteen, and children as young as eight often worked twelve hours a day, six days a week. As a result, they received little or no education.

Factories, mills, mines, and canneries were especially dangerous for children, who suffered three times as many accidents as adult workers and higher rates of respiratory diseases. A child working in a southern textile mill was only half as likely to reach the age of twenty as a child who did not.

**ORGANIZED LABOR** The efforts of the working poor to form unions to improve their pay and working conditions faced formidable obstacles during the Gilded Age. Many executives fought against unions. They "blacklisted" union organizers by circulating their names to keep them from being hired, fired labor leaders, and often hired "scabs" (nonunion workers) to replace workers who went on strike. Another factor impeding the growth of unions was that many workers were immigrants who spoke different languages and often distrusted people from other ethnic groups. Nonetheless, with or without unions, workers began to stage strikes that often led to violence.

**THE GREAT RAILROAD STRIKE (1877)** After the financial panic of 1873, the major rail lines, fearful of a recession, had slashed workers' wages by 35 percent. In 1877, the companies announced another 10 percent wage cut, which led most of the railroad workers at Martinsburg, West Virginia, to walk off the job and shut down rail traffic.

The strike spread to hundreds of other cities and towns. In San Francisco, local grievances led raging trainmen, who blamed Asians for taking white jobs, to set fire to Chinese neighborhoods. Across the nation, tens of thousands of workers walked off the job. The resulting violence left more than 100 people dead, hundreds wounded, and millions of dollars in damaged property.

In Pittsburgh, thousands of striking workers burned thirty-nine buildings and destroyed more than 1,000 railcars and locomotives. The strikers also assaulted workers who refused to join them. Hundreds of looters—men, women, and children—risked their lives to grab anything of value from the freight cars before they were put to the torch. A huge crowd filled nearby hillsides and cheered as the Pennsylvania Railroad, "that damned monopoly," went up in flames.

The **Great Railroad Strike of 1877** was the first nationwide labor uprising, and it revealed how polarized the relationship between the working poor and company executives had become. Governors mobilized state militia units to suppress the rioters.

In Philadelphia, the militia dispersed a crowd at the cost of twenty-six lives, but looting and burning continued until President Rutherford B. Hayes dispatched federal troops to put down the "insurrection." It was the first time federal troops in large numbers had suppressed civilian strikers. Eventually the disgruntled workers, lacking organized bargaining power, had little choice but to return to work.

The strike had failed, but for many it raised the possibility of what a Pittsburgh newspaper saw as "a great civil war in this country between labor and capital." Many workers felt that violence was their only option. "The working people everywhere are with us," a unionist told a reporter. "They know what it is to bring up a family on ninety cents a day, to live on beans and corn meal week in and week out, to run in debt at the [company] stores until you cannot get trusted any longer, to see the wife breaking down . . . and the children growing sharp and fierce like wolves day after day because they don't get enough to eat."

Equally disturbing to those in positions of corporate and political power was the presence of many women among the protesters. A Baltimore journalist noted that the "singular part of the disturbances is the very active part taken by the women, who are the wives and mothers of the [railroad] firemen."

President Hayes wrote in his diary, "The strikes have been put down by *force*. But now for the *real* remedy. Can't something be done by education of the strikers, by judicious control of the capitalists, by wise general policy, to end or diminish the evil?" It was a fair question that largely went unanswered.

**THE SAND-LOT INCIDENT** In California, the national railroad strike indirectly gave rise to a working-class political movement. In 1877, a meeting held in a sandy San Francisco vacant lot to express sympathy for the railroad strikers ended with white laborers attacking Chinese workers who were passing by. In the so-called Sand-Lot Incident, the Chinese were handy scapegoats for frustrated whites who believed the Asians had taken their jobs.

Such anti-Chinese sentiment soon drove an Irish immigrant deliveryman in San Francisco, Denis Kearney, to organize the Workingmen's Party of California, whose platform called for the United States to stop Chinese immigration. Kearney lectured about the "foreign peril" and blasted the railroad barons for exploiting the poor. Although Kearney failed to build a lasting movement, his anti-Chinese theme became a national issue. In 1882, Congress voted to prohibit Chinese immigration for ten years.

**THE NATIONAL LABOR UNION** As the size and power of corporations increased, efforts to build a national labor union movement gained momentum. During the Civil War, because of the increased demand for skilled labor, so-called craft unions made up of workers expert at a particular handicraft or trade grew in strength and number. Yet there was no overall connection among such groups until 1866, when the **National Labor Union (NLU)** convened in Baltimore.

The NLU was more interested in improving workplace conditions than in bargaining about wages. The group promoted an eight-hour workday, workers' cooperatives (in which workers, collectively, would create and own their own large-scale manufacturing and mining operations), "greenbackism" (the printing of paper money to inflate the currency and thereby relieve debtors), and equal voting rights for women and African Americans.

Like most such organizations in the nineteenth century, however, the NLU did not allow women as members. It also discriminated against African American workers, who were forced to organize unions of their own.

After the NLU's head, William Sylvis, died suddenly in 1869, its support declined, and by 1872 the union had disbanded. It was, however, influential in persuading Congress to enact an eight-hour workday for federal employees and to repeal the 1864 Contract Labor Act, which had been passed to encourage the importation of laborers by allowing employers to pay for the passage of foreign workers to America. In exchange, the workers were committed to work for a specified number of years. Employers had taken advantage of the Contract Labor Act to recruit foreign laborers willing to work for lower wages than their American counterparts.

**THE KNIGHTS OF LABOR** In 1869, another national labor group emerged: the Noble Order of the **Knights of Labor**. Even as trade unions collapsed during the depression of the 1870s, it grew rapidly.

The Knights of Labor endorsed most of the reforms advanced by previous workingmen's groups, including the elimination of convict-labor competition, the establishment of the eight-hour day, and the greater use of paper currency. One reform the group pursued was equal pay for equal work by men and women.

The Knights of Labor wanted to transform capitalism. "We do not believe," a Knights leader explained, "that the emancipation of labor will come with increased wages and a reduction in the [working] hours of labor; we must go deeper than that, and this matter will not be settled until the wage system is abolished."

The Knights of Labor did not believe in organizing members according to their particular trade. The organization allowed as members all who had ever worked for wages, except lawyers, doctors, bankers, those who sold liquor, and the Chinese. By recruiting all types of workers, black or white, men or women, the Knights became the nation's largest labor union, but they also struggled with internal tensions.

**Knights of Labor** This national labor organization was the most egalitarian union during the Gilded Age.

In 1879, Terence V. Powderly, the thirty-year-old mayor of Scranton, Pennsylvania, became head of the Knights of Labor. He stressed winning political control of the communities where union workers lived, and the Knights owed their greatest growth to strikes that occurred under his leadership. In the early 1880s, they increased their membership from about 100,000 to more than 700,000.

**Mother Jones** The Irish-born teacher turned celebrated union activist and progressive is pictured here campaigning for the rights of workers at the White House in 1924.

**MOTHER JONES** One of the most colorful labor agitators was a remarkable woman known simply as Mother Jones. Dressed in matronly black dresses and hats, she was a tireless champion of the working poor who used fiery rhetoric to excite crowds and attract attention. She led marches, dodged bullets, served jail terms, and confronted business titans and police. In 1913, a district attorney called her the "most dangerous woman in America."

Born in Cork, Ireland, in 1837, Mary Harris was the second of five children in a poor Catholic family that fled the Irish potato famine at midcentury and settled in Toronto. In 1861, she moved to Memphis, Tennessee, and began teaching. There, as the Civil War was erupting, she met and married George Jones, an iron molder and staunch union member. They had four children, but then, in 1867, disaster struck. A yellow fever epidemic devastated Memphis, killing Mary's husband and children.

The grief-stricken thirty-seven-year-old widow moved to Chicago and took up dressmaking, only to see her shop, home, and belongings destroyed in the Great Fire of 1871. Having lost her family and her finances, and angry at the social inequality and injustices she saw around her, Mary Jones drifted into the labor movement and soon emerged as its most passionate advocate. Chicago was, at the time, the seedbed of labor radicalism, and the union culture nurtured in her a lifelong dedication to the cause of wage workers and their families.

Declaring herself the "mother" of the fledgling labor movement, she joined the Knights of Labor as an organizer and public speaker. In the late 1880s, she became an ardent advocate for the United Mine Workers (UMW), various other unions, and the Socialist party. For the next thirty years, she crisscrossed the nation, recruiting union members, supporting strikers (her "boys"), raising funds, walking picket lines, defying court injunctions, berating politicians, and spending time in prison.

Wherever Mother Jones went, she promoted higher wages, shorter hours, safer workplaces, and restrictions on child labor. During a miners' strike in West Virginia, she was arrested, convicted of "conspiracy that resulted in murder," and sentenced to twenty years in prison. The outcry over her plight helped spur a Senate committee to investigate conditions in the coal mines. The governor set her free.

In 1903, Mother Jones organized a weeklong march of child workers from Pennsylvania to the New York home of President Theodore Roosevelt. The children were physically stunted and mutilated, most of them missing fingers or hands from machinery accidents. Roosevelt refused to see them, but as Jones explained, "Our march had done its work. We had drawn the attention of the nation to the crime of child labor." Shortly thereafter, the Pennsylvania state legislature raised the legal working age to fourteen.

Mother Jones's commitment never wavered. At age eighty-three, she was arrested and jailed after joining a miners' strike in Colorado. At her funeral, in 1930, a speaker urged people to remember her famous rallying cry: "Pray for the dead and fight like hell for the living."

**ANARCHISM** One of the many challenges facing the labor union movement during the Gilded Age was growing hostility from middle-class Americans who viewed unionized workers, especially those involved in clashes with police, as violent radicals or anarchists. Anarchists believed that powerful capitalists bribed elected officials to oppress the working poor. They dreamed of the elimination of government altogether, and some were willing to use bombs and bullets to achieve their goal.

Many European anarchists, mostly Germans or Italians, immigrated to the United States during the last quarter of the nineteenth century. Although most disavowed violence, the terrorists among them ensured that the label "anarchist" provoked frightening images in the minds of many Americans. Anarchists dreamed of labor unions replacing governments, enabling workers to rule.

Labor-related violence increased during the 1880s as the gap between the rich and working poor widened. Between 1880 and 1900, some 6.6 million hourly workers participated in more than 23,000 strikes nationwide. Chicago was a hotbed of unrest and a magnet for immigrants, especially German and Irish laborers, some of whom openly endorsed violence to ignite a working-class uprising. The Chicago labor movement's foremost demand was for an eight-hour workday. What came to be called the **Haymarket riot** grew indi-rectly out of prolonged agitation for this goal.

**THE HAYMARKET RIOT (1886)** In 1886, some 40,000 Chicago workers went on strike in support of an eight-hour workday. On May 3, vio-lent clashes between strikers and nonunion scabs hired to replace the striking workers erupted outside the McCormick Harvesting Machine Company plant. The police arrived, shots rang out, and two strikers were killed. The killings infuriated leaders of the anarchist movement, who organized a mass protest the following night at Haymarket Square.

The rally was peaceful, but the speeches were not. After listening to speak-ers complain about low wages and long working hours, the crowd of angry laborers was beginning to break up when more than a hundred police arrived and ordered them to disperse. At that point, someone threw a bomb that left dozens of maimed and dying policemen in the street. The police then fired into the fleeing crowd, resulting in more casualties. Seven policemen were killed and more than a hundred more wounded in what journalists called America's first terrorist bombing.

The next day, Chicago's mayor banned all labor meetings, and newspapers printed sensational headlines about anarchists terrorizing the city. "There are no good anarchists except dead anarchists," the *St. Louis Globe-Democrat* raged. Chicago officials banned union meetings and the printing of anarchist newspapers. One New York newspaper demanded stern punishment for "the few long-haired, wild-eyed, bad-smelling, atheistic, reckless foreign wretches."

During the summer of 1886, seven anarchist leaders, all but one of them German-language speakers, were sentenced to death despite the lack of evi-dence linking them to the bomb thrower, whose identity was never deter-mined. After being sentenced to be hanged, Louis Lingg declared that he was innocent but was "in favor of using force" to end the abuses of the capitalist system.

On November 10, 1887, Lingg committed suicide in his cell. That same day, the governor of Illinois commuted the sentences of two of the convicted conspirators to life imprisonment. The next day, the four remaining con-demned men were hanged. To labor militants around the world, the executed anarchists were working-class martyrs; to the police and the economic elite in Chicago, they were demonic assassins.

**A BACKLASH AGAINST UNIONS** After the Haymarket riot, ten-sions between workers and management reached a fever pitch across the nation. In 1886 alone, there were 1,400 strikes involving 700,000 workers.

But the violence in Chicago also triggered widespread hostility to the Knights of Labor and labor groups in general. Despite his best efforts, union leader Terence Powderly could never separate in the public mind the Knights from the anarchists, since one of those convicted of conspiracy in the bombing was a member of the union.

Powderly clung to leadership until 1893, but after that the union evaporated. Yet the Knights did attain some lasting achievements, including an 1880 federal law providing for the arbitration of labor disputes and the creation of the federal Bureau of Labor Statistics in 1884. Another of their successes was the Foran Act of 1885, which, though poorly enforced, penalized employers who imported immigrant workers. By their example, the Knights spread the idea of unionism and initiated a new type of organization: the industrial union, which included all skilled and unskilled workers within a particular industry.

**GOMPERS AND THE AFL** The craft (or trade) unions, representing skilled workers, generally opposed efforts to unite with industrial unionism. Leaders of the craft unions feared that doing so would mean the loss of their identity and bargaining power. Thus, in 1886, delegates from twenty-five craft unions organized the **American Federation of Labor (AFL)**. It was a federation of many separate national unions, each of which was largely free to act on its own in dealing with business owners.

Samuel Gompers served as president of the AFL from its founding until his death in 1924. Born in England, he came to the United States as a teenager, joined the Cigar Makers' Union in 1864, and became president of his New York City local union in 1877. Unlike Terence Powderly and the Knights of Labor, Gompers focused on concrete economic gains—higher wages, shorter hours, and better working conditions.

The AFL at first grew slowly, but by the turn of the century, it claimed 500,000 members. In 1914, it had 2 million, and in 1920, it reached a peak of 4 million. But even then, the AFL included less than 15 percent of the nation's nonagricultural workers. In fact, all unions, including the so-called railroad brotherhoods that were unaffiliated with the AFL, accounted for little more than 18 percent of all workers.

Organized labor's strongholds were in transportation and the building trades. Most of the larger manufacturing industries—including steel, textiles, tobacco, and meatpacking—remained almost untouched. Gompers never opposed industrial unions, and several became important affiliates of the AFL: the United Mine Workers, the International Ladies Garment Workers, and the Amalgamated Clothing Workers.

Two incidents in the 1890s stalled the emerging industrial-union movement: the **Homestead Steel strike** of 1892 and the **Pullman strike** of 1894. These conflicts represented a test of strength for the organized labor movement. They also served to reshape the political landscape.

**THE HOMESTEAD STEEL STRIKE** The Amalgamated Association of Iron and Steel Workers, founded in 1876, was the nation's largest craft union. At the massive steel mill owned by Andrew Carnegie at Homestead, Pennsylvania, along the Monongahela River near Pittsburgh, the union had enjoyed friendly relations with management until Henry Clay Frick became chief executive in 1889. Frick prided himself on being the most anti-labor executive in the nation.

A showdown was delayed until 1892, however, when the union contract came up for renewal. Carnegie, who had previously expressed sympathy for the unions, went on a hunting trip in his native Scotland, intentionally leaving Frick to handle the difficult negotiations.

Carnegie knew what was in the works: a cost-cutting reduction in the number of highly paid skilled workers through the use of labor-saving machinery, even though the corporation was enjoying high profits. It was a deliberate attempt to smash the union. "Am with you to the end," Carnegie wrote to Frick. William Jones, the mill manager, opposed cutting wages because "our men are working hard and faithfully. . . . Now, mark what I tell you. Our labor is the cheapest in the country."

Jones's protests did little good. As negotiations dragged on, the company announced on June 25 that it would stop negotiating with the 3,800 workers in four days unless an agreement were reached. A strike—or, more properly, a lockout in which management closed down the mill to try to force the union to make concessions—would begin on June 29.

Frick ordered construction of a twelve-foot-high fence crowned with barbed wire around the plant and equipped it with watchtowers, searchlights, rifle slits, and high-pressure water cannons. He also hired a private army of 316 Pinkerton agents to protect "Fort Frick."

Before dawn on July 6, 1892, the "Pinkertons" floated up the Monongahela River on two barges pulled by a tugboat. Thousands of unionists and their supporters, many of them armed, were waiting on shore. A fourteen-hour gun battle ensued. Seven workers and four Pinkertons were killed, and dozens were wounded. Hundreds of women on shore shouted, "Kill the Pinkertons!"

In the end, the Pinkertons surrendered and were marched away to taunts from crowds lining the streets. But the celebrations were short-lived. A week later, the Pennsylvania governor dispatched 4,000 state militiamen to Homestead, where they surrounded the mill and dispersed the picketing workers. Frick then hired strikebreakers to operate the mill. He refused to resume negotiations: "I will never recognize the union, never, never!"

The strike dragged on until November, but by then the union was dead and its leaders had been charged with murder and treason. The union cause was not helped when Alexander Berkman, a Lithuanian anarchist, tried to assassinate Frick in his office on July 23, shooting him twice in the neck and stabbing him three times. Despite his wounds, Frick fought back fiercely and, with the help of staff members, subdued the would-be assassin.

After that incident, sympathy for the strikers evaporated. Penniless and demoralized, the workers ended their walkout on November 20 and accepted the company's harsh wage cuts. Only a fifth of the strikers got their jobs back; the rest were "blacklisted" to prevent other steel mills from hiring them. After the Homestead strike, none of Carnegie's steel plants employed unionized workers. Within a few years, Carnegie could confide to a friend that he was "ashamed to tell you" how large his profits were from the Homestead plant.

But his reputation was ruined. "Three months ago Andrew Carnegie was a man to be envied," wrote a St. Louis newspaper. "Today he is an object of mingled pity and contempt." The editor called him a "moral coward." A "single word from him [in Scotland] might have saved the bloodshed—but the word was never spoken."

With each passing year, Carnegie nursed regrets about how Frick had handled the Homestead strike. In the end, Frick split with Carnegie after learning that his boss had been telling lies about him and making "insults" about his character. Frick told Carnegie that he had grown "tired of your business methods, your absurd newspaper interviews and personal remarks and unwarranted interference in matters you know nothing about."

**THE PULLMAN STRIKE** The Pullman strike of 1894 paralyzed the economies of the twenty-seven states and territories in the western half of the nation. It involved a dispute at Pullman, Illinois, a "model" industrial suburb of Chicago owned by the Pullman Palace Car Company, which made passenger train cars (called "Pullmans," or "sleeping cars").

Employees were required to live in the town's 1,400 cottages, which had been built to high standards, with gas heat and indoor plumbing. With 12,000 residents, the town boasted a library, a theater, a school, parks and playgrounds, and a glass-roofed shopping mall owned by the company. There were no saloons, social clubs, newspapers, or private property not owned by the company. No political activities were allowed.

As a "company town," Pullman was of much higher quality than the villages in the South owned by textile mills. Yet over time, many workers came to resent living under the thumb of the company's owner, George Pullman.

During the depression of 1893, Pullman laid off 3,000 of his 5,800 employees and cut wages 25 to 40 percent for the rest, but he did not lower rents for housing or the price of food in the company store. In the spring of 1894, desperate workers joined the American Railway Union, founded the previous year by Eugene V. Debs.

Debs was a child of working-class immigrants in Indiana. He had quit school at age fourteen to work for an Indiana railroad before becoming a union organizer. After serving in the state legislature, he became a tireless spokesman for labor radicalism, and he worked to organize all railway workers—skilled or unskilled—into the American Railway Union, which soon became a powerful example of his idea of "One Big Union."

Debs was impossible to dislike. Even his enemies acknowledged that he was a truly good person. His essential goodness prompted him to intervene in the Pullman controversy. He urged the angry workers to obey the laws and avoid violence. After George Pullman fired three members of a workers' grievance committee, the workers went on strike on May 11, 1894.

In June, after Pullman refused Debs's plea for a negotiated settlement, the Railway Union workers stopped handling trains containing Pullman railcars.

**Eugene V. Debs** Founder of the American Railway Union, and later the presidential candidate for the Socialist Party of America.

By the end of July, they had shut down most of the railroads in the Midwest and cut off all traffic through Chicago. To keep the trains running, railroad executives hired strikebreakers, and the U.S. attorney general swore in 3,400 special deputies to protect them. Angry workers assaulted strikebreakers and destroyed property.

Finally, on July 3, President Grover Cleveland sent 2,000 federal troops to the Chicago area, claiming it was his duty to ensure delivery of the mail. Meanwhile, the attorney general convinced a federal judge to sign an *injunction* (an official court decree) prohibiting the labor union from interfering.

On July 13, the union called off the strike. A few days later, a court cited Debs for violating the injunction and sentenced him to six months in jail. Debs emerged from jail the most famous labor leader in the United States. While a prisoner, he had become a socialist; he would run for president five times.

In 1897, George Pullman died of a heart attack, and the following year, the city of Chicago annexed the town of Pullman. A reporter for the *Nation* noted that despite the town's attractive features, what the workers wanted most was the chance to own a house of their own. "Mr. Pullman," he explained, "overlooked this peculiar American characteristic."

**THE LATTIMER MASSACRE** In August 1897, the Lehigh and Wilkes-Barre Coal Company laid off anthracite coal workers from the Lattimer mine near Hazleton, Pennsylvania. Those who remained had to accept wage cuts, longer workdays, increased costs for company-owned housing and goods from the company-owned store, and dangerous working conditions. An average of three workers were killed in accidents every two days. Immigrants were assigned the most dangerous jobs.

Such conditions eventually provoked a strike by many of the 10,000 workers, most of whom were from central or eastern Europe: Poland, Slovakia, Hungary, Lithuania, and Germany. Speaking for the workers, the *Hazleton Evening Standard* issued a blunt warning: "The day of the slave driver is past, and the once ignorant foreigner will no longer tolerate it." Initially, management agreed to raise wages, only to renege on the offer. As the strike continued, the mine owners asked county sheriff James L. Martin to disperse the workers.

On September 10, Martin organized a posse of 150 armed men paid by the mine owners. They soon confronted several hundred unarmed strikers marching peacefully to the Lattimer mine, where they intended to convince Italian workers to join them. They carried an American flag.

Sheriff Martin ordered the marchers to disperse and tried to seize their flag. When a scuffle ensued, a deputy shouted, "Shoot the sons of bitches."

The posse opened fire, killing nineteen unarmed miners. At least thirty-nine others were wounded. Most of them had been shot in the back. The flag bearer was the first man killed.

Accounts of the Lattimer Massacre circulated throughout the state and nation. Thousands attended the funerals of the slain workers as newspapers expressed widespread revulsion at the "butchery." One Pittsburgh headline read: "Massacre of Slavs—In the Free-est Country under the Sun—People Are Shot like Dogs."

In early 1898, Sheriff Martin and seventy-three of his deputies were tried for murder. Martin expressed surprise, explaining that he and his men had shot "only foreigners." In closing remarks to the jury, the district attorney noted that if the deputies "had protected the lives of these poor creatures of God with the same solicitude they displayed in protecting the property of the employers there would be no case here today." All of the accused were acquitted. Within weeks after the massacre, 15,000 miners joined the United Mine Workers union.

**THE WESTERN FEDERATION OF MINERS** At the same time that Eugene Debs was mobilizing a socialist-based working-class movement, militant labor leaders in the West were organizing the Western Federation of Miners (WFM). The WFM represented smelter workers and "hard-rock" miners who worked deep underground harvesting copper, gold, silver, and lead in Montana, Colorado, Idaho, Utah, and the Dakotas.

Almost from its birth in 1883 Butte, Montana, the WFM was viewed as a radical labor union. The Western Federation was at the center of violent confrontations with mine operators who mobilized secret spies, private armies, state militias, and even federal troops against it.

That several dozen miners were killed in clashes with management helps explain why the WFM grew especially militant. At its 1901 convention, it proclaimed that a "complete revolution of social and economic conditions" was "the only salvation of the working classes." WFM leaders demanded the abolition of the wage system. By the spring of 1903, the WFM was the most militant labor organization in the country.

The group's most outspoken leader was William "Big Bill" Haywood. Born in Salt Lake City, Utah, he went to work in the Nevada silver mines at age nine. He later was a homesteader and surveyor before becoming a socialist miner and joining the union in 1896; by 1902, he was its primary spokesman.

Haywood and the WFM promoted industrial unionism, recruiting both unskilled and skilled workers. They also welcomed members of all races and ethnic groups—men and women. Perhaps most controversial was Haywood's advocacy of strikes over negotiations, a militant stance that few other unions adopted.

**THE INTERNATIONAL WORKERS OF THE WORLD** In 1905, Big Bill Haywood, Eugene Debs, Daniel De Leon (head of the Socialist Labor party), Mother Jones, and two dozen other prominent socialists and union leaders met secretly in Chicago. Their mission was to give workers more political power by forming the **International Workers of the World (IWW)**, a giant global "revolutionary labor union" ("One Big Union") open to all workers.

The "Wobblies," as IWW members were called, sought to destroy the capitalist system and replace it with workers' unions ("syndicates") that would elect their managers. De Leon argued that the IWW "must be founded on the class struggle" and "the irrepressible conflict between the capitalist class and the working class."

Not surprisingly, the IWW generated intense criticism. The *Los Angeles Times* claimed that a "vast number of I.W.W's are non-producers. I.W.W. stands for I won't work, and I want whisky. . . . The average Wobbly, it must be remembered, is a sort of half wild animal. He lives on the road, cooks his food in rusty tin cans . . . and sleeps in "jungles," barns, outhouses, freight cars. . . . They are all in all a lot of homeless men wandering about the country without fixed destination or purpose, other than destruction."

Like other radical groups, the IWW was split by sectarian disputes. Debs and De Leon withdrew because the organization refused to affiliate with their rival socialist parties.

Bill Haywood held the IWW together, recruiting tens of thousands of new members from lumberyards, farms, and factories. Tall, handsome, and muscular, he commanded attention and respect.

Haywood and the Wobblies, however, recruited members with the least power and influence, chiefly migrant workers in the West and immigrants in the East. Always ambivalent about diluting their principles, Wobblies scorned the usual labor agreements even when they participated in them. They engaged in spectacular battles with employers but scored few victories while arousing hysterical opposition. They were branded as anarchists, bums, and criminals.

The largest and most successful IWW strike was against a textile mill in Lawrence, Massachusetts, in 1912. Haywood and others forged an unlikely coalition of immigrant workers speaking as many as fifteen different languages. The organizers shrewdly captured public support by portraying the strike as a plea for basic human rights. Striking mill girls carried picket signs announcing: WE WANT BREAD AND ROSES, TOO. The strikers won the fight, as the mill owners agreed to wage increases, overtime pay, and other benefits.

## ECONOMIC SUCCESS AND EXCESS

For all the stress and strain caused by swift industrialization and labor union responses, American productivity soared in the late nineteenth century. By 1900, the United States was producing a third of the world's goods, and millions of immigrants continued to risk all in hopes of chasing the American dream. Corporate empires generated enormous fortunes for a few and real improvements in the quality of life for many. The majority of workers now labored in factories and mines rather than on farms.

The urban-industrial revolution and the gigantic new corporations it created transformed the size, scope, and power of the American economy, for good and for ill. As the twentieth century dawned, an unregulated capitalist economy had grown corrupt and recklessly out of balance—and only government intervention could restore economic fairness and social stability.

# CHAPTER REVIEW

## SUMMARY

- **The Causes of Industrial Growth**   During the late nineteenth century, agricultural and industrial production increased sharply. The national railroad network grew to nearly 200,000 miles, the most extensive in the world. The surge of industrialization expanded the use of electrical power and the application of scientific research to industrial processes. The *Bessemer converter* allowed for the mass production of steel, which was used to construct railroads, ships, bridges, and buildings.

- **The Rise of Big Business**   Many businesses grew to enormous size and power—and often ignored ethics and the law in doing so. Entrepreneurs like John D. Rockefeller, Andrew Carnegie, and J. Pierpont Morgan were extraordinarily skilled at gaining control of particular industries. Companies such as *Standard Oil* and *Carnegie Steel* practiced both *vertical integration*, through which they controlled all the enterprises needed to produce and distribute their products, and *horizontal integration*, in which they absorbed or eliminated their competitors. To consolidate their holdings and sidestep laws prohibiting *monopolies*, they created *trusts* and eventually *holding companies*. *J. Pierpont Morgan and Company*, an investment bank, pioneered methods for consolidating corporations and eliminating competition, all in an effort to bring "order and stability" to the marketplace.

- **The Alliance of Business and Politics**   The federal government encouraged economic growth after the Civil War by imposing high *tariffs* on imported products, granting public land to railroad companies and settlers in the West, establishing a stable currency, and encouraging the creation of land-grant universities to spur technical innovation and research. Equally important, local, state, and federal governments made little effort to regulate the activities of businesses. This *laissez-faire* policy allowed entrepreneurs to experiment with new methods of organization but also created conditions for rampant corruption and abuse.

- **A Changed Social Order**   While the business and financial elite showed off their new wealth with extravagant homes and parties, the urban and industrial workforce was largely composed of unskilled workers, including recent immigrants, former farmers, and growing numbers of women and children. *Child labor* sometimes involved children as young as eight working twelve-hour days. Business owners and managers showed little concern for workplace safety, and work-related accidents and diseases were common. With industrialization and the rise of Big Business also came an increase in the number of people who considered themselves middle class. Growing numbers of women went to college, took business and professional jobs, and participated in other public activities.

- **Organized Labor**   It was difficult for unskilled workers to organize effectively into unions, in part because of racial and ethnic tensions among laborers, language barriers, and the efforts of owners and supervisors to undermine unionizing efforts.

Business owners often hired "strikebreakers," usually desperate immigrant workers who were willing to take jobs at the prevailing wage. Nevertheless, several unions did advocate for workers' rights at a national level. After the violence associated with the *Great Railroad Strike of 1877*, *Haymarket riot (1886)*, the *Homestead Steel strike (1892)*, and the *Pullman strike (1894)*, many Americans grew fearful of unions and viewed them as politically radical. Craft unions made up solely of skilled workers became more successful at organizing by focusing on better working conditions and avoiding involvement in politics.

## CHRONOLOGY

| | |
|---|---|
| **1859** | First oil well is struck in Titusville, Pennsylvania |
| **1869** | First transcontinental railroad is completed at Promontory Summit, Utah |
| **1876** | Alexander Graham Bell patents his telephone |
| **1877** | Great Railroad Strike |
| **1879** | Thomas A. Edison makes the first durable incandescent lightbulb |
| **1882** | John D. Rockefeller organizes the Standard Oil Trust |
| **1886** | American Federation of Labor is organized |
| **1892** | Homestead Steel strike |
| **1894** | Pullman strike |
| **1901** | J. Pierpont Morgan creates the U.S. Steel Corporation |

## KEY TERMS

**Standard Oil Company** p. 701

**horizontal integration** p. 701

**monopoly** p. 701

**vertical integration** p. 702

**trust** p. 702

**holding company** p. 702

**Bessemer converter** p. 703

**Carnegie Steel Company** p. 704

**J. Pierpont Morgan and Company** p. 704

**tariff** p. 706

**laissez-faire** p. 708

**child labor** p. 713

**Great Railroad Strike of 1877** p. 714

**National Labor Union (NLU)** p. 715

**Knights of Labor** p. 716

**Haymarket riot (1886)** p. 719

**American Federation of Labor (AFL)** p. 720

**Homestead Steel strike (1892)** p. 721

**Pullman strike (1894)** p. 721

**International Workers of the World (IWW)** p. 726

 INQUIZITIVE

**Go to InQuizitive to see what you've learned—and learn what you've missed—with personalized feedback along the way.**

# 18 The New South and the New West

## 1865–1900

***Mining on the Comstock* (1877)** The Comstock Lode was one of the largest gold and silver mines in America, yielding more than $300 million over two decades. This illustration shows a cutaway of the Comstock Lode, revealing the complex network of shafts and supports, as well as the various tasks performed by miners within its tunnels.

After the Civil War, the devastated South and the untamed Wes were the most distinctive sections of the nation. Both eluder mapping or measuring, for they resided within powerful myth as much as physical regions.

Both also provided enticing frontiers for economic enterprise. The Sout! had to be rebuilt, while the sparsely settled territories and states west of th Mississippi River were ripe for the development of farms, businesses, railroad: and towns. Bankers and financiers in America and Europe invested heavily i both regions, but especially in the Far West between the Mississippi River an California.

Americans had long viewed the Great Plains as suitable only for Indian After 1865, however, the federal government encouraged western settlemen and economic development in what was called Indian Country. Two thirds Native Americans in 1865 still lived on the Great Plains.

The construction of transcontinental railroads, the military conquest the Indians, and the policy of distributing 270 million acres of governmen owned lands at little or no cost to settlers, including women, African Ame icans (after the passage of the 14th Amendment), and immigrants. Free lar and the possibility of finding gold or silver or starting a business lured millio: of pioneers and enterprising capitalists westward.

## focus questions

1. In what ways did a "New South" emerge in the late nineteenth centur

2. What was the crop-lien system in the South? Explain how it shaped t region after the Civil War.

3. How and why did white southerners adopt Jim Crow segregation laws and take away African Americans' right to vote at the end of the nineteenth century?

4. Who were the various groups of migrants to the West after the Civil War? Why did they move there?

5. Describe the experiences of miners, farmers, ranchers, and women the West in the late nineteenth century.

6. How did the federal government's post–Civil War policies in the We: affect Native Americans?

7. How did the South and West change by 1900?

# THE MYTH OF THE NEW SOUTH

After the Civil War, the South fought an ideological civil war over its future. Southerners devastated by defeat found solace in the "Lost Cause"—nostalgia for the mythic Old South of white-columned plantations, white supremacy, and cotton-generated wealth produced by enslaved black people. As one southerner said, his native region remained "old-fashioned, medieval, provincial, worshipping the dead."

At the same time, no region has inspired a more tenacious pride of place. Mississippi writer Eudora Welty once explained that in the South, "feelings are bound up with place." *Home* and *history* are two of the most revered words in southern life. Nineteenth-century southerners did not simply live in the present and dream of the future. They were forever glancing backward in the process of moving forward. As William Faulkner recognized in his novel *Intruder in the Dust* (1948), "The past isn't dead. It's not even past."

Some prominent southerners, however, looked more to the future. They called for a *New* South in which the Old South agricultural economy worked by slaves and dominated by the planter elite would be replaced by a society of small farms owned by blacks and whites. The New South would also boast a growing industrial sector, and race relations would become harmonious.

The champion of the New South ideal was Henry Woodfin Grady, the powerful editor of the *Atlanta Constitution* newspaper. In 1886, Grady told a New York City audience he was glad that the Union was saved and slavery was abolished, but he insisted that the "South has nothing for which to apologize. . . . The South has nothing to take back." The Old South was dead, but there "is now a New South of union and freedom—that South, thank God, is living, breathing, and growing every hour."

Grady claimed that the New South was becoming "a perfect democracy" of small farms complemented by mills, mines, factories, and cities, "a hundred farms for every plantation, fifty homes for every palace, and a diversified industry that meets the complex needs of this complex age." The postwar South, Grady claimed, would no longer be dominated by the planter aristocracy or dependent upon cotton and slave labor. No section of the nation "shows a more prosperous laboring population than the Negroes of the South; none in fuller sympathy with the employing and land-owning class." Without acknowledging his exaggeration, he insisted that the "relations of the Southern people with the Negro are close and cordial."

Many southerners shared Grady's progressive vision. The Confederacy, they concluded, had lost the war because it had relied too much on King Cotton—and slavery. In the future, the New South needed to follow the North's example ("out-Yankee the Yankees") and develop a strong industrial sector to go with its agricultural foundation. New South advocates also stressed that more-efficient farming, which used the latest machinery and technical expertise, was essential, and that widespread vocational training was urgently needed. They asserted that racial harmony built upon by black peoples' acceptance of white supremacy (a peculiar kind of "perfect democracy") would provide a stable social environment for economic growth.

**TEXTILE MILLS** The chief accomplishment of the New South's effort to industrialize was a dramatic expansion of the region's **textile industry**, which produced cotton thread, bedding, and clothing. From 1880 to 1900, the number of red-brick cotton mills in the South grew from 161 to 400, the number of mill workers (mostly whites, with women and children outnumbering men) increased fivefold, and the demand for cotton products rose eightfold. By 1900, the South had surpassed New England as the largest producer of cotton fabric in the nation.

Thousands of dirt-poor farm folk—many of them children—rushed to take jobs in the mills. Seventy percent of mill workers were younger than twenty-one, and many were under fourteen. A dawn-to-dusk job in a mill paying 50¢ a day "was much more interesting than one-horse farming," noted one worker, "because you can meet your bills." Those bills were usually paid to the mill owner, who, like a feudal baron, provided housing, food, and supplies to the workers in his village—for a fee.

Over time, mill owners hired and paid the village school teachers, doctors, and ministers. They organized dances and concerts and created sports leagues. Their paternalistic social system was in part intended to create a sense of community so strong that workers would never be tempted to organize labor unions.

**THE TOBACCO INDUSTRY** Tobacco growing and cigarette production also soared. Essential to the rise of the tobacco industry was the Duke family of Durham, North Carolina. Soon after the Civil War ended, Washington Duke took his barn load of tobacco, dried it, and, with the help of his two sons, hitched up his wagon and traveled the state, selling tobacco in small pouches. By 1872, the Dukes had a modern cigarette factory producing 125,000 pounds of tobacco annually.

**OTHER NEW SOUTH INDUSTRIES** Effective use of other natural resources also helped revitalize the South along the Appalachian chain from West Virginia to Alabama. Coal production grew from 5 million tons in 1875 to 49 million tons by 1900. At the southern end of the mountains, Birmingham, Alabama, sprang up in large part because of the massive deposits of iron ore in the surrounding ridges, leading boosters to label the steelmaking city the "Pittsburgh of the South."

Urban and industrial expansion as well as rapid population growth created a need for housing. In response to the demand, lumber production became the fastest-growing industry in the South, after 1870. Northern investors bought vast forests of yellow pine and set about clear-cutting them and hauling the logs to new sawmills, where they were milled into lumber for the construction of homes and businesses.

By 1900, southern lumber had surpassed textiles in annual economic value. Still, for all its advances, the South continued to lag behind the rest of the nation in industrial development and educational attainment.

**THE REDEEMERS**  Henry Grady's vision of a New South celebrated the **redeemers**, the conservative, pro-business, white politicians in the Democratic party who had embraced the idea of industrial progress grounded in white supremacy. Their supporters referred to them as redeemers because they supposedly saved ("redeemed") the South from Yankee domination, and what they called "black rule," during Reconstruction.

The redeemers included lawyers, merchants, railroad executives, and entrepreneurs who wanted a more diversified economy. They also sought cuts in state taxes and expenditures, including those for public-school systems started after the war. "Schools are not a necessity," claimed a Virginia governor. Black children, in particular, suffered from such cutbacks. The redeemers did not want educated African Americans. "What I want here is Negroes who can make cotton," explained a white planter, "and they don't need education to help them make cotton."

## THE FAILINGS OF THE NEW SOUTH

Despite the development of mills and factories, the South in 1900 remained the least industrial, least urban, least educated, and least prosperous region in the nation. Per capita income in the South was only 60 percent of the national average, and the region remained dependent on the North for investment capital and manufactured goods.

Cotton remained king, although it never regained the huge profitability it had generated in the 1850s. By the 1880s, southern farmers, black and white, were producing as much cotton as they had before the war but were earning far less money because the world price for cotton had declined.

**SOUTHERN POVERTY**  Henry Grady hoped that growing numbers of southern farmers would own their own land by the end of the nineteenth century. But the opposite occurred. A prolonged decline in crop prices made it more difficult than ever to buy and own land. By 1900, an estimated 70 percent of farmers did not own the land they worked.

**THE CROP-LIEN SYSTEM**  Because few southern communities had banks after the Civil War, people had to operate with little or no cash. Many rural areas adopted a barter economy in which a "crossroads" merchant would provide food, clothing, seed, fertilizer, and other items to poor farmers "on credit" in exchange for a share (or "lien") of their crops when harvested.

Southern farmers, white and black, who participated in the **crop-lien system** fell into three categories: small farm owners, sharecroppers, and tenants. The farms owned by most southerners were small and did not generate much income. As a result, even those who owned farms had to pledge a portion of their future crop to the local merchant in exchange for supplies, clothing, and food.

**"Free slaves"** Sharecroppers painstakingly pick cotton while their white overseer watches from atop his horse.

The crop-lien system was self-destructive. Planting cotton or tobacco year after year stripped the soil of its fertility and stability and led to disastrous erosion of farmland during rainstorms. Topsoil washed into nearby creeks, collapsing riverbanks and creating ever-deepening gullies. In addition, landowners required croppers and tenants to grow a "cash crop" exclusively, usually cotton or tobacco. By permitting only these cash crops, landowners prevented croppers and tenants from growing their own vegetable gardens; they had to get their food from the local merchant in exchange for promised cotton.

Because most farmers did not own the land they worked, the cabins they lived in, or the tools they used, they had little incentive to enrich the soil or maintain buildings and equipment. According to a study of southern agriculture in 1897, the tenant system had been "more wasteful and destructive than slavery was anywhere."

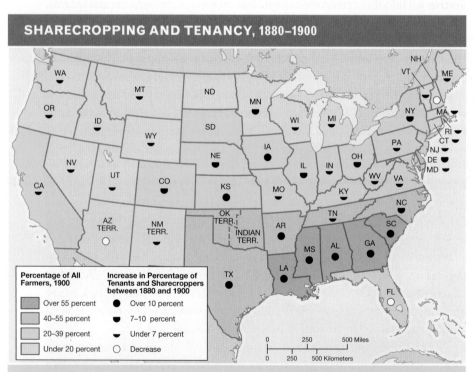

**SHARECROPPING AND TENANCY, 1880–1900**

Percentage of All Farmers, 1900
- Over 55 percent
- 40–55 percent
- 20–39 percent
- Under 20 percent

Increase in Percentage of Tenants and Sharecroppers between 1880 and 1900
- ● Over 10 percent
- ▼ 7–10 percent
- ⌄ Under 7 percent
- ○ Decrease

- Why was there a dramatic increase in sharecropping and tenancy in the late nineteenth century?
- Explain why the South had more sharecroppers than other parts of the country.

The crop-lien system was a post–Civil War version of economic slavery for poor whites as well as for blacks. The landowner, or merchant (often the same person), decided what crop would be planted and how it would be cultivated, harvested, and sold. In good times, croppers and tenants barely broke even; in bad times, they struggled to survive.

**FALLING COTTON PRICES**  As cotton production soared during the last quarter of the nineteenth century, the price paid for raw cotton fell steadily, forcing desperate farmers to plant even more cotton, which only accelerated the decline in price from 11.77¢ per pound in the 1870s to 7.72¢ in 1896.

## RACE RELATIONS DURING THE 1890S

The plight of southern farmers in the 1880s and 1890s affected race relations—for the worse. During the 1890s, white farmers and politicians demanded that blacks be stripped of their voting rights and other civil rights. What northern observers called "Negrophobia" swept across the South and much of the nation.

In part, the new wave of racism represented a revival of the idea that the Anglo-Saxon "race" of whites who originated in Germany and spread across western Europe and Great Britain was intellectually and genetically superior to blacks. Another reason was that many whites had come to resent any signs of African American financial success and political influence. An Alabama newspaper editor reported that "our blood boils when the educated Negro asserts himself politically."

**DISENFRANCHISING AFRICAN AMERICANS**  By the 1890s, a new generation of African Americans born and educated since the Civil War was determined to gain complete equality. They were more assertive and less patient than their parents. "We are not the Negro from whom the chains of slavery fell a quarter century ago, most assuredly not," a black editor announced. A growing number of young southern white adults, however, were equally determined to keep all "Negroes in their place."

Mississippi took the lead in stripping black people of their voting rights. The so-called **Mississippi Plan**, a series of amendments to the state constitution, set the pattern of disenfranchisement that nine more states would follow. The Mississippi Plan of 1890 first instituted a residence requirement for voting—two years in the state, one year in a local election district—aimed at African American tenant farmers who were in the habit of moving each year in search of better economic opportunities. Second, Mississippi disqualified black people from voting if they had committed certain crimes. Third, in order to vote, people had to have paid all taxes on time, including a so-called poll tax specifically for voting—a restriction that hurt both poor blacks and poor whites. Finally, all voters had to be able to read or at least "understand" the U.S. Constitution. White registrars decided who satisfied this requirement and usually discriminated against black people.

Other states had variations on the Mississippi Plan. In 1898, Louisiana inserted into its state constitution the "grandfather clause," which allowed illiterate whites to vote if their fathers or grandfathers had been eligible to vote on January 1, 1867, when African Americans were still disenfranchised. By 1910, Georgia, North Carolina, Virginia, Alabama, and Oklahoma had incorporated the grandfather clause.

When such "legal" means were not enough to ensure their political dominance, white candidates turned to fraud and violence. Benjamin Tillman, the white supremacist who served as South Carolina's governor from 1890 to 1894, maintained that his state's problems were caused by white farmers renting their land to "ignorant lazy negroes." With such racist comments, he gained the support of poor whites. To ensure his election, he and his followers effectively eliminated the black vote. He admitted that "we have done our level best [to prevent black people from voting] . . . We stuffed ballot boxes. We shot them. We are not ashamed of it."

By the end of the nineteenth century, widespread racial discrimination—segregation of public facilities, political disenfranchisement, and vigilante justice—had elevated government-sanctioned bigotry to an official way of life in the South. Tillman bluntly declared in 1892 that black people "must remain subordinate or be exterminated."

The efforts to suppress the black vote succeeded. In 1896, Louisiana had 130,000 registered black voters; by 1900, it had only 5,320. In Alabama in 1900, the census data indicated that 121,159 black men were literate; only 3,742, however, were registered to vote. By that year, black voting across the South had declined by 62 percent, the white vote by 26 percent.

**THE SPREAD OF SEGREGATION** At the same time that southern blacks were being shoved out of the political arena, they were also being segregated socially. The symbolic first target was the railroad passenger car. In 1885, novelist George Washington Cable noted that in South Carolina, black people "ride in first-class [rail] cars as a right" and "their presence excites no comment." Likewise, in New Orleans a visitor was surprised to find that "white and colored people mingled freely." From 1875 to 1883, in fact, any local or state law requiring racial segregation violated the federal Civil Rights Act.

In 1883, however, the U.S. Supreme Court ruled that the Civil Rights Act of 1875 was unconstitutional. In an 8-1 opinion written by Justice Joseph P. Bradley, the Court declared that neither the 13th nor the 14th Amendment gave Congress the authority to pass laws dealing with racial discrimination by private citizens or businesses. The judges explained that individuals and organizations could engage in acts of racial discrimination because the Fourteenth Amendment specified only that "no State" could deny citizens equal protection of the law.

Justice John Marshall Harlan offered a famous dissent to the Court's decision. A Kentuckian who had once owned slaves but had served in the Union army, he had opposed the emancipation of slaves and the Fourteenth and Fifteenth Amendments. After the war, however, the violent excesses of the Ku Klux Klan had convinced him to rethink his attitudes. He became a Republican in 1868 and was named to the Supreme Court by President Rutherford B. Hayes in 1877.

Harlan now argued that the 13th and 14th Amendments, as well as the Civil Rights Act of 1875, were designed to ensure African Americans the same access to public facilities that white citizens enjoyed. The federal government, he insisted, had both the authority and the responsibility to protect citizens from any actions that deprive them of their civil rights. To allow private citizens and enterprises to practice racial discrimination would "permit the badges and incidents of slavery" to remain.

The Court's interpretation in what came to be called the Civil Rights Cases left as an open question the validity of state laws requiring segregated public facilities under the principle of "separate but equal," a slogan popular in the South referring to the argument that racial segregation laws were legal as long as the segregated facilities were equal in quality. In the 1880s, Florida, Tennessee, Texas, and Mississippi required railroad passengers to ride in racially segregated cars.

When Louisiana followed suit in 1890 with a similar law, black people challenged it in the case of *Plessy v. Ferguson* (1896). The case originated in New Orleans when Homer Adolph Plessy, an "octoroon" (a racist term for a person having *one-eighth* African ancestry), refused to leave a whites-only railroad car and was convicted of violating the law.

In arguments presented to the U.S. Supreme Court, Plessy's attorney contended that the Louisiana law sought "to debase and distinguish against the inferior race." He then asked the justices to imagine a future dictated by such statutes: "Was there any limit to such laws? Why not require all colored people to walk on one side of the street and whites on the other?"

All but one justice disagreed that segregation laws necessarily "stamped the colored race with a badge of inferiority." The Court ruled that states had a right to create laws segregating public places such as schools, hotels, and restaurants.

The only justice to dissent was again John Marshall Harlan, who stressed that the Constitution is "color-blind, and neither knows nor tolerates classes among citizens. In respect of civil rights, all citizens are equal before the law." He argued that the *Plessy* ruling violated both the Thirteenth and Fourteenth Amendments. The former "not only struck down the institution of slavery" but also "any burdens or disabilities that constitute badges of slavery or servitude." Harlan concluded that the arbitrary separation of citizens, on the basis of race . . . is a badge of servitude wholly inconsistent with the civil freedom and the equality before the law established by the Constitution. It cannot be justified on any legal grounds."

Harlan feared that the Court's ruling would plant the "seeds of race hate" under "the sanction of law." That is precisely what happened. The ruling legitimized the widespread practice of racially **separate but equal** facilities. In 1900, the editor of the *Richmond Times* insisted that racial segregation "be applied in every relation of Southern life. God Almighty drew the color line, and it cannot be obliterated. The negro must stay on his side of the line, and the white man must stay on his side, and the sooner both races recognize this fact and accept it, the better it will be for both."

The new regulations came to be called "Jim Crow" laws. The name derived from "Jump Jim Crow," a song-and-dance caricature of African Americans. During the 1890s, the term *Jim Crow* became a derisive expression meaning "Negro." Signs reading "whites only" or "colored only" above restrooms and water fountains emerged as hallmarks of the Jim Crow system.

Widespread violence accompanied the Jim Crow laws. From 1890 to 1899, the United States averaged 188 racial lynchings per year, 82 percent of which occurred in the South. Lynchings usually involved a black man (or men) accused of a crime, often rape. White mobs would seize, torture, and kill the accused. Large crowds, including women and children, would watch amid a carnival-like atmosphere. The governor of Mississippi declared that "if it is necessary that every Negro in the state will be lynched, it will be done to maintain white supremacy."

**The lynching of Henry Smith** Despite a lack of evidence, Smith was convicted of murdering a white girl in Paris, Texas. A large crowd assembled to watch her family torture Smith on a platform labeled "Justice." After Smith was burned alive, the townspeople kept his charred teeth and bones as souvenirs.

**MOB RULE IN NORTH CAROLINA** In the late 1890s, a resurgent and often violent white supremacy emerged in the coastal port town of Wilmington, North Carolina, with about 20,000 residents. In 1894 and 1896, black voters, a majority in the city, elected African Americans to various municipal offices, infuriating the white elite. "We will never surrender to a ragged raffle of Negroes," warned Alfred Waddell, a former congressman and Confederate colonel, "even if we have to choke the Cape Fear River with [black] carcasses." It was not an idle threat.

On the morning of November 10, 1898, some 2,000 white men and teens rampaged through the city's streets. Armed with rifles, pistols, and even a Colt machine gun capable of firing 420 bullets per minute, they destroyed the offices of the *Daily Record*, the black-owned newspaper, then moved into African American neighborhoods, killing dozens and destroying homes and businesses.

The mob then stormed the city hall, declared that Colonel Waddell was the new mayor, and forced African American business leaders and elected officials to resign and board northbound trains. The self-appointed city government issued a "Declaration of White Independence" that stripped black people of their jobs and voting rights. Desperate black residents appealed to the governor and to President William McKinley, but received no help. The Wilmington insurrection marked the first time that a lawfully elected municipal government had been overthrown in the United States.

## THE AFRICAN AMERICAN RESPONSE

By the end of the nineteenth century, white supremacy had triumphed across the South. Some African Americans chose to leave in search of equality and opportunity. Those who stayed and resisted white supremacy—even in self-defense—were ruthlessly suppressed. When a white woman, Mrs. Pines, struck her black maid, Sarah Barnett, with a stick, Barnett fought back. Infuriated, Pines's husband shot Barnett through the shoulder. She survived, only to be convicted of assault and jailed. Another black domestic servant, Ann Beston, stabbed and killed her abusive mistress in Rome, Georgia. A mob lynched her.

Most African Americans had no choice but to adjust to the realities of white supremacy and segregation. "Had to walk a quiet life," explained James Plunkett, a Virginian. "The least little thing you would do, they [whites] would kill ya." Survival required black people to wear a mask of deference and discretion and to behave in a "servile way" when shopping at white-owned stores. News of lynchings, burnings, and beatings sent chilling reminders of the dangers they constantly faced.

Yet accommodation did not mean surrender. African Americans constructed their own lively culture. Churches continued to provide an anchor for black communities and were often the only public buildings blacks could use for large gatherings, such as club meetings, political rallies, and social events. For men especially, churches offered leadership roles and political status. Being a deacon was one of the most prestigious roles a black man could achieve. As in many white churches, men preached and governed church affairs; the women often did everything else.

One irony of Jim Crow segregation was that it opened up new economic opportunities for African Americans. Black entrepreneurs emerged to provide essential services to the black community—insurance, banking, barbering, funerals, hair salons. Blacks also formed their own social and fraternal clubs and organizations, all of which provided fellowship, mutual support, and opportunities for service.

Middle-class African American women formed a network of social clubs that served as engines of community service across the South and the nation. They cared for the aged, infirm, orphaned, and abandoned, provided homes for single mothers and nurseries for working mothers, and sponsored health clinics and classes in home economics.

In 1896, the leaders of women's clubs formed the National Association of Colored Women. The organization's first president, Mary Church Terrell, told the members they had an obligation to serve the "lowly, the illiterate, and even the vicious to whom we are bound by the ties of race and sex, and put forth every effort to uplift and reclaim them." Courageous African American women declared that black men were not providing sufficient leadership. An editorial in the *Woman's Era* called for "timid men and ignorant men" to step aside and let the women show the way.

**IDA B. WELLS** One of the most outspoken African American activists was Ida B. Wells. Born into slavery in 1862 in Mississippi, she attended a school staffed by white missionaries. In 1880, she moved to Memphis, Tennessee, where she taught in segregated schools and gained entrance to the social life of the African American middle class.

In 1883, after losing her seat on a railroad car because she was black, Wells became the first African American to file a suit challenging such discrimination. The circuit court decided in her favor and fined the railroad, but the Tennessee Supreme Court overturned the ruling. Wells thereafter discovered "[my] first and [it] might be said, my only love"—journalism—which she used to fight for justice. She became editor of *Memphis Free Speech*, a newspaper that focused on African American issues.

In 1892, after three of her friends were lynched by a white mob, Wells launched a crusade against lynching. Angry whites responded by destroying her office and threatening to lynch her. She moved briefly to New York and then settled in Chicago, where she continued to criticize Jim Crow laws and fought for the restoration of black voting rights. "Somebody must show that the Afro-American race is more sinned against than sinning," she explained, "and it seems to have fallen upon me to do so." She helped found the National Association for the Advancement of Colored People (NAACP) in 1909 and worked for women's suffrage. In promoting racial equality, Wells often found herself

**Ida B. Wells** While raising four children, Wells sustained her commitment to ending racial and gender discrimination and lynching.

in direct opposition to Booker T. Washington, the most influential African American leader of the time.

**BOOKER T. WASHINGTON** Born a slave in Virginia in 1856, the son of a black mother and a white father, Booker T. Washington at sixteen had enrolled at Hampton Normal and Agricultural Institute, one of several colleges for ex-slaves created during Reconstruction. There he met the school's founder, Samuel Chapman Armstrong, who preached moderation and urged the students: "Be thrifty and industrious," "Command the respect of your neighbors by a good record and a good character," "Make the best of your difficulties," and "Live down prejudice." Washington listened and learned.

Nine years later, Armstrong received a request from a group in northern Alabama starting a black college called Tuskegee Institute. The college needed a president, and Armstrong urged them to hire Washington. At twenty-five years old, Washington was, according to Armstrong, "a very capable mulatto, clear headed, modest, sensible, polite, and a thorough teacher and superior man."

Young Washington got the job and quickly went to work. The first students had to help construct the first buildings, making the bricks themselves. As the years passed, Tuskegee Institute became celebrated as a college dedicated to discipline and vocational training.

Over time, Washington became a skilled fundraiser, gathering substantial gifts from wealthy whites, most of them northerners. The complicated racial dynamics of the late nineteenth century required him to walk a tightrope between being candid and being an effective college president. He learned to act like a fox, masking his militancy to maintain the support of whites. As the years passed, the pragmatic Washington became a source of inspiration and hope to millions of blacks.

Washington's recurring message to black students focused on the importance of gaining "practical knowledge." In part to please his white donors, he argued that African Americans should

**Booker T. Washington** Founder of the Tuskegee Institute, a historically black vocational training school.

not focus on fighting racial segregation. They should instead work hard and avoid stirring up trouble. Their priority should be self-improvement rather than social change. Washington told them to begin "at the bottom" as well-educated, hardworking farmers, not as social activists.

In a famous speech at the Cotton States and International Exposition in Atlanta in 1895, Washington urged the African American community not to migrate to northern states or to other nations but to "Cast down your [water] bucket where you are—cast it down in making friends . . . of the people of all races by whom we are surrounded. Cast it down in agriculture, mechanics, in commerce, in domestic service, and in the professions." Fighting for "social equality" and directly challenging white rule would be "the extremest folly," and any effort at "agitation" would, he warned, backfire. African Americans first needed to become self-sufficient economically. Civil rights would have to wait.

**W. E. B. DU BOIS** Other African American leaders disagreed with Booker T. Washington's accommodationist strategy. W. E. B. Du Bois emerged as Washington's foremost rival. A native of Massachusetts, Du Bois recalled that he first experienced racial prejudice as a student at Fisk University in Nashville, Tennessee. He later studied in Germany before becoming the first African American to earn a doctoral degree from Harvard. In addition to promoting civil rights, he authored more than twenty books.

In *The Souls of Black Folk*, Du Bois highlighted the "double consciousness" felt by African Americans: "One ever feels his two-ness—an American, a Negro; two souls, two thoughts, two unreconciled strivings; two warring ideals in one dark body, whose dogged strength alone keeps it from being torn asunder." He spent his career exploring this double consciousness and how it inevitably set blacks apart. A young white visitor to Mississippi in 1910 noticed that nearly every black person he met had "two distinct social selves, the one he reveals to his own people, the other he assumes among the whites."

**W. E. B. Du Bois** A fierce advocate for black education and civil rights.

Soon after Du Bois began teaching at Atlanta University in 1897, he launched a public assault on Booker T. Washington's strategy for improving the quality of life for African Americans. Du Bois called Washington's celebrated 1895 speech "the **Atlanta Compromise**" and said that he would not "surrender the leadership of this race to cowards" who, like Washington, "accepted the alleged inferiority of the Negro" so blacks could "concentrate all their energies on industrial education, the accumulation of wealth, and the conciliation of the South." Du Bois stressed that African American leaders should adopt a strategy of "ceaseless agitation" directed at ensuring the right to vote and winning civil equality. The education of blacks, he maintained, should not be merely vocational but comparable to that enjoyed by the white elite, and it should help develop bold leaders willing to challenge Jim Crow segregation and discrimination.

The dispute between Washington and Du Bois came to define the tensions that would divide the twentieth-century civil rights movement: militancy versus conciliation, separatism versus assimilation, social justice versus economic self-reliance. What Du Bois and others did not know was that Washington secretly worked to challenge segregation and disenfranchisement, stop brutal lynchings, and increase funding for public schools. He often acted privately because he feared that public activism would trigger violence against Tuskegee and himself.

In the end, Washington wanted to engender in his students a confident faith in molding a better future. He counseled them to grasp hope rather than hate and told racist whites that "you can't keep another man in the ditch without being in the ditch yourself."

## THE SETTLING OF THE NEW WEST

In the West, the relentless march of white conquest, settlement, and exploitation continued, propelled by a special sense of "manifest destiny," a lust for land, a hope for quick fortunes, and a desire to improve one's lot in life.

Between 1870 and 1900, Americans settled more land in the West than ever before. By 1900, a third of the population lived west of the Mississippi River, and the New West came to symbolize economic opportunity and personal freedom. On another level, however, the economic exploitation of the West was a story of irresponsible behavior and abuse of nature that scarred the land, decimated its wildlife, and nearly exterminated much of Native American culture—and Native Americans.

**THE WESTERN LANDSCAPE** After midcentury, farmers and their families began spreading west across the Great Plains—western Kansas, Nebraska, Oklahoma, northern Texas, the Dakotas, eastern Colorado, Wyoming, and

Montana. From California, miners moved eastward to Utah and Nevada, drawn by one new discovery after another. From Texas, nomadic cowboys migrated northward annually onto the plains and even across the Rocky Mountains into the Great Basin of Utah and Nevada.

The settlers encountered challenges markedly different from those they had left behind. The Great Plains had little rainfall and few rivers or trees, which rendered useless the familiar trappings of the pioneer—the axe, the log cabin, the rail fence—as well as traditional methods of tilling the soil.

For a long time, the region had been called the Great American Desert; in the minds of most Americans it was unfit for human habitation, and, therefore, it was the perfect refuge for any Indians who refused to accept the white way of life. But that view changed in the last half of the nineteenth century.

With the completion of the transcontinental railroads, the diminishing threat of Indian violence, and a seemingly limitless supply of natural resources, it soon became clear that the West held the key to national prosperity. Capitalists made huge profits investing in western mines, cattle, railroads, and commercial farms. Agriculture expanded westward as the development of new techniques of dry farming and irrigation made the Great American Desert fruitful, after all.

**THE MIGRATORY STREAM** An unrelenting stream of migrants flowed into what had been the largely Indian and Hispanic West. As millions of whites, Native Americans, African Americans, Mexicans, South Americans, and European and Chinese immigrants intermingled, they transformed western life and culture.

The largest number of foreign immigrants came from northern Europe and Canada. In the northern plains (the Dakotas, Minnesota, Montana, and Wyoming), Germans, Scandinavians, and Irish were especially numerous. In Nebraska in 1870, a quarter of the 123,000 residents were foreign-born. In North Dakota in 1890, immigrants composed 45 percent of the residents.

Compared with European immigrants, those from China and Mexico were much less numerous but nonetheless significant. More than 200,000 Chinese arrived in California between 1876 and 1890, joining some 70,000 others who had come earlier to build railroads and work in mining communities. Chinese were frequently discriminated against and denied citizenship rights—and they became scapegoats whenever there was an economic downturn.

**THE AFRICAN AMERICAN MIGRATION** After the collapse of Radical Republican rule in the South, thousands of African Americans began migrating westward; some 6,000 black southerners arrived in Kansas in 1879,

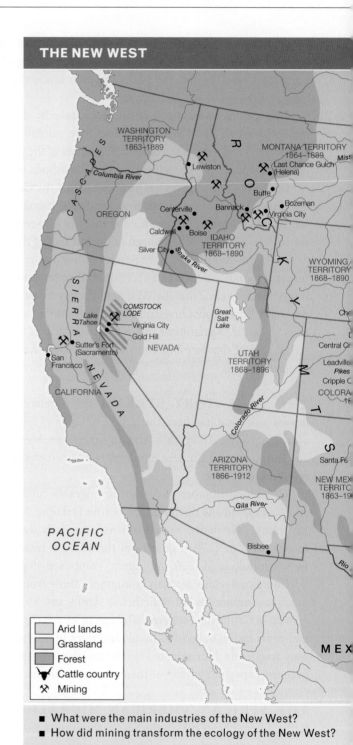

## THE NEW WEST

- What were the main industries of the New West?
- How did mining transform the ecology of the New West?

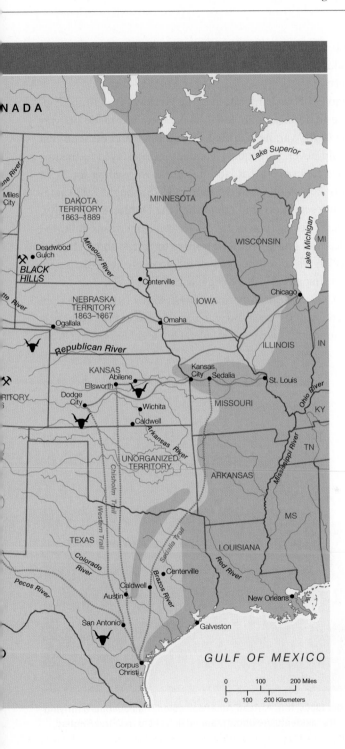

and as many as 20,000 followed the next year. They were called **Exodusters** because they were making their exodus from the South in search of a haven from racism and poverty.

The foremost promoter of black migration to the West was Benjamin "Pap" Singleton. Born a slave in Tennessee in 1809, he escaped and made his way to Michigan. After the Civil War, he returned to Tennessee and decided that African Americans could never gain equal treatment if they stayed in the former Confederacy. When he learned that land in Kansas was selling for $1.25 an acre, he led a party of 200 colonists to the state in 1878, bought 7,500 acres that had been an Indian reservation, and established the Dunlop community.

Over the next several years, thousands of African Americans followed Singleton to Kansas, leading many southern leaders to worry about the loss of black laborers. In 1879, white southerners closed access to the Mississippi River and threatened to sink all boats carrying blacks to the West.

By 1890, some 520,000 African Americans lived west of the Mississippi River. As many as 25 percent of the cowboys who participated in the Texas cattle drives were African Americans, as were many federal horse soldiers in the West.

**Nicodemus, Kansas** By the 1880s, this African American colony had become a thriving town of Exodusters. Here, its residents are photographed in front of the First Baptist Church and general store.

**WESTERN MINING** After the Civil War, the dream of striking it rich by finding gold or silver continued to be the most powerful lure to the West. The nature of mining, however, had changed drastically. Like much of western agriculture, mining had become a mass-production industry. Individual prospectors gave way to large mining companies.

The miners who first rushed to California in 1849 had sifted gold dust and nuggets out of riverbeds by means of "placer" mining, or "panning." Once the placer deposits were exhausted, however, efficient mining required large-scale operations, massive machinery, and substantial capital investment. Companies shifted from surface digging to hydraulic mining, dredging, or deep-shaft "hard-rock" mining.

Industrial miners used huge hydraulic cannons to strip canyon walls of rock and topsoil in a search for veins of gold or silver. The dirt and debris unearthed by the water cannons covered rich farmland downstream and created sandbars that clogged rivers and killed fish. All told, some 12 billion tons of earth were blasted out of the Sierra Nevada and washed into local rivers.

California farmers in the fertile Central Valley bitterly protested the damage done by the powerful industrial mining operations. In 1878, they formed the Anti-Debris Association, but their efforts to pass state legislation restricting hydraulic mining repeatedly failed because mining companies controlled the votes.

The group then turned to the courts. On January 7, 1884, they won their case when federal judge Lorenzo Sawyer, a former miner, outlawed the dumping of mining debris where it could reach farmland or navigable rivers. *Woodruff v. North Bloomfield Gravel Mining Company* became the nation's first major environmental legal victory. As a result of the ruling, hydraulic mining dried up, leaving abandoned equipment, ugly ravines, ditches, gullies, and mountains of discarded rock and gravel.

**MINING BOOMTOWNS** Tombstone, Arizona was a major silver mining site in the 1870s. Within its fourth year of existence, it was the fastest-growing boomtown in the Southwest. It boasted a bowling alley, four churches, a school, two banks, three newspapers, and an ice cream parlor alongside 110 saloons, 14 gambling halls, and numerous dance halls and brothels.

Other famous mining boomtowns included Virginia City in Nevada, Cripple Creek and Leadville in Colorado, and Deadwood in the Dakota Territory. They were male-dominated communities with a substantial population of immigrants from: China, Chile, Peru, Mexico, France, Germany, Scotland, Wales, Ireland, and England.

Ethnic prejudice was as common as violence in mining towns. Chinese, for example, were banned from laboring in the mines but were allowed to operate laundries and work in boardinghouses. Mexicans often suffered the worst treatment. "Mexicans have no business in this country," a Californian insisted. "The men were made to be shot at, and the women were made for our purposes."

Most boomtowns lasted only a few years. Once the mines played out, the people moved on. In 1870, Virginia City, Nevada, then called the richest city in America, had a population of 20,000. Today, it has fewer than 1,000 residents.

New discoveries of gold and silver occurred through the late nineteenth century. The **Comstock Lode** was found near Gold Hill, Nevada, on the eastern slope of the Sierra Nevada near the California border. Henry Comstock, a Canadian-born fur trapper, gave the discovery (actually made by other prospectors in 1859) his name. The Comstock Lode, a seam of gold and silver more than fifty feet wide and thousands of feet deep, was the most profitable mine in history to that point.

The rapid growth of mining spurred the creation of territorial governments and cries for statehood. But after Colorado's admission in 1876, there was a long pause in admitting new states because of party divisions in Congress; Democrats refused to create states out of territories that were dominated by Republicans. After the sweeping Republican victory in the 1888 legislative races, however, Congress admitted North and South Dakota, Montana, and Washington as states in 1889, and Idaho and Wyoming in 1890. Utah entered the Union in 1896 (after the Mormon church agreed to abandon the practice of polygamy). Oklahoma entered in 1907, and in 1912, Arizona and New Mexico became the forty-seventh and forty-eighth contiguous states. (The final two, Alaska and Hawaii, were added fifty years later.)

## LIFE IN THE NEW WEST

In the 1880s, James H. Kyner, a railroad builder in Oregon, described "an almost unbroken stream of emigrants from horizon to horizon." These "hardy, optimistic folk" traveled in wagons, on horses, and on foot, "going west to seek their fortunes and to settle an empire." Most thought little about forcing out the Native Americans, Chinese workers, and Hispanic cowboys who were there first. Americans claimed a special destiny to settle, develop, and dominate the entire continent.

The surge of western migration displayed some of the romantic qualities so often depicted in novels, films, and television shows. Those who braved harsh conditions and uncertain circumstances were, indeed, courageous and tenacious. Cowboys and Indians, outlaws and vigilantes, and farmers, ranchers, and herders populated the plains, while miners and trappers led nomadic lives in the hills and backwoods.

These familiar yet often romanticized images tell only part of the story, however. Drudgery and tragedy were commonplace. In contrast to the Hollywood versions of the West, settlers were a diverse lot: they included women as well as men, African Americans, Hispanics, Asians, and European immigrants. The feverish quest for quick profits also helped fuel a boom-and-bust economic cycle that injected chronic instability into the society and politics of the region.

The abuse, displacement, and relocation of Native Americans, and rapidly dwindling buffalo herds coincided with a burgeoning cattle industry in the West. Cattle were herded into the grasslands where buffalo once had roamed. For many years, wild cattle first brought to America by the Spanish had competed with buffalo in the borderlands of Texas and Arizona. Breeding them with Anglo-American domesticated cattle produced the hybrid Texas longhorn. Tough, lean, and rangy, they were noted more for speed and endurance than for yielding choice steak. By the time the Confederacy surrendered, millions of longhorn were wandering freely across Texas. They had marginal economic value because the largest urban markets for beef were so far away—that is, until the railroads arrived.

**THE CATTLE BOOM** At the end of the Civil War, Kansas Pacific Railroad crews were beginning to lay rails in the buffalo country of the southern plains, between St. Louis and Kansas City. A few entrepreneurs began to imagine how the extension of the railroad might "establish a market whereby the Southern [cattle] drover and Northern buyer would meet upon an equal footing."

That junction was Abilene, in eastern Kansas, a "very small, dead place, consisting of about one dozen log huts." Once the rail lines reached Kansas from Missouri, Joseph G. McCoy, an Illinois livestock dealer, recognized the possibilities of driving vast herds of cattle raised in Texas northward to Kansas, where they would be loaded onto freight cars and sent to the rest of the nation.

In 1867, McCoy bought 250 acres in Abilene and built a stockyard, barn, office building, livestock scales, hotel, and a bank. He then sent an agent to Texas to convince the owners of herds bound north to go through Abilene. When the cattle reached Abilene in August 1867, they were loaded onto railcars and shipped to Chicago stockyards, where they were slaughtered and then sent (as sides of beef) around the nation.

Abilene flourished, and by 1871, an estimated 700,000 steers passed through the town every year. Moreover, the ability to ship large numbers of cattle by rail transformed ranching into a huge national industry and turned Kansas into a major economic crossroads.

Other cattle towns sprouted along the rail line: Ellsworth, Wichita, Caldwell, Dodge City. None lasted more than a few years. Once people bought farms nearby, they lobbied successfully to stop the Texas herds from coming through their area.

In response, cattlemen developed new routes north to new cow towns and rail hubs in Colorado, Wyoming, and Montana. Soon, those states had their own cattle ranches. By 1883, there were half a million cattle in eastern Montana alone, as the disappearing buffalo herds gave way to steers and sheep.

Cattle ranchers were forced to meet and develop their own code of laws and ways to enforce them. As cattle often wandered onto other ranchers' land, cowboys would "ride the line" to keep the animals off the adjoining ranches. In the spring, the cowboys would "round up" the herds, which invariably got mixed up, and sort out ownership by identifying the distinctive ranch symbols "branded," or burned, into the cattle.

**Herding cattle** Cowboys on horseback herd cattle into a corral beside the Cimarron River in 1905.

All that changed in 1873, when Joseph Glidden, an Illinois farmer, developed the first effective and inexpensive form of barbed-wire fencing. Soon the **open range**, where a small rancher could graze his cattle anywhere, was no more. Barbed-wire fences triggered "range wars," where small ranchers fought to retain the open range. The widespread use of barbed wire also ravaged Native American culture by denying Indians access to their ancestral lands.

**CHICAGO**  The rise of the cattle industry helped make Chicago the fastest-growing city in the nation. Located on Lake Michigan and served by several rivers and nine railroads in 1865, Chicago was the gateway to the western economy. It was a crossroads where city and frontier intersected. Its lumber yards, grain elevators, stockyards, and slaughterhouses became magnets for immigrants seeking jobs.

The meatpacking industry in places like Cincinnati and Chicago had started not with cattle but with hogs, in part because pork could be preserved longer (with salt and smoking) than beef. Since colonial days, pork packing had been one of the earliest and most important frontier industries. Hogs reproduce much faster than cattle, and they thrive on corn. As a nineteenth-century economist explained, "What is a hog, but fifteen or twenty bushels of corn on four legs?"

In 1850, Chicago slaughterhouses butchered and packed 20,000 hogs. By contrast, Cincinnati (called "Porkopolis") processed 334,000 each year. That changed as the federal government ordered vast quantities of pork for its armies. By 1862, Chicago had displaced Cincinnati as the world's largest pork-processing center. By the 1870s, thanks to the railroad connections, the city was processing more than 2 million hogs per year. The use of ice cut from frozen Lake Michigan and placed in freight trains enabled Chicago pork to be shipped all the way to the East Coast.

But there was no ice in the summer. This challenge led Gustavus F. Swift to begin experimenting with ways to "refrigerate" railcars year round. Within a few years, Swift and his main competitor, Philip Armour, had developed refrigerated freight cars that enabled them to ship processed meat, rather than live hogs and cattle.

This key innovation enabled Chicago to add beef packing to its hog-processing operations. "The refrigerator car," announced Swift and Company, "is one of the vehicles on which the packing industry has ridden to greatness." By the end of the nineteenth century, the economies of scale enjoyed by the four dominant Chicago meatpacking corporations drove most local butchers across the nation out of business.

**Innovative farming** Powered by more than a dozen horses and driven by two men, this early-nineteenth-century "combine" machine could, at the same time, cut, thresh, bag, and weigh wheat.

Swift and Armour became two of the richest men in the world. They soon branched out and became traders in grain—wheat and corn. They also built packing plants in cattle towns such as Kansas City and Omaha, and soon were processing almost half as much meat as Chicago.

**HOMESTEADERS** The first homesteaders in the Great Plains were mostly landless folk eager to try farming. Many had never used a hoe or planted a seed. "I was raised in Chicago without so much as a back yard to play in," said a Montana homesteader, "and I worked 48 hours a week for $1.25. When I heard you [a married couple] could get 320 acres just by living on it, I felt that I had been offered a kingdom." By 1900, the federal government had awarded some 270 million acres to 1.6 million people.

Yet they faced a grim struggle. Although land was essentially free through the Homestead Act (1862), horses, livestock, wagons, wells, lumber, fencing, seed, machinery, and fertilizer were not. Freight rates and interest rates were criminally high. Declining crop prices produced chronic indebtedness, leading strapped farmers to embrace virtually any plan to increase the money supply and thus pay off their debts with inflated currency. The virgin land itself, although fertile, resisted planting; the heavy sod woven with tough grass roots broke many a plow. Since wood and coal were rare on the prairie, pioneer families initially had to use buffalo chips (dried dung from buffaloes and cattle) for fuel.

Farm families also fought constant battles with tornadoes, hailstorms, windstorms, droughts, prairie fires, blizzards, wolves, and hostile Indians. Swarms of locusts often clouded the horizon; a Wichita newspaper reported in 1878 that they destroyed "every plant that is good for food or pleasant to the eyes." In the late 1880s, a prolonged drought forced many homesteaders to give up. In the end, two thirds of the people who gained land under the Homestead Act failed to become self-sustaining farmers.

**COMMERCIAL FARMING** Eventually, as the railroads brought lumber from the East, farmers could upgrade their houses built of sod ("Kansas brick") into more-comfortable wood-framed dwellings. New machinery and equipment, for those who could afford them, improved productivity. In 1868, James Oliver, a Scottish immigrant living in Indiana, made a sturdy chilled-iron "sodbuster" plow that greatly eased the task of preparing land for planting. New threshing machines, hay mowers, planters, manure spreaders, and other equipment also lightened the burden of farm labor but often deepened the debts that farmers owed.

Although the overall value of farmland and farm products increased, small farmers did not keep up. Their numbers grew in size but decreased in proportion to the population at large. Wheat in the western states, like cotton in the antebellum South, was the export crop that spurred economic growth. Few small farmers prospered, however, and by the 1890s, they were in open revolt against the "system" of corrupt processors (middlemen) and "greedy" bankers and railroaders who they believed conspired against them.

**WOMEN IN THE WEST** The West remained a largely male society. Most women in mining towns provided domestic services: cooking, cleaning, doing laundry. They were as valued as gold, since many mining towns had a male-to-female ratio as high as 9 to 1.

In both mining and farming communities, women were prized as spouses, in part because farming required help. But women pioneers continued to face many of the same legal barriers and social prejudices prevalent in the East. A wife could not sell property without her husband's approval. Texas women could not sue except for divorce, nor could they serve on juries, act as lawyers, or witness a will.

The constant fight for survival west of the Mississippi, however, made men and women there more equal partners than was typical in the East. Many women who lost their mates to the deadly toil of "sod busting" assumed responsibility for their farms. In general, women on the prairie became more independent than women leading domestic lives back East. A Kansas woman recalled "that the environment was such as to bring out and develop the dominant qualities of individual character. Kansas women of that day learned at an early age to depend on themselves—to do whatever work there was to be done, and to face danger when it must be faced, as calmly as they were able."

It was not coincidental, then, that the new western territories and states were among the first to allow women to vote and hold office—in the hopes that by doing so, they would attract more women settlers. In 1890, Wyoming was admitted to the Union as the first state that allowed women to vote. Utah, Colorado, and Idaho followed soon thereafter.

## THE FATE OF WESTERN INDIANS

As settlers spread across the continent, some 250,000 Native Americans, many of them originally from east of the Mississippi, were forced into what was supposed to be their last refuge, the Great Plains and mountain regions of the Far West. By signing the 1851 Fort Laramie Treaty, Plains Indians accepted tribal boundaries and allowed white pioneers to travel across their lands. Yet as the numbers of white settlers increased, fighting resumed.

**INDIAN RELATIONS IN THE WEST** From the early 1860s until the late 1870s, the trans-Mississippi West, often called "Indian Country," raged with the so-called **Indian wars**. Although the U.S. government had signed numerous treaties with Indian nations giving them ownership of reservation lands for "as long as waters run and the grass shall grow," those commitments were repeatedly violated by buffalo hunters, miners, ranchers, farmers, railroad surveyors—and horse soldiers.

In the 1860s, the federal government ousted numerous tribes from lands they had been promised would be theirs forever. A Sioux chieftain named Spotted Tail expressed the anger felt by many Indians when he asked, "Why does not the Great Father [U.S. president] put his red children on wheels so that he can move them as he will?"

In the two decades before the Civil War, the U.S. Army's central mission in the West was to protect pioneers traveling on the major Overland Trails. During and after the war, the mission changed to ensuring that Native

Americans stayed on the reservations and that settlers or miners did not trespass on Indian lands.

Emigrants, however, repeatedly violated the agreements. The result was simmering frustration punctuated by outbreaks of tragic violence. In the summer of 1862, an uprising by Sioux warriors in the Minnesota Valley resulted in the deaths of 644 white traders, settlers, government officials, and soldiers. It was the first of many clashes between settlers and miners and the Indians living on reservations.

**THE SAND CREEK MASSACRE**  Two years later, a horrible incident occurred in Colorado as a result of the influx of white miners. After Indians murdered a white family near Denver, John Evans, the territorial governor, called on whites to "kill and destroy" the "hostile Indians on the plains." At the same time, Evans persuaded "friendly Indians" (mostly Cheyenne and Arapaho) to gather at "places of safety" such as Fort Lyon, in southeastern Colorado near the Kansas border, where they were promised protection.

Despite that promise, at dawn on November 29, 1864, while most of the Indian men were off hunting, Colonel John M. Chivington's 700 militiamen attacked a camp of Cheyennes and Arapahos along Sand Creek, about forty miles from Fort Lyon. Black Kettle, the chief, waved first an American flag and then a white flag, but the soldiers paid no heed. Over seven hours, the Colorado militiamen slaughtered, scalped, and mutilated 165 peaceful Indians—men, women, children, and the elderly. Chivington, a former abolitionist and Methodist minister (the "Fighting Parson"), had told his men to "kill and scalp all [Indians], big and little, you come across."

In his report to army officials, Chivington claimed a great victory against 1,000 entrenched Cheyenne warriors. He was greeted as a hero back in Denver. "Colorado soldiers have again covered themselves in glory," the *Rocky Mountain News* initially proclaimed.

Then the truth about Sand Creek began to come out. Captain Silas Soule had witnessed the massacre, but, along with his company of soldiers, had disobeyed orders to join the attack. "I refused to fire and swore [to my men] that none but a coward" would shoot unarmed women and children.

Three weeks after the massacre, Soule wrote a letter to a superior officer revealing what had actually happened: "Hundreds of women and children were coming toward us, and getting on their knees for mercy," only to be murdered and "have their brains beat out by men professing to be civilized." Far from being a hero, Soule added, Chivington encouraged the slaughter through his *lack* of leadership: "There was no organization among our troops, they were a perfect mob—every man on his own hook." He predicted that "we will have a hell of a time with Indians this winter" because of the Sand Creek Massacre.

Congress and the army launched lengthy investigations, and Captain Soule was called to testify in January 1865. The eventual congressional report concluded that Chivington had "deliberately planned and executed a foul and dastardly massacre," murdering "in cold blood" Indians who "had every reason to believe they were under [U.S.] protection." An army general described the massacre as the "foulest and most unjustifiable crime in the annals of America."

Chivington resigned from the militia to avoid a military trial. He soon became the Denver sheriff. On April 23, 1865, Soule was shot and killed in Denver. One of his murderers—never prosecuted—was identified as one of Chivington's soldiers.

**SPREADING CONFLICT** The **Sand Creek Massacre** ignited warfare that raged across the central plains for the next three years, forcing the federal government to dispatch troops to the West. Arapaho, Cheyenne, and Sioux war parties attacked ranches and stagecoach stations, killing hundreds of white men and kidnapping many white women and children. The government responded by authorizing the recruitment of soldiers from among Confederate military prisoners (called "white-washed Rebels") and the creation of African American cavalry regiments.

In 1866, Congress passed legislation establishing two "colored" cavalry units and dispatched them to the western frontier. The Cheyenne nicknamed them "buffalo soldiers" because they "fought like a cornered buffalo."

The buffalo soldiers were mostly Civil War veterans from Louisiana and Kentucky. They built and maintained forts, mapped vast areas of the Southwest, strung hundreds of miles of telegraph lines, protected railroad construction crews, subdued hostile Indians, and captured outlaws and rustlers (horse and cattle thieves). Eighteen buffalo soldiers won Congressional Medals of Honor.

**INDIAN RELOCATION** A congressional committee in 1865 gathered evidence on the Indian wars and massacres. Its 1867 "Report on the Condition of the Indian Tribes" led to the creation of an Indian Peace Commission charged with removing the causes of the wars.

Congress decided that this would be best accomplished by persuading nomadic Indians yet again to move to out-of-the-way federal reservations where they could take up farming that would "civilize" them. They were to give up their ancestral lands in return for peace so that whites could move in. In 1870, Native Americans outnumbered white people in the Dakota Territory by 2 to 1; by 1880, whites, mostly gold prospectors, would outnumber Indians by more than 6 to 1. The U.S. government had decided it had no choice but to gain control of the region—by purchase if possible, by force if necessary.

In 1867, a conference at Medicine Lodge, Kansas, ended with the Kiowas, Comanches, Arapahos, and Cheyennes reluctantly agreeing to move to western Oklahoma. The following spring, the western Sioux (the Lakotas) signed the Treaty of Fort Laramie (1868). They agreed to settle within the huge Black Hills Reservation in southwestern Dakota Territory, in part because they viewed the Black Hills as sacred ground.

**GRANT'S INDIAN POLICY**  In his inaugural address in 1869, President Ulysses S. Grant urged Congress to adopt more-progressive policies toward Native Americans: "The proper treatment of *the original inhabitants of this land*" should enable the Native Americans "to become *citizens* with all the rights enjoyed by every other American."

Grant's noble intentions, however, ran afoul of longstanding prejudices and the unrelenting efforts of miners, farmers, railroaders, and ranchers to trespass on Indian lands and reservations. The president recognized the challenges; Indians, he admitted, "would be harmless and peaceable if they were not put upon by whites." Yet he also stressed that protecting the new transcontinental railroad was his top priority. In the end, however, Grant told army officers that "it is much better to support a peace commission than a [military] campaign against Indians."

Periodic clashes brought demands for military action. William T. Sherman, commanding general of the U.S. Army, directed General Philip Sheridan, head of the military effort in the West, to "kill and punish the hostiles [Indian war parties], capture and destroy the ponies" of the "Cheyennes, Arapahos, and Kiowas."

Neither Sherman nor Sheridan agreed with Grant's peace policy. In their view, the president's naive outlook reflected the distance between the Great Plains and Washington, D.C. Sherman ordered Sheridan to force all "nonhostile" Indians onto federal reservations, where they would be provided land for farming, immediate rations of food, and supplies and equipment (a promise that was rarely kept).

Some Native Americans refused to be moved again. In the southern plains of New Mexico, north Texas, Colorado, Kansas, and Oklahoma, Native Americans, dominated by the Comanches, focused on hunting buffalo. Armed clashes occurred with increasing frequency until the Red River War of 1874–1875, when Sheridan's soldiers won a series of battles in the Texas Panhandle. The defeated Comanches, Cheyennes, Kiowas, and Arapahos were forced onto reservations.

**CUSTER AND THE SIOUX**  Meanwhile, trouble was brewing again in the northern plains. White prospectors searching for gold were soon trespassing on Sioux hunting grounds in the Dakota Territory despite promises that the army would keep them out. Ohio senator John Sherman warned that nothing would stop the mass migration of Americans across the Mississippi River: "If the whole Army of the United States stood in the way, the wave of emigration would pass over it to seek the valley where gold was found."

The massive gold rush convinced some Indians to make a last stand. As Red Cloud, a Sioux chief, said, "The white men have crowded the Indians back year by year, and now our last hunting ground, the home of my people, is to be taken from us. Our women and children will starve, but for my part I prefer to die fighting rather than by starvation." Another prominent Sioux war chief, Sitting Bull, told Indians living on the Black Hills reservation that "the whites may get me at last, but I will have good times till then."

In 1875, Lieutenant Colonel George Armstrong Custer, a veteran Indian fighter driven by headstrong ambition and reckless courage, led 1,000 soldiers into the Black Hills, where he announced the discovery of gold near present-day Custer, South Dakota. The news set off a massive gold rush, and within two years, the mining town of Deadwood overflowed with 10,000 miners.

The undermanned army units in the area could not keep the miners from violating the rights guaranteed to the Sioux by federal treaties. President Grant and federal authorities tried to convince the Sioux to sell the Black Hills to the government for $6 million. Sitting Bull told the American negotiator to tell "the Great Father [Grant] that I do not want to sell any land to the government."

With that news, Custer was sent back to the Black Hills, this time to find roving bands of Sioux and Cheyenne warriors and force them back onto reservations. If they resisted, he was to kill them. It would not be easy. As General William T. Sherman said, the Sioux were the "most brave and warlike Savages of this Continent."

The colorful Custer, with his curly, golden hair and buckskin outfits, stood out among his horse soldiers. Free-spirited and fun-loving, he was one of the few soldiers who fought for the fun of it; to him, war was "glorious." President Grant, however, noted that Custer was "not a very level-headed man."

During the Civil War, Custer had earned a battlefield promotion to brevet general (a way of honoring gallantry without conferring the actual rank) at the age of twenty-three and had played an important role in the Union victory at Gettysburg by leading a gallant cavalry charge. Now he was preparing to attack the wandering bands of Sioux hunting parties, even though he recognized that intruding American miners had caused the renewal of warfare. As he told reporters, "We are goading the Indians to madness by invading their hallowed [hunting] grounds."

What became the **Great Sioux War** was the largest military campaign since the end of the Civil War. The war lasted fifteen months and entailed fifteen battles in present-day Wyoming, Montana, South Dakota, and Nebraska. In the end, more soldiers than Indians were killed, but the Native Americans were defeated.

**Battle of Little Bighorn, 1876**  Amos Bad Heart Bull, an Oglala Sioux artist and historian, painted this scene from the battle.

In June 1876, after several indecisive encounters, Custer found a large encampment of Sioux and their Northern Cheyenne and Arapaho allies on the Little Bighorn River in the southeast corner of the Montana Territory. Ignoring the warnings of his scouts, Custer split his force in two and attacked a Sioux village on June 25. "Hurrah boys, we've got them," he shouted, not realizing how outnumbered they were. Within minutes, the horse soldiers were surrounded by 2,500 warriors led by the fierce Crazy Horse, who deemed it "A good day to fight, a good day to die!"

After a half hour, the 210 horse soldiers, their ammunition exhausted, were all dead. Custer laughed as he fired his last bullet; he was then felled by shots to his head and heart. Also dead were two of his brothers, a brother-in-law, and a nephew. Afterward, Cheyenne women pierced Custer's eardrums with sewing needles because he had failed to listen to their warnings to stay out of their ancestral lands.

The Sioux had won their greatest battle, but doing so helped ensure that they would lose the war. Upon learning of the Battle of Little Bighorn ("Custer's Last Stand"), President Grant and Congress abandoned the peace policy and dispatched more supplies and troops to the plains. General Philip Sheridan now planned for "total war." Former Confederates wrote to President Grant to offer their services.

Under Sheridan's leadership, the army quickly regained the offensive and relentlessly pursued the Sioux and Cheyenne across Montana. Warriors were slain, villages destroyed, and food supplies burned.

Forced back onto reservations, the remaining Native Americans soon were struggling to survive. Many died of starvation or disease. By the end of 1876, the chiefs living on the Dakota reservation agreed to sell the Black Hills to the U.S. government.

In the spring of 1877, Crazy Horse and his people surrendered. The Great Sioux War was over, but the fate of Native Americans remained uncertain.

**THE DEMISE OF THE BUFFALO** The collapse of Indian resistance resulted as much from the decimation of the buffalo herds as from the actions of federal troops. In 1750, an estimated 30 million buffalo inhabited the plains. The herds were so vast that one traveler said they changed the color of the landscape, "blackening the whole surface of the country." By 1850, there were fewer than 10 million; by 1900, only a few hundred remained. (Today there are about 200,000.) What happened to them?

The conventional story focuses on intensive harvesting of buffalo by white commercial hunters after the Civil War. The construction of railroads through buffalo country brought hundreds of hunters who shipped huge numbers of hides to the East, where consumers developed a voracious demand for buffalo robes, buffalo leather, and trophy heads. The average commercial hunter killed 100 buffalo a day. "The buffalo," reported an army officer, "melted away like snow before a summer's sun."

The story is more complicated, however. A prolonged drought during the late 1880s and 1890s severely reduced the grasslands upon which the animals depended. At the same time, the buffalo had to compete for food with other grazing animals; by the 1880s, more than 2 million horses were roaming buffalo lands.

The Plains Indians themselves, empowered by horses and rifles and spurred by profits reaped from selling hides and meat to white traders, accounted for much of the devastation of the buffalo herds after 1840. If there had been no white hunters, the buffalo would probably have lasted only another thirty years because their numbers had been so greatly reduced by other factors. Whatever the reasons, the disappearance of the buffalo gave the Plains Indians little choice but to settle on government reservations.

**THE LAST RESISTANCE** In the Rocky Mountains and west to the Pacific Ocean, the story of courageous yet hopeless resistance to white intruders was repeated again and again. Indians were the last obstacle to white western expansion, and they suffered as a result.

The Blackfeet and Crows had to leave their homes in Montana. In a war along the California-Oregon boundary, the Modocs held out for six months in 1871–1872 before they were overwhelmed. In 1879, the Utes were forced to give up their vast territories in western Colorado. In Idaho, the peaceful Nez Perce bands refused to surrender land along the Salmon River, and prolonged fighting erupted there and in eastern Oregon.

In 1877, Joseph, a Nez Perce chief, led some 650 of his people on a 1,300-mile journey through Montana in hopes of finding safety in Canada. Just before reaching the border, they were caught by U.S. soldiers. As he surrendered, Joseph delivered an eloquent speech: "I am tired of fighting. Our chiefs are killed.... The old men are all dead.... I want to have time to look for my children, and see how

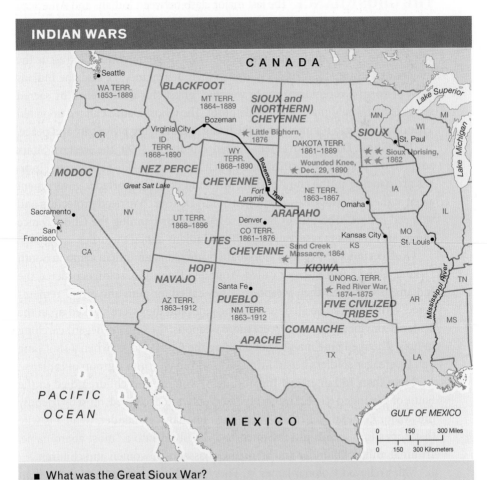

## INDIAN WARS

■ What was the Great Sioux War?
■ What happened at the Little Bighorn battle, and what were the consequences?
■ Why were hundreds of Native Americans killed at Wounded Knee?

many of them I can find. . . . My heart is sick and sad. From where the sun now stands I will fight no more forever." The Nez Perce requested that they be allowed to return to their ancestral lands in western Idaho, but they were forced to settle in the Indian Territory (Oklahoma), where many died of malaria.

A generation of Indian wars virtually ended in 1886 with the capture of Geronimo, a powerful chief of the Chiricahua Apaches, who had out-ridden, outwitted, and outfought American forces in the Southwest for fifteen years. General Nelson A. Miles, commander of the soldiers who captured Geronimo, called him "one of the brightest, most resolute, determined-looking men that I have ever encountered."

**THE GHOST DANCE**  The last major clash between Indians and American soldiers occurred near the end of the nineteenth century. Late in 1888, Wovoka (or Jack Wilson), a Paiute in western Nevada, fell ill. In a delirium, he imagined being in the spirit world, where he learned of a deliverer coming to rescue the Indians and restore their lands. To hasten their deliverance, he said, the Indians must perform a ceremonial dance wearing "ghost shirts" enlivened by sacred symbols that would make them bulletproof. The Ghost Dance cult fed upon old legends of the dead reuniting with the living and bringing prosperity and peace.

The **Ghost Dance movement** spread rapidly. In 1890, the western Sioux adopted the practice with such passion that it alarmed white authorities. "Indians are dancing in the snow and are wild and crazy," reported a government agent at the Pine Ridge Reservation in South Dakota. "We need protection and we need it now." The Indian Bureau responded by banning the Ghost Dance ceremony on Lakota reservations, but the Indians defied the order.

On December 29, 1890, a bloodbath occurred at an Indian camp in South Dakota, along a frozen creek called Wounded Knee. U.S. soldiers ordered the Indians to surrender their weapons. "They called for guns and arms," remembered White Lance, "so all of us gave the guns and they were stacked up in the center." Convinced that there were more weapons, the soldiers began searching in tipis. The medicine man began dancing the Ghost Dance when a shot rang out. Overeager soldiers began firing indiscriminately into a group of Indians.

More than 150 unarmed Indians, men, women, and children died in the Battle of Wounded Knee. Twenty-five soldiers were also killed, most by friendly fire. Major General Nelson A. Miles, the regional commander, wrote his wife that hopes for a peaceful settlement had dissolved into a "most abominable, criminal military blunder and a horrible massacre of women and children."

Miles relieved Colonel James W. Forsyth of his command and ordered an immediate inquiry into what had happened, for he was convinced that Forsyth's actions were "about the worst I have ever known." Yet the court of inquiry exonerated Forsyth and covered up the massacre, much to the chagrin of General Miles. Some twenty soldiers received the Congressional Medal of Honor.

**A CENTURY OF DISHONOR** The Indian wars ended with character-istic brutality and misunderstanding. General Philip Sheridan, overall com-mander of U.S. troops, was acidly candid in summarizing how whites had treated the Indians: "We took away their country and their means of support, broke up their mode of living, their habits of life, introduced disease and decay among them, and it was for this and against this that they made war. Could anyone expect less?"

Many politicians and religious leaders condemned the persistent mistreat-ment of Indians. In his annual message of 1877, President Rutherford B. Hayes joined the protest: "Many, if not most, of our Indian wars have had their origin in broken promises and acts of injustice on our part." Helen Hunt Jackson, a novelist and poet, focused attention on the Indian cause in *A Century of Dishonor* (1881), a book that powerfully detailed the sad history of America's exploitation of Native Americans.

In part as a reaction to Jackson's book, U.S. policies gradually improved but did little to enhance the Indians' difficult living conditions and actually helped destroy remnants of their culture. The reservation policy inaugurated by the Peace Commission in 1867, though partly humanitarian in motive, also saved money; housing and feeding Indians on reservations cost less than fighting them.

Well-intentioned but biased white reformers sought to "Americanize" Indi-ans by forcing them to become self-reliant farmers owning their own land rather than allowing them to be members of nomadic bands or tribes holding property in common. Such reform efforts produced the **Dawes Severalty Act** of 1887 (also called the General Allotment Act), the most sweeping policy directed at Native Americans in U.S. history. Sponsored by Senator Henry L. Dawes of Mas-sachusetts, it divided tribal lands and "allotted" them to individuals, granting 160 acres to each head of a family and lesser amounts to others.

White Bear, a Kiowa chief, said that his people did "not want to settle down in houses you [the federal government] would build for us. I love to roam over the wild prairie. There I am free and happy." But his preferences were ignored. Between 1887 and 1934, Indians lost an estimated 86 million of their 130 million acres. As Henry Teller, a congressman from Colorado, pointed out, the allot-ment policy was designed solely to strip the "Indians of their lands and to make them vagabonds on the face of the earth."

# THE END OF THE FRONTIER

The end of Native American resistance was one of several developments that suggested the New West was indeed different from the Old West. Other indicators of the region's transformation led some scholars to conclude that American society itself had reached a turning point.

**FREDERICK JACKSON TURNER** The 1890 national census data indicated that the frontier era was over; Americans had spread across the entire continent. This news led Frederick Jackson Turner, a historian at the University of Wisconsin, to announce in 1893 his "frontier thesis," which argued that more than slavery or any other single factor, "the existence of an area of free land, its continuous recession, and the advance of American settlement westward, explain American development." The experience of taming and settling the frontier, he added, had shaped the national character in fundamental ways. It was

> to the frontier [that] the American intellect owes its striking characteristics. That coarseness and strength combined with acuteness and acquisitiveness; that practical, inventive turn of mind, quick to find expedients; that masterful grasp of material things, lacking in the artistic but powerful to effect great ends; that restless, nervous energy; that dominant individualism, working for good and for evil, and withal that buoyancy and exuberance which comes with freedom—these are traits of the frontier, or traits called out elsewhere because of the existence of the frontier.

Now, however, Turner stressed, "the frontier has gone and with its going has closed the first period of American history."

Turner's view of the frontier gripped the popular imagination. But the frontier experience that he described was in many respects a self-serving myth involving only Christian white men and devoid of towns and cities, which grew *along* with the frontier—not after it had been tamed. He virtually ignored the role of women, African Americans, Native Americans, Hispanics, and Asians in shaping the western United States. Moreover, Turner downplayed the vivid evidence of greed, exploitation, and the failure of many dreamers in the settling of the West.

He also implied that America would be fundamentally different after 1890 because the frontier experience was essentially over. In many respects, however, the West has retained the qualities associated with the rush for land, gold, timber, and water rights. The mining frontier, as one historian recently wrote, "set a mood that has never disappeared from the West: the attitude of every extractive industry—get in, get rich, get out."

**DISCONTENTED FARMERS** By 1900, both the South and West were quite different from what they had been in 1865. In both cases, changed economic conditions spurred the emergence of a New South and a New West.

In the West, mechanized commercial agriculture changed the dynamics of farming. By the end of the nineteenth century, many homesteaders had been

**Chinese immigrants in Wyoming** These Chinese immigrants were paid lower wages than their white counterparts in the mines of Rock Springs, Wyoming. They continued to work in the mines through a wave of anti-Chinese violence that included the Rock Springs massacre of 1885.

forced to abandon their farms and become wage-earning laborers, migrant workers moving with the seasons to different states to harvest crops produced on large commercial farms or ranches. They were often treated as poorly as the white and black sharecroppers in the South. One western worker complained that the landowner "looked at me, his hired hand, as if I was just another workhorse."

As discontent rose among farmers and farmworkers in the South and the West, many joined the People's party, whose followers were known as Populists, a grassroots social and political movement that was sweeping the poorest rural regions of the nation. In 1892, a Minnesota farm leader named Ignatius Donnelly told Populists at their national convention: "We meet in the midst of a nation brought to the verge of moral, political, and material ruin." He affirmed that Populism sought "to restore the Government of the Republic to the hands of the 'plain people' with whom it originated."

The Populist movement would tie the South and West together in an effort to wrest political control from Republicans in the Northeast and Midwest. That struggle would come to define the 1890s and determine the shape of twentieth-century politics.

# CHAPTER REVIEW

## SUMMARY

- **The New South**   Many southerners embraced the vision of the New South promoted by Henry Grady and others, who called for a more diverse economy with greater industrialization, more vocational training, and widespread acceptance of white supremacy. But agriculture—and especially cotton—still dominated the southern economy, much as it had before the Civil War. Under the *crop-lien system*, large landowners rented land to cash-poor tenant farmers or sharecroppers (the latter usually African Americans) in return for a "share" of the cotton they grew each year.

- **Jim Crow Policies in the South**   During the 1890s, southern states disenfranchised the vast majority of African American voters and instituted a series of policies known as Jim Crow laws segregating blacks and whites in public facilities. State governments across the South passed a series of measures that included poll taxes, grandfather clauses, literacy tests, and residency requirements, making voting nearly impossible for most African Americans and some poor whites. Disenfranchisement was followed by legalized segregation (*separate but equal*), ruled constitutional by the Supreme Court in *Plessy v. Ferguson* (1896). African Americans who resisted were often the target of violence at the hands of whites, the most gruesome form being organized lynching. African Americans in the South responded by turning inward and strengthening their own social institutions.

- **Western Migrants**   Life in the West was often harsh, but the promise of cheap land or wealth from mining drew settlers from the East. Although most westerners were white Protestant Americans or immigrants from Germany and Scandinavia, Mexicans, African Americans (the *Exodusters*), and Chinese, as well as many other nationalities, contributed to the West's diversity. About three fourths of those who moved to the West were men.

- **Miners, Farmers, Ranchers, and Women**   Many migrants to the West were attracted to opportunities to mine, ranch, farm, or work on the railroads. Miners were drawn to the discovery of precious minerals such as silver at the *Comstock Lode* in Nevada in 1861. But most miners and cattle ranchers did not become wealthy, because mining and raising cattle, particularly after the development of barbed wire and the end of the *open range*, became large-scale enterprises. Farmers on the Great Plains were able to produce wheat for export, but declining grain prices and the need for expensive machinery and transportation meant that only large-scale farms owned by a wealthy few could sustain real profits.

- **Indian Wars and Policies**   By 1900, Native Americans were no longer free to roam the plains, as the influx of miners, ranchers, farmers, and soldiers had curtailed their traditional way of life. Instances of armed resistance, such as the *Great*

*Sioux War (1876–1877)*, were crushed. Beginning in 1887 the *Dawes Severalty Act* forced Indians to relinquish their traditional culture and adopt the "American way" of individual landownership. The prevailing attitude of most whites in the West was to displace or exterminate the Native Americans. After the *Sand Creek Massacre* in 1864, conflicts between U.S. Army units and Native Americans, called the *Indian wars*, continued for most of the century. The last major conflict at Wounded Knee resulted from the *Ghost Dance movement*.

- **The South and West in 1900**   In 1893, Frederick Jackson Turner, a prominent historian, declared that the frontier had been the nation's primary source of democratic politics and rugged individualism. By 1900, however, the frontier era was over. The West resembled the South, where agricultural resources were concentrated in the hands of a few. In the 1890s, poor farmers in the West joined tenant farmers in the South to support the People's party or the Populist movement.

## CHRONOLOGY

| | |
|---|---|
| **1862** | Congress passes the Homestead Act |
| **1864** | Sand Creek Massacre |
| **1876** | Battle of Little Bighorn |
| **1880s** | Henry Grady spreads the New South idea |
| **1886** | Capture of Geronimo marks the end of the Indian wars |
| **1890** | Battle of Wounded Knee |
| **1893** | Frederick J. Turner outlines his "frontier thesis" |
| **1896** | *Plessy v. Ferguson* mandates "separate but equal" racial facilities |

## KEY TERMS

**textile industry** p. 733

**redeemers** p. 734

**crop-lien system** p. 735

**Mississippi Plan (1890)** p. 737

**separate but equal** p. 740

**Atlanta Compromise (1895)** p. 746

**Exodusters** p. 750

**Comstock Lode** p. 752

**open range** p. 755

**Indian wars** p. 758

**Sand Creek Massacre (1864)** p. 760

**Great Sioux War** p. 762

**Ghost Dance movement** p. 766

**Dawes Severalty Act (1887)** p. 767

 INQUIZITIVE

Go to InQuizitive to see what you've learned—and learn what you've missed—with personalized feedback along the way.

# 19 Political Stalemate and Rural Revolt

## 1865–1900

***New York, 1911*** This scene of early-twentieth-century life in New York City by George Wesley Bellows captures people of all walks of life converging on a busy, vibrant downtown intersection.

Within three decades after the Civil War, American life had experienced a stunning transformation. An agricultural society long rooted in the soil and little involved in global issues had become an urban, industrialized nation deeply entwined in world markets and international politics.

The period from the end of the Civil War to the beginning of the twentieth century brought a widening social, economic, and political gap between the powerful and powerless, the haves and have-nots. It was labeled the **Gilded Age** for its greed and vulgarity, as the newly rich flaunted their personal wealth— the same wealth that financed extensive political and corporate corruption.

## URBAN AMERICA

Between 1865 and 1900, the United States became a nation dominated by rapidly growing cities. The urban population skyrocketed from 8 million to 30 million. European and Asian immigrants, as well as migrants from America's rural areas, streamed into cities, attracted by plentiful jobs. Many had been pushed off the land by new agricultural machinery that reduced the need for farmworkers. Still others, bored by rural or small-town life, moved to cities in search of more excitement.

### *focus questions*

**1.** What were the effects of urban growth during the Gilded Age? What problems did it create?

**2.** Who were the "new immigrants" of the late nineteenth century? How were they viewed by American society?

**3.** How did urban growth and the increasingly important role of science influence leisure activities, cultural life, and social policy in the Gilded Age?

**4.** How did the nature of politics during the Gilded Age contribute to political corruption and stalemate?

**5.** How effective were politicians in developing responses to the major economic and social problems of the Gilded Age?

**6.** Why did the money supply become a major political issue, especially for farmers, during the Gilded Age? How did it impact American politics?

Whatever the reasons, America increasingly became an urban society. "We cannot all live in cities," cautioned Horace Greeley, the New York newspaper editor and 1872 Democratic presidential candidate, "yet nearly all seem determined to do so."

While the Far West had the greatest proportion of urban dwellers, concentrated in cities such as San Francisco and Denver, the Northeast and Midwest held far more people in huge cities—New York, Boston, Philadelphia, Pittsburgh, Chicago, Cincinnati, St. Louis, and others. Most city dwellers had little money and nothing but their labor to sell. And they were forced to live in congested, germ-ridden hovels that seemed like prison cells.

Fortunately, researchers were making discoveries that improved living conditions, public health, economic productivity, and communications. Advances in science stimulated public support for higher education but also created doubts about many long-accepted "truths" and religious beliefs.

**GROWTH IN ALL DIRECTIONS** Advances in technology helped cities hold their surging populations. In the 1870s, heating innovations, such as steam radiators, made the construction of much larger apartment buildings financially feasible, because expensive coal-burning fireplaces and chimneys were no longer needed in each apartment. During the 1880s, engineers developed cast-iron and steel-frame construction techniques that allowed for taller structures known as "skyscrapers." When the Otis Elevator Company installed the first electric elevator in 1889, taller buildings were immediately more practical to design and inhabit.

Cities grew out as well as up, as horse-drawn streetcars and commuter railways allowed people to live farther away from their workplaces. In 1873, San Francisco became the first city to use cable cars that clamped onto a moving underground cable driven by a central power source. Some cities ran steam-powered trains on elevated tracks, but by the 1890s, electric trolleys were preferred. Mass transit received an added boost from underground subway trains built in Boston, New York City, and Philadelphia.

Commuter trains and trolleys allowed a growing middle class of business executives and professionals (accountants, doctors, engineers, sales clerks, teachers, store managers, and attorneys) to retreat from crowded downtowns to quieter, tree-lined "streetcar suburbs." But the working poor could rarely afford to leave the inner cities. As their populations grew, cities became dangerously congested and plagued with fires, violent crimes, and disease.

**CROWDS, DIRT, AND DISEASE** The wonders of big cities— electric lights, streetcars, telephones, department stores, theaters, and other attractions—lured rural dwellers bored by isolated farm life. Yet they often

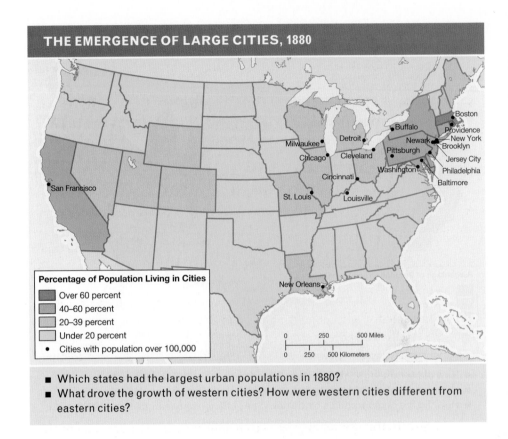

**THE EMERGENCE OF LARGE CITIES, 1880**

Percentage of Population Living in Cities
- Over 60 percent
- 40–60 percent
- 20–39 percent
- Under 20 percent
- Cities with population over 100,000

■ Which states had the largest urban populations in 1880?
■ What drove the growth of western cities? How were western cities different from eastern cities?

traded one set of problems for another. In New York City in 1900, some 2.3 million people—two thirds of the city's population—lived in overcrowded apartments called **tenements** that bred disease, frustration, and crime.

Tenement buildings were usually five to six stories tall, lacked elevators, and were jammed so tightly together that most of the apartments had little or no natural light or fresh air. They typically housed twenty-four to thirty-two families, whose children had few places to play except in the streets. On average, only one toilet (called a *privy*) served every twenty people.

Late nineteenth-century cities were filthy and disease-ridden. Streets were filled with contaminated water, horse urine and manure, and roaming pigs. Sidewalks were festooned with tobacco spit, which spread tuberculosis. Garbage and raw sewage were dumped into streets and waterways, causing epidemics of infectious diseases such as cholera, typhoid fever, and yellow fever. The child-mortality rate in tenements was as high as 40 percent. In one poor Chicago district, three of every five babies died before their first birthday.

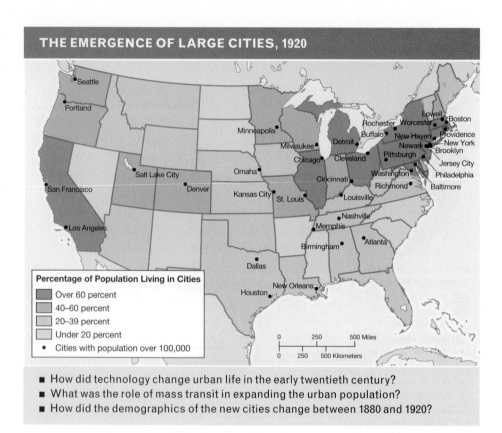

## THE EMERGENCE OF LARGE CITIES, 1920

**Percentage of Population Living in Cities**

- Over 60 percent
- 40–60 percent
- 20–39 percent
- Under 20 percent
- • Cities with population over 100,000

- How did technology change urban life in the early twentieth century?
- What was the role of mass transit in expanding the urban population?
- How did the demographics of the new cities change between 1880 and 1920?

So-called sanitary reformers—public health officials and engineers—eventually developed regulations requiring more space per resident, as well as more windows and plumbing facilities. While pushing successfully for modern water and sewage systems and regular trash collection, reformers also lobbied to ban slaughterhouses and hogs and cattle within city limits, and to replace horse-drawn trolleys with electric-powered streetcars.

## THE NEW IMMIGRATION

America's roaring prosperity and promise of political and religious freedom attracted waves of immigrants after the Civil War. By 1900, nearly 30 percent of city residents were foreign-born. Most were desperately poor and eager to pursue the American dream. They brought with them a distinctive work ethic. Working only to survive is often wretched. Working for a better life for oneself and one's family gives labor a fierce dignity. That dignity, infused with energy and aspiration, endowed the immigrants with resilience and determination. In providing much-needed labor for the growing economy, however, the influx of immigrants also sparked racial and ethnic tensions.

**A SURGE OF NEWCOMERS** Immigration has always been one of the most powerful and controversial forces in shaping America. This was especially true between 1860 and 1900, as more and more foreigners arrived from eastern and southern Europe. The number of immigrants rose from just under 3 million annually in the 1870s to nearly 9 million annually in the first decade of the twentieth century. In 1890, four out of five New Yorkers were foreign-born, a higher proportion than in any city in the world.

Rapidly growing industries—including mines, railroads, mills, and factories—sought low-wage workers; they sent agents abroad to lure immigrants to the United States. Under the Contract Labor Act of 1864, the federal government helped pay for immigrants' travel expenses to America. The law was repealed in 1868, but not until 1885 did the government stop companies

**Ellis Island** To accommodate the soaring numbers of immigrants passing through New York City, Congress built a reception center on Ellis Island, near the Statue of Liberty. Pictured here is its registry room, where immigrants awaited close questioning by officials.

from importing foreign laborers, a practice that put immigrant workers under the control of their employers.

The so-called "old immigrants" who came before 1880 were mainly Protestants and Roman Catholics from northern and western Europe. Germans were the single largest ethnic population in America by 1900, and most of them eventually settled in the Midwest.

The traditional pattern of immigration changed, however, as the proportion of immigrants from southern and eastern Europe, especially Russia, Poland, Greece, and Italy, rose. The languages and cultural backgrounds of these "**new immigrants**" were markedly different from those of previous immigrants or of most native-born Americans. The dominant religions of new immigrants, for example, were Judaism, Eastern Orthodox, and Roman Catholicism, whereas Protestants still formed a large majority of the U.S. population.

While many immigrants gravitated to large cities in the East and Midwest, others headed West. By 1890, an estimated 45 percent of people living in North Dakota were foreign-born. In South Dakota, California, and Washington, nearly 30 percent of residents were immigrants, and in virtually every western state the foreign-born made up more than 20 percent of the population.

The percentage of foreign-born residents in the South, however, declined between 1860 and 1900. By 1910, only 2 percent of southerners were immigrants, compared to the national average of 15 percent. Newcomers avoided the South because of its low wages, racial dynamics, and widespread poverty.

In 1907, Congress appointed the Dillingham Commission to examine the changes in immigration patterns. In its lengthy report, released in 1911, the commission concluded that immigrants from southern and eastern Europe posed a social and cultural threat to America's future. They were "far less intelligent than the old, approximately one-third of all those over 14 years of age when admitted being illiterate. Racially, they are for the most part essentially unlike the British, German and other peoples who came during the prior period to 1880, and generally speaking they are actuated in coming by different ideals."

Immigrants were usually desperately poor and needed to find jobs—quickly. And since most of them knew little if any English and nothing about American employment practices, they were easy targets for exploitation. Many unwittingly lost a healthy percentage of their wages to unscrupulous hiring agents in exchange for a bit of whiskey and a job. Companies gave immigrants train tickets to inland cities such as Buffalo, Pittsburgh, Cleveland, Chicago, Milwaukee, Cincinnati, and St. Louis.

Most immigrants naturally wanted to live in neighborhoods populated by people from their homeland. The largest cities had vibrant districts with

**Mulberry Street, 1900** This colorized photograph captures the many Italian immigrants who made Mulberry Street in downtown New York City their home at the turn of the century. Horse-drawn carts weave through crowds shopping, socializing, and people gazing.

names such as Little Italy, Little Hungary, and Chinatown, where immigrants practiced their native religions and customs and spoke and read newspapers in their native languages. But they paid a price for such solidarity. When new immigrants moved into an area, the previous residents often moved out, taking with them whatever social prestige and political influence they had achieved.

**THE NATIVIST RESPONSE** Then, as now, many native-born Americans saw immigrants as a threat to their jobs and way of life. Many "**nativists**" were racists who believed that "Anglo-Saxon" Americans—people of British or Germanic background—were superior to the Slavic, Italian, Greek, and Jewish arrivals.

During the late nineteenth century, anti-immigrant prejudice took an ugly turn against Chinese people, most of whom lived in California. The first non-European and non-African group to migrate in large numbers to America, Chinese were easy targets for discrimination; they were not white, they were not Christian, and many could not read or write. Whites resented them for taking their jobs, although in many instances Chinese laborers were willing to do work that whites refused to do.

**Chinese Exclusion Act** Chinese caricature "John Chinaman" is escorted out of America by Lady Liberty with his ironing board and opium pipe, while other accepted minorities look on.

Until 1875, immigration policies had been left to the states. In that year, however, Congress passed the Page Act, the first federal law intended to restrict "undesirable" immigration. It prohibited Asian prostitutes, convicts, and anyone entering the country under an arrangement of "forced labor" (a form of slavery).

Seven years later, in 1882, anti-Chinese sentiment on the West Coast led to the passage of the **Chinese Exclusion Act**. It was the first federal law to restrict the immigration of free people on the basis of race and class. The act, which barred Chinese laborers ("yellow hordes") from entering the country for ten years, was periodically renewed before being extended indefinitely in 1902. Not until 1943 were barriers to Chinese immigration finally removed.

Chinese were not the only group targeted. In 1887, Protestant activists in Iowa formed the American Protective Association (APA), a secret organization whose members pledged never to employ or vote for a Roman Catholic. Working often within local Republican party organizations, the APA quickly enlisted 2.5 million members and helped shape the 1894 elections in Ohio, Wisconsin, Indiana, Missouri, and Colorado.

In 1891, nativists in New England formed the Immigration Restriction League to, in their words, "save" the Anglo-Saxon "race" from being "contaminated" by "alien" immigrants, especially Roman Catholics and Jews. The League convinced Congress to ban illiterate immigrants. Three presidents vetoed such bills: Grover Cleveland in 1897, William Howard Taft in 1913, and Woodrow Wilson in 1915 and 1917. The last time, however, Congress overrode the veto, and illiterate immigrants were banned.

## CULTURAL LIFE

The flood of people into cities brought changes in recreation and leisure. Middle- and upper-class families, especially those in the suburbs, often spent free time at home, singing around a piano, reading, or playing games. In urban

**Vaudeville** For as little as 1¢ for admission, vaudeville shows aimed to please the tastes of their wildly diverse audiences with a great range of entertainment.

areas, politics as a form of public entertainment attracted large crowds. New forms of mass entertainment—movie theaters; music halls; vaudeville shows featuring singers, dancers, and comedians; art museums, symphonies, sporting events; Wild West shows; and circuses—drew a broad cross-section of residents. In large cities, streetcars allowed people to travel easily to sporting events, and rooting for the home team helped unify ethnic and racial groups and social classes. At the end of the century, sports of all kinds had become a major part of popular culture.

By encouraging what one writer called a "mania for facts," scientists also generated changes in social, intellectual, and cultural life. Scientific research led to transformational technologies such as electric power and lights, telephones, phonographs, motion pictures, bicycles, and automobiles.

Although only men could vote in most states, both men and women flocked to political meetings. In the largest cities, membership in a political party offered many social benefits. As labor unions became increasingly common, they took on social roles for working-class men.

**SALOONS** The most popular leisure destinations for urban wage workers were **saloons**, beer gardens, and dance halls. By 1900, the United States had more saloons (more than 325,000) than grocery stores and meat markets. New York City alone had 10,000 saloons, one for every 500 residents.

Saloons were especially popular among immigrants seeking companionship. In cities such as New York, Boston, Philadelphia, and Chicago, the customers were disproportionately Irish, German, and Italian Catholics. Politics was often the topic of intense discussions in saloons. In New York City in the 1880s, saloons doubled as polling places during elections. Men also went to saloons to check job postings, participate in labor unions, cash paychecks, mail letters, read newspapers, and gossip. Patrons could play chess, billiards, darts, cards, dice, or even handball, since many saloons included gymnasiums. Because saloons were heated and had restrooms, they served as refuges for the homeless, especially in the winter.

Although saloons were for men only, women and children could use a side door to buy a pail of beer to carry home (a task called "rushing the growler"). Some saloons also provided "snugs," separate rooms for women customers. "Stall saloons" included "wine rooms" where prostitutes worked.

**LEISURE FOR WOMEN**  Married working-class women had even less leisure time than working-class men did. Many were working for pay themselves, and even those who were not were frequently overwhelmed by housework and child-rearing responsibilities. As a social worker noted, "The men have the saloons, political clubs, trade-unions or [fraternal] lodges for their

**Steeplechase Park, Coney Island, Brooklyn, New York**  Members of the working class could afford the inexpensive rides at this popular amusement park.

recreation . . . while the mothers have almost no recreation, only a dreary round of work, day after day, with occasionally doorstep gossip to vary the monotony of their lives."

Married working-class women often used the streets as their public space. Washing clothes, supervising children at play, or shopping at the local market provided opportunities for socializing.

Single women, many of them housekeepers ("maids"), had more free time than working mothers. They flocked to dance halls, theaters, amusement parks, and picnic grounds. With the advent of movie theaters, the cinema became the most popular form of entertainment for working women. As an advertisement promised, "If you are tired of life, go to the movies. If you are sick of troubles rife, go to the picture show. You will forget your unpaid bills, rheumatism and other ills, if you stow your pills and go to the picture show."

## THE IMPACT OF DARWINISM

Virtually every field of thought felt the impact of natural scientist Charles Darwin's *On the Origin of Species* (1859), one of the most influential books ever written. Basing his conclusions on extensive yet "imperfect" field research conducted around the world, Darwin showed how the chance processes of evolution give energy and unity to life. At the center of his concept was "natural selection." He demonstrated that most organisms produce many more off-spring than can survive. The offspring with certain favorable characteristics adapt and live, while the others die from starvation, disease, or predators.

This "struggle for existence" drove the process of natural selection, Darwin said. Over many millions of years, modern species "evolved" from less complex forms of life; individuals and species that had characteristics advantageous for survival reproduced, while others died off. As Darwin wrote, "the vigorous, the healthy, and the happy survive and multiply."

Darwin's theory was shocking bec-ause most people still embraced a literal interpretation of the biblical creation

**Charles Darwin** Darwin's scientific theories influenced more than a century of political and social debate.

story, which claimed that God created all species at the same moment and they remained the same thereafter. Although Darwin was reluctant to be drawn into religious controversy, his biological findings suggested to many, then and since, that there was no providential God controlling the universe. People were no different from plants and animals; they too evolved by trial and error rather than by God's purposeful hand.

Many Christians charged that Darwin's ideas led to atheism, a denial of the existence of God, while others found their faith severely shaken. Most of the faithful, however, decided that the process of evolutionary change in nature must be God's doing.

**SOCIAL DARWINISM**    Although Darwin's theory of evolution applied only to biological phenomena, many applied it to human society. Englishman Herbert Spencer, a leading social philosopher, was the first major prophet of what came to be called **social Darwinism**.

Spencer argued that society and its institutions, like the organisms studied by Darwin, evolved through natural selection. The "survival of the fittest," in Spencer's chilling phrase, was the engine of social progress. By encouraging people, ideas, and nations to compete for dominance, society would generate "the greatest perfection and the most complete happiness."

Darwin dismissed Spencer's theories as "unconvincing." He did not believe that the evolutionary process had any relevance to human social institutions. Others, however, eagerly endorsed social Darwinism.

Social Darwinism implied the need for hands-off, laissez-faire government policies; it argued against the regulation of business or of required minimum standards for sanitation and housing. To Spencer, the only acceptable charity was voluntary, and even that was of dubious value. He warned that "fostering the good-for-nothing [people] at the expense of the good, is an extreme cruelty" to the health of civilization.

For Spencer and his many supporters, successful businessmen and corporations provided proof of the concept of survival of the fittest. Oil tycoon John D. Rockefeller revealed his embrace of social Darwinism when he told his Baptist Sunday-school class that the "growth of a large business is merely a survival of the fittest. . . . This is not an evil tendency in business. It is merely the working-out of a law of nature and a law of God."

In 1872, Spencer's chief academic disciple, William Graham Sumner, began teaching at Yale University, where he preached the gospel of natural selection. Sumner's most lasting contribution, made in his book *Folkways* (1907), was to argue that it would be a mistake for government to try to promote equality, since doing so would interfere with the "survival of the fittest."

**REFORM DARWINISM** Sumner's efforts to use Darwinism to promote "rugged individualism" and oppose government regulation of business prompted an alternative use of Darwinism in the context of human society. What came to be called **reform Darwinism** found its major advocate in Lester Frank Ward, a government employee who fought his way up from poverty and never lost his empathy for the underdog.

Ward's *Dynamic Sociology* (1883) singled out one aspect of evolution that both Darwin and Spencer had neglected: the human brain. True, as Sumner claimed, people, like animals, compete. But, as Ward explained, people also collaborate. Unlike animals, people can plan for the future; they are capable of shaping and directing social change. Far from being the helpless object of irresistible evolutionary forces, Ward argued, humanity could actively control social evolution through long-range planning.

Ward's reform Darwinism held that *cooperation*, not *competition*, would better promote social progress. Government, in Ward's view, should pursue two main goals: alleviating poverty, which impeded the development of the mind, and promoting the education of the masses. Intellect, informed by science, could foster social improvement. Reform Darwinism would prove to be one of the pillars of the progressive movement during the late nineteenth century and after.

## Realism in Literature and Art

Before the Civil War, Romanticism had dominated American literature and painting. The New England transcendentalists had believed that fundamental truths rested in the unseen world of ideas and spirit. They viewed nature—woods, fields, valleys, and mountains—as a springboard to the sacred and took notice of the divinity residing in outdoor scenes.

During the second half of the nineteenth century, however, writers and artists calling themselves "realists" began to challenge the "sentimentality" and nature-worshipping credo of the Romantic tradition. A writer in *Putnam's Monthly* noted in 1854 a growing emphasis on "the real and the practical." This emphasis on "realism" matured into a full-fledged cultural force, as more and more writers and artists focused on depicting the actual aspects of urban-industrial America: scientific research and technology, factories and railroads, cities and immigrants, labor unions and social tensions.

For many, the horrors of the Civil War had led to a more realistic view of life. An editor attending an art exhibition in 1865 sensed "the greater reality of feeling developed by the war. We have grown more sober, perhaps, and less patient of romantic idealism."

Another factor contributing to the rise of realism was the impact of science. The "stupendous power of Science," announced one editor, would rid American thought of "every old-time idea, every trace of old romance and art, poetry and romantic or sentimental feeling" and wash away the "ideal . . . and visionary."

Embracing realism, as writer Fanny Bates stressed, meant that stories and novels should be fed by facts and enlivened by textured social details. Authors should cast a roving eye on daily life and tell about life as it *is*, rather than how it should be. The tone of such writing and art appealed especially to people living in busy, swarming cities.

The worship of money was the most common theme in realistic novels, short stories, and portraits during the Gilded Age. In William Dean Howells's *The Rise of Silas Lapham* (1885), Bromfield Corey announces that money "is the romance, the poetry of our age." Lily Bart, the heroine of Edith Wharton's *The House of Mirth* (1905), declares that she "must have a great deal of money" to be happy.

***Stag at Sharkey's* (1909)** New York painter George Bellows witnessed fierce boxing matches across the street from his studio, at the saloon of retired heavyweight boxer "Sailor" Sharkey. Bellows is one of the most famous artists from the Ashcan School, which was committed to capturing the gritty reality of the urban scene.

City streets, sidewalks, and parks provided countless scenes of *real* life to depict on canvas and in words. Novelist Henry James said that the urban scene unleashed a "flood of the real" to study and portray. John Sloan, a New York City painter, confided in his diary that he was addicted to "watching every bit of human life" through his windows and along the sidewalks.

Others shared Sloan's "spectatorial" sensibility. "My favorite pastime," writer Theodore Dreiser remembered, "was to walk the city streets and view the lives and activities of others." In Dreiser's influential novel *Sister Carrie* (1900), Carrie Meeber uses her "gift of observation" to view strangers through the windows of shops, offices, and factories, imagining what "they deal with, how they labored, to what end it all came."

The realists' approach grew out of the scientific spirit. Just as scientists sought verifiable facts and transformed them into knowledge, cultural realists studied the world and expressed what they saw in art and literature. Like a gust of fresh air, they made Americans aware of the significance of all aspects of their everyday surroundings.

## GILDED AGE POLITICS

The Gilded Age brought more political corruption than political innovation. In 1879, Woodrow Wilson, then a young college graduate, described the political system as having "no leaders, no principles."

Political parties were more powerful than presidents during the Gilded Age, and business tycoons were more powerful than parties. So-called captains of industry used their wealth to "buy" elections and favors. Jay Gould, one of the most aggressive railroad tycoons, admitted that he elected "the [New York] legislature with my own money."

By the end of the nineteenth century, however, new movements and parties were pushing to reform the excesses and injustices created by the corrupt political system. As reformer Lyman Abbott maintained, "Politically America is a democracy; industrially America is an aristocracy."

**LOCAL POLITICS AND PARTY LOYALTIES** Perhaps the most important feature of Gilded Age politics was its local focus. Most political activity occurred at the state and local levels; the federal government was an insignificant force in the daily lives of most citizens, in part because it was so small. In 1871, the federal civilian workforce totaled 51,000 (most of them postal workers), of whom only 6,000 actually worked in Washington, D.C. Not until the twentieth century did the importance of the federal government begin to surpass that of local and state governments.

Americans were intensely loyal to their chosen political party, which they joined as much for the fellowship and networking connections as for its positions on issues. Unlike today, party members paid dues to join, and party leaders regularly demanded large campaign contributions from the captains of industry and finance. Collis Huntington, a California railroad tycoon, admitted that bribery in the form of campaign contributions was expected: "If you have to pay money to have the right thing done, then it is only just and fair to do it." Roscoe Conkling, a Republican senator from New York, was equally candid: "Of course, we do rotten things in New York. . . . Politics is a rotten business."

In cities crowded with new immigrant voters, politics was usually controlled by "rings"—small groups who shaped policy and managed elections. Each ring typically had a powerful "boss" who used his "machine"—a network of neighborhood activists and officials—to govern.

Colorful, larger-than-life figures such as New York City's William "Boss" Tweed ruled, plundered, and occasionally improved municipal government, often through dishonest and unethical means. Until his arrest in 1871 and conviction in 1873, Tweed used the Tammany Hall ring to dole out contracts to business allies and jobs to political supporters.

Although the various city rings and bosses were often corrupt, they did bring structure, stability, and services to rapidly growing inner-city communities, many of which were composed of immigrants newly arrived from Ireland, Germany, and, increasingly, from southern and eastern Europe.

The party in power expected the government employees it appointed to do the bidding of **party bosses**, who often decided who the candidates would be and commanded loyalty and obedience by rewarding and punishing party members. They helped settle local disputes, provided aid for the poor, and distributed government jobs and contracts to loyal followers and corporate donors through the **patronage** system. President Ulysses S. Grant's secretary told a Republican party boss that he hoped "you will distribute the patronage in such a manner as will help the Administration."

Throughout the Gilded Age, almost every government job—local, state, and federal—was subject to the latest election results. The jobs given to party loyalists ranged from cabinet posts to courthouse clerk positions. The largest single source of political jobs was the postal service, which accounted for half of all federal civilian employees. Those who were awarded government jobs (patronage) were expected to contribute a percentage of their salary to their party.

The corruption associated with the patronage system eventually drew criticism from civil service reformers, progressives who pushed through legislation designed to limit such patronage. They advocated a "merit system" for government employment based on ability and experience.

**"'Coming Out'—For Harrison"** This 1888 cartoon depicts efforts by employers to force the working class to vote for the Republican party ticket, including presidential nominee Benjamin Harrison.

**NATIONAL POLITICS** Several factors gave national politics in the Gilded Age its distinctive texture. First in importance was the close division between Republicans and Democrats in Congress. Because neither party was dominant, both avoided controversial issues or bold initiatives for fear of losing a close election. Yet, paradoxically, voter intensity at all levels peaked during the Gilded Age; voter turnout was commonly about 70 to 80 percent. (By contrast, the turnout for the 2016 U.S. presidential election was 61 percent.)

Most voters cast their ballots for the same party year after year, and party loyalty was often an emotional choice. In the 1870s and 1880s, for example, people continued to fight the Civil War during political campaigns. Republican candidates regularly took credit for abolishing slavery and saving the Union while accusing Democrats of having caused "secession and civil war."

Democrats, especially in the South, responded by reminding voters that they stood for limited government, states' rights, and white supremacy. Third parties, such as Greenbackers, Populists, and Prohibitionists, appealed to specific interests and issues—currency inflation, railroad regulations, or legislation to restrict alcohol consumption.

Party loyalties reflected religious, ethnic, and geographic divisions. The Republican party remained strongest in New England, upstate New York, Pennsylvania, Ohio, and the Midwest. Republicans tended to be Protestants of English or Scandinavian descent. As the party of Abraham Lincoln (the "Great Emancipator") and Ulysses S. Grant, Republicans could also rely upon the votes of African Americans in the South (until their right to vote was taken away by Jim Crow laws) and the support of a large bloc of Union veterans of the Civil War.

The Democrats were a more diverse coalition of conservative southern whites, northern Catholics of Irish or German backgrounds, and others repelled by the Republicans' claim to be the "party of morality." As one Chicago Democrat explained, "A Republican is a man who wants you t' go t' church every Sunday. A Democrat says if a man wants to have a glass of beer on Sunday he can have it."

During the 1880s, Protestant Republicans infuriated many immigrants and Catholics of Irish, Italian, or German background by promoting efforts to limit or prohibit the consumption of alcoholic beverages. They also pushed for nativist policies designed to restrict immigration and the employment of foreigners.

Carrie Nation, the most colorful member of the Women's Christian Temperance Union (WCTU), became a national celebrity known for her attacks on saloons with a hatchet. Saloons, she argued, stripped a married woman of everything by turning husbands into alcoholics, as had happened with her first husband: "Her husband is torn from her, she is robbed of her sons, her home, her food, and her virtue."

Between 1869 and 1913, from the first term of Ulysses S. Grant through the election of William Howard Taft, Republicans monopolized the White House except for two nonconsecutive terms of New York Democrat Grover Cleveland. Otherwise, national politics was remarkably balanced. Between 1872 and 1896, *no* president won a majority of the popular vote. In each of those elections, sixteen states invariably voted Republican, and fourteen, including every southern state (the "Solid South"), voted Democratic. That left six "swing" (closely contested) states to determine the outcome. Two of those states, New York and Ohio, decided the election of eight presidents from 1872 to 1908.

All presidents during the Gilded Age, both Republican and Democrat, deferred to their party leaders in the Senate and House of Representatives. The chief executives believed that Congress, not the White House, should formulate policies that the president would implement. As Senator John Sherman of Ohio stressed, "The President should merely obey and enforce the law" as laid out by Congress.

## HAYES TO HARRISON

While both political parties had their share of officials willing to buy and sell government jobs or legislative votes, each developed factions promoting honesty in government. The struggle for "clean" government became one of the foremost issues of the Gilded Age.

## HAYES AND CIVIL SERVICE REFORM

President Rutherford B. Hayes brought to the White House in 1877 both a lingering controversy over his disputed election results (critics called him "His Fraudulency" or "His Accidency") and an uprightness that offered a sharp contrast to the scandals of Ulysses S. Grant's presidency. Hayes appointed a Democrat as postmaster general in an effort to clean up an office infamous for trading jobs for political favors.

Hayes had been the compromise presidential nominee of two factions fighting for control of the Republican party: the so-called Stalwarts and Half-Breeds, led, respectively, by Senators Roscoe Conkling of New York and James Gillespie Blaine of Maine. The Stalwarts had been "stalwart" in their support of President Grant during the furor over the misdeeds of his cabinet members. Further, they had mastered the patronage (spoils) system of distributing political jobs to party loyalists. The Half-Breeds supposedly were only *half* loyal to Grant and *half* committed to reform of the spoils system. But in the end, the two factions existed primarily to advance the careers of Conkling and Blaine, who detested each other.

To his credit, Hayes tried to stay above the bickering and admitted that his party "must mend its ways" by focusing on Republican principles rather than fighting over the spoils of office. It was time "for **civil service** [government jobs] **reform.**" He appointed a committee to consider a merit system for hiring government employees and also fired Chester A. Arthur, a Stalwart Republican who ran the New York Customs House, for abusing the patronage system in ways that, Hayes said, promoted "ignorance, inefficiency, and corruption."

Hayes's actions enraged Republican leaders. In 1879, Ohio congressman James Garfield warned Hayes that "if he wishes to hold any influence" with fellow Republicans, he "must abandon some of his notions of Civil Service reform." For his part, Hayes confessed that he had little hope of success because he was "opposed by . . . the most powerful men in my party."

On economic issues, Hayes held to a conservative line. His answer to demands for expansion of the nation's money supply was a resounding no: he vetoed the Bland-Allison Act (1878), a bipartisan effort to increase the supply of silver coins. (More money in circulation was generally believed to raise farm prices and help those trying to pay off debts.) Hayes believed only in "hard money"—gold coins.

When the Democrat-controlled Congress convinced many Republicans to help overturn the veto, Hayes wrote in his diary that he had become a president without a party. In 1879, he was ready to leave the White House. "I am now in my last year of the Presidency," he wrote a friend, "and look forward to its close as a schoolboy longs for the coming vacation."

## GARFIELD, ARTHUR, AND THE PENDLETON ACT

With Rutherford B. Hayes choosing not to pursue a second term, the Republican presidential nomination in 1880 was up for grabs. In the end, the Stalwarts and Half-Breeds were forced to select a compromise candidate, Congressman James A. Garfield of Ohio.

Garfield had been a minister, lawyer, professor, and college president before serving in the Civil War as a Union army general. In an effort to please the Stalwarts and also win the crucial state of New York, the Republicans named Chester A. Arthur, whom Hayes had fired as head of the New York Customs House, as their candidate for vice president.

The Democrats nominated Winfield Scott Hancock, a retired Union general who had distinguished himself at the Battle of Gettysburg but done little since. In large part, the Democrats selected Hancock to help deflect the Republicans' attacks on them as the party of the Confederacy. Yet Hancock undermined that effort by supporting southern efforts to strip blacks of voting rights.

In an election marked by widespread bribery, Garfield eked out a popular-vote plurality of only 39,000, or 48.5 percent out of some 9 million votes. He won a more comfortable margin of 214 to 155 in the electoral college. Republicans took control of Congress as well.

Embedded in the voting, however, was a worrisome pattern: The Democrats won all the southern states, and the Republicans won all the northern states. Politically, the Civil War was not over. Moreover, in future presidential elections during the nineteenth century, if the Republicans lost New York State, they would lose the White House. Securing the nation's most-populous state thus became central to Republican strategy.

**A PRESIDENCY CUT SHORT** In his 1881 inaugural address, President Garfield argued that the "elevation of the negro race from slavery to the full rights of citizenship is the most important political change we have known since the adoption of the Constitution of 1787." The end of slavery, he said, "has added immensely to the moral and industrial forces of our people. It has liberated the master as well as the slave from a relation which wronged and enfeebled both." He also confirmed, however, that efforts to reconstruct the former Confederacy were over. Southern blacks had been "surrendered to their own guardianship."

Garfield was old-school in many respects. He opposed labor unions and the idea of an eight-hour workday, and he viewed voting rights for women as "atheistic, and destructive of marriage and family." Presidents, he argued, should defer to Congress, and the federal government should "keep the peace" and stay out of the way of the states.

In the continuing feud between the Half-Breeds and Stalwarts, Garfield sided with the Half-Breeds. He appointed James G. Blaine as secretary of state over Grant's objection, leading the former president to tell reporters that Garfield "is a man without backbone. A man of fine ability but lacking stamina. He wants to please everybody."

Garfield would have no time to prove himself, however. On July 2, 1881, after only four months in office, he was walking through the Washington, D.C., railroad station when he was shot twice by Charles Guiteau, a thirty-nine-year-old Republican office-seeker. Guiteau had earlier visited Garfield to ask for a job in the U.S. consulate in Paris, only to be turned down. As a policeman wrestled the assassin to the ground, Guiteau shouted: "Yes! I have killed Garfield! [Chester] Arthur is now President of the United States. I am a Stalwart!" That declaration would eventually destroy the Stalwart wing of the Republican party.

On September 19, after seventy-nine days of struggle, Garfield died of infection resulting from inept medical care. "MURDERED BY THE SPOILS SYSTEM," exclaimed a *New York Tribune* headline. During a sensational ten-week trial, Guiteau claimed that God had ordered him to kill Garfield. The jury, however, refused to believe that he was insane and pronounced him "devilishly depraved" and guilty of murder. On June 30, 1882, Guiteau was hanged; an autopsy revealed that his brain was diseased.

**THE CIVIL SERVICE COMMISSION** People saw little potential in the new president, Chester A. Arthur, who had been Roscoe Conkling's trusted lieutenant. Yet Arthur surprised most observers by distancing himself from Conkling and the Stalwarts and becoming a civil service reformer. Throughout his presidency, he kept a promise not to remove any federal office holder for political reasons. He also made cabinet appointments based on merit rather than partisanship. One of Arthur's former New York associates, a Stalwart, grumbled that "he has done less for us than Garfield, or even Hayes."

Little is known about Chester Arthur. Unlike most presidents, there is no library or museum dedicated to his career. Just before he died, he had all his official papers and correspondence burned. What we do know is that he did not invest much time in his role as chief executive. He worked only from ten to four each day and took Sundays and Mondays off. One of his clerks noted that Arthur "never did today what he could put off until tomorrow."

In 1883, momentum against the spoils system generated by Garfield's assassination enabled George H. Pendleton, a Democratic senator from Ohio, to convince Congress to establish a Civil Service Commission, the first federal regulatory agency. Because of the Pendleton Civil Service Reform Act, at least 15 percent of federal jobs would now be filled based on competitive tests (the merit system) rather than political favoritism. In addition, federal employees running for office were prohibited from receiving political contributions from government workers.

The Pendleton Act was a limited first step in cleaning up the patronage process. It was sorely needed, in part because the federal government was expanding rapidly. By 1901, there would be 256,000 federal employees, five times the number in 1871. A growing portion of these workers were women, who by 1890 held a third of the government's clerical jobs.

## The Campaign of 1884

Chester Arthur's efforts to clean up the spoils system did not please Republican leaders. So in 1884, the Republicans dumped the ailing president (he had contracted a kidney disease) and chose as their nominee James G. Blaine of Maine, the handsome secretary of state, former senator, and longtime leader of the Half-Breeds.

Blaine inspired the party faithful with his electrifying speeches, and he knew how to make backroom deals. One critic charged that Blaine "wallowed in spoils like a rhinoceros in an African pool." Newspapers soon uncovered evidence of his corruption in the so-called Mulligan letters, which revealed that, as Speaker of the House, Blaine had secretly sold his votes on measures favorable to a railroad corporation.

During the presidential campaign, more letters surfaced linking Blaine to shady deal making. In one of them, Blaine told the recipient: "Burn this letter!" For the reform element of the Republican party, this was too much. Many independent-minded Republicans refused to endorse Blaine's candidacy. "We are Republicans but we are not slaves," said one. He insisted that the party of Lincoln must recommit itself to "retrenchment, purity and reform." Party regulars scorned such critics as "goo-goos"—the "good-government" crowd who were outraged by the corrupting influence of money in politics. The editor of a New York newspaper jokingly called anti-Blaine Republicans **Mugwumps**, after an Algonquian Indian word meaning "big chief."

The Mugwumps, a self-appointed group of reformers, saw the election as a "moral rather than political" contest. Centered in the large cities and major universities of the northeast, the Mugwumps were mostly professors, editors, and writers who sought to reform the patronage system by declaring that *all* federal jobs be filled solely on the basis of merit. The rise of the Mugwumps, as well as growing national concerns about corruption, prompted the Dem-

**Grover Cleveland** As president, Cleveland made the issue of tariff reform central to the politics of the late 1880s.

ocrats to nominate New Yorker Grover Cleveland, a massive figure with a bull neck, strong jaw, and overflowing moustache that made him resemble a walrus.

Cleveland had first attracted national attention in 1881, when he was elected mayor of Buffalo on an anti-corruption platform. Elected governor of New York in 1882, he fought the corrupt Tammany Hall ring. As mayor and governor, he repeatedly vetoed bills that he felt served private interests at the expense of the public good. He supported civil service reform, opposed expanding the money supply, and preferred free trade rather than high tariffs.

Although Cleveland was known for his honesty and integrity, two personal issues hurt him: the discovery that he had paid for a substitute to take his place in the Union army during the Civil War, and a juicy sex scandal that erupted when a Buffalo newspaper revealed that Cleveland, a bachelor, had seduced an attractive widow named Maria Halpin, who named him the father of her baby born in 1874. Cleveland had refused to marry her but had provided financial support for the child.

The escapades of Blaine and Cleveland inspired some of the most colorful battle cries in political history: "Blaine, Blaine, James G. Blaine, the continental liar from the state of Maine," Democrats chanted. Republicans countered with "Ma, ma, where's my Pa? Gone to the White House—Ha! Ha! Ha!"

Near the end of the campaign, Blaine and his supporters committed two fateful blunders in the crucial state of New York. The first occurred at

New York City's Delmonico's restaurant, where Blaine went to a private dinner with 200 of the nation's wealthiest business leaders to ask them to help finance his campaign. Accounts of the unseemly event appeared in the newspapers for days afterward. One headline blared: "Blaine Hobnobbing with the Mighty Money Kings!" The article explained that the banquet was intended to collect contributions for a "Republican corruption fund."

Blaine's second blunder occurred when a Protestant minister visiting Republican headquarters in New York referred to the Democrats as the party of "rum, Romanism, and rebellion [the Confederacy]." Blaine, who was present, let pass the implied insult to Catholics—a fatal oversight, since he had cultivated Irish American support. Democrats claimed that Blaine was, at heart, anti-Irish and anti-Catholic.

The two incidents may have tipped the election. The electoral vote was 219 to 182 in Cleveland's favor, but the popular vote ran far closer: Cleveland's plurality was fewer than 30,000 votes out of 10 million cast. Cleveland won New York by only 1,149 votes out of 1,167,169 cast.

The Republicans charged that the Democrats had paid so many voters in New York that it had cost Blaine the White House. Yet Blaine refused to challenge the results, in part because the Republicans were buying votes too. Doing so, explained a journalist, "is considered a necessary part of 'practical politics,' and to be applauded in proportion to their success." By hook or by crook, a Democrat was back in the White House.

## Cleveland's Reform Efforts

During his first few months in office, President Cleveland struggled to keep Democratic leaders from reviving the patronage system. In a letter to a friend, Cleveland reported that he was living in a "nightmare," that "dreadful, damnable, office-seeking hangs over me and surrounds me" and made him "feel like resigning." Democratic newspapers heaped scorn on him for refusing to award federal jobs to his supporters. Despite the president's best efforts, however, about two thirds of the 120,000 federal jobs went to Democrats as patronage during his administration.

Cleveland was an old-style Democrat who believed in minimal government activity. During his first term, he vetoed over 400 acts of Congress, more than twice as many as all previous presidents combined. In 1887, he illustrated his "do as little as possible" philosophy by vetoing a congressional effort to provide Texas farmers with seeds in the aftermath of a terrible drought. "Though the people support the government, the government should not support the people," Cleveland asserted.

**RAILROAD REGULATION** For all his commitment to limited government, President Cleveland urged Congress to adopt an important new policy: federal regulation of the rates charged by interstate railroads (those whose tracks crossed state lines) to ship goods, crops, or livestock. States had passed laws regulating railroads since the late 1860s, but in 1886, the Supreme Court declared in *Wabash, St. Louis, and Pacific Railroad Company v. Illinois* that no state could regulate the rates charged by railroads engaged in interstate traffic. Because most railroads crossed state lines, Cleveland urged Congress to close the loophole.

Congress followed through, and in 1887, Cleveland signed an act creating the **Interstate Commerce Commission** (ICC), the first federal agency designed to regulate business activities. The law empowered the ICC's five members to ensure that railroad freight rates were "reasonable and just." But one senator called the agency "a delusion and a sham" because its members tended to be former railroad executives. Moreover, the commission's actual powers were weak when challenged in the courts. Over time, the ICC came to be ignored, and the railroads continued to charge high rates while making secret pricing deals with large shippers.

**TARIFF REFORM AND THE ELECTION OF 1888** President Cleveland's most dramatic challenge to Big Business focused on **tariff reform**. During the late nineteenth century, the government's high-tariff policies, shaped largely by the Republican party, had favored American manufacturers by effectively shutting out foreign imports, thereby enabling U.S. corporations to dominate the marketplace and charge higher prices for their products. Tariffs on some 4,000 imported items had also brought in more revenue from foreign manufacturers than the federal government spent. As a result, the tariff revenues were producing an annual government surplus, which proved to Cleveland and the Democrats that the rates were too high.

In 1887, Cleveland argued that Congress should reduce both the tariff rates and the number of imported goods subject to tariffs, which would enable European companies to compete in the American marketplace (and bring down prices for consumers). His stance set the stage for his reelection campaign in 1888.

To oppose Cleveland, the Republicans, now calling themselves the GOP (Grand Old Party) to emphasize their longevity, turned to the obscure Benjamin Harrison, whose greatest attributes were his availability and the fact that he was from Indiana, a pivotal state. The grandson of President William Henry Harrison, he had a modest political record; he had lost a race for governor and had served one term in the U.S. Senate (1881–1887). Stiff and formal, Harrison was labeled the "human iceberg."

**"King of the World"** Reformers targeted the growing power of monopolies.

Theodore Roosevelt held him in contempt, once calling him a "cold-blooded, narrow-minded, prejudiced, obstinate, timid old psalm-singing Indianapolis politician." To the party leadership, however, Harrison had the most important attribute: He would do as he was told.

The Republicans enjoyed a huge advantage in campaign funding thanks to the generous support of business executives. Still, the election outcome was incredibly close. Cleveland won the popular vote by the thinnest of margins—5,540,329 to 5,439,853—but Harrison carried New York State and the electoral college, 233 to 168. "Providence," said the new president, "has given us the victory." Matthew Quay, the powerful Republican boss of Pennsylvania who had managed Harrison's campaign, knew better. Harrison, he muttered, "ought to know that Providence hadn't a damned thing to do with it! [A] number of men were compelled to approach the penitentiary to make him President."

Quay's decision to distribute campaign money in key states and promise federal jobs to loyalists also helped Republicans gain control of the House and the Senate. *Frank Leslie's Illustrated Newspaper*, co-edited by Harrison's son Russell, made clear the new president's priorities: "This is to be a businessman's Administration," and "businessmen will be thoroughly well content with it."

## REPUBLICAN ACTIVISM UNDER HARRISON

The Republicans took advantage of their control of Congress by passing significant legislation in 1890: the Sherman Anti-Trust Act, the Sherman Silver Purchase Act, the McKinley Tariff Act; and the admission of Idaho and Wyoming into the Union—all on the heels of North and South Dakota, Montana, and Washington becoming states in 1889.

The Sherman Anti-Trust Act, named for Ohio senator John Sherman, prohibited corporations from "conspiring" to establish monopolies or "restrain trade."

It made the United States the first nation in the world to outlaw monopolistic business practices.

Though badly needed, the Sherman Anti-Trust Act was a toothless hoax intended to make it appear that Congress was clamping down on gigantic corporations. Critics called it the "Swiss Cheese Act" because it had so many holes in its language. As the *New York Times* recognized in 1890, the "so-called Anti-Trust law" was passed "to deceive the people" and prepare the way for a much higher tariff bill. Sherman, the article added, supported the law so that party spokesmen "might say 'Behold! We have attacked the trusts. The Republican Party is the enemy of all such rings.'"

The Sherman Anti-Trust Act was rarely enforced, in large part because of its vague definitions of trusts and monopolies. From 1890 to 1901, only eighteen lawsuits were filed. Four of them targeted labor unions rather than corporations, claiming that striking workers were conspiring to restrain trade.

The Sherman Silver Purchase Act (1890), which required the Treasury to purchase 4.5 million ounces of silver each month to convert into dollar coins, was an effort to please the six new western states that had numerous silver mines. Senator Sherman admitted that he proposed it only to defuse cries for the "unlimited coinage" of silver. "I voted for it," he confessed, "but the day it became law I was ready to repeal it." The act helped set the stage for the "money problem" to eclipse all others during the financial panic that would sweep the country in 1893.

As for tariff policy, Republicans viewed their electoral victory as a mandate to reward the support of large corporations by raising tariff rates. Piloted through Congress by Ohio representative William McKinley, the McKinley Tariff Act of 1890 raised duties (taxes) on imported manufactured goods to their highest level and, to appease farmers, added many agricultural products to the tariff list. Its passage encouraged many businesses to raise prices because their European competitors were now effectively shut out of the U.S. market. The *New York Times* expressed the indignation of many voters when it charged in a huge headline, "MCKINLEY'S PICKPOCKETS [WERE] PAYING A PARTY DEBT" to large corporate donors by passing the new tariff bill.

The Republican efforts to reward Big Business backfired, however. In the November 1890 congressional elections, Democrats regained control of the House by a 3 to 1 margin. McKinley lost his seat (although the following year he would be elected Ohio's governor). In the Senate, the Republican majority was reduced to four. Republicans were "astounded and dazed" by the shellacking. Even more worrisome was the emergence of the Populists, a new political party representing disgruntled farmers and wage laborers. Revolution was in the air.

## FARMERS AND THE "MONEY PROBLEM"

More than tariffs, trusts, and efforts to clean up political corruption, national politics during the Gilded Age was preoccupied with monetary issues. The nation's money supply had not grown with the expanding economy and population. From 1865 to 1890, the amount of money in circulation (both coins and paper currency) actually *decreased* about 10 percent.

Such currency deflation raised the cost of borrowing, as the shrinking money supply enabled lenders to hike interest rates on loans. Creditors—bankers and others who loaned money—supported a "sound money" policy limiting the currency supply as a means of increasing their profits. By contrast, farmers, ranchers, miners, and others who had to borrow money to make ends meet claimed that the sound money policy lowered prices for their crops and herds and drove them deeper into debt. They demanded more paper money and the increased coinage of silver, which would inflate the currency supply, raise commodity prices, and provide them more income.

In 1873, the Republican-controlled Congress had declared that only gold could be used for coins. This decision (called "the Crime of '73" by critics) occurred just when silver mines in the western states had begun to increase their production, and deposits of gold were drying up.

In 1874, several farm organizations had organized the independent Greenback party to promote the benefits of paper money. "Greenbackers" won fifteen seats in Congress in 1878. Although the party died out, demands for increasing the money supply survived. All six western states admitted to the Union in 1889 and 1890 had substantial silver mines, and their new congressional delegations—largely Republican—wanted the federal government to buy more silver for minting as coins.

**AGRICULTURAL UNREST** The 1890 congressional elections revealed a deep-seated unrest in the farming communities of the South, on the plains of Kansas and Nebraska, and in the mining towns of the Rocky Mountain region. Over the previous twenty years, overproduction and growing international competition had caused corn prices to fall by a third, wheat by more than half, and cotton by two-thirds. The vast new lands brought under cultivation in the plains as a result of the extension of rail lines and the use of new farm machinery poured an ever-increasing supply of grain into world markets, driving prices down.

Meanwhile, farmers had become increasingly indebted to banks or merchants who loaned them money at high interest rates to buy seed, fertilizer, tools, and other supplies. As crop prices dropped, however, so did farmers' incomes, thus preventing them from paying their debts on time.

In response, most farmers had no choice but to grow even more wheat, cotton, or corn, but the increased supply further reduced prices and incomes. High tariffs on imported goods also hurt farmers because they allowed U.S. companies to raise the prices of manufactured goods needed by farm families.

Besides bankers, merchants, and high tariffs, struggling farmers blamed the railroads, warehouse owners, and food processors—the so-called middlemen—who helped get crops and livestock to market. Farmers especially resented that railroads, most of which had a monopoly over the shipping of grain and animals, charged such high shipping rates.

At the same time that farm income was dropping, successive years of parched summers and bitterly cold winters had destroyed harvests in many states. "This season is without parallel in this part of the country," reported the editor of a Nebraska agricultural journal in 1891. "The hot winds burned up the entire crop, leaving thousands of families wholly destitute" and vulnerable to the "money loaners and sharks" charging criminal rates of interest.

In drought-devastated Kansas in 1890, Populists won five congressional seats from Republicans. In early 1891, the newly elected Populists and Democrats took control of Congress just as an acute economic crisis appeared on the horizon: farmers' debts were mounting as crop prices continued to fall.

**THE GRANGER MOVEMENT** When the Department of Agriculture sent Oliver H. Kelley on a tour of the South in 1866, he was struck by the social isolation of people living on small farms. To address the problem, Kelley helped found the National Grange of the Patrons of Husbandry, better known as the Grange (an old word for places where crops were stored).

The Grange grew quickly, reaching a membership of 858,000 by 1875. It started out offering social events and educational programs for farmers and their families, but as it grew, it began to promote *cooperatives* where farmers could join together to store and sell their crops to avoid the high fees charged by brokers and other middlemen.

In five Midwest states, Grange chapters persuaded legislatures to pass "Granger laws" establishing state commissions to regulate the prices charged by railroads and grain warehouses (called "elevators"). Farmers rented space in the grain elevators to store their harvested crop before it was sold and shipped by railroads. Many elevator operators were corrupt, however, and secretly conspired to "fix" the storage rates charged farmers. Railroads also squeezed the farmers. Since they usually had a monopoly in a given agricultural community, railroads could charge whatever they wanted to ship grain, and they discriminated in favor of the largest farms.

To address the concerns of grain growers, the Illinois legislature in 1871 established regulations prohibiting railroads from charging different freight rates and establishing rates for grain elevator storage. The state created a Board of Railroad and Warehouse Commissioners to enforce the new regulations. Other states soon passed similar laws.

Railroad and warehouse owners challenged and often defied the laws, arguing that efforts to regulate them were forms of socialism. In *Munn v. Illinois* (1877), however, the Supreme Court ruled 7–2 that the Constitution sanctioned regulation of businesses that operated in the public interest. In response, Chicago grain elevators lowered their storage fees. Nine years later, however, the Court threw out the *Munn* ruling, finding in *Wabash v. Illinois* that only Congress, not states, could regulate industries involved in *interstate* commerce.

**FARMERS' ALLIANCES** The Granger movement failed to address the foremost concerns of farmers: declining crop prices and the inadequate amount of money in circulation. As a result, people shifted their allegiance to a new organization called the Farmers' Alliance. Like the Grange, the Farmers' Alliance organized social and recreational activities for small farmers and their families while emphasizing political action and economic cooperation to address the hardships caused by chronic indebtedness, declining crop prices, and droughts.

Emerging first in Texas, the Southern Alliance movement swept across the South, Kansas, Nebraska, and the Dakotas. By 1890, the white Alliance movement had about 1.5 million members nationwide. The Southern Alliance refused to allow blacks to join, not only because of racism but also because most black farmers were tenants and sharecroppers rather than landowners. Although many landless farmers supported the Alliances, the majority of members were landowners who sold their crops in the marketplace. In 1886, a white minister in Texas responded to the appeals of African American farmers by organizing the Colored Farmers' National Alliance. By 1890, it would claim more than 1 million members.

In 1886, a white minister in Texas responded to the appeals of African American farmers by organizing the Colored Farmers' National Alliance. By 1890, the white Alliance movement had about 1.5 million members, and the Colored Farmers' National Alliance claimed more than 1 million members. But most white Alliance members refused to integrate their efforts with blacks, not only because of racism but also because most black farmers were tenants and sharecroppers rather than landowners. Although many landless farmers supported the Alliances, the majority of members were landowners who sold their crops in the marketplace.

**"I Feed You All!" (1875)**  The farmer is the cornerstone of American society, according to this Granger-inspired poster. Without the food he produces, no man in any occupation can do his job—including the railroad magnate (left) and warehouse owners who try to exploit him.

West of the Mississippi River, political activism intensified after record blizzards in 1887, which killed most of the cattle and hogs across the northern plains, and a prolonged drought two years later that destroyed millions of acres of corn, wheat, and oats. Distressed farmers lashed out against what they considered a powerful conspiracy of eastern financial and industrial interests.

The Alliances called for the federal government to take ownership of the railroads and create an income tax on wealthy Americans. They also organized economic cooperatives for collective bargaining strength in negotiations with warehouse owners and railroads. In 1887, Charles W. Macune, the Southern Alliance president, exhorted Texas farmers to create their own Alliance Exchange to free themselves from dependence on commercial warehouses, grain elevators, food processors, and banks. Members of the Alliance Exchange would pool their resources to borrow money from banks and purchase goods and supplies from a new corporation created by the Alliance in Dallas. The exchange would also build warehouses to store and market members' crops. With these crops as collateral, members would receive loans to buy household goods and agricultural supplies. Once the farmers sold their crops, they would repay the loans.

This *cooperative* scheme collapsed when Texas banks refused to accept paper money. Undaunted, Alliance members then focused on what Macune called a subtreasury plan, whereby they would store their crops in federally funded and *government*-run warehouses and obtain loans for up to 80 percent of the crops' value. Besides providing immediate cash, the subtreasury warehouses would allow farmers to store a crop in hopes of getting a better price later.

Congress, however, nixed the subtreasury plan in 1890. Its defeat, as well as setbacks to other Alliance proposals, convinced many farm leaders that they needed more political power to secure the reforms they believed were necessary: railroad regulation, currency inflation, state departments of agriculture, anti-trust laws, and more accessible farm-based credit (loans).

The Alliance welcomed rural women and men over sixteen years of age who displayed a "good moral character," believed in God, and demonstrated "industrious habits." A North Carolina woman relished the "grand opportunities" the Alliance provided women, allowing them to emerge from household drudgeries. "Drudgery, fashion, and gossip," she declared, "are no longer the bounds of woman's sphere." One Alliance publication made the point explicitly: "The Alliance has come to redeem woman from her enslaved condition, and place her in her proper sphere." Many women assumed key leadership roles in the "grand army of reform."

**NEW THIRD PARTIES**  The Alliances called for third-party political action. In 1890, farm activists in Colorado joined with miners and railroad workers to form the Independent party, and Nebraska farmers formed the People's Independent party. When Leonidas Polk, head of the North Carolina Alliance, traveled to Kansas, he was so impressed by the size of the open-air farm rallies that he declared that farmers across the nation "have risen up and inaugurated a movement such as the world has never seen."

In the South, the Alliance movement elected four Democrats as governors, forty-four as congressmen, and several as U.S. senators, as well as seven pro-Alliance state legislatures. Among the most respected of the Southern Alliance leaders was Thomas E. Watson, a lawyer from Georgia. The son of prosperous slaveholders who had lost everything after the Civil War, Watson took the lead in urging black and white tenant farmers to join forces to resist the power of the wealthy political elite. "You are [racially] kept apart," he told blacks and whites, "that you may be separately fleeced of your earnings."

In Kansas, Mary Elizabeth Lease emerged as a fiery speaker for the farm protest movement. Born in Pennsylvania to Irish immigrants, Lease migrated to Kansas, taught school, raised a family, and failed at farming in the mid-1880s. She then studied law and became one of the state's first female attorneys.

Lease gave rousing speeches on behalf of struggling farmers. "The people are at bay," she warned; "let the bloodhounds of money beware." She urged farmers to take control "with the ballot if possible, but if not that way then with the bayonet."

Lease viewed eastern financiers as the enemy. "Wall Street owns the country. It is no longer a government of the people, by the people, and for

**Mary Elizabeth Lease** A charismatic leader in the farm protest movement.

the people, but a government of Wall Street, by Wall Street, and for Wall Street." The two political parties "lie to us" in blaming farmers for overproduction, "when 10,000 little children starve to death every year in the United States."

**THE 1892 ELECTION**  In 1892, Alliance leaders organized a convention in Omaha, Nebraska, at which they formed the **People's party (Populists)**. Their platform called for unlimited coinage of silver, a *progressive* income tax whose rates would rise with income levels, and federal ownership of the railroads and telegraph systems. The Populists also endorsed the eight-hour workday and laws restricting "undesirable" immigration. "We meet in the midst of a nation brought to the verge of moral, political, and material ruin," they announced. "The fruits of toil of millions are boldly stolen to build up colossal fortunes for a few. . . ." They called for the "power of government" to be expanded to assault "oppression, injustice, and poverty."

The party's platform turned out to be more exciting than its presidential candidate: Iowa's James B. Weaver, a former Union army officer who had headed the Greenback party ticket twelve years earlier. The major parties renominated the same candidates who had run in 1888: Democrat Grover Cleveland and Republican president Benjamin Harrison. Each major candidate received more than 5 million votes, but Cleveland won a majority of the electoral college. Weaver received more than 1 million votes and carried Colorado, Kansas, Nevada, and Idaho.

## THE DEPRESSION OF 1893 AND THE "FREE SILVER" CRUSADE

While farmers were funneling their discontent into politics, a fundamental weakness in the economy was about to cause a major collapse and a social rebellion. Just ten days before Grover Cleveland was inaugurated in the winter of 1893, the Philadelphia and Reading Railroad declared bankruptcy, setting off a financial crisis, now called the **Panic of 1893**. It grew into the worst depression the nation had experienced.

Other overextended railroads collapsed, taking many banks with them. European investors withdrew their funds. A quarter of unskilled urban workers lost their jobs, and many others had their wages cut. By the fall of 1893, more than 600 banks had closed, and 15,000 businesses had failed. Farm foreclosures soared, and by 1900, a third of all American farmers rented their land rather than owned it.

By 1894, the economy had reached bottom. But the depression lasted another four years, with unemployment hovering at 20 percent.

President Cleveland's response was to convince Congress to return the nation's money supply to a gold standard by repealing the Sherman Silver Purchase Act of 1890. The move made the depression worse. The weak economy needed *more* money in circulation, not *less*. Investors rushed to exchange their silver dollars for gold, further constricting the money supply.

Hard times triggered unrest. In 1894, some 750,000 workers went on strike. One protest group, called Coxey's Army, was led by "General" Jacob S. Coxey, a wealthy Ohio quarry owner turned Populist who demanded that the federal government provide the unemployed with meaningful work. Coxey, his wife, and their son, Legal Tender Coxey, rode in a carriage ahead of some 400 protesters who marched to Washington, D.C., where police arrested Coxey for walking on the grass. Although the ragtag army dispersed peacefully, the march, as well as the growing strength of Populism, struck fear into the hearts of many conservatives.

Republicans portrayed Populists as "tramps" and "hayseed socialists" whose election would endanger the capitalist system. The Populists responded by charging that Americans were divided into "tramps and millionaires."

In this climate of class warfare and social anxiety, the 1894 congressional elections devastated President Cleveland and the Democrats. The Republicans

**Coxey's Army, 1894** A subset of Coxey's Army, mid-march, on the outskirts of Washington D.C. Coxey's economic ideology was popular with immigrants.

gained 118 seats in the House, the largest increase ever. Populists, who emerged with six senators and seven representatives, expected the festering discontent to carry them to national power in 1896. Their hopes would be dashed, however.

**SILVERITES VERSUS GOLDBUGS** Cleveland's decision to repeal the Sherman Silver Purchase Act created an irreparable division in his party. One pro-silver Democrat labeled the president a traitor. Politicians from western states with large silver mines increased their demands for "unlimited" coinage of silver, presenting a strategic dilemma for Populists: Should the party promote the long list of reforms it had originally advocated, or should it try to ride the silver issue into power?

Populist leaders decided to hold their 1896 nominating convention *after* the two major-party conventions, confident that the Republicans and Democrats would at best straddle the silver issue and enable the Populists to lure away pro-silver advocates from both. The major parties, however, took opposite positions.

The Republicans, as expected, nominated William McKinley, a former congressman and governor of Ohio, on a platform committed to gold coins

**William Jennings Bryan** His "cross of gold" speech at the 1896 Democratic Convention secured him the party's presidential nomination.

as the only form of currency. After the convention, a friend told McKinley that the "**money question**" would determine the election. He was right.

The Democratic convention was one of the great turning points in political history. The pro-silver, largely rural delegates surprised the party leadership and the "Gold Democrats," or "goldbugs," by capturing control of the convention.

**WILLIAM JENNINGS BRYAN** Thirty-six-year-old William Jennings Bryan of Nebraska gave the final speech at the Democratic convention before balloting began. A fiery evangelical moralist, Bryan was a two-term congressman who had lost a race for the Senate in 1894. In the months before the convention, he had traveled throughout the South and West, speaking passionately for the unlimited coinage of silver, attacking Cleveland's "do-nothing" response to the depression, and endorsing Democrats and Populists who embraced "free silver."

In his carefully crafted, well-rehearsed convention speech, Bryan, a compelling speaker, claimed that two ideas about the role of government were competing for the American voter. The Republicans, he said, believed "that if you just legislate to make the well-to-do prosperous, that their prosperity will leak through on those below." The Democrats, by contrast, believed "that if you legislate to make the masses prosperous their prosperity will find its way up and through every class that rests upon it." For his part, Bryan spoke for the "producing masses of this nation" against the eastern "financial magnates" who had "enslaved" them by manipulating the money supply to ensure high interest rates.

As Bryan brought his electrifying twenty-minute speech to a climax, he fused Christian imagery with Populist anger:

> I come to speak to you in defense of a cause as holy as the cause of liberty—the cause of humanity. . . . We have petitioned, and our petitions have been scorned. . . . We have begged, and they have mocked when our calamity came. We beg no longer; we entreat no more; we petition no more. We defy them!

Bryan then identified himself with Jesus Christ. Sweeping his fingers across his forehead, he shouted: "You shall not press down upon the brow of labor this crown of thorns. You shall not crucify mankind upon a cross of gold!"—at which point he extended his arms straight out from his sides, as if he were being crucified. As he strode triumphantly off the stage, the delegates erupted in wild applause. "Everybody seemed to go mad at once," reported the *New York World*.

Republicans were not amused by Bryan's antics. A Republican newspaper observed that no political movement had "ever before spawned such hideous and repulsive vipers." Theodore Roosevelt claimed that Bryan was a demagogue with an "unsound mind" who was promoting mob rule.

The next day, Bryan won the presidential nomination on the fifth ballot, but in the process the Democratic party was fractured. Democrats who had supported Grover Cleveland were so alienated by Bryan's positions and rhetoric that they walked out of the convention and nominated their own candidate, Senator John M. Palmer of Illinois. "Fellow Democrats," Palmer announced, "I will not consider it any great fault if you decide to cast your vote for William McKinley."

When the Populists gathered for their nominating convention two weeks later, they faced an impossible choice. They could name their own candidate and divide the pro-silver vote with the Democrats, or they could endorse Bryan and probably lose their identity. In the end, they backed Bryan but chose their own vice-presidential candidate, Thomas E. Watson, and invited the Democrats to drop their vice-presidential nominee. Bryan refused.

**THE ELECTION OF 1896** The election of 1896 was one of the most dramatic in history, in part because of the striking contrast between the candidates and in part because the terrible economic depression had made the stakes so high. One observer said the campaign "took the form of religious frenzy." Indeed, Bryan campaigned like the evangelist he was. He was the first major candidate since Andrew Jackson to champion the poor, the discontented, and the oppressed. He excited struggling farmers, miners, and union members, and he was the first leader of a major party to call for the expansion of the federal government to help the working class.

Bryan traveled some 18,000 miles by train, visiting 26 states and 250 cities and towns. His populist crusade was for whites only, however. Like so many otherwise progressive Democratic leaders, Bryan never challenged the practices of racial segregation and violence against blacks in the solidly Democratic South. And he alienated many working-class Catholics in northern states by supporting prohibition of alcoholic beverages.

McKinley, meanwhile, stayed at home and kept his mouth shut, letting other Republicans speak for him. He knew he could not compete with Bryan as a

**Presidential campaign badges**
On the left wings of the "goldbug" and "silverite" badges are McKinley (top) and Bryan (bottom), with their running mates on the right.

speaker, so he conducted a "front-porch campaign," welcoming supporters to his home in Canton, Ohio. He gave only prepared statements to the press, most of which warned middle-class voters of Bryan's "dangerous" ideas. McKinley's brilliant campaign manager, Marcus "Mark" Hanna, shrewdly portrayed Bryan as a "Popocrat," a radical whose "communistic spirit" would ruin the capitalist system and stir up a class war. Hanna convinced the Republican party to declare that it was "unreservedly for sound money"—meaning gold coins.

The Republicans raised vast sums from corporations and wealthy donors to finance an army of 1,400 speakers who traveled the country promoting McKinley. It was the most sophisticated—and expensive—presidential campaign to that point.

In the end, Bryan won the most votes of any candidate in history— 6.5 million—but McKinley won even more: 7.1 million. The better-organized and better-financed Republicans won the electoral college vote, 271 to 176.

Bryan carried most of the West and all of the South but found little support in the North and East. In the critical Midwest, he did not win a state. His evangelical Protestantism repelled many Roman Catholics, who were normally drawn to the Democrats. Farmers in the Northeast, moreover, were less attracted to radical reform than were farmers in the West and South. Workers in the cities found it easier to identify with McKinley's focus on reviving the industrial economy than with Bryan's farm-based, free-silver evangelism. Of the nation's twenty largest cities, Bryan won only New Orleans.

Although Bryan lost, he launched the Democratic party's shift from pro-business conservatism to its eventual twentieth-century role as a party of liberal reform. The Populist party, however, virtually disintegrated. Conversely, McKinley's victory climaxed a generation-long struggle for political control

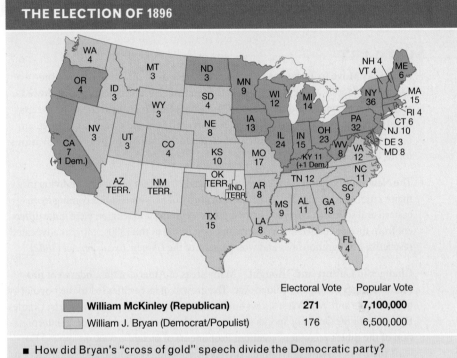

**THE ELECTION OF 1896**

| | Electoral Vote | Popular Vote |
|---|---|---|
| ◼ **William McKinley (Republican)** | 271 | 7,100,000 |
| ◻ William J. Bryan (Democrat/Populist) | 176 | 6,500,000 |

- How did Bryan's "cross of gold" speech divide the Democratic party?
- How did McKinley's campaign strategy differ from Bryan's?
- Why was Bryan able to carry the West and the South but unable to win in cities and the Northeast?

of an industrialized urban America. The Republicans would be dominant for sixteen years.

By 1897, when McKinley was inaugurated, economic prosperity was returning. Part of the reason was inflation of the currency, which bore out the arguments of the Greenbackers and silverites that the nation's money supply had been inadequate during the Gilded Age. Inflation came, however, not from the influx of more greenbacks or silver dollars but from a flood of gold discovered in South Africa, northwest Canada, and Alaska. In 1900, Congress passed a bill affirming that the nation's money supply would be based only on gold.

Even though the Populist movement faded after William Jennings Bryan's defeat, most of the ideas promoted by Bryan Democrats and Populists, dismissed as too radical in 1896, would be implemented over the next two decades by a more diverse coalition of Democrats and Republicans who would call themselves "progressives." The volcanic turmoil of the 1890s set the stage for the twentieth century's struggles and innovations.

# CHAPTER REVIEW

## Summary

- **America's Move to Town**   America's cities grew in all directions during the *Gilded Age (1860–1896)*. Electric elevators and steel-frame construction allowed architects to extend buildings upward, and mass transit enabled the middle class to retreat to suburbs. Crowded *tenements* bred disease and crime and created an opportunity for urban *party bosses* to accrue power, in part by distributing various forms of assistance to the poor.

- **The New Immigration**   By 1900, an estimated 30 percent of Americans living in major cities were foreign-born, with the majority of *new immigrants* coming from eastern and southern Europe. Their languages, culture, and religion were quite different from those of native-born Americans. Beginning in the 1880s, *nativists* advocated restrictive immigration laws and won passage of the *Chinese Exclusion Act (1882)*.

- **Changes in Culture and Thought**   Many areas of American life underwent profound changes during the Gilded Age. The growth of large cities led to the popularity of vaudeville and Wild West shows and to the emergence of spectator sports. Charles Darwin's *On the Origin of Species* shocked people who believed in a literal interpretation of the Bible's account of creation. Proponents of *social Darwinism* applied Darwin's theory of evolution to human society by equating economic and social success with "survival of the fittest."

- **Gilded Age Politics**   Huge corporations corrupted politics and bought political influence. Republicans were especially identified with promoting high *tariffs* on imported goods. Americans were intensely loyal to the two major parties, whose local "bosses" and "machines" won votes by distributing *patronage* jobs and contracts to members, as well as charitable relief. The major parties were so balanced that neither wanted to risk alienating voters by taking bold stands.

- **Corruption and Reform**   National politics during the Gilded Age focused on tariffs, the regulation of corporations, and *civil service reform*. The passage of the Pendleton Civil Service Reform Act in 1883 began the professionalization of federal workers. In the 1884 presidential election, Republicans favoring reform, the *Mugwumps*, helped elect Democrat Grover Cleveland. As president, he signed the 1887 act creating the *Interstate Commerce Commission (ICC)* to regulate railroads. In 1890, under President Benjamin Harrison, Republicans passed the Sherman Anti-Trust Act, the Sherman Silver Purchase Act, and the McKinley Tariff Act.

- **Inadequate Currency Supply and Unhappy Farmers**   Over the course of the late nineteenth century, the *money problem* had become a central political issue. The supply of money had not increased as the economy had grown. Many farmers believed that the coinage of silver, rather than a gold standard system, would result in inflation, which in turn would increase the value of their crops and reduce their debts. In the aftermath of the *Panic of 1893* and the ensuing depression, farmers and others dissatisfied with the Republican and Democratic parties formed a series of political parties and alliances, one of which, the *People's party (Populists)*, briefly operated as a national third party. In the election of 1896, the Democratic party nominated William Jennings Bryan, who adopted the coinage of silver as his crusade. He was opposed by Republican William McKinley, who supported the gold standard. McKinley won the election in part by appealing to the growing number of city dwellers and industrial workers.

## CHRONOLOGY

| | |
|---|---|
| **1859** | Charles Darwin's *On the Origin of Species* is published |
| **1882** | Congress passes the Chinese Exclusion Act |
| **1883** | Congress passes the Pendleton Civil Service Reform Act |
| **1886** | Supreme Court issues *Wabash, St. Louis, and Pacific Railroad Company v. Illinois* decision |
| **1887** | Interstate Commerce Commission is created |
| **1890** | Congress passes the Sherman Anti-Trust Act, the Sherman Silver Purchase Act, and the McKinley Tariff Act |

## KEY TERMS

**Gilded Age** p. 773

**tenements** p. 775

**new immigrants** p. 778

**nativists** p. 779

**Chinese Exclusion Act (1882)** p. 780

**saloons** p. 781

**social Darwinism** p. 784

**reform Darwinism** p. 785

**party bosses** p. 788

**patronage** p. 788

**civil service reform** p. 791

**Mugwumps** p. 795

**Interstate Commerce Commission (ICC)** p. 797

**tariff reform** p. 797

**People's party (Populists)** p. 805

**Panic of 1893** p. 806

**money problem** p. 808

 INQUIZITIVE

**Go to InQuizitive to see what you've learned—and learn what you've missed—with personalized feedback along the way.**

*part six*

# MODERN AMERICA

The United States entered the twentieth century on a wave of unrelenting
change. The nation was on the thresh-
old of modernity, which both excited and scared Americans.
Old truths and beliefs clashed with unsettling scientific discoveries and social practices. People debated the legitimacy
of Darwinism, the existence of God, the dangers of jazz, and
the federal effort to prohibit the sale of alcoholic beverages.

The advent of automobiles and airplanes helped shrink distance,
and such communications innovations as radio and film helped

strengthen the sense that America now had a *national* culture. William McKinley was the first president to ride in an automobile, appear in motion pictures, and use the telephone to plot political strategy.

Spurred by its growing industrial power, the United States began to emerge from its isolationist shell. Previously, presidents and statesmen had sought to insulate America from the intrigues and conflicts of European powers. Non-involvement in foreign wars and nonintervention in the internal affairs of foreign governments formed the pillars of U.S. foreign policy. During the 1890s, however, expanding commercial interests led Americans to broaden their global commitments.

Imperialism was the focus of the major European powers, and a growing number of expansionists demanded that the United States join in the hunt for new territories and markets beyond North America. Others believed that America should support democratic ideals abroad. Such mixed motives helped spark the Spanish-American War (more recently called the War of 1898) and justify the resulting acquisition of colonies. Entangling alliances with European powers soon followed.

The outbreak of the Great War in Europe in 1914 posed an even greater challenge to America's tradition of nonintervention. The prospect of a German victory over the French and British threatened the balance of power in Europe, which had long ensured the security of the United States. By 1917, it appeared that Germany might triumph and begin to menace the Western Hemisphere. When German submarines began sinking American merchant ships, President Woodrow Wilson's patience ran out, and in April 1917, the United States entered the Great War.

Wilson's crusade to transform international affairs in accordance with his idealistic principles dislodged American foreign policy from its isolationist moorings. It also spawned a prolonged debate about the nation's role in world affairs—a debate that World War II would resolve (for a time) on the side of internationalism.

While the United States was becoming a formidable military power, cities and factories were sprouting across the nation's landscape, and an abundance of jobs and affordable farmland attracted millions of foreign immigrants. They were not always welcomed, nor were they readily assimilated. Ethnic and racial strife grew, as did labor agitation.

In the midst of such social turmoil and unparalleled economic development, reformers made their first sustained attempt to adapt political and social institutions to the realities of the industrial age. The worst excesses of urban-industrial development—corporate monopolies, child labor, political corruption, hazardous working conditions, urban ghettos—were finally addressed.

During the Progressive Era (1890–1920), local, state, and federal governments sought to rein in industrial capitalism and develop a more rational and efficient public policy.

A conservative Republican resurgence challenged the notion of the new regulatory state during the 1920s, and free enterprise and corporate capitalism enjoyed a dramatic revival. But the stock market crash of 1929 helped propel the United States and the world into the worst economic downturn in history. The severity of the Great Depression renewed demands for federal programs to protect the general welfare. The many New Deal initiatives and agencies instituted by President Franklin Delano Roosevelt and his Democratic administration created the framework for a welfare state that has since served as the basis for public policy.

The New Deal revived public confidence and put people back to work, but it took a second world war to end the Great Depression and restore full employment. The necessity of mobilizing the nation to support the war also accelerated the growth of the federal government, and the unparalleled scope of the war helped catapult the United States into a leadership role in world politics. The development of atomic bombs ushered in a new era of nuclear diplomacy that held the fate of the world in the balance. For all the new creature comforts associated with modern life, Americans in 1945 found themselves living with an array of new anxieties.

# 20 Seizing an American Empire

## 1865–1913

**The Charge of the Rough Riders of San Juan Hill** (1898)  Before Frederic Remington became a professional artist, he had unsuccessful forays into hunting, ranching, and even the saloon business in the West. His intimacy with the Western way of life, along with his technical skill and keen sense of observation, were not lost on Theodore Roosevelt, who invited Remington to travel with the Rough Riders during the Spanish-American War.

A fter the Civil War, a mood of isolationism—a desire to stay out of conflicts elsewhere in the world—dominated American public opinion. The nation's geographic advantages encouraged this attitude: oceans to the east and west, and militarily weak neighbors in the Western Hemisphere. That the powerful British navy protected the shipping lanes between the United States and the British Isles gave Americans a heightened sense of security.

By the end of the nineteenth century, however, people had become aware that America was a world power with global responsibilities and imperial ambitions. As a Kentucky newspaper editor proclaimed in 1893, the United States was "the most advanced and powerful" nation in the world, an "imperial Republic" destined to shape the "future of the world." The *Washington Post* agreed, saying that "the Taste of Empire is in the mouth of the people."

While still wanting to stay out of European conflicts, a growing number of Americans urged officials to acquire territory outside North America. The old idea of "manifest destiny"—that the United States had been blessed by God (was "destined") to expand its territory westward across the continent—was broadened to justify American control of other regions of the Western Hemisphere, stretching as far as the Pacific and Asia. Americans embraced a new form of expansionism that sought distant territories as colonies, with no intention of admitting them to the nation as states. The new manifest destiny, in other words, became a justification for imperialism.

## *focus questions*

**1.** What factors motivated America's new imperialism after the Civil War?

**2.** How and why did America expand its influence in the Pacific before the Spanish-American War (War of 1898)?

**3.** What were the causes of the Spanish-American War (War of 1898)? What were its major events?

**4.** What were the consequences of the Spanish-American War (War of 1898) for American foreign policy?

**5.** What was behind Theodore Roosevelt's rapid rise to the presidency? What were the main elements of his foreign policies?

**6.** How did presidents Roosevelt, Taft, and Wilson expand America's international involvement?

Manifest destiny also took on a racial meaning. Many Americans agreed with future president Theodore Roosevelt that the United States needed to expand "on behalf of the *destiny* of the [Anglo-Saxon] race." Roosevelt and others believed that the Americans and British were at the top of the racial pyramid, superior to all others in intellect, ambition, and creativity.

Political and business leaders argued that America's rapid industrial development required the addition of foreign territories—by conquest if necessary—to gain easier access to vital raw materials such as rubber, tin, copper, palm oil, and various dyes. At the same time, manufacturers and commercial farmers had become increasingly dependent on international trade, which required an expanded force of warships to protect oceangoing U.S. freighters. And a modern, steam-powered navy needed bases in the Caribbean and Pacific, where its warships could replenish their supplies of coal and water.

For these and other reasons, America expanded its military presence and territorial possessions. In 1898, as the result of a one-sided war against Spain, the United States, born in a revolution against British colonial rule, would become an imperial ruler of colonies around the world.

## Toward the New Imperialism

The United States was a latecomer to global **imperialism**. By the 1880s, the British, French, Belgians, Italians, Dutch, Spanish, and Germans had subjugated most of Africa and Asia. Often competing with one another for territories, they had established colonial governments to rule over the native populations and exploited the colonies economically. Each imperial nation dispatched missionaries to convert conquered peoples to Christianity. By 1900, some 18,000 Protestant and Catholic evangelicals were scattered around the world.

A small yet influential group of American officials demanded expansion beyond North America. In addition to Theodore Roosevelt, they included naval captain Alfred Thayer Mahan, president of the U.S. Naval War College, and Senators Albert J. Beveridge of Indiana and Henry Cabot Lodge of Massachusetts. Referring to European imperialism, Lodge said, "We must not be left behind."

In 1890, Mahan published *The Influence of Sea Power upon History, 1660–1783*, in which he argued that national greatness flowed from naval power, as the British had demonstrated. Mahan insisted that modern industrial development required a powerful navy centered on huge battleships, foreign commerce, colonies to provide raw materials and new markets, and global naval bases.

Mahan championed America's "destiny" to control the Caribbean Sea, build a canal across Central America to connect the Atlantic and Pacific Oceans, acquire Hawaii and the Philippine Islands, and spread Christian values and American investments across the Pacific. His ideas were widely circulated. By 1896, the United States had built eleven new battleships, making its navy the third most powerful in the world, behind those of Great Britain and Germany.

Claims of racial superiority reinforced the new imperialist spirit. Many Americans and Europeans readily assumed that the Anglo-Saxon race was dominant and others were clearly inferior (Indians, Africans). Such racist notions were given "scientific" authority by researchers at universities throughout Europe and America.

Prominent Americans used the arguments of social Darwinism to justify economic exploitation and territorial conquest abroad and racial segregation at home. Among nations as among individuals, they claimed, only the strongest survived. John Fiske, a Harvard historian, proclaimed the superior character of "Anglo-Saxon" institutions and peoples. The English-speaking "race," he argued, was destined to dominate the globe and transform the institutions, traditions, language, and even the blood of the world's "backward" races.

Such theories were often used to justify armed conquest. Theodore Roosevelt, for example, loved war and considered it necessary to maintain racial supremacy. He described warfare as the best way to promote "the clear instinct for race selfishness" and stressed that "the most ultimately righteous of all wars is a war with savages."

## EXPANSION IN THE PACIFIC

For John Fiske and other imperialists, Asia offered an especially attractive target. In 1866, Secretary of State William H. Seward had predicted that the United States must inevitably impose its economic domination "on the Pacific Ocean, and its islands and continents." To take advantage of the Asian markets, Seward believed that the United States first had to remove foreign powers from its northern Pacific coast and gain access to the region's valuable ports. To that end, he tried to acquire British Columbia, sandwiched between Russian-owned Alaska and the Washington Territory.

Late in 1866, while encouraging British Columbia to consider becoming a U.S. territory, Seward learned of Russia's desire to sell Alaska. He leaped at the opportunity, thinking the purchase might influence British Columbia's decision. In 1867, the United States bought Alaska for $7.2 million, thus removing the threat of Russian imperialism in North America. Critics scoffed at "Seward's folly," but the purchase of Alaska proved to be the best bargain since the Louisiana Purchase, in part because of its vast deposits of gold and oil.

Seward's successors at the State Department sustained his expansionist vision. Their major focus was acquiring key ports in the Pacific Ocean. Two island groups occupied especially strategic positions: Samoa and Hawaii (the Sandwich Islands). Both had major harbors, Pago Pago and Pearl Harbor, respectively. In the years after the Civil War, American interest in those islands deepened.

**SAMOA**  In 1878, the Samoans signed a treaty that granted the United States a naval base at Pago Pago. The treaty also granted extraterritoriality for Americans (meaning that in Samoa, Americans remained subject only to U.S. law), exchanged trade concessions, and called for the United States to help resolve any disputes with other nations. The following year, the German and British governments worked out similar arrangements with other islands in the Samoan group. There matters rested until civil war broke out in Samoa in 1887. A peace conference in Berlin in 1889 established a protectorate over Samoa, with Germany, Great Britain, and the United States in an uneasy partnership administering the island nation.

**Queen Liliuokalani** The Hawaiian queen sought to preserve her nation's independence.

**HAWAII**  The Hawaiian Islands, a unified kingdom since 1795, had a sizable population of American Christian missionaries and a profitable crop, sugarcane. In 1875, Hawaii had signed a reciprocal trade agreement allowing its sugar to enter the United States duty free in exchange for a promise that none of its territory would be leased or granted to a third power.

This agreement led to a boom in sugar production based on cheap immigrant labor, mainly Chinese and Japanese workers, and American sugar planters soon formed an economic elite. By the 1890s, the native Hawaiian population had been reduced to a minority by smallpox and other diseases, and Asian immigrants had become the largest ethnic group.

Beginning in 1891, Queen Liliuokalani, the Hawaiian ruler, tried to restrict the growing political power of American planters. Two years later, however, Hawaii's white population (called *haoles*) overthrew the monarchy with the help of U.S. Marines brought in by John L. Stevens, the U.S. ambassador. Stevens reported that the "Hawaiian pear is now fully ripe, and this is the golden hour for the United States to pluck it." Within a month, a committee representing the *haoles* asked the U.S. government to annex the islands. President Benjamin Harrison sent an annexation treaty to the Senate just as he was leaving the presidency in early 1893.

**"Our New Senators"** Mocking the Alaska Purchase, this political cartoon shows President Andrew Johnson and Secretary of State William Seward welcoming two new senators from Alaska: an Eskimo and a penguin.

To investigate the situation, the new president, Grover Cleveland, sent a special commissioner, who reported that the Americans in Hawaii had acted improperly and that most native Hawaiians opposed annexation. Cleveland tried to restore the queen to power but met resistance from the *haoles*. On July 4, 1894, the government they controlled created the Republic of Hawaii, which included in its constitution a provision for American annexation.

In 1897, when William McKinley became president, he was looking for an excuse to annex the islands. "We need Hawaii," he claimed. "It is [America's] manifest destiny." The United States annexed Hawaii in the summer of 1898 over the protests of native Hawaiians.

# The Spanish-American War (The War of 1898)

The annexation of Hawaii set in motion efforts to create a much larger American presence in Asia. Ironically, this imperialist push originated in Cuba, a Spanish colony ninety miles south of Florida. Even more ironically, the chief motive for intervention in Cuba was outrage at Spain's brutal imperialism.

"**FREE CUBA**" Throughout the second half of the nineteenth century, Cubans had repeatedly revolted against Spanish rule, only to be ruthlessly suppressed. As one of Spain's oldest colonies, Cuba was a major market for Spanish goods. Powerful American sugar and mining companies had also invested heavily in Cuba. In fact, the United States traded more with Cuba than Spain did, and American owners of sugar plantations in Cuba had grown increasingly concerned about the security of their investments.

On February 24, 1895, Cubans began a guerrilla war against Spanish troops. During what became the Cuban War for Independence (1895–1898), tens of thousands of Cubans died in Spanish detention camps.

Americans followed the conflict through the newspapers. Two of the largest newspapers, William Randolph Hearst's *New York Journal* and Joseph Pulitzer's *New York World*, were locked in fierce competition for readers. Each strove to outdo the other with sensational headlines about Spanish atrocities, real or invented.

Hearst explained that the role of newspapers was not simply to report on events but to shape public opinion and legislation. Newspapers, he boasted, had the power to "declare wars." Reporters in Cuba were encouraged to distort, exaggerate, or make up stories to attract more readers. Hearst's effort to manipulate public opinion was called **yellow journalism.**

In addition to boosting the *Journal*'s circulation, Hearst wanted a war against Spain to propel the United States to world-power status. Once war was declared, he took credit for it; one headline blared, "HOW DO YOU LIKE THE JOURNAL'S WAR?" Many Protestant ministers and publications also campaigned for war, in part because of antagonism toward Catholic Spain.

**THE POLITICAL PATH TO WAR**  At the outset of the Cuban War for Independence, President Grover Cleveland tried to protect U.S. business interests while avoiding military involvement. Public sympathy for the rebel cause prompted growing concern in Congress, however. By concurrent resolutions on April 6, 1896, the House and Senate endorsed granting official recognition to the Cuban rebels.

After his inauguration in March 1897, President William McKinley continued the policy of neutrality while taking a sympathetic stance toward the rebels. Later that year, Spain offered Cubans autonomy (self-government without formal independence) in return for ending the rebellion, but the Cubans rejected the offer.

Early in 1898, two events pushed Spain and the United States into a war that neither wanted. On January 25, the **U.S. battleship *Maine*** docked in Havana, the Cuban capital, supposedly on a courtesy call. On February 9, the *New York Journal* released the text of a letter from Dupuy de Lôme, Spanish ambassador to the United States, to a friend in Havana, summarizing McKinley's annual message to Congress. In the **de Lôme letter**, the Spaniard called McKinley "weak and a bidder for the admiration of the crowd, besides being a would-be politician who tries to leave a door open behind himself while keeping on good terms with the jingoes [warmongers] of his party."

Six days later, at 9:40 on the night of February 15, the *Maine* exploded. Within minutes, its ruptured hull filled with water. Many sailors, most of whom were asleep, drowned as the ship sank. Of the 354 on board, 260 died. (Half of the sailors were foreign-born immigrants.) Years later, the sinking was ruled an accident resulting from an on-board coal explosion, but in 1898, those eager for war were convinced that the Spanish had sunk the ship.

Theodore Roosevelt, the assistant secretary of the navy, called the sinking "an act of dirty treachery" and told a friend that he "would give anything if President McKinley would order the fleet to Havana tomorrow." The United States, he insisted, "needs a war."

Congress authorized $50 million to prepare for combat, but McKinley, who assumed that the sinking was an accident, resisted demands for war while negotiating with the Spanish. As the days passed, Roosevelt told his war-hungry friends that McKinley had "no more backbone than a chocolate éclair." With Roosevelt's encouragement, the public's antagonism toward Spain grew, stirred by the popular saying "Remember the *Maine*, to Hell with Spain!"

At first, the Spanish government grudgingly agreed to every major American demand, but the weight of public opinion, the outcry from Democratic leaders, and the influence of Republican jingoists eroded McKinley's neutrality.

On April 11, he asked Congress for authority to use the armed forces to end the fighting in Cuba. On April 20, Congress declared Cuba independent from Spain and demanded the withdrawal of Spanish forces. The Spanish government quickly broke diplomatic ties with the United States. After U.S. ships began blockading Cuban ports, Spain declared war on April 24. The next day, Congress passed its own declaration of war. The **Teller Amendment** to the war resolution denied any U.S. intention to annex Cuba.

"We are all jingoes now," trumpeted the *New York Sun*, "and the head jingo is the Hon. William McKinley." McKinley called for 125,000 volunteers to supplement the 28,000 men already serving in the U.S. Army. Among the first to enlist was Roosevelt, who resigned from his government post and told his tailor to make him a dashing army uniform. To him, combat would help America reclaim "the stern and manly qualities which are essential to the well-being of a masterful race."

Never had an American war generated such unexpected and far-reaching consequences. McKinley soon saw it as an opportunity to acquire overseas territories. "While we are conducting war and until its conclusion," he wrote privately, "we must keep all we get; when the war is over we must keep what we want." (What had long been called the Spanish-American War has been renamed the War of 1898 because it involved not just Spanish and American combatants, but Cubans, Filipinos, and Puerto Ricans.)

## "A Splendid Little War"

The war with overmatched Spain lasted only 114 days, but it set the United States on a course that would transform its role in the world. The conflict was barely under way before the U.S. Navy produced a spectacular victory 7,000 miles away, at Manila Bay in the Philippine Islands, a colony controlled by Spain for more than 300 years. Just before war was declared, Theodore

Roosevelt, who was still assistant secretary of the navy, ordered Commodore George Dewey, commander of the U.S. Asiatic Squadron, to engage Spanish warships in the Philippines in case of war in Cuba.

Dewey arrived in Manila Bay on April 30 with six modern fleet, which quickly destroyed or captured the outdated Spanish vessels there. An English reporter called it "a military execution rather than a real contest." News of the battle set off wild celebrations in America.

Dewey, however, had no soldiers to go onshore. He and his fleet stayed in Manila Bay for several months waiting for reinforcements while German and British warships cruised offshore, ready to seize the Philippines if the United States did not.

In the meantime, Emilio Aguinaldo, leader of the Filipino nationalist movement, declared the Philippines independent on June 12, 1898. With Aguinaldo's help, Dewey's forces entered Manila on August 13 and accepted the surrender of the Spanish troops, who had feared for their lives if they surrendered to the Filipinos.

**THE CUBAN CAMPAIGN** At the start of the war, the Spanish army in Cuba was five times as large as the entire U.S. Army. McKinley's call for volunteers, however, inspired nearly a million men to enlist. Among the new recruits were some 10,000 African American soldiers, mostly northerners determined to "show our loyalty to our land." In the Jim Crow South, however, blacks were less eager to enlist because, as a Richmond newspaper editor observed, they suffered "a system of oppression as barbarous as that which is alleged to exist in Cuba."

In the meantime, the U.S. Navy blockaded the Spanish fleet inside Santiago Harbor while some 17,000 American troops assembled at Tampa, Florida. One prominent unit was the First Volunteer Cavalry, better known as the Rough Riders, a special regiment made up of former Ivy League athletes; Irish policemen; ex-convicts; cowboys from Oklahoma and New Mexico; Texas Rangers; and Cherokee, Choctaw, Chickasaw, Pawnee, and Creek Indians. All were "young, good shots, and good riders."

The Rough Riders are best remembered because Theodore Roosevelt was second in command. One Rough Rider said that Roosevelt was "nervous, energetic, virile [manly]. He may wear out some day, but he will never rust out."

When the 578 Rough Riders, accompanied by a gaggle of reporters and photographers, landed on June 22, 1898, at the undefended southeastern tip of Cuba, chaos followed. Except for Roosevelt's horse, most of the unit's horses and mules had been mistakenly sent elsewhere, leaving the Rough Riders to become the "Weary Walkers." Nevertheless, land and sea battles around Santiago quickly broke Spanish resistance.

**Colonel Roosevelt**  With hand on hip, Roosevelt led the Rough Riders in Cuba. He recruited most of his regiment from Arizona, New Mexico, and Texas because the southwestern climate resembled that of Cuba.

On July 1, about 7,000 U.S. soldiers took the fortified village of El Caney. While a much larger force attacked San Juan Hill, a smaller unit, led by Roosevelt on horseback and including the Rough Riders on foot, prepared to seize nearby Kettle Hill. Situated in a field of tall grass, the frustrated Americans were being shot by Spanish snipers while waiting to attack. Captain Bucky O'Neill decided to boost morale by strolling among the men while smoking a cigarette. When one of them shouted, "Captain, a bullet is sure to kill you," O'Neill replied, "Sergeant, the Spanish bullet ain't made that will kill me"— whereupon a Spanish bullet struck him in the jaw, killing him instantly.

O'Neill's death prompted Roosevelt to mount his horse and order his men to rise and charge the Spaniards. Although shot in the arm, Roosevelt kept moving, and his headlong gallop toward the Spanish lines made him a home-front legend. The *New York Times* reported that he had led the charge with "bulldog ferociousness." Roosevelt boasted that nobody "else could have handled this regiment quite as I handled it."

Being a military hero was Roosevelt's lifelong dream. According to the *New York World,* he had become "more talked about than any man in the country." Roosevelt crowed that he had "killed a Spaniard with my own hand—like a jack rabbit" and requested a Congressional Medal of Honor for his exploits.

It did not come. (President Bill Clinton finally awarded the medal posthumously in 2001.)

While Colonel Roosevelt was basking in the glory of battle, other U.S. soldiers in Cuba were less enthusiastic about modern warfare. Walter Bartholomew, a private from New York, reported that the war was so "much more hideous than my wildest imagination that I have not yet recovered from the shock." A soldier standing beside him had "the front of his throat torn completely off" by a Spanish bullet. As his unit was charging up San Juan Hill, they "became totally disorganized and thrown into utter confusion" amid the intense shooting. He discarded all he carried except for his rifle "in the mad scramble to get out of the valley of death."

**SPANISH DEFEAT AND CONCESSIONS** On July 3, the Spanish navy trapped at Santiago attempted to evade the American fleet blockading the harbor. But they were quickly destroyed; 474 Spaniards were killed or wounded, while the Americans suffered only two casualties. Spanish officials surrendered on July 17. On July 25, an American force moved into Spanish-held Puerto Rico, meeting only minor resistance.

The next day, the Spanish government sued for peace. A cease-fire agreement was signed on August 12. In Cuba, the Spanish formally surrendered and sailed for home. Excluded from the ceremony were the Cubans, for whom the war had supposedly been fought.

On December 10, 1898, the United States and Spain signed the Treaty of Paris. Under its terms, Cuba was to become independent and the United States was to annex Puerto Rico and Guam (a Spanish-controlled island between Hawaii and the Philippines) as new American territories. The United States would continue to occupy Manila, pending a transfer of power to the United States in the Philippines. Thus the Spanish Empire in the Americas, initiated by the voyages of Christopher Columbus some four centuries earlier, came to a humiliating end. The United States was ready to create its own empire.

During the four-month War of 1898 (Spanish-American War), more than 60,000 Spanish soldiers and sailors died of wounds or disease—mostly malaria, typhoid, dysentery, or yellow fever. Some 10,500 Cubans died. Among Americans, 5,462 died, but only 379 in battle; most died from disease. At such a cost, the United States imposed its will as a great power, with all the benefits—and burdens—that come with being an imperial nation.

Halfway through the fighting, John Hay, the U.S. ambassador to Great Britain who would soon become secretary of state, wrote to Roosevelt, calling the conflict "a splendid little war, begun with the highest motives, carried on with magnificent intelligence and spirit, favored by that fortune which loves the brave." By contrast, Spaniards referred to the war as "The Disaster," because the humiliating defeat called into question Spain's status as a world power.

## CONSEQUENCES OF VICTORY

Victory in the War of 1898 boosted American self-confidence and reinforced the self-serving belief that the United States had a manifest destiny to reshape the world in its own image.

In 1885, the Reverend Josiah Strong wrote a best-selling book titled *Our Country* in which he used a Darwinian argument to strengthen the appeal of manifest destiny. The "wonderful progress of the United States," he boasted, was an illustration of Charles Darwin's concept of "natural selection," since Americans had demonstrated that they were a "superior" civilization that represented "the largest liberty, the purest Christianity, the highest civilization." Strong asserted that the United States had a Christian duty and economic opportunity to expand "Anglo-Saxon" influence across the world. A growing international trade, he noted, would emerge from America's missionary evangelism and racial superiority. "Can anyone doubt," he asked, "that this race . . . is destined to dispossess many weaker races, assimilate others, and mold the remainder until . . . it has Anglo-Saxonized mankind?"

Europeans agreed that the United States had made a forceful entrance onto the world stage. The *Times* of London announced that the American victory over Spain must "effect a profound change in the whole attitude and policy of the United States. In the future America will play a part in the general affairs of the world such as she has never played before."

## TAKING THE PHILIPPINES

The United States soon substituted its own imperialism for Spain's. If the war had saved many lives by ending the insurrection in Cuba, it had also led the United States to take many lives in suppressing the anti-colonial insurrection in the Philippines. The acquisition of America's first imperial colonies created a host of moral and practical problems, from the difficulties of imposing U.S. rule on native peoples to those of defending far-flung territories.

**McKINLEY'S MOTIVES** The Treaty of Paris had left the political status of the Philippines unresolved. American business leaders wanted the United States to keep the islands so that they could more easily penetrate the markets of nearby China. As Mark Hanna, President McKinley's top adviser, stressed, controlling the Philippines would enable the United States to "take a large slice of the commerce of Asia." American missionary organizations, mostly Protestant, also favored annexation; they viewed the Philippines as a base from which to bring Christianity to "the little brown brother."

Not long after the United States took control, American authorities ended the Roman Catholic Church's status as the Philippines' official religion and made English the official language, thus opening the door for Protestant missionaries in the region.

These factors helped convince McKinley of the need to annex "those darned islands." He explained that

> one night late it came to me this way—I don't know how it was, but it came: (1) that we could not give them back to Spain—that would be cowardly and dishonorable; (2) that we could not turn them over to France or Germany—our commercial rivals in the Orient—that would be bad business and discreditable; (3) that we could not leave them to themselves—they were unfit for self-government—and they would soon have anarchy and misrule over there worse than Spain's was; and (4) that there was nothing left for us to do but to take them all, and to educate the Filipinos, and uplift and civilize and Christianize them, and by God's grace do the very best we could by them, as our fellowmen for whom Christ also died. And then I went to bed, and went to sleep and slept soundly.

In this brief statement, McKinley had summarized the motivating ideas of American imperialism: (1) national glory, (2) commerce, (3) racial superiority, and (4) evangelism. American negotiators in Paris finally offered Spain $20 million for the Philippines, Puerto Rico, and Guam, which would serve as a coaling station for ships headed across the Pacific.

Meanwhile, in addition to annexing Hawaii in 1898, the United States also claimed Wake Island, between Guam and Hawaii, which would become a vital link in a future transpacific telegraph cable. In 1899, Germany and the United States agreed to divide the Samoa Islands.

**DEBATING THE TREATY** By early 1899, the Senate had yet to ratify the Treaty of Paris with Spain because of growing opposition to a global American empire. Anti-expansionists argued that annexing the former Spanish colonies would violate the longstanding American principle embodied in the Constitution that people should be self-governing rather than colonial subjects. Senator Albert Beveridge of Indiana, however, argued that the ideal of democracy "applies only to those who are capable of self-government." In his view, the Filipinos were incapable. Theodore Roosevelt put it more bluntly. The Filipinos, he declared, were "wild beasts" who would benefit from American-imposed discipline: "There must be control! There must be mastery!"

The opposition might have killed the treaty had not the most prominent Democratic leader, William Jennings Bryan, argued that ending the war would open the way for the future independence of the Philippines. His position convinced enough Senate Democrats to support the treaty on February 6, 1899, by the narrowest of margins: only one vote more than the necessary two thirds majority.

President McKinley, however, had no intention of granting independence to the Philippines. He insisted that the United States take control of the islands as an act of "benevolent assimilation" of the native population. A California newspaper gave a more candid explanation: "WE DO NOT WANT THE FILIPINOS. WE WANT THE PHILIPPINES."

Many Filipinos had a different vision. In January 1899, they declared again their independence and named twenty-nine-year-old Emilio Aguinaldo president. The following month, an American soldier outside Manila fired on Aguinaldo's nationalist forces, called *insurrectos*, killing two. The next day, the U.S. Army commander, without investigating the shooting, ordered his troops to assault the *insurrectos*, thus igniting a full-scale conflict that continued for weeks. General Elwell S. Otis rejected Aguinaldo's proposals for a truce, saying that "fighting, having begun, must go on to the grim end." He would accept only unconditional surrender.

On June 2, 1899, the Philippine Republic declared war against the United States. Since the *insurrectos* more or less controlled the Philippines outside Manila, what followed was largely a war of conquest at odds with the founding principle of the United States: that people have the right to govern themselves. The war would rob the Filipinos of the chance to be their own masters.

**THE PHILIPPINE-AMERICAN WAR (1899–1902)** The effort to crush Filipino nationalism lasted three years and involved some 126,000 U.S. troops. It cost the American government $600 million and took the lives of 200,000 Filipinos (most of them civilians) and 4,234 American soldiers.

It was a brutal conflict fought in tropical heat and humidity. Racism spurred numerous atrocities by the Americans, many of whom referred to the Filipinos as "niggers." U.S. troops burned villages, tortured and executed prisoners, and imprisoned civilians in overcrowded concentration camps. A reporter for the *Philadelphia Ledger* noted that U.S. soldiers had "killed to exterminate men, women, children, prisoners and captives, active insurgents and suspected people from lads of ten up, the idea prevailing that the Filipino as such was little better than a dog."

Both sides used torture to gain information. A favorite method employed by Americans was the "water cure," a technique to simulate drowning developed in the Spanish Inquisition during the sixteenth century. (Today it is called waterboarding.) A captured insurgent would be placed on his back on the ground. While soldiers stood on his outstretched arms and feet, they pried his mouth open and held it in place with a bamboo stick. They then poured salt water into the captive's mouth and nose until his stomach was bloated, whereupon they would stomp on his abdomen, forcing the water, now mixed with gastric juices, out of his mouth. They repeated the process until the captive told the soldiers what they wanted to know—or died. "It is not civilized warfare," wrote the *Philadelphia Ledger*, "but we are not dealing with civilized people."

Organized Filipino resistance collapsed by the end of 1899, but sporadic clashes continued for months thereafter. On April 1, 1901, Aguinaldo swore an oath accepting the authority of the United States and pledging his allegiance to the U.S. government.

Against this backdrop, the debate over imperialism continued in the United States. In 1899, several groups combined to form the **American Anti-Imperialist League**. Andrew Carnegie footed the bills for the League and even offered $20 million to buy independence for the Filipinos. Other prominent anti-imperialists included author Mark Twain, college presidents Charles Eliot of Harvard and David Starr Jordan of Stanford, and social reformer Jane

**Turmoil in the Philippines** Emilio Aguinaldo (seated third from right) and other leaders of the Filipino insurgence.

Addams. Even former presidents Grover Cleveland and Benjamin Harrison urged President McKinley to withdraw U.S. forces from the Philippines.

The conflict to suppress Filipino independence had become "a quagmire," said Mark Twain, and the United States should "not try to get them under our heel" or intervene "in any other country that is not ours." He "opposed" the American eagle "putting its talons on any other land." Harvard philosopher William James was even more emphatic, arguing that imperialism had caused the United States to "puke up its ancient soul."

Senator George Frisbie Hoar led the opposition in Congress to annexation of the Philippines. Under the Constitution, he pointed out, "no power is given the Federal government to acquire territory to be held and governed permanently as colonies" or "to conquer alien people and hold them in subjugation."

Ministers denounced imperialism as un-Christian. Charles Ames, a prominent Unitarian leader, predicted that American imperialism would "put us into a permanent attitude of arrogance, testiness, and defiance towards other nations. . . . We shall be one more bully among bullies." Southern Democrats feared that giving civil rights to people of color would undermine white supremacy in America.

Samuel Gompers, the union leader, opposed converting the former Spanish colonies into American colonies because he was convinced that immigrants would lower wage levels: "If these new islands are to become ours . . . can we hope to close the floodgates of immigration from the hordes of Chinese and the semisavage races coming from what will then be part of our own country?"

## ORGANIZING THE NEW COLONIES

In the end, the imperialists won the debate. Senator Albert J. Beveridge boasted in 1900: "The Philippines are ours forever. And just beyond the Philippines are China's illimitable markets. . . . The power that rules the Pacific is the power that rules the world." He added that the U.S. economy was producing "more than we can consume, making more than we can use. Therefore we must find new markets for our produce." American-controlled colonies would make the best new markets. Without acknowledging it, Beveridge and others were using many of the same arguments that England had used in founding the American colonies in the seventeenth century.

On July 4, 1901, the U.S. military government in the Philippines gave way to civilian control, and William Howard Taft became the civil governor. In 1902, Congress passed the Philippine Government Act, which declared the islands an "unorganized territory"—in essence, an American colony not eligible for

## U.S. INTERESTS IN THE PACIFIC

SOVIET UNION

PRIBILOF ISLANDS 1910

ALASKA 1867

CANADA

BERING SEA

ALEUTIAN ISLANDS 1889

UNITED STATES

LIAO-TUNG PENINSULA
Port Arthur (Lü-shun)
SHAN-TUNG PEN.
Wei-hai

KOREA

CHINA

JAPAN

PACIFIC OCEAN

HONG KONG

FORMOSA (TAIWAN)

BONIN ISLANDS

MIDWAY ISLANDS 1867

HAWAIIAN ISLANDS 1898

PESCADORES (PÖENG-HU)

Kwangchow Bay

MARIANA ISLANDS

WAKE ISLAND 1898

JOHNSTON ATOLL 1858

PHILIPPINE ISLANDS 1898

GUAM 1898

MARSHALL ISLANDS

KINGMAN REEF 1858

PALMYRA ATOLL 1898

CAROLINE ISLANDS

GILBERT ISLANDS

HOWLAND ISLAND 1857

BAKER ISLAND 1857

Equator

DUTCH EAST INDIES (INDONESIA)

SOLOMON ISLANDS

SAMOA ISLANDS 1889

NEW HEBRIDES (VANUATU)

FIJI ISLANDS

AUSTRALIA

- Why was President McKinley eager to acquire territory in the Pacific and the Caribbean?
- What kind of political system did the U.S. government create in Hawaii and in the Philippines?
- How did Filipinos and Hawaiians resist the Americans?

statehood. In 1917, the Jones Act affirmed America's intention to grant the Philippines independence, but that would not happen until 1946.

Closer to home, Puerto Rico had been acquired in part to serve as a U.S. outpost guarding the Caribbean Sea. On April 12, 1900, the Foraker Act established a government on the island, and its residents were declared citizens of Puerto Rico; they were not made citizens of the United States until 1917.

In Cuba, the United States finally fulfilled the promise of independence after restoring order, organizing schools, and improving sanitary conditions.

**"Well, I hardly know which to take first!"** With a growing appetite for foreign territory, Uncle Sam browses his options: Cuba Steak, Puerto Rico Pig, Philippine Floating Islands, and others. An expectant President McKinley waits to take his order.

The problem of widespread disease prompted the work of Dr. Walter Reed. Named head of the Army Yellow Fever Commission in 1900, he proved that mosquitoes carry yellow fever. The commission's experiments led the way to effective control of the disease worldwide.

In 1900, on President McKinley's order, Cubans drafted a constitution modeled on that of the United States. The following year, however, the Platt Amendment sharply restricted the Cuban government's independence by requiring that Cuba never sign a treaty with a third power, that it keep its debt within the government's power to repay it out of ordinary revenues, and that it acknowledge the right of the United States to intervene whenever it saw fit. Finally, Cuba had to sell or lease to the United States lands to be used for coaling or naval stations, a stipulation that led to a U.S. naval base at Guantánamo Bay that still exists today.

## IMPERIAL RIVALRIES IN EAST ASIA

While the United States was conquering the Philippines, other nations were threatening to carve up China. After Japan defeated China in the First Sino-Japanese War (1894–1895), European nations set out to exploit the weakness of the virtually defenseless nation. By the end of the century, Russia, Germany, France, and Great Britain had each established spheres of influence in China—territories that they controlled but did not formally annex.

In 1898 and again in 1899, the British asked the American government to join them in preserving the territorial integrity of China against further imperialist actions. Both times, however, the Senate rejected the request because the United States as yet had no strategic investment in the region. The American outlook changed with the defeat of Spain and the acquisition of the Philippines. Instead of acting jointly with Great Britain, however, the U.S. government decided to act alone (unilaterally).

What came to be known as the **Open Door policy** was outlined in Secretary of State John Hay's Open Door Note, dispatched in 1899 to his European counterparts. Without consulting the Chinese, Hay announced that China should remain an "Open Door" to European and American trade and that other nations should not try to take control of Chinese ports or territory. None of the European powers except Britain accepted Hay's principles, but none rejected them, either. So, Hay announced that all major powers involved in China had accepted the policy.

The Open Door policy was rooted in the desire of American businesses to exploit and ultimately dominate Chinese markets. It also appealed to those who opposed imperialism because it pledged to keep China from being carved up by powerful European nations.

The policy had little legal standing, however. When the Japanese became concerned about growing Russian influence in Manchuria (in northeast China) and asked how the United States intended to enforce the policy, Hay replied that America was "not prepared . . . to enforce these views." So the situation would remain for forty years, until continued Japanese military expansion in China would bring about a diplomatic dispute with America that would lead to war.

**THE BOXERS** A new Asian crisis arose in 1900 when Chinese nationalists known to the Western world as Boxers—they called themselves the "Fists of Righteous Harmony"—rebelled against foreign involvement in China, especially Christian missionary efforts, and laid siege to foreign embassies in Peking (now known as Beijing). An expedition of British, German, Russian, Japanese, and American soldiers was organized to rescue international diplomats and their staffs. Hay, fearful that the intervention might become an excuse for other nations to dismember China, took the opportunity to refine the Open Door policy. The United States, he said, sought a solution that would "preserve Chinese territorial and administrative integrity" as well as "equal and impartial trade with all parts of the Chinese Empire." Six weeks later, the foreign military expedition reached Peking and ended the Boxer Rebellion.

# Roosevelt's "Big-Stick" Diplomacy

On September 6, 1901, while President McKinley was shaking hands in a reception line at the Pan-American Exposition in Buffalo, New York, a twenty-eight-year-old unemployed anarchist (one who does not believe in governments or rulers), approached with a concealed gun and fired twice at point-blank range. One bullet was deflected by the president's coat button and breastbone, but the other tore through his abdomen and lodged in his back.

For several days, doctors issued optimistic reports about McKinley's condition, but after a week, the president knew he was dying. "It is useless, gentlemen," he told the doctors. "I think we ought to have a prayer." Then he said, "Goodbye, goodbye to all." Leon Czolgosz (pronounced chol-GOTS), was convicted of murder and executed in an electric chair, a new invention.

Vice President Theodore Roosevelt became president on September 14, 1901. His infusion of "manly energy" would transform the modern presidency. The nation had emerged from the War of 1898 a world power with major international responsibilities. To ensure that Americans accepted their new global role, Roosevelt stretched both the Constitution and executive power to the limit. In the process, he pushed a reluctant nation onto the center stage of world affairs.

# A "Rocket" Rise to Prominence

Born in 1858 to a family of wealth and stature, "Teedie" Roosevelt enjoyed a privileged life in New York City. He visited Europe as a child, studied with a personal tutor, spoke German fluently, and graduated from Harvard with honors in 1880. A frail, puny boy, nearly blind in one eye and weakened by chronic asthma, he followed his father's order to "make your own body." He compulsively lifted weights in a gym his father installed in their mansion, wrestled, hiked, rowed, swam, boxed, played tennis, rode horses, became a crack shot, and climbed mountains, all in an effort to build himself into an intellectual athlete.

Roosevelt transformed himself into a barrel-chested man of almost superhuman energy who fiercely championed the "strenuous life." He told his children that he would rather see them dead than grow up to be "weaklings" and "sissies."

Roosevelt also displayed extraordinary intellectual curiosity. He became a voracious reader and talented writer, a natural scientist, a dedicated bird watcher, a renowned historian and essayist, and a zealous moralist who divided the world into two camps: good and evil. Roosevelt's zest for life and his combative spirit were contagious, and he was ever eager to express an opinion on any subject.

Within two years after graduating from Harvard, Roosevelt, a reform-minded Republican, won election as the youngest member of the New York legislature. He could not be bought, nor did he tolerate the excesses of the spoils system. "Though I am a strong party man," he warned, "if I find a corrupt public official, I would take off his head."

With the world seemingly at his feet, however, disaster struck. In 1884, his mother, Mittie, only forty-eight years old, died of typhoid fever. Eleven hours later, his "bewitchingly pretty," twenty-two-year-old wife, Alice, died in his arms of kidney failure, having given birth to their only child just two days earlier. The "light has gone out of my life," Roosevelt noted in his diary.

Shaken by his "strange and terrible fate," Roosevelt turned his newborn daughter over to his sister, quit his political career, sold the family house, and moved to a cattle ranch in the Dakota Territory, where he stayed for two years. He threw himself into roping and branding steers, shooting buffalo and bears, capturing outlaws, fighting Indians, and reading by campfire. He was, by his own admission, a poor shot, a bad roper, and an average rider, but he loved his western life. He would write in his memoirs that "I owe more than I can express to the West."

Back in New York City, Roosevelt remarried and ran unsuccessfully for mayor in 1886. He later served as a U.S. Civil Service commissioner and as the city's police commissioner. In 1896, he campaigned energetically for William McKinley, and the new president rewarded him with the position of assistant secretary of the navy. Roosevelt lusted to be "one of the governing class," so he took full advantage of the celebrity he had gained with the Rough Riders in Cuba to win the governorship of New York in 1898. By then, he had become the most visible young Republican in the nation. Two years later, party leaders were urging him to become the running mate for McKinley, who was hoping for a second term.

## FROM VICE PRESIDENT TO PRESIDENT

In the 1900 presidential contest, the Democrats turned again to William Jennings Bryan, who wanted to make American imperialism the "paramount issue" of the campaign. The party's platform condemned the conflict with Filipino nationalists as "an unnecessary war" that had placed the United States "in the false and un-American position of crushing with military force the efforts of our former allies to achieve liberty and self-government."

The Republicans renominated McKinley and named Roosevelt their candidate for vice president. Roosevelt crisscrossed the nation condemning Bryan's "communistic and socialistic doctrines" promoting higher taxes and the unlimited coinage of silver. In the end, McKinley and Roosevelt won by

7.2 million to 6.4 million popular votes and 292 to 155 electoral votes. Bryan even lost Nebraska, his home state.

On September 14, 1901, McKinley died from his assassin's bullet. "Now look," exclaimed Mark Hanna, who had been McKinley's political manager, "that damned cowboy is President of the United States!"

Six weeks short of his forty-third birthday, Roosevelt, known affectionately as TR, was the youngest man to become president. But he had more experience in public affairs than most new presidents, and more vitality than any. One observer compared his boundless personality and energy to Niagara Falls—"both great wonders of nature." TR's glittering spectacles, glistening teeth, and overflowing enthusiasm were like divine gifts to political cartoonists, as was his motto, an old African proverb: "Speak softly, and carry a big stick."

For Roosevelt, the presidency was, as he put it, a "bully pulpit"—an inviting platform for delivering fist-pumping speeches on the virtues of honesty, courage, and civic duty.

Like many of his political friends and associates, Roosevelt was convinced that the "civilized" and "barbarian" people of the world faced inevitable conflict, not unlike the fate of the Native Americans pushed off their ancestral lands by Americans. In 1899, he argued that the United States needed to conquer other regions to bring "law, order, and righteousness" to "backward peoples." He believed that American imperialists would be missionaries of civic virtue, spreading the merits of their "race" to "savages."

**THE PANAMA CANAL** After the Spanish-American War (the War of 1898), one issue overshadowed every other in the Caribbean: the proposed Panama Canal. By enabling ships to travel from the Pacific Ocean directly into the Gulf of Mexico, such a canal would cut the travel distance between San Francisco and New York City by almost 8,000 miles.

The nation of Panama had been a major concern of Americans since the late 1840s, when it became an important overland link in the sea route from the East Coast to the California goldfields. Two treaties dating from that period loomed as obstacles to the construction of a canal. The Bidlack Treaty with Colombia (then called New Granada) guaranteed Colombia's control over Panama. In the Clayton-Bulwer Treaty, the British had agreed to acquire no more Central American territory, and the United States joined them in agreeing to build or fortify a canal only by mutual consent.

Secretary of State John Hay asked the British for consent to build a canal. The outcome was the Hay-Pauncefote Treaty of 1901. Other obstacles remained, however. From 1881 to 1887, a French company led by Ferdinand

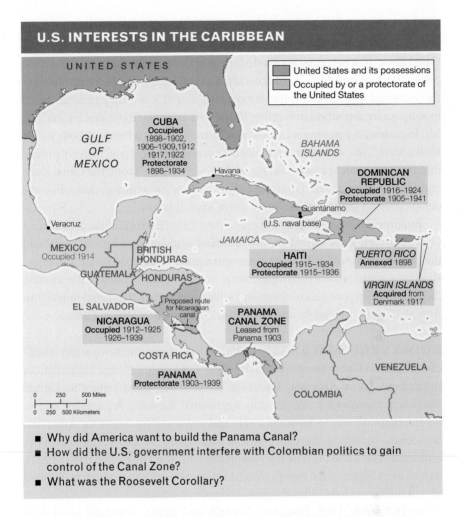

## U.S. INTERESTS IN THE CARIBBEAN

UNITED STATES

- United States and its possessions
- Occupied by or a protectorate of the United States

GULF OF MEXICO

**CUBA**
Occupied
1898–1902,
1906–1909,1912
1917,1922
Protectorate
1898–1934

Havana

BAHAMA ISLANDS

**DOMINICAN REPUBLIC**
Occupied 1916–1924
Protectorate 1905–1941

Guantánamo
(U.S. naval base)

Veracruz

JAMAICA

**MEXICO**
Occupied 1914

BRITISH HONDURAS

**HAITI**
Occupied 1915–1934
Protectorate 1915–1936

**PUERTO RICO**
Annexed 1898

GUATEMALA    HONDURAS

EL SALVADOR

Proposed route for Nicaraguan canal

**VIRGIN ISLANDS**
Acquired from Denmark 1917

**NICARAGUA**
Occupied 1912–1925
1926–1939

**PANAMA CANAL ZONE**
Leased from Panama 1903

COSTA RICA

VENEZUELA

**PANAMA**
Protectorate 1903–1939

COLOMBIA

0    250    500 Miles

0    250    500 Kilometers

- Why did America want to build the Panama Canal?
- How did the U.S. government interfere with Colombian politics to gain control of the Canal Zone?
- What was the Roosevelt Corollary?

de Lesseps, who had engineered the Suez Canal in Egypt, had already spent nearly $300 million and some 20,000 lives to dig a canal a third of the way across Panama, which was still under Colombian control. The company convinced the United States to purchase the partially completed canal.

In return for acquiring a canal zone six miles wide, the United States agreed to pay Colombia $10 million. The U.S. Senate ratified the Hay-Herrán Treaty in 1903, but the Colombian Senate held out for $25 million. As President Roosevelt raged against the "foolish and homicidal corruptionists in Bogotá," the Panamanians revolted against Colombian rule. Roosevelt aided the Panamanians and signed a treaty with the newly independent nation that extended the Canal Zone from six to ten miles wide.

For a $10 million down payment and $250,000 a year, the United States received "in perpetuity the use, occupation and control" of the fifty-mile-long Canal Zone. Not everyone applauded the president's actions. A Chicago newspaper attacked him for his "rough-riding assault upon another republic over the shattered wreckage of international law." The U.S. attorney general, asked to supply a legal opinion upholding Roosevelt's actions, responded wryly, "No, Mr. President, if I were you I would not have any taint of legality about it." He then added, "You were accused of seduction and you have conclusively proved that you were guilty of rape." Roosevelt later explained, "I took the Canal Zone and let Congress debate [about the legitimacy of his actions]; and while the debate goes on the [construction of the] Canal does also."

Building the Panama Canal was one of the greatest engineering feats in history. Over ten years, some 60,000 mostly unskilled workers from Europe, Asia, and the Caribbean, as well as U.S. engineers and managers, used dynamite and steam shovels to gouge out the canal from dense jungle. Almost a third of the workers died from malaria or yellow fever. But with great fanfare, the canal opened on August 15, 1914, two weeks after the outbreak of the Great War in Europe.

**ROOSEVELT AND LATIN AMERICA**  Theodore Roosevelt's "theft" of the Panama Canal Zone created decades of ill will toward the United States throughout Latin America. Constant interference from both the United States and European countries only aggravated tensions. A frequent excuse for intervention was to promote a safe and stable environment for American businesses, including the collection of debts owed by Latin American governments. The Latin Americans responded with the Drago Doctrine (1902), named after Argentinian foreign minister Luis María Drago, which prohibited armed intervention by other countries to collect debts.

In December 1902, however, German and British warships blockaded Venezuela to force the repayment of debts in defiance of both the Drago Doctrine and the Monroe Doctrine, the U.S. policy dating to 1823 that prohibited European intervention in the Western Hemisphere. Roosevelt decided that if the United States were to keep European nations from intervening militarily in Latin America, "then sooner or later we must keep order [there] ourselves."

In 1904, a crisis over the debts of the Dominican Republic prompted Roosevelt to send two warships to the island nation and issue what came to be known as the **Roosevelt Corollary** to the Monroe Doctrine: the principle, in short, that in certain circumstances, the United States was justified in intervening in Latin America to prevent Europeans from doing so. Thereafter, U.S. presidents would repeatedly use force to ensure that Latin American nations paid their debts.

## RELATIONS WITH JAPAN

While wielding a "big stick" in Latin America, President Roosevelt was playing the role of peacemaker in East Asia. In 1904, the rivalry between Russia and Japan flared into the Russo-Japanese War over Japan's attempts to expand its influence in China and Korea.

On February 8, Japanese warships devastated the Russian fleet. The Japanese then occupied the Korean peninsula and drove the Russians back into Manchuria. When the Japanese signaled that they would welcome a negotiated settlement, Roosevelt sponsored a peace conference in Portsmouth, New Hampshire. In the Treaty of Portsmouth, signed on September 5, 1905, Russia acknowledged Japan's "predominant political, military, and economic interests in Korea." (Japan would annex the kingdom in 1910.) Both powers agreed to leave Manchuria.

Japan's show of strength raised concerns among U.S. leaders about the security of the Philippines. During the Portsmouth talks, Roosevelt sent William Howard Taft to meet with the Japanese foreign minister. They

THE BIG STICK IN THE CARIBBEAN SEA

**Big-stick diplomacy** President Theodore Roosevelt wields "the big stick," symbolizing his aggressive diplomacy. As he stomps through the Caribbean, he drags a string of American warships behind him.

negotiated the Taft-Katsura Agreement of July 29, 1905, in which the United States accepted Japanese control of Korea in exchange for Japan acknowledging U.S. control of the Philippines. Three years later, the Root-Takahira Agreement, negotiated by Secretary of State Elihu Root and the Japanese ambassador to the United States, reinforced "the independence and integrity of China" and "the principle of equal opportunity for commerce and industry in China."

Behind the outward appearances of goodwill, however, lay distrust. For many Americans, the Russian threat in East Asia gave way to concerns about the "yellow peril." Racial conflict on the West Coast, especially in California, helped sour relations with Japan. In 1906, San Francisco's school board ordered students of Asian descent to attend a separate public school from "Americans." When the Japanese government protested, President Roosevelt persuaded the school board to change its policy, but only after making sure that Japanese authorities would stop encouraging unemployed Japanese "laborers" to go to America. This "Gentlemen's Agreement" of 1907 halted the influx of Japanese immigrants to California.

**Japanese immigration** Japanese immigrants disembark a steamship and arrive at the Immigration Station on Angel Island in San Francisco, California. Many other Japanese immigrants settled in Hawaii.

# The Great White Fleet

After Theodore Roosevelt's election to a full term as president in 1904, he celebrated America's rise as a world power. In 1907, without consulting Congress or his cabinet, he sent the entire U.S. fleet of warships, by then second in strength only to Britain's Royal Navy, on a fourteen-month world tour to demonstrate America's power and to show that "the Pacific is as much our home waters as the Atlantic."

At every port of call—down the Atlantic coast of South America, then up the Pacific coast, out to Hawaii, and down to New Zealand and Australia—the "Great White Fleet" of eighteen gleaming battleships, eight armored cruisers, and assorted support ships received a rousing welcome. The triumphal procession continued to Japan, China, and the Philippines, then to Egypt, through the Suez Canal and across the Mediterranean Sea before steaming back to Virginia in early 1909, just in time to close Roosevelt's presidency.

Roosevelt's success in expanding U.S. power abroad would have mixed consequences, however, because underlying his imperialism was a militantly racist view of the world. Roosevelt and others believed that the world included "civilized" societies, such as the United States, Japan, and the nations of Europe, and those they described as "barbarous," "backward," or "impotent." It was the responsibility of the "civilized" nations to exercise control of the "barbarous" peoples, by force if necessary.

**TAFT'S "DOLLAR DIPLOMACY"** Republican William Howard Taft, who succeeded Roosevelt as president in 1909, continued to promote America's economic interests abroad, practicing what Roosevelt called "**dollar diplomacy**." Taft used the State Department to help American companies and banks invest in foreign countries, especially in East Asia and the less developed nations of Latin America and the Caribbean. To ensure the stability of those investments, Taft did not hesitate to intervene in nations experiencing political and economic turmoil. In 1909, he dispatched U.S. Marines to support a revolution in Nicaragua. Once the new government was formed, Secretary of State Philander C. Knox helped U.S. banks negotiate loans to prop it up. Two years later, Taft again sent American troops to restore political stability. This time they stayed for more than a decade.

**WILSON'S INTERVENTIONISM** In 1913, the new Democratic president, Woodrow Wilson, attacked dollar diplomacy as a form of economic imperialism. He promised to treat Latin American nations "on terms of equality and honor." Yet Wilson, along with William Jennings Bryan, his secretary of state, dispatched American military forces to Latin America more often than Taft and Roosevelt combined. Wilson argued that the United States must intervene to stabilize weak governments in the Western Hemisphere to keep European nations from doing so.

In 1915, when the Dominican Republic refused to sign a treaty that would have given the United States a "special" role in governing the island nation, Wilson sent in Marines, who established a military government and fought a nasty guerrilla war against anti-American rebels. That same year, Wilson intervened in Haiti, next door to the Dominican Republic. He argued that his actions were justified because the "necessity for exercising control there is immediate, urgent, imperative."

**THE UNITED STATES IN MEXICO** Mexico was a much thornier problem for Woodrow Wilson. In 1910, Mexicans had revolted against the dictatorship of Porfirio Díaz, who had given foreign corporations a free rein in developing the nation's economy. After occupying Mexico City in 1911, the victorious rebels began squabbling among themselves. The leader of the rebellion, Francisco Madero, was overthrown by his chief of staff, General

**Intervention in Mexico** U.S. Marines enter Veracruz, Mexico, in 1914.

Victoriano Huerta, who assumed power in early 1913 and then had Madero and thirty other political opponents murdered.

President Wilson refused to recognize "a government of butchers." Huerta ignored the criticism and established a dictatorship. Wilson decided that Huerta must be removed and ordered U.S. warships to halt shipments of foreign weapons to the new government. Meanwhile, several rival revolutionary Mexican armies, the largest of which was led by Francisco Pancho Villa, began trying to unseat Huerta.

On April 9, 1914, nine American sailors were arrested in Tampico, Mexico, while trying to buy supplies. Mexican officials quickly released them and apologized to the U.S. naval commander. There the incident might have ended, but the imperious U.S. admiral demanded that the Mexicans fire a twenty-one-gun salute to the American flag. After they refused, Wilson sent U.S. troops ashore at Veracruz on April 21, 1914. They occupied the city at a cost of 19 American lives; at least 300 Mexicans were killed or wounded.

For seven months, the Americans governed Veracruz. They left in late 1914 after Huerta was overthrown by Venustiano Carranza. Still, the problems south of the border continued. In 1916, Pancho Villa launched raids into Texas and New Mexico in a deliberate attempt to trigger U.S. intervention. On March 9, he and his men attacked Columbus, New Mexico, three miles across the border. His army of 500 revolutionaries burned the town and killed seventeen Americans.

A furious Wilson sent General John J. Pershing to Mexico with 6,000 soldiers. For nearly a year, Pershing's troops chased Villa's army through the mountains of northern Mexico. As Pershing muttered, "It's like trying to chase a rat in a cornfield." In 1917, the American troops were ordered home. The elusive Villa, meanwhile, named his mule "President Wilson." By then, however, Wilson paid little notice, for he was distracted by a much greater threat: war in Europe.

# CHAPTER REVIEW

## SUMMARY

- **Toward the New Imperialism**   Near the end of the nineteenth century, the idea that America had a manifest destiny to expand its territory abroad, combined with industrialists' desire for new markets for their goods, helped fuel America's new *imperialism*. White Americans believed that their advanced industrial development proved their racial superiority, and by conquering "backward peoples," the United States was simply enacting the theory of survival of the fittest. Evangelical Protestants also thought they had a duty to Christianize and "uplift" people throughout the world.

- **Expansion in the Pacific**   Business leaders hoped to extend America's commercial reach across the Pacific to exploit vast Asian markets. The Alaska Purchase (1867) initiated the effort to acquire Pacific ports. American planters in the Kingdom of Hawaii developed a thriving sugar industry using Asian laborers, which increased Hawaii's commercial connections to the United States. In 1894, Hawaii's minority white population *(haoles)* ousted the native Hawaiian queen, declared a republic, and requested that Hawaii be annexed by the United States. In 1898, President William McKinley agreed to annex the islands.

- **The Spanish-American War (The War of 1898)**   When Cubans revolted against Spanish colonial rule in 1895, many Americans supported their demand for independence. *Yellow journalism* sensationalizing the Spanish suppression of the revolt further aroused Americans' sympathy. Early in 1898, the publication of the *de Lôme letter,* followed by the sinking of the *U.S. battleship Maine* in Havana Harbor, helped propel America into war with Spain. The war lasted only 114 days. Under the Treaty of Paris ending the war, Cuba became independent and the United States annexed Spain's other Caribbean possession, Puerto Rico, which it had occupied. In the Spanish colony of the Philippine Islands, America's Pacific naval fleet under Commodore George Dewey defeated the Spanish in the Battle of Manila Bay.

- **Consequences of Victory**   A vicious guerrilla war followed in the Philippines when Filipinos rebelled against American control. The rebellion was suppressed, and President McKinley announced that the United States would annex the Philippines. The *American Anti-Imperialist League* and others argued that acquiring overseas territories violated American principles of self-determination and independence. In the end, the imperialists won the debate, and Congress set up a government in the Philippines and in Puerto Rico. The United States also annexed Hawaii, Guam, Wake Island, and some of the Samoa Islands during or shortly after the Spanish-American War (the War of 1898). In East Asia, Secretary of State John Hay promoted the *Open Door policy (1899)* of preserving China's territorial integrity and equal access by all nations to trade with China.

- **Theodore Roosevelt and Big-Stick Diplomacy**   Theodore Roosevelt pursued an imperialist foreign policy that confirmed the United States' new role as a world

848

power. He helped negotiate the treaty that ended the Russo-Japanese War, seized control of the Panama Canal, and sent the navy's fleet of battleships around the world as a symbol of American might. He also proclaimed the *Roosevelt Corollary (1904)* to the Monroe Doctrine, asserting that the United States would intervene in Latin America as necessary to prevent European intervention.

- **Taft and Wilson's Interventionism Abroad** William Howard Taft and Woodrow Wilson continued Roosevelt's pattern of intervening in the internal affairs of other nations, especially in Latin America and the Caribbean. What Taft called *dollar diplomacy* involved the U.S. government fostering American investments in less developed nations and then using U.S. military force to protect those investments. Wilson's frustrations at the instability of the Mexican government led him to intervene there with American troops twice. In both cases, the presence of U.S. soldiers only deepened the resentment of "Yankee imperialism" throughout Latin America.

## CHRONOLOGY

| | |
|---|---|
| **1894** | Republic of Hawaii is proclaimed |
| **1898** | U.S. battleship *Maine* explodes in Havana Harbor |
| | The Spanish-American War (War of 1898) |
| | United States annexes Hawaii |
| **1899** | U.S. Senate ratifies the Treaty of Paris, ending the War of 1898 |
| **1899–1902** | Insurgents resist U.S. conquest of the Philippines |
| **1901** | President McKinley assassinated; Theodore Roosevelt becomes president |
| **1914** | Panama Canal opens |
| **1909–1917** | U.S. military interventions in Mexico and Latin America |

## KEY TERMS

imperialism p. 820

yellow journalism p. 825

U.S. battleship *Maine* p. 825

de Lôme letter p. 825

Teller Amendment p. 826

American Anti-Imperialist League p. 833

Open Door policy p. 837

Roosevelt Corollary p. 842

dollar diplomacy p. 845

---

 INQUIZITIVE

**Go to InQuizitive to see what you've learned—and learn what you've missed—with personalized feedback along the way.**

# 21 The Progressive Era
## 1890–1920

**"Votes For Us When We Are Women!"**  Parades organized by women's suffrage groups attracted women of all ages and social classes. Here, from a patriotically outfitted automobile, some young suffragists ask their many spectators for "votes for us when we are women."

Theodore Roosevelt's emergence as a national leader coincided with the onset of what historians have labeled the Progressive Era (1890–1920), an extraordinary period of social activism and political innovation during which compelling public issues forced profound changes in the role of government and presidential leadership. Millions of middle-class progressives believed that America was experiencing a crisis of democracy because of the urban-industrial revolution. Widespread inner-city poverty, children laboring in unregulated mines and factories, tainted food, miserable working conditions, and low pay, progressives insisted, required bold action by churches, charitable organizations, experts, and individuals—and an expanded role for governments.

One of the major concerns was continuing evidence of fraudulent conduct by elected officials. As Amos Pinchot, a progressive attorney and reformer from New York City, said, corruption was "destroying our respect for government, uprooting faith in political parties, and causing every precedent and convention of the old order to strain at its moorings."

The widening gap between rich and poor had become another major issue. Walter Weyl, a progressive economist, insisted that "we shall not advance far in working out our American ideals without striking hard at . . . inequality." Political equality, he added, "is a farce and a peril unless there is at least some measure of economic equality." The growth of industries like railroading, steel, coal, and oil had attracted waves of poor farm folk and foreign immigrants to

## focus questions

**1.** What were the motives of progressive reformers?

**2.** Which sources of thought and activism contributed to the progressive movement?

**3.** What were the specific goals of progressive reformers, and how did they address them?

**4.** What contributions did Presidents Theodore Roosevelt and William Howard Taft make to the progressive movement? How and why did these men come to disagree about the best ways to advance progressive ideals?

**5.** Which policies of President Woodrow Wilson were influenced by the progressive movement? How and why did they differ from the policies of Roosevelt and Taft?

cities, where basic social services—food, water, housing, education, sanitation, transportation, and medical care—could not keep pace with the rate of urban growth.

Between 1890 and 1920, progressive reformers attacked the problems created by political corruption, unregulated industrialization, and unplanned urbanization. They insisted that something must be done to control the powerful corporations that dominated the economy and corrupted U.S. political life.

By the beginning of the twentieth century, progressivism had become the most dynamic social and political force in the nation. In 1910, Woodrow Wilson told a gathering of clergymen that progressivism had generated "an extraordinary awakening in civic consciousness."

## THE PROGRESSIVE IMPULSE

Progressives were liberals, not revolutionaries. Liberalism in the twentieth century referred to those who believed that governments must exercise greater power on behalf of society in regulating the behavior of businesses and ensuring the welfare of the people. They wanted to reform and regulate capitalism, not destroy it. Most were Christian moralists who felt that politics had become a contest between good and evil, honesty and corruption. What they all shared was the assumption that governments—local, state, and national—must become more active in addressing the problems created by rapid urban and industrial growth.

Progressivism was more a widespread impulse supported by elements of both major political parties than it was a single movement with a common agenda. Theodore Roosevelt called it the "forward movement" because it promoted positive changes led by people "who stand for the cause of progress, for the cause of the uplift of humanity and the betterment of mankind."

Unlike Populism, whose grassroots appeal centered on farming regions in the South and Midwest, progressivism was a national movement. It was based in large cities but also popular in rural areas. Progressive activists came in all stripes: men and women; Democrats, Republicans, Populists, and socialists; labor unionists and business executives; teachers, engineers, editors, and professors; social workers, doctors, ministers, and journalists; farmers and homemakers; whites and blacks; clergymen, atheists, and agnostics. Their combined efforts led to significant social reforms and government regulations of businesses.

To make governments more efficient and businesses more honest, progressives drew upon the new "social sciences"—sociology, political science, psychology, public health, and economics—being developed at research universities. The progressive approach was to appoint social scientists to "investigate, educate, and legislate." Activist Florence Kelley voiced the era's widespread belief that once people knew "the truth" about social ills, "they would act upon it."

Yet progressivism also had flaws, inconsistencies and hypocrisies. Progressives' "do-good" perspective was often limited by racial and ethnic prejudices, as well as by social and intellectual snobbery. The goals of upper-class white progressives rarely included racial equality, for example. Many otherwise progressive people, including Theodore Roosevelt and Woodrow Wilson, believed in the supremacy of the "Anglo-Saxon race." They assumed that the forces shaping modern society were too complicated for the "ignorant" masses to understand, much less improve, without direction by those who knew better.

## SOURCES OF PROGRESSIVISM

During the last quarter of the nineteenth century, progressives began to attack corrupt political bosses and irresponsible corporate barons. They sought a more honest and efficient government, more-effective regulation of big businesses ("the trusts"), and better living and working conditions for the laboring poor. Only by expanding the scope of local, state, and federal governments, they believed, could these goals be attained.

**ECONOMIC DEPRESSION AND DISCONTENT** More than any factor, the devastating economic depression of the 1890s ignited the progressive spirit of reform. The depression brought massive layoffs; nearly a quarter of adults in the workforce lost their jobs.

Although the United States boasted the highest per capita income in the world ($428 in 1900; about $15,000 today), it also had some of the highest concentrations of poverty. In 1900, the U.S. population numbered 82 million, of which an estimated 10 million were living in poverty. The devastating effects of the depression prompted many upper-middle-class urban reformers— lawyers, doctors, executives, social workers, teachers, professors, journalists, and college-educated women—to organize efforts to help those in need and to keep them from becoming social revolutionaries or anarchists.

**POPULISM** Populism was another thread in the fabric of progressivism. The Populist party platforms of 1892 and 1896 included reforms intended to give more power to the people, such as the "direct" election of U.S. senators by voters rather than by state legislatures. Although William Jennings Bryan's loss in the 1896 presidential campaign ended the Populist party as a serious political force, many reforms pushed by Populists were implemented by progressives.

**"HONEST GOVERNMENT"** The Mugwumps—"gentlemen" reformers who had fought the patronage system and insisted that government jobs be awarded on the basis of merit—supplied progressivism with another key goal: the "honest government" ideal. Over the years, the good-government movement expanded to address persistent urban issues such as crime, unequal access to electricity, clean water and municipal sewers, mass transit, and garbage collection.

**SOCIALISM** The Socialist Party of America, supported mostly by militant farmers and German/Jewish immigrants, served as the radical wing of progressivism. Socialists focused on improving working conditions and closing the widening income gap between rich and poor through progressive taxation, whereby tax rates would rise with income. Most progressives were capitalist reformers, not socialist radicals. They rejected the extremes of both socialism and laissez-faire individualism, preferring a new, regulated capitalism "softened" by humanitarianism.

**Ludlow Street cellar habitation** This December 1895 photograph from Jacob Riis's *How the Other Half Lives* revealed the cramped and unsanitary living conditions faced by many immigrants living in tenements on New York City's lower East Side.

**MUCKRAKING JOURNALISM** Progressivism depended upon the press—newspapers and magazines—to inform the public about political corruption and social problems. The so-called **muckrakers** were America's first investigative journalists. Their aggressive reporting played a crucial role in educating readers about political and corporate wrongdoing and revealing "how the other half lives," the title of an influential exposé of the terrible living conditions experienced by immigrants in New York City, written by the Danish immigrant photojournalist Jacob Riis.

The muckrakers got their nickname from Theodore Roosevelt, who said that crusading journalists were "often indispensable to . . . society, but only if they know when to stop raking the muck." By uncovering political corruption and writing about social ills, muckrakers gave journalism a new political role. Roosevelt, both as governor of New York and as president of the United States, frequently used muckrakers to drum up support for his policies; he corresponded with them, invited them to the White House, and used them to help shape public opinion.

The golden age of muckraking began in 1902, when Samuel S. McClure, owner of *McClure's* magazine, recruited idealistic journalists to expose corruption in politics and corporations. McClure editorialized that the "vitality of democracy" depended upon educating the public about "complex questions." *McClure's* and other muckraking magazines investigated corporate monopolies and crooked political machines while exposing the miserable conditions in which the working poor lived and labored.

Muckrakers Lincoln Steffens, Ray Stannard Baker, and Ida Tarbell led the way in promoting reforms of all sorts. Steffens focused his investigative reporting on political corruption while Baker concentrated on railroad abuses. Ida Tarbell spent years investigating and writing about the unethical and illegal means by which John D. Rockefeller had built his gigantic Standard Oil Trust. At the end of her series of nineteen articles in *McClure's*, she asked readers: "And what are we going to do about it?" She stressed that it was "the people of the United States, and nobody else, [who] must cure whatever is wrong in the industrial situation."

**Ida Tarbell** An author, teacher, and pioneer of investigative journalism in the United States.

Without the muckrakers, progressivism would never have achieved widespread popular support. Investigative journalism became such a powerful force for change that one editor said that Americans were benefiting from "Government by Magazine."

## RELIGIOUS ACTIVISM AND SOCIAL RESPONSIBILITY

Still another stream flowing into progressivism was religious activism directed at achieving social justice—the idea that society had an ethical obligation to help its most vulnerable members. A related ideal was the **social gospel**, the belief that religious institutions and individual Christians must help bring about the "Kingdom of God" on earth.

Rugged individualism may have been the path to wealth, they argued, but "Christian socialism" offered hope for unity among all classes. "Every religious and political question," said George Herron, a religion professor at Grinnell College, "is fundamentally economic." And the solution to economic tensions was social solidarity.

In many respects, the progressive movement formed a new phase of Christian spiritual revival—an energetic form of public outreach focused not so much on individual conversion and salvation as on social reform. "We believe," as the Religious Education Association explained, "that the age of sheer individualism is past, and the age of social responsibility has arrived."

**THE SOCIAL GOSPEL**  During the last quarter of the nineteenth century, many churches and synagogues began emphasizing community service to address the needs of the unfortunate. New organizations made key contributions to the movement. The Young Men's Christian Association (YMCA) and a similar group for women, the YWCA, both entered the United States from England in the 1850s and grew rapidly after 1870. The Salvation Army, founded in London in 1878, came to the United States a year later.

The YMCA and YWCA combined religious evangelism with social services and fitness training in community centers, which were segregated by race and gender. Intended to provide low-cost housing and exercise in a "safe Christian environment" for young men and women from rural areas or foreign countries, the YMCA/YWCA centers often included libraries, classrooms, and kitchens. "Hebrew" counterparts—YMHAs and YWHAs—provided similar facilities in cities with large Jewish populations. Salvation Army centers offered soup kitchens to feed the poor and day nurseries for the children of working mothers.

The major forces behind the social gospel movement were Protestants and Catholics who charged that Christianity had become too closely associated with the upper and middle classes. In 1875, Washington Gladden, a pastor in Springfield, Massachusetts, published *Working People and Their Employers* (1876), which argued that true Christianity was based on the principle that "thou shalt love thy neighbor as thyself." Gladden rejected the view of social

Darwinists that the poor and disabled deserved their fate and should not be helped. He argued that helping the poor was an essential element of the Christian faith. To that end, he became the first prominent religious leader to support the rights of workers to form unions. He also condemned racial segregation and discrimination against immigrants.

Gladden's efforts helped launch a new era in which churches engaged with the problems created by a rapidly urbanizing and industrializing society. He and other social gospelers reached out to the working poor who lived in grossly substandard housing, lacked the legal right to form unions, and had no insurance for on-the-job accidents.

Walter Rauschenbusch, a German-born Baptist minister serving immigrant tenement dwellers in the Hell's Kitchen neighborhood of New York City, became the greatest champion of the social gospel. In 1907, he published *Christianity and the Social Crisis*, in which he argued that "whoever uncouples the religious and social life has not understood Jesus." The Christian emphasis on personal salvation, he added, must be linked with an equally passionate commitment to social justice. Churches must embrace "the social aims of Jesus," for Christianity was intended to be a "revolutionary" faith.

In Rauschenbusch's view, religious life needed the social gospel to revitalize it and make it socially relevant: "We shall never have a perfect social life, yet we must seek it with faith." His message resonated with Theodore Roosevelt, Woodrow Wilson, and many others. Years later, Rev. Martin Luther King Jr. said that *Christianity and the Social Crisis* "left an indelible imprint on my thinking."

**SETTLEMENT HOUSES** Among the most visible soldiers in the social gospel movement were those who volunteered in innovative community centers called settlement houses. Hull House was a dilapidated two-story mansion converted into a settlement house in a shabby Chicago neighborhood. Two college-educated women from privileged backgrounds, Jane Addams and Ellen Gates Starr, founded Hull House to address the needs of the unskilled working poor, especially newly arrived European immigrants. Some 50,000 working poor circulated through Hull House in its first year. By 1940, the annual number was 320,000.

Addams and Starr were driven by an "impulse to share the lives of the poor" and to make social service "express the spirit of Christ." Besides a nursery for the infant children of working mothers, Hull House sponsored health clinics, lectures, music lessons and art studios, men's clubs, an employment bureau, job training, a gymnasium, a coffeehouse, a savings bank, and a public bath. Classes were offered in acting, weaving, carpentry, art history, philosophy,

**Jane Addams** By the end of the century, thanks to the efforts of Jane Addams and others, religious groups were joining the settlement house movement.

and music. All residents were treated as equals. By the early twentieth century, there were hundreds of settlement houses in cities across the United States, most of them in the Northeast and Midwest.

Addams and other settlement house leaders soon realized, however, that their work was like bailing out the ocean with a teaspoon. They thus added political reform to their agenda and began lobbying for city parks and playgrounds, neighborhood clean-up days, and laws and regulations to improve living conditions in poor neighborhoods.

As her influence grew in Chicago, Jane Addams served on governmental and community boards, focusing her radiant personality and powerful convictions on improving public health and food safety. She pushed for better street lighting and police protection in poor neighborhoods, and sought to reduce the misuse of narcotics. An ardent pacifist and outspoken advocate for *suffrage* (voting rights) for women, Addams would become the first American woman to win the Nobel Peace Prize.

## THE WOMEN'S SUFFRAGE MOVEMENT

From 1880 to 1910, the number of employed women tripled from 2.6 million to 7.8 million. As college-educated women became more involved in the world of work and wages, the suffrage movement grew.

In 1869, Susan B. Anthony and Elizabeth Cady Stanton had founded the National Woman Suffrage Association (NWSA) to promote a **women's suffrage** amendment to the Constitution. They condemned both the Fourteenth and Fifteenth Amendments for limiting "citizenship" and voting rights to men only. They also campaigned for laws requiring higher pay for working women and making it easier for abused wives to get divorces.

Other suffrage activists insisted that pursuing multiple issues hurt their cause, however. In 1869, Julia Ward Howe and Lucy Stone formed the

**East meets West**  San Francisco suffragists calling for a constitutional amendment marched across the country in 1915 to deliver a petition with more than 500,000 signatures to Congress in Washington, D.C. Along the way, they were warmly received by other suffragists, like those of New Jersey, pictured here.

American Woman Suffrage Association (AWSA). Based in Boston, it focused solely on voting rights and included men among its leaders.

In 1890, the two groups united as the National American Woman Suffrage Association (NAWSA). That same year, the Wyoming Territory became a state—the first to give full voting rights to women. It was in the territories and states west of the Mississippi River that the suffrage movement had its earliest successes. In those areas, where Populism found its strongest support, women were more engaged in grassroots political activities than they were in the East. In addition, the mostly male settlers in the western territories hoped that providing suffrage would encourage more women to settle in the region.

Between 1890 and 1896, the suffrage cause won three more victories in western states—Utah, Colorado, and Idaho. In 1912, five more western states embraced women voters: Washington, California, Arizona, Kansas, and Oregon. Yet not until New York acted in 1917 did a state east of the Mississippi River allow women to vote in all elections.

Many advocates for women's suffrage argued that the right to vote and hold office was a matter of simple justice: women were just as capable as men of exercising the rights and responsibilities of citizenship. Others insisted that women were morally superior to men and would better promote the welfare

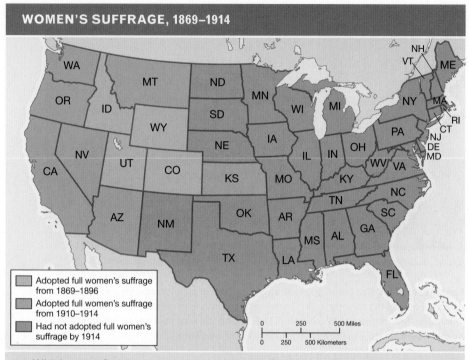

**WOMEN'S SUFFRAGE, 1869–1914**

Legend:
- Adopted full women's suffrage from 1869–1896
- Adopted full women's suffrage from 1910–1914
- Had not adopted full women's suffrage by 1914

0     250     500 Miles
0     250     500 Kilometers

- Which states first gave women the right to vote?
- Why did it take fifty-one years—from Wyoming's grant of full suffrage to women until ratification of the Nineteenth Amendment—for women to receive the right to vote in both state and national elections?
- How was suffrage part of a larger women's reform movement?

of society as a whole. One activist explicitly linked women's suffrage with the social gospel, declaring that women followed the teachings of Christ more faithfully than men did. If they were elected to public office, they would "far more effectively guard the morals of society and the sanitary conditions of cities."

The women's suffrage movement was not free from social, ethnic, and racial prejudices. After the Civil War, suffragists had hoped that the Fifteenth Amendment, which guaranteed voting rights for African American men, would aid their own efforts to gain the vote. Some believed that they should be granted the vote before freedmen. The majority of men, however, still insisted that women stay out of politics because it would supposedly corrupt their moral purity.

At the end of the nineteenth century, suffragists lashed out at Congress for allowing illiterate immigrant men to vote but not well-educated women.

Carrie Chapman Catt, who became president of the National American Woman Suffrage Association in 1900, warned of the danger that "lies in the votes possessed by the males in the slums of the cities, and the ignorant foreign [immigrant] vote." She added that the nation, with "ill-advised haste," had given "the foreigner, the Negro and the Indian" the vote but still withheld it from white women. Throughout the country, most suffrage organizations barred African American women from joining.

# PROGRESSIVES' AIMS AND ACHIEVEMENTS

The progressive movement grew out of what Theodore Roosevelt called the public's "fierce discontent with evil" at the start of the twentieth century. Progressives focused on numerous social and political ills, from corrupt politicians to too-powerful corporations, from economic distress on small farms and in big cities to the general feeling that "the people" had lost control to the special interests—businesses and their leaders who were solely interested in "money-getting" at the expense of public welfare.

## POLITICAL REFORMS

Progressivism set in motion the two most important political developments of the twentieth century: the rise of direct democracy and the expansion of federal government power. In his monthly articles in *McClure's* magazine, Lincoln Steffens, a leading muckraker, regularly asked: "Will the people rule? Is democracy possible?" Steffens and other progressives often stressed that the way to improve America's democracy was to make it even more democratic.

To empower citizens to clean up the political system, progressives pushed to make the political process more open and transparent. One proposal was the *direct primary*, which would allow all members of a party to vote on the party's nominees, rather than the traditional practice in which an inner circle of party leaders chose the candidates, often behind closed doors. In 1896, South Carolina became the first state to adopt a statewide primary. Within twenty years, nearly every state had done so.

Progressives also developed other ways to increase public participation in the political process ("direct democracy") so as to curb the influence of corporate bosses on state legislatures. In 1898, South Dakota became the first state to adopt the *initiative* and *referendum*, procedures that allowed voters to create laws directly rather than having to wait for legislative action. Citizens could sign petitions to have a proposal put on the ballot (the initiative) and then vote it up or down (the referendum). Still another progressive innovation was the *recall*, whereby corrupt or incompetent elected officials could be removed by a public petition and vote. By 1920, nearly twenty states had adopted the initiative and referendum, and nearly a dozen had sanctioned the recall procedure.

Progressives also fought to change how U.S. senators were elected. Under the Constitution, state legislatures elected senators, a process frequently corrupted by lobbyists and vote buying. In 1913, thanks to the efforts of progressives, the **Seventeenth Amendment**, providing for the direct election of senators, was ratified and became law.

## THE EFFICIENCY MOVEMENT

A second major theme of progressivism was the "gospel of efficiency." The champion of progressive efficiency was Frederick Winslow Taylor, an industrial engineer who became a celebrated business consultant, helping business owners implement "scientific management."

The nation's first "efficiency expert," Taylor showed employers how to cut waste and improve productivity. By breaking down work activities (filling a wheelbarrow, driving a nail, shoveling coal) into a sequence of mechanical steps and using stopwatches to measure the time it took each worker to perform each step, Taylor established detailed performance standards (and cash rewards) for each job classification, specifying how fast people should work and when they should rest. His book, *The Principles of Scientific Management* (1911), influenced business organizations for decades.

The goal of what came to be called **Taylorism** was to usher in a "mental revolution" in business management that would improve productivity and profits, raise pay for the most efficient workers, and reduce the likelihood of worker strikes. As Taylor wrote, "Men will not do an extraordinary day's work for an ordinary day's pay."

Many workers, however, resented Taylor's innovations, seeing them as just a tool to make people work faster at monotonous tasks. "We object to being reduced to a scientific formula," an Iowa machinist thundered. Yet Taylor's "scientific" approach to industrial management became one of the most important contributions to capitalist economies in the twentieth century and brought solid, measurable improvements in productivity.

Political progressives applied Taylorism to the operations of government by calling for the reorganization of state and federal agencies to eliminate duplication, to establish clear lines of authority, and to replace political appointees with trained specialists. By the early twentieth century, many complex functions of government had come to require specialists with technical expertise.

As Woodrow Wilson wrote, progressive ideals could be achieved only if government agencies at all levels was "informed and administered by experts." Many cities set up "efficiency bureaus" to identify government waste and apply more cost-effective best practices.

**MUNICIPAL REFORM**  Two Taylorist ideas to reform city and county governments emerged in the first decade of the new century. One, the commission system, was first adopted in 1901 by the city of Galveston, Texas, after the local government collapsed following a devastating hurricane and tidal wave that killed more than 8,000 people—the largest natural disaster in American history. The commission system placed ultimate authority in a board composed of commissioners who combined both legislative and executive powers in heading up city departments (sanitation, police, utilities, and so on). By 1911, more than sixty cities had adopted the commission system of government.

Even more popular was the city-manager plan, under which an appointed administrator ran a city or county government in accordance with policies set by the elected council and mayor. Staunton, Virginia, adopted the first city-manager plan in 1908.

Yet the efforts to make local governments more "businesslike" and professional had a downside. Shifting control from elected officials representing individual neighborhoods to at-large commissioners and nonpartisan specialists separated local government from party politics, which for many working-class voters had been their primary civic activity. In addition, running a city like a business led commissioners and managers to focus on reducing expenses rather than expanding services, even when such expansion was clearly needed.

**THE WISCONSIN IDEA**  At the state level, the ideal of efficient government run by nonpartisan experts was pursued most notably by progressive Republican governor Robert M. La Follette of Wisconsin. "Fighting Bob" La Follette declared war on "vast corporate combinations" and political corruption by creating a nonpartisan state government that would become a "laboratory for democracy." He established a Legislative Reference Bureau, which provided elected officials with nonpartisan research, advice, and help in drafting legislation. La Follette used the bureau's reports to enact such reforms as the direct primary, stronger railroad regulation, the conservation of natural resources, and workmen's compensation programs to support people injured on the job. The "Wisconsin idea" was widely copied by other progressive governors.

**REGULATION OF BUSINESS** Of all the problems facing American society, one towered above all: the regulation of giant corporations. The threat of corporate monopolies increased during the depression of the 1890s as struggling companies were gobbled up by larger ones. Between 1895 and 1904, some 157 new holding companies gained control of 1,800 different businesses. Almost 50 of these giant holding companies controlled more than 70 percent of the market in their respective industries. In 1896, fewer than a dozen companies other than railroads were worth $10 million or more. By 1903, that number had soared to 300.

Concerns over the concentration of economic power in trusts and other forms of monopolies had led Congress to pass the Sherman Anti-Trust Act in 1890, but it proved ineffective. In addition, government agencies responsible for regulating businesses were often headed and staffed by men who had worked in the very industries they were supposed to regulate. Congress, for instance, appointed retired railroad executives to the Interstate Commerce Commission (ICC), which had been created to regulate railroads. The issue of regulating the regulators has never been fully resolved.

## SOCIAL JUSTICE

The progressive movement also set its sights on improving social justice for the working poor, the jobless, and the homeless. In addition to their work in settlement houses and other areas, many progressives formed advocacy organizations such as the National Consumers League, led by Florence Kelley, which promoted safer and less exploitative working conditions for women by educating consumers about harsh work life in factories and mills and the widespread use of child workers.

Other organizations, such as the General Federation of Women's Clubs, insisted that civic life needed female leadership. Women's clubs across the country sought to clean up slums by educating residents about personal and household hygiene (what women reformers called "municipal housekeeping"), urging construction of sewer systems, and launching public-awareness campaigns about the connection between unsanitary tenements and streets and disease. Women's clubs also campaigned for child-care centers, kindergartens, government inspection of food processing plants, stricter housing codes, laws protecting women in the workplace, and more social services for the poor, sick, disabled, and abused. Still others addressed prostitution and alcohol abuse.

**THE CAMPAIGN AGAINST DRINKING** Middle-class women were the driving force behind efforts to stop the sale and consumption of alcoholic beverages. Founded in Cleveland, Ohio, in 1874, the Women's Christian Temperance Union (WCTU) became the largest women's group in the nation, boasting 300,000 members. While some members were motivated by Protestant beliefs that consuming alcohol was a sin, most saw excessive drinking, especially in saloons, as a threat to social progress and family stability.

By attacking drunkenness and closing saloons, temperance reformers hoped to (1) improve family life by preventing domestic violence, (2) reduce crime in the streets, and (3) remove one of the worst tools of corruption—free beer on Election Day, which was used to "buy" votes among the working class. As a Boston sociologist concluded, the saloon had become "the enemy of society because of the evil results produced upon the individual."

Initially, WCTU members met in churches to pray and then marched to saloons to try to convince their owners to close. They promoted *temperance*— the reduction of alcohol consumption. But they also urged individuals to embrace *abstinence* and refuse to drink any alcoholic beverages.

Under the leadership of Frances Willard, president of the WCTU between 1879 and 1898, the organization began promoting legislation to ban alcohol ("prohibition"). Willard also pushed the WCTU to lobby for an eight-hour workday, the regulation of child labor, government-funded kindergartens, the right to vote, and federal inspections of the food industry.

The battle against alcoholic beverages took on new strength in 1893 with the formation of the Anti-Saloon League, an organization based in churches that pioneered the strategy of the single-issue political pressure group. The bipartisan league, like the WCTU, initially focused on closing down saloons rather than abolishing alcohol. Eventually, however, it decided to force the prohibition issue into the forefront of state and local elections. At its "Jubilee Convention" in 1913, the league endorsed an amendment to the Constitution prohibiting the manufacture, sale, and consumption of alcoholic beverages, which Congress approved in 1917.

**LABOR LEGISLATION**  In 1890, almost half of wage workers toiled up to twelve hours a day—sometimes seven days a week—in unsafe, unsanitary, and unregulated conditions. Legislation to ensure better working conditions and limit child labor was perhaps the most significant reform to emerge from the drive for progressive social justice.

At the end of the nineteenth century, fewer than half of working families lived solely on the husband's earnings. Many married women engaged in "homework"—making clothes, selling flower arrangements, preparing food for others, and taking in boarders. Children of poor families frequently dropped out of school and went to work in factories, shops, mines, mills, canneries, and on farms. In 1900, some 1.75 million children between ten and fifteen were working outside the home.

Many progressives argued that children, too, had rights. In southern textile mills, a third of the workers were children. In several southern states, children worked sixty-six hours a week. "I regard my employees," a manager said, "as I regard my machinery. So long as they can do my work for what I choose to pay them, I keep them, getting out of them all I can." The National Child Labor Committee campaigned for laws prohibiting the employment of children. Within ten years, most states had passed such laws, although some were lax in enforcing them.

Reformers also sought to regulate the length of the workday for women, in part because some working mothers were pregnant and others had children at home with inadequate supervision. Spearheaded by Florence Kelley, progressives convinced many state governments to ban the hiring of children below a certain age, and to limit the hours that women and children could work.

**Child labor** Child workers shuck oysters in 1913 at the Varn & Platt Canning Company in Bluffton, South Carolina.

It took a tragedy, however, to spur meaningful government regulation of dangerous workplaces. On March 25, 1911, a fire broke out at the Triangle Shirtwaist factory (called a "sweatshop" because of its cramped, unventilated work areas) in New York City. Escape routes were limited because the owner kept the stairway door locked to prevent theft, and 146 workers trapped on the upper floors of the ten-story building died or leaped to their deaths. The victims were mostly young, foreign-born women in their teens, almost all Jewish, Italian, or Russian immigrants. In the fire's aftermath, dozens of city and state regulations dealing with fire hazards, dangerous working conditions, and child labor were enacted across the nation.

The Supreme Court was inconsistent in its rulings on state labor laws. In *Lochner v. New York* (1905), the Court decided that a state law limiting bakers to a sixty-hour workweek was unconstitutional because it violated workers' rights to accept any job they wanted, no matter how bad the working conditions or how low the pay. Three years later, in *Muller v. Oregon* (1908), the Court changed its mind. Based on evidence that long working hours increased the chances of health problems, the Court approved an Oregon law restricting the workday for women to no more than ten hours.

**THE "PROGRESSIVE" INCOME TAX**  The cost of fighting the Civil War had led the federal government to institute the first income tax, but it was repealed in 1872. Thereafter, it relied on tariff revenues (45 percent) and taxes on liquor and tobacco (43 percent) to fund the government.

Progressives, however, believed that a "progressive" federal income tax—so called because tax rates "progress," or rise, as income levels rise, thus forcing the rich to pay more—would close the gap between rich and poor. Such a graduated or progressive tax system was the climax of the progressive movement's commitment to a more equitable distribution of wealth.

The progressive income tax was an old idea. In 1894, William Jennings Bryan had persuaded Congress to approve a 2 percent tax on corporations and individuals earning more than $4,000 a year (the approximate equivalent of $110,000 today). Soon after the tax became law, however, the Supreme Court, in *Pollock v. Farmers' Loan Company* (1895), declared it unconstitutional, claiming that only the states could levy income taxes.

Still, progressives continued to believe that a graduated income tax would help slow the concentration of wealth in the hands of the richest Americans. In 1907, President Theodore Roosevelt announced his support. Two years later, his successor, William Howard Taft, endorsed a constitutional amendment allowing such a tax, and Congress agreed. This taxation became law in 1913 with state ratification of the **Sixteenth Amendment**.

# Progressivism under Roosevelt and Taft

Most progressive legislation originated at the state and local levels. Federal reform efforts began in earnest only when Theodore Roosevelt (TR) became president in 1901. "A great democracy," he said, "has got to be *progressive* or it will soon cease to be great or a democracy."

TR was a force of nature, an American original blessed with a triumphant grin and an oversized intellect and ego. His contradictions were maddening, but his exuberance, charm, energy, and humor made up for them. Woodrow Wilson confessed after meeting Roosevelt, "You can't resist the man."

On his first day in the White House, Roosevelt announced that he intended to use the presidency as his "bully pulpit." He would educate Americans about the new realities facing their society. He tackled his duties with self-described "strenuosity."

Roosevelt loved power, and he was certain that he knew best how to lead the nation. Congress, he decided, had grown too dominant and too corrupt. He therefore abandoned the Gilded Age tradition in which presidents had deferred to Congress. In his view, the problems caused by explosive industrial growth required substantial responses, and he was unwilling to wait for Congress to act. "I believe in a strong executive [president]," he asserted. "I believe in power." During his administration, the president, not Congress, became the source of policy making.

Like his hero Abraham Lincoln, Roosevelt believed that great presidents must take "noble risks," even if it meant stretching the limits of the Constitution. Joseph "Joe" Cannon, the Republican Speaker of the House, complained that Roosevelt had "no more use for the Constitution than a tomcat has for a marriage license."

**TAMING BIG BUSINESS**   Roosevelt was the first president to use executive power to rein in Big Business. As governor of New York, he had pushed for legislation to regulate sweatshops, institute state inspections of factories and slaughterhouses, and limit the workday to eight hours. He was willing to adopt radical methods to ensure that the social unrest caused by the insensitivity of business owners to the rights of workers and the needs of the poor did not mushroom into a revolution.

TR applauded the growth of industrial capitalism but declared war on corruption and cronyism, or the awarding of political appointments, government contracts, and other favors to politicians' personal friends. He endorsed a **Square Deal** for "every man, great or small, rich or poor." His Square Deal program featured the "Three Cs": greater government *control* of corporations, enhanced *conservation* of natural resources, and new regulations to protect *consumers* against contaminated food and medications.

**CURBING THE TRUSTS** In December 1901, just a few months after entering the White House, President Roosevelt declared that it was time to deal with the "grave evils" resulting from huge corporations exercising dominance over their industries and the nation's economic life. In his view, the federal government had an obligation to curb the excesses of Big Business.

Roosevelt believed that governments must ensure fairness. To that end, he declared war against robber barons who displayed "swinish indifference" to the public good and "unscrupulous politicians" whose votes could be bought and sold by corporate lobbyists.

Early in 1902, the president shocked the business community when he ordered his attorney general to break up the Northern Securities Company. Organized by Wall Street titan, J. P. Morgan, this immense holding company comprised a vast network of railroads and steamships in the Pacific Northwest.

Morgan could not believe the news. He rushed to the White House and told the president, "If I have done anything wrong, send your man to my man and they can fix it up." But the attorney general, who also attended the meeting, told Morgan: "We don't want to 'fix it up.' We want to stop it." Morgan then asked Roosevelt if he planned to attack his other trusts, such as U.S. Steel and General Electric. "Certainly not," Roosevelt replied, "unless we find out that . . . they have done something wrong." After Morgan left, the president told the attorney general to file the anti-trust paperwork.

In 1904, the Supreme Court would rule in a 5–4 decision that the Northern Securities Company was indeed a monopoly and must be dismantled, thereby opening the way for more-aggressive enforcement of the Sherman Anti-Trust Act (1890). Roosevelt recognized the benefits of large-scale capitalism and thought the rise of Big Business was the inevitable result of the industrial era. He did not want to

**Square Deal** This 1906 cartoon likens Roosevelt to the Greek legend Hercules, who as a baby strangled snakes sent from hell to kill him. Here, the serpents are pro-corporation senator Nelson Aldrich and Standard Oil's John D. Rockefeller.

destroy the titans of industry and finance, but he insisted that they be regulated for the public good.

Altogether, he approved about twenty-five anti-trust suits against oversized corporations. Roosevelt also sought stronger regulation of railroads. By their very nature, railroads often exercised a monopoly over the communities they served, enabling them to gouge customers. In 1903, the Elkins Act made it illegal for railroads to give secret rebates (cash refunds) on freight charges to high-volume business customers. That same year, Congress approved Roosevelt's request that a federal Department of Commerce and Labor be formed, within which a Bureau of Corporations would monitor big businesses.

**THE 1902 COAL STRIKE**  On May 12, 1902, more than 100,000 members of the United Mine Workers (UMW) labor union walked off the job in Pennsylvania and West Virginia. The miners were seeking a wage increase and a shorter workday. The union also sought official recognition by the mine owners, who refused to negotiate and instead chose to shut down the coal mines. The miners, mostly immigrants from southern and eastern Europe, were in a bind. One owner expressed the ethnic prejudices shared by many of his colleagues when he proclaimed, "The miners don't suffer—why, they can't even speak English."

By October, the lengthy shutdown had caused the price of coal to soar, and hospitals and schools reported empty coal bins as winter approached. In many northern cities, poor households had run out of coal. "The country is on the verge of a vast public calamity," warned Walter Rauschenbusch. The Reverend Washington Gladden led a petition drive urging Roosevelt to mediate the strike.

The president invited leaders of both sides to a conference in Washington, D.C., where he appealed to their "patriotism, to the spirit that sinks personal considerations and makes individual sacrifices for the public good." The mine owners, however, refused to speak to the UMW leaders.

Roosevelt, infuriated by what he called the "extraordinary stupidity" of the "wooden-headed" and "arrogant" owners, threatened to declare a national emergency so that he could take control of the mines and use soldiers to run them. When a congressman questioned the constitutionality of such a move, Roosevelt roared, "To hell with the Constitution when the people want coal!"

The president's threat worked; the strike ended on October 23. The miners won a nine-hour workday and a 10 percent wage increase. Roosevelt was the first president to use his authority to referee a dispute between management and labor—believing that both sides deserved a fair hearing. His predecessors had responded to strikes by sending federal troops to shoot union activists.

## ROOSEVELT'S REELECTION

Theodore Roosevelt's forceful leadership won him friends and enemies. As he prepared to run for reelection in 1904, he acknowledged that the "whole Wall Street crowd" would do all they could to defeat him. Nevertheless, he won the Republican nomination.

The Democrats, having lost twice with William Jennings Bryan, essentially gave the election to Roosevelt and the Republicans by nominating the virtually unknown Alton B. Parker, chief justice of the New York Supreme Court. Parker was the dullest—and most forgettable—presidential candidate in history. One journalist called him "the enigma from New York." The most interesting item in Parker's campaign biography was that he had trained his pigs to come when called by name.

The Democrats suffered their worst election defeat in thirty-two years. After winning the electoral vote 336 to 140, Roosevelt told his son it was his "greatest triumph." Having succeeded to the presidency after William McKinley's assassination, he had now won election on his own and, in his view, had a mandate to do great things.

**PROGRESSIVE REGULATION** Theodore Roosevelt launched his second term with an even stronger commitment to regulating corporations and their corrupt owners (the "criminal rich") who exploited workers and tried to eliminate competition. His comments irked many of his corporate contributors and congressional Republican leaders. Said Pittsburgh steel baron Henry Frick, "We bought the son of a bitch, and then he did not stay bought."

To promote the "moral regeneration of business," Roosevelt first took aim at the railroads. In 1906, he persuaded Congress to pass the Hepburn Act, which gave the federal Interstate Commerce Commission the power to set maximum freight rates for the railroad industry.

Under Roosevelt's Square Deal programs, the federal government also assumed oversight of key industries affecting public health: meat-packers, food processors, and makers of drugs and patent medicines. Muckraking journalists had revealed all sorts of unsanitary and dangerous activities in the preparation of food and drug products. Perhaps the most powerful blow against these abuses was struck by Upton Sinclair's novel *The Jungle* (1906), which told the story of a Lithuanian immigrant working in a filthy Chicago meatpacking plant:

> It was too dark in these storage places to see well, but a man could run
> his hand over these piles of meat and sweep off handfuls of the dried

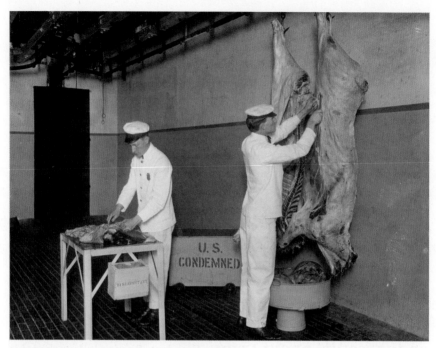

**Bad meat** Government inspectors examine sides of beef at a meatpacking plant.

dung of rats. These rats were nuisances, and the packers would put poisoned bread out for them, they would die, and then rats, bread, and meat would go into the hoppers [to be ground up] together.

After reading *The Jungle*, Roosevelt urged Congress to pass the Meat Inspection Act of 1906. It required the Department of Agriculture to inspect every hog and steer whose carcass crossed state lines. The Pure Food and Drug Act (1906), enacted the same day, required the makers of prepared food and medicines to host government inspectors—and label the ingredients in their products.

**ENVIRONMENTAL CONSERVATION** Theodore Roosevelt was passionately committed to environmental conservation. An avid outdoorsman, hunter, and naturalist, he championed efforts to protect wilderness areas and preserve the nation's natural resources. He created fifty federal wildlife refuges, approved five new national parks and fifty-one federal bird sanctuaries, and designated eighteen national monuments, including the Grand Canyon.

In 1898, Roosevelt had endorsed the appointment of his friend Gifford Pinchot, the nation's first professionally trained forest manager, as head of the Department of Agriculture's Division of Forestry. Pinchot, like Roosevelt, believed in economic growth as well as environmental preservation. Pinchot said that the conservation movement promoted the "greatest good for the greatest number for the longest time."

Roosevelt and Pinchot used the Forest Reserve Act (1891) to protect 172 million acres of federally owned forests from loggers. The owners of lumber companies were furious, but the president held firm, declaring, "I hate a man who skins the land." Overall, Roosevelt set aside more than 234 million acres of federal land for conservation purposes and created forty-five national forests. As Pinchot recalled, "Launching the conservation movement was the most significant achievement of the TR Administration, as he himself believed."

**ROOSEVELT AND RACE** Roosevelt's most significant failures were his refusal to endorse women's suffrage and to confront racism. Like Populists, progressives worked to empower "the people." For many of them, however, "the people" did not include African Americans, Native Americans, or some immigrant groups. Most white progressives ignored or even endorsed the passage of Jim Crow laws in the South that prevented blacks from voting and subjected them to rigid racial separation.

Hundreds of African Americans were being lynched each year across the South, where virtually no blacks were allowed to serve on juries or work in law enforcement. A white candidate for governor in Mississippi in 1903 announced that he believed "in the divine right of the white man to rule, to do all the voting, and to hold all the offices, both state and federal." The South, wrote W. E. B. Du Bois, then a young black sociologist at Atlanta University, "is simply an armed camp for intimidating black folk."

At the same time, few progressives questioned the many informal and private patterns of segregation and prejudice in the North and West. "The plain fact is," muckraking journalist Ray Stannard Baker admitted in 1909, "most of us in the North do not believe in any real democracy between white and colored men." Roosevelt confided to a friend in 1906 his belief that "as a race and in the mass," African Americans "are altogether inferior to whites."

Yet he had made a few exceptions. On October 16, 1901, Roosevelt invited Booker T. Washington, the nation's most prominent black leader, to the White House for dinner. White southerners exploded with fury. The *Memphis Scimitar* screamed that inviting a "nigger" to dine in the White House was "the most damnable outrage that has ever been perpetrated by a citizen of the United

**Theodore Roosevelt and Booker T. Washington**  Roosevelt addresses the National Negro Business League in 1900 with Washington seated to his left.

States." South Carolina senator Benjamin R. Tillman threatened that "a thousand niggers in the South will have to be killed to teach them 'their place' again."

Roosevelt gave in to the criticism. Never again would he host a black leader. During a tour of the South in 1905, he pandered to whites by highlighting his own southern ancestry (his mother was from Georgia) and expressing his admiration for the Confederacy and Robert E. Lee. His behavior, said a black leader, was "national treachery to the Negro."

**THE BROWNSVILLE RIOT**  In 1906, a violent racial incident occurred in Brownsville, Texas, where a dozen or so members of an African American army regiment shot several whites who had been harassing them outside a saloon. One white bartender was killed, and a police officer was seriously wounded. An investigation concluded that the soldiers were at fault, but no one could identify the shooters and none of the soldiers was willing to talk.

Roosevelt responded by dishonorably discharging the entire regiment of 167 soldiers, several of whom had been awarded the Congressional Medal of Honor for their service in Cuba during the War of 1898. Critics flooded the White House with angry telegrams. Secretary of War William H. Taft urged the president to reconsider, but Roosevelt refused to show any mercy to "murderers, assassins, cowards, and comrades of murderers." (Sixty years later, the U.S. Army "cleared the records" of the black soldiers.)

## TAFT AND RETRENCHMENT

After his 1904 election victory, Theodore Roosevelt had said he would not run for president again, in part because he did not want to be the first president to serve the equivalent of three terms. "No president has ever enjoyed himself as much as I enjoyed myself," he reflected. "I have used every ounce of power there was in the office, and I have not cared a rap for the criticisms of those who spoke of my 'usurpation of power.'" The strength of the United States depended upon having a "strong central executive," he declared. Now he was ready to leave the White House and go hunting for big game in Africa.

Unlike most presidents, however, Roosevelt would leave with regret, for he was loved by his party, who gave him a roaring ovation at the 1908 Republican nominating convention. When the cheers subsided, he urged the delegates to nominate his long-time friend, Secretary of War William Howard Taft, which they did on the first ballot.

The Democrats again chose William Jennings Bryan, who still retained a faithful following. Taft promised to continue Roosevelt's policies, and the Republican platform endorsed the president's progressive program. The Democratic platform echoed the Republican emphasis on regulation of business but called for a lower tariff. Bryan struggled to attract national support and was defeated for a third time, as Taft swept the electoral college, 321 to 162.

**A LIFE OF PUBLIC SERVICE**   On paper, William Howard Taft was superbly qualified to be president. Born in Cincinnati in 1857, the son of a prominent attorney who had served in President Grant's cabinet, Taft had graduated second in his class at Yale University and become a leading legal scholar, serving on the Ohio Supreme Court. In 1900, President McKinley appointed him the first American governor-general of the Philippines, and three years later Theodore Roosevelt named him secretary of war.

Until becoming president, Taft had never held elected office, nor was he ever sure he wanted to be chief executive. His preference was to be a justice on the U.S. Supreme Court. Running for president, he once confessed, was "a nightmare," for politics "makes me sick."

Unlike the robust, athletic Roosevelt, Taft struggled with obesity, topping out at 332 pounds. A special bathtub had to be installed in the White House to accommodate him. While serving as governor-general of the Philippines, he had cabled Secretary of War Elihu Root: "Took long horseback ride today, feeling fine." Root cabled back: "How is the horse?"

Taft's primary sin, he confessed, was laziness. He often fell asleep at cabinet meetings, banquets, and public events. Although good-natured and easygoing, Taft never managed to escape the shadow of his charismatic predecessor. "When I hear someone say 'Mr. President,'" he confessed, "I look around expecting to see Roosevelt."

Taft was a cautious, conservative progressive who embraced "strict construction" of the Constitution, which meant that he believed the founders had intentionally limited the powers of each of the three government branches—executive, legislative, and judicial. Unlike Roosevelt, who insisted that the president could take any action not explicitly prohibited by the Constitution, Taft believed that the president's authority should be limited to what the Constitution specified and that the president should have no role in the development of legislation, which was solely the responsibility of Congress.

Taft explained that his focus was to "complete" the programs and policies Roosevelt had initiated. He vowed to preserve capitalism by protecting "the right of private property" and the "right of liberty." In practice, this meant that he was even more determined than Roosevelt to support "the spirit of commercial freedom" against monopolistic trusts, but he was not interested in pushing for additional reforms or exercising extraordinary presidential power.

Taft viewed himself as a judge-like administrator, not an innovator. (After leaving the White House, he got the job he had always wanted: chief justice of the U.S. Supreme Court.) He was neither as energetic nor as wide-ranging as Roosevelt in his role as a reformer president—a difference that would lead to a fateful break between the two men.

**TAFT AND THE TARIFF** President Taft displayed his credentials as a progressive Republican by supporting *lower* tariffs on imports. But he proved less skillful than Roosevelt in dealing with Congress. Taft also discontinued Roosevelt's practice of using interviews with journalists to influence congressmen.

In the end, Taft's failure of leadership allowed Congress to pass the flawed Payne-Aldrich Tariff (1909), which did little to change federal policies. Taft's failure to gain real reform and his lack of a "crusading spirit" angered progressive, pro-Roosevelt Republicans, whom Taft called "assistant Democrats." He gravitated to the "Old Guard" Republican conservatives. Roosevelt was not happy.

**THE BALLINGER–PINCHOT CONTROVERSY** In 1910, the split between the conservative and progressive Republican factions was widened into a chasm by the Ballinger-Pinchot controversy. President Taft's secretary of the interior, Richard A. Ballinger, opened to commercial development millions of acres of federal lands that Roosevelt had ordered protected. Chief of forestry Gifford Pinchot complained about the "giveaway," but Taft refused to intervene. When Pinchot made his opposition public early in 1910, the president fired him. In doing so, Taft ignited a feud with Roosevelt that would eventually end their friendship—and cost him reelection.

**THE TAFT–ROOSEVELT FEUD** In 1909, soon after Taft became president, Roosevelt and his son Kermit had sailed to Africa, where they would spend nearly a year hunting big-game animals. The pair was supported by 250 porters and guides. (When business tycoon J. Pierpont Morgan heard about the extended safari, he expressed the hope that "every lion would do its duty" by eliminating Roosevelt.)

Roosevelt had left the White House assuming that Taft would continue to promote a progressive agenda. But by filling the cabinet with corporate lawyers and firing Gifford Pinchot, Taft had, in Roosevelt's view, failed to "carry out my work unbroken."

Roosevelt's rebuke of Taft was in some ways undeserved. Taft had at least attempted tariff reform, which Roosevelt had never dared. Although Taft had fired Pinchot, he had replaced him with another conservationist. Taft's administration actually preserved more federal land in four years than Roosevelt's had in nearly eight, and it filed twice as many anti-trust suits, including one that led to the breakup of the Standard Oil Company in 1911. Taft also supported giving women the right to vote and workers the right to join unions.

None of that satisfied Roosevelt, however. On August 31, 1910, the former president, eager to return to the political spotlight, gave a speech at Osawatomie, Kansas, in which he announced his latest progressive proposals—his "New Nationalism." He explained that he wanted to go beyond ensuring a Square Deal in which corporations were forced to "play by the rules"; he now promised to "change the rules" to force corporations to promote social welfare and serve the needs of working people.

To save capitalism from the threat of a working-class revolution, Roosevelt called for tighter federal regulation of "arrogant" corporations that too often tried to "control and corrupt" politics; for a federal income tax (the Sixteenth Amendment had still not become law); and for federal laws regulating child labor. "What I have advocated," he explained, "is not wild radicalism. It is the highest and wisest kind of conservatism."

Then, on February 24, 1912, Roosevelt announced his entry into the race for that year's Republican presidential nomination. He dismissed the "second-rate" Taft as a "hopeless fathead" and "flubdub" who had "sold the Square Deal down the river." Taft responded by calling Roosevelt a "dangerous egotist" and a "demagogue." Thus began a bitter war in which Roosevelt had the better weapons, not the least of which was his love of a good fight.

By 1912, a dozen or so states were letting citizens vote for presidential candidates in party primaries instead of following the traditional practice in which party leaders chose the nominee behind closed doors. Roosevelt decided that if he won big in the Republican primaries, he could claim to be "the people's choice." Yet even though he won all but two primaries, including the one in Taft's home state of Ohio, his popularity was no match for Taft's authority as party leader. In the thirty-six states that chose candidates by conventions dominated by party bosses, the Taft Republicans prevailed. At the Republican National Convention, Taft won easily.

Roosevelt was furious. He denounced Taft and his supporters as thieves and stormed out of the convention along with his delegates—mostly social workers, teachers, professors, journalists, and urban reformers, along with a few wealthy business executives.

**THE PROGRESSIVE PARTY** Six weeks later, Theodore Roosevelt urged the breakaway faction of Republicans to reconvene in Chicago to create the **Progressive party**. They enthusiastically nominated him as their candidate. He assured the delegates that he felt "fit as a bull moose," leading journalists to nickname the new party the "Bull Moose party." Progressives adored Roosevelt because he showed what a government dedicated to the public good might achieve. He loved to campaign because it enabled him to engage the people in the democratic process. "The first duty of the American citizen," he stressed, "is that he shall work in politics."

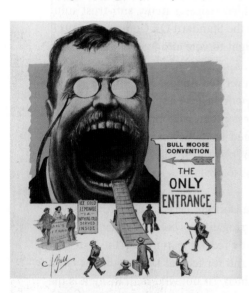

**Sideshow Ted** This 1912 cartoon criticizes the Bull Moose party for being just a sideshow (with suffragists selling lemonade outside) and points out the menacing ego of Roosevelt.

The Progressive party platform, audacious for its time, revealed Roosevelt's growing liberalism. It supported a minimum "living wage" for hourly workers; an eight-hour workday; women's suffrage and "an equal voice with women in every phase of party management"; campaign finance reform; and a system of "social security" insurance to protect people against sickness, unemployment, and disabilities. It also pledged to end the boss system governing state and local politics and destroy the "unholy alliance between corrupt business and corrupt politics." Conservative critics called Roosevelt "a socialist," a "revolutionist," "a virtual traitor to American institutions," and a "monumental egotist."

Roosevelt charged that President Taft was not a progressive because he had tried to undo efforts at environmental conservation and had failed to fight for social justice or against the special interests. Instead, Roosevelt said that Taft had aligned himself with the privileged political and business leaders who steadfastly opposed "the cause of justice for the helpless and the wronged."

# WOODROW WILSON: A PROGRESSIVE SOUTHERNER

The fight between William Howard Taft and Theodore Roosevelt gave hope to the Democrats, whose presidential nominee, New Jersey governor Woodrow Wilson, had enjoyed remarkable success in his brief political career. Until his nomination and election as governor in 1910, Wilson had been a college professor and then president of Princeton University, where he had become a popular speaker promoting progressive political reforms and government regulation of corporations.

Wilson had never run for political office or worked in business. He was a man of ideas, with a keen intellect and "a first class mind" bolstered by an analytical temperament, a tireless work ethic, an inspiring speaking style, and a strong conviction that he knew what was best for the nation.

**TO SERVE HUMANITY** Born in Staunton, Virginia, in 1856, the son, grandson, nephew and son-in-law of Presbyterian ministers, Thomas Woodrow Wilson had grown up in Georgia and the Carolinas during the Civil War and Reconstruction. The South, he once said, was the only part of the

**Woodrow Wilson** The first president to hold a doctoral degree.

nation where nothing had to be explained to him. Tall and slender, with a long, chiseled face, he developed an unquestioning religious faith. Driven by a consuming sense that God had selected him to serve humanity, he often displayed an unbending self-righteousness and a fiery temper, qualities that would prove to be his undoing as president.

Wilson graduated from Princeton in 1879. After law school at the University of Virginia, he briefly worked as an attorney before enrolling at Johns Hopkins University to study history and political science. He earned one of the nation's first doctoral degrees, became an expert in constitutional government, and taught at several colleges before becoming president of Princeton in 1902.

Eight years later, Wilson accepted the support of New Jersey Democrats for the gubernatorial nomination. He harbored higher ambitions, however. If he could become governor, he said, "I stand a very good chance of being the next President of the United States." Like Roosevelt, Wilson was intensely ambitious and idealistic; he felt destined to preside over America's emergence as the greatest world power.

After winning the governorship by a landslide, Wilson persuaded the state legislature to adopt an array of progressive reforms to curb the power of party bosses and corporate lobbyists. "After dealing with college politicians," he joked, "I find that the men who I am dealing with now seem like amateurs."

Wilson soon attracted national attention. At the 1912 Democratic convention, he faced stiff competition from several veteran party leaders for the presidential nomination. But with the support of William Jennings Bryan, he won on the forty-sixth ballot.

**THE 1912 ELECTION** The 1912 presidential campaign was one of the most exciting in history. It involved four distinguished candidates: Democrat Woodrow Wilson, Republican William Howard Taft, Socialist Eugene V. Debs, and Progressive Theodore Roosevelt. For all their differences, the candidates shared a basic progressive assumption that modern social problems could be resolved only through active governmental intervention.

No sooner did the formal campaign open than Roosevelt's candidacy almost ended. While on his way to deliver a speech in Milwaukee, Wisconsin, he was shot by John Schrank, a deranged man who believed that any president seeking a third term should be killed. The bullet went through Roosevelt's overcoat, a steel eyeglasses case, and fifty-page speech, then fractured a rib before nestling just below his right lung, an inch from his heart.

Refusing medical attention, Roosevelt insisted on delivering his eighty-minute speech to 10,000 supporters. In a dramatic gesture, he showed the audience his bloodstained shirt and punctured text, explaining that "the bullet is in me now, so I cannot make a very long speech." Then, grinning, he vowed, "It takes more than this to kill a bull moose." When he finished, he went directly to a hospital, where he stayed for a week.

As the campaign developed, Taft quickly lost ground and essentially gave up. "There are so many people in the country who don't like me," he lamented. The contest settled into a debate over Roosevelt's New Nationalism and Wilson's **New Freedom**. The New Freedom, designed by Louis Brandeis, favored small government and states' rights, arguing that federal intervention should be a last resort. It aimed to restore economic competition by eliminating *all* trusts rather than just those that misbehaved. Where Roosevelt admired the power and efficiency of law-abiding corporations, no matter how large, Brandeis and Wilson were convinced that huge, "heartless" industries needed to be broken up.

On Election Day, Wilson won handily, collecting 435 electoral votes to 88 for Roosevelt and just 8 for Taft, who said he had only one consolation: "No candidate was ever elected ex-President by such a large majority."

After learning of his election, Wilson told the chairman of his campaign committee, "I owe you nothing. God ordained that I should be the next president of the United States. Neither you nor any other mortal could have prevented that."

Had the Republicans not divided their votes between Taft and Roosevelt, however, Wilson would have lost. His was the victory of a minority candidate over a divided opposition.

The election of 1912 profoundly altered the character of the Republican party. The defection of the Bull Moose progressives had weakened the progressive wing of the Republican party. Upon returning to power in the 1920s, its platform would be more conservative in tone and temperament.

**EUGENE DEBS** The real surprise of the 1912 election was the strong showing of the Socialist party candidate, Eugene V. Debs, running for the fourth time. The tall, blue-eyed idealist had devoted his career to fighting the "monstrous system of capitalism" on behalf of the working class, first as a labor union official, then as a socialist promoting government ownership of railroads and the sharing of profits with workers.

Debs promoted a brand of socialism that was flexible rather than rigid, Christian rather than Marxist, democratic rather than totalitarian. He believed in political transformation, not violent revolution. As one of his supporters said, "That old man with the burning eyes actually believes that there can be such a thing as the brotherhood of man. And that's not the funniest part of it. As long as he's around I believe it myself."

## THE ELECTION OF 1912

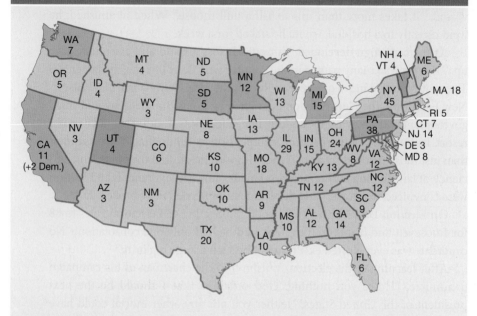

| | | Electoral Vote | Popular Vote |
|---|---|---|---|
| | **Woodrow Wilson (Democratic)** | **435** | **6,300,000** |
| | Theodore Roosevelt (Progressive) | 88 | 4,100,000 |
| | William H. Taft (Republican) | 8 | 3,500,000 |
| | Eugene V. Debs (Socialist) | 0 | 900,000 |

- Why was Taft so unpopular?
- How did the split between Roosevelt and Taft give Wilson the presidency?
- Why was Wilson's victory in 1912 especially significant?

Debs became the symbol of a diverse movement that united West Virginia coal miners, Oklahoma sharecroppers, Pacific Northwest lumberjacks, and immigrant workers in New York City sweatshops. In 1912, some 1,150 Socialists won election to local and state offices across the nation, including eighteen mayoral seats.

To many voters, the Socialist party, whose 118,000 dues-paying members in 1912 were double the number from the year before, offered the only real alternative to a stalemated political system in which the two major parties had few real differences. But fear of socialism was also widespread. Theodore Roosevelt warned that the rapid growth of the Socialist party was "far more ominous than any Populist or similar movement in the past."

In 1912, Debs crisscrossed the nation giving fiery speeches. He dismissed Roosevelt as "a charlatan, mountebank [swindler], and fraud" whose progressive promises were nothing more than "the mouthings of a low and utterly unprincipled self-seeker and demagogue." Debs won more than 900,000 votes, twice as many as he had received four years earlier.

## A Burst of Reform Bills

On March 4, 1913, a huge crowd surrounded the Capitol in Washington, D.C., to watch Woodrow Wilson's inauguration. The new president declared that it was not "a day of triumph" but "a day of dedication." Blessed with Democratic majorities in the House and Senate, Wilson promised to lower "the stiff and stupid" Republican tariff, create a new national banking system, strengthen anti-trust laws, and establish an administration "more concerned about human rights than about property rights."

Wilson worried about being compared to Roosevelt: "He appeals to their imagination; I do not. He is a real, vivid person. . . . I am a vague, conjectural [philosophical] personality, more made up of opinions and academic prepossessions than of human traits and red corpuscles."

Roosevelt had been a strong president by force of personality; Wilson became a strong president by force of conviction. "I have a strong instinct for leadership," he stressed, and he sincerely believed he was being directed by God.

Despite their differences, Wilson and Roosevelt shared a belief that national problems demanded national solutions. Together they set in motion the modern presidency, expanding the scope of the executive branch at the expense of Congress.

Like Roosevelt, Wilson was an activist president: He was the first to speak to the nation over the radio and to host weekly press conferences. As a political scientist (and the first president with a doctoral degree), Wilson was an expert at the processes of government. During his first two years, he pushed through Congress more new bills than any previous president. Like "most reformers," however, Wilson "had a fierce and unlovely side," according to the president of Harvard University. The president found it hard to understand—much less work with—people who disagreed with him.

His victory, coupled with majorities in the House and Senate, gave Democrats effective national power for the first time since the Civil War—and also gave southerners a significant national role for the first time since the war. Five of Wilson's ten cabinet members were born in the South.

**COLONEL HOUSE** Woodrow Wilson's closest adviser was "Colonel" Edward M. House of Texas, who held no official government position but was the president's constant companion. House was one of the most skilled political operators in history, and he and Wilson developed the most famous political partnership of the twentieth century. The president described House as "my second personality. He is my independent self. His thoughts and mine are one."

House told Wilson that the theme of his presidency should be a form of Christian democracy. The "strong should help the weak, the fortunate should aid the unfortunate, and business should be conducted upon a higher and more humane plane." He helped steer Wilson's proposals through a Congress in which southerners, by virtue of their seniority, held the lion's share of committee chairmanships. As a result, much of the progressive legislation of the Wilson era would bear the names of southern Democrats.

**THE TARIFF AND THE INCOME TAX**  Like Taft, Wilson pursued tariff reform, but with greater success. By 1913, the federal tariff included hundreds of taxes on different imported goods, from oil to nails. The president believed that U.S. corporations were misusing the tariff to keep out foreign competitors and create monopolies that held consumer prices artificially high.

To lower tariff rates and thereby lower prices to consumers, Wilson summoned Congress for what came to be the longest special session in history. Over that eighteen months, Wilson addressed Congress in person—the first president to do so since John Adams.

The new tariff bill passed the House easily. The crunch came in the Senate, where swarms of lobbyists grew so thick, Wilson said, "a brick couldn't be thrown without hitting one of them." By publicly criticizing the "industrious and insidious" tariff lobby, Wilson finally convinced Congress to support his approach.

The Underwood-Simmons Tariff Act (1913) lowered tariff rates on almost 1,000 imported products. To compensate for the reduced tariff revenue, the bill created the first income tax allowed under the newly ratified Sixteenth Amendment: the initial tax rates were 1 percent on income more than $3,000 ($4,000 for married couples) up to a top rate of 7 percent on annual income of $500,000 or more. Most workers paid no income tax because they earned less than $3,000 a year.

**THE FEDERAL RESERVE ACT**  No sooner did the new tariff pass than the administration proposed the first major banking reform since the Civil War. Ever since Andrew Jackson had killed the Second Bank of the United States in the 1830s, the nation had been without a central bank. Instead, the money supply was chaotically "managed" by thousands of local and state banks.

Such a decentralized system was unstable and inefficient because, during financial panics, fearful depositors eager to withdraw their money would create "runs" that often led to the failure of smaller banks because they would run out of cash. The primary reason for a new central bank was to prevent such panics, which had occurred five times since 1873. President Wilson believed the banking system needed a central reserve agency that, in a crisis, could distribute emergency cash to stressed banks. Any new system, however, must be overseen by the government rather than by bankers themselves. Wilson wanted a central bank that would benefit the entire economy, not just the large banks headquartered on Wall Street in New York City.

After much dickering, Congress passed the **Federal Reserve Act** on December 23, 1913. It created a national banking system with twelve regional districts, each of which had its own Federal Reserve Bank owned by member banks in the district. All nationally chartered banks had to be members of the Federal Reserve System. State-chartered banks—essentially unregulated—did not (and, indeed, two thirds of the nation's banks chose not to become members of the Federal Reserve System). The twelve regional Federal Reserve banks were supervised by a central board of directors in Washington, D.C.

The overarching purpose of the Federal Reserve System was to adjust the nation's currency supply to promote economic growth and ensure the stability and integrity of member banks. When banks were short of cash, they could borrow from the Federal Reserve. Each of the regional banks issued Federal Reserve notes (currency) to member banks in exchange for their loans. By doing so, "the Fed," as the system came to be called, promoted economic growth and helped preserve the stability of banks during panics. The Federal Reserve board required member banks to have a certain percentage of their total deposits in cash on hand ("reserve") at all times.

One conservative Republican called the Federal Reserve Act "populistic, socialistic, half-baked, destructive, and unworkable." The system soon proved its worth, however, and the criticism eased. The Federal Reserve Act was the most significant new program of Wilson's presidency.

**ANTI-TRUST ACTIONS** Woodrow Wilson made "trust-busting" the focus of his New Freedom program. Giant corporations had continued to grow despite the Sherman Anti-Trust Act (1890) and the Bureau of Corporations, the federal watchdog agency created by Theodore Roosevelt.

The **Clayton Anti-Trust Act** of 1914 exempted labor unions from anti-trust laws and revived the Populists' demand that companies, such as railroads, be prohibited from charging different prices to different customers. It also banned corporate directors from serving on the boards of competing companies.

Wilson decided to make a strong **Federal Trade Commission** (FTC) the cornerstone of his anti-trust program. Created in 1914, the five-member FTC replaced Theodore Roosevelt's Bureau of Corporations and assumed powers to define "unfair trade practices" and issue "cease and desist" orders when it found evidence of such practices. Wilson explained that the purpose of the FTC was to "destroy monopoly and maintain competition as the only efficient instrument of business liberty." His goal was to prevent monopolistic trusts, not to regulate them.

## WILSON DECLARES VICTORY

In November 1914, just two years after his election, President Wilson announced that he had accomplished the major goals of progressivism. Through his effective leadership, he had fulfilled his audacious promises to lower the tariff, create a national banking system, and strengthen the anti-trust laws. The New Freedom was now complete, he wrote, for he had no desire to continue increasing the power of the federal government. "The history of liberty," he stressed, "is the history of the limitation of governmental power, not the increase of it."

Wilson's victory declaration bewildered many progressives, especially those who had long advocated additional social-justice legislation that the president had earlier supported. Herbert Croly, editor of the *New Republic* magazine, wondered how the president could assert "that the fundamental wrongs of a modern society can be easily and quickly righted as a consequence of [passing] a few laws." Wilson's about-face, he concluded, "casts suspicion upon his own sincerity [as a progressive] or upon his grasp of the realities of modern social and industrial life."

**PROGRESSIVISM FOR WHITES ONLY** African Americans continued to resent the racial conservatism of most progressives. Carter Glass, the Virginia senator largely responsible for developing the Federal Reserve Act in 1913, was an enthusiastic supporter of his state's efforts to disenfranchise black voters. When questioned by a reporter about being a racist progressive, Glass embraced the label: "Discrimination! Why that is exactly what we propose. To remove every Negro voter who can be gotten rid of."

Similarly, Woodrow Wilson shared many of the racist attitudes common at the time. As a student at Princeton, he had dismissed African Americans as "an ignorant and inferior race." As a politician, Wilson courted African American voters, but he rarely consulted or associated with black leaders.

**New freedom, old rules**  Woodrow Wilson and his wife Edith ride in a carriage with African American drivers.

Josephus Daniels, a North Carolina newspaper editor who became Wilson's secretary of the navy, was a white supremacist who stressed that "the subjection of the negro, politically, and the separation of the negro, socially, are paramount to all other considerations in the South."

Daniels and other cabinet members racially segregated the employees in their offices, dining halls, and restrooms. Wilson endorsed the policy, claiming that racial segregation "is not humiliating but a benefit." To him, "separate but equal" was the best way to resolve racial tensions. He was the first president since the Civil War who openly endorsed discrimination against African Americans. In his 1902 book, *A History of the American People*, Wilson had praised the restoration of white supremacy in the South for ridding the electoral process of the "ignorant and hostile [Negro] vote."

In November 1914, a delegation of concerned African American leaders met with Wilson to ask how a "progressive" president could adopt such "regressive" policies. Wilson responded that both races benefited from the policies because they eliminated "the possibility of friction." William Monroe Trotter, a Harvard-educated African American newspaper editor who had helped found the National Association for the Advancement of Colored People (NAACP), scolded the president: "Have you a 'new freedom' for white Americans, and a new slavery for 'your Afro-American fellow citizens' [a phrase Wilson had used in a speech]? God forbid."

A furious Wilson told the visitors to leave, saying their unchristian "tone offends me." In 1916, when Wilson campaigned for a second term, not a single African American leader endorsed him. "You have grievously disappointed us," W. E. B. Du Bois said.

**THE VOTE FOR WOMEN** Activists for women's suffrage were also disappointed in President Wilson. Despite having two daughters, Eleanor and Jessie, who were suffragists, he insisted that the issue of women's voting rights should be left to the states rather than embodied in a constitutional amendment.

Wilson's lack of support led some leaders of the suffrage movement to revise their tactics. In 1910, social worker Alice Paul, a New Jersey–born

**Alice Paul** Sewing a suffrage flag—orange and purple, with stars—that she and other suffragists often waved at strikes and protests.

Quaker, returned to the United States from working with militant suffragists in England, where she had engaged in hunger strikes and been jailed. She joined the National American Woman Suffrage Association (NAWSA) and urged activists to use more aggressive tactics: picketing state legislatures, "punishing" politicians who failed to endorse suffrage, chaining themselves to public buildings, inciting police to arrest them, and launching hunger strikes. Eventually, NAWSA decided Paul was too militant and expelled her from their ranks. She responded in 1913 by forming the Congressional Union for Woman Suffrage and starting *Suffragist* magazine.

Early that March, Paul organized 5,000 suffragists to protest at Wilson's inauguration. Spectators "taunted, spat upon, and roughed up" the marchers, while police did little to control the crowds. The War Department dispatched a cavalry unit to restore order. Wilson ordered his driver to avoid the rally, for he could not stand hearing "women speak in public."

A few days later, Paul and three others met Wilson in the White House. They warned that if he continued to oppose an amendment providing the vote to women, thousands of suffragists would campaign against his reelection. "If they did that," Wilson replied, "they would not be as intelligent as I believe they are."

Four years later, having formed the National Woman's Party, Paul urged suffragists to do something even more dramatic: picket the White House. Beginning on January 11, 1917, from 10 A.M. to 5 P.M., five days a week, Paul and her followers (the "Silent Sentinels") took turns carrying signs reading: "MR. PRESIDENT! HOW LONG MUST WOMEN WAIT FOR LIBERTY?"

They picketed for six months, until Wilson ordered their arrest. Some sixty middle-class suffragists were jailed. At their trials, the women found their voices. Florence Bayard Hilles, daughter of a former secretary of state, expressed all suffragists' outrage: "What a spectacle it must be to the thinking people of this country to see us urged to go to war for democracy in a foreign land and to see women thrown into prison who plead for the same cause at home."

Paul was sentenced to seven months in prison. She went on a hunger strike, leading prison officials to force-feed her raw eggs through a rubber tube inserted in her nose. She recalled, "It was shocking that a government of men could look with such extreme contempt on a movement that was asking nothing except such a simple little thing as the right to vote." Buffeted by negative press coverage and public criticism, Wilson pardoned Paul and the other activists.

**PROGRESSIVISM RENEWED**  By 1916, Woodrow Wilson's determination to win reelection revived his commitment to progressive activism. The president nominated Bostonian Louis D. Brandeis, the "people's attorney," to the Supreme Court. Brandeis was not just a famed defender of unions against big businesses; he would also be the first Jewish member of the Supreme Court.

Progressives viewed the nomination as a "landmark in the history of American democracy." Others disagreed. Former president Taft dismissed Brandeis as "a muckraker, an emotionalist for his own purposes, a socialist . . . who is utterly unscrupulous." The Senate, however, confirmed Brandeis's appointment.

**FARM LEGISLATION**  President Wilson also urged Congress to pass the first federal legislation directed at assisting farmers. He supported a proposal to set up rural banks to provide long-term farm loans. The Federal Farm Loan Act became law in 1916. Under the control of the Federal Farm Loan Board, twelve Federal Land banks offered loans to farmers for five to forty years at low interest rates. At about the same time, a dream long advocated by Populists— federal loans to farmers on the security of their crops stored in warehouses— finally came to fruition when Congress passed the Warehouse Act of 1916.

Farmers also benefited from the Smith-Lever Act of 1914, which provided programs to educate farmers about new machinery and new ideas related to agricultural efficiency, and the Smith-Hughes Act (1917), which funded agricultural and mechanical education in high schools. Farmers with new-fangled automobiles had more than a passing interest as well in the Federal Highways Act of 1916, which helped finance new roads, especially in rural areas.

**LABOR LEGISLATION**  One of the long-standing goals of progressive Democrats was a *federal* child-labor law. When Congress passed the Keating-Owen Act in 1916, banning products made by child workers under fourteen from being shipped across state lines, Wilson expressed doubts about its constitutionality but eventually signed it.

Another landmark law was the Adamson Act of 1916, which resulted from a threatened strike by railroad unions demanding an eight-hour day and other concessions. Wilson, who objected to some of the unions' demands, nevertheless asked Congress to approve the Adamson Act. It required time-and-a-half pay for overtime work beyond eight hours and appointed a commission to study working conditions in the railroad industry.

## ASSESSING PROGRESSIVISM

Progressivism—and its notion that the quality of life could be improved by government action—reached its peak during Woodrow Wilson's two terms as president. After decades of political upheaval and social reform, progressivism had shattered the laissez-faire notion that government had no role in protecting the public welfare through regulating the economy or improving quality of life. Progressives demonstrated that people of good will could make a difference in improving social conditions for all.

Progressives established the principle that governments—local, state, and federal—had a responsibility to ensure that Americans were protected from abuse by powerful businesses and corrupt politicians. As a Texas progressive said in 1910, most Americans now acknowledged that governments must protect "the weak against the encroachments of the strong."

Ultimately, progressivism faded as an organized political movement because international issues pushed aside domestic concerns. By 1916, the optimism of a few years earlier had disappeared in the wake of the Great War in Europe. "We are at the dead season of our fortunes," wrote British economist John Maynard Keynes, contemplating the horrific scale of the war. "Never in the lifetime of men now living has the universal element in the soul of man burnt so dimly." Along with millions of soldiers, faith in the beneficence of progress died in the war's muddy trenches.

The twentieth century, which had dawned with such bright hopes, held in store episodes of unprecedented brutality that would call into question whether progress was even possible anymore.

# CHAPTER REVIEW

## Summary

- **The Progressive Impulse**    Progressives were mostly middle-class idealists of both political parties who promoted reform and government regulation to ensure social justice. Many progressives wished to restrict the powers of local political machines and establish honest and efficient government. They called for legislation to end child labor, promote workplace safety, ban the sale of alcoholic beverages, regulate or eliminate trusts and other monopolies, and grant *women's suffrage*.

- **The Varied Sources of Progressivism**    Many religious reformers, such as those involved in the *social gospel* movement, urged their fellow Protestants to reject social Darwinism and do more to promote a better life for the urban poor. The settlement house movement spread through urban America as college-educated middle-class women formed community centers in poverty-stricken neighborhoods. Progressives drew inspiration from the women's suffrage movement, as more women became involved in social reform efforts and in the workplace. Many progressive ideas arose from the efforts of reformers to end political corruption. Progressives, while not radicals, also responded to the growing socialist movement and its calls for economic justice for the working class. *Muckrakers*—investigative journalists who exposed political and corporate corruption—further fueled the efforts to address abuses of power in American society.

- **Progressives' Aims and Achievements**    Progressives focused on stopping corruption in politics. They advanced reforms such as the direct primary; the initiative, referendum, and recall at the state level; and the direct election of U.S. senators through the passage of the *Seventeenth Amendment (1913)*. Other progressives focused on incorporating new modes of efficiency and scientific management in business, known as *Taylorism*, into government. Their efforts inspired many cities and counties to adopt the commission system and the city-manager plan. Still other progressives focused on legislation and bureaucratic oversight to control or eliminate trusts and other forms of monopolies.

- **Progressivism under Roosevelt and Taft**    The administrations of Theodore Roosevelt and William H. Taft increased the power of the presidency and the federal government to regulate corporations and improve the lives of many Americans. Roosevelt promoted his *Square Deal* program, which included regulating trusts through the creation of the Bureau of Corporations, arbitrating the 1902 coal strike, persuading Congress to regulate the railroads through the Elkins and Hepburn Acts, and to clean up the meat and drug industries with the Meat Inspection and Pure Food and Drug Acts. Roosevelt also initiated an environmental conservation campaign to preserve the nation's natural resources.

- **Woodrow Wilson's Progressivism**  Wilson's *New Freedom* program included lower tariffs and anti-trust regulations. He established a central banking system with the *Federal Reserve Act (1913)*, and launched a rigorous anti-trust program with the passage of the *Clayton Anti-Trust Act (1914)* and the creation of the *Federal Trade Commission (1914)*. But he opposed a constitutional amendment guaranteeing women's suffrage. A southerner, he believed black people were inferior, and he supported segregation in the federal workforce.

## CHRONOLOGY

| | |
|---|---|
| 1901 | William McKinley is assassinated; Theodore Roosevelt becomes president |
| | Galveston, Texas, adopts the commission system of city government |
| 1902 | Justice Department breaks up the Northern Securities Company |
| 1903 | Congress passes the Elkins Act and creates the Bureau of Corporations |
| 1906 | Upton Sinclair's *The Jungle* is published |
| | Congress passes the Meat Inspection Act and the Pure Food and Drug Act |
| 1909 | William Howard Taft inaugurated |
| 1911 | Triangle Shirtwaist fire |
| | Frederick Taylor's *The Principles of Scientific Management* is published |
| 1912 | Woodrow Wilson wins four-way presidential election |
| 1913 | Alice Paul and 5,000 suffragists protest Wilson's inauguration |
| | Sixteenth and Seventeenth Amendments ratified |
| | Underwood-Simmons Tariff and Federal Reserve Act passed |
| 1914 | Congress passes the Clayton Anti-Trust Act |

## KEY TERMS

muckrakers p. 854

social gospel p. 856

women's suffrage p. 858

Seventeenth Amendment (1913) p. 862

Taylorism p. 862

Sixteenth Amendment (1913) p. 867

Square Deal p. 868

Progressive party p. 878

New Freedom p. 881

Federal Reserve Act (1913) p. 885

Clayton Anti-Trust Act (1914) p. 885

Federal Trade Commission (1914) p. 886

 INQUIZITIVE

Go to InQuizitive to see what you've learned—and learn what you've missed—with personalized feedback along the way.

# 22 America and the Great War

## 1914–1920

THE NAVY NEEDS YOU! DON'T **READ** AMERICAN HISTORY— **MAKE IT!**

**Make American History** In this U.S. Navy recruiting poster in New York City, a sailor encourages a young man to play an active role in the Great War.

Throughout the nineteenth century, the Atlantic Ocean had protected America from wars fought on the continent of Europe. During the early twentieth century, however, the nation's global isolation ended. Ever-expanding world trade entwined U.S. interests with the international economy. In addition, the development of steam-powered ships and submarines meant that foreign navies could directly threaten U.S. security.

At the same time, the election of Woodrow Wilson in 1912 brought to the White House a self-righteous moralist determined to impose his standards on what he saw as renegade nations. This combination of circumstances made the outbreak of the "Great War" in Europe in 1914 a profound crisis for the United States. The first world war would become the defining event of the early twentieth century.

For almost three years, President Wilson maintained America's stance of "neutrality" toward the war while providing increasing amounts of food and supplies to Great Britain and France. In 1917, however, German submarine attacks on U.S. ships forced Congress to declare war.

Once America entered the war, almost 5 million men joined the military, including 400,000 African Americans. The departure of so many men from civilian life opened up new jobs across the nation for men and women. Recruited by businesses, some 1.6 million mostly rural African Americans moved to cities outside the South to work in defense industries in what was called the Great Migration. The prospect of higher-paying jobs stimulated

## focus questions

1. What caused the outbreak of the Great War, and why did the United States join the conflict? What was distinctive about the fighting on the Western Front?

2. How did the Wilson administration mobilize the home front? How did these mobilization efforts affect society?

3. What were the major events of the war after the United States entered the conflict? How did the American war effort contribute to the defeat of the Central Powers?

4. How did Wilson promote his plans for a peaceful world order as outlined in his Fourteen Points?

5. What were the consequences of the war at home and abroad?

the mass migration, but African Americans were also eager to get away from the often violent racism and rigid Jim Crow segregation they suffered under in the southern states.

## AN UNEASY NEUTRALITY

Woodrow Wilson once declared that he had "a first-class mind." He was indeed intelligent, thoughtful, principled, and courageous. For all his accomplishments and abilities, however, Wilson had no experience or expertise in international relations before becoming president. "It would be an irony of fate," he confessed, "if my administration had to deal chiefly with foreign affairs." Ironic or not, when war erupted in Europe during the summer of 1914, he shifted his attention from the New Freedom's progressive reforms to foreign affairs.

Wilson believed God was directing him to help create a new world order governed by morality and ideals rather than by selfish national interests. Both Wilson and William Jennings Bryan, his first secretary of state, believed that America had a God-given duty to promote democracy and Christianity around the world. "Every nation of the world," Wilson declared, "needs to be drawn into the tutelage [guidance] of America."

## THE GREAT WAR

Woodrow Wilson faced his greatest challenge beginning in the summer of 1914, when the "dreadful conflict" in Europe exploded suddenly, like "lightning out of a clear sky," as a North Carolina congressman said. Unfortunately, the outbreak of war coincided with a rapid decline in the health of Wilson's wife Ellen, who died on August 6, 1914. "God has stricken me," the president wrote a friend, "almost beyond what I can bear."

Wilson would also have trouble bearing the horrors of the war. Lasting more than four years, from 1914 to 1918, the so-called Great War (a future generation would call it the First World War) would involve more nations and cause greater destruction than any previous conflict: 20 million military and civilian deaths, and 21 million more wounded. The Great War would topple monarchs, destroy empires, create new nations, and set in motion a series of events that would lead to an even costlier war in 1939.

CAUSES The Great War resulted from long-simmering national rivalries and ethnic conflicts in Europe, as powerful imperial nations competed for foreign colonies and military supremacy. There had not been a major European war in more than forty years, but the great powers, driven by a lusty sense of hypernationalism aggravated by ethnic hatreds and racist beliefs, had been preparing for one. Germany's determination to have its "place in the sun" at the expense of Great Britain was only one of several threats to peace and stability.

Growing tensions during the early twentieth century spawned a furious arms race and the creation of two competing military alliances: the **Central Powers** (Germany, Austria-Hungary, Bulgaria, and Turkey [the Ottoman Empire]), and the **Allied Powers** (France, Great Britain, and Russia). The members of these two alliances pledged to come to the defense of their partners should they be attacked, thus dividing Europe into two armed camps.

At the core of the tensions was the "powder keg of Europe," the Austro-Hungarian (Habsburg) Empire, an unstable collection of eleven nationalities whose leaders were determined to suppress their southern neighbor and long-standing enemy, Serbia. Serbian nationalists (Pan-Slavists) had long hoped to create "Yugoslavia," a nation encompassing all ethnic Slavic peoples from throughout the Austro-Hungarian Empire. Russia, home to millions of Slavs, supported the Pan-Slavic movement.

A recklessly militaristic Germany, led by Kaiser (Emperor) Wilhelm II, had been a latecomer to industrialization and nationalism, having become a united nation only in 1871. Its leaders yearned to catch up with Great Britain and France. By 1892, German steel production had surpassed that of Britain and by 1910 had doubled it. Germany had also created its own colonial empire in Africa and Asia while building a navy powerful enough to challenge British supremacy on the seas and an army capable of defeating its old enemies, the Russian Empire and France. Now, Kaiser Wilhelm wanted to be like Napoléon Bonaparte, a military conqueror.

These factors—militarism, alliances, imperialism, and nationalism—created a combustible situation. All that was needed to ignite it was a spark.

**FIGHTING ERUPTS**  That spark came in the Balkan Peninsula, a volatile region of southeastern Europe on the southern border of the Austro-Hungarian Empire. There, for centuries, the Austrian and Russian monarchies and the Ottoman Empire had competed for control. Six years before, in 1908, Austria had annexed Bosnia from the Ottoman Empire, infuriating Serbian nationalists.

On June 28, 1914, the heir to the Austro-Hungarian throne, Archduke Franz Ferdinand, and his pregnant wife Sophie, visited Sarajevo (the capital of Austrian-controlled Bosnia). When the Archduke's driver took a wrong turn and was forced to back the motorcar slowly down a crowded street, Gavrilo Princip, a nineteen-year-old Serbian nationalist, shot the imperial couple at point-blank range. They both died.

To avenge the murders, Austria-Hungary, with Germany's approval, resolved to bring Serbia under its control—or destroy it. To that end, it humiliated Serbia by issuing deliberately unreasonable ultimatums. Serbia agreed to most of them, but Austria-Hungary mobilized for war anyway. Russia responded by mobilizing its army to defend Serbia, triggering reactions by other members of the rival European military alliances. In late 1918, just after the war ended, an Austrian diplomat confessed, "We began the war, not the Germans."

Germany, expecting a limited war and quick victory, declared war on Russia on August 1, 1914, and on France two days later. German troops then invaded neutral Belgium to get at France, murdering or deporting thousands of Belgian civilians in the process. The "rape of Belgium" brought Great Britain into the war on August 4 on the **Western Front**, the line of fighting in northern France and Belgium.

On the evening of August 4, as five global empires—Austria-Hungary, France, Germany, Great Britain, and Russia—mobilized for war, the British foreign minister, Sir Edward Grey, expressed the fears of many when he observed that "the lamps are going out all over Europe; we shall not see them lit again in our time."

On the sprawling Eastern Front, Russian armies clashed with German and Austro-Hungarian forces as well as those of the Turkish (Ottoman) Empire. Within five weeks of the assassination in Sarajevo, a "great war" had consumed all of Europe. In 1915, Italy would join the Allied Powers in fighting Germany and Austria-Hungary.

## An Industrial War

The Great War required the total mobilization of economies and civilians, as well as soldiers and sailors. Of the approximately 70 million soldiers and sailors who fought on both sides, more than half were killed, wounded, imprisoned, or unaccounted for.

The staggering human casualties and physical destruction resulted from powerful new weapons, which dramatically changed the nature of warfare. Machine guns, submarines, aerial bombing, poison gas, flame throwers, land mines, mortars, long-range artillery, and armored tanks produced horrifying casualties and widespread destruction. On August 22, 1914, for example, the French army lost 27,000 men. An average of 900 Frenchmen and 1,300 Germans died *every* day on the Western Front.

**TRENCH WARFARE** In the early weeks of the war, German armies swept quickly across Belgium and northeastern France, only to bog down in nightmarish **trench warfare** that came to symbolize a brutal war of futility. Both

**THE GREAT WAR IN EUROPE, 1914**

- Central Powers (Triple Alliance)
- Allied Powers (Triple Entente)
- Neutral countries

0        250        500 Miles
0        250        500 Kilometers

- How did the European system of military alliances spread conflict?
- How was the Great War different from previous wars?
- How did the war in Europe lead to ethnic tensions in the United States?

sides dug in and fought a grinding war of attrition, gaining little territory in the process.

During 1914–1915, the two sides built a network of zigzagging trenches from the coast of Belgium some 460 miles across northeastern France to the border of Switzerland. Some trenches measured forty feet deep and swarmed with rats and lice. "When all is said and done," grumbled an English infantry officer, "the war was mainly a matter of holes and ditches."

Soldiers often ate, slept, lived, and died without leaving their underground homes. A French soldier described life in the trenches as a "physical, almost animal" existence in which "the primitive instincts of the race have full sway: eating, drinking, sleeping, fighting—everything but loving."

The object was not so much to gain ground as to inflict death and destruction on the enemy until its resources were exhausted. In one assault against the Germans in Belgium, the British lost 13,000 men in three hours—and gained only 100 yards. As the war ground on, both sides found themselves using up their available men, resources, courage, and cash.

From 1914 to 1918, the opposing armies in northeastern France attacked and counterattacked along the Western Front, gaining little ground while casualties soared into the millions. Time and again, inept generals sent their troops "over the top," climbing up and out of waterlogged trenches carrying sixty pounds of gear.

The soldiers who made it out of the trenches had to slog across "No Man's Land" between the opposing entrenchments. Their lives depended on navigating through webs of barbed wire and devastating fire from machine guns and high-powered rifles, all the while being showered by constant artillery shelling. During the Battle of Verdun, which lasted from February to December 1916, some 32 million artillery shells streaked across the landscape—1,500 shells for every square yard of that battlefield in northeastern France. The casualties were so numerous that French soldiers began to mutiny.

The hellish nature of trench warfare posed extraordinary psychological challenges for the combatants on both sides. Thousands of soldiers fell victim to "shell shock," now known as post–traumatic stress disorder. "It was a horrible thing," explained a nurse. "They became quite unconscious, with violent shivering and shaking."

In 1917, George Barnes, a British official whose son had been killed in the war, went to speak at a military hospital in London, where injured soldiers were being fitted with artificial limbs. At the appointed hour, the men, in wheelchairs and on crutches, all with empty sleeves or pants, arrived to hear the speaker. Yet when Barnes rose to talk, he found himself speechless—literally. As the minutes passed, tears rolled down his cheeks. Finally, without having said a word, he simply sat down. What the mutilated soldiers heard was not a war-glorifying speech but the muted pity of grief. The war's mindless horrors had come home.

## INITIAL AMERICAN REACTIONS

When war erupted in Europe, American officials were stunned. But shock mingled with relief that a wide ocean stood between America and the killing fields. President Wilson, an avowed pacifist, maintained that the United

States "was too proud to fight" in Europe's war, "with which we have nothing to do, whose causes cannot touch us." He repeatedly urged Americans to remain "neutral in thought as well as in action." Privately, however, he sought to ensure that the United States could provide Great Britain and France as much financial assistance and supplies as possible.

That most Americans wanted the nation to stay out of the fighting did not keep them from choosing sides. More than a third of the nation's citizens were first- or second-generation immigrants still loyal to their homelands. Nine million German-born Americans lived in the United States in 1914, and there were more than 500 German-language newspapers across the country. Most of the 4.5 million Irish-born Americans detested England, which had ruled Ireland for centuries. For the most part, these groups supported the Central Powers, while others, largely of British origin, supported the Allied Powers.

**SUPPORTING THE ALLIES** By the spring of 1915, the Allied Powers' need for food, supplies, and weapons had generated an economic windfall for American businesses, bankers, and farmers. Exports to France and Great Britain quadrupled from 1914 to 1916, and America's manufacturing capacity soon surpassed that of Great Britain, the world's leader. Farm income soared 25 percent. The Allies, especially Britain and France, needed loans from U.S. banks and "credits" from the U.S. government, which would allow them to pay for their purchases later.

**"The Sandwich Man"** To illustrate America's biased brand of neutrality, this political cartoon shows Uncle Sam wearing a sandwich board that advertises the nation's conflicting desires.

Early in the war, Secretary of State William Jennings Bryan, a strict pacifist, took advantage of President Wilson's absence from Washington following the death of the First Lady to tell J. Pierpont Morgan, the world's richest banker, that loans to any nations at war were "inconsistent with the true spirit of neutrality."

Upon his return to the White House, an angry Wilson reversed Bryan's policy by removing all restrictions on loans to the warring nations. The president was determined that America avoid the war's horrors while reaping its economic benefits. Banks and other investors would eventually send more than $2 billion to the Allies before the United States entered the fighting while offering only $27 million to Germany. What Bryan feared, and what Wilson did not fully realize, was that the more Britain and France borrowed and purchased, the harder it became for America to remain neutral.

Despite the disproportionate financial assistance provided to the Allies, the Wilson administration maintained its stance of neutrality for thirty months. In particular, Wilson tried valiantly to defend the age-old principle of "freedom of the seas," arguing that the ships of neutral nations had the right to trade with warring nations without fear of being attacked.

On August 6, 1914, Bryan urged the warring countries to respect the rights of neutral nations to ship goods across the Atlantic. The Central Powers agreed, but the British refused. In November, the British ordered the ships of neutral nations to submit to searches to discover if cargoes were bound for Germany. A few months later, the British announced that they would seize any ships carrying goods to Germany.

**NEUTRAL RIGHTS AND SUBMARINE ATTACKS** With its warships bottled up by a British blockade of its ports, the German government announced a "war zone" around the British Isles. All ships in those waters would be attacked by submarines, the Germans warned, and "it may not always be possible to save crews and passengers."

The German use of submarines, or **U-boats** (*Unterseeboot* in German), violated the long-established wartime custom of stopping an enemy vessel and allowing the passengers and crew to board lifeboats before sinking it. During 1915, German U-boats sank 227 British ships in the Atlantic Ocean and North Sea.

The United States called the attacks "an indefensible violation of neutral rights," and Wilson warned that he would hold Germany to "strict accountability" for the loss of lives and property. Then, on May 7, 1915, a German submarine off the Irish coast sank the British ship **Lusitania**, the foremost luxury liner in the world. Of the 1,198 persons on board who died, 128 were Americans. Fifty of the dead were infants.

The sinking of the *Lusitania*, asserted Theodore Roosevelt, called for an immediate declaration of war. Wilson, however, urged patience: "There is such a thing as a man being too proud to fight. There is such a thing as a nation being so right that it does not need to convince others by force that it is right."

Roosevelt dismissed the president's words as "unmanly," called the president a "jackass," and threatened to "skin him alive if he doesn't go to war." General John Pershing, who would later command U.S. forces in France, told his wife that Wilson was a "weak, chicken-hearted, white-livered" president. Wilson privately admitted that the fainthearted language had "occurred to me while I was speaking, and I let it out. I should have kept it in."

Wilson's earlier threat of "strict accountability" now required a tough response. On May 13, Secretary of State Bryan demanded that the Germans stop unrestricted submarine warfare, apologize, and pay the families of those killed on the *Lusitania*. The Germans countered that the ship was armed (which was false) and secretly carried rifles and ammunition (which was true); they further declared it was transporting hundreds of Canadian soldiers (which was true). On June 9, Wilson dismissed the German claims and reiterated that the United States was "contending for nothing less high and sacred than the rights of humanity."

Bryan resigned as secretary of state in protest of Wilson's pro-British stance. Upon learning of Bryan's departure, Edith Bolling Galt, soon to be Wilson's second wife, shouted: "Hurrah! Old Bryan is out!" She called the former secretary of state an "awful Deserter." The president confided that he viewed Bryan as a "traitor."

Stunned by the global outcry over the *Lusitania* sinking, the German government told its U-boat captains to stop attacking passenger vessels. Despite the order, however, a German submarine sank the British liner *Arabic*, and two Americans on board were killed. The Germans paid a cash penalty to the families of the deceased and issued what came to be called the *Arabic* Pledge on September 1, 1915: "Liners will not be sunk by our submarines without warning and without safety of the lives of non-combatants, provided that the liners do not try to escape or offer resistance."

In early 1916, Wilson again sent Colonel Edward House to London, Paris, and Berlin in hopes of stimulating peace talks, but the mission failed. So the killing continued. On March 24, 1916, a U-boat sank the French passenger ferry *Sussex*, killing eighty passengers and injuring two Americans. After Wilson threatened to end relations with Germany, its leaders again promised not to sink merchant and passenger ships. The *Sussex* Pledge implied the virtual abandonment of submarine warfare. Colonel House noted in his diary that Americans were "now beginning to realize that we are on the brink of war and what war means."

**PREPARING FOR WAR** On December 1, 1914, a "preparedness" movement, led by Theodore Roosevelt and Henry Cabot Lodge, created the National Security League to convince Congress and the president to begin preparing for war. The growing scope of the conflict in Europe and the quarrels over trading with belligerent nations contributed to a demand in the United States for a stronger army and navy.

After the *Lusitania*'s sinking, Wilson asked the War and Navy Departments to develop plans for a $1 billion military expansion. Many Americans—pacifists, progressives, and midwestern Republicans—opposed the professed preparedness effort, seeing it as a propaganda campaign to benefit businesses that made weapons and other military equipment. Some charged that Wilson was secretly plotting to enter the war.

Others, however, insisted that Wilson's proposal fell short of what the nation needed in the likelihood that it was drawn into the war. The secretary of war and his assistant resigned in protest.

Despite opposition, Congress in 1916 passed the National Defense Act, which provided for the expansion of the U.S. Army from 90,000 to 223,000 men over the next five years. While some complained that Wilson wanted to "drag this nation into war," the president told an aide that he was determined not to "be rushed into war, no matter if every damned congressman and senator stands up on his hind legs and proclaims me a coward."

Opponents of preparedness insisted that the expense of military expansion should rest upon the wealthy munitions makers who were profiting from trade with the Allies. Congress decided to use the income tax as its weapon to deter war-related profiteering. The Revenue Act of 1916 doubled the income tax rate from 1 to 2 percent, created a 12.5 percent tax on munitions makers, and added a new tax on "excessive" corporate profits. The new taxes were the culmination of the progressive legislation that Wilson had approved to strengthen his chances in the upcoming presidential election. Fearing that Theodore Roosevelt would be the Republican presidential candidate, Colonel House believed that the "Democratic Party must change its historic character and become the progressive party in the future."

## THE 1916 ELECTION

As the 1916 election approached, Theodore Roosevelt hoped to become the Republican nominee. But his decision in 1912 to run as a third-party candidate had alienated many powerful members of his party, and his eagerness to enter the war scared many voters. So instead, the Republicans nominated Supreme Court Justice Charles Evans Hughes, a progressive who had served as governor of New York from 1907 to 1910.

The Democrats, staying with Wilson, adopted a platform centered on social-welfare legislation and prudent military preparedness. The peace theme, refined in the slogan "He kept us out of war," became the campaign's rallying cry, although the president acknowledged that the nation could no longer refuse to play the "great part in the world which was providentially cut out for her. . . . We have got to serve the world." Colonel House was more blunt. He told Secretary of State Robert Lansing that they "could not permit the Allies to go down in defeat, for if they did, we would follow."

The two candidates were remarkably similar. Both Wilson and Hughes were sons of preachers; both were attorneys and former professors; both had been progressive governors; both were known for their integrity. Hughes called for higher tariffs, attacked Wilson for being hostile to Big Business, and implied that Wilson was not neutral enough in responding to the war. Roosevelt called the bearded Hughes a "whiskered Wilson." Wilson, however, proved to be the better campaigner—barely.

By midnight on election night, Wilson went to bed assuming that he had lost. Roosevelt was so sure Hughes had won that he sent him a congratulatory telegram. At 4 A.M., however, the results from California showed that Wilson had eked out a victory in that state by only 4,000 votes, and thus had become the first Democrat to win a second consecutive term since Andrew Jackson in 1832. His pledge of "peace, prosperity, and progressivism" won him the western states, Ohio, and the solidly Democratic South.

## AMERICA GOES TO WAR

On January 31, 1917, German military leaders renewed unrestricted submarine warfare in the Atlantic. All vessels from the United States headed for Britain, France, or Italy would be sunk without warning. "This was practically ordering the United States off the Atlantic," said William McAdoo, Wilson's secretary of the Treasury.

Germany's decision, Colonel House wrote in his journal, left Wilson "sad and depressed," for the president knew it meant war. For their part, the German leaders underestimated the American reaction. The United States, the German military newspaper proclaimed, "not only has no army, it has no artillery, no means of transportation, no airplanes, and lacks all other instruments of modern warfare." When his advisers warned that German submarines might cause the United States to enter the war, Kaiser Wilhelm scoffed, "I don't care."

**THE ZIMMERMANN TELEGRAM** On February 3, President Wilson informed Congress that he had formally ended diplomatic relations with the German government to preserve the "dignity and honor of the United States." Three weeks later, on February 25, he learned that the British had intercepted a coded telegram from Germany's foreign minister, Arthur Zimmermann, to the German ambassador in Mexico City. The telegram said that Germany would begin "unrestricted submarine warfare on February 1." If war erupted with the United States, the ambassador was instructed to offer the Mexican government an alliance: If the United States entered the war in Europe, Mexican forces would invade the United States. In exchange, Germany would return to Mexico its "lost territory in Texas, New Mexico, and Arizona."

On March 1, newspapers broke the news of the notorious **Zimmermann telegram**. The Mexican government immediately disavowed any support for the Germans. Infuriated Americans called for war. A New York newspaper said the Zimmermann telegram was "final proof that the German government has gone stark mad."

**AMERICA ENTERS THE WAR** In March 1917, German submarines torpedoed five U.S. ships in the North Atlantic. For Wilson, this was the last straw. On April 2, he called on Congress to declare war against the German Empire and its allies.

In one of his greatest speeches, Wilson acknowledged that it was "a fearful thing to lead this great peaceful people into war," but "the world must be made safe for democracy." He warned that it would require mobilizing "all the material resources of the country," and he called for 500,000 men to bolster the armed forces. The nation's motives, he insisted, were pure. The United States was entering the war not so much to defend its honor as to lead a "great crusade" for the "ultimate peace of the world and for the liberation of its peoples."

Congress erupted with approval. Two days later, the Senate passed the war resolution by a vote of 82 to 6. The House followed, 373 to 50, and Wilson signed the measure on April 6.

Opposing the war resolution were thirty-two Republicans, sixteen Democrats, one Socialist, and one independent. Among the "No" votes was Republican Jeannette Rankin of Montana, the first woman elected to the House of Representatives. "Peace is a woman's job," she said. "You can no more win a war than you can win an earthquake. I want to stand by my country, but I cannot vote for war."

Like Rankin, Wilson had doubts about joining the war. The president feared—accurately, as it turned out—that mobilizing the nation for war and stamping out dissent would destroy the ideals and momentum of progressivism: "Every reform we have made will be lost if we go into this war." Yet in the end, he saw no choice.

America's long embrace of isolationism was over. The nation had reached a turning point in its relations with the world that would test the president's political and diplomatic skills—and his stamina.

# Mobilizing a Nation

In April 1917, the U.S. Army remained small, untested, and poorly armed. With just 127,000 men, it was only the seventeenth largest army in the world. Now the Wilson administration needed to recruit, equip, and train an army of millions and transport them across an ocean infested with German submarines. On May 18, 1917, Congress passed the Selective Service Act, which instructed local boards to register men ages twenty-one to thirty for the draft (later expanded to eighteen to forty-five years old). Community draft boards were supposed to be impartial; many were not. An Atlanta board exempted 526 out of 815 white men but only 6 out of 202 black men.

**RECRUITING AN ARMY** Many men did not wait to be drafted; they rushed to enlist. Even recently arrived immigrants felt inspired to fight. Tony Monanco, a "diminutive Italian" who worked as a water boy, showed up early one morning at the recruiting office in Buffalo, New York. When a clerk asked him what he wanted, Monanco replied, "My name is Tony Monanco. I have been in this country six months. Give me a gun."

Twenty percent of those who joined the army were immigrants. Some 31 percent of them were illiterate. Polish immigrants were especially eager to serve because of their harsh treatment by the Germans over the years. Although they represented only 4 percent of the national population, some 40 percent of the first 100,000 U.S. service enlistees were Polish.

The challenge of training recruits of many different languages led the army to create the Foreign-Speaking Soldier Subsection to bridge the communication gap. An army officer said the foreign-born recruits "obeyed orders better and were less complaining than the native-born Americans."

**MANAGING THE HOME FRONT** Mobilizing the nation for war led to an unprecedented expansion of federal authority. Congress approved the Lever Act, which gave the president authority to manage the nation's supplies of food and fuels (oil/gasoline), and to take over factories, railroads, mines, warehouses, and telephone and telegraph systems. Federal agencies could also set prices for wheat and coal. "Laissez faire is dead," rejoiced a progressive. "Long live social control."

Soon after the United States declared war, President Wilson called for complete economic mobilization and created new agencies to coordinate the effort. The War Industries Board (WIB) soon became the most important of all the federal mobilization agencies. Bernard Baruch, a savvy financier, headed the

FOOD WILL WIN THE WAR
You came here seeking Freedom
You must now help to preserve it
WHEAT is needed for the allies
Waste nothing

UNITED   STATES   FOOD   ADMINISTRATION

**The immigrant effort** This Food
Administration poster emphasizes that
"wheat is . . . for the allies," an important
message to immigrants from Germany
and Austria.

WIB, which had the unprecedented
authority to ration raw materials, construct factories, and set prices.

Wilson appointed business magnate Herbert Hoover to lead the new
Food Administration, whose slogan
was, "Food will win the war." The
bureau's purpose was to increase agricultural production while reducing
civilian food consumption, since Great
Britain and France needed massive
amounts of corn and wheat. Hoover
organized a huge group of volunteers
who fanned out across the country
to urge families and restaurants to
participate in "Wheatless" Mondays,
"Meatless" Tuesdays, and "Porkless"
Thursdays and Saturdays. In crises
such as war, Hoover declared, democracies must show "a willingness to yield
to dictatorship."

The Great War would cost the U.S.
government $30 billion, which was
more than thirty times the federal
budget in 1917. In addition to raising
taxes to finance the war effort, the Wil-
son administration launched a nationwide campaign to sell "liberty bonds,"
government certificates that guaranteed the purchaser a fixed rate of return.
The government recruited dozens of celebrities to promote bond purchases,
arguing that a liberty bond was both patriotic and a smart investment. Even
the Boy Scouts and Girl Scouts sold bonds, using advertising posters that said,
"Every Scout to Save a Soldier." By war's end, the government had sold more
than $20 billion in bonds, most of which were purchased by banks and invest-
ment houses rather than by individuals.

**A NEW LABOR FORCE** Removing 4.7 million people from the workforce to serve in the armed forces created an acute labor shortage. It was made
worse because the European war shut off the flow of immigration to the United
States. To address the shortfall of workers, women were encouraged to take
jobs that had been held primarily by men.

**At the munitions factory** Women played crucial roles in the war effort, from building airplanes to cooking for soldiers overseas. Here, women use welding torches to fabricate bombs.

Initially, most women had supported the war effort in traditional ways. They helped organize fund-raising drives, donated canned food and war-related materials, volunteered for the Red Cross, and joined the army nurse corps. As the scope of the war widened, however, women were recruited to work on farms, loading docks, and railway crews, as well as in the armaments industry, machine shops, steel and lumber mills, and chemical plants. "At last, after centuries of disabilities and discrimination," noted a speaker at a Women's Trade Union League meeting in 1917, "women are coming into the labor [force] and festival of life on equal terms with men."

The changes turned out to be limited and brief, however. About a million women participated in "war work," but most were young, single, and already working outside the home. Most returned to their previous jobs once the war ended. In fact, after the war, male-dominated unions encouraged women to go back to domestic roles.

The Great War also generated dramatic changes for many minority groups. Hundreds of thousands of African American men joined the military, where they were required to serve in racially segregated units commanded by white officers, as in the Civil War half a century earlier.

On the home front, northern businesses sent recruiting agents into the largely rural and agricultural southern states to find workers for factories and mills. For the first time, such employment efforts were directed at African Americans as well as whites. More than 400,000 black southerners, mostly sharecroppers, joined what came to be known as the **Great Migration**, a mass movement of people that would continue through the 1920s and reshape the political and social chemistry of northern and western cities. By 1930, the number of African Americans living in the North had tripled that of 1910. A rural people had become urban; an oppressed people had gained opportunities for equality.

Recruiting agents and newspaper editors, both black and white, portrayed the North and West as the "land of promise" for African American southerners. Jobs in northern steel mills, factories, and railroads were plentiful and paid well by southern standards, and racism was less obvious and violent—at least at first. A black migrant from Mississippi wrote from Chicago in 1917 that he wished he had moved north twenty years earlier. "I just begin to feel like a man [here]," he explained. "It's a great deal of pleasure in knowing that you have some privilege. My children are going to the same school with the whites, and I don't have to be humble to no one."

Many Mexican Americans found similar opportunities to improve their status. Between 1917 and 1920, some 100,000 job-hungry Mexicans crossed the border into the United States. Some joined the military. David Barkley Hernandez had to drop his last name when he enlisted in San Antonio, Texas, because the local draft board was not accepting Mexicans. In 1918, just two days before the war ended, he died in France while returning from a dangerous mission behind German lines. Hernandez became the first person of Mexican descent in the U.S. Army to win the Congressional Medal of Honor.

But the newcomers were often resented. J. Luz Saenz, a Mexican American from Texas, noted in his diary that it took only three days after he was discharged from the army to have whites "throw us out from restaurants and deny us service as human beings." In 1917, more than forty African Americans and nine whites were killed during a riot in a weapons plant in East St. Louis, Illinois. Two years later, a Chicago race riot left twenty-three African Americans and fifteen whites dead.

**WAR PROPAGANDA** The war effort also led the government to mobilize public opinion. On April 14, 1917, eight days after the declaration of war, President Wilson established the Committee on Public Information (CPI), composed of the secretaries of state, war, and the navy. Its executive director, George Creel, convinced Wilson that the best way to influence public opinion was with propaganda. To that end, Creel organized a propaganda machine to explain the Allies' war aims to the people and, above all, to the enemy, where it might help sap their morale. To generate support, Creel gathered a remarkable group of journalists, photographers, artists, and entertainers.

Creel organized the CPI into four divisions. The Speaking Division recruited 75,000 public lecturers known as "Four-Minute Men" for their ability to compress the war's objectives into a few words. They gave some 7.5 million speeches to civic groups, churches, synagogues, fraternal lodges, union halls, colleges, and schools. The Film Division produced short films with titles such as *Pershing's Crusaders* and *America's Answer*, all celebrating the U.S. war effort. The Foreign Language Division monitored U.S. newspapers published in languages other than English, and the Division of Pictorial Publicity recruited an army of artists to produce patriotic posters.

Creel insisted his committee's work was not simply propaganda, but he admitted his job was to shape public perceptions. The CPI was "a plain publicity proposition, a vast enterprise in salesmanship, the world's greatest adventure in advertising."

**A LOSS OF CIVIL LIBERTIES** Once the United States entered the war, Americans equated anything German with disloyalty. Towns, streets, businesses, and even families with German names were renamed. Berlin, Iowa, became Lincoln, and East Germantown, Indiana, became Pershing, in honor of the military leader. Many quit drinking beer because German Americans owned most of the breweries. Symphonies refused to perform music by Bach and Beethoven, schools canceled German language classes, patriots burned German books, and grocers renamed *sauerkraut* "liberty cabbage." Mobs killed several German Americans accused of spying. Dozens of others were tarred and feathered.

In passing the Espionage and Sedition Acts, Congress authorized the most outrageous violations of civil liberties since the 1798 Alien and Sedition Acts. The Espionage Act of 1917 stipulated that anyone who helped the enemy, encouraged insubordination, disloyalty, or refusal of duty in the armed services, or interfered with the war effort in other ways, could be imprisoned for up to twenty years.

A year later, Congress amended the Espionage Act with the Sedition Act. It outlawed saying, writing, or printing anything "disloyal, profane, scurrilous, or abusive" about the American form of government, the Constitution, or the army and navy.

The effort to squelch free speech provoked sharp criticism. Senator George Norris, a progressive Republican from Nebraska, wondered why the nation should fight a war for democracy abroad if Congress were going to interfere "with the very fundamental principles of human liberty and human freedom on which our great Commonwealth is founded."

During the U.S. involvement in the war, courts convicted 1,055 people under the Espionage Act. Most were simply critics of the war. On June 16, 1918, Socialist leader Eugene V. Debs, the 63-year-old pacifist who had run against Wilson in 1912, gave a speech in Canton, Ohio, in which he stressed that the war was inherently unfair. It was, he said, "the working class who fight all the battles, the working class who make the supreme sacrifices, the working class who freely shed their blood and furnish the corpses, have never yet had a voice in either declaring war or making peace. It is the ruling class that invariably does both. They alone declare war and they alone make peace."

Government agents recorded the speech, and two weeks later they arrested Debs. After being convicted of violating the Espionage Act for expressing sympathy for men jailed for encouraging others to avoid the draft, he was sentenced to ten years in prison. He told the court he was exercising his rights of free speech under the First Amendment and would always criticize wars imposed by the "master" class: "While there is a lower class, I am in it. While there is a criminal element, I am of it. While there is a soul in prison, I am not free." In 1919, the Supreme Court unanimously approved Debs's conviction, and Woodrow Wilson refused every plea from supporters to release him.

Debs was sent first to the West Virginia State Prison, then to the federal penitentiary near Atlanta. The West Virginia warden wrote to the Atlanta warden: "I never in my life met a kinder man [Debs]. He is forever thinking of others, trying to serve them, and never thinking of himself." In the federal prison, he charmed prisoners and

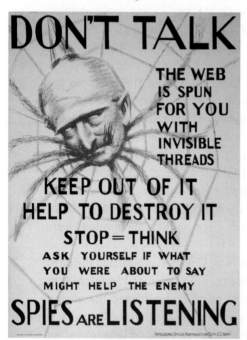

**Keep out of it** In this 1918 war poster, the kaiser—with his famous moustache and spiked German helmet—is depicted as a spider, spinning an invisible web to catch the stray words of Allied civilians.

guards alike and radiated warmth and fellowship. In 1920, the Socialist party nominated him for the fifth time as its presidential candidate. Even though he was a prisoner, he would receive more than 900,000 votes.

THE "POISON OF DISLOYALTY" President Wilson was equally resolute in prosecuting immigrants who supported America's enemies. From colonial days, Americans had always recruited, yet feared, immigrants. Now, fear took over. As Wilson warned, "there are citizens of the United States, I blush to admit, born under other flags . . . who have poured the poison of disloyalty into the very arteries of our national life. . . . Such creatures of passion, disloyalty, and anarchy must be crushed out."

Others were determined to shut off immigration altogether, especially from southern and eastern Europe. In 1916, Madison Grant, a New York attorney, published a hugely influential book, *The Passing of the Great Race*. Grant was a fervent eugenicist (a believer in the pseudoscience of racial breeding). During the early twentieth century, the popularity of eugenics prompted thirty states to pass laws requiring compulsory sterilization of the insane, the "feeble-minded," the "dependent," and the "diseased."

In *The Passing of the Great Race*, Grant claimed that racial purity was the foundation of great nations. Yet America's once-dominant Nordic stock, he warned, was committing "race suicide" by interbreeding with African Americans and an "increasing number of the weak, the broken, and the mentally crippled of all the races drawn from the lower stratum of the Mediterranean basin and the Balkans, together with hordes of the wretched, submerged populations of the Polish Ghettos." He railed against "the maudlin sentimentalism" that welcomed these "worthless race types" from Europe, for they were "sweeping the nation toward a racial abyss."

Such notions led Congress in 1917 to revive the idea of requiring a literacy test of immigrants. Three times before, Congress had passed similar legislation, only to see Presidents Cleveland, Taft, and Wilson (1915) veto it. Now, in response to theories of racial superiority and pleas from labor union leaders concerned about an influx of unskilled "aliens," overwhelming majorities in both the House and Senate overrode Wilson's veto of the first widely restrictive immigration law.

The Immigration Act of 1917 required immigrants over 16 years old to take a literacy test to demonstrate basic reading ability in any language. It also increased the "head tax" immigrants paid upon arrival to $8 (about $160 today) and allowed immigration officials to exercise more discretion in excluding newcomers. It specifically denied entry to "idiots, imbeciles, feeble-minded persons, epileptics, insane persons, paupers, beggars, vagrants, alcoholics, prostitutes, persons afflicted with disease, criminals, polygamists, and anarchists."

Finally, the Immigration Act of 1917 was much more restrictive than the 1882 Chinese Exclusion Act because it excluded *all* Asians except for Japanese and Filipinos. In 1907, the Japanese Government had voluntarily limited Japanese immigration to the United States in the so-called Gentlemen's Agreement with President Roosevelt. Because the Philippines was a U.S. colony, its citizens were U.S. nationals and could travel freely to the United States. Senator Ellison "Cotton Ed" Smith, a South Carolina Democrat who chaired the Immigration Committee, stressed "the necessity for a pure, homogeneous American people." He and other advocates of the literacy test believed it would reduce the number of immigrants from eastern and southern Europe by more than 40 percent. In reality, only a small number of immigrants were turned away because of illiteracy. Still, America's open-door tradition was closing.

**WAGING WAR ON LABOR**    President Wilson was concerned about the loyalty of other Americans, too. Hundreds of local and state officials belonged to the Socialist party, which opposed U.S. involvement in the war. And thousands of wage workers were "Wobblies," members of the radical Industrial Workers of the World (IWW), who supported the battle between labor and management, not the war in Europe.

The IWW was devastated by the Great War, when hundreds of Wobblies were jailed, beaten, shot, and tortured for opposing the conflict. Federal agents raided forty-eight IWW offices across the country. They confiscated filing cabinets filled with correspondence and records and arrested 165 Wobblies. A hundred were eventually tried for sedition, and all were convicted and imprisoned.

# THE AMERICAN ROLE IN THE WAR

In 1917, America's war strategy focused on helping the struggling French and British armies on the Western Front. The Allied leaders stressed that they needed at least a million U.S. troops, but it would take months to recruit, equip, and train that many new soldiers.

On December 21, 1917, French premier Georges Clemenceau urged the Americans to rush their army, called the American Expeditionary Force (AEF), to France. "A terrible blow is imminent," he told a journalist about to leave Paris. "Tell your Americans to come quickly." Clemenceau was referring to the likelihood of a massive German attack, made more probable by the end of the fighting on the Eastern Front following the Bolshevik Revolution in Russia in November 1917.

**THE BOLSHEVIK REVOLUTION**  Among the many casualties of the Great War, none was greater than the destruction of the Russian Empire and its incompetent monarchy. It was the first nation to crack under the prolonged strain of the war.

Ravaged by widespread starvation and united by a desire for change, the Russian people launched a revolution in the bitterly cold winter of 1917. On February 23, crowds of women factory workers gathered in the streets of Petrograd (formerly St. Petersburg). More workers, male and female, joined in. On March 1, the rebels formed a "provisional government," eventually led by Alexander Kerensky, who demanded that the inept tsar, Nicholas II, give up the throne.

On March 2, 1917, Nicholas II, having presided over a war that had ruined his nation's economy and transportation system, abdicated his throne and turned the nation over to the provisional government. Within months, Russia was a republic committed to continuing the war.

The fall of the tsar created the illusion that all the major Allied powers—including Russia—were now fighting for the ideals of constitutional democracy. Through the summer and into the fall of 1917, Woodrow Wilson and his advisers assumed that Kerensky would democratize Russian institutions, rebuild morale, and make Russia a worthy partner in making the world safe for democracy.

That illusion was shattered after the Germans helped an exiled Marxist radical named Vladimir Ilyich Lenin board a sealed train to Russia from Switzerland. For years, Lenin had been biding his time, waiting for the war to devour the German and Russian monarchs.

The Germans hoped that Lenin would cause turmoil in his homeland. He did much more than that. As the train left Zurich, he leaned out a window to say goodbye to a friend. "Either we'll be swinging from the gallows in three months," he predicted, "or we shall be in power."

On the night of April 16, 1917, the forty-seven-year-old Lenin, a man of iron will and ruthless determination, arrived in Petrograd. A huge crowd welcomed him. Climbing atop an armored car, he pledged to withdraw Russia from the hated war and to eliminate private property. "The people," he shouted, "need peace, the people need bread, the people need land." The provisional government, he charged, "gives you war, hunger, no bread. We must fight for the social revolution" until the "complete victory of the proletariat. Long live the worldwide Socialist revolution!"

Lenin saw power lying in the streets, waiting to be picked up. To do so, he mobilized the Bolsheviks, a group of cold-blooded Communist revolutionaries convinced that they were in the vanguard of the irresistible force of history. The Bolsheviks promised to end Russia's involvement in the war and to institute a Communist system of government.

During the night of October 25, armed Bolsheviks took over train stations, post offices, and telegraph offices. Others stormed the Petrograd Winter Palace, seized power from the provisional government, established a dictatorship, and called for a quick end to the war. As a disillusioned Bolshevik noted, Lenin's dictatorship, "a government that promised freedom for all working people, had created a tyranny" that soon unleashed a reign of terror.

For the first time in history, a government—the Bolsheviks—announced that it was both infallible and rooted in atheism. Lenin pledged to hang, shoot, and destroy anyone foolish enough to oppose the revolution. He took control of banks, businesses, church properties, and great landed estates, censored newspapers, shut down the legal system, jailed opponents, and created a brutal secret police force. "To us," Lenin announced, "all is permitted. . . . Blood? Let there be blood."

The Bolshevik Revolution triggered a chaotic civil war throughout Russia, with the anti-Bolshevik White army fighting the Communist Red army—and many other groups choosing or switching sides. In mid-August 1918, President Wilson, horrified at the idea of a Communist Russia, sent 8,000 U.S. soldiers to Siberia. The Siberian Expeditionary Force went to Vladivostok on Russia's Pacific coast, ostensibly to retrieve military supplies sent to the prerevolutionary Russians. Its commanding general pledged to take no part in any "crusade" against Bolshevism.

Walter Lippmann, editor of the *New Republic* magazine, warned Wilson that he should stick to his original position of "no interference in Russia's internal affairs" and not embroil U.S. troops in the Russian civil war. Yet Wilson intervened anyway. After nineteen months of unsuccessful military efforts against the Bolsheviks, U.S. troops returned to America in April 1920. Thereafter, Russian Communists steadfastly believed that America had tried to overturn their revolution.

**FOURTEEN POINTS** Woodrow Wilson was determined to ensure that the Great War would be the last world war. To that end, in September 1917, he appointed a group of 150 experts in politics, history, geography, and foreign policy, called the Inquiry, to draft a peace plan. America, according to Wilson, had no selfish goals; it was simply "one of the champions of the rights of mankind." Drawing upon the Inquiry's advice, Wilson developed the

**Fourteen Points**, a comprehensive list of provisions intended to shape the peace treaty and the postwar world.

Wilson made a dramatic presentation of his Fourteen Points to a joint session of Congress on January 8, 1918, describing his proposal as "the only possible program" for peace. The first five points endorsed the open conduct of diplomacy rather than backroom deals and secret treaties, the recognition of neutral nations' right to continue maritime commerce in time of war ("freedom of the seas"), the removal of international trade barriers ("free trade"), and the worldwide reduction of armaments.

Most of the other points dealt with territorial claims. Wilson demanded that, in redrawing the map of Europe, the victors follow the principle of "self-determination," allowing overlapping nationalities and ethnic groups to develop their own independent, democratic nations. Point thirteen created a new nation for Poland, long dominated by the Russians in the east and the Germans in the west. Point fourteen, the capstone of Wilson's postwar scheme, called for a permanent "league" of nations to preserve global peace.

Overall, the reaction was positive. The headline of a *New York Times* editorial proclaimed: "The President's Triumph." When the Fourteen Points were made public, however, African American leaders asked the president to add a fifteenth point: an end to racial discrimination. Wilson did not respond.

Meanwhile, the war ground on with no diplomatic solution in sight. In Germany, food and fuel shortages led to growing discontent. Workers went on strike, and soldiers and sailors mutinied and deserted. "The Monarchy," said a German official, "is lurching toward the edge of the abyss."

**RUSSIA SURRENDERS** Conditions were even worse in Russia. When Vladimir Lenin took power in 1917, some 4 million ill-clad, poorly equipped, and half-starved Russian soldiers had been killed or wounded in the war. Lenin declared that the world would be freed from war only by a global revolution in which capitalism was replaced by communism. To that end, he wanted Russia out of the war as soon as possible.

On March 3, 1918, Lenin signed a humiliating peace agreement with Germany, the Treaty of Brest-Litovsk. The treaty forced Russia to transfer vast territories to Germany and Turkey and to recognize the independence of the Ukraine region, thereby depriving Russia of much of its population, coal and wheat production, and heavy industry. In addition, Russia had to pay $46 million to Germany. Lenin was willing to accept such a harsh peace because he needed to concentrate on the ongoing Russian civil war.

With Russia out, the Germans could focus on the Western Front. Erich Ludendorff, the German army commander, said the ability to move hundreds of thousands of soldiers from the Russian front to France would give him numerical superiority for the first time and enable him to "deal an annihilating blow to the British before American aid can become effective."

**AMERICANS ON THE WESTERN FRONT** On March 21, 1918, the Germans began the first of several offensives in France and Belgium designed to win the war before the American Expeditionary Force could arrive. By May, the Germans had advanced within fifty miles of Paris, and the British Fifth army was destroyed.

In early April, however, the Germans suddenly lost their momentum. On April 5, the German commander called a halt because so many soldiers were exhausted and demoralized, convinced, as one officer admitted, that their "hope [for victory] had been dashed" by their inability to sustain the supply lines needed for such a widespread advance.

In May, French and British leaders pressed Wilson to hurry troops into the fighting. By the end of the month, some 650,000 American soldiers were in Europe. In June, they were ready to fight.

**Meuse-Argonne Offensive** Soldiers of the 23rd Infantry, 2nd Division, fire machine guns at the Germans from what was left of the Argonne Forest in France.

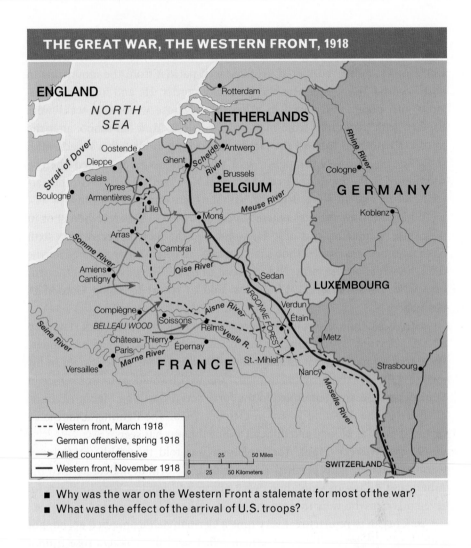

**THE GREAT WAR, THE WESTERN FRONT, 1918**

- - - Western front, March 1918
——— German offensive, spring 1918
——▶ Allied counteroffensive
———— Western front, November 1918

0    25    50 Miles
0    25    50 Kilometers

■ Why was the war on the Western Front a stalemate for most of the war?
■ What was the effect of the arrival of U.S. troops?

At the month-long Battle of Belleau Wood, U.S. forces commanded by General John J. "Black Jack" Pershing joined the French in driving the Germans back. A French officer remarked that the Americans were providing "a wonderful transfusion of blood" for the Allied cause.

During the ferocious fighting, a French officer urged an American unit to retreat. In a famous exchange, U.S. Marine Captain Lloyd W. Williams refused the order, saying: "Retreat? Hell, we just got here." Two days later, in the midst of an intense German bombardment, an American sergeant rallied his men by barking, "Come on, you sons-of-bitches! Do you want to live forever?"

**AN AMERICAN HERO** Among the millions who served in the Great War, one stood out: Sergeant Alvin York, an American original. Born in 1887, he was a tall, red-haired, freckle-faced pacifist from the mountains in north-central Tennessee, near the Kentucky border. He and his deeply religious, dirt-poor family lived in a log cabin whose windswept walls were papered with pages torn from mail-order catalogs. York left school after the third grade to help support the family by working in his father's blacksmith shop. As a teen, he went through a "wild" phase, but his hijinks ended when he succumbed to the appeals of an evangelist on New Year's Day in 1915. Thereafter, he swore off "smoking, drinking, gambling, cussing, and brawling."

When the United States entered the war in 1917, York, the best shot in Tennessee, wanted no part of it. He worshiped the Bible, especially the sixth commandment that said, "Thou shalt not kill." So when York registered for the draft, he wrote on the form, "I don't want to fight." The government thought otherwise. In November 1917, he was told to report to Camp Gordon in Georgia.

After basic training, as his unit prepared to head overseas, York stayed up all night praying. By morning, he had made up his mind: "I begun to understand that no matter what a man is forced to do, so long as he is right in his own soul, he remains a righteous man. I knowed I would go to war." Once in France, York became embroiled in the forty-seven-day-long Meuse-Argonne offensive in the Argonne Forest in October 1918. The fighting, a journalist reported, was "as bloody and difficult as any the war has seen."

On the Western Front, York's platoon was told to assault three dozen German machine guns perched along a ridge. A storm of bullets stymied the Americans, killing or wounding every officer and leaving York in charge of seven privates who were trapped in "No Man's Land."

York began to return fire. Every time a German helmet popped up, he shot with deadly accuracy. Then, a German officer and five soldiers rose from a trench twenty-five yards away and charged York, who dropped his rifle and pulled out a pistol. He shot the last man first, then the next farthest from him, and the next, just like "the way we shoot wild turkeys at home." York killed all six, which led others to surrender.

By then, York had killed twenty-one Germans using only twenty shots, one of which killed two men. He and his surviving comrades then marched their prisoners to the rear, capturing and killing more Germans along the way. When a lieutenant counted the prisoners, the number was 132.

Word spread quickly that York had singlehandedly "captured the whole damned German army." The Allied nations showered him with their highest military honors, and the United States awarded him the Congressional Medal of Honor. After appearing before Congress, York returned to his simple home along the Tennessee-Kentucky border.

**ENDING THE WAR** In a massive Allied offensive, begun on September 26, 1918, U.S. troops joined British and French armies in a drive toward Sedan, France, and its strategic railroad, which supplied the German army occupying northern France. With 1.2 million soldiers involved, it was the largest U.S. action of the war, and it resulted in 117,000 casualties, including 26,000 dead. The Allied offensive sent the outnumbered Germans reeling in retreat. "America," wrote German general Erich Ludendorff, "became the decisive power in the war."

On October 6, the German government asked Wilson for peace negotiations based on his Fourteen Points. British and French leaders accepted the Fourteen Points as a basis of negotiations, but with two significant reservations. The British insisted on the right to discuss limiting freedom of the seas to preserve their naval dominance, and the French demanded massive reparations (payments from the vanquished to the victors) from Germany and Austria for war damages.

**THE GERMAN COLLAPSE** By the end of October 1918, Germany was on the verge of collapse. Revolutionaries rampaged through the streets. Sailors mutinied. Germany's allies (Bulgaria, Turkey, and Austria-Hungary) dropped out of the war, and military leaders demanded that the civilian government ask for an armistice (cease-fire agreement). On November 9, the German kaiser resigned, and a republic was proclaimed.

Early on the morning of November 11, an official cease-fire took effect. The Germans were required to evacuate all captured territory and turn over 150,000 railroad freight cars, 5,000 locomotives, 5,000 trucks, 1,700 warplanes, and 25,000 machine guns. In exchange, they were assured that President Wilson's Fourteen Points would be the basis for the upcoming peace conference.

Six hours later, at the eleventh hour of the eleventh day of the eleventh month, and after 1,563 days of terrible warfare, the most needless of wars was finally over. That morning, Harry Truman, an artillery officer who would become America's president in 1945, could see in the distance a seated German soldier manning a machine gun. At 11 A.M., the German stood, took off his helmet, bowed toward the American lines, and walked away.

From Europe, Colonel Edward House sent Wilson a telegram: "Autocracy [government by an individual with unlimited power] is dead; long live democracy and its immortal leader." The end of the war triggered frenzied celebrations throughout the world. "The world awakes," wrote African American activist

***Armistice Night in New York* (1918)** George Luks, known for his vivid paintings of urban life, captured the unbridled outpouring of patriotism and joy that extended into the night of Germany's surrender.

W. E. B. Du Bois. "The long, horrible years of dreadful night are passed. Behold the sun!" Wilson was not as joyful. The Great War, he said, had dealt a grievous injury to civilization "which can never be atoned for or repaired."

The United States lost 53,402 servicemen in combat during its nineteen months in the war. Another 63,114 Americans died of various diseases, the largest number of casualties the result of the deadly influenza epidemic that swept through the world in 1918. Some 200,000 Americans were wounded. Germany's war dead totaled 1.6 million; France lost nearly 1.4 million, Great Britain 658,000, and Russia 1.7 million.

While decimating a generation of young men, the war also ruined the economies of Europe. The new Europe would be very different: much poorer, more violent, more polarized, more cynical, less sure of itself, and less capable of decisive action. The United States, for good or ill, emerged as the world's dominant power.

## The Politics of Peace

On June 25, 1918, Colonel House wrote Woodrow Wilson from France, urging him to take charge of the peacemaking process. "It is one of the things with which your name should be linked during the ages." House was right. Wilson and the peace agreement ending the Great War would be forever linked, but not in the positive light they assumed.

In the making of the peace agreement, Wilson showed himself both at his best and worst. The Fourteen Points embodied his vision of a better world governed by fairer principles. In promoting his peace plan, he felt guided "by the hand of God." A peacekeeping "League of Nations" was, in his view, the key element to a "secure and lasting peace" and the "most essential part of the peace settlement." If the diplomats gathering to draft the peace treaty failed to follow his plans to reshape the world in America's image, he warned, "there will be another world war" within a generation. In the end, however, Wilson's grand efforts at global peacemaking failed—not abroad—but at home, and because of his own faults.

## WILSON'S KEY ERRORS

Whatever the merits of President Wilson's peace plan, his efforts to implement it proved clumsy and self-defeating. He made several decisions that would come back to haunt him. First, against the advice of his staff and of European leaders, he decided to attend the peace conference in Paris that opened on January 18, 1919. Never before had a president left the United States for such a prolonged period (six months). During his time abroad, Wilson lost touch with political developments at home.

His second error of judgment involved politics. In the congressional election campaign of 1918, Wilson defied his advisers and political tradition by urging voters to elect a Democratic Congress as a sign of their approval of his policies in handling the war—and the peace. He "begged" the public not to "repudiate" his leadership.

Republicans, who for the most part had backed Wilson's war measures, were not pleased. Theodore Roosevelt called Wilson's self-serving appeal "a cruel insult to every Republican father or mother whose sons have entered the Army or Navy." Voters were not impressed, either, especially western farmers upset with government price ceilings placed on wheat.

In the elections, the Democrats lost control of both houses of Congress. It was a bad omen for Wilson's peacemaking efforts, since any treaty to end the war would have to be approved by at least two thirds of the Senate, now controlled by Republicans. Roosevelt said that Wilson could no longer claim "to speak for the American people." The former president and his friend Henry Cabot Lodge thereafter did their best to undermine Wilson's negotiating strength with the Allies.

Meanwhile, Wilson had dispatched Colonel House and several aides to Europe to begin convincing Allied leaders to embrace the Fourteen Points.

The lopsided losses in the elections, said House, "made his difficulties enormously greater." Gordon Auchincloss, House's son-in-law who assisted him in Europe, displayed the brash confidence of many American diplomats when he boasted that "before we get through with these fellows over here, we will teach them how to do things and to do them quickly." It would not be so easy.

Wilson's efforts were further weakened when he refused to appoint a prominent Republican to the peace delegation. House had urged him to appoint Roosevelt or Lodge, the president's archenemy and the leading Republican in Congress, but Wilson refused. In the end, he appointed Harry White, an obscure Republican. Former president William Howard Taft groused that Wilson's real intention in going to Paris was "to hog the whole show."

Wilson's participation in the Paris Peace Conference would be an opportunity for him to convince Europe to follow him in creating a very different postwar world. As Wilson prepared to head for Europe, muckraking journalist Ray Stannard Baker wrote that the president "has yet to prove his greatness. The fate of a drama lies in its last act, and Wilson is now coming to that."

Initially, Wilson's entrance on the European stage in December 1918 was triumphant. Millions of grateful Europeans greeted him as an almost mystical hero, even as their savior. An Italian mayor described Wilson's visit as the "second coming of Christ." Others hailed him as the "God of peace."

The adoration reinforced Wilson's belief that only he could guide the peacemaking efforts. Claiming that he was now "at the apex of my glory in the hearts of these people," he was committed to shaping a peace treaty and postwar world based on principles of justice, fairness, and self-determination.

From such a height, there could only be a fall. Although popular with the European people, Wilson had to negotiate with tough-minded, wily statesmen who resented his efforts to forge a peace settlement modeled on American values. That Wilson had not bothered to consult them about his Fourteen Points proposal before announcing it to the world did not help. In the end, the European leaders would force the American president to abandon many of his ideals.

## THE PARIS PEACE CONFERENCE

The Paris Peace Conference lasted from January to June 1919. The participants had no time to waste. The German, Austro-Hungarian, and Ottoman Empires were in ruins. Across much of Europe, food was scarce and lawlessness rampant. The threat of revolution hung over Central Europe as Communists jostled to take control of the defeated, war-torn nations.

The peace conference dealt with immensely complex and controversial issues (including the need to create new nations and redraw the maps of Europe and the Middle East) that required both political statesmanship and technical expertise. The British delegation alone included almost 400 members, many of them specialists in political geography or economics.

**THE BIG FOUR** From the start, the Paris Peace Conference was controlled by the Big Four: the prime ministers of Britain, France, and Italy, and the president of the United States. Neither Germany nor its allies were allowed to attend. Communist Russia was also not invited.

Georges Clemenceau, the seventy-seven-year-old French premier known as "The Tiger," had little patience with President Wilson's idealistic preaching. In response to Wilson's claim that "America is the only idealistic nation in the world," Clemenceau grumbled that talking with Wilson was like talking to Jesus Christ. "God gave us the Ten Commandments and we broke them," the French leader sneered. "Wilson gave us the Fourteen Points—we shall see."

The Big Four fought in private and in public. The French and British, led by Prime Minister David Lloyd George, insisted that Wilson agree to their proposals to weaken Germany economically and militarily, while Vittorio Orlando, prime minister of Italy, focused on gaining territories from defeated Austria.

**THE LEAGUE OF NATIONS** Although suffering from chronic health issues, including hypertension and blinding headaches, Wilson lectured the other statesmen about the need to embrace his beloved **League of Nations**, which he insisted must be the "keystone" of any peace settlement. He believed that a world peace organization would abolish war by settling international disputes and mobilizing united action against aggressors. Article X of the charter, which Wilson called "the heart of the League," allowed member nations to impose military and economic sanctions, or penalties, against military aggressors. The league, Wilson predicted, would have such moral influence that it would make military action to preserve peace unnecessary.

On February 14, 1919, Wilson presented the final draft of the league covenant to the Allies and left Paris for a ten-day visit home, where he faced growing opposition among Republicans. The League of Nations, Theodore Roosevelt complained, would revive German militarism and undermine American morale. "To substitute internationalism for nationalism," Roosevelt argued, "means to do away with patriotism."

Henry Cabot Lodge, chairman of the Senate Foreign Relations Committee, who despised Wilson, also opposed the League of Nations because, he claimed, it would potentially involve sending U.S. troops to foreign conflicts without Senate approval. On March 3, 1919, Lodge presented a resolution on the Senate floor that the "League of Nations in the form as now proposed . . . should not be accepted by the United States." He then announced that thirty-seven Republicans endorsed his resolution—more than enough to block ratification of Wilson's treaty.

## THE TREATY OF VERSAILLES

Henry Cabot Lodge's preemptive action undermined President Wilson's leverage with the British and French. When he returned to Paris in the spring of 1919, Wilson was forced to concede many controversial issues to ensure that the Europeans would approve his League of Nations.

He yielded to French demands that Germany transfer territory to France on its west and to Poland on its east and north. In other territorial matters, Wilson had to abandon his principle of national self-determination, whereby every ethnic group would be allowed to form its own nation. As Secretary of State Robert Lansing correctly predicted, preaching self-determination would only "raise hopes which can never be realized." (Wilson later told the Senate that he wished he had never said that all nations have a right to self-determination.)

In their efforts to allow for some degree of ethnic self-determination in multiethnic regions, the statesmen at Versailles transformed Europe from a continent of empires to one of nations. They created Austria, Hungary, Poland, Yugoslavia, and Czechoslovakia in Central Europe and four new nations along the Baltic Sea: Finland, Estonia, Lithuania, and Latvia.

The victorious Allies, however, did not create independent nations out of the colonies of the defeated and now defunct European empires. Instead, they assigned the former German colonies in Africa and the Turkish colonies in the Middle East to France and Great Britain for an unspecified time, while Japan took control of the former German colonies in the Pacific.

The issue of reparations—payments by the vanquished to the victors— triggered bitter arguments. The British and the French (on whose soil much of the war was fought) wanted Germany to pay the entire cost of the war, including their military veterans' pensions.

On this point, Wilson made perhaps his most fateful concessions. Although initially opposed to reparations, he eventually agreed to a crucial clause that forced Germany to accept responsibility for the war and its entire expense. The "war guilt" clause so offended Germans that it became a major factor in the rise of Adolf Hitler and the Nazi party during the 1920s. Wilson himself privately admitted that if he were a German, he would refuse to sign the treaty.

Colonel Edward House privately blamed Wilson for many problems associated with the treaty, saying that the president "speaks constantly of teamwork but seldom practices it." Wilson was "becoming stubborn and angry, and he never was a good negotiator."

On May 7, 1919, the victorious powers presented the treaty to the German delegates, who returned three weeks later with 443 pages of criticism. Among other things, they noted that Germany would lose 13 percent of its territory, 10 percent of its population, and all its colonies in Asia and Africa. The German president called the treaty's terms "unrealizable and unbearable." He resigned rather than sign it.

A few minor changes were made, but when the Germans still balked, the French threatened to launch a new military attack. Finally, on June 28, the Germans gave up and signed the treaty in the glittering Hall of Mirrors at Versailles, the magnificent palace built by King Louis XIV in the late seventeenth century. Thereafter, the agreement was called the **Treaty of Versailles**. It was signed exactly five years after the assassination of Archduke Franz Ferdinand.

None of the peacemakers was fully satisfied. As France's Georges Clemenceau observed, the treaty "was not perfect," but it was, after all, the "result of human beings. We did all we could to work fast and well." British diplomat Harold Nicolson predicted that historians would "come to the conclusion that we were very stupid men [in creating the Versailles Treaty]. I think we were."

When Adolf Hitler learned of the treaty's provisions, he vowed a ghastly and pitiless revenge. "It cannot be that two million Germans have fallen in vain," he screamed during a speech in Munich in 1922. "We demand vengeance!"

**THE TREATY DEBATE** On July 8, 1919, Woodrow Wilson arrived back in Washington, D.C., to pursue Senate approval of the treaty. Before leaving Paris, he had assured a French diplomat that he would not allow changes to the treaty: "The Senate must take its medicine." Thus began one of the most partisan and bitterly personal disputes in history.

On July 10, Wilson called upon both parties to accept their "great duty" and ratify the treaty. He then grew needlessly confrontational, dismissing critics as "blind and little provincial people." The world, he claimed, was relying on the United States to sign the treaty: "Dare we reject it and break the heart of the world?"

Yes, answered Senate Republicans, who had decided that Wilson's commitment to the League of Nations was a reckless threat to America's independence. Henry Cabot Lodge denounced the treaty's "scheme of making mankind suddenly virtuous by a statute or a written constitution." Lodge's strategy was to delay a vote on the treaty in hopes that public opposition would grow. To do so,

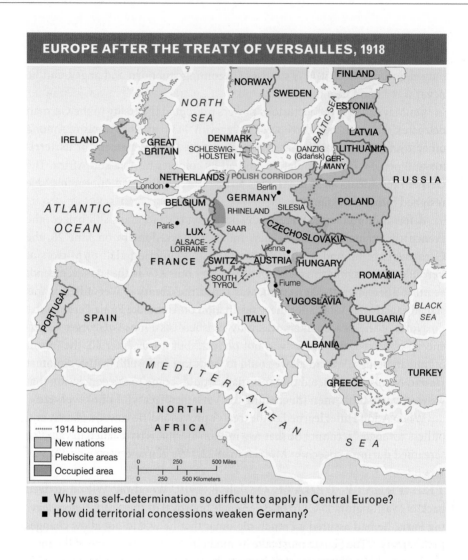

**EUROPE AFTER THE TREATY OF VERSAILLES, 1918**

Legend:
- 1914 boundaries
- New nations
- Plebiscite areas
- Occupied area

0    250    500 Miles
0    250    500 Kilometers

■ Why was self-determination so difficult to apply in Central Europe?

■ How did territorial concessions weaken Germany?

he took six weeks to read aloud the text of the treaty to the Foreign Relations Committee. He then organized a parade of expert witnesses, most of whom opposed the treaty, to appear at the hearings on ratification.

In the Senate, a group of "irreconcilables," fourteen Republicans and two Democrats, refused to support membership in the league. They were mostly western and midwestern isolationists who feared that such sweeping foreign commitments would threaten domestic reforms.

Lodge belonged to a larger group called the "reservationists," who insisted upon limiting American participation in the League of Nations in exchange for approving the rest of the treaty. The only way to get Senate approval was for

Wilson to agree to revisions, the most important of which was the requirement that Congress authorize any American participation in a league-approved war.

Colonel Edward House urged the president to "meet the Senate in a conciliatory spirit." Wilson replied that he had long ago decided that you "can never get anything in this life that is worthwhile without fighting for it." House courageously disagreed, reminding Wilson that American civilization was "built on compromise." It was the last time the two men would speak to or see each other.

The self-righteous president was temperamentally incapable of compromising. He refused to negotiate, declaring that "if the Treaty is not ratified by the Senate, the War will have been fought in vain."

**LET THE PEOPLE DECIDE** In September 1919, after a summer of fruitless debate, an exhausted Wilson decided to take his case directly to the voters. On September 2, against doctor's orders and the advice of his wife and aides, he boarded a train and left Washington for a grueling 10,000-mile tour through the Midwest to the West Coast. He planned to visit twenty-nine cities and deliver nearly 100 speeches on behalf of the treaty.

No president had ever made such an effort to win public support. Enormous crowds greeted him in Columbus, Kansas City, Des Moines, Omaha, and other stops. In St. Louis, Wilson said that he had returned from Paris "bringing one of the greatest documents of human history," which was now in danger of being rejected by the Senate. He pledged to "fight for a cause . . . greater than the Senate. It is greater than the government. It is as great as the cause of mankind."

Despite suffering from pounding headaches, Wilson spoke as many as four times a day. By the time his train reached Spokane, Washington, he was visibly fatigued. Still, he kept going, through Oregon and California. Some 200,000 people greeted him in Los Angeles.

Then disaster struck. After delivering an emotional speech on September 25, 1919, in Pueblo, Colorado, Wilson collapsed from severe headaches. His left side was paralyzed, and one side of his face was palsied, limp, and expressionless. "I seem to have gone to pieces," he sighed. The presidential train, its blinds drawn, raced back to Washington, D.C.

**A STRICKEN PRESIDENT** A week later, the president suffered a stroke (cerebral hemorrhage) that left him paralyzed on his left side and partially blind; he could barely speak. Ray Stannard Baker visited Wilson in the White House and came away stunned. The president, Baker gasped, had become "a broken, ruined old man, shuffling along, his left arm inert, the fingers drawn up like a claw, the left side of his face sagging frightfully. His voice is not human: it gurgles in his throat."

For five months, from the autumn of 1919 and into early 1920, the president lay in bed while his doctor issued reassuring medical bulletins. Wilson "lived on, but oh, what a wreck of his former self!" said a White House staff member. "He had changed from a giant to a pygmy." If a document needed Wilson's signature, his wife guided his hand, leading a senator to complain that the nation now had a "petticoat government."

Secretary of State Robert Lansing urged the president's aides to declare him disabled and appoint Vice President Thomas Marshall in his place. They angrily refused. Soon thereafter, Wilson replaced Lansing.

Wilson became emotionally unstable and began displaying signs of paranoia. A visitor found the president bitter and brooding, full of self-pity and anger. For the remaining seventeen months of his second term, Wilson's wife, along with aides and trusted cabinet members, kept him isolated from all but the most essential business. When a group of Republican senators visited the White House, one of them said: "Well, Mr. President, we have all been praying for you." Wilson replied, "Which way, Senator?"

**THE TREATY UNDER ATTACK** Such humor was rare, however. President Wilson's hardened arteries seemed to have hardened his judgment as well. For his part, Henry Cabot Lodge pushed through the Senate fourteen changes (the number was not coincidental) in the draft of the Treaty of Versailles.

The exiled Colonel Edward House became so concerned that he wrote Edith Wilson a letter in which he said how "vital" it was for some form of the treaty to be approved, since the president's "place in history is in the balance." House pleaded for Wilson to negotiate a compromise. The First Lady refused to share his concerns with her husband.

In the end, Wilson rejected any proposed changes to the treaty. As a result, his supporters in the Senate were thrown into an unlikely alliance with the irreconcilables, who opposed the treaty under *any* circumstances. The final Senate vote in 1920 on Lodge's revised treaty was 39 in favor and 55 against. On the question of approving the original treaty without changes, the irreconcilables and the reservationists, led by Lodge, combined to defeat ratification, with 38 for and 53 against.

Woodrow Wilson's grand effort at global peacemaking had failed. (He did receive the Nobel Peace Prize for his efforts.) When told of the final Senate vote, he said it "would have been better if I had died last fall."

After refusing to ratify the treaty, Congress tried to declare an official end to the war by a joint resolution on May 20, 1920, which Wilson vetoed. It was not until July 2, 1921, four months after he had left office and almost eighteen months after the fighting had stopped, that another joint resolution officially ended the state of war with Germany and Austria-Hungary. Separate peace treaties with Germany, Austria, and Hungary were ratified on October 18, 1921. By then, Warren G. Harding was president.

The U.S. failure to ratify the Versailles Treaty was a defining moment in world history, helping to trigger a chain of events that would contribute to a second world war twenty years later. The United States never joined the League of Nations. With Great Britain and France too exhausted and too timid to keep Germany weak and isolated, a dangerous power vacuum would emerge in Europe, one that Adolf Hitler and the Nazis would fill.

# STUMBLING FROM WAR TO PEACE

In America, celebrations over the war's end soon gave way to widespread inflation, unemployment, labor unrest, socialist and Communist radicalism, race riots, terrorist bombings, and government tyranny. With millions of servicemen returning to civilian life, war-related industries shutting down, and wartime price controls ending, unemployment and prices for consumer goods spiked.

Bedridden by his stroke, President Wilson became increasingly distant, depressed, and peevish. His administration was in disarray, he had never been so unpopular, and the Democratic party was floundering along with him.

**THE SPANISH FLU**  Beginning in 1918, many Americans confronted an infectious enemy that produced far more casualties than the war and in much shorter time. It became known as the "Spanish" influenza (although it did not originate in Spain), and it spread around the globe.

The disease appeared suddenly in January 1918 at a Kansas army camp and spread quickly to Europe with the U.S. troops. By June, the pandemic stretched from Algeria to New Zealand. Its initial outbreak lasted a year and killed between 50 million and 100 million people worldwide, two or three times as many as had died in the war. In the United States alone, it infected 26 million people, some 670,000 of whom died, more than ten times the number of U.S. combat deaths in France. The public health system was strained to the breaking point. Hospitals ran short of beds, nurses, and doctors; funeral homes ran out of coffins.

Fear seized the population. Schools and churches closed, and people ignored desperate appeals for hospital volunteers for fear of becoming infected themselves. In Goldsboro, North Carolina, Dan Tonkel remembered, "We were actually almost afraid to breathe. You were afraid to go out. The fear was so great people were actually afraid to leave their home . . . afraid to talk to one another."

By the spring of 1919, the pandemic had run its course. Although another outbreak occurred in the winter of 1920, people had grown more resistant to it. No disease in human history—indeed, no war, famine, or natural catastrophe—had killed so many in such a short time.

**SUFFRAGE AT LAST** As the first outbreak of the Spanish flu was ending, women finally gained a constitutional guarantee of their right to vote. After six months of delay, debate, and failed votes, Congress passed the **Nineteenth Amendment** in the spring of 1919 and sent it to the states for ratification.

Tennessee's legislature was the last of thirty-six state assemblies to approve the amendment, and it did so in dramatic fashion. As thousands of supporters and opponents mobilized in Knoxville, the state capital, the outcome was uncertain.

**Their first votes** Women of New York City's East Side vote for the first time in the presidential election of 1920.

The initial vote was 48–48. Then a twenty-four-year-old Republican legislator named Harry T. Burn changed his no vote to yes at the insistence of his strong-willed mother, Phoebe Ensminger Burn. She had written her son a note admonishing him to be a "good boy" and vote for suffrage. "Don't keep them in doubt!" He did as she directed, and the Nineteenth Amendment became official on August 18, 1920, making the United States the twenty-second nation to allow women's suffrage. Josephine Pearson, the most vocal Tennessee anti-suffragist, labeled Burn a "traitor to manhood's honor."

Women's suffrage was the climactic achievement of the Progressive Era. Suddenly, 9.5 million women were eligible to vote in national elections; in the 1920 presidential election, they would make up 40 percent of the electorate. "The greatest thing to come out of the war," said suffragist Carrie Chapman Catt, "was the emancipation of women, for which no man fought."

**ECONOMIC TURBULENCE** As consumer prices rose, discontented workers, released from wartime controls on wages, grew more willing to go on strike. In 1919, more than 4 million hourly wage workers, 20 percent of the workforce, participated in 3,600 strikes. Most wanted nothing more than higher wages and shorter workweeks, but their critics linked them with the worldwide Communist movement. Charges of a Communist conspiracy were greatly exaggerated, however. In 1919, fewer than 70,000 people nationwide belonged to the Communist party.

The most controversial labor dispute was in Boston, where police went on strike on September 9, 1919. Massachusetts governor Calvin Coolidge mobilized the National Guard to maintain order. After four days during which looters panicked the city, the striking police offered to return, but Coolidge ordered that they all be fired. When labor leaders appealed for their reinstatement, Coolidge responded in words that made him an instant national hero: "There is no right to strike against the public safety by anybody, anywhere, any time."

**RACE RIOTS** The end of the Great War brought fresh hopes that African Americans might gain full equality. Herbert Seligmann, a journalist who served on the board of the NAACP, maintained that the war "has meant a vital change in the position of the Negro and in his own feeling about the position." Yet Seligmann warned that "if the white man tries to 'show the nigger his place' by flogging and lynching him, the Negro, when the government does not defend him, will purchase arms to defend himself."

Seligmann's greatest fear was realized. The end of the war brought a wave of racist assaults. As more and more African Americans, including many of the 367,000 who were war veterans, developed successful careers and asserted their civil rights, resentful whites reacted with an almost hysterical brutality. In 1919 alone, seventy-six black people, including nine military veterans, were killed by southern whites.

What African American leader James Weldon Johnson called the Red Summer (*red* signifying blood) began in July, when a mob of whites invaded the black neighborhood in Longview, Texas, angry over rumors of interracial dating. They burned shops and houses and ran several black residents out of town. A week later, in Washington, D.C., false reports of black assaults on white women stirred up white mobs, and gangs of rioters waged a race war in the streets until soldiers and driving rains ended the fighting.

The worst was yet to come. In late July, 38 people were killed and 537 injured in five days of rioting in Chicago, where some 50,000 African Americans, mostly migrants from the South, had moved during the war, leading to tensions with local whites over jobs and housing. White unionized workers especially resented blacks who were hired as strikebreakers.

Altogether, twenty-five race riots erupted in 1919, and eighty African Americans were lynched, including eleven war veterans. In August, the NAACP sent President Wilson a telegram "respectfully enquiring how long the Federal Government under your administration intends to tolerate anarchy in the United States?" The White House chose not to reply.

The riots were indeed a turning point for many African Americans, but not a happy one. "We made the supreme sacrifice," a black veteran told poet-journalist Carl Sandburg. "Now we want to see our country live up to the Constitution and the Declaration of Independence." Another ex-soldier noted how much the war experience had changed the outlook of black people: "We were determined not to take it anymore."

Many blamed the riots on socialist and Communist agitators. "Reds Try to Stir Negroes to Revolt," and "Radicals Inciting Negro to Violence," cautioned the *New York Times* in July 1919. The *New York Tribune* followed suit, announcing that a "Plot to Stir Race Antagonism in United States Charged to Soviets." By December 1919, the *Times* had decided that "no element in this country is so susceptible to organized propaganda . . . as the least informed class of Negroes." It warned that "Bolshevist[s] . . . are winning many recruits among the colored races."

**THE FIRST RED SCARE** With so many people convinced that the strikes and riots were inspired by Communists and anarchists (two different groups who shared a hatred for capitalism), a New York journalist reported that Americans were "shivering in their boots over Bolshevism, and they are far more scared of [Vladimir] Lenin than they ever were of the [German] Kaiser. We seem to be the most frightened victors the world ever saw."

Fears of revolution were fueled by the violent actions of a few militants. In early 1919, the Secret Service discovered a plot by Spanish anarchists to kill President Wilson and other government officials. In April 1919, postal workers intercepted nearly forty homemade mail bombs addressed to government officials. One mail bomb, however, blew off the hands of a Georgia senator's maid.

In June, a twenty-four-year-old Italian anarchist named Carlo Valdinoci used a suitcase filled with dynamite to blow up Attorney General A. Mitchell Palmer's home in Washington, D.C. The bomb exploded prematurely when Valdinoci tripped and fell as he approached the house. A neighbor, Assistant Secretary of the Navy Franklin Roosevelt, was walking with his wife Eleanor when the bomb exploded. The blast shattered windows and knocked neighbors

**Safe, briefly** Escorted by a police officer, an African American family moves its belongings from their home, likely destroyed by white rioters, and into a protected area of Chicago.

out of their beds. Valdinoci's collarbone landed on the Roosevelts' front steps, and his scalp ended up on their roof.

The bombing transformed Attorney General Palmer. "I remember . . . the morning after my house was blown up, I stood in the middle of the wreckage of my library with Congressmen and Senators, and without a dissenting voice they called upon me in strong terms to exercise all the power that was possible . . . to run to earth the criminals who were behind that kind of outrage."

At the same time, other anarchist bombers were setting off explosives in New York City, Boston, Pittsburgh, Philadelphia, Cleveland, and Washington, D.C. Palmer, who had ambitions to succeed Wilson as president, concluded that a "Red Menace," a Communist "blaze of revolution," was "sweeping over every American institution of law and order."

That August, Palmer appointed a twenty-four-year-old attorney named J. Edgar Hoover to lead the new General Intelligence Division within the Justice Department to collect information on radicals. Hoover and others in the Justice Department worked with a network of 250,000 informants in 600 cities, all of them members of the American Protective League, which had been founded during the war to root out "traitors" and labor radicals.

On November 7, 1919, in what came to be called the "Palmer raids," federal agents rounded up 450 alien "radicals," most of whom were law-abiding Russian immigrants. All were deported to Russia without a court hearing. On January 2, 1920, federal agents and police in dozens of cities arrested 5,000 more suspects. The raids were disasters. Poor communications, faulty planning, and murky intelligence created chaos and confusion.

The **First Red Scare** (another would occur in the 1950s) represented one of the largest violations of civil liberties in history. In 1919, novelist Katharine Fullerton Gerould announced in *Harper's Magazine* that, as a result of the government crackdown, America "is no longer a free country in the old sense." Panic about possible foreign terrorists and American radicals erupted across the nation as vigilantes took matters into their own hands.

At a patriotic pageant in Washington, D.C., a sailor shot a spectator who refused to rise for "The Star-Spangled Banner"; the crowd cheered. In Hammond, Indiana, a jury took two minutes to acquit a man who had murdered an immigrant for yelling "To hell with the U.S." In Waterbury, Connecticut, a salesman was sentenced to six months in jail for saying that Lenin was "one of the brainiest" of the world's leaders.

By the summer of 1920, the Red Scare had begun to subside. But it left a lasting mark by strengthening the conservative crusade for "100 percent Americanism" and new restrictions on immigration.

## EFFECTS OF THE GREAT WAR

The extraordinary turbulence in 1919 and 1920 was an unmistakable indication of how the Great War had changed the shape of modern history. It had destroyed old Europe—its cities, people, economies, and four grand empires. The war also changed Europe's self-image as the center of civilized Western culture. Winston Churchill, the future British prime minister, called postwar Europe "a crippled, broken world."

Peace brought festering resentment among the vanquished. Most Germans and Austrians believed they were the victims of a harsh peace, and many wanted revenge. At the same time, the war had hastened the Bolshevik Revolution that caused Russia to exit the war, abandon its western European allies, and, in 1922, re-emerge as the Union of Soviet Socialist Republics (USSR). Thereafter, Soviet communism would be one of the most powerful forces shaping the twentieth century.

Postwar America was a much different story. For the first time, the United States had decisively intervened in a major European war. After a sharp but brief postwar recession, the economy entered a period of unprecedented prosperity. During the twenties, the United States became the world's dominant power. What came to be called the "American Century" was at hand.

# CHAPTER REVIEW

## SUMMARY

- **An Uneasy Neutrality**  After war erupted in Europe in 1914, the Western Front bogged down in horrific *trench warfare*, in which both sides were stalemated yet absorbed horrific losses. The Wilson administration declared the United States neutral but allowed businesses to extend loans to the warring nations, principally the *Allied Powers* (Britain, France, and Russia), to purchase food and military supplies. Very little aid was provided the *Central Powers* (Germany, Austria-Hungary, and Turkey). Americans were outraged by the Germans' use of submarine (*U-boat*) warfare, especially after the sinking of the *Lusitania*. In 1917, submarine attacks and the publication of the *Zimmermann telegram*, which revealed that Germany had tried to encourage Mexico to wage war against the United States, led America to enter the Great War.

- **Mobilizing a Nation**  The Wilson administration drafted young men into the army and created new agencies such as the War Industries Board and the Food Administration to coordinate industrial production and agricultural consumption. As white workers left their factory jobs to join the army, hundreds of thousands of African Americans migrated from the rural South to the urban North as part of the *Great Migration (1914-1920)*. Many white southerners and Mexican Americans also relocated to industrial centers. One million women participated in war work but were encouraged to leave those jobs as soon as the war ended. The federal government severely curtailed civil liberties, and the Espionage and Sedition Acts of 1917 and 1918 criminalized virtually any opposition to the war.

- **The American Role in Fighting the War**  Communists seized power in November 1917 in Russia and negotiated a separate peace treaty with Germany, thus freeing the Germans to focus on the *Western Front*. By 1918, however, the arrival of U.S. troops turned the tide of the war. German leaders sued for peace, and an armistice was signed on November 11, 1918. Woodrow Wilson insisted that the United States wanted a new democratic Europe. His *Fourteen Points (1918)* speech outlined his ideas for a *League of Nations* to promote peaceful resolutions to future conflicts.

- **The Fight for the Peace**  At the Paris Peace Conference, President Wilson was only partially successful. The *Treaty of Versailles (1919)* did create a League of Nations but included a "war guilt clause" that forced Germany to pay reparations for war damages to France and Britain. In the end, Wilson's illness following a stroke, his refusal to compromise on the terms of the treaty, and his alienation of Republican senators resulted in the Senate voting against ratification.

- **Lurching from War to Peace**  The United States struggled with its new status as the leading world power and with changes at home. As wartime industries shifted to peacetime production, wage and price controls ended. As former soldiers reentered the workforce, unemployment rose and consumer prices increased,

938

provoking labor unrest. Many believed these problems were part of a Bolshevik plot. Several incidents of domestic terrorism provoked what would be known as the *First Red Scare (1919–1920)*, during which the Justice Department illegally arrested and deported many suspected radicals, most of whom were immigrants. At the same time, race riots broke out as resentful white mobs tried to stop African Americans from exercising their civil rights. The summer of 1919 also brought Congressional passage of the *Nineteenth Amendment (1919)* to the Constitution, which gave women the right to vote once ratified by the states the following year.

## CHRONOLOGY

| | |
|---|---|
| 1914 | The Great War (World War I) begins in Europe |
| 1915 | The *Lusitania* is torpedoed by a German U-boat |
| February 1917 | Germany announces unrestricted submarine warfare |
| March 1917 | Zimmermann telegram disclosed in the press |
| April 1917 | United States enters the Great War |
| January 1918 | Woodrow Wilson delivers Fourteen Points speech |
| November 11, 1918 | Representatives of warring nations sign armistice |
| 1919 | Paris Peace Conference convenes |
| | Race riots break out during the Red Summer |
| 1919–1920 | First Red Scare leads to arrests and deportations of suspected radicals |
| | Woodrow Wilson suffers stroke |
| 1920 | The Senate rejects the Treaty of Versailles |
| | The Nineteenth Amendment is ratified by the states |

## KEY TERMS

Central Powers p. 897

Allied Powers p. 897

Western Front p. 898

trench warfare p. 898

U-boats p. 902

*Lusitania* p. 902

Zimmermann telegram p. 906

Great Migration p. 910

Fourteen Points (1918) p. 917

League of Nations p. 925

Treaty of Versailles (1919) p. 927

Nineteenth Amendment (1920) p. 932

First Red Scare (1919–1920) p. 936

---

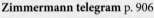 **INQUIZITIVE**

Go to InQuizitive to see what you've learned—and learn what you've missed—with personalized feedback along the way.

# 23 A Clash of Cultures

## 1920–1929

***Nightclub*** **(1933)** The roar of the twenties subsided for some at the heart of it all. In this painting by American artist Guy Pène du Bois, flappers and their dates crowd into a fashionable nightclub, yet their loneliness amid the excitement is deafening.

T he decade between the end of the Great War and the onset of the Great Depression at the end of 1929 was perhaps the most dynamic in American history, a period punctuated by rapid urbanization, technological innovation, widespread prosperity, social rebelliousness, cultural upheaval, and political conservatism.

The Eighteenth Amendment ("Prohibition") outlawed alcoholic beverages in 1920, setting off an epidemic of lawbreaking throughout the twenties, as many people defied the ban, smuggling, producing, and consuming "bootleg" liquor in violation of the law. At the same time, the Nineteenth Amendment allowed women to vote and to experience many freedoms previously limited to men. Despite some improvement in employment opportunities, Jim Crow laws continued to prevent most African Americans in the South, women and men, from voting.

Cultural conflicts resulted largely from tensions between rural and urban ways of life. For the first time in the nation's history, more people lived in cities than in rural areas, but old farm folkways lived on for almost half the population.

While the urban middle class prospered, farmers suffered as the wartime boom in exports of grains and livestock to Europe ground to a halt. Four million people moved from farms to cities, in part because of the better quality of life and in part because of the prolonged agricultural recession. Amid this massive population shift, bitter fights erupted between traditionalists and modernists, small towns and big cities, as old and new values fought a cultural civil war that continues today.

The postwar wave of strikes, bombings, anti-Communist hysteria, and race riots created a widespread sense of alarm that led many to cling to traditional religious beliefs and "native" ways of life. America during the twenties, said

## focus questions

**1.** Assess the impact of the consumer culture during the 1920s. What contributed to its growth?

**2.** What were the other major social and cultural trends and movements that became prominent during the twenties? How did they challenge traditional standards and customs?

**3.** What does "modernism" mean in intellectual and artistic terms? How did the modernist movement influence American culture in the early twentieth century?

one social commentator, was the most "volcanic of any area on earth." All of the changes created what one historian called a "nervous generation" of Americans "groping for what certainty they could find."

**MODERNITY VERSUS TRADITION** During the twenties, the new and unusual clashed openly with the conventional and commonplace. Modernists and traditionalists waged cultural warfare with one another, one group looking to the future for inspiration and the other looking to the past for guidance.

The scope and pace of societal changes were bewildering, as a national entertainment culture emerged. Radio networks and motion pictures, mass ownership of automobiles, and national chain stores, combined with the soaring popularity of spectator sports and the rise of mass marketing and advertising, transformed America into the world's leading consumer society. The culture of mass consumption ignited the growth of middle-class urban life while assaulting traditional virtues such as frugality, prudence, and religiosity.

In the political arena, reactionaries and rebels battled for control. The brutal fight between Woodrow Wilson and the Republican-led Senate over the Treaty of Versailles, coupled with the administration's crackdown on dissenters and socialists, had weakened an already fragmented progressivism. As reformer Amos Pinchot bitterly observed, President Wilson had "put his enemies in office and his friends in jail." By 1920, many disillusioned progressives had grown skeptical of any politician claiming to be a reformer or an idealist. Social reformer Jane Addams sighed that the 1920s, dominated politically by a Republican party devoted to the interests of Big Business, were "a period of political and social sag."

The desire to restore traditional values and social stability led voters to elect Republican Warren G. Harding president in 1920. He promised to return America to "normalcy." Both major parties still included progressive wings, but they were shrinking. The demand for honest, efficient government and public services remained strong; the impulse for social reform, however, shifted into a drive for moral righteousness and social conformity. By 1920, many progressives had withdrawn from public life.

Mainstream Americans were also shocked by "modernist" forms of artistic expression and sexual liberation. Mabel Dodge Luhan, a leading promoter of modern art and literature, described the literary and artistic rebels that emerged during and after the war as being determined to overthrow "the old order of things."

In sum, postwar life in America and Europe was fraught with turbulent changes, contradictory impulses, superficial frivolity, and seething tensions. As

French painter Paul Gauguin acknowledged, the upheavals of cultural modernism and the chaotic aftermath of the war produced "an epoch of confusion."

## THE NATION IN 1920

The 1920 census reported that 106 million people lived in the United States, a third of the number today. More than half were under the age of twenty-five. The average life expectancy was just fifty-six years for men and fifty-eight for women.

American society remained overwhelmingly white—90 percent. (Persons of Latino origin were considered white.) African Americans were 9 percent, and Native Americans and Asian Americans made up most of the rest. Almost half the white population were immigrants or the children of immigrants, the highest percentage since the late eighteenth century.

For the first time, more than half the population resided in "cities" of more than 2,500 residents. Some 16 million Americans lived in the ten largest cities, such as New York, Boston, Chicago, and Philadelphia. The South remained the most rural and poorest region. Only half of southern farmers owned their land, compared to three quarters of farmers in the rest of the nation. The others were either tenants who rented or sharecroppers who gave the landowner a share of the harvested crop in exchange for access to land. Most sharecroppers, especially black sharecroppers, remained grimly poor, in large part because of low crop prices during the twenties.

## A "NEW ERA" OF CONSUMERISM

America experienced so many dramatic changes during the twenties that people referred to it as a "New Era." Following the brief postwar recession in 1920–1921, economic growth soared to record levels. By 1929, the United States enjoyed the highest standard of living in the world.

Construction led the way. By 1921, a building boom was under way that would last the rest of the decade. At the same time, the remarkable growth of the automotive industry created an immediate need for roads, highways, service stations, and "motels" (motor hotels). New construction and new cars stimulated other industries such as lumber, steel, concrete, rubber, gasoline, and furniture.

Technology also played a key role in the prosperity by enabling mass production through the assembly-line process. Manufacturing grew more mechanized and efficient. Powerful new machines (electric motors, steam turbines, dump trucks, tractors, bulldozers, steam shovels) and more-efficient ways of operating farms, factories, plants, mines, and mills generated dramatic increases in productivity. In 1920, the nation's factories produced 5,000 electric refrigerators; in 1929, they produced almost a million.

## A Growing Consumer Culture

In the late nineteenth century, the U.S. economy had been driven by commercial agriculture and large-scale industrial production—the building of railroads and bridges, the manufacture of steel, and the construction of housing and businesses in cities. During the twenties, an explosion of new consumer goods made available through a national marketplace revolutionized the lives of the middle class.

The success of mass production made mass consumption more important than ever. A 1920 newspaper editorial insisted that the American's "first importance to his country is no longer that of citizen but that of *consumer*." To keep factory production humming required converting once-frugal people into enthusiastic shoppers. "People may ruin themselves by saving instead of spending," warned one economist.

During the Great War, the government had urged Americans to work long hours, conserve resources, and live simply. After the war, a new **consumer culture** encouraged carefree spending. "During the war," a journalist noted in 1920, "we accustomed ourselves to doing without, to buying carefully, to using economically. But with the close of the war came reaction. A veritable orgy of extravagant buying is going on. Reckless spending takes the place of saving, waste replaces conservation."

To keep people buying, businesses developed new ways for consumers to finance purchases over time ("layaway") rather than pay cash up front ("buy now, pay later"). Traditional notions such as paying with cash and staying out of debt were now dismissed as needlessly old-fashioned. Consumer debt almost tripled. By 1929, almost 60 percent of purchases were made on the installment plan.

Advertising became a huge enterprise, especially with the advent of the radio, which aired its first commercial in 1922. President Calvin Coolidge declared that advertising had become "the most potent influence in adopting and changing the habits and modes of life, affecting what we eat, what we wear, and the work and play of the whole nation."

The visibility of ads helped shape how people behaved and how they defined the pursuit of happiness. Zelda Sayre Fitzgerald, the writer and wife of popular novelist F. Scott Fitzgerald, recalled that "we grew up founding our dreams on the infinite promises of American advertising." In a 1923 interview, she embraced the culture of consumption: "I don't mean that money means happiness, necessarily. But having things, just things, objects, makes a woman happy. The right kind of perfume, the smart pair of shoes." Her husband chimed in: "Women care for 'things,' clothes, furniture, for themselves . . . and men [do too], in so far as they contribute to their vanity." The Fitzgeralds spoke for many Americans who assumed that social status was measured in dollars.

New weekday radio programs popular with middle-class housewives, for example, were often sponsored by national companies advertising laundry detergent and hand soap—hence the term *soap operas*. Because women purchased two thirds of consumer goods, advertisers aimed commercials at them.

The huge jump in the use of electricity was also a transformational force. In 1920, only 35 percent of homes had electricity; by 1930, the number was 68 percent. Similar increases occurred in the number of households with indoor plumbing, washing machines, and automobiles. Moderately priced creature comforts and conveniences such as flush toilets, electric irons and fans, hand-held cameras, wristwatches, cigarette lighters, vacuum cleaners, and linoleum floors, became more widely available, especially among the urban middle class. As always, the poor, with little discretionary income, remained on the margins.

**Does the Home You Love Love You?**

# Westinghouse

**A modern home** This 1925 Westinghouse ad urges homemakers to buy its "Cozy Glow, Jr." heater and "Sol-Lux Luminaire" lamp, among other new electrical appliances that would "do anything for you in return."

## THE RISE OF MASS CULTURE

The consumer culture helped create a marketplace of retail stores and national brands (Kellogg's Corn Flakes, General Electric toasters, etc.) in which local and regional businesses were increasingly squeezed out by giant department stores and "chain" stores. By the 1920s, Woolworth's, for example, had 1,500 stores across the country; Walgreen's had 525. National retailers bought goods in such large quantities that they were able to get discounted prices that they passed on to consumers.

Mass advertising and marketing campaigns increasingly led to a *mass culture*: more and more people saw the same advertisements and bought the same products at the same stores. They also read the same magazines, listened to the same radio programs, drove the same cars, adored the same sports stars and celebrities, and watched the same movies.

**MOVIE-MADE AMERICA** In 1896, a New York audience viewed the first moving-picture show. By 1924, there were 20,000 theaters showing 700 new "silent" films a year, and the movie business had become the nation's chief form of mass entertainment. Hollywood, California, emerged as the international center of movie production, grinding out Westerns, crime dramas, murder mysteries, and the comedies of Mack Sennett's Keystone Company, in which a raft of slapstick comedians, notably London-born Charlie Chaplin, perfected their art, transforming it into a form of social criticism.

Movie attendance during the 1920s averaged 80 million people a week. It surged even more after 1927 with the appearance of movies with sound ("talkies"). Americans spent ten times as much on movies as they did on tickets to baseball and football games.

Movies did much more than entertain, however. They helped expand the consumer culture by setting standards and tastes in fashion, music, dancing, and hairstyles. As producer-director D.W. Griffith claimed in 1917, "The cinema is the agent of Democracy. It levels barriers between races and classes."

Popular films also helped stimulate the sexual revolution. One boy admitted that the movies taught him how "to kiss a girl on her ears, neck, and cheeks, as well as on the mouth." A researcher concluded that movies made young Americans more "sex-wise, sex-excited, and sex-absorbed" than previous generations.

**Charlie Chaplin** An English-born actor who rose to international fame as the "Tramp," pictured above in the 1921 silent film *The Kid*.

**RADIO**   Radio broadcasting enjoyed even more spectacular growth. Between 1920 and 1930, the number of families owning a radio soared from 15,000 to nearly 14 million. Almost two thirds of homes had at least one radio.

The radio changed the patterns of everyday life. At night after dinner, families gathered to listen to music, speeches, news broadcasts, weather forecasts, and comedy shows. One ad claimed that the radio "is your theater, your college, your newspaper, your library."

In 1920, some 41 million radios were manufactured in the United States. Calvin Coolidge was the first president to address the nation by radio, and his monthly talks paved the way for Franklin Delano Roosevelt's influential "fireside chats" during the thirties.

Radio transformed jazz music into a national craze. Big band leaders Paul Whiteman, Guy Lombardo, Duke Ellington, Glenn Miller, and Tommy and Jimmy Dorsey regularly performed live over the radio. Country music also developed a national following as a result of radio broadcasts. In 1925, WSM, a station in Nashville, Tennessee, began offering a weekly variety show, *The Grand Ole Opry*, which featured an array of country music stars.

**Radio broadcasting**   Radio players act out 'Rip Van Winkle' in a sound effects studio during a broadcast from Schenectady, New York, circa 1926.

**FLYING MACHINES** Advances in transportation were as significant as the impact of commercial radio and movies. In 1903, Wilbur and Orville Wright, owners of a bicycle shop in Dayton, Ohio, had built and flown the first "flying machine" at Kitty Hawk, North Carolina.

The development of airplanes advanced slowly until the outbreak of war in 1914, when Europeans began using the airplane as a military weapon. When the United States entered the war, it had no combat planes; American pilots flew British or French warplanes. An American aircraft industry arose during the war but collapsed in the postwar demobilization. Under the Kelly Act of 1925, however, the federal government began to subsidize the industry through airmail delivery contracts. The Air Commerce Act of 1926 provided federal funds for the advancement of air transportation and navigation, including the construction of airports.

The aviation industry received a huge psychological boost in May 1927 when twenty-six-year-old Charles A. Lindbergh Jr., a St. Louis–based pilot blessed with extraordinary courage and endurance, made the first *solo* transatlantic flight, traveling from New York City to Paris in thirty-three and a half hours through thunderstorms, ice clouds, and dense fog.

A handsome, daring college dropout, Lindbergh oversaw a fanatical effort to reduce the weight of his plane so as to accommodate the 2,500 pounds of fuel—heavier than the plane itself—needed for the crossing. He used a wicker basket for a seat, removed the radio, and modified the tail section to make the plane hard to control so as to ensure he did not fall asleep.

When Lindbergh, known as the "Lone Eagle," landed in France, 150,000 people greeted him with thunderous cheers. The New York City parade honoring his accomplishment surpassed the celebration of the end of the Great War. A new dance, the Lindy Hop, was named for him, and a popular song, "Lucky Lindy," celebrated his "peerless, fearless" feat. (When Lindbergh met Britain's King George V soon after his long flight, the monarch asked him, "How did you pee?" "In paper cups," the pilot answered.) Lindbergh's flight redefined the potential of "flying machines" to transform transportation and compress distance.

No sooner did Lindbergh return to America than promoters began looking for a female pilot to equal his feat. In June 1928, Kansas-born Amelia Earhart, who had dropped out of college during the Great War to nurse wounded soldiers, joined two male pilots in being the first woman to cross the Atlantic in an airplane—as a passenger. "Stultz did all the flying — had to," she said. "I was just baggage, like a sack of potatoes. Maybe someday I'll try it alone."

Thereafter, Earhart launched a national organization of female pilots, solo piloted a plane non-stop coast to coast across the United States, and set several speed records for women pilots. In 1932, Earhart climbed into her candy apple red Lockheed Vega and equaled Lindbergh by flying solo from Canada to

Northern Ireland in fifteen hours, thereby becoming one of the most famous women in the world.

In 1937, Earhart set out with a male navigator to fly around the globe at the equator, long before radar was developed. They would use the sun and stars to guide them the 30,000 miles. Just before taking off, she told reporters, "I won't feel completely cheated if I fail to come back." While crossing the South Pacific, she lost radio contact and was never heard from again.

**THE CAR CULTURE**  By far the most significant economic and social development of the early twentieth century was the emergence of a car-centered culture. The motor car came to symbolize the twentieth-century machine age, which transported people into modernity. In 1924, when asked about the changes transforming American life, a resident of Muncie, Indiana, replied: "I can tell you what's happening in just four letters: A-U-T-O."

In 1900, the United States had produced 5,000 automobiles. By 1910, that number had spiked to 137,000. Ten years later, there were 8.1 million cars motoring across America, and half of all families owned at least one.

The first cars were handmade, expensive, and designed for the wealthy. Henry Ford changed all that beginning in 1903 by pledging to build "a car for the multitude." He vowed "to democratize the automobile. When I'm through, everybody will be able to afford one, and about everyone will have one."

Ford's Model T, the celebrated "Tin Lizzie," appeared in 1908 at a price of $850 (about $22,000 today). By 1924, as a result of Ford's increasingly efficient production techniques, the same car sold for $290 (less than $4,000 today). The Model T, "built to last forever," changed little from year to year, and it came in one color: black. Selling millions of identical cars at a small profit allowed Ford to keep prices low and wages high—the perfect formula for a mass-consumption economy.

Other automakers followed Ford's production model. By 1929, there were more than 23 million registered cars and trucks. The automobile revolution was in part propelled by the discovery of vast oil fields in Texas, Oklahoma, Wyoming, and California. By 1920, the United States produced two thirds of the world's oil and gasoline. By 1930, an estimated 10 percent of America's workforce was centered on the production of automobiles.

The automobile industry also became the leading example of modern, mechanized, mass-production techniques. Ford's Highland Park plant outside Detroit was the largest factory in the world. It employed 68,000 workers and used a moving conveyor system that pulled the car chassis down an assembly line of sequential workstations. Each worker performed a single task, such as installing a fender or a wheel, as the car-in-process moved down the line.

**Ford Motor Company's Highland Park plant, 1913** Gravity slides and chain conveyors contributed to the mass production of automobiles.

Through this monotonous yet efficient technique, a new car could be pieced together in ninety-three minutes.

Just as the railroad helped transform the pace and scale of life in the late nineteenth century, the automobile changed social life during the twentieth century. Americans developed a love affair with cars. In the words of one male driver, young people viewed the car as "an incredible engine of escape" from parental control and a safe place to "take a girl and hold hands, neck, pet, or . . . go the limit."

Cars and networks of new roads enabled people to live farther away from their workplaces, thus encouraging suburban sprawl. Cars also helped fuel the economic boom of the 1920s by creating tens of thousands of new jobs and a huge demand for steel, glass, rubber, leather, oil, and gasoline. The car culture stimulated road construction, sparked a real estate boom in Florida and California, and dotted the landscape with gasoline stations, traffic lights, billboards, and motor hotels. By 1929, the federal government was constructing 10,000 miles of paved highways each year.

**SPECTATOR SPORTS** Automobile ownership and rising incomes changed the way people spent their leisure time. Americans fell in love with spectator sports; people in cities could drive into the countryside, visit friends and relatives, and go to ballparks, stadiums, or boxing rings.

Baseball had become the "national pastime." With larger-than-life heroes such as New York Yankee legends George Herman "Babe" Ruth and Henry Louis "Lou" Gehrig, baseball teams attracted intense interest and huge crowds.

Ruth may well have been the most famous athlete of all time. In 1920, more than a million spectators attended his games.

Two years later, the Yankees built a new stadium, dubbing it the "House That Ruth Built." They went on to win World Series championships in 1923, 1927, and 1928. More than 20 million people attended professional games in 1927, the year that Ruth, the "Sultan of Swat," set a record by hitting sixty home runs. Because baseball remained a segregated sport, so-called Negro Leagues were organized for African Americans.

Football, especially at the college level, also attracted huge crowds. It, too, benefited from outsized heroes such as running back Harold Edward "Red" Grange of the University of Illinois, the first athlete to appear on the cover of *Time* magazine. In a 1924 game against the University of Michigan, the "Galloping Ghost" scored a touchdown the first four times he carried the ball. After Illinois won, students carried him on their shoulders for two miles across the campus. When Grange signed a contract with the Chicago Bears in 1926, he single-handedly made professional football competitive with baseball as a spectator sport.

What Ruth and Grange were to their sports, William Harrison "Jack" Dempsey was to boxing. In 1919, he won the world heavyweight title from Jess Willard, a giant of a man weighing 300 pounds and standing six and a half feet tall. Dempsey knocked him down seven times in the first round. Willard gave up in the fourth round, and Dempsey became a dominant force in boxing. The "Manassa Mauler" was especially popular with working-class men, for he had been born poor and lived for years as a hobo, wandering the rails in search of work and challenging toughs in bars to fight for money.

Dempsey was more than a champion; he was a hero to millions. In 1927, when James Joseph "Gene" Tunney defeated Dempsey, more than 100,000 people attended, including 1,000 reporters, 10 state governors, and numerous Hollywood celebrities. Some 60 million people listened to the fight over the radio.

## THE "JAZZ AGE"

While the masses of Americans devoted their free time to spectator sports, radio programs, and movies, many young people, especially college students, focused on social and cultural rebellion—trying daring new fads and fashions, new music, new attitudes, and new ways of having fun.

F. Scott Fitzgerald became the self-infatuated "voice of his generation" after his best-selling first novel, *This Side of Paradise* (1920), portrayed rowdy student life at Princeton University, which he had attended. "No one else," Fitzgerald announced, "could have written so searchingly the story of the youth of our generation." Fitzgerald fastened upon the "**Jazz Age**" as the evocative label for the rebelliousness and spontaneity displayed by American youth during the "greatest, gaudiest spree in history."

## THE BIRTH OF JAZZ

F. Scott Fitzgerald's Jazz Age label referred to the popularity of jazz music, a dynamic blend of several musical traditions. It had first emerged as piano-based "ragtime" at the end of the nineteenth century. Thereafter, African American musicians such as Jelly Roll Morton, Duke Ellington, Louis Armstrong, and Bessie Smith (known as the "Empress of the Blues") combined the energies of ragtime with the emotions of the blues to create *jazz*, originally an African American slang term meaning sexual intercourse. With its improvisations, variations, and sensual spontaneity, jazz appealed to people of all ethnicities and ages because it celebrated pleasure and immediacy.

Louis Armstrong, an inspired trumpeter with a unique, froggy voice, was the Pied Piper of jazz, an inventive and freewheeling performer who reshaped the American music scene. Born in a New Orleans shack in 1900, the grandson of slaves, he was abandoned by his father and raised by his prostitute mother, who was just fifteen when he was born. As a youth, he experienced the mean and ugly side of America. "I seen everythin' from a child comin' up," he said once. "Nothin' happen I ain't never seen before."

**Duke Ellington and his band** Jazz emerged in the 1920s as a uniquely American expression of the modernist spirit. African American artists bent musical conventions to give freer rein to improvisation and sensuality.

Then he found music, using his natural genius to explore the fertile possibilities of jazz. As a teen, he sneaked into music halls to watch Joe "King" Oliver and other early jazz innovators. In 1922, Armstrong moved to Chicago, where he delighted audiences with his passionate trumpet performances and open-hearted personality. He radiated a joy that reflected his faith in the power of music and laughter to promote racial harmony.

The culture of jazz quickly spread from its origins in New Orleans, Kansas City, Memphis, and St. Louis to the African American neighborhoods of Harlem in New York City and

Chicago's South Side. Large dance halls met the demand for jazz music and the dances it inspired, like the Charleston and the Black Bottom. Affluent whites flocked to the dance halls as well as to "black" nightclubs and "jazz joints." People spoke of "*jazzing* something up" (invigorating it) or "jazzing around" (acting youthfully and energetically).

Many Americans, however, were not fans of jazz ("the devil's music") or the suggestive dances it inspired. Dr. Francis E. Clark, a Christian moralist, denounced "indecent dance" as "an offense against womanly purity." In 1921, the *Ladies' Home Journal* discouraged jazz dancing because of its "direct appeal to the body's sensory centers," and Princeton professor Henry van Dyke dismissed jazz as "merely an irritation of the nerves of hearing, a sensual teasing of the strings of physical passion."

Such criticism, however, failed to stem the growing worldwide popularity of jazz. As celebrated symphony conductor Leopold Stokowski acknowledged, "Jazz has come to stay because it is an expression of the times, of the breathless, energetic, superactive times in which we are living."

## A Sexual Revolution?

What was most shocking during the Jazz Age was a defiant sexual revolution among young people, especially those on college campuses. "None of the Victorian mothers—and most of the mothers were Victorian—had any idea how casually their daughters were accustomed to being kissed," wrote F. Scott Fitzgerald in *This Side of Paradise*.

During the twenties, Americans learned about the hidden world of "flaming youth" (the title of a popular novel): wild "petting parties," free love, speakeasies, "joyriding," and skinny-dipping. A promotional poster for the 1923 silent film *Flaming Youth* asked: "How Far Can a Girl Go?" Other ads claimed the movie appealed especially to "neckers, petters, white kisses, red kisses, pleasure-mad daughters, [and] sensation-craving mothers."

**THE IMPACT OF SIGMUND FREUD** The increasingly frank treatment of sex resulted in part from the influence of Sigmund Freud, the Austrian founder of modern psychoanalysis. Freud explored the human psyche, determined to legitimize psychoanalysis as a professional field anchored in clinical research. Yet he was a reckless and unethical scientist. He lied, manipulated or invented data, made unsubstantiated assertions, and stole ideas from others. He also relied upon a handful of questionable clinical cases to justify his insistence that the mind is baffling in its opaqueness and unpredictability, mysteriously "conflicted" by often unconscious efforts to repress powerful impulses and sexual desires ("libido"). Yet Freud created a new vocabulary for mapping the inner lives of people, explaining the complex dynamics of the ego, the id, and, after 1914, the superego.

Freud dismissed all forms of traditional religion as irrational responses to infantile fears and father worship. "Science," he stressed, "is no illusion," but religious faith was an illusion—and nothing more. Freud came to see psychoanalysis as the modern successor to religion. It could provide the answers to the fundamental questions that for thousands of years religion had claimed authority over: How should we live? Why does happiness elude us? What really matters?

In 1899, the cocaine-addicted Freud (cocaine was then legal) had published *The Interpretation of Dreams*, a pathbreaking book that stressed the crucial role of the subconscious in shaping behavior and moods. He claimed that dreams provide the "royal road to the unconscious" by revealing the psyche as a roiling snake pit of "repressed" sexual yearnings and aggressions, many of which result from early childhood experiences with repressed erotic feelings toward our parents. Dreams, slips of the tongue, and neurotic symptoms, Freud concluded, were the mind's most important activity, for they reveal what we truly desire. The role of psychotherapy was thus to help patients discover their hidden selves and suppressed desires.

Women and men, Freud argued, are endowed with equal sexual energy, and human behavior is driven by a variety of intense sexual desires, repressed memories, and efforts to release pent-up aggression. These natural human conflicts cause unhappiness because people desire more pleasures than they can attain.

It did not take long for Freud's ideas to penetrate society at large. By 1909, when he first visited the United States to lecture at Clark University in Massachusetts, he was surprised to find himself famous "even in prudish America." Books, movies, and plays included frequent references to his ideas and phrases (Oedipus complex, penis envy, the death drive, the superego, talk therapy), and some of the decade's most popular magazines—*True Confessions, Telling Tales,* and *True Story*—focused on Freud-inspired romance and sex. Likewise, the most popular female movie stars—Madge Bellamy, Clara Bow, and Joan Crawford—projected images of sensual freedom, rebellious energy, and feisty independence.

Traditionalists bristled at the scandalous behavior of rebellious young women. "One hears it said," lamented a Baptist magazine, "that the girls are actually tempting the boys more than the boys do the girls, by their dress and conversation."

Psychoanalysis, whose purpose is to explain activities in the mind, soon became the world's most celebrated—and controversial—technique for helping troubled people come to grips with the psychic demons haunting them by using "talk therapy"—getting patients to tell the story of their lives, inner frustrations, and repressed fears and urges. By 1916, there were some 500 psychoanalysts in New York City alone.

For many young Americans, Sigmund Freud seemed to provide scientific justification for rebelling against social conventions and indulging in sex. Some oversimplified his theories by claiming that sexual pleasure was essential for emotional health, that all forms of sexual activity were good, and that all inhibitions about sex were bad.

**MARGARET SANGER AND BIRTH CONTROL**  Perhaps the most controversial women's issue of the Jazz Age was birth control. Christians—both Protestants and Catholics—opposed it as a violation of God's law. Other crusaders viewed it differently.

Margaret Sanger, a nurse and midwife in the working-class tenements of Manhattan, saw many young mothers struggling to provide for their families. One of eleven children born to Irish immigrants, she herself had experienced the poverty often faced by large immigrant families. "Our childhood," she remembered, "was one of longing for things that were always denied."

In her work, Sanger witnessed the consequences of unwanted pregnancies, miscarriages, and amateur abortions. To her, the problems had an obvious solution: *birth control*, a term she and friends coined in 1914.

In 1911, Sanger and her husband joined the Socialist party, and their home became a gathering place for journalists, anarchists, labor leaders, and feminists. The party hired Sanger to promote women's suffrage, but she decided that birth control was more important to poor women than the vote. In 1912, she began to distribute birth-control information to working-class women and resolved to spend the rest of her life helping women gain control of their bodies. To do so, she began publishing a magazine called *Woman Rebel* in which she promoted women's suffrage, workers' rights, and contraception.

In 1916, Sanger was arrested and charged with disseminating obscenity

**Margaret Sanger**  The American sex educator, nurse, and birth control activist circa 1925.

through the mail, but the case was eventually dropped. She then opened the nation's first birth-control clinic, in Brooklyn, serving 464 clients before police shut it down.

In 1921, Sanger organized the American Birth Control League, which in 1942 would change its name to Planned Parenthood. The Birth Control League distributed information to doctors, social workers, women's clubs, the scientific community, and to thousands of women.

Sanger, however, alienated supporters of birth control by endorsing sterilization for the mentally incompetent and for people with certain hereditary conditions. Birth control, she stressed, was "the most constructive and necessary of the means to racial health."

Although Sanger did not succeed in legalizing the distribution of contraceptives and contraceptive information through the mail, she laid the foundation for such efforts. In 1936, a federal court ruled that physicians could prescribe contraceptives. Before Sanger died in 1966 at the age of eighty-seven, the U.S. Supreme Court, in *Griswold v. Connecticut* (1965), declared that women had a constitutional right to use contraceptives as a form of birth control.

THE "NEW WOMEN" New clothing fashions reflected the rebellion against traditional female roles in an especially powerful way. Emancipated "new women" seized the right to vote while discarding the confining wardrobe of their "frumpy" mothers—pinched-in corsets and choking girdles, layers of petticoats, and floor-length dresses. In 1919, skirt hems were typically six inches above the ground; by 1927, they were at the knee. The Utah legislature in 1921 debated a bill that would have jailed women wearing "skirts higher than three inches above the ankle."

The shortest skirts were worn by so-called **flappers**, impetuous young women eager to defy prevailing social conventions. F. Scott Fitzgerald defined the flappers (the name derived from the flapping sound made by the unfastened rubber galoshes they wore over their shoes in wet weather) as "young things with a splendid talent for living." Usually thin, long-legged, and precocious, flappers were daring pleasure-seekers who loved short dresses and plunging necklines while wearing minimal underclothing, gauzy fabrics, sheer stockings, dangling pearl necklaces, and plenty of makeup. They often joined young men in smoking cigarettes, drinking, gambling, and shaking and shimmying to the sensual energies of jazz music.

Flappers attracted enormous attention in part because they were both defiantly independent and desperately seductive. After interacting with flappers in New York City, British novelist Elinor Glyn asked: "Has the American girl no innate modesty—no sub-conscious self-respect, no reserve, no dignity?"

Others, however, embraced "flapperism." Charles W. Hoffman, a Cincinnati judge, celebrated the flapper for "standing on her own feet, with the right to be free from the pretentious mastery of men." When a Pennsylvania high school PTA met to pass restrictions on the behavior of student flappers, girls in the crowd shouted defiance: "I can show my shoulders, I can show my knees, I'm a free-born American, and can show what I please."

Flappers were hell-bent on defying traditional standards for women. They wanted more out of life than conventional marriage and motherhood. Their carefree feminism was fun-loving, self-indulgent, and often self-destructive.

The craziness of flappers shocked and scared observers. A Catholic priest in Brooklyn complained that the rebelliousness of young women

**The "new woman" of the 1920s**
Two risk-taking flappers dance atop the Hotel Sherman in Chicago.

during the 1920s had provoked a "pandemonium of powder, a riot of rouge, and a moral anarchy of dress."

**NOT SO NEW WOMEN** Most women in the 1920s were not flappers, however. Lillian Symes, a longtime activist, stressed that her "generation of feminists" had little in common with the "spike-heeled, over-rouged flapper of today." Although more middle-class women attended college in the 1920s than ever before, a higher percentage of them married soon after graduation than had been the case in the nineteenth century.

Women were discouraged from enrolling in coeducational colleges and universities, however. Male doctors warned that mixed-gender classrooms hindered childbearing potential in women by "forcing their blood to nourish their brain instead of their ovaries." Prolonged academic study made women "mannish."

The conservative political mood helped steer women who had worked for the war effort back into their traditional roles as homemakers, and college curricula began to shift accordingly. At Vassar College, an all-women's school outside New York City, students took domestic courses such as "Husband and Wife," "Motherhood," and "The Family as an Economic Unit."

At the same time, fewer college-educated women pursued careers outside the home. The proportion of physicians who were women fell during the twenties, and similar reductions occurred among dentists, architects, and chemists. A student at all-female Smith College in Massachusetts expressed frustration "that a woman must choose between a home and her work, when a man may have both. There must be a way out, and it is the problem of our generation to find the way."

As before, most women who worked outside the home labored in unskilled, low-paying jobs. Only 4 percent of working women were salaried professionals. Some moved into new vocations, such as accounting assistants and department-store clerks. The number of beauty shops soared from 5,000 in 1920 to 40,000 in 1930, creating jobs for hair stylists, manicurists, and cosmeticians.

The majority of women, however, remained either full-time wives and mothers or household servants. The growing availability of electricity and electrical appliances—vacuum cleaners, toasters, stoves, refrigerators, washing machines, irons—made housework easier. Likewise, "supermarkets" offered year-round access to fruits, vegetables, and meats, which greatly reduced the traditional tasks of food preparation—canning, baking bread, and plucking chickens.

African American and Latino women faced the greatest challenges. As a New York City newspaper observed, they did the "work which white women will not do." Women of color usually worked as maids, laundresses, or seamstresses, or on farms.

**THE COLOR LINE** Racism also continued to limit the freedom of women. For example, in 1919, an interracial couple from Ayer, Massachusetts, Mabel Puffer, a wealthy college graduate, and Arthur Hazzard, a handyman, decided to get married in Concord, New Hampshire. They checked into separate rooms in a hotel, then walked three blocks to the courthouse to apply for a marriage license, only to be told that there was a five-day waiting period. So they waited and made preparations for the wedding. The mayor of Concord agreed to perform the service.

When news of the interracial couple strolling the streets of Concord reached the Boston newspapers, the headline in the *Boston Traveller* read: "Will Marry Negro in 'Perfect Union': Rich Ayer Society Woman Determined to Wed Servant Although Hometown Is Aflame with Protest." The news outraged many residents of Ayer. The next day, the *Boston Evening Globe* ran the now provocative story on its front page. The headline was sensational: "Hope to Prevent White Woman Wedding Negro: Two Friends of Mabel E. Puffer Have Gone to Concord, N.H."

Suddenly, the mayor of Concord announced he could not perform the wedding. The betrothed couple, after being turned down several times, finally found a minister willing to marry them. But the night before the wedding, the Ayer police chief arrested Hazzard on a charge of "enticement" and took Puffer into custody because she had been deemed "insane." The nation that Woodrow Wilson had led into war to "make the world safe for democracy" remained an unsafe place for those bold enough to cross the color line.

## African American Life

The most significant development in African American life during the early twentieth century was the **Great Migration** northward from the South. The mass movement accelerated in 1915–1916, when rapidly expanding war industries needed new workers. It continued throughout the twenties, as almost a million African Americans, mostly sharecroppers, boarded trains bound for what they called the "promised land" up north.

Many landed in large cities—New York City, Chicago, Detroit, Cleveland, Washington, D.C., Philadelphia, and others—producing dramatic social, economic, and political changes. In 1900, only 740,000 African Americans lived outside the South, just 8 percent of the nation's black population. By 1970, more than 10.6 million African Americans lived outside the South, 47 percent of the nation's total.

They were lured by what writer Richard Wright called the "warmth of other suns"—better living conditions and better-paying jobs. In the North, for the most part, they were able to speak more freely and were treated better than in the South, although not equally, and educational opportunities for children were much better. Collectively, blacks gained more political leverage by settling in populous states like New York, Pennsylvania, Ohio, and Illinois, with many electoral votes. The political effects of the Great Migration were evident in 1928 when a Chicago Republican, Oscar De Priest, became the first black elected to Congress since Reconstruction and the first ever from a northern district.

The difficult decision to leave their native South ended one set of troubles but created others. "Never in history," said Richard Wright, "has a more utterly unprepared folk wanted to go to the city." They were strangers in a strange land, and they were not always welcomed. In densely populated northern cities, blacks who moved into established neighborhoods sometimes clashed with local ethnic groups, especially Irish and Italians who feared that the newcomers would take their jobs. Many southern blacks, ignorant of city ways, were taken advantage of by white landlords, realtors, and bankers; they were often forced into substandard and segregated housing and were paid lower wages than whites.

But northern discrimination still paled beside the injustices of the segregated South. "If all of their dream does not come true," a black newspaper in Chicago stressed, "enough will come to pass to justify their actions." Black poet Langston Hughes spoke for many when he wrote that he was "fed up / With Jim Crow laws, / People who are cruel / And afraid, / Who lynch and run, / Who are scared of me / And me of them." Over time, the transplanted African Americans built new lives, new churches, new communities, new families, even new cultures.

**THE NAACP** The mass migration of southern blacks northward helped spur the creation of the **National Association for the Advancement of Colored People (NAACP)**, founded in 1910 by African American activists and white progressives. W. E. B. Du Bois became the organization's director of publicity and research and editor of its journal, *The Crisis.*

The NAACP focused its political strategy on legal action to bring the Fourteenth and Fifteenth Amendments back to life. One early victory came with *Guinn v. United States* (1915), in which the Supreme Court struck down Oklahoma's efforts to deprive African Americans of the vote. In *Buchanan v. Warley* (1917), the Court invalidated a residential segregation ordinance in Louisville, Kentucky. In 1919, the NAACP launched a national campaign against lynching. An anti-lynching bill to make mob murder a federal crime passed the House in 1922 but was defeated by southerners in the Senate.

**THE HARLEM RENAISSANCE** So many African Americans converged in New York City during the twenties that they inspired the **Harlem Renaissance**, the nation's first black literary and artistic movement. It started in the community of Harlem in northern Manhattan. In 1890, one in seventy people in Manhattan had been African American; by 1930, it was one in nine.

The "great, dark city" of Harlem, in poet Langston Hughes's phrase, contained more blacks per square mile than any urban neighborhood in the nation. Their numbers generated a sense of common identity, power, and distinctive self-expression that transformed Harlem into the cultural capital of African American life. Writer James Weldon Johnson described "Black Manhattan" as a "typically Negro" community of 175,000 in that it featured "movement, color, gaiety, singing, dancing, boisterous laughter, and loud talk."

Dotted with lively taverns, lounges, supper clubs, dance halls, and saloons ("speakeasies") where writers and painters listened to jazz and drank illegal booze, Harlem became what journalists called the "Nightclub Capital of the World." Hughes explained that Harlem writers and artists were ready "to express our individual dark-skinned selves without fear or shame. If white people are pleased, we are glad. If they are not, it doesn't matter. We know we are beautiful. And ugly too."

In poetry and prose, Harlem Renaissance writers celebrated African American culture, especially jazz and the blues, which featured deep emotional roots in black history. As Hughes wrote, "I am a Negro—and beautiful. . . . The night is beautiful. So [are] the faces of

***Into Bondage*** This painting by Aaron Douglas exemplifies how black artists in the Harlem Renaissance used their African roots and collective history as inspiration.

my people." But while Hughes loved Africa and its cultural heritage, his outlook emphatically "was not Africa. I was [shaped by] Chicago and Kansas City and Broadway and Harlem."

Women were active in the Harlem Renaissance. In January 1925, a thirty-four-year-old African American woman named Zora Neale Hurston arrived in Harlem from Eatonville, an all-black community in rural central Florida. An aspiring writer and inventive storyteller, she became the first African American to enroll at Barnard College, the woman's college of Columbia University, where she majored in cultural anthropology.

Hurston had mastered the art of survival by learning to reinvent herself as the need arose. Motherless at nine and a runaway at fourteen, she became a calculating opportunist blessed with remarkable willpower. She came to Harlem to immerse herself in the "clang and clamor" of city life.

Within a few months, Hurston was behaving, in her words, as the queen of the Harlem Renaissance, writing short stories and plays about the "Negro furthest down" while positioning herself at the center of the community's raucous social life. Her outspokenness invited controversy, as when she claimed that she "did not belong to the sobbing school of Negrohood who hold that nature somehow has given them a lowdown dirty deal and whose feelings are all hurt about it." Hurston went on to become an anthropologist, folklorist, and novelist, expert at describing the ways in which African Americans in the Lower South forged cohesive communities in the face of white bigotry and violence. She also spoke out on behalf of poor African Americans who, "having nothing, still refused to be humble."

By 1930, Harlem Renaissance writers had produced dozens of novels and volumes of poetry, several Broadway plays, and a flood of short stories, essays, and films. A people capable of producing such great art and literature, Johnson declared, should never again be "looked upon as inferior."

**GARVEYISM** The celebration of black culture found much different expression in what came to be called **black nationalism**, which promoted black separatism from mainstream American life. Its leader was Marcus Garvey, who claimed to speak for all 400 million blacks worldwide. In 1916, Garvey brought to Harlem the headquarters of the Universal Negro Improvement Association (UNIA), which he had started in his native Jamaica two years before.

Garvey insisted that blacks had *nothing* in common with whites and called for racial separation. "The black skin," he stressed, "is not a badge of shame, but rather a glorious symbol of national greatness." Garvey urged African Americans to cultivate black solidarity and "black power."

The UNIA quickly became the largest black political organization in U.S. history. By 1923, Garvey claimed the UNIA had as many as 4 million members served by 800 offices. His goal was to build an all-black empire in Africa. To that end, he called himself the "Provisional President of Africa," raised funds to send Americans to Africa, and expelled any UNIA member who married a white.

**Marcus Garvey** The Jamaican-born founder of the Universal Negro Improvement Association and leading spokesman for "Negro nationalism" in the 1920s.

Garvey's message of black nationalism and racial solidarity appealed especially to poor blacks in northern cities, but he also had supporters across the rural South. Garveyism, however, appalled some black leaders. W. E. B. Du Bois labeled Garvey "the most dangerous enemy of the Negro race. . . . He is either a lunatic or a traitor." An African American newspaper pledged to help "drive Garvey and Garveyism in all its sinister viciousness from the American soil."

Garvey's crusade collapsed in 1923 when he was convicted of fraud for overselling shares of stock in a steamship corporation, the Black Star Line, which he had founded to transport American blacks to Africa. Sentenced to five years in prison, he was pardoned in 1927 by President Calvin Coolidge on the condition that he be deported to Jamaica. Upon arrival there, he received a hero's welcome. Garvey died in obscurity in 1940, but the memory of his movement kept alive an undercurrent that would re-emerge in the 1960s under the slogan "black power."

# THE MODERNIST REVOLT

During the twenties, a cultural civil war erupted between modernists eager to "make it new" and traditionalists anchored in what experimental poet Ezra Pound called "a botched civilization." Modernists were intellectuals, writers, and artists who used new modes of expression and behavior to illustrate that they were living in an era of confusion and possibility that demanded new ways of thinking and behaving. They saw the start of the twentieth century as a historical hinge opening the way for a new world view that rejected conventional notions of reality and values (progress, reason, and even God).

The modernists adopted radical new forms of artistic expression. In 1922, Irish modernist James Joyce published his pathbreaking novel *Ulysses,* and Anglo-American poet T. S. Eliot wrote "The Waste Land," in which he claimed to speak for a postwar culture in crisis.

Critics charged that Eliot, Joyce, and other self-described modernists were "ruining" literature. Modernists fought back, claiming that they were simply acknowledging the arrival of an unsettling new way of viewing life and expressing its raucous energies.

## ALBERT EINSTEIN

During a century remarkable for its disorienting discoveries and technological advances, one modernist genius stands out: Albert Einstein, who precipitated a fundamental change in understanding the operations of the universe. In

1905, the German-born Einstein, then a twenty-six-year-old physicist working in Switzerland, published several papers that changed science forever while at times defying common sense.

The first paper, which would earn him the Nobel Prize in 1921, revealed that nothing could travel faster than light and that light was not simply a wave of continuous energy but a stream of tiny particles, called *quanta* (now called *photons*). This breakthrough would provide the theoretical basis for quantum physics and lead to new electronic technologies such as television, laser beams, and semiconductors used to make computers and cell phones.

In his second research paper, Einstein confirmed the existence of molecules and atoms by showing how their random collisions explained the jerky motions of minute particles in water.

Einstein's third paper overturned traditional notions of the universe by introducing his special theory of relativity, which explains that no matter how fast one is moving toward or away from a source of light, the speed of that light beam will appear the same, a constant 186,000 miles per second. Space and time, however, will appear relative to the speed of light. So if a train were traveling at the speed of light, time would slow down from the perspective of those watching, and the train itself would get shorter and heavier. Space and time, in other words, are not independent of one another. They instead form the fabric of space-time within which matter resides.

It took Einstein ten more years to devise a *general theory of relativity*. It maintains that the fundamental concepts of space, time, matter, and energy are not distinct, independent entities with stable and permanent dimensions, as Sir Isaac Newton had assumed in the eighteenth century. Instead, they are interacting elements constantly changing one another.

Einstein's discoveries revolutionized the way scientists perceived the universe. A British newspaper said the general theory of relativity was "one of the most momentous . . . pronouncements of human thought."

## MODERNIST ART AND LITERATURE

The scientific breakthroughs associated with Sigmund Freud, Albert Einstein, and others helped to inspire and shape a "modernist" cultural revolution. **Modernism** as a movement appeared first in the capitals of Europe in the 1890s. By the second decade of the twentieth century, cultural modernism had spread to the United States.

Put most simply, modernism was the widespread awareness that new ideas and ways of doing things were making a sharp break with tradition, and that new technologies, modes of transportation and communication, and scientific discoveries were transforming the nature of everyday life and the way people "saw" the world.

The horrors of the Great War accelerated and expanded the appeal of modernism. To be modern was to take chances, violate artistic rules and moral restrictions, and behave in deliberately shocking ways. "Art," said a modernist painter, "is meant to disturb."

Modernism was loosely based on three unsettling assumptions: (1) God did not exist; (2) reality was not rational, orderly, or obvious; and, in the aftermath of the Great War, (3) social progress could no longer be taken for granted. These premises led writers, artists, musicians, designers, and architects to rebel against good taste, old-fashioned morals, and old-time religion.

***Russian Ballet*** **(1916)** Jewish American artist Max Weber's painting is a modernist take on a traditional subject. Splicing the scene of the performance into overlapping planes of jarring colors, this painting exemplifies the impact of psychoanalysis and the theory of relativity on the arts.

Modernists refused to be conventional. Poet Ezra Pound, a militant propagandist for the modernist movement, believed that he and other cultural rebels were "saving civilization" from the dictatorship of tradition: "We are restarting civilization."

Like many previous cultural movements, modernism involved a fresh way of *seeing* the world, led by a new intellectual and cultural elite determined to capture and express the hidden realm of imagination and dreams. Doing so, however, often made their writing, art, music, and dance difficult to understand, interpret, or explain. "The pure modernist is merely a snob," explained a British writer.

But for many modernists, being misunderstood was a badge of honor. American experimentalist writer Gertrude Stein, for example, declared that a novel "which tells about what happens is of no interest." Instead of depicting real life or telling recognizable stories, she was interested in playing with language. Words, not people, are the characters in her writings.

Until the twentieth century, most writers and artists had taken for granted an identifiable real world that could be readily observed, scientifically explained, and accurately represented in words or paint or even music. Modernists, however, applied Einstein's ideas about relativity to a world in which reality no longer had an objective or recognizable basis. They agreed with Freud that reality was an intensely inward and subjective experience— something deeply personal that was to be imagined and expressed by one's innermost being. Walter Pach, an early champion of modern art, explained that modernism resulted from the discovery of "the role played by the unconscious in our lives."

**THE ARMORY SHOW** The crusade to bring European-inspired modernism to the United States reached a climax in the **Armory Show** of 1913, the most scandalous event in the history of American art. Mabel Dodge, one of the organizers, wrote to Gertrude Stein that the exhibition would cause "a riot and revolution and things will never be the same afterwards."

The Armory Show, officially known as the International Exhibition of Modern Art, opened February 17, 1913, in the vast 69th Army Regiment Armory in New York City. It featured 1,200 works and created an immediate sensation. One prominent critic grumbled that modernism "is nothing else than the total destruction of the art of painting." The *New York Times* warned visitors that they would enter "a stark region of abstractions" at the "lunatic asylum" show that was "hideous to our unaccustomed eyes."

The experimentalist ("avant-garde") artists whose works were on display (including painters Vincent Van Gogh, Paul Gauguin, Henri Matisse, Paul Cezanne, and Picasso) were "in love with science but not with objective reality," the *Times* critic complained, and had produced paintings "revolting in their inhumanity." Former president Theodore Roosevelt dismissed the show as "repellent from every standpoint."

Yet it also generated excitement. "A new world has arisen before our eyes," announced an art magazine. "To miss modern art," a critic stressed, "is to miss one of the few thrills that life holds." From New York, the show went to Chicago and Boston, where it aroused similar responses and attracted overflow crowds.

After the Armory Show, many people discovered a new faith in the disturbing powers of art. "America in spite of its newness," predicted Walt Kuhn, a painter who helped organize the exhibition, "is destined to become the coming center" of modernism. Indeed, the Museum of Modern Art, founded in New York City in 1929, came to house the world's most celebrated collection of avant-garde paintings and sculpture.

**POUND, ELIOT, AND STEIN** The leading American champions of modern art and literature lived in England and Europe: Idaho-born Ezra Pound and St. Louis–born T. S. Eliot in London, and Californian Gertrude

Stein in Paris. They were self-conscious revolutionaries concerned with creating strange, new, and often beautifully difficult forms of expression, and they found more inspiration and more receptive audiences in Europe.

As the foreign editor of the Chicago-based *Poetry* magazine, Pound became the cultural impresario of modernism. In bitter poems and earnest essays denouncing war and commercialism, he displayed an uncompromising urgency to transform the literary landscape. An English poet called him a "solitary volcano." Eliot claimed that Pound was single-handedly responsible for the modernist movement in poetry.

Pound recruited, edited, published, and reviewed the best among the modernist writers, improving their writing, bolstering their courage, and propelling their careers. In his own poetry, he expressed the feeling of many that the Great War had wasted a generation of young men who died in defense of a "botched civilization."

One of the young American writers Pound took under his wing was Eliot, who had recently graduated from Harvard. Within a few years, Eliot surpassed Pound to become the leading American modernist.

Eliot's epic 433-line poem *The Waste Land* (1922), which Pound edited, became a monument of modernism. It expressed a sense of postwar disillusionment and melancholy that had a powerful effect on other writers. As a poet and critic for the *Criterion,* a poetry journal he founded in 1922, Eliot became the arbiter of modernist taste in Anglo-American literature.

Gertrude Stein was the self-appointed champion of the American modernists living in Paris. Long regarded as simply the literary eccentric who wrote, "Rose is a rose is a rose is a rose," Stein was in fact one of the chief promoters of the triumphant subjectivity undergirding modernist expression. She sought to capture in words the equivalent of abstract painting and its self-conscious revolt against portraying recognizable scenes from real life. Stein hosted a cultural salon in Paris that became a gathering place for American and European modernists.

**THE "LOST GENERATION"**    The arts and literature of the twenties were also greatly influenced by the dreadfulness of the Great War. F. Scott Fitzgerald wrote in *This Side of Paradise* that the "sad young men" who had fought to "make the world safe for democracy" had "grown up to find all Gods dead, all wars fought, all faiths in man shaken."

Cynicism had supposedly displaced idealism in the wake of the war's horrific senselessness. Frederic Henry, a character in Ernest Hemingway's novel *A Farewell to Arms* (1929), declares that "abstract words such as *glory, honor, courage* . . . were obscene" in the context of the war's colossal casualties.

Hemingway, Fitzgerald, and other young modernists were labeled the **Lost Generation**—those who had lost faith in the values and institutions of Western civilization and were frantically looking for new gods to worship. In 1921, Gertrude Stein told Hemingway that he and his dissolute friends who had served in the war as soldiers or ambulance drivers "are a lost generation." When Hemingway objected, she held her ground. "You are [lost]. You have no respect for anything. You drink yourselves to death."

In his first novel, *The Sun Also Rises* (1926), Hemingway used the phrase "lost generation" in the book's opening quotation. The novel centers on Jake Barnes, a young American castrated by a war injury. His impotence leads him to wander the cafes and nightclubs of postwar Europe with his often-drunk friends, who acknowledge that they are all wounded and sterile in their own way. They have lost their innocence, their illusions, and their motivation to do anything with their lives.

Hemingway sought "in all my stories to get the feeling of the actual life across—not just to depict life—but to actually make it alive. So that when you have read something by me you actually experience the thing."

Hemingway's friend and rival, Fitzgerald, shared a similar goal. He was the self-appointed chronicler of the Lost Generation. Like his fictional characters, Fitzgerald blazed up brilliantly, delighted in the hard-drinking, party-going pace of the Jazz Age, and then flickered out in a fog of drunkenness. (He would die in 1940 at age forty-four.) A fellow writer called Fitzgerald "our darling, our genius, our fool." He used his writings to depict the frivolity of the "upper tenth" of American society and to reveal his own shortcomings and failures, guilt and shame.

In 1924, while drafting *The Great Gatsby*, Fitzgerald announced his intention to "write a novel better than any novel ever written in America." The novel dealt with the misfortunes of the fortunate: self-indulgent and self-destructive wealthy people who drank and partied as a means of medicating themselves to the pointlessness of their shallow lives.

What gave depth to the best of Fitzgerald's stories was what a character in *The Great Gatsby* called "a sense of the fundamental decencies" amid all the superficial merriment and fanatical materialism—and a sense of impending doom in a world that had lost its meaning through the disorienting discoveries of modern science and the horrors of war.

Just six months after the stock market crashed in October 1929, Zelda Fitzgerald experienced the first of several nervous breakdowns triggered by schizophrenia and punctuated by attempted suicide. She and Scott, drinking heavily and fighting viciously, experienced the "crack up" of their hopes and sanity at the same time that the world careened into the Great Depression.

The gaiety of the Jazz Age, F. Scott Fitzgerald noted, "leaped to a spectacular death in October 1929," with the collapse of the stock market. In 1931, he recalled that the Roaring Twenties "was an age of miracles, an age of art, it was an age of excess, and it was an age of satire." It "bore him up, flattered him and gave him more money than he had dreamed of, simply for telling people that he felt as they did, that something had to be done with all the nervous energy stored up and unexpended in the War."

To be sure, the twenties roared only for a small group of affluent Americans, but those years involved something soon inconceivable—the belief in freedom at all costs; freedom for the sake of nothing but the enjoyment of one's freedom; freedom that endowed life with vitality, ingenuity, and openness to new experience that had defined the American myth since colonial days.

The title of one of Fitzgerald's earliest novels seemed to have predicted the collapse of the Jazz Age and all of its hollowness and aimlessness. It was called *The Beautiful and the Damned* (1922).

# CHAPTER REVIEW

## SUMMARY

- **A "New Era" of Consumerism**  The American economy grew at its fastest rate in history during the 1920s, led by an explosion in mass production and sales of new consumer goods. Innovations in production, advertising, and financing, and a sharp rise in the use of electricity, enabled and encouraged millions of Americans to purchase automobiles, radios, and other electrical appliances. Ford Motor Company pioneered mass production using moving assembly lines, a highly efficient method that helped make its cars affordable for a majority of Americans. The new *consumer culture* valued leisure, self-expression, and self-indulgence. During the twenties, consumer debt tripled. Innovations in communications (especially the growth in radio ownership), transportation, finance, and advertising also brought about a mass culture, as more and more Americans purchased national brand-name items from retail chain stores, listened to the same radio shows, watched the same movies, and followed the lives and careers of national celebrities and superstars.

- **The "Jazz Age"**  Other new social and cultural trends and movements rapidly challenged the traditional order. The carefree fads and attitudes of the 1920s, perhaps best represented by the frantic rhythms of jazz music, led writer F. Scott Fitzgerald to call the decade the *Jazz Age*. A "new woman" appeared, best represented by *flappers*—impetuous young women eager to define their own identity by challenging prewar restrictions with their short hemlines, drinking, smoking, and open discussions of sex. The majority of women, however, remained full-time housewives and mothers or domestic servants, and fewer young women pursued professional careers. With the *Great Migration* continuing, African Americans in northern cities felt freer to speak out against racial injustice and express pride in their race. The *Harlem Renaissance* movement gave voice to African American literature and music. Racial separatism and *black nationalism* grew popular under the leadership of Marcus Garvey, while other African Americans joined white supporters in the *National Association for the Advancement of Colored People (NAACP)* and supported its efforts to undo racism through education, legislation, and court challenges.

- **The Modernist Revolt**  Some American artists and intellectuals alienated by the horrors of the Great War and the collapse of many traditional ideals coalesced into what was called the *Lost Generation*. Others were attracted to *modernism*, a movement that had begun in Europe before the Great War and reflected new developments in science, particularly Albert Einstein's theory of relativity and Sigmund Freud's exploration of how the subconscious mind shapes human behavior. To be "modern" meant to break free of tradition, violate restrictions, shock the public, and make one's works difficult to explain or interpret. Americans were first exposed to modern art in a substantial way with the *Armory Show* of 1913.

970

# CHRONOLOGY

| | |
|---|---|
| **1903** | Wright Brothers fly first motorized airplane |
| | Ford Motor Company is founded |
| **1910** | National Association for the Advancement of Colored People (NAACP) is founded |
| **1913** | Armory Show introduces Americans to modern art |
| **1916** | Marcus Garvey brings Universal Negro Improvement Association to New York |
| **1920** | Prohibition begins |
| | F. Scott Fitzgerald's *This Side of Paradise* is published |
| | Warren G. Harding is elected president |
| **1921** | Albert Einstein receives Nobel Prize in physics |
| **1922** | First radio commercial is aired |
| **1927** | Charles A. Lindbergh Jr. makes first solo transatlantic airplane flight |

## KEY TERMS

**consumer culture** p. 944

**Jazz Age** p. 952

**flappers** p. 956

**Great Migration** p. 959

**National Association for the Advancement of Colored People (NAACP)** p. 960

**Harlem Renaissance** p. 960

**black nationalism** p. 962

**modernism** p. 964

**Armory Show** p. 966

**Lost Generation** p. 968

 **INQUIZITIVE**

Go to InQuizitive to see what you've learned—and learn what you've missed—with personalized feedback along the way.

# 24 The Reactionary Twenties

**Black Tuesday** In this photograph, crowds panicked by the news of the plummeting stock market take to Wall Street on the morning of Tuesday, October 29, 1929. An account of the crash in the *New York Times* reported that "the streets were crammed with a mixed crowd—agonized little speculators, . . . sold-out traders, . . . inquisitive individuals and tourists seeking . . . a closer view of the national catastrophe. . . . Where was it going to end?"

The self-indulgent excesses of the Lost Generation and the frivolities associated with the Jazz Age made little sense to most Americans during the twenties. They were not disillusioned, self-destructive, or defiantly modernist. Most people still led traditional lives; they aggressively defended established values, old certainties, and the comfort of past routines, and they were shocked by the decade's social turmoil and cultural rebelliousness.

In national politics, the small-town backlash against modern city life—whether represented by immigrants plotting revolution, liberal churches embracing evolution, or jazzed-up flappers swilling cocktails—mirrored Republican efforts to reverse the progressivism of Theodore Roosevelt and Woodrow Wilson.

By 1920, the progressive political coalition that had reelected Wilson in 1916 had fragmented. The growing middle class had become preoccupied less with reform than with enjoying America's economic prosperity, the outcome of increased mass production, mass consumption, and labor-saving electrical appliances.

Many Americans traced the germs of dangerous radicalism (the Red Scare) to cities teeming with immigrants and foreign ideas such as socialism, communism, anarchism, and labor union militancy. Others feared the erosion of traditional religious beliefs in the face of secular modernism. People were convinced that dangers from abroad and at home must be vigorously resisted. This reactionary conservatism of the 1920s fed on the popularity of **nativism**—the prejudice against immigrants from countries outside of

## focus questions

**1.** How did the reactionary conservatism during the 1920s manifest itself in social life and governmental policies?

**2.** To what extent did the policies of the Republican party dominate the federal government during the twenties? In what ways were these policies a rejection of progressivism?

**3.** What were the major causes of the Great Depression?

**4.** How did the Great Depression impact the American people?

**5.** In what ways did Hoover fail to address the human distress caused by the Great Depression?

western Europe—and a militant Protestantism that sought to restore the primacy of traditional Christian morality.

## REACTIONARY CONSERVATISM AND IMMIGRATION RESTRICTION

After the end of the Great War, masses of people emigrated from Europe to the United States. Between 1919 and 1924, more than 600,000 people from southern and eastern Europe, most of them Italians, entered the United States, along with 150,000 Poles and 50,000 Russians. At the same time, some 150,000 Mexicans crossed the border; most settling in the Southwest and California. In the early 1920s, more than half of the white men and a third of the white women working in mines, mills, and factories were immigrants. Some had retained a passion for socialism or anarchism—as well as a willingness to use violence to achieve their political goals.

Nativists alarmed by the surge in immigration realized the literacy test added in 1917 was not excluding enough newcomers, for between 1920 and 1921 some 1,235,000 foreigners entered the United States. Fears of an invasion of foreign radicals led Congress to pass the Emergency Immigration Act of 1921, which limited *total* immigration to 150,000 a year and restricted newcomers from each European country to 3 percent of the total number of that nationality represented in the 1910 census.

Three years later, Congress responded to complaints that too many eastern and southern Europeans were still being admitted by passing the **Immigration**

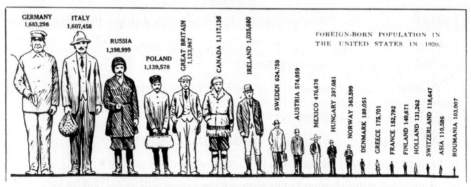

**Immigration Act of 1924** This immigration chart illustrates the nationalities of the foreign-born population in the United States in 1920, which formed the basis of the quota system introduced in the Johnson-Reed Act.

**Act of 1924** (the Johnson-Reed Act). The bill, set to take effect in 1929, reduced the number ("quota") of visas from 3 to 2 percent of the total number of people of each nationality in the United States as of the 1890 rather than the 1910 national census, since there were far fewer eastern and southern Europeans in the nation in 1890. It also banned most immigrants from Asia.

The purpose of placing a numerical ceiling or quota on immigrants was to shrink the total number of newcomers, to favor immigrants from northern and western Europe, and to reduce those from southern and eastern Europe, especially Jews, Italians, Poles, Turks, and Russians. The intent was openly racist. Congressman Fred S. Purnell of Indiana urged legislators to stop the "stream of irresponsible and broken wreckage that is pouring into the life-blood of America the social and political diseases of the Old World."

President Calvin Coolidge agreed. "America," he emphasized, "must be kept for Americans." He readily signed the immigration restriction bill, which remained in force until 1965. Its impact was immediate. Under the quota system, more than 50,000 Germans could enter the nation annually, while fewer than 4,000 Italians were allowed, compared to the more than 2 million Italians who had arrived between 1910 and 1920. Not even Adolf Hitler's persecution of Jews could persuade Congress to raise the quota for Europeans.

The Immigration Act of 1924, however, placed no quota on immigrants from countries in the Western Hemisphere, particularly Mexico. Responding to the lobbying efforts of railroads and commercial farm owners in the West, Congress sought to ensure an adequate supply of low-paid Latino laborers from Mexico, Puerto Rico, and Cuba. An unintended result of the 1924 immigration act was that people of Latin American descent became the fastest-growing ethnic minority during the twenties.

**SACCO AND VANZETTI** The nativism embedded in the new immigration laws reinforced the connection between European immigrants and political radicalism. That connection erupted in the most widely publicized criminal case of the twenties.

On May 5, 1920, two Italian immigrants who described themselves as revolutionary anarchists eager to topple the American government were arrested outside Boston, Massachusetts. Shoemaker Nicola Sacco and fish peddler Bartolomeo Vanzetti were accused of stealing $16,000 from a shoe factory and killing the paymaster and a guard. Both men were armed with loaded pistols when arrested, both lied to the police, and both were identified by eyewitnesses. The stolen money, however, was never found, and several people claimed that they were with Sacco and Vanzetti far from the scene of the crime when it occurred.

The **Sacco and Vanzetti case** occurred at the height of Italian immigration to the United States and against the backdrop of numerous terror attacks by anarchists, some of which Sacco and Vanzetti had participated in. The charged atmosphere, called "the Red hysteria" by one journalist, ensured that the men's trial would be a public spectacle.

In July 1921, Sacco and Vanzetti were convicted and sentenced to death. Their legal appeals lasted six years before they were electrocuted on August 23, 1927, still claiming innocence. To millions around the world, they were victims of capitalist injustice. People still debate their guilt or innocence.

**THE NEW KLAN** The most violent of the reactionary conservative movements during the twenties was a revived Ku Klux Klan, the infamous post–Civil War group of racists that had re-created itself in 1915. By 1920, the Invisible Empire of the Knights of the Ku Klux Klan was a *nationwide* organization devoted to "the maintenance of White Supremacy" and "100 percent Americanism." Only "natives"—meaning white, "Anglo-Saxon," evangelical Protestants born in the United States—could be members. At its peak in 1924, the new Klan numbered more than 4 million members, making it the largest far-right movement in history. (It is no coincidence that 1924 was the same year

**Ku Klux Klan rally** In 1925, the KKK marched down Pennsylvania Avenue in Washington, D.C.

in which numerous states erected memorial statues celebrating Confederate generals such as Robert E. Lee.)

Klan leader Hiram Wesley Evans explained that the organization embodied "an idea, a faith, a purpose, an organized crusade" against "that which is corrupting and destroying the best in American life." It embraced militant patriotism, restrictions on immigration and voting, and strict personal morality. It opposed illegal ("bootleg") liquor and labor unions and preached hatred against African Americans, Roman Catholics, Jews, immigrants, Communists, atheists, prostitutes, and adulterers.

The Klan became infamous for its blanket assaults on various categories of Americans. In the Southwest, Klansmen directed their anger at Mexicans; in the Pacific Northwest, Japanese people were the enemy; in New York, the targets were primarily Jews and Catholics. Klan members were elected governor in Oregon, Texas, and Colorado; others were mayors in Portland, Oregon, and Portland, Maine. The Klan became so "respectable" in the eyes of many that none of the presidents during the twenties—Wilson, Coolidge, or Hoover—spoke out against it.

White-robed bigotry also became big business. Members of local "klaverns" paid a $10 initiation fee and $5 in annual dues; they were required to buy an official Klan robe, a pointed hood, and other accessories. Protestant ministers received free membership. Whole families attended Klan gatherings, "klasping" hands while listening to violent speeches, watching fireworks, and burning crosses.

In Texas, Klan members used harassment, intimidation (often in the form of burning crosses), beatings, and "tar and feathers" to discipline alcoholics, gamblers, adulterers, and other sinners. In the spring of 1922 alone, the Dallas Klan flogged sixty-eight men.

The reborn Klan grew rapidly, especially in the rural Midwest. During the twenties, 40 percent of its "Anglo-Saxon" members were in three midwestern states: Illinois, Indiana, and Ohio. Only 16 percent were in the former Confederate states. Recruiters, called Kleagles, were told to "play upon whatever prejudices were most acute in a particular area."

Most Klan members were small farmers, sharecroppers, or wage workers, but the organization also attracted clergymen, engineers, doctors, lawyers, accountants, business leaders, and teachers. Defying class lines, Klan membership grew to include judges, mayors, sheriffs, state legislators, six governors, and three U.S. senators. In 1924, the Klan mobilized to lobby Congress for tighter restrictions on immigration, especially with regard to Asians, Jews, and Roman Catholics.

David C. Stephenson, the Grand Dragon of Indiana and a sly con man, became so influential in electing local and state officials (the "kluxing" of America, as he called it) that he boasted, "I am the law in Indiana!" Klan-endorsed candidates won the Indiana governorship and controlled the state legislature.

At the 1924 Republican State Convention, Stephenson patrolled the aisles with a pistol. He later confessed that he "purchased the county and state officials." Stephenson, who had grown wealthy by skimming from the dues he collected from Klan members as well as selling robes and hoods, planned to run for president.

In August 1925, some 25,000 Klansmen paraded down Pennsylvania Avenue in the nation's capital, dressed in their white-hooded regalia. The Klan's influence began to crumble, however, after Stephenson was arrested and sentenced to life in prison in 1925 for kidnapping, raping, and mutilating a twenty-eight-year-old female staff member, who then committed suicide.

Stephenson assumed the governor would pardon him. When that did not happen, he told police about the widespread political bribery he had engaged in. As a result, the governor, the Indianapolis mayor, the county sheriff, congressmen, and other officeholders were indicted. Many ended up in prison.

News of the scandal caused Klan membership to tumble. More than a dozen Klan offices and meeting places across the country were bombed, burned, or blasted by shotguns. Several states passed anti-Klan laws, and others banned the wearing of masks and burning of crosses. By 1930, nationwide Klan membership had dwindled to 100,000, mostly southerners.

Yet the impulse underlying the Klan lived on, fed by deep-seated fears and hatreds that have yet to disappear. On Memorial Day in 1927, a throng of 1,000 white-robed Klansmen paraded through the Jamaica neighborhood in Queens, a borough of New York City. A confrontation with police grew into a brawl, and six Klansmen were arrested. Another "berobed" man was jailed for "refusing to disperse," although the charge was later dropped. His name was Fred C. Trump, who later would father a son named Donald, a future president.

## FUNDAMENTALISM

While the Klan fought against what they viewed as the nation's "growing immorality" and the "alien menace," they also defended "old-time religion" against dangerous ideas circulating in progressive or liberal Protestant churches. The most threatening of those ideas were that the Bible was not literally the word of God and that Charles Darwin's theories of biological evolution were true.

Conservative Protestants embraced a militant fundamentalism, distinctive for its hostility toward such liberal beliefs and its insistence on the literal truth of the Bible.

The result was a religious civil war that divided congregations and entire denominations. A burst of Protestant fundamentalism swept the country, largely as a conservative reaction to the spread of modernism in mainline Protestantism, which sought to accommodate Christian teaching with modern science.

In a famous 1922 sermon titled "Shall the Fundamentalists Win?" Harry Emerson Fosdick, the progressive pastor at New York City's First Presbyterian Church, dismissed biblical fundamentalism as "immeasurable folly." The Bible, he explained, was not literally the "word of God" but a representation of God's wonders. Christianity had nothing to fear from Darwinian evolution or modern science, he argued, for liberal Christianity "saves us from the necessity of apologizing for immature states in the development of the biblical revelation." Fosdick, an outspoken critic of racism and social injustice, outraged fundamentalists, who launched an effort to "try" him for heresy. He decided to resign instead.

Among national leaders, however, only the "Great Commoner," William Jennings Bryan, the former Democratic congressman, secretary of state, and three-time presidential candidate, had the support, prestige, and eloquence to transform fundamentalism into a popular crusade. Bryan was a strange bird, a liberal progressive and pacifist Populist in politics and a right-wing religious crusader who believed in the literal Bible.

Bryan supported new state laws banning the teaching of evolution in public schools. He passionately condemned Darwin's theory of evolution, which suggested that human beings had evolved from monkeys and apes. "Darwinism is not science at all," he maintained. "It is guesses strung together."

**THE SCOPES TRIAL** During the 1920s, bills banning the teaching of Darwinian evolution in public schools were introduced in numerous state legislatures, but the only victories came in the South—and there were few of them. The dramatic highpoint of the fundamentalist war on Darwinism came in Tennessee, where in 1925 the legislature outlawed the teaching of evolution in public schools and colleges.

In the small mining town of Dayton, in eastern Tennessee, civic leaders eager to create money-making publicity for their depressed economy persuaded John T. Scopes, a twenty-four-year-old substitute high-school science teacher, to become a test case against the new law. He was arrested for "teaching" Darwin's theory of evolution.

**Monkey trial** In this snapshot of the courtroom, John T. Scopes (far left) clasps his face in his hands and listens to one of his attorneys (second from right). Clarence Darrow (far right), too, listens on, visibly affected by the sweltering heat.

The **Scopes Trial** did indeed bring worldwide publicity to Dayton, but not the kind town leaders had anticipated. Before the start of the trial on July 10, 1925, the sweltering streets of Dayton overflowed with sightseers, evangelists, atheists, and some 200 newspaper and radio reporters. Main Street merchants festooned their shop windows with pictures of apes and monkeys lampooning Darwinian evolution. A man tattooed with Bible verses preached on a street corner while a live piano-playing monkey was paraded about town. Ministers harangued passersby about the evils of coffee, ice cream, and Coca-Cola ("a hell-sent narcotic").

The two warriors pitting science against fundamentalism were both national celebrities: William Jennings Bryan, who had offered his services to the prosecution, and Chicagoan Clarence Darrow, the nation's foremost defense attorney and a tireless defender of the rights of the working class, who had volunteered to defend Scopes.

Temperatures surpassed 100 degrees as the trial began. Bryan insisted that the trial was about a state's right to determine what was taught in the public schools. It was a "contest between evolution and Christianity, a duel to the death." Darrow countered: "Scopes is not on trial. Civilization is on trial." His goal was to prevent "bigots and ignoramuses from controlling the education of the United States" by proving that America was "founded on liberty and not on narrow, mean, intolerable and brainless prejudice of soulless religio-maniacs."

On July 20, the seventh day of the trial, the defense called Bryan as an expert witness on biblical interpretation. Darrow began by asking him about biblical stories. Did he believe that Jonah was swallowed by a whale and that Joshua made the sun stand still? Yes, Bryan replied, as beads of sweat streamed down his face. All things were possible with God.

Darrow pressed on relentlessly. What about the great flood and Noah's ark? Was Eve really created from Adam's rib? Bryan hesitated, and the crowd grew uneasy as the hero of fundamentalism crumpled in the heat. Bryan appealed to the judge, claiming that the Bible was not on trial, only to have Darrow yell: "I am examining you on your fool ideas that no intelligent Christian on earth believes." A humiliated Bryan claimed that Darrow was insulting Christians. Darrow, his thumbs clasping his colorful suspenders, shot back: "You insult every man of science and learning in the world because he does not believe in your fool religion." At one point, the men lunged at each other, prompting the judge to adjourn court for the day.

Journalist H. L. Mencken called the legal proceedings a "universal joke." Bryan, he said, was a "charlatan, a mountebank, a zany," and the residents of Dayton ("Monkey Town") were "gaping primates" and "rustic ignoramuses."

As the trial ended, the judge said that the only question for the jury was whether John T. Scopes had taught evolution. No one had denied that he had done so. The jurors did not even sit down before deciding, in nine minutes, that Scopes was guilty. But the Tennessee Supreme Court, while upholding the anti-evolution law, waived Scopes's $100 fine on a technicality. Both sides claimed victory.

Five days after the trial ended, the sixty-five-year-old Bryan died in his sleep. Scopes left Dayton to study geology at the University of Chicago; he became a petroleum engineer.

The Scopes Trial symbolized the waning of an old order in America and the rise of a *modern* outlook—more pluralistic, diverse, and skeptical, more tolerant of controversial ideas, and less obsessed with intellectual control. Still, the debate between fundamentalism and modernism continues today.

## PROHIBITION

William Jennings Bryan died in 1925 knowing that one of his crusades had succeeded: On December 18, 1917, Congress had sent to the states the Eighteenth Amendment. Ratified by all but two states by January 1919, the amendment banned "the manufacture, sale, and transportation of intoxicating liquors," effective one year later. Prior to ratification, alcohol-related problems had become widespread and were seen as an urgent social issue. Per capita beer consumption between 1840 and 1910 had soared more than 1,000 percent. Excessive drinking, said the *Nashville Banner*, was the largest "producer of disease, crime, and poverty."

During the Great War, rationing dictated the need to use grain for food rather than for making booze. That, combined with a backlash against the majority of beer brewers because of their German background, transformed the cause of Prohibition into a virtual test of American patriotism. Victory in the Great War led many to assume that the federal government could play a greater role in reforming society—including the banning of alcohol.

The movement to prohibit the sale of beer, wine, and liquor forged an unusual alliance between rural and small-town Protestant evangelicals and urban political progressives: between believers in religious fundamentalism who opposed drinking as sinful and progressive social reformers, mostly women, who were convinced that **Prohibition** would reduce prostitution, domestic abuse, and workplace violence. The result was the largest social reform movement since abolitionism.

Billy Sunday, a Christian evangelist who described himself as a "temperance Republican down to my toes," told 10,000 people gathered at his tabernacle that the age of righteousness was at hand: "Men will walk upright now; women will smile and the children will laugh." Former president William Howard Taft, soon to be chief justice of the Supreme Court, had a different perspective. "No tendency is quite so strong in human nature," he said, "as the desire to lay down rules of conduct for other people."

Ethnic and social prejudices drove the Prohibition crusade. The head of the Anti-Saloon League, for example, declared that German Americans "eat like gluttons and drink like swine." For many such nativists, in fact, the primary goal of Prohibition was to police the behavior of the foreign-born, the working class, African Americans, and poor whites.

Many leaders of the Prohibition movement also supported immigration restrictions. Charles Eliot, president of Harvard University, declared that alcoholism "threatened the destruction of the white race." Likewise, Frances Willard, head of the Women's Christian Temperance Union, believed Prohibition was essential in the war against foreign invaders, many of whom were Catholics. "Alien illiterates rule our cities today," she exclaimed. "The saloon is their place; the toddy stick [a utensil used to make toddy, a hot rum drink] their sceptre."

Prohibition took effect in January 1920. For a time, it worked. Neighborhood saloons closed, and drinking among the working poor dropped by half.

With each passing month, however, people found ways to defy the law. Passenger ships anchored just offshore to serve as floating saloons, and commercial bootleggers sprouted like mushrooms.

Over time, Prohibition proved to be a colossal and costly failure. In 1923, a federal agent said it would take a visitor in any city less than thirty minutes to find a drink. In New Orleans, he added, it would take only thirty-five seconds.

**All's fair in drink and war** Torpedoes filled with malt whiskey were discovered in New York Harbor in 1926, an elaborate attempt by bootleggers to smuggle alcohol during Prohibition. Each "torpedo" had an air compartment so it could be floated to shore.

The National Prohibition Act of 1919 (commonly called the Volstead Act) outlined the rules and regulations needed to enforce the Eighteenth Amendment. Yet it had so many loopholes that it virtually guaranteed failure. Technically, it never stated that *drinking* alcohol was illegal, only the manufacture, distribution, and sale of alcoholic beverages.

In addition, individuals and organizations were allowed to keep and drink any liquor owned on January 16, 1919. Not surprisingly, people stocked up before the law took effect. The Yale Club in New York City stored so much liquor that it never ran out during the thirteen years of Prohibition. Farmers were allowed to "preserve" their fruits by fermenting them, which resulted in barns stockpiled with "hard cider" and homemade wine. So-called medicinal liquor remained legal, which meant that physicians (and even veterinarians) wrote numerous prescriptions for "medicinal" brands such as Old Grand-Dad and Jim Beam whiskies.

Thousands of people set up home breweries, producing 700 million gallons of beer in 1929 alone. Wine was made just as easily, and "bathtub gin" was the simplest of all, requiring little more than a one-gallon still and some fruit, grain, or potatoes. Two thirds of illegal liquor came from Canada, with most of the rest from Mexico or overseas. Yet this bootleg alcohol became notoriously dangerous because of its high alcohol content. Tens of thousands were killed or disabled by deadly batches of illegal alcohol.

The new law was too sweeping to enforce and too inconveniencing for most Americans to respect. It also had unexpected consequences. The loss of liquor taxes cost the federal government 10 percent of its annual revenue, and the closing of breweries, distilleries, and saloons eliminated thousands of jobs. Prohibition also spurred a dramatic increase in the size and scope of the federal government. Enforcement agents had to be hired, prisons needed to be built to house violators, federal police powers were expanded, and civil liberties were violated.

Yet for all the increases in federal power, Congress never supplied adequate funding to implement the Volstead Act. The Prohibition Unit, a new agency within the U.S. Treasury Department, had 3,000 employees to police the nation, five times the number at the new Federal Bureau of Investigation, yet not nearly enough to enforce Prohibition. New York's mayor said it would require 250,000 police officers in his city alone. In working-class and ethnic-rich Detroit, the bootleg industry was second in size only to the auto industry. In Virginia, jails could not contain the 20,000 Prohibition-related arrests each year.

Moreover, many prominent Americans regularly broke the anti-liquor law. President Warren G. Harding drank and served bootleg liquor in the White House, explaining that he was "unable to see this as a great moral issue." The largest bootlegger in Washington, D.C., reported that "a majority of both houses" of Congress were regular customers. Secretary of Commerce Herbert Hoover often slipped into the Belgian Embassy to satisfy his thirst for fine wines.

The efforts to defy Prohibition generated widespread police corruption and boosted organized crime. Many activities and images associated with the Roaring Twenties were fueled by bootleg liquor supplied by crime syndicates and sold in saloons called speakeasies, which police often ignored in exchange for bribes. Well-organized crime syndicates controlled the entire stream of liquor's production, pricing, distribution, and sales. As a result, the Prohibition era was a thirteen-year orgy of unparalleled criminal activity. By 1930, more than one third of federal prisoners were Prohibition violators.

Although total alcohol consumption did decrease during the twenties, as did the number of deaths from alcohol abuse, in many cities drinking actually *increased*. As humorist Will Rogers quipped, "Prohibition is better than no liquor at all."

Outlawing alcohol became a prime example of unintended consequences. Prohibition, for example, generated enormous income for organized crime. The most notorious Prohibition-era gangster was Alphonse Capone, the son of poor Italian immigrants. As a teenager, he shined shoes on a street corner in Brooklyn, New York, where he saw local mobsters at work. Soon, he organized a ring to extort money from other shoeshine boys.

In 1917, a neighborhood gangster hired seventeen-year-old Capone as bartender and bouncer at the Harvard Inn on Coney Island. One night, Capone insulted a woman at the bar. Her brother punched Capone, then slashed him across the face with a knife, leaving three scars that inspired his nickname, "Scarface." By 1925, Capone had assumed control of a mob in Chicago.

Two years later, Capone's bootlegging, prostitution, and gambling empire brought him an annual income of $60 million. His army of 700 gangsters was involved in 200 murders (none solved). The worst was the St. Valentine's Day Massacre, when his hit men, disguised as cops, drove up to a garage where seven members of a rival gang were awaiting a shipment of bootleg liquor. Capone's men murdered them with machine guns.

Capone, however, was a hero to many. He dressed in expensive, colorful suits; rode in a custom-built, armor-plated Cadillac with bulletproof glass; telephoned his mother and wife every day; gave huge tips to waiters, newsboys, and hatcheck girls; and provided a soup kitchen that served 3,000 of Chicago's poorest residents daily. When criticized for his shady dealings, he claimed to be providing the public with the goods and services it demanded: "Some call it bootlegging. Some call it racketeering. I call it business. They say I violate the prohibition law. Who doesn't?"

Capone neglected to add that he had also beaten to death several police officers; ordered the execution of dozens of rivals; and bribed mayors, judges, and police officers. Law-enforcement officials led by FBI agent Eliot Ness began to smash Capone's bootlegging operations in 1929. In the end, he was convicted on charges of tax evasion and sentenced to eleven years in prison. After only eight years, however, he died in prison of cardiac arrest.

# A REPUBLICAN RESURGENCE

After the Great War, most Americans had endured enough of Wilson's crusading idealism and spurned any leader who promoted sweeping reforms. Wilson, who despite his poor health wanted a third presidential term, recognized the shifting public mood. "It is only once in a generation," he remarked, "that a people can be lifted above material things. That is why conservative government is in the saddle two-thirds of the time."

Progressivism lost its impetus for several reasons. For one thing, its leaders were no more. Roosevelt died in 1919, just as he was beginning to campaign for the Republican presidential nomination, and Wilson's stroke had left him broken physically and mentally.

In addition, organized labor resented the Wilson administration's crackdown on striking workers in 1919–1920. Farmers in the Great Plains and West thought wartime price controls had discriminated against them. Liberal intellectuals became disillusioned with grassroots democracy because of popular support for Prohibition, the Ku Klux Klan, and religious fundamentalism.

Progressivism did not disappear, however. Progressive Republicans and Democrats dominated key leadership positions in Congress during much of the 1920s. The progressive impulse for honest, efficient government and regulation of business remained strong, especially at the state and local levels, where efforts to improve public education, public health, and social-welfare programs gained momentum. At the national level, however, conservative Republicans returned to power.

**HARDING AND "NORMALCY"**  In 1920, Republican leaders turned to a likeable mediocrity as their presidential candidate: Warren G. Harding, a dapper, silver-haired U.S. senator from Ohio. One Republican senator explained that the party chose Harding not for his abilities or experience (which were minimal) but because he was from a key state and looked presidential. Harding, he said, was "the best of the second–raters." Harding admitted as much. When he asked his campaign manager, Harry Daugherty, if he had the abilities to be president, Daugherty laughed: "The day of giants in the presidential chair is passed."

Even Harding's wife, Florence, was wary. After learning that her husband had been nominated, she told a journalist, "I can see but one word written over the head of my husband if he is elected—and that word is tragedy." The irreverent H. L. Mencken was much less sympathetic: "No other such complete and dreadful nitwit is to be found in the pages of American history."

Harding set the conservative tone of his campaign when he pledged to "safeguard America first . . . to exalt America first, to live for and revere America first." America, Harding concluded, needed not "heroics, but healing; not nostrums, but normalcy; not revolution, but restoration; not agitation, but adjustment; not surgery, but serenity; not the dramatic, but the dispassionate."

At their convention, the Democrats quickly rejected Wilson's desire for a third term and chose Ohioan James Cox, a former newspaper publisher and three-term governor of the state. For vice president, they selected New Yorker Franklin Delano Roosevelt, who as assistant secretary of the navy occupied the same position his Republican cousin Theodore Roosevelt had once held. Handsome, vigorous, and a stirring speaker, he would deliver more than 1,000 speeches during the campaign.

Cox's campaign was disorganized and underfunded, however, and the Democrats struggled against the conservative postwar mood. In the words of progressive journalist William Allen White, Americans were "tired of issues, sick at heart of ideals, and weary of being noble."

Harding won big, getting 16 million votes to 9 million for Cox, and the Republicans increased their majority in both houses of Congress. Harding's victory led Clarence Darrow to quip that he had grown up hearing that "anybody can become president. I'm beginning to believe it." Franklin Roosevelt predicted that the Democratic party could not hope to return to power until the Republicans led the nation "into a serious period of depression and unemployment." He was right.

The one-sided election was significant in another way: it was the first presidential contest in which women voted in all forty-eight states. (In the 1916 presidential election, about thirty states had permitted women to participate.) Still, not all women found voting easy. In North Carolina, Blanche Benton remembered that many men "said if their wives voted, they would leave them. Even my mother didn't want to vote the first time." She told the *Charlotte Observer* that many women voted like their husbands or fathers in the beginning, but she voted her conscience. "My husband, he said to vote the way I wanted, and he would vote the way he wanted."

**"JUST A PLAIN FELLOW"** Harding's vanilla promise of a "**return to normalcy**" reflected his unexceptional background and limited abilities. One of his speechwriters admitted that Harding was both "indolent" and "ignorant of most of the big questions that would confront him." A farmer's son and newspaper editor, Harding described himself as "just a plain fellow" who was "old-fashioned and even reactionary in matters of faith and morals" and had pledged "total abstinence" from alcohol.

In fact, however, Harding drank outlawed liquor in the White House, smoked and chewed tobacco, hosted twice-weekly poker games, had numerous affairs, and even fathered children with women other than his domineering wife, Florence. The president's dalliances brought him much grief, however. One of his mistresses blackmailed him, demanding money for her silence—which she received. Another, after his death in 1923, wrote a tell-all account of their affair titled *The President's Daughter*.

The public, however, saw Harding as a handsome, charming politician who looked the part of a leader. Yet privately, he worried about his limitations. "I am not fit for this office and should never have been here," he once admitted. "I cannot hope to be one of the great presidents, but perhaps I may be remembered as one of the best loved."

Harding in office had much in common with Ulysses S. Grant. His cabinet, like Grant's, mixed some of the "best minds" in the party with a few of the worst. Charles Evans Hughes, like Grant's Hamilton Fish, became a distinguished secretary of state. Herbert Hoover in the Commerce Department,

Andrew W. Mellon in the Treasury, and Henry C. Wallace in the Agriculture Department made policy on their own. Other cabinet members and administrative appointees, however, were not so conscientious. The secretary of the interior landed in prison, and the attorney general narrowly escaped serving time. Many lesser offices went to members of the "Ohio gang," a group of Harding's drinking buddies.

Harding was no reformer. He set out to reverse the progressive activism of Woodrow Wilson and Theodore Roosevelt and reassert the primacy of Congress over the presidency. He and his lieutenants dismantled or neutralized many progressive regulatory laws and agencies. His four Supreme Court appointments were all conservatives, including Chief Justice William Howard Taft, who announced that he had been "appointed to reverse a few decisions." During the 1920s, the Taft-led court struck down a federal child-labor law and a minimum-wage law for women, issued numerous injunctions against striking unions, and passed rulings limiting the powers of federal agencies that regulated big businesses.

**ANDREW MELLON AND THE ECONOMY**  The Harding administration inherited a slumping economy burdened by high wartime taxes and a national debt that had ballooned from $1 billion in 1914 to $27 billion in 1920 because of the expenses associated with the war. Unemployment was at nearly 12 percent.

To generate economic growth, Secretary of the Treasury Andrew Mellon called for reducing federal spending and lowering tax rates. Mellon persuaded Congress to pass the landmark Budget and Accounting Act of 1921, which created a Bureau of the Budget to streamline the process of preparing an annual federal budget to be approved by Congress. The bill also created a General Accounting Office to audit spending by federal agencies. The act fulfilled a long-held progressive desire to bring greater efficiency and nonpartisanship to the budget preparation process.

Mellon also proposed sweeping tax reductions. By 1918, the wartime tax rate on the highest income bracket had risen to 73 percent. Mellon believed the high rates were pushing wealthy Americans to avoid paying taxes by investing their money in foreign countries or tax-free government bonds. His policies systematically reduced tax rates while increasing tax revenues. He convinced Congress to cut the top rate from 73 percent in 1921 to 24 percent in 1929, and rates for individuals with the lowest incomes were also cut substantially, helping the working poor. By 1929, barely 2 percent of American workers had to pay any income tax.

At the same time, Mellon helped Harding reduce the federal budget. Government expenditures fell, as did the national debt, and the economy soared. Unemployment plummeted to 2.4 percent in 1923. Mellon's supporters labeled him the greatest Treasury secretary since Alexander Hamilton in the late eighteenth century.

In addition to tax cuts, Mellon promoted the long-standing Republican policy of high tariffs on imported goods. The Fordney-McCumber Tariff of 1922 increased rates on imported chemical and metal products to help prevent the revival of German corporations that had dominated those industries before the Great War. To please commercial farmers, the new act included tariffs on agricultural imports.

**REDUCED REGULATION** The Republican economic program also sought to dismantle or neutralize many progressive regulatory laws and agencies. President Harding appointed commissioners to federal agencies who would promote "regulatory capitalism" and policies "friendly" to business interests. Republican senator Henry Cabot Lodge, who influenced Harding's choices to lead the regulatory agencies, boasted that "we have torn up Wilsonism by the roots."

**RACIAL PROGRESSIVISM** In one area, however, conservative Warren G. Harding proved to be more progressive than Woodrow Wilson. He reversed Wilson's segregationist policy of excluding African Americans from federal government jobs. He also spoke out against the vigilante racism that had flared up across the country during and after the war.

In his first speech to a joint session of Congress in 1921, Harding insisted that the nation must deal with the festering "race question." He attacked the Ku Klux Klan for fomenting "hatred and prejudice and violence" and urged Congress "to wipe the stain of barbaric lynching from the banners of a free and orderly, representative democracy." Harding supported an anti-lynching bill that passed the House but was killed by southern Democrats in the Senate.

In October 1921, Harding became the first president to deliver a speech focused on race in the former Confederacy. In Birmingham, Alabama, to celebrate the city's fiftieth anniversary, the president shocked whites among the 100,000 in attendance by demanding complete economic and political rights for African Americans: "I say let the black man vote when he is fit to vote; prohibit the white man voting when he is unfit to vote." As whites in the segregated audience responded with icy silence, Harding abandoned his prepared text and lectured them: "Whether you like it or not, our democracy is a lie unless you stand for that equality." He then stressed that he did not endorse "social equality" for blacks and whites: by which he meant intermarriage and the desegregation of schools, restaurants, hotels, and other public places. "Racial amalgamation can never come in America," he stressed.

After reading the text of the president's speech, Marcus Garvey, president of the Universal Negro Improvement Association, sent a telegram to Harding in which he applauded his speech "on behalf of four hundred million negroes of the world." Garvey added that "all true negroes are against social equality, believing that all races should develop on their own social lines. Only a few selfish members of the negro race believe in the social amalgamation of black and white." Harding's unprecedented speech also delighted W. E. B. Du Bois, head of the NAACP. Writing in *The Crisis*, he stressed that Harding's address, "like sudden thunder in blue skies, ends the hiding and drives us all into the clear light of truth."

Few southerners agreed, however. Pat Harrison, a Democratic senator from Mississippi, warned that if Harding's speech "were carried to its ultimate conclusion, that means that the black man can strive to become president of the United States!" Likewise, Senator J. Thomas Heflin of Alabama reminded the president that white southerners "hold to the doctrine that God Almighty has fixed the limits and boundaries between the two races, and no Republican living can improve upon His work."

**SETBACKS FOR UNIONS** Urban workers shared in the affluence of the 1920s. Nonfarm workers gained about 30 percent in real wages between 1921 and 1928, but farm income rose only 10 percent, and organized labor suffered. Although President Harding endorsed collective bargaining and tried to reduce the twelve-hour workday and six-day workweek to give the working class "time for leisure and family life," he ran into stiff opposition in Congress. The widespread strikes of 1919 had created fears that unions promoted radical socialism.

Between January 1920 and August 1921, the national unemployment rate jumped from 2 percent to 14 percent, and industrial production fell by 23 percent. The brief postwar depression so weakened unions that in 1921 business groups in Chicago designated the **open shop** to be the "American plan" of employment. Unlike the closed shop, which forced businesses to hire only union members, the open shop gave an employer the right to hire anyone.

Employers often required workers to sign "yellow-dog" contracts, which forced them to agree not to join a union, leaving them feeling as mistreated as a yellow dog. Owners also used spies, blacklists, and intimidation to block unions. Some employers tried to kill the unions with kindness by introducing programs of "industrial democracy" guided by company-sponsored unions, or various schemes of "welfare capitalism," such as profit sharing, bonuses, pensions, health programs, and recreational activities.

Such anti-union efforts paid off for employers. Union membership dropped from about 5 million in 1920 to 3.5 million in 1929 as industrial production soared and joblessness fell to 3 percent. But the anti-union effort, led by businesses that wanted to keep wages low and unions weak, unwittingly helped create a "purchasing-power crisis" whereby the working poor were not earning enough to buy the goods being churned out by increasingly productive industries. Executives used company profits to pay dividends to stockholders, invest in new equipment, and increase their own salaries, while doing little to help wage earners. In 1929, an estimated 5 percent of the nation's corporate executives received one third of the nation's income.

In other words, the much-trumpeted "new economy" was not benefiting enough working-class Americans to be sustainable. The gap between income levels and purchasing power would be a major cause of the Great Depression, as the Republican formula of high tariffs, low wages, low taxes, little regulation, and anti-unionism would eventually implode.

## ISOLATIONISM IN FOREIGN AFFAIRS

In addition to the Senate's rejection of American membership in the League of Nations, the postwar spirit of isolation found other expressions. George Jean Nathan, a drama critic, expressed the sentiments of many when he announced that the "great problems of the world—social, political, economic and theological—do not concern me in the slightest. . . . What concerns me alone is myself, and the interests of a few close friends."

Yet the desire to stay out of foreign wars did not mean that the United States could ignore its expanding global interests. The Great War had made the United States the world's chief banker, and American investments and loans enabled foreigners to purchase U.S. exports.

**WAR DEBTS AND REPARATIONS** Nothing did more to heighten America's isolationism—and anti-American feelings among Europeans—than the complex issue of paying off war debts. In 1917, when France and Great Britain ran out of money to pay for military supplies, the U.S. government had advanced them massive loans, first for the war effort and then for postwar reconstruction projects.

Most Americans expected the debts to be repaid, but Europeans thought differently. The European Allies had held off the German invasion at great cost while the United States was raising an army in 1917. The British also noted that after the American Revolution, the newly independent United States had repudiated old debts to British investors. The French likewise pointed out that they had never been repaid for helping the Americans win the Revolution.

Throughout the 1920s, the British and French were in a complex financial bind. To get U.S. dollars with which to pay their war-related debts, European nations had to sell their goods to the United States. However, soaring American tariff rates made imported European goods more expensive for wage-stagnant U.S. consumers, so the war-related debts became harder to pay. The French and British insisted that they could repay their debts only if they could collect the $33 billion in reparations owed them by Germany. The German economy, however, was in shambles.

Twice during the 1920s, the financial strain on Germany brought the structure of international payments to the verge of collapse, and both times the international Reparations Commission called in private American bankers to work out rescue plans. Loans provided by U.S. banks thus propped up the German economy so that Germany could pay its reparations to Britain and France, thereby enabling them to pay their debts to the United States.

**ATTEMPTS AT DISARMAMENT** After the Great War, many Americans decided that the best way to keep the peace was to limit the size of armies and navies. The United States had no intention of maintaining a large army after 1920, but under the shipbuilding program begun in 1916, it had constructed a powerful navy second only to that of Great Britain. Although neither the British nor the Americans wanted a naval armaments race, both were worried about the growth of Japanese power in Asia and the Pacific.

To address the problem, President Harding in 1921 invited diplomats from eight nations to a peace conference in Washington, D.C., at which Secretary of State Charles Evans Hughes made a blockbuster proposal. The only way out of an expensive naval arms race, he declared, "is to end it now" by eliminating scores of existing warships. He pledged that America would junk thirty battleships and cruisers and then named thirty-six British and Japanese warships that would also be destroyed. The stunned audience stood and roared its approval. In less than fifteen minutes, one journalist reported, Hughes had destroyed more warships "than all the admirals of the world have sunk in a cycle of centuries."

At the Washington Naval Conference (1921–1922), delegates from the United States, Britain, Japan, France, and Italy signed the Five-Power

Treaty (1922), which limited the size of their navies. It was the first disarmament treaty in history. The agreement also, in effect, divided the world into spheres of influence: U.S. naval power became supreme in the Western Hemisphere, Japanese power in the western Pacific, and British power from the North Sea to Singapore.

**THE KELLOGG-BRIAND PACT** During and after the Great War, many Americans embraced the fanciful idea of abolishing war with a stroke of a pen. In 1921, a wealthy Chicagoan founded the American Committee for the Outlawry of War. "We can outlaw this war system just as we outlawed slavery and the saloon," said an enthusiastic convert.

The seductive notion of simply abolishing war culminated in the signing of the Kellogg-Briand Pact. In 1927, French foreign minister Aristide Briand proposed to U.S. Secretary of State Frank B. Kellogg that the two countries agree never to go to war against each other.

Kellogg countered with a plan to have *all* nations sign the pact. The General Treaty for Renunciation of War as an Instrument of National Policy, or the Kellogg-Briand Pact, signed on August 27, 1928, declared that the signatories renounced war "as an instrument of national policy." Eventually, sixty-two nations, including all the great powers, signed the pact, but all reserved the right of "self-defense." The U.S. Senate ratified the agreement by a vote of 85 to 1.

A senator who voted for "this worthless, but perfectly harmless peace treaty" wrote a friend later that he feared it would "confuse the minds of many good people who think that peace may be secured by polite professions of neighborly and brotherly love." In a more pointed assessment, British writer George Orwell said that outlawing war was one of those "ideas so absurd only an intellectual could believe them."

The treaty went into effect July 24, 1929, after which Japan invaded Manchuria (1931); Italy invaded Ethiopia (1935); Japan invaded China (1937); Germany invaded Poland (1939); the Soviet Union invaded Finland (1939); Germany invaded Denmark, Norway, Belgium, the Netherlands, Luxembourg, and France, and attacked Great Britain (1940); and Japan attacked the United States (1941), culminating in a global war that resulted in more than 60 million deaths. All these nations had signed the Kellogg-Briand Pact. So much for outlawing war.

**THE WORLD COURT** The isolationist mood in the United States was no better illustrated than in the repeated refusal by the Senate to approve

American membership in the World Court, formally called the Permanent Court of International Justice, at The Hague in the Netherlands. Created in 1921 by the League of Nations, the World Court was intended to arbitrate disputes between nations. During the 1920s, Presidents Harding, Coolidge, and Hoover had each asked the Senate to approve American membership in the World Court, but the legislative body refused, for the same reasons that it had refused to sign the Versailles treaty: it did not want the United States to be bound in any way by an international organization.

**IMPROVING RELATIONS IN LATIN AMERICA** The isolationist attitude during the 1920s led Republican presidents Harding, Calvin Coolidge, and Herbert Hoover to soothe tensions with America's neighbors to the south. The Harding administration agreed in 1921 to pay the $25 million that the republic of Colombia had demanded for America having seized the Panama Canal Zone. In 1924, American troops left the Dominican Republic after eight years of intervention. U.S. Marines left Nicaragua in 1925 but returned a year later at the outbreak of disorder and civil war. There, in 1927, the Coolidge administration brought both parties into an agreement for U.S.-supervised elections, but one rebel leader, César Augusto Sandino, held out, and the marines stayed until 1933.

The troubles in Nicaragua increased strains between the United States and Mexico. Relations had already soured after repeated Mexican threats to expropriate American oil properties in Mexico. In 1928, however, the U.S. ambassador negotiated an agreement protecting American rights acquired before 1917. Expropriation did in fact occur in 1938, but the Mexican government agreed to reimburse American owners.

## THE HARDING SCANDALS

As time passed, President Harding found himself increasingly distracted by scandals within his administration. Early in 1923, the head of the Veterans Bureau resigned when faced with an investigation for stealing medical and hospital supplies intended for former servicemen. A few weeks later, the legal adviser to the bureau killed himself.

Soon thereafter, it was learned that Jesse Smith, a colleague of Attorney General Harry M. Daugherty, was illegally selling federal paroles, pardons, and judgeships from his Justice Department office. When Harding learned of his escapades, he called Smith to the Oval Office and dressed him down. The next day, Smith killed himself in Daugherty's apartment. Then, Daugherty was accused of selling, for his personal gain, German assets seized after the war. When asked to testify about the matter, he refused on the grounds that doing so might incriminate him.

The most serious scandal was the **Teapot Dome Affair**. The Teapot Dome was a government-owned oil field in Wyoming managed by the Department of the Interior. Secretary of the Interior Albert B. Fall, deeply in debt and eight years overdue in paying his taxes, began selling the oil to close friends who were executives of petroleum companies. In doing so, Fall took bribes of about $400,000 from an oil tycoon. Convicted of conspiracy and bribery and sentenced to a year in prison, Fall was the first former cabinet official to serve time because of misconduct in office.

**Teapot Dome scandal** In this 1924 political cartoon, Republican officials try to outrun the Teapot Dome scandal, represented by a giant steamrolling teapot, on an oil-slicked highway.

How much Harding knew of the scandals is unclear, but he knew enough to be troubled. As he confided to a journalist, "I have no trouble with my enemies; I can take care of my enemies all right. But my damn friends, my God-damn friends. . . . They're the ones that keep me walking the floor nights!"

In 1923, Harding left on what would be his last journey, a trip to the West Coast and the Alaska Territory. Along the way, he asked Herbert Hoover, the secretary of commerce, what he should do about the Fall scandal. Hoover gave the correct response: "Publish it, and at least get credit for integrity on your side." Before Harding had time to act, he suffered an attack of food poisoning in Seattle. After showing signs of recovering, he died in San Francisco. He was fifty-seven years old.

Largely as a result of Harding's corrupt associates, his administration came to be viewed as one of the worst in history. Even Hoover admitted that Harding was not "a man with either the experience or the intellectual quality that the position needed."

More recent assessments, however, suggest that the scandals obscured Harding's accomplishments. He led the nation out of the turmoil of the postwar years and helped create the economic boom of the 1920s. He endorsed diversity and civil rights and was a forceful proponent of women's rights. Yet even Harding's foremost scholarly defender admits that he lacked good judgment and "probably should never have been president."

## Coolidge Conservatism

The news of President Harding's death reached Vice President Calvin Coolidge when he and his wife were visiting his father in Plymouth Notch, Vermont. "Guess we'd better have a drink," said Coolidge upon being awakened to learn the news. At 2:47 A.M. on August 3, 1923, Colonel John Coolidge, a farmer, merchant, and notary public, issued the presidential oath of office to his son by the light of a kerosene lamp.

Calvin Coolidge, born on the fourth of July in 1872, was a throwback to an earlier era. A puritan in his personal life, he was horrified by the jazzed-up Roaring Twenties. He believed in the ideals of personal integrity and devotion to public service, and, like Harding, he was an evangelist both for capitalism and minimal government regulation of business.

**A DO-NOTHING PRESIDENT—BY DESIGN**  Although Coolidge had won every political race he had entered, he had never loved the limelight. Shy and awkward, he was a man of famously few words—hence his nickname, "Silent Cal." After being reelected president of the Massachusetts State Senate in

1916, he gave a four-sentence inaugural address that concluded with, "above all things, be brief." He later explained that he had "never been hurt by what he had not said."

Coolidge demanded that his wife, Grace, a gregarious college graduate of "vastly different temperament and taste," speak less and do less than he did. He prohibited the First Lady from giving interviews, driving a car, flying in an airplane, cutting her hair, smoking in public, or giving opinions on national affairs. Grace Coolidge accepted her subordinate role. She once proudly revealed that she never entered the President's office and "knew nothing of what took place there."

**Calvin Coolidge** "Silent Cal" was so inactive as president that when he died in 1933, American humorist Dorothy Parker remarked, "How could they tell?"

Coolidge's conventional views about gender roles did not faze voters. Most people liked his uprightness and personal humility. He was a simple, direct man who championed self-discipline and hard work. Alice Roosevelt Long-worth, the outspoken daughter of Theodore Roosevelt, said the atmosphere in the Coolidge White House compared to that of Harding was "as different as a New England front parlor is from the back room in a speakeasy."

As a state senator in Massachusetts, Coolidge had often aligned himself with Republican progressives. He voted for women's suffrage, a state income tax, a minimum wage for female workers, and salary increases for public school teachers. By the time he entered the White House, however, he had abandoned most of those causes.

Coolidge was determined *not* to be an activist president. He noted that his greatest accomplishment was "minding my own business," and he believed that "four-fifths of our troubles would disappear if we would sit down and keep still." Following his own logic, he insisted on twelve hours of sleep *and* a lengthy afternoon nap. Journalist H. L. Mencken claimed that Coolidge "slept more than any other president."

**EVANGELIST FOR CAPITALISM**  Even more than Harding, Coolidge linked the nation's welfare with the success of Big Business. "The chief business of the American people is business," he preached. "The man who builds a factory builds a temple. The man who works there worships there." Coolidge famously claimed that "wealth is the *chief* end of man."

With the help of Treasury secretary Andrew Mellon and Republican-controlled Congresses, Coolidge continued Harding's efforts to lower tax rates. Where Harding had sought to balance the interests of labor, agriculture, and industry, Coolidge focused on promoting industrial development by limiting federal regulation of business and industry. The nation had too many laws, Coolidge insisted, and "we would be better off if we did not have any more." True to his word, he vetoed fifty acts of Congress.

Coolidge was also "obsessed" with reducing federal spending, even to the point of issuing government workers one pencil at a time—and only after they turned in the stub of the old pencil. His penny-pinching, pro-business stance led the *Wall Street Journal* to rejoice: "Never before, here or anywhere else, has a government been so completely fused with business."

**THE ELECTION OF 1924**  Calvin Coolidge restored the dignity of the presidency while holding warring Republican factions together. He easily gained the party's 1924 presidential nomination. Soon thereafter, he invited reporters to the White House. One reporter asked, "Have you any statement on the campaign?" Coolidge said, "No." Another reporter tried: "Can you tell us about the world situation?" Again the president said, "No." After someone asked about Prohibition, the reply was the same: "No." As the frustrated reporters left, Coolidge yelled, "Now remember—don't quote me."

Meanwhile, the Democratic party's nominating convention in New York City illustrated the deep divisions between urban and rural America. One of the leading contenders, lawyer William McAdoo, Woodrow Wilson's son-in-law, was endorsed by the Ku Klux Klan. The other front-runner, New York governor Al Smith, was an Irish Catholic who led the party's anti-Klan, anti-Prohibition wing.

Neither McAdoo nor Smith could gain the nomination. The fragmented Democrats took a record 103 ballots over sixteen broiling summer days before deciding on a compromise candidate: John W. Davis, a little-known lawyer from West Virginia who could nearly outdo Coolidge in his conservatism.

While the Democrats bickered, rural Populists and urban progressives decided to abandon both major parties, as they had done in 1912. Reorganizing the old Progressive party, they nominated Wisconsin's Robert M. "Fighting Bob" La Follette. As a Republican senator, La Follette had voted against the 1917 declaration of war against Germany. Now, in addition to the progressives, he won the support of the Socialist party and the American Federation of Labor.

In the 1924 election, Coolidge swept both the popular and electoral votes. Davis and the Democrats took only the southern states, and La Follette carried only Wisconsin, his home state. The popular vote went 15.7 million for Coolidge, 8.4 million for Davis, and 4.8 million for La Follette—the largest popular vote ever polled by a third-party candidate up to that time. Coolidge viewed his landslide as a mandate to continue his efforts to shrink the federal government. If it disappeared, he predicted, most voters "would not detect the difference."

Coolidge's victory represented the height of postwar political conservatism. Business executives interpreted the election results as an endorsement of their influence on government policy, and Coolidge saw the economy's surging prosperity as confirmation of his support of Big Business. The United States, he proclaimed in his 1925 inaugural address, had reached "a state of contentment seldom before seen." His duty was to do nothing that might undermine such contentment.

## THE RISE OF HERBERT HOOVER

During the twenties, the drive for industrial efficiency, which had been a prominent theme among progressives, powered the wheels of mass production and consumption and became a cardinal belief of Republican leaders. Herbert Hoover, secretary of commerce in the Harding and Coolidge cabinets, embodied the dream of organizational efficiency, for he himself was a remarkable success story.

Born into a devout Quaker family in Iowa in 1874, he was orphaned at age nine, and raised by stern uncles in Iowa and Oregon. He was a shy "loner" who studied geology and mechanical engineering at Stanford University, where he determined that he was smarter, more energetic, and more disciplined than others. After graduating, he became a world-renowned mining engineer, harvesting gold in Australia, coal in China, and zinc in Burma. He went on to prosper as an oil tycoon and financial wizard, and was a multimillionaire before the age of forty.

Hoover's meteoric success and ruthless genius for managing difficult operations bred in him a self-confidence verging on conceit. In his twenties, he began planning to be president of the United States.

**A PROGRESSIVE CONSERVATIVE** With the outbreak of war in 1914, Herbert Hoover exchanged his business career for one in public service. He organized the evacuation of tens of thousands of Americans stranded in Europe by the German invasion of France, then led a massive program to provide food to 7.5 million starving civilians in German-occupied Belgium.

The "Great Humanitarian" also applied his managerial skills to the Food Administration and served with the U.S. delegation at the Versailles peace conference. Hoover idolized Woodrow Wilson and supported American membership in the League of Nations. Franklin Roosevelt, then assistant secretary of the navy, stood in awe of Hoover. In 1920, Roosevelt said that Hoover was "certainly a wonder [boy], and I wish we could make him President of the United States. There would not be a better one."

Hoover, however, soon disappointed Roosevelt by declaring himself a Republican "progressive conservative." In a book titled *American Individualism* (1922), Hoover wrote of an "ideal of *service*" that went beyond "rugged individualism" to promote the greater good. He wanted government officials to encourage business leaders to forgo "cutthroat competition" and engage in "voluntary cooperation" by forming trade associations that would share information and promote standardization—all in an effort to increase efficiency and productivity.

As secretary of commerce during the 1920s, Hoover transformed the small department into the government's most dynamic agency. He looked for new markets for business, created a Bureau of Aviation to promote the new airline industry, and established the Federal Radio Commission. When the Mississippi River flooded in 1927, devastating much of the Midwest and Gulf states, Hoover organized the massive recovery effort, despite President Coolidge's indifference.

**THE BUSINESS OF FARMING** During the 1920s, agriculture remained the weakest sector of the economy. The wartime boom fed by agricultural exports lasted into 1920 before commodity prices collapsed as European agricultural production returned to prewar levels. Lower prices for crops persisted into 1923, and after that, improvement was spotty. A bumper cotton crop in 1926 resulted only in a price collapse and an early taste of depression in much of the South, where foreclosures and bankruptcies spread.

The most successful farms, like the most successful corporations, were getting larger, more efficient, and more mechanized. By 1930, about 13 percent of all farmers had tractors; the proportion was even higher on the western plains. Better plows, harvesters, combines, and other machines improved crop yields, fertilizers, and methods of animal breeding.

Most farmers, however, were struggling to survive. They asked for help, and in 1924, Senator Charles L. McNary of Oregon and Representative Gilbert N. Haugen of Iowa introduced the first McNary-Haugen bill, which sought to secure "equality for agriculture in the benefits of the protective tariff."

The proposed bill called for surplus American crops to be sold on the world market. The goal was to raise prices at home so that farmers would have the same purchasing power relative to the prices they had enjoyed between 1909 and 1914, a time viewed as a golden age of American agriculture.

The McNary-Haugen bill passed Congress in 1927 but was vetoed by President Coolidge, who dismissed it as unsound and unconstitutional. The process was repeated in 1928. In a broader sense, however, McNary-Haugenism did not fail. The debates over the bill made the "farm problem" a national issue and defined it as a matter of managing surpluses. Moreover, the evolution of the McNary-Haugen plan revived the idea of a political alliance between the rural South and the West, a coalition that in the next decade would have a dominant influence on national farm policy.

**THE 1928 ELECTION: HOOVER VERSUS SMITH** On August 2, 1927, while on vacation in the Black Hills of South Dakota, President Coolidge announced, "I do not choose to run for President in 1928." His unexpected decision reflected his continuing grief at the death of his sixteen-year-old son in 1924 from an infected foot. He also was wary of becoming the longest-serving president in history, fearing that critics would claim he was pursuing a dictatorship.

Coolidge's decision cleared the way for Herbert Hoover to win the Republican nomination. The party's platform took credit for the nation's longest period of sustained prosperity, the government's cost cutting, debt and tax reduction, and the high tariffs ("as vital to American agriculture as . . . to manufacturing") designed to "protect" American businesses from foreign competition.

The Democrats nominated four-term New York governor Alfred E. Smith, called the "Happy Warrior" by Franklin D. Roosevelt in his nominating speech. The candidates presented sharply different images: Hoover, the successful businessman and bureaucratic manager from an Iowa farm, and Smith, a professional Irish American politician from New York City's Lower East Side. To working-class Democrats in northern cities, Smith was a hero, the poor grandson of Irish Catholic immigrants who had become governor of the most populous state. His outspoken criticism of Prohibition also endeared him to the Irish, Italians, Germans, and others.

**Herbert Hoover** "I have no fears for the future of our country," Hoover told the nation at his inauguration in 1929.

On the other hand, as the first Roman Catholic nominated for president by a major party, a product of New York's machine-run politics, and a "wet" on Prohibition (in direct opposition to his party's platform), Smith represented all that was opposed by southern and western rural Democrats—as well as most rural and small-town Republicans. A Kansas newspaper editor declared that the "whole puritan civilization, which has built a sturdy, orderly nation, is threatened by Smith." The Ku Klux Klan issued a "Klarion Kall for a Krusade" against him, mailing thousands of postcards proclaiming that "Alcohol" Smith, the Catholic New Yorker, was the Antichrist. While Hoover stayed above the fray, Smith was forced to deal with constant criticism.

No Democrat could have beaten Hoover in 1928, however. The nation was prosperous and at peace, and Hoover seemed the best person to sustain the good times. He was perhaps the best-trained economic mind ever to run for president, and he was widely viewed as a brilliant engineer and humanitarian, a genius "who never failed."

On Election Day, Hoover, the first Quaker to be president, won in a landslide, with 21 million popular votes to Smith's 15 million and an electoral college majority of 444 to 87. Hoover even penetrated the Democrats' Solid South, winning Virginia, North Carolina, Tennessee, Florida, and Texas. Republicans also kept control of both houses of Congress.

Hidden in the results, however, was a glimmer of hope for Democrats. Overall, Smith's vote total, especially strong in the largest cities, doubled that of John Davis four years earlier. In 1932, Franklin D. Roosevelt would build upon that momentum to win back the presidency for the Democrats.

Calvin Coolidge was skeptical that Hoover could sustain the good times. He quipped that the "Wonder Boy" had offered him "unsolicited advice for six years, all of it bad." Coolidge's doubts about Hoover's political abilities would prove accurate, as the new president would soon confront an economic earthquake that would test all of his skills—and expose his weaknesses.

## 1929—A Turning Point

Rarely had a new president entered office with greater expectations. In fact, Herbert Hoover was worried that people mistakenly viewed him as "a superman; that no problem is beyond my capacity."

He was right to be concerned. People saw in him a dedicated public servant whose proven organizational skills and business savvy would ensure continued prosperity. In 1929, Americans were fully employed and earning record levels of income. But that was about to change.

## The Onset of the Great Depression

Herbert Hoover's election boosted the hopes of Wall Street investors in what had come to be called "the Great Bull Market." Since 1924, the prices of stock shares invested in U.S. companies had steadily risen. Beginning in 1927, prices soared further on wings of reckless speculation. In 1919, some 317 million shares of stock changed hands; in 1929, the number was more than a billion. Treasury secretary Andrew W. Mellon's tax reductions had given people more money, and much of it went into the stock market. In April 1929, Hoover voiced concern about the "orgy of mad speculation" and urged investors to be more cautious—while privately telling his broker to sell many of his stock holdings. He saw disaster coming.

**THE STOCK MARKET** What made it so easy for so many to invest in stocks was the common practice of buying "on margin"—that is, an investor could make a small cash down payment (the "margin") on shares of stock and borrow the rest from a bank or a stockbroker, who held the stock certificates as security in case the share price plummeted. If stock prices rose, as they did in 1927, 1928, and most of 1929, the investor made enough profits to pay for the "margin loan" and reinvest the rest.

Yet if the stock price declined and the buyer failed to pay off the broker's loan, the broker could sell the stock at a much lower price to cover the loan. By August 1929, stockbrokers were lending investors more than two thirds of the face value of the stocks they were buying. Yet few people seemed concerned, and stock prices kept rising.

There were signs that the economy was weakening. By 1927, steel production, residential construction, and automobile sales were slowing, as was the rate of consumer spending. By mid-1929, industrial production, employment, and other measures of economic activity were also declining. Still, the stock market rose.

Then, in early September 1929, the stock market fell sharply. By the middle of October, world exchanges had gone into a steep decline. Still, most investors remained upbeat. The nation's foremost economist, Irving Fisher of Yale University, told investors on October 17, "Stock prices have reached what looks like a permanently high plateau."

**THE CRASH** The next week, however, stock market values wobbled, then tumbled again, triggering a wild scramble among terrified investors. As they rushed to sell their shares, the decline in stock prices accelerated. On what came to be called Black Tuesday, October 29—the worst day in the stock market's history—prices went into free fall, and brokers found themselves flooded with stocks they could not sell. On that day, investors lost $15 billion. By the end of the month, they had lost $50 billion.

Suddenly, the carefree indulgences of the Jazz Age had ended with the nerve-shattering crash on Wall Street. Fear and uncertainty spread like a virus across the nation and the world.

Rumors circulated of fortunes lost and careers ruined. Investors who had borrowed heavily to buy stocks were now forced to sell their holdings at huge losses so they could pay their debts. Some stockbrokers and investors committed suicide. In New York, the president of a bankrupt cigar company jumped off a hotel window ledge, and two business partners joined hands and leaped to their deaths from the Ritz Hotel. Room clerks in Manhattan hotels started asking registering guests if they wanted a room for jumping or sleeping.

The economy began to sputter. In 1930, at least 26,355 businesses shut down; even more failed the following year. The resulting economic slowdown

**Bank run** As news of the Great Crash spread across the world, people rushed to banks to withdraw their deposits. The line at this branch of the American Union Bank wraps around the building.

became so severe and long-lasting that it came to be known as the Great Depression.

The collapse of the stock market did not *cause* the **Great Depression**, however. Rather, it revealed that the prosperity of the 1920s had been built on weak foundations. As F. Scott Fitzgerald observed in *Echoes of the Jazz Age* (1931), the twenties were an "age of excess" that could not last.

The stock market crash had the added effect of creating a psychological panic that accelerated the economic decline. Frightened of losing everything, people rushed to remove their money from banks and the stock market. This only made things worse. By 1932, more than 9,000 banks had closed as the nation's economy experienced a shocking collapse.

## Why the Economy Collapsed

What were the underlying *causes* of the Great Depression? Most scholars emphasize a combination of interrelated elements. The once roaring economy had actually begun to fall into a recession months *before* the stock market crash because of *overproduction* and *underconsumption*. During the twenties, manufacturing production increased 43 percent, but the purchasing power of consumers did not grow nearly as fast. In essence, the economy was turning out more products than consumers could buy, and too many people had been borrowing too much money for unproductive purposes, such as speculating in the stock market.

At the same time, many business owners had taken large profits while denying wage increases to employees. By plowing profits into business expansion, executive salaries, and stock dividends, employers created an imbalance between production and consumption. Because union membership had plummeted, organized labor no longer exerted as much leverage with management over wage increases. Two thirds of families in 1929 earned less than $2,000 annually, an amount said by economists to provide "only basic necessities."

As the stock market was crashing, factories were reducing production or shutting down altogether. From 1929 to 1933, U.S. economic output dropped by almost 27 percent. And by 1933, a quarter of the workforce was jobless.

At the same time, the farm sector stagnated. Farm incomes had soared during the Great War because the European nations needed American grains, beef, and pork. Eager to sustain their prosperity, farmers took out mortgages to buy more acreage or equipment to boost output. However, without European demand, increased production during the twenties led to *lower* prices for grains and livestock. To make matters worse, record harvests in the summer and fall of 1929 caused prices for corn, wheat, and cotton to fall precipitously, pinching the income of farmers who had taken on mounting debts.

**GOVERNMENT'S ROLE** Government policies also contributed to the Depression. Like most Republican presidents, Herbert Hoover supported raising tariffs on imported goods to keep out foreign competition.

The Smoot-Hawley Tariff of 1930, authored by Republicans Reed Owen Smoot and Willis C. Hawley, sought to help the farm sector by raising tariff duties on agricultural products imported into the United States. As so often happens, however, a swarm of corporate lobbyists convinced Congress to add thousands of non-agricultural items to the tariff bill. The average tariff rate jumped from an already high 25 percent to 50 percent, making it the highest in history.

More than 1,000 economists petitioned Hoover to veto the bill because its logic was flawed: By trying to "protect" farmers from foreign competition, it would actually raise prices on most raw materials and consumer products. And by reducing European imports into the United States, the bill would make it much harder for France, Great Britain, and Germany to repay their war debts.

On June 17, 1930, however, Hoover, pressured by Republicans, signed the bill, causing another steep drop in the stock market. As predicted, the Smoot-Hawley Tariff prompted other countries to retaliate by passing tariffs of their own, thereby making it more difficult for American farms and businesses to sell their products abroad. U.S. exports plummeted along with international trade in general, worsening the Depression.

Another factor contributing to the Great Depression was the stance of the Federal Reserve Board, the government agency that serves as a "central bank" by managing the nation's money supply and interest rates. Instead of expanding the money supply to generate growth, the Federal Reserve tightened it out of concern for possible inflation in consumer prices. Between 1929 and 1932, the money supply shrank by a third, leading almost 10,000 small banks to close—and take millions of their depositors with them into bankruptcy.

**THE IMPACT OF EUROPE** The Depression was also fueled by the chaotic state of the European economy, which had never fully recovered from the Great War or from the punitive provisions of the Versailles treaty. During the late 1920s, nations such as Great Britain, France, Spain, and Italy slowed their purchases of American goods as their economies began recovering. Meanwhile, the German economy continued to flounder, drained by the war reparations it was forced to pay France and Great Britain.

A related factor was the inability of the victorious Allied nations to pay their war debts to each other—and to the United States. The American government insisted that the $11 billion it had loaned the Allies be repaid, but Great Britain and France had no money. They were forced to borrow billions of dollars from U.S. banks, which only increased their overall indebtedness. After the stock market crash, American banks could no longer prop up the European economies.

The Federal Reserve's tight monetary policy also slowed the amount of American money going abroad. The German economy, which had grown dependent on loans from American banks, was devastated as American loans dried up. Then the Smoot-Hawley Tariff made it even more difficult for European nations to sell their products in the United States. As the European economy stumbled, it subsequently deepened the American depression.

## The Human Toll of the Depression

The Great Depression was an international catastrophe that brought the worst of times. No business slump had been so deep, so long, or so painful. By 1932, one of every four Americans was unemployed, most of them wage workers. In many large cities, nearly *half* the adults were out of work. Millions of others saw their working hours and wages reduced. Some 500,000 people lost homes or farms because they could not pay their mortgages.

Amid such turmoil, the carefree optimism and indulgence of the twenties disappeared. Grassroots protests erupted; hungry people looted grocery stores, angry mobs stopped sheriffs from foreclosing on farms, and judges were threatened at bankruptcy hearings.

## The Farmers' Holiday Association

In Iowa in 1932, a growing number of farmers were unable to make their mortgage payments. Before long, sheriffs were showing up at farms with foreclosure papers. Frustrated farmers formed the Farmers' Holiday Association to make their case for government assistance. If their demands were not met, they threatened to go on strike ("holiday"), withholding their crops, milk, and livestock from the nation's markets. Before the Association could mobilize, however, scattered groups of farmers took direct action, blockading roads and preventing the movement of milk and grains.

Some launched a "Cornbelt Rebellion," invading courthouses and intimidating judges. On April 27, 1933, angry farmers broke through a line of deputies outside the O'Brien County Court House, entered the courtroom, and demanded that the judge stop signing farm eviction orders. When he refused, they dragged him outside along with the county sheriff and deputies, and forced them to kneel and kiss the U.S. flag. A few days later, a mob almost lynched still another judge.

Iowa's governor responded by mobilizing the National Guard and declaring martial law in several rural counties. The lawlessness subsided, and the farm protest movement gave way to hopes for agricultural improvement under a new presidential administration.

## RISING UNEMPLOYMENT AND DEMANDS FOR ASSISTANCE
As the economy spiraled downward, growing numbers of city workers were fired or had their wages cut. Unemployment soared to 4 million in 1930, to 8 million in 1931, and to 12 million by 1932.

As record numbers found themselves out of work and money, many people grew desperate. "Hold-ups and killings are becoming more frequent," a man wrote in his diary, "and it becomes dangerous to walk the streets." Unemployed city dwellers became street-corner merchants. Some 6,000 jobless New Yorkers sold apples on street corners to survive. Their motto was, "Buy an apple a day and eat the Depression away."

Many struggling business executives and professionals—lawyers, doctors, dentists, accountants, stockbrokers, teachers, nurses, and engineers—went without food and medical care to save money and avoid the humiliation of "going on relief"—seeking assistance from churches, charitable organizations, and soup kitchens. The sense of shame cut across class lines. In *The Grapes of Wrath* (1939), John Steinbeck's novel about the victims of the Depression, a poor but proud woman is disgraced by accepting "charity" from the Salvation Army: "We was hungry. They made us crawl for our dinner. They took our dignity."

**HUNGER** Surveys of children in the nation's public schools in 1932 showed that one-quarter suffered from malnutrition. The U.S. Public Health Service revealed that the families of unemployed workers had 66 percent more illnesses than those of employed workers. In 1931, New York City hospitals reported about 100 cases of death by starvation.

Millions lined up at neighborhood soup kitchens and breadlines, where churches and charities distributed free food and water. In Detroit, "we saw the city at its worst," wrote Louise V. Armstrong. "We saw a crowd of some fifty men fighting over a barrel of garbage which had been set outside the back door of a restaurant. American citizens fighting over scraps of food like animals!"

**HOMELESSNESS** The contraction of the economy squeezed homeowners who had monthly mortgages to pay. A thousand Americans per day lost their homes to foreclosure, and millions were forced to move in with relatives or friends. At first, those made homeless by the Depression were placed in almshouses, also called *poorhouses* or *workhouses*.

By 1933, however, the swelling numbers of homeless people overwhelmed the public facilities. People were forced to live in culverts, under bridges, on park benches, and in doorways and police stations. To make matters worse, the poor were subject to frequent abuse and arrest. Fourteen states banned paupers from voting.

Millions of homeless people, mostly men, took to living on the road or the rails. These hobos walked, hitchhiked, or sneaked onto empty railway cars and rode from town to town. One railroad, the Missouri Pacific, counted 200,000 vagrants living in its empty boxcars in 1931. The following year, the Southern Pacific Railroad reported that it had evicted 683,457 people from its freight trains. A black military veteran recalled life as a hobo: "Black and white, it didn't make any difference who you were, 'cause everybody was poor. . . . They didn't have no mothers or sisters, they didn't have no home; they were dirty, they had overalls on, they didn't have no food, they didn't have anything."

**The morning news in a Chicago shantytown** In response to the economic devastation of the Great Depression, numerous shantytowns emerged in cities across the country to house the homeless. Here, a man reads a newspaper outside his makeshift dwelling in Chicago.

In New York City, hundreds of homeless people lived on subway trains. One of them, Karl Monroe, an unemployed reporter, discovered that he could pay a nickel and ride the subway all night, sleeping in his seat. "A good corner seat" on a subway train, he explained, "gives the rider a chance to get a fair nap, and the thing can be repeated endlessly." In 1932, the *New York Times* reported the arrest of fifty-four men for "idling" in a subway. Most of them celebrated, for in going to jail they would get free meals and a bed.

**DESPERATE RESPONSES** As always, those hardest hit were the most disadvantaged groups—immigrants, women, children, farmers, the urban unemployed, Native Americans, and African Americans. Desperate conditions led desperate people to do desperate things. Crime soared, as did street-corner begging, homelessness, and prostitution.

Although the divorce rate dropped, in part because couples could not afford to live separately or pay legal fees, many jobless husbands simply deserted their wives and children. "You don't know what it's like when your husband's out of work," a woman told a reporter. "He's gloomy and unhappy all the time. Life is terrible. You must try all the time to keep him from going crazy."

With their future so uncertain, married couples often decided not to have children, and birth rates plummeted. Many struggling parents sent their children to live with relatives or friends. Some 900,000 children simply left home and joined the growing army of homeless wanderers. During the Great Depression, for the first time ever, more people left the United States than arrived as immigrants.

**PLIGHT OF WORKING WOMEN** The Depression put women in a peculiar position. By 1932, an estimated 20 percent of working women were unemployed, a slightly lower percentage than men. Because women held a disproportionate number of the lowest-paying jobs, they were often able to keep them. Even so, many women also had the added burden of keeping their families together emotionally. Magazines published numerous articles about the challenge of maintaining households when the husband had been "unmanned" by losing his job.

As the Depression deepened, however, married women became the

**Just dropping off a résumé** In 1938, when the federal government opened six custodian positions, 15,000 African American women lined up overnight to turn in their applications. Pictured here is a policeman leaping over a hedge to control the crowd.

primary targets of layoffs. Some twenty-six states passed laws prohibiting their employment, the reasoning being that a married woman—who presumably had a husband to take care of her—should not "steal" a job from a man who may be a husband and father. In a desperate attempt to create jobs for unemployed men, many employers and even whole states adopted policies barring married women from employment. For example, three fourths of the public school systems across the nation during the Great Depression fired women teachers who got married. As a legislator commented, the working woman in Depression-era America was "the first orphan in the storm."

It was acceptable for single white women to find jobs that were considered "women's work": as salesgirls, beauticians, schoolteachers, secretaries, and nurses. The job market for African American women was even more restricted, with most of them limited to working as maids, cooks, or laundresses.

**MINORITIES** Most African Americans still lived in the states of the former Confederacy, where the farm-dominated economy was depressed before 1929 and worsened during the Great Depression. African Americans in the South continued to earn meager livelihoods as tenants and sharecroppers. Pervasive racial discrimination consigned them to the most menial, lowest-paying jobs.

They also continued to be victims of violence and intimidation. Jim Crow laws still excluded most African Americans from voting, and public places like hotels and trains were segregated. Black people were among the hardest hit by the Depression. As a blues song called "Hard Times Ain't Gone Nowhere" revealed, "Hard times don't worry me; I was broke when it first started out." Some 3 million rural southern blacks lived in cramped cabins without electricity, running water, or bathrooms.

In the mills, factories, mines, and businesses of the North, the philosophy of "last hired, first fired" meant that the people who could least afford to be jobless were fired first. Black workers who had left the South to take factory jobs in the North were among the first to be laid off; and this group had the highest rate of joblessness in the early years of the Great Depression. "At no time in the history of the Negro since slavery," reported the Urban League, "has his economic and social outlook seemed so discouraging." Churches and other charity organizations gave aid, but some refused to provide support for minority groups.

Impoverished whites found themselves competing with Latino and Asian farmhands for seasonal work on large corporate farms. Many Chinese, Japanese, and Filipino farm laborers moved to cities. Mexicans, who had come to the United States during the 1920s, were also mostly migrant farmworkers, traveling from farm to farm to work during harvest and planting seasons.

They settled in California, New Mexico, Arizona, Colorado, Texas, and the midwestern states. As economic conditions worsened, government officials called for the deportation of Mexican-born Americans to avoid the cost of providing them with public services. By 1935, more than 500,000 Mexican Americans (250,000 from Texas alone) and their American-born children were deported to Mexico.

Everywhere one looked in the early 1930s, people were suffering. City, county, and state governments proved incapable of managing the misery. As Americans turned to the federal government for answers, Herbert Hoover, the "Great Engineer," struggled to provide them.

# FROM HOOVERISM TO THE NEW DEAL

The Great Depression revealed Herbert Hoover to be a brilliant mediocrity. His initial response to the crisis was denial; there was no calamity, he insisted. All that was needed, he and others in his administration argued, was to let the economy cure itself. The best policy, Treasury secretary Andrew Mellon advised, would be to "liquidate labor, liquidate stocks, liquidate the farmers, liquidate real estate." Letting events run their course, he claimed, would "purge the rottenness out of the [capitalist] system."

Mellon's do-nothing approach did not work, however. Falling wages and declining land and home values made it even harder for struggling farmers, businesses, and households to pay their bills. With so many people losing jobs and income, consumers and businesses simply could not buy enough goods and services to reenergize the economy.

## HOOVER'S EFFORTS AT RECOVERY

As the months passed, President Hoover proved less willing than Andrew Mellon to sit by and let events take their course. He invited business, labor, government, and agricultural leaders to a series of conferences in which he urged companies to maintain employment and wage levels, asked unions to end strikes, and pleaded with state governors to accelerate planned construction projects so as to keep people working. He also formed committees and commissions to study various aspects of the economic calamity.

**UPBEAT MESSAGES** President Hoover became an ineffective cheerleader for capitalism. In early May 1930, he told the U.S. Chamber of Commerce that he was "convinced we have passed the worst and with continued effort we shall rapidly recover." A few weeks later, Hoover assured a group of bankers that the "depression is over." His administration also circulated upbeat slogans such as "Business IS Better" and "Keep Smiling."

Uplifting words were not enough, however, and Hoover never felt comfortable reassuring a desperate nation. His recurring statement—"No one is actually starving. The hoboes . . . are better fed than they have ever been"—was hardly helpful, or, as it turned out, accurate.

**SHORT-SIGHTED TAX INCREASES** The Great Depression was the greatest national emergency since the Civil War, and the nation was woefully unprepared to deal with it. As personal income plummeted, so did government tax revenues. President Hoover insisted on trying to balance the federal budget by raising taxes and cutting budgets—precisely the wrong prescription. He pushed through Congress the Revenue Act of 1932, the largest—and most poorly timed—peacetime tax increase in history, raising the top rate from 24 percent to 63 percent. By taking money out of consumers' pockets, the higher taxes accelerated the economic slowdown. People had less money to spend when what the economy most needed was increased consumer spending.

**HOOVER'S REACTION TO THE SOCIAL CRISIS** By the fall of 1930, many cities were buckling under the strain of lost revenue and human distress. State and local governments cut spending, worsening the economic situation, and the federal government had no programs to deal with homelessness and joblessness. Shantytowns sprouted in vacant lots. People called their makeshift villages *Hoovervilles* to mock the president. To keep warm, they wrapped themselves in newspapers, calling them *Hoover blankets*.

The president's unwillingness to address the social crisis reflected his fear that the nation would be "plunged into socialism" if the government provided direct support to the poor. He still trumpeted the virtues of self-reliance, claiming that government assistance would rob people of the desire to help themselves.

Hoover hoped that the "natural generosity" of the American people and charitable organizations would be sufficient, and he believed that volunteers (the backbone of charity organizations) would relieve the social distress. But his faith in traditional "voluntarism" was misplaced. Local and state relief agencies were overwhelmed by the crisis, as were churches and charitable organizations like the Salvation Army and the Red Cross.

## RISING CRITICISM OF HOOVER

That the economic collapse was so unexpected and intense made people all the more insecure and anxious, and Herbert Hoover increasingly became the target of their frustration. The Democrats shrewdly exploited his predicament. In November 1930, they gained their first national off-year election victory since 1916, winning a majority in the House and a near majority in the Senate.

Hoover refused to see the elections as a warning. Instead, he grew more resistant to calls for federal intervention. The *New York Times* concluded that Hoover had "failed as a party leader. He has failed as an economist. . . . He has failed as a business leader. . . . He has failed as a personality because of [his] awkwardness of manner and speech and lack of mass magnetism." When Hoover asked Treasury secretary Andrew Mellon for a nickel to phone a friend, the secretary replied, "Here are two nickels—call all of them."

**CONGRESSIONAL INITIATIVES**  With a new Congress in session in 1932, demands for federal action forced President Hoover to do more. That year, Congress approved his request to create the **Reconstruction Finance Corporation (RFC)** to make emergency loans to banks, life-insurance companies, and railroads. If the federal government could help huge banks and railroads, asked New York Democratic senator Robert F. Wagner, why not "extend a helping hand to that forlorn American, in every village and every city of the United States, who has been without wages since 1929?" Hoover, however, signed only the Emergency Relief Act (1932), which authorized the RFC to make loans to states for infrastructure projects. Critics called the RFC a "breadline" for businesses while the unemployed went hungry.

**VETERANS IN PROTEST**  Fears of organized revolt arose when almost 20,000 Great War veterans and their families converged on the nation's capital in the spring of 1932. The "**Bonus Expeditionary Force**" pressed Congress to pay the cash bonuses owed to nearly 4 million veterans, many of them now homeless and jobless. In 1924, Congress had passed the Adjusted Compensation Act, which agreed to pay veterans in 1945 a bonus for their war service. Now, in 1932, the House authorized the payments immediately, but the Senate said no because they would have forced a tax increase.

Most of the veterans went home. The rest, along with their families, having no place to go, camped in vacant federal buildings and in a shantytown within sight of the Capitol. They became the first large-scale example of nonviolent protest in the nation's capital.

Eager to remove the veterans, Hoover persuaded Congress to pay for their train tickets home. More left, but hundreds stayed, hoping to meet with the president. Late in July, Attorney General William D. Mitchell ordered the government buildings cleared.

The secretary of war dispatched 700 soldiers to remove the "Bonus Army." The soldiers, commanded by the army chief of staff, General Douglas MacArthur, used horses, tanks, tear gas, and bayonets to disperse the unarmed veterans and their families. Then, exceeding orders, the soldiers burned the makeshift camp. Fifty-five veterans were injured and 135 arrested. The grandstanding MacArthur held a press conference at which he assured the nation that he had suppressed the "insurrectionists" who were spreading a "spirit of revolution."

The attack on the Bonus Army was a public relations disaster and led even more people to view Hoover and the Republicans as heartless. Unbeknownst to the nation, the president had sent a message to MacArthur ordering him not to send his troops in. Hoover, however, perhaps out of embarrassment, took responsibility for MacArthur's assault on the Bonus Army: "Thank God," he declared, "we still have a government in Washington that knows how to deal with a mob."

The Democratic governor of New York was horrified by the assault on the Bonus Army. "Well," Franklin Roosevelt told an aide, "this elects me" as the next president. (The veterans finally received their "bonus" payment in 1936.)

**HOOVER'S PREDICAMENT** The stress of the nation's plight sapped Hoover's health and morale. "I am so tired," he said, "that every bone in my body aches." When aides urged him to be more of a public leader, he replied, "I have no Wilsonian qualities." He hated giving speeches, and when he did he came across as cold and uncaring. He also got along badly with journalists, who often highlighted his sour demeanor and dull, monotone voice. A sculptor claimed that "if you put a rose in Hoover's hand, it would wilt."

The organization genius who had promised Americans "permanent prosperity" became a laughingstock. Unemployment continued to rise, wage levels continued to fall, and millions struggled simply to survive. In the end, Hoover failed because he never understood or acknowledged the seriousness of the nation's economic problems and social distress.

**THE 1932 ELECTION** In June 1932, glum Republicans gathered in Chicago to nominate Herbert Hoover for a second term. By contrast, the Democrats arrived in Chicago a few weeks later confident that they would nominate the next president. Fifty-year-old New York governor Franklin Delano Roosevelt won on the fourth ballot.

Roosevelt—charming, witty, energetic, and eloquent—broke precedent by traveling to Chicago to accept the nomination in person. He told the cheering delegates: "I pledge you, I pledge myself to a *new deal* for the American people" that would "break foolish traditions" and create a new, enlightened administration "of competence and courage." The contest against Hoover, he said, would be "more than a political campaign; it is a call to arms."

Throughout the campaign, Roosevelt stressed that the struggling economy required new ideas and aggressive action. "The country needs, and . . . the country demands bold, persistent experimentation," he said. "Above all, try something." There were "many ways of going forward," but "only one way of standing still."

In contrast to Roosevelt, Hoover lacked vitality and vision. He warned that Roosevelt's proposals for unprecedented government action "would destroy the very foundations of our American system." The election, he said, was a battle "between two philosophies of government" that would decide "the direction our nation will take over a century to come."

On Election Day, voters swept Roosevelt into office, 23 million to 16 million. In 1928, Hoover had carried forty states; four years later, he won but six. Roosevelt had promised Americans a vague "New Deal." Now he had to fashion one.

# CHAPTER REVIEW

## SUMMARY

- **The Reactionary Twenties**   With the end of the Great War, a renewed surge of immigration led to another wave of *nativism*. To Americans who feared that many immigrants were political radicals, the *Sacco and Vanzetti case (1921)* confirmed their suspicions. Nativists persuaded Congress to restrict future immigration, particularly from eastern and southern Europe, in the *Immigration Act of 1924*. Other reactionary movements reflected the feeling of many white Protestants that their religion and way of life were under attack. A revived Ku Klux Klan promoted hatred of Catholics, Jews, immigrants, Communists, and liberals, as well as African Americans. Fundamentalist Protestants campaigned against teaching evolution in public schools. Their efforts culminated in the 1925 *Scopes Trial*. Along with progressive reformers, conservative Protestants supported the nationwide *Prohibition (1920–1933)* of alcoholic beverages. Union membership declined in the 1920s as businesses adopted new techniques (such as the so-called *open shop*) to resist unions.

- **Republican Resurgence**   Although the Eighteenth Amendment (paving the way for Prohibition) and the Nineteenth Amendment (guaranteeing women's right to vote) marked the culmination of progressivism, the movement lost much of its appeal as disillusionment with the Great War and its results created a public preference for disarmament and isolationism, stances reflected in the Five-Power Treaty of 1922. Warren G. Harding's landslide presidential victory in 1920 was based on his call for a *return to normalcy*. Harding and his fellow Republicans, including his vice president and successor, Calvin Coolidge, followed policies advocated by Secretary of the Treasury Andrew Mellon that emphasized lowering taxes and government spending as well as raising tariffs to protect domestic industries. The plan revived the economy. Harding died suddenly in 1923. Coolidge restored trust in the presidency and won reelection in a landslide in 1924. In the 1928 presidential election, Herbert Hoover, secretary of commerce under Harding and Coolidge, won a third straight decisive victory for the Republicans.

- **The Great Depression**   The 1929 stock market crash revealed the structural flaws in the economy, but it was not the only cause of the *Great Depression (1929–1941)*. During the twenties, business owners did not provide adequate wage increases for workers, thus preventing consumers' "purchasing power" from keeping up with increases in production. The nation's agricultural sector also suffered from overproduction. Government policies—such as high tariffs that helped to reduce international trade and the reduction of the nation's money supply as a means of dealing with the financial panic—worsened the emerging economic depression.

- **Hoover's Failure**   Hoover's philosophy of voluntary self-reliance prevented him from using federal intervention to relieve the nation's suffering. When thousands of out-of-work veterans of the Great War protested in Washington, D.C., demanding that Congress pay the cash bonus owed them, their efforts ended in violence. In March 1933, Franklin D. Roosevelt assumed the presidency and set in motion a New Deal that entailed scores of new federal agencies and programs designed to end the depression and put people back to work.

## CHRONOLOGY

| | |
|---|---|
| 1920 | Prohibition begins |
| | Warren G. Harding is elected president |
| 1921 | Congress passes Emergency Immigration Act |
| | Washington Naval Conference |
| 1922 | Five-Power Treaty |
| 1923 | Teapot Dome scandal becomes public |
| | President Harding dies in office and is succeeded by Calvin Coolidge |
| 1924 | Congress passes Immigration Act (Johnson-Reed Act) |
| | Coolidge is reelected president |
| 1925 | Scopes "monkey trial" |
| 1928 | Herbert Hoover is elected president |
| 1929 | Stock market crashes in late October |

## KEY TERMS

nativism p. 973

Immigration Act of 1924 p. 974

Sacco and Vanzetti case (1921) p. 976

Scopes Trial (1925) p. 980

Prohibition (1920–1933) p. 982

return to normalcy p. 987

open shop p. 990

Teapot Dome Affair (1923) p. 995

Great Depression (1929–1941) p. 1004

Reconstruction Finance Corporation (1932) p. 1013

Bonus Expeditionary Force (1932) p. 1013

 INQUIZITIVE

**Go to InQuizitive to see what you've learned—and learn what you've missed—with personalized feedback along the way.**

# 25 The New Deal

## 1933–1939

***Construction of a Dam*** **(1939)** One of the most famous and controversial of the
artists commissioned by the New Deal's Works Progress Administration was William
Gropper, the son of Jewish immigrants who became a Communist sympathizer during
the twenties and thirties. In 1939, he painted this mural displayed in the Department
of the Interior building in Washington, D.C. Based on his observations of dam
construction on the Columbia and Colorado Rivers, Gropper illustrates the sense of
triumph and brotherhood that emerged from the New Deal's massive public projects
during the Great Depression.

The Great Depression was not simply an American event; it was a worldwide economic disaster whose global scale increased its severity and complicated efforts to address its impact. In 1929, Europe was still reeling from the financial effects of the Great War. Once the American economy tumbled, it sent shock waves throughout the world. Economic distress fed the rise of totalitarian regimes—fascism and Nazism in Italy and Germany, communism in the Soviet Union. "Capitalism is dying," theologian Reinhold Niebuhr proclaimed. "Let no one delude himself by hoping for reform from within."

Yet that is exactly what Franklin Delano Roosevelt sought to do in 1933. He would save capitalism by transforming it from within. Like his cousin and hero, Theodore Roosevelt, he believed that the basic problem of twentieth-century life was the excessive power of large corporations. Only the federal government and an active president could regulate corporate capitalism for the public benefit.

Few leaders have taken office in more dire circumstances. Yet within days of becoming president, Roosevelt, often called FDR, took dramatic steps that forever changed the scope and role of the federal government while keeping the nation from fragmenting. He believed that America's democratic form of government had the responsibility to help people who were in distress. With the help of a supportive Congress, he set about enacting dozens of measures to relieve human suffering and promote economic recovery.

FDR was an inspiring personality, overflowing with cheerfulness, strong convictions, and an unshakeable confidence in himself and in the resilience of the American people. He was not committed to any particular ideology; instead, he was a pragmatist willing to try different approaches. As a consequence, his program for economic recovery, the New Deal, was a series of trial-and-error actions rather than a comprehensive scheme. None of the many

## focus questions

1. What were the accomplishments and criticisms of the First New Deal?

2. Analyze why FDR launched a Second New Deal in 1935. How did it differ from the first?

3. What was the purpose and structure of the Social Security system?

4. How did the New Deal transform the role of the federal government in American life?

initiatives worked perfectly, and some failed miserably. Yet their combined effect restored hope and energy to a nation eager for dynamic leadership.

# ROOSEVELT'S NEW DEAL

Franklin Roosevelt promised voters a "New Deal," and within hours of being inaugurated, he and his aides set about creating a "new order of competence and courage." The federal government assumed responsibility for national economic planning and for restoring prosperity and ensuring social security—for all. What Roosevelt called the "forgotten man" (by which he meant the working poor, both men and women) would no longer be forgotten.

**ROOSEVELT'S RISE**  Born in 1882, the only child of wealthy, aristocratic parents, young Franklin Roosevelt enjoyed a pampered life. He was educated by tutors at Springwood, a Hudson River manor near Hyde Park, north of New York City. At age fourteen, he boarded his father's private railroad car and traveled to Massachusetts, where he enrolled in the exclusive Groton school. He then attended Harvard College and Columbia University Law School, where he did not earn a degree. While a law student in 1905, he married Anna Eleanor Roosevelt, his distant cousin and the favorite niece of President Theodore Roosevelt. Eleanor's father, Elliott, was Theodore's alcoholic brother who died in 1894 at age thirty-four.

In 1910, twenty-eight-year-old Franklin Roosevelt won a Democratic seat in the New York State Senate. Tall, handsome, and athletic, he seemed destined for greatness. In 1913, President Woodrow Wilson appointed him assistant secretary of the navy. Seven years later, Roosevelt became James Cox's vice presidential running mate on the Democratic ticket.

**TRIAL BY FIRE**  Then a tragedy occurred. In 1921, at age thirty-nine, Franklin Roosevelt contracted polio, an infectious neuromuscular disease that left him permanently disabled. He would never walk again unaided. Roosevelt fought back, however. For seven years, with his wife Eleanor's help, he strengthened his body to compensate for his disability. The exhausting daily exercise and the awareness that his disability would be permanent transformed him. He became less pompous, more considerate, more focused, and more able to identify with the problems of people facing hard times.

**THE 1933 INAUGURATION**  Inaugurated in March 1933, Franklin Delano Roosevelt assumed leadership during a profound national crisis that threatened the very fabric of American capitalism and unleashed the possibility of widespread civil unrest. "The situation is critical, Franklin," journalist Walter Lippmann warned. "You may have to assume dictatorial powers"—as had happened in Germany, Italy, and the Soviet Union.

Roosevelt did not become a dictator, but he did take extraordinary steps while assuring Americans "that the only thing we have to fear is fear itself." He confessed in his inaugural address that he did not have all the answers, but he did know that "this nation asks for action, and action now." He asked Congress for "a broad Executive power to wage a war against the emergency" just as "if we were in fact invaded by a foreign foe." Roosevelt's uplifting speech won rave reviews. Even the pro-Republican *Chicago Tribune* praised his "courageous confidence."

**THE FIRST HUNDRED DAYS** In March 1933, President Roosevelt confronted four major challenges: reviving the industrial economy, addressing the needs of record numbers of jobless and homeless Americans, rescuing the ravaged farm sector, and reforming those defects of the capitalist system that had contributed to the Depression. The new president admitted that he would try several different "experiments." Some would succeed, and others would fail, but the important thing was to do something bold—and fast. It was no time for timid leadership or paralyzing doubts. The defining characteristic of Roosevelt's approach to presidential leadership was *action*. To advise him, Roosevelt assembled a "brain trust" of specialists—professors, journalists, economists, social workers, and others. "I'm not the smartest fellow in the world," Roosevelt admitted, "but I sure can pick smart colleagues."

**Franklin Delano Roosevelt** Preparing to deliver the first of his popular "fireside chats" to a national radio audience. This message focused on measures to reform the American banking system.

The president and his advisers settled on a three-pronged strategy to revive the economy and help those in need. First, they would tackle the banking crisis and provide short-term emergency relief for the jobless. Roosevelt said, "Our greatest primary task is putting people to work." Second, they would encourage agreements between management and unions designed to keep businesses from failing. Third, they would raise depressed commodity prices (corn, cotton, wheat, beef, pork, etc.) by paying farmers "subsidies" to *reduce* the sizes of their crops and herds so that prices would *rise* and thereby increase farm income over time, even if it meant higher food prices for consumers.

The new Congress was ready to take action. From March 9, when the session opened, to June 16, the so-called First Hundred Days, Congress approved fifteen major pieces of legislation proposed by Roosevelt. Several of these programs comprised what came to be called the **First New Deal** (1933–1935).

## Shoring Up the Financial System

Money is the lubricant of capitalism, and money was fast disappearing from circulation by 1933. Since the stock market crash of 1929, panicky depositors had been withdrawing their money from banks and the stock market—and hoarding gold. Taking so much money out of circulation worsened the Depression and brought the banking system to the brink of collapse.

**BANKING REGULATION** On March 5, 1933, his first full day in office, Franklin Roosevelt called on Congress to convene in emergency session. He asked the legislators to pass the Emergency Banking Relief Act, which declared a four-day bank holiday to allow the financial panic to subside. For the first time, all U.S. banks closed their doors.

Roosevelt's financial experts drafted the Emergency Banking Act of 1933 to restore confidence in banks and inject $2 billion of new cash into the economy. On March 12, in the first of his many radio "fireside chats" to the nation, the president assured his 60 million listeners that it was safer to "keep your money in a reopened bank than under the mattress." The following day, people took their money back to the banks. "Capitalism was saved in eight days," said one of Roosevelt's advisers.

On June 5, 1933, Roosevelt shocked the financial world and earned the scorn of bankers by taking the United States off the gold standard, whereby the amount of dollars in circulation was governed by the amount of gold in government vaults. Dropping the gold standard enabled the president to increase the currency supply and ward off deflation while encouraging the public to spend, which would foster economic growth. As it turned out, the sooner countries abandoned the gold standard, the more quickly their economies recovered. By 1936, most nations had done so.

On June 16, Roosevelt signed the Glass-Steagall Banking Act of 1933. It created the **Federal Deposit Insurance Corporation (FDIC)**, which insured

**The galloping snail**  A vigorous Roosevelt drives Congress to action in this *Detroit News* cartoon from March 1933.

customer bank accounts up to $2,500, thus reducing the likelihood of future panics. The Glass-Steagall Act also called for the separation of commercial banking from investment banking to prevent banks from investing the savings of depositors in the risky stock market. Only banks that specialized in investment could trade shares in the stock market after 1933. In addition, the Federal Reserve Board was given more authority to intervene in future financial emergencies. These steps effectively ended the banking crisis.

**REGULATING WALL STREET**  Before the Great Crash in 1929, there was little government oversight of the securities (stocks and bonds) industry. In 1933, President Roosevelt's administration developed two important pieces of legislation intended to regulate the operations of the stock market and eliminate fraud and abuses.

The Securities Act of 1933 was the first major federal legislation to regulate the sale of stocks and bonds. It required every corporation that issued stock for public sale to disclose all relevant information about the operations and management of the company so that investors could know what they were buying. The second bill, the Securities Exchange Act of 1934, established the **Securities and Exchange Commission** to enforce the new laws and regulations governing the issuance and trading of stocks and bonds.

**THE FEDERAL BUDGET** As part of the breathless pace of the First Hundred Days, FDR convinced Congress to pass the Economy Act allowing him to cut government workers' salaries, reduce payments to military veterans for non-service-connected disabilities, and reorganize federal agencies—all designed to reduce government expenses. He then took the dramatic step of ending Prohibition—in part because it was so widely violated, in part because most Democrats wanted to end it, and in part because he wanted to regain the federal tax revenues from the sale of alcoholic beverages. The Twenty-First Amendment, ratified on December 5, 1933, ended Prohibition.

## Helping the Unemployed and Homeless

Another top priority was relieving the human distress caused by joblessness and homelessness. With a sense of urgency that Herbert Hoover had never summoned, President Roosevelt pushed through a series of programs that created what came to be called the "welfare state." He insisted that the federal government help the unemployed and homeless by providing them jobs. For the first time, the federal government took responsibility for assisting the most desperate Americans.

**PUTTING PEOPLE TO WORK** The Federal Emergency Relief Administration (FERA), headed by Harry L. Hopkins, was Roosevelt's first effort to deal with massive unemployment. It sent money to the states to spend on the unemployed and homeless. After the state-sponsored programs proved inadequate, Congress created the Civil Works Administration (CWA) in November 1933. It marked the first large-scale *federal* effort to put people directly on the government payroll at competitive wages: 40¢ an hour for unskilled workers, $1 for skilled.

The CWA provided 4 million federal jobs during the winter of 1933–1934 and organized a variety of useful projects: repairing 500,000 miles of roads, laying sewer lines, constructing or improving more than 1,000 airports and 40,000 public schools, and providing 50,000 teaching jobs that helped keep small rural public schools open. When the program's cost soared, however, Roosevelt ordered the CWA dissolved. By April 1934, 4 million workers were again unemployed.

**THE CCC** The most successful New Deal jobs program was the Civilian Conservation Corps (CCC), managed by the War Department. It built 2,500 camps in forty-seven states to house up to half a million unemployed, unmarried young men ages seventeen to twenty-seven. The CCC also recruited 150,000 jobless military veterans and 85,000 Native Americans. Congress

**Federal relief programs** Civilian Conservation Corps enrollees in 1933, on a break from work. Directed by army officers and foresters, the CCC camps were operated like military bases.

passed the CCC bill only after Oscar De Priest, an African American legislator from Illinois, introduced an amendment requiring that the agency not discriminate on account of race, color, or creed. Women were excluded from working in the CCC; African Americans and Native Americans were housed in segregated facilities.

Over the next nine years, the 2.5 million CCC enrollees were provided shelter in barracks, given uniforms, food, and a small wage of $30 a month ($25 of which had to be sent home to their families). The young men could also earn high-school diplomas.

CCC workers cleared brush; constructed roads, bridges, campgrounds, fire towers, fish hatcheries, and 800 parks; planted 3 *billion* trees; taught farmers how to control soil erosion; built 13,000 miles of trails, including the Appalachian Trail from Georgia to Maine; and fought fires. Roosevelt, a dedicated conservationist, saw the New Deal as an opportunity to reinvigorate the movement to preserve America's natural resources. He believed that a "nation that destroys its soils destroys itself. Forests are the lungs of our land, purifying the air and giving fresh strength to our people."

**SAVING HOMES** In 1933, an estimated 1,000 homes or farms were being foreclosed upon each day because people could not pay their monthly mortgages. President Roosevelt convinced Congress to create the Home Owners'

Loan Corporation, which helped people refinance their mortgages at lower interest rates. In 1934, Roosevelt created the Federal Housing Administration (FHA), which offered mortgages of much longer duration (twenty years) to reduce monthly payments. Prior to that, typical home mortgages had terms of less than ten years.

**REVIVING THE INDUSTRIAL SECTOR** The centerpiece of the New Deal's efforts to revive the industrial economy was the National Industrial Recovery Act (NIRA) of 1933. It created massive public-works construction projects funded by the federal government. The NIRA started the Public Works Administration (PWA), granting $3.3 billion for the construction of government buildings, highways, bridges, dams, port facilities, and sewage plants. Among its noteworthy projects were the Blue Ridge Parkway in North Carolina and the Grand Coulee Dam in Washington State. The PWA also built forty-seven public housing projects for low-income Americans, all of them segregated by race.

A second, more controversial part of the NIRA created the **National Recovery Administration (NRA)**. The NRA represented a radical shift in the federal government's role in the economy. Never before in peacetime had Washington bureaucrats taken charge of setting prices, wages, and standards for working conditions.

The primary purpose of the NRA was to promote economic growth by ignoring anti-trust laws and allowing executives of competing businesses to negotiate among themselves and with labor unions to create "codes of fair competition" that would set prices, production levels, minimum wages, and maximum hours within each industry, no matter how small. In New York City, for example, women who made their living as burlesque-show strippers agreed to an NRA code limiting the number of performers on stage and the number of performances they could provide each night.

The NRA codes included "fair labor" policies long sought by unions and social progressives: a national forty-hour workweek with a maximum eight-hour workday, minimum weekly wages of $13 ($12 in the South, where living costs were lower), and a ban on the employment of children under the age of sixteen. The NRA also guaranteed the right of workers to organize unions.

For a time, the downward spiral of wages and prices subsided. As soon as economic recovery began, however, small business owners complained that the NRA's price-fixing robbed small producers of the chance to compete with large corporations. And because NRA wage codes excluded agricultural and domestic workers (at the insistence of southern Democrats), few African Americans derived any benefit. When the Supreme Court declared the NRA unconstitutional in May 1935 for assigning lawmaking powers to the NRA in violation of the Constitution's allocation of such authority only to Congress, few regretted its demise.

Despite being declared unconstitutional, some NRA policies that remained in place had lasting effects. New workplace standards, such as the forty-hour workweek; a national minimum wage; and restrictions that ended child labor were part of the NRA legacy. Its endorsement of collective bargaining spurred the growth of unions. Yet, as 1934 ended, industrial recovery was still feeble.

**AGRICULTURAL ASSISTANCE** In addition to rescuing the banks and providing jobs to the unemployed, Franklin Roosevelt created the Farm Credit Administration to help farmers deal with their debts and lower their mortgage payments to avoid bankruptcy.

The **Agricultural Adjustment Act** of 1933 created the Agricultural Adjustment Administration (AAA), which sought to raise prices for crops and herds by paying farmers to cut production. The money came from a tax on the businesses that processed food crops and certain agricultural commodities—cotton gins, flour mills, and slaughterhouses.

By the time the AAA was created, however, the spring planting season was under way. The prospect of another bumper cotton crop forced the AAA to pay farmers to "plow-under" the sprouting seeds in their fields.

By the end of 1934, the AAA efforts had worked. Wheat, cotton, and corn production had declined, and prices for those commodities had risen. Farm income increased by 58 percent between 1932 and 1935.

**A NEW ROLE FOR GOVERNMENT** At the end of the First Hundred Days of Franklin Roosevelt's presidency, the principle of an *activist* federal government had been established. While journalists characterized the AAA, NRA, CCC, CWA, and other New Deal programs as "alphabet soup," and conservative critics warned that Roosevelt was leading America toward fascism or communism, the president had become the most popular man in the nation.

**DUST BOWL MIGRANTS** At the same time that the agricultural economy was struggling, a terrible drought created an ecological catastrophe known as the **Dust Bowl**. Colorado, New Mexico, Kansas, Nebraska, Texas, Arkansas, and Oklahoma were hardest hit. With little rain for months, crops withered, and income plummeted. Strong winds swept across the treeless plains, scooping up tons of parched topsoil into billowing dark clouds, called black blizzards, which engulfed farms and towns. By 1938, topsoil had disappeared from more than 25 million acres of prairie land.

**"Okies" on the run** A sharecropping family reaches its destination of Bakersfield, California, in 1935, after "we got blowed out in Oklahoma."

Farmers could not pay their debts, and banks foreclosed on family farms. Suicides soared, and millions abandoned their farms and headed toward California, where jobs were said to be plentiful. Disparagingly called "Okies" or "Arkies," most of the Dust Bowl refugees were from Arkansas, Texas, Missouri, and Oklahoma. During the 1930s and 1940s, some 800,000 people, mostly whites, headed to the Far West.

Most of them went to California's urban areas—Los Angeles, San Diego, or San Francisco. Others moved into the San Joaquin Valley, the state's agricultural heartland. There they discovered that California was no paradise. Most had to work as farm laborers. Living in tents or crude cabins, they suffered from exposure to the elements, poor sanitation, and social abuse. As one transplanted worker from Oklahoma reported, when the big farmers "need us they call us *migrants*, and when we've picked their crop, we're *bums* and we got to get out."

**THE TENNESSEE VALLEY AUTHORITY** Early in his presidency, Franklin Roosevelt declared that the "South is the nation's number one economic problem." Indeed, since the end of the Civil War, the economy and quality of life in the southern states had lagged far behind the rest of the nation. That gap only widened during the Great Depression.

To help, Roosevelt created one of the most innovative programs of the First New Deal: the Tennessee Valley Authority (TVA), which brought electrical power, flood control efforts, and jobs to Appalachia, the desperately poor mountainous region that stretched from West Virginia through western Virginia and North Carolina, Kentucky, eastern Tennessee, and northern Georgia and Alabama.

By 1940, the TVA, a multipurpose public corporation, had constructed twenty-one hydroelectric dams that created the "Great Lakes of the South" in Kentucky, Tennessee, North Carolina, Georgia, and Alabama, and produced enough electricity to power the entire region, at about half the average national rate. The TVA also dredged rivers to allow for boat and barge traffic, promoted soil conservation and forestry management, attracted new industries, and improved schools and libraries. It provided 1.5 million isolated farms with electricity and indoor plumbing.

Building those huge dams in Appalachia and the resulting lakes, however, meant displacing thousands from homes and villages that were destroyed to make way for progress. "I don't want to move," said an elderly East Tennessee woman. "I want to sit here and look out over these hills where I was born."

Yet overall, the First New Deal programs—and Roosevelt's leadership—had given Americans a renewed faith in the future. In the congressional elections of 1934, the Democrats increased their majority in Congress.

**ELEANOR ROOSEVELT**  One of the reasons for FDR's popularity was his energetic wife, Eleanor, who would prove to be one of the most influential leaders of the twentieth century. Never had a first lady been so engaged in public life or so widely beloved. She was her husband's moral compass, prodding him about social-justice issues while steadfastly supporting his political ambitions and policies.

Soon after she married Franklin in 1905, Eleanor learned that his domineering mother, Sara Delano Roosevelt, would always be the most important woman in his life. (Sara once had workers erect a ladder to Franklin's boarding school window so that she could climb up and care for him during an illness.) "He might have been happier with a wife who was completely uncritical," Eleanor wrote later. "That I was never able to be, and he had to find it in other people."

Eleanor was dedicated to progressive and humanitarian causes. While raising six children, she worked tirelessly on behalf of women, African Americans, and youth, giving voice to the voiceless and hope to the hopeless. Her

**Eleanor Roosevelt** Intelligent, principled, and a political figure in her own right, she is pictured here addressing the Red Cross Convention.

compassion resulted in large part from the self-doubt and loneliness she had experienced as the ignored child of an alcoholic father and an aloof mother. Throughout her life, she fought a paralyzing fear of being unloved.

In September 1918, the Roosevelts' marriage changed forever when Eleanor, while unpacking Franklin's suitcase after a trip, discovered love letters he had exchanged with Lucy Mercer, her friend and personal secretary. As Eleanor read the letters, "the bottom dropped out" of her world.

Eleanor offered Franklin a divorce, but he knew that would end his political future since divorce was not a socially accepted practice at the time. So they decided to maintain their marriage as a political partnership. As their son James said, the relationship became an "armed truce"—more a merger than a marriage.

Franklin and Eleanor were both concerned for each other's happiness while acknowledging their inability to provide it. In the White House, they lived apart, rarely seeing each other except for formal occasions and public events. As Eleanor confided to a friend, "There is no fundamental love to draw on," no passion or intimacy, "just respect and affection."

Over time, Eleanor compensated for her cooled relationship with Franklin by nurturing "a life of my own" and forming "special friendships" with men and women.

Lorena "Hick" Hickok, the first female journalist to have her byline featured on the front page of the *New York Times* and the only female reporter on Franklin's 1932 "Roosevelt Special" campaign train, had asked the Associated Press to assign her to cover the First Lady. Within weeks, the women fell deeply in love, and Eleanor proudly wore an emerald ring Hick had given her as proof of their special relationship. "Remember," Eleanor told Hick in early 1933, "no one is just what you are to me."

By then, Hickok had quit her job in order to become Eleanor's nearly constant traveling companion. When separated, they wrote letters, more than 3,000 of them during their thirty-year-long relationship. "I wish I could lie down beside you tonight & take you in my arms," Eleanor wrote Hick one night. The two women became so infatuated that Eleanor convinced Hick to move into the White House, assuming a post in the Federal Emergency Relief Administration.

During the summer of 1933, Eleanor and Hick drove around New England in a blue convertible, surprising desk clerks at motels when they showed up without reservations. Two years later, however, Eleanor ended their relationship.

While redefining the role of the First Lady, Eleanor Roosevelt became an outspoken and relentless social activist: the first woman to address a national political convention, write a nationally syndicated newspaper column, and hold press conferences. She crisscrossed the nation, speaking in support of the New Deal, meeting with African American leaders, supporting equal access for women in the workforce and in labor unions, and urging Americans to live up to their humanitarian ideals. She helped convince her husband to reverse Woodrow Wilson's policy of segregation of federal government agencies and offices.

**Eleanor and Hick** Here, Roosevelt and Hickok walk side by side during an inspection trip to Puerto Rico.

In 1933, Eleanor convened a White House conference on the emergency needs of women. It urged the Federal Emergency Relief Administration (FERA) to ensure that "women are employed wherever possible." Within six months, some 300,000 women were at work on various federal government projects.

Eleanor Roosevelt had become, said a journalist, "the most influential woman of our times." A popular joke claimed that the president's nightly prayer was: "Dear God, please make Eleanor a little tired." In fact, however, he was deeply dependent on his wife. She was the impatient agitator dedicated to what *should* be done; he was the calculating politician concerned with what *could* be done.

## THE NEW DEAL UNDER FIRE

By 1934, Franklin Roosevelt had become the best loved and most hated president of the twentieth century. He was loved because he believed in and fought for the common people. The president, said a southern white tenant farmer, "is as good a man as ever lived." A textile mill worker reinforced the point by declaring that Roosevelt "is the biggest-hearted man we ever had in the White House."

He was also loved for what a French leader called his "glittering personality." Roosevelt, with his famously arched eyebrows, upturned chin, and twinkling eyes, radiated optimism and confidence, courage in a crisis, and a self-assurance bordering on arrogance. "Meeting him," said British prime minister Winston Churchill, "was like uncorking a bottle of champagne." Roosevelt, he added, was "the greatest man I have ever known."

Roosevelt was the most visible and accessible of all U.S. presidents. Twice a week he held press conferences, explaining new legislation, addressing questions and criticisms, and winning over most journalists while befuddling his opponents. Huey Long, a Democratic senator from Louisiana and one of Roosevelt's harshest critics, complained that the president could charm a snake: "You go in there [the White House] and see FDR wanting to tear him apart. You come out whistling 'Dixie.'"

But even Roosevelt's charm had its limits. He was despised by business leaders and political conservatives who believed the New Deal and the higher taxes it required were moving America toward socialism. Some called Roosevelt a "traitor to his [aristocratic] class."

Others, on the left, hated him for not doing enough to end the Depression. By the mid-1930s, the early New Deal programs had slowed the economy's downward slide, but prosperity remained elusive. "We have been patient and long suffering," said a farm leader. "We were promised a New Deal. . . . Instead, we have the same old stacked deck."

In many respects, the contrasting opinions of Roosevelt reflected his own divided personality and erratic management style. He was both a man of idealistic principles and a practical politician prone to snap judgments, capable of both compromise and contradictory actions. He once admitted to an aide that to implement the New Deal he had to "deceive, misrepresent, leave false impressions . . . and trust to charm, loyalty, and the result to make up for it. . . . A great man cannot be a good man."

## CONTINUING HARDSHIPS

Economic growth during FDR's first term averaged 9 percent, a peacetime record, but extensive suffering persisted. As late as 1939, some 9.5 million workers (17 percent of the labor force) remained unemployed.

**IMMIGRATION AND THE GREAT DEPRESSION** There was no New Deal for immigrants. Hard times had always provoked anti-immigration feelings, and the Great Depression was no exception. Nativist prejudices prevailed as people blamed "aliens" for taking "Americans' jobs." In 1935, the *New York American* newspaper declared that "existing immigration laws ought to be strengthened not weakened."

Congressman Martin Dies of Texas, a powerful Democrat, blamed the Depression itself on immigration. "If we had refused admission to the 16,500,000 foreign-born who are living in this country today, we would have no unemployment problem to distress and harass us." Dies was an ardent nativist who viewed immigration as the nation's greatest threat. "There is no middle ground or compromise" on the issue, he argued. "Either we are for or against America. If we are for America, we must be for the exclusion of these new-seed immigrants and the deportation of those unlawfully here."

Opposing such efforts was Congressman Vito Marcantonio, the son of Italian immigrants whose New York City district was filled with immigrants from Italy and Puerto Rico. "Let us legislate not by hysteria but with common sense," he told the House of Representatives. Marcantonio expressed his sorrow and disbelief that congressmen "would dare talk disparagingly about any racial group in the United States where, after all, we are all of alien stock." His strenuous opposition to anti-immigrant bills prevented their passage during the mid-1930s, a development all the more remarkable for the failure of Franklin Roosevelt to speak out on the issue. He refused to take political risks by protecting immigrants. The president was fearful of losing Democratic support in the South.

**AFRICAN AMERICANS AND THE NEW DEAL** The New Deal also had blind spots. Franklin Delano Roosevelt was never as progressive on social issues as most people assumed. A northern senator was shocked to hear the president speak of "the nigger vote." FDR showed little interest in the plight of African Americans, even as black voters were shifting from the Republicans (the "party of Lincoln") to the Democrats. And like Woodrow Wilson before him, he failed to address long-standing patterns of racism and segregation in the South for fear of angering conservative southern Democrats in Congress.

As a result, many New Deal programs discriminated against African Americans. As Mary White Ovington, treasurer of the National Association for the Advancement of Colored People (NAACP), stressed, the racism in any agency "varies according to the white people chosen to administer it, but always there is discrimination."

**"There's no way like the American way"** Margaret Bourke-White's famous 1937 photograph of desperate people waiting in a disaster-relief line in Louisville, Kentucky, captures the continuing racial divide of the era and the elusiveness of the "American Dream" for many minorities.

For example, the payments from the AAA to farm owners to take land *out* of production in an effort to raise prices for farm products forced hundreds of thousands of tenant farmers and sharecroppers, both black and white, off the land. In addition, the FHA refused to guarantee mortgages on houses purchased by African Americans in white neighborhoods, and both the CCC and the TVA practiced racial segregation within their facilities.

The NAACP waged an energetic campaign against racial prejudice throughout the 1930s, as did Eleanor Roosevelt, and the president did appoint more African Americans to significant government positions than had any of his predecessors. One of the most visible was Mary McLeod Bethune, the child of slaves from South Carolina, who had founded Bethune-Cookman College in Daytona Beach, Florida, and served as head of the NAACP in the 1920s. In 1935, Roosevelt named her director of the Division of Negro Affairs within the National Youth Administration, an agency that provided jobs to unemployed young Americans.

**COURT CASES AND CIVIL LIBERTIES** Racial prejudice in the South remained unabated. In a 1931 Alabama case, an all-white jury, on flimsy, conflicting testimony, convicted nine black boys and young men, ranging in age from thirteen to twenty-one, of raping two white women while riding a freight train. Eight of the "Scottsboro Boys" were sentenced to death as white spectators cheered. In his award-winning novel *Native Son* (1940), African American writer Richard Wright recalled the "mob who surrounded the Scottsboro jail with rope and kerosene."

The injustice of the Scottsboro case sparked protests throughout the world. The two white women, it turned out, had been selling sex to white and black teens on the train. One of the women eventually recanted and began appearing at rallies on behalf of the defendants.

No case in legal history produced as many trials, appeals, reversals, and retrials as the Scottsboro case. Further, it prompted two important rulings. In *Powell v. Alabama* (1932), the U.S. Supreme Court overturned the original convictions and ordered new trials because the judge had not ensured that the accused were provided adequate defense attorneys. In *Norris v. Alabama* (1935), the Court ruled that the systematic exclusion of African Americans from Alabama juries had denied the Scottsboro defendants equal protection under the law—a principle that had widespread impact on state courts by opening up juries to African Americans.

Although Alabama eventually dropped the charges against the four youngest Scottsboro defendants and granted paroles to the others, their lives were ruined. The last defendant left prison in 1950.

**Scottsboro case** Haywood Patterson (center), one of the defendants in the case, with his attorney, Samuel Leibowitz (left) in Decatur, Alabama, in 1933.

**NATIVE AMERICANS AND THE DEPRESSION** The Great Depression also ravaged Native Americans. Some were initially encouraged by President Roosevelt's appointment of John Collier as commissioner of the Bureau of Indian Affairs (BIA). Collier steadily increased the number of Native Americans employed by the BIA and ensured that all Indians gained access to New Deal relief programs.

Collier's primary objective, however, was passage of the Indian Reorganization Act. Designed to reinvigorate Native American cultural traditions by restoring land to tribes, the proposed law would have granted them the right to start businesses, establish self-governing constitutions, and receive federal funds for vocational training and economic development. The act that Congress passed, however, was a much-diluted version, and the "Indian New Deal" brought only partial improvements. It did, however, spur several tribes to revise their constitutions so as to give women the right to vote and hold office.

**"Indian New Deal"** Arrayed in traditional dress, several Hopi Native American chiefs visiting from Arizona are honored at a ceremony of the new Interior Department building in Washington, D.C. Seated left to right: Chief Loma Haftowa, Chief Kol Chaf Towa, and United States Indian Commissioner John Collier.

## CULTURAL LIFE DURING THE DEPRESSION

One might have expected the onset of the Great Depression to have deepened the despair of the Lost Generation of writers, artists, and intellectuals during the 1920s. Instead, it brought them a renewed sense of militancy and affirmation. By the summer of 1932, even the "golden boy" of the Lost Generation, F. Scott Fitzgerald, had declared that "to bring on the revolution, it may be necessary to work within the Communist party."

Few Americans remained members of the Communist party for long, however. Most writers rebelled at demands to hew to a shifting party line, and many abandoned communism by the end of the decade upon learning that Soviet leader Josef Stalin practiced a tyranny more horrible than that of the Russian czars.

**LITERATURE AND THE DEPRESSION** Among the writers who addressed themes of social significance during the 1930s, two deserve special notice: John Steinbeck and Richard Wright. To capture the ordeal of the Depression in *The Grapes of Wrath* (1939), Steinbeck traveled with displaced "Okies" driven from the Dust Bowl to chase the false rumor that good jobs were to be had for the taking in the fields of California's Central Valley. This firsthand experience allowed Steinbeck to create a vivid tale of the Joad family's gritty struggle for survival. To him, the solidarity of struggling people was the theme of the Depression. As Tom Joad promises, "Wherever there's a fight so hungry people can eat, I'll be there."

Among the most talented novelists to emerge in the 1930s was Richard Wright. The grandson of former slaves and the son of a Mississippi sharecropper who deserted his family, Wright ended his formal schooling with the ninth grade (as valedictorian of his class). He then worked in Memphis and devoured books he borrowed on a white friend's library card, all the while saving to go north. In Chicago, his period as a Communist, from 1934 to 1944, gave him an intellectual framework for his powerful novels centered on the quest for social justice.

*Native Son* (1940), Wright's masterpiece, focuses on the forgotten Americans at the bottom of the heap. It's the story of twenty-year-old Bigger Thomas, a black pool shark and petty thief imprisoned in a Chicago ghetto by virtue of his birth. "Bigger, sometimes I wonder why I birthed you," his God-fearing mother tells him. "Honest, you the most no-countest man I ever seen in all my life." Bigger fears and envies whites. "Every time I get to thinking about me being black and they being white, me being here and they being there," he explains, "I feel like something awful's going to happen to me."

And something awful does happen. An accidental murder and its cover-up lead him to more heinous crimes, all of which, Wright suggests, resulted from the racism in American society. At Bigger's murder trial, his attorney, Mr. Max, pleads for African Americans in general: "They are not simply twelve million people; in reality they constitute a separate nation, stunted, stripped and held captive *within* this nation." Many of them are overflowing with "balked longing for some kind of fulfilment and exultation"; and their seething futility is "what makes our future seem a looming image of violence."

**POPULAR CULTURE** While many writers and artists dealt with the suffering and social tensions aroused by the Great Depression, the more popular cultural outlets, such as radio programs and movies, provided a welcome escape. In 1930, more than 10 million families owned a radio; by the end of the decade, the number had tripled.

Movies were transformed by the introduction of sound. The "talkies" made movies the most popular form of entertainment during the 1930s, and the introduction of double features in 1931 and the construction of outdoor drive-in theaters in 1933 boosted interest and attendance. More than 60 percent of the population—70 million people—paid a quarter to see at least one movie each week.

The movies rarely dealt directly with hard times. People wanted to be entertained and uplifted. In *Stand Up and Cheer!* (1934), featuring child star Shirley Temple, President Roosevelt appoints a Broadway producer to his cabinet as Secretary of Amusement. His goal is to use entertainment to distract people from the ravages of the Depression.

Most feature films transported viewers into the escapist realms of adventure, spectacle, and fantasy. *Gone with the Wind* (1939), based on Margaret Mitchell's Pulitzer Prize-winning novel, was a good example, as were *The Wizard of Oz* (1939) and Walt Disney's Mickey Mouse cartoons. Moviegoers also relished shoot-'em-up gangster films, extravagant musicals (especially those starring dancers Fred Astaire and Ginger Rogers), "screwball" romantic comedies like *It Happened One Night* (1934), *My Man Godfrey* (1936), and *Mister Deeds Goes to Town* (1936), and horror films such as *Dracula* (1931), *Frankenstein* (1931), *The Mummy* (1932), *King Kong* (1933), *The Invisible Man* (1933), and *Werewolf of London* (1935).

Perhaps the best way to escape the Depression was to watch the zany comedies of the Marx Brothers. As one Hollywood official explained, the movies of the 1930s were intended to "laugh the big bad wolf of the depression out of the public mind." *The Cocoanuts* (1929), *Animal Crackers* (1930), *Monkey Business* (1931), *Horse Feathers* (1932), and *Duck Soup* (1933) introduced moviegoers to the anarchic antics of Chico, Groucho, Harpo, and Zeppo Marx, who combined slapstick humor with verbal wit to create plotless masterpieces of irreverent satire.

*A Paramount Picture* (1934)  The glamor of actress Claudette Colbert's Cleopatra is sharply contrasted with the exhaustion of the average theatergoer in this painting by Reginald Marsh. The growing popularity of movies offered Americans escape from the daily challenges of the Great Depression, although Marsh's work suggests that this was fleeting at best.

## CRITICS ASSAULT THE NEW DEAL

For all their criticisms of New Deal programs, Native Americans and African Americans still voted in large majorities for Franklin Roosevelt. Other New Deal critics, however, hated Roosevelt and despised his policies. Many Republican business executives were so angered by the president's promotion of a welfare state and support for labor unions that they refused to use his name, calling him instead "that man in the White House."

**HUEY LONG** Others criticized Roosevelt for not doing enough to help the common people. The most potent of the president's "populist" opponents was Huey Pierce Long Jr., the flamboyant Democratic senator from Louisiana. A short, colorful man with wild, curly hair, Long was a classic demagogue, a theatrical politician who appealed to the raw emotions of the masses (populism). The swaggering son of a backwoods farmer, he sported pink suits and pastel shirts, red ties, and two-toned shoes. Long claimed to be leading a crusade to serve the poor, arguing that Louisiana would be a place where "every man [is] a king, but no one wears a crown."

First as Louisiana's governor, then as its powerful U.S. senator, Long came to view the state as his personal empire. Reporters called him the "dictator of Louisiana." True, he reduced state taxes, improved roads and schools, built charity hospitals, and provided better public services. But in the process, he used bribery, intimidation, and blackmail to get his way.

**Huey Long** As the powerful governor of Louisiana, Long was a shrewd lawyer and "wheeler-dealer" politician.

In 1933, Long arrived in Washington as a supporter of Roosevelt and the New Deal, but he quickly grew suspicious of the NRA's efforts to cooperate with Big Business. Having developed presidential aspirations, he also grew jealous of Roosevelt's popularity.

To launch his presidential candidacy, Long devised a simplistic plan that he called the Share-the-Wealth Society. Long wanted to raise taxes on the wealthiest Americans and redistribute the money to "the people"—giving every poor family $5,000 and every wage worker an annual income of $2,500, providing pensions to retirees, reducing working hours, paying bonuses to military veterans, and enabling every qualified student to attend college. It did not matter that his plan would have spent far more money than his proposed taxes would have raised. As he told a group of Iowa farmers, "Maybe somebody says I don't understand it [government finance]. Well, you don't have to. Just shut your damn eyes and believe it. That's all."

By early 1935, Long claimed to have enough support to unseat Roosevelt: "He's a phony. . . . He's scared of me. I can outpromise him, and he knows it. People will believe me, and they won't believe him." Long's antics led Roosevelt to declare that the Louisiana senator was "one of the two most dangerous men in the country." (The other was General Douglas MacArthur.)

**THE TOWNSEND PLAN** Another critic of Roosevelt who championed a form of populist capitalism was Francis E. Townsend, a retired California doctor. Shocked by the sight of three elderly women digging through garbage cans for food scraps, he began promoting the Townsend Recovery Plan in 1934. He wanted the federal government to pay $200 a month to every American over age sixty who agreed to quit working. The recipients would have to spend the money each month.

Townsend claimed that his plan would create jobs for young people by giving older people the means to retire, and it would energize the economy by enabling retirees to buy more products. But like Long's Share-the-Wealth scheme, the numbers in Townsend's plan did not add up. It would have paid retirees, only 9 percent of the population, more than half the total national income.

Townsend, like Long, didn't care about his plan's cost. Not surprisingly, it attracted great support among Americans sixty years and older. Advocates flooded the White House with letters urging Roosevelt to enact it.

**FATHER COUGHLIN** A third outspoken critic of FDR and New Deal was Father Charles E. Coughlin, a Canadian-born Roman Catholic "radio priest" in Detroit, Michigan. In fiery weekly broadcasts that attracted as many as 40 million listeners nationwide, he assailed President Roosevelt as "anti-God" and claimed that the New Deal was a Communist conspiracy. Coughlin wanted to put all banks, utilities, oil companies, and "our God-given natural resources" under government control.

During the 1930s, as Fascism and Nazism gained power in Europe, Coughlin became rabidly anti-Semitic, claiming that Roosevelt was a tool of "international Jewish bankers" and relabeling the New Deal the "Jew Deal." He praised Adolf Hitler and the Nazis for killing Jews because they were all Communists. During the 1940 presidential campaign, Coughlin gave a Nazi salute and bragged, "When we get through with the Jews in America, they'll think the treatment they received in Germany was nothing."

Such threats finally galvanized opposition groups across the country, both Jewish and non-Jewish. They exerted enough pressure to force radio stations to drop his weekly broadcast. By late 1940, Coughlin's radio program went off the air.

In the mid-thirties, however, Coughlin was at the peak of his influence, and, along with Francis Townsend and Huey Long, they formed a powerful threat to Roosevelt's reelection. A 1935 poll showed that Long could draw more than 5 million votes as a third-party candidate for president, perhaps enough to prevent Roosevelt's reelection. General Hugh S. Johnson, head of the NRA, warned corporate executives, "You can laugh at Father Coughlin. You can snort at Huey Long—but this country was never under a greater menace."

Roosevelt decided to "steal the thunder" from his three most visible critics by instituting an array of new programs. "I'm fighting Communism, Huey Longism, Coughlinism, Townsendism," he told a reporter in early 1935. He explained that he needed "to save our system, the capitalist system" from such "crackpot ideas."

## OPPOSITION FROM THE COURT

The growing opposition to the New Deal came from all directions. By the mid-1930s, businesses were filing lawsuits against various elements of the New Deal, and some of them made their way to the U.S. Supreme Court.

On May 27, 1935, the Court killed the National Industrial Recovery Act (NIRA) by a unanimous vote. In *Schechter Poultry Corporation v. United States*, the justices ruled that Congress had given too much authority to the president when the National Recovery Administration (NRA) brought business and labor leaders together to create "codes of fair competition" for their industries—an activity that violated federal anti-trust laws.

On January 6, 1936, in *United States v. Butler*, the Supreme Court declared the Agricultural Adjustment Act's tax on "middle men," the companies that processed food crops and warehoused commodities like cotton, unconstitutional. In response, the Roosevelt administration passed the Agricultural Adjustment Act of 1938, which reestablished the earlier crop-reduction payment programs but left out the tax on processors. Although the AAA helped boost the overall farm economy, conservatives criticized its sweeping powers.

By the end of its 1936 term, the Supreme Court had ruled against New Deal programs in seven of nine major cases. Similar conservative judicial reasoning, Roosevelt warned, might endanger other New Deal programs—if he did not prevent it.

# THE SECOND NEW DEAL

To rescue his legislative program from judicial and political challenges, President Roosevelt launched in January 1935 the second, more radical phase of the New Deal, explaining that "social justice . . . has become a definite goal" of his administration. In his effort to undermine Long's appeal, the president called on Congress to pass legislation that included another federal construction program to employ the jobless; banking reforms; higher taxes on the wealthy; and "social security" programs to protect people during unemployment, old age, and illness. Roosevelt's closest aide, Harry L. Hopkins, told the cabinet: "Boys—this is our hour. We've got to get everything we want—a [public] works program, social security, wages and hours, everything—now or never."

**THE WPA** In the first three months of 1935, dubbed the Second Hundred Days, Roosevelt convinced Congress to pass most of the **Second New Deal**'s "must" legislation. The results of the Second New Deal (1935-1938) would change the face of American life.

**Federal art project** A group of WPA artists at work on *Building the Transcontinental Railroad*, a mural celebrating the contributions of foreign newcomers that appears in the immigrants' dining hall on Ellis Island, outside New York City.

The first major initiative was the $4.8 billion Emergency Relief Appropriation Act. The largest peacetime spending bill in history to that point, it included an array of job programs managed by a new agency, the **Works Progress Administration (WPA)**.

The WPA quickly became the nation's largest employer, hiring an average of 2 million people annually over four years. WPA workers built New York's LaGuardia Airport; restored the St. Louis riverfront; and employed a wide range of writers, artists, actors, and musicians in new cultural programs: the Federal Theatre Project, the Federal Art Project, the Federal Music Project, and the Federal Writers' Project.

The National Youth Administration (NYA), also under the WPA, provided part-time employment to students and aided jobless youths. Two future presidents were among the beneficiaries: Twenty-seven-year-old Lyndon B. Johnson directed an NYA program in Texas, and Richard M. Nixon, a Duke University law student, found work through the NYA at 35¢ an hour. The WPA helped some 9 million people before it expired in 1943.

**THE WAGNER ACT** Another major element of the Second New Deal was the National Labor Relations Act, often called the **Wagner Act** in honor of the New York senator, Robert Wagner, who drafted it and convinced Roosevelt to support it. The Wagner Act guaranteed workers the right to organize unions and bargain directly with management about wages and other issues. It also created a National Labor Relations Board to oversee union activities and ensure that management bargained with them in good faith.

**SOCIAL SECURITY** The Great Depression hit the oldest Americans and those with disabilities especially hard. To address these problems, FDR proposed the **Social Security Act** of 1935. Social Security, he announced, was the "cornerstone" and "supreme achievement" of the New Deal.

The basic concept of government assistance to the elderly was not new. Progressives during the early 1900s had proposed a federal system of social security for the aged, poor, disabled, and unemployed, and other nations had already enacted such programs. The hardships caused by the Great Depression revived the idea, and Roosevelt masterfully guided the legislation through Congress.

The Social Security Act, designed by Secretary of Labor Frances Coralie Perkins, the first woman cabinet member in history, included three major provisions. Its centerpiece was a federal retirement fund for people over sixty-five. Beginning in 1937, workers and employers contributed payroll taxes to establish the fund. Most of the collected taxes funded pension payments to retirees;

the rest went into a trust fund for the future.

Roosevelt stressed that Social Security would not guarantee everyone a comfortable retirement. Rather, it would supplement other sources of income and protect the elderly. Not until the 1950s did voters and politicians come to view Social Security as the *primary* source of retirement income for working-class Americans.

The Social Security Act also set up a shared federal–state unemployment-insurance program, financed by a payroll tax paid by employers. In addition, it committed the national government to a broad range of social-welfare activities based upon the assumption that "unemployables"—people who were unable to work—would remain a state responsibility while the national government would provide work relief for the able-bodied. To that end, the Social Security Act provided federal funding for three state-administered programs—old-age assistance, aid to dependent children, and aid for the blind—and further aid for maternal, child-welfare, and public health services.

**Social Security** A poster distributed by the government to educate the public about the new Social Security Act.

When compared with similar programs in Europe, the U.S. Social Security system was—and remains—conservative. It is the only government-managed retirement program in the world financed by taxes on the earnings of workers; most other countries funded such programs out of general government revenues.

The Social Security payroll tax was also a regressive tax because it used a single withholding tax *rate* for everyone, regardless of income level. It thus pinched the poor more than the rich and hurt efforts to revive the economy because it removed from circulation a significant amount of money. In addition, the Social Security system *excluded* 9.5 million low-paid workers who most needed it: farm laborers, domestic workers (maids and cooks), and the self-employed, a disproportionate percentage of whom were African Americans.

Treasury officials cited a practical reason for this exclusion: how could they collect Social Security taxes from people earning "irregular" wages paid in cash rather than through a weekly payroll system. Others, however, argued that the exclusion was made at the insistence of powerful southern Democrats in Congress afraid of the federal government gaining influence in the South through such "welfare" programs.

Roosevelt regretted the Social Security Act's limitations, but he saw them as necessary compromises to gain congressional approval and withstand court challenges. As he told an aide who criticized funding the program out of employee contributions:

> I guess you're right on the economics, but those taxes were never a problem of economics. They are politics all the way through. We put those payroll contributions there so as to give the contributors a moral, legal, and political right to collect their pensions and their unemployment benefits. With those taxes in there, no damn politician can ever scrap my Social Security program.

FDR also preferred that workers fund their own Social Security pensions because he wanted Americans to view their retirement checks as an *entitlement*—as something that they had paid for and deserved.

Conservatives condemned the Social Security Act as another "tyrannical" expansion of government power. The head of the National Association of Manufacturers told Congress that Social Security would lead to "ultimate socialist control of life and industry." Former president Herbert Hoover refused to apply for a Social Security card because of his opposition to the "radical" program. He received a Social Security number anyway.

**A NEW DIRECTION FOR UNIONS** The New Deal reinvigorated the labor union movement. When the National Industrial Recovery Act (NIRA) demanded that industry fairness codes affirm workers' rights to organize, unionists quickly translated it to mean "the president wants you to join the union." John L. Lewis, head of the United Mine Workers (UMW), was among the first to capitalize on the pro-union spirit of the NIRA. He rebuilt the UMW from 150,000 members to 500,000 within a year.

Encouraged by Lewis's success, Sidney Hillman of the Amalgamated Clothing Workers and David Dubinsky of the International Ladies Garment Workers organized clothing industry workers into an industrial union (composed of all types of workers, skilled and unskilled). Opposing them were the smaller craft unions (composed of skilled male workers only, with each union serving just one trade).

In 1935, with the passage of the Wagner Act, industrial unions formed a Committee for Industrial Organization (CIO) to represent their interests. In 1936, the American Federation of Labor (AFL) expelled the CIO unions, which then formed a permanent structure of their own called the Congress of Industrial Organizations (also known by the initials CIO). The rivalry spurred both groups to greater efforts.

The Congress of Industrial Organizations focused on organizing the automobile and steel industries. Until the Supreme Court upheld the Wagner Act in 1937, however, companies used various forms of intimidation to fight the unions. Early in 1937, automobile workers tried a new tactic, the "sit-down strike," in which they refused to leave a workplace until employers had granted them collective-bargaining rights.

Led by the fiery Walter Reuther, thousands of employees at the General Motors plant in Flint, Michigan, stopped production and locked themselves in the plant. "She's ours," yelled one worker participating in the sit-down strike. Company officials responded by turning off the heat to the plant, called in police to harass the strikers with tear gas and cut off their food supply, and threatened to fire the workers. They also pleaded with President Roosevelt to dispatch federal troops. He refused but expressed his displeasure with the strike.

The standoff lasted more than a month before the company relented and signed a contract recognizing the United Automobile Workers (UAW) as a legitimate union. Dubbed the "strike heard round the world," the successful takeover of automobile plants inspired workers to join unions. In the year following the strike, the UAW's membership soared from 30,000 to 500,000.

## ROOSEVELT'S SECOND TERM

On June 27, 1936, Franklin Delano Roosevelt accepted the Democratic party's nomination for a second term as president. The Republicans chose Governor Alfred M. Landon of Kansas, a progressive who had endorsed many New Deal programs. "We cannot go back to the days before the depression," Landon scolded conservative Republicans. "We must go forward, facing our new problems."

The Republicans hoped that the followers of Huey Long, Charles E. Coughlin, Francis E. Townsend, and other Roosevelt critics would combine to draw enough Democratic votes away from the president to give Landon a winning margin. That possibility faded, however, when an assassin shot and killed the forty-two-year-old Long in 1935.

In the 1936 election, Roosevelt carried every state except Maine and Vermont, with a popular vote of 27.7 million to Landon's 16.7 million, the largest margin of victory to that point. Democrats would also dominate the new Congress, by 77 to 19 in the Senate and 328 to 107 in the House.

Roosevelt had forged a new electoral coalition that would affect national politics for years to come. While holding the support of most traditional Democrats, North and South, he made strong gains in the West. In the northern cities, he held on to the ethnic groups helped by New Deal welfare policies. Many middle-class voters flocked to support him, as did intellectuals stirred by the ferment of new ideas. The revived labor union movement also threw its support to Roosevelt, and, in the most meaningful shift of all, a majority of African Americans voted for a Democratic president.

**THE COURT-PACKING PLAN** President Roosevelt's landslide victory emboldened him to pursue even more radical efforts to end the Great Depression. One major roadblock stood in the way: the conservative Supreme Court. In Roosevelt's view, it had become an outdated "horse-and-buggy" court made up of "nine old men" (average age: seventy-one) determined to thwart Roosevelt's attempts to expand executive authority to deal with the economic crisis.

Lawsuits challenging the constitutionality of the Social Security and Wagner Acts were pending. Given the Court's conservative bent and its earlier anti–New Deal rulings, Roosevelt feared that the Second New Deal was in danger of being nullified.

For that reason, he hatched a clumsy plan to "reform" the Supreme Court by enlarging it. Congress, not the Constitution, determines the size of the Court, which over the years had numbered between six and ten justices. In 1937, the number was nine. On February 5, 1937, Roosevelt asked Congress to name up to six new justices, one for each of the current justices over seventy years old, explaining that the aging members of the Court were falling behind in their work and needed help.

The **"Court-packing" plan**, as opponents labeled the scheme, backfired, however, and ignited a profound debate among the three branches of government—executive, legislative, and judicial. For the next 168 days, the nation was preoccupied with the constitutionality of Roosevelt's proposal. In the end, both Republicans and Democrats decided that the Court-packing scheme was too manipulative and far too political.

As it turned out, several Supreme Court decisions during the spring of 1937 *upheld* disputed provisions of the Wagner and Social Security Acts. In addition, a conservative justice resigned, and Roosevelt replaced him with a New Dealer, Senator Hugo Black of Alabama.

Still, Roosevelt insisted on forcing his Court-packing bill through Congress. The Senate Judiciary Committee described it as "a measure which should be so emphatically rejected that its parallel will never again be presented to the free representatives of the free people of America." On July 22, 1937, the Senate overwhelmingly voted it down.

It was the worst political blunder and greatest humiliation of Roosevelt's career. The episode fractured the Democratic party and damaged the president's prestige, but the bill's defeat preserved the institutional integrity of the Supreme Court.

**A SLUMPING ECONOMY** During 1935 and 1936, the economy finally began showing signs of revival. By the spring of 1937, industrial output had risen above the 1929 level before the Stock Market crash. In 1937, however, President Roosevelt, worried about federal budget deficits and rising inflation, ordered sharp cuts in government spending. The economy stalled, then slid into a slump nearly as deep as that of 1929 after the Wall Street crash. In only three months, unemployment rose by 2 million. When the spring of 1938 failed to bring recovery, Roosevelt reversed himself and asked Congress for a new federal spending program. Congress approved $3.3 billion in new expenditures. The increase in government spending helped, but only during the Second World War would employment again reach pre-1929 levels.

The Court-packing fight, the sit-down strikes, and the 1937 recession all undercut Roosevelt's prestige and power. When the 1937 congressional session ended, the only major New Deal initiatives were the Wagner-Steagall National Housing Act and the Bankhead-Jones Farm Tenant Act. The Housing Act, developed by Senator Robert F. Wagner, set up the United States Housing Authority within the Department of Interior. It extended long-term loans to cities to build high-rise public housing projects in blighted neighborhoods and provide subsidized rents for low-income residents. Later, during the Second World War, it would finance housing for employees working in new defense plants.

The Farm Tenant Act created the Farm Security Administration (FSA), which provided loans to keep farmers from losing their land to bankruptcy. It also made loans to tenant farmers to enable them to purchase farms. In the end, however, the FSA did little more than tide a few farmers over during difficult times. A more effective answer to the sluggish economy eventually arrived in the form of national mobilization for war, which landed many struggling tenant farmers in military service or the defense industry, broadened their horizons, and taught them new skills.

In 1938, Congress enacted the Fair Labor Standards Act. It replaced many of the provisions that had been in the NIRA, which were deemed unconstitutional. Like the NIRA, it established a minimum wage of 40¢ an hour and a maximum workweek of forty hours. The act, which applied only to businesses engaged in *interstate* commerce, also prohibited the employment of children under the age of sixteen.

**SETBACKS FOR THE PRESIDENT** During the late 1930s, Democrats in Congress increasingly split into two factions, with conservative southerners on one side and liberal northerners on the other. Many southern Democrats balked at the party's growing dependence on the votes of northern union members and African Americans. Senator Ellison "Cotton Ed" Smith of South Carolina and several other southern delegates walked out of the 1936 Democratic party convention, with Smith declaring that he would not support any party that views "the Negro as a political and social equal." Other critics believed that President Roosevelt was exercising too much power and spending too much money. Some southern Democrats began to work with conservative Republicans to block proposed New Deal programs.

The congressional elections of November 1938 handed the administration another setback when the Democrats lost seven seats in the Senate and 80 in the House. In his State of the Union message in 1939, Roosevelt for the first time spoke of the need "to *preserve* our reforms" rather than add to them. The conservative coalition of Republicans and southern Democrats had stalemated him.

**A HALFWAY REVOLUTION** The New Deal's political momentum petered out in 1939 just as a new world war was erupting in Europe and Asia. What, then, was its impact? In hindsight, it had more energy than coherence. Many New Deal programs failed or were poorly conceived and implemented. But several programs changed life for the better: Social Security, federal regulation of stock markets and banks, minimum wage levels for workers, federally insured bank accounts, and government-sanctioned labor unions.

The greatest triumph of the New Deal, however, was its demonstration that American democracy could cope with the collapse of capitalism. A self-proclaimed "preacher President," Franklin Roosevelt raised the nation's spirits and its income through his relentless optimism and unprecedented activism. As a CCC worker recalled late in life, Roosevelt "restored a sense of confidence and morale and hope—hope being the greatest of all." New Deal programs provided stability for tens of millions of people. "We aren't on relief anymore," one woman noted with pride. "My husband is working for the government."

The greatest failure of the New Deal was its inability to restore prosperity and end record levels of unemployment. In 1939, an estimated 10 million

Americans—nearly 17 percent of the workforce—remained jobless. Only the Second World War would finally produce full employment.

Roosevelt was an idealist without illusions. Energetic pragmatism was his greatest strength—and weakness. He admitted that he often acted out of conflicting convictions. "I am a juggler," he explained. "I never let my right hand know what my left hand does." He sharply increased the regulatory powers of the federal government and laid the foundation for what would become an expanding system of social welfare programs.

The result was, paradoxically, both revolutionary and conservative. New Deal initiatives left a legacy of unprecedented innovations: a joint federal-state system of unemployment insurance; a compulsory, federally administered retirement system; financial support for families with dependent children; maternal and child-care programs; and several public health programs. The New Deal also improved working conditions and raised wage levels for millions.

Roosevelt had sought to preserve the basic capitalist economic structure while providing protection to the most vulnerable. In this sense, the New Deal represented a "halfway revolution" that permanently altered the nation's social and political landscape. "During the ten years between 1929 and 1939," marveled an appreciative social worker in 1940, "more progress was made in public welfare and relief than in the three hundred years after this country was first settled." In a time of peril, Roosevelt created for Americans a more secure future.

# CHAPTER REVIEW

## Summary

- **The First New Deal**  During his early months in office, Franklin Roosevelt pushed through Congress the *First New Deal (1933–1935)*, which propped up the banking industry with the *Federal Deposit Insurance Corporation (1933)*, provided short-term emergency work relief and promoted industrial recovery with the *National Recovery Administration (1933)*, raised agricultural prices with the *Agricultural Adjustment Act (1933)*, and enforced new laws and regulations on Wall Street with the *Securities and Exchange Commission (1934)*. Most of the early New Deal programs helped end the economy's downward spiral but still left millions unemployed and mired in poverty, despite the earnest efforts of First Lady Eleanor Roosevelt, who became justly famous for her strenuous efforts to help the poor, minorities, and refugees.

- **New Deal under Fire**  The Supreme Court ruled that many of the First New Deal programs were unconstitutional violations of private property and states' rights. Conservatives criticized the New Deal for expanding the scope and reach of the federal government so much that it was steering the nation toward socialism. The "radio priest," Father Charles E. Coughlin, charged that the New Deal was a Jewish-atheist-Communist conspiracy. Other critics did not think New Deal reforms went far enough. Senator Huey Long of Louisiana and Dr. Francis Townsend of California proposed radical plans to reshape the distribution of wealth from the rich to the poor. African Americans criticized the widespread racial discrimination in New Deal policies and agencies.

- **The Second New Deal and the New Deal's Legacy**  Roosevelt responded to the criticism and continuing economic hardship with a *Second New Deal (1935–1938)*, which sought to reshape the nation's social structure by expanding the role of the federal government. Many of the programs making up the Second New Deal, such as the *Works Progress Administration*, *Social Security*, and the *Wagner Act*, aimed to achieve greater social justice by establishing new regulatory agencies and laying the foundation of a federal social welfare system. Frustrated by the Supreme Court's opposition to the First New Deal, Roosevelt proposed his *Court-packing scheme (1937)*, but it was rejected by the Senate. Support for the New Deal began to lose steam in the late 1930s amid the lingering effects of the Great Depression. However, the New Deal established the idea that the federal government should provide at least a minimal quality of life for all Americans, and it provided people with some security against a future crisis, reaffirming for millions a faith in American capitalism.

# Chronology

| | |
|---|---|
| **November 1932** | Franklin D. Roosevelt is elected president |
| **March 1933** | Congress passes the Emergency Banking Relief Act |
| | Congress establishes the Civilian Conservation Corps |
| **May 1933** | Congress creates the Tennessee Valley Authority and the Agricultural Adjustment Act |
| **June 1933** | Congress establishes the Federal Deposit Insurance Corporation (Glass-Steagall Banking Act) and passes the National Industrial Recovery Act |
| **December 1933** | Prohibition repealed with the passage of the Twenty-First Amendment to the Constitution |
| **May 1935** | Supreme Court finds the National Industrial Recovery Act unconstitutional |
| **1935** | Roosevelt creates the Works Progress Administration |
| **1936** | Roosevelt is reelected in a landslide |
| **1937** | Social Security taxes and payments begin |

# Key Terms

**First New Deal (1933–1935)** p. 1022

**Federal Deposit Insurance Corporation (FDIC) (1933)** p. 1022

**Securities and Exchange Commission (1934)** p. 1024

**National Recovery Administration (NRA) (1933)** p. 1026

**Agricultural Adjustment Act (1933)** p. 1027

**Dust Bowl** p. 1027

**Second New Deal (1935–1938)** p. 1043

**Works Progress Administration (WPA) (1935)** p. 1044

**Wagner Act (1935)** p. 1044

**Social Security Act (1935)** p. 1044

**Court-packing scheme (1937)** p. 1048

 INQUIZITIVE

Go to InQuizitive to see what you've learned—and learn what you've missed—with personalized feedback along the way.

# 26 The Second World War

## 1933–1945

***Raising the Flag on Iwo Jima* (February 23, 1945)** Five members of the United States Marine Corps raise the U.S. flag on Mount Suribachi, during the Battle of Iwo Jima. Three of them would die within days after this photograph was taken. The image earned photographer Joe Rosenthal the Pulitzer Prize. A bronze statue of this scene is the centerpiece of the Marine Corps War Memorial in Virginia.

W hen Franklin Roosevelt became president in 1933, he shared with most Americans a determination to stay out of international disputes. While the United States had become deeply involved in global trade during the twenties, it had remained aloof from global conflicts. So-called isolationists insisted that there was no justification for America to become embroiled in international affairs, much less another major war. With each passing year during the 1930s, however, Germany, Italy, and Japan threatened the peace and stability of Europe and Asia.

Roosevelt strove to keep the United States out of what he called the "spreading epidemic of world lawlessness" as fascist dictatorships in Germany and Italy and ultranationalist militarists in Japan violated international law by invading neighboring countries. By the end of the thirties, Roosevelt had decided that the only way for the United States to avoid another war was to offer all possible assistance to Great Britain, France, and China.

Roosevelt's efforts to stop what he called "aggressor nations" ignited a fierce debate between isolationists and interventionists that ended suddenly on December 7, 1941, when Japan staged a surprise attack against U.S. military bases at Pearl Harbor in Hawaii. America was again involved in a world war. It would become the most significant event of the twentieth century, engulfing five continents and leaving few people untouched.

The Japanese attack unified the country as never before. Men and women rushed to join the armed forces. Eventually, 16.4 million Americans would

## focus questions

**1.** How did German and Japanese actions lead to the outbreak of war in Europe and Asia?

**2.** How did President Roosevelt and Congress respond to the outbreak of wars in Europe and Asia between 1933 and 1941?

**3.** What were the effects of the Second World War on American society?

**4.** What major factors enabled the United States and its allies to win the war in Europe?

**5.** How were the Japanese defeated in the war in the Pacific?

**6.** How did President Roosevelt and the Allies work to shape the postwar world?

serve in the military during the war, including 350,000 women. The massive government spending required to wage total war boosted industrial production and wrenched the economy out of the Great Depression.

The United States and its allies emerged victorious in the costliest and most destructive war in history. More than 50 million people were killed in the war between 1939 and 1945—perhaps 60 percent of them civilians, including millions of Jews and other ethnic and social minorities in Nazi death camps and Soviet concentration camps.

The scope and scale of the Second World War transformed America's role in the world. Isolationism gave way to internationalism. By 1945, America was the world's most powerful nation, with new international interests and responsibilities. Instead of bringing peace, however, the end of the fighting led to a new "cold war" between two former allies, the United States and the Soviet Union.

## THE RISE OF FASCISM IN EUROPE

In 1917, Woodrow Wilson had led the United States into the Great War to make the world "safe for democracy." In fact, though, democracy was in retreat after 1919, while Soviet communism was on the march. So, too, was **fascism**, a radical form of totalitarian government in which a dictator uses propaganda and brute force to seize control of all aspects of national life—the economy, the armed forces, the legal and educational systems, and the press. Fascism in Germany and Italy thrived on a violent ultranationalist patriotism and almost hysterical emotionalism built upon claims of racial superiority and the simmering resentments that grew out of defeat in the Great War.

At the same time, halfway around the world, the Japanese government fell under the control of expansionists eager to conquer China and most of Asia. Japanese leaders were convinced that theirs was a "master race" with a mission to lead a resurgent Asia, just as Adolf Hitler claimed that Germany's mission was to use its supposed racial supremacy to dominate Europe. By 1941, there would be only a dozen or so democratic nations left on earth.

**ITALY AND GERMANY** In 1922, Benito Mussolini and 40,000 of his black-shirted supporters seized control of Italy, taking advantage of a government incapable of dealing with widespread unemployment, runaway inflation, mass strikes, and fears of communism. By 1925, Mussolini was wielding dictatorial power as "Il Duce" (the Leader). He called his version of antisocialist totalitarian nationalism *fascism*. He eliminated all political parties except the Fascists and ordered his political opponents murdered. There was something clownish about the strutting, chest-thumping Mussolini, who claimed that "my animal instincts are always right," when in fact he was at best a mediocre statesman.

There was nothing amusing, however, about his German counterpart, the Austrian-born Adolf Hitler, whom Mussolini privately described as "an aggressive little man . . . probably a liar, and certainly mad."

Hitler's transformation during the 1920s from social misfit to head of the National Socialist German Workers' (Nazi) party startled the world and led many to underestimate the man and his appeal. As late as 1930, a German magazine editor dismissed Hitler as a "half-insane rascal," a "pathetic dunderhead," and a "nowhere fool" whose Nazi organization had "no future at all."

Yet Hitler used his talents at demagoguery, lying, and showmanship to organize a grassroots movement through nativist appeals to the masses.

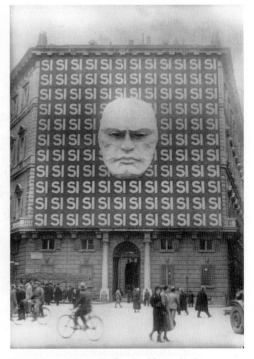

**Fascist propaganda** Benito Mussolini's headquarters in Rome's Palazzo Braschi, which bore an oversized reproduction of his head.

Hitler and the Nazis claimed that they represented a German master race whose "purity and strength" were threatened by liberals and other "inferior" peoples: Jews, socialists, Communists, Romani (gypsies), and homosexuals. "Democracy must be destroyed," he shouted.

Hitler promised to make Germany strong again by renouncing the Versailles treaty, defying the limits on its armed forces, and establishing a Greater German Empire that would give the nation what Hitler called "living space" to expand, dominate "lesser" races, and rid the continent of Jews. He was appointed chancellor on January 30, 1933.

Like Mussolini, Hitler was idolized by the masses. He declared himself absolute leader, or *Führer*, and in 1934 became president and supreme commander of the armed forces. All the while, he was imposing a totalitarian regime. He banned all political parties except the Nazis, had his opponents jailed or killed, created a secret police force (the *Gestapo*), and stripped people of voting rights. There would be no more elections, labor unions, or

**Adolf Hitler** Hitler performs the Nazi salute at a rally. The giant banners, triumphant music, powerful oratory, and expansive military parades were all designed to stir excitement and allegiance among Nazis.

strikes. All non-German books were burned, and Jews were blamed for most of Germany's problems.

Hitler's Nazi police state employed tyranny and terrorism, propaganda and censorship to impose absolute control over Germany. Two million brown-shirted thugs ("storm troopers") fanned out across the nation, burning books and persecuting, imprisoning, and murdering Communists, Jews, Gypsies—and their sympathizers.

Most Germans gloried in Hitler's ruthless aggressiveness in crushing any opposition. At a famous rally in Nuremburg, his supporters screamed: "We want one leader! Nothing for us! Everything for Germany!"

**THE EXPANDING AXIS** As the 1930s unfolded, a catastrophic series of events sent the world hurtling toward disaster. In 1931–1932, some 10,000 Japanese troops had occupied Manchuria, in northeast China, a territory rich in raw materials; mineral deposits, including iron ore and coal; and farm-land needed for Japanese expansion. At the time, China was fragmented by civil war between Communists led by Mao Zedong and Nationalists led by Chiang Kai-shek. The Japanese took advantage of China's weakness to pro-claim Manchuria's independence, renaming it the "Republic of Manchukuo."

While Japan was expanding its control in Asia, Mussolini was on the march. In 1935, he launched a reconquest of Ethiopia, a nation in eastern Africa that Italy had controlled until 1896. When the League of Nations retaliated by imposing economic sanctions on Italy, Mussolini expressed surprise that European leaders would prefer a "horde of barbarian Negroes" in Ethiopia over Italy, the "mother of civilization."

In 1935, Hitler, in flagrant violation of the Versailles treaty, began rebuilding Germany's armed forces. He reinstated compulsory military service and built an air force. The next year, he sent 35,000 soldiers into the Rhineland, the demilitarized buffer zone between France and Germany. In a staged vote, 99 percent of the Germans living in the Rhineland approved Hitler's action. The failure of France and Great Britain to counter these moves convinced Hitler that the western democracies were cowards and would not try to stop him.

The year 1936 also witnessed the outbreak of the Spanish Civil War, which began when Spanish troops (the Nationalists) loyal to General Francisco Franco, with the support of the Roman Catholic Church, revolted against the fragile new democratic government (the Republicans). Hitler and Mussolini rushed German and Italian troops (called "volunteers" to disguise their purpose), warplanes, and military and financial aid to support Franco's fascist insurgency. Some 2,800 American volunteers joined in defense of Spain's republican government, supported by weapons from the Soviet Union.

While peace in Europe was unraveling, the Japanese government fell under the control of aggressive militarists. On July 7, 1937, Japanese and Chinese soldiers clashed at China's Marco Polo Bridge, near Beijing. The incident quickly escalated into the Sino-Japanese War.

By December, the Japanese had captured the Nationalist Chinese capital of Nanjing. They looted the city and murdered and tortured as many as 300,000 civilians in what came to be called the Rape of Nanjing. Thereafter, the Sino-Japanese War bogged down into a stalemate.

## FROM ISOLATIONISM TO INTERVENTION

Most Americans responded to the mounting world crises by deepening their commitment to isolationism. In his 1933 inaugural address, President Roosevelt announced that he would continue to promote what Woodrow Wilson had earlier called "the good neighbor policy" in the Western Hemisphere, declaring that no nation "has the right to intervene in the internal or external affairs of another."

The nation's isolationist mood was reinforced by a Senate inquiry into the role of bankers and businesses in the American decision to enter the Great War, Chaired by Senator Gerald P. Nye of North Dakota, the "Nye Committee" concluded that weapons makers and bankers (the "merchants of death") had spurred U.S. intervention in 1917 and were continuing to "help frighten nations into military activity."

**U.S. NEUTRALITY** In 1935, *Christian Century* magazine declared that "ninety-nine Americans out of a hundred would today regard as an imbecile anyone who might suggest that, in the event of another European war, the United States should again participate in it."

Such isolationism led President Roosevelt to sign the first of several **"neutrality laws"** to help avoid the supposed mistakes that had led the nation into the Great War. The Neutrality Act of 1935 prohibited American manufacturers from selling weapons to nations at war ("belligerents") and banned citizens from traveling on ships owned by belligerents. In 1936, Congress revised the Neutrality Act by banning loans to warring nations.

Roosevelt, however, was not so sure that the United States could or should remain neutral. In October 1937, he delivered a speech in Chicago, the heartland of isolationism, in which he called for international cooperation to "quarantine the aggressors." But his appeal fell flat as isolationists warned he would get America embroiled in another war.

The Neutrality Act of 1937 allowed Roosevelt to sell nonmilitary goods to warring nations on a "cash-and-carry" basis—that is, a nation would have to pay cash and then carry the U.S.-made goods in its own ships. This would preserve America's profitable trade with warring nations without running the risk of being drawn into the fighting.

**THE AXIS ALLIANCE** In 1937, Japan joined Germany and Italy in establishing the Rome-Berlin-Tokyo **"Axis" alliance** because they claimed that all other nations would be forced to revolve around the "axis" created by those three dominant nations. Hitler and Mussolini vowed to create a "new order in Europe," while Japanese imperialists pursued their "divine right" to control east Asia by creating what they called the Greater East Asia Co-Prosperity Sphere.

*ANSCHLUSS* Hitler's madness broke over Europe in dark waves. In March 1938, he forced the *Anschluss* (union) of Austria with Germany. His triumphant return to his native country delighted crowds waving Nazi flags and tossing flowers. Soon, "Jews not Wanted" signs appeared in Austrian cities.

A month later, after arresting more than 70,000 anti-Nazis, German leaders announced that 99.75 percent of Austrian voters had "approved" the forced union with Germany. (In fact, it was a sham election, since some 400,000 Austrians, mostly liberals and Jews, were prevented from voting.)

Soon the Nazi government in Austria began arresting or murdering opponents and imprisoning or exiling Jews, including the famed psychiatrist Sigmund Freud.

Again, no nation stepped up to oppose Hitler, in part because it was so hard to assess the German leader's motives, predict his moves, and understand his ambition—or his lunacy.

**THE MUNICH PACT (1938)** Hitler turned next to the Sudeten territory (Sudetenland), a mountainous region in western Czechoslovakia along the German border where more than 3 million ethnic Germans lived. It was also where the Czechs had positioned their defensive positions in the event of a war with Germany. Hitler threatened to ignite a European war unless the Sudetenland was ceded to Germany. In response, timid British and French leaders tried to "appease" Hitler, hoping that if they agreed to his demands for the Sudeten territory he would stop his aggressions.

On September 30, 1938, the British prime minister, Neville Chamberlain, and the French prime minister, Édouard Daladier, joined Mussolini and Hitler in signing the notorious Munich Pact, which transferred the Sudetenland to Germany. As pawns in the chess game of European politics, the Czechs now faced a grim future. President Roosevelt privately grumbled that Britain and France had left Czechoslovakia "to paddle its own canoe" and predicted that they would "wash the blood from their Judas Iscariot hands."

The naive Chamberlain claimed that the Munich treaty had provided "peace for our time. Peace with honor." Winston Churchill, a member of the British Parliament who would become prime minister in May 1940, strongly disagreed. In a speech to the House of Commons, he claimed that "England has been offered a choice between war and shame. She has chosen shame, and will get war. . . . This is only the beginning of the reckoning."

Churchill was right. Hitler never intended to honor the Munich Pact. Although the Nazi tyrant had promised that the Sudetenland would be his last territorial demand, he scrapped his pledge in March 1939 and sent German tanks and soldiers to conquer the remainder of the Czech Republic. The European democracies, having shrunk their armies after the Great War, continued to cower in the face of his seemingly unstoppable military advances.

After German troops seized Czechoslovakia on March 15, 1939, Hitler called it "the greatest day of my life." He immediately set about oppressing the

263,000 Jews living in Czechoslovakia, lumping them together with "thieves, criminals, swindlers, insane people, and alcoholics." By the end of May, the Nazis were filling prisons with Czechs who resisted or resented the German occupation.

Hitler's conquest of Czechoslovakia convinced Roosevelt that fascism and Nazism must be stopped. Hitler and Mussolini were "madmen" who "respect force and force alone." Throughout late 1938 and 1939, Roosevelt tried to persuade Congress to increase military spending in anticipation of a possible war.

**THE CONQUEST OF POLAND** In 1939, Hitler, having decided that he had "the world in my pocket," turned to Poland, Germany's eastern neighbor. Conquering Poland would give the German army a clear path to invade the Soviet Union, especially the fertile Ukraine region, where much of the world's grains were grown.

To ensure that the Soviets did not interfere, Hitler camouflaged his intentions. On August 23, 1939, he shocked the world by signing the Nazi-Soviet Non-Aggression Pact with Josef Stalin, the brutish, antifascist Soviet premier.

Stalin had become the Soviet leader after Vladimir Lenin's death in 1924. Soon after, he had launched a Great Purge, in which some 8 million "critics" were executed and millions more exiled to forced labor camps. Two thirds of the Communist party leadership and some 35,000 army officers were victims of Stalin's reign of terror.

The announcement of the Nazi-Soviet treaty surprised a world that had assumed fascism and communism were mortal enemies. Stalin and Hitler agreed to divide northern and eastern Europe between them. The Germans took most of Poland, and the Soviet Union claimed a "sphere of interest" in Estonia, Latvia, Finland, and a portion of Lithuania.

Just nine days later, at dawn on September 1, an estimated 1.5 million German troops invaded Poland from the north, south, and west. Hitler ordered them "to kill without mercy men, women, and children of the Polish race or language." He also directed that all terminally ill patients in German hospitals be killed to make room for soldiers wounded in Poland.

The invasion of Poland was the final straw for the western democracies. On September 3, Great Britain and France declared war against Germany. The nations making up the British Empire and Commonwealth—Canada, India, Australia, New Zealand—joined the war as Americans watched in horror. "This nation," declared Franklin Roosevelt, "will remain a neutral nation, but I cannot ask that every American remain neutral in thought as well. Even a neutral cannot be asked to close his mind or conscience."

Sixteen days after German troops stormed across the Polish border, the Soviet Union invaded Poland from the east. Pressed from all sides, 700,000 poorly equipped Polish soldiers surrendered after a few weeks. On October 6, 1939, the Nazis and Soviets divided Poland between them.

Hitler's goal was to obliterate Polish civilization, especially the Jewish population, and to Germanize the country. For his part, Stalin wanted to recapture Polish territory lost during the Great War. Over the next five years, millions of Poles were arrested, deported, enslaved, and murdered. In April and May 1940, the Russians executed some 22,000 Polish military officers to ensure that its conquered neighbor would never mount a rebellion.

In late November 1939, the Soviets invaded neighboring Finland, leading President Roosevelt to condemn their "wanton disregard for law." Outnumbered five to one, Finnish troops held off the invaders for three months before being forced to negotiate a treaty that gave the Soviet Union a tenth of Finland.

**REVISING THE NEUTRALITY ACT** In September 1939, President Roosevelt decided that the United States must do more to stop "aggressor" nations. He summoned Congress into special session to revise the Neutrality Act.

The Neutrality Act of 1939 allowed Britain and France to send freighters to the United States to bring back American military supplies. It was, said Roosevelt, the best way "to keep us out of war." Public opinion supported such measures as long as other nations did the fighting.

**WAR IN EUROPE** The war in Europe settled into a three-month stalemate during early 1940, as Hitler's generals waited out the winter. Then, at dawn on April 9, Germany attacked again, invading Denmark and landing along the Norwegian coast. German paratroopers, the first used in warfare, seized Norway's airports. Denmark fell in a day, Norway within a few weeks. On May 10, German forces invaded the Low Countries—Belgium, Luxembourg, and the Netherlands (Holland). Luxembourg fell the first day, the Netherlands three days later. Belgium held out until May 28.

A few days later, German tanks roared into northern France. "The fight beginning today," Hitler declared, "decides the fate of the German nation for the next thousand years!" His blitzkrieg ("lightning war") strategy centered on speed. Columns of tanks, motorized artillery, and truck-borne infantry, all supported by warplanes and paratroopers, moved so fast they stunned their opponents. Winston Churchill called the Allied performance "a colossal military disaster."

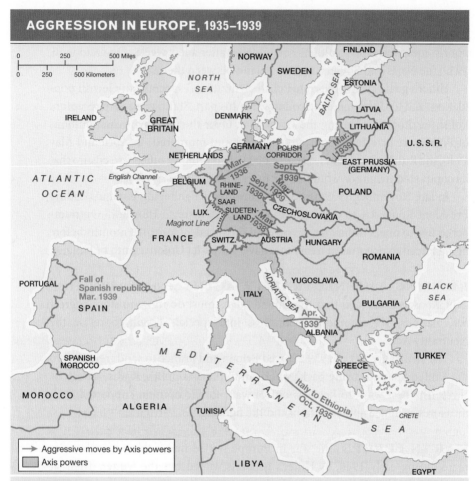

## AGGRESSION IN EUROPE, 1935–1939

0    250    500 Miles
0    250    500 Kilometers

FINLAND

NORWAY

SWEDEN

NORTH
SEA

BALTIC SEA

ESTONIA

LATVIA

IRELAND

GREAT
BRITAIN

DENMARK

LITHUANIA

U.S.S.R.

GERMANY    POLISH
CORRIDOR

NETHERLANDS

Mar.
1939

EAST PRUSSIA
(GERMANY)

ATLANTIC
OCEAN

English Channel

BELGIUM

Mar.
1936

Sept.
1939

RHINE-
LAND

Sept. 1939

POLAND

SAAR

1938

LUX.    SUDETEN-
LAND

Maginot Line

CZECHOSLOVAKIA

Mar.
1939

FRANCE    SWITZ.    AUSTRIA    HUNGARY

ROMANIA

PORTUGAL

Fall of
Spanish republic
Mar. 1939

YUGOSLAVIA

ADRIATIC SEA

ITALY

BLACK
SEA

SPAIN

BULGARIA

Apr.
1939

ALBANIA

SPANISH
MOROCCO

M E D I T E R R A N E A N

GREECE

TURKEY

MOROCCO

ALGERIA

TUNISIA

Italy to Ethiopia,
Oct. 1935

CRETE

S E A

→ Aggressive moves by Axis powers

Axis powers

LIBYA

EGYPT

- Keeping in mind the terms of the Treaty of Versailles ending the First World War, explain why Hitler began his campaign of expansion by invading the Rhineland and the Sudetenland.
- Why did the German attack on Poland begin the Second World War, whereas Hitler's previous invasions of Austria and Czechoslovakia did not?

A British force sent to help the Belgians and French fled along with French troops toward the coast, with the Germans in hot pursuit. On May 26, Churchill organized a desperate weeklong evacuation of British, Belgian, Canadian, and French soldiers from the beaches at Dunkirk. Despite attacks by German warplanes, some 338,000 soldiers escaped in 700 warships and an array of privately-owned vessels volunteered for the emergency: fishing trawlers, barges, yachts and other pleasure craft. The fleeing troops left behind vast stockpiles of vehicles, weaponry, and ammunition. "Wars are not won by evacuations," observed Prime Minister Churchill, "but there was a victory inside this deliverance."

While the evacuation was unfolding, German forces decimated the remaining French armies. Tens of thousands of panicked refugees and soldiers clogged the roads to Paris. Mussolini also declared war on France and Great Britain, which he dismissed as "the reactionary democracies of the West."

On June 14, 1940, German soldiers marched unopposed through the streets of Paris. Eight days later, French leaders officially surrendered, whereupon the Germans established a puppet fascist French government in the city of Vichy.

The rapid fall of France astonished the world. In the United States, complacency about the Nazis turned to fear and even panic as people realized the Germans, who now ruled most of western Europe, could eventually assault America. Great Britain stood alone against Hitler's relentless military power. "The war is won," an ecstatic Hitler bragged to Mussolini. "The rest is only a matter of time."

**PREPARING AMERICA FOR WAR** The United States was in no condition to wage war. After the First World War, the U.S. Army was reduced to a small force; by 1939, it numbered only 175,000. By contrast, Germany had almost 5 million soldiers. In May 1940, President Roosevelt called for increasing the size of the army and adding 50,000 war planes.

Roosevelt also responded to Winston Churchill's repeated requests for assistance by increasing military shipments to Great Britain and promising to provide all possible "aid to the Allies short of war." Churchill focused on one strategic objective: to convince, coax, bluff, seduce, or frighten the United States into entering the war.

**THE MANHATTAN PROJECT** Adding to President Roosevelt's concerns was the possibility that Germany might have a secret weapon. The famous physicist Albert Einstein, an Austrian Jew who had fled Nazism, had alerted Roosevelt in late 1939 that the Germans were trying to create atomic bombs. In June 1940, Roosevelt established the National Defense Research Committee to coordinate a top-secret effort—the Manhattan Project—to develop an atomic bomb before the Germans did. Almost 200,000 people worked on the Manhattan Project, including Dr. J. Robert Oppenheimer, who led the team of scientists scattered among thirty-seven secret facilities in thirteen states.

**THE BATTLE OF BRITAIN** Having conquered western Europe, Hitler began preparing to invade Great Britain ("Operation Sea Lion"). He launched the Battle of Britain, as the Germans sought to destroy the Royal Air Force (RAF). The Nazis deployed some 2,500 warplanes, outnumbering the RAF two to one. "Never has a nation been so naked before its foes," Winston Churchill admitted.

**The London "Blitz"** An aerial photograph of London set aflame by German bombing raids in 1940. Winston Churchill responded, "We shall never surrender."

Churchill became the symbol of Britain's determination to stop Hitler. With his bulldog face, ever-present cigar, and "V for Victory" gesture, he urged the citizenry to make the defense of their homeland "their finest hour." He breathed defiance as the British built fortifications, laid mines, dug trenches, and mobilized for war. The British, Churchill pledged, would confront Hitler's invaders with "blood, toil, tears, and sweat." They would "never surrender."

In July and August 1940, the German air force (*Luftwaffe*) launched raids against military targets across southeast England. RAF pilots employed radar, a new technology, to fend off the assault, ultimately destroying 1,700 German warplanes.

Hitler then ordered his bombers to target civilians and cities (especially London) in night raids designed to terrorize civilians and force a surrender. In what came to be called "the Blitz" during September and October 1940, German bombers destroyed a million homes and killed 40,000 civilians. "The last three nights in London," reported the U.S. ambassador to Great Britain on September 10, "have been simply hell."

The Blitz, however, enraged rather than demoralized the British. A London newspaper headline summarized the nation's courage and mood: "Is That the Best You Can Do, Adolf?" The British success in the air proved decisive. Hitler scrapped his invasion plans and turned his attention to the Soviet Union. It was the first battle he had lost, and it was Britain's finest hour.

**"ALL AID SHORT OF WAR"** During the Battle of Britain, Franklin Roosevelt began an urgent and eloquent campaign to convince Americans that isolationism was impractical and even dangerous. His phrase, "all aid short of war," became the label for his efforts to help Great Britain.

Roosevelt was especially concerned about a German invasion of the British Isles. "It is now most urgent," Prime Minister Churchill cabled Roosevelt, "that you let us have the destroyers" needed to stop such an invasion.

To address the challenge, Roosevelt and Churchill negotiated a trade on September 2, 1940, called the Destroyers for Bases Agreement, by which fifty old U.S. warships went to the British Royal Navy in return for allowing the United States to build military bases on British island colonies in the Caribbean.

Two weeks later, on September 16, 1940, a reluctant Congress approved the first peacetime conscription (military draft) in American history. The Selective Training and Service Act, passed by a single vote, required all 16 million men ages twenty-one to thirty-five to register for the draft at one of 6,500 local draft boards. (The minimum age was later reduced to eighteen and the maximum increased to forty-five.)

**A SAVAGE DEBATE** The world crisis transformed Franklin Roosevelt. Having been stalemated for much of his second term by congressional opposition to the New Deal, he was revitalized by the need to stop Nazism. Yet his efforts outraged isolationists. A prominent Democrat remembered that the dispute between isolationists and so-called interventionists was "the most savage political debate during my lifetime."

Isolationists, mostly midwestern and western Republicans, formed the America First Committee to oppose "military preparedness." Charles Lindbergh, the first man to fly solo across the Atlantic Ocean, led the effort. Openly sympathetic to Nazism and fascism, he charged that Roosevelt's efforts to help Britain were driven by Jews who owned "our motion pictures, our press, our radio, and our government." Were it not for the Jews in America, Lindbergh claimed, "we would not be on the verge of war today." He assured Americans that Britain was doomed and that they should join hands with Hitler: "Democracy as we know it is a thing of the past," and "one of the first steps must be to disenfranchise the Negro."

**ROOSEVELT'S THIRD TERM** Charles Lindbergh and other isolationists sought to make the 1940 presidential campaign a debate about the war. The Republicans nominated Wendell L. Willkie of Indiana, a plainspoken corporate lawyer and former Democrat who had voted for FDR in 1932.

Willkie called Roosevelt a "warmonger" and predicted that "if you re-elect him, you may expect war in April, 1941." Roosevelt responded that he had "said this before, but I shall say it again and again and again: Your boys are not going to be sent into any foreign wars." In November 1940, Roosevelt won an unprecedented third term by 27 million votes to Willkie's 22 million and by an even more decisive margin, 449 to 82, in the electoral college. Winston Churchill wrote Roosevelt that he had "prayed for your success and I am truly thankful for it."

**THE LEND-LEASE ACT** Once reelected, Roosevelt found an ingenious way to provide more aid to Britain, whose cash was running out. The **Lend-Lease Act** (officially "An Act to Promote the Defense of the United States"), introduced in Congress on January 10, 1941, allowed the president to lend or lease military equipment to "any country whose defense the President deems vital to the defense of the United States." It was a bold challenge to the isolationists. As Senator Hiram Johnson of California claimed, "This bill is war." Roosevelt told critics that "no nation can appease the Nazis. No man can turn a tiger into a kitten by stroking it." The United States, he added, would provide everything the British needed while doing the same for China in its war against Japan, all in an effort to keep Americans from going to war themselves. Churchill shored up the president's efforts by announcing that Britain did not need American troops to defeat Hitler: "Give us the tools and we will finish the job." In early March, 1941, Congress approved the Lend-Lease Act. "Let not the dictators of Europe or Asia doubt our unanimity now," Roosevelt declared.

Between 1941 and 1945, the Lend-Lease program would ship $50 billion worth of supplies to Great Britain, the Soviet Union, France, China, and other Allied nations. Churchill called it the most generous "act in the history of any nation."

**GERMANY INVADES THE SOVIET UNION** While Americans continued to debate President Roosevelt's efforts to help Great Britain, the European war expanded. In the spring of 1941, German troops joined Italian armies in Libya, forcing the British army in North Africa to withdraw to Egypt. In April 1941, Nazi armies overwhelmed Yugoslavia and Greece. With Hungary, Romania, and Bulgaria also under Nazi control, Hitler ruled most of Europe. His ambition was unbounded, however, and he remained dangerously unpredictable.

On June 22, 1941, Hitler launched "Operation Barbarossa," a shocking invasion of the Soviet Union, his supposed ally. His objective was to destroy communism (his long-standing obsession), enslave the vast population of the Soviet Union, open up new lands for German settlement, and exploit Russia's considerable natural resources.

Hitler's decision was the defining moment of the European war. The 3 million German soldiers sent to the Soviet Union would be worn down and thrown back. At first, however, the invasion seemed a great success, as entire Soviet armies and cities were destroyed. During the second half of 1941, an estimated 3 million Soviet soldiers—50 percent of the Soviet army—were captured. For four months, the Soviets retreated in the face of the German blitzkrieg.

During the summer of 1941, German forces surrounded Leningrad (now called St. Petersburg) and lay siege to the city. Food and supplies became scarce; hunger alone would kill 800,000 Russians. As a bitterly cold winter set in, corpses were left to freeze in the snow. Still, Leningrad held out and became known as the city that refused to die. By December 1941, other German armies had reached the suburbs of Moscow, 1,000 miles east of Berlin.

To American isolationists, Germany's invasion of Russia confirmed that the United States should stay out of the war and let the two dictatorships bleed each other to death. Roosevelt, however, insisted on including the Soviet Union in the Lend-Lease agreement. He and Churchill were determined to keep the Russians fighting so that Hitler could not concentrate on Great Britain. In 1941 alone, America sent thousands of trucks, tanks, guns, and warplanes to the Soviet Union, along with food (especially Spam) and enough blankets, shoes, and boots to clothe every Soviet soldier.

Gradually, Josef Stalin slowed the Nazi advance by forcing the Russian people to fight—or be killed. During the Battle of Moscow, Soviet defenders executed 8,000 civilians charged with "cowardice." Stalin ordered that Soviet soldiers who surrendered be classified as traitors. In 1941, when the Germans captured Stalin's eldest son, Yakov, Stalin had his son's wife arrested, separated from her three-year-old daughter, and imprisoned for two years as punishment for her husband's "cowardice" in surrendering. "There are no prisoners of war," Stalin explained, "only traitors to their homeland." While still a prisoner-of-war, Yakov committed suicide in 1943 by throwing himself onto an electric fence.

By the winter of 1941–1942, Hitler's generals were learning the same bitter lesson that the Russians had taught Napoléon and the French in 1812: invading armies must contend not only with Russia's ferocious fighters and enormous population but also vast distances, deep snow, and subzero temperatures.

**THE ATLANTIC CHARTER** By late summer 1941, the United States was no longer a neutral nation. In August, Roosevelt and Churchill met on a warship off the Canadian coast and drew up a joint statement of "common principles" known as the **Atlantic Charter**. The agreement pledged that after the "final destruction of the Nazi tyranny," the victors would promote the self-determination of all peoples, economic cooperation, freedom of the seas, and a new multination system of international security to be called the United Nations. Within weeks, eleven anti-Axis nations, including the Soviet Union, had endorsed the Atlantic Charter.

**WAR IN THE ATLANTIC** No sooner had Franklin Roosevelt signed the Atlantic Charter than U.S. warships came under fire. On September 4, 1941, the *Greer* was tracking a German submarine ("U-boat") off the coast of Iceland and sharing the information with British warplanes when it was attacked. In response, Roosevelt began an undeclared war in the Atlantic by ordering warships to protect shipping convoys all the way to Iceland.

Six weeks later, on October 17, 1941, a German U-boat sank the U.S. warship *Kearny*. Eleven sailors died. Two weeks later, the *Reuben James* was torpedoed and sunk while escorting a convoy near Iceland, with a loss of 115 seamen.

The attacks spurred Congress to change the 1939 Neutrality Act by allowing freighters and oil tankers to be armed and to enter combat zones and the ports of nations at war ("belligerents"). Step by step, the United States was engaging in naval warfare against Nazi Germany. Still, Americans hoped to avoid all-out war.

## THE STORM IN THE PACIFIC

In 1940, Japan and the United States had begun to move closer to war. The Japanese had built airfields in French Indochina (now Cambodia, Laos, and Vietnam). The United States responded with the Export Control Act of July 2, 1940, which authorized President Roosevelt to restrict the export of military supplies and other strategic materials to Japan. Three weeks later, on July 26, Roosevelt ordered that all Japanese assets in the United States be frozen and that oil shipments be stopped.

**THE TRIPARTITE PACT**  On September 27, 1940, the Imperial Japanese government signed a Tripartite Pact with Nazi Germany and fascist Italy, by which each pledged to declare war on any nation that attacked any of them. Roosevelt called the pact an "unholy alliance" designed to "dominate and enslave the entire human race." Several weeks later, the United States expanded its trade embargo against Japan to include iron ore, copper, and brass, deliberately leaving oil as the remaining bargaining chip, for it was the commodity Japan most needed to sustain its war against China.

In July 1941, Japan announced that it was taking complete control of French Indochina and thereby gaining access to the raw materials denied it by the United States. Roosevelt responded by restricting oil exports to Japan. *Time* magazine claimed that Roosevelt was "waging the first great undeclared war in U.S. history."

**THE ATTACK ON PEARL HARBOR**  On October 16, 1941, Hideki Tōjō became the Japanese prime minister. He ordered a fleet of Japanese warships to prepare for a surprise attack on Hawaii's Pearl Harbor, the most important U.S. military base in the Pacific. The Japanese naval commander, Admiral Isoroku Yamamoto, knew that his country could not defeat the United States in a long war. Its only hope was "to decide the fate of the war on the very first day" by launching a "fatal attack."

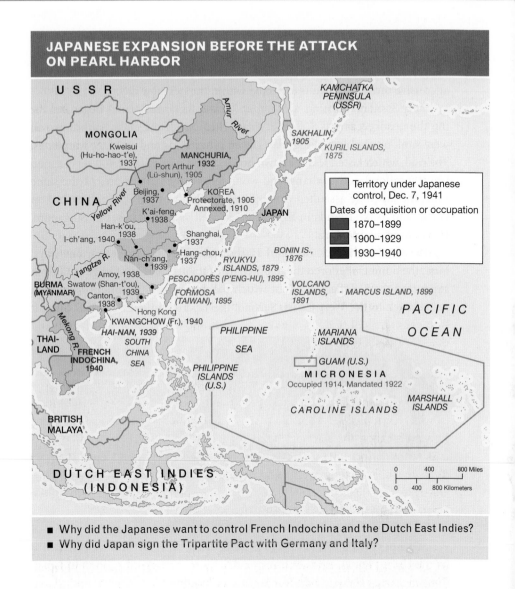

## JAPANESE EXPANSION BEFORE THE ATTACK ON PEARL HARBOR

Territory under Japanese control, Dec. 7, 1941

Dates of acquisition or occupation
- 1870–1899
- 1900–1929
- 1930–1940

USSR

KAMCHATKA PENINSULA (USSR)

MONGOLIA

Kweisui (Hu-ho-hao-t'e), 1937

MANCHURIA, 1932

Port Arthur 1932 (Lü-shun), 1905

SAKHALIN, 1905

KURIL ISLANDS, 1875

Amur River

CHINA

Beijing, 1937

KOREA Protectorate, 1905 Annexed, 1910

JAPAN

Yellow River

K'ai-feng, 1938

Han-k'ou, 1938

I-ch'ang, 1940

Shanghai, 1937

Hang-chou, 1937

BONIN IS., 1876

Yangtze R.

Nan-ch'ang, 1939

RYUKYU ISLANDS, 1879

Amoy, 1938

PESCADORES (P'ENG-HU), 1895

VOLCANO ISLANDS, 1891

MARCUS ISLAND, 1899

BURMA (MYANMAR)

Swatow (Shan-t'ou), 1939

FORMOSA (TAIWAN), 1895

Canton, 1938

Hong Kong

KWANGCHOW (Fr.), 1940

Mekong R.

HAI-NAN, 1939

SOUTH CHINA SEA

PHILIPPINE SEA

MARIANA ISLANDS

PACIFIC OCEAN

THAI-LAND

FRENCH INDOCHINA, 1940

GUAM (U.S.)

PHILIPPINE ISLANDS (U.S.)

MICRONESIA Occupied 1914, Mandated 1922

MARSHALL ISLANDS

CAROLINE ISLANDS

BRITISH MALAYA

DUTCH EAST INDIES (INDONESIA)

0    400    800 Miles
0    400    800 Kilometers

- Why did the Japanese want to control French Indochina and the Dutch East Indies?
- Why did Japan sign the Tripartite Pact with Germany and Italy?

On November 5, 1941, the Japanese asked the Roosevelt administration to end its embargo or "face conflict." Secretary of State Cordell Hull responded on November 26 that Japan must remove its troops from China before the United States would lift its embargo. The Japanese government then secretly ordered a fleet of warships to begin steaming toward Hawaii. By this time, political and military leaders on both sides considered war inevitable. Yet Hull continued to meet with Japanese diplomats in Washington, privately dismissing them as being as "crooked as a barrel of fish hooks."

Roosevelt and others expected the Japanese to strike Singapore or the Philippines. The U.S. Navy Department sent an urgent message to its commanders in the Pacific: "Negotiations with Japan . . . have ceased, and an aggressive move by Japan is expected within the next few days."

Early Sunday morning, December 7, 1941, Japanese planes began bombing the unsuspecting U.S. fleet at **Pearl Harbor**. Of the eight battleships, all were sunk or disabled, along with eleven other ships and 180 U.S. warplanes. The raid, which lasted less than two hours, killed more than 2,400 servicemen (mostly sailors) and civilians, and wounded nearly 1,200 more. At the same time, the Japanese assaulted U.S. military facilities in the Philippines and on Guam and Wake Islands in the Pacific, as well as British bases in Singapore, Hong Kong, and Malaya.

The shocking attack on Pearl Harbor fell short in two important ways. First, the bombers ignored the maintenance facilities and oil storage tanks that supported the U.S. fleet, without which the surviving ships might have been forced back to the West Coast. Second, the Japanese missed the U.S. aircraft

**Explosion of the USS *Shaw*** The destroyer exploded after being hit by Japanese warplanes at Pearl Harbor. It was repaired shortly thereafter and went on to earn eleven battle stars in the Pacific campaign.

carriers that had left port a few days earlier. In the naval war to come, aircraft carriers, not battleships, would prove to be decisive.

In a larger sense, the attack on Pearl Harbor was a spectacular miscalculation, for it destroyed the American isolationist movement. As the Japanese admiral who planned the attack said, "I fear that we have only succeeded in awakening a sleeping tiger." After learning of the Japanese attack, Winston Churchill, who desperately wanted the United States to enter the war, wrote that he "slept the sleep of the saved and thankful."

At half past noon on December 8, President Roosevelt delivered his war message to Congress: "Yesterday, December 7, 1941—a date which will live in infamy—the United States of America was suddenly and deliberately attacked by naval and air forces of the Empire of Japan." He asked Congress to declare a "state of war." The Senate approved the resolution twenty-five minutes after Roosevelt finished speaking; the House followed immediately thereafter.

Three days later, on December 11, Germany and Italy declared war on what Hitler called the "half Judaized and the other half Negrified" United States. The separate wars in Asia, Europe, and Africa had now become one global conflict. Roosevelt told the American people in a radio address that "we are going to win, and we are going to win the peace that follows."

## ARSENAL OF DEMOCRACY

Waging war against Germany and Japan required harnessing all of America's population and industrial capacity. On December 18, 1941, Congress passed the War Powers Act, which gave the president far-reaching authority to reorganize government agencies and create new ones, regulate business and industry, and even censor mail and other forms of communication.

With the declaration of war, millions of men and women began enlisting in the armed services. The average male U.S. soldier or sailor was twenty-six years old, stood five feet eight, and weighed 144 pounds, an inch taller and eight pounds heavier than the typical recruit in the First World War. Only one in ten had attended college, and only one in four had graduated from high school.

**MILITARY PRODUCTION** After the attack on Pearl Harbor, President Roosevelt told Congress that the nation's "powerful enemies must be outfought and outproduced." In 1940, Adolf Hitler had scoffed at the idea that the United States could produce 50,000 warplanes a year, claiming that America

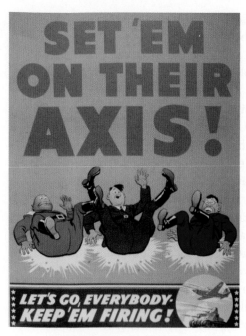

**War Production Board** This 1942 poster features caricatures of Mussolini, Hitler, and Tōjō, who—according to the poster—will fall on their "axis" if Americans continued their relentless production of military equipment.

was nothing but "beauty queens, millionaires, and Hollywood." By the end of 1942, however, U.S. war production exceeded the *combined* output of Germany, Japan, and Italy.

The **War Production Board**, created by Roosevelt in 1942, directed the conversion of industries to war production. In 1941, more than 3 million automobiles were manufactured; only 139 were built during the next four years, as automobile plants were reorganized to produce huge numbers of tanks, jeeps, trucks, and warplanes.

The Roosevelt administration transformed the nation's war economy into the world's most efficient military machine. By 1945, America would be manufacturing half the goods produced in the world. Factories, many running twenty-four hours a day, seven days a week, produced 300,000 warplanes, 89,000 tanks, 3 million machine guns, and 7 million rifles.

**FINANCING THE WAR**  To cover the war's huge cost (more than $3 trillion in today's values), Congress passed the Revenue Act of 1942 (Victory Tax), which required most workers to begin paying taxes. In 1939, only about 4 million people (about 5 percent of the workforce) earned enough to file tax returns; by the end of the war, 90 percent of workers were paying income tax. Tax revenues covered about 45 percent of military costs from 1939 to 1946; the government borrowed the rest, mostly by selling $185 billion worth of government war bonds, which paid interest to purchasers. By the end of the war, the national debt was six times what it had been at the start.

The size of the federal government soared. More than a dozen new federal agencies managed the war effort, and the number of civilian federal workers quadrupled to 4 million.

Jobs were suddenly plentiful, as millions quit work to join the military. The unemployment rate plummeted from 14 percent in 1940 to 2 percent in 1943.

People who had long lived on the margins of the economic system, especially women, now entered the labor force in large numbers. For most civilians, especially those who had lost their jobs and homes in the Depression, the war spelled a better life.

**ECONOMIC CONTROLS** The United States not only had to equip and feed its military forces but also needed to provide massive amounts of food, clothing, and weapons to its allies. This created shortages at home that caused sharp price increases in consumer goods. In 1942, Congress ordered the Office of Price Administration to set price ceilings. With prices frozen, basic goods had to be allocated through rationing, with coupons doled out for limited amounts of sugar, coffee, gasoline, automobile tires, and meat.

The government urged every family to become a "fighting unit on the home front." Posters featured slogans such as "Save Your Stuff to Make Us Tough," "Use it up, wear it out, make it do, or do without," and "Save Your Scraps to Beat the Japs." People collected scrap metal, tin foil, rubber, and cardboard for military use.

Businesses and workers often grumbled about the wage and price controls, but the system succeeded. By the end of the war, consumer prices had risen about 31 percent, far less than the increase of 62 percent during the First World War.

## THE DISRUPTIVE EFFECTS OF WORLD WAR

The Second World War transformed domestic life. Housewives went to work as welders and riveters (workers who connected sheets of metal together with metal pins) at aircraft factories and defense plants. Some 3.5 million rural southerners left farms for cities outside the South. The federal government paid for a national day-care program for young children to enable their mothers to work full-time. The dramatic changes affected many areas of social life, and their impact would last long after the war's end.

**WOMEN IN THE WAR** The war marked a watershed in the status of women. Nearly 350,000 women served in the U.S. armed forces. They enlisted in the **Women's Army Corps (WAC)**; the navy's equivalent, Women Accepted for Volunteer Emergency Service (WAVES); and in the Marine Corps, the Coast Guard, and the Army Air Force.

With millions of men going into military service, more than 8 million women entered the civilian workforce. To help recruit women for traditionally male jobs, the government launched a promotional campaign featuring the

**Women of the workforce, 1942**  At the Douglas Aircraft Company in Long Beach, California, three women assemble the tail section of a Boeing B-17 Flying Fortress bomber.

story of "Rosie the Riveter," a woman named Rosina Bonavita, who excelled as a riveter at an airplane factory.

Many men opposed women taking traditionally male jobs. A disgruntled male legislator asked: "Who will do the cooking, the washing, the mending, the humble homey tasks to which every woman has devoted herself; who will rear and nurture the children?" Many women, however, were eager to escape the grinding routines of domestic life and earn good wages. A female welder remembered that her wartime job "was the first time I had a chance to get out of the kitchen and work in industry and make a few bucks. This was something I had never dreamed would happen."

**AFRICAN AMERICANS DURING THE WAR**  Although Americans found themselves fighting the racial bigotry celebrated by fascism and Nazism, the war did not end racism in the United States. The Red Cross, for example, initially refused to accept blood donated by black people, and the president of North American Aviation announced that "we will not employ

Negroes." Black workers were often limited to the lowest-paid, lowest-skilled jobs.

African Americans noted the irony of the United States fighting racism abroad while tolerating it at home. "The army is about to take me to fight for democracy," a black draftee said, "but I would [rather] fight for democracy right here." During the summer of 1943 alone, there were 274 race-related incidents in almost fifty cities. In Detroit, racial tensions escalated into a full-fledged riot. Fighting raged for two days until federal troops arrived. Twenty-five black and nine white people were killed, and more than 700 people were injured.

More than a half-million African Americans left the South for better opportunities during the war years, and more than a million blacks joined the industrial workforce for the first time, lured by jobs and higher wages in military-related plants and factories. During the war years, the number of

**Bigotry at home**  During the Detroit Riots of 1943, police officers do nothing when a white thug hits a black man.

African Americans rose sharply in cities such as Chicago, Detroit, Seattle, Portland, and Los Angeles.

The war also provided a boon to southern textile mills by requiring millions of uniforms and blankets. Manufacturing jobs led thousands of "dirt poor" sharecroppers and tenant farmers to pursue the steady work offered in new mills and factories. Sixty of the nation's 100 army camps were in southern states, further transforming local economies. During the war, the U.S. rural population decreased by 20 percent.

**RACIAL TENSIONS** The most volatile social issue ignited by the war was African American participation in the military. Although the armed forces were still racially segregated in 1941, African Americans rushed to enlist after the attack on Pearl Harbor. As Joe Louis, the heavyweight boxing champion, explained, "Lots of things [are] wrong with America, but Hitler ain't going to fix them." Altogether, about a million African Americans—men and women—served in the armed forces during the war.

**Tuskegee Airmen** The Tuskegee Airmen were the first African American military pilots. Here, the first graduates are reviewed at Tuskegee, Alabama, in 1941.

Black soldiers and sailors were initially excluded from combat units. They loaded ships, drove trucks, dug latrines, and handled supplies and mail. Black officers could not command white soldiers or sailors. Henry L. Stimson, the secretary of war, claimed that "leadership is not embedded in the negro race." Military bases had segregated facilities to prevent the "intermingling" of "colored and white" troops.

In late 1944, however, the need for more troops led the government to revisit its racial policies. General Dwight Eisenhower, commander of U.S. forces in Europe, agreed to let black volunteers fight in all-black fifty-man platoons commanded by white officers.

The black soldiers became known as fierce fighters. The same was true of some 600 African American pilots trained in Tuskegee, Alabama. The **Tuskegee Airmen** flew more than 15,000 missions, and their undeniable excellence spurred military and civilian leaders to desegregate the armed forces after the war. At war's end, however, the U.S. Army reimposed segregation. It would be several more years before the military was truly integrated.

**MEXICAN AMERICANS DURING THE WAR** As rural dwellers moved west, many farm counties experienced a labor shortage. In an ironic about-face, local and federal authorities who before the war had forced migrant laborers back across the Mexican border now recruited them to harvest crops on American farms. The Mexican government would not consent to provide the laborers, however, until the United States promised to ensure them decent working and living conditions.

The result was the creation in 1942 of the Emergency Farm Labor Program, soon dubbed the **bracero program** (for a Spanish word meaning manual laborer). Under the program, Mexico agreed to provide about 70,000 seasonal farmworkers on year-long contracts between 1942–1945. At least that many more crossed the border as undocumented workers. They were not considered immigrants since they were supposed to return to Mexico when the war ended. The success of the program led to its extension after the war, and the annual numbers of seasonal migrant workers soared.

Even though some 300,000 Mexican Americans served in the war and earned a higher percentage of Congressional Medals of Honor than any other minority group, racial prejudices against Mexicans and other Latinos persisted, especially in the Far West. In southern California, for example, there was constant conflict between white servicemen and Mexican American gang members and teenage "zoot-suiters." (Zoot suits were flamboyant clothing worn by some young Mexican American men.) In 1943, several thousand

**Navajo code talkers** Here, a code talker relays messages for U.S. Marines in the Battle of Bougainvilie in the South Pacific in 1943.

off-duty sailors and soldiers, joined by hundreds of whites, rampaged through Los Angeles, assaulting people of color: Latinos, African Americans, and Filipinos. The weeklong violence came to be called the "Zoot Suit Riots."

**NATIVE AMERICANS IN THE MILITARY** Amerindians supported the war effort more fully than any other group. Almost a third of eligible Native American men served in the armed forces. Unlike their African American counterparts, Indian servicemen were integrated into regular units with whites. Many others worked in defense-related industries, and thousands of Indian women volunteered as nurses or joined the WAVES. As was the case with African Americans, Native Americans benefited from the experiences afforded by the war by gaining vocational skills they would transfer to civilian jobs after the war.

Why did so many Native Americans fight for a nation that had stripped them of their land and ravaged their heritage? Some felt that they had no choice. Mobilization for the war ended many New Deal programs that had provided them with jobs. At the same time, many viewed the Nazis and Japanese as threats to their own homeland.

Whatever their motivations, Indians distinguished themselves in the military. Perhaps their most distinctive role was serving as "code talkers." As had occurred during the First World War, every military branch used Indians, especially Navajos, to encode and decipher messages using Indian languages unknown to the Germans and Japanese.

**DISCRIMINATION AGAINST JAPANESE AMERICANS** After Pearl Harbor, widespread fear of a Japanese attack on the U.S. mainland fueled a hunger for vengeance against the Nisei—people of Japanese descent living in the United States. "A Jap's a Jap," declared Lieutenant General John L. DeWitt, head of West Coast defense efforts. "It makes no difference whether he's an American [citizen] or not." Signs appeared in storefronts declaring, "No Japs Wanted." Banks stopped cashing the checks of Japanese Americans, and grocers refused to sell food to them.

Such bigotry helps explain why the U.S. government sponsored one of the worst violations of civil liberties in history when armed soldiers forcibly removed more than 112,000 Nisei from their homes and transported them to ten "**war relocation camps**." These were hastily constructed tent cities in remote areas guarded by sentry towers and soldiers with machine guns.

President Roosevelt initiated the incarceration of Japanese Americans, 70 percent of whom were already U.S. citizens, when he issued Executive Order 9066 on February 19, 1942. There were no trials, no "due process," no concerns about violations of civil rights. Roosevelt called the program a "military necessity," although not a single incident of espionage involving Japanese Americans was proved. Only later did government documents reveal that the motive for the mass removal of Japanese Americans was to quell fears among the general public after the attack on Pearl Harbor.

On Evacuation Day, Burt Wilson, a white schoolboy in Sacramento, California, was baffled as soldiers ushered the Nisei children out of his school:

> We wondered what had happened. They took somebody out of eighth grade, a boy named Sammy, who drew wonderful cartoons. He was my friend, and one day he was there and the next day he was gone.

**A farewell to civil rights** American troops escorted Japanese Americans by gunpoint to remote war relocation camps, some of which were horse-racing tracks, whose stables served as housing.

> And that was very difficult for us to understand because we didn't see
> Sammy or any Japanese American—at least I didn't—as the enemy.

Some 39,000 Japanese Americans served in the U.S. armed forces during the war, and others worked as interpreters and translators. All were victims of racial and fear-based prejudice.

Not until 1983 did the U.S. government acknowledge the injustice of the incarceration policy. Five years later, the Civil Liberties Act granted those Nisei still living $20,000 each in compensation, a minor sum relative to what they had lost during four years of confinement. "The internment of Americans of Japanese ancestry," explained President George H. W. Bush in 1991, "was a great injustice, and it will never be repeated."

# THE ALLIED DRIVE TOWARD BERLIN

By mid-1942, U.S. naval forces had become increasingly successful at destroying German U-boats off the Atlantic coast. Up to that point, German submarines had sunk hundreds of Allied cargo vessels, killing 2,500 sailors. Stopping the submarine attacks was important because the Grand Alliance—Great Britain, the United States, and the Soviet Union—called for the defeat of Germany first. Defeating the Japanese could wait.

## WAR AIMS AND STRATEGY

A major consideration for Allied military strategy was the clash of massive armies on the vast Eastern Front in the Soviet Union. The Soviet population— by far—bore the brunt of the war against the Nazis, leading Josef Stalin to insist that the Americans and British attack the Germans in western Europe, thereby forcing Hitler to pull units away from the Russian Front.

Meanwhile, with most of the German army deployed on the Russian Front, the British and American air forces, flying from bases in England, would bomb military and industrial targets in German-occupied western Europe, and in Germany itself, while making plans to attack Nazi troops in North Africa, Italy, and France.

Franklin Roosevelt and Winston Churchill agreed that they needed to create a second front in western Europe, but they could not agree on the timing or location of an invasion. U.S. planners wanted to attack the Germans in France before the end of 1942. The British, however, were wary of moving too fast. An Allied defeat on the French coast, Churchill warned, was "the only way in which we could possibly lose this war." Finally, Roosevelt decided to accept

Churchill's proposal for a joint Anglo-American invasion of North Africa, which was then controlled by German and Italian armies not nearly as strong as those in Europe.

**THE NORTH AFRICA CAMPAIGN** On November 8, 1942, the Americans and British landed 100,000 troops in Morocco and Algeria on the North African coast ("Operation Torch"). U.S. general Dwight D. Eisenhower led the assault. After the Americans lost badly in early battles, Eisenhower, soon known as "Ike," found a brilliant field commander in General George Patton, who said he loved war "more than my life."

Brimming with bravado, Patton showed American troops how to fight a modern war of speed and daring. On May 12, 1943, some 250,000 Germans and Italians surrendered, leaving North Africa in Allied control. The "continent had been redeemed," said Winston Churchill.

**THE CASABLANCA CONFERENCE** Five months earlier, in January 1943, Franklin Roosevelt, Winston Churchill, and the Anglo-American military chiefs met at a seaside resort near Casablanca in French Morocco. Stalin chose to stay in the Soviet Union, but he again urged the Allies to invade Nazi-controlled western Europe to relieve the pressure on the Russians.

At the conference, the British convinced the Americans to assault the Italian island of Sicily. Roosevelt and Churchill also decided to step up the bombing of Germany and to increase shipments of military supplies to the Soviet Union and the Nationalist Chinese forces fighting the Japanese.

Before leaving the conference, Roosevelt announced, with Churchill's blessing, that the war would end only with the "unconditional surrender" of all enemy nations. This decision was designed to ease Soviet suspicions that the Americans and British might negotiate separately with Hitler to end the war in western Europe. The announcement also reflected Roosevelt's determination that "every person in Germany should realize that this time Germany is a defeated nation."

**THE BATTLE OF THE ATLANTIC** While fighting raged in North Africa, the Battle of the Atlantic reached its climax. Great Britain desperately needed more food and military supplies from the United States, but German submarines were sinking British vessels faster than shipyards could replace them. By July 1942, some 230 Allied ships and almost 5 million tons of war supplies had been lost. "The only thing that ever frightened me during the war," recalled Churchill, "was the U-boat peril."

By the end of 1942, however, the British and Americans had cracked the German naval radio codes, enabling Allied convoys to steer clear of U-boats or hunt them down with warplanes (called "subchasers") and anti-submarine weapons deployed on warships. New technology also helped, as sonar and radar allowed Allied ships to track submarines. In May 1943, the Allies destroyed fifty U-boats. Thereafter, Allied shipping losses fell significantly— just as hundreds of thousands of American troops and equipment were being transported across the Atlantic.

**SICILY AND ITALY**  On July 10, 1943, following the Allied victory in North Africa, about 250,000 British and American troops landed on the coast of Sicily. General Eisenhower called it the "first page of the liberation of the European continent." The island was in Allied hands by August 17, bringing to an end Benito Mussolini's twenty years of fascist rule in Italy.

On July 25, 1943, the Italian king had dismissed Mussolini as prime minister and had him arrested. The new Italian government then startled the Allies when it offered to switch sides in the war. Hitler responded by sending German armies into Italy.

The Italian campaign thereafter became a series of stalemated battles. Winter came early to southern Italy, making life even more miserable for the soldiers. The Germans positioned themselves behind formidable defenses and rugged terrain that enabled them to slow the Allied advance to a crawl. "Italy was one hill after another," said a U.S. soldier, "and when it was wet, you were either going up too slow or down too fast, but always the mud. And every hill had a German [machine] gun on it." Allied casualties soared.

By February 1944, the two sides were, in the words of U.S. commander Mark W. Clark, like "two boxers in the ring, both about to collapse." Mussolini, plucked from prison by a daring German airborne commando raid, became head of a fascist government in northern Italy as Allied forces finally took control of the rest of the country. On June 4, 1944, the U.S. Fifth Army entered Rome.

**THE TEHRAN CONFERENCE**  Late in the fall of 1943, in Tehran, Iran, Winston Churchill and Franklin Roosevelt had their first joint meeting with Josef Stalin. Their discussions focused on the planned invasion of Nazi-controlled France and a simultaneous Russian offensive across eastern Europe. The three leaders agreed to create an international organization—the United Nations—to maintain peace after the war. By the end of the conference, Roosevelt told a cabinet officer that he had grown to like Stalin and had forged a close working relationship with the Soviet leader. Stalin knew this, too, for he had told his secret police to bug Roosevelt's rooms.

**THE STRATEGIC BOMBING OF EUROPE** Months of preparation
went into the Allied invasion of German-occupied France. While waiting for
D-day (the day the invasion would begin), the U.S. Army Air Force tried to
pound Germany into submission. Although the air offensive, while killing
350,000 civilians, failed to shatter German morale or war-related production,
it did force the Germans to commit precious resources to air-raid defense and
eventually wore down their air force. With Allied air supremacy assured by
1944, the much-anticipated invasion of Hitler's "Fortress Europe" could move
forward.

**PLANNING AN INVASION** In early 1944, Dwight D. Eisenhower
arrived in London with a new title: Supreme Commander of the Allied Expeditionary Force (AEF). He faced the daunting task of planning **Operation
Overlord**, the daring assault on Hitler's "Atlantic Wall," an array of mines,
machine guns, barbed wire, and jagged obstacles along the French coastline. The planned invasion gave Churchill nightmares: "When I think of the
beaches . . . choked with the flower of American and British youth . . . I see the
tides running red with their blood. I have my doubts. I have my doubts."

The seaborne invasion would be the greatest gamble and most complex
military operation in history. "I am very uneasy about the whole operation,"
admitted Sir Alan Brooke, head of British forces. "It may well be the most
ghastly disaster of the whole war." Eisenhower was so concerned that he carried in his wallet a note to be circulated if the Allies failed. It read: "If any
blame or fault attaches to the attempt, it is mine alone."

**D-DAY AND AFTER** Operation Overlord succeeded in part because it
surprised the Germans. The Allies positioned British decoy troops and made
misleading public statements to fool the Nazis into believing that the invasion would come at Pas-de-Calais, on the French-Belgian border, where the
English Channel was narrowest. Instead, the landings would actually occur
along 50 miles of shoreline in northern Normandy, a French coastal region
almost 200 miles south.

On the blustery evening of June 5, 1944, General Eisenhower visited some
of the 16,000 U.S. paratroopers preparing to drop behind German lines. The
soldiers, noticing Eisenhower's concerned demeanor, tried to lift his spirits.
"Now quit worrying, General," one of them said, "we'll take care of this thing
for you." A sergeant said, "We ain't worried. It's Hitler's turn to worry."

After the planes took off, Eisenhower confided to an aide: "I hope to God
I know what I'm doing." Others were concerned too. As he got into bed that
night, Winston Churchill, with tears running down his cheeks, asked his

**General Eisenhower** Eisenhower visiting with U.S. paratroopers before they began the night assault in Operation Overlord.

wife: "Do you know that by the time you wake up in the morning, 20,000 men may have been killed?"

As the planes carrying the para-troopers arrived over coastal France, thick clouds and German anti-aircraft fire disrupted the formations. Some soldiers were dropped miles from their landing sites, some were dropped far out at sea, and some were dropped so low that their parachutes never opened.

Yet those among the U.S. 82nd and 101st Airborne Divisions who landed safely outfought three German divisions during the night and prepared the way for the main invasion by destroying bridges and capturing artillery positions and key road junctions.

**THE NORMANDY LANDINGS** As the gray, misty light of dawn broke on D-day, June 6, 1944, the biggest invasion fleet in history—some 5,300 Allied ships carrying 370,000 soldiers and sailors—filled the horizon off the Normandy coast. Sleepy German soldiers awoke to the breathtaking array of ships. "I saw an armada like a plague of locusts," said a German officer. "The number of ships was uncountable."

When Hitler learned of the Allied landings, he boasted that "the news couldn't be better. As long as they [the Allied armies] were in Britain, we couldn't get at them. Now we have them where we can destroy them." In the United States, word that the long-anticipated liberation of Nazi Europe had begun captured the nation's attention. Businesses closed, church bells tolled, and people prayed in the streets.

During the first day of Operation Overlord, foul weather and rough seas caused injuries and seasickness and capsized dozens of the boxy, flat-bottomed landing craft. More than 1,000 soldiers, weighed down by seventy pounds of equipment, drowned as they stepped into water above their heads.

The noise was deafening as shells exploded across the beaches and in the surf. Bodies piled up amid wrenching cries for help. "As our boat touched sand and the ramp went down," Private Harry Parley remembered, "I became a vis-itor to Hell."

The first U.S. units ashore at Omaha Beach, beneath 130-foot-tall cliffs defended by German machine guns and mortars, lost more than 90 percent of their men. Officers struggled to rally the troops. "Two kinds of men are staying on this beach," shouted cigar-smoking Colonel George Taylor. "The dead and those who are going to die. Get up! Move in! Goddammit! Move in and die! Get the hell out of here!"

Inch by inch, U.S. troops pushed across the beach and up the cliffs. By nightfall, 170,000 Allied soldiers—57,000 of them Americans—were scattered across fifty miles of the windswept Normandy coastline. So too were the bodies of 10,724 dead or wounded Allied soldiers.

Within three weeks, the Allies had landed more than a million troops, 566,000 tons of supplies, and 171,000 vehicles. "Whether the enemy can still be stopped at this point is questionable," German army headquarters near Paris warned Hitler. "The enemy air superiority is terrific and smothers almost every one of our movements. . . . Losses in men and equipment are extraordinary."

Operation Overlord was the greatest seaborne invasion in the history of warfare, but it was small when compared with the offensive launched by the Soviet army a few weeks later. Between June and August 1944, the Soviets killed, wounded, or captured more German soldiers (350,000) than were stationed in all of western Europe.

**The landing at Normandy** D-Day, June 6, 1944. Before they could huddle under a seawall and begin to dislodge the Nazi defenders, U.S. soldiers on Omaha Beach had to cross a fifty-yard stretch that exposed them to machine guns housed in concrete bunkers.

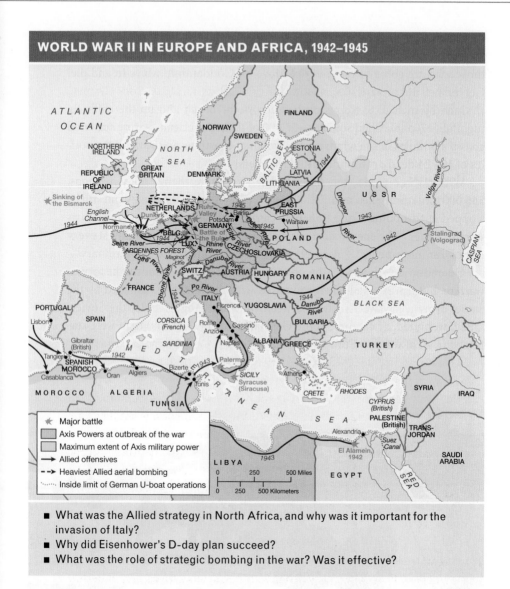

## WORLD WAR II IN EUROPE AND AFRICA, 1942–1945

- What was the Allied strategy in North Africa, and why was it important for the invasion of Italy?
- Why did Eisenhower's D-day plan succeed?
- What was the role of strategic bombing in the war? Was it effective?

Still, the Normandy invasion was a turning point in the war. With the beachhead secured, the Allied leaders knew that final victory was just a matter of time, as Hitler's armies were caught between the Soviets advancing from the east and the Allied forces from the west and south. "What a plan!" Churchill exclaimed to the British Parliament.

**THE LIBERATION OF PARIS** It would take seven more weeks and 37,000 more lives for the Allied troops to gain control of Normandy. The Germans lost more than twice that many, and some 19,000 French civilians were killed. Then, on July 25, American armies headed east from Normandy toward Paris. On August 15, a joint American-French force landed on the Mediterranean coast and raced up the Rhone Valley in eastern France.

German resistance collapsed after only ten weeks. On D-day, one German unit, the 21st Panzer Division, boasted 12,000 men and 127 tanks; ten weeks later, having retreated across France, it had just 300 men and 10 tanks left. A division of the Free French Resistance, aided by American units, liberated Paris on August 25. As U.S. soldiers marched through the cheering crowds, a reporter said that he had never "seen in any place such joy as radiated from the people of Paris this morning."

By mid-September, most of France and Belgium had been cleared of German troops. Meanwhile, the Soviet army moved relentlessly westward along a 1,200-mile front, pushing the fleeing Germans out of Russia. Between D-day and the end of the war in Europe a year later, 1.2 million German soldiers were killed or wounded.

**ROOSEVELT'S FOURTH TERM** In 1944, war or no war, the calendar required another presidential election. This time the Republicans nominated New York governor Thomas E. Dewey, who argued that it was time for a younger man to replace the "tired" Democratic leader.

Franklin Roosevelt was not only tired; he was seriously ill. In March, the president's physician had said that Roosevelt would not survive another four years in office. The next day, the president, determined to guide the nation to victory and create a stable postwar world, announced that he would accept his party's nomination for a fourth term. The public knew nothing about his failing health. On November 7, 1944, Roosevelt won yet again, this time by a popular vote of 25.6 million to 22 million and an electoral vote of 432 to 99.

**THE RACE TO BERLIN** By the time Franklin Roosevelt was reelected, Allied armies were approaching the German border from the east and the west. Winston Churchill was worried that if the Soviets arrived first in Berlin, the German capital, Josef Stalin would control the postwar map of Europe. Churchill urged Eisenhower to beat the Soviets to Berlin. Eisenhower, however, decided it was not worth the estimated 100,000 American casualties such an operation would cost.

**GERMAN COUNTERATTACK: THE BATTLE OF THE BULGE** As the Anglo-American armies approached the German border in mid-December 1944, a desperate Hitler sprang a surprise. He dispatched most of his army's reserves and 1,800 tanks to the Ardennes Forest in Belgium, where they launched a counterattack intended to split the Allied advance and retake

**Battle of the Bulge**  Two U.S. soldiers stand out sharply against snow-covered ground and a night sky alight with a barrage of artillery fire.

the Belgian port of Antwerp. "This battle is to decide whether we shall live or die," Hitler told his officers.

The Battle of the Bulge involved a million combatants and almost changed the course of the war. Initially, the counterattack surprised Allied commanders, punched a hole in the overstretched Allied lines, and drove the British and U.S. forces back fifty miles, thus creating the "bulge" on the map that gave the battle its name. Eight days of bad weather complicated matters, as frigid temperatures, blinding snow, winter fog, and thick clouds prevented Allied warplanes from supporting the troops.

General Eisenhower remained calm. He saw the massive assault as "an opportunity" to destroy much of the German army. The heaviest fighting centered on Bastogne, where seven key roads converged. There, some 18,000 U.S. infantry and paratroopers found themselves hopelessly surrounded. For more than a week, as they ran low on supplies, they held off a much larger force of Germans as General George S. Patton's Third Army, some ninety miles away, raced to the rescue with 250,000 soldiers.

On December 22, the German commander encircling Bastogne sent his American counterpart, General Anthony McAuliffe, a demand to surrender within two hours or be "annihilated." McAuliffe's one-word reply ("Nuts!") confused the Germans. An American officer then explained to the German representative that "Nuts" meant the same as "Go to Hell." And, he added, "we will kill every goddamned German who tries to break into the city."

The weather cleared the next morning, enabling U.S. planes to bring desperately needed supplies to the units trapped in Bastogne. A few days later, the advance guard of Patton's relief force arrived. Bastogne was no longer surrounded. For three more weeks, the Germans repeatedly tried to take the town, but without success. Throughout the region, wave after wave of American and British warplanes assaulted German forces in what one observer called "a great slaughter."

Hitler's gamble had failed. The Germans at the Battle of the Bulge lost more than 100,000 men—killed, wounded, or captured. American casualties were also high—81,000—but it was clear that Germany was teetering toward defeat. "Now," Patton wrote in his diary, "we are going to attack until the war is over."

## THE YALTA CONFERENCE

As the Allied armies converged on Berlin, Josef Stalin hosted Franklin Roosevelt and Winston Churchill at the **Yalta Conference** (February 4–11, 1945) in Crimea, a seaside resort on the Black Sea. The "Big Three" agreed that, once Germany surrendered, the Soviets would occupy eastern Germany, and the Americans and British would control western Germany. Berlin, the German capital within the Soviet zone, would be subject to joint occupation.

Stalin's goals were to retrieve former Russian territory transferred to Poland after the First World War and impose Soviet control over eastern and central Europe. Churchill and Roosevelt urged Stalin to allow Poland, then occupied by the Red Army, to become a self-governing democracy. Stalin refused, explaining

**The Yalta Conference** Churchill, Roosevelt, and Stalin (with their respective foreign ministers behind them) confer on plans for the postwar world in February 1945.

that Soviet control of Poland was more important to him than participation in the United Nations, Roosevelt's proposed international peacekeeping organization.

Stalin also knew that the Americans needed Soviet support in the ongoing war with Japan. Military analysts estimated that Japan could hold out for eighteen months after the defeat of Germany unless the Soviets joined the war in Asia. Stalin agreed to do so, but the price was high: he demanded territories from Japan and China.

As a face-saving gesture, Roosevelt and Churchill convinced Stalin to sign the Yalta Declaration of Liberated Europe, which called for free and open elections in the liberated nations of eastern Europe. Nevertheless, Stalin would fail to live up to his promises. When the Soviet Red Army "liberated" Hungary, Romania, Bulgaria, Czechoslovakia, Poland, and eastern Germany, it plundered and sent back to Russia anything of economic value, dismantling thousands of factories and mills and rebuilding them in the Soviet Union. To ensure control over eastern Europe, the Soviets shipped off to prison anyone who questioned the new Communist governments they installed.

At Yalta, the three leaders agreed to hold organizational meetings for the United Nations beginning on April 25, 1945. Like Woodrow Wilson, Roosevelt was determined to replace America's "outdated" isolationism with an engaged internationalism. But to get Stalin's approval of the UN, Roosevelt gave in to the Soviet leader's demands for territory held by Japan in northeast Asia.

Admiral William D. Leahy, the president's chief of staff, complained to Roosevelt that the agreement's language on Poland was "so elastic that the Russians can stretch it all the way from Yalta to Washington without ever technically breaking it." Some blamed Roosevelt's unwillingness to force Stalin to create democracies in the liberated nations on his declining health. (He would die in a few weeks.)

But even a robust Roosevelt could not have dislodged the Soviet army from its control of eastern Europe. The course of the war shaped the outcome at Yalta, and the United States had no real leverage. As a U.S. diplomat admitted, "Stalin held all the cards." Roosevelt agreed. "I didn't say the result was good," Roosevelt said after returning from the Yalta Conference. "I said it was the best I can do for Poland at this time."

**DEATH OF A PRESIDENT**    By early 1945, Nazi Germany was on the verge of defeat, but sixty-three-year-old Franklin Roosevelt would not live to join the victory celebrations.

In the spring of 1945, he went to the "Little White House" in Warm Springs, Georgia. On April 12, 1945, just eighty-two days into his fourth term, he complained of a headache but seemed to be in good spirits. It was nearly lunchtime when he said to an artist painting his portrait, "Now we've got just about 15 minutes more to work." Then, while reading some documents, Roosevelt groaned, saying that he had "terrific pain" in the back of his head. He slumped over, fell into a coma, and died two hours later.

On hand to witness the president's death was Lucy Mercer Rutherford, the woman with whom Roosevelt had an affair thirty years before. Eleanor Roosevelt was in Washington, D.C., when Franklin died, unaware of the president's guest. Although Franklin had promised in 1918 to end all communications with Mercer, he had in fact secretly stayed in touch, even enabling her to attend his presidential inauguration in 1933.

Roosevelt's death shocked and saddened the world. Even his sharpest critics were devastated. Ohio senator Robert Taft, known as "Mr. Republican," said, "The President's death removes the greatest figure of our time at the very climax of his career. . . . He dies a hero of the war, for he literally worked himself to death in the service of the American people."

Children took Roosevelt's death especially hard. It was "catastrophic" news for twelve-year-old Burt Wilson of Sacramento, California. "My parents were Republicans and hated Roosevelt, but I loved him. And most of us kids loved him, I believe, because he was the face of America that was saying, 'Hey, things are going to get better.'"

**THE COLLAPSE OF NAZISM** Adolf Hitler's Nazi empire collapsed less than a month later. In Berlin on April 28, as Soviet troops entered the German capital, Hitler married his mistress, Eva Braun, in an underground bunker. That same day, Italian freedom fighters captured Mussolini. Despite his plea to "Let me live, and I will give you an empire," Mussolini and his mistress were shot and hung by their heels from a girder above a Milan gas station. On April 30, Hitler and his wife retired to their underground bedroom, where she poisoned herself and he put a bullet in his head. Their bodies were taken outside, doused with gasoline, and burned.

On May 2, Berlin fell. Axis forces in Italy surrendered the same day. Five days later, on May 7, the chief of staff of the German armed forces agreed to unconditional surrender. So ended the Nazi domination of Europe, just over twelve years after Hitler had proclaimed his "Thousand-Year Reich."

On May 8, V-E day ("Victory in Europe") generated massive celebrations. In Paris, an American bomber pilot flew his plane through the arch of the Eiffel Tower. In New York City, 500,000 people celebrated in the streets. The elation, however, was tempered by the ongoing war against Japan and the immense challenges of helping Europe rebuild. The German economy had to be revived, a new democratic government had to be formed, and millions of displaced Europeans had to be clothed, housed, and fed.

**THE HOLOCAUST** The end of the war in Europe revealed to the world the horrific extent of the **Holocaust**, Hitler's systematic program to destroy Jews, whom he hated and blamed for most of Germany's problems. Reports of the Nazis' methodical slaughter of Jews had appeared as early as 1942, but the ghastly stories of millions killed in gas chambers seemed beyond belief until the Allied armies liberated the death camps in central and eastern Europe. There the Germans had imposed their "Final Solution": the wholesale extermination of at least 6 million Jews, and many millions more non-Jewish peoples deemed unworthy of living within the German Reich.

The Allied troops were stunned at what they discovered in the extermination camps, where as many as 24,000 Jews a day had been killed, week after week, month after month. Bodies were piled as high as buildings; survivors were living skeletons. General Eisenhower reported that the "things I saw beggar description." Everywhere, the "starvation, cruelty, and bestiality were so

**Holocaust survivors** American troops liberate survivors of the Mauthausen, Austria concentration camp in May 1945. The Nazis tattooed the prisoners with identification numbers on their wrists or chests, as seen on the man at left.

overpowering as to leave me a bit sick. In one room, where they were piled up twenty or thirty naked men, killed by starvation, [General] George Patton would not even enter. He said that he would get sick if he did so. I made the visit deliberately, in order to be in a position to give first-hand evidence of these things if ever, in the future, there develops a tendency to charge these allegations merely to 'propaganda.'"

American government officials had dragged their feet in acknowledging the Holocaust for fear that relief efforts for Jewish refugees might stir up anti-Semitism at home. At the same time, several key figures in the State Department proved to be anti-Semitic themselves, and they balked at bringing more refugees to America. Under pressure from Jewish groups and his own wife, President Roosevelt had created a War Refugee Board early in 1944 to rescue European Jews at risk of extermination. The War Refugee Board managed to rescue about 200,000 European Jews and some 20,000 other refugees. But the administration refused appeals from Jewish leaders to bomb the concentration camp at Auschwitz, arguing that doing so would kill many Jews, be ineffective (the Nazis would simply build another one), and distract resources from the priority of defeating Hitler's war machine. In 1944, Churchill called the Holocaust the "most horrible crime ever committed in the history of the world." He did not know at the time that Stalin's death camps killed more people than Hitler's.

## THE PACIFIC WAR

For months after the attack on Pearl Harbor at the end of 1941, the news from the Pacific was "all bad," as President Roosevelt acknowledged. With stunning speed, the Japanese had captured numerous territories in Asia, including the British colonies of Hong Kong, Burma, Malaya, and Singapore, and the French colony of Indochina.

**THE PHILIPPINES** In the Philippines, U.S. forces and their Filipino allies were overwhelmed. On April 10, 1942, the Japanese gathered some 12,000 captured American troops along with 66,000 Filipinos and forced them to march sixty-five miles in six days up the Bataan peninsula. Already underfed and ravaged by disease, the prisoners were brutalized in what came to be known as the Bataan Death March. Those who fell out of line were bayoneted or shot. Others were beaten, stabbed, or shot for no reason. More than 10,000 died along the way. News of the Bataan Death March outraged Americans and contributed to the Pacific war's emotional intensity and mutual atrocities.

By the summer of 1942, Japan was on the verge of assaulting Australia when its naval leaders succumbed to what one admiral called "victory disease." Intoxicated with easy victories and lusting for more, they pushed into the South Pacific, intending to isolate Australia and strike again at Hawaii.

**CORAL SEA AND MIDWAY** During the spring of 1942, U.S. forces in the Pacific finally had some success. In the Battle of the Coral Sea (May 2–6), U.S. warplanes forced a Japanese fleet headed toward the island of New Guinea to turn back after sinking an aircraft carrier and destroying seventy planes.

A few weeks later, Admiral Yamamoto steered his main Japanese fleet of eighty-six warships and 700 warplanes toward Midway, the westernmost of Hawaii's inhabited islands, from which he hoped to strike Pearl Harbor again. This time, however, the Japanese were the ones who were surprised. In a crucial breakthrough, Americans had cracked the Japanese military radio code, allowing Admiral Chester Nimitz, commander of the U.S. central Pacific fleet, to learn where Yamamoto's fleet was heading.

The Japanese hit Midway hard on June 4, 1942, but at the cost of about a third of their warplanes. American planes then struck back, crippling the Japanese fleet.

The **Battle of Midway** was the first major defeat for the Japanese navy in 350 years and a turning point of the Pacific war. The American victory blunted Japan's military momentum, eliminated the threat to Hawaii, and bought time for the United States to organize its massive industrial productivity for a wider war.

**MacARTHUR'S PACIFIC STRATEGY** American and Australian forces were jointly under the command of General Douglas MacArthur, an egotistical military genius who irritated his superiors with his "unpleasant personality" and constant self-promotion. MacArthur had retired in 1937 but was called back into service in mid-1941. In 1942, he assumed command of the Allied forces in the southwest Pacific.

On August 7, 1942, some 19,000 U.S. Marines landed on Guadalcanal Island, where the Japanese had an air base. Savage fighting lasted through February 1943, but it resulted in the Japanese army's first defeat, with a loss of 20,000 men compared to 1,752 Americans. Said a U.S. Marine, "These people refuse to surrender."

The suicidal intensity of the Japanese led MacArthur and Admiral Chester Nimitz to adopt a "leapfrogging" or "island-hopping" strategy whereby they liberated the most important islands and bypassed the others, leaving isolated Japanese bases to "wither on the vine," as Nimitz put it.

**BATTLES IN THE CENTRAL PACIFIC** On June 15, 1944, U.S. forces liberated Tinian, Guam, and Saipan in the Mariana Islands. Saipan was strategically important because it allowed new B-29 Superfortress bombers, the largest in the war, to strike Japan itself. The struggle for Saipan lasted three weeks. Some 20,000 Japanese were killed compared to 3,500 Americans. But 7,000 more Japanese soldiers committed suicide upon the order of their commanding general, who killed himself with his sword.

General MacArthur's forces invaded the Philippines on October 20. The Japanese, knowing that the loss of the Philippines would cut them off from essential raw materials, brought in warships from three directions.

The four battles fought in the Philippine Sea from October 23 to October 26, 1944, known collectively as the Battle of Leyte Gulf, marked the largest naval engagement in history and the worst Japanese defeat of the war. Some 216 U.S. warships converged to engage 64 Japanese ships. By the end of the battle's last day, thirty-six Japanese warships, including four aircraft carriers, had been destroyed.

The Battle of Leyte Gulf included the first Japanese *kamikaze* ("divine wind") attacks, in which pilots deliberately crashed their bomb-laden planes into American warships. From the fall of 1944 to the war's end in the summer of 1945, an estimated 4,000 kamikaze pilots died on suicide missions. "Kamikazes just poured at us, again and again," a sailor remembered. "It scared the shit out of us."

As MacArthur waded ashore with the U.S. troops liberating the Philippines, he reminded reporters of his 1942 pledge—"I shall return"—when he was evacuated in the face of the Japanese invasion. Now he announced: "People of the Philippines, I have returned! The hour of your redemption is here. . . . Rally to me."

**A WAR TO THE DEATH** The closer the Allied forces got to Japan, the fiercer the resistance they encountered. While fighting continued in the Philippines, 30,000 U.S. Marines landed on Iwo Jima, a volcanic atoll 760 miles from Tokyo, which the Americans wanted as an airbase for fighter planes to escort bombers over Japan. It took almost six weeks to secure the tiny island at a cost of nearly 7,000 American lives—and 21,000 of the 22,000 Japanese soldiers. In the end, the air base never materialized.

The assault on Okinawa was even bloodier. Only 360 miles from the main Japanese islands, Okinawa was strategically important because it would serve as the staging area for the planned Allied invasion of Japan. The conquest of Okinawa was the largest amphibious operation of the Pacific war, involving some 300,000 troops and requiring almost three months of brutal fighting.

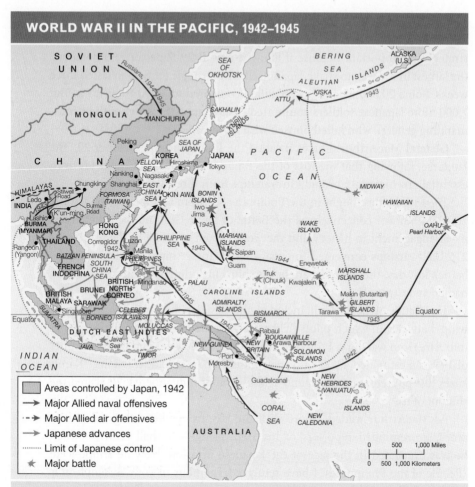

## WORLD WAR II IN THE PACIFIC, 1942–1945

Areas controlled by Japan, 1942
→ Major Allied naval offensives
·-→ Major Allied air offensives
→ Japanese advances
······· Limit of Japanese control
✳ Major battle

- What was MacArthur's "leapfrogging" strategy? Why were the battles in the Marianas a major turning point in the war?
- What was the significance of the Battle of Leyte Gulf?
- How did the battle at Okinawa affect both Japanese and American military strategists?

More than 150,000 Japanese were killed; some 49,000 Americans were killed, wounded, or missing, a 35 percent casualty rate. A third of U.S. pilots and a quarter of submariners lost their lives.

As the fighting raged on Okinawa, Allied commanders began planning Operation Downfall—the invasion of Japan itself. To weaken Japanese defenses, destroy their war-related industries, and erode civilian morale, the

Allied command stepped up bombing raids in the summer of 1944. Then, in early 1945, General Curtis Lemay, head of the U.S. Bomber Command, ordered devastating "firebomb" raids upon Japanese cities: "Bomb and burn 'em till they quit."

On March 9, some 300 B-29 bombers dropped napalm bombs on Tokyo. The attack incinerated sixteen square miles of the city and killed some 100,000 people while rendering a million people homeless. By then, American military leaders had lost all moral qualms about targeting civilians. The kamikaze attacks, the Japanese savagery toward prisoners of war, the burning of Manila that had killed 100,000 civilians, and the "rape" of China had eroded almost all sympathy.

By August 1945, sixty-six Japanese cities had been firebombed. Secretary of War Henry Stimson called the lack of public outcry in the United States over the raids "appalling."

**THE ATOMIC BOMB** Still, the Japanese refused to surrender. In early 1945, new U.S. president Harry S. Truman, the vice president who became president upon Roosevelt's death on April 12, learned of the first successful test of an atomic bomb in New Mexico. Now that military planners knew the bomb would work, they selected two Japanese cities as targets. The first was **Hiroshima**, a port city and army headquarters in southern Japan. On July 25, 1945, Truman, who knew nothing about the devastating effects of radiation poisoning, ordered that the atomic bomb be dropped if Japan did not surrender before August 3.

Although an intense debate emerged over the decision (General Eisenhower argued that the "Japanese were ready to surrender," and he "hated to see our country be the first to use such a weapon"), Truman later recalled, "We faced half a million casualties trying to take Japan by land. It was either that or the atom bomb, and I didn't hesitate a minute, and I've never lost any sleep over it since."

To Truman and others, the use of atomic bombs seemed a logical next step to end the war. As it turned out, scientists greatly underestimated the bomb's power. Their prediction that 20,000 people would be killed proved much too low.

In mid-July 1945, the Allied leaders met in Potsdam, Germany, near Berlin. Josef Stalin demanded, according to Truman, that the United States and Great Britain "recognize the new puppet governments" the Soviets had created in Romania, Bulgaria, and Hungary. Truman responded that the United States would do so only after the Soviets allowed "free access" to them and adopted "democratic" processes. Until that happened, America would veto efforts to allow such Soviet-dominated nations to participate in the new United Nations.

The conference deadlocked over the issue of Soviet control of eastern Europe. The allies did issue the Potsdam Declaration, which demanded that Japan surrender by August 3 or face "prompt and utter destruction." Truman left Potsdam optimistic about postwar relations with the Soviet Union. "I can deal with Stalin," he wrote. "He is honest—but smart as hell." (Truman would soon change his mind about Stalin's honesty.)

The deadline calling for Japan's surrender passed, and on August 6, 1945, a B-29 bomber piloted by Colonel Paul Tibbets (the plane was named *Enola Gay* after Tibbets' mother) took off at 2 A.M. from the island of Tinian, headed for Hiroshima. At 8:15 A.M., flying at 31,600 feet, the bombardier aboard the *Enola Gay* released the five-ton, ten-foot-long uranium bomb nicknamed "Little Boy."

**Bombing of Nagasaki** A 52,000-foot tall mushroom cloud enveloped the city of Nagasaki after the atomic bombing on August 9, 1945.

Forty-three seconds later, the bomb exploded at an altitude of 1,900 feet, creating a blinding flash of light followed by a fireball towering to 40,000 feet. The tail gunner on the *Enola Gay* described the scene: "It's like bubbling molasses down there . . . the mushroom is spreading out . . . fires are springing up everywhere . . . it's like a peep into hell."

The bomb's shock wave and firestorm killed some 78,000 people, including thousands of Japanese soldiers and twenty-three American prisoners of war. By the end of the year, the death toll would reach 140,000, as people died of injuries or radiation poisoning. In addition, the bomb destroyed 76,000 buildings.

President Truman was returning from the Potsdam conference when news arrived that the atomic bomb had been dropped. "This is the greatest thing in history!" he repeatedly exclaimed. In the United States, Americans greeted the news with similar joy.

"No tears of sympathy will be shed in America for the Japanese people," the *Omaha World-Herald* predicted. "Had they possessed a comparable weapon at Pearl Harbor, would they have hesitated to use it?" Others reacted by pointing to the implications of atomic warfare. "Yesterday," journalist Hanson Baldwin wrote in the *New York Times*, "we clinched victory in the Pacific, but we sowed the whirlwind."

Two days after the Hiroshima bombing, an opportunistic Soviet Union entered the war in the Pacific by sending hundreds of thousands of troops into Japanese-occupied Manchuria, along the border between China and the Soviet Union. Truman and his aides, frustrated by the refusal of Japanese leaders to surrender and fearful that the Soviet Union's entry would complicate negotiations, ordered a second atomic bomb ("Fat Man") to be dropped.

On August 9, the city of Nagasaki, a shipbuilding center, experienced the same nuclear devastation that had destroyed Hiroshima. An estimated 71,000 people were killed in the city of some 240,000 residents. Five days later, on August 14, 1945, the Japanese emperor accepted the terms of surrender. The formal surrender ceremony occurred on an American warship in Tokyo Bay on September 2, 1945, a date quickly known as V-J Day.

## A NEW AGE IS BORN

Thus ended the costliest war in history. Including deaths from war-related disease and famine, some 50 million civilians and 22 million combatants had died.

The Second World War was more costly for the United States than any other foreign war: 292,000 combat deaths and 114,000 noncombat deaths among soldiers, sailors, airmen, and marines. A million more were wounded, with half of them seriously disabled.

In proportion to its population, however, the United States suffered far fewer losses than did the other major Allies or their enemies. For every American killed in the Second World War, for example, some fifty-nine Soviets died.

The war was the pivotal event of the turbulent twentieth century. It engulfed five continents, leveled cities, reshaped societies, transformed international relations, and destroyed German and Italian fascism and Japanese militarism. It set in motion the fall of China to communism in 1949 and the outbreak of the Korean War a year later. Colonial empires in Africa and Asia rapidly crumbled as the conflict unleashed independence movements. The Soviet Union emerged as a new global superpower, while the United States, as Winston Churchill told the House of Commons, stood "at the summit of the world."

**WHY DID THE ALLIES WIN?**  Many factors contributed to the Allied victory. Franklin Roosevelt and Winston Churchill were better at coordinating military efforts and maintaining national morale than were Hitler, Mussolini, and the Japanese emperor, Hirohito. By 1944, Hitler had grown increasingly unstable and more withdrawn, especially after a failed attempt by high-ranking officers to assassinate him in July by placing a bomb under his desk. The blast shattered Hitler's eardrums, riddled his body with wooden splinters, and caused a nervous breakdown that left him paranoid, anxious, and addicted to cocaine injections.

In the end, however, what turned the tide was the awesome productivity of American industry and the ability of the Soviet Union to absorb the massive German invasion and push the Nazis back to Berlin. By the end of the war, Japan had run out of food and Germany had run out of fuel. By contrast, the United States was churning out more of everything. As early as 1942, just a few weeks after the Japanese attack on Pearl Harbor, Fritz Todt, a Nazi engineer, told Hitler that the war against the United States was already lost because of America's ability to outproduce all the other warring nations combined.

**A TRANSFORMATIONAL WAR** The Second World War shattered the old world order and created a new international system. Nations such as France, Germany, Great Britain, and Japan were left devastated or impoverished.

Henry Luce, publisher of *Time* magazine, said that the war had demonstrated the "moral and practical bankruptcy of all forms of Isolationism." Internationalism was now dominant, and most Americans acknowledged that the United States had profound responsibilities for global stability and security. It had emerged from the war with the most powerful military in the world—and as the only nation with atomic weapons.

The expansion of the federal government spurred by the war effort continued after 1945, and presidential authority increased enormously at the expense of congressional and state power. The war also ended the Great Depression and launched a long period of unprecedented prosperity and global economic domination.

Big businesses grew into gigantic corporations as a result of huge government contracts for military weapons and supplies. New technologies and products developed for military purposes—radar, computers, electronics, plastics and synthetics, jet engines, rockets, atomic energy—transformed the private sector, as did new consumer products generated from war-related innovations. And the opportunities created for women as well as African Americans, Mexican Americans, and other minorities set in motion social changes that would culminate in the civil rights movement of the 1960s and the feminist movement of the 1970s.

In August 1945, President Truman announced that the United States had "emerged from this war the most powerful nation in this world—the most powerful nation, perhaps, in all history." But the Soviet Union, despite its human losses and physical destruction, had gained much new territory, built massive armed forces, and enhanced its international influence, making it the greatest power in Eurasia. A little over a century after Frenchman Alexis de Tocqueville had predicted that Europe would eventually be overshadowed by the United States and Russia, his prophecy had come to pass.

# CHAPTER REVIEW

## SUMMARY

- **Fascism and the Start of the War**   In Italy, Benito Mussolini and his *Fascist* party assumed control in 1922 by promising law and order. Adolf Hitler rearmed Germany in defiance of the Treaty of Versailles. By March 1939, Nazi Germany had annexed Austria and seized Czechoslovakia. Hitler then invaded Poland with the *blitzkrieg* strategy after signing a non-aggression pact with the Soviet Union. The British and French governments declared war.

- **America Goes to War**   The United States issued *neutrality laws (1935–1939)* to avoid being drawn into wars in Europe and Asia, but after the fall of France in 1940, President Roosevelt accelerated military aid to Great Britain through the *Lend-Lease Act (1941)*. In 1941, the United States and Great Britain signed the *Atlantic Charter*. After Japan joined with Germany and Italy to form the *Axis alliance,* Roosevelt froze Japanese assets in the United States and restricted oil exports to Japan, which led the frustrated Japanese government to launch a surprise attack at *Pearl Harbor (1941)* in Hawaii.

- **The Second World War and American Society**   The war had profound social effects. Americans—white, black, and brown—enlisted in the military, went to work in defense plants, and migrated west to take jobs in factories. Farmers recovered, supported by Mexican labor through the *bracero program (1942–1945)*. The federal government, through agencies such as the *War Production Board*, took control of managing the economy. Many women took nontraditional jobs, including service in the military. More than 150,000 joined the *Women's Army Corps (WAC)*. About a million African Americans served in the military in segregated units, the most famous of which was the *Tuskegee Airmen*. More than 100,000 Japanese Americans were forcibly interned in *war relocation camps*.

- **Road to Allied Victory in Europe**   By 1943, the Allies had defeated the German and Italian armies occupying North Africa. From there, they launched attacks on Sicily and then the mainland of Italy. *Operation Overlord,* the invasion of Western Europe, began June 6, 1944. German resistance slowly crumbled. The "Big Three"—Roosevelt, Churchill, and Stalin—met at the *Yalta Conference* in February 1945, where they decided that a conquered Germany would be divided into four occupation zones. In May, Soviet forces captured Berlin, and Germany surrendered. After the war, Allied forces discovered the extent of the *Holocaust*—the Nazis' systematic effort to exterminate European Jews and other minority groups.

- **The Pacific War**   The Japanese advance across the Pacific was halted in June 1942 at the *Battle of Midway*. Fierce Japanese resistance at Iwo Jima and Okinawa and Japan's refusal to surrender after the firebombing of Tokyo led the new president, Harry S. Truman, to order the use of atomic bombs on the cities of *Hiroshima* and Nagasaki in August 1945.

- **Postwar World** The Soviet Union and United States emerged from the war as global superpowers, with the United States possessing the world's strongest economy. The opportunities for women and minorities during the war would contribute to the emergence of the civil rights and feminist movements.

## CHRONOLOGY

| | |
|---|---|
| 1933 | Adolf Hitler becomes chancellor of Germany |
| 1937 | War between China and Japan begins |
| September 1939 | German troops invade Poland |
| 1940 | Battle of Britain |
| June 1941 | Germany invades Soviet Union |
| August 1941 | United States and Great Britain sign the Atlantic Charter |
| December 7, 1941 | Japanese launch surprise attack at Pearl Harbor, Hawaii |
| June 1942 | Battle of Midway |
| June 6, 1944 | D-day |
| February 1945 | Yalta Conference |
| April 1945 | Roosevelt dies; Hitler commits suicide |
| May 7–8, 1945 | Nazi Germany surrenders; V-E day |
| August 1945 | Atomic bombs dropped on Hiroshima and Nagasaki |
| September 2, 1945 | Japan surrenders; V-J day |

## KEY TERMS

fascism p. 1056

neutrality laws p. 1060

Axis alliance p. 1060

Lend-Lease Act (1941) p. 1067

Atlantic Charter (1941) p. 1069

Pearl Harbor (1941) p. 1072

War Production Board p. 1074

Women's Army Corps p. 1075

Tuskegee Airmen p. 1079

bracero program (1942) p. 1079

war relocation camps p. 1081

Operation Overlord p. 1085

Yalta Conference (1945) p. 1091

Holocaust p. 1094

Battle of Midway (1942) p. 1096

Hiroshima (1945) p. 1099

 INQUIZITIVE

**Go to InQuizitive to see what you've learned—and learn what you've missed—with personalized feedback along the way.**

# part seven

# THE AMERICAN AGE

As the Second World War was ending in 1945, President Franklin D. Roosevelt, like Woodrow Wilson before him, staked his hopes for a peaceful future on a new international organization.

On April 25, 1945, two weeks after Roosevelt's death and two weeks before the German surrender, delegates from fifty nations met in San Francisco to draw up the Charter of the United Nations. It gave the UN Security Council "primary responsibility for the maintenance of international peace and security." The Security Council included five permanent members: the United States, the Soviet Union (replaced by the Russian Federation in 1991), Great Britain, France, and the Republic of China (replaced by the People's Republic of China in 1971). Each could *veto* any proposed action by the United Nations.

It soon became evident, however, that the United States and the Soviet Union had such intense differences of opinion about international policies that the United Nations was largely impotent in dealing with the emerging cold war between the competing ideologies of communism and capitalism.

The United States emerged from the Second World War as the dominant nation. It was the world's preeminent military and economic power, and the only nation with atomic weapons. While much of Europe, Asia, and Africa struggled to recover from the war's destruction, the United States emerged from the conflict relatively unscathed, its economic infrastructure intact and operating at peak efficiency. Jobs were available for the taking. By 1955, the United States, with only 6 percent of the world's population, was producing half the world's goods.

However, the deepening cold war between democratic and Communist nations cast a cloud over the postwar world. The tense ideological contest with the Soviet Union produced numerous crises and sparked a witch hunt for Communists in the United States. After 1945, Republican and Democratic presidents sought to "contain" the spread of communism; this bedrock assumption embroiled the United States in costly wars in Korea and in Southeast Asia.

A backlash against the Vietnam War (1964–1973) inflamed a rebellious countercultural movement in which young idealists opposed to the war also provided much of the energy for many overdue social reforms. An array of social justice and liberation movements emerged during the sixties, including racial and ethnic equality, gay rights (known as LGBTQ rights since the 1990s), feminism, and environmentalism. The anti-war movement destroyed Lyndon Johnson's presidency in 1968 and provoked a conservative counterattack. President Richard Nixon's paranoid reaction to his critics led to the Watergate affair and the destruction of his presidency.

Through all this turmoil, however, the expanding role of the federal government that Franklin Roosevelt and his New Deal programs had initiated remained essentially intact. With only a few exceptions, both Republicans and Democrats after 1945 acknowledged that the federal government must assume greater responsibility for the welfare of individuals. Yet this fragile consensus on public policy collapsed, along with the cold war, by the late 1980s amid stunning international developments and social changes at home. The implosion and dissolution of the Soviet Union in 1989 left the United States as the world's only superpower, lowered the threat of nuclear war, and reduced public interest in foreign affairs.

Numerous ethnic, nationalist, and separatist conflicts, however, brought constant international instability. The United States found itself drawn into political and military crises in Bosnia, Somalia, Afghanistan, Iraq, Ukraine, and Syria.

Throughout the 1990s, the United States waged a difficult struggle against many groups engaged in organized terrorism. The challenges of tracking the movements of foreign terrorists became tragically evident in 2001. At 8:46 on the morning of September 11, 2001, the world watched in horror as hijacked commercial airplanes slammed into the World Trade Center in New York City and the Pentagon in Washington, D.C.

Officials identified the hijackers as members of al Qaeda (Arabic for "the Base"), a well-financed network of Islamic terrorists led by a wealthy Saudi renegade, Osama bin Laden. President George W. Bush responded by declaring a "war on terror." With the passage of the so-called Patriot Act, Congress gave the president authority to track down and imprison terrorists at home and abroad. Militarily, the war on terror began with assaults first on terrorist bases in Afghanistan and then on Saddam Hussein's dictatorship in Iraq (Operation Iraqi Freedom).

Frustrated by the expense and casualties of the ongoing wars in Iraq and Afghanistan, American voters elected Democrat Barack Obama in the 2008 presidential contest. He pledged to end the wars, create a national health-care system, unite the polarized nation, and provide jobs to the unemployed. As the first African American U.S. president, Obama symbolized the societal changes transforming national life.

Upon taking office, President Obama inherited the worst economic slow-down since the Great Depression. What came to be called the Great Recession dominated both terms of his presidency. For all its economic power and military might, the United States in the twenty-first century has not eliminated the threat of terrorism or unlocked the mystery of sustaining prosperity and reducing economic inequality.

That many Americans did not share in the economic recovery and were frustrated by the continuing influx of immigrants, especially Mexicans, helps explain the remarkable presidential candidacy of brash real-estate developer Donald Trump. As a self-described "disruptive" political force, he seized control of the 2016 presidential campaign by turning conventional assumptions of America's role abroad and its priorities at home topsy-turvy.

# 27 The Cold War and the Fair Deal

## 1945–1952

**Duck and cover** A "duck-and-cover" air-raid drill in 1951 that was commonplace in schools during the cold war. The drills began in 1949, when the Soviet Union set off its first nuclear weapon. Pictured above are schoolchildren practicing ducking and covering in February 1951.

No sooner did the Second World War end than a tense cold war erupted between communism and capitalism, totalitarianism and democracy. For over forty years after 1945, the Soviet Union and the United States engaged in a relentless war of words as each sought to gain influence around the world for its way of life. The awkward wartime alliance between the United States and the Soviet Union collapsed during the spring and summer of 1945. With the elimination of German Nazism, the two nations became fierce rivals who could not bridge their ideological differences over basic issues such as human rights, individual liberties, democratic elections, and religious freedom. As President Harry Truman said, the most important issue facing the postwar world was the contest between "tyranny or freedom."

Mutual suspicion and a race to gain influence over "nonaligned" nations in Asia, Africa, the Middle East, and Central and South America further distanced the two former allies. The defeat of Japan and Germany had created power vacuums in Europe and Asia that sucked the Soviet Union and the United States into a contest for global influence and control.

The postwar era also brought anti-colonial liberation movements that would soon strip Great Britain, France, the Netherlands, and the United States of their global empires. The emergence of Communist China (the People's Republic) in 1949 further complicated global politics and cold war dynamics.

In the unstable postwar world, international tensions shaped domestic politics and foreign relations. The advent of atomic weapons (weapons of mass destruction) made the very idea of warfare unthinkably horrific,

## *focus questions*

1. Why and how did the cold war between the United States and the Soviet Union develop?

2. What was the impact of U.S. efforts to contain the Soviet Union and the growth of global communism during Harry Truman's presidency?

3. How did Truman expand the New Deal? How effective was his Fair Deal agenda?

4. What were the major international developments during 1949–1950, and how did they alter U.S. foreign policy?

5. How did the Red Scare emerge? How did it impact American politics and society?

which in turn made national leaders more cautious so as not to trigger a third world war.

## TRUMAN AND THE COLD WAR

In April 1945, less than three months after Harry S. Truman had begun his new role as vice president, Eleanor Roosevelt calmly informed him, "Harry, the President is dead." When Truman asked how he could help her, the First Lady replied: "Is there anything we can do for *you*? For you are the one in trouble now."

Born in 1884 in western Missouri, Truman grew up in Independence, near Kansas City. During the First World War, he served in France as captain of an artillery battery. Afterward, he and a partner started a clothing business, but it failed in the recession of 1922, leaving him in debt for twenty years. Truman, who did not attend college, then entered politics as a Democrat. In 1934, Missouri sent him to the U.S. Senate.

On his first full day as president, Truman was awestruck. "Boys, if you ever pray, pray for me now," he told reporters. "I don't know whether you fellows ever had a load of hay fall on you, but when they told me yesterday what had happened, I felt like the moon, the stars and all the planets had fallen on me."

An unreflective man rarely troubled by doubts or moral ambiguities, Truman was famously short-tempered, profane, and dismissive. His press conferences were known for confrontations. ("If you ask smart-aleck questions, I'll give you smart-aleck answers.") He called publisher William Randolph Hearst "the number one whore monger of our time," columnist Westbrook Pegler "the greatest character assassin in the United States," and Richard Nixon "a shifty-eyed god-damned liar." The president's behavior, said the *Chicago Tribune*, called into question his "mental competence and emotional stability."

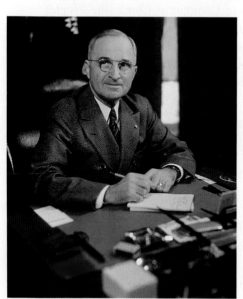

**Harry S. Truman** The successor to Franklin Roosevelt who led the United States out of the Second World War and into the cold war.

Although Washington politicos had low expectations for the new president, Truman did better than anyone expected. He rose above his limitations and never pretended to be something he was not. During a visit in 1952, British leader Winston Churchill confessed to Truman that initially he had held him "in very low regard. I loathed your taking the place of Franklin Roosevelt. I misjudged you badly. Since that time, you, more than any other man, have saved Western civilization."

**ORIGINS OF THE COLD WAR** Historians have long debated the unanswerable question: Was the United States or the Soviet Union more responsible for the onset of the cold war? The conventional view argues that the Soviets, led by Josef Stalin, set out to dominate the globe after 1945. The United States had no choice but to defend democratic capitalist values.

Historians critical of this explanation insist that the United States unnecessarily antagonized the Soviet Union. Instead of continuing Franklin Roosevelt's collaborative efforts with the Soviets, Truman pursued a confrontational foreign policy that focused on stopping the spread of communism, a policy that only aggravated tensions. For example, the United States in 1947 and 1948 secretly intervened in elections in France and Italy to ensure that Communist candidates were defeated. American agents gave bags of money to anti-Communist candidates, provided campaign advisers, and publicly threatened to cut off aid to the governments if Communists were elected.

In retrospect, the onset of the cold war seems to have been an unavoidable result of the ideological competition between capitalism and communism and their opposing views of what the postwar world should become. America's commitment to free-enterprise capitalism, political self-determination, and religious freedom conflicted with the Soviet Union's preference for controlling its neighbors, ideological conformity, and prohibiting religious practices.

Insecurity drove much of Soviet behavior. Russia, after all, had been invaded by Germany twice in the first half of the twentieth century, and some 23 million people died as a result. Soviet leaders were determined to dominate nations on their borders and in their region, just as the United States had been doing for decades in Central and South America.

The people of Eastern Europe were caught in the middle, and the cold war soon came to dominate global politics. We are still living in its shadow.

**CONFLICTS WITH THE SOVIETS** The wartime military alliance against Nazism disintegrated after 1945 as the Soviet Union violated the promises it had made at the Yalta Conference. The USSR imposed military control and a Communist political system on the nations of Eastern Europe that it had liberated from Nazi control. On May 12, 1945, four days after victory in Europe, Winston Churchill asked Truman: "What is to happen about [Eastern] Europe? An **iron curtain** is drawn down upon [the Russian] front. We do not know what is going on behind [it]." Churchill and Truman wanted to lift the iron curtain and help those nations develop democratic governments. Events during the second half of 1945, however, dashed those expectations.

Beginning in the spring of 1945 and continuing for the next two years, the Soviet Union systematically imprisoned half the European continent and installed puppet governments across Central and Eastern Europe (Albania, Bulgaria, Czechoslovakia, East Germany, Hungary, Poland, Romania, and Yugoslavia). The Soviets eliminated all political parties except the Communists; created secret police forces; took control of intellectual and cultural life, including the mass media; and organized a process of ethnic cleansing whereby whole populations—12 million Germans, as well as Poles and Hungarians—were relocated, usually to West Germany or to prisons. Anyone who opposed the Soviet-installed regimes was exiled, silenced, executed, or imprisoned.

Stalin's promise at the Yalta Conference to allow open elections in the nations controlled by Soviet armies had turned out to be a lie. In a fit of candor, he admitted that "a freely elected government in any of these countries would be anti-Soviet, and that we cannot allow."

U.S. Secretary of State James F. Byrnes tried to use America's monopoly on the atomic bomb to pressure the Soviets. In April 1945, he suggested to President Truman that nuclear weapons "might well put us in position to dictate our own terms [with the Soviets] at the end of the war." The Soviets, however, paid little attention, in part because their spies had kept them informed of what U.S. scientists had been doing and in part because they were developing their own atomic bombs.

In April 1945, a few days before the opening of the conference to organize the United Nations, Truman met with Soviet foreign minister Vyacheslav Molotov. Truman directed Molotov to tell Stalin that the United States expected the Soviet leader to live up to his agreements. "I have never been talked to like that in my life," Molotov angrily replied. "Carry out your agreements," Truman snapped, "and you won't get talked to like that."

That July, when Truman met Stalin at the Potsdam conference, he wrote that he had never seen "such pig-headed people as are the Russians." He later acknowledged that they broke their promises "as soon as the unconscionable Russian Dictator [Stalin] returned to Moscow!" Truman added, with a note of embarrassment, "And I liked the little son of a bitch."

## The Containment Policy

In February 1946, Stalin had proclaimed the superiority of the Soviet Communist system of government and declared that peace was impossible "under the present capitalist development of the world economy." By the beginning of 1947, relations with the Soviet Union had grown ice cold. Stalin's provocative statement against capitalism led the State Department to ask for an analysis of Soviet communism from George Frost Kennan, the best-informed expert on the Soviet Union, who was then working in the U.S. embassy in Moscow.

Kennan responded on February 22, 1946, with a 5,000-word "Long Telegram." He predicted that the Soviets would never embrace a "permanent happy coexistence" of the socialist and capitalist worlds.

Kennan explained that the Soviet Union was founded on a rigid ideology (Marxism-Leninism), which saw a fundamental global conflict between Communist and capitalist nations. The Soviet goal, according to Kennan, was to build military strength while subverting the stability of capitalist democracies. He advised that the strategic **containment** of Soviet expansionism was the best way for the United States to deal with such an ideological foe—and that could best be achieved through patient, persistent tactical efforts. Creating "unalterable counterforce" to Communist expansionism, Kennan predicted, would eventually cause "either the breakup or the gradual mellowing of Soviet power" because communism was inherently unstable and would eventually collapse.

New secretary of state George C. Marshall, the distinguished commander of the U.S. armed forces during the war, was so impressed by Kennan's analysis that he put him in charge of the State Department's Policy Planning office. No other diplomat at the time forecast so accurately what would happen to the Soviet Union some forty years later.

But how were the United States and its allies to *contain* the Soviet Union's expansionist tendencies? How should the United States respond to Soviet aggression? Kennan left the task of containing communism to Truman and his advisers, most of whom, unlike Kennan, considered containment to be as much a *military* doctrine as a *political* strategy. As Truman insisted, the Soviets understood only one language: military power.

In 1946, civil war broke out in Greece between the monarchy backed by the British and a Communist-led insurgency supported by the Soviets. On February 21, 1947, the British informed the U.S. government that they could no longer provide economic and military aid to Greece and would withdraw their 40,000 troops in five weeks. Truman quickly conferred with congressional leaders. One of them, Republican senator Arthur Vandenberg of Michigan, warned the president that he would need to "scare the hell out of the American people" about the menace of communism to gain public support for any new aid program.

**THE TRUMAN DOCTRINE** On March 12, 1947, President Truman gave a national radio speech in which he asked Congress to provide $400 million for economic and military assistance to Greece and Turkey. More important, he announced what came to be known as the **Truman Doctrine**, which would guide American foreign policy for the next two decades. To ensure congressional support, he exaggerated the danger of a Communist takeover in Greece. Like a row of dominoes, Truman predicted, the fall of Greece would topple the other nations of the eastern Mediterranean, then Western Europe. To prevent such a catastrophe, he said, the United States must "support free peoples who are resisting attempted subjugation by armed minorities or by outside pressures."

In this single sentence, Truman in essence declared war on communism everywhere. In his view, shared by later presidents, the assumptions of the "domino theory" made an aggressive containment strategy a necessity.

Truman's speech generated widespread public support. The *New York Times* said that his message was clear: "The epoch of isolation is ended. It is being replaced by an epoch of American responsibility." At the State Department, Secretary of State Marshall announced that "we are now concerned with the peace of the entire world."

Still, the secretary of state and others privately feared that Truman's speech was unnecessarily provocative. Marshall believed that the president was overstating the Soviet threat. Others expressed concern about the scope and vagueness of the Truman Doctrine. Bernard Baruch, a prominent political adviser, charged that Truman's speech represented a "declaration of . . . an ideological or religious war" against the Soviet Union.

George Kennan similarly cringed at the president's "grandiose" commitment to contain communism *everywhere*. In Kennan's view, Truman's "militarized view of the Cold War" was an open-ended ideological confrontation rather than a *policy* with an accompanying program of steps capable of implementation. Efforts to contain communism needed to be selective rather than universal, political and economic rather than military. The United States could not intervene in every "hot spot" around the world.

Truman and his advisers rejected such concerns. In 1947, Congress approved the president's request for aid to Greece and Turkey.

**THE MARSHALL PLAN** In the spring of 1947, most postwar European governments remained insolvent, shattered, and desperate, and political unrest was growing. By 1947, Socialist and Communist parties were forming in many European nations, including Italy, France, and Belgium. The crises among these struggling democracies required bold action.

The United States stepped into the breach. In May 1947, Secretary of State Marshall, building upon suggestions from George Kennan and others, called for a massive U.S. program to provide financial and technical assistance to rescue Europe, including the Soviet Union.

What came to be known as the **Marshall Plan** was intended to reconstruct the European economy, neutralize Communist insurgencies, and build up foreign markets for U.S. products. As Truman said, "the American [capitalist] system can survive only if it is part of a world system." The Marshall Plan was about more than economics, however. It was part of Truman's effort to contain the expansionist tendencies of the Soviet Union by reestablishing a strong Western Europe anchored in American values.

In December 1947, Truman submitted Marshall's proposal to Congress, saying that "if Europe fails to recover" from the war's devastation, voters might be won over by Communist parties, which would deal a "shattering blow to peace and stability."

Initially, Republican critics dismissed the Marshall Plan as "New Dealism" for Europe, a "costly boondoggle" that smacked of socialism. However, two months later, on February 25, 1948, a Communist-led coup in Czechoslovakia, the last nation in Eastern Europe with a democratic government, ensured the Marshall Plan's passage.

From 1948 until 1951, the Marshall Plan provided $13 billion to sixteen European nations. The Soviet Union, however, refused to participate and forced the Eastern European countries

**"It's the same thing"** The Marshall Plan, which distributed massive amounts of economic aid throughout postwar Europe, is represented in this 1949 cartoon as a modern tractor driven by a prosperous farmer. In the foreground, a poor, overworked man is yoked to an old-fashioned "Soviet" plow, forced to go over the ground of the "Marshal Stalin Plan," while Stalin himself tries to persuade others that "it's the same thing without mechanical problems."

under its control—Albania, Bulgaria, Poland, Romania, Yugoslavia—to refuse as well.

The Marshall Plan (officially called the European Recovery Plan) worked as hoped. By 1951, Western Europe's industrial production had soared to 40 percent above prewar levels, and its farm output was larger than ever. England's *Economist* magazine called the Marshall Plan "an act without peer." It became the most successful peacetime diplomatic initiative in history.

**DIVIDED GERMANY** Although the Marshall Plan drew the nations of Western Europe closer together, it increased tensions with the Soviet Union. The breakdown of the wartime alliance between the United States and the Soviet Union also left the problem of postwar Germany unsettled. In 1945, Berlin, the German capital, had been divided into four sectors, or zones, each governed by one of the four principal allied nations—the United States, France, Great Britain, and the Soviet Union.

The German economy continued to languish, requiring the U.S. Army to provide food and supplies to millions of civilians. Slowly, the Allied occupation zones evolved into functioning governments. In 1948, the British, French, and Americans united their three administrative zones into one and developed a common currency for West Germany and West Berlin, a city of 2.5 million people, which was more than 100 miles inside the Soviet occupation zone of East Germany. The West Germans also organized state governments and began drafting a federal constitution.

The political unification and economic recovery of West Germany infuriated Stalin, and the status of divided Berlin had become a powder keg. In March 1948, Stalin prevented the new West German currency from being used in Berlin. Then, on June 23, he stopped all road and rail traffic into West Berlin, hoping to force the United States and its allies to leave the divided city.

Americans interpreted Stalin's blockade as a tipping point in the cold war. "When Berlin falls," predicted General Lucius D. Clay, the U.S. Army commander in Germany, "western Germany will be next. Communism will run rampant." The United States thus faced a dilemma: risk a third world war by using force to break the Soviet blockade or begin a humiliating retreat from West Berlin.

Truman, who prided himself on his decisiveness, made clear his stance: "We stay in Berlin—period." The United States announced an embargo against all goods exported from Soviet-controlled eastern Germany and began organizing a massive airlift to provide food and supplies to West Berliners.

By October 1948, U.S. and British air forces were flying in 7,000 tons of food, fuel, medicine, coal, and equipment to Berlin each day. To support the

**Through the iron curtain** German children greet a U.S. cargo plane as it flies into West Berlin to drop off much-needed food and supplies.

airlift and prepare for a possible war, thousands of former military pilots were called back into service. Truman revived the military draft, and Congress provided emergency funds to increase military spending. The world watched as the two superpowers teetered on the edge of conflict.

For all the threats and harsh words, however, the **Berlin airlift** went on for 321 days without shots being fired. Finally, on May 12, 1949, the Soviets lifted their blockade, in part because bad Russian harvests had made them desperate for food grown in western Germany.

The Berlin airlift was the first major "victory" for the West in the cold war, and the unprecedented efforts of the United States and Great Britain to supply West Berliners transformed most of them into devoted allies. In May 1949, the Federal Republic of Germany (West Germany) was founded. In October, the Soviet-controlled German Democratic Republic (East Germany) came into being.

**FORMING ALLIANCES** The Soviet blockade of Berlin convinced the United States and its allies that they needed to act together to stop further Communist expansion into Western Europe. On April 4, 1949, representatives of twelve nations signed the North Atlantic Treaty: the United States, Great Britain, France, Belgium, the Netherlands, Luxembourg, Canada, Denmark, Iceland, Italy, Norway, and Portugal. Greece and Turkey joined the alliance in 1952, West Germany in 1955, and Spain in 1982.

**THE OCCUPATION OF GERMANY AND AUSTRIA**

■ How did the Allies decide to divide postwar Germany at the Yalta Conference?
■ What was the "iron curtain"?
■ Why did the Allies airlift supplies to West Berlin?

The **North Atlantic Treaty Organization (NATO)**, the largest defensive alliance in the world, declared that an attack against any of the members would be an attack against all. The creation of NATO marked the high point of efforts to contain Soviet expansion. By joining NATO, the United States committed itself to go to war on behalf of its allies. Isolationism was dead.

**REORGANIZING THE MILITARY** The onset of the cold war and the emergence of nuclear weapons led President Truman to sign the **National Security Act (1947)**, which reorganized the armed forces and intelligence agencies. It created a Department of Defense led by a new cabinet officer, the secretary of defense; a Joint Chiefs of Staff to oversee the three military branches—the army, navy, and the newly created air force; and established the National Security Council (NSC), a group of top specialists in international relations appointed to advise the president. The act also established the Central Intelligence Agency (CIA) to coordinate global intelligence-gathering activities. The following year, the NSC gave the CIA permission to launch covert operations abroad to undermine governments that threatened American interests.

**A JEWISH NATION: ISRAEL** At the same time that the United States was forming new alliances, it was helping to form a new nation. Palestine, the biblical Holy Land, had been a British protectorate since 1919. For hundreds of years, Jews throughout the world had dreamed of returning to their ancestral homeland of Israel and its ancient capital Zion, a part of Jerusalem. Many Zionists—Jews who wanted a separate Jewish nation—had migrated there. More arrived during and after the Nazi persecution of European Jews. Hitler's effort to exterminate Jews convinced many that their only hope for a secure future was to create their own nation.

Late in 1947, the United Nations voted to divide ("partition") Palestine into separate Jewish and Arab states. The Jews agreed to the partition, but the Arabs opposed it. Palestine was their ancestral home, too; Jerusalem was as holy to Muslims and Christians as it was to Jews.

Arabs viewed the creation of a Jewish nation in Palestine as an act of war, and they attacked Israel in early 1948. Hundreds were killed before the Haganah (Jewish militia) won control of most of Palestine. When British oversight of Palestine officially expired on May 14, 1948, David Ben-Gurion, the Jewish leader in Palestine, proclaimed Israel's independence. President Truman officially recognized the new Israeli nation within minutes, as did the Soviet Union.

One million Jews, most of them European immigrants, now had their own nation. Early the next morning, however, the Arab League nations—Lebanon, Syria, Iraq, Jordan, and Egypt—invaded Israel. Mediators from the United Nations gradually worked out a truce, restoring an unstable peace by May 11, 1949, when Israel joined the United Nations. Israel kept all its conquered territories, including the whole Palestine coast.

The Palestinian Arabs lost everything. Most became stateless refugees who scattered into neighboring Lebanon, Jordan, and Egypt. Stored-up resentments and sporadic warfare between Israel and the Arab states have festered since, complicating U.S. foreign policy, which has tried to maintain friendships with both sides but has usually tilted toward Israel.

# EXPANDING THE NEW DEAL

For the most part, Republicans and Democrats in Congress cooperated with President Truman on issues related to the cold war. On domestic issues, however, Truman faced widespread opposition. The cost-cutting Republicans in Congress hoped that they could end the New Deal as the Second World War drew to a close.

**FROM WAR TO PEACE**  In September 1945, Truman called Congress into a special emergency session at which he presented a twenty-one-point program to guide the nation's "reconversion" from wartime back to peacetime. His greatest challenge was to ensure that the peacetime economy absorbed the millions of men and women who had served in the armed forces and were now seeking civilian jobs.

That would not be easy. The day after the war in Asia ended, the Springfield Armory, which had made weapons for the army, fired every worker. Other military-dependent companies also announced layoffs. The nation faced a crisis as some 12 million men and women in uniform left military service and returned to an economy careening into recession.

Fears of massive unemployment in defense-related industries prompted concerns about another depression. Truman called for unemployment insurance to cover more workers, a higher minimum wage, construction of massive public-housing projects, regional development projects to put military veterans to work, and much more.

Truman's primary goal was to "prevent prolonged unemployment" while avoiding the "bitter mistakes" that had produced wild price inflation and a recession after the First World War. He also wanted to retain, for a while, the wartime controls on wages, prices, and rents, as well as the rationing of scarce food items. Most of all, he wanted to ensure that military veterans found civilian jobs. Truman called on Congress to *guarantee* every American a job.

Congress refused to go that far. Instead, it approved the Employment Act of 1946, which called on the federal government "to promote maximum employment, production, and purchasing power." Liberals were disappointed by Truman's inability to win over skeptical legislators. "What one misses," said journalist Max Lerner, "is the confident sense of direction that Roosevelt gave, despite all the contradictions of his policy."

Throughout 1946, Republicans and conservative southern Democrats in Congress balked at Truman's efforts to revive or expand New Deal programs. The Great Depression was over, critics stressed. Different times demanded different programs—or none at all.

The end of the war caused short-term economic problems. The federal government immediately canceled 100,000 contracts for military supplies and equipment. Many women who had been recruited to work in wartime defense industries were shoved out as men took off uniforms and looked for jobs. At a shipyard in California, a foreman gathered women workers and told them to welcome the troop ships as they pulled into port from Asia. The next day, the women were laid off to make room for male veterans.

**Drugstore in Bronxville, NY** America quickly demobilized after the long war effort, turning its attention to the pursuit of abundance.

Still, several shock absorbers cushioned the economic impact of demobilization. They included federal unemployment insurance (and other Social Security benefits) and the Servicemen's Readjustment Act of 1944, known as the GI Bill of Rights, under which the federal government provided $13 billion for veterans to use for education, vocational training, medical treatment, unemployment insurance, and loans for building houses and starting new businesses.

Veterans eagerly returned to colleges, jobs, wives or husbands, and babies. Marriage rates soared. So, too, did population growth, which had dropped off sharply in the 1930s. Americans born during the postwar period (roughly 1946–1964) composed the "baby boom generation," a disproportionately large group that would shape the nation's social and cultural life throughout the second half of the twentieth century and after.

**WAGES, PRICES, AND LABOR UNREST** The most acute economic problem Harry Truman faced was the postwar spike in prices for consumer goods. During the war, the government had frozen wages and prices and banned strikes by labor unions. Truman's decision in June 1946 to remove wartime controls on wages and consumer prices caused consumer prices to spike, which led labor unions to demand pay increases. When management balked, more than 4,000 strikes at automobile plants, steel mills, coal mines, and railroads erupted in 1945–1946, involving some 5 million workers. Never before or since had so many employees walked off the job in one year.

Labor disputes crippled the crucial coal and railroad industries. Like Theodore Roosevelt before him, Truman grew frustrated with the stubbornness of both management and labor leaders. He took federal control of the coal mines, whereupon the mine owners agreed to union demands. In May 1946, Truman threatened to use soldiers to operate the trains and to draft striking railroad workers into the military if they did not go back to work, for the entire national rail system had been forced to shut down. In a speech to Congress, Truman declared that "this is no longer a dispute between labor and management. It has now become a strike against the United States government itself." His threat, probably unconstitutional, did the trick, but it embittered many union members who had long voted Democratic.

The backlash over postwar inflation led Truman to restore government controls on particular consumer items such as meat. This only led to more complaints. Ranchers were so upset that they refused to sell their cattle for slaughter. Suddenly, there was a "beefsteak" crisis as consumers complained that the supply of food was worse than it had been during the war. *Time* magazine's Washington-based political reporter alerted his editor that Truman was so unpopular "he could not carry Missouri now."

**POLITICAL COOPERATION AND CONFLICT** During the congressional election campaigns in 1946, Republicans adopted a simple, four-word slogan: "Had Enough? Vote Republican!" Using loudspeakers, Republicans drove through city streets saying, "Ladies, if you want meat, vote Republican." A union leader tagged Truman "the No. 1 Strikebreaker," while much of the public, upset by the unions, price increases, food shortages, and scarcity of automobiles and affordable housing, blamed the strikes on the White House.

Labor unions had emerged from the war with more power than ever, for blue-collar workers were essential to military victory. The National Labor Relations Act (NLRA) of 1935 had also helped ensure the rights of workers to form and join unions. As a consequence, by 1945 some 14.5 million workers, more than a third of the workforce, were now unionized. Members had tended to vote Democratic, but not in the 1946 elections, for union members viewed Truman as their enemy. Their votes gave the Republicans majorities in both houses of Congress for the first time since 1928. Even many Democrats had soured on Truman, circulating a slogan that expressed their frustration: "I'm just Mild about Harry."

Tired of strikes and labor unrest, the Republican Congress that convened in early 1947 sought to curb the power of unions by passing the **Taft-Hartley Labor Act** (officially called the Labor-Management Relations Act). The law gutted many of the provisions of the NLRA by allowing employers to campaign against efforts to form unions and outlawed unions from coercing workers to join or refusing to negotiate grievances.

The Taft-Hartley Act also required union leaders to take "loyalty oaths" declaring that they were not members of the Communist party, banned strikes by federal government employees, and imposed a "cooling-off" period of eighty days on any strike that the president deemed dangerous to the public welfare. Yet the most troubling element of the new bill for unions was a provision that ended the practice of forcing all workers to join a union once a majority voted to unionize. William Green, the president of the American Federation of Labor (AFL) proclaimed that the true purpose of the Taft-Hartley Act was "to destroy unions and to wreck collective bargaining."

Truman vetoed the Taft-Hartley Act, denouncing it as "bad for labor, bad for management, and bad for the country." Working-class Democrats were delighted. Many unionists who had voted Republican in 1946 returned to the Democrats. Journalist James Wechsler reported that "Mr. Truman has reached the crucial fork in the road and turned unmistakably to the left."

Congress, however, overturned the president's veto, and Taft-Hartley became law, largely because southern Democrats overwhelmingly supported it. Southern conservatives adamantly opposed the formation of unions. They feared that unions would disrupt the profitability of the southern textile industry and exert pressure against the tradition of racial segregation.

Vance Muse, a prominent Texas business executive, lobbyist, and white supremacist, hated unions because they encouraged workers to organize across racial lines. His own grandson described him as "a white supremacist, an anti-Semite, and a Communist-baiter, a man who beat on labor unions not on behalf of working people, as he said, but because he was paid to do so." Without the right-to-work provisions of the Taft-Hartley Act, Muse warned, "white women and white men will be forced into organizations with black African apes whom they will have to call 'brother' or lose their jobs."

The number of strikes dropped sharply as a result of the Taft-Hartley Act, and representatives of management and labor learned to work together. By 1954, fifteen state legislatures, mainly in the South and West, had used the Taft-Hartley Act to pass right-to-work laws. Those states thereafter recruited industries to relocate because of their low wages and nonunion policies. As the Republicans celebrated, however, they did not realize that the Taft-Hartley Act would cause most union members to vote Democratic in 1948.

**CIVIL RIGHTS AMID A CHANGING SOCIETY** President Truman was also forced to confront the bigotry faced by returning African American soldiers. When one black veteran arrived home in a uniform decorated with combat medals, a white neighbor yelled, "Don't you forget . . . that you're still a nigger." Another black veteran was yanked off a bus in South Carolina and beaten so badly that he was blinded.

The Second World War had changed America's racial landscape in important ways, however. As a *New York Times* editorial explained in early 1946, "This is a particularly good time to campaign against the evils of bigotry, prejudice, and race hatred because we have witnessed the defeat of enemies who tried to found a mastery of the world upon such cruel and fallacious policy."

African Americans had fought to overthrow the Nazi regime of government-sponsored racism, and many returning black veterans were unwilling to put up with racial abuse at home. The cold war also gave political leaders added incentive to improve race relations. The Soviets often compared racism in the United States to the Nazis' brutalization of Jewish people. In the ideological contest against capitalism, Communists highlighted examples of racism to win influence among newly emerging African nations.

Black veterans who spoke out often risked their lives. In 1946, a white mob in rural Georgia gunned down two African American couples. One of the murderers explained that George Dorsey, one of the victims, was "a good nigger" until he went into the army. "But when he came out, he thought he was as good as any white people."

In the fall of 1946, a delegation of civil rights activists urged President Truman to condemn the Ku Klux Klan and the lynching of African Americans. The delegation graphically described incidents of torture and intimidation against blacks in the South. Truman was horrified: "My God! I had no idea that it was as terrible as that! We've got to do something."

Truman thereupon appointed a Commission on Civil Rights. A year later, with the president's endorsement, the commission issued a report, *To Secure These Rights*, which called for a federal anti-lynching bill, abolition of the poll tax designed to keep poor black people from voting, a voting rights act, an end to racial segregation in the armed forces, and a ban on racial segregation in public transportation.

Southern Democrats were furious. A Mississippi congressman claimed that Truman "had seen fit to run a political dagger into our backs." A South Carolina legislator said his friends and neighbors were now "more afraid of Truman than of Russia."

On July 26, 1948, Truman took a bolder step by banning racial discrimination throughout the federal government. Four days later, he issued an executive order ending racial segregation in the armed forces. Desegregating the military was, Truman claimed, "the greatest thing that ever happened to America." Southerners disagreed. Democratic congressman Mendel Rivers of

South Carolina boasted that Truman "is a dead bird" as far as being reelected. "We in the South are going to see to that."

**JACKIE ROBINSON**   Meanwhile, racial segregation was being dismantled in a much more public area: professional baseball. In April 1947, the Brooklyn Dodgers roster included the first African American to play major league baseball: Jack Roosevelt "Jackie" Robinson. He was born in 1919 in a Georgia sharecropper's cabin, the grandson of slaves. Six months later, his father left, never to return. Robinson's mother moved the family to Pasadena, California, where he became a marvelous all-around athlete. After serving in the army during World War II, Robinson began playing professional baseball in the so-called Negro Leagues. Major league scouts reported that he could play in the big leagues.

At that point, Branch Rickey, president and general manager of the Brooklyn Dodgers, interviewed Robinson for three hours on August 28, 1945. Rickey asked Robinson if he could face racial abuse without losing his temper. Robinson

**Jackie Robinson**   Robinson's unfaltering courage and superior athletic skills prompted the integration of sports, drawing African American and Latino spectators to the games. Here, he greets his Dominican fans at Trujillo High School in Santo Domingo.

was shocked: "Are you looking for a Negro who is afraid to fight back?" Rickey replied that he needed a "Negro player" with "guts enough *not* to fight back." Robinson assured him he was the best candidate to integrate baseball. After signing Robinson to a contract for $600 a month, Rickey explained to his critics that he had found a terrific player of incomparable courage capable of looking the other way when provoked. And Robinson was often provoked.

Soon after Robinson arrived for preseason practice, many of his white teammates refused to take the field with him. Manager Leo Durocher told the team, "I don't care if the guy is yellow or black, or if he has stripes . . . I'm the manager of this team, and I say he plays."

During the 1947 season, teammates and opposing players viciously baited Robinson. Pitchers hit him, baserunners spiked him, and spectators booed him and even threatened to kill him. Hotels refused him rooms, and restaurants denied him service. Hate mail arrived by the bucketful. One sportswriter called Robinson "the loneliest man I have ever seen in sports."

On the other hand, black spectators loved Robinson's courageous example and turned out in droves to watch him play. A headline in a Boston newspaper expressed the prevailing sentiment: "Triumph of Whole Race Seen in Jackie's Debut in Major League Ball."

As time passed, Robinson won over many fans and players with his courage, wit, grit, and talent. Sportswriter Red Smith observed that Robinson was an example of "the unconquerable doing the impossible." During his first season with the Dodgers, Robinson led the National League in stolen bases and was named Rookie of the Year. Between 1949 and 1954, he had a batting average of .327, among the best in baseball. Robinson's very presence on the field forced spectators sitting in racially divided bleachers to confront the hypocritical reality of segregation. Other teams soon began signing black players. In 1947, Robinson was voted the second most popular American, behind singer Bing Crosby. "My life," Robinson remembered, "produced understanding among whites, and it gave black people the idea that if I could do it, they could do it, too, that blackness wasn't subservient to anything."

**MEXICAN AMERICANS AND CIVIL RIGHTS** In the Far West, Mexican Americans (often grouped with other Spanish-speaking immigrants as *Hispanics* or *Latinos*) continued to experience ethnic prejudice. Schools in Arizona, New Mexico, Texas, and California routinely segregated Mexican American children from whites. The 500,000 Latino military veterans were especially frustrated that their efforts in the war did not bring equality at home. They were frequently denied access to educational, medical, and housing benefits available to white veterans.

To fight such treatment, Mexican American veterans led by Dr. Hector Perez Garcia, a U.S. Army major who had served as a combat surgeon, organized the GI Forum in Texas in 1948. Soon there were branches across the nation.

Garcia, born in Mexico in 1914 and raised in Texas, stressed the importance of formal education. At a time when Mexican Americans in Texas averaged no more than a third-grade education, Garcia and five of his siblings had completed medical school. Yet upon his return from the war, he encountered "discrimination everywhere. We had no opportunities. We had to pay [poll taxes] to vote. We had segregated schools. We were not allowed to go into public places."

Garcia and the GI Forum initially focused on veterans' issues but soon expanded the organization's scope to include fostering equal treatment for all people. The GI Forum lobbied to end poll taxes, sued for the right of Latinos to serve on juries, and developed schools for jobless veterans. In 1984, Garcia received the Presidential Medal of Freedom, the nation's highest civilian honor.

**SHAPING THE FAIR DEAL** During 1947, after less than three years in the White House, President Truman had yet to shake the widespread impression that he was not up to the job. Critics proclaimed, "To err is Truman." The editors of *Time* magazine reflected the national sentiment when they wrote, "Mr. Truman has often faced his responsibilities with a cheerful, dogged courage. But his performance was almost invariably awkward, uninspired, and above all, mediocre." Voters, they added, believed that Truman "means well, but he doesn't do well."

Most political analysts assumed that the president would lose the next election. Truman feared the same thing. In July 1947, he met with Dwight D. Eisenhower. Worried that General Douglas MacArthur might be the Republican presidential nominee in 1948, Truman urged Eisenhower to run as the Democratic nominee and even offered to be his vice-presidential running mate. Eisenhower declined, explaining that he was going to become president of Columbia University in New York City.

With Truman's popularity sinking, the Democratic party was about to split in two. While southern conservatives resented the president's outspoken support of civil rights, the left wing of the party resented the firing of Secretary of Commerce Henry A. Wallace for criticizing the administration's anti-Soviet policies. Wallace had said that the United States had "no more business in the *political affairs* of Eastern Europe than Russia has in the *political affairs* of Latin America." The danger of another world war, he said, "is much less from communism than it is from [American] imperialism." Wallace's comments so outraged the leaders of the State Department that Truman fired him, even though the president had preapproved his controversial remarks.

Despite the gloomy predictions for 1948, Truman mounted an energetic reelection campaign. His first step was to shore up the major elements of the New Deal coalition of working-class voters: farmers, labor unionists, and African Americans.

In his 1948 State of the Union message, Truman announced that the programs he would later call his **Fair Deal** would build upon the efforts of Roosevelt's New Deal. The first goal, Truman said, was to ensure civil rights for everyone. He added proposals to increase federal aid to education, expand unemployment and retirement benefits, create a comprehensive system of national health insurance, enable more rural people to connect to electricity, and increase the minimum wage.

**THE ELECTION OF 1948** The Republican-controlled Congress dismissed President Truman's proposals, an action it would later regret. At the Republican convention, moderate New York governor Thomas E. Dewey, who had lost to Roosevelt in 1944, won the presidential nomination on the third ballot. While the party's platform endorsed most New Deal reforms and approved the administration's bipartisan foreign policy, Dewey promised to run things more efficiently and promote civil rights for all.

In July, glum Democrats gathered in Philadelphia. A reporter wrote that they behaved "as though they [had] accepted an invitation to a funeral." At the convention, some party leaders, including Franklin Roosevelt's son James, a California congressman, tried again to convince Dwight Eisenhower to accept the Democratic presidential nomination. The popular war hero declined.

Delegates who expected to do little more than go through the motions of nominating Truman were doubly surprised, first by the battle on the convention floor over civil rights and then by Truman's endorsement of civil rights in his acceptance speech. Liberal Democrats led by Minnesota's Hubert Humphrey commended Truman "for his courageous stand" and declared that the "time has arrived for the Democratic party to get out of the shadow of civil rights." White delegates from Alabama and Mississippi walked out in protest. The solidly Democratic South had fractured over race.

On July 17, a group of rebellious southern Democrats organized their own convention in Birmingham, Alabama. While waving Confederate flags and singing "Dixie," they nominated South Carolina's segregationist governor, Strom Thurmond, on a States' Rights Democratic party ticket, whose members were quickly dubbed the "**Dixiecrats**." Thurmond, a cocky white supremacist, had secretly fathered a child with a black housekeeper. He later

**Birth of the Dixiecrats** Alabama delegates stand to boo Truman's call for civil rights before they walked out of the 1948 Democratic National Convention.

paid hush money to his biracial daughter, denounced Truman's civil rights initiatives, and championed states' rights against federal efforts to change the tradition of white supremacy in the South. He warned that there were "not enough troops in the U.S. Army to force the Southern people to . . . admit the Negro race into our theaters, into our swimming pools, into our homes and into our churches."

On July 23, the left wing of the Democratic party gathered in Philadelphia to form a new Progressive third party and nominate for president Henry A. Wallace, FDR's former vice president, whom Truman had fired as secretary of commerce. Wallace charged that both major parties were recklessly provoking a confrontation with the Soviet Union.

The splits in the Democratic ranks seemed to spell doom for Truman, but he refused to give in. He aroused the faithful by promising, "I will win this election and make the Republicans like it!" He pledged to bring Congress into special session and demand that it confront the housing crisis and boost the minimum wage.

Within days, Truman set out on a 22,000-mile "whistle-stop" train tour, making 271 speeches scolding the "do-nothing" Republicans. The plain-talking president attracted huge crowds. The Republicans, he charged, "have the propaganda and the money, but we have the people, and the people have the votes. *That's* why we're going to win." Friendly audiences loved his fighting spirit and dogged courage, shouting, "Pour it on, Harry!" and "Give 'em hell, Harry." Truman responded: "I don't give 'em hell. I just tell the truth and they think it's hell."

The polls predicted a sure win for Dewey, but on Election Day Truman pulled off the biggest upset ever, taking 24.2 million votes (49.5 percent) to Dewey's 22 million (45.1 percent) and winning a thumping margin of 303 to 189 in the electoral college. Democrats also regained control of both houses

## THE ELECTION OF 1948

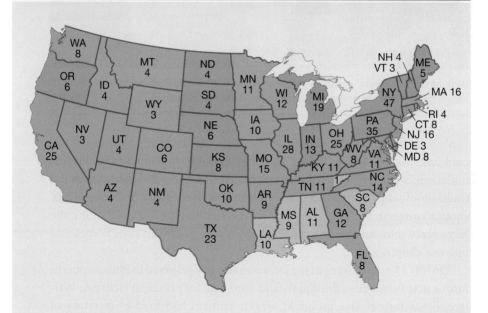

|  | | Electoral Vote | Popular Vote |
|---|---|---|---|
| | **Harry S. Truman (Democrat)** | **303** | **24,200,000** |
| | Thomas E. Dewey (Republican) | 189 | 22,000,000 |
| | J. Strom Thurmond (States' Rights Democrat) | 39 | 1,200,000 |
| | Henry A. Wallace (Progressive) | 0 | 1,160,000 |

- Why did the political experts predict a Dewey victory?
- Why was civil rights such a divisive issue at the Democratic convention?
- How did the candidacies of Strom Thurmond and Henry Wallace end up helping Truman?

of Congress. Thurmond and Wallace each received more than a million votes. The president was helped by black voters who, angered by the Dixiecrats, turned out in record numbers to support him, while the Progressive party's radicalism made it hard for Republicans to tag Truman as a communist sympathizer. Thurmond carried only four southern states (South Carolina, Mississippi, Alabama, and Louisiana).

**THE FAIR DEAL REJECTED** Harry Truman viewed his victory in 1948 as a mandate for expanding the social welfare programs established by Franklin Roosevelt. "Every segment of our population and every individual," he declared, "has a right to expect from our government a *fair deal*." Truman's Fair Deal promised "greater economic opportunity for the mass of the people."

Yet there was little new in Truman's Fair Deal proposals. Most of them were simply extensions or enlargements of New Deal programs: a higher minimum wage, expansion of Social Security coverage to 10 million workers not included in the original 1935 bill, and a large slum-clearance and public-housing program.

Despite enjoying Democratic majorities in Congress, however, Truman ran up against the same alliance of conservative southern Democrats and Republicans who had worked against Roosevelt in the late 1930s. The bipartisan coalition rejected several civil rights bills, national health insurance, federal aid to education, and a new approach to subsidizing farmers. It also turned down Truman's requested repeal of the anti-union Taft-Hartley Act.

Yet the Fair Deal was not a complete failure. It laid the foundation for programs that the next generation of reformers would promote.

# The Cold War Heats Up

Global concerns during Harry Truman's second term would again distract him from domestic issues. In his 1949 inaugural address, Truman called for a vigilant anti-Communist foreign policy resting on three pillars: the United Nations, the Marshall Plan, and NATO. None of them could help resolve the civil war in China, however.

**"LOSING" CHINA** One of the thorniest postwar problems, the Chinese civil war, was fast coming to a head. Chinese Nationalists, led by Chiang Kai-shek, had been fighting Mao Zedong and the Communists since the 1920s. After the Second World War, the Communists won over most of the peasants. By the end of 1949, the Nationalist government had fled to the island of Formosa, which it renamed Taiwan.

President Truman's critics—mostly Republicans—asked, "Who lost China to communism?" What they did not explain was how Truman could have prevented a Communist victory without a massive U.S. military intervention, which would have been risky, unpopular, and expensive. After 1949, the United States continued to recognize the Nationalist government on Taiwan island as the official government of China, delaying formal relations with the People's Republic of China ("Red China") for thirty years.

**THE SOVIETS DEVELOP ATOMIC BOMBS**  As the Communists were gaining control of China in 1949, news that the Soviets had detonated a nuclear weapon led Truman to accelerate the design of a hydrogen "super-bomb," a weapon far more powerful than the atomic bombs dropped on Japan. That the Soviets now possessed atomic weapons intensified every cold war confrontation. "There is only one thing worse than one nation having an atomic bomb," said Nobel Prize–winning physicist Harold C. Urey, who helped develop the first atomic bomb. "That's two nations having it."

*NSC-68*  In January 1950, President Truman grew so concerned about the Soviets possessing atomic weapons that he asked the National Security Council to assess America's readiness to contain communism. Four months later, the Council submitted a top-secret report, *NSC-68*, which called for an even more robust effort and revealed the major assumptions that would guide U.S. foreign policy for the next twenty years: "The issues that face us are momentous, involving the fulfillment or destruction not only of this Republic but of civilization itself."

*NSC-68* endorsed George Kennan's containment strategy. But where he had focused on political and economic counterpressure, the report called for a massive military buildup and "a policy of calculated and gradual coercion" against Soviet expansionism—everywhere.

Paul Nitze, Kennan's successor as director of policy planning for the State Department, wrote *NSC-68*. He claimed that the Soviets were becoming increasingly "reckless" and would invade Western Europe by 1954, by which time they would have enough nuclear weapons to destroy the United States. *NSC-68* became the guidebook for future American policy, especially as the United States became involved in an unexpected war in Korea that ignited into open combat the smoldering animosity between communism and capitalism around the world.

# WAR IN KOREA

By the mid-1950s, tensions between the United States and the Soviet Union in Europe had temporarily eased as a result of the "balance of terror" created by both sides having atomic weapons. In Asia, however, the situation remained turbulent. Communists had gained control of mainland China and were threatening to destroy the Chinese Nationalists, who had taken refuge on the island of Taiwan.

Japan, meanwhile, was experiencing a dramatic recovery from the devastation caused by the Second World War. Douglas MacArthur showed deft leadership as the consul in charge of U.S.-occupied Japan. He oversaw the disarming of the Japanese military, the drafting of a democratic constitution, and the nation's economic recovery, all of which were turning Japan into America's friend.

To the east, however, tensions between North and South Korea threatened to erupt into civil war. The Japanese had occupied the Korean Peninsula since 1910, but after they were defeated and withdrew in 1945, the victorious Allies had faced the difficult task of creating an independent Korean nation.

**A DIVIDED KOREA** Complicating that effort was the presence of Soviet troops in northern Korea. They had accepted the surrender of Japanese forces above the 38th parallel, which divides the Korean Peninsula, while U.S. forces had overseen the surrender south of the line. The Soviets quickly organized a Communist government, the Democratic People's Republic of Korea (North Korea). The Americans countered by helping to establish a democratic government in the more populous south, the Republic of Korea (South Korea). By the end of 1948, Soviet and U.S. forces had withdrawn, and some 2 million North Koreans had fled to South Korea.

**WAR ERUPTS** On January 12, 1950, Secretary of State Dean Acheson gave a speech in which he said he was often asked, "Has the State Department got an Asian policy?" He stressed that the United States had assumed "the necessity of . . . the military defense of Japan." Acheson then added that America had created a "defensive perimeter" running along the Aleutian Islands off the coast of Alaska to Japan to the Ryukyu Islands to the Philippines. Where "other areas in the Pacific are concerned," Acheson added, "it must be clear that no person can guarantee these areas against military attack."

Acheson's statement came back to haunt him. On June 24, 1950, he telephoned President Truman to report, "The North Koreans have invaded South Korea." With the encouragement of the Soviet Union and Communist China, the Soviet-equipped North Korean People's Army—135,000 strong—had forced the South Korean defenders into a headlong retreat. Within three days, Seoul, the South Korean capital, was captured, and only 22,000 of the 100,000 South Korean soldiers were still capable of combat. People then and since have argued that Acheson's clumsy reference to the limits of the "defensive perimeter" in Asia may have convinced the North Koreans and Soviets that the United States would not resist an invasion of South Korea.

When reporters asked Truman how he would respond, the president declared: "By God, I'm going to let them have it!" Without consulting the Joint Chiefs of Staff or Congress, he decided to wage war through the backing of the United Nations rather than by seeking a declaration of war from Congress, which the Constitution requires. He suspected that a congressional debate would take so long that, once finished, it might then be too late to stop the Communists.

An emergency meeting of the UN Security Council in late June 1950 censured the North Korean "breach of peace." By sheer coincidence, the Soviet delegate, who held a veto power, was at the time boycotting the council because it would not seat Communist China in place of Nationalist China. On June 27, the Security Council called on UN members to "furnish such assistance to the Republic of Korea as may be necessary to repel the armed attack and to restore international peace and security in the area."

Truman then ordered U.S. air, naval, and ground forces into action and appointed seventy-year-old Douglas MacArthur supreme commander of the UN forces.

The Korean conflict was the first military action authorized by the United Nations, and some twenty other nations participated along with the United States. For the first time, soldiers fought under an international flag. The United States provided the largest contingent by far, some 330,000 troops. The defense of South Korea set a worrisome precedent: war by order of a president—rather than by a vote of Congress. Truman dodged the issue by calling the conflict a "police action" rather than a war. Critics labeled it "Mr. Truman's War."

**TURNING THE TABLES**  The Korean War featured brutal combat in terrible conditions punctuated by heavy casualties and widespread destruction. For the first three months, the fighting went badly for the Republic of Korea (ROK) and the UN forces. By September 1950, South Korean troops were barely hanging on at Pusan, at the southern tip of the Korean Peninsula. Then, in a brilliant maneuver on September 15, General MacArthur staged a surprise amphibious landing behind the North Korean lines at Inchŏn, the port city for Seoul, some 150 miles north of Pusan. UN troops drove a wedge through the North Korean army. Days later, South Korean troops recaptured Seoul.

At that point, an overconfident MacArthur hatched a grandiose plan to rid North Korea of the "red menace," even if this meant expanding the war into China. Truman foolishly approved MacArthur's request to advance into North Korea so as to destroy its armies and enable the unification of both Koreas.

**THE CHINESE INTERVENE**  By October 1950, UN forces were about to capture the North Korean capital, P'yŏngyang. President Truman, concerned that General MacArthur's move would provoke Communist China to enter the war, repeatedly asked the U.S. commander to meet with him, only to be rebuffed. Finally, the president flew 7,000 miles to Wake Island to meet with MacArthur, who contemptuously refused to salute his commander in chief.

At the meeting on October 15, MacArthur dismissed Chinese threats to intervene, even though they had massed troops on the Korean border. That same day, the Chinese Communist government announced that it "cannot stand idly by" as its North Korean allies were humiliated. On October 20, UN forces entered the North Korean capital, and six days later, advance units reached Ch'osan on the Yalu River, North Korea's border with China.

MacArthur predicted total victory by Christmas. He could not have been more wrong. On the night of November 25, some 500,000 Chinese "volunteers" crossed into Korea and surprised MacArthur, sending the U.S. forces in retreat. MacArthur called for more troops and suggested that atomic weapons be used. Truman wrote in his diary that it "looks like World War III is here."

By January 15, the Communist Chinese and North Koreans had recaptured Seoul, the South Korean capital. What had started as a defensive war against North Korean aggression had become an unlimited war against the North Koreans and China's People's Liberation Army.

**MACARTHUR CROSSES THE LINE**  In late 1950, the UN forces rallied. By January 1951, they had secured their lines below Seoul and launched a counterattack.

When President Truman began negotiations with North Korea to restore the prewar boundary, General MacArthur undermined him by issuing an ultimatum for China to make peace or suffer an attack. On April 5, on the floor of Congress, the Republican minority leader read a letter from MacArthur that criticized the president and said that "there is no substitute for victory." Such open insubordination left Truman only two choices: He could accept MacArthur's aggressive demands, or fire him. Secretary of State Dean Acheson warned Truman that "if you relieve MacArthur, you will have the biggest fight of your administration."

**THE KOREAN WAR, 1950 AND 1950–1953**

- How did the surrender of the Japanese in Korea during 1945 set up the conflict between Soviet-influenced North Korea and U.S.-influenced South Korea?
- What was General MacArthur's strategy for winning the Korean conflict?
- Why did President Truman remove General MacArthur from command?

**SACKING A HERO** On April 11, 1951, Truman removed MacArthur and replaced him with General Matthew B. Ridgway, who better understood how to conduct a modern war in pursuit of limited objectives. "I believe that we must try to limit the war to Korea," Truman explained in a speech to Congress. "A number of events have made it evident that General MacArthur did not agree with that policy. I have therefore considered it essential to relieve General MacArthur so that there would be no doubt or confusion as to the real purpose and aim of our policy."

Truman's sacking of MacArthur, the army's only five-star general, divided the nation. "Seldom had a more unpopular man fired a more popular one," *Time* magazine reported. Senator Joseph McCarthy called the president a "son of a bitch," and an editorial in the *Chicago Tribune* demanded that Truman "be impeached and convicted." Sixty-six percent of Americans initially opposed Truman's decision.

Douglas MacArthur was greeted by adoring crowds upon his return to the United States, but Truman stood firm: "I fired him because he wouldn't respect the authority of the President. I didn't fire him because he was a dumb son of a bitch, although he was, but that's not against the law for generals. If it was, half to three-quarters of them would be in jail." That all of the top military leaders supported Truman's decision deflated much of the criticism. "Why, hell, if MacArthur had had his way," the president warned, "he'd have had us in the Third World War and blown up two-thirds of the world."

**A CEASE-FIRE**  On June 24, 1951, the Soviet representative at the United Nations proposed a cease-fire in Korea along the 38th parallel, the original dividing line between North and South. Secretary of State Acheson accepted the cease-fire (armistice) with the consent of the United Nations. China and North Korea responded favorably.

Truce talks that started on July 10, 1951, dragged on for two years while sporadic fighting continued. The chief snags were exchanges of prisoners (many captured North Korean and Chinese soldiers did not want to go home) and South Korea's insistence on unification of the two Koreas.

By the time a truce was reached, on July 27, 1953, Truman had retired and Dwight D. Eisenhower was president. No peace treaty was ever signed, and Korea, like Germany, remained divided. The inconclusive war cost the United States more than 33,000 battle deaths and 103,000 wounded or missing. South Korean casualties were about 2 million, and North Korean and Chinese casualties were an estimated 3 million.

**THE IMPACT OF THE KOREAN WAR**  Harry Truman's assumption that Stalin and the Soviets were behind the invasion of South Korea deepened his commitment to stop communism. Fearful that the Soviets would use the Korean conflict as a diversion to invade Western Europe, he ordered a major expansion of U.S. military forces around the world. Truman also increased assistance to French troops fighting a Communist independence movement in the French colony of Indochina (which included Vietnam), starting America's military involvement in Southeast Asia.

# ANOTHER RED SCARE

The Korean War sparked another Red Scare at home, as the **House Committee on Un-American Activities (HUAC)** claimed that Communist agents had infiltrated the federal government.

On March 21, 1947, President Truman sought to blunt conservative Republicans' attacks on the patriotism of left-wing Democrats by signing an executive order (known as the Loyalty Order). It required all 2 million federal government workers to undergo a background investigation to ensure they had no ties to Communists or other "subversive" groups.

Truman was responding to pressure from FBI director J. Edgar Hoover and Attorney General Tom Clark, both of whom believed that there were numerous spies working inside the federal government. Truman was also eager to reduce criticism that he was not doing enough to ensure that Soviet sympathizers were not working in government.

Privately, however, Truman thought that concerns about Communist subversives were exaggerated. As he wrote to Pennsylvania governor George Earle, "I am of the opinion that the country is perfectly safe so far as Communism is concerned." By early 1951, the federal Civil Service Commission had cleared more than 3 million government workers, while only 378 had been dismissed for doubtful loyalty. In 1953, President Eisenhower revoked the Loyalty Order.

**THE HOLLYWOOD TEN** Charges that the Hollywood movie industry was a "hotbed of communism" led HUAC to launch a full-blown investigation. The committee subpoenaed dozens of actors, producers, and directors to testify at hearings held in Los Angeles in October 1947. Ten witnesses refused to testify, arguing that the questioning violated their First Amendment rights. A member of the so-called Hollywood Ten, screenwriter Dalton Trumbo, shouted as he left the hearings, "This is the beginning of an American concentration camp." All ten were cited for contempt of Congress, given prison terms, and blacklisted (banned) from the film industry.

The witch hunt launched by the HUAC inspired Arthur Miller, who himself was blacklisted, to write *The Crucible*, an award-winning play produced in 1953. His dramatic account of the witch trials in Salem, Massachusetts, at the end of the seventeenth century, was intended to alert audiences to the dangers of anti-Communist hysteria.

**ALGER HISS** The spy case most damaging to the Truman administration involved Alger Hiss, president of the Carnegie Endowment for International

Peace. Whittaker Chambers, a former Soviet spy who reversed himself and became an informer testifying against supposed Communists in the government, told the HUAC in 1948 that Hiss had given him secret documents ten years earlier, when Chambers was spying for the Soviets and Hiss was working in the State Department. Hiss sued Chambers for libel, and Chambers produced microfilm of the State Department documents that he said Hiss had passed to him. Although Hiss denied the accusation, he was convicted in 1950. The charge was perjury, but he was convicted of lying about espionage, for which he could not be tried because the statute of limitations on the crime had expired.

More cases of Communist infiltration surfaced. In 1949, eleven top leaders of the Communist party of the United States were convicted under the Smith Act of 1940, which outlawed any conspiracy to advocate the overthrow of the government. The Supreme Court upheld the law under the doctrine of a "clear and present danger," which overrode the right to free speech.

**ATOMIC SPYING** In 1950, the FBI unearthed a spy network involving American and British Communists who had secretly passed information about the development of the atomic bomb to the Soviet Union. The disclosure led to the arrest of Klaus Fuchs, a German-born English nuclear physicist who had worked in the United States and helped to develop the atomic bomb.

As it turned out, a New York couple, former Communists Julius and Ethel Rosenberg, were part of the same Soviet spy ring. Their claims of innocence were undercut by Ethel's brother, who admitted he was a spy along with his sister and brother-in-law.

The convictions of Fuchs and the Rosenbergs fueled Republican charges that Truman's administration was not doing enough to hunt down Communist agents. The case, called the crime of the century by J. Edgar Hoover, also heightened fears that a vast Soviet network of spies and sympathizers was operating in the United States. Irving Kaufman, the federal judge who sentenced the Rosenbergs to death, explained that "plain, deliberate murder is dwarfed . . . by comparison with the crime you have committed." They were the first Americans executed for spying.

**MCCARTHY'S WITCH HUNT** Evidence of Soviet spying encouraged some to exploit fears of the Communist menace. Early in 1950, a little-known Republican senator, Joseph R. McCarthy of Wisconsin, surfaced as the most ruthless manipulator of anti-Communist anxieties.

McCarthy, eager to attract media attention through his "bare-knuckle," red-baiting tactics, delivered a fiery speech in Wheeling, West Virginia, on

**Joseph R. McCarthy** The senator who was determined to "sweep" Communists out of the federal government.

February 9, 1950, in which he charged that the State Department was infested with Communists. He claimed to have their names, although he never provided them.

McCarthy's stunt got him what he wanted most: publicity. During the next four years, McCarthy made more irresponsible accusations, initially against many Democrats, whom he smeared as "dupes" or "fellow travelers" of the "Commies," then, unbelievably, against officers in the U.S. Army.

McCarthy enjoyed the backing of fellow Republicans eager to hurt Democrats in the 1950 congressional elections. By the summer of 1951, however, **McCarthyism** spun out of control when the zealous senator accused George Marshall, the former secretary of state and war hero, of "being an instrument of the Communist conspiracy." Concerns about truth or fair play did not faze McCarthy; his goal was to create a reign of terror. President Truman called him a "pathological character assassin."

For all his boasting, McCarthy never uncovered a single Communist agent within the federal government. Yet his smear campaign, which tarnished many reputations and had a chilling effect on free speech, went largely unchallenged until the end of the Korean War. During the Red Scare, thousands of left-wing activists were blacklisted from employment because of past political associations, real or rumored. Movies with titles like "I Married a Communist" fed the hysteria, and magazine stories warned of "a Red under every bed."

**THE McCARRAN ACT** Fears of Soviet spies working with American sympathizers led Congress in 1950 to pass, over President Truman's veto, the McCarran Internal Security Act, which made it unlawful "to combine, conspire, or agree with any other person to perform any act which would substantially contribute to . . . the establishment of a totalitarian dictatorship." The legislation, proposed by Nevada Democratic senator Pat McCarran, required Communist organizations to register with the Justice Department. Immigrants who had belonged to totalitarian parties in their home countries were barred from entering the United States, and during any future national emergencies, Communists were to be herded into concentration camps. The McCarran Internal Security Act, Truman said in his veto message, would "put the government into the business of thought control."

Concerns about Communist infiltration also shaped immigration policy. In 1952, Senator McCarran pushed through the Immigration and Nationality Act of 1952 (the McCarran-Walter Act). While reducing the number of immigrants admitted each year, it renewed the national origins quota system established by the Immigration Act of 1924, which favored newcomers from northern and western Europe. As a result, the act allocated 85 percent of the 154,277 annual visas to people from northern and Western European nations. It also introduced a system of preferences based on skills and family ties and removed the ban on Asian immigrants. Yet the number of Asians allowed into the United States remained small (only 100 a year). Finally, it barred suspected "subversives" and the "immoral," including gays and lesbians. Truman vetoed the bill, but Congress overrode him again.

**McCarran-Walter Act** The German-born wife and daughter of an American GI are interrogated by immigration inspectors at Ellis Island after being detained under the McCarran-Walter Act.

**THE RED SCARE AND THE COLD WAR** The Red Scare ended up violating the civil liberties of innocent people. President Truman may have erred in 1947 by creating a government loyalty program that aggravated the anti-Communist hysteria. He also overstretched resources when he pledged to contain communism everywhere. Containment's chief theorist, George F. Kennan, later confessed that he had failed to clarify the limits of the containment policy and to stress that the United States needed to prioritize its responses to Soviet adventurism.

**A COLD WAR GOVERNMENT** Having taken on global burdens after the Second World War, the United States became committed to a large military establishment, along with shadowy new government agencies such as the National Security Council (NSC), the National Security Agency (NSA), and the Central Intelligence Agency (CIA).

The federal government—and the presidency—grew larger, more powerful, and more secretive, fueled by the actions of both major political parties as well as by the intense lobbying efforts of what Dwight D. Eisenhower would later call the *military-industrial complex*—defense contractors, lobbyists, and influential legislators.

Republicans used the Red Scare to claim that Democrats were soft on communism and to encourage widespread conformity of thought and behavior. By 1950, it had become dangerous to criticize anything associated with the American way of life.

**ASSESSING HARRY TRUMAN** On March 30, 1952, Harry Truman announced that he would not seek another presidential term, in part because it was unlikely he could win. Fewer than 25 percent of voters surveyed thought he was doing a good job, the lowest presidential approval rating in history. The unrelenting war against communism, at home and abroad, led people to question Truman's strategy. Negotiations to end the war in Korea had bogged down, the "red-baiting" of McCarthyism was expanding, and conservative southern Democrats had defeated most of his Fair Deal proposals. The war had also brought higher taxes and higher prices for consumers, many of whom blamed the president. Only years later would people (and historians) fully appreciate how effectively Truman had dealt with so many complex problems.

To the end of his presidency, Truman viewed himself as an ordinary person operating in extraordinary times. "I have tried my best to give the nation everything I have in me," Truman told reporters at one of his last press conferences.

"There are a great many people . . . who could have done the job better than I did it. But I had the job and had to do it." At the end of one difficult day in the White House, Truman growled: "They [his critics] talk about the power of the President, how I can just push a button to get things done. Why, I spend most of my time kissing somebody's ass."

By the time he left the White House in early 1953, the cold war had become an accepted part of the American way of life. But fears about the spread of communism were counterbalanced by the joys of unexpected prosperity. Toward the end of Truman's presidency, the economy began to grow at the fastest rate in history, transforming social and cultural life and becoming the marvel of the world.

# CHAPTER REVIEW

## SUMMARY

- **The Cold War**   The cold war was an ideological contest between the Western democracies (especially the United States) and Communist countries. At the end of the Second World War, the Soviet Union established "friendly" (puppet) governments in the Eastern European countries it occupied behind an *iron curtain* of totalitarian control and secrecy.

- **Containment**   President Truman responded to the Soviet occupation of Eastern Europe with the policy of *containment*. With the *Truman Doctrine (1947)*, he proposed giving economic and military aid to countries facing Communist insurgencies; he also convinced Congress to approve the *National Security Act*, which reorganized the U.S. armed forces and created the Central Intelligence Agency. With the *Marshall Plan (1948)*, Truman offered redevelopment aid to all European nations. In 1949, the United States became a founding member of the *North Atlantic Treaty Organization (NATO)*.

- **Truman's Fair Deal**   Truman's proposed *Fair Deal (1949)* would have expanded the New Deal despite intense Republican opposition in Congress. Truman could not stop the *Taft-Hartley Act*, a Republican-backed measure to curb the power of labor unions. Truman was more successful in expanding Social Security, desegregating the military, and banning racial discrimination in the hiring of federal employees. After winning a second term in 1948, he proposed a civil rights bill, national health insurance, federal aid to education, and new farm subsidies. Despite the Democrats' majority in Congress, however, conservative Republicans and southern Democrats (*Dixiecrats*) joined forces to defeat these initiatives.

- **The Korean War**   Containment policies proved less effective in East Asia, as Communists won a long civil war in China in 1949 and ignited a war in Korea. In 1950, Truman authorized *NSC-68* in response—a comprehensive blueprint for foreign and defense policies that called for a dramatic increase in military spending and nuclear arms. When North Korean troops invaded South Korea in June 1950, Truman quickly decided to go to war under the auspices of the United Nations. A truce was concluded in July 1953 and established a demilitarized zone in Korea.

- **The Red Scare**   The onset of the cold war inflamed another Red Scare. Investigations by the *House Committee on Un-American Activities (HUAC)* sought to find "subversives" within the federal government. Starting in 1950, Senator Joseph R. McCarthy exploited fears of Soviet spies infiltrating the highest levels of the U.S. government. *McCarthyism* flourished in the short term because the threat of a world dominated by Communist governments seemed all too real.

# Chronology

| | |
|---|---|
| **November 1946** | Republicans win control of both houses of Congress |
| **February 1946** | George Kennan urges a containment policy toward the Soviet Union |
| **March 1947** | The Truman Doctrine promises financial and military assistance to countries resisting Communist takeover |
| **May 1947** | The Marshall plan calls for massive financial assistance to European nations |
| **June 1947** | Congress passes the Taft-Hartley Labor Act |
| **July 1947** | National Security Council (NSC) is established |
| **May 1948** | Israel is proclaimed an independent nation |
| **July 1948** | Truman's executive order ends segregation in the U.S. armed forces |
| **October 1948** | United States and Great Britain begin airlifting supplies to West Berlin |
| **November 1948** | Truman defeats Dewey in the presidential election |
| **April 1949** | North Atlantic Treaty Organization (NATO) is created |
| **October 1949** | China "falls" to communism |
| **February 1950** | Senator Joseph McCarthy begins his crusade against suspected Communists in the federal government |
| **June 1950** | United States and other UN members go to war in Korea |

# Key Terms

iron curtain p. 1114

containment p. 1115

Truman Doctrine (1947) p. 1116

Marshall Plan (1948) p. 1117

Berlin airlift (1948) p. 1119

North Atlantic Treaty Organization (NATO) p. 1120

National Security Act p. 1120

Taft-Hartley Labor Act (1947) p. 1124

Fair Deal (1949) p. 1130

Dixiecrats p. 1130

NSC-68 (1950) p. 1134

House Committee on Un-American Activities (HUAC) p. 1140

McCarthyism p. 1142

 INQUIZITIVE

Go to InQuizitive to see what you've learned—and learn what you've missed—with personalized feedback along the way.

# 28 America in the Fifties

**The art of consumerism**  The United States experienced unprecedented prosperity after the Second World War, enabling many Americans in the 1950s to engage in carefree consumption—and personal indebtedness.

In the summer of 1959, a survey revealed that most Americans believed that a nuclear holocaust was "likely." To highlight the possibility, newlyweds Melvin and Maria Mininson spent their two-week honeymoon in an underground bomb shelter in their Miami backyard. *Life* magazine showcased their 18-by-24-foot "fallout" shelter twelve feet underground. Weighing twenty tons, the steel and concrete bunker held enough food and water to survive an atomic attack.

The image of newlyweds seeking sheltered security in a new age of nuclear terror symbolized America in the 1950s. The deepening cold war with the Soviet Union cast a frightening shadow over the nation's traditionally sunny optimism.

Still, most Americans had emerged from the Second World War proud of their country's military strength, international stature, and industrial might. As the editors of *Fortune* magazine proclaimed in 1946, "This is a dream era. . . . The Great American Boom is on."

So it was, at least for white, middle-class Americans. During the late 1940s and throughout the 1950s, the United States enjoyed unprecedented economic growth, and most people were content. Divorce and homicide rates fell, and people lived longer, on average, thanks in part to medical breakthroughs, including new antibiotics and the vaccine invented by Dr. Jonas Salk that ended the menace of polio. The idealized image of America in the fifties as an innocent, prosperous nation awash in good times and enlivened by teenage energies contains a kernel of truth. But life was actually much more complicated—even contradictory and hypocritical at times.

## focus questions

**1.** What were President Eisenhower's political philosophy and priorities?

**2.** What factors contributed to America's postwar prosperity? To what extent did all benefit from it?

**3.** What were the criticisms of postwar society and culture? What were the various forms of dissent and anxiety?

**4.** What were the goals and strategies of the civil rights movement? What was its impact?

**5.** What were President Eisenhower's foreign policy priorities? What was his influence on global affairs?

# MODERATE REPUBLICANISM

Dwight David Eisenhower dominated politics during the 1950s. He was the nation's most famous figure, a model of moderation, modesty, stability, and optimism, celebrated for his genial personality and irresistible grin. He was a soldier who hated war, a politician who hated politics. If forced to choose, he preferred golf over governance. Committed to what he called **moderate Republicanism**, Eisenhower promised to restore the authority of state and local governments and restrain the federal government from engaging in political and social "engineering." In the process, he sought to renew traditional virtues and inspire Americans with a vision of a brighter future.

"TIME FOR A CHANGE" By 1952, the Truman administration was the target of growing public criticism. The conflict in Korea had stalled, the economy was sputtering, and President Truman was put on the defensive by the disclosure that corrupt lobbyists had rigged military contracts related to the Korean War. The scandal led him to fire nearly 250 Internal Revenue Service employees, but doubts lingered that he would ever finish the housecleaning. Critics charged that the slogan for his administration was "plunder at home, blunder abroad."

Public sentiment turned toward Republicans. Beginning in the late 1940s, both Republican and Democratic leaders, including Truman, recruited Eisenhower to be their presidential candidate. Eisenhower, known as "Ike," had displayed remarkable organizational and diplomatic skill in coordinating the Allied invasion of Nazi-controlled Europe. In 1952, after serving as president of Columbia University, he had moved to Paris to become supreme commander of NATO forces in Europe. His decision

**Dwight D. Eisenhower** His many supporters wore "I Like Ike" hats, pins, and even nylon stockings, speaking to the consumer culture's impact on politics.

to run for president as a Republican was wildly popular. Bumper stickers announced, "I Like Ike."

At the 1952 convention, Eisenhower was nominated on the first ballot. Republican leaders then tried to reassure party conservatives by balancing the ticket with a youthful running mate: Richard M. Nixon, a thirty-nine-year-old California senator known for his shrewd opportunism and combative temperament. Nixon was an aggressive anti-Communist; his dogged pursuit of the Alger Hiss spying case had brought him national prominence.

The Republican platform declared that the Democratic emphasis on containing communism was "negative, futile, and misguided." If elected, Eisenhower would bring "genuine independence" to the oppressed people of Eastern Europe.

**THE ELECTION OF 1952** The presidential campaign featured contrasting personalities. Dwight Eisenhower was an international figure and a man of readily acknowledged decency and integrity. He pledged to clean up "the mess in Washington" and to travel to Korea to secure "an early and honorable" end to the prolonged conflict.

Illinois governor Adlai Stevenson, the Democratic candidate, was virtually unknown outside his home state. Although brilliant and witty, he came across as more an aloof intellectual than a leader. Republicans labeled him an "egghead" (meant to suggest a balding professor with more intellect than common sense). Even Harry Truman grumbled that Stevenson "was too busy making up his mind whether he had to go to the bathroom or not."

Stevenson was outmatched. On election night, Eisenhower triumphed in a landslide, gathering nearly 34 million votes to Stevenson's 27 million. The electoral vote was more lopsided: 442 to 89. Stevenson even failed to win his home state of Illinois. More important, by securing four southern states, Eisenhower had cracked the solidly Democratic South.

Yet voters liked Eisenhower more than they liked other Republican candidates. In the 1952 election, Democrats kept control of most governorships, lost control in the House by only eight seats, and broke even in the Senate.

**A "MIDDLE WAY" PRESIDENCY** Dwight Eisenhower was the first professional soldier elected president since Ulysses S. Grant in 1868. During his campaign, he appealed to the "middle-of-the-road voter" and progressive moderates. Once elected, he promised to pursue a "middle way" between conservatism and liberalism. He was a pragmatist who liked to be called a "responsible progressive." Rather than dismantle all the New Deal and Fair Deal programs, he wanted to end the "excesses" resulting from twenty years of Democratic control of the White House.

Eisenhower pledged to shrink the federal bureaucracy and make it more efficient while restoring the balance between the executive and legislative branches. He also promised to reduce the national debt, cut military expenses, balance the federal budget, and trim taxes. At the same time, however, he insisted that workers had a right to form unions and bargain with management. He added that employees needed to be paid enough to afford the comforts of a good life. "We all—workers and farmers, foremen and financiers, technicians and builders—all must produce, produce more, and produce yet more," he said. Peace would be maintained "not by weapons of war but by wheat and cotton, by milk and wool, by meat and by timber and by rice." He hated the arms race because "every gun that is made, every warship launched,

## THE ELECTION OF 1952

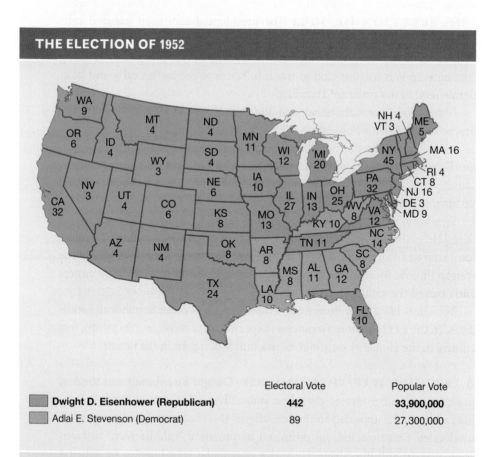

|  | Electoral Vote | Popular Vote |
|---|---|---|
| ■ **Dwight D. Eisenhower (Republican)** | **442** | **33,900,000** |
| □ Adlai E. Stevenson (Democrat) | 89 | 27,300,000 |

■ Why was the contest between Adlai Stevenson and Dwight D. Eisenhower so lopsided?

■ Why was Eisenhower's victory in several southern states remarkable?

every rocket fired signifies, in the final sense, a theft from those who hunger and are not fed, those who are cold and are not clothed."

Eisenhower's cautious personality and genial public face fit the prevailing mood of most voters. He inspired trust, sought consensus, and avoided confrontation. He also championed the nineteenth-century view that Congress should make policy and the president should carry it out. Like Calvin Coolidge, Eisenhower said his administration searched for "things it can stop doing rather than new things for it to do."

**"DYNAMIC CONSERVATISM" AT HOME** President Eisenhower labeled his domestic program "dynamic conservatism," by which he meant being "conservative when it comes to money and liberal when it comes to human beings." He kept intact the basic structure of the New Deal, even convincing Congress to establish a federal Department of Health, Education, and Welfare and to extend Social Security benefits to millions of workers formerly excluded: white-collar professionals, housekeepers and sales clerks, farmworkers, and members of the armed forces. Eisenhower also approved increases in the minimum wage and additional public-housing projects for low-income occupants.

Conservative Republicans charged that he was being too liberal. He told his brother Edgar in 1954 that if the "stupid" right wing of the Republican party tried "to abolish Social Security and eliminate labor laws and farm programs, you would not hear of that party again in our political history."

**TRANSPORTATION IMPROVEMENTS** Under Dwight Eisenhower, the federal government launched two huge construction projects: the St. Lawrence Seaway and the Interstate Highway System, both of which resembled the public works projects constructed under the New Deal during the 1930s. The St. Lawrence Seaway project (in partnership with Canada) opened the Great Lakes to oceangoing ships.

The **Federal-Aid Highway Act** (1956) created a network of interstate highways to serve the needs of commerce and defense, as well as the public. The $32 billion interstate highway system, funded largely by federal gasoline taxes, took twenty-five years to construct and was the largest federal project in history. It stretched for 47,000 miles and required 55,512 bridges.

Highway construction generated what economists call "multiplier effects." It created jobs; stimulated economic growth; and spurred the tourism, motor hotel ("motel"), billboard, fast-food, and long-haul trucking industries. Interstates transformed the way people traveled and where they lived, while creating a new form of middle-class leisure—the family vacation by car. In 1956, writer Bernard De Voto exclaimed that "a new highway is not only a measure of progress, but a true index of our culture."

**THE CAR CULTURE** "The American," novelist William Faulkner observed in 1948, "really loves nothing but his automobile." Thanks to the highway system, said President Eisenhower, cars would provide "greater convenience, greater happiness, and greater standards of living." In 1948, only 60 percent of families owned a car; by 1955, some 90 percent owned a car, and many households had two.

Americans had always cherished personal freedom and mobility, rugged individualism and masculine force. Automobiles embodied all these qualities and more. Cars were much more than a form of transportation; they provided social status, freedom, and a wider range of choices—where to travel, where to work and live, where to seek pleasure and recreation. The car culture prompted the creation of "convenience stores," drive-in movies, and fast-food restaurants. Even more important, the interstate highway system and the car

**1950s car culture** In this 1958 advertisement for Plymouth Belvedere convertibles, a family gets ready to enjoy a picnic lunch in the countryside.

culture weakened public transit systems (buses and subways), accelerated the movement of white people from cities to suburbs, and caused a surge in environmental pollution.

**THE END OF McCARTHYISM** Republicans thought their presidential victory in 1952 would curb the efforts of Wisconsin senator Joseph R. McCarthy to ferret out Communist spies in the federal government. Instead, the publicity-seeking senator's behavior grew even more outlandish, in part because reporters loved his theatrics and in part because he became a master at telling outrageous lies. President Eisenhower despised McCarthy but refused to criticize him in public, explaining that he did not want to "get into a pissing contest with that skunk."

McCarthy finally committed political suicide when he made the absurd charge that the U.S. Army was soft on communism. For thirty-six days in the spring of 1954, the Army-McCarthy hearings provided television viewers with a fantastic spectacle. The unkempt McCarthy was at his worst, browbeating high-ranking officers, shamelessly promoting himself, and producing little evidence to back up his charges. "You are a disgrace to the uniform," he told General Ralph Zwicker. "You're shielding Communist conspirators. You're not fit to be an officer. You're ignorant. You are going to be put on public display."

McCarthy was finally outwitted by the deliberate, reasoned counterattacks of the army's legal counsel, Joseph Welch. When McCarthy tried to smear one of Welch's associates, the attorney exploded: "Until this moment, Senator, I think I never really gauged your cruelty or your recklessness. . . . Have you no sense of decency, sir, at long last?" When the audience burst into applause, the confused senator was reduced to whispering, "What did I do?"

On December 2, 1954, the Senate voted 67 to 22 to "condemn" McCarthy. Soon thereafter, his influence collapsed. His crusade against Communists had catapulted him into the limelight and captured the nation's attention, but he had trampled upon civil liberties. His rapid demise helped the Democrats capture control of both houses of Congress in the 1954 elections. In 1957, at the age of forty-eight, he died of liver inflammation brought on by years of alcohol abuse.


# A PEOPLE OF PLENTY

What most distinguished the United States from the rest of the world after the Second World War was what one journalist called America's "screwball materialism." The economy soared to record heights as businesses shifted from wartime production to the construction of new housing and the manufacture of mass-produced consumer goods. The quarter century from 1948 to 1973 witnessed the greatest economic growth in history. In 1957, *U.S. News and World Report* magazine declared that "never had so many people, anywhere, been so well off."

## POSTWAR PROSPERITY

Several factors led to the nation's extraordinary prosperity. First, huge federal expenditures during the Second World War and Korean War propelled the economy out of the Great Depression. Unemployment was virtually nonexistent. High government spending continued in the 1950s, thanks to the construction of highways, bridges, airports, and ports, and the global arms race. The military budget after 1945 represented 60 percent of the national budget and was by far the single most important stimulant to the economy.

The superior productivity of American industries also contributed to economic growth. No sooner was the war over than the government transferred many federal defense plants to civilian owners who retooled them for peacetime manufacturing. Military-related research helped stimulate new glamour industries: chemicals (including plastics), electronics, and aviation. By 1957, the aircraft industry was the nation's largest employer.

The economy also benefited from the emergence of new technologies, including the first generation of computers. Factories and industries became increasingly automated. At the same time, the oil boom in Texas, Wyoming, and Oklahoma continued to provide low-cost fuel to heat buildings and power cars and trucks.

Another reason for the record-breaking economic growth was the lack of foreign competition. Most of the other major industrial nations—Great Britain, France, Germany, Japan, and the Soviet Union—had been physically devastated during the Second World War, leaving American manufacturers with a virtual monopoly on international trade that lasted well into the 1950s.

## THE CONSUMER CULTURE

What differentiated the postwar era from earlier periods of prosperity was the large number of people who shared in the rising standard of living. *Consumerism* became America's secular religion.

Most Americans had money to spend during the fifties, and they did so with gusto. Between 1947 and 1960, the average income for the working class increased by as much as it had in the previous *fifty* years. More and more blue-collar Americans, especially unionized automotive and steel workers, moved into the middle class. George Meany, the leading union spokesman during the 1950s, declared in 1955 that his members "never had it so good." A marketing consultant stressed that the new economy required "that we convert the buying and use of goods into [religious] rituals, that we seek our spiritual satisfaction, our ego satisfaction, in consumption."

**A BUYING SPREE**  Innovations in financing made it easier to buy things. The first credit card appeared in 1949; soon, "buying with plastic" had become the new norm. Personal indebtedness doubled, and frugality became unpatriotic. As television personality Hugh Downs remembered, "those were exciting days . . . of hope and optimism . . . when the sky was the limit."

What most Americans wanted to buy was a new house. In 1945, only 40 percent of Americans owned homes; by 1960, the number had increased to 60 percent. New homes featured the latest electrical appliances—refrigerators, dishwashers, washing machines, vacuum cleaners, electric mixers, carving knives, even shoe polishers.

The use of electricity tripled, in part because of the popularity of television, which displaced listening to the radio and going to the movies as the most popular way to spend free time. Between 1946 and 1960, the number of homes with TV sets soared from 8,000 to 46 million. In 1954, grocery stores

**Family, modified**  The dynamics of American family life changed with the onslaught of new products. In this 1959 advertisement for TV dinners, a family eats out of disposable containers in front of the television.

began selling frozen "TV dinners" to be heated and consumed while watching popular shows such as *Father Knows Best, I Love Lucy, Leave It to Beaver,* and *The Adventures of Ozzie and Harriet,* all of which idealized the child-centered world of suburban white families.

The popularity of television provided a powerful medium for advertisers to promote a new phase of the consumer culture that reshaped the contours of postwar life: the nature of work, where people lived and traveled, how they interacted, and what they valued. It also affected class structure, race relations, and gender roles.

**THE GI BILL OF RIGHTS** As World War II came to an end, fear that a sudden influx of veterans into the workforce would produce widespread unemployment led Congress in 1944 to pass the Servicemen's Readjustment Act, nicknamed the **GI Bill of Rights**. ("GI" meant "government issue," a phrase stamped on military uniforms and equipment that became slang for "serviceman.")

The GI Bill's package of benefits for veterans included unemployment pay for one year, preference to those applying for federal government jobs, loans for home construction or starting a business, access to government hospitals, and generous subsidies for education. Some 5 million veterans bought homes with the assistance of GI Bill mortgage loans, which required no down payment. Almost 8 million took advantage of GI Bill benefits to attend college or enroll in job-training programs.

Before the Second World War, about 160,000 Americans had graduated from college each year. By 1950, the figure had risen to 500,000. In 1949, veterans accounted for 40 percent of college enrollments, and the United States could boast the world's best-educated workforce, largely because of the GI Bill.

For African American veterans, however, most colleges and universities remained racially segregated and refused to admit blacks. Those that did often discriminated against them. African Americans attending white colleges or universities were barred from playing on athletic teams, attending social events, and joining fraternities or sororities. Even with GI Bill mortgage loans, black veterans were often prevented from buying homes in white neighborhoods. Although women veterans were eligible for the GI Bill, there were so few of them that the program had the unintended effect of widening the income gap between men and women, since the much more numerous male veterans had greater access to education and housing.

**COOLING THE SUBURBAN FRONTIER** The second half of the twentieth century brought a mass migration to a new frontier—the suburbs. An acute postwar housing shortage sparked the escape from inner cities to the sprawling suburbs emerging in the countryside, just outside of city or town limits. Of the 13 million homes built between 1948 and 1958, more than 11 million were in the suburbs. Many among the exploding middle-class white population moved to what were called the Sun Belt states—California, Arizona, Florida, Texas—as well as to the Southeast, where rapid population growth and new highways generated an economic boom.

The first air-conditioning system was designed in 1902 by inventor Willis Carrier. The earliest home unit was installed in 1914, but it utilized hazardous chemicals and was too bulky and noisy to become widely applicable. Advances in technology eventually produced the more convenient window air conditioner in the late 1930s, though it remained too costly for most residents.

Most Americans first encountered air conditioning while sitting in movie theaters and walking through department stores. In 1951, inexpensive window units were invented, and soon thousands of homes featured dripping, humming metal boxes hanging out bedroom windows.

As air conditioning became common across the Sun Belt, the appeal of living in warmer climates soared. California led the way. In 1940, it was the fifth most-populous state; by 1963, it held first place. And, by 1960, for the first time since the Civil War, more people moved into the South than moved out.

**SUBURBAN CULTURE** Suburbia met an acute need (affordable housing) and fulfilled a common dream—personal freedom and family security within commuting distance of cities. In the half century after the Second World War, the suburban "good life" included a big home with a big yard on a big lot accessed by a big car—or two. By 1970, more people lived in suburbs than in cities.

A brassy New York real estate developer, William Levitt, led the suburban revolution. Between 1947 and 1951, on 6,000 acres of Long Island farmland east of New York City, he built 17,447 small (750 square feet), sturdy, two-bedroom homes to house more than 82,000 mostly lower-middle-class people. Levitt believed he was enabling the American dream. "No man who owns his own lot and his own house can be a communist," he said.

The planned community, called Levittown, included schools, parks, swimming pools, shopping centers, and playing fields. The look-alike houses came in three styles—the Cape Cod, the Rancher, and the Colonial. All sold for the same low price—$6,990, with no down payments for veterans—and featured the same floor plan and accessories. Each had a living room with a picture window and a television set, a bathroom, two bedrooms, and a kitchen equipped with an electric refrigerator, oven, and washing machine. Homeowners were required to cut their grass once a week and prohibited from hanging laundry on outside clotheslines on weekends.

**Levittown** Identical mass-produced houses in Levittown, New York, and other suburbs across the country provided veterans and their families with affordable homes.

When the first houses in Levittown went on sale, people, especially military veterans, stood in long lines to buy one. Levitt soon built three more Levittowns in Pennsylvania, New Jersey, and Puerto Rico. They and other planned suburban communities benefited greatly from government assistance. Federal and state tax codes favored homeowners over renters, and local governments paid for the infrastructure the subdivisions required: roads, water and sewer lines, fire and police protection. By insuring loans for up to 95 percent of the value of a house, the Federal Housing Administration (FHA) made it easy for builders to construct low-cost homes and for people to purchase them.

Initially, the contracts for houses in Levittown specifically excluded "members of other than the Caucasian race." When asked about this "racial covenant," Levitt said that "if we sell one house to a Negro family, then 90 to 95 percent of our white customers will not buy into the community." His policy was: "We can solve a housing problem or we can try to solve a racial problem. But we can't combine the two." It wasn't long, however, before the U.S. Supreme Court ruled in *Shelley v. Kraemer* (1948) that such racial restrictions were illegal.

The Court ruling, however, did not end segregated housing practices; it simply made them more discreet. In 1953, when the original Levittown's population reached 70,000, it was the largest community in the nation without an African American resident. Although Jewish himself, Levitt discouraged Jews from living in his communities. "As a Jew," he explained, "I have no room in my heart for racial prejudice. But the plain fact is that most whites prefer not to live in mixed communities. This attitude may be wrong morally, and someday it may change. I hope it will."

Other developers soon mimicked Levitt's efforts. In 1955, *House and Garden* magazine declared that suburbia had become the "national way of life." By 1960, however, only 5 percent of African Americans lived in suburbs.

**PEOPLE OF COLOR ON THE MOVE** The mass migration of rural southern blacks to the urban North, Midwest, and West after the Second World War was much larger than the migration after the First World War,

**The Second Great Migration** African American families, such as the New Jersey–bound family pictured here, moved to northern urban centers in droves following the end of World War II.

and its social consequences were even more dramatic. After 1945, more than 5 million blacks left the South in search of better jobs and housing, higher wages, and greater civil rights.

By 1960, for the first time in history, more African Americans were living in urban areas than in rural areas. As people of color moved into cities, however, many white residents left for the suburbs ("white flight"). Between 1950 and 1960, some 3.6 million whites left the nation's largest cities for suburban neighborhoods, while 4.5 million blacks moved into the cities.

Through organizations such as the National Association for the Advancement of Colored People (NAACP), the Congress of Racial Equality (CORE), and the National Urban League, blacks sought to change the hearts and minds of their white neighbors. However, for all the racism that black migrants encountered, most of them preferred their new lives to the enforced segregation and often violent abuse in the South.

Just as African Americans were on the move, so, too, were Mexicans and Puerto Ricans. Congress renewed the *bracero* program, begun during the Second World War, which enabled Mexicans to work as wage laborers in the

**Hollywood homemakers** TV shows, movies, and plays in the fifties were outlets for homemakers' anxieties and fantasies. Left: *Leave It to Beaver* (1957) was a popular comedy about a young boy and his happy-go-lucky family living in suburban America. Right: Domestic bliss was out of reach for African American female characters. In the award-winning Broadway production of *Porgy and Bess* (1959), Dorothy Dandridge plays an addict so lost in the vice of New Orleans that even her self-sacrificing disabled lover (Sidney Poitier) cannot save her.

United States, often as migrant workers. Mexicans streamed across the nation's southwest border. By 1960, Los Angeles had the largest concentration of Mexican Americans in the nation.

Mexican Americans, Puerto Ricans, and other Latinos who served in the military also benefited from the GI Bill. Many of them—and their families— were able to relocate to the mainland United States because of the educational and housing programs provided veterans through the federal government. Between 1940 and 1960, nearly a million Puerto Ricans, mostly small farmers and agricultural workers, moved into American cities, especially New York City. By the late 1960s, more Puerto Ricans (who enjoy dual citizenship of the Commonwealth of Puerto Rico and the United States) lived in New York City than in San Juan, the capital of Puerto Rico.

**SHIFTING WOMEN'S ROLES** During the Second World War, millions of women had assumed traditionally male jobs in factories and mills. After the war, the influx of men returning to the job force led many employers to push working women back into traditional homemaking roles. A 1945 article in *House Beautiful* magazine informed women that the returning war veteran was "head man again. . . . Your part in the remaking of this man is to fit his home to him, understanding why he wants it this way, forgetting your own preferences."

Advertisements in popular magazines often targeted middle-class women, depicting them happily bound to the house, at work in the kitchen in dresses adorned with jewelry (usually pearl necklaces) and high heels, conversing with children, serving dinner, cleaning, and otherwise displaying the joy of a clean home or the latest kitchen appliance.

During the 1950s, the U.S. marriage rate reached an all-time high, and the average age of marriage for women plummeted to nineteen. There was enormous social pressure on teenaged girls to get married quickly; if a woman wasn't engaged or married by her early twenties, she was in danger of becoming an "old maid." In 1956, one-fourth of white college women wed while still enrolled in school, and most dropped out before receiving a degree. A common joke was that women went to college to get an "M.R.S. degree"—that is, a husband. Female college students were encouraged to take such courses as home economics, interior decoration, and family finance.

Despite this "modern" version of the nineteenth century's cult of domesticity, many women did work outside the home. In 1950, women comprised 29 percent of the workforce, and that percentage rose steadily throughout the decade. Some 70 percent of employed women worked in clerical positions—as secretaries, bank tellers, or sales clerks—or on assembly lines or in the service industry (waitresses, laundresses, housekeepers). African American and women of color had even fewer vocational choices and were mostly delegated to low-paying service jobs such as maids and cooks.

**THE CHILD-CENTERED FIFTIES** With the war over, millions of military veterans eagerly returned to civilian life in America with its schools, jobs, wives, and growing families. The record number of Americans born during the postwar period (roughly 1941–1964) composed what came to be known as the "**baby boom** generation," which would shape the nation's social and cultural life throughout the second half of the twentieth century and after.

The fifties was the ideal decade to be a child. Social life became centered on the needs of children because there were so many of them. Between 1946 and 1964, the birth of 76 million Americans reversed a century-long decline in the nation's birthrate and created a demographic upheaval whose repercussions are still being felt. The baby boom peaked in 1957, when a record 4.3 million births occurred. From 1940 to 1960, the number of families with three children doubled, and the number with four quadrupled.

Postwar babies initially created a surge in demand for diapers, washing machines, and baby food, then required the construction of thousands of new schools—and the hiring of teachers to staff them. Children's needs drove much of the economy's growth.

That so many women were having babies and raising children necessarily shaped societal attitudes toward them—and vice versa. A special issue of *Life* in 1956 featured the "ideal" middle-class woman: a thirty-two-year-old "pretty and popular" white suburban housewife, mother of four, who had married at age sixteen. She was described as an excellent wife, mother, volunteer, and "home manager." She made her own clothes, hosted dozens of dinner parties each year, sang in her church choir, and was devoted to her husband. "In her daily round," *Life* reported, "she attends club or charity meetings, drives the children to school, does the weekly grocery shopping, makes ceramics, and is planning to study French."

The soaring birthrate reinforced the notion that a woman's place was in the home. "Of all the accomplishments of the American woman," *Life* proclaimed, "the one she brings off with the most spectacular success is having babies."

**Roadside service** Drive-in churches offered members the comfort of listening to Sunday Mass from their cars. Here, the pastor of New York's Tremont Methodist Church greets a member of his four-wheeled congregation.

## A Religious Nation

After the Second World War, Americans joined churches and synagogues in record numbers. In 1940, less than half the adult population belonged to a church; by 1960, more than 65 percent were members of churches or synagogues. The cold war provided a stimulant to Christian evangelism. A godly nation, it was assumed, would better withstand the march of "godless" communism.

President Eisenhower promoted a patriotic religious crusade. "Recognition of the Supreme Being," he declared, "is the first, the most basic, expression of Americanism. Without God, there could be no American form of government, nor an American way of life." In 1954, Congress added the phrase "[one nation] under God" to the Pledge of Allegiance. In 1956, it made the statement "In God We Trust" the nation's official motto, and Eisenhower ordered it displayed on all currency. "Today in the United States," *Time* magazine claimed in 1954, "the Christian faith is back at the center of things."

## CRACKS IN THE PICTURE WINDOW

In contrast to the "happy days" image of the fifties, there was also anxiety, dissent, and diversity. In *The Affluent Society* (1958), economist John Kenneth Galbraith attacked the prevailing notion that sustained economic growth was solving social problems. He reminded readers that the nation had yet to eradicate poverty, especially among minorities in inner cities; female-led households; Mexican American migrant farmworkers; Native Americans; and rural southerners, both black and white.

**POVERTY AMID PROSPERITY** Uncritical praise for the "throwaway" culture of consumption masked the nation's chronic poverty amid its mythic plenty. In 1959, a quarter of the population had *no* financial assets, and more than half had no savings accounts or credit cards. Poverty afflicted nearly half of African Americans, compared to only a quarter of whites. At least 40 million people had incomes below the poverty line during the 1950s.

The "promised land" in the North was not perfect. Because those who left the South were often undereducated, poor, and black, they were regularly denied access to good jobs, good schools, and good housing. Although states in the North, Midwest, and Far West were not as blatantly discriminatory as in the South, African Americans still encountered racism and discrimination.

**LITERATURE AS SOCIAL CRITICISM** Many critics, writers, and artists rejected America's social complacency and worship of consumerism. Playwright Thornton Wilder labeled young adults of the fifties the "Silent Generation" because of their self-centered outlook, and writer Norman Mailer said the 1950s was "one of the worst decades in the history of man" because so many Americans embraced a bland conformity. The most powerful novels of the postwar period emphasized the individual's struggle for survival amid the smothering forces of mass society. Books such as James Jones's *From Here to Eternity* (1951), Ralph Ellison's *Invisible Man* (1952), Saul Bellow's *Seize the Day* (1956), J. D. Salinger's *Catcher in the Rye* (1951), William Styron's *Lie Down in Darkness* (1951), and John Updike's *Rabbit, Run* (1961) feature restless, tormented souls who can find neither contentment nor respect in a superficial world.

The upper-middle-class white suburbs and the culture of comfortable conformity were frequent literary targets. John Cheever set most of his short stories in suburban neighborhoods—"cesspools of conformity." The typical suburban dweller, one critic charged in 1956, "buys the right car, keeps his lawn like his neighbor's, eats crunchy breakfast cereal, and votes Republican."

In his vicious satire of affluent suburbia, *The Crack in the Picture Window* (1956), John Keats charged that "miles of identical boxes are spreading like gangrene" across the nation, producing "haggard" businessmen, "tense and anxious" housewives, and "the gimme kids" who, after unwrapping the last Christmas gift, "look up and ask whether that is all." He dismissed Levittowns as residential "developments conceived in error, nurtured by greed, corroding everything they touch. They destroy established cities and trade patterns, pose dangerous problems for the areas they invade, and actually drive mad myriads of housewives shut up in them."

**Art ache** The Beat community fostered a frenzied desire to experience life in all of its intensity and spontaneity, including the cultural realm. In this 1959 photograph, poet Tex Kleen reads verse in a bathtub at Venice Beach, California, while artist Mad Mike paints trash cans.

**THE BEATS** A small but highly controversial group of young writers, poets, painters, and musicians rejected the consumer culture and the traditional responsibilities of middle-class life. They were known as the **Beats**. To be "beat" was likened to being "upbeat" and even "beatific," as well as being "on the beat" in "real cool" jazz music. But the Beats also liked the name because it implied "weariness," being "exhausted" or "beaten down," qualities which none of them actually exhibited.

Jack Kerouac, Allen Ginsberg, William Burroughs, Neal Cassady, Gary Snyder, and other Beats rebelled against conventional literary and artistic expression and excelled at often purposeless and even criminal behavior. In nurturing their alienation from mainstream life, the mostly male Beats were nomadic seekers, restless and often tormented souls who stole cars and cash and sought solace in booze, mind-altering drugs, carefree sex, and various forms of risk-taking behavior. A drunk Burroughs, for example, tried to shoot an apple off his wife's head and missed, killing her instantly.

The Beats emerged from the bohemian underground in New York City's Greenwich Village. Ginsberg called them "angelheaded hipsters burning for the ancient heavenly connection." An anarchic boys club, the Beats were masters at outrageous behavior: they were serial misogynists who viewed women as second-class accessories. Carolyn Cassady said that "the boys didn't know where they were going. . . . They just knew they wanted to *go.*"

The Beat hipsters wanted their art and literature to change consciousness rather than address social ills. During three feverish weeks, Kerouac typed nonstop on a continuous roll of teletype paper the manuscript of his remarkable novel *On the Road* (1957), an account of a series of frenzied cross-country trips he and others made between 1948 and 1950.

Kerouac and the Beats were, at heart, outlandish romantics searching for an authentic sense of self in a nation absorbed in consumerism, conformism, and anti-communism.

The Beats were as much a force for social change as they were a cultural movement. Many Beats, notably Allen Ginsberg and his life-long partner, poet Peter Orlovsky, were gay or bisexual during an era when homosexuality continued to be scorned as "deviant" behavior. Ginsberg and Orlovsky termed their relationship a marriage, and by doing so the two men were social pioneers, the first gay "married" couple that many people had ever encountered. They remained partners for more than forty years, until Ginsberg's death in 1997.

Ginsberg's provocative jazzed-up prose-poem, "Howl," which applauded the defiant alienation of the Beats, openly celebrated erotic homosexuality. It was so stippled with vivid sexual references that copies of the poem were impounded by United States Customs agents and its publisher, poet Lawrence Ferlinghetti, was charged with obscenity. After a long trial, Ferlinghetti was acquitted after the judge ruled that the poem was neither obscene nor without "redeeming social importance." Thereafter, "Howl" served as a manifesto for the sexual revolution.

The raucous rebelliousness of the Beats set the stage for the more widespread youth revolt of the 1960s and the flowering of the hippies.

**ROCK 'N' ROLL** The millions of children making up the first wave of baby boomers became adolescents in the late 1950s. People began calling them teenagers, and a distinctive teen subculture began to emerge, as did a wave of juvenile delinquency. By 1956, more than a million teens were being arrested each year. One contributing factor was access to automobiles, which enabled them to escape parental control and, in the words of one journalist, provided "a private lounge for drinking and for petting [embracing and kissing] or sex episodes."

Many blamed teen delinquency on rock 'n' roll, a new form of music. Alan Freed, a Cleveland disc jockey, coined the term *rock 'n' roll* in 1951. He had noticed that white teenagers buying rhythm and blues (R&B) records preferred the livelier recordings by African Americans and Latino Americans. Freed began playing R&B songs on his radio show, but he called the music rock 'n' roll (a phrase used in African American communities to refer to dancing and sex). By 1954, Freed had moved to New York City, where his program helped bridge the gap between "white" and "black" music.

African American singers such as Chuck Berry, Little Richard, and Ray Charles, along with Latino American performers such as Ritchie Valens (Richard Valenzuela), captivated young, white, middle-class audiences. At the same time, Sam Phillips, a disk jockey in Memphis, Tennessee, was searching for a particular type of pop singer. "If I could find a white man with a Negro sound," Phillips said, "I could make a billion dollars."

He found him in Elvis Presley, the lanky son of poor Mississippi farmers. In 1956, the twenty-one-year-old Presley, by then a regional star famous for his long, unruly hair, sullen yet sensual sneer, and swiveling hips, released his smash-hit recording "Heartbreak Hotel." Over the next two years, he emerged as the most popular musician in American history, carrying rock 'n' roll across the race barrier and assaulting the bland conformity of fifties culture. Presley's gyrating performances (his nickname was "Elvis the Pelvis") and incomparable voice drove young people wild and earned him millions of fans. His movements, said one music critic, "suggest, in a word, sex."

Cultural conservatives urged parents to destroy Presley's records. A Roman Catholic official denounced Presley as a symptom of a teenage "creed of dishonesty, violence, lust and degeneration." Patriotic groups claimed that rock 'n' roll music was part of a Communist plot to corrupt America's youth. Writing in the *New York Times*, a psychiatrist characterized it as a "communicable disease." A U.S. Senate subcommittee warned that Presley was threatening "to rock-n-roll the juvenile world into open revolt against society. The gangster of tomorrow is the Elvis Presley type of today."

Yet rock 'n' roll flourished in part because it was so controversial. It gave teenagers a sense of belonging to a tribal social group. More important, it brought together, on equal terms, musicians (and their audiences) of varied races and backgrounds.

# THE CIVIL RIGHTS MOVEMENT

Soon after the cold war began, Soviet diplomats began to use America's widespread racial discrimination against African Americans as a propaganda tool to illustrate the defects of the American way of life. Under the Jim Crow system in southern states, blacks still risked being lynched if they registered to vote. They were forced to use separate facilities—water fountains, restrooms, hotels, theaters, parks—and attend segregated schools. In the North, discrimination was not officially sanctioned but it was equally real, especially in housing and employment. President Eisenhower had an opportunity to exercise transformational leadership in race relations; his unwillingness to do so was his greatest failure. As *Time* magazine noted in 1958, Eisenhower "overlooked the fact that the U.S. needed [his] moral leadership in fighting segregation."

**EISENHOWER AND RACE**  Eisenhower had entered the White House committed to civil rights in principle, and he pushed for improvements in some areas. During his first three years, public facilities (parks, playgrounds, libraries, restaurants) in Washington, D.C., were desegregated, and he intervened to end discrimination at military bases in Virginia and South Carolina. Beyond that, however, he refused to make civil rights for African Americans a moral crusade. Pushing too hard, he believed, would "raise tempers and increase prejudices."

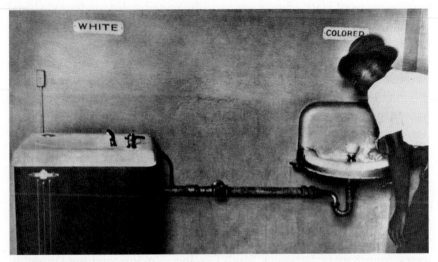

**Fountains of truth** An Alabama motel offers its white patrons chilled water from a cooler, while its African American guests are limited to a simple drinking fountain.

Two aspects of Eisenhower's political philosophy limited his commitment to racial equality: his preference for state or local action over federal involvement and his doubt that laws could change attitudes. His passivity meant that governmental leadership on civil rights would come from the judiciary more than from the executive or legislative branches.

In 1953, Eisenhower appointed Republican Earl Warren, former governor of California, as chief justice of the U.S. Supreme Court, a decision he later said was the "biggest damn fool mistake I ever made." Warren, who had seemed safely conservative while in elected office, displayed a social conscience and a streak of libertarianism on the bench. Under his leadership (1953–1969), the Supreme Court became a powerful force for social and political change.

**AFRICAN AMERICAN ACTIVISM** The most-crucial leaders of the civil rights movement came from those whose rights were most often violated: African Americans, Latino Americans, Asian Americans, and others. Courageous blacks led what would become the most important social movement in twentieth-century America. They fought in the courts, at the ballot box, and in the streets.

Although many African Americans had moved to the North and West, a majority remained in the South, where they still faced a rigidly segregated society. In the 1952 presidential election, for example, only 20 percent of eligible African Americans were registered to vote. And although the public schools, especially in the South, were supposedly racially separate but equal in quality, many all-black schools were actually underfunded, understaffed, and overcrowded.

In the mid-1930s, the National Association for the Advancement of Colored People (NAACP) challenged the **separate-but-equal** judicial doctrine that had preserved racial segregation since the *Plessy* decision by the Supreme Court in 1896. It took almost fifteen years, however, to convince the courts that racial segregation must end. Finally, in *Sweatt v. Painter* (1950), the Supreme Court ruled that a separate black law school in Texas was *not* equal in quality to the state's whites-only schools. The Court ordered Texas to remedy the situation. It was the first step toward dismantling America's tradition of racial segregation.

**THE *BROWN* DECISION** By the early 1950s, people were challenging state laws requiring racial segregation in the public schools. Five such cases, from Kansas, Delaware, South Carolina, Virginia, and the District of Columbia—usually cited by reference to the first, ***Brown v. Board of Education of Topeka, Kansas***—went to the Supreme Court in 1952. President Eisenhower gutlessly told the attorney general that he hoped the justices would postpone dealing with the case "until the next Administration took over." When it became obvious that the Court was moving forward, Eisenhower urged Chief Justice Warren to side with segregationists. Warren was not swayed: "You mind your business," he told the president, "and I'll mind mine."

Warren wrote the pathbreaking opinion, delivered on May 17, 1954, in which the Court declared that "in the field of public education the doctrine of 'separate but equal' has no place." The justices used a variety of sociological and psychological findings to show that even if racially separate schools were equal in quality, the very practice of separating students by race caused feelings of inferiority among black children. A year later, the Court directed that racial *integration* should move forward "with all deliberate speed."

Eisenhower refused to endorse or enforce the Court's ruling. He grumbled in private "that the Supreme Court decision set back progress in the South at least fifteen years." He even refused to condemn the lynching of fourteen-year-old Emmett Till, an African American whose mutilated body was found in a Mississippi River after he had supposedly whistled at a white woman.

While token racial integration began as early as 1954 in northern states and the border states of Kentucky and Missouri, hostility mounted in the Lower South and Virginia. The Alabama State Senate and the Virginia legislature both passed resolutions "nullifying" the Supreme Court's decision, arguing that racial integration was an issue of states' rights. Arkansas governor Orval Faubus insisted that the "federal government is a creature of the states. . . . We must either choose to defend our rights or else surrender."

In 1954, Harry F. Byrd, a Virginia senator and former governor, called for "**massive resistance**" against federal efforts to enforce integration in the South. Senator James O. Eastland of Mississippi, a notorious racist whose father had lynched a black couple, told the Senate that "the Negro race is an inferior race" and that the South was determined to maintain white supremacy.

The grassroots opposition among southern whites to the *Brown* case was led by newly formed Citizens' Councils, middle-class versions of the Ku Klux Klan that spread quickly and eventually enrolled 250,000 members. The Councils, which used economic coercion against blacks who crossed racial boundaries, grew so powerful in some communities that membership became almost a necessity for an aspiring white politician.

One hundred one members of Congress signed a Declaration of Constitutional Principles ("Southern Manifesto") in 1956, deploring the *Brown* decision as "a clear abuse of judicial power" that had created an "explosive and dangerous condition" in the South. Only three southern Democrats refused to sign. One of them, Senator Lyndon B. Johnson of Texas, would become president seven years later. In six southern states at the end of 1956, two years after the *Brown* ruling, no black children attended school with whites. By 1960, only 765 of 6,676 school districts in the South had desegregated.

**THE MONTGOMERY BUS BOYCOTT** While mobilizing white resistance, the *Brown* case also inspired many blacks (and white activists) by suggesting that the federal government was finally beginning to confront racial discrimination. Yet the essential role played by the NAACP and the courts in the civil rights movement often overshadows the courageous contributions of individual African Americans who took great risks to challenge segregation.

For example, in Montgomery, Alabama, on December 1, 1955, Mrs. Rosa Parks, a forty-two-year-old seamstress who was a determined activist for racial justice, boarded the Cleveland Avenue bus and sat in the third row. As white passengers boarded, the driver, James Blake, told Parks she had to move to the back, as the city required blacks to do. She refused. Blake then demanded, "Why don't you stand up?" Parks calmly replied, "I don't think I should have to stand up." When the driver told her that "niggers must move back" or he would have her arrested, she replied, "You may do that." She was "tired of giving in," she recalled. Police then arrested her. In holding her ground, Parks had unwittingly launched the modern civil rights movement.

The next night, black community leaders met at Dexter Avenue Baptist Church to organize a long-planned boycott of the city's bus system, most of whose riders were African Americans. Student and faculty volunteers from Alabama State University stayed up all night to distribute 35,000 flyers denouncing the arrest of Rosa Parks and urging support for the **Montgomery bus boycott**.

**MARTIN LUTHER KING JR.** In the Dexter Avenue church's twenty-six-year-old pastor, Martin Luther King Jr., the boycott movement found a brave and charismatic leader. The grandson of a slave and son of a prominent minister, King was an eloquent speaker. "We must use the weapon of love," he told supporters. "We must realize so many people are taught to hate us that they are not totally responsible for their hate."

To his foes, King warned, "We will soon wear you down by our capacity to suffer, and in winning our freedom we will so appeal to your heart and conscience that we will win you in the process." He preached **nonviolent civil disobedience**, the tactic of defying unjust laws through peaceful actions, but he also valued militancy, for without crisis and confrontation there would be no progress.

The Montgomery bus boycott was a stunning success. For 381 days, African Americans, women and men, organized carpools, used black-owned taxis, hitchhiked, or simply walked. White supporters also provided rides.

**Civil disobedience** Martin Luther King Jr. is arrested for "loitering" in 1958. He was arrested thirty times for defying racist laws.

The unprecedented mass protest infuriated many whites; police harassed and ticketed black carpools, and white thugs attacked black pedestrians. Ku Klux Klan members burned black churches and bombed houses. King himself was arrested twice.

On December 20, 1956, the Montgomery boycotters won a federal case they had initiated against racial segregation on public buses. The Supreme Court affirmed that "the separate but equal doctrine can no longer be safely followed as a correct statement of the law." The next day, King and other African Americans boarded the city buses. They showed that well-coordinated, nonviolent black activism could trigger major changes. Among African Americans, hope replaced resignation, and action supplanted passivity. The boycott also catapulted King into the national spotlight.

And what of Rosa Parks? She and her husband lost their jobs. Hate mail, death threats, and firebombings forced them to leave Alabama eight months after her arrest. They moved to Detroit, where they remained fully engaged in the evolving civil rights movement. "Freedom fighters never retire," she explained.

**THE CIVIL RIGHTS ACTS OF 1957 AND 1960** In 1956, hoping to exploit divisions between northern and southern Democrats and reclaim some of the black vote for Republicans, congressional leaders agreed to support what became the Civil Rights Act of 1957.

The first civil rights law passed since 1875, it finally got through the Senate, after a year's delay, with the help of majority leader Lyndon B. Johnson, a Texas Democrat who knew that he could never be elected president if he was viewed as just another racist white southerner. The bill was intended to ensure that all Americans, regardless of race or ethnicity, were allowed to vote. Johnson won southern acceptance of the bill by watering down its enforcement provisions.

The Civil Rights Act established the Civil Rights Commission and a new Civil Rights Division in the Justice Department intended to prevent interference with the right to vote. Yet by 1959, not a single southern black voter had been added to the rolls. The Civil Rights Act of 1960, which provided for federal courts to register African Americans to vote in districts where there was a "pattern and practice" of racial discrimination, also lacked teeth and depended upon vigorous presidential enforcement to achieve any tangible results.

**DESEGREGATION IN LITTLE ROCK**   A few weeks after the Civil Rights Act of 1957 was passed, Arkansas's Democratic governor, Orval Eugene Faubus, a rabid segregationist, called a special session of the state legislature. He asked the legislators to pass a series of bills designed to give him sweeping

**"Lynch her!"** A determined Elizabeth Eckford endures the hostile screams of future classmates as she enters Central High School in Little Rock, Arkansas.

powers to close public schools threatened with integration and to transfer funds from public schools facing federally enforced integration to private "segregation academies."

In the fall of 1957, Faubus defied a federal court order by using the state's National Guard to prevent nine black students from enrolling at Little Rock's Central High School. When one of the students, fifteen-year-old Elizabeth Eckford, tried to enter the school, National Guardsmen barred the door. All alone, she headed back to the bus stop, only to be confronted by a mob of jeering white mothers and schoolgirls shrieking, "Lynch her! Lynch her!" Eckford recalled, "They moved closer and closer. . . . I tried to see a friendly face somewhere in the crowd—someone who maybe could help. I looked into the face of an old woman and it seemed a kind face, but when I looked at her again, she spat at me."

The mayor of Little Rock frantically called the White House "pleading" for federal troops. At that point, President Eisenhower, who had resisted all appeals for federal action, reluctantly dispatched 1,000 army paratroopers to protect the brave black students as they entered the school. "Mob rule," he told the nation, "cannot be allowed to overrule the decisions of our courts."

It was the first time since the 1870s that federal troops had been sent to the South to protect African Americans. Dunbar Ogden, a Presbyterian minister in Little Rock, found a ray of hope in the ugly confrontation: "This may be looked back upon by future historians as the turning point—for good—of race relations in this country."

With television cameras sending dramatic images across the country, paratroopers used bayonets and rifle butts to disperse the angry crowd. The nine black students attended their first classes with soldiers patrolling the halls.

The soldiers stayed in Little Rock through the school year. To a man, unyielding southern governors and congressmen furiously lashed out at Eisenhower, charging that he was violating states' rights. The president had "lit the fires of hate," claimed Senator James Eastland. Many southern politicians called for the president's impeachment and removal. Eisenhower, who had grown up in an all-white Kansas town and spent his military career in a segregated army, stressed that his use of federal troops had little to do with "the integration or segregation question" and everything to do with maintaining law and order. Although Eisenhower favored equality of opportunity, he explained to an aide that equality did not mean "that a Negro should court my daughter."

In Eisenhower's view, the gleaming bayonets in Little Rock showed that the United States was a government of law, that the Constitution remained the supreme law of the land, and that the U.S. Supreme Court was the final interpreter of the Constitution. Martin Luther King Jr. forced the president out of his comfort zone. He told Eisenhower that the "overwhelming majority of southerners, Negro and white, stand behind your resolute action to restore law and order in Little Rock."

In the summer of 1958, Governor Faubus closed the Little Rock high schools rather than allow racial integration. The governor of Virginia did the same. Their actions led Jonathan Daniels, editor of the Raleigh (North Carolina) *News & Observer*, to write that closing public schools is "something beyond secession from the Union; [it] is secession from civilization."

Court proceedings in Arkansas dragged into 1959 before the schools reopened. Resistance to integration in Virginia collapsed when state and

federal courts struck down state laws that had cut off funds to integrated public schools. Thereafter, massive resistance to racial integration was confined
mostly to the Lower South, where five states—from South Carolina westward
through Louisiana—still opposed even token integration. Not a single pupil in
those states attended an integrated school. Faubus went on to serve six terms
as governor of Arkansas.

**SOUTHERN CHRISTIAN LEADERSHIP CONFERENCE** After
Little Rock, progress toward greater civil rights seemed agonizingly slow. Frustrated African Americans began blaming the NAACP for relying too much on
the courts.

The widespread sense of disappointment gave Martin Luther King's
nonviolent civil rights movement even greater visibility. As King explained,
"We were confronted with blasted hopes, and the dark shadow of a deep
disappointment settled upon us. So we had no alternative except that of
preparing for direct action, whereby we would present our very bodies as
a means of laying our case before the conscience of the local and national
community."

On January 10, 1957, King invited about sixty black ministers and leaders to Ebenezer Church in Atlanta. Their goal was to form an organization
to promote nonviolent civil disobedience as a method of desegregating bus
systems across the South. A new organization soon emerged: the **Southern
Christian Leadership Conference (SCLC)**, with King as its president. Unlike
the NAACP, which recruited individual members, SCLC coordinated activities on behalf of a cluster of organizations, mostly individual churches or
community groups. Because King pushed for direct action, only a few African
American ministers were initially willing to affiliate with SCLC, for fear of a
white backlash.

King persisted, however, and over time SCLC grew into a powerful organization. The activists knew that violence awaited them. Roy Wilkins, head of
the NAACP, noted that "the Negro citizen has come to the point where he is
not afraid of violence. He no longer shrinks back. He will assert himself, and
if violence comes, so be it."

Thus began the second phase of the civil rights movement. It would come
to fruition in the 1960s as African American activists showed the courage to
resist injustice, the power to love everyone, and the strength to endure dis-
couragement and opposition. They did so without the president's support. As
Wilkins asserted: "President Eisenhower was a fine general and a good, decent
man, but if he had fought World War II the way he fought for civil rights, we
would all be speaking German today."

# FOREIGN POLICY IN THE FIFTIES

The Truman administration's commitment to contain communism focused on the Soviet threat to Western Europe. During the 1950s, the Eisenhower administration, especially Secretary of State John Foster Dulles, determined that containment was no longer enough; instead, the United States must develop a "dynamic" foreign policy that would "roll back" communism around the world.

Dulles's goal was to "liberate" people under Communist rule rather than merely contain its expansion. "For us," he said, "there are two kinds of people in the world. There are those who are Christians and support free enterprise, and there are the others." He soon discovered, however, that the complexities of world affairs and the realities of Soviet and Communist Chinese power made his moral commitment to manage the destiny of the world unrealistic—and costly.

**CONCLUDING AN ARMISTICE**  In Korea, President Eisenhower faced three choices: increase the war effort, continue the military stalemate, or pursue a negotiated settlement. Eisenhower chose the third option, but he first had to convince John Foster Dulles that negotiations were warranted. In April 1953, Eisenhower told Dulles that he was not willing to prolong the military effort, but he was comfortable using the threat of nuclear weapons to reach a settlement.

In May, Eisenhower took the bold step of intensifying the aerial bombardment of North Korea. He let it be known that he would use nuclear weapons if a truce were not forthcoming. Thereafter, negotiations moved quickly toward an armistice (cease-fire agreement) on July 26, 1953. It ended "all acts of armed force" and reaffirmed the historical border between the two Koreas just above the 38th parallel until both sides could arrive at a "final peaceful settlement." Other factors in bringing about the armistice were China's rising military losses in the conflict and the spirit of uncertainty felt by the Soviet Communists after the death of Josef Stalin on March 5, 1953.

The Korean War was the first in which helicopters were used in combat, and it ushered in the era of jet fighters. It transformed the United States into the world's police officer by convincing American political and military leaders that communism was indeed a global threat. Within a few years, the United States would create scores of permanent military bases around the world and organize a national security apparatus in Washington to manage its new responsibilities—not the least of which was a growing stockpile of nuclear weaponry.

**DULLES AND MASSIVE RETALIATION**  Like Woodrow Wilson, Secretary of State Dulles was a Presbyterian minister's son. He believed that the United States was "born with a sense of destiny and mission" to defeat communism.

Dulles (and Eisenhower) insisted that containing communism was immoral because it did nothing to free people from oppression. America, he argued, should work toward the liberation of the "captive peoples" of Eastern Europe and China. When State Department analyst George F. Kennan, architect of the containment doctrine, dismissed Dulles's rhetoric as lunacy, Dulles fired him.

Eisenhower, however, understood Kennan's objections. He stressed that the so-called liberation doctrine would not involve military force. Instead, he would promote the removal of Communist control "by every peaceful means, but only by peaceful means." Yet he did nothing to temper Dulles's rhetoric and praised his secretary of state's moral fervor.

Dulles and Eisenhower knew they could not win a ground war against the Soviet Union or Communist China, whose armies had millions more soldiers than did the United States. Nor could the administration afford—politically or financially—to sustain military expenditures at the levels required during the Korean War. So they crafted a strategy that came to be called "**massive retaliation**," which meant using the threat of nuclear warfare to prevent Communist aggression. The strategy, they argued, would provide a "maximum deterrent at bearable cost," or "more bang for the buck."

Massive retaliation had major weaknesses, however. By the mid-1950s, both the United States and Soviet Union had developed hydrogen bombs that were 750 times as powerful as the atomic bombs dropped on Japan in 1945. A single hydrogen bomb would have a devastating global impact, yet war planners envisioned using hundreds of them. "The necessary art," Dulles explained, was in the *brinkmanship*, "the ability to get to the verge without getting into war. . . . If you are scared to go to the brink, you are lost."

**THE CIA'S FOREIGN INTERVENTIONS** While publicly promoting the liberation of Communist nations and massive retaliation as a strategy against the Soviets, President Eisenhower and Secretary of State Dulles were secretly using the **Central Intelligence Agency (CIA)** to manipulate world politics in covert ways that produced unintended consequences—all of them bad.

The anti-colonial independence movements unleashed by the Second World War led to nationalist groups around the globe revolting against British and French rule. In May 1951, the Iran parliament seized control of the nation's British-run oil industry. The following year, prime minister Mohammed Mossadegh cut diplomatic ties with Great Britain and insisted that Iran, not Britain, should own, sell, and profit from Iranian oil. Dulles predicted that Iran was on the verge of falling under Communist control. The CIA and the British intelligence service, MI6, then launched Operation Ajax to oust Mossadegh.

The CIA bribed Iranian army officers and hired Iranian agents to arrest Mossadegh, who was then convicted of high treason. Thereafter, in return for access to Iranian oil, the U.S. government provided massive support for the anti-Communist (and increasingly authoritarian) regime of the shah (king) of Iran, Mohammad Reza Pahlavi, who seized power. The Iranians would not forget that the Americans had put the hated shah in power.

The success of the CIA-engineered coup emboldened Eisenhower to authorize other secret operations to undermine "unfriendly" government regimes, even if it meant aligning with corrupt dictatorships. In 1954, the target was Guatemala, a poor Central American country led by Colonel Jacobo Arbenz Guzman. Arbenz's decision to take over U.S.-owned property and industries convinced Dulles that Guatemala was falling victim to "international communism." Dulles persuaded Eisenhower to approve a CIA operation to organize a secret Guatemalan army in Honduras.

On June 18, 1954, aided by CIA-piloted warplanes, 150 paid "liberators" forced Arbenz Guzman into exile in Mexico. The United States then installed a new ruler in Guatemala who eliminated all political opposition.

By secretly overthrowing elected governments to ensure that they did not join the Soviet bloc, however, the CIA destabilized Iran and Guatemala and created resentments in the Middle East and Central America that would eventually come back to haunt the United States.

**INDOCHINA** During the 1950s, the United States also became embroiled in Southeast Asia. Indochina, created by French imperialists in the nineteenth century out of the old kingdoms of Cambodia, Laos, and Vietnam, offered a distinctive case of anti-colonial nationalism. During the Second World War, after Japanese troops had occupied the region, the Viet Minh (League for the Independence of Vietnam) waged a guerrilla resistance movement led by Ho Chi Minh, a seasoned revolutionary and passionate nationalist.

"Uncle Ho," a wispy man weighing barely 100 pounds, had a single goal for his country: independence. At the end of the war against Japan, the Viet Minh controlled part of northern Vietnam. On September 2, 1945, Ho Chi Minh proclaimed the creation of a Democratic Republic of Vietnam, with its capital in Hanoi.

The French, like the Americans would later, underestimated the determination of the Vietnamese nationalists to maintain their independence. In 1946, the First Indochina War erupted when Ho's fighters resisted French efforts to restore the colonial regime. French forces quickly regained control of the cities, while the Viet Minh controlled the countryside. Ho predicted that his forces would absorb more losses, but the French would give in first.

When the Korean War ended, the United States continued its efforts to strengthen French control of Vietnam. By the end of 1953, the Eisenhower administration was paying nearly 80 percent of the cost of the French military effort.

In December 1953, some 12,000 French soldiers parachuted into **Dien Bien Phu**, a cluster of villages in a valley ringed by mountains in northwestern Vietnam. Their plan was to lure Viet Minh guerrillas into the open and then overwhelm them with superior firepower. The French assumed that the surrounding forested hills were impassable. Their strategy, however, backfired.

Slowly, more than 55,000 Viet Minh fighters took up positions atop the ridges overlooking the French base. They laboriously dug trenches and tunnels down into the valley. By March 1954, the French found themselves surrounded.

As the weeks passed, the French government pleaded with the United States to relieve the pressure on Dien Bien Phu. The National Security Council—John Foster Dulles, Vice President Nixon, and the chairman of the Joint Chiefs of Staff—urged President Eisenhower to use atomic bombs to aid the French. Eisenhower snapped back: "You boys must be crazy. We can't use those awful things against Asians for the second time in less than ten years. My God!"

The president opposed U.S. intervention unless the British joined the effort. When they refused, Eisenhower told the French that U.S. military action was "politically impossible." On May 7, 1954, the Viet Minh fighters overwhelmed the last French resistance. The catastrophic defeat at Dien Bien Phu signaled the end of French colonial rule in Asia.

On July 20, 1954, representatives of France, Britain, the Soviet Union, the People's Republic of China, and the Viet Minh signed the Geneva Accords, which gave Laos and Cambodia their independence and divided Vietnam at the 17th parallel of latitude. The Viet Minh Communists were given control in the North, with the French remaining south of the line until nationwide elections in 1956. Ho Chi Minh took charge of the government in North Vietnam, executing thousands of Vietnamese he deemed opponents.

In South Vietnam, power gravitated to a new premier chosen by the French at American urging: Ngo Dinh Diem, a Catholic nationalist who had opposed both the French and the Viet Minh. In 1954, Eisenhower began providing military and economic aid to Diem. Yet Diem's autocratic efforts to eliminate all opposition played into the hands of the Communists, who found eager recruits among the discontented South Vietnamese. By 1957, Communist guerrillas known as the **Viet Cong** were launching attacks on the Diem government. As the warfare intensified, the Eisenhower administration concluded that its only option was to "sink or swim with Diem."

Eisenhower had used what he called the **"falling-domino" theory** to explain why the United States needed to fight communism in Vietnam: "You have a row of dominos set up, you knock over the first one, and what will

## POSTWAR ALLIANCES: THE FAR EAST

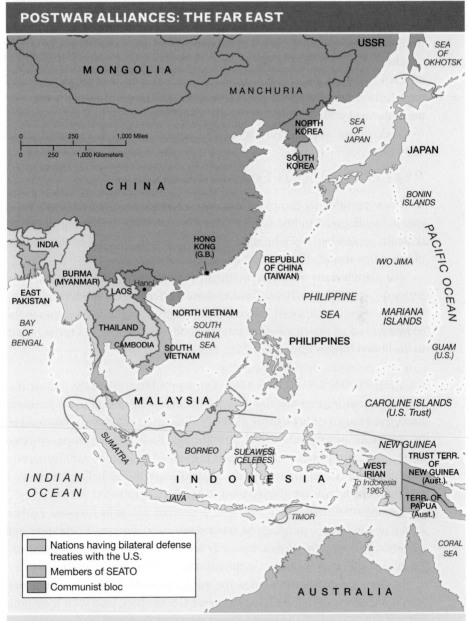

USSR

SEA OF OKHOTSK

MONGOLIA

MANCHURIA

NORTH KOREA

SEA OF JAPAN

JAPAN

0    250    1,000 Miles

0    250    1,000 Kilometers

SOUTH KOREA

CHINA

BONIN ISLANDS

INDIA

HONG KONG (G.B.)

REPUBLIC OF CHINA (TAIWAN)

IWO JIMA

PACIFIC OCEAN

BURMA (MYANMAR)

Hanoi

LAOS

EAST PAKISTAN

NORTH VIETNAM

PHILIPPINE SEA

MARIANA ISLANDS

BAY OF BENGAL

THAILAND

SOUTH CHINA SEA

PHILIPPINES

GUAM (U.S.)

CAMBODIA    SOUTH VIETNAM

MALAYSIA

CAROLINE ISLANDS (U.S. Trust)

SUMATRA

BORNEO    SULAWESI (CELEBES)

NEW GUINEA

INDIAN OCEAN

I N D O N E S I A

WEST IRIAN
To Indonesia 1963

TRUST TERR. OF NEW GUINEA (Aust.)

JAVA

TERR. OF PAPUA (Aust.)

TIMOR

CORAL SEA

☐ Nations having bilateral defense treaties with the U.S.

☐ Members of SEATO

☐ Communist bloc

AUSTRALIA

- How did the United States become increasingly involved in Vietnam during the fifties?
- Why did the installation of Ngo Dinh Diem by the French and the Americans backfire and generate more conflict in Vietnam?

happen to the last one is the certainty that it will go over very quickly." If South Vietnam were to fall to communism, he predicted, the rest of Southeast Asia would soon follow.

The domino analogy assumed that communism was a global movement directed by Soviet leaders in Moscow. Yet anti-colonial insurgencies resulted more from nationalist motives than Communist ideology. The domino analogy thus informed policy and meant that the United States had to police the entire world. As a consequence, *every* insurgency mushroomed into a strategic crisis.

## REELECTION AND FOREIGN CRISES

As a new presidential campaign unfolded in 1956, Dwight Eisenhower still enjoyed widespread public support. But his health was beginning to deteriorate. In September 1955, he suffered a heart attack, the first of three major illnesses that would affect the rest of his presidency.

The Republicans eagerly renominated Eisenhower and Vice President Richard Nixon. The party platform endorsed Eisenhower's moderate Republicanism, meaning balanced budgets, reduced government intervention in the economy, and an internationalist foreign policy. The Democrats turned again to the liberal Illinois leader, Adlai Stevenson.

**REPRESSION IN HUNGARY** During the last week of the presidential campaign, fighting erupted along the Suez Canal in Egypt and in the streets of Budapest, Hungary. On October 23, 1956, Hungarian nationalists, encouraged by American propaganda broadcasts through Radio Free Europe, revolted against Communist troops. The Soviets responded by killing 2,000 Hungarian freedom fighters and forcing nearly 200,000 more to flee before installing a new puppet government. The revolution had been smothered in twelve days.

Eisenhower's strategy in dealing with such crises was, as he later said, "Take a hard line—and bluff." Although he avoided war over Hungary, Eisenhower had allowed administration officials, especially Secretary of State Dulles, to make reckless pledges about "rolling back" communism and "liberating" Eastern Europe.

In Hungary, the Soviets called the administration's bluff. The Hungarian freedom fighters, having been led to expect U.S. support, paid with their lives. Richard Nixon cynically reassured Eisenhower that the Soviet crackdown would be beneficial in showing the world the ruthlessness of communism. The president felt guilty about failing to support the rebels, but Dulles showed little concern, reminding the president that "we always have been against violent rebellion."

**THE SUEZ WAR** President Eisenhower was more successful in handling an unexpected crisis in Egypt. In 1952, Egyptian army officer Gamal Abdel

Nasser had overthrown King Farouk and set out to become the leader of the Arab world. To do so, he promised to destroy the new Israeli nation, created in 1948, and to end British and French imperialism in the region. Nasser, with Soviet support, first sought to take control of the Suez Canal, the internationally managed waterway in Egypt connecting the Mediterranean to the Red Sea and Indian Ocean.

The canal had opened in 1869 as a joint French–Egyptian venture. From 1882 on, British troops had protected it as the British Empire's "lifeline" to oil in the Middle East and to India and its other Asian colonies. When Nasser's regime pressed for the withdrawal of the British forces, an Anglo-Egyptian treaty provided for their withdrawal within twenty months.

In 1955, Nasser, adept at playing both sides, announced a huge arms deal with the Soviet Union. The United States countered by offering to help Egypt finance a massive hydroelectric dam at Aswan on the Nile River. In 1956, after Nasser increased trade with the Soviet bloc and recognized the People's Republic of China, John Foster Dulles abruptly canceled the Aswan Dam offer.

Unable to retaliate directly against the United States, Nasser seized control of the French-owned Suez Canal Company and denied Israel-bound ships access through the canal. For Egyptians, this was their declaration of independence from European colonialism. The British and French were furious, for two thirds of Europe's oil came through the canal, but they needed a pretext for military action. Israel soon provided one.

On September 30, 1956, Israeli, British, and French officials secretly hatched a plan: Israel would invade Egypt and race west to the Suez Canal. The French and British would then send troops to the canal zone, posing as peacekeepers.

On October 29, 1956, Israeli paratroopers dropped into Egypt. The British and French then issued an ultimatum demanding that the fighting cease. When Egypt rejected the ultimatum, British warplanes began bombing Egyptian airfields. On November 5, British and French soldiers invaded the canal zone. Nasser responded by sinking all forty international ships then in the Suez Canal. A few days later, Anglo-French commandos and paratroopers took control of the canal.

Eisenhower was furious that the three nations had attacked Egypt without informing the American government. He resolved to put a stop to the invasion, for he believed the Egyptians had the right to control the Suez Canal, since it was entirely within their boundaries. "How could we possibly support Britain and France," he asked, "if in doing so we lose the whole Arab world?"

Eisenhower demanded that the British and French withdraw and that the Israelis evacuate the Sinai Peninsula—or face severe economic sanctions. The three aggressor nations grudgingly complied on November 7.

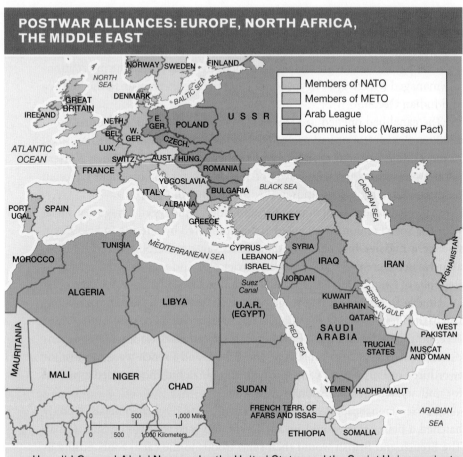

## POSTWAR ALLIANCES: EUROPE, NORTH AFRICA, THE MIDDLE EAST

Legend:
- Members of NATO
- Members of METO
- Arab League
- Communist bloc (Warsaw Pact)

- How did General Abdel Nasser play the United States and the Soviet Union against each other in pursuing Egypt's goals?
- Why did the Israelis, French, and British attack Egypt?
- How was the Suez War resolved?

The Suez debacle led to the resignation of Prime Minister Anthony Eden and hastened the process of independence among Great Britain's remaining colonies. But perhaps its major result was that the British government realized the risk of acting independently of the United States. Egypt reopened the Suez Canal, and, as Eisenhower had predicted, operated it in a professional, nonpolitical manner.

The **Suez crisis** and the Hungarian revolt led Democrat Adlai Stevenson to declare the Eisenhower administration's foreign policy "bankrupt." Most Americans, however, reasoned that the crises actually affirmed the nation's status as *the* global superpower. Voters handed Eisenhower an even more lopsided victory than the one in 1952. Eisenhower carried all but seven states and won the electoral vote 457 to 73. His decisive victory, however, failed to swing a congressional majority for his party in either house.

*SPUTNIK* On October 4, 1957, the Soviets shocked the world when they announced the launch of the first communications satellite, called *Sputnik* (*"traveling companion"*). Americans panicked, believing that if the Soviets could put a satellite in orbit, they could also fire a rocket with a nuclear warhead across the Pacific Ocean and detonate it on the West Coast. Senator Lyndon B. Johnson warned that the Russians would soon be "dropping bombs on us from space like kids dropping rocks on cars from freeway overpasses."

The Soviet success in space also dealt a severe blow to the prestige of American science and technology and changed the military balance of power. Democrats charged that the Soviets had "humiliated" the United States and launched a congressional investigation to assess the new threat.

"*Sputnik*-mania" led the United States to increase defense spending and enhance science education. In 1958, Congress created the National Aeronautics and Space Administration (NASA) to coordinate research and development related to outer space. The same year, Congress, with President Eisenhower's support, enacted the National Defense Education Act (NDEA), which authorized large federal grants to colleges and universities to enhance education and research in mathematics, science, and modern languages, as well as for student loans and fellowships.

**THE EISENHOWER DOCTRINE** In the aftermath of the Suez crisis, President Eisenhower decided that the United States must replace Great Britain and France as the guarantor of Western interests in the Middle East. In 1958, Congress approved what came to be called the Eisenhower Doctrine, which promised to extend economic and military aid to Arab nations and to use armed force if necessary to assist any such nation against Communist aggression.

**CRISIS IN BERLIN** Since the Second World War, West Berlin had become an oasis of Western democracy and prosperity, while East Berlin continued to be administered by the Soviet Union. West Berlin served as an enticing alternative to life behind the iron curtain. Each year, thousands of East Germans escaped to West Berlin.

On November 10, 1958, Soviet leader Nikita Khrushchev threatened to give East Germany control of East Berlin and of the air lanes into West Berlin. After the deadline he set (May 27, 1959), Western authorities would have to deal with the Soviet-controlled East German government or face the possibility of another blockade of the city.

Eisenhower told Khrushchev that he "would hit the Russians" with every weapon in the American arsenal if they persisted in their efforts to intimidate West Berlin. At the same time, however, Eisenhower sought a settlement. The negotiations distracted attention from the May 27 deadline, which passed almost unnoticed. In September 1959, Khrushchev and Eisenhower agreed to a summit meeting.

**THE U-2 SUMMIT** The summit meeting literally crashed and burned, however, when on Sunday morning, May 1, 1960, a Soviet rocket brought down a U.S. spy plane (called the U-2) flying at 70,000 feet over the Soviet Union. Khrushchev, embarrassed by the ability of U.S. spy planes to enter Soviet airspace, then sprang a trap on Eisenhower. The Soviets announced only that the plane had been shot down. The U.S. government, not realizing that the Soviets had captured the pilot, lied about the incident and claimed that it was missing a weather-monitoring plane over Turkey. Khrushchev then announced that the Soviets had American pilot Francis Gary Powers "alive and kicking" and also had the photographs Powers had taken of Soviet military installations.

On May 11, Eisenhower took personal responsibility for the spying program, explaining that such illegally obtained intelligence information was crucial to national security. At the testy summit in Paris five days later, Khrushchev lectured Eisenhower for forty-five minutes before walking out because the U.S. president refused to apologize. Later, in 1962, Powers would be exchanged for a captured Soviet spy.

**COMMUNIST CUBA** President Eisenhower's greatest embarrassment was Fidel Castro's new Communist regime in Cuba, which came to power on January 1, 1959, after two years of guerrilla warfare against the U.S.-supported dictator, Fulgencio Batista. The bearded, cigar-smoking Castro embraced Soviet support as he systematically imprisoned hundreds of opponents, canceled elections, and staged public executions. A CIA agent predicted, "We're going to take care of Castro just like we took care of Arbenz [in Guatemala]." The Soviets warned that American intervention in Cuba would trigger a military response.

One of Eisenhower's last acts as president, on January 3, 1961, was to suspend diplomatic relations with Cuba. He also authorized a secret CIA operation to train a force of Cuban refugees to oust Castro, but the final decision on the use of the invasion force would rest with the next president, John F. Kennedy.

## EVALUATING THE EISENHOWER PRESIDENCY

During President Eisenhower's second term, Congress added Alaska and Hawaii as the forty-ninth and fiftieth states (1959), while the nation experienced its worst economic slump since the Great Depression. Volatile issues such as civil rights, defense policy, and corrupt aides compounded the administration's troubles. The president's desire to avoid divisive issues led him at times to value harmony and popularity over justice. One observer called the Eisenhower years "the time of the great postponement."

Opinion of Eisenhower's presidency has improved with time, however. He presided with steady self-confidence over a prosperous nation. In dealing with crises, he displayed good judgment and firmness of purpose. He fulfilled his pledge to end the war in Korea, refused to intervene militarily in Indochina, and maintained the peace in the face of explosive global tensions.

Eisenhower's greatest decisions were the wars he chose to avoid. After the truce in Korea, not a single American soldier died in combat during his two administrations, something no president since has achieved. For the most part, he acted with poise, restraint, and intelligence in managing an increasingly complex cold war.

If Eisenhower refused to take the lead in addressing social and racial problems, he did balance the budget while sustaining the major reforms of the New Deal. If he tolerated unemployment of as much as 7 percent, he saw to it that inflation remained minimal.

Still, it is fair to ask what might have happened if Eisenhower had invested his enormous prestige and popularity in the civil rights movement. Because he did not, his successors were forced to try to improve race relations in a much more volatile political and social climate.

Eisenhower's January 17, 1961, farewell address focused on the threat posed to government integrity by "an immense military establishment and a large arms industry." It was striking for Eisenhower, a celebrated military leader, to highlight the dangers of a large "military-industrial complex" exerting "unwarranted influence" in Congress and the White House.

Eisenhower confessed that his greatest disappointment was that he could affirm only that "war has been avoided," not that "a lasting peace is in sight." Eisenhower, who never promoted warfare as an instrument of foreign policy, pledged to "do anything to achieve peace within honorable means. I'll travel anywhere. I'll talk to anyone." His successors would not be as successful in keeping war at bay.

# CHAPTER REVIEW

## SUMMARY

- **Eisenhower's Dynamic Conservatism**  President Eisenhower promoted *moderate Republicanism*, or "dynamic conservatism." While critical of excessive government spending on social programs, he expanded Social Security coverage and launched ambitious public works programs, such as the *Federal-Aid Highway Act (1956)*. Interstate highways helped stimulate the rise of *suburbia*, which transformed social life for many Americans and contributed to a declining quality of life in inner cities. The need for more housing in the fifties was in part a function of the *baby boom*.

- **Growth of the U.S. Economy**  High levels of federal spending continued during the postwar period. The *GI Bill of Rights (1944)* boosted home buying and helped many veterans attend college and enter the middle class. Consumer demand for homes, cars, and household goods fueled the economy.

- **Critics of Mainstream Culture**  The *Beats* and many other writers and artists rejected what they claimed was the suffocating conformity of middle-class life. Adolescents rebelled through acts of juvenile delinquency and a new form of sexually provocative music called rock 'n' roll. Pockets of chronic poverty persisted despite record-breaking economic growth, and people of color did not prosper to the extent that white Americans did.

- **Civil Rights Movement**  During the early 1950s, the NAACP mounted legal challenges to states that refused to create racially segregated public schools. In *Brown v. Board of Education (1954)*, the U.S. Supreme Court nullified the *separate-but-equal* doctrine. Many white southerners adopted a strategy of *massive resistance* against court-ordered desegregation. In response, civil rights activists used *nonviolent civil disobedience* to force local and state officials to allow integration, as demonstrated in the *Montgomery bus boycott (1955–1956)* in Alabama and the forced desegregation of public schools in Little Rock, Arkansas. Martin Luther King organized the *Southern Christian Leadership Conference (SCLC)* after white violence against activists in Little Rock. In 1957, Congress passed a Civil Rights Act intended to stop discrimination against black voters in the South, but it was rarely enforced.

- **American Foreign Policy in the 1950s**  Eisenhower's first major foreign-policy accomplishment was to end the fighting in Korea. Thereafter, he kept the United States out of war and relied on secret *Central Intelligence Agency (CIA)* intervention, financial and military aid, and threats of *massive retaliation* to stem the spread of communism.  Eisenhower's belief in the *falling-domino theory* deepened U.S. support for the government in South Vietnam in its war with North Vietnam and the Communist *Viet Cong* insurgents. In 1956, Eisenhower opposed the invasion of Egypt by Israeli, French, and British forces determined to take control of the strategic Suez Canal. The *Suez crisis (1956)* was resolved when the invaders withdrew from Egypt in response to U.S. pressure.

# CHRONOLOGY

| | |
|---|---|
| **1944** | Congress passes the GI Bill of Rights |
| **1951** | Alan Freed coins the term rock 'n' roll |
| **1952** | Eisenhower wins the presidency |
| **July 1953** | Armistice is reached in Korea |
| **1954** | Supreme Court decides *Brown v. Board of Education of Topeka, Kansas* |
| **July 1954** | Geneva Accords adopted |
| **December 1955** | Montgomery, Alabama, bus boycott begins |
| **1956** | Congress passes the Federal-Aid Highway Act |
| | Soviets suppress Hungarian revolt |
| **1957** | Federal troops sent to protect students attempting to integrate Central High School in Little Rock, Arkansas |
| | Soviet Union launches *Sputnik* satellite |
| **1960** | U-2 Incident |

## KEY TERMS

**moderate Republicanism** p. 1150

**Federal-Aid Highway Act (1956)** p. 1153

**GI Bill of Rights (1944)** p. 1158

**suburbia** p. 1159

**baby boom (1946–1964)** p. 1163

**Beats** p. 1166

**separate-but-equal** p. 1170

***Brown v. Board of Education* (1954)** p. 1170

**massive resistance** p. 1171

**Montgomery bus boycott (1955–1956)** p. 1172

**nonviolent civil disobedience** p. 1172

**Southern Christian Leadership Conference (SCLC)** p. 1176

**massive retaliation** p. 1178

**Central Intelligence Agency (CIA)** p. 1178

**Dien Bien Phu (1954)** p. 1180

**Viet Cong** p. 1180

**falling-domino theory** p. 1180

**Suez crisis** p. 1184

 INQUIZITIVE

**Go to InQuizitive to see what you've learned—and learn what you've missed—with personalized feedback along the way.**

# 29 A New Frontier and a Great Society

## 1960–1968

**March on Washington** Marchers hold aloft picket signs calling for "INTEGRATED SCHOOLS NOW!," "EQUAL RIGHTS," "JOBS FOR ALL," and CIVIL RIGHTS LAWS NOW." They were among the more than 250,000 people nationwide who joined the March on Washington for Jobs and Freedom on August 28, 1963. The march was televised extensively, and was host to Martin Luther King Jr.'s landmark "I Have a Dream" speech. At the time, it was the largest protest ever held in the nation's capital.

For those who considered the fifties dull, the following decade provided a striking contrast. The 1960s were years of extraordinary social turbulence and liberal activism, tragic assassinations and painful trauma, cultural conflict and youth rebellion, civil rights and civil unrest. Assassins killed four of the most important leaders of the time: John F. Kennedy, Malcolm X, Martin Luther King Jr., and Robert F. Kennedy.

The "politics of expectation" that a British journalist said shone brightly in John Kennedy's short tenure as president did not die with him in November 1963. Instead, his idealistic commitment to improving America's quality of life—for everyone—was given new meaning by his successor, Texan Lyndon B. Johnson, whose war on poverty and Great Society programs outstripped Franklin Roosevelt's New Deal in their scope and promises.

Johnson's energy and legislative savvy resulted in a blizzard of new programs as many social issues that had been ignored or postponed for decades—civil rights for people of color, equality for women, gay and lesbian rights, medical insurance, federal aid to the poor—forced their way to the forefront of national concerns.

In the end, however, Johnson promised too much. The Great Society programs fell victim to unrealistic hopes, poor execution, and the nation's expanding involvement in Vietnam. The deeply entrenched assumptions of the cold war led the nation into the longest, most controversial, and least successful war in its history.

## focus questions

**1.** How did President John F. Kennedy try to contain communism abroad and pursue civil rights and other social programs at home?

**2.** What were the strategies and achievements of the civil rights movement in the 1960s? What divisions emerged among its activists?

**3.** What were President Lyndon B. Johnson's major war on poverty and Great Society initiatives? How did they impact American society?

**4.** What were Kennedy's and Johnson's motivations for deepening America's military involvement in the Vietnam War?

**5.** What issues propelled Richard Nixon to victory in the 1968 presidential election?

# THE NEW FRONTIER

In his 1960 speech accepting the Democratic presidential nomination, John F. Kennedy (JFK) showcased the muscular language that would characterize his campaign and his presidency: "We stand today on the edge of a **New Frontier**—the frontier of unknown opportunities and perils—a frontier of unfulfilled hopes and threats." He wanted Americans to explore "science and space, unsolved problems of peace and war, unconquered pockets of ignorance and prejudice, unanswered questions of poverty and surplus."

Kennedy and his staff fastened upon the frontier metaphor as the label for their proposed domestic programs because they believed Americans had always been eager to conquer and exploit new frontiers. Kennedy promised to get the country "moving again" and to be more aggressive in waging the cold war with the Soviet Union than Dwight Eisenhower had been.

**KENNEDY VERSUS NIXON**   In 1960, the presidential election featured two candidates—Vice President Richard M. Nixon and Massachusetts senator John F. Kennedy—of similar ages and life experiences. Both were elected to Congress in 1946, both were Navy veterans, and both preferred foreign affairs over domestic issues.

But in fact, they were more different than alike. Although Nixon was Dwight Eisenhower's vice president for two terms, Eisenhower had grave misgivings about him. When asked by reporters to name a single major accomplishment of his vice president, Ike replied: "If you give me a week, I might think of one."

The two Republican leaders had long had a testy relationship. Nixon once called Eisenhower "a goddamned old fool," while the president dismissed his vice president as a man who couldn't "think of anything but politics." On more than one occasion, Eisenhower had sought to dump Nixon in favor of other Republicans whom he respected.

A native of California, the forty-seven-year-old Nixon was the son of a shopkeeper. All his life he had fought to be a success, first as an attorney, then as a congressman. He had come to Washington after the Second World War eager to reverse the tide of New Deal liberalism. His visibility among Republicans rose when he led the anti-Communist hearings in Congress during the McCarthy hysteria.

Nixon—graceless, awkward, and stiff—proved to be one of the most complicated political figures in American history. By 1960, he had become known as "Tricky Dick," a cunning deceiver who concealed his real ideas and bigoted attitudes. Kennedy told an aide that "Nixon doesn't know who he

**The Kennedy–Nixon debates** Nixon's decision to debate his less prominent opponent on television backfired.

is . . . so every time he makes a speech he has to decide which Nixon he is, and that will be very exhausting."

Unlike Nixon, the forty-three-year-old Kennedy lit up a room with his smile and zest for life. More pragmatic than principled, more personality than character, he was handsome, articulate, and blessed with youthful energy and wit. Coolly analytical and dangerously self-absorbed, he was a contradictory and elusive political celebrity. But this much is certain: Kennedy had a bright, agile mind; a Harvard education; a record of heroism in the Second World War; a rich and powerful Roman Catholic family; and a beautiful and accomplished young wife. In the words of a southern senator, Kennedy combined "the best qualities of Elvis Presley and Franklin D. Roosevelt"—a combination that played well in the first-ever televised presidential debate.

Some 70 million people tuned in to watch the debate. They saw an uncomfortable Nixon, ill with a virus and perspiring heavily; he looked pale, haggard, and as a number of viewers described, even somewhat menacing. By contrast, Kennedy looked tanned and confident. He offered crisp answers that made him appear qualified for the nation's highest office. The morning after the debate, his approval ratings skyrocketed. The *Chicago Daily News* asked, "Was Nixon Sabotaged by TV Makeup Artists?"

Kennedy's political rise owed much to the public relations campaign engineered by his father, Joseph, a self-made tycoon with a genius for promotion who believed that *image* was much more important than substance. "Can't you get it into your head," he told his son John, "that it's not important what you *really* are? The only important thing is what people *think* you are." The elder Kennedy hired talented writers to produce his son's two books, paid a publisher to print them, purchased thousands of copies to make them "best sellers," and helped engineer his son's elections to the House and Senate.

John Kennedy was a relentless presidential campaigner, traveling 65,000 miles, visiting twenty-five states, and making more than 350 speeches. In an address to Protestant ministers in Texas, he neutralized concerns about his being a Roman Catholic by stressing that the pope would never "tell the President—should he be a Catholic—how to act."

Kennedy emphasized that he was tired of reading about what Soviet and Cuban leaders were doing. He wanted to read about what the U.S. president was doing to combat communism. "The enemy," Kennedy said in 1960, "is the Communist system itself—implacable, insatiable, increasing in its drive for world domination." He saw the cold war as a "struggle for supremacy between two conflicting ideologies: freedom under God versus ruthless, godless tyranny."

Although Kennedy worked to increase voter registration among African Americans, his response to the growing civil rights movement was ambivalent. Like Eisenhower, Kennedy believed racial unrest needed to be handled with caution. To him, racial justice was less an urgent moral crusade than a potential barrier to his election. He understood the injustices of bigotry and segregation, but he needed the votes of southern whites to win the presidency.

During the campaign, Kennedy won the hearts of many black voters by helping to get Martin Luther King Jr. discharged from a Georgia prison after King had been convicted of trespassing in an all-white restaurant in a downtown department store, where he and members of the Student Nonviolent Coordinating Committee (SNCC) had organized a sit-in. On the Sunday before Election Day, a million leaflets describing Kennedy's effort to release King from prison were distributed in African American churches across the nation.

In November, Kennedy and his running mate, Texas senator Lyndon B. Johnson, won one of the closest presidential elections in history. Their margin was only 118,574 votes out of more than 68 million cast, a record turnout.

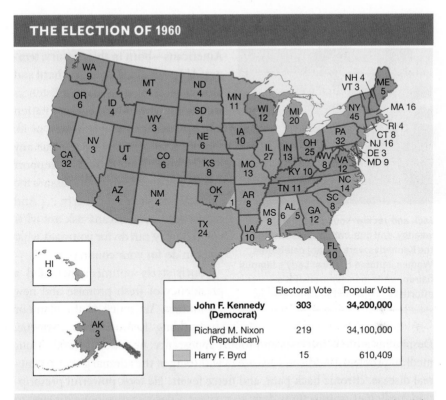

## THE ELECTION OF 1960

| | Electoral Vote | Popular Vote |
|---|---|---|
| **John F. Kennedy (Democrat)** | **303** | **34,200,000** |
| Richard M. Nixon (Republican) | 219 | 34,100,000 |
| Harry F. Byrd | 15 | 610,409 |

■ How did the election of 1960 represent a sea change in American presidential politics?

■ How did John F. Kennedy win the election in spite of winning fewer states than Richard M. Nixon?

Nixon won more states, but Kennedy captured 70 percent of the black vote, which proved decisive in at least three key states. Nixon convinced himself that the Democrats had stolen the election through chicanery in Illinois and Texas, but recounts confirmed the vote totals.

**A VIGOROUS NEW ADMINISTRATION** John F. Kennedy was the youngest person and the first Roman Catholic elected president. His inauguration ceremony on a cold, sunny, blustery January day introduced the nation to his distinctive elegance and flair. In his speech, he focused almost entirely on foreign affairs. He accepted the responsibility of "defending freedom in its hour of maximum danger" and promised to keep America strong while seeking to reduce friction with the Soviet Union: "Let us never negotiate out of fear, but let us never fear to negotiate."

**Jack and Jackie** Young, dashing, wealthy, and culturally sophisticated, the Kennedys were instant celebrities. Women imitated the First Lady's famous hairdo, while men admired JFK's effortless "cool" and youthful energy.

Kennedy claimed "that the torch has been passed to a new generation of Americans—born in this century, tempered by war, disciplined by a hard and bitter peace," and he dazzled listeners with uplifting words: "Let every nation know, whether it wishes us well or ill, that we shall pay any price, bear any burden, meet any hardship, support any friend, oppose any foe, to assure the survival and success of liberty. . . . And so, my fellow Americans: ask not what your country can do for you—ask what *you* can do for your country."

Such steely optimism heralded a presidency of fresh promise and new beginnings. Yet much of the glamour surrounding Kennedy was cosmetic. Despite his athletic interests and robust appearance, he suffered from serious medical problems: Addison's disease (a withering of the adrenal glands), venereal disease, chronic back pain, and fierce fevers. He took powerful prescription medicines or injections daily to manage a degenerative bone disease, to deal with anxiety, to help him sleep, and to control his allergies. (All the medications gave Kennedy the perpetual tan that the public interpreted as a sign of good health.) Kennedy and his associates also hid both his physical ailments and his often reckless sexual dalliances in the White House with a galaxy of women, including actress Marilyn Monroe and Judith Campbell Exner, the girlfriend of a Chicago mob boss.

Kennedy represented a new wave of political figures who had fought in the Second World War. Known as the "pragmatic generation," they were decisive, bold, and prized courage and conviction in the face of the cold war and the threat of nuclear conflict. With at times an almost dismissive arrogance, Kennedy frequently complained about "academics" who criticized statesmen without exercising responsibility themselves. In the White House, he observed, he and others could not afford to be professorial. The Oval Office was "where decisions have to be made."

Kennedy appointed his younger brother Robert ("Bobby") as attorney general even though he had never tried a case or even practiced law. The *New York Times* called the younger Kennedy's qualifications "insufficient," and the *Wall*

*Street Journal* predicted he would be an "unmitigated disaster." The president, however, assured skeptics that his brother could learn "on the job."

**A BALKY CONGRESS** President Kennedy had a difficult time launching his New Frontier domestic program. Conservative southern Democrats joined Republicans in blocking Kennedy's efforts to increase federal aid to education, provide medical insurance for the aged, and establish a cabinet-level department of urban affairs and housing to address inner-city poverty. In his first year, Kennedy submitted 355 legislative requests; Congress approved only half of them. He complained that he "couldn't get a Mother's Day resolution through the goddamned Congress."

Legislators did approve increasing the minimum wage; a Housing Act that earmarked nearly $5 billion for new public-housing projects in poverty-stricken inner-city areas; the Peace Corps, which recruited idealistic young volunteers who would provide educational and technical service abroad; and the Alliance for Progress, a financial assistance program to Latin American countries intended to blunt the appeal of communism. In 1963, Kennedy also signed the Equal Pay Act, which required that women performing the same jobs as men be paid the same. But his efforts to provide more assistance for educational programs and for medical care for the elderly never got out of committees.

News that the Soviets had launched the first manned space flight in 1961 prompted Kennedy's greatest legislative success. He convinced Congress to commit $40 billion to put an American on the moon within ten years. (The goal was achieved in 1969.)

**JFK AND CIVIL RIGHTS** The most important developments in domestic life during the sixties occurred in civil rights. Like Franklin D. Roosevelt and Dwight Eisenhower, President Kennedy celebrated racial equality but did little to promote it until forced to do so.

Although racial segregation remained firmly in place in the South, Kennedy was reluctant to challenge conservative southern Democrats on this explosive issue. Both he and his brother Bobby, his closest adviser, had to be dragged into supporting the civil rights movement. After appointing Harris Wofford, a white law professor and campaigner for racial equality, as the special presidential assistant for civil rights, President Kennedy told him "to make substantial headway against . . . the nonsense of racial discrimination," but to do so with "minimum civil rights legislation [and] maximum Executive action." Such an approach led Martin Luther King Jr. to comment that

Kennedy had great political skill but no "moral passion" about the need to end racial injustice.

**CATASTROPHE IN CUBA** Kennedy's performance in foreign relations was spectacularly mixed. Although he had told a reporter that he wanted to "break out of the confines of the cold war," he quickly found himself reinforcing its ideological assumptions. While still a senator, Kennedy had blasted President Eisenhower for not being tough enough with the Soviets and for allowing Fidel Castro and his Communist followers to take over Cuba, just ninety miles from the southern tip of Florida.

Soon after his inauguration, Kennedy learned that Eisenhower had approved a secret CIA operation to train some 1,500 anti-Castro Cubans to invade their homeland in hopes of triggering a mass uprising against Castro. U.S. military leaders assured Kennedy that the invasion plan, called Operation Trinidad, was feasible; CIA analysts and the Joint Chiefs of Staff naively predicted that news of the invasion would inspire anti-Castro Cubans to rebel. Secretary of Defense Robert McNamara, National Security Advisor McGeorge Bundy, and Bobby Kennedy endorsed the plan, as did the new president.

The ragtag group of Miami-based Cuban exiles, trained by the CIA and transported on American ships, landed before dawn at the **Bay of Pigs** on Cuba's south shore on April 17, 1961. Having been tipped off by spies, Castro had 20,000 soldiers waiting. Kennedy panicked when he realized the operation was failing, and he refused pleas from the rebels for support from U.S. warplanes that Kennedy had promised. General Lyman Lemnitzer, chair of the Joint Chiefs of Staff, said that Kennedy's "pulling out the rug [on the Cuban invaders] was . . . absolutely reprehensible, almost criminal." More than a hundred of the invaders were killed and more than 1,200 were captured. (Kennedy later paid $53 million for their release.)

The failed operation humiliated Kennedy and elevated Castro in the eyes of the world. A *New York Times* columnist reported that the Americans "looked like fools to our friends, rascals to our enemies, and incompetents to the rest." In Moscow, Nikita Khrushchev asked if Kennedy could "really be that indecisive?"

To his credit, Kennedy admitted that the Bay of Pigs invasion was a "colossal mistake." Only later did he learn that the planners had assumed that he would commit American forces if the invasion effort failed. He said that after the initial disastrous reports from the Bay of Pigs, "we all looked at each other and asked, 'How could we have been so stupid?'"

**THE VIENNA SUMMIT** Just weeks after the Bay of Pigs invasion, President Kennedy met Soviet premier Khrushchev at a summit conference in Vienna, Austria. Khrushchev badgered Kennedy, bragged about the superiority of communism, and threatened to take full control of Berlin, the divided city inside Communist East Germany. Kennedy confided to a journalist that the summit "was awful. Worst thing of my life. He rolled right over me—he thinks I'm a fool—he thinks I'm weak. . . . He treated me like a little boy." When asked what he planned to do next, Kennedy replied: "I have to confront them [the Soviets] someplace to show that we're tough."

The first thing Kennedy did upon returning to the White House was to request an estimate of how many Americans might be killed in a nuclear war with the Soviet Union. The answer was chilling: 70 million. Kennedy, desperate not to appear weak in the face of Khrushchev's aggressive actions in Germany, asked Congress for additional spending on defense and called up 156,000 members of the Army Reserve and National Guard to protect West Berlin. He also ordered an armed military convoy to travel from West Germany across East Germany to West Berlin to show the Soviets that he would use force to protect the city. "West Berlin," he declared, "has become . . . the great testing place of Western courage and will."

The Soviets responded on August 13, 1961. They stopped all traffic between East and West Berlin and began erecting the twenty-seven-mile-long **Berlin Wall** to separate East Berlin from West Berlin, where thousands of refugees were fleeing communism each week. For the United States, the wall became a powerful propaganda weapon in the cold war. As Kennedy said, "Freedom has many difficulties and democracy is not perfect, but we have never had to put up a wall to keep our people in."

The Berlin Wall demonstrated the Soviets' willingness to challenge American resolve in Europe. In response, Kennedy gave a televised address alerting the nation to the significance of the Berlin crisis. Then, he and Secretary of Defense Robert McNamara embarked upon the most intensive arms race in history. The administration increased the number of nuclear missiles fivefold, added 300,000 men to the armed forces, and created the U.S. Special Forces (Green Berets), an elite group of commandos who specialized in guerrilla warfare and could provide a "more flexible response" to hot spots around the world.

In contrast to the Eisenhower–Dulles emphasis on "massive retaliation," Kennedy sought more military flexibility: "We intend to have a wider choice than humiliation or all-out war." He and McNamara also launched a civil defense program focused on the construction of nuclear fallout shelters.

**Severed ties** Two West Berliners climb the newly constructed Berlin Wall to talk with a family member at an open window.

Secretly, they commissioned an analysis of the implications of launching a full-scale nuclear strike against the Soviet Union in response to any effort to invade West Berlin.

**THE CUBAN MISSILE CRISIS** In the fall of 1962, Nikita Khrushchev and the Soviets decided to challenge President Kennedy again. To protect Communist Cuba and show critics at home that he was not afraid of the Americans, Khrushchev approved the secret installation of Soviet missiles on the island nation. The Soviets felt justified in doing so because Kennedy, after the Bay of Pigs invasion, had ordered that U.S. missiles with nuclear warheads be installed in Turkey, along the Soviet border.

On October 16, 1962, Kennedy learned that photos taken by U.S. spy planes showed some forty Soviet missile sites and twenty-five jet bombers in Cuba. Somehow, the president had to convince the Soviets to remove the missiles. But how? As the air force chief of staff told Kennedy, "You're in a pretty bad fix, Mr. President."

Over the next thirteen days, Kennedy and the National Security Council (NSC) considered several possible responses. The world held its breath as the NSC discussed the unthinkable possibility of a nuclear exchange with the Soviets.

Eventually, the NSC fastened on two options: (1) a "surgical" air strike on the missiles, followed, if necessary, by an invasion, or (2) a naval blockade of Cuba in which U.S. warships would stop Soviet vessels and search them for missiles. Although most of the military advisers supported the first option, Kennedy chose the blockade, prompting a general to shout, "You're screwed! You're screwed!"

But Kennedy had been burned by overconfident military advisers during the Bay of Pigs operation, and he was not going to let it happen again. He also feared that an American attack on Cuba would give the Soviets an excuse to take control of West Berlin.

On October 22, Kennedy delivered a televised speech of the "highest national urgency," announcing that the U.S. Navy was establishing a "quarantine" of Cuba to prevent Soviet ships from delivering more weapons to the island nation. Kennedy added that he had "directed the armed forces to prepare for any eventuality." He closed by urging the Soviets to "move the world back from the abyss of destruction." Tensions grew, and some 200,000 U.S. soldiers made their way to southern Florida.

Khrushchev replied that Soviet ships would ignore the quarantine and accused Kennedy of "an act of aggression propelling humankind into the abyss of a world nuclear-missile war." Despite such rhetoric, however, on Wednesday, October 24, five Soviet ships, presumably with more missiles aboard, stopped well short of the quarantine line.

Two days later, Khrushchev, knowing that the United States enjoyed a 5 to 1 advantage in nuclear weapons, offered a deal. Neither he nor Kennedy wanted to be the first to launch nuclear missiles. The Soviets would agree to remove the missiles already in Cuba in return for a *public* pledge by the United States never to invade Cuba—and a *secret* agreement to remove U.S. missiles from Turkey. Kennedy agreed. Secretary of State Dean Rusk stressed to a newscaster, "Remember, when you report this, [say] that eyeball to eyeball, they [the Soviets] blinked first."

In the aftermath of the **Cuban missile crisis,** cold war tensions subsided, in part because of several symbolic steps: an agreement to sell the Soviet Union surplus American wheat, the installation of a "hotline" telephone between Washington and Moscow to provide instant contact between the heads of government, and the removal of U.S. missiles from Turkey, Italy, and Britain.

**"PEACE FOR ALL TIME"** Approaching the brink of nuclear war led President Kennedy and others in the administration to soften their cold war rhetoric and pursue other ways to reduce the threat of atomic warfare. Kennedy told an audience at American University on June 10, 1963, that his new goal was "peace for all men and women, not merely peace in our time but peace for all time."

Soon thereafter, the president began discussions with Soviet and British leaders to reduce the risk of nuclear war. The discussions resulted in the Limited Nuclear Test Ban Treaty, ratified in September 1963, which banned the testing of nuclear weapons in the atmosphere. It was the first joint agreement of the cold war and an important move toward improved relations with the Soviet Union. As Kennedy put it, using an ancient Chinese proverb: "A journey of a thousand miles begins with one step."

**VIETNAM**  As tensions with the Soviet Union eased, events in Southeast Asia were moving toward what would become the greatest American foreign-policy calamity of the century. Throughout the fifties, U.S. officials increasingly came to view the preservation of anticommunist South Vietnam as the critical test of American willpower in the cold war. As a senator in 1956, John F. Kennedy described South Vietnam as the "cornerstone of the free world in Southeast Asia."

Yet the situation in South Vietnam had worsened under the corrupt leadership of Premier Ngo Dinh Diem and his family. Diem had backed away from promised social and economic reforms, and his repressive tactics, directed not only against Communists but also against the Buddhist majority and other critics, played into the hands of his enemies.

President Eisenhower had provided more than $1 billion in aid to Diem's government during the late fifties. Kennedy sent even more weapons, money, and some 16,000 military "advisers" to South Vietnam to help shore up the government. (They were called advisers to avoid the impression that U.S. soldiers were doing the fighting.) "If I tried to pull out," Kennedy explained, "we would have another Joe McCarthy red scare on our hands," with Republicans accusing him of "losing" Vietnam to communism. To withdraw "would be a great mistake."

In the countryside of South Vietnam, the National Liberation Front (NLF), a left-wing nationalist movement backed by Communist North Vietnam, had launched a violent insurgency in which guerrilla fighters known as the Viet Cong (VC) were winning the fight against the South Vietnamese government. American military advisers began relocating Vietnamese peasants to "strategic hamlets"—new villages ringed by barbed wire—where the VC could not receive assistance.

By the fall of 1963, Kennedy acknowledged that Diem was "out of touch with his people" and had to be removed. On November 1, Vietnamese generals, with the approval of U.S. officials in Saigon, seized control of the government. They then took a step that Kennedy had neither intended nor expected: they murdered Diem and his brother.

The rebel generals soon began fighting one another, leaving Vietnam even more vulnerable to the Communist insurgency. Thereafter, for the next several years, South Vietnam essentially became an American colony. The United States put Vietnamese generals in power, gave them orders, and provided massive financial support, much of which was diverted into the hands of corrupt politicians and their families.

By September 1963, Kennedy had developed doubts about his ability to defend the South Vietnamese. "In the final analysis," he told aides, "it's their war. . . . We can help them as advisers but they have to win it." Yet only a week later, in a televised interview, Kennedy reiterated the domino theory endorsed by Presidents Truman and Eisenhower, saying that if South Vietnam fell to communism, the rest of Southeast Asia would follow. He stressed that "we should stay [in South Vietnam]. We should use our influence in as effective a way as we can, but we should not withdraw."

**KENNEDY'S ASSASSINATION** What Kennedy would have done in Vietnam has remained a matter of endless discussion, because his presidency was brought to an untimely end. At noon on November 22, 1963, while riding in an open car through Dallas, Texas, he was shot and killed by Lee Harvey Oswald, a twenty-four-year-old ex-Marine turned Communist. Oswald idolized Fidel Castro and hated the United States. As he fled after shooting Kennedy, he also killed a Dallas policeman.

Kennedy seemed to have had a premonition of his death. "We're heading into nut country today," he warned his wife that morning. "But Jackie, if somebody wants to shoot me from a window with a rifle, nobody can stop it, so why worry about it?"

Debate still swirls about whether Oswald, who had lived in the Soviet Union and had met with officials in Cuba, acted alone or as part of a conspiracy, because he did not live long enough to tell his story. As Oswald was being transported to a court hearing, Jack Ruby, a Dallas nightclub owner distraught over Kennedy's death, shot and killed Oswald as a nationwide television audience watched.

Kennedy's assassination and heartrending funeral enshrined the president in the public imagination as a martyred leader cut down in the prime of life. He came to have a stronger reputation after his death than he enjoyed in life. "That debonair touch, that shock of chestnut hair, that beguiling grin, that shattering understatement—these are what we shall remember," wrote newspaper columnist Mary McGrory.

Kennedy's thousand-day presidency had flamed up and out like a comet hitting the earth's atmosphere. Yet all the transformational events of the later

1960s—the Vietnam War, the civil rights revolution, and the youth rebellion—were set in motion during his brief time in the White House. With his death, Americans wept in the streets, and the world was on edge as the nation buried its fallen president.

## CIVIL RIGHTS TRIUMPHANT

During the sixties, Martin Luther King Jr. remained the face and heart of the civil rights movement. He was an uplifting example of fortitude and dignity in confronting brutality and oppression; he had an astonishing capacity for forgiveness and a deep understanding of the dynamics of political power and social change. Yet he was also immensely complicated and contradictory, even hypocritical, as the FBI discovered by subjecting him to relentless electronic surveillance and even blackmail.

King was neither a genius nor a saint, but his shortcomings pale when compared to his achievements. He was an inspiring example of courage, conviction, and dignity in the face of often violent prejudice and persecution. With the help of those he led, King changed the trajectory of American history—for the better. Alas, like the Kennedy brothers, he did not live to see the promised land made possible by his actions.

**SIT-INS**    The civil rights movement gained momentum when four African American college students sat down and ordered coffee and doughnuts at an "all-white" Woolworth's lunch counter in Greensboro, North Carolina, on February 1, 1960. The clerk refused to serve them, explaining that blacks had to eat standing up or take their food outside.

The Greensboro Four, as the students came to be called, waited forty-five minutes and then returned the next day with two dozen more students. As they sat for hours, fruitlessly waiting to be served, some read Bibles; others read Henry David Thoreau's famous essay on civil disobedience. They returned every day for a week, patiently tolerating the hostility of white hooligans.

Within two months, similar sit-ins—involving 50,000 blacks and whites, men and women, young and old—had occurred in more than 100 cities. Black comedian Dick Gregory participated in several sit-ins. When the managers told him, "We don't serve Negroes," he replied: "No problem, I don't eat Negroes." Some 3,600 people were arrested nationwide, but the sit-ins worked. By the end of July 1960, officials in Greensboro lifted the whites-only policy.

**Civil rights and its peaceful warriors** Joseph McNeil, Franklin McCain, Billy Smith, and Clarence Henderson (listed from left) await service on day two of their sit-in at the Woolworth's in Greensboro, North Carolina. A painful irony of the Jim Crow system was how African Americans could work at diners but not eat there.

In April 1960, some 200 student activists, black and white, converged in Raleigh, North Carolina, to form the **Student Nonviolent Coordinating Committee (SNCC—**pronounced "snick"). Their goal was to intensify the effort to dismantle segregation. SNCC expanded the sit-ins to include "kneel-ins" at all-white churches and "wade-ins" at segregated public swimming pools. In many communities, demonstrators were pelted with rocks, burned with cigarettes, and even killed by white racists. As a Florida hog farmer named Holstead "Hoss" Manucy told a journalist, "I ain't got no bad habits. Don't smoke. Don't cuss. My only bad habit is fightin' niggahs."

**FREEDOM RIDES** In 1961, civil rights leaders decided to focus on integrating public transportation, namely buses and trains. Their larger goal was to force President Kennedy to embrace the cause of civil rights in the South. On May 4, the New York–based Congress of Racial Equality (CORE), led by James Farmer, decided to put "the civil rights movement on wheels" when a courageous group of eighteen black and white **Freedom Riders**, as they were called,

**Freedom Riders** On May 14, 1961, a white mob in Alabama assaulted a Freedom Bus, flinging fire bombs into its windows and beating the activists as they emerged. Here, the Freedom Riders sit outside the burnt shell of their bus.

boarded two buses traveling from Washington, D.C., through the Lower South to New Orleans. They wanted to test a federal court ruling that banned racial segregation on buses and trains, and in terminals.

On May 14, a mob of white racists in rural Alabama, many of them Klansmen, surrounded the Greyhound bus carrying the Freedom Riders. After throwing a firebomb into the bus, the mob barricaded its door. "Burn them alive," one yelled. "Fry the damned niggers." The riders were able to escape the bus, only to be battered with metal pipes, chains, and clubs.

A few hours later, Freedom Riders on a second bus were beaten after entering whites-only waiting rooms at a terminal in Birmingham, Alabama. Even journalists covering the incident were beaten and their cameras destroyed. The city police, it turned out, had encouraged the assaults. The brutality, displayed on television, caused national outrage. The Freedom Riders wanted to continue their trip, but the bus drivers refused out of concern for their own safety.

When Diane Nash, a black college student and SNCC leader in Nashville, Tennessee, heard about the violence in Birmingham, she recruited new riders. President Kennedy called her, warning that she could "get killed if you do this." Her response: "It doesn't matter if we're killed. Others will come—others will come."

On May 17, Nash and ten other students took a bus to Birmingham, where they were arrested. While in jail, they sang "freedom songs," many of which were versions of old gospel hymns or spirituals: "We'll Never Turn Back," "Ain't Gonna Let Nobody Turn Me Around," "We Shall Overcome." Their joyous rebelliousness so frustrated Eugene "Bull" Connor, the city's racist police chief, that he drove them in the middle of the night to the Tennessee state line and dropped them off to walk. Instead of going back to Nashville, however, the students returned to Birmingham.

To President Kennedy, the Freedom Riders were a "pain in the ass." He called them "publicity seekers" who were threatening to embarrass him and the United States on the eve of his summit meeting with Soviet leader Nikita Khrushchev. Kennedy ordered Harris Wofford, his special assistant on civil rights, to end the freedom rides: "Can't you get your goddamned friends off those buses? Stop them!"

When Kennedy suggested to several civil rights leaders that they allow things to "cool off," James Farmer replied that blacks had been "cooling off for a hundred years. . . . If we got any cooler, we'd be in the deep freeze."

The activists finally forced the president to provide another bus, which enabled them to renew the journey to New Orleans. When the new group of riders reached Montgomery, the capital of Alabama, white racists attacked them. The next night, civil rights activists, including Martin Luther King Jr., gathered at a Montgomery church to honor the Freedom Riders. But their meeting was interrupted by a mob of whites armed with rocks and fire bombs.

Ministers made frantic appeals to the White House. Kennedy responded by urging the Alabama governor to intervene. After midnight, national guardsmen arrived. The Freedom Riders continued into Mississippi, where they were jailed. They never made it to New Orleans.

Still, their courage and principled resistance—along with that of federal judges whose rulings supported integration efforts—prompted the Interstate Commerce Commission (ICC) in September 1961 to order that all interstate transportation facilities be integrated. Equally important, the Freedom Riders kindled the rapid growth of civil rights groups. The freedom rides were a crucial turning point in the civil rights movement.

Despite the court rulings, white segregationists remained violently opposed to racial equality. In Birmingham in September 1962, King was speaking at the meeting of the Southern Christian Leadership Conference when a white member of the American Nazi party jumped to the stage and punched him in the face. King simply dropped his hands and allowed the man to hit him again. "Don't touch him," King yelled. "We have to pray for him." King was determined, as an aide said, to "love segregation to death." His home was bombed three times, and he was arrested fourteen times, yet he kept telling people to use "the weapon of nonviolence, the breastplate of righteousness, the armor of truth, and just keep marching."

**JAMES MEREDITH** In the fall of 1962, James Meredith, an African American student and air force veteran whose grandfather had been a slave, tried to enroll at the all-white University of Mississippi in Oxford. Ross Barnett, the governor of Mississippi, refused to allow Meredith to register. Breathing defiance, Barnett vowed "to rot in jail" rather than "let one Negro ever darken the sacred threshold of our white schools."

U.S. Attorney General Robert F. Kennedy dispatched federal marshals to enforce the law, but when they were assaulted by a white mob shouting "Go to Hell, JFK," the president sent National Guard troops. Their arrival ignited rioting that left two dead and dozens injured. Once the violence subsided, Meredith was registered at the university. "Only in America," a reporter noted, "would the federal government send thousands of troops to enforce the right of an otherwise obscure citizen to attend a particular university."

**BIRMINGHAM** In early 1963, in conjunction with the celebration of the 100th anniversary of Abraham Lincoln's Emancipation Proclamation, Martin Luther King Jr. organized a massive series of demonstrations in Birmingham. Alabama was now led by George Wallace, an openly racist governor who had vowed to protect "segregation now, segregation tomorrow, segregation forever!"

King knew that weeks of public demonstrations would likely provoke violence and result in thousands of arrests, but a victory in Birmingham, he felt, would "break the back of segregation all over the nation" by revealing southern "brutality openly—in the light of day—with the rest of the world looking on" through television cameras.

The Birmingham campaign began with sit-ins at restaurants, picket lines at segregated businesses, and a march on city hall. The police arrested and jailed hundreds of activists. Each day, however, more demonstrators, black and white, joined the efforts. As thousands of demonstrators marched through Birmingham streets on May 7, the all-white police force led by "Bull" Connor used snarling dogs, tear gas, electric cattle prods, and high-pressure fire hoses on the protesters. Millions of Americans were outraged when they saw the ugly confrontations on television. "The civil rights movement," President Kennedy observed, "owes Bull Connor as much as it owes Abraham Lincoln." It also owed a lot to the power of television.

**Bull's dogs** Eugene "Bull" Connor ordered Birmingham police to unleash their dogs and nightsticks on civil rights demonstrators in May 1963.

More than 3,000 demonstrators were arrested, including King and several white ministers. In his cell, King wrote a "Letter from Birmingham Jail," a stirring defense of **nonviolent civil disobedience** that has become a classic document of the civil rights movement. "One who breaks an unjust law," King stressed, "must do so openly, lovingly, and with a willingness to *accept the penalty.*" In a reference to President Kennedy's timid support, King wrote that the most perplexing foe of equal justice was not the southern white bigot but "the white moderate, who is more devoted to 'order' than to justice . . . who constantly says, 'I agree with you in the goal you seek, but I cannot agree with your methods.'"

King's efforts prevailed when Birmingham officials finally agreed to end their segregationist practices. But throughout 1963, whites in the Lower South continued to defy efforts at racial integration, while blacks and white activists organized demonstrations across the nation. In 1963, Alabama was the only state where black and white students did not attend the same schools or colleges. On June 11, 1963, Alabama governor George Wallace theatrically blocked the door at the University of Alabama as African American students tried to register for classes. Wallace finally stepped aside in the face of insistent federal marshals.

That night, President Kennedy finally decided he needed to lead. In a hastily arranged televised speech, he announced that he would soon submit to Congress a major new civil rights bill that would remove race as a consideration "in American life or law." He stressed that "a great change is at hand," and he was determined to make "that change, that [civil rights] revolution," peaceful and constructive. "We are confronted primarily with a moral issue," the president said in language King had been urging him to invoke for years. "It is as old as the Scriptures and is as clear as the American Constitution. The heart of the question is whether all Americans are to be afforded equal rights and equal opportunities." He asked "every American, regardless of where he lives," to "stop and examine his conscience," for America, "for all its hopes and all its boasts, will not be fully free until all its citizens are free."

That same night, in Mississippi, a thirty-seven-year-old African American activist, Medgar Evers, listened to the president's speech in his car. Kennedy's remarks so excited him that he turned around and went home so that he could discuss the speech with his children. When Evers arrived at his house in Jackson at midnight, he was shot by a white racist lying in ambush. He died before reaching a hospital.

The killing of Medgar Evers led President Kennedy to host his first meeting of civil rights leaders in the White House.

**"I HAVE A DREAM!"**    For weeks, southern Democrats in the House of Representatives blocked President Kennedy's civil rights bill. The standoff led African American leaders to take a bold step. On August 28, some 250,000 blacks and whites, many of them schoolchildren brought in on buses, marched arm in arm down the Mall in Washington, D.C., chanting "Equality Now!" and singing "We Shall Overcome."

The **March on Washington** for Jobs and Freedom was the largest political demonstration in American history. "When you looked at the crowd," remembered a U.S. Park Service ranger, "you didn't see blacks or whites. You saw America." For almost six hours, prominent entertainers sang protest songs, and civil rights activists gave speeches calling for racial justice.

Then something remarkable happened. On the steps of the Lincoln Memorial, thirty-four-year-old Martin Luther King Jr. came to the podium. He started awkwardly. Noticing his nervousness, someone urged him to "tell 'em about the dream, Martin."

As if suddenly inspired, King set aside his prepared remarks and delivered an extraordinary sermon in the form of a speech, using righteousness and passion to inspire his listeners to action. He started slowly and picked up speed, as if he were speaking at a revival, giving poetic voice to the hopes of millions as he stressed the "fierce urgency of now" and the unstoppable power of "meeting physical force with soul force."

King then shared his dream for an America in which equality would be realized:

> In spite of the difficulties and frustrations of the moment, I still have a *dream*. It is a *dream* deeply rooted in the American dream. I have a *dream* that one day this nation will rise up and live out the true meaning of its creed: 'We hold these truths to be self-evident; that all men are created equal.' I have a *dream* that one day . . . the sons of former slaves and the sons of former slaveowners will be able to sit together at the table of brotherhood.

King summoned the nation to justice: "So let freedom ring!" he shouted, for "when we allow freedom to ring from every town and every hamlet, from every state and every city, we will be able to speed up the day when *all* God's children—black men and white men, Jews and Gentiles, Protestants and Catholics—will be able to join hands and sing in the words of the old Negro spiritual, *Free at last, free at last, thank God Almighty, we are free at last!*"

As King finished, there was a startling hush, then a deafening ovation. The crowd spontaneously joined hands and began singing "We Shall Overcome." "I have never been so proud to be a Negro," said baseball superstar Jackie Robinson. "I have never been so proud to be an American." President Kennedy, who had tried to convince organizers to call off the march, was watching on TV at the White House, just a mile away. As King spoke, the president told an aide that "he's damn good."

But King's dream remained just that—a dream deferred. Eighteen days later, four Klansmen in Birmingham detonated a bomb in a black church, killing four young girls. The murders sparked a new wave of indignation across the country and the world. The editors of the *Milwaukee Sentinel* stressed that the bombing "should serve to goad the conscience. The deaths . . . in a sense are on the hands of each of us."

**THE WARREN COURT** The civil rights movement depended as much on the courts as it did on the leadership of Martin Luther King, Rosa Parks, and others. Federal judges kept forcing states and localities to integrate schools and other public places. Under Chief Justice Earl Warren, the U.S. Supreme Court also made landmark decisions in other areas of American life.

In 1962, the Court ruled in *Engel v. Vitale* that an official statewide school prayer adopted by the New York State Board of Regents violated the constitutional prohibition against government-supported religion. In *Gideon v.*

*Wainwright* (1963), the Court required that every felony defendant be provided a lawyer regardless of the defendant's ability to pay. In 1964, the Court ruled in *Escobedo v. Illinois* that a person accused of a crime must be allowed to consult a lawyer before being interrogated by police.

Two years later, in *Miranda v. Arizona* (1966), the Court ordered that an accused person in police custody must be informed of certain basic rights: the right to remain silent; the right to know that anything said to authorities can be used against the individual in court; and the right to have a defense attorney present during interrogation. These requirements have come to be known as Miranda rights.

**FREEDOM SUMMER** During late 1963 and throughout 1964, the civil rights movement continued to grow. Racism, however, remained entrenched in the Lower South. White officials kept African Americans from voting by charging them poll taxes, forcing them to take difficult literacy tests, making the application process inconvenient, and intimidating them through arson, beatings, and lynchings.

In early 1964, Robert "Bob" Moses, a black New Yorker who had resigned from the SCLC to head the Student Nonviolent Coordinating Committee (SNCC) office in Mississippi, decided it would take "an army" to force the state to give voting rights to blacks. So he set about recruiting black and white volunteers who would live with rural African Americans, teach them in "freedom schools," and help them register to vote.

Most of the recruits for what came to be called Freedom Summer were idealistic white college students, many of them Jewish. Mississippi's white leaders prepared for "the nigger-communist invasion" by doubling the state police force and stockpiling tear gas, electric cattle prods, and shotguns.

In mid-June, the volunteer activists met at an Ohio college to learn about southern racial history, nonviolent civil disobedience, and the likely abuses they would suffer. On the final evening of training, Moses pleaded with anyone who feared heading to Mississippi to go home; several did. The next day, the volunteers boarded buses and headed south.

In all, forty-one freedom schools taught thousands of Mississippi children math, writing, and history. They also tutored black adults about the complicated process of voter registration. Stokely Carmichael, an African American student from Trinidad studying at Howard University, wrote that black Mississippians "took us in, fed us, instructed and protected us, and ultimately civilized, educated, and inspired the smartassed college students."

The Ku Klux Klan, local police, and other white racists harassed, arrested, and assaulted many of the volunteers. But the worst incident occurred on

June 21, 1964, just two days after Congress approved the Civil Rights Act, when three young SNCC workers—James Earl Chaney, Andrew Goodman, and Michael "Mickey" Schwerner—disappeared after going to investigate the burning of an African American church. Their decomposed, bullet-riddled bodies were found two months later buried in a dam at a cattle pond. They had been abducted and murdered by Klan members. While searching for the missing men, authorities found the bodies of eight black males in rivers and swamps who also had been killed. The murders, said one volunteer, were "the end of innocence," after which "things could never be the same." A growing number of black activists began to call into question Martin Luther King's nonviolent strategy.

**BLACK POWER** Racism was not limited to the South. By the mid-1960s, about 70 percent of the nation's African Americans were living in blighted urban areas, and many young blacks were losing faith in the strategy of Christian nonviolence. Inner-city poverty and frustration cried out for its own social justice movement.

The fragmentation of the civil rights movement was tragically evident on August 11, 1965, when Watts, the largest black neighborhood in Los Angeles, exploded in rioting and looting that left 34 dead, almost 4,000 in jail, and widespread property damage. Dozens of other cities experienced similar riots in the summer of 1966. Between 1965 and 1968, nearly 300 racial uprisings rocked urban America.

The violence revealed the growing civil war within the civil rights movement. As Gil Scott-Heron, a black musician, sang: "We are tired of praying and marching and thinking and learning / Brothers want to start cutting and shooting and stealing and burning." What came to be called "black power" began to compete with the integrationist, nonviolent philosophy espoused by Martin Luther King and the SCLC.

**MALCOLM X AND BLACK POWER** The most visible spokesman for the **Black Power movement** was Malcolm X, born in 1925 in Omaha, Nebraska, as Malcolm Little. His father, a Baptist minister, and his West Indian mother, supported Marcus Garvey's crusade for black nationalism in the 1920s, and his childhood home was burned to the ground by white racists. His father was killed when Malcolm was six, perhaps by white supremacists. Afterward, Malcolm's mother suffered a breakdown and was institutionalized for the rest of her life. Young Malcolm was placed in foster care, but after being expelled from school in the ninth grade, he drifted from Detroit to New York City to Boston.

**Malcolm X** The Black Power movement's most influential spokesman.

By age nineteen, Malcolm, now known as Detroit Red, had become a thief, drug dealer, and pimp. He spent seven years in Massachusetts prisons, where he joined a small Chicago-based religious sect, the Nation of Islam (NOI), whose members were called Black Muslims. The organization had little to do with Islam and everything to do with its domineering leader, Elijah Muhammad. Muhammad dismissed whites as "devils" and championed black nationalism, racial pride, self-respect, and self-discipline. By 1953, a year after leaving prison, Malcolm Little was calling himself Malcolm X in tribute to his lost African name, and he had become a full-time NOI minister famous for electrifying speeches attacking white racism and black powerlessness.

Malcolm X dismissed Martin Luther King and other mainstream civil rights leaders as "nothing but modern Uncle Toms" who "keep you and me in check, keep us under control, keep us passive and peaceful and nonviolent." He insisted that there "was no such thing as a nonviolent revolution." His militant speeches inspired thousands of mostly urban blacks to join the Nation of Islam.

Malcolm X expressed the emotions and frustrations of the inner-city African American working poor. Yet at the peak of his influence, and just as he was moderating his militant message, he became embroiled in a conflict with Elijah Muhammad that proved fatal. NOI assassins killed Malcolm X in Manhattan on February 21, 1965.

Black militancy did not end with Malcolm X, however. By 1966, "black power" had become a rallying cry for many young militants. When Stokely Carmichael became head of the Student Nonviolent Coordinating Committee (SNCC), he ousted whites from the organization. "When you talk of black power," Carmichael shouted, "you talk of bringing this country to its knees, of building a movement that will smash everything Western civilization has created." Having been beaten by whites and having seen fellow volunteers killed, Carmichael rejected the nonviolent philosophy of the civil rights movement.

**THE BLACK PANTHER PARTY** Brown and Carmichael spoke to the seething rage of the young black underclass. Soon, they and others would move from SNCC to the Black Panther Party for Self Defense (BPP), a group of black revolutionaries founded in 1966 by Huey P. Newton and Bobby Seale in Oakland, California. Newton and Seale, both college-educated, were community workers in a federal anti-poverty program. They decided to form a militant self-defense organization (the BPP) after San Francisco police killed Matthew Johnson, an unarmed black teen. The BPP called for an end to "police terrorism," full employment for African Americans, decent housing, and the release of all "black men" from prison.

Wearing black berets, leather coats, and sunglasses, and armed with rifles and shotguns, cartridge belts, a menacing swagger, and a clenched fist black power salute, Black Panthers rejected the integrationist philosophy of Martin Luther King Jr. in favor of revolutionary violence. "We do not believe in passive and nonviolent tactics," Newton explained. "They haven't worked for us black people. They are bankrupt" in the inner cities of America. "Force, guns, and arms are the real political arena." The "racist" police "in our communities are not there to protect us. They are here to contain us, to oppress us, to brutalize us."

The Black Panthers intended to "police the police" in their communities while addressing the pressing needs of their inner-city neighborhoods. They sought to become self-governing communities. To that end, they organized Free Breakfast for Children programs, offered job-training programs, and created free community health clinics. Soon, more than forty Black Panther chapters emerged in cities across America: New York, Los Angeles, Chicago, Boston, Philadelphia, and Seattle, among others.

The Black Panthers insisted that they had a right to defend themselves from police harassment and brutality. A gun battle with police in which an officer was shot and killed landed Newton in jail. Between 1967 and 1969, nine police officers and ten Black Panthers were killed in shootouts. FBI Director J. Edgar Hoover labeled the Black Panthers terrorists who constituted the "greatest threat to the internal security of the country." To meet the threat of "black nationalist hate groups," he organized a comprehensive program to undermine the Black Panther party. The efforts of the FBI, along with infighting and drug abuse among the members, destroyed the Black Panthers by 1982.

For all their violent and self-destructive behavior, the Black Panthers infused the civil rights movement with powerful insights and constructive beliefs. They affirmed that the necessary first step for African Americans seeking true equality was first to learn to love oneself and then to love and protect each other, regardless of age, gender, or sexual preference.

Audre Lorde, a powerful New York writer, the child of West Indian immigrants who described herself as a black lesbian feminist, mother, warrior, and poet, credited the Black Panthers with helping to expand the civil rights movement to include other "disenfranchised" groups such as women and gays/lesbians. Huey Newton, for example, urged the BPP "to form a working coalition with the Gay Liberation and Women's Liberation groups."

Lorde emphatically agreed, noting that people "don't lead single-issue lives." Creating a truly powerful movement for social change thus required connecting across difference to link organizations that speak to different constituencies. Activists must learn "how to take our differences and make them strengths."

The men who founded the Black Panther party proclaimed themselves "the cream of Black Manhood" who would protect and defend "our Black community." Initially, the role of female Panthers was to "stand behind black men" and be supportive. Yet despite such masculine bravado, the majority of Black Panthers were women. "The women who were drawn to the Black Panther Party were all feminists," explained Ericka Huggins, a leader of the organization. By 1969, the Black Panther Party newspaper declared that men and women were now equal members of the organization and instructed male members to treat women as equals.

Alabama-born Angela Davis, a Phi Beta Kappa graduate of Brandeis University who earned a doctoral degree in philosophy from Humboldt University in Germany and taught at the University of California at Los Angeles (UCLA), was a radical feminist aligned with SNCC, the Black Panthers, and the Communist Party. California governor Ronald Reagan ordered the Board of Regents to fire Davis for using "inflammatory language," for she repeatedly referred to police officers as "pigs."

A formidable speaker, Davis became an outspoken activist for an array of causes. She opposed the Vietnam War, racism, sexism, and the "prison-industrial complex." She also supported gay/lesbian rights and other social justice movements. "I am no longer accepting

**Panther power** Black Panthers issue a black power salute outside a San Francisco Liberation School, where activists raised awareness and appreciation of African American history, a topic often ignored by white, mainstream curricula.

the things I cannot change," she declared. "I am changing the things I cannot accept."

**THE EFFECT OF BLACK POWER**  Although widely covered in the media, the Black Power movement never attracted more than a small minority of African Americans. Still, it forced Martin Luther King and other mainstream civil rights leaders to shift their focus from the rural South to inner-city neighborhoods in the North and West.

The time had come, King declared while launching his "Poor People's Campaign" in December 1967, for radical new measures "to provide jobs and income for the poor." Yet as he and others stressed, the war in Vietnam was taking funds away from federal programs serving the poor, and black soldiers were dying in disproportionate numbers in Southeast Asia.

The Black Power movement also motivated African Americans to push for black studies programs in schools and colleges, the celebration of African cultural and artistic traditions, the organizing of inner-city voters to elect black mayors, laws forcing landlords to treat blacks fairly, and the creation of grassroots organizations and community centers in black neighborhoods. As an NOI minister, Malcolm X had insisted that blacks call themselves *African Americans* as a symbol of pride and as a spur to learn more about their history.

## THE GREAT SOCIETY

Stronger federal support for civil rights came from an unlikely source: the white Texan who succeeded John F. Kennedy in the White House. Lyndon B. Johnson, known as "LBJ," took the presidential oath on board the plane that brought Kennedy's body back to Washington from Dallas.

Johnson, who was fifty-five years old and stood six feet, four inches tall, had risen to be one of the most powerful Democratic leaders ever in the Senate during his twenty-six years in Washington. Now, this legislative magician was the first southern president since Woodrow Wilson.

Johnson's transition to the presidency was not easy. The Kennedy brothers despised him and his hardscrabble background. JFK had warned aides that Johnson was "a very insecure, sensitive man with a huge ego," and he had directed them to "kiss his ass from one end of Washington to the other." Not surprisingly, Johnson had come to hate the Kennedys.

Like Kennedy, Johnson was one of the most complex men to occupy the White House. Unlike Kennedy, however, Johnson's was a rags-to-riches story. He had worked his way out of rural Texas poverty during the Great Depression to become one of the Senate's dominant figures.

**The oath of office** Less than ninety minutes after John Kennedy's death, Lyndon Johnson took the presidential oath aboard Air Force One between his wife, Lady Bird (left), and Jacqueline Kennedy (right), before flying out of Dallas for Washington, D.C.

LBJ's personality largely shaped his successes and failures. His ego and insecurities were as massive as his vanity and ambition. He could not stand being alone, and he insisted on always being the center of attention. At press conferences, he referred to "my Vietnam policy," "my Security Council," "my Cabinet," "my legislation," and "my boys" fighting in Southeast Asia.

George Reedy, his press secretary, described Johnson as a "man of too many paradoxes." Ruthless and often bullying, needy and warmhearted, Johnson was a crude idealist and brutal optimist so thin-skinned that he took all criticism personally. In his vengeful view, people were either with him or against him, and he was rabidly impatient with anyone who dissented or diverged from his agenda.

At bottom, psychologists believed, Johnson suffered from narcissism and bipolar disorder. Being respected was not enough; he needed to be adored. Famous for his dramatic mood swings and coarse behavior, he often berated his aides with cutting profanity and belittling humor. "There's only two kinds at the White House," he told the staff. "There's elephants and there's pissants. And I'm the only elephant." Reedy described Johnson as "a miserable person— a bully, sadist, lout, and egoist."

Most of all, Johnson yearned to be recognized as a transformational leader. And, like the Kennedy brothers, he had a weakness for attractive women. He often bragged about how many women he had bedded, and when aides mentioned Kennedy's escapades, Johnson would claim that he "had more women by accident than Kennedy ever had on purpose." Early in his presidency, LBJ alerted reporters that they should ignore him "coming in and out of a few women's bedrooms while in the White House." His long-suffering wife, Claudia "Lady Bird" Johnson, explained that "Lyndon loved the human race, and half of the human race are women."

Johnson wanted to be the greatest American president, the one who did the most good for the most people by creating the most new programs. He promised to "help every child get an education, to help every Negro and every

American citizen have an equal opportunity, to help every family get a decent home, and to help bring healing to the sick and dignity to the old."

Those who dismissed him as a traditional southern conservative failed to appreciate his genuine compassion for the poor and his embrace of civil rights. "I'm going to be the best friend the Negro ever had," Johnson bragged.

His commitment to civil rights was in part motivated by politics, in part by his desire to bring the South into the mainstream of American life, and in part by his life experiences. His first teaching job was at an elementary school in Texas that served Mexican American children. His experiences created in him a lifelong desire to help "those poor little kids. I saw hunger in their eyes and pain in their bodies. Those little brown bodies had so little and needed so much."

## Politics and Poverty

Lyndon Johnson maneuvered legislation through Congress better than any president in history. He was a consummate wheeler-dealer. In 1964, he took advantage of widespread public support in the aftermath of Kennedy's death to push through Congress the fallen president's stalled measures for tax reductions and civil rights. He later said that he wanted to take Kennedy's incomplete program "and turn it into a martyr's cause."

The Revenue Act of 1964 provided a 20 percent reduction in tax rates. (The top rate was then a whopping 91 percent, compared to 37 today.) It was intended to give consumers more money to spend so as to boost economic growth and create new jobs, and it worked. Unemployment fell from 5.2 percent in 1964, to 4.5 percent in 1965, and to 3.8 percent in 1966.

**THE CIVIL RIGHTS ACT** Long thwarted by southern Democrats in Congress, the **Civil Rights Act of 1964** finally became law on July 2. It guaranteed equal treatment for *all* Americans and outlawed discrimination in public places on the basis of race, sex, or national origin. It also prohibited discrimination in the buying, selling, and renting of housing, as well as in the hiring and firing of employees.

Johnson pursued its passage with an urgent sense of purpose. He lobbied key legislators one-on-one over drinks and cigarettes in his office, his outsized presence overwhelming any opposition. One senator who survived the "Johnson treatment" said that the president would "twist your arm off at the shoulder and beat your head with it" if you did not agree to vote as he wanted.

People from all walks of life helped Johnson convince Congress to pass the Civil Rights Act—Senator Hubert Humphrey, congressional committee chairs (both Republicans and Democrats), labor unions, church leaders, and civil rights organizations. Their efforts produced what is arguably the most important piece of legislation in the twentieth century. The passage of the Civil Rights Act marked one of those extraordinary moments when the ideals of democracy, equal opportunity, and human dignity were affirmed.

The Civil Rights Act dealt a major blow to racial segregation while giving the federal government new powers to bring lawsuits against organizations or businesses that violated constitutional rights. It also established the Equal Employment Opportunities Commission to ensure that employers treated job applicants equally, regardless of race, gender, or national origin.

On the night after signing the bill, Johnson predicted that "we have just delivered the South to the Republican party for a long time to come." He feared that his commitment to civil rights would cost him the election of 1964.

**A WAR ON POVERTY** In addition to fulfilling President Kennedy's legislative priorities that had stalled in Congress, Lyndon Johnson launched an elaborate legislative program of his own, declaring "unconditional war on poverty in America." Elected officials had "rediscovered" poverty in 1962 when social critic Michael Harrington published a powerful exposé, *The Other America,* in which he revealed that more than 40 million people were mired in an invisible "culture of poverty." Poverty led to poor housing conditions, which in turn led to poor health, poor attendance at school or work, alcohol and drug abuse, unwanted pregnancies, and single-parent families. Harrington added that poverty was much more extensive than people realized because much of it was hidden from view in isolated rural areas or inner-city slums. He pushed for a "comprehensive assault on poverty."

Kennedy had read Harrington's book and had asked his advisers in the fall of 1963, just before his assassination, to investigate the problem and suggest solutions. Upon becoming president, Johnson announced that he wanted an anti-poverty legislative package "with real impact." He was determined to help the "one-fifth of all American families with incomes too small to even meet their basic needs." Money for the program would come from the tax revenues generated by corporate profits made possible by the tax reduction of 1964, which had led to one of the longest sustained economic booms in history.

Johnson knew that the "war" on poverty would be long and costly. He did not expect to "wipe out poverty" in "my lifetime. But we can minimize it, moderate it, and in time eliminate it." His war on poverty would not give people handouts but open "the door of opportunity" for them.

The **Economic Opportunity Act** of 1964 was the primary weapon in Johnson's war on poverty. It created an Office of Economic Opportunity (OEO) to administer eleven new community-based programs, many of which still exist. They included a Job Corps training program for the long-term unemployed; an Upward Bound program to excite inner-city youth about attending college; a Head Start educational program for disadvantaged preschoolers; a Legal Services Corporation to provide legal assistance for low-income Americans; financial-aid programs for low-income college students; grants to small farmers and rural businesses; loans to businesses that hired the chronically unemployed; the Volunteers in Service to America program (VISTA) to combat inner-city poverty; and the Community

**War on poverty** In 1964, President Johnson visited Tom Fletcher, a father of eight children living in a tar-paper shack in rural Kentucky. Fletcher became a "poster father" for the war on poverty, although his life benefited little from its programs.

Action Program, which would allow the poor "maximum feasible participation" in organizing and directing their own neighborhood programs. In 1964, Congress also approved the Food Stamp Act to help poor people afford groceries.

**THE ELECTION OF 1964** President Johnson's successes aroused a conservative Republican counterattack. Arizona senator Barry Goldwater, a wealthy department-store owner, emerged as the square-jawed, blunt-talking leader of the growing right wing of the Republican party. He was one of only six Republican senators to vote against the Civil Rights Act and warned that the bill would lead to a "federal police state."

In his best-selling book *The Conscience of a Conservative* (1960), Goldwater had called for ending the income tax and drastically reducing federal entitlement programs such as Social Security. Conservatives controlled the Republican National Convention when it gathered in San Francisco in the early summer of 1964, and they ensured Goldwater's nomination. "I would remind you," Goldwater told the delegates, "that extremism in the defense of liberty is no vice." He later explained that his objective was like that of Calvin Coolidge in the 1920s: "to reduce the size of government. Not to pass laws, but repeal them."

Goldwater was refreshingly candid. A rugged outdoorsman, he was quick to smile and easy to like, but he was out of his depth as a presidential candidate. He frightened many voters by urging wholesale bombing of North Vietnam and suggesting the use of atomic weapons. He criticized Johnson's war on poverty as a waste of money, told students that the federal government should not provide assistance for education, and opposed the nuclear test ban treaty. To Republican campaign buttons that claimed, "In your heart, you know he's right," Democrats responded, "In your guts, you know he's nuts."

Johnson, by comparison, portrayed himself as a responsible centrist. He chose as his running mate Hubert H. Humphrey of Minnesota, a prominent liberal senator who had long promoted civil rights, and pledged that he was "not about to send American boys nine or ten thousand miles from home to do what Asian boys ought to be doing for themselves."

The election was not close. Johnson won 61 percent of the popular vote and dominated the electoral vote, 486 to 52. Goldwater captured only Arizona and five states in the Lower South. In the Senate, the Democrats increased their majority by two (68 to 32) and in the House by thirty-seven (295 to 140).

But Goldwater's success in the Lower South accelerated the region's shift to the Republican party, and his candidacy proved to be a turning point in the development of the national conservative movement by inspiring a generation of young activists and the formation of conservative organizations that would transform the dynamics of American politics during the 1970s and 1980s. Their success would culminate in the presidency of Ronald Reagan, the Hollywood actor who co-chaired the "California for Goldwater" campaign in 1964.

## THE GREAT SOCIETY

Lyndon Johnson misread his lopsided victory in 1964 as a mandate for massive changes. He knew, however, that his popularity could quickly fade. "Every day I'm in office," he told his aides, "I'm going to lose votes. I'm going to alienate somebody. . . . We've got to get this legislation fast. You've got to get it during my honeymoon."

As Johnson's war on poverty gathered momentum, his ambitions grew. He resolved to finish FDR's New Deal by creating what he called the **Great Society**. In May 1964, he announced his intention to develop an array of programs designed to "move not only toward the rich society and the powerful society, but upward to the Great Society" which would end poverty and racial injustice and provide "abundance and liberty for all."

Johnson viewed the federal government as the magical lever for raising the quality of life for all Americans. "Hell, we're the richest country in the world, the most powerful," Johnson told an aide. "We can do it all."

Soon, Johnson was working to gain congressional approval for dozens of new bills and federal programs. He eventually convinced the Democrat-controlled Congress to approve a torrent of legislative requests focused on education, health care, civil rights, urban renewal, rural poverty, transportation, and even cultural offerings such as government-funded public television and radio programming. The Great Society also featured dozens of initiatives to enhance the environment, including an Air Quality Act, a Wilderness Act, an Endangered Species Act, a Scenic Rivers Act, and a National Trails Act.

**HEALTH INSURANCE, HOUSING DEVELOPMENT, AND HIGHER EDUCATION** Lyndon Johnson's first priorities among his Great Society programs were federal health insurance and aid for young people to pursue higher education—all liberal proposals that had first been suggested by President Truman in 1945 but were rejected by conservative southern Democrats and Republicans in Congress. For twenty years, the steadfast opposition of the American Medical Association (AMA) had stalled a comprehensive medical-insurance program. Now that Johnson and the Democrats had the votes, however, the AMA joined Republicans in supporting a bill serving only those over age sixty-five.

The act created not just a **Medicare** health insurance program for the elderly but also a **Medicaid** program of federal grants to states to help cover medical expenses for the poor of all ages. Johnson signed the bill on July 30, 1965, in Independence, Missouri, with eighty-one-year-old Harry Truman looking on.

The Higher Education Act of 1965 increased federal grants to universities, created scholarships for low-income students, provided low-interest loans for students, and established a National Teachers Corps. "Every child," Johnson asserted, "must be encouraged to get as much education as he has the ability to take."

The momentum generated by the Higher Education and Medicare Acts helped carry many more Great Society bills through Congress. Among them was the Appalachian Regional Development Act of 1966, which allocated $1 billion for programs in impoverished mountain areas. The Housing and Urban Development Act of 1965 provided $3 billion for urban renewal projects in inner cities. Funds to help low-income families pay their rent followed in 1966, and the same year a new Department of Housing and Urban Development was established, headed by Robert C. Weaver, the first African American cabinet member.

**THE IMMIGRATION ACT**  Little noticed in the stream of Great Society legislation was the Immigration and Nationality Services Act of 1965 (also called the **Hart-Celler Act**), which Johnson signed in a ceremony at the base of the Statue of Liberty in New York Harbor. It was the most sweeping revision in immigration policies in decades, and both Democrats and Republicans supported it. In his speech, Johnson stressed that the law would redress the wrong done to those "from southern and eastern Europe" and the "developing continents" of Asia, Africa, and Latin America.

The old system, dating to 1924, greatly favored immigrants from Great Britain and the countries of western and northern Europe over those from southern and eastern Europe, Asia, and Africa. The new law ended discriminatory national-origins quotas and created hemispheric ceilings on visas issued: 170,000 for persons from outside the Western Hemisphere, 120,000 for persons from within. It also stipulated that no more than 20,000 people could come from any one country each year.

The 290,000 immigrants admitted annually were to be accepted under seven "preference" quotas. First and second preferences—40 percent of the total—were provided for unmarried adult sons and daughters of citizens and documented resident immigrants. (Spouses, minor children, and parents of citizens were not counted in the quotas.) The third preference, 10 percent, went to "members of the professions and scientists and artists of exceptional ability." The fourth, 10 percent, went to adult married children of U.S. citizens, and the fifth, 24 percent, to brothers and sisters of citizens. The sixth, 10 percent, was for "skilled labor in great demand" and "unskilled workers in occupations for which labor is in short supply." The final preference, 6 percent, was for specifically defined refugees from political tyranny.

Johnson explained that the new law "repairs a deep and painful flaw in the fabric of American life. . . . The days of unlimited immigration are past. But those who come will come because of what they are—not because of the land from which they sprung."

Johnson's insistence that the new law was not "revolutionary" has been proven wrong. During the 1960s and since, Europeans dropped to less than 10 percent of the total immigrants. Asians and Latin Americans became the largest cohort of new Americans. More than 80 million immigrants have come to America since 1965, most of them from Mexico, the Philippines, Cuba, South Korea, China, and Taiwan.

**VOTING RIGHTS LEGISLATION** Building upon the successes of Freedom Summer, Martin Luther King Jr. organized an effort in early 1965 to register the 3 million unregistered African American voters in the South. On February 6, the White House announced that it would urge Congress to enact a voting rights bill.

Activists converged on Selma, Alabama, where only 250 of the 15,000 blacks of voting age were registered voters. King told his staff on February 10 that to get the voting rights bill passed, "we need to make a dramatic" statement. That drama occurred three weeks later.

On Sunday, March 7, hundreds of black and white civil rights activists assembled near the Edmund Pettus Bridge to begin a fifty-four-mile march to the state capitol in Montgomery. Before reaching the bridge, however, the marchers were assaulted by state troopers and local police using billy clubs, tear gas, and bull whips. In what came to be called "Bloody Sunday," the violence was televised for all to see. Fifty marchers were hospitalized.

King, torn between congressional appeals to call off the march and the demands of militants that it continue, announced that a second march would be held. A federal judge agreed to allow the marchers to continue once President Johnson agreed to provide soldiers and federal marshals for their protection.

By March 25, when the demonstrators reached Montgomery, some 25,000 people were with them. King delivered a rousing address in which he said, "the battle is in our hands. And we can answer with creative nonviolence the call to higher ground to which the new directions of our struggle summons us."

Several days earlier, President Johnson had urged Congress to "overcome the crippling legacy of bigotry and injustice" by making the cause of civil rights "our cause too." He concluded by slowly speaking the words of the movement's hymn: "And we *shall* overcome."

The resulting **Voting Rights Act of 1965** was a momentous legislative accomplishment. It ensured *all* citizens the right to vote and authorized the attorney general to send federal officials to register voters in areas that had long experienced racial discrimination. The act banned the various methods, like requiring literacy tests, that local officials had used to keep black and Latino citizens from voting.

By the end of the year, some 250,000 African Americans were newly registered to vote in several southern states. By 1968, an estimated 53 percent of blacks in Alabama were registered, compared to only 14 percent in 1960. In this respect, the Voting Rights Act was even more important than the Civil Rights Act because it empowered black voters in the South, thereby transforming the white-dominated politics in the region and making possible the

**Voting Rights Act of 1965**  President Johnson gifts the Reverend Martin Luther King Jr. with a souvenir pen—one of those used to sign the bill into law.

election of black public officials. Yet by enabling southern blacks—most of whom preferred Democratic candidates—to vote, it also helped turn the once-solidly Democratic South into a Republican stronghold, as many white voters switched parties.

**THE GREAT SOCIETY IN PRACTICE**  The scope of Lyndon Johnson's Great Society programs exceeded Franklin Roosevelt's New Deal in part because of the nation's booming prosperity during the mid-1960s. Whereas Roosevelt passed fifteen major bills in his First Hundred Days, Johnson told an aide in 1966, he had "passed two hundred in the last two years." "This country," Johnson proclaimed, "is rich enough to do anything it has the guts to do and the vision to do and the will to do."

That proved *not* to be the case, however. As *Time* magazine reported, "No matter how much Lyndon gets, he asks for more." Soon there was no more money to spend. In 1966, Johnson warned that if taxes were not raised, the economy would suffer a "ruinous spiral of inflation" and "brutally higher interest rates."

The Great Society and war on poverty did not end urban blight or rural poverty or stubborn social problems, in part because the Vietnam War soon took priority and siphoned away funding, and in part because neither Johnson nor his congressional supporters understood the complexity of chronic poverty.

The Great Society programs have led to several triumphs since their enactment, however. Infant mortality has dropped, college completion rates have soared, malnutrition has virtually disappeared, and far fewer elderly Americans live below the poverty line and without access to health care. The federal guarantee of civil rights and voting rights remains in place. Medicare and Medicaid have become two of the most appreciated—and expensive—government programs. Consumers now have a federal agency protecting them. Head Start programs providing preschool enrichment activities for poor students have produced long-term benefits. The federal food stamp program has improved the nutrition and health of children living in poverty. Finally, scholarships for low-income college students have made access to higher education possible for millions.

Several of Johnson's most ambitious programs, however, were ill-conceived. Others were vastly underfunded, and many were mismanaged and even corrupt. Some of the problems they were meant to address actually worsened. Medicare, for example, removed incentives for hospitals to control costs, thereby contributing to skyrocketing medical bills. In addition, food stamp fraud occurred as people took advantage of a program intended to ensure healthy nutrition. A final example has been the challenge of single-parent households. In 1960, about 5 percent of children were born to single mothers. Today, the number has soared to 40 percent, in part because of federal programs that provide child support.

Overall, Great Society programs helped reduce poverty from 19 percent in 1964 to 10 percent in 1973, but it did so largely by providing federal welfare payments, not by finding people jobs. In 1966, middle-class resentment over the cost and excesses of the Great Society programs generated a conservative backlash that fueled a Republican resurgence. In the congressional elections of 1966, only thirty-eight of the seventy-one Democrats elected to the House in 1964 won reelection.

## THE TRAGEDY OF VIETNAM

In foreign affairs, Lyndon Johnson was, like Woodrow Wilson, a novice. He admitted that he was "not temperamentally equipped to be commander in chief." And, again like Wilson, his presidency would become a victim of his crusading idealism.

In early 1965, LBJ confided to friends that the "Vietnam thing" was "wearing him down." As racial violence erupted in America's cities, the war in Vietnam reached new levels of destruction. Using weapons and supplies from China and the Soviet Union, North Vietnam provided massive support to the Viet Cong—the guerrillas fighting in South Vietnam to overthrow the U.S.-backed government and to unify the divided nation under Communist control.

Johnson inherited a long-standing U.S. commitment to prevent a Communist takeover in Vietnam. Beginning with Harry S. Truman, U.S. presidents had done just enough to avoid being charged with having "lost" Vietnam. Johnson initially sought to do the same. His path, however, took the United States into a deeper military commitment.

When John F. Kennedy was assassinated in November 1963, there were 16,000 U.S. military advisers in South Vietnam. As vice president, Johnson had told Kennedy, "If we don't stop the Reds in South Vietnam, tomorrow they will be in Hawaii, and next week they will be in San Francisco."

Johnson, however, soon came to doubt that South Vietnam was worth more extensive military involvement. In May 1964, he told his national security adviser, McGeorge Bundy: "It looks to me like we are getting into another Korea. . . . I don't think it's worth fighting for. And I don't think we can get out. It's just the biggest damned mess that I ever saw." Yet Johnson's fear of appearing weak outweighed his misgivings.

**ESCALATION IN VIETNAM** The official justification for the military *escalation*—a Defense Department term—was the **Tonkin Gulf Resolution**, passed by the Senate on August 7, 1964. On that day, President Johnson, unknowingly acting on false information provided by Secretary of Defense Robert McNamara, reported that on August 2 and 4, North Vietnamese torpedo boats had attacked two U.S. warships in the Gulf of Tonkin, off the coast of North Vietnam. He called it "naked aggression on the high seas." As it turned out, however, the American vessels had actually fired first in support of South Vietnamese attacks against two North Vietnamese islands—attacks planned by American advisers. (Whether the American warships were actually fired upon remains in dispute).

The Tonkin Gulf Resolution empowered Johnson to "take all necessary measures" to protect U.S. forces and "prevent further aggression." Only two senators voted against the resolution. Johnson interpreted the support as equivalent to a congressional declaration of war, since it allowed him to wage war as he saw fit.

It would be no small war, however. Soon after the landslide victory over Barry Goldwater in November 1964, Johnson committed America to full-scale war in Vietnam. On February 5, 1965, Viet Cong guerrillas attacked a U.S. military base near Pleiku, in South Vietnam, killing and wounding more than 100 Americans. More attacks led Johnson to approve Operation Rolling Thunder, the first sustained U.S. bombing of North Vietnam. Thereafter, there were essentially two fronts in the war: one, in North Vietnam, where U.S. warplanes conducted a massive bombing campaign, and the other, in South Vietnam, where nearly all the ground combat occurred.

In March 1965, the U.S. commander, General William C. Westmoreland, greeted the first American combat troops in Vietnam. His strategy was focused on waging a war of attrition, using overwhelming U.S. firepower to produce so many casualties that the Viet Cong and North Vietnamese would give up.

Soon, U.S. forces launched "search and destroy" operations against VC guerrillas throughout South Vietnam. But the Viet Cong, made up of both men and women, wore no uniforms and dissolved by day into the villages, hiding among civilians. Their elusiveness exasperated American soldiers, most of whom were not trained for such unconventional warfare in Vietnam's dense jungles and intense heat and humidity.

The escalating war brought rising U.S. casualties (the number of killed, wounded, and missing), which were announced each week on the television news programs. Criticism of the war grew, but LBJ stood firm. "We will not be defeated," he told the nation. "We will not grow tired. We will not withdraw."

Johnson viewed the war as a test of his manliness. He vowed to an aide that he was not going to let a "raggedy-ass little fourth-rate country" like North Vietnam push him around.

Yet he greatly underestimated the tenacity and ingenuity of the North Vietnamese. On July 20, 1965, Robert McNamara told Johnson that "the situation in South Vietnam is worse than a year ago (when it was worse than the year before that)." The South Vietnamese army seemed inept, and the U.S. bombing campaign was ineffective.

McNamara posed three options: (1) "cut our losses and withdraw"; (2) "continue about the present level"; or, (3) "expand promptly and substantially the U.S. pressure." LBJ chose the third option, and the American buildup in Vietnam began. By the end of 1965, there were 184,000 U.S. troops in Vietnam; in 1966, there were 385,000; by 1969, at the height of the war effort, 542,000.

What the public did not know was that Johnson never thought the war was winnable. He told Lady Bird in July 1965 that escalating the war was "like being in an airplane and I have to choose between crashing the plane or jumping out. I do not have a parachute."

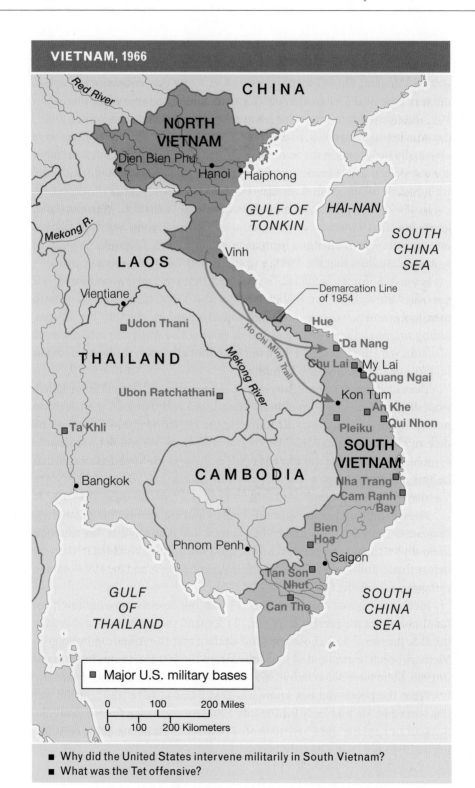

VIETNAM, 1966

Major U.S. military bases

■ Why did the United States intervene militarily in South Vietnam?
■ What was the Tet offensive?

**THE CONTEXT FOR POLICY** President Johnson's decision to "Americanize" the war flowed directly from the assumptions that had long guided U.S. foreign policy during the cold war. The commitment to contain the spread of communism guided Johnson as well. "Why are we in Vietnam?" the president asked during a speech in 1965. "We are there because we have a promise to keep. . . . To leave Vietnam to its fate would shake the confidence of all these people in the value of American commitment." What Johnson did not say was that he dreaded being blamed for "losing Vietnam" to communism.

Johnson's military advisers also believed that U.S. military force would defeat the Viet Cong. Yet the president insisted that the war effort not reach levels that would cause the Chinese or Soviets to become involved—which meant, as it turned out, that a military victory was never possible. The United States was not fighting to "win" but to prevent the North Vietnamese and Viet Cong from winning and, eventually, to force them to sign a negotiated settlement. This meant that the United States would have to maintain a military presence as long as the enemy retained the will to fight.

**RESISTANCE GROWS** As the war ground on, opposition grew fierce. In 1965, college campuses began hosting "teach-ins" critical of the war effort. Professors gathered with students to discuss "a better policy" in Vietnam. In April 1965, some 20,000 students converged on Washington, D.C., where they picketed the White House before moving to the Washington Monument, where they carried signs saying: "GET OUT OF SAIGON AND INTO SELMA," "FREEDOM NOW IN VIETNAM," "WAR ON POVERTY NOT PEOPLE." The crowd then went to the Capitol, where it demanded that Congress "end, not extend, the war in Vietnam."

The following year, Senator J. William Fulbright of Arkansas, chairman of the Senate Foreign Relations Committee, began congressional investigations into American policy in Vietnam. George F. Kennan, the former State Department diplomat who had inspired the containment policy, told the committee that the containment doctrine was appropriate for Europe but not for Southeast Asia, which was not a region vital to American security. Johnson labeled his political critics and anti-war protesters "Communists" and used government agencies to punish them.

Still, the resistance grew. By 1967, anti-war demonstrations were commonplace. Americans began dividing into "hawks" who supported the war and "doves" who opposed it. Nightly television accounts of the fighting—Vietnam was the first war to receive extended television coverage and hence was dubbed the "living-room war"—called into question the accuracy of statements by military and government officials claiming the Americans were winning. Journalists called it a "credibility crisis." But Johnson insisted that there would be no withdrawal from Vietnam.

As American military involvement deepened and criticism of the war mounted, Johnson grew more frustrated and depressed. "I can't get out [of Vietnam]. I can't finish it with what I got. So what the hell can I do?" His wife recalled that Vietnam became a "hell of a thorn stuck in his throat. It wouldn't come up; it wouldn't go down. . . . It was pure hell." White House aides became so concerned about Johnson's mental stability that they consulted psychiatrists.

**THE TET OFFENSIVE**  On January 31, 1968, the first day of the Vietnamese New Year (Tet), some 70,000 Viet Cong and North Vietnamese troops unleashed surprise attacks on U.S. and South Vietnamese forces throughout South Vietnam. Within a few days, American firepower turned the tables, but the damage had been done.

Although General Westmoreland proclaimed the **Tet offensive** a major defeat for the Viet Cong, its *political* impact in the United States was dramatic; it decisively turned Americans against the war. The scope and intensity of the Tet offensive contradicted upbeat claims by U.S. commanders. "What the hell is going on?" CBS newscaster Walter Cronkite demanded. "I thought we were winning this war." After the Tet offensive, Johnson's popularity plummeted.

**Whose war?** President Johnson lowers his head in disappointment as he listens to a commander's report from Vietnam.

Equally disturbing to LBJ was Westmoreland's unexpected request for more than 200,000 additional U.S. troops. The request stunned Clark Clifford, the new defense secretary who replaced McNamara in March 1968. He told the president that the military leaders "don't know what they're talking about." Instead of winning the war, he added, the United States had become mired in a sinkhole with "no end in sight."

Civil rights leaders and social activists felt betrayed as federal funds earmarked for the war on poverty were gobbled up by the war. By 1967, the United States was spending some $2 billion each month in Vietnam, about $322,000 for every VC killed. Anti-poverty programs at home received only $53 per person. Martin Luther King Jr. pointed out that "the bombs in Vietnam explode at home—they destroy the hopes and possibilities for a decent America."

Senator Eugene McCarthy of Minnesota took advantage of the consternation caused by the Tet offensive to ramp up his anti-war challenge to Johnson in the Democratic primaries. With students rallying to his "Dump Johnson" candidacy, McCarthy polled a stunning 42 percent of the vote to Johnson's 48 percent in New Hampshire's March primary. "Dove bites Hawk," a reporter quipped.

McCarthy's success in New Hampshire convinced Robert F. Kennedy, now a New York senator, to launch his own challenge to Johnson's reelection. That members of his own party were opposing his reelection devastated Johnson.

The growing opposition to the Vietnam war was even a worse blow. During a private meeting with military leaders, the president acknowledged that "the country is demoralized. . . . Most of the press is against us. . . . We have no support for the war." Johnson had also grown concerned about his own health. Lady Bird told him to think about retiring after one term.

On March 31, 1968, Johnson appeared on national television to announce a limited halt to the bombing of North Vietnam to enable a negotiated cease-fire agreement with the Communists. Then, he made an astounding announcement: "I shall not seek, and I will not accept, the nomination of my party for another term as your President." As his daughter explained, the "agony of Vietnam" had engulfed her father.

The problem with Johnson's attempt to fight a "limited war" in Vietnam was that the Vietnamese Communists fought an absolute war in defense of their country. Among other things, the war revealed that the capabilities of the United States, including its military power, were limited; the nation could not simply have its way around the world.

Now there were three candidates for the Democratic nomination: McCarthy, Kennedy, and Vice President Hubert Humphrey. Many anti-war Democrats expected McCarthy to drop out in favor of Kennedy, but the Minnesota senator, buoyed by his success and convinced of his moral superiority, refused to leave the race. For his part, Kennedy, with his long hair and boyish faith, appealed to the idealism of America's youth: "Some men see things as they are and ask, why? I dream things that never were and say, why not?"

## THE TURMOIL OF THE SIXTIES

By the late 1960s, traditional notions of authority were under attack. The spirit of resistance was especially evident among disaffected youth who called into question not only the Vietnam War and the credibility of the Johnson administration but virtually every aspect of mainstream life, including the traditional family structure, the middle-class work ethic, universities, religion, and the nonviolent integrationist philosophy underpinning the civil rights movement. Many alienated young Americans, often lumped together as "hippies," felt that they were part of "the Revolution," a magical force that would overthrow a corrupt and outdated way of life.

**1968: A TRAUMATIC YEAR** All the turbulent elements affecting American life came to a head in 1968, the most traumatic year in a traumatic decade. As *Time* magazine reported, "Nineteen sixty-eight was a knife blade that severed past from future." It was "one tragic, surprising, and perplexing thing after another."

On April 4, James Earl Ray, a petty thief, drifter, and white racist, shot and killed Martin Luther King Jr. as the African American leader stood outside the Lorraine Motel in Memphis, Tennessee. Ray had earlier vowed that he was going "to get the big nigger."

King's murder ignited a wave of violence. Riots erupted in more than 100 cities, but the damage was especially devastating in Chicago, Baltimore, and Washington. Forty-six people were killed, all but five of them black. Some 20,000 army soldiers and 34,000 National Guard troops eventually helped stop the violence across the country, and 21,000 people were arrested.

The night that King died, Robert Kennedy was in Indianapolis, Indiana. Upon hearing the news, he stood on a flatbed truck to speak to a grieving crowd of African Americans. "Those of you who are black can be filled with hatred, with bitterness and a desire for revenge," he said. "We can move toward further polarization. Or we can make an effort, as Dr. King did, to understand, to reconcile ourselves and to love."

Two months after King's death, after midnight on June 6, 1968, Kennedy appeared at the Ambassador Hotel in Los Angeles to celebrate his victory over Eugene McCarthy in the California presidential primary. Kennedy closed his remarks by pledging that "we can end the divisions within the United States, end the violence."

After the applause subsided, Kennedy walked through the hotel kitchen on his way to the press room for interviews. Along the way, a Jordanian Arab named Sirhan Sirhan, resentful of the senator's strong support of Israel, pulled out a pistol and fired eight shots, hitting Kennedy in the head and wounding three others. Kennedy died the next morning. Only forty-two years old, he was buried beside his brother John in Arlington National Cemetery outside of Washington, D.C.

The assassinations of the Kennedys, Martin Luther King, and Malcolm X came to frame the sixties. With their deaths, a wealth of idealism died too—the idealism that Bobby Kennedy had hoped would put a fragmented America back together again. Having lost the leading voices for real change, a growing number of young people lost hope in democracy and turned to radicalism and violence—or dropped out of society.

**CHICAGO AND MIAMI** In August 1968, the nation's social unrest came to a head at the **Chicago Democratic National Convention**, where delegates gathered to nominate Johnson's faithful vice president, Hubert H. Humphrey, as the party's candidate for president. LBJ had endorsed Humphrey as his successor despite criticizing him in private as "all heart and no balls."

Outside the Chicago convention hall, almost 20,000 police officers and National Guard soldiers confronted thousands of anti-war protesters who taunted the police with obscenities. Richard J. Daley, Chicago's gruff Democratic mayor, warned that he would not tolerate disruptions. Nonetheless, riots broke out and were televised nationwide. As police used tear gas and clubs to pummel the demonstrators, others chanted, "The whole world is watching." The *New York Times* reported, "Those were our children in the streets, and the Chicago police beat them up." Nationally, the Democratic party began to fragment as a result of the chaos in Chicago.

Three weeks earlier, the Republicans had gathered in Miami Beach to nominate Richard Nixon. In 1962, after losing the California governor's race, Nixon had vowed never again to run for public office. By 1968, however, he had changed his mind and become a self-appointed spokesman for the values of "middle America." He and the Republicans claimed they would "end the war" in Vietnam and "win the peace" while bringing law and order to the nation's streets.

Nixon appealed to what he called the "**silent majority**" of working- and middle-class Americans who viewed the "rabble rousing" protesters with contempt. In accepting the nomination, Nixon pledged to listen to "the voice of the great majority of Americans, the forgotten Americans, the non-shouters, the non-demonstrators, that are not racists or sick, that are not guilty of the crime that plagues the land."

Former Alabama governor George Wallace, an outspoken segregationist, ran on the American Independent party ticket. Wallace mounted a crusade on behalf of "common folks" against blacks, political elites, and "little pinkos." He promised to get tough on "scummy anarchists" and bring stability to the nation. He appealed even more forcefully than Nixon to working-class voters' disgust with anti-war protesters, the mushrooming federal welfare system, the growth of the federal government, forced racial integration, and rioting in the inner cities.

Wallace displayed a savage wit, once saying that the "only four-letter words that hippies did not know were w-o-r-k and s-o-a-p." He predicted that on Election Day, the nation would realize that "there are a lot of rednecks in this country." His candidacy generated considerable appeal outside his native South, especially among white working-class communities. Wallace hoped to deny Humphrey and Nixon an electoral majority and throw the choice into the House of Representatives, which would have provided a fitting climax to a chaotic year.

## THE ELECTION OF 1968

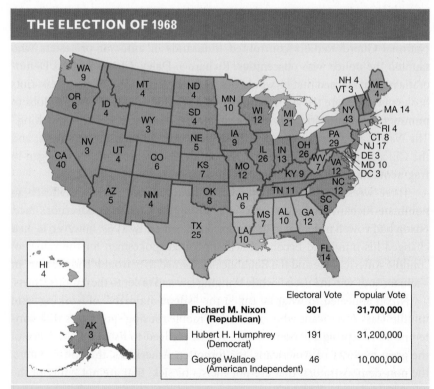

| | Electoral Vote | Popular Vote |
|---|---|---|
| **Richard M. Nixon (Republican)** | **301** | **31,700,000** |
| Hubert H. Humphrey (Democrat) | 191 | 31,200,000 |
| George Wallace (American Independent) | 46 | 10,000,000 |

- How did the riots at the Chicago Democratic National Convention affect the 1968 presidential campaign?
- What does the electoral map reveal about the support for each of the three major candidates?
- How was Richard Nixon able to win enough electoral votes in such a close, three-way presidential race?
- What was George Wallace's appeal to 10 million voters?

Nixon resolved to do anything to win, including violating the Logan Act, which prohibits private citizens from communicating with foreign governments about controversial issues. Just weeks before the election, Nixon ordered an aide to "monkey wrench" President Johnson's last-minute efforts to end the Vietnam War. Nixon used an intermediary to let South Vietnamese officials know they should stall the ongoing negotiations because Nixon, if elected, would provide them better terms.

When Johnson learned, through CIA surveillance, of Nixon's efforts to subvert the negotiations, he was furious, shouting that the Republican presidential candidate had committed "treason." But he did not have enough proof to share with the public.

While it remains an open question whether Johnson could have negotiated a deal to end the war before the election, Nixon's most recent biographer, John A. Farrell, concluded that "of all of Richard Nixon's actions in a lifetime of politics, this was the most reprehensible," for he chose winning an election over the possibility of ending a war. In what one journalist called an "uncommon act of political decency," Humphrey decided not to make Nixon's efforts to sabotage the peace a last-minute election issue.

**NIXON TRIUMPHANT** On November 5, 1968, Richard Nixon and Governor Spiro Agnew of Maryland, his acid-tongued running mate, eked out a narrow victory of some 500,000 votes, a margin of about 1 percentage point. The electoral vote was more decisive: 301 for Nixon and 191 for Hubert Humphrey; the 46 electoral votes for George Wallace all came from the Lower South.

Embedded in the election returns was a sobering development for Democrats. White wage workers, the backbone of the party since FDR and the New Deal, were shifting to the Republicans. Both Ohio and New Jersey, traditional Democratic strongholds, went for Nixon. And more southern whites voted Republican than Democrat, a trend that has continued to this day.

So at the end of 1968, the century's most turbulent year, a divided society looked to Richard Nixon to fulfill his promises to bring "peace with honor" in Vietnam and to "bring us together" as a nation. Nixon privately admitted that he was a polarizing figure. In his first week in the White House, he told an aide that "I've got to put on my nice-guy hat . . . but let me make it clear that's not my nature."

# CHAPTER REVIEW

## SUMMARY

- **Kennedy's New Frontier**   President John F. Kennedy promised a *New Frontier* in 1961, but many of his domestic policies stalled in Congress. The *Bay of Pigs* fiasco led the Soviet premier, Nikita Khrushchev, to erect the *Berlin Wall* and install nuclear-armed missiles in Cuba. Kennedy in October 1962 ordered a naval "quarantine" of Cuba that led Khrushchev to withdraw the missiles. During his presidency, Kennedy deepened America's commitment in South Vietnam.

- **Civil Rights' Achievements**   At the beginning of the decade, growing numbers of African Americans and whites staged acts of *nonviolent civil disobedience* to protest racial discrimination in the South. In 1960, activists formed the *Student Nonviolent Coordinating Committee (SNCC)* to intensify efforts to dismantle desegregation. In 1961, courageous *Freedom Riders* attempted to integrate public transportation in the South. At the 1963 *March on Washington* for Jobs and Freedom, Martin Luther King Jr. delivered his famous "I Have a Dream" speech. Later, the *Black Power movement* emerged and emphasized militancy, black nationalism, separatism, and, often, violence.

- **Johnson's Great Society**   Lyndon Johnson forced the *Civil Rights Act of 1964* through Congress and then declared "war" on poverty by persuading Congress to pass the *Economic Opportunity Act (1964)*. Johnson's *Great Society* included hundreds of initiatives to expand federal social-welfare programs, most noticeably the *Voting Rights Act of 1965*, *Medicare*, and *Medicaid*. Johnson also ended national quotas in immigration law through the *Hart-Celler Act*. Yet his massive expansion of the Vietnam War eventually siphoned resources away from the war on poverty.

- **The Vietnam War**   The *Tonkin Gulf Resolution (1964)* gave the administration the power to wage war in Southeast Asia without a congressional declaration of war. During early 1965, the United States began escalating its role in Vietnam. By 1968, more than 500,000 U.S. military personnel were in South Vietnam. Claims that the Americans were winning were upended by the *Tet offensive (1968)*. Its initial success led many Americans to decide that the war could not be won. Resistance to "Johnson's War" thereafter steadily increased.

- **1968 Presidential Election**   Frustrated by his failures in Vietnam and aware that he had lost public support, Johnson chose not to seek reelection in 1968. Anti-war Democrats rallied around senators Eugene McCarthy and Robert Kennedy. In April, Martin Luther King Jr. was assassinated, setting off riots in urban black neighborhoods across the country. Two months later, Robert Kennedy was assassinated. Ultimately, the Democrats selected Johnson's loyal vice president, Hubert Humphrey, as their nominee, provoking angry protests by anti-war demonstrators at the *1968 Chicago Democratic National Convention*. As they had in 1960, the Republicans nominated Richard Nixon, who claimed to represent the *silent majority*. In the end, Nixon narrowly beat Humphrey.

# CHRONOLOGY

| | |
|---|---|
| **February 1960** | Students in Greensboro, North Carolina, stage sit-in |
| **April 1960** | Student Nonviolent Coordinating Committee formed |
| **November 1960** | John F. Kennedy elected president |
| **April 1961** | Bay of Pigs invasion fails |
| **May 1961** | Freedom Rides begin |
| **August 1961** | Soviets erect the Berlin Wall |
| **October 1962** | Cuban missile crisis |
| **August 1963** | March on Washington for Jobs and Freedom |
| **November 1963** | John F. Kennedy is assassinated |
| **June 1964** | Congress passes the Civil Rights Act |
| **November 1964** | Lyndon B. Johnson is elected to a full presidential term |
| **February 1965** | Malcolm X is assassinated |
| **August 1965** | Congress passes the Voting Rights Act |
| **January 1968** | Viet Cong stage the Tet offensive |
| **April 1968** | Martin Luther King Jr. is assassinated |
| **November 1968** | Richard Nixon is elected president |

## KEY TERMS

New Frontier p. 1192

Bay of Pigs (1961) p. 1198

Berlin Wall p. 1199

Cuban missile crisis (1962) p. 1201

Student Nonviolent Coordinating Committee (SNCC) p. 1205

Freedom Riders p. 1205

nonviolent civil disobedience p. 1209

March on Washington (1963) p. 1210

Black Power movement p. 1213

Civil Rights Act of 1964 p. 1219

Economic Opportunity Act (1964) p. 1221

Great Society p. 1222

Medicare and Medicaid p. 1223

Hart-Celler Act p. 1224

Voting Rights Act of 1965 p. 1225

Tonkin Gulf Resolution (1964) p. 1228

Tet offensive (1968) p. 1232

Chicago Democratic National Convention p. 1235

silent majority p. 1235

 INQUIZITIVE

**Go to InQuizitive to see what you've learned—and learn what you've missed—with personalized feedback along the way.**

# 30 Rebellion and Reaction

## 1960s and 1970s

**Rebels with a cause** Established in 1967, the Vietnam Veterans Against the War (VVAW) grew quickly during the sixties and early seventies. Here, a former Marine throws his service jacket and medals onto the Capitol steps on April 23, 1971, as part of a protest against the U.S. invasion of Laos.

As Richard M. Nixon entered the White House in early 1969, the nation's social fabric was in tatters. The traumatic events of 1968 had revealed how deeply divided American society had become and how difficult a task Nixon faced in carrying out his campaign pledge to restore social harmony.

Ironically, many of the forces that had contributed to the complacent prosperity of the fifties—the baby boom, the cold war, and the growing consumer culture—helped generate the social upheaval of the sixties and early seventies. The civil rights movement inspired efforts to ensure equal treatment for other minorities, from African Americans to women, gays and lesbians, bisexuals, Native Americans, Latinos, and people with disabilities. At the same time, intense opposition to the Vietnam War helped launch an unprecedented countercultural "youth revolt" that encompassed a unique blend of idealism, opportunism, and goofiness.

Despite Nixon's promise to restore the public's faith in the integrity of its leaders, he ended up aggravating the growing cynicism about the motives and methods of government officials. During 1973 and 1974, the Watergate scandal resulted in the greatest constitutional crisis since the impeachment of President Andrew Johnson in 1868, and it ended with the first resignation of a U.S. president.

## *focus questions*

**1.** How did the origins of the youth revolt shape the New Left and the counterculture?

**2.** How did the youth revolt and early civil rights movement influence other protest movements? How did new protest movements affect social attitudes and public policy?

**3.** How did the political environment of the late sixties influence Richard Nixon's election strategy and domestic policy?

**4.** How and why did Nixon and Henry Kissinger change military and political strategies to end America's involvement in the Vietnam War?

**5.** What was the international strategy brought about by Nixon's and Kissinger's diplomacy and foreign policy during the 1970s?

**6.** How did the Watergate scandal unfold? What was its political significance?

# "Forever Young": The Youth Revolt

The Greensboro sit-ins in 1960 not only launched a decade of civil rights activism but also signaled an end to the complacency that had characterized the fifties. Rennie Davis, a sophomore at Ohio's Oberlin College in 1960, remembered that the Greensboro student activists inspired him and many others: "Here were four students from Greensboro who were suddenly all over *Life* magazine. There was a feeling that they were us and we were them, and a recognition that they were expressing something we were feeling as well."

The sit-ins, marches, protests, and sacrifices associated with the civil rights movement inspired other groups—women, Native Americans, Latinos, gays and lesbians, and people with disabilities—to demand justice, freedom, and equality. Many idealistic young people decided that they could no longer ignore the widespread injustice and inequality staining the American dream.

A full-fledged youth revolt erupted. "Your sons and your daughters are beyond your command," sang Bob Dylan in "The Times They Are a-Changin." By 1970, more than half of Americans were under thirty. These baby boomers, who unlike their parents had experienced neither an economic depression nor a major war, were now attending colleges and universities in record numbers; enrollment quadrupled between 1945 and 1970.

Many universities had become gigantic institutions dependent upon huge research contracts from corporations and the federal government, especially the Defense Department. As these "multiversities" grew larger and more bureaucratic, they became targets for students wary of what President Dwight D. Eisenhower had labeled "the military-industrial complex." As criticism of U.S. military involvement in Vietnam mounted, disillusioned young people flowed into two distinct yet frequently overlapping movements: the New Left and the counterculture.

**THE NEW LEFT**   The political arm of the youth revolt originated in 1962 when Tom Hayden and Alan Haber, two University of Michigan students, convened a meeting of sixty young activists at Port Huron, Michigan, and formed Students for a Democratic Society (SDS). Their goal was ambitious: to quit reading history in order to *make* history, and to remake the United States into a more democratic society. Several participants were the children of former leftists or Communists; even more were Jewish.

At the gathering, Hayden, a veteran of the civil rights struggle in the South, drafted an impassioned document known as the "Port Huron Statement." It began: "We are the people of this generation, bred in at least moderate comfort, housed in universities, looking uncomfortably to the world we inherit." Only by giving "power to the people," the manifesto insisted, could America restore its founding principles. Inspired by African American civil rights activists, Hayden declared that college campuses would become the crossroads of social change. College students would snatch "control of the educational process from the administrative bureaucracy."

Hayden and others adopted the term **New Left** to distinguish their efforts at grassroots democracy from those of the "Old Left" of the 1930s, which had embraced an orthodox Marxism. Hayden's proposed revolution would be energized by hope and change, not abstract theories. Within a few years, more than 1,000 campuses hosted SDS chapters, and the organization began publishing its own underground newspaper, *The Rag*.

In the fall of 1964, students at the University of California at Berkeley took Hayden's New Left program to heart. Several had spent the summer working with the Student Nonviolent Coordinating Committee's (SNCC) voter-registration project in Mississippi (freedom summer), where three volunteers had been killed by Klansmen and many others had been arrested or harassed. When the university's chancellor announced that campus political demonstrations were banned, thousands of students staged a sit-in. After a thirty-two-hour standoff, the administration relented. Student groups then formed the free-speech movement (FSM).

Led by Mario Savio, who had participated in freedom summer in Mississippi, the FSM initially protested on behalf of students' rights, but it quickly mounted more general criticisms of the university and what Savio called the "depersonalized, unresponsive bureaucracy" stifling free speech on many campuses. In 1964, Savio led hundreds of students into Sproul Hall, UC Berkeley's administration building, and organized another sit-in. At 4 A.M., 600 state police arrested the protesters.

A few hours later, some 7,000 students filled Sproul Plaza, circulating leaflets and joining folk singer Joan Baez in singing "We Shall Overcome." Finally, the university's president gave in and revoked the ban on political demonstrations.

**ANTI-WAR PROTESTS** By 1965, the growing U.S. involvement in Vietnam had changed the New Left's agenda as millions of young men suddenly faced the prospect of being drafted to fight in the increasingly unpopular conflict.

The Vietnam War was primarily a poor man's fight. Most college students were able to postpone military service until they received their degree or reached the age of twenty-four. From 1965 through 1966, college students made up only 2 percent of military inductees. African Americans and Latinos

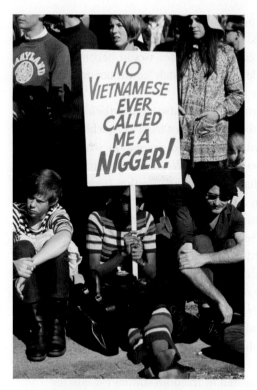

**All that rises must converge** This protester's sign at a Washington, D.C., demonstration bridged the civil rights and anti-war movements, which pursued many of the same racial and political goals.

were twice as likely to be drafted as whites.

As the war dragged on, opposition to U.S. involvement exploded. Some 200,000 young men ignored their draft notices, and some 4,000 served prison sentences for doing so. Another 56,000 qualified for conscientious objector (CO) status, meaning that they presented evidence to officials authenticating their moral, ethical, or religious opposition to war and/or the military. If granted, a CO had to perform alternative civilian service, often in hospitals or clinics. Others defied the draft by burning their draft cards while shouting "Hell No, We Won't Go!" Still others fled to Canada or Sweden to avoid military service or found creative ways to flunk the physical examination.

**RISING VIOLENCE** Throughout 1967 and 1968, the anti-war movement grew more violent as inner-city neighborhoods in Cleveland, Detroit, Newark, and other large urban areas exploded in flames fanned by racial injustice. Frustration over discrimination in employment and housing, as well as staggering rates of joblessness among inner-city African American youths, ignited the rage. "There was a sense everywhere, in 1968," journalist Garry Wills wrote, "that things were giving way."

During the eventful spring of 1968—when Lyndon Johnson announced that he would not run for reelection and Martin Luther King Jr. and Robert F. Kennedy were assassinated—campus unrest boiled over. The turmoil reached a climax at Columbia University, where SDS student radicals and black militants occupied the president's office and classroom buildings. They renamed the administration building Malcolm X Hall.

Mark Rudd, the campus SDS leader, called his parents to report, "We took a building." His father, Jacob Rudd, a retired army officer and a real estate investor, replied, "Well, give it back." After a failed attempt to negotiate an end to the takeover, the university's president canceled classes and called in the New York City police. More than 100 students were injured, 700 were arrested, and the leaders of the uprising were expelled. President Nixon declared that the rebellion was "the first major skirmish in a revolutionary struggle to seize the universities."

The events at Columbia inspired similar clashes at Harvard, Cornell, and San Francisco State, among others. Vice President Spiro Agnew dismissed the militants as "impudent snobs who characterize themselves as intellectuals" and condemned the "circuit-riding, Hanoi-visiting . . . caterwauling, riot-inciting, burn-America-down" anti-war protesters, whom he labeled "thieves and traitors" and "nattering nabobs of negativism."

**THE WEATHER UNDERGROUND** A small group of radical militants called the Revolutionary Youth Movement (RYM) emerged during the summer of 1969. They wanted to move political radicalism from "protest to resistance." At the SDS convention in Chicago on June 18, 1969, RYM members distributed a position paper titled "You don't need a weatherman / To know which way the wind blows," a line from Bob Dylan's 1965 song "Subterranean Homesick Blues."

The document called for a "white fighting force" to ally with the Black Panthers and others to destroy "U.S. imperialism and achieve a classless world: world communism." By embracing revolutionary violence, however, the so-called Weathermen essentially committed suicide. They killed SDS by abandoning the pacifist principles that had given the movement moral legitimacy.

Members of the Weather Underground took to the streets of Chicago in October 1969 to assault police and trash the city. Their goal was "to lead white kids into armed revolution." Almost 300 were arrested. During the so-called Days of Rage between September 1969 and May 1970, 250 draft board offices, ROTC buildings (for military training on university campuses), federal government facilities, and corporate headquarters were bombed. In March 1970, three members of the Weather Underground in New York City died when a bomb they were making exploded prematurely.

The Weathermen and other radical groups were forced underground by the aggressive efforts of federal law enforcement agencies. Their momentum diminished as President Nixon ended the draft and withdrew U.S. troops from Vietnam. Mark Rudd, who became one of the Weathermen organizers, later confessed that they intended to destroy SDS "because it wasn't revolutionary enough for us. I am not proud of this history." The Weathermen's "hyper-militancy" and bombings weakened "the larger anti-war movement and demoralized many good people." Blowing things up "got us isolated" by the media and "smashed" by the FBI.

**THE COUNTERCULTURE** Looking back over the 1960s, Tom Hayden, the founder of SDS, recalled that most rebellious young Americans "were not narrowly political. Most were not so interested in attaining [elected] office but in changing lifestyles." Hayden acknowledged that the shocking events of 1968 led disaffected young rebels—so-called hippies—to embrace the **counterculture**, an unorganized rebellion against mainstream institutions, values, and behavior that focused more on cultural change than political activism. (The term was coined by Theodore Roszak in his 1969 book, *The Making of a Counter Culture.*)

In pursuing personal liberation, hippies strove to exceed limits, trespass across boundaries, and heighten sensibilities. They rejected the pursuit of wealth and careers and embraced plain living, authenticity, friendship, peace, and, especially, *freedom.* In a 1967 cover story, the editors of *Time* magazine suggested that "in their independence of material possessions and their emphasis on peacefulness and honesty, hippies lead considerably more virtuous lives than the great majority of their fellow citizens. . . . In the end, it may be that the hippies have not so much dropped out of American society as given it something to think about."

Both the counterculture and the New Left rejected the status quo, but most hippies preferred to "drop out" of mainstream society rather than try to change the political system. Their preferred slogan was "Make Love, Not War." Like the Beats of the fifties, hippies created their own subculture that promoted freedom from all traditional constraints. In all their technicolor variety, they were defiant, innocent, egalitarian, optimistic, and indulgent as they rejected the authority of the nation's core institutions: the family, government, political parties, corporations, the military, and colleges and universities. "Do Your Own Thing" became their unofficial motto.

The counterculture lifestyle included an array of popular ideals and activities: peace, love, harmony, rock music, mystical religions, mind-altering drugs, casual sex, yoga, vegetarianism, organic food, and communal living. Hippie fashion featured rebelliously long hair for both women and men and casual clothing that was striking, unusual, or, God forbid, comfortable: flowing cotton dresses, granny gowns, ragged bell-bottom blue jeans, tie-dyed T-shirts, love beads, Tibetan bells, peace symbols, black boots, and sandals. Young men grew beards and women stopped wearing makeup as badges of difference (or indifference).

Underground newspapers celebrating the counterculture appeared in every large city, many of them with defiant names such as *Fuck You: A Magazine of the Arts.* A hippie magazine called *Avatar* asked, "Who is the underground?" Its answer: "You are, if you think, dream, work, and build towards the improvements and changes in your life, your social and personal

**Flower power** Hippies let loose at a 1967 love-in, one of many such gatherings that celebrated world peace, free love, and nontheological spirituality, often as a gesture of protest.

environments, towards the expectations of a better existence. . . . Think, look around, maybe in a mirror, maybe inside."

**DO YOUR OWN THING** The countercultural rebels were primarily middle-class whites alienated by the Vietnam War, racism, political corruption, and parental authority. In their view, a superficial materialism had settled over mainstream life, which they defied by embracing the pathway to freedom popularized by former Harvard psychology professor Timothy Leary: "Tune in, turn on, drop out." He added that "your only hope is dope." If it had not been for marijuana, said one hippie, "I'd still be wearing a crew cut and saluting the flag."

Leary, the self-styled high priest of the psychedelic revolution, had been dismissed by Harvard in 1963 for using students in experiments with hallucinatory drugs (one high student tried to eat the bark off a tree). In 1966, Leary formed the League of Spiritual Discovery (LSD) to lobby for decriminalization of mind-altering drugs. He promised his mostly young supporters that "proper drugs and rock music can make everybody young forever." He assured audiences that he had "a blueprint [for a new mind-altering religion], and we're going to change society in the next ten years."

Leary's crusade on behalf of expanded consciousness frightened most Americans, for LSD ruined many young people, some of whom committed suicide under its influence. President Richard Nixon called Leary "the most dangerous man in America." Leary responded by announcing his candidacy for the governorship of California, Nixon's home state. John Lennon of the Beatles wrote his campaign song, "Come Together."

Soon thereafter, however, Leary was forced to give up politics and psychedelics for a long prison sentence, having been convicted in California of possessing marijuana. The judge called him "an insidious menace" to society and a "pleasure–seeking, irresponsible, Madison Avenue advocate of the free use of LSD." Six months later, however, prisoner Leary pulled off a dramatic penitentiary escape and with the help of friends left the country. He was ultimately captured in Afghanistan and returned to prison in California, where he was a jailmate of mass murderer Charles Manson.

"**EIGHT MILES HIGH**" As Leary hoped, illegal drugs—marijuana, amphetamines, cocaine, peyote, hashish, heroin, and LSD, the "Acid Test"— became commonplace within the counterculture. Said Todd Gitlin, a former SDS president, "More and more, to get access to youth culture" in the late 1960s, "you had to get high." The Byrds sang about getting "Eight Miles High," and Bob Dylan proclaimed that "everybody must get stoned!"

Getting stoned was one of the favorite activities of the millions who participated in the 1967 Summer of Love, a series of nationwide events protesting the Vietnam War and celebrating the youth revolt.

The most publicized activity of the "Summer of Love" occurred in San Francisco, where more than 100,000 hippies ("flower children") converged in search of tribal intimacy. As author P. J. O'Rourke recalled, "You name it and I believed it" that summer. "I believed love was all you need. . . . I believed drugs could make you a better person. I believed I could hitchhike to California with 35 cents and people would be glad to feed me. . . . I believed the Age of Aquarius was about to happen. . . . With the exception of anything my parents said, I believed everything."

The loosely organized "Council for the Summer of Love" intended the gathering to be the first step in a grassroots revolution opposing the war in Vietnam by celebrating "hippiedom" and other alternative lifestyles.

**THE YIPPIES** The countercultural alternative to SDS and the New Left was the Youth International party, better known as the Yippies, founded in New York City on December 31, 1967, by two irreverent pranksters, Jerry Rubin and Abbie Hoffman. The Yippies were countercultural comedians bent on thumbing their noses at the "absurdity" of conventional laws and behavior and mocking capitalism and the consumer culture. Utterly alienated from mainstream life, they wanted "to offer the people an alternative lifestyle. Something to do other than conform or die." Their notion of community was modeled after their skewed understanding of Native Americans: "a whole bunch of people living together, having children, none of them married."

Hoffman explained that their "conception of revolution is that it's fun." They wanted to form an alliance between hippies and Weathermen, a "blending of pot and politics," and overthrow the power structure. Rubin claimed that "the first part of the Yippie program is to kill your parents," since they are "our first oppressors." He added that the use of "psychedelic" drugs "signifies the total end of the Protestant ethic: screw work, we want to know ourselves." The Yippie platform called for peace in Vietnam, absolute personal freedom, free birth control and abortions, and legalization of marijuana and LSD.

The anarchistic Yippies organized marijuana "smoke-ins," threw pies at political figures, nominated a squealing pig for the presidency, urged voters to cast their ballots for "None of the Above," and threatened to put LSD in Chicago's water supply during the 1968 Democratic National Convention. When asked what being a Yippie meant, Hoffman replied, "Energy–fun–fierceness–exclamation point!"

**COMMUNES** For some, the counterculture involved experimenting with alternative living arrangements, especially "intentional communities" or "communes." Communal living in urban areas such as San Francisco's Haight-Ashbury district, New York's Greenwich Village, Chicago's Uptown, and Atlanta's 14th Street neighborhood were popular for a time, as were rural communes. Thousands of hippie romantics flocked to the countryside, eager to live in harmony with nature, coexist in love and openness, deepen their sense of self, and forge authentic community ties.

Yet all but a handful of the back-to-the-land experiments collapsed within a few months or years. Almost none of the participants knew how to sustain a farm, and many were unwilling to do the hard work that living off the land required. In 1968, *Newsweek* magazine reported "Trouble in Hippieland," noting that most flower children were "seriously disturbed youngsters" incapable of sustaining an alternative to mainstream life. A resident of Paper Farm in northern California, which started in 1968 and collapsed a year later, said of its participants: "They had no commitment to the land—a big problem. All would take food from the land, but few would tend it. . . . We were entirely open. We did not say no [to anyone]. We felt this would make for a more dynamic group. But we got a lot of sick people."

**WOODSTOCK** The sixties counterculture thrived on music—initially folk "protest" songs and later psychedelic rock music. During the early sixties, Pete Seeger; Joan Baez; Peter, Paul, and Mary; and Bob Dylan, among others, produced powerful songs intended to spur social reform. In Dylan's "The Times They Are a-Changin'," he warns: "There's a battle outside and it's ragin' / It'll soon shake your windows and rattle your walls / For the times, they are a-changin.'"

Within a few years, however, the hippies' favorite performers were those under the influence of mind-altering drugs, especially the San Francisco–based "acid rock" bands: Jefferson Airplane, Big Brother and the Holding Company, and the Grateful Dead. "Rock 'n roll was the tribal telegraph," remembered Jann Wenner, founder of *Rolling Stone* magazine.

Huge outdoor concerts—music-infused psychedelic picnics—were wildly popular. The largest and most publicized was the sprawling Woodstock Music and Art Fair ("Aquarian Exposition"). In mid-August 1969, more than 400,000 mostly young people converged on a 600-acre farm near the tiny rural town of Bethel, New York, for what was billed as the world's "largest happening," three days "of peace and music."

The festival boasted an all-star cast of musicians, among them Jimi Hendrix, Jefferson Airplane, Janis Joplin, Santana, the Who, Joan Baez, and Crosby, Stills and Nash. For three days amid heat, rain storms, and rivers of mud, the assembled flower children "grooved" on music, beer and booze, cheap marijuana, and casual sex. Baez described Woodstock as a "technicolor, mud-splattered reflection of the 1960s."

Woodstock's carefree "spirit of love" was short-lived, however. Just four months later, when other concert promoters tried to replicate the experience at the Altamont Speedway Free Festival near San Francisco, the counterculture fell victim to the criminal culture.

The Rolling Stones foolishly hired the Hells Angels motorcycle gang to provide "security" for their show. During the band's performance of "Under My Thumb," a drunken Hells Angel stabbed to death an eighteen-year-old African American man wielding a gun in front of the stage. Three other spectators were killed that night. Much of the vitality and innocence of the counterculture died with them.

After 1969, the hippie phenomenon began to fade as the spirit of liberation ran up against the hard realities of poverty, drug addiction, crime, and mental and physical illness among the flower children. Yet strands of the counterculture survive in the popularity of ecology; yoga; meditation; "health foods" and organic farming, food co-ops; craft guilds; and digital social media promoting connectedness, sharing, and collaboration.

# Social Activism Spreads

The same liberationist ideals that prompted young people to revolt against mainstream values and protest against the Vietnam War led many of them to embrace other causes. The civil rights movement inspired women, Latinos and Native Americans, gays and lesbians, the elderly, and people with physical and mental disabilities to demand equal opportunities and equal rights. Still others joined the emerging environmental movement or groups working on behalf of consumers.

## The New Feminism

The first wave of the women's movement in the late nineteenth and early twentieth centuries had focused on gaining the right to vote. The second wave of the feminist movement, in the sixties and seventies, challenged the conventional ideal of female domesticity and worked to ensure that women gained equal treatment in the workplace.

Many women in the early 1960s, however, did not view gender equality as possible or even desirable. In 1962, more than two thirds of women surveyed agreed that the most important family decisions "should be made by the man of the house." Although the Equal Pay Act of 1963 had made it illegal to pay women less than men for doing the same job, discrimination and harassment continued. Women, who were 51 percent of the nation's population and held 37 percent of the jobs, were paid 42 percent less than men on average.

Betty Friedan, a forty-two-year-old mother of three from Peoria, Illinois, who supplemented her husband's income by writing articles for women's magazines, emerged as one of the leaders of the postwar **women's movement**. As a brilliant student at all-female Smith College in Massachusetts, she had edited the campus newspaper, arguing for non-intervention in the

**Betty Friedan** Author of *The Feminine Mystique* and the first president of NOW.

Second World War and unionization for the campus housekeepers. After the war, she worked as a journalist for progressive publications promoting labor unions. In her articles, Friedan called for equal pay for equal work and an end to gender and race-based discrimination in hiring and housing. Then, in 1963, she published her searing first book, *The Feminine Mystique*, which helped launch the second phase of the feminist movement. Rarely has a single book exercised such a transformational influence.

Friedan argued that her generation of upper- and middle-class college-educated white mothers and wives (she did not discuss working-class women, women of color, or women without husbands or suburban homes) had actually lost ground after the Second World War, when many left wartime employment and settled in suburbia as full-time wives and mothers, only to suffer from the "happy homemaker" syndrome that undermined their intellectual capacity and public aspirations. Suburban women of privilege, like herself, Friedan observed, "seemed suddenly incapable of any ambition, any vision, any passion, except the pursuit of a wedding ring."

She blamed the "enforced domesticity" of postwar America on a massive propaganda campaign by advertisers and women's magazines that brainwashed women to embrace the "feminine mystique," in which fulfillment came only with marriage and motherhood. Women, Friedan claimed, "were being duped into believing homemaking was their natural destiny."

*The Feminine Mystique*, an immediate best seller, forever changed American society by defining "the problem that has no name." Friedan inspired many well-educated, unfulfilled middle- and upper-class white women who felt trapped by household drudgery.

Moreover, Friedan discovered that there were far more women working outside the home than she had assumed. Many were frustrated by the demands of holding "two full-time jobs instead of just one—underpaid clerical worker and unpaid housekeeper." Perhaps most important, Friedan helped empower women to achieve their "full human capacities"—in the home, in schools, in offices, on college campuses, and in politics.

In 1966, Friedan and other activists founded the National Organization for Women (NOW). It promoted "true equality for all women in America . . . as part of the worldwide revolution of human rights now taking place." It sought to end gender discrimination in the workplace and spearheaded efforts to legalize abortion and obtain federal and state support for child-care centers. Change came slowly, however. By 1970, there was still only one woman in the U.S. Senate, ten in the House of Representatives, and none on the Supreme Court or in the president's cabinet.

**GLORIA STEINEM** The women's movement received a boost from the energetic leadership provided by Gloria Steinem, who founded, with others, *Ms.* magazine in 1971. It was the first feminist periodical with a national readership. Its first edition of 300,000 copies sold out in eight days, and at the end of the first year it enjoyed half a million subscribers. By writing scores of hard-hitting essays in *Ms.* and other national magazines, Steinem expanded the scope of feminism beyond what Betty Friedan and others had started.

Born in Toledo, Ohio, in 1934, Steinem grew up in a poor, dysfunctional family. By age ten, she became her family's primary caregiver. Gloria did not spend a full year in school until she was twelve, but by then she was reading a book a day on her own. To supplement her family's meager finances, she performed as a tap dancer and sales clerk before she earned a scholarship to Smith College, where she majored in government and political affairs. She graduated with honors in 1956 and earned a two-year fellowship for study in India.

Upon her return to America, Steinem began a career as a hard-nosed freelance investigative journalist living in New York City. In 1963, *Show* magazine hired her to go undercover as a scantily-clad Playboy "Bunny" at the New York City Playboy Club. The resulting article ("I Was a Playboy Bunny") detailed the degrading treatment and inequitable wages she and others received as sex objects wearing rabbit ears and cottontails. It also made Steinem famous. In 1968, she helped found *New York* magazine, which enabled her, the only woman on the staff, to write about political topics and progressive social issues.

A year later, in 1969, Steinem attended an event in Greenwich Village sponsored by the Redstockings, a radical feminist group, at which women stood and recounted their experience with abortion. Having had an illegal abortion in London at age twenty-two on her way to India, Steinem stood and told her story to the group of strangers. "Why should each of us," she asked, "be made to feel criminal or alone?"

That event proved to be life-changing, as Steinem sensed "a great blinding lightbulb" coming on in her head. She committed herself that night to advancing the women's liberation movement through advocacy journalism that gave voice to the voiceless. She resolved to engage in "outrageous acts and everyday rebellions."

Steinem thereafter became a prolific writer, fundraiser, and speaker, addressing numerous rallies, sit-ins, demonstrations, corporations, and organizations. She donated half her speaking fees to women's organizations and insisted on sharing the lectern with at least one woman of color to demonstrate that the women's liberation movement encompassed many diverse feminisms.

"For twenty years," she recalled, "not a week went by when I wasn't on a plane" headed to give another public address.

Steinem soon became the public face and voice of the women's liberation movement, its celebrity diva and the icon of feminism. She was usually the first choice of reporters eager for provocative interviews and comments. As feminist scholar Rebecca Traister explained, Steinem was "young and white and pretty, and she looked great on magazine covers. I'm not deriding her. She tells this story about herself." Steinem testified before a Senate committee in 1970 on behalf of the Equal Rights Amendment, and co-founded the Women's Action Alliance, and the National Women's Political Caucus in 1971.

Steinem then joined forces with fellow journalists Patricia Carbine and Letty Cottin Pogrebin to launch *Ms.* magazine in December 1971 because there was "nothing for women to read that was controlled by women." The masthead of the first issue listed the editors alphabetically so as not to imply a hierarchy, because hierarchies were male and hence undesirable. The first issue included stories titled "Sisterhood," "Raising Kids without Sex Roles," and "Women Tell the Truth about Their Abortions." Just a few months later, *Ms.* shocked the publishing world in 1972 when it revealed the names of women who admitted to having had an abortion when the procedure was still illegal in most states.

Unlike other women's magazines, *Ms.* focused on controversial topics such as gender bias, sexual harassment, abortion, pornography, workplace equality, same-sex marriage, and college curricula. "We need Women's Studies courses just as much as Black Studies," Steinem insisted in 1971.

**INNER TURMOIL** Like every other movement for social justice, the feminist movement experienced internal tensions. Betty Friedan, famous for her prickly claim to the leadership spotlight of the feminist movement, grew jealous of Steinem's celebrity status and her hip glamour. Steinem had become famous for her tinted aviator glasses, belted mini-dresses, backless blouses, long brown hair streaked with signature blond highlights, white lipstick, and romances with powerful men. More important, Friedan accused Steinem and others of practicing a "female chauvinism" that was "corrupting our move-ment for equality." She bristled at Steinem's dismissal of conventional marriage as a form of "prostitution." Steinem replied that she was puzzled by Friedan's broadside. Male critics had long "falsely" accused her of liking men too much, yet now Friedan was falsely accusing her "of not liking them enough."

Other criticisms were more worrisome. The much-celebrated African American writer Alice Walker, an early *Ms.* contributor, resigned from the staff because the magazine covers featured too many whites and not enough blacks. Steinem persevered in the face of attacks from all sides. She was a gifted conciliator who always sought common ground in dealing with her critics.

**What women want** The Women's Strike for Equality brought tens of thousands of women together on August 26, 1970, to march for gender equality and celebrate the fiftieth anniversary of the Nineteenth Amendment.

**FEMINIST VICTORIES** In the early 1970s, Steinem joined members of Congress, the Supreme Court, and NOW in advancing the cause of gender equality. A major victory occurred with the Congressional passage of Title IX of the Educational Amendments of 1972. It barred gender discrimination in any "education program or activity receiving federal financial assistance." Most notably applied to athletics, Title IX spurred female participation in high school sports to increase nearly tenfold and to almost double at the college level.

Congress also overwhelmingly approved an equal-rights amendment (ERA) to the U.S. Constitution, which, if ratified by the states, would have required equal treatment for women throughout society and politics. By mid-1973, twenty-eight states had approved the amendment, ten short of the thirty-eight needed for approval.

In 1973, the Supreme Court, in its *Roe v. Wade* decision, struck down state laws forbidding abortions during the first three months of pregnancy. The Court ruled that women have a fundamental "right to choose" whether to bear a child or not, since pregnancy necessarily affects a woman's health and well-being. The *Roe v. Wade* decision, and the ensuing success of NOW's efforts to liberalize local and state abortion laws, generated a powerful conservative backlash, especially among Roman Catholics and evangelical Protestants, who mounted a "right-to-life" crusade that helped fuel the conservative political resurgence in the seventies and thereafter.

**RADICAL FEMINISM** During the late sixties, a new wave of younger, more militant feminists emerged. They sought "women's liberation" from all forms of sexism (also called "male chauvinism" or "male oppression").

Many of the new feminists, often called "women's libbers," were veterans of the civil rights and anti-war movements. Having come to realize that male revolutionaries could be sexists, too, the women began meeting in small groups to discuss their opposition to the war and racism, only to discover at such "consciousness-raising" sessions that what bound them together was their shared grievances as women in a "man's world."

To gain true liberation, many of them decided, required exercising "sexual politics" whereby women would organize their own political movement. Writer Robin Morgan captured this newly politicized feminism in the slogan, "The personal is political," a radical notion that Betty Friedan rejected. When lesbians and bisexual women demanded a public role in the feminist movement, Friedan deplored the "lavender menace" of lesbianism as a divisive distraction that would only enrage their homophobic opponents. By 1973, however, NOW had endorsed gay and lesbian rights.

Friedan failed to dampen or deflect the younger generation of women activists, just as Martin Luther King Jr. had failed to suppress the Black Power movement. The goal of the women's liberation movement, said Susan Brownmiller, was to "go beyond a simple concept of equality. NOW's emphasis on legislative change left the radicals cold."

For women to be truly equal, many new feminists believed, *every* aspect of society needed to be transformed: child rearing, entertainment, domestic duties, business, and the arts. In pursuit of their goal, they took direct action, such as picketing the 1968 Miss America Pageant, burning copies of *Playboy* and other men's magazines, and tossing their bras and high-heeled shoes into "freedom cans."

**FRACTURED FEMINISM** By the end of the seventies, sharp disputes between moderate and radical feminists had fractured the women's movement in ways similar to the fragmentation experienced by civil rights organizations a decade earlier. The movement's failure to broaden its appeal much beyond white middle class heterosexual women also caused reform efforts to stall.

Ratification of the Equal Rights Amendment ("Equality of rights under the law shall not be denied or abridged by the United States or by any State on account of sex") was stymied in several state legislatures by conservative groups. By 1982, it had died, three states short of ratification. Conservatives saw the defeat of the ERA as a triumph. They drew much of their strength from the backlash against changing social attitudes about women's roles.

Yet the successes of the women's movement endured, as it called attention to issues long hidden or ignored. In 1970, for example, 36 percent of the nation's "poor" families were headed by women, as were most urban families dependent on federal welfare services. Nearly 3 million poor children needed access to day-care centers, but there were places for only 530,000.

The feminist movement helped women achieve mass entry into the labor market and enjoy steady improvements toward equal pay and treatment. In 1960, some 38 percent of women were working outside the home; by 1980, an estimated 52 percent were doing so.

Their growing presence in the labor force brought women a greater share of economic and political influence. By 1976, more than half of married women, and nine of ten female college graduates, were employed outside the home, a development that one economist called "the single most outstanding phenomenon of this century." Women also enrolled in graduate and professional schools in record numbers. During the 1970s, women began winning elected offices at the local, state, and national levels.

**THE SEXUAL REVOLUTION AND THE PILL**  The feminist movement coincided with the so-called sexual revolution. Americans became more tolerant of premarital sex, and women became more sexually active. Between 1960 and 1975, the number of college women engaging in heterosexual intercourse doubled, to 50 percent.

Enabling this change, in large part, was the birth-control pill, approved for public use by the Food and Drug Administration in 1960. Widespread access to the pill gave women a greater sense of sexual freedom and led to more-open discussion of birth control, reproduction, and sexuality in general. Although the pill contributed to a rise in sexually transmitted diseases, many women viewed it as an inexpensive, nonintrusive way to gain better control over their bodies, their careers, and their futures.

## LATINO RIGHTS

The activism of student revolts, the civil rights movement, and the crusade for women's rights soon spread to various ethnic groups. The word *Latino*, referring to people who trace their ancestry to Spanish-speaking Latin

America, came into increasing use after 1945 in conjunction with growing efforts to promote economic and social justice.

Labor shortages during the Second World War had led defense industries to offer Latino Americans their first significant access to skilled-labor jobs. And as with African Americans, service in the military helped to heighten an American identity among Latino Americans and increase their desire for equal rights and social opportunities.

Social equality, however, remained elusive. After the Second World War, Latino Americans still faced widespread discrimination in hiring, housing, and education. Latino American activists denounced segregation, called for improved public schools, and struggled to increase their political influence, economic opportunities, and visibility in the curricula of schools and colleges.

Latino civil rights leaders faced an awkward dilemma: what should they do about the stream of undocumented Mexicans flowing across the border into the United States? Many Latino Americans argued that their hopes for economic advancement and social equality were threatened by the influx of Mexican laborers willing to accept low-paying jobs. In 1964, Latino American leaders helped end the *bracero* program, which trucked in contract day-laborers from Mexico during harvest season.

**THE UNITED FARM WORKERS** In the early 1960s, Mexican American workers formed their own civil rights organization, the **United Farm Workers (UFW)**. Its founder was the charismatic Cesar Chavez. Born in 1927 in Yuma, Arizona, the son of Mexican immigrants, Chavez spent his youth shuttling with his family to various farm camps. The family often earned only a dollar a day as fruit pickers. Chavez and his siblings went barefoot and attended 40 different schools. During the Second World War, he served in the U.S. Navy. Afterward, he was a migrant laborer and community organizer focused on registering Latinos to vote.

In 1962, Chavez formed the Farm Workers' Association. Like the earlier farm Alliances, it was more than a union. It was *La Causa*, a broad social movement intended to enhance the solidarity and dignity of migrant farm workers. By 1965, he and Dolores Huerta converted the Farm Workers' Association into the United Farm Workers (UFW), a union for migrant lettuce workers and grape pickers, many of them undocumented immigrants who could be deported at any time. Over the next ten years, Chavez led some of the poorest workers in the nation in a series of nonviolent protest marches, staged hunger strikes, and managed nationwide boycotts. Workers were spellbound by his humility, his integrity, and his sincere dedication to improving the quality of their lives.

**Cesar Chavez** The usually energetic Chavez is visibly weakened from what would be a twenty-five-day hunger strike in support of the United Farm Workers Union in March 1968. Robert F. Kennedy, a great admirer of Chavez, is seated to his right.

The United Farm Workers gained national attention in September 1965 when it joined with Filipino migrant workers in organizing a strike (*la huelga*) against grape growers in California's San Joaquin Valley. Their grievance focused on wages; they earned about $1,350 a year. As Huerta explained, "We have to get farmworkers the same type of benefits, the same type of wages, and the respect that they deserve because they do the most sacred work of all. They feed our nation every day."

Chavez's relentless energy and deep Catholic faith, his insistence upon nonviolent tactics, his reliance upon college-student volunteers, his skillful alliance with organized labor and religious groups, and his simple lifestyle attracted popular support in a strike that would last five years.

In 1968, Chavez began a twenty-five-day hunger strike to raise national attention for his efforts. On the day he broke his fast, the first to greet him was Robert F. Kennedy, then campaigning for the Democratic presidential nomination. "The world must know, from this time forward, that the migrant farm worker, the Mexican-American, is coming into his own rights," Kennedy declared, adding that the farmworkers were gaining "a special kind of citizenship . . . . You are winning it for yourselves—and therefore no one can ever take it away."

Finally, in 1970, the grape growers agreed to raise wages, offer health benefits, and improve working conditions. Chavez then turned his attention to political activism, organizing voter registration drives and advocating laws to protect the civil rights of migrant workers.

As Chavez recognized, the chief strength of the Latino rights movement lay in the rapid growth of the Latino American population. From 1970 to 2015, their numbers grew from 9 million (4.8 percent of the total population) to 55 million, making them the nation's largest minority group (17 percent). The increased population of Latinos in key electoral states has given them significant political clout.

## NATIVE AMERICANS' QUEST FOR EQUALITY

American Indians—many of whom began calling themselves *Native Americans*—also emerged as a political force in the late 1960s. Two conditions combined to make Indian rights a priority. First, many whites felt guilty for the destructive actions of their ancestors toward a people who had, after all, been here first. Second, Indian unemployment was ten times the national rate, life expectancy was twenty years lower than the national average, and the suicide rate was a hundred times higher than the rate for whites.

Although President Lyndon Johnson attempted to funnel federal anti-poverty-program funds to reservations, many Native American activists grew impatient with the pace of change. Those promoting **"Red Power"** organized protests and demonstrations against local, state, and federal agencies.

On November 20, 1969, fourteen Red Power activists occupied Alcatraz Island near San Francisco. Over the next several months, hundreds of others, mostly students, joined them. The Nixon administration responded by cutting off electrical service and telephone lines. Stranded without power and fresh water, most of the protesters left the island. Finally, on June 11, 1971, the government removed the remaining fifteen Native Americans.

In 1968, the year before the Alcatraz occupation, George Mitchell and Dennis Banks, two Chippewas (or Ojibwas) living in Minneapolis, founded the American Indian Movement (AIM). In October 1972, AIM organized the Trail of Broken Treaties caravan, which traveled by bus and car from the West Coast to Washington, D.C., to draw attention to the federal government's broken promises. When Nixon administration officials refused to meet with them, the protesters barged into the offices of the Bureau of Indian Affairs. The sit-in ended when government negotiators agreed to renew discussions of Native American grievances.

In 1973, AIM led 200 Sioux in the occupation of the tiny South Dakota village of Wounded Knee, where the U.S. Seventh Cavalry had massacred an entire Sioux village in 1890. Newly outraged by the light sentences given a group of local whites who had killed a Sioux just a year earlier, the organizers sought to draw attention to the plight of Native Americans and took eleven hostages.

Federal marshals and FBI agents surrounded the encampment. When AIM leaders tried to bring in food and supplies, a shoot-out erupted, with two activists killed and a U.S. marshal shot and paralyzed. The confrontation ended with a government promise to reexamine Indian treaty rights.

Indian protesters subsequently discovered a more effective tactic: they went into federal courts armed with copies of old treaties and demanded that the documents become the basis for financial restitution for the lands taken from them. In Alaska, Maine, South Carolina, and Massachusetts, the groups won substantial settlements that officially recognized their tribal rights and helped to upgrade the standard of living on several reservations.

## GAY AND LESBIAN RIGHTS

The liberationist impulses of the sixties also encouraged gay, lesbian, and transgender people, long defamed as sinful or mentally unbalanced, to assert their right to be treated as equals. Throughout the 1960s, this population continued to encounter social and institutional discrimination. Many local ordinances and state laws deemed non-heterosexual behavior a vice crime, meaning an activity deemed illegal because it "offended" the moral standards of the community.

On Saturday night, June 28, 1969, New York City police vice officers raided the Stonewall Inn, a popular gay bar in Greenwich Village. The patrons, led by transgender women of color, drag queens, and street people, fought back, and the struggle spilled outside, forcing the outnumbered police to take shelter inside the bar. One participant described the rioting as "a public assertion of real anger by gay people that was just electric."

The **Stonewall riots** lasted five days, during which the Stonewall Inn burned down. When the turmoil ended, gays had forged a sense of solidarity embodied in two new organizations, the Gay Liberation Front and the Gay Activists' Alliance, both of which focused on ending discrimination and harassment against gay, lesbian, bisexual, and transgender people.

As news of the Stonewall rebellion spread, the gay rights movement grew. By 1973, almost 800 organizations supporting sexual orientation and gender identification rights had emerged. That year, the American Psychiatric

**Gay pride in the seventies** Activists march in the Annual Gay Pride Day demonstration, commemorating the fifth anniversary of the Stonewall riots that jumpstarted what became the modern LGBTQ (lesbian, gay, bisexual, transgender, and queer) rights movement in the United States.

Association removed homosexuality from its official diagnostic manual of mental disorders. Colleges and universities began offering courses and majors in gay and lesbian studies (also called queer studies), and groups began pushing for official government recognition of same-sex marriages. As with the civil rights and women's movements, however, the campaign for gay and lesbian rights soon suffered from internal divisions and a conservative counterattack.

# Nixon and the Revival of Conservatism

The turmoil of the sixties spawned a cultural backlash from what President Richard Nixon called the "great silent majority" of middle-class Americans that had propelled him to victory in 1968. He had been elected as the representative of middle America—voters fed up with liberal politics, hippies, radical feminism, gay and lesbian rights, and **affirmative-action** programs that gave preferential treatment to people of color and women to atone for past injustices.

**THE CONSERVATIVE BACKLASH** Alabama's Democratic governor, George Wallace, led the conservative white backlash. "Liberals, intellectuals, and long hairs," he shouted, "have run the country for too long." He repeatedly attacked "welfare queens," unmarried African-American mothers whom he claimed "were breeding children as a cash crop" to receive federal child-support checks. Wallace became the voice for many working-class whites fed up with political liberalism and social radicalism.

*All in the Family*, the most popular television show in the 1970s, showcased the decade's culture wars. In the much-celebrated sitcom, the Bunker family lived in a working-class suburb of New York City. Semiliterate Archie Bunker (played by Carroll O'Connor), a Polish American loading-dock worker, was the gruff but lovable head of the family, a proud Republican, Nixon supporter, and talkative member of the silent majority who railed against blacks, Jews, Italians, gays, feminists, hippies, and liberals (including his live-in daughter and her hippie husband). At one point, he said: "I ain't no bigot. I'm the first guy to say, 'It ain't your fault that youse are colored.'"

The producer of the series, Norman Lear, sought to provoke viewers to question their own prejudices. In fact, however, many of the 50 million people watching each Saturday night identified *with* Archie's values.

**RICHARD NIXON** Richard Nixon courted working- and middle-class whites who feared that America was being corrupted by permissiveness, anarchy, and the tyranny of the rebellious minority. He explicitly appealed to voters "who did not break the law, people who pay their taxes and go to work, people who send their children to school, who go to their churches, people who are not haters, people who love this country." Above all, he promised to restore "law and order," which to him and his followers meant "cracking down" on anti-war protesters, civil rights demonstrators, and activists who challenged traditional gender roles.

A grocer's son from Whittier, California, Nixon was a humorless man of fierce ambition and extraordinary perseverance. Raised in a family that struggled with poverty, he nursed a deep resentment of people who had enjoyed an easier time (the "moneyed class").

Like Lyndon Johnson, Nixon was a paradoxical character. He was smart, cunning, and doggedly determined to succeed in politics. Cold and calculating, he saw enemies around every corner and allowed his paranoia and vengefulness to isolate him from political reality—and from his family. He and his wife, Pat, had separate bedrooms for most of their marriage. He even wrote sterile memos to her with the salutation, "To Mrs. Nixon, from the President."

Nixon displayed violent mood swings (punctuated by alcohol abuse), raging temper tantrums, profanity, and anti-Semitic outbursts. He was driven as much by anger and resentment as by civic duty. Critics nicknamed him "Tricky Dick" because he excelled at deceit. In his speech accepting the Republican nomination in 1968, Nixon pledged "to find the truth, to speak the truth, and live with the truth." In fact, however, he often did the opposite. One of his presidential aides admitted that "we did often lie, mislead, deceive, try to use [the media], and to con them."

**NIXON'S APPOINTMENTS** In his first term, Nixon selected for his cabinet and staff only white men who would blindly carry out his orders. John Mitchell, the gruff attorney general who had been a senior partner in Nixon's New York law firm, was his closest confidant. H. R. (Bob) Haldeman, a former advertising executive, served as chief of staff. Nixon called him his "chief executioner." John Ehrlichman, a Seattle attorney and college schoolmate of Haldeman, was chief domestic-policy adviser. John W. Dean III, an associate deputy in the office of the U.S. Attorney General, became the White House legal counsel.

Nixon tapped as secretary of state his friend William Rogers, who had served as attorney general under Dwight D. Eisenhower. The president, however, virtually ignored Rogers while forging an unlikely partnership with Dr. Henry Kissinger, a brilliant German-born Jew and Harvard political scientist who had become the nation's leading foreign-policy expert. Kissinger's thick accent, owlish appearance, and outsized ego had helped to make him an international celebrity, courted by presidents of both parties. In 1969, Nixon named Kissinger his national security adviser, and in 1973 Kissinger became secretary of state, although in private Nixon called him "my Jew-boy."

Both Nixon and Kissinger were outsiders who preferred operating in secret; both were insecure and even paranoid at times; and both mistrusted and envied the other's power and prestige. Nixon would eventually tire of Kissinger's efforts at self-promotion and frequent threats to resign.

For his part, Kissinger lavished praise on Nixon in public, but in private he dismissed the president as an insecure man with a "meatball mind" who went on frequent stress-induced drinking binges. (To his aides, Kissinger frequently referred to Nixon as "our drunken friend.") Yet for all their differences, they worked well together, in part because they both loved intrigue, power politics, and diplomatic flexibility, and in part because of their shared vision of a multipolar world order that was beginning to replace the bipolar cold war.

**THE SOUTHERN STRATEGY** A major reason for Nixon's election victories in 1968 and 1972 was his shrewd southern strategy, designed to win over white southern Democrats angered by the civil rights revolution. The majority of white southern voters were religious and patriotic, fervently anti-Communist and anti-union, and skeptical of social-welfare programs benefiting people of color.

For a century, whites in the South had steadfastly voted for Democrats. This trend reflected lingering resentments, dating to the Civil War and Reconstruction, against Abraham Lincoln and his Republican successors for imposing northern ways of life on the South, including racial integration. During the late 1960s and 1970s, however, a surging economy and a spurt of population growth began to transform the South.

Between 1970 and 1990, the South's population grew by 40 percent, a rate of more than twice the national average. The region's warm climate, low cost of living, absence of labor unions, low taxes, and government incentives for economic development convinced waves of businesses to relocate there. During the 1970s, the rate of job growth in the South was seven times greater than in New York and Pennsylvania.

Southern "redneck" culture suddenly became the rage as the nation embraced stock car racing, cowboy boots, pickup trucks, barbecue, and country music. Rapid population growth—and the continuing spread of air-conditioning—brought the sunbelt states of the South, the Southwest, and California more congressional seats and more electoral votes. Every president elected between 1964 and 2008 had roots in the Sun Belt.

Nixon's favorite singer, country star Merle Haggard, crooned in his smash hit, "Okie from Muskogee": "We don't smoke marijuana in Muskogee / We don't take our trips on LSD / We don't burn our draft cards down on Main Street / We like livin' right and bein' free." Haggard's conservative working-class fans bristled at anti-war protesters, hippies, rising taxes, social-welfare programs, and civil rights activism. The alienation of many blue-collar whites from the Democratic party, the demographic changes transforming sunbelt states, and the white backlash against court-ordered integration created a fertile opportunity to gain southern votes that the Republican party eagerly exploited.

In the 1968 presidential campaign, Nixon won over traditionally Democratic working-class white voters. He cleverly "played the race card," assuring white conservatives that he would appoint justices to the Supreme Court who would undermine federal enforcement of civil rights laws, such as mandatory school busing to achieve racial integration and affirmative-action programs that gave women and people of color priority in hiring decisions and the awarding of government contracts. Nixon also appealed to the economic concerns of middle-class southern whites by promising lower tax rates and less government regulation.

In the 1972 election, Nixon easily carried every southern state. The Republican takeover of the once Solid South was the greatest realignment in American politics since Franklin D. Roosevelt's election in 1932. It was also an unlikely coalition, for it brought together traditional "country club" Republicans—corporate executives, financiers, and investors—with poor, rural, fundamentalist southerners who had always voted for segregationist Democrats. What they shared was a simmering hatred for what the Democratic party had become.

**NIXON'S DOMESTIC AGENDA**  As president, Richard Nixon was less a rigid conservative ideologue than a crafty politician. Forced to deal with a Congress controlled by Democrats, he chose his battles carefully and showed surprising flexibility, leading journalist Tom Wicker to describe him as "at once liberal and conservative, generous and begrudging, cynical and idealistic, choleric and calm, resentful and forgiving."

Nixon focused during his first term on developing policies and programs that would please conservatives and ensure his reelection. To recruit conservative Democrats, he touted his New Federalism, which sent federal money to state and local governments to spend as they saw fit. He also disbanded the core agency of Lyndon Johnson's war on poverty—the Office of Economic Opportunity—and cut funding to several Great Society programs.

At the same time, Democrats in Congress passed significant legislation that Nixon signed: the right of eighteen-year-olds to vote in national elections (1970) and in all elections under the Twenty-Sixth Amendment (1971); increases in Social Security benefits and food-stamp funding; the Occupational Safety and Health Act (1970) to ensure safer workplace environments; and the Federal Election Campaign Act (1971), which modified the rules governing corporate financial donations to political campaigns.

**NIXON AND CIVIL RIGHTS**  During his first term, President Nixon followed through on campaign pledges to blunt the momentum of the civil rights movement. He appointed no African Americans to his cabinet and refused to meet with the all-Democratic Congressional Black Caucus.

He also launched a concerted effort to block congressional renewal of the Voting Rights Act of 1965 and to delay implementation of federal court orders requiring the racial desegregation of school districts in Mississippi.

Sixty-five lawyers in the Justice Department signed a letter protesting Nixon's stance. The Democratic-controlled Congress extended the Voting Rights Act over Nixon's veto.

The Supreme Court also thwarted Nixon's efforts to slow desegregation. In its first decision under the new chief justice, Warren Burger—a Nixon appointee—the Court ordered the racial integration of the Mississippi public schools in *Alexander v. Holmes County Board of Education* (1969). During Nixon's first term, more schools were desegregated under court order than in all the Kennedy–Johnson years combined.

**Off to school**  Because of violent protests by whites against forced desegregation, school buses in Boston were escorted by police in 1974.

The Burger Court also ruled unanimously in *Swann v. Charlotte-Mecklenburg Board of Education* (1971) that school systems must bus students out of their neighborhoods if necessary to achieve racially integrated schools. Protests over busing erupted in the North, the Midwest, and the Southwest, as white families denounced the destruction of "the neighborhood school."

**NIXON AND ENVIRONMENTAL PROTECTION** During the seventies, dramatic increases in the price of oil and gasoline fueled a major energy crisis. Natural resources grew limited—and increasingly precious. Nixon recognized that the public mood had shifted in favor of greater federal environmental protections, especially after two widely publicized environmental events in 1969.

The first was a massive oil spill off the coast of Santa Barbara, California, when a slick of crude oil contaminated 200 miles of California beaches, killing thousands of sea birds and marine animals. Six months later, on June 22, 1969, the Cuyahoga River, an eighty-mile-long stream that slices through Cleveland, Ohio, spontaneously caught fire. Fouled with oil and grease, bubbling with subsurface gases, and littered with debris, the river burned for five days.

The images of the burning river helped raise environmental awareness. A 1969 survey of college campuses by the *New York Times* revealed that many young people were transferring their idealism from the anti-war movement to the environmental movement.

Nixon knew that if he vetoed legislative efforts to improve environmental quality, the Democratic majorities in Congress would overrule him, so he chose not to stand in the way. In late 1969, he signed the amended Endangered Species Preservation Act and the National Environmental Policy Act. The latter became effective on January 1, 1970, the year that environmental groups established an annual Earth Day celebration. In 1970, Nixon signed an executive order that created two federal agencies, the **Environmental Protection Agency (EPA)** and the National Oceanic and Atmospheric Administration (NOAA) and signed the Clean Air Act. Two years later, he vetoed a new clean water act, only to see Congress override him. He also undermined many new environmental laws by refusing to spend money appropriated by Congress to fund them.

"STAGFLATION" The major domestic development during the Nixon administration was a floundering economy. The accumulated expense of the Vietnam War and the Great Society programs helped quadruple the annual inflation rate from 3 percent in 1967 to 12 percent in 1974. Meanwhile, unemployment, at only 3.3 percent when Nixon took office, hit 6 percent by the end of 1970.

Economists coined the term "**stagflation**" to describe the simultaneous problems of stalled economic growth (stagnation), rising inflation, and high unemployment. Consumer prices usually rose with a rapidly growing economy and rising employment. This was just the reverse, and there were no easy ways to fight the unusual combination of recession and inflation.

Stagflation had at least three causes. First, the Johnson administration had financed both the Great Society social-welfare programs and the Vietnam War without a major tax increase, thereby generating large federal deficits, a major expansion of the money supply, and price inflation. Second, U.S. companies were facing stiff competition from West Germany, Japan, and other emerging international industrial powers. Third, America's prosperity since 1945 had resulted in part from the ready availability of cheap sources of energy. No other nation was more dependent upon the automobile, and no other nation was more wasteful in its use of fossil fuels. During the seventies, however, oil and gasoline became scarcer and costlier. High energy prices and oil shortages took their toll on the economy.

It was oil that complicated U.S. foreign policies in the Middle East. The longstanding American commitment to the security of Israel clashed with Arab countries determined to engineer the Jewish nation's destruction. In late

May 1967, Israeli intelligence services discovered that Egypt, Jordan, Iraq, and Palestinian forces were preparing an attack. On June 5, Israeli forces launched a surprise preemptive air strike, destroying most of Egypt's and Syria's warplanes. Israeli tanks and infantry then captured the Gaza Strip, much of Egypt's Sinai Peninsula, the West Bank of the Jordan River, and East Jerusalem.

After just six days of fighting, the Arab nations requested a cease fire, which the United Nations helped to negotiate. Egypt, Syria, and Jordan had suffered more than 18,000 killed or wounded, compared with only 700 casualties for Israel.

The lopsided Six-Day War had long-range consequences, as the Israelis took control of strategic Syrian and Egyptian territories that almost doubled the nation's size. More important, the war launched a new phase in the perennial conflict between Israel and the nation-less Palestinians. The brief conflict uprooted hundreds of thousands of Palestinian refugees and brought more than one million Palestinians in the occupied territories under Israeli rule.

In 1973, tensions between Israel and its Arab neighbors again boiled over, and the United States was caught in the crossfire. When Egypt and Syria attacked Israel on Yom Kippur, the holiest day on the Jewish calendar, President Nixon sent massive aid to Israel.

In response, the Arab members of the Organization of Petroleum Exporting Countries (OPEC) convinced the group to cut off oil shipments to America.

President Nixon warned Americans that the nation was facing "the most acute shortage of energy since World War II." He asked commercial airlines to reduce flights, lowered the speed limit on federal highways from 70 to 55, halted plans to convert electricity-generating plants from coal to oil, and urged all Americans to conserve energy.

The Arab oil embargo caused gasoline shortages and skyrocketing prices. Motorists suddenly faced mile-long lines at gas stations. To manage the crisis, the federal government created

**Oil crisis, 1973** The embargo of imported Arab oil forced the rationing of gasoline. Gas stations, such as this one in Colorado, closed on Sundays to conserve supplies.

a gas-rationing program: Service stations would be open on alternate days to drivers with license plates ending in odd or even numbers.

Another condition leading to stagflation was the flood of new workers—mainly baby boomers and women. From 1965 to 1980, the workforce grew by almost 30 million, but there weren't enough new jobs to keep up with demand, so many were left unemployed.

The Nixon administration responded erratically and ineffectively to the stagflation crisis. First, the president sought to reduce the federal deficit by raising taxes and cutting the budget. When the Democratic Congress refused to cooperate, he encouraged the Federal Reserve Board to reduce the nation's money supply by raising interest rates. The stock market immediately nose-dived, and the economy plunged into the "Nixon recession."

In 1969, when asked about the possibility of imposing government caps on wages and prices, Nixon had been clear: "Oh, my God, no! . . . We'll never go to controls." In 1971, however, he reversed himself and froze wages and prices for ninety days, arguing that doing so would generate a "new prosperity: more jobs, more incomes, more profits, without inflation and without war." But the economy remained sluggish.

## "Peace with Honor": Ending the Vietnam War

Since 1945, the United States had lost its monopoly on nuclear weapons, its overwhelming economic dominance, and much of its geopolitical influence. The rapid rise of competing power centers in Europe, China, and Japan further complicated international relations and the cold war.

Richard Nixon and Henry Kissinger developed a comprehensive goal of a new world order in which they envisioned defusing the cold war by pursuing peaceful coexistence with the Soviets and Chinese. Preoccupied with secrecy, they bypassed the State Department and Congress between 1969 and 1973 in their efforts to take advantage of shifting world events.

Their immediate task was to end the war in Vietnam. Until all troops had returned home, the social harmony that Nixon had promised would remain elusive. Privately, he had decided by 1969 that "there's no way to win the war," so he sought what he and Kissinger called "peace with honor." That is, the United States needed to withdraw in a way that upheld the credibility of its military alliances around the world. Peace, however, was long in coming, not honorable, and shockingly brief.

GRADUAL WITHDRAWAL (1969-1973) The Vietnam policy implemented by Nixon and Kissinger moved along three fronts in 1969. First, U.S. negotiators in Paris demanded the withdrawal of Viet Cong forces from South Vietnam and the preservation of the U.S.-backed government of President Nguyen Van Thieu. The North Vietnamese and Viet Cong negotiators insisted on retaining a Communist military presence in the south and reunifying the Vietnamese people under a government dominated by the Communists. Hidden from public awareness and from America's South Vietnamese allies were secret meetings between Kissinger and the North Vietnamese.

On the second front, Nixon sought to steadily reduce the number of U.S. troops in Vietnam, justifying the reduction as the natural result of **"Vietnamization"**—the equipping and training of South Vietnamese soldiers and pilots to assume the burden of combat. The president began withdrawing U.S. troops while expanding the bombing of North Vietnam to buy time for the transition. From a peak of 560,000 American troops in January 1969, only 50,000 remained in Vietnam by 1973.

In 1969, Nixon also established a draft lottery whereby the birthdates of nineteen-year-old men were randomly selected and assigned a number between 1 and 366. Those with low lottery numbers would be the first drafted into military service. The lottery system eliminated many inequities and clarified the likelihood of being drafted. Four years later, in 1973, the president ended the draft by creating an all-volunteer military.

These initiatives, coupled with the troop withdrawals, defused the antiwar movement, and opinion polls showed strong support for Nixon's war policies. "We've got those liberal bastards on the run now," the president gloated.

On the third front, Nixon and Kissinger greatly intensified the bombing of North Vietnam in hopes of pressuring the Communist leaders to end the war. Kissinger felt that "a fourth-rate power" like North Vietnam must have a "breaking point." Nixon agreed, suggesting that they let the North Vietnamese leaders know that he was so "obsessed about Communism" that he might use the "nuclear button" if necessary.

In March 1969, Nixon approved a secret fourteen-month-long bombing campaign aimed at Vietnamese forces using neighboring Cambodia as a base for raids into South Vietnam. The total tonnage of bombs dropped was four times that dropped on Japan during the Second World War. Still, Hanoi's leaders did not flinch.

Then, over a year later, on April 30, 1970, Nixon announced a U.S. military incursion into "neutral" Cambodia to "clean out" hidden Communist military bases, even though he knew that sending troops into Cambodia would reignite the anti-war movement. Secretary of State William Rogers predicted that "this will make the [anti-war] students puke."

**DIVISIONS AT HOME** Strident public opposition to the war and Nixon's slow withdrawal of combat forces devastated the military's morale and reputation. "No one wants to be the last grunt to die in this lousy war," said one soldier. Between 1969 and 1971, there were 730 reported fragging incidents (efforts by troops to kill or injure their officers). In 1971, four times as many troops were hospitalized for drug overdoses as for combat-related wounds.

Revelations of atrocities committed by U.S. soldiers caused even the staunchest supporters of the war to wince. Late in 1969, the story of the My Lai Massacre exposed the country to the tale of William L. "Rusty" Calley, a twenty-six-year-old army lieutenant who ordered the massacre of 347 Vietnamese civilians in the village of My Lai in 1968. One soldier described it as "point-blank murder, and I was standing there watching it."

Newsmagazines published gruesome photos of the massacre, and Americans debated the issues it raised. A father in northern California grumbled that Calley "would have been a hero" in the Second World War. His son shot back: "Yeah, if you were a Nazi." Twenty-five army officers were charged with complicity in the massacre and subsequent cover-up, but only Calley was convicted. Nixon later granted him parole.

**Hidden** A Vietnamese mother hides with her child in the bushes near My Lai in 1968 after U.S. soldiers murdered Vietnamese villagers.

The escalation of the air war in Vietnam and the extension of the war into Cambodia triggered widespread anti-war demonstrations. The president, however, was unmoved. "As far as this kind of activity is concerned," he gruffly explained, "we expect it; however, under no circumstances will I be affected whatever by it."

The news of the American invasion ("incursion") of Cambodia set off explosive demonstrations on college campuses. At Kent State University, the Ohio National Guard mobilized on May 4. As protesters hurled insults and

**Shooting at Kent State** Mary Ann Vecchio, a teenage runaway participating in the anti-war demonstration, decries the killing of a Kent State student after the National Guard fired into the crowd.

rocks at them, the poorly trained guardsmen panicked and opened fire. Four people, all bystanders, were killed, and thirteen students were wounded.

The killings at Kent State added new fury to the anti-war and anti-Nixon movements. That spring, demonstrations occurred on more than 350 campuses.

A presidential commission charged with investigating the shootings concluded that they were "unnecessary and unwarranted." Not all agreed. A resident of Kent told a reporter that "anyone who appears on the streets of a city like Kent with long hair, dirty clothes, or barefooted deserves to be shot. . . . It would have been better if the Guard had shot the whole lot of them."

Singer Neil Young had a different view. Shortly after the killings, he composed a song called "Ohio":

Tin soldiers and Nixon's coming.
We're finally on our own.
This summer I hear the drumming.
Four dead in Ohio.

The Ohio governor banned radio stations from playing the song, which only made it more popular.

Eleven days after the Kent State tragedy, on May 15, Mississippi highway patrolmen riddled a dormitory at predominantly black Jackson State College with 460 bullets, killing two students and wounding twelve. The tragedy was brought on by chronic tensions between white police and black students. Charles Evers, mayor of a nearby town, said: "If Jackson State had been a white campus, not a single bullet would have been fired."

In New York City, anti-war demonstrators were attacked by conservative "hard-hat" construction workers, many of them shouting "All the way, USA" and "America: Love It or Leave It." They forced the protesters to disperse, then marched on City Hall to raise the U.S. flag, which had been lowered to half-staff in mourning for the Kent State victims.

In June 1971, the *New York Times* began publishing excerpts from *The History of the U.S. Decision-Making Process of Vietnam Policy,* a secret Defense Department study commissioned by Robert McNamara before his resignation as secretary of defense in 1968. The so-called Pentagon Papers, leaked to the press by Daniel Ellsberg, a former Marine and Defense Department official, confirmed what many critics of the war had long suspected: Congress and the public had not received the full story about the Gulf of Tonkin incident of 1964. Plans for the U.S. entry into the war were being drawn up even as President Johnson was promising that combat troops would never be sent to Vietnam.

Although the Pentagon Papers dealt with events only up to 1965, the Nixon administration blocked their publication, arguing that their release would endanger national security and prolong the war. By a vote of 6 to 3, the Supreme Court ruled against the government. Newspapers began publishing the documents the next day. A furious Nixon ordered the FBI to find out who had leaked the Pentagon Papers. When the agency identified Ellsberg as the culprit, the president launched a crusade to destroy him, including a botched effort to break in to his psychiatrist's office.

**WAR WITHOUT END** In the summer of 1972, Henry Kissinger renewed private meetings with the North Vietnamese negotiators in Paris. He dropped his insistence upon the removal of all North Vietnamese troops from South Vietnam before the withdrawal of the remaining U.S. troops. On October 26, a week before the U.S. presidential election, a jubilant Kissinger announced that "Peace is at hand."

As it turned out, however, this was a cynical ploy to win votes for Nixon's reelection bid. Several days earlier, the Thieu regime in South Vietnam had rejected the Kissinger plan for a cease-fire, fearful that allowing North Vietnamese troops to remain in the south would guarantee a Communist victory. The peace talks broke off on December 16, and two days later the newly reelected Nixon ordered massive bombings of Hanoi and Haiphong, the two largest cities in North Vietnam.

The so-called Christmas bombings and the simultaneous U.S. decision to place explosive underwater mines in North Vietnam's Haiphong harbor to prevent ships from offloading their cargoes aroused worldwide protests. Yet the talks in Paris soon resumed, and on January 27, 1973, the United States, North and South Vietnam, and the Viet Cong signed an "agreement on ending the war and restoring peace in Vietnam," known as the Paris Peace Accords.

In fact, however, the agreement was a carefully disguised surrender that enabled the United States to end its combat role. While Nixon and Kissinger claimed that the bombings had brought North Vietnam to its senses, in truth the North Vietnamese never altered their basic stance; they kept 150,000 troops in South Vietnam and remained committed to the reunification of Vietnam under one government. What had changed was the willingness of the South Vietnamese leaders, who had not been allowed to participate in the negotiations, to accept the agreement on the basis of Nixon's personal promise that the United States would respond "with full force" to any Communist violation of the agreement.

Between the time Nixon took office in 1969 and the signing of the Paris Peace Accords in 1973, another 20,000 American troops had died; the morale of the U.S. military had been shattered; and millions of Southeast Asians had been killed, wounded, or displaced. Fighting soon broke out again in both Vietnam and Cambodia. In the end, the diplomatic efforts gained nothing the president could not have accomplished in 1969 by ending the war on similar terms.

**THE COLLAPSE OF SOUTH VIETNAM** On March 29, 1973, the last U.S. combat troops left Vietnam. The same day, the North Vietnamese released almost 600 U.S. prisoners of war. Within months, however, the cease-fire collapsed, the war resumed, and Communist forces gained the upper hand. In Cambodia (renamed the Khmer Republic after a 1970 military coup) and Laos, where fighting had been sporadic, a Communist victory seemed inevitable.

In 1975, the North Vietnamese launched a full-scale invasion of South Vietnam, sending the country into headlong panic. President Thieu appealed to Washington for the U.S. assistance promised in the Paris Peace Accords. But Congress, weary of spending dollars and lives in Vietnam, refused. On April 21, Thieu resigned and flew to Taiwan.

In the end, "peace with honor" had given the United States just enough time to remove itself before the collapse of the South Vietnamese government.

On April 30, 1975, Americans watched on television as North Vietnamese tanks rolled into Saigon, soon to be renamed Ho Chi Minh City, and military helicopters airlifted U.S. embassy and South Vietnamese officials and their families to warships offshore.

The longest, most controversial, and least successful war in American history to that point was finally over. It left a bitter legacy. During the period of U.S. involvement, the combined death count for combatants and civilians reached nearly 2 million. North Vietnam absorbed incredible losses—some 600,000 soldiers and countless civilians. South Vietnam lost 240,000 soldiers, and more than 500,000 Vietnamese became refugees in the United States. More than 58,000 Americans died; another 300,000 were wounded, 2,500 were declared missing, and almost 100,000 returned missing one or more limbs. The United States spent more than $699 billion on the war.

Vietnam veterans (average age nineteen, compared to twenty-six in the Second World War) had "lost" a war in which their country had lost interest. When they returned, many found even their families unwilling to talk about

**Leave with honor** Hundreds of thousands of terrified South Vietnamese tried to flee the Communist forces with evacuating Americans. Here, a U.S. official punches a Vietnamese man trying to join his family in an overflowing airplane at Nha Trang.

what the soldiers had experienced, or they themselves were embarrassed about their involvement in the war. "I went over there thinking I was doing something right and came back a bum," said Larry Langowski from Illinois.

The Vietnam War, initially described as a crusade for democratic ideals, revealed that America's form of democracy was not easily transferable to regions of the world that lacked democratic traditions. And, as critics noted, imposed democracy is not democratic. Fought to contain the spread of communism, the war instead fragmented the national consensus that had governed U.S. foreign affairs since 1947, when President Truman developed policies to contain communism around the world.

Not only had a decade of American effort in Vietnam proved costly and futile, but the Khmer Rouge, the insurgent Cambodian Communist movement, had also won a resounding victory over the U.S.-backed Khmer Republic, plunging the country into a horrific bloodbath. The maniacal Khmer Rouge leaders renamed the country Kampuchea and organized a campaign to destroy all their opponents, killing almost a third of the total population.

## THE NIXON DOCTRINE AND A THAWING COLD WAR

Richard Nixon greatly preferred foreign policy to domestic policy (which he compared to building "sewer projects"), and his greatest successes were in international relations. Nixon was an expert in foreign affairs, and he benefited greatly from the strategic vision of Henry Kissinger. Their grand design for U.S. foreign policy after the Vietnam War centered on developing friendly relations with the Soviet Union and Communist China.

**THE CIA IN CHILE** Henry Kissinger pressed for a return to an Eisenhower-era approach to foreign policy that entailed using the Central Intelligence Agency (CIA) to pursue America's strategic interests covertly while reducing large-scale military interventions.

Since Fidel Castro and his supporters gained control of Cuba in 1959, American presidents had been determined to prevent any more Communist insurgencies in the Western Hemisphere. In 1970, Salvador Allende, a Socialist party leader, friend of Castro, and critic of the United States, was a leading presidential candidate in Chile. Kissinger and President Nixon knew that, if elected, Allende planned to take control of Chilean industries owned by U.S. corporations, just as Fidel Castro had done after seizing power in Cuba in 1959.

Nixon urged the CIA to do anything to prevent an Allende presidency. Although CIA agents provided campaign funds to his opponents, Allende was democratically elected on October 24, 1970. The CIA then encouraged Chilean military leaders to oust him. In September 1973, the army took control, Allende either committed suicide or was murdered, and General Augusto Pinochet, a ruthless dictator supposedly friendly to the United States, declared himself head of the government. Within a few months, Pinochet had taken over dozens of U.S.-owned businesses in Chile and executed thousands of political opponents. Kissinger, now secretary of state, told Nixon that the CIA "didn't do it," but "we helped" put Pinochet in office by creating the conditions that made the coup possible.

**THE NIXON DOCTRINE** In July 1969, while announcing the first troop withdrawals from Vietnam, President Nixon unveiled what came to be called the Nixon Doctrine. Unlike John F. Kennedy, who had declared that the United States would "pay any price, bear any burden" to win the cold war, Nixon explained that "America cannot—and will not—conceive *all* the plans, design *all* the programs, execute *all* the decisions, and undertake *all* the defense of the free nations of the world." Under the Nixon Doctrine, the United States would provide weapons and money to fend off Communist insurgencies, but not troops.

At the same time, Nixon announced that he would pursue partnerships with Communist countries in areas of mutual interest. That Nixon, with his history of rabid anti-communism, would embrace such a policy of **détente** (a French word meaning "easing of relations") shocked many and demonstrated yet again his pragmatic flexibility.

**THE PEOPLE'S REPUBLIC OF CHINA** Richard Nixon had an exquisite gift for doing the unexpected. In 1971, Nixon sent Henry Kissinger on a secret trip to Beijing to explore the possibility of U.S. recognition of Communist China. Since 1949, when Mao Zedong's revolutionary movement established control, the United States, with Richard Nixon's hearty support, had refused even to recognize the People's Republic of China, preferring to regard Chiang Kai-shek's exiled regime on Taiwan as the legitimate Chinese government.

Now, however, the time seemed ripe for a bold renewal of ties. Both the United States and Communist China were exhausted from domestic strife (anti-war protests in America, the Cultural Revolution in China), and both were eager to resist Soviet expansionism. Nixon also relished the shock effect of his action, which he told senior aide John Ehrlichman would "discombobulate" the "god-damned liberals."

Nixon's bombshell announcement on July 15, 1971, that Kissinger had just returned from Beijing and that the president himself would be going to China the following year, sent shock waves around the world. Nixon became the first U.S. president to use the term *People's Republic of China*, a symbolic step in normalizing relations. The Nationalist Chinese on Taiwan felt betrayed, and the Japanese, historic enemies of China, were furious. In October 1971, the United Nations voted to admit the People's Republic of China and expel Taiwan.

**Nixon goes to China** President Nixon and Chinese premier Zhou Enlai toast each other at a farewell banquet in Shanghai celebrating the historic visit.

On February 21, 1972, during the "week that changed the world," Nixon arrived in Beijing. Americans watched on television as the president shook hands and drank toasts with Prime Minister Zhou Enlai and Communist party Chairman Mao Zedong. In one simple but astonishing stroke, Nixon and Kissinger had ended two decades of diplomatic isolation of the People's Republic of China.

During the president's week-long visit, the two nations agreed to scientific and cultural exchanges, steps toward resuming trade, and the eventual reunification of Taiwan with the mainland. A year later, "liaison offices" that served as unofficial embassies were established in Washington and Beijing. In 1979, diplomatic recognition was officially formalized.

As a conservative anti-Communist, Nixon had accomplished a diplomatic feat that his Democratic predecessors could not have attempted for fear of being branded "soft" on communism. Nixon's and Kissinger's bold move gave them leverage with the Soviet Union, which was understandably nervous about a U.S.–Chinese alliance.

**EMBRACING THE SOVIET UNION** China welcomed the breakthrough because of tensions with the Soviet Union, with which it shared a long but contested border. By 1972, the Chinese had become more fearful of the Soviet Union than the United States.

The Soviets were also eager to ease tensions with the Americans. In 1972, President Nixon again surprised the world by announcing that he would visit

Moscow for discussions with Leonid Brezhnev, the Soviet premier. The high drama of the China visit was repeated in Moscow, with toasts and dinners attended by world leaders who had previously regarded each other as incarnations of evil.

Nixon and Brezhnev signed the pathbreaking **Strategic Arms Limitation Treaty (SALT I)**, which negotiators had been working on since 1969. The agreement did not end the nuclear arms race, but it did limit the number of missiles with nuclear warheads and prohibited the construction of missile-defense systems. The Moscow summit also produced new trade agreements, including an arrangement whereby the United States sold almost a quarter of its wheat crop to the Soviets at a favorable price

The summit resulted in a dramatic easing of tensions. As Nixon told Congress upon his return, "never before have two adversaries, so deeply divided by conflicting ideologies and political rivalries, been able to limit the armaments upon which their survival depends."

Over time, détente with the Soviet Union would help end the cold war by lowering Soviet hostility to Western influences, which in turn slowly eroded Communist rule from the inside.

**SHUTTLE DIPLOMACY** The Nixon–Kissinger initiatives in the Middle East were less dramatic and less conclusive than those in China and the Soviet Union, but they showed that the United States at last recognized the legitimacy of Arab interests in the region and its own dependence upon Middle Eastern oil.

On October 6, 1973, Syria and Egypt, backed by Saudi Arabia and armed with Soviet weapons, attacked Israel, igniting what became the Yom Kippur War. It created the most dangerous confrontation between the United States and the Soviet Union since the Cuban missile crisis.

When the Israeli army, with weapons supplied by the United States, launched a fierce counterattack that appeared likely to overwhelm Egypt, the Soviets threatened to intervene militarily. Nixon, whose presidency was increasingly at risk because of the Watergate investigations, was bedridden because he was drunk, according to Henry Kissinger and other aides, so Kissinger, as secretary of state, presided over a National Security Council meeting that placed America's military forces on full alert.

On October 20, Kissinger flew to Moscow to meet with Soviet premier Brezhnev. Kissinger skillfully negotiated a cease-fire agreement and exerted pressure on the Israelis to prevent them from taking additional Arab territory, and in an attempt to broker a lasting settlement, he made numerous flights among the capitals of the Middle East. His "shuttle diplomacy" won acclaim from all sides, although he failed to find a comprehensive formula for peace. He did, however, lay the groundwork for an important treaty between Israel and Egypt in 1977.

## WATERGATE

Nixon's foreign policy achievements allowed him to stage the presidential campaign of 1972 as a triumphal procession. Early on, the main threat to his reelection came from George Wallace, who had the potential as a third-party candidate to deprive the Republicans of conservative southern votes and thereby throw the election to the Democrats. That threat ended, however, on May 15, 1972, when Wallace was shot in an assassination attempt. Although he survived, he was left paralyzed below the waist and had to withdraw from the campaign. Nixon ordered aides to plant a false story that Democrats had orchestrated Wallace's assassination.

Meanwhile, the Democrats nominated Senator George McGovern of South Dakota, an anti-war liberal. "George is the most decent man in the Senate," Robert Kennedy had said. "As a matter of fact, he is the only decent man."

Decency does not win elections, however. McGovern was a poor campaigner, and many dismissed him as a left-wing extremist. Nixon also defused the Vietnam War as the central issue in the campaign, emphasizing that he had brought more than 500,000 troops home from Vietnam. By Election Day, only 20,000 U.S. military personnel remained in South Vietnam.

Nixon won the greatest victory of any Republican presidential candidate in history, capturing 520 electoral votes to only 17 for McGovern. The popular vote was equally decisive: 46 million to 28 million, a proportion of the total vote (60.8 percent) second only to Lyndon Johnson's victory over Barry Goldwater in 1964. The only downside for the Republicans was that the Democrats maintained control of Congress.

For all of Nixon's abilities and accomplishments, however, he remained chronically insecure. He began keeping a secret "enemies list" and approved plans to break into the offices of some of his opponents. Little did he know that such behavior would bring him crashing down.

**"DIRTY TRICKS"**  By the spring of 1972, Nixon aide John Ehrlichman was overseeing a secret team of agents who performed various acts of partisan sabotage, such as falsely accusing Democratic senators Hubert H. Humphrey and Henry Jackson of sexual improprieties, forging press releases, setting off stink bombs at Democratic campaign events, and planting spies on George McGovern's campaign plane. Charles "Chuck" Colson, one of the most active "dirty tricksters," admitted that "we did a hell of a lot of things and never got caught."

But others were caught. On June 17, 1972, police in Washington, D.C., captured five burglars breaking into the Democratic National Committee headquarters in the **Watergate** hotel-apartment-office complex. The burglars were all former CIA agents; four were Miami-based Cuban exiles, and the other, James W. McCord, was the Nixon campaign's security director. Two others were also arrested—Gordon Liddy and E. Howard Hunt—who were directing the break-in from a hotel across the street. The police found wads of hundred-dollar bills on the burglars. When the bungled break-in was first reported, McGovern's complaints about it seemed like sour grapes from a candidate running far behind in the polls.

Nixon and his staff did their best to dismiss the incident as a "third-rate burglary." The president denied any involvement, but he was lying; he told Alexander Haig, then his national security adviser, that "we will cover up [the Watergate burglary] until hell freezes over."

To protect Nixon, White House aides secretly provided $350,000 in "hush money" to the jailed burglars, only to learn that it was not enough—they wanted $1 million. Nixon and his aides also discussed using the CIA to derail the Justice Department's investigation of the burglary. Bob Haldeman, Nixon's chief of staff, told the FBI to quit investigating the incident, falsely claiming that it involved a super-secret CIA operation. White House spokesmen lied to journalists and destroyed evidence.

Nixon encouraged the cover-up, stressing that his "main concern is to keep the White House out of it." In August 1972, he told reporters that his own investigation into the Watergate incident had confirmed that no one in the White House or the administration was involved—when in fact, there was no such investigation.

**UNCOVERING THE COVER-UP** During the trial of the accused Watergate burglars in January 1973, relentless questioning by federal judge John J. Sirica, a Nixon supporter and a hard-nosed jurist with the nickname "Maximum John" because of his history of issuing harsh sentences, led one of the accused to tell the full story. James W. McCord, security chief of the Committee to Re-Elect the President (CREEP), was the first in what would become a long line of informers to reveal the systematic efforts of Nixon and his aides to create an "imperial presidency." By the time of the Watergate break-in, money to finance such dirty tricks was being illegally collected through CREEP and controlled by the White House staff.

The trail of evidence was pursued first by Sirica, then by a grand jury, and then by a Senate committee headed by Democrat Samuel J. Ervin Jr. of North Carolina. The investigations led directly to what White House legal counsel John Dean called a "cancer close to the Presidency." By this point, Nixon was using his presidential powers to block the investigation. He ordered the CIA to keep the FBI off the case and coached his aides on how to lie under oath. Most alarming, as it turned out, the Watergate burglary was merely part of a larger pattern of corruption and criminality sanctioned by the White House.

The cover-up crumbled as people involved began to cooperate with prosecutors. James McCord admitted to Judge Sirica that the White House had provided the burglars hush money and that witnesses had lied at the trial. He then named names before the Ervin committee. Other White House aides also confessed their roles in the burglary and cover-up.

The cover-up unraveled further in 1973 when L. Patrick Gray, acting director of the FBI, resigned after confessing that he had destroyed incriminating documents at the behest of the president. On April 30, Ehrlichman and Haldeman resigned (they would later serve time in prison), as did Attorney General Richard Kleindienst. A few days later, Nixon nervously assured the public in a television address, "I am not a crook." Then John Dean, the White House legal counsel whom Nixon had dismissed because of his cooperation with prosecutors, shocked the nation. He told the Ervin committee that there had been a White House cover-up approved by the president himself.

Nixon thereafter behaved like a cornered lion. He refused to provide Senator Ervin's committee with documents it requested, citing "executive privilege" to protect national security. Then, in another shocking disclosure, a White House aide told the committee that Nixon had installed a secret taping system in the White House, meaning that many of the conversations about the Watergate burglary and cover-up had been recorded.

The bombshell news set off a legal battle for the "Nixon tapes." Harvard law professor Archibald Cox, whom Nixon's new attorney general, Elliot Richardson, had appointed as special prosecutor to investigate the Watergate case, took the president to court in October 1973 to obtain the tapes. Nixon refused to release the recordings and ordered Cox fired.

On October 20, in what became known as the "Saturday Night Massacre," Richardson and his deputy, William Ruckelshaus, resigned rather than fire Cox. (Solicitor General Robert Bork finally fired him.) Cox's dismissal produced a firestorm of public indignation. Numerous newspapers and magazines, as well as a growing chorus of legislators, called for the president to resign or be impeached for obstructing justice. A Gallup poll revealed that Nixon's approval rating had plunged to 17 percent, the lowest in presidential history.

The new special prosecutor, Leon Jaworski, a prominent Texas attorney, also took the president to court. In March 1974, the Watergate grand jury indicted Ehrlichman, Haldeman, and former attorney general John Mitchell for obstruction of justice and named Nixon an "unindicted co-conspirator."

On April 30, Nixon, still refusing to turn over the tapes, released 1,254 pages of transcribed recordings that he had edited himself, often substituting the phrase "expletive deleted" for his vulgar language and anti-Semitic rants. ("People said my language was bad," Nixon later rationalized, "but Jesus, you should have heard LBJ!"). The transcripts revealed a president whose conversations were so petty, self-serving, bigoted, and profane that they degraded the stature of the office. At one point in the transcripts, the president told his aides to have frequent memory lapses when testifying.

By the summer of 1974, Nixon was in full retreat. He became alternately combative, melancholy, and petty, and his efforts to orchestrate the cover-up obsessed, unbalanced, and unhinged him. Henry Kissinger found him increasingly unstable and drinking heavily. After meeting with the president, Senator Barry Goldwater reported that Nixon "jabbered incessantly, often incoherently." He seemed "to be cracking."

On July 24, 1974, the Supreme Court ruled unanimously that the president must surrender *all* the tape recordings. A few days later, the House Judiciary Committee voted to recommend three articles of impeachment: obstruction of justice through the payment of hush money to witnesses and the withholding of evidence; abuse of power through the use of federal agencies to deprive citizens of their constitutional rights; and defiance of Congress by withholding the tapes. The president, chief of staff Alexander Haig confided to White House aides, was "guilty as hell." He then told Nixon that he did not "see how we can survive this one."

Before the House of Representatives could vote on impeachment, Nixon grudgingly handed over the tapes. The drama continued, however, when investigators learned that segments of several recordings were missing, including eighteen minutes of a conversation in June 1972 during which Nixon first mentioned the Watergate burglary.

The president's loyal secretary took the blame for the erasure, claiming that she had accidentally pushed the wrong button, but technical experts later concluded that the missing segments had been intentionally deleted. The other recordings, however, provided more than enough evidence of Nixon's involvement in the cover-up. At one point, he had yelled at aides who were asking what they and others should say to Watergate investigators: "I don't give a shit what happens. I want you all to stonewall it, let them plead the Fifth Amendment, cover up or anything else."

The incriminating recordings led Republican leaders to urge the embattled president to quit rather than face an impeachment trial in the Senate. "There are only so many lies you can take and now there has been one too many," Senator Barry Goldwater concluded. "Nixon should get his ass out of the White House—today."

On August 9, 1974, Nixon did just that. He resigned from office, the only president to do so.

Nixon had begun his presidency hoping to heal a fractured America. Now he left the White House for a self-imposed exile at his home in San Clemente, California, having deeply wounded the nation. A London news-paper explained that America had digressed "from George Washington, who could not tell a lie, to Richard Nixon, who could not tell the truth."

**V for "Victory"** Before boarding the White House helicopter following his resignation, Nixon flashes a bright smile and his trademark V-sign to the world on August 9, 1974.

The Watergate affair's clearest lesson was that not even a president is above the law. But while the system worked by calling a president to justice, many Americans lost faith in the credibility of elected officials. The *New York Times* reported that people "think and feel differently from what they once did" as a result of the Watergate crisis. "They ask questions, they reject assumptions, they doubt what they are told."

**WATERGATE AND THE PRESIDENCY** If there was a silver lining in the dark cloud of Watergate, it was the vigor and resilience of the institutions that had brought a rogue president to justice—the press, Congress, the courts, and public opinion.

In the aftermath of the scandal, Congress passed several pieces of legislation designed to curb executive power. Nervous about possible efforts to renew military assistance to South Vietnam, the Democratic Congress passed the **War Powers Act** (1973), which requires a president to inform Congress within forty-eight hours if U.S. troops are deployed in combat abroad and to withdraw them after sixty days unless Congress specifically approves their stay.

Then, to correct abuses in the use of campaign funds, Congress enacted legislation in 1974 that set new ceilings on political campaign contributions and expenditures. And in reaction to the Nixon claim of "executive privilege" as a means of withholding evidence, Congress strengthened the 1966 Freedom of Information Act to require prompt responses to requests for information from government files and to place on government agencies the burden of proof for classifying information as secret.

**AN UNELECTED PRESIDENT** During Richard Nixon's last year in office, the Watergate crisis so dominated national politics that major domestic and foreign problems received little attention.

Vice President Spiro Agnew had himself been forced to resign in October 1973 for accepting bribes from Maryland contractors before and during his term in office. The vice president at the time of Nixon's resignation was Gerald Rudolph Ford, a square-jawed, plain-speaking former House minority leader from Michigan whom Nixon had appointed to succeed Agnew under the provisions of the Twenty-Fifth Amendment.

**Gerald Ford** The 38th president is pictured listening apprehensively to reports of rising rates of unemployment and inflation in 1974.

On August 9, 1974, Ford, an honest and decent man who held a law degree from Yale, was sworn in as the nation's chief executive, the only person in history to serve as both vice president and president without having been elected to those offices. "I am acutely aware that you have not elected me as your President by your ballots," Ford said in a televised address. "So I ask you to confirm me as your President with your prayers." He then assured the nation that "our long national nightmare [Watergate] is over."

But less than a month after taking office, Ford reopened the wounds of Watergate by issuing Nixon a "full, free, and absolute pardon" for any crimes he may have committed while in office.

Ford's pardon unleashed a storm of controversy. "Jail Ford!" yelled protesters outside the White House. A House subcommittee grilled the new president, wanting to know whether Nixon had made a secret deal for the pardon. Ford vigorously denied the charge, but others wondered why he had pardoned someone who had not been charged with a crime. The *Washington Post* declared that Ford's decision was "nothing less than the continuation of a cover-up," while the *New York Times* dismissed the pardon as "profoundly unwise, divisive, and unjust."

The controversial pardon hobbled Ford's presidency. Doing what he had thought was the right thing made him suspect in the eyes of many voters. His approval rating plummeted from 71 percent to 49 percent in one day, the steepest drop ever recorded. His press secretary resigned in protest of the "Nixon pardon."

**THE FORD YEARS** As president, Gerald Ford adopted the posture he had developed as minority leader in the House of Representatives: naysaying head of the opposition who believed the federal government exercised too much power. In his first fifteen months as president, Ford vetoed thirty-nine bills passed by the Democratic-controlled Congress, outstripping Herbert Hoover's all-time veto record in less than half the time.

By far the most important issue during Ford's brief presidency was the struggling economy. In the fall of 1974, the nation entered its deepest recession since the Great Depression. Unemployment jumped to 9 percent in 1975, the rate of inflation reached double digits, and the federal budget deficit soon hit a record. Ford announced that inflation had become "Public Enemy No. 1," but instead of taking bold action, he launched a timid public relations campaign featuring lapel buttons that simply read WIN, symbolizing the administration's determination to "Whip Inflation Now."

The WIN buttons became a national joke and a symbol of Ford's ineffectiveness in the fight against stagflation. He later admitted that they were a failed "gimmick."

**Whip Inflation Now!** Initial excitement about the program, which was ultimately unsuccessful, generated great quantities of WIN-themed collectibles. These items included stickers, buttons, clothing, and even earrings.

In his State of the Union address in 1975, Ford conceded that "the state of the union is not good." The economic recession was now his greatest concern, not inflation. In March 1975, Ford signed a tax reduction bill that failed to stimulate economic growth. The federal budget deficit grew from $53 billion in 1975 to $74 billion in 1976.

In foreign policy, Ford retained Henry Kissinger as secretary of state (while stripping him of his dual role as national security adviser). He continued to pursue Nixon's goals of stability in the Middle East, friendly relations with China, and détente with the Soviet Union. Kissinger's tireless Middle East diplomacy produced an important agreement: Israel promised to return to Egypt most of the Sinai territory captured in the 1967 war, and the two nations agreed to rely on diplomacy rather than force to settle future disagreements.

These limited but significant achievements, however, were drowned in the criticism over the collapse of the South Vietnamese government in the face of the North Vietnamese invasion. At the same time, conservative Republicans led by Ronald Reagan lambasted Ford and Kissinger for their policy of détente toward the Soviet Union. Reagan argued that the efforts of Nixon, Kissinger, and Ford were helping to ensure the continued existence of the Soviet Union rather than accelerating its self-destruction.

**THE ELECTION OF 1976** Both political parties were in disarray as they prepared for the 1976 presidential election. Gerald Ford had to fend off a challenge from the darling of the Republican party's growing conservative wing, Ronald Reagan, a former two-term California governor and Hollywood actor.

The Democrats chose a little-known candidate: James "Jimmy" Carter Jr., who had served one term as governor of Georgia. When Carter told his mother he was running for president, she replied: "President of *what*?" Tip O'Neill, the Democratic Speaker of the House, dismissed Carter as "a complete unknown."

Yet Carter did have several assets. A former naval officer and engineer turned peanut farmer, he was one of several Democratic southern governors who sought to move their party away from its traditional "tax and spend" liberalism. The federal government, he charged, was a "horrible, bloated, confused . . . bureaucratic mess." The Great Society social-welfare programs created by LBJ were a "failure" that were in "urgent need of a complete overhaul."

Carter capitalized on post-Watergate cynicism by promising that he would "never tell a lie to the American people." He also trumpeted his status as a political "outsider," and reporters covering the campaign marveled at a Southern Baptist candidate who was a "born again" Christian.

A poll found that voters viewed Ford as "a nice guy," but "not . . . very smart about the issues the country is facing." Ford reinforced that impression during a televised debate with Carter when he mistakenly claimed that "there is no Soviet domination of Eastern Europe."

Carter revived the New Deal voting alliance of southern whites, blacks, urban labor unionists, and ethnic groups like Jews and Latinos to eke out a narrow win, receiving 41 million votes to Ford's 39 million. A heavy turnout of African Americans in the South enabled Carter to sweep every state in the region except Virginia. He also benefited from the appeal of Walter F. Mondale, his liberal running mate and a favorite among blue-collar workers and the urban poor. Ford was the first president to lose his bid for reelection since Herbert Hoover in 1932.

The most significant story of the election, however, was the low voter turn-out. Almost half the eligible voters chose to sit out the election, the lowest turnout since the Second World War.

In explaining why he had not voted, one man noted that he was "a three-time loser. In 1964 I voted for the peace candidate—Johnson—and got war. In '68 I voted for the law-and-order candidate—and got crime. In '72 I voted for Nixon again, and we got Watergate." Such an alienated voter was not a good omen for a new Democratic president about to begin his first term as head of the nation.

# CHAPTER REVIEW

## SUMMARY

- **Youth Revolt**  Civil rights activism inspired a heightened interest in social causes during the 1960s, especially among the young. Students for a Democratic Society (SDS) embodied the *New Left* ideology, and their ideas and tactics spread to many campuses. By 1970, a distinctive *counterculture* had emerged among disaffected youth ("hippies").

- **The Inspirational Effects of the Civil Rights Movement**  The civil rights movement inspired many social reform movements including the youth revolt, *women's movement*, the *Red Power* movement among Native Americans, and the *United Farm Workers* (UFW). The *Stonewall riots* in New York City in 1969 marked a militant new era for gay and lesbian rights.

- **Reaction and Domestic Agenda**  Richard Nixon's southern strategy drew conservative southern white Democrats to the Republican party. As president, he sought to slow the momentum of the civil rights movement, including *affirmative-action* programs. Congress overrode his veto of the Voting Rights Act of 1968. Nixon did grudgingly support new federal environmental policies, such as the creation of the *Environmental Protection Agency* (EPA) in 1970. During Nixon's second term, the economy struggled with *stagflation*. In a landmark decision, the Supreme Court in *Roe v. Wade* (1973) struck down state laws forbidding abortions during the first three months of pregnancy.

- **End of the Vietnam War**  In 1968, Nixon campaigned for the presidency pledging to secure "peace with honor" in Vietnam, but years would pass before the war ended. Nixon implemented the *Vietnamization* of the war, which involved increasing economic and military aid to the South Vietnamese, reducing U.S. ground forces, and escalating the bombing of North Vietnam (and Cambodia), while attempting to negotiate a cease-fire agreement. The publication of the Pentagon Papers in 1971 and the intense bombing of North Vietnam in December 1972 aroused more protests, but a month after the bombings began, North and South Vietnam agreed to a cease-fire called the Paris Peace Accords. In November 1973, Congress passed the *War Powers Act*, which requires the president to notify Congress within 48 hours of committing armed forces to military action and forbids armed forces from remaining for more than 60 days without Congressional approval or a declaration of war.

- **Détente**  Nixon's greatest accomplishments were in foreign policy. He opened diplomatic relations with Communist China and pursued *détente* with the Soviet Union, focusing on areas of shared agreement with the 1972 *Strategic Arms Limitation Treaty* (SALT I) treaty. He and Henry Kissinger also helped ease tensions in the Middle East.

- **Watergate**  During the 1972 presidential campaign, burglars were caught breaking into the Democratic party's national campaign headquarters at the *Watergate* complex in Washington, D.C. Nixon tried to block congressional investigations, which eventually led to calls for his impeachment for obstruction of justice. Nixon resigned in 1974 and was succeeded by Vice President Gerald Ford.

# CHRONOLOGY

| | |
|---|---|
| 1965 | Vietnam War expands |
| 1966 | National Organization for Women (NOW) founded |
| 1967 | Six-Day War in Middle East |
| 1968 | Richard M. Nixon elected president |
| June 1969 | Stonewall riots in New York City |
| August 1969 | Woodstock music festival attracts 400,000 people |
| 1970 | EPA created and Clean Air Act passed |
| | Shooting of students at Kent State University |
| 1971 | Ratification of the Twenty-Sixth Amendment |
| 1972 | Nixon wins reelection and visits Communist China |
| | Nixon visits USSR and signs SALT I treaty |
| 1972–1974 | Watergate scandal unfolds |
| January 1973 | Cease-fire declared in Vietnam War |
| | Nixon ends the military draft (June) |
| | Congress passes War Powers Act (November) |
| 1973 | Supreme Court overturns anti-abortion laws in Roe v. Wade |
| 1974 | Gerald Ford becomes president after Nixon's resignation |
| April 1975 | Saigon falls to the North Vietnamese |
| November 1976 | Democrat Jimmy Carter defeats Gerald Ford |

# KEY TERMS

New Left p. 1243

counterculture p. 1246

women's movement p. 1251

*Roe v. Wade* (1973) p. 1255

United Farm Workers (UFW) p. 1258

Red Power p. 1260

Stonewall riots (1969) p. 1261

affirmative action p. 1262

Environmental Protection Agency (EPA) (1970) p. 1268

stagflation p. 1268

Vietnamization p. 1271

détente p. 1278

Strategic Arms Limitation Treaty (SALT I) p. 1280

Watergate (1972–1974) p. 1282

War Powers Act (1973) p. 1285

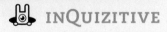 INQUIZITIVE

Go to InQuizitive to see what you've learned—and learn what you've missed—with personalized feedback along the way.

# 31 Conservative Revival

## 1977–1990

**Feels good to be Right** This proud Republican lets her hat adorned with campaign buttons speak for her at the 1980 Republican National Convention. Held in Detroit, Michigan, the convention nominated former California governor Ronald Reagan, who promised to "make America great again."

During the 1970s, the United States lost much of its self-confidence as it confronted difficult lessons about the limits of its power and financial resources and the pitfalls of greed and corruption. The failed Vietnam War; the Watergate scandal; and the spike in oil prices, interest rates, and consumer prices frustrated Americans. For a country accustomed to economic growth and carefree consumerism, the persistence of stagflation and gasoline shortages was exasperating. In July 1976, as the United States celebrated the bicentennial of its independence, many people were downsizing their expectations of the American dream.

Jimmy Carter, the first president from the Lower South, took office in 1977 promising a government that would be "competent" as well as "decent, open, fair, and compassionate." After four years, however, Carter had little to show for his efforts. The economy remained sluggish, consumer prices continued to increase, and failed efforts to free Americans held hostage in Iran prompted critics, including Democrats, to denounce Carter's administration as indecisive and inept. In the end, Carter's inability to mobilize support for an ill-fated energy program and his call for "a time of national austerity" revealed both his clumsy legislative skills and his misreading of the public mood.

The Republicans capitalized on public frustration by electing Ronald Reagan president in 1980. The new president promised to revive the capitalist spirit, restore national pride, and regain international respect. He did all of

## focus questions

**1.** Why did Jimmy Carter have such limited success as president?

**2.** What factors led to the election of Ronald Reagan, the rise of the conservative movement, and the resurgence of the Republican party?

**3.** What is "Reaganomics"? What were its effects on American society and the economy?

**4.** How did Reagan's Soviet strategy help end the cold war?

**5.** What social and economic issues and innovations emerged during the 1980s?

**6.** What was the impact of the end of the cold war and the efforts of President George H. W. Bush to create a post–cold war foreign policy?

that and more, as he inspired a conservative resurgence, helped raise morale, and accelerated the forces that would cause the collapse of the Soviet Union and bring an end to the cold war.

## THE CARTER PRESIDENCY

James ("Jimmy") Earl Carter Jr. won the 1976 election because he convinced voters that he was a man of pure motives, a "born-again" Christian who would restore integrity and honesty to the presidency. A former governor of Georgia (1971–1975), he represented a new generation of moderate southern Democrats who were committed to restraining "big-government" spending. In his inaugural address, Carter confessed that he had no grand "vision." Unlike his predecessors, he highlighted America's limitations rather than its potential: "We have learned that 'more' is not necessarily 'better,' that even our great nation has its recognized limits, and that we can neither answer all questions nor solve all problems."

Carter later admitted that his re-marks about dialing back national expectations were "politically unpopular," for "Americans were not accustomed to limits—on natural resources . . . or on the power of our country to . . . control international events."

### JIMMY WHO?

Jimmy Carter's public modesty masked a complex and, at times, contradictory personality. No modern president was as openly committed to his Christian faith as Carter. At the same time, few presidents were as tough on others as Carter was.

Carter, who came out of nowhere to win the presidency ("Jimmy Who?"), displayed an "almost arrogant self-confidence," as *Time* magazine described it. All his life he had shown a fierce determination to succeed and he expected those around him to show the same tenacity. Carter and his closest aides ("the Georgia Mafia") arrived in Washington, D.C., convinced that they would clean up the "mess" made by politicos and bureaucrats within the federal government. Congress, Carter noted in his diary, "was disgusting." Yet his naive dismissal of Congress would prove to be his downfall.

Carter wanted to be a "strong, aggressive president," an incorruptible outsider who would make the federal government run more smoothly at less expense to taxpayers by eliminating waste and providing expert management. Yet he could not inspire people. Democratic senator Eugene McCarthy described Carter as an "oratorical mortician," while a journalist stressed that "there's no music in him." He was, as he acknowledged, a manager rather than a visionary.

In 1977, Carter faced formidable challenges. Americans expected him to restore U.S. stature abroad, cure the stubborn economic recession, and reduce both unemployment and inflation at a time when industrial economies around the world were struggling.

Carter was also expected to lift the national spirit in the wake of the Watergate scandal. Meeting such daunting expectations would be miraculous, and Carter displayed a sunburst smile and flinty willpower, but he was no miracle worker.

**The Carters** After his inauguration in 1977, President Jimmy Carter forgoes the traditional limousine and walks down Pennsylvania Avenue with his wife, Rosalynn.

**EARLY SUCCESS** During the first two years of his presidency, Carter enjoyed several successes, both symbolic and real. To demonstrate his frugality, he took the symbolic step of selling the presidential yacht, cut the White House staff by a third, told cabinet officers to give up their government cars, and installed solar panels on the White House roof to draw attention to the nation's need to become energy independent. His administration included more African Americans and women than any before.

More tangibly, Carter fulfilled a campaign pledge by offering amnesty (forgiveness) to the thousands of young men who had fled the country rather than serve in Vietnam. He also reorganized the executive branch and reduced government bureaucracy.

Carter pushed several significant environmental initiatives through the Democratic-controlled Congress, including stricter controls over the stripmining of coal, the creation of a $1.6 billion "Superfund" to clean up toxic chemical waste sites, and a bill protecting more than 100 million acres of Alaskan land from development. He also deregulated the trucking, airline, and financial industries in an effort to restore competition. At the end of his first 100 days in office, Carter enjoyed a 75 percent public approval rating.

**CARTER'S LIMITATIONS** Yet Jimmy Carter's successes were short-lived. Instead of focusing on a few priorities, he tried to do too much too fast, and his inexperienced team of senior aides was often more a burden than a blessing. Worst of all, the self-proclaimed "outsider" president saw little need to consult with Democratic leaders, which helps explain why many of his legislative requests got nowhere.

Ultimately, Carter's inability to revive the economy crippled his presidency. He first attacked unemployment, authorizing some $14 billion in federal spending to trigger job growth while cutting taxes by $34 billion. His actions helped generate new jobs but also caused a spike in consumer prices from 5 percent when he took office to as much as 13 percent during 1980. The result was a deepening recession and rising unemployment.

Carter was also hampered by the worsening global "energy crisis." He claimed that America was the "most wasteful nation on earth." Since the Arab oil embargo in 1973, the price of imported oil had doubled, while U.S. dependence on foreign oil had grown from 35 to 50 percent of its annual needs. In April 1977, Carter presented Congress with a comprehensive energy proposal designed to cut oil consumption. Legislators, however, turned down most of the bill's key elements when the National Energy Bill was finally passed in 1978.

In 1979, the energy crisis grew more troublesome when Islamic fundamentalists assumed power in oil-rich Iran. They shut off the supply of Iranian oil to the United States, creating gasoline shortages and higher prices. Warning that the "growing scarcity in energy" would paralyze the U.S. economy, Carter asked Congress for a more comprehensive energy bill, but again the legislators rejected its conservation measures.

**A "CRISIS OF CONFIDENCE"** By July 1979, President Carter had grown so discouraged with both public and private efforts to reduce U.S. oil consumption that for eleven days he holed up at Camp David, the presidential retreat in the Maryland mountains. There he met privately with some 150 representatives from business, labor, education, politics, religion, even psychiatrists—all the while keeping the media at bay.

On July 15, he returned to the White House and delivered a televised speech in which he sounded more like an angry preacher than a president. He declared that a "crisis of confidence" was paralyzing the nation. The people had lost confidence in his leadership, and America had become rudderless, with no "sense of purpose" other than "to worship self-indulgence and consumption." He repeatedly blamed the citizenry for the nation's problems. "All the legislation in the world can't fix what's wrong with America," Carter stressed. Americans had become preoccupied with "owning and consuming things" at the expense of "hard work, strong families, close-knit communities, and our faith in God."

The nation was at a crossroads, Carter concluded. Americans could choose continued self-indulgence and political stalemate, or they could revive traditional values such as thrift, mutual aid, simple living, and spirituality. "We can take the first step down that path as we begin to solve our energy problem. Energy will be the immediate test of our ability to unite this nation."

Carter failed that test, however. An Arizona newspaper grumbled that "the nation . . . wanted answers. It did not get them." Even Democrats lambasted the speech. Arkansas governor Bill Clinton said that Carter was behaving more like a "17th century New England Puritan than a 20th century Southern Baptist."

It did not help when, two days after the speech, Carter asked more than thirty government officials, including his entire cabinet, to resign. He accepted the resignations of five cabinet officers. In doing so, he reinforced the public image of a White House out of control.

Carter's inept legislative relations ensured that his new energy proposals got nowhere in Congress. By the fall of 1979, his poll ratings were among the lowest in history. Former president Gerald Ford observed that if Nixon had created "an imperial presidency," Carter had fashioned "an imperiled presidency."

## CARTER'S FOREIGN POLICY

Carter's greatest success was facilitating a 1978 peace agreement between Prime Minister Menachem Begin of Israel and President Anwar Sadat of Egypt. When the two foreign leaders, bitter enemies, arrived in September at Camp David, Maryland, they refused to be in the same room together. After twelve days, however, Carter's patience paid off when the parties signed two landmark treaties, thereafter called the **Camp David Accords**.

The first provided the framework for an eventual peace treaty. The Israelis pledged to end their military occupation of the Sinai region of Egypt, and the Egyptians promised to restore Israeli access to the Suez Canal. The second treaty called for a comprehensive settlement based on Israel's willingness to allow the Palestinians living in the Israeli-controlled West Bank and Gaza Strip to govern themselves.

Sadat's willingness to recognize the legitimacy of the Israeli nation and sign the two treaties sparked violent protests across the Arab world. The Arab League representing twenty-two Arab nations expelled Egypt and announced an economic boycott, and the Israelis later backtracked on aspects of the agreements. Sadat, however, paid the highest price, as Islamist extremists assassinated him in 1981. Still, Carter's diplomacy made war between Israel and the Arab world less likely.

**HUMAN RIGHTS** Carter stumbled again, however, when he vowed that "the soul of our foreign policy" should be an absolute "commitment to human rights" abroad, drawing a direct contrast between his international "idealism" and the geopolitical "realism" practiced by Richard Nixon and Henry Kissinger. Carter created an Office of Human Rights within the State Department and selectively cut off financial assistance to some repressive governments.

Critics noted that the United States had its own human rights issues, including the plight of Native Americans and African Americans, and that Carter ignored abuses by key allies, such as the shah of Iran. Others asserted that the president's definition of human rights was so vague and sweeping that few nations could meet its benchmark. Critics on the right argued that the president was sacrificing America's global interests to promote an impossible standard of international moral purity, while critics on the left highlighted his seeming hypocrisy in pursuing human rights in a few nations but not everywhere.

**THE PANAMA CANAL** Similarly, Carter's decision to turn over control of the ten-mile-wide Panama Canal Zone to the Panamanian government aroused intense criticism. He argued that Panama's deep resentment of America for taking control of the Canal Zone during the presidency of Theodore Roosevelt left him no choice.

Conservatives blasted Carter's "giveaway." In Ronald Reagan's view, "We bought it, we paid for it, it's ours." Legal scholars and the Panamanian government disagreed, however. No Panamanian had signed the 1903 document granting the United States perpetual control of the strategic waterway. The new agreement called for the Canal Zone to be transferred to Panama at the end of 1999. Carter said the exchange reflected the American belief that "fairness, not force, should lie at the heart of our dealings with the world."

**AFGHANISTAN** In late December 1979, President Carter faced another crisis when 100,000 Soviet soldiers invaded Afghanistan, a remote, mountainous country where a faltering Communist government was being challenged by Islamist *jihadists* ("holy warriors") and ethnic warlords. It was the first Soviet army deployment outside Europe since the Second World War, and the forces soon found themselves mired in what some called the Soviet Vietnam.

Carter responded with a series of steps. In January 1980, he refused to sign a Strategic Arms Limitation Talks (SALT II) treaty with the Soviets, suspended U.S. grain shipments to the Soviet Union, began using the CIA to supply Afghan "freedom fighters" with weapons, requested large increases in U.S. military spending, required all nineteen-year-old men to register for the military draft, and called for an international boycott of the 1980 Olympic Games, which were to be held that summer in Moscow. Some sixty nations joined the United States in the boycott. Still, the Soviets persisted in their intervention for nine years. It ultimately cost 15,000 Soviet lives.

The Soviet invasion of Afghanistan also prompted Carter to announce what came to be called the Carter Doctrine, in which he threatened to use military force to prevent any nation from gaining control of the Persian Gulf waterways, through which most of the oil from the Middle East made its way to foreign ports.

**CRISIS IN IRAN** Then came the **Iranian hostage crisis**, a series of dramatic events that illustrated the inability of the United States to control world affairs.

In January 1979, Islamist revolutionaries had ousted the pro-American government led by the hated shah of Iran, Mohammad Reza Pahlavi. The rebel leaders executed hundreds of the shah's former officials. Thousands more Iranians were imprisoned, tortured, or executed for refusing to abide by strict Islamic social codes. The turmoil led to a sharp drop in oil production, driving up gasoline prices worldwide. By the spring of 1979, Americans were again waiting in long lines for limited amounts of high-priced gasoline.

In October, the Carter administration allowed the deposed shah to come to the United States to receive medical treatment for cancer. What Carter called this humanitarian decision enraged Iranian revolutionaries. On November 4, 1979, a frenzied mob stormed the U.S. embassy in Tehran and seized sixty-six diplomats, Marines, and staff, including fifty-two American citizens. Iranian leader Ayatollah Ruhollah Khomeini demanded the return of the shah (and all his wealth) in exchange for the release of the hostages. Nightly television coverage in the United States generated a near obsession with the fate of the hostages.

Angry Americans, including many in Congress, demanded a military response. Carter appealed to the United Nations, but Khomeini scoffed at UN efforts. Carter then froze all Iranian financial assets in America and asked Europe to join in a trade embargo of Iran. But because America's allies were not willing to lose access to Iranian oil, the trade restrictions were only partially effective.

As the crisis continued and gasoline prices rose to record levels, Carter authorized a risky rescue attempt by U.S. commandos on April 24, 1980. (His

**A king's ransom** An Iranian militant holds a group of U.S. embassy staff members hostage in Tehran, Iran, in 1979.

secretary of state, Cyrus Vance, resigned in protest because he thought the military action would be counter-productive.) As it turned out, the raid had to be aborted when several helicopters developed mechanical problems; it ended with the deaths of eight U.S. soldiers when a helicopter collided with a transport plane in the Iranian desert.

For fourteen months, the Iranian hostage crisis paralyzed Carter's ability to lead. For many, the prolonged standoff became a symbol of his failed presidency. A Democrat in Congress reported that Carter "hasn't a single friend up here. Not one soul."

The Iranian crisis finally ended after 444 days, on January 20, 1981, when Carter, just hours before leaving office, released several billion dollars of Iranian assets to ransom the hostages.

## THE RISE OF RONALD REAGAN

No sooner had Jimmy Carter been elected in 1976 than conservative Republicans (the "New Right") began working to ensure that he would not win a second term. Their plans centered on the tall, square-shouldered, plain-speaking

Ronald Reagan, the handsome actor, two-term California governor, and prominent political commentator. Reagan was not a deep thinker, but he was a superb reader of the public mood, an outspoken patriot, and a committed champion of conservative principles.

## The Actor Turned President

Born in Tampico, Illinois, in 1911, the son of an often-drunk, Irish Catholic shoe salesman and a devout, Bible-quoting mother, Ronald Reagan earned a football scholarship to attend tiny Eureka College during the Great Depression; he washed dishes in the dining hall to pay for his meals. After graduation, Reagan worked as a radio sportscaster before starting a movie career in Hollywood. He served three years in the army during the Second World War, making training films. At that time, as he recalled, he was a Democrat, "a New Dealer to the core."

After the war, Reagan became president of the acting profession's union, the Screen Actors Guild (SAG), where he honed his negotiating skills and fended off Communist efforts to infiltrate the union. Reagan supported Democrat Harry S. Truman in the 1948 presidential election, but during the fifties he decided that federal taxes were too high. In 1960, he campaigned as a Democrat for Richard Nixon, and two years later he joined the Republican party. "I didn't leave the Democratic party," Reagan explained, "the Democratic party left me."

Reagan achieved political stardom in 1964 when he delivered a rousing speech on national television on behalf of Barry Goldwater's presidential candidacy. Wealthy admirers convinced him to run for governor of California in 1966, and he won by a landslide.

As the Republican presidential nominee in 1980, Reagan set about contrasting his optimistic vision of America's future with Jimmy Carter's bleak outlook and "mediocre leadership." Reagan insisted that there was "nothing wrong with the American people" and that there were

**Ronald Reagan** The "Great Communicator" flashes his charming, trademark smile.

"simple answers" to the complex problems facing the country, although they were not *easy* answers. He pledged to slash many social-welfare programs, increase military spending to "win" the cold war, dismantle the "bloated" federal bureaucracy, restore states' rights, reduce taxes and government regulation of businesses, and appoint conservative judges to the federal courts. He also promised to affirm old-time religious values by banning abortions and reinstituting prayer in public schools.

Reagan's popularity resulted in part from his skill as a speaker (journalists dubbed him the "Great Communicator") and his commitment to a few basic principles and simple themes. Blessed with a reassuring baritone voice and a wealth of entertaining stories, he rejected Carter's assumption that Americans needed "to start getting along with less, to accept a decline in our standard of living."

## THE RISE OF THE NEW RIGHT

By 1980, an increase in the number of senior citizens, a group that tends to be more politically and socially conservative, and the steady migration of people—especially older Americans—to the conservative Sun Belt states were shifting the political balance of power. Fully 90 percent of the nation's population growth during the 1980s occurred in southern or western Sun Belt states, while the Northeast and industrial states of the Midwest—Ohio, Michigan, Illinois, Pennsylvania, and West Virginia (called the Rust Belt)—experienced economic decline, factory closings, and population losses.

A related development was a growing tax revolt. As consumer prices and home values rose, so did property taxes. In California, Ronald Reagan's home state, skyrocketing property taxes threatened to force many working-class people from their homes. This spurred efforts to cut back on the size and cost of government to enable reductions in property taxes. In June 1978, tax rebels, with Reagan's support, succeeded in putting an initiative known as Proposition 13 on the state ballot. An overwhelming majority of voters approved the measure, which slashed property taxes by 57 percent and amended the state constitution to make it more difficult to raise taxes. The "Prop 13" tax revolt soon spread across the nation, leading the *New York Times* to call it a "modern Boston Tea Party."

**THE CHRISTIAN RIGHT** Conservatives promoting a faith-based political agenda formed the strongest grassroots movement of the late twentieth century. By the 1980s, Catholic conservatives and Protestant evangelicals owned television and radio stations, operated their own schools and universities, and organized megachurches from which televangelists such as the Reverend Jerry Falwell launched a cultural crusade against the "demonic" forces of liberalism at home and communism abroad.

**Look on the Right side** The rise of the Religious Right brought protests against Supreme Court rulings that reinforced the separation of church and state. Here, in a 1984 rally organized by the Moral Majority, students chant "Kids want to pray!" in support of an amendment to reinstate prayer in public schools. (The effort failed.)

In 1979, Falwell formed the **Moral Majority** (later renamed the Liberty Alliance) to campaign for the political and social goals of the Christian Right: The economy should operate without "interference" by the government, which should be reduced in size; the Supreme Court decision in *Roe v. Wade* (1973) legalizing abortion should be reversed; Darwinian evolution should be replaced in school textbooks by the biblical story of creation; daily prayer should return to public schools; women should submit to their husbands; and communism should be opposed as a form of pagan totalitarianism.

That Ronald Reagan became the hero of the Christian Right was a tribute to his political skills, for he rarely attended church and had no strong religious affiliations. Jimmy Carter, though famous as a born-again Baptist Sunday-school teacher, lost the support of religious conservatives because he was not willing to ban abortions or restore prayers in public schools. His push for state ratification of the Equal Rights Amendment (ERA) also cost him votes among conservatives.

**ANTI-FEMINIST BACKLASH** By the late 1970s, a well-organized, well-financed backlash against the feminist movement reinforced the rise of the New Right. Activists like Republican Phyllis Schlafly, a conservative Catholic attorney from Illinois, stopped the ERA from being ratified by the required thirty-eight states. Schlafly's STOP (Stop Taking Our Privileges) ERA organization warned that the ERA would allow husbands to abandon their wives, force women into military service, and give gay "perverts" the right to marry. She and others stressed that the gender equality promised by the proposed amendment violated biblical teachings about women's "God-given" roles as nurturers and helpmates.

Many of Schlafly's supporters also participated in the growing anti-abortion, or "pro-life," movement. The emotional intensity of the issue made it a powerful political force.

**FINANCING CONSERVATISM** The business community had also become a source of conservative activism. In 1972, leaders of the nation's largest corporations formed the Business Roundtable to promote their interests in Congress. Within a few years, many of them had created political action committees (PACs) to distribute money to pro-business political candidates. Corporate donations also helped fund conservative "think tanks," such as the American Enterprise Institute, the Cato Institute, and the Heritage Foundation. By 1980, the conservative insurgency had become a powerful political force.

**THE ELECTION OF 1980** Ronald Reagan's supporters loved his simple solutions and genial, upbeat personality, and they responded passionately to his recurring question: "Are you better off than you were four years ago?" Their answer was a resounding "No!" Jimmy Carter had not been able to gain the release of the Americans held hostage in Iran, nor had he improved the economy. His approval ratings had sunk below those of Richard Nixon.

On Election Day, Reagan swept to a lopsided victory, with 489 electoral votes to 49 for Carter, who carried only six states. (It was the second worst defeat for an incumbent president in the twentieth century, behind William Howard Taft in 1912). The popular vote was 44 million (51 percent) for Reagan to Carter's 35 million (41 percent), with 7 percent going to John Anderson, a moderate Republican who ran as an independent. Reagan's victory signaled a major realignment of voters in which many so-called Reagan Democrats—conservative white southern Protestants and blue-collar northern Catholics—crossed over to the Republican party.

# THE REAGAN REVOLUTION

Democrats who dismissed sixty-nine-year-old Ronald Reagan, the oldest man to assume the presidency, as a mental lightweight underrated him. Few people in public life had Reagan's presence—or confidence. His ability to revitalize the

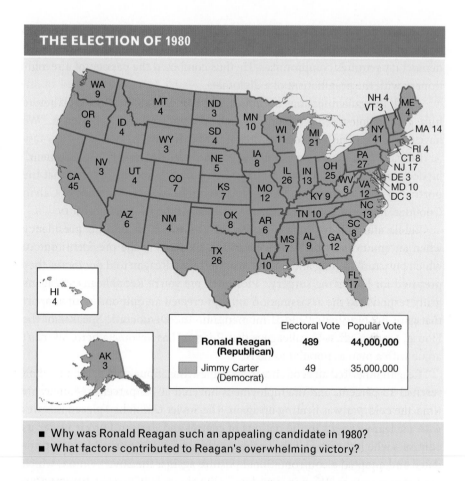

## THE ELECTION OF 1980

| | Electoral Vote | Popular Vote |
|---|---|---|
| **Ronald Reagan (Republican)** | 489 | 44,000,000 |
| Jimmy Carter (Democrat) | 49 | 35,000,000 |

■ Why was Ronald Reagan such an appealing candidate in 1980?
■ What factors contributed to Reagan's overwhelming victory?

American dream won him the 1980 and 1984 presidential elections and ensured the victory of his anointed successor, Vice President George H. W. Bush, in 1988. Reagan's actions and beliefs set the tone for the decade's political and economic life.

## REAGAN'S FIRST TERM

"Fellow conservatives," President Reagan said in a speech in 1981, "our moment has arrived." In his inaugural address, he promised to help Americans "renew our faith and hope" in their nation as a "shining city on a hill" for the rest of the world to emulate.

Reagan succeeded where Carter failed for three main reasons. First, he focused on a few priorities like slowing the rate of inflation, lowering tax rates, reducing the scope of the federal government, increasing military spending, and conducting an anti-Soviet foreign policy.

Second, he was a shrewd negotiator with congressional leaders and foreign heads of state. He also recognized early on that governing a representative democracy requires compromises. He thus combined the passion of a revolutionary with the pragmatism of a diplomat.

Third, Reagan's infectious optimism, like that of Franklin Roosevelt before him, gave people a sense of common purpose and renewed confidence. "We have every right," he stressed, "to dream heroic dreams."

Reagan's first step as president was to freeze federal hiring. "Government," he declared, "*is* the problem." To drive home that theme, he ordered that the portrait of Harry Truman in the Cabinet Room be replaced with one of Calvin Coolidge, the most anti-government president of the twentieth century.

Public affection for Reagan spiked just two months into his presidency when an emotionally disturbed man fired six shots at the president, one of which punctured a lung and lodged near his heart. Reagan told doctors as they prepared for life-saving surgery, "Please tell me you're Republicans." Reagan's gritty response to the assassination attempt created an outpouring of support that gave his presidency added momentum. The Democratic Speaker of the House, Tip O'Neill, told colleagues that Reagan "has become a hero. We can't argue with a man as popular as he is."

Reagan inherited an economy in shambles. The annual rate of inflation had reached 13 percent, and unemployment hovered at 7.5 percent. At the same time, the cold war was heating up again. The Soviet Union had placed missiles with nuclear weapons in the nations of central and Eastern Europe under its control—which threatened the entire continent. Reagan refused to be intimidated and adopted a confrontational posture against the Soviet Union, which he summarized as, "We win, you lose." He convinced Congress to support a huge increase in the military budget, deployed U.S. missiles in Europe, and sought to root out Communist insurgencies in Central America.

**REAGANOMICS** On August 1, 1981, President Reagan signed the Economic Recovery Tax Act (ERTA), which cut personal income taxes by 25 percent, lowered the maximum tax rate from 70 to 50 percent for 1982, and offered a broad array of tax concessions. The bill was the centerpiece of Reagan's "common sense" economic plan. While theorists called the philosophy behind the plan supply-side economics, journalists dubbed the president's proposals **Reaganomics**.

Simply put, Reaganomics argued that the stagflation of the seventies had resulted from excessive corporate and personal income taxes, which weakened incentives for individuals and businesses to increase productivity, save money, and reinvest in economic expansion. The solution was to slash tax rates,

**A miss for Reaganomics**  More than 5,000 senior citizens staged a demonstration in downtown Detroit against Reagan's decision to make cuts in Social Security and other federal programs supporting the elderly in 1982.

especially on the wealthy, in the belief that they would spend their savings on business expansion and consumer goods (the "supply side" of the economy). Such spending, advocates believed, would provide "trickle down" benefits to the masses. Reaganomics promised to produce enough new tax revenues from rising corporate profits and personal incomes to pay for the tax cuts. In the short term, however, ERTA did not work as planned. The federal budget deficit grew, and by November 1981, the economy was officially in recession.

**MANAGING THE BUDGET**  To offset the loss of government tax revenues, David Stockman, President Reagan's budget director, proposed sharp reductions in federal spending, including Social Security and Medicare, the two most expensive—and most popular—federal social welfare programs. Liberal Democrats howled, and Reagan responded that he was committed to maintaining the "safety net" of government services for the "truly needy."

Within a year, Stockman realized that the actual cuts in domestic spending had fallen far short of what the president had promised. Massive increases in military spending complicated the situation. Over the next five years, the administration would spend $1.2 *trillion* on military expenses. Something had to give.

In the summer of 1981, Stockman warned that "we're heading for a crash landing on the budget. We're facing potential deficit numbers so big that they could wreck the president's entire economic program." The fast-growing federal deficit, which had helped trigger the worst recession since the 1930s, was Reagan's greatest failure. During 1982, an estimated 10 million Americans were jobless, more than 10 percent of the workforce,. "The stench of failure hangs over Ronald Reagan's White House," declared the *New York Times*.

Stockman and other aides finally convinced the president that the government needed "revenue enhancements" (tax increases). With Reagan's support, Congress passed a tax bill in 1982 that would raise almost $100 billion, but the economic slump persisted. In the 1982 congressional midterm elections, Democrats picked up twenty-six seats in the House of Representatives.

Over time, however, Reagan's determination to "stay the course" began to pay off. By the summer of 1983, a robust economic recovery was underway, in part because of increased government spending and lower interest rates and in part because of lower tax rates. Inflation subsided, as did unemployment. Reaganomics was not helping to balance the budget as promised, however. In fact, the federal deficits had grown larger—so much so that the president had run up an accumulated debt larger than that of all his predecessors combined.

**REAGAN'S ANTI-LIBERALISM** During Ronald Reagan's presidency, organized labor suffered severe setbacks. In 1981, he fired members of the Professional Air Traffic Controllers Organization who had participated in an illegal strike intended to shut down air travel. (Air traffic controllers were deemed essential to public safety and therefore were prohibited from striking.) Reagan's actions broke the political power of the American Federation of Labor–Congress of Industrial Organizations (AFL-CIO), the national confederation of labor unions that traditionally supported Democratic candidates. Although record numbers of jobs were created during the 1980s, union membership steadily dropped. By 1987, unions represented only 17 percent of the nation's full-time workers, down from 24 percent in 1979.

**Sandra Day O'Connor** Her Supreme Court confirmation hearing in September 1981 was picketed by conservatives who decried her pro-abortion stance.

Reagan also opposed the Equal Rights Amendment, abortion rights, and proposals from women's rights organizations to require comparable pay for jobs of comparable worth. He cut funds for civil rights enforcement and the Equal Employment Opportunity Commission, and he opposed renewal of the Voting Rights Act of 1965.

He did name Sandra Day O'Connor, an Arizona judge, as the first woman Supreme Court justice in 1981, despite the Religious Right's objections that O'Connor supported abortion rights for women.

**THE ELECTION OF 1984** By 1983, Reagan's supply-side economics was at last working as advertised—except for the growing federal budget deficits. Reporters began to speak of the "Reagan Revolution." In 1984, the slogan at the Republican National Convention was, "America is back and standing tall."

The Democrats' presidential nominee, Walter Mondale, Jimmy Carter's vice president, was endorsed by the AFL-CIO, the National Organization for Women (NOW), and many prominent African Americans. He made history by choosing as his running mate Geraldine Ferraro, a New York congresswoman.

A bit of frankness in Mondale's acceptance speech ended up hurting his campaign. "Mr. Reagan will raise taxes [to reduce budget deficits], and so will I," he told the convention. "He won't tell you. I just did." Reagan responded by vowing never to approve another tax increase (a promise he could not keep). Reagan also repeated a theme he had used against Carter: "It's morning again in America," and record numbers of Americans were finding jobs. In the end, Reagan took 59 percent of the popular vote and lost only Minnesota (Mondale's home state) and the District of Columbia. It was the worst defeat ever for a Democratic candidate.

## REAGAN'S SECOND TERM

Spurred by his landslide reelection, Ronald Reagan called for "a Second American Revolution of hope and opportunity." Through much of 1985, he drummed up support for a tax-simplification plan. After vigorous debate, Congress passed a comprehensive Tax Reform Act in 1986. It cut the number of federal tax brackets from fourteen to two and reduced rates from the maximum of 50 percent to 15 and 28 percent—the lowest since Calvin Coolidge was president in the 1920s.

**REAGAN'S HALF-HEARTED REVOLUTION** Although Ronald Reagan had promised to "curb the size and influence of the federal establishment," the number of federal employees actually *grew* during his two terms as president. Neither Social Security nor Medicare, the two largest federal social programs, was overhauled, and the federal agencies that Reagan had threatened to abolish, such as the Department of Education, not only survived but saw their budgets grow.

The federal deficit almost tripled during Reagan's two terms. He blamed Congress for the problem, "since only Congress can spend money," but the legislators essentially approved the budgets Reagan submitted to them. As Dick Cheney, a future Republican vice president, quipped, "Reagan showed that deficits don't matter."

The cost of Social Security, the most expensive "entitlement" program, grew by 27 percent under Reagan, as some 6,000 people each day turned sixty-five years old. Moreover, he failed to fulfill his campaign promises to the Religious Right, such as reinstituting daily prayer in public schools and banning abortion. Reagan did follow through on his pledge to reshape the federal court system. He appointed 368 mostly conservative judges, including Supreme Court justices Antonin Scalia and Anthony Kennedy.

Reagan also ended the prolonged period of stagflation and set in motion what economists called the "Great Expansion," an unprecedented twenty-year burst of productivity and prosperity. True, Reagan's presidency left the nation with a massive debt burden that would cause major problems, but the Great Communicator also renewed the nation's strength, self-confidence, and soaring sense of possibilities.

## AN ANTI-SOVIET FOREIGN POLICY

In foreign affairs, President Reagan promoted what he called his "peace through strength" strategy. Through a series of bold steps, he would eventually build up the U.S. military to the point that it would overwhelm the Soviet Union, both financially and militarily.

What came to be called the Reagan Doctrine pledged to combat Soviet adventurism throughout the world, even if it meant partnering with brutal dictatorships. Reagan believed that aggressive CIA-led efforts to stymie Soviet expansionism would eventually cause the unstable Soviet system to implode "on the ash heap of history."

**A MASSIVE DEFENSE BUILDUP** Ronald Reagan long believed that Richard Nixon and Gerald Ford (who followed Henry Kissinger's advice) had been too soft on the Soviets. Kissinger's emphasis on détente, Reagan said, had been a "one-way street" favoring the Soviets. Reagan wanted to reduce the risk of nuclear war by convincing the Soviets that they could not win such a conflict.

To do so, he and Secretary of Defense Caspar Weinberger embarked upon a major buildup of nuclear and conventional weapons. Defense spending came to represent a fourth of all federal government expenditures. To critics who complained about the spending, Reagan replied, "It will break the Soviets." It did.

"STAR WARS" On March 23, 1983, two weeks after denouncing the Soviet Union as "the focus of evil in the modern world," Reagan escalated the nuclear arms race when he announced that he was authorizing the Defense Department to develop a **Strategic Defense Initiative (SDI).** The complex antimissile defense system featured satellites equipped with laser weapons that would "intercept and destroy" Soviet missiles in flight before they could harm the United States. The program was controversial because it relied upon untested technology and violated a 1972 U.S.–Soviet treaty banning such anti-missile defensive systems.

Despite skepticism among journalists, scientists, and even government officials that such an expensive defense system (dubbed "Star Wars" by the media) could be built, Congress approved the first stage of funding, eventually allocating $30 billion to the program. Although SDI was never implemented, it did force the Soviets to launch an expensive research and development effort of their own, which helped bankrupt their economy. As a Soviet foreign minister later admitted, Reagan's commitment to SDI "made us realize we were in a very dangerous spot."

**COMMUNIST INSURGENCIES IN CENTRAL AMERICA** President Reagan's foremost international concern was Central America. The tiny nation of El Salvador was caught up in a brutal struggle between Communist-supported revolutionaries and the right-wing military government, which received U.S. economic and military assistance. Critics argued that U.S. involvement ensured that the revolutionary forces would gain favor among the people by capitalizing on "anti-Yankee" sentiment. Reagan's supporters countered that a victory by the revolutionaries would lead Central America into the Communist camp (a new "domino" theory). By 1984, the U.S.-backed government of President José Napoleón Duarte had brought some stability to El Salvador.

More troubling to Reagan was the situation in Nicaragua. The State Department claimed that the Cuban-sponsored Sandinista socialist government, which had seized power in 1979, was sending arms to leftist Salvadoran rebels. In response, the Reagan administration ordered the CIA to train, equip, and finance anti-Communist Nicaraguans, or Contras (short for *contrarevolucionarios*, or "counterrevolutionaries"), who staged attacks on Sandinista bases.

In supporting these "freedom fighters," Reagan sought to impede the traffic in arms to Salvadoran rebels and to replace the Sandinistas with a democratic government. Yet his anti-Communist interventionism fostered a prolonged civil war that killed tens of thousands of Nicaraguans on both sides. Critics accused the Contras of being right-wing fanatics who killed indiscriminately. They also feared that the United States might eventually commit its own combat forces, leading to a Vietnam-like intervention. Reagan warned that if the Communists prevailed in Central America, "our credibility would collapse, our alliances would crumble, and the safety of our homeland would be jeopardized."

**STRIFE IN THE MIDDLE EAST** The Middle East remained a tinderbox of conflict during the 1980s. In September 1980, the Iraqi despot, Saddam Hussein, had attacked his neighbor, Iran. The brutal war involved the extensive use of chemical weapons and generated hundreds of thousands of casualties on both sides, but showed no sign of ending. In 1984, both sides began to attack tankers in the Persian Gulf, a major source of the world's oil. Nor was any cease-fire imminent in Afghanistan, where Soviet occupation forces had bogged down as badly as the Americans had in Vietnam.

American administrations continued to consider Israel the strongest and most reliable ally in the volatile region, while still seeking to encourage moderate Arab groups. But the forces of moderation were dealt a blow during the mid-1970s when Lebanon, long an enclave of peace, collapsed into an anarchy of warring groups. The most powerful of the rival factions was the Palestine Liberation Organization (PLO). Founded in 1964, the PLO sought the "liberation of Palestine" from Israeli control through armed struggle, with much of its violence aimed at Israeli civilians on Lebanon's southern border.

In 1982, Israeli forces pushed the PLO from southern Lebanon north to Beirut, where they began shelling PLO strongholds. The United States sent a special ambassador to negotiate a settlement. Israeli troops moved into Beirut and looked the other way when Christian militiamen slaughtered Muslim women and children in Palestinian refugee camps. French, Italian, and U.S. forces then moved into Lebanon as "peacekeepers," but in such small numbers as to become targets themselves. Muslims resentful of Western troops in their homeland constantly harassed them. American warships and planes responded by bombing Muslim positions in the highlands behind Beirut.

By 1983, Israel had driven the PLO from Beirut, but the city became increasingly unstable. In April, Islamist suicide bombers drove a truck laden with explosives into the U.S. embassy compound in Beirut, detonated it, and killed forty people, including seventeen Americans. On October 23, 1983, an

Islamist suicide bomber attacked U.S. Marine headquarters at the Beirut airport; the explosion left 241 Americans and 58 Frenchmen dead. In early 1984, Reagan announced that the Marines remaining in Lebanon would be redeployed to warships offshore. The Israeli forces pulled back to southern Lebanon, while the Syrians remained in eastern Lebanon. Peaceful coexistence in the region proved to be an elusive dream.

**U.S. INVASION OF GRENADA** Fortune, as it happened, presented Ronald Reagan the chance for an easy triumph closer to home that eclipsed news of the debacle in Lebanon. On the tiny Caribbean island of Grenada, the smallest independent country in the Western Hemisphere, a leftist government had admitted Cuban workers to build a new airfield and signed military agreements with Communist countries. In 1983, an even more radical military council seized power and killed the prime minister. Appeals from neighboring islands convinced Reagan to send 1,900 Marines to invade Grenada, depose the new military government, and evacuate a small group of American students at the country's medical school. The UN General Assembly condemned the U.S. invasion, but it was popular among Grenadians and their neighbors and in the United States. (The date of the invasion is now a national holiday in Grenada, called Thanksgiving Day.) The decisive move served as notice to Latin American revolutionaries that Reagan might use military force elsewhere in the region.

**THE IRAN-CONTRA AFFAIR** During the fall of 1986, Democrats regained control of the Senate and picked up six seats in the House, increasing their already comfortable margin to 259–176. The election results meant that Reagan would face a Democrat-led Congress during the last two years of his presidency.

Worse for the administration were reports that surfaced in late 1986 finding the United States had been secretly selling arms to U.S.-hating Iran in the hope of securing the release of American hostages held in Lebanon by extremist groups sympathetic to Iran. Such action contradicted Reagan's insistence that his administration would never negotiate with terrorists. The disclosures angered America's allies as well as many Americans who vividly remembered the 1979 Iranian hostage situation.

Over the next several months, revelations emerged about a complicated series of covert activities carried out by administration officials. At the center of what came to be called the **Iran-Contra affair** was Marine Lieutenant Colonel Oliver North, a National Security Council aide who specialized in counterterrorism. Working from the basement of the White House, North had secretly sold military supplies to Iran and used the proceeds to support the

**Iran-Contra hearings** Admiral John Poindexter listens warily to a question from the congressional investigation committee on July 21, 1987.

Contra rebels in Nicaragua at a time when Congress had banned such aid.

North's activities, it turned out, had been approved by national security adviser Robert McFarlane; McFarlane's successor, Admiral John Poindexter; and CIA director William Casey. After information about the secret dealings surfaced, North and others erased incriminating computer files and destroyed documents. McFarlane attempted suicide before being convicted of withholding information from Congress. Poindexter resigned, and North, described by the White House as a "loose cannon," was fired.

Facing a barrage of criticism, Reagan appointed a commission, led by former Republican senator John Tower, to investigate the scandal. The Tower Commission issued a devastating report early in 1987 that placed much of the responsibility for the Iran-Contra affair on Reagan's loose management style. When asked if he had known of Colonel North's illegal actions, the president simply replied, "I don't remember." During the spring and summer of 1987, a joint House-Senate committee held hearings into the Iran-Contra affair. In his testimony, North claimed that he thought "he had received authority from the President."

The investigations led to six indictments in 1988. A jury found North guilty of three minor charges but innocent of nine more serious counts because he had acted as an agent of higher-ups. An appellate court later overturned his conviction. Of those involved, only John Poindexter received a jail sentence—six months for obstructing justice and lying to Congress.

**A HISTORIC TREATY** The most notable achievement at the end of Reagan's second term was a surprising arms-reduction agreement with the Soviet government. Under Mikhail Gorbachev, who came to power in 1985, the Soviets pursued three dramatic initiatives. They renewed the policy of détente, encouraging a reduction of tensions with the United States, so that they could subsequently reduce military spending and focus on more-pressing problems, chiefly an inefficient economy and a losing war in Afghanistan.

Gorbachev also instituted what he called *perestroika* (restructuring) to make the Soviet government bureaucracy more efficient. Third, he encouraged *glasnost* (openness), a radical reappraisal of the Soviet system that allowed for open debate and shared information. In the end, however, the forces of modernization that Gorbachev helped unleash would end up dismantling the Soviet Union.

**THE REYKJAVIK SUMMIT** In October 1986, Ronald Reagan and Mikhail Gorbachev met for the first time in Reykjavik, Iceland, to discuss ways to reduce the threat of nuclear war. At one point, Reagan shocked Gorbachev and the Soviets by saying, "It would be fine with me if we eliminated all nuclear weapons." Equally shocking was Gorbachev's reply: "We can do that."

By the end of the meeting, however, the two sides remained far apart, and Gorbachev privately called Reagan a "feebleminded cave man." The main sticking point was Reagan's refusal to call off the Strategic Defense Initiative (SDI, or "Star Wars").

**Mikhail Gorbachev** Deputy chairman, and later, president of the Soviet Union in 1988.

**THE INF TREATY** The logjam in the disarmament negotiations suddenly broke in 1987, when Mikhail Gorbachev announced that he was willing to consider mutual reductions in nuclear weaponry. A member of the Soviet negotiating team acknowledged Ronald Reagan's role in the breakthrough. The U.S. president, he explained, "takes you by the arm, walks you to the cliff's edge, and invites you to step forward for the good of humanity."

After nine months of negotiations, Reagan and Gorbachev met in Washington, D.C., on December 9, 1987, and signed the **Intermediate-Range Nuclear Forces (INF) Treaty**, an agreement to eliminate intermediate-range (300- to 3,000-mile) missiles. The treaty marked the first time that the two nations had agreed to destroy a whole class of weapons systems and produced the most sweeping cuts in nuclear weaponry in history.

**REAGAN'S GLOBAL LEGACY** Ronald Reagan achieved the unthinkable by helping to end the cold war. Although his massive defense buildup almost bankrupted the United States, it forced the Soviet Union to the bargaining table. By negotiating the nuclear disarmament treaty and lighting the fuse of democratic freedom in Soviet-controlled East Germany, Hungary, Poland, and Czechoslovakia, Reagan set in motion events that would lead to the collapse of the Soviet Union.

In June 1987, Reagan visited the Berlin Wall in East Germany and, in a dramatic speech, called upon the Soviet Union to allow greater freedom within the countries under its control. "General Secretary Gorbachev, if you seek peace, if you seek prosperity for the Soviet Union and Eastern Europe, if you seek liberalization: Come here to this gate! Mr. Gorbachev, open this gate! Mr. Gorbachev, tear down this wall!" It was great theater and good politics.

## THE CHANGING ECONOMIC AND SOCIAL LANDSCAPE

During the 1980s, the U.S. economy went through a wrenching transformation. The nations most devastated by the Second World War—France, Germany, the Soviet Union, Japan, and China—had now developed formidable economies with higher levels of productivity than the United States. Increasingly more U.S. companies shifted their production overseas to take advantage of lower labor costs, accelerating the transition of the economy from its once-dominant industrial base to a more services-oriented approach. Driving these changes were the impact of the computer revolution and the development of the internet.

**THE COMPUTER REVOLUTION** The idea of a programmable machine that would rapidly perform mental tasks had been around since the eighteenth century, but it took the Second World War to gather the intellectual and financial resources needed to create such a "computer."

In 1946, a team of engineers at the University of Pennsylvania developed ENIAC (electronic numerical integrator and computer), the first all-purpose, all-electronic digital computer. It required 18,000 vacuum tubes to operate and an entire room to house it. The following year, researchers at Bell Telephone Laboratories invented the transistor, which replaced the bulky vacuum tubes and enabled much smaller, yet more-powerful, computers—as well as being the foundation for new devices such as hearing aids and transistor radios.

The next major breakthrough was the invention in 1971 of the **microprocessor**—virtually a tiny computer on a silicon chip. The microprocessor chip revolutionized computing by allowing for the storage of far more data in much smaller machines.

The microchip made possible the personal computer. In 1975, an engineer named Ed Roberts developed the Altair 8800, the prototype of the personal computer. Its potential excited a Harvard University sophomore named Bill Gates, who improved the software of the Altair 8800, dropped out of college, and formed a company called Microsoft.

During the 1980s, IBM (International Business Machines), using a microprocessor made by the Intel Corporation and an operating system provided by Microsoft, helped transform the personal computer into a mass consumer product. In 1963, a half-million computer chips were sold worldwide; by 1970, the number was 300 million.

Computer chips transformed a variety of electronic products—televisions, calculators, wristwatches, clocks, ovens, phones, laptops, and automobiles—while facilitating efforts to land astronauts on the moon and launch satellites into space. The development of the internet, email, and cell-phone technology during the 1980s and '90s allowed for instantaneous communication, thereby accelerating the globalization of the economy and dramatically increasing productivity in the workplace.

**CAREFREE CONSUMERS AND THE STOCK MARKET PLUNGE**  In the late 1970s, Jimmy Carter had urged Americans to lead simpler lives, reduce energy use, and invest more time in faith and family. During the 1980s, Ronald Reagan reduced tax rates so people would have more money to spend. Americans preferred Reagan's emphasis on prosperity to Carter's focus on propriety.

Reagan, however, succeeded too well in shifting the public mood back to the "bigger is better" tradition of heedless consumerism. During the "age of Reagan," advertisements celebrated instant gratification. Many consumers went on self-indulgent spending sprees, and the more they bought, the more they wanted. As the stock market soared, the number of multimillionaires working on Wall Street and in the financial industry mushroomed as income inequality in the United States widened. The national economy during the 1980s shifted from manufacturing to service industries, where wages were lower (a process known as "deindustrialization"). Most new jobs created during the 1980s paid only the minimum wage.

Yet affluent Americans showed little concern about those struggling to make ends meet. The money fever was contagious. Compulsive shoppers donned T-shirts proclaiming: "Born to Shop." By 1988, 110 million Americans had an average of seven credit cards each. Money—lots of it—came to define the American dream.

During the 1980s, many Americans began spending more than they earned. All categories of debt dramatically increased. Americans in the 1960s had saved, on average, 10 percent of their income; in 1987, the figure was less than 4 percent. The federal debt more than tripled, from $908 billion in 1980 to $2.9 trillion at the end of the 1989 fiscal year.

On October 19, 1987, the bill collector suddenly arrived at the nation's doorstep. On that "Black Monday," the stock market experienced a tidal wave of selling reminiscent of the 1929 crash, as investors worried that the United States would never address its massive budget deficits. The Dow Jones Industrial Average plummeted 22.6 percent, nearly doubling the 12.8 percent fall on October 28, 1929. Wall Street's selling frenzy sent stock prices plummeting in Tokyo, London, Paris, and Toronto.

In the aftermath of Black Monday, fears of an impending recession led business leaders and economists to attack President Reagan for allowing such huge budget deficits. He responded by agreeing to work with Congress to develop a deficit-reduction package. For the first time, Reagan indicated a willingness to increase taxes to help reduce the deficit. The eventual compromise plan, however, was so modest that it did little to restore investor confidence.

**THE POOR** Despite unprecedented prosperity in the eighties, homelessness became an acute social issue. An estimated 400,000 people were dispossessed by the end of the decade. Several factors had led to a shortage of low-cost housing. The government had given up on building public housing, urban-renewal programs had demolished blighted areas but provided no housing for those who were displaced, and owners had abandoned unprofitable buildings in poor inner-city neighborhoods or converted them into expensive condominiums for high-income city dwellers, a process called gentrification.

In addition, the working poor during the 1980s saw their incomes decline at the same time that the Reagan administration was making deep cuts in federal social welfare programs. By 1983, over 15 percent of adults were living below the poverty line, even though half of them lived in households where at least one person worked. Still another factor affecting the homelessness epidemic was the unintended effects of new medications that allowed some patients to be discharged from mental institutions. Once released, many of them ended up on the sidewalks of America, homeless and without care, because promised mental-health services failed to materialize. Between 1982 and 1985, federal programs targeted to the poor were reduced by $57 billion.

The culture of homelessness often sent victims on a downward spiral. Drug and alcohol abuse were rampant among the homeless. In Los Angeles County, for example, there were 400,000 cocaine addicts and 200,000 other drug addicts in need of treatment by the late 1980s. An estimated 100,000 of them were homeless or poor. Nationwide, a quarter of the homeless (about 100,000 people) had spent time in mental institutions, and some 40 percent had spent time in jail.

**THE AIDS EPIDEMIC** Still another group of outcasts included those suffering from a new disease called AIDS (acquired immunodeficiency syndrome). At the beginning of the 1980s, public health officials had reported that gay men and intravenous drug users were especially at risk for developing AIDS. People contracted the human immunodeficiency virus (HIV), which causes AIDS, through contact with the blood or body fluids of an infected person. Those infected with the virus showed signs of extreme fatigue, developed a strange combination of infections, and soon died.

The Reagan administration showed little interest in AIDS in part because it was viewed as a "gay" disease. Reagan himself did not specifically mention AIDS in public until 1985, even though some 5,000 Americans had died of the disease. Patrick Buchanan, who served as Reagan's director of communications, said that gays had "declared war on nature, and now nature is extracting an awful retribution." Buchanan and others convinced Reagan not to engage in the **HIV/AIDS** issue. As a result, by 2000, AIDS had claimed almost 300,000 American lives, and it had become the leading cause of death among men ages twenty-five to forty-four.

Frustrated by the lack of concern shown by the Reagan administration, activists founded the AIDS Coalition to Unleash Power (ACT UP) in 1987. It has since become the most effective voice for fighting AIDS. In large part because of its advocacy, the number of

**Act Up!** Members of the influential AIDS activist group Act Up! demonstrate for increased availability of life-saving medication.

newly reported AIDS cases has significantly declined from nearly 200,000 a year in 1988 to 40,000 in 2016.

## THE PRESIDENCY OF GEORGE H. W. BUSH

In his farewell address in January 1989, Ronald Reagan said with a smile, "My friends, we did it. We . . . made a difference." Over his two terms, Reagan had become a transformational president. While restoring the stature of the presidency, helping to defuse the cold war, and reviving the economy, he had accelerated the nation's shift toward conservatism and rejuvenated the Republican party after the Watergate scandal. He put the Democrats on the defensive and forced conventional New Deal "liberalism" into retreat. For the next twenty years or so, his anti-government, anti-tax agenda would dominate the political landscape.

He would be a tough act to follow. His two-term vice president, George H. W. Bush, won the Republican presidential nomination in 1988 because he pledged to create an ethical government, be a more "hands-on" president than Reagan, and promote "a more compassionate conservatism." It was time to deal more seriously with the thorny problems of inner-city poverty, homelessness, and drug abuse.

Born into a prominent New England family, the son of a U.S. senator, George H. W. Bush had, at the age of eighteen, enlisted in the U.S. Navy at the start of the Second World War, becoming the youngest combat pilot to have flown in the U.S. military. After his distinguished military service, Bush graduated from Yale University and became a wealthy oil executive in Texas before entering government service. He served first as a member of the U.S. House of Representatives and then as U.S. ambassador to the United Nations. He was elected chair of the Republican National Committee, became a diplomat in China, and was appointed director of the CIA before becoming Reagan's loyal vice president.

In all those roles, Bush had displayed intelligence, integrity, and courage, but he lacked Reagan's charm and eloquence. One Democrat described Bush as being born "with a silver foot in his mouth."

A centrist Republican, Bush promised to use the White House to fight bigotry, illiteracy, and homelessness. "I want a kinder, gentler nation," Bush said in accepting the Republican nomination. Yet his most memorable line in his speech was a defiant statement ruling out tax increases: "The Congress will push me to raise taxes, and I'll say no, and they'll push, and I'll say no, and they'll push again. And I'll say to them: Read my lips. No new taxes."

**THE ELECTION OF 1988**

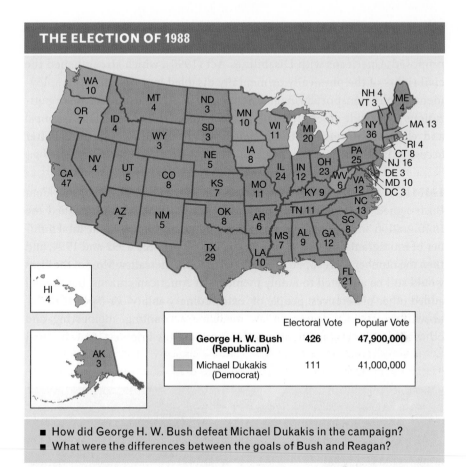

| | | Electoral Vote | Popular Vote |
|---|---|---|---|
| ■ | **George H. W. Bush** (Republican) | **426** | **47,900,000** |
| □ | Michael Dukakis (Democrat) | 111 | 41,000,000 |

■ How did George H. W. Bush defeat Michael Dukakis in the campaign?
■ What were the differences between the goals of Bush and Reagan?

In the end, Bush won decisively over the Democratic nominee, Massachusetts governor Michael Dukakis. Dukakis carried only ten states plus the District of Columbia. Bush won with a margin of about 54 percent to 46 percent in the popular vote and 426 to 111 in the electoral college, but the Democrats retained control of the House and Senate.

As the new president, George H. W. Bush felt the need to show that he was his own man, not a Reagan clone. To that end, he replaced Calvin Coolidge's portrait in the White House with one of Theodore Roosevelt, and he ordered all Reagan appointees to submit their resignation. Bush ended support for the Contras in Nicaragua and abandoned Reagan's unworkable "Star Wars" missile defense program.

Yet, for the most part, Bush sought to consolidate the initiatives that Reagan had put in place rather than launch his own array of programs and policies. "We don't need to remake society," he announced. As an example of his compassionate conservatism, Bush supported the Democratic-proposed Americans with Disabilities Act (1990), which strengthened the civil rights of the physically or mentally disabled in areas such as employment, public transportation, and housing. The ADA also required organizations to provide amenities such as mechanized doors, wheelchair ramps, and elevators to ensure that people with disabilities could have better access to facilities.

**IMMIGRATION ACT OF 1990** On November 29, 1990, President Bush signed the bipartisan Immigration Act of 1990, which amended the Immigration and Nationality Act of 1965. It initially increased the total number of immigrants allowed each year to 700,000 between 1992 and 1994, and then the number was capped at an annual 675,000 thereafter. Most of the visas would still be allocated to family members of American citizens, but the bill added other preferences: people of "extraordinary ability" or "special skills," or with professional degrees in law, medicine, accounting, engineering, and other fields, all designed to attract the "best and the brightest" in the global

**Immigration Act of 1990** New citizens wait to be sworn in at a United States Citizenship Ceremony in Los Angeles, California.

labor market. In addition, the amendment introduced a "diversity lottery" system to assign visas to immigrants randomly, regardless of their country of origin. The act also lifted the 1965 ban on suspected gay and lesbian immigrants.

In signing the legislation, President Bush described it as the most comprehensive revision of immigration laws in decades and applauded its emphasis on ensuring greater diversity among immigrants being welcomed into the United States. He added that he was "also pleased to note that this Act facilitates immigration not just in numerical terms, but also in terms of basic entry rights of those beyond our borders." The new immigration act had a greater impact than its proponents imagined. During the 1990s, more immigrants entered the country than in any previous decade.

**THE FEDERAL DEBT AND RECESSION** The biggest problem facing the Bush administration was the huge national debt, which stood at $2.6 trillion in 1989, nearly three times its 1980 level. President Bush's pledge not to increase taxes made it all the more difficult to reduce the deficit or trim the debt. Likewise, Bush was not willing to make substantial spending cuts to defense or social-welfare programs like Social Security, Medicare, and food stamps. As a result, by 1990 the country faced "a fiscal mess."

During the summer of 1990, Bush proposed several tax increases, which he had sworn to avoid. His reversal set off a revolt among conservative Republicans. A Republican-aligned newspaper expressed its views with a banner headline: "READ MY LIPS: I LIED."

Congressional Republicans were so angry that they joined with Democrats in nixing Bush's budget proposal. With Congress and the White House unable to reach agreement, the federal government shut down. The public was furious, and its anger forced Bush to sign a resolution that reopened government offices. To do so, however, he had to agree to a new budget drafted by Democrats. It replaced his proposed gasoline tax with an increase in the top income tax rate, from 28 to 31 percent. Only a fourth of Republicans supported the idea, but the Democrats marshaled enough votes for it to become law in October 1990.

The budget fiasco and tax increase created a lasting divide between congressional Republicans and President Bush. Even more worrisome was that the economy barely grew during the first three years of the Bush administration— the worst record since the end of the Second World War. By 1991, the economy was in a recession, the unemployment rate had spiked to 8 percent, and public disapproval of the president had risen accordingly.

**THE DEMOCRACY MOVEMENT ABROAD** George H. W. Bush entered the White House with more foreign-policy experience than most presidents, and, like Nixon, he preferred to deal with international relations rather than domestic problems, especially since Democrats controlled Congress.

In the Soviet Union, with his nation's economy failing, Mikhail Gorbachev accelerated the implementation of policies designed to democratize Soviet life. His foreign policy sought harmony and trade with the West, staking his nation's future on cooperation and trade with its cold war enemies.

Early in 1989, Soviet troops left Afghanistan. Gorbachev then renounced Soviet intervention in the internal affairs of other Communist countries. His foreign minister, Eduard Shevardnadze, told the Soviet legislature that the nations of Eastern Europe had "absolute freedom" to choose their own form of government.

**A hammer to the Soviet empire**
A West German demonstrator pounds away at the Berlin Wall on November 11, 1989, while East German border guards look on. Two days later, all the crossings between East and West Germany were opened.

Soon thereafter, Communist regimes in Eastern Europe were toppled, first in Poland and Hungary, then in Czechoslovakia and Bulgaria. In Romania, the people joined the army in a bloody uprising against Nicolae Ceauşescu, the country's brutal dictator. He and his wife were captured and tried, then executed on Christmas Day. Although the new democratic governments faced immense economic and social challenges, Europe had been born anew.

**THE DESTRUCTION OF THE BERLIN WALL** The most spectacular event in the collapse of the Soviet empire came on November 9, 1989, when tens of thousands of East Germans gathered at the Berlin Wall and demanded that the border guards open the gates to West Berlin. The guards reluctantly did so, and soon Germans on both sides began tearing the wall down. What Germans called the "peaceful revolution" had occurred with dramatic suddenness. With the borders to West Germany now fully open, the Communist government of

East Germany collapsed. On October 3, 1990, the five states of East Germany were united with West Germany.

The reform impulse sped out of control within the Soviet Union itself, however. Gorbachev had proven unusually adept at political restructuring and building a presidential system that gave him, if anything, increased powers. His skills, however, could not salvage an antiquated economy that resisted change.

**COMMUNIST COUP FAILS** Mikhail Gorbachev's popularity shrank in the Soviet Union as it grew abroad. On August 18, 1991, a group of "old guard" political and military leaders accosted him at his vacation retreat in Crimea and demanded that he proclaim a state of emergency and transfer his powers to them so that they could restore the supremacy of the Communist party. He replied, "Go to hell," whereupon he was placed under house arrest.

The coup, however, was poorly planned and clumsily implemented. The plotters failed to arrest popular leaders such as Boris Yeltsin, the feisty president of the Russian Republic. They also neglected to close airports or cut off telephone and television communications, and they were opposed by key elements of the military and KGB (the Soviet secret police).

On August 20, President Bush responded favorably to Yeltsin's request for support and persuaded other leaders to join him in refusing to recognize the new Soviet government. The next day, word began to seep out that the plotters were fleeing. Several committed suicide, and a freed Gorbachev ordered the others arrested. Although Gorbachev reclaimed the title of president, he was forced to resign as head of the Communist party and admit that he had made a mistake in appointing the men who had turned against him. Yeltsin emerged as the most popular political figure in the country.

What had begun as a reactionary coup turned into a powerful accelerant for the "Soviet Disunion," as one journalist termed it. Most of the fifteen Soviet republics proclaimed their independence from Russia, with the Baltic states of Latvia, Lithuania, and Estonia regaining the status of independent nations. The Communist party was dismantled, prompting celebrating crowds to topple statues of Lenin and other Communist heroes.

**U.S. INVASION OF PANAMA** The end of the cold war and the implosion of the Soviet Union did not spell the end of international tensions, however. Before the close of 1989, U.S. troops were engaged in battle in Panama.

In 1983, General Manuel Noriega had become the ruthless leader of the Panamanian Defense Forces, which made him head of the government in fact if not in title. In 1988, federal grand juries in Florida indicted Noriega and fifteen others on charges of conspiring with Colombia's drug lords to ship cocaine through Panama to the United States. The next year, the Panamanian president tried to fire Noriega, but the National Assembly ousted the president and named Noriega "maximum leader." The legislators then declared Panama "in a state of war" with the United States.

On December 16, 1989, a U.S. Marine in Panama was killed. President Bush thereupon ordered an invasion ("Operation Just Cause") to capture Noriega and install a government to be headed by Guillermo Endara, who had won the presidency in an election that had been nullified by Noriega.

Early on December 20, U.S. troops struck at strategic targets. Noriega surrendered within hours. Twenty-three U.S. servicemen were killed; estimates of Panamanian casualties were as high as 4,000, including civilians. In April 1992, Noriega was convicted in the United States on eight counts of racketeering and drug distribution.

**THE GULF WAR**   On August 2, 1990, Saddam Hussein, dictator of Iraq, focused U.S. attention back upon the Middle East when his army suddenly invaded its tiny neighbor, Kuwait. Kuwait had increased its oil production, contrary to agreements with the Organization of the Petroleum Exporting Countries (OPEC). The resulting drop in global oil prices offended the Iraqi regime, which was deeply in debt and heavily dependent upon oil revenues.

President Bush condemned Iraq's "naked aggression" and dispatched warplanes and troops to Saudi Arabia, on the southern border of Iraq and Kuwait. British forces soon joined in, as did Arab units from Egypt, Morocco, Syria, Oman, the United Arab Emirates, and Qatar. Iraq refused to yield, and on January 12, 1991, Congress authorized the use of U.S. armed forces.

Four days later, U.S. forces and those from thirty-three other nations, including ten Islamic countries, launched **Operation Desert Storm** against Iraq. During the next six weeks, Iraqi soldiers surrendered by the thousands, and on February 28, Bush called for a cease-fire. The Iraqis accepted. There were 137 American fatalities; the lowest estimate of Iraqi deaths, civilian and military, was 100,000. But although coalition forces occupied about a fifth of Iraq, Hussein's tyrannical regime remained intact.

What came to be called the First Gulf War was thus a triumph without victory. Hussein had been defeated, but he was allowed to escape and remained in power. The consequences of the brief but intense war would be played out in the future, as Arabs humiliated by the American triumph began plotting revenge that would spiral into a new war of terrorism.

**Operation Desert Storm**  Allied soldiers patrol the southern Iraqi town of Salman on February 27, 1991. On the side of a building is a propaganda mural of dictator Saddam Hussein in military uniform.

**BUSH'S "NEW WORLD ORDER"**  After the First Gulf War, President Bush's public approval rating soared to 91 percent, even though Saddam Hussein's iron grip on Iraq was still intact. On December 25, 1991, the Soviet flag over the Kremlin was replaced by the flag of the Russian Federation. The cold war had ended with the dismemberment of the Soviet Union and its fifteen republics.

Containment of the Communist Soviet Union, the bedrock of U.S. foreign policy for more than four decades, had suddenly become irrelevant. For all its potential horrors, the cold war had brought stability; the two superpowers, the United States and the Soviet Union, had restrained themselves from an all-out nuclear war. Now the world would witness a growing number of unresolved crises and unstable regimes, some of which had access to weapons of mass destruction—nuclear as well as chemical and biological.

Bush spoke of a "new world order" but never defined it, admitting he had trouble with "the vision thing." He faced a challenge for the 1992 Republican presidential nomination from Patrick Buchanan, the conservative commentator and former White House aide, who adopted the slogan "America First" and called on Bush to "bring home the boys."

The excitement over the victory in the Gulf War also gave way to anxiety over the depressed economy. Bush tried a clumsy balancing act, acknowledging that "people are hurting" while telling Americans that "this is a good time to buy a car." By 1991, the public approval rating of his economic policy had plummeted to 18 percent.

**THE ELECTION OF 1992** At the 1992 Republican National Convention, Patrick Buchanan, who had won about a third of the votes in the party's primaries, blasted Bush for breaking his pledge not to raise taxes and for becoming the "biggest spender in American history." As the 1992 election unfolded, however, Bush's real problem proved to be his failure to improve the economy. In reflection of the high unemployment rate, a popular bumper sticker mirrored the public's frustration: "Saddam Hussein still has his job. What about you?"

In contrast, the Democrats presented an image of moderate forces in control. For several years, the Democratic Leadership Council, led by Arkansas governor William Jefferson Clinton, had been pushing the party from the liberal left to the center. The 1992 campaign also featured a third-party candidate, H. Ross Perot, a puckish Texas billionaire who found a large audience for his criticism of Reaganomics as "voodoo economics" (a phrase originally used by Bush in the 1980 Republican primary before he was named the vice-presidential candidate).

Born in 1946 in Hope, Arkansas, Bill Clinton never knew his biological father, who died before his son was born. As a teenager, Clinton yearned to be a national political leader. He attended Georgetown University in Washington, D.C., won a Rhodes Scholarship to Oxford University, and earned a law degree from Yale University, where he met his future wife, Hillary Rodham. Clinton returned to Arkansas and won election as the state's attorney general. By 1979, at age thirty-two, he was the youngest governor in the country. He served three more terms as governor and emerged as a dynamic leader of the "**New Democrats**," who were committed to winning back the middle-class whites ("Reagan Democrats") who had voted Republican during the 1980s.

In seeking the Democratic nomination, Clinton promised to cut the defense budget, provide tax relief, and create a massive economic aid package to help the former republics of the Soviet Union forge democratic societies. Witty, intelligent, optimistic, and charismatic, with an in-depth knowledge of public policy, Clinton reminded many of John F. Kennedy, his boyhood hero.

But beneath Clinton's charisma and expertise were several flaws. The *New York Times* explained that Clinton was "emotionally needy, indecisive, and undisciplined." He had also earned a well-deserved reputation for half-truths, exaggerations, and talking out of both sides of his mouth. Clinton used opinion polls to shape his stances on issues, pandered to special-interest groups, and flip-flopped on controversial subjects, leading critics to label him "Slick Willie." Even more enticing to the media were charges that Clinton was a chronic adulterer and that he had manipulated the Reserve Officers' Training Corps (ROTC) program during the Vietnam War to avoid military service. Clinton's evasive denials could not dispel lingering mistrust.

After a series of closely contested primaries, Clinton won the Democratic nomination and promised to restore the "hopes of the forgotten middle class." He chose Senator Albert "Al" Gore Jr. of Tennessee as his running mate. The Clinton-Gore team hammered Bush on economic issues. Clinton pledged that, if elected, he would cut the federal budget deficit in half in four years while reducing taxes on middle-class Americans.

The 1992 campaign also featured a third-party candidate, H. Ross Perot, a puckish Texas billionaire who found a large audience ("Perotistas") for his criticism of Reaganomics as "voodoo economics" (a phrase originally used by Bush in the 1980 Republican primary before he was named the vice-presidential candidate). Perot appealed to those fed up with government "gridlock" created by the polarization of the two major parties. As the CEO of a high-tech company, Perot initially won support for a unique proposal: an electronic town hall that would enable voters to express their preferences for major policies through instantaneous digital polling.

As political experts predicted, Perot's on-again, off-again candidacy helped elect Bill Clinton by drawing Republican votes away from Bush. Clinton won only 43 percent of the popular vote but garnered 370 electoral votes. Bush received 168 electoral votes and 39 percent of the vote. Perot won 19 percent of the popular vote, more than any third-party candidate since Theodore Roosevelt ran as a Progressive in 1912.

As 1992 came to an end, Bill Clinton, the "New Democrat," prepared to lead the United States. "The urgent question of our time," he said, "is whether we can make change our friend and not our enemy." Clinton would embrace unexpected changes while ushering America into the twenty-first century.

# CHAPTER REVIEW

## SUMMARY

- **The Carter Presidency**   While Jimmy Carter had some notable achievements, such as the *Camp David Accords (1978)*, his administration suffered from legislative inexperience, a deepening economic recession, soaring inflation, and the *Iranian hostage crisis (1979)*.

- **The Rise of Conservatism**   The Republican insurgency, beginning with Reagan's election, was dominated by Christian conservatives like those who made up the *Moral Majority*. The migration of older Americans and others to conservative southern and western states increased the voting power of the so-called Sun Belt.

- **Reaganomics**   Reagan introduced a "supply-side" economic philosophy, commonly called *Reaganomics*, that championed tax cuts for the rich, reductions in government regulations, cuts to social-welfare programs, and increased defense spending. Reagan was unable to cut domestic spending, however, and the tax cuts failed to pay for themselves as promised. The result was a dramatic increase in the national debt.

- **The End of the Cold War**   Reagan's military buildup, including the *Strategic Defense Initiative (SDI) (1983)*, helped force the Soviets to the negotiating table to conclude the *Intermediate-Range Nuclear Forces (INF) Treaty (1987)*—the beginning of the end of the cold war. But Reagan's foreign-policy efforts were tarnished by the *Iran-Contra affair (1987)*, in which members of his administration sold American-made armaments to Iran in exchange for Iranian influence to secure the release of American hostages held in Lebanon.

- **America in the 1980s**   Americans in the eighties not only experienced unprecedented prosperity but also rising poverty and homelessness. Conservatives condemned (and dismissed) *HIV/AIDS* as a "gay" disease. The development of the *microprocessor* paved the way for the computer revolution. Consumerism flourished, resulting in massive public and private debt. Two major initiatives in 1990 transformed the quality of life for many: the Immigration Act and the Americans with Disabilities Act (ADA).

- **A New World Order**   Republican George H. W. Bush won the presidency in 1988. At the end of the 1980s, democratic political movements emerged across Eastern Europe. In the Soviet Union, Mikhail Gorbachev's steps to restructure the economy (*perestroika*) and promote more open policies (*glasnost*) led to further reform and the collapse of the Soviet empire. But new trouble spots quickly emerged. Iraq, led by Saddam Hussein, invaded neighboring Kuwait in 1990. President Bush ordered American-led allied forces to launch *Operation Desert Storm*, and the Iraqis surrendered within six weeks. Despite the success of the first Gulf War, the sluggish economy and President Bush's decision to raise taxes led to his defeat by Democrat Bill Clinton in 1992.

# CHRONOLOGY

| | |
|---|---|
| **1978** | President Carter helps negotiate the Camp David Accords |
| **November 1979** | Iranian hostage crisis |
| **1980** | Ronald Reagan elected president |
| **1981** | President Reagan enacts major tax cuts |
| **1983** | President Reagan authorizes development of the Strategic Defense Initiative (SDI) |
| **1987** | Reagan delivers his famous Berlin Wall speech |
| **1988** | George H.W. Bush is elected president |
| **November 1989** | Berlin Wall is torn down |
| **December 1989** | U.S. troops invade Panama and capture Manuel Noriega |
| **1991** | Iraq forced from Kuwait in the First Gulf War |
| | Breakup of the USSR |
| **1992** | Bill Clinton is elected president |

# KEY TERMS

**Camp David Accords (1978)** p. 1297

**Iranian hostage crisis (1979)** p. 1299

**Moral Majority** p. 1303

**Reaganomics** p. 1306

**Strategic Defense Initiative (SDI) (1983)** p. 1311

**Iran-Contra affair (1987)** p. 1313

*perestroika* p. 1314

*glasnost* p. 1314

**Intermediate-Range Nuclear Forces (INF) Treaty (1987)** p. 1315

**microprocessor** p. 1316

**HIV/AIDS** p. 1319

**Operation Desert Storm (1991)** p. 1326

**New Democrats** p. 1328

---

 INQUIZITIVE

Go to InQuizitive to see what you've learned—and learn what you've missed—with personalized feedback along the way.

# 32 Twenty-First-Century America

## 1993–Present

**March for Our Lives** Throngs of people on Pennsylvania Avenue hold up home-made signs in support of gun control at the student-led rally on Saturday, March 24, 2018 after another tragic school shooting. Some 800 sister events to the Washington, D.C. rally took place in the United States and across the world. Two of the signs read: LOVE OVER LEAD and KIDS OVER CAMPAIGN DONATIONS.

The United States entered the final decade of the twentieth century triumphant. American persistence in the cold war had brought about the collapse of the Soviet Union and the birth of democracy and capitalism in Eastern Europe. During the 1990s, the U.S. economy became the marvel of the world, as remarkable gains in productivity boosted by new digital technologies led to the greatest prosperity in modern history.

Yet America's sense of physical security and material comfort was soon shattered by terrorist assaults on New York City and Washington, D.C., in 2001. The attacks killed thousands, deepened the recession, and raised profound questions about national security, personal safety, and civil liberties.

In leading the fight against global terrorism, the United States became embroiled in long, costly, and controversial wars in Iraq and Afghanistan. Opposition to those wars would provide much of the momentum for Democrat Barack Obama's election in 2008 as the nation's first African American president. Obama entered the White House at the same time that the United States and Europe were experiencing the Great Recession, a prolonged economic downturn that threatened the global banking system, caused widespread unemployment, and ignited social unrest and political tensions.

## *focus questions*

**1.** What were the major population trends (demographics) in the United States during the twenty-first century? How did they influence the nation's politics?

**2.** What were the accomplishments and setbacks of Bill Clinton's presidency?

**3.** What was the impact of global terrorism during the presidency of George W. Bush? How effective was his "war on terror"?

**4.** What were the issues and developments during Bush's second term that helped lead to Barack Obama's historic victory in the 2008 presidential election?

**5.** What were President Obama's priorities at home and abroad? How effective were his efforts to pursue them?

**6.** What were the factors that led to Donald Trump's 2016 presidential election and how would you assess his early presidency?

Eight years later, those political tensions gave rise to an unconventional Republican presidential candidate, billionaire New York real-estate developer Donald Trump. In 2016, he would surprise mainstream Republican leaders, pundits, and pollsters by winning the Republican nomination and then stunned pollsters by narrowly defeating Democrat Hillary Clinton in the general election.

## America's Changing Population

The United States in the twenty-first century experienced dramatic social changes. By 2019, America's population had surpassed 330 million, more than 80 percent of whom lived in cities or suburbs.

Even more important, the nation's racial and ethnic composition was changing rapidly. In 1980, the national population was 80 percent white. By 2019, that percentage had fallen below 60 percent. Hispanics/Latinos in 2019 represented 19 percent of the population, African Americans 13 percent, Asians about 5 percent, and Native Americans 1 percent. The rate of increase among those four groups was increasing twice as fast as it had during the 1980s. In 2005, Latinos surpassed African Americans as the nation's largest minority group (and salsa replaced ketchup as the nation's top condiment). Latinos were two-thirds of the population of Miami, nearly half of Los Angeles, and over one-fifth of New York City and Chicago.

Yet the fastest-growing group in the United States was composed of the nearly 10 million people who described themselves as "multiracial" and who represented more than 3 percent of the population.

This dramatic change in the nation's ethnic mix was the result of an immigration surge during the late twentieth and early twenty-first centuries. In 1996, immigration reached its highest level since before the First World War. By 2019, the United States had more foreign-born residents than ever—more than 46 million, 11 million of whom were undocumented immigrants (formerly classified as "illegal aliens"). In the first decade of the twenty-first century, the United States became home to more than twice as many immigrants as in *all* other countries combined. And for the first time, the majority of immigrants to America came not from Europe but from other parts of the world: Asia, Latin America, and Africa. Mexicans made up the largest share of Latinos, followed by Puerto Ricans and Cubans. Asian Americans increased their numbers at a faster rate than any other ethnic group, largely because of a surge in Chinese immigrants.

In 1980, Latinos lived mainly in five states: California, Arizona, New Mexico, Texas, and Florida. By 2019, every state had a rapidly growing Latino population. Demographers projected that by 2044, whites would become a minority in the United States.

Immigration also had potent political effects, as almost 1 million Latinos reached voting age each year. In 1980, six Latino Americans served in the U.S. Congress. By 2010, there were more than five times as many. In 1992, Latinos constituted only 2 percent of American voters; by 2019, they were nearly 13 percent.

By 2016, only 23 percent of baby boomers born during and after the Second World War considered the surge in American diversity a "change for the better." They worried that Latinos would never truly assimilate into mainstream American culture but would constitute a permanent underclass of people tied closely to their ancestral homelands.

Yet such concerns were countered by growing evidence during the twenty-first century that Latinos were successfully integrating into American society and embracing its ideals. High school graduation and college-enrollment rates among Latinos rose, teen pregnancy fell, and more and more learned English. In recent years, more than a quarter of Latino marriages involved a non-Latino partner.

Far from being a disaster, the growing Latino population provided the nation with a surge of youthful energy and vitality—and demonstrated such traditional American attributes as self-reliance, rugged individualism, thrift, close family ties, strong religious beliefs, support for the military, and an ethic of hard work.

The nation's African American population also experienced significant changes in the early twenty-first century. In a reverse of the Great Migration of the 1920s and after, a steady stream of young blacks moved out of rust belt states like Michigan and Illinois to the South. Atlanta replaced Chicago as the metro area with the largest population of African Americans. By 2010, some 57 percent of African Americans lived in the states of the former Confederacy, the highest percentage in fifty years.

# THE CLINTON PRESIDENCY (1993–2001)

Bill Clinton brought to the White House extraordinary gifts—and robust weaknesses. At forty-six years old, he was the third-youngest president in history. Like Ronald Reagan, Clinton charmed people, and his speeches inspired them. Wickedly smart and politically shrewd, he embraced politics as a civic duty and painstakingly learned the details of major policies and programs while mastering the personal touch.

While graced with charm and a common touch, Clinton was also prone to self-absorption, self-deception, and self-inflicted wounds. Eager to please and be loved, he often decided his stances on issues by studying focus-group interviews and public-opinion surveys. He at times seemed less a president than a flawed good ol' boy capable of self-righteousness and shameless misbehavior.

In sum, Clinton was a bundle of warring impulses whose faults often confounded his talents. Yet he displayed legendary energy and resilience— his nicknames were "Slick Willie" and the "Comeback Kid"—and he seemed to thrive amid controversy and setbacks. One of his advisers predicted that Clinton would make every mistake possible, "but he will only make it once."

Clinton's inexperience in international affairs and congressional maneuvering led to several missteps in his first year as president. Like George H. W. Bush before him, he reneged on several campaign promises. In a bruising battle with Congress, he was forced to abandon his proposed middle-class tax cut in order to keep another campaign promise to reduce the federal deficit. Then he dropped his promise to allow gays, lesbians, and bisexuals to serve openly in the armed forces after military commanders expressed strong opposition. He later announced an ambiguous policy called "don't ask, don't tell" (DADT), which allowed gays, lesbians, and bisexuals to serve in the military but only if they kept their sexual orientation secret (DADT did not mention transgender service members). "I got the worst of both worlds," Clinton later confessed. "I lost the fight, and the gay community was highly critical of me for the compromise."

**THE ECONOMY**    As a candidate, Bill Clinton had pledged to reduce the federal deficit without damaging the economy or hurting the nation's most vulnerable people. To this end, he proposed $241 billion in higher taxes for corporations and for the wealthiest individuals over four years, and $255 billion in spending cuts over the same period. The hotly contested bill passed the Democratic-controlled Congress by the slimmest of margins: 218 to 216 in the House and 51 to 50 in the Senate, with Vice President Al Gore providing the tie-breaking vote.

For virtually the first time since 1945, Congress had passed a major bill without a single Republican vote, a troubling indication of the nation's growing partisan divide. Clinton's deficit-reduction effort worked as planned, however. It led to lower interest rates, which, along with low energy prices, helped spur economic growth.

Equally difficult was gaining congressional approval of the **North American Free Trade Agreement (NAFTA)**, which the Bush administration had negotiated with Canada and Mexico. In 1994, Clinton urged Congress to approve NAFTA, which would make North America the largest free-trade zone in the world. Opponents favored tariffs to discourage the importation of cheaper foreign products, especially from Mexico. Yet Clinton prevailed

**NAFTA protesters** Protesters going to a rally against NAFTA, the controversial free-trade agreement for North America.

with solid Republican support. A sizable minority of Democrats, mostly labor unionists and southerners, opposed NAFTA, fearing that textile mills would lose business (and millions of jobs) to "cheap labor" countries—as they did.

**HEALTH-CARE REFORM** Clinton's primary public-policy initiative was an ambitious plan to overhaul the nation's health-care system. Public support for government-administered health insurance had increased as medical costs skyrocketed and some 37 million Americans, most of them poor or unemployed, went without coverage.

The Clinton administration argued that providing medical insurance to everyone, regardless of income, would reduce the costs of health care, but critics questioned the savings—and the ability of the federal government to manage such a huge program. The grand plan, known as the Health Security Act, called for large corporations to pay most of the medical insurance expenses of their employees and required small businesses to form "health alliances" so that they, too, could provide subsidized health insurance to their workers.

By the summer of 1994, Clinton's plan, developed by a task force headed by First Lady Hillary Rodham Clinton, was doomed, in part because the president opposed any changes and in part because, as one of Hillary Clinton's aides confessed, the "ludicrously complex report . . . had something in it to piss everybody off. So by the time it goes up to the Hill, it's dead on arrival." Congress voted down the bill in August 1994, and the controversial Clinton health plan turned many away from the Democratic party.

**LANDSLIDE REPUBLICAN VICTORY** The health-care disaster and the growing federal budget deficit played a dramatic role in the 1994 mid-term elections. In the most astonishing congressional victory of the twentieth century, the Republicans captured both houses of Congress for the first time since 1953 and won thirty-two governorships, including those in the most populous states of California, New York, and Texas, where George W. Bush, son of the former president and a future president himself, won handily.

The Republican victory was led by a combative Georgia conservative named Newton ("Newt") Leroy Gingrich. In early 1995, he became the first Republican Speaker of the House in forty-two years. Gingrich, a former history professor with a lust for controversy and an unruly ego, was a superb tactician who had helped mobilize conservatives associated with the Christian Coalition.

The Christian Coalition, organized by television evangelist Pat Robertson in 1989 to replace Jerry Falwell's Moral Majority (which had disbanded that year), was pro–school prayer, anti-abortion, anti-feminist, and anti–LGBTQ (lesbian, gay, bisexual, transgender, queer) rights. In many respects, the Religious Right took control of the political and social landscape in the nineties.

In 1994, Gingrich and other Republican candidates rallied conservative voters by lambasting Bill Clinton as "the enemy of normal Americans" and promised to bring forward a **Contract with America**, a pledge to dismantle the "corrupt liberal welfare state" created by Democrats.

The ten-point, anti-big-government "contract" promised a smaller federal government by reducing taxes and regulations, requiring term limits for members of Congress, slashing social-welfare programs, and passing a constitutional amendment requiring a balanced federal budget. As Texan Tom DeLay, a leading House Republican, explained, "You've got to understand, we are ideologues. We have an agenda. We have a philosophy."

Yet the much-trumpeted Contract with America quickly fizzled. The conservatives pushed too hard and too fast, realizing too late that their slim majority in Congress could not launch a revolution.

Gingrich's heavy-handed methods contributed to the disintegration of the Contract with America. He was too ambitious, too abrasive, too divisive.

**Newt Gingrich** Joined by 160 of his fellow House Republicans, Gingrich promotes the Contract with America in April 1995.

When Clinton refused to go along with Republican demands for a balanced-budget pledge, Gingrich twice shut down the federal government during the fall of 1995, sending 800,000 employees home and closing national parks, Social Security offices, and other agencies. The tactic backfired. By 1996, Republicans had abandoned its Contract with America.

**THE SUPREME COURT AND RACE**   The conservative mood also revealed itself in Supreme Court rulings that undermined affirmative-action programs, which gave African American students special consideration in college admissions and financial-aid awards. Between 1970 and 1977, African American enrollment in colleges and universities doubled, even as white students and their parents complained about "reverse discrimination."

Two major 1996 rulings affected affirmative action in college admissions. In *Hopwood v. Texas*, a federal court ruled that race could not be used as a consideration for admission. Later that year, California voters passed Proposition 209 (also known as the California Civil Rights Initiative, or CCRI), which ruled out preferential treatment (affirmative action) in government hiring, government contracting, and public schools and universities based on race, sex, ethnicity, or national origin.

Similar complaints were directed against affirmative-action programs that awarded government contracts to businesses owned by women and people of color. In 1995, the Court in *Adarand Constructors v. Peña* declared that affirmative-action programs had to be "narrowly tailored" to serve a "compelling national interest." The implication of such vague language was clear: the mostly conservative members of the Court had come to share the growing public suspicion of the legitimacy of programs designed to benefit a particular race, gender, or ethnic group.

**LEGISLATIVE BREAKTHROUGH**   After the surprising 1994 Republican takeover of Congress, Bill Clinton shrewdly resolved to reinforce his claim that he was a "centrist." He co-opted much of the energy of the conservative movement by announcing that "the era of big government is over" and by reforming the federal system of welfare payments to the poor.

Late in the summer of 1996, the Republican Congress passed a comprehensive welfare-reform measure, the **Personal Responsibility and Work Opportunity Act of 1996 (PRWOA)**. It illustrated Clinton's efforts to move the Democratic party away from the liberalism it had promoted since the 1930s. PRWOA abolished the Aid to Families with Dependent Children (AFDC) program, which had provided poor families almost $8,000 a year, and replaced it with the Temporary Assistance for Needy Families program, which limited the duration of welfare payments to two years in an effort to encourage unemployed people to get self-supporting jobs.

Liberal Democrats bitterly criticized Clinton's "welfare reform" deal. Yet it was a statistical success. Both the number of welfare recipients and poverty rates declined during the late 1990s, leading the editors of the left-leaning *New Republic* to report that the PRWOA had "worked much as its designers had hoped."

**THE 1996 CAMPAIGN** The Republican takeover of Congress in 1994 gave the party hope that it could prevent President Clinton's reelection. After clinching the GOP presidential nomination in 1996, Senate majority leader Bob Dole resigned his seat to devote his attention to the campaign. Clinton, however, maintained a large lead in the polls.

Concern about Dole's age (73) and his gruff personality, as well as tensions between economic and social conservatives over volatile issues such as abortion and gun control, hampered Dole's efforts to generate widespread support, especially among independent voters. Dole portrayed himself as a pragmatist willing to "downsize government, [but] not devastate it." Clinton, however, framed the election as a stark choice between Dole's desire to build a bridge to the past and Clinton's promise to build a bridge to the future.

On November 5, 1996, Clinton won with an electoral vote victory of 379 to 159 and 49 percent of the popular vote. Dole received 41 percent of the popular vote. Third-party candidate Ross Perot got 8 percent.

**THE "NEW ECONOMY"** Bill Clinton's presidency benefited from a prolonged period of unprecedented prosperity. During his last three years in office (1998–2000), the federal government generated unheard-of budget *surpluses*. What came to be called the "new economy" featured high-flying electronics, computer, software, telecommunications (cell phones, cable TV, etc.), and e-commerce internet firms called "dot-com" companies.

These dynamic tech enterprises helped the U.S. economy set records in every area: low inflation, low unemployment, corporate profits, and personal fortunes. Alan Greenspan, the Federal Reserve Board chairman, suggested that "we have moved beyond history" into an economy that seemed only to grow. He would soon be proven wrong.

**GLOBALIZATION** Another feature of the new economy was **globalization**. The end of the cold war and the disintegration of the Soviet Union opened many opportunities for U.S. companies in international trade. In addition, new globe-spanning communication technologies and massive new container-carrying ships and cargo jets shortened time and distance, enabling multinational companies to conduct more business abroad.

By 2000, more than a third of the production of U.S. multinational companies was occurring abroad, compared with 9 percent in 1980. In 1970, there were 7,000 American multinational companies; by 2000, there were 63,000. Many pursued controversial *outsourcing* strategies—moving their production "offshore" to nations such as Mexico and China to take advantage of lower labor costs and fewer workplace and environmental regulations. At the same time, many European and Asian companies, especially automobile manufacturers, built large plants in the United States to reduce the shipping expenses required to get their products to American markets.

## FOREIGN POLICY IN THE NINETIES

Unlike George H. W. Bush, Bill Clinton had little interest in global politics. Untrained and inexperienced in international relations, he sought to create opportunities around the world for U.S. business expansion. Yet, as international analyst Leslie Gelb cautioned Clinton, "A foreign economic policy is not a foreign policy, and it is not a national security strategy." Events soon forced Clinton to intervene to help foreign nations in crisis.

**THE MIDDLE EAST** During the 1990s, the Middle East remained a region fractured by ethnic and religious conflict and stubbornly composed of authoritarian regimes. President Clinton continued George H. W. Bush's policy of orchestrating patient negotiations between the Arabs and the Israelis. A new development was the inclusion of the Palestine Liberation Organization (PLO) in the discussions.

In 1993, secret talks between Israeli and Palestinian representatives resulted in a draft agreement that provided for the restoration of Palestinian self-rule in the occupied Gaza Strip and in Jericho, in the West Bank, in a "land for peace" exchange as outlined in United Nations Security Council resolutions. A formal signing occurred at the White House on September 13, 1993.

However, the Middle East peace process suffered a terrible blow in early November 1995, when Israeli Prime Minister Yitzhak Rabin was assassinated by a countryman because of his efforts to negotiate with the Palestinians. Seven months later, conservative hard-liner Benjamin Netanyahu narrowly defeated the U.S.–backed Shimon Peres in the Israeli national elections. Nevertheless, in October 1998, Clinton brought Yasir Arafat, Netanyahu, and King Hussein of Jordan together to reach an agreement. Under the Wye River Accords, Israel agreed to surrender land in return for security guarantees by the Palestinians.

**Clinton and the Middle East** President Clinton presides as Israeli prime minister Yitzhak Rabin (left) and PLO leader Yasir Arafat (right) agree to a pathbreaking peace accord between Israel and the Palestinians, September 1993.

**THE BALKANS** President Clinton also felt compelled to address turmoil in the Eastern European nations recently freed from Soviet domination. In 1991, Yugoslavia had disintegrated into ethnic warfare as four of its six multiethnic republics declared their independence. Serb minorities, backed by the new Republic of Serbia, stirred up civil wars in neighboring Croatia and Bosnia. In Bosnia, the conflict involved systematic efforts to eliminate Muslims. Clinton decided that the situation was "intolerable" because the massacres of thousands of people "tore at the very fabric" of human decency. He ordered food and medical supplies sent to Bosnian Muslims and dispatched warplanes to stop the massacres.

In 1995, U.S. negotiators finally persuaded the foreign ministers of Croatia, Bosnia, and Yugoslavia (by then a loose federation of the Republics of Serbia and Montenegro) to agree to a comprehensive peace plan. Bosnia would remain a single nation divided into two states: a Muslim-Croat federation controlling 51 percent of the territory, and a Bosnian-Serb republic controlling the rest. To enforce the agreement, 60,000 NATO peacekeeping troops were dispatched to Bosnia.

In 1998, the Balkan tinderbox flared up again, this time in the Yugoslav province of Kosovo, long considered sacred ground by Christian Serbs, although 90 percent of the 2 million Kosovars were in fact Albanian Muslims. In 1998, Yugoslav president Slobodan Milošević began a program of "**ethnic cleansing**" whereby Yugoslav forces burned Albanian villages, murdered men, raped women, and displaced hundreds of thousands of Muslim Kosovars.

On March 24, 1999, NATO, relying heavily upon U.S. military support, launched air strikes against Yugoslavian military targets. After seventy-two days of bombardment, Milošević sued for peace on NATO's terms, in part because his Russian allies had abandoned him. An agreement was reached on June 3, 1999, and Clinton pledged extensive U.S. aid to help the Yugoslavs rebuild.

## THE SCANDAL MACHINE

For a time, Bill Clinton's preoccupation with foreign crises helped deflect attention from several investigations into his personal conduct. During his first term, he was dogged by old charges about investments he and his wife had made in Whitewater, a planned resort development in Arkansas. The project turned out to be a fraud and a failure, and people accused the Clintons of conspiring with the developer. In 1994, Kenneth Starr, a former judge and a conservative Republican, was appointed to investigate the Whitewater case.

Starr found no evidence that the Clintons were involved in the Whitewater fraud, but he soon happened upon evidence of a White House sex scandal. For years, rumors had circulated about the president's dalliances with women. James Carville, Clinton's political consultant, once asked Clinton about his sexual risk-taking. "Well," Clinton replied, "they haven't caught me." He spoke too soon.

MONICAGATE Between 1995 and 1997, President Clinton had engaged in a sexual affair with an unpaid, twenty-two-year-old White House intern, Monica Lewinsky. More disturbing, he had pressed her to lie about their relationship, even under oath. Clinton initially denied the affair, telling the nation in late January 1998 that "I did not have sexual relations with that woman, Miss Lewinsky."

Yet the scandal would not disappear, and for the next thirteen months, the media circus surrounding the "Monicagate" or "Zippergate" affair captured public attention like a daily soap opera. (Since the Watergate affair in 1973–1974, journalists have routinely attached the suffix "-gate" to scandals.) Other women stepped forward to claim that Clinton had engaged in improper relations with them, charges that the president denied.

The First Lady, Hillary Clinton, grimly stood by her husband, declaring that the rumors were the result of a "vast right-wing conspiracy." With the economy booming, Clinton's public approval ratings actually rose during 1998. In August, however, the scandal revived when Lewinsky provided a federal grand jury with a detailed account of her relationship with the president.

Soon thereafter, Clinton became the first president to testify before a grand jury. On August 17, he admitted having "inappropriate, intimate physical contact" with Lewinsky, and he acknowledged that it was "wrong." He also admitted that he had misled the American people. The president insisted, however, that he had done nothing illegal.

Public reaction was mixed. A majority expressed sympathy for Clinton because of his humiliation and because the Lewinsky affair was a private act of consensual sex. Others, however, were eager to see the president resign. Republicans were convinced they could impeach him.

**THE IMPEACHMENT OF CLINTON** On September 9, 1998, Special Prosecutor Kenneth Starr submitted to Congress thirty-six boxes of documents that included graphic accounts of the president's encounters with Monica Lewinsky. The report claimed that there was "substantial and creditable" evidence of presidential wrongdoing (perjury, obstructing justice, and abuse of power). The Starr report prompted the Republican-dominated House of Representatives on October 8 to begin a wide-ranging impeachment inquiry, which led Bill Clinton to claim that he was the victim of a rogue prosecutor run amok. "When this thing is over," Clinton said, "there's only going to be one of us left standing. And it's going to be me."

On December 19, 1998, William Jefferson Clinton was impeached (accused of "high crimes and misdemeanors") by the House of Representatives. The House charged Clinton with obstructing justice and lying under oath to a federal grand jury.

House Speaker Newt Gingrich led the impeachment effort, even though he himself was, at the time, secretly engaged in a longstanding affair with a congressional staff member. (Gingrich resigned as speaker in November 1998 and left both the House and his wife, escaping with his new wife from elected office altogether.) Journalists began calling Clinton's Senate trial the "soap opera" impeachment after Gingrich's successor as Speaker, Robert Livingston of Louisiana, suddenly resigned after admitting that he, too, had engaged in adulterous affairs.

The Senate impeachment trial began on January 7, 1999. Five weeks later, on February 12, Clinton was acquitted, largely on a party-line vote. A majority of senators, Democrats and a few Republicans (55–45), decided that Clinton had not committed the "high crimes and misdemeanors" required to remove a president from office.

Most Americans agreed. As historian Steven Gillon observed, "The only thing most Americans disliked more than a devious middle-aged man lying about sex was moralizing, self-righteous hypocrites telling other people how to lead their lives."

Although the impeachment effort failed, the scandal tainted Clinton's final eighteen months in office.

**ASSESSING THE CLINTON PRESIDENCY** For all his faults, Bill Clinton presided over an unprecedented period of prosperity (115 consecutive months of economic growth and the lowest unemployment rate in 30 years), generated record budget surpluses, and passed a welfare-reform measure with support from both parties. In the process, he revitalized the Democratic party by moving it from the left to the "vital center" of the political spectrum. Clinton also helped bring peace and stability to the Balkans.

At times, however, his boundless self-confidence led to arrogant recklessness. He debased the presidency with his sexual escapades, and his effort to bring health insurance to the uninsured was a clumsy failure. Yet in 2000, his last year in office, his public approval rating was 65 percent, the highest end-of-term rating since President Dwight D. Eisenhower. Bill Clinton's popularity was not enough, however, to ensure the election of his vice president, Al Gore, as his successor.

# A CHAOTIC START TO A NEW CENTURY

Wild celebrations ushered in the year 2000, and Americans led the cheering. The cold war was over, the United States was the world's only superpower, and the high-tech U.S. economy dominated global trade. But the joyous mood did not last. Powerful and unstable forces were emerging, the most dangerous of which were sophisticated global networks of Islamist terrorists eager to disrupt and destroy American values and institutions.

## A DISPUTED ELECTION

The presidential election of 2000 proved to be one of the closest and most controversial in history. The two major-party candidates, Vice President Albert Gore Jr., the Democrat, and Texas governor George W. Bush, son of the former Republican president, offered contrasting views on the role of the federal government, tax cuts, environmental policies, and the best way to preserve Social Security and Medicare.

## THE ELECTION OF 2000

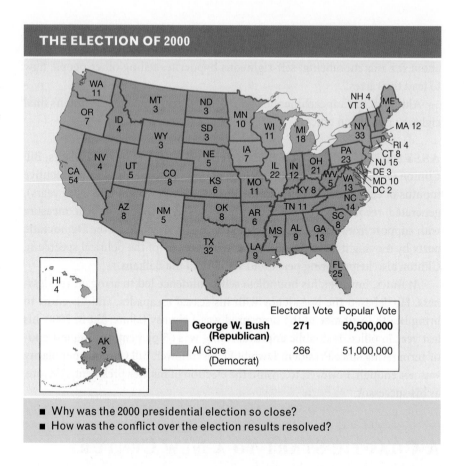

| | Electoral Vote | Popular Vote |
|---|---|---|
| **George W. Bush (Republican)** | **271** | **50,500,000** |
| Al Gore (Democrat) | 266 | 51,000,000 |

- Why was the 2000 presidential election so close?
- How was the conflict over the election results resolved?

Gore, a Tennessee native and Harvard graduate whose father had been a U.S. senator, favored an active federal government that would do more to protect the environment.

Bush, on the other hand, campaigned on a theme of "compassionate conservatism." He also promised to restore "honor and dignity" to the White House after the Clinton scandal, and he proposed transferring power from the federal government to the states. A born-again Christian with degrees from Yale University and Harvard Business School, he also urged a more "humble" foreign policy that would end U.S. efforts at "nation-building," whereby American officials sought to install democratic governments in undemocratic societies.

The November election results created high drama. The television networks initially reported that Gore had narrowly won the state of Florida and its decisive twenty-five electoral votes. Later in the evening, however, they reversed themselves, saying that Florida was too close to call. In the chaotic early-morning hours, the networks declared that Bush had been elected president. The final tally showed Bush with a razor-thin lead, but Florida law required a recount. For the first time in 125 years, the results of a presidential election remained in doubt for weeks.

As a painstaking hand recount proceeded, the two sides sparred in court, each accusing the other of trying to steal the election. The drama lasted for five weeks, until, on December 12, a divided U.S. Supreme Court ruled 5–4 that the recount be halted. Bush was declared the winner in Florida by 537 votes. Gore had amassed a 540,000-vote lead nationwide, but losing Florida meant he lost the electoral college by two votes. Although Gore "strongly disagreed" with the Supreme Court's decision, he asked voters to rally around Bush and move forward. "Partisan rancor," he urged, "must be put aside."

The ferocious sparring between the two national parties was not put aside, however, in part because Bush chose as key advisers men known for their strong ideological convictions. One of them, Richard "Dick" Cheney, a former Wyoming congressman and influential member of the Nixon, Ford, and George H. W. Bush administrations, quickly became the most powerful vice president in modern history. The secretive Cheney used his long experience with government bureaucracy to fill the administration with like-minded associates who helped him control the flow of information to the president. He became a domineering influence on the inexperienced Bush.

**The recount** In yet another recount, Judge Robert Rosenberg examines a ballot with a magnifying glass. That Florida's voting machines were so unreliable introduced doubt about the legitimacy of the close results in the November 2000 election.

## A CHANGE OF DIRECTION

George W. Bush had promised to cut taxes for the wealthy, increase military spending, and eliminate overly strict environmental regulations.

First, however, he had to deal with a sputtering economy, which in March 2001 was in recession for the first time in more than a decade. Bush decided that cutting taxes was the best way to boost economic growth and to generate jobs for the growing number of unemployed. On June 7, 2001, he signed the Economic Growth and Tax Relief Act, which cut $1.35 trillion in taxes.

Instead of paying for themselves in renewed economic growth, however, the tax cuts led to a sharp drop in federal revenue, producing in turn a fast-growing budget deficit as the Clinton surpluses were quickly used up. Huge increases in the costs of Medicare and Medicaid resulting from the aging of the baby boom generation contributed to the deficit, as did military expenditures caused by an unexpected war against global terrorism.

Bush was also distracted by global crises. Islamist militants around the world bitterly resented what they viewed as the "imperial" globalization of U.S. culture and power. With increasing frequency, they used terrorism, including suicide bombings, to gain notoriety, exact vengeance, and generate fear and insecurity.

Throughout the 1990s, the United States had fought a losing struggle against global terrorist groups. The ineffectiveness of U.S. intelligence agencies in tracking the movements and intentions of militant extremists became tragically evident in the late summer of 2001.

**9/11—A NEW DAY OF INFAMY** Early on the morning of September 11, 2001, Islamist terrorists hijacked a U.S. airliner in Boston. They flew it to New York City, where at 8:44 A.M. they slammed the fuel-laden jet into the north tower of the World Trade Center in the heart of the nation's financial district. The twin towers, each 110 stories tall and filled with Wall Street investment companies, had been viewed as the cathedrals of capitalism, and now they were being toppled.

Eighteen minutes after the first tower was hit, a second hijacked jumbo jet crashed into the Trade Center's south tower. The two skyscrapers, filled with 50,000 workers, burned fiercely. The televised images were heartbreaking. Hundreds of trapped occupants, many of them on fire, saw no choice but to jump to their deaths. One couple held hands as they plummeted to the ground.

The mammoth steel structures quickly collapsed from the intense inferno, destroying surrounding buildings and killing nearly 3,000 people, including more than 400 firefighters, police officers, and emergency responders. One of the dead, the Reverend Mychal Judge, was a fire department chaplain who was killed by falling debris as he administered last rites to an injured fireman. The southern end of Manhattan—"ground zero"—became a hellish scene of raging fires, twisted steel, broken concrete, suffocating smoke, wailing sirens,

**September 11** Smoke pours out of the north tower of the World Trade Center as the south tower bursts into flames after being struck by a second hijacked airplane. Both iconic buildings would collapse within an hour.

blood-covered streets, victims in agony, and thousands of panicked people fleeing the island.

While the catastrophic drama in New York City was unfolding, a third hijacked plane crashed into the Pentagon in Washington, D.C. A fourth hijacked airliner, most likely aimed toward the White House, missed its mark when passengers—who had heard reports of the earlier hijackings via cell phones—assaulted the knife-wielding hijackers to prevent the plane from being used as a weapon. During the struggle, the plane went out of control and plummeted into the ground near Shanksville, Pennsylvania, killing all aboard.

Within hours of the hijackings, the nineteen dead terrorists, fifteen of them from Saudi Arabia, were identified as members of al Qaeda (Arabic for "the Base"), a well-financed network of Islamist extremists led by a wealthy Saudi renegade, Osama bin Laden. Years before, bin Laden had declared *jihad* ("holy war") on the United States, Israel, and the Saudi monarchy in his effort to create a single Islamist caliphate ("global empire"). He used remote bases in Sudan and Afghanistan as training centers for jihadist fighters recruited from around the world. Collaborating with bin Laden's terrorist network was Afghanistan's ruling Taliban, a coalition of ultraconservative Islamists who provided bin Laden a safe haven.

The governments of Islamic nations worldwide condemned the 9/11 attacks, but al Qaeda was not a nation. Instead it was a new and extremely dangerous type of organization—a shadowy virtual terrorist state, borderless yet global in its reach, and populated by multinational Islamist zealots. As religious terrorists, they were the products of failed societies that bred their anger and their hatred of the West—and of America in particular because of its steadfast support of Israel. As a Pakistani newspaper asserted, "September 11 was not a mindless terrorism for terrorism's sake. It was reaction and revenge, even retribution" for America's pro-Israeli policies in the Middle East. The suicide terrorists viewed themselves as God's people doing holy work. Killing "infidels" (Americans and their allies) was a sacred act that would earn heavenly rewards. Bin Laden told his followers that it was their religious duty "to kill the Americans and their allies, civilian and military, in any country."

## THE "WAR ON TERROR"

The 9/11 assault on the United States, like the Japanese attack on Pearl Harbor on December 7, 1941, changed the course of modern life. Many Americans were initially paralyzed by grief, confusion, and fear. As the shock wore off, however, Americans were consumed by blinding anger and a feverish quest for retaliation and revenge, the same emotions that had propelled the terrorists.

**War fever** President George W. Bush addresses members of the Special Forces in July 2002 as part of an appeal to Congress to increase defense spending after the September 11 terrorist attacks.

George W. Bush suddenly found his presidential voice and purpose as he forged a coalition of allied nations committed to a global **war on terror** "to answer these attacks and rid the world of evil. . . . We will not waver, we will not tire, we will not falter, and we will not fail." He warned other nations that they needed to make a grave decision: "either you are with us or you are with the terrorists." The war, Bush stressed, would begin with al Qaeda but would "not end until every terrorist group of global reach has been found, stopped, and defeated."

A wave of patriotic fervor swept the nation after Bush's declaration of war. In just 48 hours, Walmart sold more than 300,000 U.S. flags. People formed long lines to donate blood, and many men and women signed up for military service.

President Bush led the military campaign to ferret out the al Qaeda terrorists and destroy their networks and infrastructure. That required ousting the Taliban movement, for it hosted al Qaeda. Bush demanded that Afghanistan's Taliban government surrender the al Qaeda terrorists or risk military attack. The Taliban refused, and on October 7, 2001, the United States and its allies launched an invasion of Afghanistan dubbed Operation Enduring Freedom. Bush pledged that American forces would stay until they finished the job. (The war is now in its eighteenth year.)

On December 9, the Taliban regime collapsed, and the United States inherited a failed nation. Afghanistan was a desperately poor country with a dysfunctional and corrupt government and inhabited by a largely rural population whose life expectancy was forty-seven and literacy rate was thirty-eight percent. The United States proved unable to improve the Islamic nation's quality of life, and, as a result, the war in Afghanistan transitioned into a high-stakes manhunt for the elusive Osama bin Laden.

**FIGHTING TERROR AT HOME** While the fighting continued in Afghanistan, officials in Washington worried that terrorists might attack the United States with biological, chemical, or even nuclear weapons. To address the threat and help restore public confidence, President Bush exercised extraordinary executive powers as commander in chief. Without congressional approval, he established the Office of Homeland Security and gave it sweeping authority to spy on Americans. Another new federal agency, the Transportation Security Administration (TSA), assumed responsibility for screening airline passengers for weapons and bombs.

At the same time, Bush and a supportive Congress created the **USA Patriot Act**, which gave government agencies the right to eavesdrop on confidential conversations between prison inmates and their lawyers, and permitted suspected terrorists to be tried in secret military courts. Civil liberties groups voiced concerns that the measures jeopardized constitutional rights and protections, but most people supported them.

What the public did not know was that Vice President Cheney, Secretary of Defense Donald Rumsfeld, and other so-called neoconservatives ("neocons") in the Departments of State and Defense had convinced Bush to authorize the use of torture ("enhanced interrogation techniques") in interviewing captured terrorist suspects. Such tactics violated international law and compromised human rights. When asked about this approach, Cheney scoffed that America sometimes had to work "the dark side": "We've got to spend time in the shadows in the intelligence world."

**THE BUSH DOCTRINE**   In the fall of 2002, George Bush unveiled a dramatic new national security policy. The **Bush Doctrine** said that the growing menace posed by "shadowy networks" of terrorist groups and unstable rogue nations with "**weapons of mass destruction**" (often referred to as WMDs) required the United States at times to use *preemptive* military action and to act unilaterally if necessary to defuse threats. "If we wait for threats to fully materialize," or wait for allies to join America, he explained, "we will have waited too long. In the world we have entered, the only path to safety is the path of action. And this nation will act."

The sweeping Bush Doctrine promised to "extend the benefits of freedom across the globe . . . for all peoples everywhere" without mentioning the potential human and financial cost of such an open-ended commitment.

**THE SECOND IRAQ WAR**   During 2002 and 2003, Iraq emerged as the focus of the Bush administration's policy of preemptive military action. Vice President Cheney, Secretary of Defense Rumsfeld, and Deputy Defense Secretary Paul Wolfowitz urged the president to use U.S. power to reshape the world in America's image. This included sponsoring "regime change" in authoritarian nations lacking "political and economic freedom" so as to create a new world order "friendly to our security, our prosperity, and our principles." They convinced Bush that the dictatorial Iraqi regime of Saddam Hussein represented a "grave and gathering danger" because of its supposed possession of biological and chemical weapons of mass destruction.

On March 17, 2003, Bush issued Hussein an ultimatum: leave Iraq within forty-eight hours or face a United States–led invasion. Hussein refused. Two days later, on March 19, American and British forces (the "coalition of the willing") attacked Iraq. They did so, according to Bush, because Saddam "promotes international terror" and "seeks nuclear weapons."

The Second Iraq War began with a massive bombing campaign, followed by a fast-moving invasion from bases in Kuwait. On April 9, after three weeks of intense fighting, U.S. forces captured Baghdad, the capital of Iraq. Hussein's regime and his demoralized army collapsed a week later.

The six-week war was ferociously efficient: among the 300,000 allied troops less than 200 were killed compared to more than 2,000 Iraqi combat deaths;

civilian casualties numbered in the tens of thousands. President Bush staged a celebration onboard a U.S. aircraft carrier at which he announced victory under a massive banner proclaiming "MISSION ACCOMPLISHED."

But the president, as he later admitted, spoke too soon; the initial military triumph carried with it the seeds of deception and disaster, as no weapons of mass destruction were to be found in Iraq. Bush said that the absence of WMDs left him with a "sickening feeling," for he knew that his primary justification for the war had evaporated.

**REBUILDING IRAQ**  It proved far easier to win the brief war than to rebuild Iraq in America's image. Unprepared U.S. officials faced the daunting task of installing a democratic government in a nation fractured by religious feuds, and with ethnic tensions made worse by the breakdown in law and order caused by the allied invasion. Large parts of the war-torn country fell into civil war as sectarian tribalism replaced the dictatorship. As a result of the U.S. invasion, the entire Middle East was further destabilized.

Rather than reducing the number of Islamist terrorists, the U.S. intervention in Iraq served to increase them. And soon Iraq became a quagmire for American forces reminiscent of the Vietnam War. Within weeks of the U.S. invasion, vengeful Islamist radicals streamed into Iraq to wage a campaign of terror, sabotage, and suicide bombings.

Bush's macho reaction—"Bring 'em on!"—revealed how uninformed he was about the fast-deteriorating situation. The leader of the new Iraqi government, Prime Minister Nouri al-Maliki, quickly imposed his own authoritarian, Shiite-dominated regime, which discriminated against the Sunnis, the Kurds, and other ethnic and religious minorities. Soon the chaotic conflict had grown beyond America's capacity to control or end.

By the fall of 2003, Bush admitted that substantial numbers of American troops (around 150,000) would have to remain in Iraq much longer than anticipated. He also acknowledged that rebuilding Iraq would take years and cost almost a trillion dollars.

**Freedom for whom?** The American torture of Iraqis in Abu Ghraib prison only exacerbated the anger and humiliation that Iraqis experienced since the First Gulf War. In response to America's incessant promises of peace and autonomy, a Baghdad mural fires back: "That Freedom for B[u]sh."

Americans grew more and more dismayed as the number of casualties and the expense of the military occupation in Iraq soared. The nation became more alienated from the Iraqi intervention when journalists revealed graphic pictures of U.S. soldiers abusing and torturing Arab detainees in the Abu Ghraib prison near Baghdad. "When you lose the moral high ground," an army general observed, "you lose it all." By 2004, a Republican journalist dismissed Bush's Middle East strategy as "shiftless, reactive, irrelevantly grandiose; our war aims undefined; our preparations insufficient; our civil defense neglected."

Regardless, President Bush still insisted that a democratic Iraq would bring stability to the Middle East and blunt the momentum of Islamist terrorism. Yet even though Saddam Hussein was captured in December 2003 and later hanged, Iraq seemed less secure than ever.

By the beginning of 2004, some 1,000 Americans had died in the conflict, more than 10,000 had been wounded, and many other veterans of the conflict suffered from post–traumatic stress disorder (PTSD). The ethnic and religious tensions only worsened as Sunni jihadists allied with al Qaeda to undermine the new Iraqi government and assault U.S. forces.

The U.S. effort in Iraq was the wrong war in the wrong place fought in the wrong way. It forced Bush to spend government funds at a rate faster than any president since Lyndon Johnson, and it distracted attention from the revival of the Taliban and other terrorist groups in Afghanistan. Journalist Roger Cohen distilled perhaps the most important lesson from the wars in Iraq and Afghanistan when he said that the American ideal of democracy "can still resonate" with people around the world, but U.S. leaders "must embody it rather than impose it."

**THE ELECTION OF 2004** Growing concern about Iraq complicated George W. Bush's campaign for a second presidential term in 2004. The Democratic nominee, Senator John Kerry of Massachusetts, condemned Bush for misleading the nation about weapons of mass destruction and for his slipshod handling of the reconstruction of postwar Iraq. Kerry also highlighted the Bush administration's record budget deficits. Bush countered that the tortuous efforts to create a democratic government in Iraq would enhance America's long-term security.

On Election Day, November 2, 2004, exit polls suggested a Kerry victory, but in the end the election hinged on the crucial swing state of Ohio, where late returns tipped the balance toward Bush, even as rumors of electoral "irregularities" began to circulate. Nevertheless, Kerry conceded. "The outcome," he stressed, "should be decided by voters, not a protracted legal battle."

## THE ELECTION OF 2004

| | Electoral Vote | Popular Vote |
|---|---|---|
| **George W. Bush** (Republican) | **286** | **60,700,000** |
| John Kerry (Democrat) | 251 | 57,400,000 |

- How did the war in Iraq polarize American politics?
- In what ways did the election of 2004 give Republicans a mandate for change?

By winning Ohio, Bush captured 286 electoral votes to Kerry's 251. Yet in some respects, the election was not so close. Bush received 3.5 million more votes nationwide than Kerry, and Republicans increased their majorities in both houses of Congress. Bush pledged to bring democracy and stability to Iraq, trim the federal deficit, pass a major energy bill, create more jobs, and "privatize" Social Security funds by investing them in the stock market. "I earned capital in the campaign, political capital, and now I intend to spend it," he told reporters.

## SECOND-TERM BLUES

George Bush's second term was beset by thorny political problems, a sluggish economy, and continuing turmoil in Iraq. In 2005, he pushed through Congress an energy bill and a Central American Free Trade Act (CAFTA). But his effort to privatize Social Security retirement accounts by enabling individuals to invest their accumulated pension dollars themselves went nowhere, and soaring budget deficits made many fiscal conservatives feel betrayed by the supposedly "conservative" Bush.

**HURRICANE KATRINA** In late August 2005, President Bush's eroding public support suffered another blow in the form of a natural disaster. When killer-hurricane Katrina slammed into the Gulf coast, it devastated large areas of Alabama, Mississippi, and Louisiana. Katrina left more than 1,500 dead and many thousands more homeless and hopeless, especially in New Orleans. Local officials and the Federal Emergency Management Agency (FEMA) were caught unprepared, and confusion and incompetence abounded. President Bush seemed listless, confused, and tone-deaf as the storm took its tragic toll. In the face of blistering criticism, he accepted responsibility for the balky federal response and accepted the resignation of the FEMA director.

The backlash over the federal response to Katrina contributed to a devastating defeat for Republicans in the November 2006 congressional elections. The Democrats won control of the House of Representatives, the Senate, and a majority of governorships and state legislatures. The election also included a significant milestone: Californian Nancy Pelosi, leader of the Democrats in the

**The aftermath of Hurricane Katrina** Two men use boards to paddle through high water in flood-devastated New Orleans.

House of Representatives, became the highest-ranking woman in the history of the U.S. Congress upon her election as House Speaker in January 2007.

**THE "SURGE" IN IRAQ**   George W. Bush bore the brunt of public indignation over the bungled response to Katrina. He also received the blame for the costs and casualties of the unending war in Iraq, where the violence increased throughout the fall of 2006. Bush eventually responded to declining public and political support by creating the Iraq Study Group, a bipartisan task force that surprised the president by issuing a report recommending the withdrawal of combat forces from a "grave and deteriorating Iraq" by the spring of 2008.

Bush disagreed with those who urged a phased withdrawal. On January 10, 2007, he announced that he was sending a "surge" of 20,000 (eventually 30,000) more troops to Iraq, bringing the total to almost 170,000. From a military perspective, the surge succeeded. By the fall of 2008, violence in Iraq had declined dramatically, and the Iraqi government had grown in stature and confidence.

The U.S. general who masterminded the increase in troops admitted that the gains were "fragile and reversible," however. As the number of U.S. combat deaths in Iraq passed 4,000, Bush acknowledged that the conflict was "longer and harder and more costly than we anticipated." By 2008, more than 60 percent of Americans believed the Iraqi invasion had been a mistake and that the conflict had become a war without end.

**ECONOMIC SHOCK**   After the intense but brief 2001 recession, the boom/bust economy had begun another period of prolonged expansion. Between 1997 and 2006, home prices in the United States rose 85 percent, leading to a frenzy of irresponsible mortgage lending—whereby homebuyers were often freed from making down payments or demonstrating creditworthiness—and a debt-financed consumer spending spree. Tens of millions of people bought houses they could not afford, refinanced their mortgages, or tapped home-equity loans to make discretionary purchases. The irrational confidence that housing prices would steadily continue to inflate also led regulatory agencies and mortgage lenders to ease credit restrictions so that unqualified people could buy homes without making any down payment.

Then in 2007, the huge housing-price bubble burst and home values and real-estate sales began a sharp decline. The loss of trillions of dollars in home values set off a seismic shock across the economy, as record numbers of borrowers defaulted on their mortgage payments. Foreclosures and bankruptcies soared, and banks lost billions, first on the shaky mortgages, then on other categories of overleveraged debt: credit cards, car loans, student loans, and commercial mortgage-backed securities.

The economy fell into a recession in 2008, and some of the nation's most prestigious banks, investment firms, and insurance companies went belly up. Neither politicians nor government regulators were prepared for the financial calamity that quickly threatened to turn into a depression. The price of food and gasoline spiked. Unemployment soared. What had begun as a sharp decline in home prices became a global economic meltdown.

The economic crisis demanded decisive action to stem the panic and restore confidence. On October 3, 2008, President Bush signed into law the Troubled Asset Relief Program (TARP), which called for the Treasury Department to spend $700 billion to keep big banks and other large financial institutions afloat, since they were deemed "too big to fail." Yet given its ambitious goal, the TARP program did little to restore confidence in the economy.

In early October, stock markets around the world began to crash with the onset of what came to be called the **Great Recession**, which technically lasted from December 2007 to January 2009 and forced almost 9 million people out of work. Federal Reserve chairman Ben Bernanke called it "the worst financial crisis in modern history."

The effects of the Great Recession lasted long thereafter. The economic recovery that began in June 2009 would be the weakest since the end of the Second World War. Between 2009 and 2013, economic growth averaged just 2.2 percent, barely half the 4.2 percent average of the seven previous recoveries.

Why was the recovery so tepid? Consumers were burdened by too much household debt; businesses were unable or unwilling to make new capital investments; and the damaged financial system continued to stifle commercial and personal loans.

Taken together, the wars in Afghanistan and Iraq, coupled with a slumping economy, shattered public support for the Bush administration. During Bush's last year in office, his approval rating was an abysmal 25 percent, just one point higher than Richard Nixon's during the Watergate investigations.

Bush's failed presidency weakened the Republican party, strained the nation's military, eroded American prestige, and created the largest budget deficits in history by cutting taxes while increasing spending.

## A HISTORIC NEW PRESIDENCY

Democrats were excited about the possibility of regaining the White House in 2008. The early front-runner for their party's nomination was New York senator Hillary Rodham Clinton, the spouse of ex-president Bill Clinton, who enjoyed the support of the most powerful Democratic leaders. Like her husband, she displayed an impressive command of policy issues and mobilized a well-funded campaign team. Moreover, as the first woman with a serious chance of gaining the presidency, she had widespread support among voters eager for female leadership.

In the end, however, an overconfident Clinton lost the nomination to Barack Obama of Illinois, a little-known first-term senator. Young, handsome, and intelligent, a vibrant mixture of idealism and pragmatism, coolness and passion, Obama was an inspiring speaker who promised a "politics of hope," the "energy of change," and the revival of bipartisanship. In early June 2008, he gained enough delegates to secure the nomination, with veteran Senator Joseph Biden of Delaware as his running mate.

Obama, the first African American presidential nominee of either party, was the biracial son of a white mother from Kansas and a black father from Kenya who left the household and returned to Africa when Barack was a toddler. Obama eventually graduated from Columbia University before earning a law degree from Harvard. The forty-seven-year-old senator presented himself as a leader who could inspire, unite, and forge collaborations across the partisan divide. He promised to end the wars in Afghanistan and Iraq, stop the use of torture in the war on terror, reduce nuclear weapons, tighten regulation of the banking industry, secure the border with Mexico, enable a path to citizenship for undocumented immigrants, and provide medical coverage to the millions of uninsured.

Candidate Obama radiated poise, confidence, and energy. He and his strategists mastered the use of social media to organize rock-concert-like campaign rallies and turned his vitality and political inexperience into strengths at a time when voter disgust with politics was widespread.

By contrast, his Republican opponent, seventy-two-year-old Arizona senator John McCain, was the oldest presidential candidate in history. A twenty-five-year veteran of Congress, McCain had developed a reputation as a bipartisan "maverick" willing to work with Democrats to achieve legislative goals. His impolitic and unpredictable running mate, former Alaska governor

**Barack Obama** The president-elect and his family wave to supporters in Chicago's Grant Park.

## THE ELECTION OF 2008

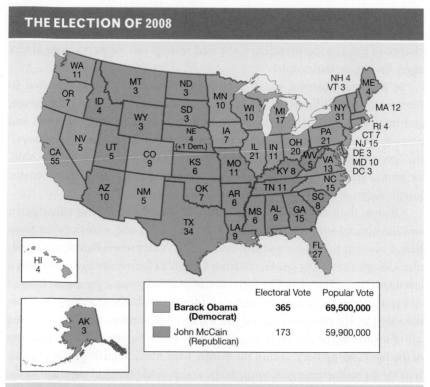

|  | Electoral Vote | Popular Vote |
|---|---|---|
| **Barack Obama** (Democrat) | 365 | 69,500,000 |
| John McCain (Republican) | 173 | 59,900,000 |

- How did the economic crisis affect the outcome of the election?
- What are the similarities and differences between the map of the 2004 election and the map of the 2008 election?

Sarah Palin, did not help McCain's chances when she revealed to a reporter that she could not recall reading any newspapers or magazines.

On November 4, 2008, Obama made history by becoming the first person of color to be elected president. He won the popular vote by 53 percent to 46 percent, and the electoral college 365 to 173. He also helped the Democrats win solid majorities in both houses of Congress.

Obama considered his election a "defining moment" in political history. "It's been a long time coming, but tonight . . . change has come to America." He urged Americans to "resist the temptation to fall back on the same partisanship and pettiness and immaturity that has poisoned our politics for so long." It was one of those uplifting sentiments that sounded great but had no chance of unifying America's polarized electorate.

**OBAMA'S FIRST TERM** In his 2009 inaugural address, President Obama acknowledged that America was in a crisis forged by a staggering number of challenges. The new administration inherited two unpopular wars, rising unemployment, and a staggering national debt. The economy was the weakest it had been in eighty years, and health care was too costly for most Americans.

Yet the new president pledged to lead the nation out of the paralyzing sense of crisis. To do so, he promised to inaugurate "a new politics for a new time"—without explaining what that meant or how he planned to implement it. In the end, Obama would prove to be more inspirational than effective as the nation's chief executive.

Obama's most pressing challenge was to keep the Great Recession from becoming a prolonged depression. Unemployment had passed 8 percent and was still rising. The financial sector remained paralyzed, and public confidence in the economy had plummeted.

The Obama administration continued the Bush TARP program, which provided massive government bailouts to the largest banks and financial institutions. Both the Left and the Right attacked the bailouts as deeply unfair to most Americans. Treasury Secretary Timothy Geithner later explained, "We had to do whatever we could to help people feel their money was safe in the [banking] system, even if it made us unpopular." Had they not saved the big banks, Obama and Geithner argued, the economy would have crashed.

Preserving the banking system did not create many jobs, however. To do so, in mid-February 2009, Congress passed, and Obama signed, an $832 billion economic-stimulus bill called the American Recovery and Reinvestment Act. The bill included cash distributions to states for construction projects to renew the nation's infrastructure (roads, bridges, levees, government buildings, and the electricity grid), money for renewable-energy systems, and $212 billion in tax reductions for individuals and businesses, as well as funds for food stamps and unemployment benefits. It was the largest government infusion of cash into the economy in history. Although Obama's actions did not generate a robust economic recovery, they did save the nation—and the world economy—from a financial meltdown.

**HEALTH-CARE REFORM** From his first day in office, Barack Obama stressed his intention to reform a health-care system that was "bankrupting families, bankrupting businesses, and bankrupting our government at the state and federal level." The United States was the only developed nation without a national health-care program. Since 1970, the number of uninsured people had been steadily rising, as had health care costs. In 2010, roughly

**Go Obama Go**  A Democrat holds up a sign in support of the Affordable Care Act, more commonly known as Obamacare, in a march in Washington, D.C., in 2010.

50 million Americans (16 percent of the population), most of them poor, young, or people of color, had no health insurance.

The president's goal in creating the Patient Protection and **Affordable Care Act (ACA)**, which critics labeled "**Obamacare**," was to make health insurance more affordable and health care accessible to everyone.

The $940 billion law, proposed in 2009 and debated for a year, centered on the so-called individual mandate, which required uninsured adults to purchase an approved private insurance policy through state-run exchanges (websites where people could shop for insurance), or pay a tax penalty. Low-income Americans could receive federal subsidies to help pay for their coverage, and insurance companies could no longer deny coverage to people with preexisting illnesses. Companies that did not offer health insurance would have to pay higher taxes, and drug companies and manufacturers of medical devices would have to pay annual government fees. Everyone would pay higher Medicare payroll taxes to help fund the changes.

The idea of forcing people to buy health insurance flew in the face of such ideals as individual freedom and personal responsibility. Critics questioned not only the individual mandate but the administration's projections that the program would reduce federal expenditures over the long haul.

Republicans mobilized to defeat the ACA, but it passed with narrow party-line majorities in both houses of Congress. Obama signed it into law on March 23, 2010. Its complex provisions, to be implemented over a four-year period, would bring health insurance to 32 million people, half of whom would be covered by expanded Medicaid and the other half by the individual mandate. In the end, about half those numbers enrolled. In its scope and goals, the ACA was a landmark in the history of health and social welfare—as well as the expansion of the federal government.

**REGULATING WALL STREET** The near collapse of the nation's financial system beginning in 2008 prompted calls for overhauling the financial regulatory system. On July 21, 2010, Obama signed the Wall Street Reform and Consumer Protection Act, also called the Dodd-Frank bill after its two congressional sponsors. The 2,319-page law required government agencies to exercise greater oversight over complex new financial transactions and protected consumers from unfair practices in loans and credit cards by establishing the Consumer Financial Protection Bureau.

## FOREIGN AFFAIRS

President Obama had more success in dealing with foreign affairs than in reviving the American economy. What journalists came to call the Obama Doctrine was much like the Nixon Doctrine, stressing that the United States could not afford to police the world.

**THE OBAMA DOCTRINE** The loosely defined Obama Doctrine grew out of efforts to end the costly wars in Iraq and Afghanistan. In essence, the president wanted to replace confrontation and military intervention with a stance of cooperation and negotiation.

On February 27, 2009, President Obama announced that all 142,000 U.S. troops would be withdrawn from Iraq by the end of 2011, as the Iraqi government and the Bush administration had agreed in 2008. True to his word, the last U.S. combat troops left Iraq in December 2011. Their departure marked the end of a bitterly divisive war that had raged for nearly nine years, killed more than 110,000 Iraqis, and left the nation shattered and unstable, despite Obama's claim that the U.S. forces were "leaving behind a sovereign, stable, and self-reliant Iraq with a representative government."

The war had cost more than 4,500 American lives, 30,000 wounded (many grievously so), and $2 trillion. Perhaps the greatest embarrassment was that the Iraqi government the United States left in power was inept and unfriendly to American interests.

**Home from Iraq** U.S. troops returned from Iraq to few celebrations.

The long and chaotic war was an expensive mistake. As it turned out, there were no weapons of mass destruction, nor was there a direct link between the al Qaeda terrorists and Saddam Hussein. Al Qaeda, in fact, did not arrive in Iraq until after the American invasion. "The first Iraq war, in which I led a tank platoon, was necessary," said John Nagel, a retired army officer. "This one was not."

American efforts at nation building had failed. Obama's hopes that the United States could avoid fighting in the Middle East and that the Iraqis could sustain a stable government in the face of terrorist incursions and sectarian fighting proved fruitless. Iraq's woeful government and constant sectarian strife required continued infusions of U.S. military assistance, daily bombing raids, and massive economic aid.

"SURGE" IN AFGHANISTAN At the same time that President Obama was ending U.S. military involvement in Iraq, he dispatched 21,000 additional troops to Afghanistan and changed the U.S. commander on the ground in what had become the nation's longest war. While doing so, however, he narrowed the focus of the U.S. mission to suppressing terrorists rather than transforming the strife-torn country into a stable capitalist democracy.

The surge worked as hoped. By the summer of 2011, Obama announced that the "tide of war was receding" and that the United States had largely achieved its goals, setting in motion a substantial withdrawal of forces that lasted until 2014. "We will not try to make Afghanistan a perfect place," Obama said. "We will not police its streets or patrol its mountains indefinitely. That is the responsibility of the Afghan government."

Since then, however, the situation has deteriorated, and substantial American forces remain in place. The Taliban have increased the amount of territory they control, and the Afghan government continues to be ineffective, unstable, and corrupt.

**THE DEATH OF OSAMA BIN LADEN** Ever since the attacks of 9/11, Osama bin Laden, tall and thin with a scraggly beard, had eluded an intensive manhunt. In August 2010, however, U.S. intelligence analysts discovered his sanctuary outside Abbottabad, Pakistan. On May 1, 2011, President Obama authorized a daring night raid by a U.S. Navy SEAL team transported by helicopters from Afghanistan. After a brief firefight, the SEALs killed bin Laden. His death was a watershed moment, but it did not spell the end of Islamist terrorism.

**THE "ARAB AWAKENING"** In late 2010 and early 2011, spontaneous uprisings erupted throughout much of the Arab world as long-oppressed peoples rose up against authoritarian regimes. Young idealists inspired by the hope of democracy and connected by social media forced corrupt tyrants from power. The essentially leaderless uprisings seemed to herald a new era in the Middle East.

Yet building new democratic governments proved much harder than expected. The Middle East had no models of open societies to follow, and the essential elements of democratic governance had to be established from scratch. As a result, the grassroots revolutionary movements in most Arab nations stalled by 2014. Egypt reverted to an even harsher authoritarian government, Libya lapsed into chaos, and Yemen exploded in civil war.

**LIBYA OUSTS GADDAFI** The pro-democracy turmoil in North Africa engulfed oil-rich Libya, long governed by Colonel Muammar Gaddafi, the Arab world's most violent dictator. Anti-government demonstrations began on February 15, 2011, prompting Gaddafi to order Libyan soldiers and mercenaries (paid foreign soldiers) to suppress the rebellious "rats." By the end of February, what began as a peaceful pro-democratic uprising had turned into a full-scale civil war that provided the first real test of the Obama Doctrine.

True to his word, the president refused to act alone in helping the Libyan rebels. Instead, he encouraged European allies to take the lead. On March 19, France and Great Britain, with American support, began bombing Gaddafi's military strongholds. In late August, rebel forces captured the capital of Tripoli, ending Gaddafi's forty-two-year dictatorship. On October 20, rebel fighters killed Gaddafi, but stability remained elusive.

**THE CUBAN THAW**  At the end of 2014, President Obama surprised the world by announcing that the United States and Cuba would restore normal relations after more than fifty years of bitter hostility. As a first step, Obama relaxed restrictions on American tourists visiting Cuba. Six months later, in mid-2015, the two nations reestablished embassies in each other's capital cities.

The powerful Cuban community in south Florida fiercely criticized Obama's decision, and congressional Republicans threatened to block the appointment of a U.S. ambassador to Cuba because of its Communist government. But the president insisted that isolating Cuba had not worked. "Americans and Cubans alike are ready to move forward," he said in July 2015. "I believe it's time for Congress to do the same."

## POLARIZED POLITICS

Barack Obama had campaigned in 2008 on the promise of bringing dramatic change while reducing the partisan warfare between the two national parties. By the end of his first year in office, however, a Gallup poll found that he had become the most polarizing president in modern history. In part, the partisan civil war resulted from Obama's detached style. Like Jimmy Carter, he did not like to lobby and horse-trade his way to legislative approval. Republican senator John McCain quipped that Obama preferred "leading from behind." Even Democrats criticized his "aloofness."

Yet the standoff with Congress was not solely his fault. His Republican opponents had no interest in negotiating with him, and American political culture had become so polarized that it resembled two separate nations. Each party had its own cable-news station and rabidly partisan commentators, its own newspapers, its own think tanks, and its own billionaire donors. Governing, Obama quickly discovered, is far more difficult than campaigning.

**THE TEA PARTY**  No sooner was Barack Obama sworn in than grassroots conservatives mobilized against the "tax-and-spend" liberalism he represented in their eyes. In January 2009, a New York stock trader named

**The Tea Party movement** Tea Party supporters gather outside the New Hampshire Statehouse for a tax-day rally.

Graham Makohoniuk urged people to send tea bags to their congressional representatives to symbolize the Boston Tea Party of 1773, when American colonists protested against British tax policies.

Within a year or so, the revolt against big government had become a national **Tea Party** movement, with chapters in all fifty states. The Tea Party was not so much a cohesive political organization as it was an attitude and an ideology, a collection of self-described "disaffected," "angry," and "very conservative" activists, mostly white, male, married, middle-class Republicans over forty-five years of age who had grown incensed by the corporate bailouts and unprecedented federal government spending (by both Bush and Obama) to check the Great Recession. Tea Party members tended to focus more on bloated governments and reckless spending than on religious or cultural issues such as abortion or LGBTQ rights.

To the anti-tax rebels, the bailouts were a form of "crony capitalism" whereby the political "elite" rewarded big companies that had funded their campaigns, colluding for power and profit at the expense of common folk. Tea Party members demanded a radically smaller federal government (although most of them supported Social Security and Medicare, the most expensive federal social programs). Democrats, including Obama, initially dismissed the Tea Party as a fringe group, but the 2010 election results proved it had become a fast-brewing political force, mobilizing almost 25 percent of voters.

Democratic House and Senate candidates (as well as moderate Republicans), including many long-serving leaders, were defeated in droves when conservative Republicans, many of them aligned with the Tea Party, gained sixty-three seats to recapture control of the House of Representatives. They won a near majority in the Senate as well. It was the most lopsided midterm election since 1938.

Still, mainstream Republicans remained wary of the Tea Partiers, for they seemed determined to transform the party into one embroiled in perpetual civil war. "If the Republicans don't come through on their promises," threatened Colleen Conley of Rhode Island, "maybe the party needs to be blown up." Her take-no-prisoners outlook galvanized Congressman Mike Pence of Indiana: "There will be no compromise on stopping runaway spending, deficits, and debt. There will be no compromise on repealing Obamacare."

**Occupy Wall Street** The Manhattan-born grassroots movement grew rapidly from rallies to massive marches in financial districts nationwide, like this demonstration in Los Angeles.

**OCCUPY WALL STREET** The emergence of the Tea Party was mirrored on the left by the Occupy Wall Street (OWS) movement, mobilized in the fall of 2011 when a call went out over the internet to "Occupy Wall Street. Bring tent." Dozens, then hundreds, then thousands of people, many of them unemployed young adults, converged on Zuccotti Park in lower Manhattan to "occupy" Wall Street, protesting the "tyrannical" power of major banks and investment companies.

The protesters described themselves as the voice of the 99 percent of Americans who were being victimized by the 1 percent—the wealthiest and most politically connected Americans who controlled 38 percent of the nation's wealth. Unlike the Tea Party, however, OWS did not have staying power. Within a year, its energies and visibility had waned, in part because of mass arrests and in part because it was an intentionally "leaderless" movement more interested in saying what it was against than explaining what it was for.

## Bold Decisions

For all the political sniping, however, attitudes toward some hot-button cultural values were slowly changing. In December 2010, Congress repealed the "don't ask, don't tell" (DADT) military policy that, since 1993, had resulted in some 9,500 gays and lesbians being discharged from the armed forces. A year later, a report by army officers concluded that the repeal "had no overall negative impact on military readiness or its component dimensions, including cohesion, recruitment, retention, assaults, harassment, or morale."

**MARRIAGE EQUALITY** In May 2012, President Obama became the first sitting president to support the right of gay and lesbian couples to marry. That his statement came a day after the North Carolina legislature voted to ban all rights for couples of the same sex, illustrated how incendiary the issue was. While asserting that it was the "right" thing to do, Obama knew that endorsing **marriage equality** had powerful political implications. The LGBTQ community would come to play an energetic role in the 2012 presidential election, and the youth vote—the under-thirty electorate who most supported marriage equality—would be crucial. No sooner had Obama made his announcement than polls showed that American voters were, for the first time, evenly split on the charged issue, with Democrats and independent voters providing the bulk of support for marriage equality.

**THE DREAM ACT** In 2012, the Census Bureau reported that 39.5 million residents, some 13 percent of the total population, had been born outside the United States. In June 2012, Obama again bypassed the Republican-controlled Congress and issued an executive order called the Development, Relief and Education for Alien Minors Act (soon labeled the DREAM Act) that allowed 1.5 million undocumented immigrants (Dreamers) brought to the United States as children (under the age of sixteen) to remain as residents and pursue formal citizenship. The policy had been debated in Congress since 2001 but had never been passed. Obama decided to break the legislative logjam by using an executive order to implement the policy. His unanticipated decision thrilled Latino supporters who were discouraged by his failure to convince Congress to support more-comprehensive immigration reform.

The DREAM Act, however, had unexpected consequences. It excited masses of Central Americans willing to endure enormous risks to migrate to America. Panicked parents in El Salvador, Guatemala, and Honduras, worried about widespread drug-related gang violence, sent their children through Mexico to the United States in hopes of connecting with relatives and being granted citizenship. At the same time, the Obama administration was deporting record numbers of undocumented immigrants (more than 2 million by the end of 2014), some of whom had been working in the nation for decades, in what was called the "great expulsion." Obama, called the "Deporter in Chief" by critics, claimed that he was only following the laws written by anti-immigration Republicans.

At the same time, however, Obama continued to use his administrative authority to address the growing issue of undocumented immigrant children. On June 15, 2012, Janet Napolitano, Secretary of Homeland Security, announced a new agency policy called Deferred Action for Childhood Arrivals (DACA). An exercise of prosecutorial discretion, DACA provided temporary relief from deportation ("deferred action") to undocumented immigrants brought to the United States as children. DACA enabled almost 800,000 eligible young adults to work lawfully, attend school, and pursue their dreams without the threat of deportation. However, as an administrative policy DACA did not provide permanent legal status to individuals and had to be renewed every two years (the policy would be rescinded by the Trump administration in 2017).

## THE SUPREME COURT IN THE TWENTY-FIRST CENTURY

The Supreme Court surprised observers in 2013 by overturning the Defense of Marriage Act (DOMA) of 1996, which had denied gay and lesbian couples who married in states allowing such unions the right to federal benefits. In *United States v. Windsor,* the Court voted 5–4 that the federal government could not withhold spousal benefits from couples of the same sex who had been legally married. But the justices did not rule that same-sex marriage was a right guaranteed under the Constitution. That issue would have to be resolved by a future Court. In the meantime, each state could decide whether to allow such marriages. During 2014, however, federal courts repeatedly overturned state laws banning marriage between same-sex couples.

While the Supreme Court disappointed social conservatives with its *Windsor* decision, its five conservative justices continued to restrict the powers of the federal government. In June 2013, in *Shelby County v. Holder,* the Court gutted key provisions of the 1965 Voting Rights Act (VRA), which had outlawed discrimination toward voters "on account of race or color." The majority opinion declared that in five of the six southern states originally covered by the VRA, black voter turnout now exceeded white turnout. To the judges, this seemed to prove that there was no evidence of continuing racial discrimination. Today's laws "must be justified by current needs," Chief Justice John Roberts wrote.

Soon after the Court's ruling, counties and states in the South pushed through new laws that had the effect of making voting more difficult for people of color, poor people, and immigrants by reducing voting hours or requiring that driver's licenses or other government-issued identification cards be shown on voting days. That there was in fact little evidence of voter fraud to justify such new restrictions led critics to charge that the new requirements were in fact intended to suppress Democratic votes.

**THE 2012 ELECTION** The 2012 presidential election would be the most expensive election ever, in part because the Supreme Court had ruled in *Citizens United v. Federal Elections Committee* (2010) that corporations could spend as much as they wanted in support of candidates.

Mitt Romney, a governor of Massachusetts (2003–2007) and former corporate executive, emerged as the Republican nominee. Two factors eventually hurt his candidacy. The first was his decision to please right-wing voters by opposing immigration reforms that might allow undocumented immigrants a pathway to citizenship. The second was the disclosure of a recording in which he had privately told a group of wealthy contributors that he "did not care" about the 47 percent of Americans who failed "to take personal responsibility and care for their lives."

The Obama campaign seized on the impolitic statement and demonized Romney as an uncaring elitist. On Election Day, Obama won with 66 million votes to Romney's 61 million, and 332 electoral votes to 206.

Nearly 60 percent of white voters chose Romney. But the nation's fastest-growing groups—Latinos, Asian Americans, and African Americans—voted overwhelmingly for Obama, as did college-educated women. David Frum, a prominent Republican speechwriter and columnist, confessed that his party was becoming "increasingly isolated and estranged from modern America."

**BLACK LIVES MATTER** In 2013, three African American activists— Alicia Garza, Patrisse Cullors, and Opal Tometi—created a civil rights organization called Black Lives Matter to address mounting evidence that African Americans were being treated unfairly by law enforcement officers and the judicial system. In 2012, 31 percent of people killed by police were African American (often unarmed), even though blacks made up just 13 percent of the total population.

Using social media as their primary recruiting tool, Garza, Cullors, Tometi, and others generated widespread support. Black Lives Matter, the organizers explained, "is an ideological and political intervention in a world where Black lives are systematically and intentionally targeted for demise. It is an affirmation of Black folks' humanity, our contributions to this society, and our resilience in the face of deadly oppression."

The Black Lives Matter movement gained added urgency on August 9, 2014, when Michael Brown, an unarmed black teenager, was shot and killed by a white police officer in Ferguson, Missouri, a St. Louis suburb. The failure of a grand jury to indict the police officer prompted civil unrest and organized protests around the country. In the process, the phrase "Black Lives Matter" became a rallying cry for millions of Americans who had grown convinced that police brutality against people of color had become commonplace. "We have made enormous progress in race relations over the course of the past several decades," President Obama said in response to the Missouri case. "But

**Black Lives Matter** The founders of the movement stand with arms linked at a protest in Cleveland, Ohio. Left to right: Opal Tometi, Alicia Garza, and Patrisse Cullors.

what is also true is that there are still problems, and communities of color aren't just making these problems up."

**OBAMACARE ON THE DEFENSIVE**  President Obama's proudest achievement, the Affordable Care Act, was so massive and complicated that it took four years before it was ready to roll out. In the fall of 2013, the federal online health insurance "exchange," where people without insurance could sign up, opened with great fanfare. Obama assured Americans that using the online registration system would be "real simple."

It was not. On October 1, millions tried to sign up; only six succeeded. The website had never been properly tested, and it was hobbled with technical glitches. It also became evident that Obama had misled the nation when he told voters that if they liked their current health-insurance plan, they could, under Obamacare, "keep that insurance. Period. End of story." As it turned out, many saw their policies canceled by insurers.

Eventually, the ACA website was fixed, and by August 2014, more than 9 million people, well above the original target number, had signed up for health insurance. "The Affordable Care Act is here to stay," Obama said. But public skepticism about the government's ability to manage the program continued.

## NEW GLOBAL CHALLENGES IN AN AGE OF INSECURITY

In 2013, the United States held its first high-level talks with Iran since 1979, when Iranian militants took U.S. embassy employees in Tehran hostage. On November 23, Secretary of State John Kerry reached a multinational agreement with Iran to scale back its nuclear development program for six months as a first step toward a more comprehensive agreement not to develop nuclear weapons.

At the same time, an increasingly bloody civil war in Syria was beginning to have major international repercussions. U.S. intelligence analysts confirmed that the Syrian government, ruled with an iron fist by Bashar al-Assad, had used chemical weapons to kill 1,400 people, many of them children.

President Obama had repeatedly warned that the use of weapons of mass destruction was a "red line" that would trigger international military intervention of "enormous consequences." In late August, he (and the French government) hesitantly began preparing for a military strike against Syria, but his failure to follow through led his former secretary of defense, Leon Panetta, to argue that backing off the threat "was a blow to American credibility. When the president as commander in chief draws a red line, it is critical that he act if the line is crossed."

On September 9, Kerry defused the crisis by signing an agreement with Russia to dispose of Syria's chemical weapons. By the end of October, the chemical weapon stockpiles had supposedly been destroyed or dismantled, but the civil war raged on.

**RUSSIA'S ANNEXATION OF CRIMEA**    For nearly a quarter of a century, Russian president Vladimir Putin had viewed the disintegration of the Soviet Union as the "greatest geopolitical catastrophe of the century." To restore Russian influence over its neighbors and to divide NATO and the European Union, he exerted economic and political pressure on the republics of the former Soviet Union.

On February 27, 2013, Putin sent troops into Crimea, a part of Ukraine, a former Soviet republic. A week later, the Crimean parliament voted to become part of the Russian Federation. Putin, claiming that Crimea had "always been an inseparable part of Russia," made the illegal annexation official by positioning Russian troops there, even though he denied their presence.

The speed and ruthlessness with which Putin seized control of Crimea, mobilized 40,000 Russian troops on the Ukrainian border, and cut off Ukraine's access to Russian natural gas surprised President Obama and European leaders. It may not have been the start of a new cold war, but it put an end to hope that Russia would become a cordial partner of the United States and the European democracies. By 2014, Putin was displaying a raw and resentful anti-Americanism.

In response, the United States and the European Union organized diplomatic efforts to de-escalate the crisis. They refused to recognize the annexation of Crimea and announced economic sanctions against Russia while pledging financial assistance to Ukraine. By a vote of 100–11, the United Nations General Assembly also opposed the annexation.

In April 2014, heavily armed pro-Russian separatists, as many as a third of whom were Russian soldiers and agents, seized control of several cities in eastern Ukraine. They declared a "people's republic" and called for secession.

After a Malaysian passenger jet flying across eastern Ukraine was shot down by a Russian-made rocket in July 2014, killing all 298 on board, the United States and its allies slammed Russia with more economic sanctions. But Putin showed no sign of backing away. In fact, his popularity in Russia soared, leaving the United States once again in the position of trying to contain Russia's expansionist ambitions.

**THE BURDENS OF LEADERSHIP**    Rarely are presidents more popular than on their first day in office. To govern requires making decisions, and decisions in democratic nations inevitably produce disappointments, disagreements, and criticism.

During his presidency, Barack Obama discovered how hard it was to lead the world's economic and military superpower in the post–cold war era. He struggled to stabilize a cluster of unstable nations—Iraq, Afghanistan, Libya, Ukraine, and Syria—that craved U.S. resources but resented American meddling.

Overall, Obama adopted a posture of restraint in world affairs. He was determined to "avoid stupid errors," wind down the wars in Iraq and Afghanistan, and reduce the use of U.S. military power abroad.

Yet he and others were naive to think that the United States could avoid the burdens of being the only superpower in a post–cold war world of growing anarchy and violence. Democratic senator Diane Feinstein of California wondered in September 2014 if Obama had become "too cautious" about the use of force in world affairs.

**ISLAMISTS ON THE MOVE**    Unexpected events during the summer of 2014 gave Barack Obama the opportunity to take decisive action. In June, the volatile Middle East took a sudden turn for the worse when Sunni jihadists who had been fighting in Syria invaded northern Iraq and announced the creation of their own caliphate called the Islamic State (ISIS). ISIS quickly emerged as the largest, best-financed, most heavily armed, and most brutal of the jihadist terrorist groups.

ISIS represented both the culmination of decades of Arab Islamist rage against Europe and the United States and the collapse of effective government and security in Syria and Iraq. Once American forces left Iraq and Sunnis grew frustrated with the Shiite-dominated government, ISIS swept in. Sadistic ISIS fighters seized huge tracts of territory in Syria and Iraq while enslaving, terrorizing, raping, massacring, crucifying, or beheading thousands of men, women, and children.

In August 2014, after ISIS terrorists gruesomely beheaded two captured Americans, Obama ordered systematic airstrikes, first in Iraq and later in Syria, as ISIS fighters assaulted Christians, Yazidis, and Kurds in the region. If George W. Bush had plunged U.S. power too deeply into Iraq, Obama seemed to have withdrawn U.S. power too quickly. One overreached, the other undershot.

## THE AGE OF GRIDLOCK

American politics has always been chaotic and combative; its raucous energy is one of its great strengths. During Barack Obama's two terms as president, however, compromise and moderation became dirty words. Republican efforts to reject any and all proposals from the Obama White House meant stalemate had become the controlling political principle.

Intense partisanship dominated the 2014 congressional elections, when Republicans gained control of the Senate for the first time since 2006. They also strengthened their hold on the House, added governorships, and tightened their control of state legislatures. Republicans campaigned on a single theme: the "failure" of President Obama and the "disaster" of Obamacare.

Political moderates became a dying breed. By late 2014, the percentage of voters who described themselves as liberals or conservatives had doubled since 1994, and more than twice as many Democratic and Republican voters as in 1994 had a "very unfavorable" view of the other party. Congress included mostly Republicans on the far right, Democrats on the far left, and hardly anyone in the middle. "That alignment," said Gerald Seib of the *Wall Street Journal*, created a Congress "that does less, and does it less well, than any time in memory."

Voters hoping for a more energetic and engaged Obama after his reelection were disappointed. He seemed disheartened by the "gap between the magnitude of our challenges and the smallness of our politics" and blamed Republicans for stalemating his second term. But the president was not blameless. As Ian Bremmer, a political scientist specializing in foreign policy, said, "George W. Bush was a leader who didn't like to think. Barack Obama is a thinker who doesn't like to lead."

**RENEWED ENERGY** Yet during the summer of 2015, in the sunset of his presidency, Obama regained his energy. He also benefited from two surprising U.S. Supreme Court rulings.

For years, Republicans had waged all-out war on the Affordable Care Act. Unable to halt the implementation of the new program in Congress, critics turned to the courts to challenge the health-care law. The claim raised in *King v. Burwell* (2015)—that individuals who purchase insurance on the federal government's health-care exchange are not entitled to the tax subsidies available to those purchasing on state exchanges—would, if accepted by the Court, have greatly weakened ACA.

In a surprising 6–3 decision, the Supreme Court saved the controversial law Chief Justice John Roberts explained in the majority opinion that some of the sloppy language in the original legislation should not be used to destroy the program. "Congress passed the Affordable Care Act to improve health insurance markets, not to destroy them," Roberts stressed. "If at all possible, we must interpret the Act in a way that is consistent with the former, and avoids the latter."

Just a day later, the Supreme Court issued another bombshell ruling when it announced a 5–4 decision in *Obergefell v. Hodges*, which banned states from preventing marriages between same-sex couples. The landmark decision infuriated the Religious Right. Rick Scarborough, a Baptist minister in Texas, vowed that he and others would "denounce this practice in our [religious] services, we will not teach it in our schools, we will refuse to officiate at this type of wedding, and we will not accept any encroachments on our First Amendment rights."

Yet the Supreme Court's affirmation of same-sex marriage reflected the profound change in public attitudes toward LGBTQ rights during the early twenty-first century. In 2008, presidential candidate Barack Obama had felt the need to disavow support for marriage equality. By 2012, he had reversed himself by embracing the right to marriage between same-sex couples. His change of mind reflected a resurgent social transformation in American life. Cultural

**Married with pride** A California couple pose in front of the United States Supreme Court building in Washington, D.C., while the justices hear arguments on the constitutional right for same-sex couples to wed in April 2015. On June 26, 2015, in a landmark 5–4 decision, the Court ruled in favor of upholding marriage equality in all fifty states.

diversity, like Obamacare, was here to stay. Obama had appointed two women to the U.S. Supreme Court, including the first Latina justice. He also ended the ban on lesbian, gay, and bisexual people serving openly in the military.

The momentum of the Court decisions in June 2015 bolstered Obama's efforts in foreign policy. In his 2009 inaugural address, he had vowed to international enemies that "we will extend a hand if you are willing to unclench your fist." That effort finally paid off in 2015, not only with the normalizing of relations with Cuba but also when the United States and other major world powers (Russia, China, Germany, Britain, France, and the European Union) announced a draft treaty with Iran intended to thwart its efforts to develop a nuclear weapon. In exchange for ending the international trade embargo against Iran, the agreement called for the Iranians to dismantle much of their nuclear program and allow for international inspectors to confirm their actions. Obama warned congressional critics that any attempt to veto the treaty (called the Joint Comprehensive Plan of Action) would mean "a greater chance of war in the Middle East." In July 2015 the Iran nuclear deal was formalized.

## The "Angry" 2016 Election

In 1780, future president John Adams proclaimed that "division of the republic into two great parties, each arranged under its leader. . . . is to be dreaded as the greatest political evil under our Constitution." His fears were well founded. Because of over-the-top partisanship, many party followers—even young people—distrust, disdain, or even smear the opposition party. They do not acknowledge its legitimacy, much less respect it.

A study commissioned by the Pew Foundation found that 38 percent of Democrats and 43 percent of Republicans display a "very unfavorable" view of the other party, triple the numbers from just twenty years before. People with strong political views today tend to believe that the opposition has no redeeming virtues. Politics has devolved into an "us versus them" zero-sum game, a death match between good and evil energized by mutual contempt. There is no room for compromise or bargaining because there are few negotiable principles, just intense team loyalties.

Embedded in the 2017 Pew survey on the partisan divide, however, is a surprising and perhaps encouraging trend: record numbers of Americans are declaring their independence and rejecting both the Republican and Democratic parties. In fact, there are more Independents than Democrats or Republicans. Independent voters tend to be closer on economic issues to Republicans and closer to Democrats on social issues, and their growing numbers represent a direct reaction against the unprecedented polarization of the two parties.

**THE 2016 PRESIDENTIAL PRIMARIES** The ferocious polarization of American society and politics was on full display during the 2016 presidential campaign. The contest featured a seething sense of anger at the federal government among voters furious at cultural liberalism, bureaucratic incompetence, and the self-serving focus of party leaders. "Both parties have failed us," observed a lifelong conservative.

Surveys showed that Americans were more divided about partisan politics than they were about race, class, gender, and age. Republicans self-identify as conservative and 87 percent of them are non-Hispanic whites, with an average age of fifty. Over half of Democrats call themselves liberals. They are more racially diverse than ever and less likely to belong to a church or synagogue or to have "old-fashioned values about family and marriage."

The *emotional* discord of growing partisanship is revealed in a single data point: in 1960, only 5 percent of Republicans and 4 percent of Democrats said they would oppose their child marrying someone with the opposing party affiliation. A 2010 survey found that 49 percent of Republicans said they would resist their child marrying a Democrat, and 33 percent of Democrats said they would oppose their child marrying a Republican.

As the 2016 presidential campaign began, many working-class whites felt left behind by the economic recovery. Some had seen their factory jobs go offshore through globalization. Others had seen their wages stagnate, their prospects diminished, their hopes crushed. Although unemployment nationally was low, about one-third of U.S. adults faced financial insecurity in 2016 and often struggled to pay unexpected expenses. Three in ten adults saw their monthly incomes fluctuate—often because of unstable work schedules—and that caused about one in ten Americans to miss bill payments. Many blamed their troubles on an economic system that favored the wealthy, government-subsidized minorities, low-wage immigrant labor, and the political elite. Their shared anxieties and resentments had coalesced into a grassroots nationalist backlash against the multiculturalism evident during Obama's presidency.

**CLINTON VERSUS SANDERS** A handful of Democrats emerged as presidential candidates in 2015, but the race soon narrowed to two: Hillary Rodham Clinton, the former First Lady who had served as a U.S. senator from New York and as secretary of state in the Obama administration, and seventy-four-year-old Vermont senator Bernie Sanders. The policy-fluent Clinton, a

**Democratic campaigns, 2016** Democrats in the 2016 primary election had two very different candidates to choose between. (Left) Hillary Rodham Clinton, the first woman ever to be nominated by a major political party, was saddled with a long history of establishment politics. (Right) Bernie Sanders, in contrast, was viewed as an outsider who represented a progressive, socialist platform.

supreme political insider, represented the party establishment. Sanders, a rumpled, white-haired socialist and grandfather of seven, surprisingly appealed most to younger, progressive Democrats who viewed Clinton as too conservative and too scripted.

Sanders portrayed Clinton as a fraud who claimed to be a friend of the common folk but actually preferred hobnobbing with the rich and famous, and who promised to protect American jobs while supporting free-trade pacts that shut down plants and factories. In the end, Clinton emerged on top and became the first female major-party nominee in history.

**TRUMP THE OUTSIDER** The Republican contest was more a carnival than a campaign. Seventeen candidates competed for the nomination— governors, senators, corporate executives—but one was unique: New Yorker Donald Trump, a billionaire real-estate developer and reality-television star who had never held elected office but, unlike the other candidates, had national name recognition. As he claimed, "There's nobody like me. Nobody."

The wealthiest of the contenders and the only one who refused to disclose his tax returns, Trump was a charismatic if sometimes crude and impulsive showman possessed of the ruthless skill to skewer his opponents and the mainstream media. He was both volatile and competitive, always on the go, and, like Bill Clinton, eager to be both loved and adored.

Trump positioned himself as an "outsider," promising to "drain the swamp" of corruption created by political insiders in Washington, D.C. He skillfully exploited the emotions of people who felt left behind by the economic recovery and resentful of "unregulated immigration" by campaigning against career politicians and Washington bureaucrats.

"MAKE AMERICA GREAT AGAIN" Americans had never seen a candidate as unconventional and unpredictable as Donald John Trump, yet his entertaining shoot-from-the-hip candor and combativeness appealed to voters fed up with conventional politics and to journalists eager to cover his latest controversial statement.

Born in 1946 in Queens, a borough of New York City, Trump attended Fordham University for two years before transferring to the Wharton School of Business at the University of Pennsylvania, where he earned a degree in economics in 1968. After graduating from college, Trump parlayed a large loan from his wealthy father into a successful real-estate development business, called the Trump Organization.

Thereafter, Trump expanded his business empire into the casino gambling industry and later acquired numerous golf resorts around the world. All the while, he focused on building the Trump brand, despite numerous business failures and bankruptcies. Trump's visibility earned him a starring role in a popular NBC television reality series called *The Apprentice*, in which contestants vied for a management position within the Trump Organization.

**Republican rally** Donning his "Make America Great Again" baseball cap, Donald Trump speaks at a rally in Orlando, Florida, six days before the presidential election.

A master at the use of social media, Trump was one of the few candidates to embrace those living in the left-behind parts of the country, including people suffering from the opioid drug epidemic, declining manufacturing jobs, and the rising cost of health care. More people were living in poverty in 2016 than ever before. Many of them had grown up assuming that America was the most powerful and prosperous nation on earth, famous for the upward mobility it provided its citizens. Now they worried that was no longer true. For adults in their thirties, the chance of earning more than their parents over their lifetimes dropped to 50 percent from 90 percent just two generations earlier. For these reasons and others, many working-class Americans and farmers were angry; they wanted someone to blame and that someone was the party in power: Democrats.

Trump appealed directly to such disgruntled voters, many of them independents or members of the Tea Party. He depicted a declining America besieged by cheap Chinese imports, Muslim terrorists, and illegal immigrants ("bad dudes") and poorly led by self-serving liberal "elites" who championed unconstrained diversity at the expense of national security.

Trump vowed to "Make America Great Again." He promised to end Obamacare, cut taxes, abandon the "unfair" NAFTA and TPP (Trans-Pacific Partnership) trade deals, reverse the Obama administration's environmental protections, and increase funding for the military. Most of all, he repeatedly lashed out at "illegal immigrants," promising to build a towering, "beautiful" wall along the entire border with Mexico—and make the Mexican government pay for it.

Trump overflowed with confidence as he was swept along by a tidal wave of populist rage. "I alone can fix" America's problems, he shouted, claiming that he was the best, the smartest, and the toughest candidate. Trump offered simplistic solutions to complex problems. On the campaign trail, he preferred spontaneous remarks over prepared speeches, and he became notorious for his exaggerations, half-truths, outright falsehoods, and praise for white supremacists and foreign dictators.

Trump's nontraditional campaign also benefited from the surging influence of social media such as Twitter and Facebook. People could now discuss politics in an unmediated way, reading and expressing themselves in the language of resentment not allowed on television or in newspapers.

To the surprise of pundits and the chagrin of party leaders, Trump won the Republican nomination in July 2016. The raucous outsider and his populist insurgency had overturned the party establishment and fractured the conservative movement. Many leading Republicans, including former presidents George H. W. Bush and George W. Bush, and former presidential nominees John McCain and Mitt Romney, were so alienated by Trump's boorish behavior and disrespectful treatment that they refused to attend the Republican nominating convention or to campaign for him.

Such opposition within his own party never fazed Trump. In fact, he loved the challenge of running against two parties, for he knew his supporters were passionately committed to him. "I could stand in the middle of Fifth Avenue and shoot somebody, and I wouldn't lose [my] voters," Trump boasted.

**A CAMPAIGN LIKE NO OTHER**   The 2016 contest between Donald Trump and Hillary Clinton was more memorable for its drama and insults than its issues or proposals. Trump dismissed "crooked Hillary" as a "nasty woman," calling her the "most corrupt person ever to seek the presidency." He lampooned her as a creature of the Washington and Wall Street elite who masqueraded as a friend of the people while raking in millions of dollars for the Clinton Foundation. If elected president, he promised, he would "put her in jail," leading his supporters to wear T-shirts saying, "Lock Her Up."

For her part, Clinton dismissed Trump as unfit for the highest office in the land, labeling him as dangerous, unpredictable, and lacking the temperament demanded of the U.S. president. She hurt her cause when, in a fit of frustration, she claimed that "you could put half of Trump's supporters into what I call the 'basket of deplorables.'"

The fall campaign featured one startling surprise after another. On October 7, 2016, just two days before the candidates' second televised debate, the *Washington Post* released a videotape from 2005 that showed a married Trump lewdly describing his unsolicited kissing and groping of women he had just met. "You know I'm automatically attracted to beautiful women," he bragged. "I just start kissing them. It's like a magnet. Just kiss. I don't even wait [to be asked]. And when you're a star [like me], they let you do it. You can do anything [to them]." A media furor ensued, but Trump barreled on, dismissing his comments as simply "locker room banter" that he claimed all men engage in.

Hillary Clinton confronted her own scandals. In March 2015, the *New York Times* reported that Clinton, as secretary of state between 2009 and 2013, had used her family's email server for official communications rather than the State Department server. Doing so violated departmental protocols, created a security risk that confidential ("classified") diplomatic emails might be hacked by foreign agents (as they were). After an exhaustive investigation, the FBI director, James B. Comey, concluded publicly that Clinton had been "extremely careless" in handling her email, but saw no point in prosecuting her. Republican critics used the issue to call into question Clinton's honesty and reliability. Trump charged that Clinton's use of a personal email server was "worse than Watergate."

**James Comey in Congress** FBI Director James Comey swears an oath before the House Oversight Committee on July 7, 2016, two days after announcing that he would not recommend pressing criminal charges against Hillary Clinton, after all.

Then came more surprises. During the summer of 2016, agents of the Russian government "hacked" the email system of the Democratic National Committee and forwarded the data to WikiLeaks, which collaborated with Russian agents to release tens of thousands of confidential messages intended to embarrass and distract the Clinton campaign and thereby help to elect Trump.

On October 28, 2016, just eleven days before the presidential election, FBI director Comey violated FBI protocols to keep the bureau out of national elections when he informed Congress that "in connection with an unrelated case, the FBI has learned of the existence of emails that appear pertinent to the investigation" of Clinton's use of her personal email server.

This revelation hit the Clinton campaign like a bomb. It raised new questions about her presidential fitness and revealed that the ongoing investigation into her emails would last beyond Election Day. Clinton would later claim that Comey's "October surprise" cost her the election.

Clinton's narrow loss to Trump on November 8 surprised virtually everyone. All major polls predicted a narrow Democratic victory. Yet Trump won 309 electoral votes to her 228. True, Clinton attracted 3 million more votes than Trump out of the 136 million cast, but she lost by 78,000 votes the crucial swing states of Michigan, Ohio, Pennsylvania, and Wisconsin.

Candidate Clinton struggled as a lackluster defender of more government as the solution to the nation's problems. Throughout the campaign, she failed to articulate a unifying vision of America's future or fashion a compelling explanation for why she should be president. At the close of her campaign, she could only offer a limp promise: "I'm not him." Shannon Goodin, a twenty-four-year-old first-time voter in Michigan, explained that Trump won her vote by being a "big poster child for change." She added that traditional "politicians don't appeal to us. Clinton would go out of her way to appeal to minorities, immigrants, but she didn't really care for everyday Americans."

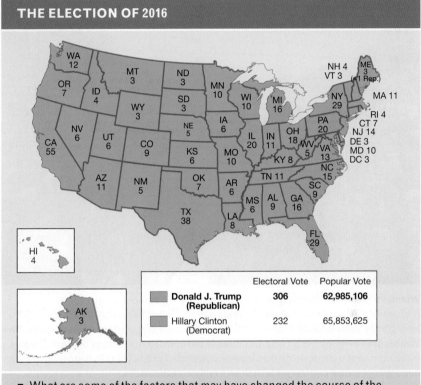

THE ELECTION OF 2016

| | Electoral Vote | Popular Vote |
|---|---|---|
| **Donald J. Trump (Republican)** | 306 | **62,985,106** |
| Hillary Clinton (Democrat) | 232 | 65,853,625 |

- What are some of the factors that may have changed the course of the election?
- What does the map reveal, or conceal, about the disconnect between the popular vote and the electoral college?

# A POPULIST PRESIDENT

President-elect Trump could claim several firsts. He was the first president never to have served in the military or to have held public office, and at seventy-one, he was the oldest president on Inauguration Day.

Yet Trump was also the most unpopular new president in history. His 40 percent approval rate upon taking office was the lowest ever. A majority of Americans voted against him, and no sooner was he elected than his opponents mobilized to contest his presidency. In more than 50 cities and towns, demonstrators took to the streets, stopping traffic and chanting, "We reject the president-elect!"

The grassroots opposition to President Trump soon had a name—The Resistance—and it quickly became a significant political force. Women upset by

**Women's March on Washington**  On January 21, 2017, demonstrators flooded the National Mall in support of women's rights and reproductive justice, health-care and immigration reform, racial justice, LGBTQ rights, and other interconnected issues. The Washington demonstration was grounded in the nonviolent ideology of the civil rights movement, and went down as the largest coordinated protest in U.S. history; along with hundreds of global counterparts, it drew 5 million participants.

Trump's election organized mass demonstrations in January 2017 on behalf of women's rights, immigrants and refugees, improved health care, reproductive rights, LGBTQ rights, racial equality, freedom of religion, and workers' rights. At the Women's March on Washington, D.C., which included a half a million protesters, twice the number of those who attended Trump's inauguration, feminist leader Gloria Steinem, directed her comments at President Trump: "Our Constitution does not begin with 'I, the President.' It begins with, 'We, the People.'"

Trump, whom more than a dozen women had accused of sexual misconduct, also fell afoul of the Me Too crusade against widespread sexual assault and abuse. Started in 2007 by Tarana Burke, an African American civil rights activist, the small Me Too organization suddenly gained national support in October 2017 when dozens of actresses and female staffers accused Harvey Weinstein, a prominent movie producer, of rape, sexual assault, and sexual abuse over many years.

The widely publicized scandal prompted a wave of similar allegations against powerful men—politicians, CEOs, actors, sports stars, and celebrities of all sorts. Growing numbers of women and men came forward to share on social media under the hashtag MeToo their own experiences of sexual assault, harassment, or rape.

## A CHAOTIC FIRST 100 DAYS

Trump's supporters were enthusiastic about a future of unconventional presidential action designed to end their alienation and nurture their bitterness. In his inaugural address, Trump assured the nation that his swearing-in ceremony would be "remembered as the

**Me Too** The creator of the movement Tarana Burke (center) and others lead the #MeToo Women's March in Los Angeles on November 12, 2017.

day the people became the rulers of this nation again." An unapologetic and aggressive hypernationalism would be the theme of his administration: "From this day forward, it is going to be only America first—America first."

In December 2015, Florida Republican Jeb Bush made a prediction about then candidate Donald Trump. "Donald, you know, is great at the one-liners," Bush quipped. "But, he's a chaos candidate. And he'd be a chaos president."

Indeed, chaos characterized Trump's presidency. He forged an unstable cabinet dominated by family members and wealthy loyalist ideologues, bankers, businessmen, and billionaires, mostly older white men with little government experience. Some of his closest aides, such as Steve Bannon, his chief strategist, and senior policy adviser Stephen Miller, were leaders of "alt-right" (alternative right), hypernationalist organizations that promoted white supremacy, anti-immigrant nativism, and America-first trade policies while rejecting multiculturalism and political correctness.

An unprecedented number of Trump's cabinet members and senior aides did not last long in their new government jobs. The president's national security adviser, Michael Flynn, a former army general who had led the Defense Intelligence Agency before being fired by President Obama, was forced to resign after lying to Vice President Mike Pence and the FBI about secret conversations he had with the Russian ambassador about lifting U.S. sanctions. He had also violated protocols and laws by failing to disclose huge payments in 2015 from foreign companies linked to Russia and Turkey.

In 2017, Flynn offered to testify to congressional committees investigating Russian efforts to influence the 2016 presidential election in exchange for immunity from prosecution. Even more worrisome for the Trump administration was news that the FBI was investigating the possibility that people associated with the Trump campaign had secretly collaborated with Russia to torpedo Hillary Clinton's campaign.

Trump vigorously denied that he or his campaign staff ever "colluded" with Russian officials to benefit his election, and rejected any suggestion that his new administration was anything but perfect. As journalist Timothy Noah explained, however, "the Trump administration in its infancy [was] creating enough blunders, scandals, and controversies to strain the resources" of the White House press corps.

**AN ACTIVIST PRESIDENT**    To generate momentum for his presidency, Donald Trump in his first year declared a freeze on most federal hiring, cut aid payments to foreign governments, pressured several U.S. companies to abandon plans to build plants or factories overseas, and curbed federal efforts to constrict the coal industry. His greatest success early in his presidency was the appointment of a conservative justice to the Supreme Court. Although most Democrats opposed the nomination of Neil Gorsuch, a federal court of appeals judge with a sterling reputation, the Republican majority revised the Senate filibuster rules to ensure his confirmation.

The irony of this procedure is that the same Republican Congressional leaders who engineered the confirmation of Gorsuch had denied President Obama the same opportunity to fill the Supreme Court vacancy before he left office. In 2018, President Trump seized the opportunity presented by the retirement announcement of Justice Anthony Kennedy to nominate another conservative Republican judge, Brett Kavanaugh, to be confirmed by the Senate.

In his first year, Trump signed thirty-two executive orders *removing* federal protections for consumers, the environment, food safety, internet privacy, transgender Americans, and victims of sexual abuse.

**ABANDONING THE CLIMATE COMMITMENT**    On June 1, 2017, President Trump announced that the U.S., the world's second largest polluter, would cease all participation in the 2015 Paris Climate Agreement addressing climate change. He claimed that the agreement, signed by 195 nations, imposed grossly unfair environmental standards on American businesses and workers. He vowed to stand with the people of the United States against what he called a "draconian" international deal. Trump's withdrawal from the global climate agreement represented his most sweeping assertion of an "America First" foreign policy. Others disagreed. "Removing the United States from the Paris agreement is a reckless and indefensible action," asserted Al Gore, the former vice president who has become an evangelist for fighting climate change. "It undermines America's standing in the world and threatens to damage humanity's ability to solve the climate crisis in time."

## BANNING MUSLIMS OR SECURING THE BORDERS?

Trump's most controversial executive order was a temporary ban on immigrants and refugees from seven nations with large Muslim populations. The resistance to Trump's proposal was immediate and widespread. Tens of thousands of Americans organized protests at airports across the nation while lawyers for various organizations filed suits to stop the executive order from taking effect. Even Dick Cheney, the hardnosed former Republican vice president, declared that Trump's proposed travel ban "went against everything we stand for." The acting attorney general, Sally Yates, refused to enforce the new policy. Trump fired her.

Within days, federal judges dismissed the travel ban as an unconstitutional assault on a particular religious group. A furious Trump scorned the "ridiculous" ruling and pledged to overturn it. The pro-Trump editors of the *Wall Street Journal* described the immigration order as "so poorly explained and prepared for, that it has produced fear and confusion at airports, an immediate legal defeat, and political fury at home and abroad."

Yet Trump persisted in his efforts to stop Muslims from entering the United States. On March 6, 2017, he issued a revised executive order, but it too was staunchly opposed and rejected by federal judges as discriminatory. In mid-2018, the U.S. Supreme Court by a 5-4 vote in *Trump v. Hawaii* approved a revised ban on immigrants from seven Muslim nations because the president

**Muslim Ban**  A crowd of protesters gather at the Los Angeles International Airport on January 29, 2017, speaking out against President Trump's executive order to ban immigrants from certain Muslim-majority countries from entering the United States.

deemed them terrorist risks. Speaking for the majority, Chief Justice John Roberts acknowledged that the court had "no view on the soundness of the policy," but insisted that the president had the authority to impose such a ban for national security reasons. In her dissenting opinion, Justice Sonia Sotomayor argued that any "reasonable observer" would conclude that the travel ban was "motivated by anti-Muslim animus."

A similar battle with the courts greeted Trump's announcement reversing Barack Obama's decision in 2016 to allow transgender people to serve openly in the military. The United States "will not accept or allow" transgender people in the military "in any capacity," Trump tweeted in July 2017, without having consulted with his defense secretary, James Mattis. He added that the military "cannot be burdened with the tremendous medical costs and disruption that transgender in the military would entail."

Congressman Ted Lieu of California, himself a military veteran, was one of many legislators and military leaders who opposed the new policy affecting some 15,000 personnel. "We're discriminating against people who want to sacrifice for their country. What's worse, we're doing it for no measurable reason. It's transphobia masked as policy and it's disgraceful as much as it's unconstitutional." Lawsuits filed in several federal courts delayed implementation of the ban. In issuing an injunction against the ban, U.S. District Court Judge Colleen Kollar-Kotelly found "absolutely no support for the claim that the ongoing service of transgender people would have any negative effects on the military."

**TRUMP'S ASSAULT ON OBAMACARE** Eventually, Trump could not govern simply by issuing executive orders; he had to negotiate the passage of legislation. Throughout the presidential campaign, he had lambasted Obamacare, promising to replace it "on day one" with a much better healthcare program "at a tiny fraction of the cost, and it is going to be so easy." To that end, he and House speaker Paul Ryan unveiled in early 2017 the American Health Care Act (AHCA). It would have removed many of the pillars of Obamacare, including phasing out Medicaid subsidies that had enabled millions of people to gain coverage for the first time.

Yet surveys showed that only 17 percent of voters liked the new bill. For that reason and others, Trump and Ryan could not get the Republican majority in the House to support "Trumpcare." The Republican leadership in Congress withdrew the AHCA without a formal vote. Trump, the self-described wizard at "deal-making," had been unable to strike a deal with members of his own party. He expressed surprise "that health care could be so complicated," but he remained committed to the destruction of Obamacare.

**Trumpcare** Speaker of the House Paul Ryan holds up a copy of the American Health Care Act on March 7, 2017. The Republican's bill to replace the Affordable Care Act was supremely unpopular.

**BUILDING A WALL** Trump's other showcase campaign promise proved equally difficult to implement: building a "huge" anti-immigrant wall along the 2,000 mile-long Mexican border and forcing Mexico to pay for it. In late April 2017, the president acknowledged that he could not convince Congress to finance the wall. In 2018, Congress approved limited funds for a small portion of the complete wall Trump had demanded. Rebuffed by Capitol Hill, Trump redirected his anti-immigrant crusade to federal enforcement. He vowed to triple the number of Immigration and Customs Enforcement (ICE) officers and expand the Border Patrol.

**FORGING FOREIGN POLICIES** In foreign affairs, Donald Trump's early actions were equally minimal, in part because he had so little preparation for global leadership. Other than hosting several foreign dignitaries, talking tough toward rogue nations North Korea and Iran, and twice launching a volley of cruise missiles at Syrian air bases in retaliation for chemical attacks by the Syrian government on its own civilians, the president's view of America's role in the world remained confusing.

In 2013, for example, when Syria had first used chemical weapons against its opponents, killing a thousand people, Trump had urged President Obama: "Do not attack Syria. There is no upside and tremendous downside." Similarly, during his campaign against Clinton, he had told Reuters news service that "we should not be focusing on Syria. You're going to end up in World War III over Syria if we listen to Hillary Clinton." He saw no need to explain his change of heart as president.

# The 100-Day Mark

By the end of his first 100 days in office, President Trump was floundering as a result of self-inflicted wounds, missteps, contradictions, and his naive understanding of the political process. Candidate Trump had promised ten significant pieces of legislation by the end of April 2017. In fact, however, he had no major legislation to his credit and the lowest public approval rating (37 percent) of any first-term president.

In an early assessment of the Trump presidency, Jennifer Rubin, a conservative columnist, saw "nothing much of substance" accomplished because of "an unhinged president, too many weak aides, and an administration that cannot control itself." Trump, in her view, had overpromised and underdelivered. He had become "all flash and big talk."

**LEGAL ISSUES** Nothing was easy for the Trump administration. In May 2017, the president stunned the nation by firing James Comey, the FBI director, who was leading the agency's investigation into contacts between Trump campaign officials and Russia. White House aides initially claimed that Trump had acted on the advice of the deputy attorney general, only to have the president contradict them the next day when he acknowledged that he had grown frustrated by Comey's Russia investigation.

Only days later, the *New York Times* reported that Comey had created detailed summaries of his meetings with the president, one of which revealed that Trump on February 14 had urged the FBI director to drop the investigation into Michael Flynn's illegal interactions with Russian officials, pressuring him to "let this go." On May 18, 2017, after Jeff Sessions, the attorney general, had recused himself because of his own contacts with Russian officials during the 2016 campaign, Rod Rosenstein, the deputy attorney general, appointed a special counsel, Robert Mueller III. A former FBI director held in high esteem by both Democrats and Republicans, Mueller was asked to lead a criminal investigation into Russian involvement in the 2016 campaign.

Trump's response to the investigation was consistently combative. On May 18, he tweeted that his administration was the victim of the greatest "witch hunt" in history. Almost daily, he attacked the media, calling its stories about him and his administration "fake news." Witch hunt or not, Trump faced the prospect of a prolonged criminal investigation shrouding the White House and playing havoc with his efforts to fulfill his campaign promises.

Equally challenging to the new president was the constant turnover within the senior administration. By early 2018, nearly half of Trump's inner circle of aides and cabinet members had resigned or been fired. The departed included the secretary of state; the secretary of human services; the secretary of veterans affairs; the national security adviser and deputy national security adviser; the FBI director; the chief strategist; the chief of staff and deputy chief of staff; the chief economic adviser; the administrator of the Environmental Protection Agency; the press secretary, and several members of his personal legal team.

**TAX REFORM VICTORY** President Trump finally achieved a major legislative victory with the passage of a comprehensive tax cut at the end of 2017. It was one of his primary campaign promises and marked the first major reduction in federal taxes in more than thirty years.

On December 22, 2017, the president signed the Tax Cuts and Jobs Act, which the Republican-controlled Congress passed without a single Democratic vote. In the belief that lower business taxes would boost economic growth, it cut the corporate tax rate from 35 percent to 21 percent, beginning in 2018. The bill lowered income tax rates overall, doubled the standard deduction, and eliminated personal exemptions.

The Congressional Budget Office estimated that the Trump tax cut would add $1.455 trillion to the national debt over ten years. Republicans, who for years had stressed the importance of reducing the federal deficit and balancing budgets, abandoned such priorities in approving the tax cut without any offsetting spending cuts. Just seven months after the tax cut was implemented, the Federal Reserve Bank of San Francisco announced that Trump's key piece of legislation would trigger much less economic growth than anticipated—and perhaps none at all, for it appeared as the economy was already robust.

**A UNIQUE PRESIDENCY** As Donald Trump entered his second year as president, he remained the most unique person ever to occupy the Oval Office. His intentionally disruptive behavior continued to entertain and perplex observers while roiling financial markets. He often seemed angry and isolated; he lashed out at friends and enemies and was exasperated by daily leaks from his staff to the press.

In March 2018, Trump abruptly announced punitive tariffs on imported steel and aluminum, catching his aides and fellow Republicans off guard and infuriating America's most reliable global trading partners, who predicted a no-win, tit-for-tat, retaliatory trade war resulting from his actions. His own economic adviser, who resigned in protest, dismissed the tariffs as "obviously stupid."

Trump, however, responded that "trade wars are good, and easy to win," which stunned economists and Republicans in Congress. Over a hundred Republicans in the House of Representatives urged the president to reconsider launching a trade war, claiming that no nation wins such vengeful efforts.

Just weeks later, on May 8, 2018, President Trump again angered America's western European allies when he announced that the United States would withdraw from the Joint Comprehensive Plan of Action (JCPA) agreement with Iran and reinstitute economic sanctions. It was Trump's most consequential foreign policy action, and it baffled observers, since the United Nations had verified that Iran was abiding by the agreement. Trump's withdrawal from the JCPA called into question the U.S. government's commitment to other treaties around the world. Britain, France, and Germany admonished Trump and vowed to honor the deal.

Soon after, Trump again surprised the world when he announced that he and North Korean leader Kim Jong-un would hold a summit meeting to discuss the future of nuclear weapons in the Communist nation. On June 12, Trump and Kim Jong-un met in Singapore and announced that discussions

**North Korea summit** President Trump poses alongside North Korean leader Kim Jong-un at a photo session during their one-on-one summit in Singapore.

would continue "to work toward complete denuclearization of the Korean Peninsula." Ten days later, President Trump claimed that North Korea had begun to dismantle its nuclear test sites, only to be contradicted by his secretary of defense, James Mattis, who said there was no evidence of North Korea taking any concrete steps to denuclearize.

Also in June 2018 the Trump administration ignited a firestorm of criticism over its zero-tolerance policy on undocumented immigrants crossing into the United States from Mexico, many of them seeking asylum from political tyranny abroad, coming from strife-torn Central America. The Department of Homeland Security and the U.S. Border Patrol began separating hundreds of

**Families separated at the border** U.S. Border Patrol agents detain undocumented asylum seekers in steel cages at the Central Processing Center in McAllen, Texas in June 2018. 2,000 children were separated from their parents during a six-week period under the Trump administration.

detainee parents from their children while the parents were being prosecuted and potentially deported. When large numbers of Republican legislators condemned the new approach to detainees, President Trump reversed himself on June 20, 2018, signing an executive order meant to end the separation of families at the border.

This much seemed certain as 2018 unfolded: Donald Trump would continue to please or irritate Americans with his efforts to stop the flow of "illegal immigrants" into the country, his biting criticism of America's allies and his unsettling praise of tyrants and dictators, his contradictory stances toward rogue nations like North Korea, and his decision to withdraw the United States from some of its major treaty commitments like the JCPA with Iran and the North American Free Trade Act.

Yet amid all the fury and furor of the Trump White House, the president continued to enjoy intense support among his "base"—those loyal voters who carried him into office. They seemed uninterested in the ongoing investigation of Russian interference in the 2016 election headed by special counsel Robert Mueller, the constant turnover and factional drama among Trump's aides, and the group of aggrieved women claiming the president had abused or engaged in affairs with them before his election. The president—a man celebrated for his resilience—seemed determined to fend off all challenges by staying on the offensive, dismissing his critics as morons and scorning journalists as liars. What the future of his presidency would hold remained predictably unpredictable.

# CHAPTER REVIEW

## SUMMARY

- **Changing Demographics**  From 1980 to 2019, the population of the United States grew by 40 percent, reaching 330 million. A wave of immigration from Latin America allowed Latinos to surpass African Americans as the nation's largest minority. By 2018, the U.S. population included more foreign-born and first-generation residents than ever.

- **Divided Government**  Just two years after the election of "New Democrat" Bill Clinton in 1992, Republican Speaker of the House Newt Gingrich crafted his *Contract with America* and achieved a Republican landslide victory in the midterm elections of 1994. Despite the bipartisan success of the *North American Free Trade Agreement (NAFTA)* and the *Personal Responsibility and Work Opportunity Act of 1996*—and a prosperous, high-tech "new economy" that helped balance the federal budget—Clinton's private life produced a sex scandal that resulted in impeachment.

- **Global Terrorism**  The 9/11 attacks led President George W. Bush to declare a *war on terror* that commenced with the U.S. invasion of Afghanistan to capture Osama bin Laden and oust the Islamist Taliban government. The *Bush Doctrine* declared America's right to initiate preemptive military strikes against terrorists or rogue nations possessing *weapons of mass destruction (WMDs)*. In 2003, Bush invoked this doctrine against Saddam Hussein, the leader of Iraq. The ensuing Second Iraq War removed Hussein from power but turned up no WMDs.

- **A Historic Election**  The 2008 presidential primary campaigns featured Democratic senators Hillary Rodham Clinton, the first formidable female candidate, and Barack Obama, the first truly contending African American candidate, as well as Republican senator John McCain, the oldest candidate in history. Obama won his party's nomination and went on to take the election in large part due to public dismay about the *Great Recession (2007–2009)*.

- **Obama's Priorities**  Obama's first priority was to shore up the failing economy, which he attempted through controversial Wall Street "bailouts" and a huge "economic stimulus" package. Yet the recovery remained slow and unequal, widening the economic divide and spawning the short-lived Occupy Wall Street movement. The *Affordable Care Act (ACA)* incited increasingly bitter opposition from the conservative *Tea Party*. Obama was more successful in winning public support to reduce American military deployment abroad, remove all combat troops from Iraq in 2011, and downsize their presence in Afghanistan.

- **A Populist President**  The election of Donald Trump in 2016 in part reflected how divided American society had become over the last four decades. His promise to "Make America Great Again" appealed to voters who felt alienated as American society moved toward becoming part of an interconnected, global world.

Efforts early in his administration to enact policies to limit immigration, protect jobs, and pull out of various treaties with other nations were met with strong resistance. Eventually, the new president would be able to claim some victories: tax reform, rolling back environmental regulations, and the appointment of two new conservative U.S. Supreme Court Justices.

## CHRONOLOGY

| | |
|---|---|
| 1992 | Bill Clinton elected president |
| 1993 | Congress passes NAFTA |
| 1994 | The Contract with America |
| 1998 | President Clinton impeached and acquitted |
| 2000 | George W. Bush elected after controversial recount |
| September 11, 2001 | Terrorists attack New York City |
| October 2001 | Operation Enduring Freedom begins in Afghanistan |
| March 2003 | Iraq War begins |
| 2007 | Global financial markets collapse; Great Recession begins |
| 2009 | Barack Obama elected nation's first black president |
| | American Recovery and Investment Act |
| 2010 | Congress passes the Affordable Care Act (Obamacare) |
| May 2011 | Al Qaeda leader Osama bin Laden killed |
| 2016 | Donald Trump elected president |

## KEY TERMS

North American Free Trade Agreement (NAFTA) p. 1337

Contract with America p. 1338

Personal Responsibility and Work Opportunity Act of 1996 (PRWOA) p. 1339

globalization p. 1340

ethnic cleansing p. 1343

war on terror p. 1350

USA Patriot Act (2001) p. 1351

Bush Doctrine p. 1352

weapons of mass destruction (WMDs) p. 1352

Great Recession (2007–2009) p. 1358

Affordable Care Act (ACA—also called Obamacare) p. 1362

Tea Party p. 1367

marriage equality p. 1369

 INQUIZITIVE

Go to InQuizitive to see what you've learned—and learn what you've missed—with personalized feedback along the way.

# GLOSSARY

**1968 Chicago Democratic National Convention** Held August 26–29 in Chicago, Illinois, the event was infamously tumultuous. Inside the International Amphitheatre, the Democratic Party fought over its direction on Vietnam, while outside tens of thousands of Vietnam War protestors clashed with police.

**36°30'** According to the Missouri Compromise, any part of the Louisiana Purchase north of this line (Missouri's southern border) was to be excluded from slavery.

**54th Massachusetts Regiment** After President Abraham Lincoln's Emancipation Proclamation, the Union army organized all black military units, which white officers led. The 54th Massachusetts Regiment was one of the first of such units to be organized.

**Abigail Adams (1744–1818)** As the wife of John Adams, she endured long periods of separation from him while he served in many political roles. During these times apart, she wrote often to her husband, and their correspondence has provided a detailed portrait of life during the Revolutionary War.

**abolition** In the early 1830s, the anti-slavery movement shifted its goal from the gradual end of slavery to the immediate end or abolition of slavery.

**John Adams (1735–1826)** He was a signer of the Declaration of Independence and a delegate to the First and Second Continental Congresses. A member of the Federalist Party, he served as the first vice president and the second president of the United States. As president, he passed the Alien and Sedition Acts and endured a stormy relationship with France, which included the XYZ affair.

**John Quincy Adams (1767–1848)** As secretary of state, he urged President Monroe to issue the Monroe Doctrine, which incorporated his belief in an expanded use of federal powers. As the sixth president, Adams's nationalism and praise of European leaders caused a split in his party, causing some Republicans to leave and form the Democrat party.

**Samuel Adams (1722–1803)** A genius of revolutionary agitation, he believed that English Parliament had no right to legislate for the colonies. He organized the Sons of Liberty as well as protests in Boston against the British.

**Jane Addams (1860–1935)** She founded and ran of one of the best known settlement houses, the Hull House. Active in the peace and suffragist movements, she established child care for working mothers, health clinics, job training, and other social programs.

**affirmative action** Programs designed to give preferential treatment to women and people of color as compensation for past injustices.

**Affordable Care Act (ACA) (2010)** Vast health-care reform initiative signed into law and championed by President Obama, and widely criticized by Republicans, that aims to make health insurance more affordable and make health care accessible to everyone, regardless of income or prior medical conditions.

**Agricultural Adjustment Act (1933)** Legislation that paid farmers to produce less in order to raise crop prices for all; the AAA was later declared unconstitutional by the U.S. Supreme Court in the case of *United States v. Butler* (1936).

**Emilio Aguinaldo (1869?–1964)** He was a leader in the Filipino struggle for independence. During the war of 1898, Commodore George Dewey brought Aguinaldo back to the Philippines from exile to help fight the Spanish. However, after the Spanish surrendered to Americans, America annexed the Philippines and Aguinaldo fought against the American military until he was captured in 1901.

**Battle of the Alamo** Siege in the Texas War for Independence of 1836, in which the San Antonio mission fell to the Mexicans. Davy Crockett and Jim Bowie were among the courageous defenders.

**Albany Plan of Union (1754)** A failed proposal by the seven northern colonies in anticipation of the French and Indian War, urging the unification of the colonies under one Crown-appointed president.

**Alien and Sedition Acts of 1798** Four measures passed during the undeclared war with France that limited the freedoms of speech and press and restricted the liberty of noncitizens.

**alliance with France** Critical diplomatic, military, and economic alliance between France and the newly independent United States, codified by the Treaty of Amity and Commerce and the Treaty of Alliance (1778).

**Allied Powers** The nations fighting the Central Powers during the First World War, including France, Great Britain, and Russia; later joined by Italy and, after Russia quit the war in 1917, the United States.

**American Anti-Imperialist League** Coalition of anti-imperialist groups united in 1899 to protest American territorial expansion, especially in the Philippine Islands; its membership included prominent politicians, industrialists, labor leaders, and social reformers.

**American Colonization Society** Established in 1817, an organization whose mission was to return freed slaves to Africa.

**American Federation of Labor** Founded in 1881 as a national federation of trade unions made up of skilled workers.

**American Indian Movement (AIM)** Fed up with the poor conditions on Indian reservations and the federal government's unwillingness to help, Native Americans founded the American Indian Movement (AIM) in 1963. In 1973, AIM led 200 Sioux in the occupation of Wounded Knee. After a ten-week standoff with the federal authorities, the government agreed to reexamine Indian treaty rights and the occupation ended.

**American Recovery and Reinvestment Act** Hoping to restart the weak economy, President Obama signed this $787-billion economic stimulus bill in February of 2009. The bill included cash distributions to states, funds for food stamps, unemployment benefits, construction projects to renew the nation's infrastructure, funds for renewable-energy systems, and tax reductions.

**American System** Economic plan championed by Henry Clay of Kentucky that called for federal tariffs on imports, a strong national bank, and federally financed internal improvements—roads, bridges, canals—all intended to strengthen the national economy and end American dependence on Great Britain.

**American Tobacco Company** Business founded in 1890 by North Carolina's James Buchanan Duke, who combined the major tobacco manufacturers of the time, ultimately controlling 90 percent of the country's cigarette production.

**Anaconda Plan** The Union's primary war strategy calling for a naval blockade of major southern seaports and then dividing the Confederacy by gaining control of the Tennessee, Cumberland, and Mississippi Rivers.

**Annapolis Convention** In 1786, all thirteen colonies were invited to a convention in Annapolis to discuss commercial problems, but only representatives from five states attended. However, the convention was not a complete failure because the delegates decided to have another convention in order to write the constitution.

**Battle of Antietam (1862)** Turning-point battle near Sharpsburg, Maryland, leaving over 20,000 soldiers dead or wounded, in which Union forces halted a Confederate invasion of the North.

**anti-Federalists** Opponents of the Constitution as an infringement on individual and states' rights, whose criticism led to the addition of a Bill of Rights to the document. Many anti-Federalists later joined Thomas Jefferson's Democratic-Republican party.

**Anti-Masonic party** This party grew out of popular hostility toward the Masonic fraternal order and entered the presidential election of 1832 as a third party. It was the first party to run as a third party in a presidential election as well as the first to hold a nomination convention and announce a party platform.

**Appomattox Court House** Virginia village where Confederate general Robert E. Lee surrendered to Union general Ulysses S. Grant on April 9, 1865.

**Arab Awakening** A wave of spontaneous democratic uprisings that spread throughout the Arab world beginning in 2011, in which long-oppressed peoples demanded basic liberties from generations-old authoritarian regimes.

**Armory Show** A divisive and sensational art exhibition in 1913 that introduced European-inspired modernism to American audiences.

**Benedict Arnold (1741–1801)** A traitorous American commander who planned to sell out the American garrison at West Point to the British; his plot was discovered before it could be executed and he joined the British army.

**Articles of Confederation** The first form of government for the United States, ratified by the original thirteen states in 1781; weak in central authority, it was replaced by the U.S. Constitution in 1789.

**Atlanta Compromise (1895)** A speech by Booker T. Washington that called for the black community to strive for economic prosperity before attempting political and social equality.

**Atlantic Charter (1941)** Joint statement crafted by Franklin D. Roosevelt and British prime minister Winston Churchill that listed the war goals of the Allied Powers.

**Crispus Attucks (1723–1770)** During the Boston Massacre, he was supposedly at the head of the crowd of hecklers who baited the British troops. He was killed when the British troops fired on the crowd.

**Stephen F. Austin (1793–1836)** He established the first colony of Americans in Texas, which eventually attracted 2,000 people.

**Axis alliance** Military alliance formed in 1937 by the three major fascist powers: Germany, Italy, and Japan.

**Aztec Empire** Mesoamerican people who were conquered by the Spanish under Hernando Cortés, 1519–1528.

**baby boom** Markedly high birth rate in the years following World War II, leading to the biggest demographic "bubble" in U.S. history.

**Bacon's Rebellion** Unsuccessful 1676 revolt led by planter Nathaniel Bacon against Virginia governor William Berkeley's administration, which, Bacon charged, had failed to protect settlers from Indian raids.

**Bank of the United States (1791)** National bank responsible for holding and transferring federal government funds, making business loans, and issuing a national currency.

**Bank War** Political struggle in the early 1830s between President Jackson and financier Nicholas Biddle over the renewing of the Second Bank's charter.

**Barbary pirates** North Africans who waged war (1801–1805) on the United States after President Thomas Jefferson refused to pay tribute (a bribe) to protect American ships.

**Bay of Pigs** Failed CIA operation that, in April 1961, deployed a band of Cuban rebels to overthrow Fidel Castro's Communist regime.

**Battle of the Bulge** On December 16, 1944, the German army launched a counterattack against the Allied forces, which pushed them back. However, the Allies were eventually able to recover and break through the German lines. This defeat was a great blow to the Nazi's morale and their army's strength. The battle used up the last of Hitler's reserve units and opened a route into Germany's heartland.

**Bear Flag Republic** On June 14, 1846, a group of Americans in California captured Sonoma from the Mexican army and declared it the Republic of California whose flag featured a grizzly bear. In July, the commodore of the U.S. Pacific Fleet landed troops on California's shores and declared it part of the United States.

**Beats** Group of bohemian, downtown New York writers, artists, and musicians who flouted convention in favor of liberated forms of self-expression.

**beatnik** A name referring to almost any young rebel who openly dissented from the middle-class life. The name itself stems from the Beats.

**Berlin airlift (1948–1949)** Effort by the United States and Great Britain to deliver massive amounts of food and supplies flown to West Berlin in response to the Soviet land blockade of the city.

**Berlin Wall** Twenty-seven-mile-long concrete wall constructed in 1961 by East German authorities to stop the flow of East Germans fleeing to West Berlin.

**Bessemer converter** Apparatus that blasts air through molten iron to produce steel in very large quantities.

**Nicholas Biddle (1786–1844)** He was the president of the second Bank of the United States. In response to President Andrew Jackson's attacks on the bank, Biddle curtailed the bank's loans and exchanged its paper currency for gold and silver. In response, state banks began printing paper without restraint and lent it to speculators, causing a binge in speculating and an enormous increase in debt.

**Bill of Rights** First ten amendments to the U.S. Constitution, adopted in 1791 to guarantee individual rights and to help secure ratification of the Constitution by the states.

**Osama bin Laden (1957–2011)** The Saudi-born leader of al Qaeda, whose members attacked America on September 11, 2001. Years before the attack, he had declared *jihad* (holy war) on the United States, Israel, and the Saudi monarchy. In Afghanistan, the Taliban leaders gave bin Laden a safe haven in exchange for aid in fighting the Northern Alliance, who were rebels opposed to the Taliban. Following the Taliban's refusal to turn over bin Laden to the United States, America and a multinational coalition invaded Afghanistan and overthrew the Taliban. In May 2011, bin Laden was shot and killed by American special forces during a covert operation in Pakistan.

**birth rate** Proportion of births per 1,000 of the total population.

**black codes** Laws passed in southern states to restrict the rights of former slaves; to combat the codes, Congress passed the Civil Rights Act of 1866 and the Fourteenth Amendment and set up military governments in southern states that refused to ratify the amendment.

**Black nationalism** A cultural and political movement in the 1920s spearheaded by Marcus Garvey that exalted blackness, black cultural expression, and black exclusiveness.

**Black Power movement** Militant form of civil rights protest focused on urban communities in the North and led by Malcolm X that grew as a response to impatience with the nonviolent tactics of Martin Luther King Jr.

**James Gillepsie Blaine (1830–1893)** As a Republican congressman from Maine, he developed close ties with business leaders, which contributed to him losing the presidential election of 1884. He later opposed President Cleveland's efforts to reduce tariffs, which became a significant issue in the 1888 presidential election. Blaine served as secretary of state under President Benjamin Harrison.

**Bleeding Kansas (1856)** A series of violent conflicts in the Kansas Territory between anti-slavery and pro-slavery factions over the status of slavery.

**blitzkrieg (1940)** The German "lightning war" strategy characterized by swift, well-organized attacks using infantry, tanks, and warplanes.

**Bolsheviks** Under the leadership of Vladimir Lenin, this Marxist party led the November 1917 revolution against the newly formed provisional government in Russia. After seizing control, the Bolsheviks negotiated a peace treaty with Germany, the Treaty of Brest-Litovsk, and ended their participation in World War I.

**Bonus Expeditionary Force (1932)** Protest march in Washington, D.C., by thousands of World War I veterans and their families, calling for immediate payment of their service bonuses certificates; violence ensued when President Herbert Hoover ordered their tent villages cleared.

**boomtown** Town, often in the West, that developed rapidly due to the sudden influx of wealth and work opportunities; often male-dominated with a substantial immigrant population.

**Daniel Boone (1734–1820)** He found and expanded a trail into Kentucky, which pioneers used to reach and settle the area.

**John Wilkes Booth (1838?–1865)** He assassinated President Abraham Lincoln at the Ford's Theater on April 14, 1865. He was pursued and killed.

**Boston Massacre** Violent confrontation between British soldiers and a Boston mob on March 5, 1770, in which five colonists were killed.

**Boston Tea Party** Demonstration against the Tea Act of 1773 in which the Sons of Liberty, dressed as Indians, dumped hundreds of chests of British-owned tea into Boston Harbor.

**Bourbons** In post–Civil War southern politics, the opponents of the Redeemers were called Bourbons. They were known for having forgotten nothing and learned nothing from the ordeal of the Civil War.

**bracero program (1942)** System created in 1942 that permitted seasonal farm workers from Mexico to work in the United States on year-long contracts.

**Joseph Brant (1742?–1807)** Mohawk leader who led the Iroquois against the Americans in the Revolutionary War.

**brinksmanship** Secretary of State John Foster Dulles believed that communism could be contained by bringing America to the brink of war with an aggressive Communist nation. He believed that the aggressor would back down when confronted with the prospect of receiving a mass retaliation from a country with nuclear weapons.

**John Brown (1800–1859)** In response to a pro-slavery mob's sacking of the free-state town of Lawrence, Kansas, Brown went to the pro-slavery settlement of Pottawatomie, Kansas, which led to a guerrilla war in the Kansas territory. In 1859, he attempted to raid the federal arsenal at Harpers Ferry, hoping to use the stolen weapons to arm slaves, but he was captured and executed.

***Brown v. Board of Education*** (1954) Landmark Supreme Court case that struck down racial segregation in public schools and declared "separate-but-equal" unconstitutional.

**William Jennings Bryan (1860–1925)** He delivered the pro-silver "cross of gold" speech at the 1896 Democratic Convention and won his party's nomination for president. Disappointed pro-gold Democrats chose to walk out of the convention and nominate their own candidate, which split the Democratic party and cost them the White House. Bryan's loss also crippled the Populist movement that had endorsed him.

**"Bull Moose" Progressive party** *See* Progressive party

**Battles of (First and Second Manassas) Bull Run** First land engagement of the Civil War took place on July 21, 1861, at Manassas Junction, Virginia, at which surprised Union troops quickly retreated; one year later, on August 29–30, Confederates captured the federal supply depot and forced Union troops back to Washington.

**Martin Van Buren (1782–1862)** During President Jackson's first term, he served as secretary of state and minister to London. In 1836, Van Buren was elected president, and he inherited a financial crisis. He believed that the government should not continue to keep its deposits in state banks and set up an independent Treasury, which was approved by Congress after several years of political maneuvering.

**General John Burgoyne (1722–1792)** He was the commander of Britain's northern forces during the Revolutionary War. He and most of his troops surrendered to the Americans at the Battle of Saratoga.

**burial mounds** A funeral tradition, practiced in the Mississippi and Ohio Valleys by the Adena-Hopewell cultures, of erecting massive mounds of earth over graves, often in the designs of serpents and other animals.

**burned-over district** Area of western New York strongly influenced by the revivalist fervor of the Second Great Awakening; Disciples of Christ and Mormons are among the many sects that trace their roots to the phenomenon.

**Aaron Burr (1756–1836)** Even though he was Thomas Jefferson's vice president, he lost favor with Jefferson's Republican supporters. He sought to work with the Federalists and run as their candidate for the governor of New York. Alexander Hamilton opposed Burr's candidacy and his stinging remarks on the subject led to Burr challenging him to duel in which Hamilton was killed.

**George H. W. Bush (1924– )** He served as vice president during the Reagan administration and then won the presidential election of 1988. His presidency was marked by raised taxes in the face of the federal deficit, the creation of the Office of National Drug Control Policy, and military activity abroad, including the invasion of Panama and Operation Desert Storm in Kuwait. He lost the 1992 presidential election to Bill Clinton.

**George W. Bush (1946– )** In the 2000 presidential election, Texas governor George W. Bush won as the Republican nominee against Democratic nominee Vice President Al Gore. After the September 11 terrorist attacks, he launched his "war on terrorism." President Bush adopted the Bush Doctrine, and United States invaded Afghanistan and Iraq with unclear outcomes leaving the countries divided. In September 2008, the nation's economy nose-dived as a credit crunch spiraled into a global economic meltdown. Bush signed into law the bank bailout fund called Troubled Asset Relief Program (TARP), but the economy did not improve.

**Bush v. Gore (2000)** The close 2000 presidential election came down to Florida's decisive twenty-five electoral votes. The final tally in Florida gave Bush a slight lead, but it was so small that a recount was required by state law. While the votes were being recounted, a legal battle was being waged to stop the recount. Finally, the case, *Bush v. Gore*, was presented to the Supreme Court who ruled 5–4 to stop the recount and Bush was declared the winner.

**Bush Doctrine** National security policy launched in 2002 by which the Bush administration claimed the right to launch preemptive military attacks against perceived enemies, particularly outlaw nations or terrorist organizations believed to possess weapons of mass destruction.

**buying (stock) on margin** The investment practice of making a small down payment (the "margin") on a stock and borrowing the rest of the money needed for the purchase from a broker who held the stock as security against a down market. If the stock's value declined and the buyer failed to meet a margin call for more funds, the broker could sell the stock to cover his loan.

**Cahokia** The largest chiefdom and city of the Mississippian Indian culture located in present-day Illinois, and the site of a sophisticated farming settlement that supported up to 15,000 inhabitants.

**John C. Calhoun (1782–1850)** He served in both the House of Representatives and the Senate for South Carolina before becoming secretary of war under President Monroe and then John Quincy Adams's vice president. Though he started his political career as an advocate of a strong national government, he eventually believed that states' rights, limited central government, and the power of nullification were necessary to preserve the Union.

**California gold rush (1849)** A massive migration of gold hunters, mostly men, who transformed the economy of California after gold was discovered in the foothills of northern California.

**Camp David Accords (1978)** Peace agreement between Prime Minister Menachem Begin of Israel and President Anwar Sadat of Egypt, the first Arab head of state to officially recognize the state of Israel.

**"Scarface" Al Capone (1899–1947)** The most successful gangster of the Prohibition era whose Chicago-based criminal empire included bootlegging, prostitution, and gambling.

**Andrew Carnegie (1835–1919)** A steel magnate who believed that the general public benefited from big business even if these companies employed harsh business practices. This philosophy became deeply ingrained in the conventional wisdom of some Americans. After retiring, he devoted himself to philanthropy in hopes of promoting social welfare and world peace.

**Carnegie Steel Company** Corporation under the leadership of Andrew Carnegie that came to dominate the American steel industry.

**Carolina colonies** English proprietary colonies comprised of North and South Carolina, whose semitropical climate made them profitable centers of rice, timber, and tar production.

**carpetbaggers** Northern emigrants who participated in the Republican governments of the reconstructed South.

**Jimmy Carter (1924–)** Elected president in 1976, Jimmy Carter was an outsider to Washington. He created the departments of Energy and Education and signed into law several environmental initiatives. In 1978, he successfully brokered a peace agreement between Israel and Egypt called the Camp David Accords. However, his unwillingness to make deals with legislators caused other bills to be either gutted or stalled in Congress. His administration was plagued with a series of crises: a recession and increased inflation, a fuel shortage, the Soviet invasion of Afghanistan, and the overthrow of the Shah of Iran, leading to the Iran Hostage Crisis. Carter struggled to get the hostages released and was unable to do so until after he lost the 1980 election to Ronald Reagan. He was awarded the Nobel Peace Prize in 2002 for his efforts to further peace and democratic elections around the world.

**Jacques Cartier (1491–1557)** He led the first French effort to colonize North America and explored the Gulf of St. Lawrence, reaching as far as present day Montreal on the St. Lawrence River.

**Fidel Castro (1926–)** In 1959, his Communist regime came to power in Cuba after two years of guerrilla warfare against the dictator Fulgenico Batista. He enacted land redistribution programs and nationalized all foreign-owned property. The latter action as well as his political trials and summary executions damaged relations between Cuba and America. Castro was turned down when he asked for loans from the United States. However, he did receive aid from the Soviet Union.

**Central Intelligence Agency (CIA)** Intelligence-gathering government agency founded in 1947; under President Eisenhower's orders, secretly undermined elected governments deemed susceptible to communism.

**Central Powers** One of the two sides during the First World War, including Germany, Austria-Hungary, the Ottoman Empire (Turkey), and Bulgaria.

**Carrie Chapman Catt (1859–1947)** She was a leader of a new generation of activists in the women's suffrage movement who carried on the work started by Elizabeth Cady Stanton and Susan B. Anthony.

**Cesar Chavez (1927–1993)** He founded the United Farm Workers (UFW) in 1962 and worked to organize migrant farm workers. In 1965, the UFW joined Filipino farm workers striking against corporate grape farmers in California's San Joaquin Valley. In 1970, the strike and a consumer boycott on grapes compelled the farmers to formally recognize the UFW. As the result of Chavez's efforts, wages and working conditions improved for migrant workers. In 1975, the California state legislature passed a bill that required growers to bargain collectively with representatives of the farm workers.

**child labor** The practice of sending children to work in mines, mills, and factories, often in unsafe conditions; widespread among poor families in the late nineteenth century.

**Chinese Exclusion Act (1882)** Federal law that barred Chinese laborers from immigrating to America.

**Church of Jesus Christ of Latter-day Saints / Mormons** Founded in 1830 by Joseph Smith, the sect was a product of the intense revivalism of the burned-over district of New York; Smith's successor Brigham Young led 15,000 followers to Utah in 1847 to escape persecution.

**Winston Churchill (1874–1965)** The British prime minister who led the country during the Second World War. Along with Roosevelt and Stalin, he helped shape the postwar world at the Yalta Conference. He also coined the term "iron curtain," which he used in his famous "The Sinews of Peace" speech.

**citizen-soldiers** Part-time nonprofessional soldiers, mostly poor farmers or recent immigrants who had been indentured servants, who played an important role in the Revolutionary War.

**"city machines"** Local political party officials used these organizations to dispense patronage and favoritism amongst voters and businesses to ensure their loyal support to the political party.

**Civil Rights Act of 1957** First federal civil rights law since Reconstruction; established the Civil Rights Commission and the Civil Rights Division of the Department of Justice.

**Civil Rights Act of 1964** Legislation that outlawed discrimination in public accommodations and employment, passed at the urging of President Lyndon B. Johnson.

**civil service reform** An extended effort led by political reformers to end the patronage system; led to the Pendleton Act (1883), which called for government positions to be awarded based on merit rather than party loyalty.

**Henry Clay (1777–1852)** In the first half of the nineteenth century, he was the foremost spokesman for the American system. As Speaker of the House in the 1820s, he promoted economic nationalism, "market revolution," and the rapid development of western states and territories. A broker of compromise, he formulated the "second" Missouri Compromise and the Compromise of 1850. In 1824, Clay supported John Quincy Adams, who won the presidency and appointed Clay to secretary of state. Andrew Jackson claimed that Clay had entered into a "corrupt bargain" with Adams for his own selfish gains.

**Clayton Anti-Trust Act (1914)** Legislation that served to enhance the Sherman Anti-Trust Act (1890) by clarifying what constituted "monopolistic" activities and declaring that labor unions were not to be viewed as "monopolies in restraint of trade."

**Bill Clinton (1946–)** The governor of Arkansas won the 1992 presidential election against President George H. W. Bush. In his first term, he pushed through Congress a tax increase, an economic stimulus package, the adoption of the North America Free Trade Agreement, welfare reform, a raise in the minimum wage, and improved public access to health insurance. His administration also negotiated the Oslo Accord and the Dayton Accords. After his re-election in 1996, he was involved in two high-profile scandals: his investment in the fraudulent Whitewater Development Corporation (but no evidence was found of him being involved in any wrong-doing) and his sexual affair with a White House intern. His attempt to cover up the affair led to a vote in Congress on whether or not to begin an impeachment inquiry. The House of Representatives voted to impeach Clinton, but the Senate found him not guilty.

**Hillary Rodham Clinton (1947–)** In the 2008 presidential election, Senator Hillary Clinton, the spouse of former President Bill Clinton, initially was the front-runner for the Democratic nomination, which made her the first woman with a serious chance to win the presidency. However, Senator Barack Obama's Internet-based and grassroots-orientated campaign garnered him enough delegates to win the nomination. After Obama became president, she was appointed secretary of state. In 2016, Clinton ran again and won the Democratic nomination for the presidency. Although she won the popular vote, she lost the election to Donald Trump.

**clipper ships** Tall, slender, mid-nineteenth-century sailing ships that were favored over older merchant ships for their speed, but ultimately gave way to steamships because they lacked cargo space.

**Coercive Acts (1774)** Four parliamentary measures that required the colonies to pay for the Boston Tea Party's damages, imposed a military government, disallowed colonial trials of British soldiers, and forced the quartering of troops in private homes.

**coffin ships** Irish immigrants fleeing the potato famine had to endure a six-week journey across the Atlantic to reach America. During these voyages, thousands of passengers died of disease and starvation, which led to the ships being called "coffin ships."

**cold war** A state of political and ideological conflict between nations, primarily the United States, representing western-democratic nations, and the Soviet Union, representing Marxist-communist nations, marked by propaganda, threats, and other hostilities falling short of direct open warfare between the United States and Soviet Union.

**Columbian Exchange** The transfer of biological and social elements, such as plants, animals, people, diseases, and cultural practices, among Europe, the Americas, and Africa in the wake of Christopher Columbus's voyages to the "New World."

**Christopher Columbus (1451–1506)** The Italian sailor who persuaded King Ferdinad and Queen Isabella of Spain to fund his expedition across the Atlantic to discover a new trade route to Asia. Instead of arriving at China or Japan, he reached the Bahamas in 1492.

**James B. Comey (1960–)** FBI director fired by President Donald Trump in 2017.

**Committee of Correspondence** Group organized by Samuel Adams in retaliation for the *Gaspée* incident to address American grievances, assert American rights, and form a network of rebellion.

**Committee on Public Information** During the First World War, this committee produced war propaganda that conveyed the Allies' war aims to Americans as well as attempted to weaken the enemy's morale.

**Committee to Re-elect the President (CREEP)** During Nixon's presidency, his administration engaged in a number of immoral acts, such as attempting to steal information and falsely accusing political appointments of sexual improprieties. These acts were funded by money illegally collected through CREEP.

**Common Sense (1776)** Popular pamphlet written by Thomas Paine attacking British principles of hereditary rule and monarchical government, and advocating a declaration of American independence.

**Compromise of 1850** A package of five bills presented to the Congress by Henry Clay intended to avoid secession or civil war by reducing tensions between North and South over the status of slavery.

**Compromise of 1877** Deal made by a special congressional commission on March 2, 1877, to resolve the disputed presidential election of 1876; Republican Rutherford B. Hayes, who had lost the popular vote, was declared the winner in exchange for the withdrawal of federal troops from the South, marking the end of Reconstruction.

**Comstock Lode** Mine in eastern Nevada acquired by Canadian fur trapper Henry Comstock that between 1860 and 1880 yielded almost $1 billion worth of gold and silver.

**Conestoga wagons** These large horse-drawn wagons were used to carry people or heavy freight long distances, including from the East to the western frontier settlements.

**Congressional Reconstruction** Phase of Reconstruction directed by Radical Republicans through the passage of three laws: the Military Reconstruction Act, the Command of the Army Act, and the Tenure of Office Act.

**conquistadores** Spanish term for "conquerors," applied to Spanish and Portuguese soldiers who conquered lands held by indigenous peoples in central and southern America as well as the current states of Texas, New Mexico, Arizona, and California.

**consumer culture** A society in which mass production and consumption of nationally advertised products comes to dictate much of social life and status.

**containment** U.S. cold war strategy that sought to prevent global Soviet expansion and influence through political, economic, and, if necessary, military pressure as a means of combating the spread of communism.

**Continental army** Army authorized by the Continental Congress, 1775–1784, to fight the British; commanded by General George Washington.

**Contract with America** A list of conservative promises in response to the supposed liberalism of the Clinton administration, that was drafted by Speaker of the House Newt Gingrich and other congressional Republicans as the GOP platform for the 1994 midterm elections. More a campaign tactic than a practical program, few of its proposed items ever became law.

**contrabands** Slaves who sought refuge in Union military camps or who lived in areas of the Confederacy under Union control.

**Contras** The Reagan administration ordered the CIA to train and supply guerrilla bands of anti-Communist Nicaraguans called Contras. They were fighting the Sandinista government that had recently come to power in Nicaragua. The State Department believed that the Sandinista government was supplying the leftist Salvadoran rebels with Soviet and Cuban arms. A cease-fire agreement between the Contras and Sandinistas was signed in 1988.

**Calvin Coolidge (1872–1933)** After President Harding's death, his vice president, Calvin Coolidge, assumed the presidency. Coolidge believed that the nation's welfare was tied to the success of Big Business, and he worked to end government regulation of business and industry as well as reduce taxes. In particular, he focused on the nation's industrial development.

**Copperhead Democrats** Democrats in northern states who opposed the Civil War and argued for an immediate peace settlement with the Confederates; Republicans labeled them "Copperheads," because they wore copper coins on their lapels.

**Hernán Cortés (1485–1547)** The Spanish conquistador who conquered the Aztec Empire and set the precedent for other plundering conquistadores.

**General Charles Cornwallis (1738–1805)** He was in charge of British troops in the South during the Revolutionary War. His surrender to George Washington at the Battle of Yorktown ended the Revolutionary War.

**Corps of Discovery** Meriwether Lewis and William Clark led this group of men on an expedition of the newly purchased Louisiana territory, which took them from Missouri to Oregon. As they traveled, they kept detailed journals and drew maps of the previously unexplored territory. Their reports attracted traders and trappers to the region and gave the United States a claim to the Oregon country by right of discovery and exploration.

**corrupt bargain** Scandal in which presidential candidate and Speaker of the House Henry Clay secured John Quincy Adams's victory over Andrew Jackson in the 1824 election, supposedly in exchange for Clay being named secretary of state.

**cotton** White fibers harvested from cotton plants, spun into yarn, and woven into textiles that made comfortable, easy-to-clean products, especially clothing; the most valuable cash crop driving the economy in the United States and Great Britain during the nineteenth century.

**cotton gin** Hand-operated machine invented by Eli Whitney in the late eighteenth century that quickly removed seeds from cotton bolls, enabling the mass production of cotton in nineteenth-century America.

**Cotton Kingdom** Cotton-producing region, relying predominantly on slave labor, that spanned from North Carolina west to Louisiana and reached as far north as southern Illinois.

**counterculture** Unorganized youth rebellion against mainstream institutions, values, and behavior that more often focused on cultural rather than political activism.

**Court-packing scheme** President Franklin D. Roosevelt's failed 1937 attempt to increase the number of U.S. Supreme Court justices from nine to fifteen in order to save his Second New Deal programs from constitutional challenges.

**covenant theory** A Puritan concept that believed true Christians could enter a voluntary union for the common worship of God. Taking the idea one step further, the union could also be used for the purposes of establishing governments.

**crop-lien system** Credit system used by sharecroppers and share tenants who pledged a portion ("share") of their future crop to local merchants or land owners in exchange for farming supplies and food.

**"Cross of Gold" Speech** In the 1896 election, the Democratic Party split over the issue of whether to use gold or silver to back American currency. Significant to this division was the pro-silver "Cross of Gold" speech that William Jennings Bryan delivered at the Democratic convention, which was so well received that Bryan won the nomination to be their presidential candidate. Disappointed pro-gold Democrats chose to walk out of the convention and nominate their own candidate.

**Cuban missile crisis** Thirteen-day U.S.-Soviet standoff in October 1962, sparked by the discovery of Soviet missile sites in Cuba; the crisis was the closest the world has come to nuclear war since 1945.

**cult of domesticity** A pervasive nineteenth-century ideology that urged women to celebrate their role as manager of the household and nurturer of the children.

**George A. Custer (1839–1876)** He was a reckless and glory-seeking Lieutenant Colonel of the U.S. Army who fought the Sioux Indians in the Great Sioux War. In 1876, he and his detachment of soldiers were entirely wiped out in the Battle of Little Bighorn.

*Dartmouth College v. Woodward* **(1819)** Supreme Court ruling that enlarged the definition of *contract* to put corporations beyond the reach of the states that chartered them.

**Daughters of Liberty** Colonial women who protested the British government's tax policies by boycotting British products, such as clothing, and who wove their own fabric, or "homespun."

**Dawes Severalty Act (1887)** Federal legislation that divided ancestral Native American lands among the heads of each Indian family in an attempt to "Americanize" Indians by forcing them to become farmers working individual plots of land.

**D-day** June 6, 1944, when an Allied amphibious assault landed on the Normandy coast and established a foothold in Europe from which Hitler's defenses could not recover.

**Jefferson Davis (1808–1889)** He was the president of the Confederacy during the Civil War. When the Confederacy's defeat seemed invitable in early 1865, he refused to surrender. Union forces captured him in May of that year.

**Bartolomé de Las Casas (1484–1566)** A Catholic missionary who renounced the Spanish practice of coercively converting Indians and advocated their better treatment. In 1552, he wrote *A Brief Relation of the Destruction of the Indies*, which described the Spanish's cruel treatment of the Indians.

**death rate** Proportion of deaths per 1,000 of the total population; also called *mortality rate*.

**Eugene V. Debs (1855–1926)** Founder of the American Railway Union, which he organized against the Pullman Palace Car Company during the Pullman strike. Later he organized the Social Democratic party, which eventually became the Socialist Party of America. In the 1912 presidential election, he ran as the Socialist party's candidate and received more than 900,000 votes.

**Declaration of Independence** Formal statement, principally drafted by Thomas Jefferson and adopted by the Second Continental Congress on July 4, 1776, that officially announced the thirteen colonies' break with Great Britain.

**Declaration of Rights and Sentiments** Document based on the Declaration of Independence that called for gender equality, written primarily by Elizabeth Cady Stanton and signed by Seneca Falls Convention delegates in 1848.

**Declaratory Act** Following the repeal of the Stamp Act in 1766, Parliament passed this act which asserted Parliament's full power to make laws binding the colonies "in all cases whatsoever."

**Deism** Enlightenment thought applied to religion, emphasizing reason, morality, and natural law rather than scriptural authority or an ever-present God intervening in human life.

**détente** Period of improving relations between the United States and Communist nations, particularly China and the Soviet Union, during the Nixon administration.

**George Dewey (1837–1917)** On April 30, 1898, Commodore George Dewey's small U.S. naval squadron defeated the Spanish warships in Manila Bay in the Philippines. This quick victory aroused expansionist fever in the United States.

**John Dewey (1859–1952)** He is an important philosopher of pragmatism. However, he preferred to use the term *instrumentalism*, because he saw ideas as instruments of action.

**Ngo Dinh Diem (1901–1963)** Following the Geneva Accords, the French, with the support of America, forced the Vietnamese emperor to accept Dinh Diem as the new premier of South Vietnam. President Eisenhower sent advisors to train Diem's police and army. In return, the United States expected Diem to enact democratic reforms and distribute land to the peasants. Instead, he suppressed his political opponents, did little or no land distribution, and let corruption grow. In 1956, he refused to participate in elections to reunify Vietnam. Eventually, he ousted the emperor and declared himself president.

**Distribution Act (1836)** Law requiring the distribution of the federal budget surplus to the states, creating chaos among state banks that had become dependent on such federal funds.

**Dorothea Lynde Dix (1802–1887)** She was an important figure in increasing the public's awareness of the plight of the mentally ill. After a two-year investigation of the treatment of the mentally ill in Massachusetts, she presented her findings and won the support of leading reformers. She eventually convinced twenty states to reform their treatment of the mentally ill.

**Dixiecrats** Breakaway faction of southern Democrats who defected from the national Democratic party in 1948 to protest the party's increased support for civil rights and to nominate their own segregationist candidates for elective office.

**dollar diplomacy** Practice advocated by President Theodore Roosevelt in which the U.S. government fostered American investments in less developed nations and then used U.S. military force to protect those investments

**Donner party** Forty-seven surviving members of a group of migrants to California were forced to resort to cannibalism to survive a brutal winter trapped in the Sierra Nevadas, 1846–1847; highest death toll of any group traveling the Overland Trail.

**Stephen A. Douglas (1812–1861)** As a senator from Illinois, he authored the Kansas-Nebraska Act. Running for senatorial reelection in 1858, he engaged Abraham Lincoln in a series of public debates about slavery in the territories. Even though Douglas won the election, the debates gave Lincoln a national reputation.

**Frederick Douglass (1818–1895)** He escaped from slavery and become an eloquent speaker and writer against the institution. In 1845, he published his autobiography entitled *Narrative of the Life of Frederick Douglass* and two years later he founded an abolitionist newspaper for blacks called the *North Star*.

**dot-coms** In the late 1990s, the stock market soared to new heights and defied the predictions of experts that the economy could not sustain such a performance. Much of the economic success was based on dot-com enterprises, which were firms specializing in computers, software, telecommunications, and the internet. However, many of the companies' stock market values were driven higher and higher by speculation instead of financial success. Eventually the stock market bubble burst.

***Dred Scott v. Sandford* (1857)** U.S. Supreme Court ruling that slaves were not U.S. citizens and therefore could not sue for their freedom and that Congress could not prohibit slavery in the western territories.

**W. E. B. Du Bois (1868–1963)** He criticized Booker T. Washington's views on civil rights as being accommodationist. He advocated "ceaseless agitation" for civil rights and the immediate end to segregation and an enforcement of laws to protect civil rights and equality. He promoted an education for African Americans that would nurture bold leaders who were willing to challenge discrimination in politics.

**John Foster Dulles (1888–1959)** As President Eisenhower's secretary of state, he institutionalized the policy of containment and introduced the strategy of deterrence.

He believed in using brinkmanship to halt the spread of communism. He attempted to employ it in Indochina, which led to the United States' involvement in Vietnam.

**Dust Bowl** Vast area of the Midwest where windstorms blew away millions of tons of top-soil from parched farmland after a long drought in the 1930s, causing great social distress and a massive migration of farm families.

**Eastern Woodlands Peoples** Various Native American peoples, particularly the Algonquian, Iroquoian, and Muskogean regional groups, who once dominated the Atlantic seaboard from Maine to Louisiana.

**Peggy Eaton (1796–1879)** The wife of John Eaton, President Jackson's secretary of war, was the daughter of a tavern owner with an unsavory past. Supposedly her first husband had committed suicide after learning that she was having an affair with John Eaton. The wives of members of Jackson's cabinet snubbed her because of her lowly origins and past, resulting in a scandal known as the Eaton Affair.

**Economic Opportunity Act (1964)** Key legislation in President Johnson's "War on Poverty" which created the Office of Economic Opportunity and programs like Head Start and work-study.

**Jonathan Edwards (1703–1758)** New England Congregationalist minister who began a religious revival in his Northampton church and was an important figure in the Great Awakening.

**election of 1800** Presidential election between Thomas Jefferson and John Adams; resulted in the first Democratic-Republican party victory after the Federalist administrations of George Washington and John Adams.

**election campaign of 1828** Bitter presidential contest between Democrat Andrew Jackson and National Republican John Quincy Adams (running for reelection), resulting in Jackson's victory.

**election of 1864** Abraham Lincoln's successful reelection campaign, capitalizing on Union military successes in Georgia, to defeat Democratic opponent, former general George B. McClellan, who ran on a peace platform.

**election of 1912** The presidential election of 1912 featured four candidates: Wilson, Taft, Roosevelt, and Debs. Each candidate believed in the basic assumptions of progressive politics, but each had a different view on how progressive ideals should be implemented through policy. In the end, Taft and Roosevelt split the Republican party votes and Wilson emerged as the winner.

**Queen Elizabeth I of England (1533–1603)** The protestant daughter of Henry VIII, she was Queen of England from 1558–1603 and played a major role in the Protestant Reformation. During her long reign, the doctrines and services of the Church of England were defined and the Spanish Armada was defeated.

**General Dwight D. Eisenhower (1890–1969)** During the Second World War, he commanded the Allied Forces landing in Africa and was the supreme Allied commander as well as planner for Operation Overlord. In 1952, he was elected president on his popularity as a war hero and his promises to clean up Washington. His administration sought to cut the nation's domestic programs and budget, ended the fighting in Korea, and institutionalized the policies of containment and deterrence. He established the Eisenhower doctrine, which promised to aid any nation against aggression by a Communist nation.

**Ellis Island** Reception center in New York Harbor through which most European immigrants to America were processed from 1892 to 1954.

**Emancipation Proclamation (1862)** Military order issued by President Abraham Lincoln that freed slaves in areas still controlled by the Confederacy but did not free the 500,000 slaves in the four border states that remained in the Union.

**Embargo Act (1807)** A law promoted by President Thomas Jefferson prohibiting American ships from leaving for foreign ports, in order to safeguard them from British and French attacks. This ban on American exports proved disastrous to the U.S. economy.

**Ralph Waldo Emerson (1803–1882)** As a leader of the transcendentalist movement, he wrote poems, essays, and speeches that discussed the sacredness of nature, optimism, self-reliance, and the unlimited potential of the individual. He wanted to transcend the limitations of inherited conventions and rationalism to reach the inner recesses of the self.

*encomienda* A land-grant system under which Spanish army officers (*conquistadores*) were awarded large parcels of land taken from Native Americans.

**Enlightenment** A revolution in thought begun in Europe in the seventeenth century that emphasized reason and science over the authority and myths of traditional religion.

**enumerated goods** According to the Navigation Act, these particular goods, like tobacco or cotton, could only be shipped to England or other English colonies.

**Environmental Protection Agency (EPA) (1970)** Federal environmental agency created by Nixon to appease the demands of congressional Democrats for a federal environmental watchdog agency.

**Erie Canal (1825)** Most important and profitable of the barge canals of the 1820s and 1830s; stretched from Buffalo to Albany, New York, connecting the Great Lakes to the East Coast and making New York City the nation's largest port.

**ethnic cleansing** The systematic removal of an ethnic group from a territory through violence or intimidation in order to create a homogenous society; the term was popularized by the Yugoslav policy brutally targeting Albanian Muslims in Kosovo.

**Exodusters** African Americans who migrated west from the South in search of a haven from racism and poverty after the collapse of Radical Republican rule.

**Fair Deal (1949)** President Truman's proposals to build upon the New Deal with national health insurance, the repeal of the Taft-Hartley Act, new civil rights legislation, and other initiatives; most were rejected by the Republican-controlled Congress.

**Fair Employment Practices Commission** Created in 1941 by executive order, the FEPC sought to eliminate racial discrimination in jobs; it possessed little power but represented a step toward civil rights for African Americans.

**falling-domino theory** Theory that if one country fell to communism, its neighboring countries would follow suit.

**Farmers' Alliances** Like the Granger movement, these organizations sought to address the issues of small farming communities; however Alliances emphasized more political action and called for the creation of a Third Party to advocate their concerns.

**fascism** A radical form of totalitarian government that emerged in Italy and Germany in the 1920s in which a dictator uses propaganda and brute force to seize control of all aspects of national life.

**Federal-Aid Highway Act (1956)** Largest federal project in U.S. history that created a national network of interstate highways and was the largest federal project in history.

**Federal Deposit Insurance Corporation (1933)** Independent government agency, established to prevent bank panics, which guarantees the safety of deposits in citizens' savings accounts.

**Federal Reserve Act (1913)** Legislation passed by Congress to create a new national banking system in order to regulate the nation's currency supply and ensure the stability and integrity of member banks who made up the Federal Reserve System across the nation.

**Federal Trade Commission (1914)** Independent agency created by the Wilson administration that replaced the Bureau of Corporations as an even more powerful tool to combat unfair trade practices and monopolies.

**Federal Writers' Project** During the Great Depression, this project provided writers, such as Ralph Ellison, Richard Wright, and Saul Bellow, with work, which gave them employment and a chance to develop as artists.

**federalism** Concept of dividing governmental authority between the national government and the states.

***The Federalist Papers*** Collection of eighty-five essays, published widely in newspapers in 1787 and 1788, written by Alexander Hamilton, James Madison, and John Jay in support of adopting the proposed U.S. Constitution.

**Federalists** Proponents of a centralized federal system and the ratification of the Constitution. Most Federalists were relatively young, educated men who supported a broad interpretation of the Constitution whenever national interest dictated such flexibility. Notable Federalists included Alexander Hamilton and John Jay.

**Geraldine Ferraro (1935–)** In the 1984 presidential election, Democratic nominee, Walter Mondale, chose her as his running mate. As a member of the U.S. House of Representatives from New York, she was the first woman to be a vice-presidential nominee for a major political party. However, she was placed on the defensive because of her husband's complicated business dealings.

**field hands** Slaves who toiled in the cotton or cane fields in organized work gangs.

**Fifteenth Amendment (1870)** This amendment forbids states to deny any person the right to vote on grounds of "race, color or pervious condition of servitude." Former Confederate states were required to ratify this amendment before they could be readmitted to the Union.

**"final solution"** The Nazi party's systematic murder of some 6 million Jews along with more than a million other people including, but not limited to, gypsies, homosexuals, and handicap individuals.

**First New Deal (1933–1935)** Franklin D. Roosevelt's ambitious first-term cluster of economic and social programs designed to combat the Great Depression.

**First Red Scare (1919–1920)** Outbreak of anti-Communist hysteria that included the arrest without warrants of thousands of suspected radicals, most of whom (mainly Russian immigrants) were deported.

**flappers** Young women of the 1920s whose rebellion against prewar standards of femininity included wearing shorter dresses, bobbing their hair, dancing to jazz music, driving cars, smoking cigarettes, and indulging in illegal drinking and gambling.

**Food Administration** After America's entry into World War I, the economy of the home front needed to be reorganized to provide the most efficient means of conducting the war. The Food Administration was a part of this effort. Under the leadership of Herbert Hoover, the organization sought to increase agricultural production while reducing civilian consumption of foodstuffs.

**Force Bill (1833)** Legislation, sparked by the Nullification Crisis in South Carolina, that authorized the president's use of the army to compel states to comply with federal law.

**Gerald Ford (1913–2006)** He was appointed to the vice presidency under President Nixon after the resignation of Spiro Agnew, and assumed the presidency after President Nixon's resignation. He resisted congressional pressure to both reduce taxes and increase federal spending, which sent the American economy into the deepest recession since the Great Depression. Ford retained Kissinger as his secretary of state and continued Nixon's foreign policy goals. He was heavily criticized following the collapse of South Vietnam.

**Fort Laramie Treaty (1851)** Restricted the Plains Indians from using the Overland Trail and permitted the building of government forts.

**Fort Necessity** After attacking a group of French soldiers, George Washington constructed and took shelter in this fort from vengeful French troops. Washington eventually surrendered to them after a day-long battle. This conflict was a significant event in igniting the French and Indian War.

**Fort Sumter** First battle of the Civil War, in which the federal fort in Charleston (South Carolina) Harbor was captured by the Confederates on April 14, 1861, after two days of shelling.

**"forty-niners"** Speculators who went to northern California following the discovery of gold in 1848; the first of several years of large-scale migration was 1849.

**Fourteen Points (1918)** President Woodrow Wilson's proposed plan for the peace agreement after the First World War that included the creation of a "league of nations" intended to keep the peace.

**Fourteenth Amendment (1866)** Guaranteed rights of citizenship to former slaves, in words similar to those of the Civil Rights Act of 1866.

**Franciscan Missions** In 1769, Franciscan missioners accompanied Spanish soldiers to California and over the next fifty years established a chain of missions from San Diego to San Francisco. At these missions, friars sought to convert Indians to Catholicism and make them members of the Spanish empire. The friars stripped the Indians of their native heritage and used soldiers to enforce their will.

**Benjamin Franklin (1706–1790)** A Boston-born American, who epitomized the Enlightenment for many Americans and Europeans, Franklin's wide range of interests led him to become a publisher, inventor, and statesman. As the latter, he contributed to the writing of the Declaration of Independence, served as the minister to France during the Revolutionary War, and was a delegate to the Constitutional Convention.

**Free-Soil party** A political coalition created in 1848 that opposed the expansion of slavery into the new western territories.

**Freedmen's Bureau** Reconstruction agency established in 1865 to protect the legal rights of former slaves and to assist with their education, jobs, health care, and landowning.

**Freedom Riders** Activists who, beginning in 1961, traveled by bus through the South to test federal court rulings that banned segregation on buses and trains.

**John C. Frémont "the Pathfinder" (1813–1890)** He was an explorer and surveyor who helped inspire Americans living in California to rebel against the Mexican government and declare independence.

**French and Indian War (Seven Years' War) (1756–1763)** The last—and the most important—of four colonial wars fought between England and France for control of North America east of the Mississippi River.

**French Revolution** Revolutionary movement beginning in 1789 that overthrew the monarchy and transformed France into an unstable republic before Napoleon Bonaparte assumed power in 1799.

**Sigmund Freud (1865–1939)** He was the founder of psychoanalysis, which suggested that human behavior was motivated by unconscious and irrational forces. By the 1920s, his ideas were being discussed more openly in America.

**frontier revivals** Religious revival movement within the Second Great Awakening, that took place in frontier churches in western territories and states in the early nineteenth century.

**Fugitive Slave Act (1850)** Part of the Compromise of 1850, a provision that authorized federal officials to help capture and then return escaped slaves to their owners without trials.

**fundamentalism** Anti-modernist Protestant movement started in the early twentieth century that proclaimed the literal truth of the Bible; the name came from *The Fundamentals*, published by conservative leaders.

**William Lloyd Garrison (1805–1879)** In 1831, he started the anti-slavery newspaper *Liberator* and helped start the New England Anti-Slavery Society. Two years later, he assisted Arthur and Lewis Tappan in the founding of the American Anti-Slavery Society. He and his followers believed that America had been thoroughly corrupted and needed a wide range of reforms, embracing abolition, temperance, pacifism, and women's rights.

**Marcus Garvey (1887–1940)** He was the leading spokesman for Negro Nationalism, which exalted blackness, black cultural expression, and black exclusiveness. He called upon African Americans to liberate themselves from the surrounding white culture and create their own businesses, cultural centers, and newspapers. He was also the founder of the Universal Negro Improvement Association.

**Citizen Genet (1763–1834)** As the ambassador to the United States from the new French Republic, he engaged American privateers to attack British ships and conspired with frontiersmen and land speculators to organize an attack on Spanish Florida and Louisiana. His actions and the French radicals excessive actions against their enemies in the new French Republic caused the French Revolution to lose support among Americans.

**Geneva Accords** In 1954, the Geneva Accords were signed, which ended French colonial rule in Indochina. The agreement created the independent nations of Laos and Cambodia and divided Vietnam along the 17th parallel until an election in 1956 would reunify the country.

**Battle of Gettysburg (1863)** A monumental three-day battle in southern Pennsylvania, widely considered a turning point in the war, in which Union forces successfully countered a second Confederate invasion of the North.

**Ghost Dance movement** A spiritual and political movement among Native Americans whose followers performed a ceremonial "ghost dance" intended to connect the living with the dead and make the Indians bulletproof in battles to restore their homelands.

**GI Bill of Rights (1944)** Provided unemployment, education, and financial benefits for World War II veterans to ease their transition back to the civilian world.

*Gibbons v. Ogden* **(1824)** Supreme Court case that gave the federal government the power to regulate interstate commerce.

**Newt Gingrich (1943–)** He led the Republican insurgency in Congress in the mid 1990s through mobilizing religious and social conservatives. Along with other Republican congressmen, he created the Contract with America, which was a ten-point anti-big government program. However, the program fizzled out after many of its bills were not passed by Congress.

**Gilded Age** (1860–1896) An era of dramatic industrial and urban growth characterized by widespread political corruption and loose government oversight of corporations.

*The Gilded Age* Mark Twain and Charles Dudley Warner's 1873 novel, the title of which became the popular name for the period from the end of the Civil War to the turn of the century.

*glasnost* Russian term for "openness"; applied to the loosening of censorship in the Soviet Union under Mikhail Gorbachev.

**globalization** An important, and controversial, transformation of the world economy whereby the Internet helped revolutionize global commerce by creating an international marketplace for goods and services. Led by the growing number of multinational companies and the Americanization of many foreign consumer cultures, with companies like McDonald's and Starbucks appearing in all of the major cities of the world.

**Glorious Revolution (1688)** Successful coup, instigated by a group of English aristocrats, which overthrew King James II and instated William of Orange and Mary, his English wife, to the British throne.

**Barry Goldwater (1909–1998)** A leader of the Republican right whose book, *The Conscience of a Conservative*, was highly influential to that segment of the party. He proposed eliminating the income tax and overhauling Social Security. In 1964, he ran as the Republican presidential candidate and lost to President Johnson. He campaigned against Johnson's war on poverty, the tradition of New Deal, the nuclear test ban and the Civil Rights Act of 1964 and advocated the wholesale bombing of North Vietnam.

**Samuel Gompers (1850–1924)** He served as the president of the American Federation of Labor from its inception until his death. He focused on achieving concrete economic gains such as higher wages, shorter hours, and better working conditions.

**"good neighbor" policy** Proclaimed by President Franklin D. Roosevelt in his first inaugural address in 1933, it sought improved diplomatic relations between the United States and its Latin American neighbors.

**Mikhail Gorbachev (1931–)** In the late 1980s, Soviet leader Mikhail Gorbachev attempted to reform the Soviet Union through his programs of *perestroika* and *glasnost* and pursued a renewal of détente with America, signing new arms-control agreements with President Reagan. Gorbachev allowed the velvet revolutions of Eastern Europe to occur without outside interference. Eventually the political, social, and economic upheaval he had unleashed would lead to the break-up of the Soviet Union.

**Albert Gore Jr. (1948–)** He served as a senator of Tennessee and then as President Clinton's vice president. In the 2000 presidential election, he was the Democratic candidate against Governor George W. Bush. The close election came down to Florida's electoral votes. While the votes were being recounted as required by state law, a legal battle was being waged to stop the recount. Finally, the case, *Bush v. Gore*, was presented to the Supreme Court who ruled 5–4 to stop the recount and Bush was declared the winner.

**Jay Gould (1836–1892)** As one of the biggest railroad robber barons, he was infamous for buying rundown railroads, making cosmetic improvements and then reselling them for a profit. He used corporate funds for personal investments and to bribe politicians and judges.

**gradualism** This strategy for ending slavery involved promoting the banning of slavery in the new western territories and encouraging the release of slaves from slavery. Supporters of this method believed that it would bring about the gradual end of slavery.

**Granger movement** Began by offering social and educational activities for isolated farmers and their families and later started to promote "cooperatives" where farmers could join together to buy, store, and sell their crops to avoid the high fees charged by brokers and other middle-men.

**Ulysses S. Grant (1822–1885)** After distinguishing himself in the western theater of the Civil War, he was appointed general in chief of the Union army in 1864. Afterward, he defeated General Robert E. Lee through a policy of aggressive attrition. Lee surrendered to Grant on April 9th, 1865 at the Appomattox Court House. His presidential tenure suffered from scandals and fiscal problems, including the debate on whether or not greenbacks, paper money, should be removed from circulation.

**Great Awakening** Fervent religious revival movement that swept the thirteen colonies from the 1720s through the 1740s.

**Great Compromise (Connecticut Compromise)** Mediated the differences between the New Jersey and Virginia delegations to the Constitutional Convention by providing for a bicameral legislature, the upper house of which would have equal representation and the lower house of which would be apportioned by population.

**Great Depression (1929–1941)** Worst economic downturn in American history; it was spurred by the stock market crash in the fall of 1929 and lasted until the Second World War.

**Great Migration** Mass exodus of African Americans from the rural South to the Northeast and Midwest during and after the First World War.

**Great Railroad Strike of 1877** A series of demonstrations, some violent, held nationwide in support of striking railroad workers in Martinsburg, West Virginia, who refused to work due to wage cuts.

**Great Recession (2007–2009)** Massive, prolonged economic downturn sparked by the collapse of the housing market and the financial institutions holding unpaid mortgages; it lasted from December 2007 to January 2009 and resulted in 9 million Americans losing their jobs.

**Great Sioux War** Conflict between Sioux and Cheyenne Indians and federal troops over lands in the Dakotas in the mid-1870s.

**Great Society** Term coined by President Lyndon B. Johnson in his 1965 State of the Union address, in which he proposed legislation to address problems of voting rights, poverty, diseases, education, immigration, and the environment.

**Horace Greeley (1811–1872)** In reaction to Radical Reconstruction and corruption in President Ulysses S. Grant's administration, a group of Republicans broke from the party to form the Liberal Republicans. In 1872, the Liberal Republicans chose Horace Greeley as their presidential candidate who ran on a platform of favoring civil service reform and condemning the Republican's Reconstruction policy.

**greenbacks** Paper money issued during the Civil War. After the war ended, a debate emerged on whether or not to remove the paper currency from circulation and revert back to hard-money currency (gold coins). Opponents of hard-money feared that eliminating the greenbacks would shrink the money supply, which would lower crop prices and make it more difficult to repay long-term debts. President Ulysses S. Grant, as well as hard-currency advocates, believed that gold coins were morally preferable to paper currency.

**Greenback party** Formed in 1876 in reaction to economic depression, the party favored issuance of unsecured paper money to help farmers repay debts; the movement for free coinage of silver took the place of the greenback movement by the 1880s.

**General Nathanael Greene (1742–1786)** He was appointed by Congress to command the American army fighting in the South during the Revolutionary War. Using his patience and his skills of managing men, saving supplies, and avoiding needless risks, he waged a successful war of attrition against the British.

**Sarah Grimké (1792–1873)** and **Angelina Grimké (1805–1879)** These two sisters gave anti-slavery speeches to crowds of mixed gender that caused some people to condemn them for engaging in unfeminine activities. In 1840, William Lloyd Garrison convinced the Anti-Slavery Society to allow women equal participation in the organization.

**Half-Way Covenant** Allowed baptized children of church members to be admitted to a "halfway" membership in the church and secure baptism for their own children in turn, but allowed them neither a vote in the church, nor communion.

**Alexander Hamilton (1755–1804)** His belief in a strong federal government led him to become a leader of the Federalists. As the first secretary of the Treasury, he laid the foundation for American capitalism through his creation of a federal budget, funded debt, a federal tax system, a national bank, a customs service, and a coast guard. His "Reports on Public Credit" and "Reports on Manufactures" outlined his vision for economic development and government finances. He died in a duel against Aaron Burr.

**Alexander Hamilton's economic reforms** Various measures designed to strengthen the nation's economy and generate federal revenue through the promotion of new industries, the adoption of new tax policies, the payment of war debts, and the establishment of a national bank.

**Warren G. Harding (1865–1923)** In the 1920 presidential election, he was the Republican nominee who promised Americans a "return to normalcy." Once in office, Harding's administration dismantled many of the social and economic components of progressivism and pursued a pro-business agenda. Harding appointed four pro-business Supreme Court Justices, cut taxes, increased tariffs, and promoted a lenient attitude towards regulation of corporations. However, he did speak out against racism and ended the exclusion of African Americans from federal positions.

**Harlem Renaissance** The nation's first self-conscious black literary and artistic movement; it was centered in New York City's Harlem district, which had a largely black population in the wake of the Great Migration from the South.

**Hartford Convention** A series of secret meetings in December 1814 and January 1815 at which New England Federalists protested American involvement in the War of 1812 and discussed several constitutional amendments, including limiting each president to one term, designed to weaken the dominant Republican party.

**Haymarket riot (1886)** Violent uprising in Haymarket Square, Chicago, where police clashed with labor demonstrators in the aftermath of a bombing.

**headright** A land-grant policy that promised fifty acres to any colonist who could afford passage to Virginia, as well as fifty more for any accompanying servants. The headright policy was eventually expanded to include any colonists—and was also adopted in other colonies.

**Patrick Henry (1736–1799)** He inspired the Virginia Resolves, which declared that Englishmen could only be taxed by their elected representatives. In March of 1775, he met with other colonial leaders to discuss the goals of the upcoming Continental Congress and famously declared "Give me liberty or give me death." During the ratification process of the U.S. Constitution, he became one of the leaders of the anti-federalists.

*Hessians* German mercenary soldiers who are paid by the royal government to fight alongside the British army.

**Hiroshima (1945)** Japanese port city that was the first target of the newly developed atomic bomb on August 6, 1945. Most of the city was destroyed.

**Alger Hiss (1904–1996)** During the second Red Scare he had served in several government departments and was accused of being a spy for the Soviet Union and was convicted of lying about espionage. The case was politically damaging to the Truman administration because the president called the charges against Hiss a "red herring."

**Adolph Hitler (1889–1945)** The leader of the Nazis who advocated a violent anti-Semitic, anti-Marxist, pan-German ideology. He started World War II in Europe and orchestrated the systematic murder of some 6 million Jews along with more than a million others.

**HIV/AIDS** Human immunodeficiency virus (HIV) transmitted via the bodily fluids of infected persons to cause acquired immunodeficiency syndrome (AIDS), an often-fatal disease of the immune system when it appeared in the 1980s.

**holding company** A corporation established to own and manage other companies' stock rather than to produce goods and services itself.

**Holocaust** Systematic racist attempt by the Nazis to exterminate all Jews in Europe, resulting in the murder of more than 6 million Jews and more than 5 million other "undesirables."

**Homestead Act (1862)** Legislation granting "homesteads" of 160 acres of government-owned land to settlers who agreed to work the land for at least five years.

**Homestead Steel strike (1892)** Labor conflict at the Homestead steel mill near Pittsburgh, Pennsylvania, culminating in a battle between strikers and private security agents hired by the factory's management.

**Herbert Hoover (1874–1964)** Prior to becoming president, Hoover served as the secretary of commerce in both the Harding and Coolidge administrations. As president during the Great Depression, he believed that the nation's business structure was sound and sought to revive the economy through boosting the nation's confidence. He also tried to restart the economy with government constructions projects, lower taxes and new federal loan programs, but nothing worked.

**horizontal integration** The process by which a corporation acquires or merges with its competitors.

**horse** A tall, four-legged mammal (*Equus caballus*), domesticated and bred since prehistoric times for carrying riders and pulling heavy loads. The Spanish introduced horses to the Americas, eventually transforming many Native American cultures.

**House Committee on Un-American Activities (HUAC)** Committee of the U.S. House of Representatives formed in 1938; it was originally tasked with investigating Nazi subversion during the Second World War and later shifted its focus to rooting out Communists in the government and the motion-picture industry.

**Sam Houston (1793–1863)** During Texas's fight for independence from Mexico, Sam Houston was the commander in chief of the Texas forces, and he led the attack that captured General Antonio López de Santa Anna. After Texas gained its independence, he was named its first president.

*How the Other Half Lives* In this book, early muckraking journalist Jacob Riis exposed the slum conditions in New York City.

**General William Howe (1729–1814)** As the commander of the British army in the Revolutionary War, he seized New York City from Washington's army, but failed to capture it. He missed several more opportunities to quickly end the rebellion, and he resigned his command after the British defeat at Saratoga.

**Saddam Hussein (1937–2006)** The former dictator of Iraq who became the head of state in 1979. In 1980, he invaded Iran and started the eight-year-long Iran-Iraq War. In 1990, he invaded Kuwait, which caused the Gulf War of 1991. In 2003, he was overthrown and captured when the United States invaded. He was sentenced to death by hanging in 2006.

**Anne Hutchinson (1591–1643)** The articulate, strong-willed, and intelligent wife of a prominent Boston merchant, who espoused her belief in direct divine revelation.

She quarreled with Puritan leaders over her beliefs; and they banished her from the colony.

**Immigration Act of 1924** Federal legislation intended to favor northern and western European immigrants over those from southern and eastern Europe by restricting the number of immigrants from any one European country to 2 percent of the total number of immigrants per year, with an overall limit of slightly over 150,000 new arrivals per year.

**Immigration and Nationality Services Act of 1965 (Hart-Cellar Act)** Legislation that abolished discriminatory quotas based upon immigrants' national origin and treated all nationalities and races equally.

**impeachment** A formal misconduct charge made against a public official, usually the president, by the House of Representatives. The official's removal from office requires a separate process in the form of a trial facilitated by the Senate. A guilty verdict from two-thirds of the participating senators leads to a conviction.

**imperialism** The use of diplomatic or military force to extend a nation's power and enhance its economic interests, often by acquiring territory or colonies and justifying such behavior with assumptions of racial superiority.

**indentured servants** Settlers who consented to work for a defined period of labor (often four to seven years) in exchange for having their passage to the New World paid by their "master."

**Independent Treasury Act (1840)** System created by President Martin Van Buren and approved by Congress in 1840 whereby the federal government moved its funds from favored state banks to the U.S. Treasury, whose financial transactions could only be in gold or silver coins of paper currency backed by gold or silver.

**"Indian New Deal"** This phrase refers to the reforms implemented for Native Americans during the New Deal era. John Collier, the commissioner of the Bureau of Indian Affairs (BIA), increased the access Native Americans had to relief programs and employed more Native Americans at the BIA. He worked to pass the Indian Reorganization Act. However, the version of the act passed by Congress was a much-diluted version of Collier's original proposal and did not greatly improve the lives of Native Americans.

**Indian Removal Act (1830)** Law permitting the forced relocation of Indians to federal lands west of the Mississippi River in exchange for the land they occupied in the East and South.

**Indian wars** Bloody conflicts between U.S. soldiers and Native Americans that raged in the West from the early 1860s to the late 1870s, sparked by American settlers moving into ancestral Indian lands.

**Indochina** This area of Southeast Asia consists of Laos, Cambodia, and Vietnam and was once controlled by France as a colony. After the Viet Minh defeated the French, the Geneva Accords were signed, which ended French colonial rule. The agreement created the independent nations of Laos and Cambodia and divided Vietnam along the 17th parallel until an election would reunify the country. Fearing a Communist take over, the United States government began intervening in the region during the Truman administration, which led to President Johnson's full-scale military involvement in Vietnam.

**industrialization** Major shift in the nineteenth century from handmade manufacturing to mass production in mills and factories using water-, coal-, and steam-powered machinery.

**Industrial Revolution** Major shift in the nineteenth century from hand-made manufacturing to mass production in mills and factories using water-, coal-, and steam-powered machinery.

**industrial war** A new concept of war enabled by industrialization that developed from the early 1800s through the Atomic Age. New technologies, including automatic weaponry, forms of transportation like the railroad and airplane, and communication technologies such as the telegraph and telephone, enabled nations to equip large, mass-conscripted armies with chemical and automatic weapons to decimate opposing armies in a "total war."

**Industrial Workers of the World (IWW)** A radical union organized in Chicago in 1905, nicknamed the Wobblies; its opposition to World War I led to its destruction by the federal government under the Espionage Act.

**infectious diseases** Also called contagious diseases, illnesses that can pass from one person to another by way of invasive biological organisms able to reproduce in the bodily tissues of their hosts. Europeans unwittingly brought many such diseases to the Americas, devastating the Native American peoples.

*The Influence of Sea Power upon History, 1660–1783* **(1890)** Historical work in which Rear Admiral Alfred Thayer Mahan argues that a nation's greatness and prosperity comes from the power of its navy; the book helped bolster imperialist sentiment in the United States in the late nineteenth century.

**Intermediate-Range Nuclear Forces (INF) Treaty (1987)** Agreement signed by U.S. president Ronald Reagan and Soviet premier Mikhail Gorbachev to eliminate the deployment of intermediate-range missiles with nuclear warheads.

**internal improvements** Construction of roads, bridges, canals, harbors, and other infrastructural projects intended to facilitate the flow of goods and people.

**internationalists** Prior to the United States' entry in World War II, internationalists believed that America's national security depended on aiding Britain in its struggle against Germany.

**Interstate Commerce Commission (ICC) (1887)** An independent federal agency established to oversee businesses engaged in interstate trade, especially railroads, but whose regulatory power was limited when tested in the courts.

**interstate highway system** In the late 1950s, construction began on a national network of interstate superhighways for the purpose of commerce and defense. The interstate highways would enable the rapid movement of military convoys and the evacuation of cities after a nuclear attack.

**Iran-Contra affair (1987)** Reagan administration scandal over the secret, unlawful U.S. sale of arms to Iran in partial exchange for the release of hostages in Lebanon; the arms money in turn was used illegally to aid Nicaraguan right-wing insurgents, the Contras.

**Iranian hostage crisis (1979)** Storming of the U.S. embassy in Tehran by Iranian revolutionaries, who held fifty-two Americans hostage for 444 days, despite President Carter's appeals for their release as well as a botched rescue attempt.

**Irish Potato Famine** In 1845, an epidemic of potato rot brought a famine to rural Ireland that killed over 1 million peasants and instigated a huge increase in the number of Irish immigrating to America. By 1850, the Irish made up 43 percent of the foreign-born population in the United States; and in the 1850s, they made up over half the population of New York City and Boston.

**iron curtain** Term coined by Winston Churchill to describe the cold war divide between western Europe and the Soviet Union's Eastern European satellites.

**Iroquois League** An alliance of the Iroquois tribes, originally formed sometime between 1450 and 1600, that used their combined strength to pressure Europeans to work with them in the fur trade and to wage war across what is today eastern North America.

**Andrew Jackson (1767–1837)** As a major general in the Tennessee militia, he had a number of military successes. As president, he worked to enable the "common man" to play a greater role in the political arena. He vetoed the re-chartering of the Second National Bank and reduced federal spending. When South Carolina nullified the Tariffs of 1828 and 1832, Jackson requested that Congress pass a "force bill" that would authorize him to use the army to compel the state to comply with the tariffs. He forced eastern Indians to move west of the Mississippi River so their lands could be used by white settlers. Groups of those who opposed Jackson come together to form a new political party called the Whigs.

**Thomas "Stonewall" Jackson (1824–1863)** A Confederate general who was known for his fearlessness in leading rapid marches, bold flanking movements, and furious assaults. He earned his nickname at the Battle of the First Bull Run for standing courageously against Union fire. During the battle of Chancellorsville, his own men accidentally mortally wounded him.

**William James (1842–1910)** He was the founder of Pragmatism and one of the fathers of modern psychology. He believed that ideas gained their validity not from their inherent truth, but from their social consequences and practical application.

**Jay's Treaty (1794)** Agreement between Britain and the United States, negotiated by Chief Justice John Jay, that settled disputes over trade, prewar debts owed to British merchants, British-occupied forts in American territory, and the seizure of American ships and cargo.

**Jazz Age** Term coined by writer F. Scott Fitzgerald to characterize the spirit of rebellion and spontaneity among young Americans in the 1920s, a spirit epitomized by the hugely popular jazz music of the era.

**Thomas Jefferson (1743–1826)** He was a plantation owner, author, the drafter of the Declaration Independence, ambassador to France, leader of the Republican party, secretary of state, and the third president of the United States. As president, he purchased the Louisiana territory from France, withheld appointments made by President Adams leading to *Marybury v. Madison*, outlawed foreign slave trade, and was committed to a "wise and frugal" government.

**Jeffersonian Republicans** Political party founded by Thomas Jefferson in opposition to the Federalist party led by Alexander Hamilton and John Adams; also known as the Democratic-Republican party.

**Jesuits** A religious order founded in 1540 by Ignatius Loyola. They sought to counter the spread of Protestantism during the Protestant Reformation and spread the Catholic faith through work as missionaries. Roughly 3,500 served in New Spain and New France.

**"Jim Crow" laws** In the New South, these laws mandated the separation of races in various public places that served as a way for the ruling whites to impose their will on all areas of black life.

**Andrew Johnson (1808–1875)** He was elevated to the presidency after Abraham Lincoln's assassination. In order to restore the Union after the Civil War, he issued an amnesty proclamation and required former Confederate states to ratify the Thirteenth Amendment. After disagreements over the power to restore states rights, the Radical Republicans attempted to impeach Johnson but fell short on the required number of votes needed to remove him from office.

**Lyndon B. Johnson (1908–1973)** Former member of the House of Representatives and the former Majority Leader of the Senate, Vice President Lyndon B. Johnson assumed the presidency after President Kennedy's assassination. During his presidency, he passed the Civil Rights Act of 1964, declared a "war on poverty" promoting his own social program called the Great Society, and signed the Immigration and Nationality Service Act of 1965. Johnson greatly increased America's role in Vietnam.

**Johnson's Restoration Plan** Plan to require southern states to ratify the Thirteenth Amendment, disqualify wealthy ex-Confederates from voting, and appoint a Unionist governor.

**joint-stock companies** Businesses owned by investors, who purchase shares of companies' stocks and share all the profits and losses.

**Kansas-Nebraska Act (1854)** Controversial legislation that created two new territories taken from Native Americans, Kansas and Nebraska, where residents would vote to decide whether slavery would be allowed (popular sovereignty).

**Florence Kelley (1859–1932)** As the head of the National Consumer's League, she led the crusade to promote state laws to regulate the number of working hours imposed on women who were wives and mothers.

**George F. Kennan (1904–2005)** While working as an American diplomat, he devised the strategy of containment, which called for the halting of Soviet expansion. It became America's choice strategy throughout the cold war.

**John F. Kennedy (1917–1963)** He was elected president in 1960. Despite the difficulties he had in getting his legislation through Congress, he established the Alliance for Progress programs to help Latin America, the Peace Corps, the Trade Expansion Act of 1962, and funding for urban renewal projects and the space program. His foreign political involvement included the failed Bay of Pigs invasion and the missile crisis in Cuba, as well as support of local governments in Indochina. In 1963, he was assassinated by Lee Harvey Oswald in Dallas, Texas.

**Kent State** During the spring of 1970, students on college campuses across the country protested the expansion of the Vietnam War into Cambodia. At Kent State University, the National Guard attempted to quell the rioting students. The guardsmen panicked and shot at rock-throwing demonstrators. Four student bystanders were killed.

**Kentucky and Virginia Resolutions (1798–1799)** Passed in response to the Alien and Sedition Acts, the resolutions advanced the state-compact theory that held states could nullify an act of Congress if they deemed it unconstitutional.

**Francis Scott Key (1779–1843)** During the War of 1812, he watched British forces bombard Fort McHenry, but fail to take it. Seeing the American flag still flying over the fort at dawn inspired him to write "The Star-Spangled Banner," which became the American national anthem.

**Martin Luther King Jr. (1929–1968)** A central leader of the civil rights movement, he urged people to use nonviolent civil disobedience to demand their rights and bring about change. He successfully led the Montgomery bus boycott. While in jail for his role in demonstrations, he wrote his famous "Letter from Birmingham City Jail," in which he defended his strategy of nonviolent protest. In 1963, he delivered his famous "I Have a Dream Speech" from the steps of the Lincoln Memorial as a part of the March on Washington. A year later, he was awarded the Nobel Peace Prize. In 1968, he was assassinated.

**King Philip's War** A bloody, three-year war in New England (1675–1676), resulting from the escalation of tensions between Indians and English settlers; the defeat of the Indians led to broadened freedoms for the settlers and their dispossessing the region's Indians of most of their land.

**King William's War (War of the League of Augsburg)** First (1689–1697) of four colonial wars between England and France.

**Henry Kissinger (1923–)** He served as the secretary of state and national security advisor in the Nixon administration. He negotiated with North Vietnam for an end to the Vietnam War, but the cease-fire did not last; South Vietnam fell to North Vietnam. He helped organize Nixon's historic trips to China and the Soviet Union. In the Middle East, he negotiated a cease-fire between Israel and its neighbors following the Yom

Kippur War and solidified Israel's promise to return to Egypt most of the land it had taken during the 1967 war.

**Knights of Labor** A national labor organization with a broad reform platform; reached peak membership in the 1880s.

**Know-Nothings** Nativist, anti-Catholic third party organized in 1854 in reaction to large-scale German and Irish immigration.

**Ku Klux Klan** Organized in Pulaski, Tennessee, in 1866 to terrorize former slaves who voted and held political offices during Reconstruction; a revived organization in the 1910s and 1920s stressed white, Anglo-Saxon, fundamentalist Protestant supremacy; the Klan revived a third time to fight the civil rights movement of the 1950s and 1960s in the South.

**Marquis de Lafayette (1757–1834)** A wealthy French idealist excited by the American cause, he offered to serve in Washington's army for free in exchange for being named a major general. He overcame Washington's initial skepticism to become one of his most trusted aides.

**laissez-faire** An economic doctrine holding that businesses and individuals should be able to pursue their economic interests without government interference.

**Land Ordinance of 1785** Directed surveying of the Northwest Territory into townships of thirty-six sections (square miles) each, the sale of the sixteenth section of which was to be used to finance public education.

**League of Nations** Organization of nations formed in the aftermath of the First World War to mediate disputes and maintain international peace; despite President Wilson's intense lobbying for the League of Nations, Congress did not ratify the treaty and the United States failed to join.

**Mary Elizabeth Lease (1850–1933)** She was a leader of the farm protest movement who advocated violence if change could not be obtained at the ballot box. She believed that the urban-industrial East was the enemy of the working class.

**Robert E. Lee (1807–1870)** Even though he had served in the United States Army for thirty years, he chose to fight on the side of the Confederacy. Lee was excellent at using his field commanders and his soldiers respected him. However, General Ulysses S. Grant eventually wore down his army, and Lee surrendered to Grant at the Appomattox Court House on April 9, 1865.

**Lend-Lease Act (1941)** Legislation that allowed the president to lend or lease military equipment to any country whose own defense was deemed vital to the defense of the United States.

**Levittown** First low-cost, mass-produced development of suburban tract housing built by William Levitt on Long Island, New York, in 1947.

**Lewis and Clark expedition (1804–1806)** Led by Meriwether Lewis and William Clark, a mission to the Pacific coast commissioned for the purposes of scientific and geographical exploration

**Battle of Lexington and Concord** The first shots fired in the Revolutionary War, on April 19, 1775, near Boston; approximately 100 Minutemen and 250 British soldiers were killed.

*Liberator* William Lloyd Garrison started this anti-slavery newspaper in 1831 in which he renounced gradualism and called for abolition.

**Queen Liliuokalani (1838–1917)** In 1891, she ascended to the throne of the Hawaiian royal family and tried to eliminate white control of the Hawaiian government. Two years later, Hawaii's white population revolted and seized power with the support of American Marines.

**Abraham Lincoln (1809–1865)** Shortly after he was elected president in 1860, southern states began seceding from the Union, and in April of 1861 he declared war on the seceding states. On January 1, 1863, Lincoln signed the Emancipation Proclamation. At the end of the war, he favored a reconstruction strategy for the former Confederate states that did not radically alter southern social and economic life. He was assassinated by John Wilkes Booth at Ford's Theater on April 14, 1865.

**Lincoln-Douglas debates (1858)** During the Illinois race between Republican Abraham Lincoln and Democrat Stephen A. Douglas for a seat in the U.S. Senate, a series of seven dramatic debates focusing on the issue of slavery in the territories.

**John Locke (1632–1704)** An English philosopher whose ideas were influential during the Enlightenment. He argued in his *Essay on Human Understanding* (1690) that humanity is largely the product of the environment, the mind being a blank tablet, *tabula rasa*, on which experience is written.

**Henry Cabot Lodge (1850–1924)** He was the chairman of the Senate Foreign Relations Committee who favored limiting America's involvement in the League of Nations' covenant and sought to amend the Treaty of Versailles.

**de Lôme letter (1898)** Private correspondence written by the Spanish ambassador to the U.S., Depuy de Lôme, that described President McKinley as "weak"; the letter was stolen by Cuban revolutionaries and published in the *New York Journal*, deepening American resentment of Spain and moving the two countries closer to war in Cuba.

**Lone Star Republic** After winning independence from Mexico, Texas became its own nation that was called the Lone Star Republic. In 1836, Texans drafted a constitution, legalized slavery, banned free blacks, named Sam Houston president, and voted for the annexation to the United States. However, quarrels over adding a slave state and fears of instigating a war with Mexico delayed Texas's entrance into the Union until December 29, 1845.

**Huey P. Long (1893–1935)** He began his political career in Louisiana where he developed a reputation for being an unscrupulous reformer. As a U.S. senator, he became a critic of President Roosevelt's New Deal Plan and offered his alternative called the Share-the-Wealth program. He was assassinated in 1935.

**Lost Cause narrative** Southern whites' view of secession as a noble "lost cause." A revisionist version of history that glamorized plantation culture and insisted that the Civil War had little to do with slavery and everything to do with a defense of states' rights from the Republican party and the "War of Northern Aggression."

**Lost Generation** Label given to modernist writers and authors, such as F. Scott Fitzgerald and Ernest Hemingway, who had lost faith in the values and institutions of Western civilization in the aftermath of the Great War.

**Louisiana Purchase (1803)** President Thomas Jefferson's purchase of the Louisiana Territory from France for $15 million, doubling the size of U.S. territory.

**Lowell system** Model New England factory communities that during the first half of the nineteenth century provided employees, mostly young women, with meals, a boardinghouse, and moral discipline, as well as educational and cultural opportunities.

**Loyalists** Colonists who remained loyal to Great Britain before and during the Revolutionary War.

***Lusitania*** British ocean liner torpedoed and sunk by a German U-boat in 1915; the deaths of nearly 1,200 of its civilian passengers, including many Americans, caused international outrage.

**Martin Luther (1483–1546)** A German monk who founded the Lutheran church. He protested abuses in the Catholic Church by posting his Ninety-five Theses, which began the Protestant Reformation.

**General Douglas MacArthur (1880–1964)** During World War II, he and Admiral Chester Nimitz dislodged the Japanese military from the Pacific Islands they had occupied. Following the war, he was in charge of the occupation of Japan. After North Korea invaded South Korea, Truman sent the U.S. military to defend South Korea under the command of MacArthur. Later in the war, Truman expressed his willingness to negotiate the restoration of prewar boundaries which MacArthur attempted to undermine. Truman fired MacArthur for his open insubordination.

**James Madison (1751–1836)** He participated in the Constitutional Convention during which he proposed the Virginia Plan. He believed in a strong federal government and was a leader of the Federalists. However, he also presented to Congress the Bill of Rights and drafted the Virginia Resolutions. As secretary of state, he withheld a commission for William Marbury, which led to the landmark *Marbury v. Madison* decision. During his presidency, he declared war on Britain in response to violations of American shipping rights, which started the War of 1812.

**U.S. battleship *Maine*** American warship that exploded in the Cuban port of Havana on January 25, 1898; though later discovered to be the result of an accident, the destruction of the *Maine* was attributed by war-hungry Americans to Spain, contributing to the onset of the War of 1898.

**maize (corn)** The primary grain crop in Mesoamerica yielding small kernels often ground into cornmeal. Easy to grow in a broad range of conditions, it enabled a global population explosion after being brought to Europe, Africa, and Asia.

**Malcolm X (1925–1964)** The most articulate spokesman for black power. Originally the chief disciple of Elijah Muhammad, the black Muslim leader in the United States, Malcolm X broke away and founded his own organization committed to establishing relations between African Americans and the nonwhite peoples of the world. Near the end of his life, he began to preach a biracial message of social change. In 1964, he was assassinated by members of a rival group of black Muslims.

**Manchuria incident** The northeast region of Manchuria was an area contested between China and Russia. In 1931, the Japanese claimed that they needed to protect their extensive investments in the area and moved their army into Manchuria. They quickly conquered the region and set up their own puppet empire. China asked both the United States and the League of Nations for help and neither responded.

**manifest destiny** The widespread belief that America was "destined" by God to expand westward across the continent into lands claimed by Native Americans as well as European nations.

**Horace Mann (1796–1859)** He believed the public school system was the best way to achieve social stability and equal opportunity. As a reformer of education, he sponsored a state board of education, the first state-supported "normal" school for training teachers, a state association for teachers, the minimum school year of six months, and led the drive for a statewide school system.

***Marbury v. Madison* (1803)** First Supreme Court decision to declare a federal law—the Judiciary Act of 1801—unconstitutional.

**March on Washington** Civil rights demonstration on August 28, 1963, on the National Mall, where Martin Luther King Jr. gave his famous "I Have a Dream" speech.

**March to the Sea (1864)** The Union army's devastating march through Georgia from Atlanta to Savannah led by General William T. Sherman, intended to demoralize civilians and destroy the resources the Confederate army needed to fight.

**market-based economy** Large-scale manufacturing and commercial agriculture that emerged in America during the first half of the nineteenth century, displacing much of the premarket subsistence and barter-based economy and producing boom-and-bust cycles while raising the American standard of living.

**marriage equality** The legal right for gay and lesbian couples to marry; it became the most divisive issue in the culture wars of the early 2010s as more and more court rulings affirmed this right in states and municipalities across the United States. The 2015 Supreme Court case *Obergefell v. Hodges* affirmed the right to same-sex marriage, also known as marriage equality, nationally.

**George C. Marshall (1880–1959)** As the chairman of the Joint Chiefs of Staff, he orchestrated the Allied victories over Germany and Japan in the Second World War. In 1947, he became President Truman's secretary of state and proposed the massive reconstruction program for western Europe called the Marshall Plan.

**Chief Justice John Marshall (1755–1835)** During his long tenure as chief justice of the supreme court (1801–1835), he established the foundations for American jurisprudence, the authority of the Supreme Court, and the constitutional supremacy of the national government over states.

**Marshall Plan (1948)** Secretary of State George C. Marshall's post–World War II program providing massive U.S. financial and technical assistance to war-torn European countries.

**Massachusetts Bay Colony** English colony founded by English Puritans in 1630 as a haven for persecuted Congregationalists.

**massive resistance** White rallying cry disrupting federal efforts to enforce racial integration in the South.

**massive retaliation** Strategy that used the threat of nuclear warfare as a means of combating the global spread of communism.

**Mayflower Compact** A formal agreement signed by the Separatist colonists aboard the *Mayflower* in 1620 to abide by laws made by leaders of their own choosing.

**Senator Joseph R. McCarthy (1908–1957)** In 1950, this senator became the shrewdest and most ruthless exploiter of America's anxiety of communism. He claimed that the United States government was full of Communists and led a witch hunt to find them, but he was never able to uncover a single communist agent.

**McCarthyism** Anti-Communist hysteria led by Senator Joseph McCarthy's "witch hunts" attacking the loyalty of politicians, federal employees, and public figures, despite a lack of evidence.

**George B. McClellan (1826–1885)** In 1861, President Abraham Lincoln appointed him head of the Army of the Potomac and, later, general in chief of the U.S. Army. He built his army into well trained and powerful force. After failing to achieve a decisive victory against the Confederacy, he was removed from command in 1862.

**Cyrus Hall McCormick (1809–1884)** In 1831, he invented a mechanical reaper to harvest wheat, which transformed the scale of agriculture. By hand a farmer could only harvest a half an acre a day, while the McCormick reaper allowed two people to harvest twelve acres of wheat a day.

**McCormick reaper** Mechanical reaper invented by Cyrus Hall McCormick in 1831 that dramatically increased the production of wheat.

**McCulloch v. Maryland (1819)** Supreme Court ruling that prohibited states from taxing the Bank of the United States.

**William McKinley (1843–1901)** As a congressman, he was responsible for the McKinley Tariff of 1890, which raised the duties on manufactured products to their highest level ever. Voters disliked the tariff and McKinley, as well as other Republicans, lost his seat in Congress the next election. However, he won the presidential election of 1896 and raised the tariffs again. In 1898, he annexed Hawaii and declared war on Spain. The war concluded with the Treaty of Paris, which gave America control over Puerto Rico, Guam, and the Philippines. Soon America was fighting Filipinos, who were seeking independence for their country. In 1901, McKinley was assassinated.

**Robert McNamara (1916–)** He was the secretary of defense for both President Kennedy and President Johnson and a supporter of America's involvement in Vietnam.

**Medicare and Medicaid** Health-care programs designed to aid the elderly and disadvantaged, respectively, as part of President Johnson's Great Society initiative.

**Andrew W. Mellon (1855–1937)** As President Harding's secretary of the Treasury, he sought to generate economic growth through reducing government spending and lowering taxes. However, he insisted that the tax reductions mainly go to the rich because he believed the wealthy would reinvest their money. In order to bring greater efficiency and nonpartisanship to the government's budget process, he persuaded Congress to created a new Bureau of the Budget and a General Accounting Office.

**mercantilism** Policy of Great Britain and other imperial powers of regulating the economies of colonies to benefit the mother country.

**James Meredith (1933–)** In 1962, the governor of Mississippi defied a Supreme Court ruling and refused to allow James Meredith, an African American, to enroll at the University of Mississippi. Federal marshals were sent to enforce the law which led to clashes between a white mob and the marshals. Federal troops intervened and two people were killed and many others were injured. A few days later, Meredith was able to register at the university.

***Merrimack* (ship renamed the *Virginia*) and the *Monitor*** First engagement between ironclad ships; fought at Hampton Roads, Virginia, on March 9, 1862.

**Metacomet or King Philip (?–1676)** The chief of the Wampanoages, who the colonists called King Philip. He resented English efforts to convert Indians to Christianity and waged a war against the English colonists in which he was killed.

**Mexica** Otherwise known as "Aztecs," a Mesoamerican people of northern Mexico who founded the vast Aztec Empire in the fourteenth century, later conquered by the Spanish under Hernán Cortés in 1521.

**microprocessor** An electronic circuit printed on a small silicon chip; a major technological breakthrough in 1971, it paved the way for the development of the personal computer.

**Middle Passage** The hellish and often deadly middle leg of the transatlantic "Triangular Trade" in which European ships carried manufactured goods to Africa, then transported enslaved Africans to the Americas and the Caribbean, and finally conveyed American agricultural products back to Europe; from the late sixteenth to the early nineteenth centuries, some 12 million Africans were transported via the Middle Passage, unknown millions more dying en route.

**Battle of Midway** A 1942 battle that proved to be a turning point in the Pacific front during World War II; it was the Japanese navy's first major defeat in 350 years.

**militant nonviolence** After the success of the Montgomery bus boycott, people were inspired by Martin Luther King Jr.'s use of this nonviolent form of protest. Throughout the civil rights movement, demonstrators used this method of protest to challenge racial segregation in the South.

**Militia Act (1862)** Congressional measure that permitted freed slaves to serve as laborers or soldiers in the United States Army.

**Ho Chi Minh (1890–1969)** He was the Vietnamese communist resistance leader who drove the French and the United States out of Vietnam. After the Geneva Accords divided the region into four countries, he controlled North Vietnam, and ultimately became the leader of all of Vietnam at the conclusion of the Vietnam War.

**minstrelsy** A form of entertainment that was popular from the 1830s to the 1870s. The performances featured white performers who were made up as African Americans or blackface. They performed banjo and fiddle music, "shuffle" dances and lowbrow humor that reinforced racial stereotypes.

**Minutemen** Special units organized by the militia to be ready for quick mobilization.

*Miranda v. Arizona* **(1966)** U.S. Supreme Court decision required police to advise persons in custody of their rights to legal counsel and against self-incrimination.

**Mississippi Plan (1890)** Series of state constitutional amendments that sought to severely disenfranchise black voters and were quickly adopted by other southern states.

**Missouri Compromise (1820)** Legislative decision to admit Missouri as a slave state and abolish slavery in the area west of the Mississippi River and north of the parallel 36°30′.

**Model T Ford** Henry Ford developed this model of car so that it was affordable for everyone. Its success led to an increase in the production of automobiles which stimulated other related industries such steel, oil, and rubber. The mass use of automobiles increased the speed goods could be transported, encouraged urban sprawl, and sparked real estate booms in California and Florida.

**moderate Republicanism** Promise to curb federal government and restore state and local government authority, spearheaded by President Eisenhower.

**modernism** An early-twentieth-century intellectual and artistic movement that rejected traditional notions of reality and adopted radical new forms of artistic expression.

**money problem** Late-nineteenth-century national debate over the nature of U.S. currency; supporters of a fixed gold standard were generally money lenders, and thus preferred to keep the value of money high, while supporters of silver (and gold) coinage were debtors, they owed money, so they wanted to keep the value of money low by increasing the currency supply (inflation).

**monopoly** A corporation so large that it effectively controls the entire market for its products or services.

**James Monroe (1758–1831)** He served as secretary of state and war under President Madison and was elected president. As the latter, he signed the Transcontinental Treaty with Spain which gave the United States Florida and expanded the Louisiana territory's western border to the Pacific coast. In 1823, he established the Monroe Doctrine. This foreign policy proclaimed the American continents were no longer open to colonization and America would be neutral in European affairs.

**Monroe Doctrine (1823)** U.S. foreign policy that barred further colonization in the Western Hemisphere by European powers and pledged that there would be no American interference with any existing European colonies.

**Montgomery bus boycott (1955–1956)** Boycott of bus system in Montgomery, Alabama, organized by civil rights activists after the arrest of Rosa Parks.

**Moral Majority** Televangelist Jerry Falwell's political lobbying organization, the name of which became synonymous with the Religious Right—conservative evangelical Protestants who helped ensure President Ronald Reagan's 1980 victory.

**J. Pierpont Morgan (1837–1913)** As a powerful investment banker, he would acquire, reorganize, and consolidate companies into giant trusts. His biggest achievement was the consolidation of the steel industry into the United States Steel Corporation, which was the first billion-dollar corporation.

**J. Pierpont Morgan and Company** An investment bank under the leadership of J. Pierpont Morgan that bought or merged unrelated American companies, often using capital acquired from European investors.

**Mormons** Members of the Church of Jesus Christ of Latter-day Saints, which dismissed other Christian denominations, emphasizing universal salvation and a modest lifestyle; Mormons were often persecuted for their secrecy and clannishness.

**Morrill Land Grant College Act (1862)** Federal statute that allowed for the creation of land-grant colleges and universities, which were founded to provide technical education in agriculture, mining, and industry.

**Samuel F. B. Morse (1791–1872)** In 1832, he invented the telegraph and revolutionized the speed of communication.

**mountain men** Inspired by the fur trade, these men left civilization to work as trappers and reverted to a primitive existence in the wilderness. They were the first white people to find routes through the Rocky Mountains, and they pioneered trails that settlers later used to reach the Oregon country and California in the 1840s.

**muckrakers** Writers who exposed corruption and abuses in politics, business, consumer safety, working conditions, and more, spurring public interest in progressive reforms.

**Mugwumps** Reformers who bolted from the Republican party in 1884 to support Democratic Grover Cleveland for president over Republican James G. Blaine, whose secret dealings on behalf of railroad companies had brought charges of corruption.

**mulattoes** Mixed-race people who constituted most of the South's free black population.

**Benito Mussolini (1883–1945)** The Italian founder of the Fascist party who came to power in Italy in 1922 and allied himself with Adolf Hitler and the Axis powers during the Second World War.

**National Association for the Advancement of Colored People (NAACP)** Organization founded in 1910 by black activists and white progressives that promoted education as a means of combating social problems and focused on legal action to secure the civil rights supposedly guaranteed by the Fourteenth and Fifteenth Amendments.

**National Banking Act (1863)** The U.S. Congress created a national banking system to finance the enormous expense of the Civil War. It enabled loans to the government and established a single national currency, including the issuance of paper money ("greenbacks").

**National Industrial Recovery Act (1933)** Passed on the last of the Hundred Days; it created public-works jobs through the Federal Emergency Relief Administration and established a system of self-regulation for industry through the National Recovery Administration, which was ruled unconstitutional in 1935.

**National Labor Union (NLU)** A federation of labor and reform leaders established in 1866 to advocate for new state and local laws to improve working conditions.

**National Recovery Administration (NRA) (1933)** Controversial federal agency that brought together business and labor leaders to create "codes of fair competition" and "fair labor" policies, including a national minimum wage.

**National Security Act (1947)** Congressional legislation that created the Department of Defense, the National Security Council, and the Central Intelligence Agency.

**National Socialist German Workers' Party (Nazi)** Founded in the 1920s, this party gained control over Germany under the leadership of Adolf Hitler in 1933 and continued in power until Germany's defeat at the end of the Second World War. It advocated a violent anti-Semitic, anti-Marxist, pan-German ideology. The Nazi party perpetrated the Holocaust.

**National Trades' Unions** Formed in 1834 to organize all local trade unions into a stronger national association, only to be dissolved amid the economic depression during the late 1830s.

**nativism** Reactionary conservative movement characterized by heightened nationalism, anti-immigrant sentiment, and the enactment of laws setting stricter regulations on immigration.

**nativists** Members of a reactionary conservative movement characterized by heightened nationalism, anti-immigrant sentiment, and the enactment of laws setting stricter regulations on immigration.

**natural rights** An individual's basic rights that should not be violated by any government or community.

**Navigation Acts (1650–1775)** Restrictions passed by the British Parliament to control colonial trade and bolster the mercantile system.

**Negrophobia** A violent new wave of racism that spread in the late nineteenth century largely spurred by white resentment for African American financial success and growing political influence.

**neutrality laws** Series of laws passed by Congress aimed at avoiding entering a Second World War; these included the Neutrality Act of 1935, which banned loans to warring nations.

**new conservatism** The political philosophy of those who led the conservative insurgency of the early 1980s. This brand of conservatism was personified in Ronald Reagan who believed in less government, supply-side economics, and "family values."

**New Democrats** Centrist ("moderate") Democrats led by President Bill Clinton that emerged in the late 1980s and early 1990s to challenge the "liberal" direction of the party.

**"new economy"** Period of sustained economic prosperity during the nineties marked by budget surpluses, the explosion of dot.com industries, low inflation, and low unemployment.

**New France** The name used for the area of North America that was colonized by the French. Unlike Spanish or English colonies, New France had a small number of colonists, which forced them to initially seek good relations with the indigenous people they encountered.

**New Freedom** Program championed in 1912 by the Woodrow Wilson campaign that aimed to restore competition in the economy by eliminating all trusts rather than simply regulating them.

**New Frontier** Proposed domestic program championed by the incoming Kennedy administration in 1961 that aimed to jump-start the economy and trigger social progress.

**new immigrants** Wave of newcomers from southern and eastern Europe, including many Jews, who became a majority among immigrants to America after 1890.

**New Jersey Plan** The delegations to the Constitutional Convention were divided between two plans on how to structure the government: New Jersey wanted one legislative body with equal representation for each state.

**New Left** Term coined by the Students for a Democratic Society to distinguish their efforts at grassroots democracy from those of the 1930s Old Left, which had embraced orthodox Marxism.

**New Mexico** A U.S. territory and later a state in the American Southwest, originally established by the Spanish, who settled there in the sixteenth century, founded Catholic missions, and exploited the region's indigenous peoples.

**New Nationalism** Platform of the Progressive party and slogan of former President Theodore Roosevelt in the presidential campaign of 1912; stressed government activism, including regulation of trusts, conservation, and recall of state court decisions that had nullified progressive programs.

**"New Negro"** In the 1920s, a slow and steady growth of black political influence occurred in northern cities where African Americans were freer to speak and act. This political activity created a spirit of protest that expressed itself culturally in the Harlem Renaissance and politically in "new Negro" nationalism.

**New Netherland** Dutch colony conquered by the English in 1667 and out of which four new colonies were created—New York, New Jersey, Pennsylvania, and Delaware.

**Battle of New Orleans (1815)** Final major battle in the War of 1812, in which the Americans under General Andrew Jackson unexpectedly and decisively countered the British attempt to seize the port of New Orleans, Louisiana.

**New South** *Atlanta Constitution* editor Henry W. Grady's 1886 term for the prosperous post–Civil War South: democratic, industrial, urban, and free of nostalgia for the defeated plantation South.

**New York Journal** In the late 1890s, William Randolph Hearst's *New York Journal* and its rival, the *New York World*, printed sensationalism on the Cuban revolution as part of their heated competition for readership. The *New York Journal* printed a negative letter from the Spanish ambassador about President McKinley and inflammatory coverage of the sinking of the *Maine* in Havana Harbor. These two events roused the American public's outcry against Spain.

***New York World*** In the late 1890s, Joseph Pulitzer's *New York World* and its rival, the *New York Journal*, printed sensationalism on the Cuban revolution as part of their heated competition for readership.

**Admiral Chester Nimitz (1885–1966)** During the Second World War, he was the commander of central Pacific. Along with General Douglas MacArthur, he dislodged the Japanese military from the Pacific Islands they had occupied.

**Nineteenth Amendment (1920)** Constitutional amendment that granted women the right to vote.

**Richard M. Nixon (1913–1994)** He first came to national prominence as a congress-man involved in the investigation of Alger Hiss, and later served as vice president during the Eisenhower administration. After being elected president in 1968, he slowed the federal enforcement of civil rights and appointed pro-Southern justices to the Supreme Court. He began a program of Vietnamization of the war. In 1973, America, North and South Vietnam, and the Viet Cong agreed to end the war and the United States withdrew. However, the cease-fire was broken, and the South Vietnam fell to North Vietnam. In 1970, Nixon declared that America was no longer the world's policeman and he would seek some partnerships with Communist countries, historically traveling to China and the Soviet Union. In 1972, he was reelected, but the Watergate scandal erupted shortly after his victory; he resigned the presidency under threat of impeachment.

**No Child Left Behind** President George W. Bush's education reform plan that required states to set and meet learning standards for students and make sure that all students were "proficient" in reading and writing by 2014. States had to submit annual reports of students' standardized test scores. Teachers were required to be "proficient" in their subject area. Schools who failed to show progress would face sanctions. States criticized the lack of funding for remedial programs and noted that poor school districts would find it very difficult to meet the new guidelines.

**nonviolent civil disobedience** Tactic of defying unjust laws through peaceful actions championed by Dr. Martin Luther King Jr.

**Lord North (1732–1792)** The first minister of King George III's cabinet whose efforts to subdue the colonies only brought them closer to revolution. He helped bring about the Tea Act of 1773, which led to the Boston Tea Party. In an effort to discipline Boston, he wrote, and Parliament passed, four acts that galvanized colonial resistance.

**North American Free Trade Agreement (NAFTA) (1994)** Agreement eliminating trade barriers that was signed by the United States, Canada, and Mexico, making North America the largest free-trade zone in the world.

**North Atlantic Treaty Organization (NATO)** Defensive alliance founded in 1949 by ten western European nations, the United States, and Canada to deter Soviet expansion in Europe.

**Northwest Ordinance (1787)** Land policy for new western territories in the Ohio Valley that established the terms and conditions for self-government and statehood while also banning slavery from the region.

**NSC-68 (1950)** Top-secret policy paper approved by President Truman that outlined a militaristic approach to combating the spread of global communism.

**nullification** The right claimed by some states to veto a federal law deemed unconstitutional.

**Nuremberg trials** At the site of the annual Nazi party rallies, twenty-one major German offenders faced an international military tribunal for Nazi atrocities. After a ten-month trial, the court acquitted three and sentenced eleven to death, three to life imprisonment, and four to shorter terms.

**Barack Obama (1961–)** In the 2008 presidential election, Senator Barack Obama mounted an innovative Internet based and grassroots orientated campaign. As the nation's economy nose-dived in the fall of 2008, Obama linked the Republican economic philosophy with the country's dismal financial state and promoted a message of "change" and "politics of hope," which resonated with voters. He decisively won the presidency and became America's first person of color to be elected president. In 2012, Obama successfully won re-election to serve as president for a second term.

**Occupy Wall Street** A grassroots movement protesting a capitalist system that fostered social and economic inequality. Begun in Zuccotti Park, New York City, during 2011, the movement spread rapidly across the nation, triggering a national conversation about income inequality and protests of the government's "bailouts" of the banks and corporations allegedly responsible for the Great Recession.

**Sandra Day O'Connor (1930–)** She was the first woman to serve on the Supreme Court of the United States and was appointed by President Reagan. Reagan's critics charged that her appointment was a token gesture and not a sign of any real commitment to gender equality.

**Ohio gang** In order to escape the pressures of the White House, President Harding met with a group of people, called the "Ohio gang," in a house on K Street in Washington D.C. Members of this gang were given low-level positions in the American government and they used their White House connection to "line their pockets" by granting government contracts without bidding, which led to a series of scandals, most notably the Teapot Dome Scandal.

**Old Southwest** Region covering western Georgia, Alabama, Mississippi, Louisiana, Arkansas, and Texas, where low land prices and fertile soil attracted hundreds of thousands of settlers after the American Revolution.

**Frederick Law Olmsted (1822–1903)** In 1858, he constructed New York's Central Park, which led to a growth in the movement to create urban parks. He went on to design parks for Boston, Brooklyn, Chicago, Philadelphia, San Francisco, and many other cities.

**Open Door policy (1899)** Official U.S. insistence that Chinese trade would be open to all nations; Secretary of State John Hay unilaterally announced the policy in hopes of protecting the Chinese market for U.S. exports.

**open range** Informal system of governing property on the frontier in which small ranchers could graze their cattle anywhere on unfenced lands; brought to an end by the introduction of barbed wire, a low-cost way to fence off one's land.

**open shop** Business policy of not requiring union membership as a condition of employment; such a policy, where legal, has the effect of weakening unions and diminishing workers' rights.

**Operation Desert Shield** After Saddam Hussein invaded Kuwait in 1990, President George H. W. Bush sent American military forces to Saudi Arabia on a strictly defensive mission. They were soon joined by a multinational coalition. When the coalition's mission changed to the retaking of Kuwait, the operation was renamed Desert Storm.

**Operation Desert Storm (1991)** Assault by American-led multinational forces that quickly defeated Iraqi forces under Saddam Hussein in the First Gulf War, ending the Iraqi occupation of Kuwait.

**Operation Overlord** The Allies' assault on Hitler's "Atlantic Wall," a seemingly impregnable series of fortifications and minefields along the French coastline that German forces had created using captive Europeans for laborers.

**J. Robert Oppenheimer (1904–1967)** He led the group of physicists at the laboratory in Los Alamos, New Mexico, who constructed the first atomic bomb.

**Oregon Country** The Convention of 1818 between Britain and the United States established the Oregon Country as being west of the crest of the Rocky Mountains and the two countries were to jointly occupy it. In 1824, the United States and Russia signed a treaty that established the line of 54°40′ as the southern boundary of Russia's territorial claim in North America. A similar agreement between Britain and Russia finally gave the Oregon Country clearly defined boarders, but it remained under joint British and American control.

**Oregon fever** The lure of fertile land and economic opportunities in the Oregon Country that drew thousands of settlers westward, beginning in the late 1830s.

**Osceola (1804?–1838)** He was the leader of the Seminole nation who resisted the federal Indian removal policy through a protracted guerilla war. In 1837, he was treacherously seized under a flag of truce and imprisoned at Fort Moultrie, where he was left to die.

**Overland Trails** Trail routes followed by wagon trains bearing settlers and trade goods from Missouri to the Oregon Country, California, and New Mexico, beginning in the 1840s.

**Pacific Railway Act (1862)** Congress provided funding for a transcontinental railroad from Nebraska west to California.

**A. Mitchell Palmer (1872–1936)** As the attorney general, he played an active role in the government's response to the Red Scare. After several bombings across America, including one at Palmer's home, he and other Americans became convinced that there was a well-organized Communist terror campaign at work. The federal government launched a campaign of raids, deportations, and collecting files on radical individuals.

**Panic of 1819** A financial panic that began a three-year-long economic crisis triggered by a reduced demand of American imports, declining land values, and reckless practices by local and state banks.

**Panic of 1837** A financial calamity in the United States brought on by a dramatic slowdown in the British economy and falling cotton prices, failed crops, high inflation, and reckless state banks.

**Panic of 1873** A financial calamity in the United States brought on by a dramatic slowdown in the British economy and exacerbated by falling cotton prices, failed crops, high inflation, and reckless state banks.

**Panic of 1893** A major collapse in the national economy after several major railroad companies declared bankruptcy, leading to a severe depression and several violent clashes between workers and management.

**panning** A method of mining that used a large metal pan to sift gold dust and nuggets from riverbeds during the California gold rush of 1849.

**Rosa Parks (1913–2005)** In 1955, she refused to give up her seat to a white man on a city bus in Montgomery, Alabama, which a local ordinance required of blacks. She was arrested for disobeying the ordinance. In response, black community leaders organized the Montgomery bus boycott.

**Parliament** Legislature of Great Britain, composed of the House of Commons, whose members are elected, and the House of Lords, whose members are either hereditary or appointed.

**party "boss"** A powerful political leader who controlled a "machine" of associates and operatives to promote both individual and party interests, often using informal tactics such as intimidation or the patronage system.

**paternalism** A moral position developed during the first half of the nineteenth century which claimed that slaves were deprived of liberty for their own "good." Such a rationalization was adopted by some slave owners to justify slavery.

**Patriots** Colonists who rebelled against British authority before and during the Revolutionary War.

**patronage** An informal system (sometimes called the "spoils system") used by politicians to reward their supporters with government appointments or contracts.

**Alice Paul (1885–1977)** She was a leader of the women's suffrage movement and head of the Congressional Committee of National Women Suffrage Association. She instructed female suffrage activists to use more militant tactics, such as picketing state legislatures, chaining themselves to public buildings, inciting police to arrest them, and undertaking hunger strikes.

**Norman Vincent Peale (1898–1993)** He was a champion of the upbeat and feel-good theology that was popular in the 1950s religious revival. He advocated getting rid of any depressing or negative thoughts and replacing them with "faith, enthusiasm and joy," which would make an individual popular and well liked.

**Pearl Harbor (1941)** Surprise Japanese attack on the U.S. fleet at Pearl Harbor on December 7, which prompted the immediate American entry into the war.

**peculiar institution** A phrase used by whites in the antebellum South to refer to slavery without using the word slavery.

**Pentagon Papers** Informal name for the Defense Department's secret history of the Vietnam conflict; leaked to the press by former official Daniel Ellsberg and published in the *New York Times* in 1971.

**People's party (Populists)** Political party largely made up of farmers from the South and West that struggled to gain political influence from the East. Populists advocated a variety of reforms, including free coinage of silver, a progressive income tax, postal savings banks, regulation of railroads, and direct election of U.S. senators.

**Pequot War** Massacre in 1637 and subsequent dissolution of the Pequot Nation by Puritan settlers, who seized the Indians' lands.

*perestroika* Russian term for "economic restructuring"; applied to Mikhail Gorbachev's series of political and economic reforms that included shifting a centrally planned Commmunist economy to a mixed economy allowing for capitalism.

**Commodore Matthew Perry (1794–1858)** In 1854, he negotiated the Treaty of Kanagawa, which was the first step in starting a political and commercial relationship between the United States and Japan.

**John J. Pershing** United States general sent by President Wilson to put down attacks on the Mexican border led by Francisco "Pancho" Villa.

**Personal Responsibility and Work Opportunity Act of 1996 (PRWOA)** Comprehensive welfare-reform measure, passed by a Republican Congress and signed by President Clinton, that aimed to decrease the size of the "welfare state" by limiting the amount of government aid provided the unemployed so as to encourage recipients to find jobs.

**"pet banks"** During President Andrew Jackson's fight with the national bank, Jackson resolved to remove all federal deposits from it. To comply with Jackson's demands, Secretary of the Treasury Taney continued to draw on government's accounts in the national bank, but deposit all new federal receipts in state banks. The state banks that received these deposits were called "pet banks."

**Pilgrims** Puritan Separatists who broke completely with the Church of England and sailed to the New World aboard the *Mayflower*, founding Plymouth Colony on Cape Cod in 1620.

**Dien Bien Phu** Cluster of Vietnamese villages and site of a major Vietnamese victory over the French in the First Indochina War.

**Gifford Pinchot (1865–1946)** As the head of the Division of Forestry, he implemented a conservation policy that entailed the scientific management of natural resources to serve the public interest. His work helped start the conservation movement.

**Elizabeth Lucas Pinckney (1722? –1793)** One of the most enterprising horticulturists in colonial America, she began managing her family's three plantations in South Carolina at the age of sixteen. She had tremendous success growing indigo, which led to many other plantations growing the crop as well.

**Pinckney's Treaty** Treaty with Spain negotiated by Thomas Pinckney in 1795; established United States boundaries at the Mississippi River and the 31st parallel and allowed open transportation on the Mississippi.

**Francisco Pizarro (1478?–1541)** In 1531, he lead his Spanish soldiers to Peru and conquered the Inca Empire.

**plain white folk** Yeoman farmers who lived and worked on their own small farms, growing a food and cash crops to trade for necessities.

**plantation mistress** Matriarch of a planter's household, responsible for supervising the domestic aspects of the estate.

**planters** Owners of large farms in the South that were worked by twenty or more slaves and supervised by overseers.

**political "machine"** A network of political activists and elected officials, usually controlled by a powerful "boss," that attempts to manipulate local politics

**James Knox Polk "Young Hickory" (1795–1849)** As president, his chief concern was the expansion of the United States. Shortly, after taking office, Mexico broke off relations with the United States over the annexation of Texas. Polk declared war on Mexico and sought to subvert Mexican authority in California. The United States defeated Mexico; and the two nations signed the Treaty of Guadalupe Hidalgo in which Mexico gave up any claims on Texas north of the Rio Grande River and ceded New Mexico and California to the United States.

**Pontiac's Rebellion (1763)** An Indian attack on British forts and settlements after France ceded to the British its territory east of the Mississippi River, as part of the Treaty of Paris, without consulting France's Indian allies.

**popular sovereignty** Legal concept by which the white male settlers in a new U.S. territory would vote to decide whether or not to permit slavery.

**Populist/People's party** Political success of Farmers' Alliance candidates encouraged the formation in 1892 of the People's party (later renamed the Populist party); active until 1912, it advocated a variety of reform issues, including free coinage of silver, income tax, postal savings, regulation of railroads, and direct election of U.S. senators.

**Pottawatomie Massacre** In retaliation for the "sack of Lawrence," John Brown and his abolitionist cohorts hacked five men to death in the pro-slavery settlement of Pottawatomie, Kansas, on May 24, 1856, triggering a guerrilla war in the Kansas Territory that cost 200 settler lives.

**Powhatan Confederacy** An alliance of several powerful Algonquian tribes under the leadership of Chief Powhatan, organized into thirty chiefdoms along much of the Atlantic coast in the late sixteenth and early seventeenth centuries.

**Chief Powhatan Wahunsonacock** He was called Powhatan by the English after the name of his tribe, and was the powerful, charismatic chief of numerous Algonquian-speaking towns in eastern Virginia representing over 10,000 Indians.

**pragmatism** William James founded this philosophy in the early 1900s. Pragmatists believed that ideas gained their validity not from their inherent truth, but from their social consequences and practical application.

**professions** Occupations requiring specialized knowledge of some field; the Industrial Revolution and its new organization of labor created an array of professions in the nineteenth century.

**Progressive party** In the 1912 election, Theodore Roosevelt was unable to secure the Republican nomination for president. He left the Republican party and formed his own party of progressive Republicans, called the "Bull Moose" party (later Progressive party). Roosevelt and Taft split the Republican vote, which allowed Democrat Woodrow Wilson to win.

**progressivism** A sometimes grassroots and sometimes elite-driven national movement for social and political reforms that called for more government regulation of business, supported by elements of both major political parties during the Progressive Era (1890–1920).

**Prohibition** National ban on the manufacture and sale of alcohol that lasted from 1920 to 1933, though the law was widely violated and proved too difficult to enforce effectively.

**proprietary colonies** A colony owned by an individual, rather than a joint-stock company.

**Protestant Reformation** Sixteenth-century religious movement initiated by Martin Luther, a German monk whose public criticism of corruption in the Roman Catholic Church, and whose teaching that Christians can communicate directly with God, gained a wide following.

*pueblos* The Spanish term for the adobe cliff dwellings of the indigenous people of the southwestern United States.

**Pullman strike (1894)** A national strike by the American Railway Union, whose members shut down major railways in sympathy with striking workers in Pullman, Illinois; ended with intervention of federal troops.

**Puritans** English religious dissenters who sought to "purify" the Church of England of its Catholic practices.

**Quakers** George Fox founded the Quaker religion in 1647. They rejected the use of formal sacraments and ministry, refused to take oaths and embraced pacifism. Fleeing persecution, they settled and established the colony of Pennsylvania.

**race-based slavery** Institution that uses racial characteristics and myths to justify enslaving a people.

**Radical Republicans** Senators and congressmen who, strictly identifying the Civil War with the abolitionist cause, sought swift emancipation of the slaves, punishment of the rebels, and tight controls over the former Confederate states after the war.

**railroads** Steam-powered vehicles that improved passenger transportation, quickened western settlement, and enabled commercial agriculture in the nineteenth century.

**Raleigh's Roanoke Island Colony** English expedition of 117 settlers, including Virginia Dare, the first English child born in the New World; colony disappeared from Roanoke Island in the Outer Banks sometime between 1587 and 1590.

**A. Philip Randolph (1889–1979)** He was the head of the Brotherhood of Sleeping Car Porters who planned a march on Washington D.C. to demand an end to racial discrimination in the defense industries. To stop the march, the Roosevelt administration negotiated an agreement with the Randolph group. The demonstration would be called off and an executive order would be issued that forbid discrimination in defense work and training programs and set up the Fair Employment Practices Committee.

**range wars** In the late 1800s, conflicting claims over land and water rights triggered violent disputes between farmers and ranchers in parts of the western United States.

**Ronald Reagan (1911–2004)** In 1980, the former actor and governor of California was elected president. In office, he reduced social spending, cut taxes, and increased defense spending. During his presidency, the federal debt tripled, the federal deficit rose, programs such as housing and school lunches were cut, and the HIV/AIDS crisis grew to prominence in the United States. He signed an arms-control treaty with the Soviet Union in 1987, authorized covert CIA operations in Central America, and in 1986 the Iran-Contra scandal was revealed.

**Reaganomics** President Reagan's "supply-side" economic philosophy combining tax cuts with the goals of decreased government spending, reduced regulation of business, and a balanced budget.

**Reconstruction Finance Corporation (1932)** Federal program established under President Hoover to loan money to banks and other corporations to help them avoid bankruptcy.

**Red Power** Activism by militant Native American groups to protest living conditions on Indian reservations through demonstrations, legal action, and, at times, violence.

**First Red Scare** Fear among many Americans after the First World War of Communists in particular and noncitizens in general, it was a reaction to the Russian Revolution, mail bombs, strikes, and riots.

**redeemers** Post–Civil War Democratic leaders who supposedly saved the South from Yankee domination and preserved the primarily rural economy.

**Dr. Walter Reed (1851–1902)** His work on yellow fever in Cuba led to the discovery that the fever was carried by mosquitoes. This understanding helped develop more effective controls of the worldwide disease.

**reform Darwinism** A social philosophy developed by Lester Frank War that challenged the ruthlessness of social Darwinism by asserting that humans were not passive pawns of evolutionary forces. Instead, people could actively shape the process of evolutionary social development through cooperation, innovation, and planning.

**Reformation** European religious movement that challenged the Catholic Church and resulted in the beginnings of Protestant Christianity. During this period, Catholics and Protestants persecuted, imprisoned, tortured, and killed each other in large numbers.

**religious right** Christian conservatives with a faith-based political agenda that includes prohibition of abortion and allowing prayer in public schools.

**reparations** As a part of the Treaty of Versailles, Germany was required to confess its responsibility for the First World War and make payments to the victors for the entire expense of the war. These two requirements created a deep bitterness among Germans.

**Report on Manufactures** First Secretary of the Treasury Alexander Hamilton's 1791 analysis that accurately foretold the future of American industry and proposed tariffs and subsidies to promote it.

**republican ideology** Political belief in representative democracy in which citizens govern themselves by electing representatives, or legislators, to make key decisions on the citizens' behalf.

**republican simplicity** Deliberate attitude of humility and frugality, as opposed to monarchical pomp and ceremony, adopted by Thomas Jefferson in his presidency.

**Republicans** First used during the early nineteenth century to describe supporters of a strict interpretation of the Constitution, which they believed would safeguard individual freedoms and states' rights from the threats posed by a strong central government. The idealist Republican vision of sustaining an agrarian-oriented union was developed largely by Thomas Jefferson.

**return to normalcy** Campaign promise of Republican presidential candidate Warren G. Harding in 1920, meant to contrast with Woodrow Wilson's progressivism and internationalism.

**Paul Revere (1735–1818)** On the night of April 18, 1775, British soldiers marched toward Concord to arrest American Revolutionary leaders and seize their depot of supplies. Paul Revere famously rode through the night and raised the alarm about the approaching British troops.

**Roaring Twenties** The 1920s, an era of social and intellectual revolution in which young people experimented with new forms of recreation and sexuality. The Eastern, urban cultural shift clashed with conservative and insular Midwestern America, which increased the tensions between the two regions.

**Jackie Robinson (1919–1972)** In 1947, he became the first African American to play major league baseball. He won over fans and players and stimulated the integration of other professional sports.

**rock-and-roll music** Alan Freed, a disc jockey, noticed white teenagers were buying rhythm and blues records that had been only purchased by African Americans and Hispanic Americans. Freed began playing these records, but called them rock-and-roll records as a way to overcome the racial barrier. As the popularity of the music genre increased, it helped bridge the gap between "white" and "black" music.

**John D. Rockefeller (1839–1937)** In 1870, he founded the Standard Oil Company of Ohio, which was his first step in creating his vast oil empire. He perfected the idea of a holding company.

*Roe v. Wade* **(1973)** Landmark Supreme Court decision striking down state laws that banned abortions during the first trimester of pregnancy.

**Roman Catholicism** The Christian faith and religious practices of the Roman Catholic Church, which exerted great political, economic, and social influence on much of Western Europe and, through the Spanish and Portuguese Empires, on the Americas.

**Romanticism** Philosophical, literary, and artistic movement of the nineteenth century that was largely a reaction to the rationalism of the previous century; Romantics valued emotion, mysticism, and individualism.

**Eleanor Roosevelt (1884–1962)** She redefined the role of the presidential spouse and was the first woman to address a national political convention, write a nationally syndicated column and hold regular press conferences. She travelled throughout the nation to promote the New Deal, women's causes, organized labor, and meet with African American leaders.

**Franklin Delano Roosevelt (1882–1945)** Elected during the Great Depression, Roosevelt sought to help struggling Americans through his New Deal programs that created employment and social programs, such as Social Security. After the bombing of Pearl Harbor, he declared war on Japan and Germany and led the country through most of the Second World War before dying of cerebral hemorrhage.

**Theodore Roosevelt (1858–1919)** As the assistant secretary of the navy, he supported expansionism, American imperialism, and war with Spain. He led the Rough Riders in Cuba during the war of 1898 and used the notoriety of this military campaign for political gain. As President McKinley's vice president, he succeeded McKinley after his assassination. His forceful foreign policy became known as "big stick diplomacy." Domestically, his policies on natural resources helped start the conservation movement. Unable to win the Republican nomination for president in 1912, he formed his own party of progressive Republicans called the "Bull Moose" party.

**religious Right** Christian conservatives with a faith-based political agenda that includes allowing prayer in public schools and prohibition of abortion.

**Roosevelt Corollary (1904)** President Theodore Roosevelt's revision of the Monroe Doctrine (1823) in which he argued that the United States could use military force in Central and South American nations to prevent European nations from intervening in the Western Hemisphere.

**Rough Riders** The First U.S. Volunteer Cavalry, led in the War of 1898 by Theodore Roosevelt; they were victorious in their only engagement, the Battle of San Juan Hill near Santiago, Cuba, and Roosevelt was celebrated as a national hero, bolstering his political career.

**Royal Proclamation of 1763** Proclamation drawing a boundary along the Appalachian Mountains from Canada to Georgia in order to minimize occurrences of settler–Indian violence; colonists were forbidden to go west of the line.

**Rust Belt** Parts of the midwestern and northeastern United States marked by industrial decline and falling populations during the second half of the twentieth century, exemplified by steel-manufacturing cities in Ohio and Pennsylvania.

**Nicola Sacco (1891–1927)** In 1920, he and Bartolomeo Vanzetti were Italian immigrants who were arrested for stealing $16,000 and killing a paymaster and his guard. Their trial took place during a time of numerous bombings by anarchists and their judge was openly prejudicial; many liberals and radicals believe that their conviction was based on their political ideas and ethnic origin rather than the evidence against them.

**Sacco and Vanzetti case (1921)** Trial of two Italian immigrants that occurred at the height of Italian immigration and against the backdrop of numerous terror attacks by anarchists; despite a lack of clear evidence, the two defendants, both self-professed anarchists, were convicted of murder and were executed in 1927.

**saloons** Bars or taverns where mostly men would gather to drink, eat, relax, play games, and, often, to discuss politics.

**salutary neglect** Informal British policy during the first half of the eighteenth century that allowed the American colonies considerable freedom to pursue their economic and political interests in exchange for colonial obedience.

**Sand Creek Massacre (1864)** Colonel Chivington's unprovoked slaughter of the Cheyennes and Arapahos in Colorado, initially reported as a justified battle but soon exposed for the despicable massacre it was.

**Sandinista** Cuban-sponsored government that came to power in Nicaragua after toppling a corrupt dictator. The State Department believed that the Sandinistas were supplying the leftist Salvadoran rebels with Cuban and Soviet arms. In response, the Reagan administration ordered the CIA to train and supply guerrilla bands of anti-Communist Nicaraguans called Contras. A cease-fire agreement between the Contras and Sandinistas was signed in 1988.

**Sandlot Incident** Violence occurring during the Great Railroad Strike of 1877, when mobs of frustrated working-class whites in San Francisco attacked Chinese immigrants, blaming them for economic hardship.

**General Antonio López de Santa Anna (1794–1876)** In 1834, he seized political power in Mexico and became a dictator. In 1835, Texans rebelled against him and he led his army to Texas to crush their rebellion. He captured the mission called the Alamo and killed all of its defenders, which inspired Texans to continue resistance and Americans to volunteer to fight for Texas. The Texans captured Santa Anna during a surprise attack and he bought his freedom by signing a treaty recognizing Texas's independence.

**Battles of Saratoga** Decisive defeat of 5,000 British troops under General John Burgoyne in several battles near Saratoga, New York, in October 1777; the American victory helped convince France to enter the war on the side of the Patriots.

**scalawags** White southern Republicans—some former Unionists—who served in Reconstruction governments.

**Phyllis Schlafly (1924–2016)** A right-wing Republican activist who spearheaded the anti-feminism movement. She believed feminists were "anti-family, anti-children, and pro-abortion." She worked against the equal-rights amendment for women and civil rights protection for gays.

**Scopes Trial** Highly publicized 1925 trial of a high school teacher in Tennessee for violating a state law that prohibited the teaching of evolution; the trial was seen as the climax of the fundamentalist war on Darwinism.

**Winfield Scott (1786–1866)** During the Mexican War, he was the American general who captured Mexico City, which ended the war. Using his popularity from his military success, he ran as a Whig party candidate for President.

**Sears, Roebuck and Company** By the end of the nineteenth century, this company dominated the mail-order industry and helped create a truly national market. Its mail-order catalog and low prices allowed people living in rural areas and small towns to buy products that were previously too expensive or available only to city dwellers.

**secession** Shortly after President Abraham Lincoln was elected, southern states began dissolving their ties with the United States because they believed Lincoln and the Republican party were a threat to slavery.

**Second Bank of the United States (B.U.S)** Established in 1816 after the first national bank's charter expired; it stabilized the economy by creating a sound national currency, by making loans to farmers, small manufacturers, and entrepreneurs, and by regulating the ability of state banks to issue their own paper currency.

**Second Great Awakening** Religious revival movement that arose in reaction to the growth of secularism and rationalist religion; spurred the growth of the Baptist and Methodist churches.

**Second Industrial Revolution** Beginning in the late nineteenth century, a wave of technological innovations, especially in iron and steel production, steam and electrical power, and telegraphic communications, all of which spurred industrial development and urban growth.

**Second New Deal (1935–1938)** Expansive cluster of legislation proposed by President Roosevelt that established new regulatory agencies, strengthened the rights of workers to organize unions, and laid the foundation of a federal social welfare system through the creation of Social Security.

**second two-party system** The political party system in the United States between 1828 and 1854, consisting of Andrew Jackson's Democratic Party and Henry Clay's Whig Party. The first two party system consisted of the Federalist and Democratic-Republican Parties.

**Securities and Exchange Commission (1934)** Federal agency established to regulate the issuance and trading of stocks and bonds in an effort to avoid financial panics and stock market "crashes."

**Seneca Falls Convention (1848)** Convention organized by feminists Lucretia Mott and Elizabeth Cady Stanton to promote women's rights and issue the pathbreaking Declaration of Sentiments.

**separate but equal** Principle underlying legal racial segregation, which was upheld in *Plessy v. Ferguson* (1896) and struck down in *Brown v. Board of Education* (1954).

**separation of powers** Strict division of the powers of government among three separate branches (executive, legislative, and judicial) which, in turn, check and balance each other.

**September 11** On September 11, 2001, Islamic terrorists, who were members of the al Qaeda terrorist organization, hijacked four commercial airliners. Two were flown into the World Trade Center, a third into the Pentagon, and a fourth plane was brought down in Pennsylvania. In response, President George W. Bush launched his "war on terrorism." His administration assembled an international coalition to fight terrorism, which invaded Afghanistan after the country's government would not turn over Osama bin Laden. Bush and Congress passed the U.S.A. Patriot Act, which allowed government agencies to try suspected terrorists in secret military courts and eavesdrop on confidential conversations.

**settlement houses** Product of the late nineteenth-century movement to offer a broad array of social services in urban immigrant neighborhoods; Chicago's Hull House was one of hundreds of settlement houses that operated by the early twentieth century.

**Seventeenth Amendment (1913)** Constitutional amendment that provided for the direct election of senators rather than the traditional practice allowing state legislatures to name them.

**Shakers** Founded by Mother Ann Lee Stanley in England, the United Society of Believers in Christ's Second Appearing settled in Watervliet, New York, in 1774 and subsequently established eighteen additional communes in the Northeast, Indiana, and Kentucky.

**share tenants** Poor farmers who rented land to farm in exchange for a substantial share of the crop, though they would often have their own horse or mule, tools, and line of credit with a nearby store.

**sharecroppers** Poor, mostly black farmers who would work an owner's land in return for shelter, seed, fertilizer, mules, supplies, and food, as well as a substantial share of the crop produced.

**Share-the-Wealth program** Huey Long offered this program as an alternative to the New Deal. The program proposed to confiscate large personal fortunes, which would be used to guarantee every poor family a cash grant of $5,000 and every worker an annual income of $2,500. This program promised to provide pensions, reduce working hours, pay veterans' bonuses, and ensures a college education to every qualified student.

**Shays's Rebellion (1786–1787)** Storming of the Massachusetts federal arsenal by Daniel Shays and 1,200 armed farmers seeking debt relief from the state legislature through issuance of paper currency and lower taxes.

**silent majority** Term popularized by President Richard Nixon to describe the great majority of American voters who did not express their political opinions publicly—"the non-demonstrators."

**Sixteenth Amendment (1913)** Constitutional amendment that authorized the federal income tax.

**slave codes** Ordinances passed by a colony or state to regulate the behavior of slaves, often including brutal punishments for infractions.

**Alfred E. Smith (1873–1944)** In the 1928 presidential election, he won the Democratic nomination, but failed to win the presidency. Rural voters distrusted him for being Catholic and the son of Irish immigrants as well as his anti-Prohibition stance.

**Captain John Smith (1580–1631)** A swashbuckling soldier of fortune with rare powers of leadership and self-promotion, he was appointed to the resident council to manage Jamestown.

**Joseph Smith (1805–1844)** In 1823, he claimed that the Angel Moroni showed him the location of several gold tablets on which the Book of Mormon was written. Using the Book of Mormon as his gospel, he founded the Church of Jesus Christ of Latter-day Saints, or Mormons. In 1839, they settled in Commerce, Illinois, to avoid persecution. In 1844, Joseph and his brother were arrested and jailed for ordering the destruction of a newspaper that opposed them. While in jail, an anti-Mormon mob stormed the jail and killed both of them.

**social Darwinism** The application of Charles Darwin's theory of evolutionary natural selection to human society; Social Darwinists used the concept of "survival of the fittest" to justify class distinctions, explain poverty, and oppose government intervention in the economy.

**social gospel** Protestant movement that stressed the Christian obligation to address the mounting social problems caused by urbanization and industrialization.

**social justice** An important part of the Progressive's agenda, social justice sought to solve social problems through reform and regulation. Methods used to bring about social justice ranged from the founding of charities to the legislation of a ban on child labor.

**Social Security Act (1935)** Legislation enacted to provide federal assistance to retired workers through tax-funded pension payments and benefit payments to the unemployed and disabled.

**Sons of Liberty** First organized by Samuel Adams in the 1770s, groups of colonists dedicated to militant resistance against British control of the colonies.

**Hernando de Soto (1500?–1542)** A conquistador who explored the west coast of Florida, western North Carolina, and along the Arkansas river from 1539 till his death in 1542.

**Southern Christian Leadership Conference (SCLC)** Civil rights organization formed by Dr. Martin Luther King Jr., that championed nonviolent direct action as a means of ending segregation.

**"southern strategy"** This strategy was a major reason for Richard Nixon's victory in the 1968 presidential election. To gain support in the South, Nixon assured southern conservatives that he would slow the federal enforcement of civil rights laws and appoint pro-southern justices to the Supreme Court. As president, Nixon fulfilled these promises.

**Spanish Armada** A massive Spanish fleet of 130 warships that was defeated at Plymouth in 1588 by the English navy during the reign of Queen Elizabeth I.

**Spanish flu** Unprecedentedly lethal influenza epidemic of 1918 that killed more than 22 million people worldwide.

**Herbert Spencer (1820–1903)** As the first major proponent of social Darwinism, he argued that human society and institutions are subject to the process of natural selection and that society naturally evolves for the better. He was against any form of government interference with the evolution of society, like business regulations, because it would help the "unfit" to survive.

**spirituals** Songs with religious messages sung by slaves to help ease the strain of field labor and to voice their suffering at the hands of their masters and overseers.

**spoils system** The term—meaning the filling of federal government jobs with persons loyal to the party of the president—originated in Andrew Jackson's first term; the system was replaced in the Progressive Era by civil service.

**Square Deal** Roosevelt's progressive agenda of the "Three C's": control of corporations, conservation of natural resources, and consumer protection.

**stagflation** Term coined by economists during the Nixon presidency to describe the unprecedented situation of stagnant economic growth and consumer price inflation occurring at the same time.

**Joseph Stalin (1879–1953)** The Bolshevik leader who succeeded Lenin as the leader of the Soviet Union in 1924 and ruled the country until his death. During his totalitarian rule of the Soviet Union, he used purges and a system of forced labor camps to maintain control over the country, and claimed vast areas of Eastern Europe for Soviet domination.

**Stalwarts** Conservative Republican party faction during the presidency of Rutherford B. Hayes, 1877–1881; led by Senator Roscoe B. Conkling of New York, Stalwarts opposed civil service reform and favored a third term for President Ulysses S. Grant.

**Stamp Act (1765)** Act of Parliament requiring that all printed materials (e.g., newspapers, bonds, and even playing cards) in the American colonies use paper with an official tax stamp in order to pay for British military protection of the colonies.

**Stamp Act Congress** Twenty-seven delegates from nine of the colonies met from October 7 to 25, 1765 and wrote a Declaration of the Rights and Grievances of the Colonies, a petition to the King and a petition to Parliament for the repeal of the Stamp Act.

**Standard Oil Company** Corporation under the leadership of John D. Rockefeller that attempted to dominate the entire oil industry through horizontal and vertical integration.

**Elizabeth Cady Stanton (1815–1902)** A prominent reformer and advocate for the rights of women, she helped organize the Seneca Falls Convention to discuss women's rights. The convention was the first of its kind and produced the Declaration of Sentiments, which proclaimed the equality of men and women.

**staple crop** A profitable market crop, such as cotton, tobacco, or rice that predominates in a given region.

**state constitutions** Charters that define the relationship between the state government and local governments and individuals, and also protects their rights from violation by the national government.

**steamboats** Ships and boats powered by wood-fired steam engines. First used in the early nineteenth century, they made two-way traffic possible in eastern river systems, creating a transcontinental market and an agricultural empire.

**Thaddeus Stevens (1792–1868)** As one of the leaders of the Radical Republicans, he argued that the former Confederate states should be viewed as conquered provinces, which were subject to the demands of the conquerors. He believed that all of Southern society needed to be changed, and he supported the abolition of slavery and racial equality.

**Adlai E. Stevenson (1900–1965)** In the 1952 and 1956 presidential elections, he was the Democratic nominee who lost to Dwight Eisenhower. He was also the U.S. Ambassador to the United Nations and is remembered for his famous speech in 1962 before the UN Security Council that unequivocally demonstrated that the Soviet Union had built nuclear missile bases in Cuba.

**Stonewall riots (1969)** Violent clashes between police and lesbian, gay, bisexual, transgender, and queer (LGBTQ) patrons of New York City's Stonewall Inn, seen as the starting point of the modern LGBTQ rights movement.

**Stono Rebellion (1739)** A slave uprising in South Carolina that was brutally quashed, leading to executions as well as a severe tightening of the slave code.

**Strategic Arms Limitation Talks (SALT I) (1972)** Agreement signed by President Nixon and Secretary Brezhnev prohibiting the development of missile defense systems in the United States and Soviet Union and limiting the quantity of nuclear warheads for both.

**Strategic Defense Initiative (SDI) (1983)** Ronald Reagan's proposed space-based antimissile defense system, dubbed "Star Wars" by the media, that aroused great controversy and escalated the arms race between the United States and the Soviet Union.

**Levi Strauss (1829–1902)** A Jewish tailor who followed miners to California during the gold rush and began making durable work pants that were later dubbed blue jeans or Levi's.

**Student Nonviolent Coordinating Committee (SNCC)** Interracial organization formed in 1960 with the goal of intensifying the effort to end racial segregation.

**Students for a Democratic Society (SDS)** Major organization of the New Left, founded at the University of Michigan in 1960 by Tom Hayden and Al Haber.

**suburbia** Communities formed from mass migration of middle-class whites from urban centers.

**Suez crisis (1956)** British, French, and Israeli attack on Egypt after Nasser's seizure of the Suez Canal; President Eisenhower interceded to demand the withdrawal of the British, French, and Israeli forces from the Sinai Peninsula and the canal.

**Sun Belt** The label for an arc that stretched from the Carolinas to California. During the postwar era, much of the urban population growth occurred in this area.

**"surge"** In early 2007, President Bush decided he would send a "surge" of new troops to Iraq and implement a new strategy. U.S. forces would shift their focus from offensive operations to the protection of Iraqi civilians from attacks by terrorist insurgents and sectarian militias. While the "surge" reduced the violence in Iraq, Iraqi leaders were still unable to develop a self-sustaining democracy.

**Taft-Hartley Labor Act (1947)** Congressional legislation that banned "unfair labor practices" by labor unions, required union leaders to sign anti-Communist "loyalty oaths," and prohibited federal employees from going on strike.

**Taliban** A coalition of ultraconservative Islamists who rose to power in Afghanistan after the Soviets withdrew. The Taliban leaders gave Osama bin Laden a safe haven in their country in exchange for aid in fighting the Northern Alliance, who were rebels opposed to the Taliban. After they refused to turn bin Laden over to the United States, America invaded Afghanistan.

**Tammany Hall** The "city machine" used by "Boss" Tweed to dominate politics in New York City until his arrest in 1871.

**tariff** A tax on goods imported from other nations, typically used to protect home industries from foreign competitors and to generate revenue for the federal government.

**Tariff of 1816** A cluster of taxes on imports passed by Congress to protect America's emerging iron and textile industries from British competition.

**Tariff of 1832** This tariff act reduced the duties on many items, but the tariffs on cloth and iron remained high. South Carolina nullified it along with the tariff of 1828. President Andrew Jackson sent federal troops to the state and asked Congress to grant him the authority to enforce the tariffs. Henry Clay presented a plan of gradually reducing the tariffs until 1842, which Congress passed and ended the crisis.

**Tariff of Abominations (1828)** Tax on imported goods, including British cloth and clothing, that strengthened New England textile companies but hurt southern consumers, who experienced a decrease in British demand for raw cotton grown in the South.

**tariff reform (1887)** Effort led by the Democratic party to reduce taxes on imported goods, which Republicans argued were needed to protect American industries from foreign competition.

**Troubled Asset Relief Program (TARP)** In 2008 President George W. Bush signed into law the bank bailout fund called Troubled Asset Relief Program (TARP), which required the Treasury Department to spend $700 billion to keep banks and other financial institutions from collapsing.

**Zachary Taylor (1784–1850)** During the Mexican War, he scored two quick victories against Mexico, which made him very popular in America. He used his popularity from his military victories to be elected president as a member of the Whig party, but died before he could complete his term.

**Taylorism** Labor system based on detailed study of work tasks, championed by Frederick Winslow Taylor, intended to maximize efficiency and profits for employers.

**Tea Party** Right-wing populist movement, largely made up of middle-class, white male conservatives, that emerged as a response to the expansion of the federal government under the Obama administration.

**Teapot Dome Affair (1923)** Harding administration scandal in which Secretary of the Interior Albert B. Fall profited from secret leasing of government oil reserves in Wyoming to private oil companies.

**Tecumseh (1768–1813)** He was a leader of the Shawnee tribe who tried to unite all Indians into a confederation that could defend their hunting grounds. He believed that no land cessions could be made without the consent of all the tribes since they held the land in common. His beliefs and leadership made him seem dangerous to the American government and they waged war on him and his tribe. He was killed at the Battle of the Thames.

**Tecumseh's Indian Confederacy** A group of Native Americans under leadership of Shawnee leader Tecumseh and his prophet brother Tenskwatawa; its mission of fighting off American expansion was thwarted in the Battle of Tippecanoe (1811), when the confederacy fell apart.

**telegraph system** System of electronic communication invented by Samuel F. B. Morse that could be transmitted instantaneously across great distances (first used in the 1840s).

**Teller Amendment** Addition to the congressional war resolution of April 20, 1898, which marked the U.S. entry into the war with Spain; the amendment declared that the United States' goal in entering the war was to ensure Cuba's independence, not to annex Cuba as a territory.

**temperance** A widespread reform movement, led by militant Christians, focused on reducing the use of alcoholic beverages.

**tenements** Shabby, low-cost inner-city apartment buildings that housed the urban poor in cramped, unventilated apartments.

**Tenochtitlán** The capital city of the Aztec Empire. The city was built on marshy islands on the western side of Lake Tetzcoco, which is the site of present-day Mexico City.

**Tet offensive (1968)** Surprise attack by Viet Cong guerrillas and the North Vietnamese army on U.S. and South Vietnamese forces that shocked the American public and led to widespread sentiment against the war.

**Texas Revolution (1835–1836)** Conflict between Texas colonists and the Mexican government that resulted in the creation of the separate Republic of Texas in 1836.

**textile industry** Commercial production of thread, fabric, and clothing from raw cotton in mills in New England during the first half of the nineteenth century, and later in the South in the late nineteenth century.

**Thirteenth Amendment (1865)** Amendment to the U. S. Constitution that freed all slaves in the United States.

**Battle of Tippecanoe (1811)** Battle in northern Indiana between U.S. troops and Native American warriors led by Tenskwatawa, the brother of Tecumseh, who had organized an anti-American Indian confederacy to fight American efforts to settle on Indian lands.

**tobacco** A cash crop grown in the Caribbean as well as the Virginia and Maryland colonies, made increasingly profitable by the rapidly growing popularity of smoking in Europe after the voyages of Columbus.

**Gulf of Tonkin incident** On August 2 and 4 of 1964, North Vietnamese vessels attacked two American destroyers in the Gulf of Tonkin off the coast of North Vietnam. President Johnson described the attacks as unprovoked. In reality, the U.S. ships were monitoring South Vietnamese attacks on North Vietnamese islands that America advisors had planned. The incident spurred the Tonkin Gulf resolution.

**Tonkin Gulf Resolution** Congressional action that granted the president unlimited authority to defend U.S. forces abroad, passed in August 1964 after an allegedly unprovoked attack on American warships off the coast of North Vietnam.

**Tories** Term used by Patriots to refer to Loyalists, or colonists who supported the Crown after the Declaration of Independence.

**Townshend Acts** Parliamentary measures to extract more revenue from the colonies; the Revenue Act of 1767, which taxed tea, paper, and other colonial imports, was one of the most notorious of these policies.

**Trail of Tears (1832–1840)** The Cherokees' 800-mile journey from the southern Appalachians to Indian Territory (in present-day Oklahoma); 4,000 people died along the way.

**transcendentalism** Philosophy of a small group of New England writers and thinkers who advocated personal spirituality, self-reliance, social reform, and harmony with nature.

**Transcontinental railroad** First line across the continent from Omaha, Nebraska, to Sacramento, California, established in 1869 with the linkage of the Union Pacific and Central Pacific railroads at Promontory, Utah.

**Transcontinental Treaty (1819) (Adams-Onís Treaty)** Treaty between Spain and the United States that clarified the boundaries of the Louisiana Purchase and arranged the transfer of Florida to the United States in exchange for cash.

**Treaty of Ghent** Agreement between Great Britain and the United States that ended the War of 1812, signed on December 24, 1814.

**Treaty of Guadalupe Hidalgo (1848)** Treaty between United States and Mexico that ended the Mexican-American War.

**Treaty of Paris (1763)** Settlement between Great Britain and France that ended the French and Indian War.

**Treaty of Versailles** Peace treaty that ended the First World War, forcing Germany to dismantle its military, pay immense war reparations, and give up its colonies around the world.

**trench warfare** A form of prolonged combat between the entrenched positions of opposing armies, often with little tactical movement.

**Battle of Trenton** A surprising and pivotal victory for General Washington and American forces in December 1776 that resulted in major British and Hessian losses.

**triangular trade** A network of trade in which exports from one region were sold to another region, which sent its exports to a third region, which exported its own goods back to the first country or colony.

**Harry S. Truman (1884–1972)** As President Roosevelt's vice president, he succeeded him after his death near the end of the Second World War. After the war, Truman wrestled with the inflation of both prices and wages, worked with Congress to pass the National Security Act, and banned racial discrimination in the hiring of federal employees and ended racial segregation in the armed forces. In foreign affairs, he established the Truman Doctrine to contain communism, developed the Marshall Plan to rebuild Europe, and sent the U.S. military to defend South Korea after North Korea invaded.

**Truman Doctrine (1947)** President Truman's program of "containing" communism in Eastern Europe and providing economic and military aid to any nations at risk of Communist takeover.

**Donald J. Trump (1946–)** The 45th President of the United States.

**trust** A business arrangement that gives a person or corporation (the "trustee") the legal power to manage another person's money or another company without owning those entities outright.

**Sojourner Truth (1797?–1883)** She was born into slavery, but New York State freed her in 1827. She spent the 1840s and 1850s travelling across the country and speaking to audiences about her experiences as slave and asking them to support abolition and women's rights.

**Harriet Tubman (1820–1913)** She was born a slave, but escaped to the North. She then returned to the South nineteen times and guided 300 slaves to freedom.

**Frederick Jackson Turner** An influential historian who authored the "Frontier Thesis" in 1893, arguing that the existence of an alluring frontier and the experience of persistent westward expansion informed the nation's democratic politics, unfettered economy, and rugged individualism.

**Nat Turner (1800–1831)** He was the leader of the only slave revolt to get past the planning stages. In August of 1831, the revolt began with the slaves killing the members of Turner's master's household. Then they attacked other neighboring farmhouses and recruited more slaves until the militia crushed the revolt. At least fifty-five whites were killed during the uprising and seventeen slaves were hanged afterwards.

**Nat Turner's Rebellion (1831)** Insurrection in rural Virginia led by black overseer Nat Turner, who killed slave owners and their families; in turn, federal troops indiscriminately killed hundreds of slaves in the process of putting down Turner and his rebels.

**Tuskegee Airmen** U.S. Army Air Corps unit of African American pilots whose combat success spurred military and civilian leaders to desegregate the armed forces after the war.

**Mark Twain (1835–1910)** Born Samuel Langhorne Clemens in Missouri, he became a popular humorous writer and lecturer and established himself as one of the great American satirists and authors. His two greatest books, *The Adventures of Tom Sawyer* and *The Adventures of Huckleberry Finn*, drew heavily on his childhood in Missouri.

**"Boss" Tweed (1823–1878)** An infamous political boss in New York City, Tweed used his "city machine," the Tammany Hall ring, to rule, plunder and sometimes improve the city's government. His political domination of New York City ended with his arrest in 1871 and conviction in 1873.

**Twenty-first Amendment (1933)** Repealed prohibition on the manufacture, sale, and transportation of alcoholic beverages, effectively nullifying the Eighteenth Amendment.

**two-party system** Domination of national politics by two major political parties, such as the Whigs and Democrats during the 1830s and 1840s.

**U-boat** German military submarine (*Unterseeboot*) used during the First World War to attack enemy naval vessels as well as merchant ships of enemy and neutral nations.

**Underground Railroad** A secret system of routes and safe houses through which runaway slaves were led to freedom in the North.

**Unitarians** Members of the liberal New England Congregationalist offshoot, often well-educated and wealthy, who profess the oneness of God and the goodness of rational man.

**United Farm Workers (UFW)** Organization formed in 1965 to represent the interests of Mexican American migrant workers.

**United Nations Security Council** A major agency within the United Nations which remains in permanent session and has the responsibility of maintaining international peace and security. Originally, it consisted of five permanent members, (United States, Soviet Union, Britain, France, and the Republic of China), and six members elected to two-year terms. After 1965, the number of rotating members was increased to ten. In 1971, the Republic of China was replaced with the People's Republic of China and the Soviet Union was replaced by the Russian Federation in 1991.

**Universalists** Members of a New England religious movement, often from the working class, who believed in a merciful God and universal salvation.

**USA Patriot Act (2001)** Wide-reaching Congressional legislation, triggered by the war on terror, which gave government agencies the right to eavesdrop on confidential conversations between prison inmates and their lawyers and permitted suspected terrorists to be tried in secret military courts.

**utopian communities** Ideal communities that offered innovative social and economic relationships to those who were interested in achieving salvation.

**Valley Forge** American military encampment near Philadelphia, where more than 3,500 soldiers deserted or died from cold and hunger in the winter of 1777–1778.

**Cornelius Vanderbilt (1794–1877)** In the 1860s, he consolidated several separate railroad companies into one vast entity, New York Central Railroad.

**Bartolomeo Vanzetti (1888–1927)** In 1920, he and Nicola Sacco were Italian immigrants who were arrested for stealing $16,000 and killing a paymaster and his guard. Their trial took place during a time of numerous bombings by anarchists and their judge was openly prejudicial. Many liberals and radicals believe that their conviction was based on their political ideas and ethnic origin rather than the evidence against them.

**vertical integration** The process by which a corporation gains control of all aspects of the resources and processes needed to produce and sell a product.

**Amerigo Vespucci (1455–1512)** Italian explorer who reached the New World in 1499 and was the first to suggest that South America was a new continent. Afterward, European mapmakers used a variant of his first name, America, to label the New World.

**Battle of Vicksburg (1863)** A protracted battle in northern Mississippi in which Union forces under Ulysses Grant besieged the last major Confederate fortress on the Mississippi River, forcing the inhabitants into starvation and then submission.

**Viet Cong** Communist guerrillas in Vietnam who launched attacks on the Diem government.

**Vietnamization** Nixon-era policy of equipping and training South Vietnamese forces to take over the burden of combat from U.S. troops.

**Vikings** Norse people from Scandinavia who sailed to Newfoundland about a.d. 1001.

**Francisco Pancho Villa (1877–1923)** While the leader of one of the competing factions in the Mexican civil war, he provoked the United States into intervening. He hoped attacking the United States would help him build a reputation as an opponent of the United States, which would increase his popularity and discredit Mexican President Carranza.

**Virginia Company** A joint stock enterprise that King James I chartered in 1606. The company was to spread Christianity in the New World as well as find ways to make a profit in it.

**Virginia Plan** The delegations to the Constitutional Convention were divided between two plans on how to structure the government: Virginia called for a strong central government and a two-house legislature apportioned by population.

**Virginia Statute of Religious Freedom** A Virginia law, drafted by Thomas Jefferson in 1777 and enacted in 1786, that guarantees freedom of, and from, religion.

**virtual representation** The idea that the American colonies, although they had no actual representative in Parliament, were "virtually" represented by all members of Parliament.

**Voting Rights Act of 1965** Legislation ensuring that all Americans were able to vote; the law ended literacy tests and other means of restricting voting rights.

**Wagner Act (1935)** Legislation that guaranteed workers the right to organize unions, granted them direct bargaining power, and barred employers from interfering with union activities.

**George Wallace (1919–1998)** An outspoken defender of segregation. As the governor of Alabama, he once attempted to block African American students from enrolling at the University of Alabama. He ran as the presidential candidate for the American Independent party in 1968, appealing to voters who were concerned about rioting anti-war protestors, the welfare system, and the growth of the federal government.

**war hawks** In 1811, congressional members from the southern and western districts who clamored for a war to seize Canada and Florida were dubbed "war hawks."

**War of 1812 (1812–1815)** Conflict fought in North America and at sea between Great Britain and the United States over American shipping rights and British efforts to spur Indian attacks on American settlements. Canadians and Native Americans also fought in the war.

**war on terror** Global crusade to root out anti-American, anti-Western Islamist terrorist cells launched by President George W. Bush as a response to the 9/11 attacks.

**War Powers Act (1973)** Legislation requiring the president to inform Congress within 48 hours of the deployment of U.S. troops abroad and to withdraw them after 60 days unless Congress approves their continued deployment.

**War Production Board** Federal agency created by President Roosevelt in 1942 that converted America's industrial output to war production.

**war relocation camps** Detention camps housing thousands of Japanese Americans from the West Coast who were forcibly interned from 1942 until the end of the Second World War.

**Warren Court** The U.S. Supreme Court under Chief Justice Earl Warren, 1953–1969, decided such landmark cases as *Brown v. Board of Education* (school desegregation), *Baker v. Carr* (legislative redistricting), and *Gideon v. Wainwright* and *Miranda v. Arizona* (rights of criminal defendants).

**Booker T. Washington (1856–1915)** He founded a leading college for African Americans in Tuskegee, Alabama, and become the foremost black educator in America by the 1890s. He believed that the African American community should establish an economic base for its advancement before striving for social equality. His critics charged that his philosophy sacrificed educational and civil rights for dubious social acceptance and economic opportunities.

**George Washington (1732–1799)** In 1775, the Continental Congress named him the commander in chief of the Continental Army which defeated the British in the American Revolution. He had previously served as an officer in the French and Indian War. In 1787, he was the presiding officer over the Constitutional Convention, but participated little in the debates. In 1789, the Electoral College chose Washington to be the nation's first president. Washington faced the nation's first foreign and domestic crises, maintaining the United States' neutrality in foreign affairs. After two terms in office, Washington chose to step down; and the power of the presidency was peacefully passed to John Adams.

**Watergate (1972–1974)** Scandal that exposed the criminality and corruption of the Nixon administration and ultimately led to President Nixon's resignation in 1974.

**weapons of mass destruction (WMDs)** Radioactive, chemical, or biological weapons capable of unleashing mass death and damage. The Bush administration believed Saddam Hussein to possess such weapons, which it used to justify the second U.S invasion of Iraq during the War on Terror following the 9/11 terrorist bombings.

**Daniel Webster (1782–1852)** As a representative from New Hampshire, he led the New Federalists in opposition to the moving of the second national bank from Boston to Philadelphia. Later, he served as representative and a senator for Massachusetts and emerged as a champion of a stronger national government. He also switched from opposing to supporting tariffs because New England had built up its manufactures with the understanding tariffs would protect them from foreign competitors.

**Webster-Ashburton Treaty** Settlement in 1842 of U.S.–Canadian border disputes in Maine, New York, Vermont, and in the Wisconsin Territory (now northern Minnesota).

**Webster-Hayne debate** U.S. Senate debate of January 1830 between Daniel Webster of Massachusetts and Robert Hayne of South Carolina over nullification and states' rights.

**Western Front** The contested frontier between the Central and Allied Powers that ran along northern France and across Belgium.

**Whig party** Political party founded in 1834 in opposition to the Jacksonian Democrats; Whigs supported federal funding for internal improvements, a national bank, and high tariffs on imported goods.

**Whigs** Another name for revolutionary Patriots.

**Whiskey Rebellion (1794)** Violent protest by western Pennsylvania farmers against the federal excise tax on corn whiskey, put down by a federal army.

**Eli Whitney (1765–1825)** He invented the cotton gin which could separate cotton from its seeds. One machine operator could separate fifty times more cotton than worker could by hand, which led to an increase in cotton production and prices. These increases gave planters a new profitable use for slavery and a lucrative slave trade emerged from the coastal South to the Southwest.

**Wilderness Road** Originally an Indian path through the Cumberland Gap, it was used by over 300,000 settlers who migrated westward to Kentucky in the last quarter of the eighteenth century.

**Roger Williams (1603–1683)** Puritan who believed that the purity of the church required a complete separation between church and state and freedom from coercion in matters of faith. In 1636, he established the town of Providence, the first permanent settlement in Rhode Island and the first to allow religious freedom in America.

**Wendell L. Willkie (1892–1944)** In the 1940 presidential election, he was the Republican nominee who ran against President Roosevelt. He supported aid to the Allies and criticized the New Deal programs. Voters looked at the increasingly dangerous world situation and chose to keep President Roosevelt in office for a third term.

**Wilmot Proviso (1846)** Proposal by Congressman David Wilmot, a Pennsylvania Democrat, to prohibit slavery in any land acquired in the Mexican-American War.

**Woodrow Wilson (1856–1924)** In the 1912 presidential election, Woodrow Wilson ran under the slogan of New Freedom, which promised to improve of the banking system, lower tariffs, and break up monopolies. At the beginning of the First World War, Wilson kept America neutral, but provided the Allies with credit for purchases of supplies; however, the sinking of U.S. merchant ships and the Zimmerman telegram caused him to ask Congress to declare war on Germany. Wilson supported the entry of America into the League of Nations and the ratification of the Treaty of Versailles, but Congress would not approve the entry or ratification.

**John Winthrop** Puritan leader and Governor of the Massachusetts Bay Colony who resolved to use the colony as a refuge for persecuted Puritans and as an instrument of building a "wilderness Zion" in America.

**women's suffrage** Movement to give women the right to vote through a constitutional amendment, spearheaded by Susan B. Anthony and Elizabeth Cady Stanton's National Woman Suffrage Association.

**Women Accepted for Voluntary Emergency Services (WAVES)** During the Second World War, the increased demand for labor shook up old prejudices about gender roles in the workplace and in the military. Nearly 200,000 women served in the Women's Army Corps or its naval equivalent, Women Accepted for Volunteer Emergency Service (WAVES).

**Women's Army Corps** Women's branch of the United States Army; by the end of the Second World War nearly 150,000 women had served in the WAC.

**women's movement** Wave of activism sparked by Betty Friedan's *The Feminine Mystique* (1963); it argued for equal rights for women and fought against the cult of domesticity of the 1950s that limited women's roles to the home as wife, mother, and housewife.

**women's work** The traditional term referring to routine tasks in the house, garden, and fields performed by women. The sphere of women's occupations expanded in the colonies to include medicine, shopkeeping, upholstering, and the operation of inns and taverns.

**Woodstock** In 1969, roughly a half a million young people converged on a farm near Bethel, New York, for a three-day music festival that was an expression of the flower children's free spirit.

**Works Progress Administration (1935)** Government agency established to manage several federal job programs created under the New Deal; the WPA became the largest employer in the nation.

**Battle of Wounded Knee** Last incident of the Indians Wars took place in 1890 in the Dakota Territory, where the U.S. Cavalry killed over 200 Sioux men, women, and children who were in the process of surrender.

**XYZ affair** French foreign minister Tallyrand's three anonymous agents demanded payments to stop French plundering of American ships in 1797; refusal to pay the bribe led to two years of sea war with France (1798–1800).

**Yalta Conference (1945)** Meeting of the "Big Three" Allied leaders, Franklin D. Roosevelt, Winston Churchill, and Joseph Stalin, to discuss how to divide control of postwar Germany and Eastern Europe

**yellow journalism** A type of news reporting, epitomized in the 1890s by the newspaper empires of William Randolph Hearst and Joseph Pulitzer, that intentionally manipulates public opinion through sensational headlines, illustrations, and articles about both real and invented events.

**yeomen** Small landowners (the majority of white families in the South) who farmed their own land and usually did not own slaves.

**Battle of Yorktown** Last major battle of the Revolutionary War; General Cornwallis along with over 7,000 British troops surrendered to George Washington at Yorktown, Virginia, on October 17, 1781.

**Brigham Young (1801–1877)** Following Joseph Smith's death, he became the leader of the Mormons and promised Illinois officials that the Mormons would leave the state. In 1846, he led the Mormons to Utah and settled near the Salt Lake. After the United States gained Utah as part of the Treaty of Guadalupe Hidalgo, he became the governor of the territory and kept the Mormons virtually independent of federal authority.

**youth culture** The youth of the 1950s had more money and free time than any previous generation which allowed a distinct youth culture to emerge. A market emerged for products and activities that were specifically for young people such as transistor radios, rock records, *Seventeen* magazine, and Pat Boone movies.

**Zimmermann telegram** Message sent by a German official to the Mexican government in 1917 urging an invasion of the United States; the telegram was intercepted by British intelligence agents and angered Americans, many of whom called for war against Germany.

# APPENDIX

## THE DECLARATION OF INDEPENDENCE (1776)

When in the Course of human events, it becomes necessary for one people to dissolve the political bands which have connected them with another, and to assume among the powers of the earth, the separate and equal station to which the Laws of Nature and of Nature's God entitle them, a decent respect to the opinions of mankind requires that they should declare the causes which impel them to the separation.

We hold these truths to be self-evident, that all men are created equal, that they are endowed by their Creator with certain unalienable Rights, that among these are Life, Liberty and the pursuit of Happiness. —That to secure these rights, Governments are instituted among Men, deriving their just powers from the consent of the governed, —That whenever any Form of Government becomes destructive of these ends, it is the Right of the People to alter or to abolish it, and to institute new Government, laying its foundation on such principles and organizing its powers in such form, as to them shall seem most likely to effect their Safety and Happiness. Prudence, indeed, will dictate that Governments long established should not be changed for light and transient causes; and accordingly all experience hath shewn, that mankind are more disposed to suffer, while evils are sufferable, than to right themselves by abolishing the forms to which they are accustomed. But when a long train of abuses and usurpations, pursuing invariably the same Object evinces a design to reduce them under absolute Despotism, it is their right, it is their duty, to throw off such Government, and to provide new Guards for their future security.—Such has been the patient sufferance of these Colonies; and such is now the necessity which constrains them to alter their former Systems of Government. The history of the present King of Great Britain is a history of repeated injuries and usurpations, all having in direct object the establishment of an absolute Tyranny over these States. To prove this, let Facts be submitted to a candid world.

He has refused his Assent to Laws, the most wholesome and necessary for the public good.

He has forbidden his Governors to pass Laws of immediate and pressing importance, unless suspended in their operation till his Assent should be obtained; and when so suspended, he has utterly neglected to attend to them.

He has refused to pass other Laws for the accommodation of large districts of people, unless those people would relinquish the right of Representation in the Legislature, a right inestimable to them and formidable to tyrants only.

He has called together legislative bodies at places unusual, uncomfortable, and distant from the depository of their public Records, for the sole purpose of fatiguing them into compliance with his measures.

He has dissolved Representative Houses repeatedly, for opposing with manly firmness his invasions on the rights of the people.

He has refused for a long time, after such dissolutions, to cause others to be elected; whereby the Legislative powers, incapable of Annihilation, have returned to the People at large for their exercise; the State remaining in the mean time exposed to all the dangers of invasion from without, and convulsions within.

He has endeavoured to prevent the population of these States; for that purpose obstructing the Laws for Naturalization of Foreigners; refusing to pass others to encourage their migrations hither, and raising the conditions of new Appropriations of Lands.

He has obstructed the Administration of Justice, by refusing his Assent to Laws for establishing Judiciary powers.

He has made Judges dependent on his Will alone, for the tenure of their offices, and the amount and payment of their salaries.

He has erected a multitude of New Offices, and sent hither swarms of Officers to harrass our people, and eat out their substance.

He has kept among us, in times of peace, Standing Armies without the Consent of our legislatures.

He has affected to render the Military independent of and superior to the Civil power.

He has combined with others to subject us to a jurisdiction foreign to our constitution, and unacknowledged by our laws; giving his Assent to their Acts of pretended Legislation:

For quartering large bodies of armed troops among us:

For protecting them, by a mock Trial, from punishment for any Murders which they should commit on the Inhabitants of these States:

For cutting off our Trade with all parts of the world:

For imposing Taxes on us without our Consent:

For depriving us in many cases, of the benefits of Trial by Jury:

For transporting us beyond Seas to be tried for pretended offences

For abolishing the free System of English Laws in a neighbouring Province, establishing therein an Arbitrary government, and enlarging its Boundaries so as to render it at once an example and fit instrument for introducing the same absolute rule into these Colonies:

For taking away our Charters, abolishing our most valuable Laws, and altering fundamentally the Forms of our Governments:

For suspending our own Legislatures, and declaring themselves invested with power to legislate for us in all cases whatsoever.

He has abdicated Government here, by declaring us out of his Protection and waging War against us.

He has plundered our seas, ravaged our Coasts, burnt our towns, and destroyed the lives of our people.

He is at this time transporting large Armies of foreign Mercenaries to compleat the works of death, desolation and tyranny, already begun with circumstances of Cruelty & perfidy scarcely paralleled in the most barbarous ages, and totally unworthy the Head of a civilized nation.

He has constrained our fellow Citizens taken Captive on the high Seas to bear Arms against their Country, to become the executioners of their friends and Brethren, or to fall themselves by their Hands.

He has excited domestic insurrections amongst us, and has endeavoured to bring on the inhabitants of our frontiers, the merciless Indian Savages, whose known rule of warfare, is an undistinguished destruction of all ages, sexes and conditions.

In every stage of these Oppressions We have Petitioned for Redress in the most humble terms: Our repeated Petitions have been answered only by repeated injury. A Prince whose character is thus marked by every act which may define a Tyrant, is unfit to be the ruler of a free people.

Nor have We been wanting in attentions to our Brittish brethren. We have warned them from time to time of attempts by their legislature to extend an unwarrantable jurisdiction over us. We have reminded them of the circumstances of our emigration and settlement here. We have appealed to their native justice and magnanimity, and we have conjured them by the ties of our common kindred to disavow these usurpations, which, would inevitably interrupt our connections and correspondence. They too have been deaf to the voice of justice and of consanguinity. We must, therefore, acquiesce in the necessity, which denounces our Separation, and hold them, as we hold the rest of mankind, Enemies in War, in Peace Friends.

We, therefore, the Representatives of the united States of America, in General Congress, Assembled, appealing to the Supreme Judge of the world for the rectitude of our intentions, do, in the Name, and by Authority of the good People of these Colonies, solemnly publish and declare, That these United Colonies are, and of Right ought to be Free and Independent States; that they are Absolved from all Allegiance to the British Crown, and that all political connection between them and the State of Great Britain, is and ought to be totally dissolved; and that as Free and Independent States, they have full Power to levy War, conclude Peace, contract Alliances, establish Commerce, and to do all other Acts and Things which Independent States may of right do. And for the support of this Declaration, with a firm reliance on the protection of divine Providence, we mutually pledge to each other our Lives, our Fortunes and our sacred Honor.

**Georgia**
Button Gwinnett
Lyman Hall
George Walton

**North Carolina**
William Hooper
Joseph Hewes
John Penn

**South Carolina**
Edward Rutledge
Thomas Heyward, Jr.
Thomas Lynch, Jr.
Arthur Middleton

**Massachusetts**
John Hancock

**Maryland**
Samuel Chase
William Paca
Thomas Stone
Charles Carroll of
    Carrollton

**Virginia**
George Wythe
Richard Henry Lee
Thomas Jefferson
Benjamin Harrison
Thomas Nelson, Jr.
Francis Lightfoot Lee
Carter Braxton

**Pennsylvania**
Robert Morris
Benjamin Rush
Benjamin Franklin
John Morton
George Clymer
James Smith
George Taylor
James Wilson
George Ross

**Delaware**
Caesar Rodney
George Read
Thomas McKean

**New York**
William Floyd
Philip Livingston
Francis Lewis
Lewis Morris

**New Jersey**
Richard Stockton
John Witherspoon
Francis Hopkinson
John Hart
Abraham Clark

**New Hampshire**
Josiah Bartlett
William Whipple

**Massachusetts**
Samuel Adams
John Adams
Robert Treat Paine
Elbridge Gerry

**Rhode Island**
Stephen Hopkins
William Ellery

**Connecticut**
Roger Sherman
Samuel Huntington
William Williams
Oliver Wolcott

**New Hampshire**
Matthew Thornton

# ARTICLES OF CONFEDERATION (1787)

To ALL TO WHOM these Presents shall come, we the undersigned Delegates of the States affixed to our Names send greeting.

Whereas the Delegates of the United States of America in Congress assembled did on the fifteenth day of November in the Year of our Lord One Thousand Seven Hundred and Seventy-seven, and in the Second Year of the Independence of America agree to certain articles of Confederation and perpetual Union between the States of Newhampshire, Massachusetts-bay, Rhodeisland and Providence Plantations, Connecticut, New York, New Jersey, Pennsylvania, Delaware, Maryland, Virginia, North-Carolina, South-Carolina and Georgia in the Words following, viz.

Articles of Confederation and perpetual Union between the States of Newhampshire, Massachusetts-bay, Rhodeisland and Providence Plantations, Connecticut, New-York, New-Jersey, Pennsylvania, Delaware, Maryland, Virginia, North-Carolina, South-Carolina and Georgia.

ARTICLE I. The stile of this confederacy shall be "The United States of America."

ARTICLE II. Each State retains its sovereignty, freedom and independence, and every power, jurisdiction and right, which is not by this confederation expressly delegated to the United States, in Congress assembled.

ARTICLE III. The said States hereby severally enter into a firm league of friendship with each other, for their common defence, the security of their liberties, and their mutual and general welfare, binding themselves to assist each other, against all force offered to, or attacks made upon them, or any of them, on account of religion, sovereignty, trade or any other pretence whatever.

ARTICLE IV. The better to secure and perpetuate mutual friendship and intercourse among the people of the different States in this Union, the free inhabitants of each of these States, paupers, vagabonds and fugitives from justice excepted, shall be entitled to all privileges and immunities of free citizens in the several States; and the people of each State shall have free ingress and regress to and from any other State, and shall enjoy therein all the privileges of trade and commerce, subject to the same duties, impositions and restrictions as the inhabitants thereof respectively, provided that such restrictions shall not extend so far as to prevent the removal of property imported into any State, to any other State of which the owner is an inhabitant; provided also that no imposition, duties or restriction shall be laid by any State, on the property of the United States, or either of them.

If any person guilty of, or charged with treason, felony, or other high misdemeanor in any State, shall flee from justice, and be found in any of the United States, he shall upon demand of the Governor or Executive power, of the State from which he fled, be delivered up and removed to the State having jurisdiction of his offence.

Full faith and credit shall be given in each of these States to the records, acts and judicial proceedings of the courts and magistrates of every other State.

ARTICLE V. For the more convenient management of the general interests of the United States, delegates shall be annually appointed in such manner as the legislature of each State shall direct, to meet in Congress on the first Monday in November, in every year, with a power reserved to each State, to recall its delegates, or any of them, at any time within the year, and to send others in their stead, for the remainder of the year.

No State shall be represented in Congress by less than two, nor by more than seven members; and no person shall be capable of being a delegate for more than three years in any term of six years; nor shall any person, being a delegate, be capable of holding any office under the United States, for which he, or another for his benefit receives any salary, fees or emolument of any kind.

Each State shall maintain its own delegates in a meeting of the States, and while they act as members of the committee of the States.

In determining questions in the United States, in Congress assembled, each State shall have one vote.

Freedom of speech and debate in Congress shall not be impeached or questioned in any court, or place out of Congress, and the members of Congress shall be protected in their persons from arrests and imprisonments, during the time of their going to and from, and attendance on Congress, except for treason, felony, or breach of the peace.

ARTICLE VI. No State without the consent of the United States in Congress assembled, shall send any embassy to, or receive any embassy from, or enter into any conference, agreement, alliance or treaty with any king, prince or state; nor shall any person holding any office of profit or trust under the United States, or any of them, accept of any present, emolument, office or title of any kind whatever from any king, prince or foreign state; nor shall the United States in Congress assembled, or any of them, grant any title of nobility.

No two or more States shall enter into any treaty, confederation or alliance whatever between them, without the consent of the United States in Congress assembled, specifying accurately the purposes for which the same is to be entered into, and how long it shall continue.

No State shall lay any imposts or duties, which may interfere with any stipulations in treaties, entered into by the United States in Congress assembled, with any king, prince or state, in pursuance of any treaties already proposed by Congress, to the courts of France and Spain.

No vessels of war shall be kept up in time of peace by any State, except such number only, as shall be deemed necessary by the United States in Congress assembled, for the defence of such State, or its trade; nor shall any body of forces be kept up by any State, in time of peace, except such number only, as in the judgment of the United States, in Congress assembled, shall be deemed requisite to garrison the forts necessary for the defence of such State; but every State shall always keep up a well regulated and disciplined militia, sufficiently armed and accoutred, and shall provide and constantly have ready for use, in public stores, a due number of field pieces and tents, and a proper quantity of arms, ammunition and camp equipage.

No State shall engage in any war without the consent of the United States in Congress assembled, unless such State be actually invaded by enemies, or shall have received certain advice of a resolution being formed by some nation of Indians to invade such State, and the danger is so imminent as not to admit of a delay, till the United States in Congress assembled can be consulted: nor shall any State grant commissions to any ships or vessels of war, nor letters of marque or reprisal, except it be after a declaration of war by the United States in Congress assembled, and then only against the kingdom or state and the subjects thereof, against which war has been so declared, and under such regulations as shall be established by the United States in Congress assembled, unless such State be infested by pirates, in which case vessels of war may be fitted out for that occasion, and kept so long as the danger shall continue, or until the United States in Congress assembled shall determine otherwise.

ARTICLE VII. When land-forces are raised by any State of the common defence, all officers of or under the rank of colonel, shall be appointed by the Legislature of each State respectively by whom such forces shall be raised, or in such manner as such State shall direct, and all vacancies shall be filled up by the State which first made the appointment.

ARTICLE VIII. All charges of war, and all other expenses that shall be incurred for the common defence or general welfare, and allowed by the United States in Congress assembled, shall be defrayed out of a common treasury, which shall be supplied by the several States, in proportion to the value of all land within each State, granted to or surveyed for any person, as such land and the buildings and improvements thereon shall be estimated according to such mode as the United States in Congress assembled, shall from time to time direct and appoint.

The taxes for paying that proportion shall be laid and levied by the authority and direction of the Legislatures of the several States within the time agreed upon by the United States in Congress assembled.

ARTICLE IX. The United States in Congress assembled, shall have the sole and exclusive right and power of determining on peace and war, except in the cases mentioned in the sixth article—of sending and receiving ambassadors—entering into treaties and alliances, provided that no treaty of commerce shall be made whereby the legislative power of the respective States shall be restrained from imposing such imposts and duties on foreigners, as their own people are subjected to, or from prohibiting the exportation or importation of and species of goods or commodities whatsoever—of establishing rules for deciding in all cases, what captures on land or water shall be legal, and in what manner prizes taken by land or naval forces in the service of the United States shall be divided or appropriated—of granting letters of marque and reprisal in times of peace—appointing courts for the trial of piracies and felonies committed on the high seas and establishing courts for receiving and determining finally appeals in all cases of captures, provided that no member of Congress shall be appointed a judge of any of the said courts.

The United States in Congress assembled shall also be the last resort on appeal in all disputes and differences now subsisting or that hereafter may arise between two or more States concerning boundary, jurisdiction or any other cause whatever; which authority shall always be exercised in the manner following. Whenever the legislative or executive authority or lawful agent of any State in controversy with another shall present a petition to Congress, stating the matter in question and praying for a hearing, notice thereof shall be given by order of Congress to the legislative or executive authority of the other State in controversy, and a day assigned for the appearance of the parties by their lawful agents, who shall then be directed to appoint by joint consent, commissioners or judges to constitute a court for hearing and determining the matter in question: but if they cannot agree, Congress shall name three persons out of each of the United States, and from the list of such persons each party shall alternately strike out one, the petitioners beginning, until the number shall be reduced to thirteen; and from that number not less than seven, nor more than nine names as Congress shall direct, shall in the presence of Congress be drawn out by lot, and the persons whose names shall be so drawn or any five of them, shall be commissioners or judges, to hear and finally determine the controversy, so always as a major part of the judges who shall hear the cause shall agree in the determination: and if either party shall neglect to attend at the day appointed, without reasons, which Congress shall judge sufficient, or being present shall refuse to strike, the Congress shall proceed to nominate three persons out of each State, and the Secretary of Congress shall strike in behalf of such party absent or refusing; and the judgment and sentence of the court to be appointed, in the manner before prescribed, shall be final and conclusive; and if any of the parties shall refuse to submit to the authority of such court, or to appear or defend their claim or cause, the court shall nevertheless proceed to pronounce sentence, or judgment, which shall in like manner be final and decisive, the judgment or sentence and other proceedings being in either case transmitted to Congress, and lodged among the acts of Congress for the security of the parties concerned: provided that every commissioner, before he sits in judgment, shall take an oath to be administered by one of the judges of the supreme or superior court of the State where the case shall be tried, "well and truly to hear and determine the matter in question, according to the best of his judgment, without favour, affection or hope of reward:" provided also that no State shall be deprived of territory for the benefit of the United States.

All controversies concerning the private right of soil claimed under different grants of two or more States, whose jurisdiction as they may respect such lands, and the states which passed such grants are adjusted, the said grants or either of them being at the same time claimed to have originated antecedent to such settlement of jurisdiction, shall on the petition of either party to the Congress of the United States, be finally determined as near as may be in the same manner as is before prescribed for deciding disputes respecting territorial jurisdiction between different States.

The United States in Congress assembled shall also have the sole and exclusive right and power of regulating the alloy and value of coin struck by their own authority, or by that of the respective States—fixing the standard of weights and measures throughout the United States—regulating the trade and managing all affairs with the Indians, not members of any of the States, provided that the legislative right of any State within its own limits be not infringed or violated—establishing and regulating post-offices from one State to another, throughout all of the United States, and exacting such postage on the papers passing thro' the same as may be requisite to defray the expenses of the said office—appointing all officers of the land forces, in the service of the United States, excepting regimental officers—appointing all the officers of the naval forces, and commissioning all officers whatever in the service of the United States—making rules for the government and regulation of the said land and naval forces, and directing their operations.

The United States in Congress assembled shall have authority to appoint a committee, to sit in the recess of Congress, to be denominated "a Committee of the States," and to consist of one delegate from each State; and to appoint such other committees and civil officers as may be necessary for managing the general affairs of the United States under their direction—to appoint one of their number to preside, provided that no person be allowed to serve in the office of president more than one year in any term of three years; to ascertain the necessary sums of money to be raised for the service of the United States, and to appropriate and apply the same for defraying the public expenses—to borrow money, or emit bills on the credit of the United States, transmitting every half year to the respective States an account of the sums of money so borrowed or emitted,—to build and equip a navy—to agree upon the number of land forces, and to make requisitions from each State for its quota, in proportion to the number of white inhabitants in such State; which requisition shall be binding, and thereupon the Legislature of each State shall appoint the regimental officers, raise the men and cloath, arm and equip them in a soldier like manner, at the expense of the United States; and the officers and men so cloathed, armed and equipped shall march to the place appointed, and within the time agreed on by the United States in Congress assembled: but if the United States in Congress assembled shall, on consideration of circumstances judge proper that any State should not raise men, or should raise a smaller number of men than the quota thereof, such extra number shall be raised, officered, cloathed, armed and equipped in the same manner as the quota of such State, unless the legislature of such State shall judge that such extra number cannot be safely spared out of the same, in which case they shall raise officer, cloath, arm and equip as many of such extra number as they judge can be safely spared. And the officers and men so cloathed, armed and equipped, shall march to the place appointed, and within the time agreed on by the United States in Congress assembled.

The United States in Congress assembled shall never engage in a war, nor grant letters of marque and reprisal in time of peace, nor enter into any treaties or alliances, nor coin money, nor regulate the value thereof, nor ascertain the sums and expenses necessary for the defence and welfare of the United States, or any of them, nor emit bills, nor borrow money on the credit of the United States, nor appropriate money, nor agree upon the number of vessels to be built or purchased, or the number of land or sea forces to be raised, nor appoint a commander in chief of the army or navy, unless nine States assent to the same: nor shall a question on any other point, except for adjourning from day to day be determined, unless by the votes of a majority of the United States in Congress assembled.

The Congress of the United States shall have power to adjourn to any time within the year, and to any place within the United States, so that no period of adjournment be for a longer duration than the space of six months, and shall publish the journal of their proceedings monthly, except such parts thereof relating to treaties, alliances or military operations, as in their judgment require secrecy; and the yeas and nays of the delegates of each State on any question shall be entered on the Journal, when it is desired by any delegate; and the delegates of a State, or any of them, at his or their request shall be furnished with a transcript of the said journal, except such parts as are above excepted, to lay before the Legislatures of the several States.

ARTICLE X. The committee of the States, or any nine of them, shall be authorized to execute, in the recess of Congress, such of the powers of Congress as the United States in Congress assembled, by the consent of nine States, shall from time to time think expedient to vest them with; provided that no power be delegated to the said committee, for the exercise of which, by the articles of confederation, the voice of nine States in the Congress of the United States assembled is requisite.

ARTICLE XI. Canada acceding to this confederation, and joining in the measures of the United States, shall be admitted into, and entitled to all the advantages of this Union: but no other colony shall be admitted into the same, unless such admission be agreed to by nine States.

ARTICLE XII. All bills of credit emitted, monies borrowed and debts contracted by, or under the authority of Congress, before the assembling of the United States, in pursuance of the present confederation, shall be deemed and considered as a charge against the United States, for payment and satisfaction whereof the said United States, and the public faith are hereby solemnly pledged.

ARTICLE XIII. Every State shall abide by the determinations of the United States in Congress assembled, on all questions which by this confederation are submitted to them. And the articles of this confederation shall be inviolably observed by every State, and the Union shall be perpetual; nor shall any alteration at any time hereafter be made in any of them; unless such alteration be agreed to in a Congress of the United States, and be afterwards confirmed by the Legislatures of every State.

And whereas it has pleased the Great Governor of the world to incline the hearts of the Legislatures we respectively represent in Congress, to approve of, and to authorize us to ratify the said articles of confederation and perpetual union. Know ye that we the undersigned delegates, by virtue of the power and authority to us given for that purpose, do by these presents, in the name and in behalf of our respective constituents, fully and entirely ratify and confirm each and every of the said articles of confederation and perpetual union, and all and singular the matters and things therein contained: and we do further solemnly plight and engage the faith of our respective constituents, that they shall abide by the determinations of the United States in Congress assembled, on all questions, which by the said confederation are submitted to them. And that the articles thereof shall be inviolably observed by the States we respectively represent, and that the Union shall be perpetual.

In witness thereof we have hereunto set our hands in Congress. Done at Philadelphia in the State of Pennsylvania the ninth day of July in the year of our Lord one thousand seven hundred and seventy-eight, and in the third year of the independence of America.

# The Constitution of the United States (1787)

We the People of the United States, in Order to form a more perfect Union, establish Justice, insure domestic Tranquility, provide for the common defence, promote the general Welfare, and secure the Blessings of Liberty to ourselves and our Posterity, do ordain and establish this Constitution for the United States of America.

## Article. I.

**SECTION. 1.** All legislative Powers herein granted shall be vested in a Congress of the United States, which shall consist of a Senate and House of Representatives.

**SECTION. 2.** The House of Representatives shall be composed of Members chosen every second Year by the People of the several States, and the Electors in each State shall have the Qualifications requisite for Electors of the most numerous Branch of the State Legislature.

No Person shall be a Representative who shall not have attained to the Age of twenty five Years, and been seven Years a Citizen of the United States, and who shall not, when elected, be an Inhabitant of that State in which he shall be chosen.

Representatives and direct Taxes shall be apportioned among the several States which may be included within this Union, according to their respective Numbers, which shall be determined by adding to the whole Number of free Persons, including those bound to Service for a Term of Years, and excluding Indians not taxed, three fifths of all other Persons. The actual Enumeration shall be made within three Years after the first Meeting of the Congress of the United States, and within every subsequent Term of ten Years, in such Manner as they shall by Law direct. The Number of Representatives shall not exceed one for every thirty Thousand, but each State shall have at Least one Representative; and until such enumeration shall be made, the State of New Hampshire shall be entitled to chuse three, Massachusetts eight, Rhode-Island and Providence Plantations one, Connecticut five, New-York six, New Jersey four, Pennsylvania eight, Delaware one, Maryland six, Virginia ten, North Carolina five, South Carolina five, and Georgia three.

When vacancies happen in the Representation from any State, the Executive Authority thereof shall issue Writs of Election to fill such Vacancies.

The House of Representatives shall chuse their Speaker and other Officers; and shall have the sole Power of Impeachment.

**SECTION. 3.** The Senate of the United States shall be composed of two Senators from each State, chosen by the Legislature thereof for six Years; and each Senator shall have one Vote.

Immediately after they shall be assembled in Consequence of the first Election, they shall be divided as equally as may be into three Classes. The Seats of the Senators of the first Class shall be vacated at the Expiration of the second Year, of the second Class at the Expiration of the fourth Year, and of the third Class at the Expiration of the sixth Year, so that one third may be chosen every second Year; and if Vacancies happen by Resignation, or otherwise, during the Recess of the Legislature of any State, the Executive thereof may make temporary Appointments until the next Meeting of the Legislature, which shall then fill such Vacancies.

No Person shall be a Senator who shall not have attained to the Age of thirty Years, and been nine Years a Citizen of the United States, and who shall not, when elected, be an Inhabitant of that State for which he shall be chosen.

The Vice President of the United States shall be President of the Senate, but shall have no Vote, unless they be equally divided.

The Senate shall chuse their other Officers, and also a President pro tempore, in the Absence of the Vice President, or when he shall exercise the Office of President of the United States.

The Senate shall have the sole Power to try all Impeachments. When sitting for that Purpose, they shall be on Oath or Affirmation. When the President of the United States is tried, the Chief Justice shall preside: And no Person shall be convicted without the Concurrence of two thirds of the Members present.

Judgment in Cases of Impeachment shall not extend further than to removal from Office, and disqualification to hold and enjoy any Office of honor, Trust or Profit under the United States: but the Party convicted shall nevertheless be liable and subject to Indictment, Trial, Judgment and Punishment, according to Law.

**SECTION. 4.** The Times, Places and Manner of holding Elections for Senators and Representatives, shall be prescribed in each State by the Legislature thereof; but the Congress may at any time by Law make or alter such Regulations, except as to the Places of chusing Senators.

The Congress shall assemble at least once in every Year, and such Meeting shall be on the first Monday in December, unless they shall by Law appoint a different Day.

**SECTION. 5.** Each House shall be the Judge of the Elections, Returns and Qualifications of its own Members, and a Majority of each shall constitute a Quorum to do Business; but a smaller Number may adjourn from day to day, and may be authorized to compel the Attendance of absent Members, in such Manner, and under such Penalties as each House may provide.

Each House may determine the Rules of its Proceedings, punish its Members for disorderly Behaviour, and, with the Concurrence of two thirds, expel a Member.

Each House shall keep a Journal of its Proceedings, and from time to time publish the same, excepting such Parts as may in their Judgment require Secrecy; and the Yeas and Nays of the Members of either House on any question shall, at the Desire of one fifth of those Present, be entered on the Journal.

Neither House, during the Session of Congress, shall, without the Consent of the other, adjourn for more than three days, nor to any other Place than that in which the two Houses shall be sitting.

**SECTION. 6.** The Senators and Representatives shall receive a Compensation for their Services, to be ascertained by Law, and paid out of the Treasury of the United States. They shall in all Cases, except Treason, Felony and Breach of the Peace, be privileged from Arrest during their Attendance at the Session of their respective Houses, and in going to and returning from the same; and for any Speech or Debate in either House, they shall not be questioned in any other Place.

No Senator or Representative shall, during the Time for which he was elected, be appointed to any civil Office under the Authority of the United States, which shall have been created, or the Emoluments whereof shall have been encreased during such time; and no Person holding any Office under the United States, shall be a Member of either House during his Continuance in Office.

**SECTION. 7.** All Bills for raising Revenue shall originate in the House of Representatives; but the Senate may propose or concur with Amendments as on other Bills.

Every Bill which shall have passed the House of Representatives and the Senate shall, before it become a Law, be presented to the President of the United States; If he approve he shall sign it, but if not he shall return it, with his

Objections to that House in which it shall have originated, who shall enter the Objections at large on their Journal, and proceed to reconsider it. If after such Reconsideration two thirds of that House shall agree to pass the Bill, it shall be sent, together with the Objections, to the other House, by which it shall likewise be reconsidered, and if approved by two thirds of that House, it shall become a Law. But in all such Cases the Votes of both Houses shall be determined by yeas and Nays, and the Names of the Persons voting for and against the Bill shall be entered on the Journal of each House respectively. If any Bill shall not be returned by the President within ten Days (Sundays excepted) after it shall have been presented to him, the Same shall be a Law, in like Manner as if he had signed it, unless the Congress by their Adjournment prevent its Return, in which Case it shall not be a Law.

Every Order, Resolution, or Vote to which the Concurrence of the Senate and House of Representatives may be necessary (except on a question of Adjournment) shall be presented to the President of the United States; and before the Same shall take Effect, shall be approved by him, or being disapproved by him, shall be repassed by two thirds of the Senate and House of Representatives, according to the Rules and Limitations prescribed in the Case of a Bill.

**SECTION. 8.** The Congress shall have Power To lay and collect Taxes, Duties, Imposts and Excises, to pay the Debts and provide for the common Defence and general Welfare of the United States; but all Duties, Imposts and Excises shall be uniform throughout the United States;

To borrow Money on the credit of the United States;

To regulate Commerce with foreign Nations, and among the several States, and with the Indian Tribes;

To establish an uniform Rule of Naturalization, and uniform Laws on the subject of Bankruptcies throughout the United States;

To coin Money, regulate the Value thereof, and of foreign Coin, and fix the Standard of Weights and Measures;

To provide for the Punishment of counterfeiting the Securities and current Coin of the United States;

To establish Post Offices and post Roads;

To promote the Progress of Science and useful Arts, by securing for limited Times to Authors and Inventors the exclusive Right to their respective Writings and Discoveries;

To constitute Tribunals inferior to the supreme Court;

To define and punish Piracies and Felonies committed on the high Seas, and Offences against the Law of Nations;

To declare War, grant Letters of Marque and Reprisal, and make Rules concerning Captures on Land and Water;

To raise and support Armies, but no Appropriation of Money to that Use shall be for a longer Term than two Years;

To provide and maintain a Navy;

To make Rules for the Government and Regulation of the land and naval Forces;

To provide for calling forth the Militia to execute the Laws of the Union, suppress Insurrections and repel Invasions;

To provide for organizing, arming, and disciplining, the Militia, and for governing such Part of them as may be employed in the Service of the United States, reserving to the States respectively, the Appointment of the Officers, and the Authority of training the Militia according to the discipline prescribed by Congress;

To exercise exclusive Legislation in all Cases whatsoever, over such District (not exceeding ten Miles square) as may, by Cession of particular States, and the Acceptance of Congress, become the Seat of the Government of the United States, and to exercise like Authority over all Places purchased by the Consent of the Legislature of the State in which the Same shall be, for the Erection of Forts, Magazines, Arsenals, dock-Yards, and other needful Buildings;—And

To make all Laws which shall be necessary and proper for carrying into Execution the foregoing Powers, and all other Powers vested by this Constitution in the Government of the United States, or in any Department or Officer thereof.

SECTION. 9. The Migration or Importation of such Persons as any of the States now existing shall think proper to admit, shall not be prohibited by the Congress prior to the Year one thousand eight hundred and eight, but a Tax or duty may be imposed on such Importation, not exceeding ten dollars for each Person.

The Privilege of the Writ of Habeas Corpus shall not be suspended, unless when in Cases of Rebellion or Invasion the public Safety may require it.

No Bill of Attainder or ex post facto Law shall be passed.

No Capitation, or other direct, Tax shall be laid, unless in Proportion to the Census or enumeration herein before directed to be taken.

No Tax or Duty shall be laid on Articles exported from any State.

No Preference shall be given by any Regulation of Commerce or Revenue to the Ports of one State over those of another; nor shall Vessels bound to, or from, one State, be obliged to enter, clear, or pay Duties in another.

No Money shall be drawn from the Treasury, but in Consequence of Appropriations made by Law; and a regular Statement and Account of the Receipts and Expenditures of all public Money shall be published from time to time.

No Title of Nobility shall be granted by the United States: And no Person holding any Office of Profit or Trust under them, shall, without the Consent of the Congress, accept of any present, Emolument, Office, or Title, of any kind whatever, from any King, Prince, or foreign State.

**SECTION. 10.** No State shall enter into any Treaty, Alliance, or Confederation; grant Letters of Marque and Reprisal; coin Money; emit Bills of Credit; make any Thing but gold and silver Coin a Tender in Payment of Debts; pass any Bill of Attainder, ex post facto Law, or Law impairing the Obligation of Contracts, or grant any Title of Nobility.

No State shall, without the Consent of the Congress, lay any Imposts or Duties on Imports or Exports, except what may be absolutely necessary for executing it's inspection Laws: and the net Produce of all Duties and Imposts, laid by any State on Imports or Exports, shall be for the Use of the Treasury of the United States; and all such Laws shall be subject to the Revision and Controul of the Congress.

No State shall, without the Consent of Congress, lay any Duty of Tonnage, keep Troops, or Ships of War in time of Peace, enter into any Agreement or Compact with another State, or with a foreign Power, or engage in War, unless actually invaded, or in such imminent Danger as will not admit of delay.

# Article. II.

**SECTION. 1.** The executive Power shall be vested in a President of the United States of America. He shall hold his Office during the Term of four Years, and, together with the Vice President, chosen for the same Term, be elected, as follows:

Each State shall appoint, in such Manner as the Legislature thereof may direct, a Number of Electors, equal to the whole Number of Senators and Representatives to which the State may be entitled in the Congress: but no Senator or Representative, or Person holding an Office of Trust or Profit under the United States, shall be appointed an Elector.

The Electors shall meet in their respective States, and vote by Ballot for two Persons, of whom one at least shall not be an Inhabitant of the same State with themselves. And they shall make a List of all the Persons voted for, and of the Number of Votes for each; which List they shall sign and certify, and transmit sealed to the Seat of the Government of the United States, directed to the President of the Senate. The President of the Senate shall, in the Presence of the Senate and House of Representatives, open all the Certificates, and the Votes shall then be counted. The Person having the greatest Number of Votes shall be the President, if such Number be a Majority of the whole Number of Electors appointed; and if there be more than one who have such Majority, and have an equal Number of Votes, then the House of Representatives shall immediately chuse by Ballot one of them for President; and if no Person have a Majority, then from the five highest on the List the said House shall in like Manner chuse the President. But in chusing the President, the Votes shall be taken by States, the Representation from each State having one Vote; A quorum for this purpose shall consist of a Member or Members from two thirds of the States, and a Majority of all the States shall be necessary to a Choice. In every Case, after the Choice of the President, the Person having the greatest Number of Votes of the Electors shall be the Vice President. But if there should remain two or more who have equal Votes, the Senate shall chuse from them by Ballot the Vice President.

The Congress may determine the Time of chusing the Electors, and the Day on which they shall give their Votes; which Day shall be the same throughout the United States.

No Person except a natural born Citizen, or a Citizen of the United States, at the time of the Adoption of this Constitution, shall be eligible to the Office of President; neither shall any Person be eligible to that Office who shall not have attained to the Age of thirty five Years, and been fourteen Years a Resident within the United States.

In Case of the Removal of the President from Office, or of his Death, Resignation, or Inability to discharge the Powers and Duties of the said Office, the Same shall devolve on the Vice President, and the Congress may by Law provide for the Case of Removal, Death, Resignation or Inability, both of the President and Vice President, declaring what Officer shall then act as President, and such Officer shall act accordingly, until the Disability be removed, or a President shall be elected.

The President shall, at stated Times, receive for his Services, a Compensation, which shall neither be increased nor diminished during the Period for which he shall have been elected, and he shall not receive within that Period any other Emolument from the United States, or any of them.

Before he enter on the Execution of his Office, he shall take the following Oath or Affirmation:—"I do solemnly swear (or affirm) that I will faithfully execute the Office of President of the United States, and will to the best of my Ability, preserve, protect and defend the Constitution of the United States."

**SECTION. 2.** The President shall be Commander in Chief of the Army and Navy of the United States, and of the Militia of the several States, when called into the actual Service of the United States; he may require the Opinion, in writing, of the principal Officer in each of the executive Departments, upon any Subject relating to the Duties of their respective Offices, and he shall have Power to grant Reprieves and Pardons for Offences against the United States, except in Cases of Impeachment.

He shall have Power, by and with the Advice and Consent of the Senate, to make Treaties, provided two thirds of the Senators present concur; and he shall nominate, and by and with the Advice and Consent of the Senate, shall appoint Ambassadors, other public Ministers and Consuls, Judges of the supreme Court, and all other Officers of the United States, whose Appointments are not herein otherwise provided for, and which shall be established by Law: but the Congress may by Law vest the Appointment of such inferior Officers, as they think proper, in the President alone, in the Courts of Law, or in the Heads of Departments.

The President shall have Power to fill up all Vacancies that may happen during the Recess of the Senate, by granting Commissions which shall expire at the End of their next Session.

**SECTION. 3.** He shall from time to time give to the Congress Information of the State of the Union, and recommend to their Consideration such Measures as he shall judge necessary and expedient; he may, on extraordinary Occasions, convene both Houses, or either of them, and in Case of Disagreement between them, with Respect to the Time of Adjournment, he may adjourn them to such Time as he shall think proper; he shall receive Ambassadors and other public Ministers; he shall take Care that the Laws be faithfully executed, and shall Commission all the Officers of the United States.

**SECTION. 4.** The President, Vice President and all civil Officers of the United States, shall be removed from Office on Impeachment for, and Conviction of, Treason, Bribery, or other high Crimes and Misdemeanors.

## ARTICLE. III.

**SECTION. 1.** The judicial Power of the United States shall be vested in one supreme Court, and in such inferior Courts as the Congress may from time to time ordain and establish. The Judges, both of the supreme and inferior Courts, shall hold their Offices during good Behaviour, and shall, at stated Times, receive for their Services a Compensation, which shall not be diminished during their Continuance in Office.

**SECTION. 2.** The judicial Power shall extend to all Cases, in Law and Equity, arising under this Constitution, the Laws of the United States, and Treaties made, or which shall be made, under their Authority;—to all Cases affecting Ambassadors, other public Ministers and Consuls;—to all Cases of admiralty and maritime Jurisdiction;—to Controversies to which the United States shall be a Party;—to Controversies between two or more States;— between a State and Citizens of another State,—between Citizens of different States,—between Citizens of the same State claiming Lands under Grants of different States, and between a State, or the Citizens thereof, and foreign States, Citizens or Subjects.

In all Cases affecting Ambassadors, other public Ministers and Consuls, and those in which a State shall be Party, the supreme Court shall have original Jurisdiction. In all the other Cases before mentioned, the supreme Court shall have appellate Jurisdiction, both as to Law and Fact, with such Exceptions, and under such Regulations as the Congress shall make.

The Trial of all Crimes, except in Cases of Impeachment, shall be by Jury; and such Trial shall be held in the State where the said Crimes shall have been committed; but when not committed within any State, the Trial shall be at such Place or Places as the Congress may by Law have directed.

**SECTION. 3.** Treason against the United States, shall consist only in levying War against them, or in adhering to their Enemies, giving them Aid and Comfort. No Person shall be convicted of Treason unless on the Testimony of two Witnesses to the same overt Act, or on Confession in open Court.

The Congress shall have Power to declare the Punishment of Treason, but no Attainder of Treason shall work Corruption of Blood, or Forfeiture except during the Life of the Person attainted.

## ARTICLE. IV.

**SECTION. 1.** Full Faith and Credit shall be given in each State to the public Acts, Records, and judicial Proceedings of every other State. And the Congress may by general Laws prescribe the Manner in which such Acts, Records and Proceedings shall be proved, and the Effect thereof.

**SECTION. 2.** The Citizens of each State shall be entitled to all Privileges and Immunities of Citizens in the several States.

A Person charged in any State with Treason, Felony, or other Crime, who shall flee from Justice, and be found in another State, shall on Demand of the executive Authority of the State from which he fled, be delivered up, to be removed to the State having Jurisdiction of the Crime.

No Person held to Service or Labour in one State, under the Laws thereof, escaping into another, shall, in Consequence of any Law or Regulation therein, be discharged from such Service or Labour, but shall be delivered up on Claim of the Party to whom such Service or Labour may be due.

SECTION. 3. New States may be admitted by the Congress into this Union; but no new State shall be formed or erected within the Jurisdiction of any other State; nor any State be formed by the Junction of two or more States, or Parts of States, without the Consent of the Legislatures of the States concerned as well as of the Congress.

The Congress shall have Power to dispose of and make all needful Rules and Regulations respecting the Territory or other Property belonging to the United States; and nothing in this Constitution shall be so construed as to Prejudice any Claims of the United States, or of any particular States.

SECTION. 4. The United States shall guarantee to every State in this Union a Republican Form of Government, and shall protect each of them against Invasion; and on Application of the Legislature, or of the Executive (when the Legislature cannot be convened), against domestic Violence.

# ARTICLE. V.

The Congress, whenever two thirds of both Houses shall deem it necessary, shall propose Amendments to this Constitution, or, on the Application of the Legislatures of two thirds of the several States, shall call a Convention for proposing Amendments, which, in either Case, shall be valid to all Intents and Purposes, as Part of this Constitution, when ratified by the Legislatures of three fourths of the several States, or by Conventions in three fourths thereof, as the one or the other Mode of Ratification may be proposed by the Congress; Provided that no Amendment which may be made prior to the Year One thousand eight hundred and eight shall in any Manner affect the first and fourth Clauses in the Ninth Section of the first Article; and that no State, without its Consent, shall be deprived of its equal Suffrage in the Senate.

# ARTICLE. VI.

All Debts contracted and Engagements entered into, before the Adoption of this Constitution, shall be as valid against the United States under this Constitution, as under the Confederation.

This Constitution, and the Laws of the United States which shall be made in Pursuance thereof; and all Treaties made, or which shall be made, under the Authority of the United States, shall be the supreme Law of the Land; and the Judges in every State shall be bound thereby, any Thing in the Constitution or Laws of any State to the Contrary notwithstanding.

The Senators and Representatives before mentioned, and the Members of the several State Legislatures, and all executive and judicial Officers, both of the United States and of the several States, shall be bound by Oath or Affirmation, to support this Constitution; but no religious Test shall ever be required as a Qualification to any Office or public Trust under the United States.

## Article. VII.

The Ratification of the Conventions of nine States, shall be sufficient for the Establishment of this Constitution between the States so ratifying the Same.

The Word, "the," being interlined between the seventh and eighth Lines of the first Page, the Word "Thirty" being partly written on an Erazure in the fifteenth Line of the first Page, The Words "is tried" being interlined between the thirty second and thirty third Lines of the first Page and the Word "the" being interlined between the forty third and forty fourth Lines of the second Page.

Attest William Jackson Secretary

Done in Convention by the Unanimous Consent of the States present the Seventeenth Day of September in the Year of our Lord one thousand seven hundred and Eighty seven and of the Independance of the United States of America the Twelfth In witness whereof We have hereunto subscribed our Names,

G°. Washington
Presidt and deputy from Virginia

| | |
|---|---|
| **Delaware** | Geo: Read<br>Gunning Bedford jun<br>John Dickinson<br>Richard Bassett<br>Jaco: Broom |
| **Maryland** | James McHenry<br>Dan of St Thos. Jenifer<br>Danl. Carrol |
| **Virginia** | John Blair<br>James Madison Jr. |
| **North Carolina** | Wm. Blount<br>Richd. Dobbs Spaight<br>Hu Williamson |
| **South Carolina** | J. Rutledge<br>Charles Cotesworth Pinckney<br>Charles Pinckney<br>Pierce Butler |
| **Georgia** | William Few<br>Abr Baldwin |

| | |
|---|---|
| **New Hampshire** | John Langdon<br>Nicholas Gilman |
| **Massachusetts** | Nathaniel Gorham<br>Rufus King |
| **Connecticut** | Wm. Saml. Johnson<br>Roger Sherman |
| **New York** | Alexander Hamilton |
| **New Jersey** | Wil: Livingston<br>David Brearley<br>Wm. Paterson<br>Jona: Dayton |
| **Pennsylvania** | B Franklin<br>Thomas Mifflin<br>Robt. Morris<br>Geo. Clymer<br>Thos. FitzSimons<br>Jared Ingersoll<br>James Wilson<br>Gouv Morris |

# Amendments to the Constitution

## The Bill of Rights: A Transcription

**THE PREAMBLE TO THE BILL OF RIGHTS** Congress of the United States begun and held at the City of New-York, on Wednesday the fourth of March, one thousand seven hundred and eighty nine.

THE Conventions of a number of the States, having at the time of their adopting the Constitution, expressed a desire, in order to prevent misconstruction or abuse of its powers, that further declaratory and restrictive clauses should be added: And as extending the ground of public confidence in the Government, will best ensure the beneficent ends of its institution.

RESOLVED by the Senate and House of Representatives of the United States of America, in Congress assembled, two thirds of both Houses concurring, that the following Articles be proposed to the Legislatures of the several States, as amendments to the Constitution of the United States, all, or any of which Articles, when ratified by three fourths of the said Legislatures, to be valid to all intents and purposes, as part of the said Constitution; viz.

ARTICLES in addition to, and Amendment of the Constitution of the United States of America, proposed by Congress, and ratified by the Legislatures of the several States, pursuant to the fifth Article of the original Constitution.

**Note:** The first ten amendments to the Constitution were ratified December 15, 1791, and form what is known as the "Bill of Rights."

## Amendment I

Congress shall make no law respecting an establishment of religion, or prohibiting the free exercise thereof; or abridging the freedom of speech, or of the press; or the right of the people peaceably to assemble, and to petition the Government for a redress of grievances.

## Amendment II

A well regulated Militia, being necessary to the security of a free State, the right of the people to keep and bear Arms, shall not be infringed.

# AMENDMENT III

No Soldier shall, in time of peace be quartered in any house, without the consent of the Owner, nor in time of war, but in a manner to be prescribed by law.

# AMENDMENT IV

The right of the people to be secure in their persons, houses, papers, and effects, against unreasonable searches and seizures, shall not be violated, and no Warrants shall issue, but upon probable cause, supported by Oath or affirmation, and particularly describing the place to be searched, and the persons or things to be seized.

# AMENDMENT V

No person shall be held to answer for a capital, or otherwise infamous crime, unless on a presentment or indictment of a Grand Jury, except in cases arising in the land or naval forces, or in the Militia, when in actual service in time of War or public danger; nor shall any person be subject for the same offence to be twice put in jeopardy of life or limb; nor shall be compelled in any criminal case to be a witness against himself, nor be deprived of life, liberty, or property, without due process of law; nor shall private property be taken for public use, without just compensation.

# AMENDMENT VI

In all criminal prosecutions, the accused shall enjoy the right to a speedy and public trial, by an impartial jury of the State and district wherein the crime shall have been committed, which district shall have been previously ascertained by law, and to be informed of the nature and cause of the accusation; to be confronted with the witnesses against him; to have compulsory process for obtaining witnesses in his favor, and to have the Assistance of Counsel for his defence.

# AMENDMENT VII

In Suits at common law, where the value in controversy shall exceed twenty dollars, the right of trial by jury shall be preserved, and no fact tried by a jury, shall be otherwise re-examined in any Court of the United States, than according to the rules of the common law.

## AMENDMENT VIII

Excessive bail shall not be required, nor excessive fines imposed, nor cruel and unusual punishments inflicted.

## AMENDMENT IX

The enumeration in the Constitution, of certain rights, shall not be construed to deny or disparage others retained by the people.

## AMENDMENT X

The powers not delegated to the United States by the Constitution, nor prohibited by it to the States, are reserved to the States respectively, or to the people.

## AMENDMENT XI

*Passed by Congress March 4, 1794. Ratified February 7, 1795.*

**Note**: Article III, section 2, of the Constitution was modified by amendment 11.

The Judicial power of the United States shall not be construed to extend to any suit in law or equity, commenced or prosecuted against one of the United States by Citizens of another State, or by Citizens or Subjects of any Foreign State.

## AMENDMENT XII

*Passed by Congress December 9, 1803. Ratified June 15, 1804.*

**Note**: A portion of Article II, section 1 of the Constitution was superseded by the 12th amendment.

The Electors shall meet in their respective states and vote by ballot for President and Vice-President, one of whom, at least, shall not be an inhabitant of the same state with themselves; they shall name in their ballots the person voted for as President, and in distinct ballots the person voted for as Vice-President, and they shall make distinct lists of all persons voted for as President, and of all persons voted for as Vice-President, and of the number of votes for each, which lists they shall sign and certify, and transmit sealed to the seat of the government of the United States, directed to the President of the Senate; — the President of the Senate shall, in the presence of the Senate and House of Representatives, open all the certificates and the votes shall then be counted; — The person having the greatest number of votes for President, shall be the President, if such number be a majority of the whole number of Electors appointed; and if no person have such majority, then from the persons having the highest numbers not exceeding three on the list of those voted for as President, the House of Representatives shall choose immediately, by ballot, the President. But in choosing the President, the votes shall be taken by states, the representation from each state having one vote; a quorum for this purpose shall consist of a member or members from two-thirds of the states, and a majority of all the states shall be necessary to a choice. [And if the House of Representatives shall not choose a President whenever the right of choice shall devolve upon them, before the fourth day of March next following, then the Vice-President shall act as President, as in case of the death or other constitutional disability of the President. —]* The person having the greatest number of votes as Vice-President, shall be the Vice-President, if such number be a majority of the whole number of Electors appointed, and if no person have a majority, then from the two highest numbers on the list, the Senate shall choose the Vice-President; a quorum for the purpose shall consist of two-thirds of the whole number of Senators, and a majority of the whole number shall be necessary to a choice. But no person constitutionally ineligible to the office of President shall be eligible to that of Vice-President of the United States.

## AMENDMENT XIII

*Passed by Congress January 31, 1865. Ratified December 6, 1865.*

**Note**: A portion of Article IV, section 2, of the Constitution was superseded by the 13th amendment.

**SECTION 1.** Neither slavery nor involuntary servitude, except as a punishment for crime whereof the party shall have been duly convicted, shall exist within the United States, or any place subject to their jurisdiction.

**SECTION 2.** Congress shall have power to enforce this article by appropriate legislation.

---

*Superseded by section 3 of the 20th amendment.*

# AMENDMENT XIV

*Passed by Congress June 13, 1866. Ratified July 9, 1868.*

**Note**: Article I, section 2, of the Constitution was modified by section 2 of the 14th amendment.

**SECTION 1.** All persons born or naturalized in the United States, and subject to the jurisdiction thereof, are citizens of the United States and of the State wherein they reside. No State shall make or enforce any law which shall abridge the privileges or immunities of citizens of the United States; nor shall any State deprive any person of life, liberty, or property, without due process of law; nor deny to any person within its jurisdiction the equal protection of the laws.

**SECTION 2.** Representatives shall be apportioned among the several States according to their respective numbers, counting the whole number of persons in each State, excluding Indians not taxed. But when the right to vote at any election for the choice of electors for President and Vice-President of the United States, Representatives in Congress, the Executive and Judicial officers of a State, or the members of the Legislature thereof, is denied to any of the male inhabitants of such State, being twenty-one years of age,* and citizens of the United States, or in any way abridged, except for participation in rebellion, or other crime, the basis of representation therein shall be reduced in the proportion which the number of such male citizens shall bear to the whole number of male citizens twenty-one years of age in such State.

**SECTION 3.** No person shall be a Senator or Representative in Congress, or elector of President and Vice-President, or hold any office, civil or military, under the United States, or under any State, who, having previously taken an oath, as a member of Congress, or as an officer of the United States, or as a member of any State legislature, or as an executive or judicial officer of any State, to support the Constitution of the United States, shall have engaged in insurrection or rebellion against the same, or given aid or comfort to the enemies thereof. But Congress may by a vote of two-thirds of each House, remove such disability.

**SECTION 4.** The validity of the public debt of the United States, authorized by law, including debts incurred for payment of pensions and bounties for services in suppressing insurrection or rebellion, shall not be

*Changed by section 1 of the 26th amendment.*

questioned. But neither the United States nor any State shall assume or pay any debt or obligation incurred in aid of insurrection or rebellion against the United States, or any claim for the loss or emancipation of any slave; but all such debts, obligations and claims shall be held illegal and void.

**SECTION 5.** The Congress shall have the power to enforce, by appropriate legislation, the provisions of this article.

## AMENDMENT XV

*Passed by Congress February 26, 1869. Ratified February 3, 1870.*

**SECTION 1.** The right of citizens of the United States to vote shall not be denied or abridged by the United States or by any State on account of race, color, or previous condition of servitude—

**SECTION 2.** The Congress shall have the power to enforce this article by appropriate legislation.

## AMENDMENT XVI

*Passed by Congress July 2, 1909. Ratified February 3, 1913.*

**Note:** Article I, section 9, of the Constitution was modified by amendment 16.

The Congress shall have power to lay and collect taxes on incomes, from whatever source derived, without apportionment among the several States, and without regard to any census or enumeration.

## AMENDMENT XVII

*Passed by Congress May 13, 1912. Ratified April 8, 1913.*

**Note:** Article I, section 3, of the Constitution was modified by the 17th amendment.

The Senate of the United States shall be composed of two Senators from each State, elected by the people thereof, for six years; and each Senator shall have one vote. The electors in each State shall have the qualifications requisite for electors of the most numerous branch of the State legislatures.

When vacancies happen in the representation of any State in the Senate, the executive authority of such State shall issue writs of election to fill such vacancies: *Provided*, That the legislature of any State may empower the executive thereof to make temporary appointments until the people fill the vacancies by election as the legislature may direct.

This amendment shall not be so construed as to affect the election or term of any Senator chosen before it becomes valid as part of the Constitution.

## AMENDMENT XVIII

*Passed by Congress December 18, 1917. Ratified January 16, 1919. Repealed by amendment 21.*

**SECTION 1.** After one year from the ratification of this article the manufacture, sale, or transportation of intoxicating liquors within, the importation thereof into, or the exportation thereof from the United States and all territory subject to the jurisdiction thereof for beverage purposes is hereby prohibited.

**SECTION 2.** The Congress and the several States shall have concurrent power to enforce this article by appropriate legislation.

**SECTION 3.** This article shall be inoperative unless it shall have been ratified as an amendment to the Constitution by the legislatures of the several States, as provided in the Constitution, within seven years from the date of the submission hereof to the States by the Congress.

## AMENDMENT XIX

*Passed by Congress June 4, 1919. Ratified August 18, 1920.*

The right of citizens of the United States to vote shall not be denied or abridged by the United States or by any State on account of sex.

Congress shall have power to enforce this article by appropriate legislation.

## AMENDMENT XX

*Passed by Congress March 2, 1932. Ratified January 23, 1933.*

**Note**: Article I, section 4, of the Constitution was modified by section 2 of this amendment. In addition, a portion of the 12th amendment was superseded by section 3.

**SECTION 1.** The terms of the President and the Vice President shall end at noon on the 20th day of January, and the terms of Senators and Representatives at noon on the 3rd day of January, of the years in which such terms would have ended if this article had not been ratified; and the terms of their successors shall then begin.

**SECTION 2.** The Congress shall assemble at least once in every year, and such meeting shall begin at noon on the 3d day of January, unless they shall by law appoint a different day.

**SECTION 3.** If, at the time fixed for the beginning of the term of the President, the President elect shall have died, the Vice President elect shall become President. If a President shall not have been chosen before the time fixed for the beginning of his term, or if the President elect shall have failed to qualify, then the Vice President elect shall act as President until a President shall have qualified; and the Congress may by law provide for the case wherein neither a President elect nor a Vice President shall have qualified, declaring who shall then act as President, or the manner in which one who is to act shall be selected, and such person shall act accordingly until a President or Vice President shall have qualified.

**SECTION 4.** The Congress may by law provide for the case of the death of any of the persons from whom the House of Representatives may choose a President whenever the right of choice shall have devolved upon them, and for the case of the death of any of the persons from whom the Senate may choose a Vice President whenever the right of choice shall have devolved upon them.

**SECTION 5.** Sections 1 and 2 shall take effect on the 15th day of October following the ratification of this article.

**SECTION 6.** This article shall be inoperative unless it shall have been ratified as an amendment to the Constitution by the legislatures of three-fourths of the several States within seven years from the date of its submission.

# AMENDMENT XXI

*Passed by Congress February 20, 1933. Ratified December 5, 1933.*

**SECTION 1.** The eighteenth article of amendment to the Constitution of the United States is hereby repealed.

**SECTION 2.** The transportation or importation into any State, Territory, or Possession of the United States for delivery or use therein of intoxicating liquors, in violation of the laws thereof, is hereby prohibited.

**SECTION 3.** This article shall be inoperative unless it shall have been ratified as an amendment to the Constitution by conventions in the several States, as provided in the Constitution, within seven years from the date of the submission hereof to the States by the Congress.

## AMENDMENT XXII

*Passed by Congress March 21, 1947. Ratified February 27, 1951.*

**SECTION 1.** No person shall be elected to the office of the President more than twice, and no person who has held the office of President, or acted as President, for more than two years of a term to which some other person was elected President shall be elected to the office of President more than once. But this Article shall not apply to any person holding the office of President when this Article was proposed by Congress, and shall not prevent any person who may be holding the office of President, or acting as President, during the term within which this Article becomes operative from holding the office of President or acting as President during the remainder of such term.

**SECTION 2.** This article shall be inoperative unless it shall have been ratified as an amendment to the Constitution by the legislatures of three-fourths of the several States within seven years from the date of its submission to the States by the Congress.

## AMENDMENT XXIII

*Passed by Congress June 16, 1960. Ratified March 29, 1961.*

**SECTION 1.** The District constituting the seat of Government of the United States shall appoint in such manner as Congress may direct:
A number of electors of President and Vice President equal to the whole number of Senators and Representatives in Congress to which the District would be entitled if it were a State, but in no event more than the least populous State; they shall be in addition to those appointed by the States, but they shall be

considered, for the purposes of the election of President and Vice President, to be electors appointed by a State; and they shall meet in the District and perform such duties as provided by the twelfth article of amendment.

**SECTION 2.** The Congress shall have power to enforce this article by appropriate legislation.

## AMENDMENT XXIV

*Passed by Congress August 27, 1962. Ratified January 23, 1964.*

**SECTION 1.** The right of citizens of the United States to vote in any primary or other election for President or Vice President, for electors for President or Vice President, or for Senator or Representative in Congress, shall not be denied or abridged by the United States or any State by reason of failure to pay poll tax or other tax.

**SECTION 2.** The Congress shall have power to enforce this article by appropriate legislation.

## AMENDMENT XXV

*Passed by Congress July 6, 1965. Ratified February 10, 1967.*

**Note**: Article II, section 1, of the Constitution was affected by the 25th amendment.

**SECTION 1.** In case of the removal of the President from office or of his death or resignation, the Vice President shall become President.

**SECTION 2.** Whenever there is a vacancy in the office of the Vice President, the President shall nominate a Vice President who shall take office upon confirmation by a majority vote of both Houses of Congress.

**SECTION 3.** Whenever the President transmits to the President pro tempore of the Senate and the Speaker of the House of Representatives his written declaration that he is unable to discharge the powers and duties of his office, and until he transmits to them a written declaration to the contrary, such powers and duties shall be discharged by the Vice President as Acting President.

**SECTION 4.** Whenever the Vice President and a majority of either the principal officers of the executive departments or of such other body as Congress may by law provide, transmit to the President pro tempore of the Senate and the Speaker of the House of Representatives their written declaration that the President is unable to discharge the powers and duties of his office, the Vice President shall immediately assume the powers and duties of the office as Acting President.

Thereafter, when the President transmits to the President pro tempore of the Senate and the Speaker of the House of Representatives his written declaration that no inability exists, he shall resume the powers and duties of his office unless the Vice President and a majority of either the principal officers of the executive department or of such other body as Congress may by law provide, transmit within four days to the President pro tempore of the Senate and the Speaker of the House of Representatives their written declaration that the President is unable to discharge the powers and duties of his office. Thereupon Congress shall decide the issue, assembling within forty-eight hours for that purpose if not in session. If the Congress, within twenty-one days after receipt of the latter written declaration, or, if Congress is not in session, within twenty-one days after Congress is required to assemble, determines by two-thirds vote of both Houses that the President is unable to discharge the powers and duties of his office, the Vice President shall continue to discharge the same as Acting President; otherwise, the President shall resume the powers and duties of his office.

## Amendment XXVI

*Passed by Congress March 23, 1971. Ratified July 1, 1971.*

**Note**: Amendment 14, section 2, of the Constitution was modified by section 1 of the 26th amendment.

**SECTION 1.** The right of citizens of the United States, who are eighteen years of age or older, to vote shall not be denied or abridged by the United States or by any State on account of age.

**SECTION 2.** The Congress shall have power to enforce this article by appropriate legislation.

# AMENDMENT XXVII

*Originally proposed Sept. 25, 1789. Ratified May 7, 1992.*

No law, varying the compensation for the services of the Senators and Representatives, shall take effect, until an election of representatives shall have intervened.

## PRESIDENTIAL ELECTIONS

| Year | Number of States | Candidates | Parties | Popular Vote | % of Popular Vote | Electoral Vote | % Voter Participation |
|------|------|------|------|------|------|------|------|
| 1789 | 11 | **GEORGE WASHINGTON** | No party designations | | | 69 | |
| | | John Adams | | | | 34 | |
| | | Other candidates | | | | 35 | |
| 1792 | 15 | **GEORGE WASHINGTON** | No party designations | | | 132 | |
| | | John Adams | | | | 77 | |
| | | George Clinton | | | | 50 | |
| | | Other candidates | | | | 5 | |
| 1796 | 16 | **JOHN ADAMS** | Federalist | | | 71 | |
| | | Thomas Jefferson | Democratic-Republican | | | 68 | |
| | | Thomas Pinckney | Federalist | | | 59 | |
| | | Aaron Burr | Democratic-Republican | | | 30 | |
| | | Other candidates | | | | 48 | |
| 1800 | 16 | **THOMAS JEFFERSON** | Democratic-Republican | | | 73 | |
| | | Aaron Burr | Democratic-Republican | | | 73 | |
| | | John Adams | Federalist | | | 65 | |
| | | Charles C. Pinckney | Federalist | | | 64 | |
| | | John Jay | Federalist | | | 1 | |
| 1804 | 17 | **THOMAS JEFFERSON** | Democratic-Republican | | | 162 | |
| | | Charles C. Pinckney | Federalist | | | 14 | |

| Year | Number of States | Candidates | Parties | Popular Vote | % of Popular Vote | Electoral Vote | % Voter Participation |
|---|---|---|---|---|---|---|---|
| 1808 | 17 | JAMES MADISON | Democratic-Republican | | | 122 | |
| | | Charles C. Pinckney | Federalist | | | 47 | |
| | | George Clinton | Democratic-Republican | | | 6 | |
| 1812 | 18 | JAMES MADISON | Democratic-Republican | | | 128 | |
| | | DeWitt Clinton | Federalist | | | 89 | |
| 1816 | 19 | JAMES MONROE | Democratic-Republican | | | 183 | |
| | | Rufus King | Federalist | | | 34 | |
| 1820 | 24 | JAMES MONROE | Democratic-Republican | | | 231 | |
| | | John Quincy Adams | Independent | | | 1 | |
| 1824 | 24 | JOHN QUINCY ADAMS | Democratic-Republican | 108,740 | 30.5 | 84 | 26.9 |
| | | Andrew Jackson | Democratic-Republican | 153,544 | 43.1 | 99 | |
| | | Henry Clay | Democratic-Republican | 47,136 | 13.2 | 37 | |
| | | William H. Crawford | Democratic-Republican | 46,618 | 13.1 | 41 | |
| 1828 | 24 | ANDREW JACKSON | Democratic | 647,286 | 56.0 | 178 | 57.6 |
| | | John Quincy Adams | National-Republican | 508,064 | 44.0 | 83 | |

| Year | Number of States | Candidates | Parties | Popular Vote | % of Popular Vote | Electoral Vote | % Voter Participation |
|------|------------------|------------|---------|--------------|-------------------|----------------|------------------------|
| 1832 | 24 | **ANDREW JACKSON** | Democratic | 688,242 | 54.5 | 219 | 55.4 |
|      |    | Henry Clay | National-Republican | 473,462 | 37.5 | 49 | |
|      |    | William Wirt | Anti-Masonic } | 101,051 | 8.0 | 7 | |
|      |    | John Floyd | Democratic } | | | 11 | |
| 1836 | 26 | **MARTIN VAN BUREN** | Democratic | 765,483 | 50.9 | 170 | 57.8 |
|      |    | William H. Harrison | Whig } | | | 73 | |
|      |    | Hugh L. White | Whig } | 739,795 | 49.1 | 26 | |
|      |    | Daniel Webster | Whig } | | | 14 | |
|      |    | W. P. Mangum | Whig } | | | 11 | |
| 1840 | 26 | **WILLIAM H. HARRISON** | Whig | 1,274,624 | 53.1 | 234 | 80.2 |
|      |    | Martin Van Buren | Democratic | 1,127,781 | 46.9 | 60 | |
| 1844 | 26 | **JAMES K. POLK** | Democratic | 1,338,464 | 49.6 | 170 | 78.9 |
|      |    | Henry Clay | Whig | 1,300,097 | 48.1 | 105 | |
|      |    | James G. Birney | Liberty | 62,300 | 2.3 | | |
| 1848 | 30 | **ZACHARY TAYLOR** | Whig | 1,360,967 | 47.4 | 163 | 72.7 |
|      |    | Lewis Cass | Democratic | 1,222,342 | 42.5 | 127 | |
|      |    | Martin Van Buren | Free Soil | 291,263 | 10.1 | | |
| 1852 | 31 | **FRANKLIN PIERCE** | Democratic | 1,601,117 | 50.9 | 254 | 69.6 |
|      |    | Winfield Scott | Whig | 1,385,453 | 44.1 | 42 | |
|      |    | John P. Hale | Free Soil | 155,825 | 5.0 | | |
| 1856 | 31 | **JAMES BUCHANAN** | Democratic | 1,832,955 | 45.3 | 174 | 78.9 |
|      |    | John C. Frémont | Republican | 1,339,932 | 33.1 | 114 | |
|      |    | Millard Fillmore | American | 871,731 | 21.6 | 8 | |

| Year | Number of States | Candidates | Parties | Popular Vote | % of Popular Vote | Electoral Vote | % Voter Participation |
|------|------|------------|---------|--------------|-------------------|----------------|-----------------------|
| 1860 | 33 | **ABRAHAM LINCOLN** | Republican | 1,865,593 | 39.8 | 180 | 81.2 |
|      |    | Stephen A. Douglas | Democratic | 1,382,713 | 29.5 | 12 | |
|      |    | John C. Breckinridge | Democratic | 848,356 | 18.1 | 72 | |
|      |    | John Bell | Constitutional Union | 592,906 | 12.6 | 39 | |
| 1864 | 36 | **ABRAHAM LINCOLN** | Republican | 2,206,938 | 55.0 | 212 | 73.8 |
|      |    | George B. McClellan | Democratic | 1,803,787 | 45.0 | 21 | |
| 1868 | 37 | **ULYSSES S. GRANT** | Republican | 3,013,421 | 52.7 | 214 | 78.1 |
|      |    | Horatio Seymour | Democratic | 2,706,829 | 47.3 | 80 | |
| 1872 | 37 | **ULYSSES S. GRANT** | Republican | 3,596,745 | 55.6 | 286 | 71.3 |
|      |    | Horace Greeley | Democratic | 2,843,446 | 43.9 | 66 | |
| 1876 | 38 | Rutherford B. Hayes | Republican | 4,036,572 | 48.0 | 185 | 81.8 |
|      |    | Samuel J. Tilden | Democratic | 4,284,020 | 51.0 | 184 | |
| 1880 | 38 | **JAMES A. GARFIELD** | Republican | 4,453,295 | 48.5 | 214 | 79.4 |
|      |    | Winfield S. Hancock | Democratic | 4,414,082 | 48.1 | 155 | |
|      |    | James B. Weaver | Greenback-Labor | 308,578 | 3.4 | | |
| 1884 | 38 | **GROVER CLEVELAND** | Democratic | 4,879,507 | 48.5 | 219 | 77.5 |
|      |    | James G. Blaine | Republican | 4,850,293 | 48.2 | 182 | |
|      |    | Benjamin F. Butler | Greenback-Labor | 175,370 | 1.8 | | |
|      |    | John P. St. John | Prohibition | 150,369 | 1.5 | | |
| 1888 | 38 | **BENJAMIN HARRISON** | Republican | 5,477,129 | 47.9 | 233 | 79.3 |
|      |    | Grover Cleveland | Democratic | 5,537,857 | 48.6 | 168 | |
|      |    | Clinton B. Fisk | Prohibition | 249,506 | 2.2 | | |
|      |    | Anson J. Streeter | Union Labor | 146,935 | 1.3 | | |

| Year | Number of States | Candidates | Parties | Popular Vote | % of Popular Vote | Electoral Vote | % Voter Participation |
|---|---|---|---|---|---|---|---|
| 1892 | 44 | **GROVER CLEVELAND** | Democratic | 5,555,426 | 46.1 | 277 | 74.7 |
|  |  | Benjamin Harrison | Republican | 5,182,690 | 43.0 | 145 |  |
|  |  | James B. Weaver | People's | 1,029,846 | 8.5 | 22 |  |
|  |  | John Bidwell | Prohibition | 264,133 | 2.2 |  |  |
| 1896 | 45 | **WILLIAM MCKINLEY** | Republican | 7,102,246 | 51.1 | 271 | 79.3 |
|  |  | William J. Bryan | Democratic | 6,492,559 | 47.7 | 176 |  |
| 1900 | 45 | **WILLIAM MCKINLEY** | Republican | 7,218,491 | 51.7 | 292 | 73.2 |
|  |  | William J. Bryan | Democratic; Populist | 6,356,734 | 45.5 | 155 |  |
|  |  | John C. Wooley | Prohibition | 208,914 | 1.5 |  |  |
| 1904 | 45 | **THEODORE ROOSEVELT** | Republican | 7,628,461 | 57.4 | 336 | 65.2 |
|  |  | Alton B. Parker | Democratic | 5,084,223 | 37.6 | 140 |  |
|  |  | Eugene V. Debs | Socialist | 402,283 | 3.0 |  |  |
|  |  | Silas C. Swallow | Prohibition | 258,536 | 1.9 |  |  |
| 1908 | 46 | **WILLIAM H. TAFT** | Republican | 7,675,320 | 51.6 | 321 | 65.4 |
|  |  | William J. Bryan | Democratic | 6,412,294 | 43.1 | 162 |  |
|  |  | Eugene V. Debs | Socialist | 420,793 | 2.8 |  |  |
|  |  | Eugene W. Chafin | Prohibition | 253,840 | 1.7 |  |  |
| 1912 | 48 | **WOODROW WILSON** | Democratic | 6,296,547 | 41.9 | 435 | 58.8 |
|  |  | Theodore Roosevelt | Progressive | 4,118,571 | 27.4 | 88 |  |
|  |  | William H. Taft | Republican | 3,486,720 | 23.2 | 8 |  |
|  |  | Eugene V. Debs | Socialist | 900,672 | 6.0 |  |  |
|  |  | Eugene W. Chafin | Prohibition | 206,275 | 1.4 |  |  |

| Year | | Candidates | Parties | Popular Vote | % Popular Vote | Electoral Vote | % Voter Participation |
|------|---|------------|---------|--------------|----------------|----------------|------------------------|
| 1916 | 48 | **WOODROW WILSON** | Democratic | 9,127,695 | 49.4 | 277 | 61.6 |
| | | Charles E. Hughes | Republican | 8,533,507 | 46.2 | 254 | |
| | | A. L. Benson | Socialist | 585,113 | 3.2 | | |
| | | J. Frank Hanly | Prohibition | 220,506 | 1.2 | | |
| 1920 | 48 | **WARREN G. HARDING** | Republican | 16,143,407 | 60.4 | 404 | 49.2 |
| | | James M. Cox | Democratic | 9,130,328 | 34.2 | 127 | |
| | | Eugene V. Debs | Socialist | 919,799 | 3.4 | | |
| | | P. P. Christensen | Farmer-Labor | 265,411 | 1.0 | | |
| 1924 | 48 | **CALVIN COOLIDGE** | Republican | 15,718,211 | 54.0 | 382 | 48.9 |
| | | John W. Davis | Democratic | 8,385,283 | 28.8 | 136 | |
| | | Robert M. La Follette | Progressive | 4,831,289 | 16.6 | 13 | |
| 1928 | 48 | **HERBERT C. HOOVER** | Republican | 21,391,993 | 58.2 | 444 | 56.9 |
| | | Alfred E. Smith | Democratic | 15,016,169 | 40.9 | 87 | |
| 1932 | 48 | **FRANKLIN D. ROOSEVELT** | Democratic | 22,809,638 | 57.4 | 472 | 56.9 |
| | | Herbert C. Hoover | Republican | 15,758,901 | 39.7 | 59 | |
| | | Norman Thomas | Socialist | 881,951 | 2.2 | | |
| 1936 | 48 | **FRANKLIN D. ROOSEVELT** | Democratic | 27,752,869 | 60.8 | 523 | 61.0 |
| | | Alfred M. Landon | Republican | 16,674,665 | 36.5 | 8 | |
| | | William Lemke | Union | 882,479 | 1.9 | | |
| 1940 | 48 | **FRANKLIN D. ROOSEVELT** | Democratic | 27,307,819 | 54.8 | 449 | 62.5 |
| | | Wendell L. Willkie | Republican | 22,321,018 | 44.8 | 82 | |
| 1944 | 48 | **FRANKLIN D. ROOSEVELT** | Democratic | 25,606,585 | 53.5 | 432 | 55.9 |
| | | Thomas E. Dewey | Republican | 22,014,745 | 46.0 | 99 | |

| Year | Number of States | Candidates | Parties | Popular Vote | % of Popular Vote | Electoral Vote | % Voter Participation |
|---|---|---|---|---|---|---|---|
| 1948 | 48 | **HARRY S. TRUMAN** | Democratic | 24,179,345 | 49.6 | 303 | 53.0 |
| | | Thomas E. Dewey | Republican | 21,991,291 | 45.1 | 189 | |
| | | J. Strom Thurmond | States' Rights | 1,176,125 | 2.4 | 39 | |
| | | Henry A. Wallace | Progressive | 1,157,326 | 2.4 | | |
| 1952 | 48 | **DWIGHT D. EISENHOWER** | Republican | 33,936,234 | 55.1 | 442 | 63.3 |
| | | Adlai E. Stevenson | Democratic | 27,314,992 | 44.4 | 89 | |
| 1956 | 48 | **DWIGHT D. EISENHOWER** | Republican | 35,590,472 | 57.6 | 457 | 60.6 |
| | | Adlai E. Stevenson | Democratic | 26,022,752 | 42.1 | 73 | |
| 1960 | 50 | **JOHN F. KENNEDY** | Democratic | 34,226,731 | 49.7 | 303 | 62.8 |
| | | Richard M. Nixon | Republican | 34,108,157 | 49.5 | 219 | |
| 1964 | 50 | **LYNDON B. JOHNSON** | Democratic | 43,129,566 | 61.1 | 486 | 61.9 |
| | | Barry M. Goldwater | Republican | 27,178,188 | 38.5 | 52 | |
| 1968 | 50 | **RICHARD M. NIXON** | Republican | 31,785,480 | 43.4 | 301 | 60.9 |
| | | Hubert H. Humphrey | Democratic | 31,275,166 | 42.7 | 191 | |
| | | George C. Wallace | American Independent | 9,906,473 | 13.5 | 46 | |
| 1972 | 50 | **RICHARD M. NIXON** | Republican | 47,169,911 | 60.7 | 520 | 55.2 |
| | | George S. McGovern | Democratic | 29,170,383 | 37.5 | 17 | |
| | | John G. Schmitz | American | 1,099,482 | 1.4 | | |
| 1976 | 50 | **JIMMY CARTER** | Democratic | 40,830,763 | 50.1 | 297 | 53.5 |
| | | Gerald R. Ford | Republican | 39,147,793 | 48.0 | 240 | |

| Year | Number of States | Candidates | Parties | Popular Vote | % of Popular Vote | Electoral Vote | % Voter Participation |
|---|---|---|---|---|---|---|---|
| 1980 | 50 | **RONALD REAGAN** | Republican | 43,901,812 | 50.7 | 489 | 52.6 |
| | | Jimmy Carter | Democratic | 35,483,820 | 41.0 | 49 | |
| | | John B. Anderson | Independent | 5,719,437 | 6.6 | | |
| | | Ed Clark | Libertarian | 921,188 | 1.1 | | |
| 1984 | 50 | **RONALD REAGAN** | Republican | 54,451,521 | 58.8 | 525 | 53.1 |
| | | Walter F. Mondale | Democratic | 37,565,334 | 40.6 | 13 | |
| 1988 | 50 | **GEORGE H. W. BUSH** | Republican | 47,917,341 | 53.4 | 426 | 50.1 |
| | | Michael Dukakis | Democratic | 41,013,030 | 45.6 | 111 | |
| 1992 | 50 | **BILL CLINTON** | Democratic | 44,908,254 | 43.0 | 370 | 55.0 |
| | | George H. W. Bush | Republican | 39,102,343 | 37.4 | 168 | |
| | | H. Ross Perot | Independent | 19,741,065 | 18.9 | | |
| 1996 | 50 | **BILL CLINTON** | Democratic | 47,401,185 | 49.0 | 379 | 49.0 |
| | | Bob Dole | Republican | 39,197,469 | 41.0 | 159 | |
| | | H. Ross Perot | Independent | 8,085,295 | 8.0 | | |
| 2000 | 50 | **GEORGE W. BUSH** | Republican | 50,455,156 | 47.9 | 271 | 50.4 |
| | | Al Gore | Democrat | 50,997,335 | 48.4 | 266 | |
| | | Ralph Nader | Green | 2,882,897 | 2.7 | | |
| 2004 | 50 | **GEORGE W. BUSH** | Republican | 62,040,610 | 50.7 | 286 | 60.7 |
| | | John F. Kerry | Democrat | 59,028,444 | 48.3 | 251 | |
| 2008 | 50 | **BARACK OBAMA** | Democrat | 69,456,897 | 52.9 | 365 | 63.0 |
| | | John McCain | Republican | 59,934,814 | 45.7 | 173 | |
| 2012 | 50 | **BARACK OBAMA** | Democrat | 65,915,795 | 51.1 | 332 | 57.5 |
| | | Mitt Romney | Republican | 60,933,504 | 47.2 | 206 | |
| 2016 | 50 | **DONALD TRUMP** | Republican | 62,979,636 | 46.1 | 304 | 60.2 |
| | | Hillary Rodham Clinton | Democrat | 65,844,610 | 48.2 | 227 | |
| | | Gary Johnson | Libertarian | 4,489,235 | 3.3 | | |
| | | Jill Stein | Green | 1,457,226 | 1.1 | | |

Candidates receiving less than 1 percent of the popular vote have been omitted. Thus the percentage of popular vote given for any election year may not total 100 percent.

Before the passage of the Twelfth Amendment in 1804, the electoral college voted for two presidential candidates; the runner-up became vice president.

## ADMISSION OF STATES

| Order of Admission | State | Date of Admission | Order of Admission | State | Date of Admission |
|---|---|---|---|---|---|
| 1 | Delaware | December 7, 1787 | 26 | Michigan | January 26, 1837 |
| 2 | Pennsylvania | December 12, 1787 | 27 | Florida | March 3, 1845 |
| 3 | New Jersey | December 18, 1787 | 28 | Texas | December 29, 1845 |
| 4 | Georgia | January 2, 1788 | 29 | Iowa | December 28, 1846 |
| 5 | Connecticut | January 9, 1788 | 30 | Wisconsin | May 29, 1848 |
| 6 | Massachusetts | February 7, 1788 | 31 | California | September 9, 1850 |
| 7 | Maryland | April 28, 1788 | 32 | Minnesota | May 11, 1858 |
| 8 | South Carolina | May 23, 1788 | 33 | Oregon | February 14, 1859 |
| 9 | New Hampshire | June 21, 1788 | 34 | Kansas | January 29, 1861 |
| 10 | Virginia | June 25, 1788 | 35 | West Virginia | June 30, 1863 |
| 11 | New York | July 26, 1788 | 36 | Nevada | October 31, 1864 |
| 12 | North Carolina | November 21, 1789 | 37 | Nebraska | March 1, 1867 |
| 13 | Rhode Island | May 29, 1790 | 38 | Colorado | August 1, 1876 |
| 14 | Vermont | March 4, 1791 | 39 | North Dakota | November 2, 1889 |
| 15 | Kentucky | June 1, 1792 | 40 | South Dakota | November 2, 1889 |
| 16 | Tennessee | June 1, 1796 | 41 | Montana | November 8, 1889 |
| 17 | Ohio | March 1, 1803 | 42 | Washington | November 11, 1889 |
| 18 | Louisiana | April 30, 1812 | 43 | Idaho | July 3, 1890 |
| 19 | Indiana | December 11, 1816 | 44 | Wyoming | July 10, 1890 |
| 20 | Mississippi | December 10, 1817 | 45 | Utah | January 4, 1896 |
| 21 | Illinois | December 3, 1818 | 46 | Oklahoma | November 16, 1907 |
| 22 | Alabama | December 14, 1819 | 47 | New Mexico | January 6, 1912 |
| 23 | Maine | March 15, 1820 | 48 | Arizona | February 14, 1912 |
| 24 | Missouri | August 10, 1821 | 49 | Alaska | January 3, 1959 |
| 25 | Arkansas | June 15, 1836 | 50 | Hawaii | August 21, 1959 |

## POPULATION OF THE UNITED STATES

| Year | Number of States | Population | % Increase | Population per Square Mile |
|------|------------------|------------|------------|---------------------------|
| 1790 | 13 | 3,929,214 | | 4.5 |
| 1800 | 16 | 5,308,483 | 35.1 | 6.1 |
| 1810 | 17 | 7,239,881 | 36.4 | 4.3 |
| 1820 | 23 | 9,638,453 | 33.1 | 5.5 |
| 1830 | 24 | 12,866,020 | 33.5 | 7.4 |
| 1840 | 26 | 17,069,453 | 32.7 | 9.8 |
| 1850 | 31 | 23,191,876 | 35.9 | 7.9 |
| 1860 | 33 | 31,443,321 | 35.6 | 10.6 |
| 1870 | 37 | 39,818,449 | 26.6 | 13.4 |
| 1880 | 38 | 50,155,783 | 26.0 | 16.9 |
| 1890 | 44 | 62,947,714 | 25.5 | 21.1 |
| 1900 | 45 | 75,994,575 | 20.7 | 25.6 |
| 1910 | 46 | 91,972,266 | 21.0 | 31.0 |
| 1920 | 48 | 105,710,620 | 14.9 | 35.6 |
| 1930 | 48 | 122,775,046 | 16.1 | 41.2 |
| 1940 | 48 | 131,669,275 | 7.2 | 44.2 |
| 1950 | 48 | 150,697,361 | 14.5 | 50.7 |
| 1960 | 50 | 179,323,175 | 19.0 | 50.6 |
| 1970 | 50 | 203,235,298 | 13.3 | 57.5 |
| 1980 | 50 | 226,504,825 | 11.4 | 64.0 |
| 1985 | 50 | 237,839,000 | 5.0 | 67.2 |
| 1990 | 50 | 250,122,000 | 5.2 | 70.6 |
| 1995 | 50 | 263,411,707 | 5.3 | 74.4 |
| 2000 | 50 | 281,421,906 | 6.8 | 77.0 |
| 2005 | 50 | 296,410,404 | 5.3 | 77.9 |
| 2010 | 50 | 308,745,538 | 9.7 | 87.4 |
| 2015 | 50 | 321,931,311 | 4.3 | 91.1 |

## LEGAL IMMIGRATION TO THE UNITED STATES, FISCAL YEARS 1820–2016**

| Year | Number | Year | Number | Year | Number | Year | Number |
|---|---|---|---|---|---|---|---|
| **1820–1989** | **55,457,531** | **1871–80** | **2,812,191** | **1921–30** | **4,107,209** | **1971–80** | **4,493,314** |
| 1820 | 8,385 | 1871 | 321,350 | 1921 | 805,228 | 1971 | 370,478 |
| **1821–30** | **143,439** | 1872 | 404,806 | 1922 | 309,556 | 1972 | 384,685 |
| 1821 | 9,127 | 1873 | 459,803 | 1923 | 522,919 | 1973 | 400,063 |
| 1822 | 6,911 | 1874 | 313,339 | 1924 | 706,896 | 1974 | 394,861 |
| 1823 | 6,354 | 1875 | 227,498 | 1925 | 294,314 | 1975 | 386,914 |
| 1824 | 7,912 | 1876 | 169,986 | 1926 | 304,488 | 1976 | 398,613 |
| 1825 | 10,199 | 1877 | 141,857 | 1927 | 335,175 | 1976 | 103,676 |
| 1826 | 10,837 | 1878 | 138,469 | 1928 | 307,255 | 1977 | 462,315 |
| 1827 | 18,875 | 1879 | 177,826 | 1929 | 279,678 | 1978 | 601,442 |
| 1828 | 27,382 | 1880 | 457,257 | 1930 | 241,700 | 1979 | 460,348 |
| 1829 | 22,520 | **1881–90** | **5,246,613** | **1931–40** | **528,431** | 1980 | 530,639 |
| 1830 | 23,322 | 1881 | 669,431 | 1931 | 97,139 | **1981–90** | **7,338,062** |
| **1831–40** | **599,125** | 1882 | 788,992 | 1932 | 35,576 | 1981 | 596,600 |
| 1831 | 22,633 | 1883 | 603,322 | 1933 | 23,068 | 1982 | 594,131 |
| 1832 | 60,482 | 1884 | 518,592 | 1934 | 29,470 | 1983 | 559,763 |
| 1833 | 58,640 | 1885 | 395,346 | 1935 | 34,956 | 1984 | 543,903 |
| 1834 | 65,365 | 1886 | 334,203 | 1936 | 36,329 | 1985 | 570,009 |
| 1835 | 45,374 | 1887 | 490,109 | 1937 | 50,244 | 1986 | 601,708 |
| 1836 | 76,242 | 1888 | 546,889 | 1938 | 67,895 | 1987 | 601,516 |
| 1837 | 79,340 | 1889 | 444,427 | 1939 | 82,998 | 1988 | 643,025 |
| 1838 | 38,914 | 1890 | 455,302 | 1940 | 70,756 | 1989 | 1,090,924 |
| 1839 | 68,069 | **1891–1900** | **3,687,564** | **1941–50** | **1,035,039** | 1990 | 1,536,483 |
| 1840 | 84,066 | 1891 | 560,319 | 1941 | 51,776 | **1991–2000** | **9,090,857** |
| **1841–50** | **1,713,251** | 1892 | 579,663 | 1942 | 28,781 | 1991 | 1,827,167 |
| 1841 | 80,289 | 1893 | 439,730 | 1943 | 23,725 | 1992 | 973,977 |
| 1842 | 104,565 | 1894 | 285,631 | 1944 | 28,551 | 1993 | 904,292 |
|  |  | 1895 | 258,536 | 1945 | 38,119 | 1994 | 804,416 |
|  |  | 1896 | 343,267 | 1946 | 108,721 |  |  |

| Year | Number | Year | Number | Year | Number | Year | Number |
|---|---|---|---|---|---|---|---|
| 1843 | 52,496 | 1897 | 230,832 | 1947 | 147,292 | 1995 | 720,461 |
| 1844 | 78,615 | 1898 | 229,299 | 1948 | 170,570 | 1996 | 915,900 |
| 1845 | 114,371 | 1899 | 311,715 | 1949 | 188,317 | 1997 | 798,378 |
| 1846 | 154,416 | 1900 | 448,572 | 1950 | 249,187 | 1998 | 660,477 |
| 1847 | 234,968 | | | | | 1999 | 644,787 |
| 1848 | 226,527 | **1901–10** | **8,795,386** | **1951–60** | **2,515,479** | 2000 | 841,002 |
| 1849 | 297,024 | 1901 | 487,918 | 1951 | 205,717 | | |
| 1850 | 369,980 | 1902 | 648,743 | 1952 | 265,520 | **2001–10** | **10,503,454** |
| | | 1903 | 857,046 | 1953 | 170,434 | 2001 | 1,058,902 |
| **1851–60** | **2,598,214** | 1904 | 812,870 | 1954 | 208,177 | 2002 | 1,059,356 |
| 1851 | 379,466 | 1905 | 1,026,499 | 1955 | 237,790 | 2003 | 705,827 |
| 1852 | 371,603 | 1906 | 1,100,735 | 1956 | 321,625 | 2004 | 957,883 |
| 1853 | 368,645 | 1907 | 1,285,349 | 1957 | 326,867 | 2005 | 1,122,373 |
| 1854 | 427,833 | 1908 | 782,870 | 1958 | 253,265 | 2006 | 1,266,129 |
| 1855 | 200,877 | 1909 | 751,786 | 1959 | 260,686 | 2007 | 1,052,415 |
| 1856 | 200,436 | 1910 | 1,041,570 | 1960 | 265,398 | 2008 | 1,107,126 |
| 1857 | 251,306 | | | | | 2009 | 1,130,818 |
| 1858 | 123,126 | **1911–20** | **5,735,811** | **1961–70** | **3,321,677** | 2010 | 1,042,625 |
| 1859 | 121,282 | 1911 | 878,587 | 1961 | 271,344 | | |
| 1860 | 153,640 | 1912 | 838,172 | 1962 | 283,763 | **2011–15** | **5,356,671** |
| | | 1913 | 1,197,892 | 1963 | 306,260 | 2011 | 1,062,040 |
| **1861–70** | **2,314,824** | 1914 | 1,218,480 | 1964 | 292,248 | 2012 | 1,031,631 |
| 1861 | 91,918 | 1915 | 326,700 | 1965 | 296,697 | 2013 | 523,000 |
| 1862 | 91,985 | 1916 | 298,826 | 1966 | 323,040 | 2014 | 1,360,000 |
| 1863 | 176,282 | 1917 | 295,403 | 1967 | 361,972 | 2015 | 1,380,000 |
| 1864 | 193,418 | 1918 | 110,618 | 1968 | 454,448 | | |
| 1865 | 248,120 | 1919 | 141,132 | 1969 | 358,579 | | |
| 1866 | 318,568 | 1920 | 430,001 | 1970 | 373,326 | | |
| 1867 | 315,722 | | | | | | |
| 1868 | 138,840 | | | | | | |
| 1869 | 352,768 | | | | | | |
| 1870 | 387,203 | | | | | | |

Source: U.S. Department of Homeland Security.

## IMMIGRATION BY REGION AND SELECTED COUNTRY OF LAST RESIDENCE, FISCAL YEARS 1820–2015

| Region and country of last residence | 1820 to 1829 | 1830 to 1839 | 1840 to 1849 | 1850 to 1859 | 1860 to 1869 | 1870 to 1879 | 1880 to 1889 | 1890 to 1899 |
|---|---|---|---|---|---|---|---|---|
| **Total** | 128,502 | 538,381 | 1,427,337 | 2,814,554 | 2,081,261 | 2,742,137 | 5,248,568 | 3,694,294 |
| Europe | 99,272 | 422,771 | 1,369,259 | 2,619,680 | 1,877,726 | 2,251,878 | 4,638,677 | 3,576,411 |
| Austria-Hungary | — | — | — | — | 3,375 | 60,127 | 314,787 | 534,059 |
| Austria | — | — | — | — | 2,700 | 54,529 | 204,805 | 268,218 |
| Hungary | — | — | — | — | 483 | 5,598 | 109,982 | 203,350 |
| Belgium | 28 | 20 | 3,996 | 5,765 | 5,785 | 6,991 | 18,738 | 19,642 |
| Bulgaria | — | — | — | — | — | — | — | 52 |
| *Former Czechoslovakia | — | — | — | — | — | — | — | — |
| Denmark | 173 | 927 | 671 | 3,227 | 13,553 | 29,278 | 85,342 | 56,671 |
| Finland | — | — | — | — | — | — | — | — |
| France | 7,694 | 39,330 | 75,300 | 81,778 | 35,938 | 71,901 | 48,193 | 35,616 |
| Germany | 5,753 | 124,726 | 385,434 | 976,072 | 723,734 | 751,769 | 1,445,181 | 579,072 |
| Greece | 17 | 49 | 17 | 32 | 51 | 209 | 1,807 | 12,732 |
| Ireland | 51,617 | 170,672 | 656,145 | 1,029,486 | 427,419 | 422,264 | 674,061 | 405,710 |
| Italy | 430 | 2,225 | 1,476 | 8,643 | 9,853 | 46,296 | 267,660 | 603,761 |
| Netherlands | 1,105 | 1,377 | 7,624 | 11,122 | 8,387 | 14,267 | 52,715 | 29,349 |
| Norway-Sweden | 91 | 1,149 | 12,389 | 22,202 | 82,937 | 178,823 | 586,441 | 334,058 |
| Norway | — | — | — | — | 16,068 | 88,644 | 185,111 | 96,810 |
| Sweden | — | — | — | — | 24,224 | 90,179 | 401,330 | 237,248 |
| Poland | 19 | 366 | 105 | 1,087 | 1,886 | 11,016 | 42,910 | 107,793 |
| Portugal | 177 | 820 | 196 | 1,299 | 2,083 | 13,971 | 15,186 | 25,874 |
| Romania | — | — | — | — | — | — | 5,842 | 6,808 |
| Russia | 86 | 280 | 520 | 423 | 1,670 | 35,177 | 182,698 | 450,101 |
| Spain | 2,595 | 2,010 | 1,916 | 8,795 | 6,966 | 5,540 | 3,995 | 9,189 |
| Switzerland | 3,148 | 4,430 | 4,819 | 24,423 | 21,124 | 25,212 | 81,151 | 37,020 |
| United Kingdom | 26,336 | 74,350 | 218,572 | 445,322 | 532,956 | 578,447 | 810,900 | 328,759 |
| *Former Yugoslavia | — | — | — | — | — | — | — | — |
| Other Europe | 3 | 40 | 79 | 4 | 9 | 590 | 1,070 | 145 |

| | | | | | | | | |
|---|---|---|---|---|---|---|---|---|
| Asia | 34 | 55 | 121 | 36,080 | 54,408 | 134,128 | 71,151 | 61,285 |
| China | 3 | 8 | 32 | 35,933 | 54,028 | 133,139 | 65,797 | 15,268 |
| Hong Kong | — | — | 33 | 42 | 50 | 166 | 247 | 102 |
| India | 9 | 38 | — | — | — | — | — | 102 |
| Iran | — | — | — | — | — | — | — | — |
| *Israel | — | — | — | — | — | — | — | — |
| Japan | — | — | — | — | 138 | 193 | 1,583 | 13,998 |
| Jordan | — | — | — | — | — | — | — | — |
| *Korea | — | — | — | — | — | — | — | — |
| Philippines | — | — | — | — | — | — | — | — |
| Syria | — | — | — | — | — | — | — | — |
| Taiwan | — | — | — | — | — | — | — | — |
| Turkey | 19 | 8 | 45 | 94 | 129 | 382 | 2,478 | 27,510 |
| Vietnam | — | — | — | — | — | — | — | — |
| Other Asia | 3 | 1 | 11 | 11 | 63 | 248 | 1,046 | 4,407 |
| North America | 9,655 | 31,905 | 50,516 | 84,145 | 130,292 | 345,010 | 524,826 | 37,350 |
| Canada and Newfoundland | 2,297 | 11,875 | 34,285 | 64,171 | 117,978 | 324,310 | 492,865 | 3,098 |
| Mexico | 3,835 | 7,187 | 3,069 | 3,446 | 1,957 | 5,133 | 2,405 | 734 |
| Caribbean | 3,061 | 11,792 | 11,803 | 12,447 | 8,751 | 14,285 | 27,323 | 31,480 |
| Cuba | — | — | — | — | — | — | — | — |
| Dominican Republic | — | — | — | — | — | — | — | — |
| Haiti | — | — | — | — | — | — | — | — |
| Jamaica | — | — | — | — | — | — | — | — |
| Other Caribbean | 3,061 | 11,792 | 11,803 | 12,447 | 8,751 | 14,285 | 27,323 | 31,480 |
| Central America | 57 | 94 | 297 | 512 | 70 | 173 | 279 | 649 |
| Belize | — | — | — | — | — | — | — | — |
| Costa Rica | — | — | — | — | — | — | — | — |
| El Salvador | — | — | — | — | — | — | — | — |
| Guatemala | — | — | — | — | — | — | — | — |
| Honduras | — | — | — | — | — | — | — | — |
| Nicaragua | — | — | — | — | — | — | — | — |
| Panama | — | — | — | — | — | — | — | — |
| Other Central America | 57 | 94 | 297 | 512 | 70 | 173 | 279 | 649 |
| South America | 405 | 957 | 1,062 | 3,569 | 1,536 | 1,109 | 1,954 | 1,389 |
| Argentina | — | — | — | — | — | — | — | — |
| Bolivia | — | — | — | — | — | — | — | — |

| Region and country of last residence | 1820 to 1829 | 1830 to 1839 | 1840 to 1849 | 1850 to 1859 | 1860 to 1869 | 1870 to 1879 | 1880 to 1889 | 1890 to 1899 |
|---|---|---|---|---|---|---|---|---|
| Brazil | — | — | — | — | — | — | — | — |
| Chile | — | — | — | — | — | — | — | — |
| Colombia | — | — | — | — | — | — | — | — |
| Ecuador | — | — | — | — | — | — | — | — |
| Guyana | — | — | — | — | — | — | — | — |
| Paraguay | — | — | — | — | — | — | — | — |
| Peru | — | — | — | — | — | — | — | — |
| Suriname | — | — | — | — | — | — | — | — |
| Uruguay | — | — | — | — | — | — | — | — |
| Venezuela | — | — | — | — | — | — | — | — |
| Other South America | 405 | 957 | 1,062 | 3,569 | 1,536 | 1,109 | 1,954 | 1,389 |
| Other America | — | — | — | — | — | — | — | — |
| Africa | 15 | 50 | 61 | 84 | 407 | 371 | 763 | 432 |
| Egypt | — | — | — | — | 4 | 29 | 145 | 51 |
| Ethiopia | — | — | — | — | — | — | — | — |
| Liberia | 1 | 8 | 5 | 7 | 43 | 52 | 21 | 9 |
| Morocco | — | — | — | — | — | — | — | — |
| South Africa | — | — | — | — | 35 | 48 | 23 | 9 |
| Other Africa | 14 | 42 | 56 | 77 | 325 | 242 | 574 | 363 |
| Oceania | 3 | 7 | 14 | 166 | 187 | 9,996 | 12,361 | 4,704 |
| Australia | 2 | 1 | 2 | 15 | — | 8,930 | 7,250 | 3,098 |
| New Zealand | — | — | — | — | — | 39 | 21 | 12 |
| Other Oceania | 1 | 6 | 12 | 151 | 187 | 1,027 | 5,090 | 1,594 |
| Not Specified | 19,523 | 83,593 | 7,366 | 74,399 | 18,241 | 754 | 790 | 14,112 |

| Region and country of last residence | 1900 to 1909 | 1910 to 1919 | 1920 to 1929 | 1930 to 1939 | 1940 to 1949 | 1950 to 1959 | 1960 to 1969 | 1980 to 1989 |
|---|---|---|---|---|---|---|---|---|
| **Total** | 8,202,388 | 6,347,380 | 4,295,510 | 699,375 | 856,608 | 2,499,268 | 3,213,749 | 6,244,379 |
| Europe | 7,572,569 | 4,985,411 | 2,560,340 | 444,399 | 472,524 | 1,404,973 | 1,133,443 | 668,866 |
| Austria-Hungary | 2,001,376 | 1,154,727 | 60,891 | 12,531 | 13,574 | 113,015 | 27,590 | 20,437 |
| Austria | 532,416 | 589,174 | 31,392 | 5,307 | 8,393 | 81,354 | 17,571 | 15,374 |
| Hungary | 685,567 | 565,553 | 29,499 | 7,224 | 5,181 | 31,661 | 10,019 | 5,063 |
| Belgium | 37,429 | 32,574 | 21,511 | 4,013 | 12,473 | 18,885 | 9,647 | 7,028 |
| Bulgaria | 34,651 | 27,180 | 2,824 | 1,062 | 449 | 97 | 598 | 1,124 |
| *Former Czechoslovakia | — | — | 101,182 | 17,757 | 8,475 | 1,624 | 2,758 | 5,678 |
| Denmark | 61,227 | 45,830 | 34,406 | 3,470 | 4,549 | 10,918 | 9,797 | 4,847 |
| Finland | — | — | 16,922 | 2,438 | 2,230 | 4,923 | 4,310 | 2,569 |
| France | 67,735 | 60,335 | 54,842 | 13,761 | 36,954 | 50,113 | 46,975 | 32,066 |
| Germany | 328,722 | 174,227 | 386,634 | 119,107 | 119,506 | 576,905 | 209,616 | 85,752 |
| Greece | 145,402 | 198,108 | 60,774 | 10,599 | 8,605 | 45,153 | 74,173 | 37,729 |
| Ireland | 344,940 | 166,445 | 202,854 | 28,195 | 15,701 | 47,189 | 37,788 | 22,210 |
| Italy | 1,930,475 | 1,229,916 | 528,133 | 85,053 | 50,509 | 184,576 | 200,111 | 55,562 |
| Netherlands | 42,463 | 46,065 | 29,397 | 7,791 | 13,877 | 46,703 | 37,918 | 11,234 |
| Norway-Sweden | 426,981 | 192,445 | 170,329 | 13,452 | 17,326 | 44,224 | 36,150 | 13,941 |
| Norway | 182,542 | 79,488 | 70,327 | 6,901 | 8,326 | 22,806 | 17,371 | 3,835 |
| Sweden | 244,439 | 112,957 | 100,002 | 6,551 | 9,000 | 21,418 | 18,779 | 10,106 |
| Poland | — | — | 223,316 | 25,555 | 7,577 | 6,465 | 55,742 | 63,483 |
| Portugal | 65,154 | 82,489 | 44,829 | 3,518 | 6,765 | 13,928 | 70,568 | 42,685 |
| Romania | 57,322 | 13,566 | 67,810 | 5,264 | 1,254 | 914 | 2,339 | 24,753 |
| Russia | 1,501,301 | 1,106,998 | 61,604 | 2,463 | 605 | 453 | 2,329 | 33,311 |
| Spain | 24,818 | 53,262 | 47,109 | 3,669 | 2,774 | 6,880 | 40,793 | 22,783 |
| Switzerland | 32,541 | 22,839 | 31,772 | 5,990 | 9,904 | 17,577 | 19,193 | 8,316 |
| United Kingdom | 469,518 | 371,878 | 341,552 | 61,813 | 131,794 | 195,709 | 220,213 | 153,644 |
| *Former Yugoslavia | — | — | 49,215 | 6,920 | 2,039 | 6,966 | 17,990 | 16,267 |
| Other Europe | 514 | 6,527 | 22,434 | 9,978 | 5,584 | 11,756 | 6,845 | 3,447 |
| Asia | 299,836 | 269,736 | 126,740 | 19,231 | 34,532 | 135,844 | 358,605 | 2,391,356 |
| China | 19,884 | 20,916 | 30,648 | 5,874 | 16,072 | 8,836 | 14,060 | 170,897 |
| Hong Kong | — | — | — | — | — | 13,781 | 67,047 | 112,132 |
| India | 3,026 | 3,478 | 2,076 | 554 | 1,692 | 1,850 | 18,638 | 231,649 |
| Iran | — | — | 208 | 198 | 1,144 | 3,195 | 9,059 | 98,141 |
| *Israel | — | — | — | — | 98 | 21,376 | 30,911 | 43,669 |

| Region and country of last residence | 1900 to 1909 | 1910 to 1919 | 1920 to 1929 | 1930 to 1939 | 1940 to 1949 | 1950 to 1959 | 1960 to 1969 | 1980 to 1989 |
|---|---|---|---|---|---|---|---|---|
| Japan | 139,712 | 77,125 | 42,057 | 2,683 | 1,557 | 40,651 | 40,956 | 44,150 |
| Jordan | — | — | — | — | — | 4,899 | 9,230 | 28,928 |
| *Korea | — | — | — | — | 83 | 4,845 | 27,048 | 322,708 |
| Philippines | — | — | 5,307 | 391 | 4,099 | 17,245 | 70,660 | 502,056 |
| Syria | — | — | — | 2,188 | 1,179 | 1,091 | 2,432 | 14,534 |
| Taiwan | — | — | — | — | — | 721 | 15,657 | 119,051 |
| Turkey | 127,999 | 160,717 | 40,450 | 1,327 | 754 | 2,980 | 9,464 | 19,208 |
| Vietnam | — | — | — | — | — | 290 | 2,949 | 200,632 |
| Other Asia | 9,215 | 7,500 | 5,994 | 6,016 | 7,854 | 14,084 | 40,494 | 483,601 |
| North America | 277,809 | 1,070,539 | 1,591,278 | 230,319 | 328,435 | 921,610 | 1,674,172 | 2,695,329 |
| Canada and Newfoundland | 123,067 | 708,715 | 949,286 | 162,703 | 160,911 | 353,169 | 433,128 | 156,313 |
| Mexico | 31,188 | 185,334 | 498,945 | 32,709 | 56,158 | 273,847 | 441,824 | 1,009,586 |
| Caribbean | 100,960 | 120,860 | 83,482 | 18,052 | 46,194 | 115,661 | 427,235 | 790,109 |
| Cuba | — | — | 12,769 | 10,641 | 25,976 | 73,221 | 202,030 | 132,552 |
| Dominican Republic | — | — | — | 1,026 | 4,802 | 10,219 | 83,552 | 221,552 |
| Haiti | — | — | — | 156 | 823 | 3,787 | 28,992 | 121,406 |
| Jamaica | — | — | — | — | — | 7,397 | 62,218 | 193,874 |
| Other Caribbean | 100,960 | 120,860 | 70,713 | 6,229 | 14,593 | 21,037 | 50,443 | 120,725 |
| Central America | 7,341 | 15,692 | 16,511 | 6,840 | 20,135 | 40,201 | 98,560 | 339,376 |
| Belize | 77 | 40 | 285 | 193 | 433 | 1,133 | 4,185 | 14,964 |
| Costa Rica | — | — | — | 431 | 1,965 | 4,044 | 17,975 | 25,017 |
| El Salvador | — | — | — | 597 | 4,885 | 5,094 | 14,405 | 137,418 |
| Guatemala | — | — | — | 423 | 1,303 | 4,197 | 14,357 | 58,847 |
| Honduras | — | — | — | 679 | 1,874 | 5,320 | 15,078 | 39,071 |
| Nicaragua | — | — | — | 405 | 4,393 | 7,812 | 10,383 | 31,102 |
| Panama | — | — | — | 1,452 | 5,282 | 12,601 | 22,177 | 32,957 |
| Other Central America | 7,264 | 15,652 | 16,226 | 2,660 | — | — | — | — |

| | | | | | | | | |
|---|---|---|---|---|---|---|---|---|
| South America | 15,253 | 39,938 | 43,025 | 9,990 | 19,662 | 78,418 | 250,754 | 399,862 |
| Argentina | — | — | — | 1,067 | 3,108 | 16,346 | 49,384 | 23,442 |
| Bolivia | — | — | — | 50 | 893 | 2,759 | 6,205 | 9,798 |
| Brazil | — | — | 4,627 | 1,468 | 3,653 | 11,547 | 29,238 | 22,944 |
| Chile | — | — | — | 347 | 1,320 | 4,669 | 12,384 | 19,749 |
| Colombia | — | — | — | 1,027 | 3,454 | 15,567 | 68,371 | 105,494 |
| Ecuador | — | — | — | 244 | 2,207 | 8,574 | 34,107 | 48,015 |
| Guyana | — | — | — | 131 | 596 | 1,131 | 4,546 | 85,886 |
| Paraguay | — | — | — | 33 | 85 | 576 | 1,249 | 3,518 |
| Peru | — | — | — | 321 | 1,273 | 5,980 | 19,783 | 49,958 |
| Suriname | — | — | — | 25 | 130 | 299 | 612 | 1,357 |
| Uruguay | — | — | — | 112 | 754 | 1,026 | 4,089 | 7,235 |
| Venezuela | — | — | — | 1,155 | 2,182 | 9,927 | 20,758 | 22,405 |
| Other South America | 15,253 | 39,938 | 38,398 | 4,010 | 7 | 17 | 28 | 61 |
| Other America | — | — | 29 | 25 | 25,375 | 60,314 | 22,671 | 83 |
| Africa | 6,326 | 8,867 | 6,362 | 2,120 | 6,720 | 13,016 | 23,780 | 141,990 |
| Egypt | — | — | 1,063 | 781 | 1,613 | 1,996 | 5,581 | 26,744 |
| Ethiopia | — | — | — | 10 | 28 | 302 | 804 | 12,927 |
| Liberia | — | — | — | 35 | 37 | 289 | 841 | 6,420 |
| Morocco | — | — | — | 73 | 879 | 2,703 | 2,880 | 3,471 |
| South Africa | — | — | — | 312 | 1,022 | 2,278 | 4,360 | 15,505 |
| Other Africa | 6,326 | 8,867 | 5,299 | 909 | 3,141 | 5,448 | 9,314 | 76,923 |
| Oceania | 12,355 | 12,339 | 9,860 | 3,306 | 14,262 | 11,353 | 23,630 | 41,432 |
| Australia | 11,191 | 11,280 | 8,404 | 2,260 | 11,201 | 8,275 | 14,986 | 16,901 |
| New Zealand | — | — | 935 | 790 | 2,351 | 1,799 | 3,775 | 6,129 |
| Other Oceania | 1,164 | 1,059 | 521 | 256 | 710 | 1,279 | 4,869 | 18,402 |
| Not Specified | 33,493 | 488 | 930 | — | 135 | 12,472 | 119 | 305,406 |

| Region and country of last residence | 1990 to 1999 | 2000 to 2009 | 2010 | 2011 | 2012 | 2013 | 2014 | 2015 | 2016 |
|---|---|---|---|---|---|---|---|---|---|
| **Total** | 9,775,398 | 10,299,430 | 1,042,625 | 1,062,040 | 1,031,631 | 990,553 | 1,016,518 | 1,051,031 | 1,183,505 |
| Europe | 1,348,612 | 1,349,609 | 95,429 | 90,712 | 86,956 | 91,095 | 87,790 | 90,789 | 98,043 |
| Austria-Hungary | 27,529 | 33,929 | 4,325 | 4,703 | 3,208 | 2,061 | 2,058 | 2,965 | 2,620 |
| Austria | 18,234 | 21,151 | 3,319 | 3,654 | 2,199 | 1,053 | 1,088 | 1,928 | 1,621 |
| Hungary | 9,295 | 12,778 | 1,006 | 1,049 | 1,009 | 1,008 | 970 | 1,037 | 999 |
| Belgium | 7,077 | 8,157 | 732 | 700 | 698 | 803 | 775 | 809 | 821 |
| Bulgaria | 16,948 | 40,003 | 2,465 | 2,549 | 2,322 | 2,720 | 2,886 | 2,585 | 2,560 |
| *Former Czechoslovakia | 8,970 | 18,691 | 1,510 | 1,374 | 1,316 | 1,258 | 1,168 | 1,236 | 1,299 |
| Denmark | 6,189 | 6,049 | 545 | 473 | 492 | 546 | 533 | 634 | 562 |
| Finland | 3,970 | 3,970 | 414 | 398 | 373 | 360 | 368 | 397 | 512 |
| France | 35,945 | 45,637 | 4,339 | 3,967 | 4,201 | 4,668 | 4,544 | 5,034 | 5,473 |
| Germany | 92,207 | 122,373 | 7,929 | 7,072 | 6,732 | 6,880 | 6,387 | 5,965 | 5,895 |
| Greece | 25,403 | 16,841 | 966 | 1,196 | 1,264 | 1,526 | 1,388 | 1,330 | 1,664 |
| Ireland | 65,384 | 15,642 | 1,610 | 1,533 | 1,694 | 1,765 | 1,721 | 1,798 | 1,895 |
| Italy | 75,992 | 28,329 | 2,956 | 2,670 | 2,946 | 3,233 | 3,647 | 3,829 | 4,385 |
| Netherlands | 13,345 | 17,351 | 1,520 | 1,258 | 1,294 | 1,376 | 1,373 | 1,505 | 1,550 |
| Norway-Sweden | 17,825 | 19,382 | 1,662 | 1,530 | 1,441 | 1,665 | 1,479 | 1,551 | 1,729 |
| Norway | 5,211 | 4,599 | 363 | 405 | 314 | 389 | 332 | 357 | 404 |
| Sweden | 12,614 | 14,783 | 1,299 | 1,125 | 1,127 | 1,276 | 1,147 | 1,194 | 1,325 |
| Poland | 172,249 | 117,921 | 7,391 | 6,634 | 6,024 | 6,073 | 5,437 | 4,921 | 5,287 |
| Portugal | 25,497 | 11,479 | 759 | 878 | 837 | 917 | 920 | 869 | 1,017 |
| Romania | 48,136 | 52,154 | 3,735 | 3,679 | 3,477 | 3,475 | 3,022 | 3,160 | 3,322 |
| Russia | 433,427 | 167,152 | 7,502 | 8,548 | 10,114 | 10,154 | 9,455 | 9,030 | 9,280 |
| Spain | 18,443 | 17,695 | 2,040 | 2,319 | 2,316 | 2,970 | 3,341 | 3,707 | 4,018 |
| Switzerland | 11,768 | 12,173 | 868 | 861 | 916 | 1,040 | 888 | 1,007 | 1,090 |
| United Kingdom | 156,182 | 171,979 | 14,781 | 13,443 | 13,938 | 15,321 | 14,395 | 14,653 | 14,887 |
| *Former Yugoslavia | 57,039 | 131,831 | 4,772 | 4,611 | 4,488 | 4,445 | 4,321 | 4,721 | 5,392 |
| Other Europe | 29,087 | 290,871 | 22,608 | 20,316 | 16,865 | 17,839 | 17,684 | 19,083 | 22,785 |

| | | | | | | | | |
|---|---|---|---|---|---|---|---|---|
| Asia | 2,859,899 | 3,470,835 | 410,209 | 438,580 | 389,301 | 419,382 | 405,854 | 442,854 |
| China | 342,058 | 591,711 | 67,634 | 83,603 | 68,410 | 72,492 | 70,977 | 77,658 |
| Hong Kong | 116,894 | 57,583 | 3,263 | 3,149 | 2,614 | 2,515 | 2,426 | 2,982 |
| India | 352,528 | 590,464 | 66,185 | 66,331 | 65,506 | 74,451 | 61,380 | 61,691 |
| Iran | 76,899 | 76,755 | 9,078 | 9,015 | 9,658 | 8,894 | 9,074 | 9,596 |
| *Israel | 41,340 | 54,081 | 5,172 | 4,389 | 4,555 | 4,251 | 4,324 | 4,652 |
| Japan | 66,582 | 84,552 | 7,100 | 6,751 | 6,383 | 5,980 | 5,808 | 5,709 |
| Jordan | 42,755 | 53,550 | 9,327 | 8,211 | 5,949 | 9,028 | 7,835 | 7,345 |
| *Korea | 179,770 | 209,758 | 22,022 | 22,748 | 22,937 | 20,313 | 16,976 | 21,329 |
| Philippines | 534,338 | 545,463 | 56,399 | 55,251 | 52,955 | 48,633 | 54,307 | 50,609 |
| Syria | 22,906 | 30,807 | 7,424 | 7,983 | 3,999 | 4,677 | 5,459 | 3,800 |
| Taiwan | 132,647 | 92,657 | 6,785 | 6,206 | 5,336 | 4,712 | 4,814 | 5,062 |
| Turkey | 38,687 | 48,394 | 7,435 | 9,040 | 7,189 | 7,248 | 8,762 | 8,635 |
| Vietnam | 275,379 | 289,616 | 30,065 | 33,486 | 26,578 | 29,825 | 30,332 | 40,412 |
| Other Asia | 637,116 | 745,444 | 112,320 | 122,417 | 107,232 | 126,363 | 123,380 | 143,374 |
| North America | 5,137,743 | 4,441,529 | 426,981 | 423,277 | 399,380 | 400,102 | 439,228 | 502,639 |
| Canada and Newfoundland | 194,788 | 236,349 | 19,491 | 19,506 | 20,489 | 17,670 | 19,309 | 19,349 |
| Mexico | 2,757,418 | 1,704,166 | 138,717 | 142,823 | 134,198 | 133,107 | 157,227 | 172,726 |
| Caribbean | 1,004,687 | 1,053,357 | 139,389 | 133,012 | 121,349 | 133,550 | 146,086 | 180,479 |
| Cuba | 159,037 | 271,742 | 33,372 | 36,261 | 31,343 | 46,505 | 54,178 | 66,120 |
| Dominican Republic | 359,818 | 291,492 | 53,890 | 46,036 | 41,487 | 44,550 | 50,382 | 60,613 |
| Haiti | 177,446 | 203,827 | 22,336 | 21,802 | 20,083 | 15,107 | 16,787 | 23,185 |
| Jamaica | 177,143 | 172,523 | 19,439 | 19,298 | 19,052 | 18,804 | 17,362 | 22,833 |
| Other Caribbean | 181,243 | 113,773 | 10,352 | 9,615 | 9,384 | 8,584 | 7,377 | 7,728 |
| Central America | 610,189 | 591,130 | 43,597 | 43,249 | 44,056 | 43,638 | 46,556 | 54,512 |
| Belize | 12,600 | 9,682 | 997 | 933 | 969 | 823 | 804 | 878 |
| Costa Rica | 17,054 | 21,571 | 2,306 | 2,230 | 2,232 | 2,018 | 2,121 | 2,295 |
| El Salvador | 273,017 | 251,237 | 18,547 | 18,477 | 18,015 | 18,964 | 18,699 | 21,268 |
| Guatemala | 126,043 | 156,992 | 10,263 | 10,795 | 9,829 | 9,871 | 11,466 | 12,548 |
| Honduras | 72,880 | 63,513 | 6,381 | 6,053 | 8,795 | 8,025 | 9,071 | 12,996 |

| Region and country of last residence | 1990 to 1999 | 2000 to 2009 | 2010 | 2011 | 2012 | 2013 | 2014 | 2015 | 2016 |
|---|---|---|---|---|---|---|---|---|---|
| Nicaragua | 80,446 | 70,015 | 3,476 | 3,314 | 2,943 | 2,940 | 2,773 | 3,262 | 3,397 |
| Panama | 28,149 | 18,120 | 1,627 | 1,447 | 1,363 | 1,276 | 1,164 | 1,133 | 1,130 |
| Other Central America | — | | | | | | - | - | - |
| South America | 570,624 | 856,508 | 85,783 | 84,687 | 77,748 | 79,287 | 72,135 | 70,049 | 75,571 |
| Argentina | 30,065 | 47,955 | 4,312 | 4,335 | 4,218 | 4,227 | 3,757 | 3,542 | 3,783 |
| Bolivia | 18,111 | 21,921 | 2,211 | 2,113 | 1,920 | 2,005 | 1,663 | 1,549 | 1,481 |
| Brazil | 50,744 | 115,404 | 12,057 | 11,643 | 11,248 | 10,772 | 10,246 | 11,247 | 13,528 |
| Chile | 18,200 | 19,792 | 1,940 | 1,854 | 1,628 | 1,751 | 1,591 | 1,620 | 1,711 |
| Colombia | 137,985 | 236,570 | 21,861 | 22,130 | 20,272 | 20,611 | 17,614 | 16,509 | 16,830 |
| Ecuador | 81,358 | 107,977 | 11,463 | 11,068 | 9,284 | 10,553 | 10,871 | 9,816 | 10,779 |
| Guyana | 74,407 | 70,373 | 6,441 | 6,288 | 5,282 | 5,564 | 6,031 | 5,313 | 4,909 |
| Paraguay | 6,082 | 4,623 | 449 | 501 | 454 | 437 | 363 | 353 | 400 |
| Peru | 110,117 | 137,614 | 14,063 | 13,836 | 12,414 | 12,370 | 10,450 | 9,973 | 10,519 |
| Suriname | 2,285 | 2,363 | 202 | 167 | 216 | 170 | 160 | 116 | 130 |
| Uruguay | 6,062 | 9,827 | 1,286 | 1,521 | 1,348 | 1,314 | 1,098 | 1,023 | 911 |
| Venezuela | 35,180 | 82,087 | 9,497 | 9,229 | 9,464 | 9,512 | 8,289 | 8,985 | 10,590 |
| Other South America | 28 | 2 | 1 | 2 | - | 1 | 2 | 3 | - |
| Other America | 37 | 19 | 4 | - | - | 1 | 2 | 1 | 2 |
| Africa | 346,416 | 759,734 | 98,246 | 97,429 | 103,685 | 94,589 | 94,834 | 98,677 | 110,754 |
| Egypt | 44,604 | 81,564 | 9,822 | 9,096 | 10,172 | 10,719 | 12,043 | 13,907 | 13,367 |
| Ethiopia | 40,097 | 87,207 | 13,853 | 13,985 | 15,400 | 13,484 | 12,926 | 12,566 | 13,699 |
| Liberia | 13,587 | 23,316 | 2,924 | 3,117 | 3,451 | 3,036 | 3,681 | 3,580 | 3,545 |
| Morocco | 15,768 | 40,844 | 4,847 | 4,249 | 3,534 | 3,202 | 3,495 | 3,569 | 4,447 |
| South Africa | 21,964 | 32,221 | 2,705 | 2,754 | 2,960 | 2,693 | 2,871 | 3,298 | 3,441 |
| Other Africa | 210,396 | 494,582 | 64,095 | 64,228 | 68,168 | 61,455 | 59,818 | 61,757 | 72,255 |
| Oceania | 56,800 | 65,793 | 5,946 | 5,825 | 5,573 | 6,061 | 5,980 | 6,227 | 6,489 |
| Australia | 24,288 | 32,728 | 3,077 | 3,062 | 3,146 | 3,529 | 3,582 | 3,795 | 4,173 |
| New Zealand | 8,600 | 12,495 | 1,046 | 1,006 | 980 | 1,027 | 941 | 978 | 939 |
| Other Oceania | 23,912 | 20,570 | 1,823 | 1,757 | 1,447 | 1,505 | 1,457 | 1,454 | 1,377 |
| Not Specified | 25,928 | 211,930 | 5,814 | 6,217 | 9,265 | 10,127 | 8,430 | 10,256 | 22,726 |

—Represents zero or not available. *Note that a) Korea split into North Korea and South Korea in 1945; b) Czechoslovakia separated into the Czech Republic and the Slovak Republic in 1993; c) Former Yugoslavia, beginning in the 1990s, broke into the six nations of Serbia, Montenegro, Slovenia, Croatia, Macedonia, and Kosovo; d) and due to the way United States immigration statistics are recognized and collected, immigrants from the Occupied Palestinian Territories are grouped together with immigrants from Israel. **This data tracks the number of people who are annually granted legal permanent residence.

## PRESIDENTS, VICE PRESIDENTS,
## AND SECRETARIES OF STATE

| | *President* | *Vice President* | *Secretary of State* |
|---|---|---|---|
| 1. | George Washington, Federalist 1789 | John Adams, Federalist 1789 | Thomas Jefferson 1789<br>Edmund Randolph 1794<br>Timothy Pickering 1795 |
| 2. | John Adams, Federalist 1797 | Thomas Jefferson, Dem.-Rep. 1797 | Timothy Pickering 1797<br>John Marshall 1800 |
| 3. | Thomas Jefferson, Dem.-Rep. 1801 | Aaron Burr, Dem.-Rep. 1801<br>George Clinton, Dem.-Rep. 1805 | James Madison 1801 |
| 4. | James Madison, Dem.-Rep. 1809 | George Clinton, Dem.-Rep. 1809<br>Elbridge Gerry, Dem.-Rep. 1813 | Robert Smith 1809<br>James Monroe 1811 |
| 5. | James Monroe, Dem.-Rep. 1817 | Daniel D. Tompkins, Dem.-Rep. 1817 | John Q. Adams 1817 |
| 6. | John Quincy Adams, Dem.-Rep. 1825 | John C. Calhoun, Dem.-Rep. 1825 | Henry Clay 1825 |
| 7. | Andrew Jackson, Democratic 1829 | John C. Calhoun, Democratic 1829<br>Martin Van Buren, Democratic 1833 | Martin Van Buren 1829<br>Edward Livingston 1831<br>Louis McLane 1833<br>John Forsyth 1834 |
| 8. | Martin Van Buren, Democratic 1837 | Richard M. Johnson, Democratic 1837 | John Forsyth 1837 |
| 9. | William H. Harrison, Whig 1841 | John Tyler, Whig 1841 | Daniel Webster 1841 |

| | President | Vice President | Secretary of State |
|---|---|---|---|
| 10. | John Tyler, Whig and Democratic 1841 | None | Daniel Webster 1841<br>Hugh S. Legaré 1843<br>Abel P. Upshur 1843<br>John C. Calhoun 1844 |
| 11. | James K. Polk, Democratic 1845 | George M. Dallas, Democratic 1845 | James Buchanan 1845 |
| 12. | Zachary Taylor, Whig 1849 | Millard Fillmore, Whig 1848 | John M. Clayton 1849 |
| 13. | Millard Fillmore, Whig 1850 | None | Daniel Webster 1850<br>Edward Everett 1852 |
| 14. | Franklin Pierce, Democratic 1853 | William R. King, Democratic 1853 | William L. Marcy 1853 |
| 15. | James Buchanan, Democratic 1857 | John C. Breckinridge, Democratic 1857 | Lewis Cass 1857<br>Jeremiah S. Black 1860 |
| 16. | Abraham Lincoln, Republican 1861 | Hannibal Hamlin, Republican 1861<br>Andrew Johnson, Unionist 1865 | William H. Seward 1861 |
| 17. | Andrew Johnson, Unionist 1865 | None | William H. Seward 1865 |
| 18. | Ulysses S. Grant, Republican 1869 | Schuyler Colfax, Republican 1869<br>Henry Wilson, Republican 1873 | Elihu B. Washburne 1869<br>Hamilton Fish 1869 |
| 19. | Rutherford B. Hayes, Republican 1877 | William A. Wheeler, Republican 1877 | William M. Evarts 1877 |

| | President | Vice President | Secretary of State |
|---|---|---|---|
| 20. | James A. Garfield, Republican 1881 | Chester A. Arthur, Republican 1881 | James G. Blaine 1881 |
| 21. | Chester A. Arthur, Republican 1881 | None | Frederick T. Frelinghuysen 1881 |
| 22. | Grover Cleveland, Democratic 1885 | Thomas A. Hendricks, Democratic 1885 | Thomas F. Bayard 1885 |
| 23. | Benjamin Harrison, Republican 1889 | Levi P. Morton, Republican 1889 | James G. Blaine 1889 John W. Foster 1892 |
| 24. | Grover Cleveland, Democratic 1893 | Adlai E. Stevenson, Democratic 1893 | Walter Q. Gresham 1893 Richard Olney 1895 |
| 25. | William McKinley, Republican 1897 | Garret A. Hobart, Republican 1897 Theodore Roosevelt, Republican 1901 | John Sherman 1897 William R. Day 1898 John Hay 1898 |
| 26. | Theodore Roosevelt, Republican 1901 | Charles Fairbanks, Republican 1905 | John Hay 1901 Elihu Root 1905 Robert Bacon 1909 |
| 27. | William H. Taft, Republican 1909 | James S. Sherman, Republican 1909 | Philander C. Knox 1909 |
| 28. | Woodrow Wilson, Democratic 1913 | Thomas R. Marshall, Democratic 1913 | William J. Bryan 1913 Robert Lansing 1915 Bainbridge Colby 1920 |
| 29. | Warren G. Harding, Republican 1921 | Calvin Coolidge, Republican 1921 | Charles E. Hughes 1921 |
| 30. | Calvin Coolidge, Republican 1923 | Charles G. Dawes, Republican 1925 | Charles E. Hughes 1923 Frank B. Kellogg 1925 |

| | President | Vice President | Secretary of State |
|---|---|---|---|
| 31. | Herbert Hoover, Republican 1929 | Charles Curtis, Republican 1929 | Henry L. Stimson 1929 |
| 32. | Franklin D. Roosevelt, Democratic 1933 | John Nance Garner, Democratic 1933<br>Henry A. Wallace, Democratic 1941<br>Harry S. Truman, Democratic 1945 | Cordell Hull 1933<br>Edward R. Stettinius, Jr. 1944 |
| 33. | Harry S. Truman, Democratic 1945 | Alben W. Barkley, Democratic 1949 | Edward R. Stettinius, Jr. 1945<br>James F. Byrnes 1945<br>George C. Marshall 1947<br>Dean G. Acheson 1949 |
| 34. | Dwight D. Eisenhower, Republican 1953 | Richard M. Nixon, Republican 1953 | John F. Dulles 1953<br>Christian A. Herter 1959 |
| 35. | John F. Kennedy, Democratic 1961 | Lyndon B. Johnson, Democratic 1961 | Dean Rusk 1961 |
| 36. | Lyndon B. Johnson, Democratic 1963 | Hubert H. Humphrey, Democratic 1965 | Dean Rusk 1963 |
| 37. | Richard M. Nixon, Republican 1969 | Spiro T. Agnew, Republican 1969<br>Gerald R. Ford, Republican 1973 | William P. Rogers 1969<br>Henry Kissinger 1973 |
| 38. | Gerald R. Ford, Republican 1974 | Nelson Rockefeller, Republican 1974 | Henry Kissinger 1974 |
| 39. | Jimmy Carter, Democratic 1977 | Walter Mondale, Democratic 1977 | Cyrus Vance 1977<br>Edmund Muskie 1980 |

| | President | Vice President | Secretary of State |
|---|---|---|---|
| 40. | Ronald Reagan, Republican 1981 | George H. W. Bush, Republican 1981 | Alexander Haig 1981 George Schultz 1982 |
| 41. | George H. W. Bush, Republican 1989 | J. Danforth Quayle, Republican 1989 | James A. Baker 1989 Lawrence Eagleburger 1992 |
| 42. | William J. Clinton, Democratic 1993 | Albert Gore, Jr., Democratic 1993 | Warren Christopher 1993 Madeleine Albright 1997 |
| 43. | George W. Bush, Republican 2001 | Richard B. Cheney, Republican 2001 | Colin L. Powell 2001 Condoleezza Rice 2005 |
| 44. | Barack Obama, Democratic 2009 | Joseph R. Biden, Democratic 2009 | Hillary Rodham Clinton 2009 John Kerry 2013 |
| 45. | Donald J. Trump, Republican 2017 | Michael R. Pence, Republican 2017 | Rex W. Tillerson 2017 Michael R. Pompeo 2018 |

# FURTHER READINGS

## CHAPTER 1

A fascinating study of pre-Columbian migration is Gavin Menzes and Ian Hudson, *Who Discovered America?: The Untold Story of the Peopling of the Americas* (2014). Clarissa Confer's *Daily Life in Pre-Columbian Native America* (2007) reveals what life was like before the arrival of Europeans. Erik Wahlgren describes the Norse settlements in the north Atlantic in *The Vikings and America* (2000). Alice B. Kehoe's *North American Indians: A Comprehensive Account*, 3rd ed. (2005), provides an encyclopedic treatment of Native Americans. Equally valuable is Anton Truer's *Atlas of Indian Nations* (2014). See also Charles Mann's *1491: New Revelations of the Americas before Columbus* (2005) and *1493: Uncovering the New World that Columbus Created* (2011), Colin G. Calloway's *One Vast Winter Count: The Native American West* (2006), Daniel K. Richter, *Before the Revolution: America's Ancient Pasts* (2011), and Peter Silver's *Our Savage Neighbors: How Indian War Transformed Early America* (2008). On North America's largest Native American city, see Timothy R. Pauketat, *Cahokia* (2010).

The conflict between Native Americans and Europeans is in the focus of James Axtell's *The Invasion Within: The Contest of Cultures in Colonial North America* (1986) and *Beyond 1492: Encounters in Colonial North America* (1992). Colin G. Calloway's *New Worlds for All: Indians, Europeans, and the Remaking of Early America* (1997) explores the ecological effects of European settlement while Peter Mitchell's *Horse Nations* explains the transformational impact of horses on Native Americans.

On the religious turmoil of the era, see and Matthew Carr's *Blood and Faith: The Purging of Muslim Spain* (2010), Carlos M.N. Eire's *Reformations: The Early Modern World, 1450–1650* (2016), Alec Ryrie's *Protestants: The Faith That Made the Modern World* (2017), Lyndal Roper's *Martin Luther: Renegade and Prophet* (2017), John M. Todd's *Luther: A Life* (2008), and Peter H. Wilson's *Europe's Tragedy: A History of the Thirty Years' War* (2009).

For changes in science and technology, see David Wooton's *The Invention of Science* (2015).

Laurence Bergreen examines the voyages of Columbus in *Columbus: The Four Voyages* (2011). To learn about the queen who sent Columbus to the New World, see Kristin Downey's *Isabella: The Warrior Queen* (2014). For sweeping overviews of Spain's creation of a global empire, see Hugh Thomas's *Rivers of Gold: The Rise of the Spanish Empire, from Columbus to Magellan* (2004) and *World without End: Spain, Philip II, and the First Global Empire* (2016), Robert Goodwin, *Spain: The Center of the World, 1519–1682* (2015). David J. Weber examines Spanish colonization in *The Spanish Frontier in North America* (1992). On Portugal, see Roger Crowley's *Conquerors: How Portugal Forged the First Global Empire* (2016). For the French experience, see William J. Eccles's *France in America*, rev. ed. (1990). For an insightful comparison of Spanish and English modes of settlement, see J. H. Elliott, *Empires of the Atlantic World: Britain and Spain in America, 1492–1830* (2006).

## CHAPTER 2

Two excellent surveys of early American history are Peter C. Hoffer's *The Brave New World: A History of Early America*, 2nd ed. (2006), and William R. Polk's *The Birth of America: From before Columbus to the Revolution* (2006).

Bernard Bailyn's *The Barbarous Years: The Peopling of British North America: The Conflict of Civilizations, 1600–1675* (2013) tells the often brutal story of British settlement in America during the seventeenth century. On the impact of the American environment on colonial settlement, see Malcolm Gaskill's *Between Two Worlds: How the English Became Americans* (2015). The best overview of the colonization of North America is Alan Taylor's *American Colonies: The Settling of North America* (2001). On the interactions among Indian, European, and African cultures, see Andrew Lipman's *The Saltwater Frontier: Indians and the Contest for the American Coast* (2015) and Gary B. Nash's *Red, White, and Black: The Peoples of Early North America*, 5th ed. (2005).

A good overview of the founding of Virginia and Maryland is Jean and Elliott Russo's *The Early Chesapeake in British North America* (2012). For information regarding the Puritan settlement of New England, see David D. Hall's *A Reforming People: Puritanism and the Transformation of Public Life in New England* (2013). The best biography of John Winthrop is Francis J. Bremer's *John Winthrop: America's Forgotten Founding Father* (2003). On Roger Williams, see John M. Barry's *Roger Williams and the*

*Creation of the American Soul* (2012) and James A. Warren's *God, War, and Providence* (2018).

The pattern of settlement in the middle colonies is explained in Barry Levy's *Quakers and the American Family: British Settlement in the Delaware Valley* (1988). On the early history of New York, see Russell Shorto's *The Island at the Center of the World: The Epic Story of Dutch Manhattan and the Forgotten Colony That Shaped America* (2004). Settlement of the Chesapeake Bay region is traced in James Horn's *Adapting to a New World: English Society in the Seventeenth-Century Chesapeake* (1994). On North Carolina, see Noeleen McIlvenna's *A Very Mutinous People: The Struggle for North Carolina, 1660-1713* (2009).

On shifting political life in England, see Peter Ackroyd, *The History of England from James I to the Glorious Revolution* (2015) and Steve Pincus, *1688: The First Modern Revolution* (2009). For a study of race and the settlement of South Carolina, see Peter H. Wood's *Black Majority: Negroes in Colonial South Carolina from 1670 through the Stono Rebellion* (1974). On the flourishing trade in captive Indians, see Alan Gallay's *The Indian Slave Trade: The Rise of the English Empire in the American South, 1670–1717* (2002) and Andres Resendez's *The Other Slavery* (2016). On the Yamasee War, see Steven J. Oatis's *A Colonial Complex: South Carolina's Frontiers in the Era of the Yamasee War, 1680–1730* (2004) and William L. Ramsey's *The Yamasee War* (2010).

## CHAPTER 3

The diversity of colonial societies may be seen in David Hackett Fischer's *Albion's Seed: Four British Folkways in America* (1989). John Frederick Martin's *Profits in the Wilderness: Entrepreneurship and the Founding of New England Towns in the Seventeenth Century* (1991) indicates that economic concerns rather than spiritual motives were driving forces in many New England towns.

Bernard Rosenthal challenges many myths concerning the Salem witch trials in *Salem Story: Reading the Witch Trials of 1692* (1993). Mary Beth Norton's *In the Devil's Snare: The Salem Witchcraft Crisis of 1692* (2002) emphasizes the role of Indian violence, while Stacy Schiff's *The Witches* (2016) provides a riveting analysis of the many factors influencing the outbreak of anti-witch hysteria. See also Benjamin C. Ray's *Satan and Salem: The Witch-Hunt Crisis of 1692* (2015).

Discussions of women in the New England colonies can be found in Laurel Thatcher Ulrich's *Good Wives: Image and Reality in the Lives of Women in Northern New England, 1650–1750* (1980), and Mary Beth Norton, *Separated by Their Sex: Women in Public and Private in the Colonial Atlantic World* (2011). On women and religion, see Susan Juster's *Disorderly Women: Sexual Politics and Evangelicalism in Revolutionary New England* (1994). John Demos describes family life in *A Little Commonwealth: Family Life in Plymouth Colony*, new ed. (2000).

For an excellent overview of Indian relations with Europeans, see Colin G. Calloway's *New Worlds for All: Indians, Europeans, and the Remaking of Early America* (1997). For analyses of Indian wars, see Alfred A. Cave's *The Pequot War* (1996), James D. Drake's *King Philip's War: Civil War in New England* (2000), and Jill Lepore's *The Name of War: King Philip's War and the Origins of American Identity* (1998). The story of the Iroquois is told well in Daniel K. Richter's *The Ordeal of the Longhouse: The Peoples of the Iroquois League in the Era of European Colonization* (1992). Indians in the southern colonies are the focus of James Axtell's *The Indians' New South: Cultural Change in the Colonial Southeast* (1997). On the fur trade, see Eric Jay Dolan, *Fur, Fortune, and Empire: The Epic Story of the Fur Trade in America* (2010). For the Glorious Revolution, see Steve Pincus's *1688: The First Modern Revolution* (2009).

For the social history of the southern colonies, see Allan Kulikoff's *Tobacco and Slaves: The Development of Southern Cultures in the Chesapeake, 1680–1800* (1986). On the interaction of the cultures of blacks and whites, see Mechal Sobel's *The World They Made Together: Black and White Values in Eighteenth-Century Virginia* (1987). On the slave trade, see William St. Clair's *The Door of No Return* (2007). African Americans during colonial settlement are the focus of Timothy H. Breen and Stephen Innes's *"Myne Owne Ground": Race and Freedom on Virginia's Eastern Shore, 1640–1676*, new ed. (2004). David W. Galenson's *White Servitude in Colonial America: An Economic Analysis* (1981) looks at the indentured labor force.

Henry F. May's *The Enlightenment in America* (1976) and Donald H. Meyer's *The Democratic Enlightenment* (1976) examine intellectual trends in eighteenth-century America while Jonathan Israel does the same for Europe in *Enlightenment Contested: Philosophy, Modernity, and the Emancipation of Man, 1670–1752* (2006). See also Dorinda Outram's *Panorama of the Enlightenment* (2006). On the Great Awakening, see Frank Lambert's *Inventing the "Great Awakening"* (1999), and Thomas S. Kidd's *The Great Awakening: The Roots of Evangelical Christianity in Colonial America* (2007). Excellent biographies of the key revivalists are Phillip F. Gura's *Jonathan Edwards: A Life* (2003) and Thomas S. Kidd's *George Whitefield* (2015).

## CHAPTER 4

A good introduction to the imperial phase of the colonial conflicts is Douglas Edward Leach's *Arms for Empire: A Military History of the British Colonies in North America, 1607–1763* (1973). Also useful is Brendan Simms's *Three Victories and a Defeat: The Rise and Fall of the First British Empire* (2008). Fred Anderson's *Crucible of War: The Seven Years' War and the Fate of Empire in British North America, 1754–1766* (2000) is the best history of the Seven Years' War along with D. Peter MacLeod's *Northern Armageddon* (2016). For the implications of the British victory in 1763, see Colin G. Calloway's *The Scratch of a Pen: 1763 and the Transformation of North America* (2006). On the French colonies in North America, see David Hackett Fisher's *Champlain's Dream* (2008) and Allan Greer's *The People of New France* (1997).

For a narrative survey of the events leading to the Revolution, see Edward Countryman's *The American Revolution,* rev. ed. (2003) and Eric Hinderaker's *Boston's Massacre* (2017). For Great Britain's perspective on the imperial conflict, see Ian R. Christie's *Crisis of Empire: Great Britain and the American Colonies, 1754–1783* (1966). Also see Jeremy Black's *George III: America's Last King* (2007) and David Preston's *Braddock's Defeat* (2015). For the British perspective, see Nick Bunker's *An Empire on the Edge: How Britain Came to Fight America* (2015). For a social history of the Revolution, see Gary Nash's *The Unknown American Revolution* (2006).

The intellectual foundations of revolt are explored in Bernard Bailyn's *The Ideological Origins of the American Revolution* (1992). To understand how these views were connected to organized protest, see Jon Butler's *Becoming America: The Revolution before 1776* (2000) and Kevin Phillips's *1775: A Good Year for a Revolution* (2012). On the first major battle, see Nathaniel Philbrick's *Bunker Hill: A City, A Siege, A Revolution* (2013).

On the efforts of colonists to boycott the purchase of British goods, see T. H. Breen's *The Marketplace of Revolution: How Consumer Politics Shaped American Independence* (2004). For the events during the summer of 1776, see Joseph J. Ellis's *Revolutionary Summer: The Birth of American Independence.* Pauline Maier's *American Scripture: Making the Declaration of*

*Independence* (1997) remains the best analysis of the framing of that document. The best analysis of why Americans supported independence is Thomas Slaughter's *Independence: The Tangled Roots of the American Revolution* (2014).

## CHAPTER 5

Military affairs in the early phases of the Revolutionary War are the focus of John Ferling's *Almost a Miracle: The American Victory in the War for Independence* (2009). The Revolutionary War is the subject of Gordon S. Wood's *The Radicalism of the American Revolution* (1991), Holger Hoock's *Scars of Independence: America's Violent Birth* (2017) and Jeremy Black's *War for America: The Fight for Independence, 1775–1783* (1991). John Ferling's *Setting the World Ablaze: Washington, Adams, Jefferson, and the American Revolution* (2000) highlights the roles played by key leaders. For a splendid account of Washington's generalship, see Robert Middlekauf's *Washington's Revolution: The Making of America's First Great Leader* (2015).

On the social history of the Revolutionary War, see John W. Shy's *A People Numerous and Armed: Reflections on the Military Struggle for American Independence*, rev. ed. (1990). Colin G. Calloway tells the neglected story of the Indian experiences in the Revolution in *The American Revolution in Indian Country: Crisis and Diversity in Native American Communities* (1995). For a broader assessment of the Revolution, see Alan Taylor's *American Revolutions: A Continental History* (2016).

Why some Americans remained loyal to the Crown is the subject of Thomas B. Allen's *Tories: Fighting for the King in America's First Civil War* (2010) and Maya Jasanoff's *Liberty's Exiles: American Loyalists in the Revolutionary War* (2011). A superb study of African Americans during the Revolutionary era is Douglas R. Egerton's *Death or Liberty: African Americans and Revolutionary America* (2009). For insights into the role of Native Americans in the war, see Colin Calloway's *The American Revolution in Indian Country* (1995), and Joseph Glatthaar and James Kirby Martin's *Forgotten Allies: The Oneida Indians and the American Revolution* (2007). The strategic American victory at Saratoga is the focus of Richard M. Ketchum's *Saratoga: Turning Point of America's Revolutionary War* (1999).

Carol Berkin's *Revolutionary Mothers: Women in the Struggle for America's Independence* (2005) documents the role that women played in securing independence. A superb biography of Revolutionary America's most prominent woman is Woody Holton's *Abigail Adams* (2010). A fine new biography of America's commander in chief is Ron Chernow's *Washington: A Life* (2010). The best analysis of the British side of the war is Andrew Jackson O'Shaughnessy's *The Men Who Lost America: British Leadership, the American Revolution, and the Fate of Empire* (2013).

## CHAPTER 6

A good overview of the Confederation period is Richard B. Morris's *The Forging of the Union, 1781–1789* (1987). Another useful analysis of this period is Richard Buel Jr.'s *Securing the Revolution: Ideology in American Politics, 1789–1815* (1972). For the role played by key leaders, see Joseph J. Ellis's *The Quartet: Orchestrating the Second American Revolution, 1783-1789* (2016). David P. Szatmary's *Shays's Rebellion: The Making of an Agrarian Insurrection* (1980) covers that fateful incident. For a fine account of cultural change during the period, see Joseph J. Ellis's *After the Revolution: Profiles of Early American Culture* (1979).

An excellent overview of post-Revolutionary life is Joyce Appleby's *Inheriting the Revolution: The First Generation of Americans* (2000). On the political philosophies contributing to the drafting of the Constitution, see Ralph Lerner's *The Thinking Revolutionary: Principle and Practice in the New Republic* (1987). For the dramatic story of the framers of the Constitution, see Richard Beeman's *Plain, Honest Men: The Making of the American Constitution* (2009). Woody Holton's *Unruly Americans and the Origins of the Constitution* (2007) emphasizes the role of taxes and monetary policies in the crafting of the Constitution. The complex story of ratification is well told in Pauline Maier's *Ratification: The People Debate the Constitution, 1787–1788* (2010). An excellent study of James Madison's development as a political theorist is Michael Signer's *Becoming Madison* (2015).

On attitudes toward religion in the new United States, see Mark Lilla's *The Stillborn God: Religion, Politics, and the Modern West* (2007) and John Meacham's *American Gospel: God, the Founding Fathers and the Making of a Nation* (2006).

The best introduction to the early Federalists remains John C. Miller's *The Federalist Era, 1789-1801* (2011). Other works analyze the ideological debates among the nation's first leaders. Richard Buel Jr.'s *Securing the Revolution: Ideology in American Politics, 1789–1815* (1972), Joyce Appleby's *Capitalism and a New Social Order: The Republican Vision of the 1790s* (1984), and Stanley Elkins and Eric McKitrick's *The Age of Federalism: The Early American Republic, 1788–1800*

(1993) trace the persistence and transformation of ideas first fostered during the Revolutionary crisis. The best studies of Washington's political career are John Ferling's *The Ascent of George Washington: The Hidden Political Genius of an American Icon* (2009) and Edward Larson's *The Return of George Washington: Uniting the States, 1783–1789* (2015). For compelling portraits of four key leaders, see Joseph J. Ellis's *The Quartet: Orchestrating the Second American Revolution, 1783–1789* (2015).

The 1790s may also be understood through the views and behavior of national leaders. See the following biographies: Richard Brookhiser's *Founding Father: Rediscovering George Washington* (1996), *Alexander Hamilton, American* (1999), and *James Madison* (2013), and Joseph J. Ellis's *Passionate Sage: The Character and Legacy of John Adams* (1993). On social life, see Jack Larkin's *Everyday Life in America, 1790–1840* (1989).

On the formation of the federal government and its economic policies, see Thomas K. McCraw's *The Founders and Finance* (2012). Federalist foreign policy is explored in Jerald A. Comb's *The Jay Treaty: Political Battleground of the Founding Fathers* (1970) and William Stinchcombe's *The XYZ Affair* (1980).

## CHAPTER 7

Marshall Smelser's *The Democratic Republic, 1801–1815* (1968) presents an overview of the Republican administrations. Even more comprehensive is Gordon S. Wood's *Empire of Liberty: A History of the Early Republic, 1789–1815* (2010). The best treatment of the election of 1800 is Edward J. Larson's *A Magnificent Catastrophe: The Tumultuous Election of 1800* (2008).

The standard biography of Jefferson is Joseph J. Ellis's *American Sphinx: The Character of Thomas Jefferson* (1996). More recent analyses include John Boles's *Jefferson* (2017) and Andrew Burstein's *Democracy's Muse* (2015). On the life of Jefferson's friend and successor, see Drew R. McCoy's *The Last of the Fathers: James Madison and the Republican Legacy* (1989). Joyce Appleby's *Capitalism and a New Social Order: The Republican Vision of the 1790s* (1984) minimizes the impact of Republican ideology.

Linda K. Kerber's *Federalists in Dissent: Imagery and Ideology in Jeffersonian American* (1970) explores the Federalists while out of power. The concept of judicial review and the courts can be studied in Cliff Sloan and David McKean's *The Great Decision: Jefferson, Adams, Marshall, and the Battle for the Supreme Court* (2009). Milton Lomask's two volumes, *Aaron Burr: The Years from Princeton to Vice President, 1756–1805* (1979) and *The Conspiracy and the Years of Exile, 1805–1836* (1982), trace the career of that remarkable American. A more recent biography is Nancy Isenberg's *Fallen Founder: The Life of Aaron Burr* (2008).

For the Louisiana Purchase, consult Jon Kukla's *A Wilderness So Immense: The Louisiana Purchase and the Destiny of America* (2003). The development of the states bordering the Gulf of Mexico is told well in Jack E. Davis's *The Gulf: The Making of an American Sea* (2017). For a captivating account of the Lewis and Clark expedition, see Stephen Ambrose's *Undaunted Courage: Meriwether Lewis, Thomas Jefferson, and the Opening of the American West* (1996).

Burton Spivak's *Jefferson's English Crisis: Commerce, Embargo, and the Republican Revolution* (1979) discusses Anglo-American relations during Jefferson's administration; Clifford L. Egan's *Neither Peace Nor War: Franco-American Relations, 1803–1812* (1983) covers America's relations with France. An excellent revisionist treatment of the events that brought on war in 1812 is J. C. A. Stagg's *Mr. Madison's War: Politics, Diplomacy, and Warfare in the Early American Republic, 1783–1830* (1983). See also Paul A. Gilje's *Free Trade and Sailors' Rights in the War of 1812* (2013). The war itself is the focus of Donald R. Hickey's *The War of 1812: A Forgotten Conflict* (1989). For the perspective of those who fought in the war, see A. J. Langguth's *Union 1812: The Americans Who Fought the Second War of Independence* (2007). See also Alan Taylor's award-winning *The Civil War of 1812: American Citizens, British Subjects, Irish Rebels, and Indian Allies* (2011).

## CHAPTER 8

The best overview of the second quarter of the nineteenth century is Daniel Walker Howe, *What Hath God Wrought: The Transformation of America, 1815–1845* (2007). The classic study of transportation and economic growth is George Rogers Taylor's *The Transportation Revolution, 1815–1860* (1951). A more recent treatment is Sarah H. Gordon's *Passage to Union: How the Railroads Transformed American Life, 1829–1929* (1996). On the Erie Canal, see Carol Sheriff's *The Artificial River: The Erie Canal and the Paradox of Progress, 1817–1862* (1996). See also John Lauritz Larson's *Internal Improvement: National Public Works and the Promise of Popular Government in the Early United States* (2001). On the development of clipper ships, see Stephen Ujifusa's *Barons of the Sea: The Race to Build Clipper Ships* (2018).

Several books focus on social issues of the post-Revolutionary period, including *Keepers of the Revolution: New Yorkers at Work in the Early Republic*

(1992), edited by Paul A. Gilje and Howard B. Rock; Ronald Schultz's *The Republic of Labor: Philadelphia Artisans and the Politics of Class, 1720–1830* (1993); and Peter Way's *Common Labor: Workers and the Digging of North American Canals, 1780–1860* (1993).

On the industrial revolution, see Charles R. Morris's *The Dawn of Innovation: The First American Industrial Revolution* (2013). The impact of technology is examined in David J. Jeremy's *Transatlantic Industrial Revolution: The Diffusion of Textile Technologies between Britain and America, 1790–1830s* (1981). On the invention of the telegraph, see Kenneth Silverman's *Lightning Man: The Accursed Life of Samuel F. B. Morse* (2003). For the story of steamboats, see Andrea Sutcliffe's *Steam: The Untold Story of America's First Great Invention* (2004).

The outlook of the working class during this time of transition is surveyed in Edward E. Pessen's *Most Uncommon Jacksonians: The Radical Leaders of the Early Labor Movement* (1967). See also James R. Barrett's *History from the Bottom Up and Inside Out: Ethnicity, Race, and Identity in Working-Class History* (2017). Detailed case studies of working communities include Anthony F. C. Wallace's *Rockdale: The Growth of an American Village in the Early Industrial Revolution* (1978), Thomas Dublin's *Women at Work: The Transformation of Work and Community in Lowell, Massachusetts, 1826–1860* (1979), and Sean Wilentz's *Chants Democratic: New York and the Rise of the American Working Class, 1788–1850* (1984).

For a fine treatment of urbanization, see Charles N. Glaab and A. Theodore Brown's *A History of Urban America* (1967). On immigration, see John Bodnar's *The Transplanted: A History of Immigrants in Urban America* (1987), Roger Daniels's *Coming to America: A History of Immigration and Ethnicity in American Life* (2002), Leonard Dinnerstein's *Ethnic Americans: A History of Immigration* (2009), Jay P. Dolan's *The Irish Americans* (2008), and John Kelly's *The Graves Are Walking: The Great Famine and the Saga of the Irish People* (2012).

## CHAPTER 9

The standard overview of the Era of Good Feelings remains George Dangerfield's *The Awakening of American Nationalism, 1815–1828* (1965). A classic summary of the economic trends of the period is Douglass C. North's *The Economic Growth of the United States, 1790–1860* (1961). An excellent synthesis of the era is Charles Sellers's *The Market Revolution: Jacksonian America, 1815–1846* (1991).

On Monroe, see Harlow Giles Unger's *The Last Founding Father* (2010). On John Quincy Adams, see William J. Cooper's *The Lost Founding Father* (2017) and Charles N. Edel's *John Quincy Adams and the Grand Strategy of the Republic* (2014). For diplomatic relations during James Monroe's presidency, see William Earl Weeks's *John Quincy Adams and American Global Empire* (1992). For relations after 1812, see Ernest R. May's *The Making of the Monroe Doctrine* (1975). The campaign that brought Andrew Jackson to the White House is analyzed in Robert Vincent Remini's *The Election of Andrew Jackson* (1963).

## CHAPTER 10

The best comprehensive surveys of politics and culture during the Jacksonian era are Daniel Walker Howe's *What Hath God Wrought: The Transformation of America, 1815–1848* (2007) and David S. Reynolds's *Waking Giant: America in the Age of Jackson* (2008). A more political focus can be found in Harry L. Watson's *Liberty and Power: The Politics of Jacksonian America* (1990). On the rise of urban political machines, see Terry Golway's *Machine Made: Tammany Hall and the Creation of Modern American Politics* (2014).

For an outstanding analysis of women in New York City during the Jacksonian period, see Christine Stansell's *City of Women: Sex and Class in New York, 1789–1860* (1986). In *Chants Democratic: New York City and the Rise of the American Working-Class, 1788–1850* (1984), Sean Wilentz analyzes the social basis of working-class politics. More recently, Wilentz has traced the democratization of politics in *The Rise of American Democracy: Jefferson to Lincoln* (2009).

The best biography of Jackson remains Robert Vincent Remini's three-volume work: *Andrew Jackson: The Course of American Empire, 1767–1821* (1977), *Andrew Jackson: The Course of American Freedom, 1822–1832* (1981), and *Andrew Jackson: The Course of American Democracy, 1833–1845* (1984). A more critical study of the seventh president is Andrew Burstein's *The Passions of Andrew Jackson* (2003). See also Jon Meacham's *American Lion: Andrew Jackson in the White House* (2009). On Jackson and the Indians see Robert Remini's *Andrew Jackson and His Indian Wars* (2001). The story of the Trail of Tears is told in A. J. Langguth's *Driven West: Andrew Jackson and the Trail of Tears* (2011).

On Jackson's successor, consult Ted Widmer's *Martin Van Buren* (2005). Studies of other major figures of the period include John Niven's *John C. Calhoun and the Price of Union: A Biography* (1988), Merrill D. Peterson's *The Great*

*Triumvirate: Webster, Clay, and Calhoun* (1987), James C. Klotter's *Henry Clay: The Man Who Would be President* (2018), and *Daniel Webster: The Man and His Time* (1997).

The political philosophies of Jackson's opponents are treated in Michael F. Holt's *The Rise and Fall of the American Whig Party: Jacksonian Politics and the Onset of the Civil War* (1999) and Harry L. Watson's *Andrew Jackson vs. Henry Clay: Democracy and Development in Antebellum America* (1998). The outstanding book on the nullification issue remains William W. Freehling's *Prelude to Civil War: The Nullification Controversy in South Carolina, 1816–1836* (1965). John M. Belohlavek's *"Let the Eagle Soar!": The Foreign Policy of Andrew Jackson* (1985) is a thorough study of Jacksonian diplomacy.

## Chapter 11

Three efforts to understand the mind of the Old South and its defense of slavery are Eugene D. Genovese's *The Slaveholders' Dilemma: Freedom and Progress in Southern Conservative Thought, 1820–1860* (1992), William W. Freehling's *The Road to Disunion: Secessionists Triumphant, 1854–1861* (2007), and Walter Johnson's *River of Dark Dreams: Slavery and Empire in the Cotton Kingdom* (2013). Stephanie McCurry's *Masters of Small Worlds: Yeoman Households, Gender Relations, and the Political Culture of the Antebellum South Carolina Low Country* (1995) describes southern households, religion, and political culture. The best recent book on the role of slavery in creating the cotton culture is Edward E. Baptist's *The Half Has Never Been Told: Slavery and the Making of American Capitalism* (2014).

Other essential works on southern culture and society include Bertram Wyatt-Brown's *Honor and Violence in the Old South* (1986), Elizabeth Fox-Genovese's *Within the Plantation Household: Black and White Women of the Old South* (1988), Catherine Clinton's *The Plantation Mistress: Woman's World in the Old South* (1982), Joan E. Cashin's *A Family Venture: Men and Women on the Southern Frontier* (1991), and Theodore Rosengarten's *Tombee: Portrait of a Cotton Planter* (1986).

John W. Blassingame's *The Slave Community: Plantation Life in the Antebellum South*, rev. and enlarged ed. (1979), Eugene D. Genovese's *Roll, Jordan, Roll: The World the Slaves Made* (1974), and Herbert G. Gutman's *The Black Family in Slavery and Freedom, 1750–1925* (1976) all stress the theme of a persisting and identifiable slave culture.

On the question of slavery's profitability, see Sven Beckert's *Empire of Cotton: A Global History* (2014), Robert William Fogel and Stanley L. Engerman's *Time on the Cross: The Economics of American Negro Slavery* (1974), Robert Johnson's *River of Dark Dreams: Slavery and Empire in the Cotton Kingdom* (2017), and Edward E. Baptist's *The Half Has Never Been Told* (2014). Charles Joyner's *Down by the Riverside: A South Carolina Slave Community* (1984) offers a vivid reconstruction of one community.

## CHAPTER 12

Russel Blaine Nye's *Society and Culture in America, 1830–1860* (1974) provides a wide-ranging survey of the Romantic movement. On the reform impulse, consult Ronald G. Walter's *American Reformers, 1815–1860*, rev. ed. (1997). Revivalist religion is treated in Nathan O. Hatch's *The Democratization of American Christianity* (1989), Christine Leigh Heyrman's *Southern Cross: The Beginnings of the Bible Belt* (1997), and Ellen Eslinger's *Citizens of Zion: The Social Origins of Camp Meeting Revivalism* (1999). On the Mormons, see Alex Beam's *American Crucifixion: The Murder of Joseph Smith and the Fate of the Mormon Church* (2014).

The best treatments of transcendentalist thought are Paul F. Boller's *American Transcendentalism, 1830–1860: An Intellectual Inquiry* (1974) and Philip F. Gura's *American Transcendentalism: A History* (2007). On Henry D. Thoreau, see Michael Sims's *The Adventures of Henry Thoreau* (2014). Edgar Allan Poe is the subject of Jerome McGann's *The Poet Edgar Allan Poe: Alien Angel* (2015). For the war against alcohol, see W. J. Rorabaugh's *The Alcoholic Republic: An American Tradition* (1979) and Barbara Leslie Epstein's *The Politics of Domesticity: Women, Evangelism, and Temperance in Nineteenth-Century America* (1981). On prison reform and other humanitarian projects, see David J. Rothman's *The Discovery of the Asylum: Social Order and Disorder in the New Republic*, rev. ed. (2002), and Thomas J. Brown's biography *Dorothea Dix: New England Reformer* (1998).

Useful surveys of abolitionism include Manisha Sinha's *The Slave's Cause: A History of Abolition* (2017), James Brewer Stewart's *Holy Warriors: The Abolitionists and American Slavery*, rev. ed. (1997), and Julie Roy Jeffrey's *The Great Silent Army of Abolitionism: Ordinary Women in the Antislavery Movement* (1998). For the pro-slavery argument as it developed in the South, see Larry E. Tise's *Proslavery: A History of the Defense of Slavery in America, 1701–1840* (1987) and James Oakes's *The Ruling Race: A History of American*

*Slaveholders* (1982). The problems southerners had in justifying slavery are explored in Kenneth S. Greenberg's *Masters and Statesmen: The Political Culture of American Slavery* (1985). For the dramatic story of the role of the Underground Railroad in freeing slaves, see Eric Foner's *Gateway to Freedom: The Hidden History of the Underground Railroad* (2015).

## CHAPTER 13

For background on Whig programs and ideas, see Michael F. Holt's *The Rise and Fall of the American Whig Party: Jacksonian Politics and the Onset of the Civil War* (1999). On John Tyler, see Edward P. Crapol's *John Tyler: The Accidental President* (2006). On the expansionist impulse westward, see Walter Nugent's *Habits of Empire: A History of American Expansionism* (2008) and Richard White's *"It's Your Misfortune and None of My Own": A New History of the American West* (1991). On the creation of the California missions, see Steven W. Hackel's *Junipero Serra: California's Founding Father* (2013) and Gregory Orfalea's *Journey to the Sun: Junipero Serra's Dream and the Founding of California* (2014).

For the expansionism of the 1840s, see Steven E. Woodworth's *Manifest DwnbExpansion and the Road to the Civil War* (2010). The movement of settlers to the West is ably documented in John Mack Faragher's *Women and Men on the Overland Trail*, 2nd ed. (2001), David Dary's *The Santa Fe Trail: Its History, Legends, and Lore* (2000), and Rinker Buck's *The Oregon Trail* (2015). For first-hand accounts of life on the Overland Trails, see Michael L. Tate, ed., *The Great Medicine Road: Narratives of the Oregon, California, and Mormon Trails* (2014). On the Donner Party tragedy, see Michael Wallis's *The Best Land under Heaven: The Donner Party in the Age of Manifest Destiny* (2017).

Gene M. Brack's *Mexico Views Manifest Destiny, 1821–1846: An Essay on the Origins of the Mexican War* (1975) takes Mexico's viewpoint on U.S. designs on the West. For the American perspective on Texas, see Joel H. Silbey's *Storm over Texas: The Annexation Controversy and the Road to Civil War* (2005). On the siege of the Alamo, see William C. Davis's *Three Roads to the Alamo: The Lives and Fortunes of David Crockett, James Bowie, and William Barret Travis* (1998) and James Donovan's *The Blood of Heroes* (2012). An excellent biography related to the emergence of Texas is Gregg Cantrell's *Stephen F. Austin: Empresario of Texas* (1999).

On James K. Polk, see Robert W. Merry's *A Country of Vast Designs: James K. Polk, the Mexican War, and the Conquest of the American Continent* (2009). The best survey of the military conflict is John S. D. Eisenhower's *So Far from God: The U.S. War with Mexico, 1846–1848* (1989). The Mexican

War as viewed from the perspective of the soldiers is described in Richard Bruce Winders's *Mr. Polk's Army: American Military Experience in the Mexican War* (1997). On the diplomatic aspects of Mexican-American relations, see David M. Pletcher's *The Diplomacy of Annexation: Texas, Oregon, and the Mexican War* (1973).

## CHAPTER 14

The best surveys of the forces and events leading to the Civil War include James M. McPherson's *Battle Cry of Freedom: The Civil War Era* (1988) and *The War That Forged a Nation: Why the Civil War Still Matters* (2017), Stephen B. Oates's *The Approaching Fury: Voices of the Storm, 1820–1861* (1997), James Oakes's *The Scorpion's Sting: Antislavery and the Coming of the Civil War* (2015), and Bruce Levine's *Half Slave and Half Free: The Roots of Civil War* (1992). The most recent narrative of the political debate leading to secession is Michael A. Morrison's *Slavery and the American West: The Eclipse of Manifest Destiny and the Coming of the Civil War* (1997). The best brief history of the Civil War, at less than a hundred pages, is Louis Masur's *The Civil War: A Concise History* (2011).

Mark J. Stegmaier's *Texas, New Mexico, and the Compromise of 1850: Boundary Dispute and Sectional Crisis* (1996) probes that crucial dispute, while Michael F. Holt's *The Political Crisis of the 1850s* (1978) traces the demise of the Whigs. See also Fergus M. Bordewich's *America's Great Debate: Henry Clay, Stephen A. Douglas, and the Compromise That Preserved the Union* (2012). Eric Foner, in *Free Soil, Free Labor, Free Men: The Ideology of the Republican Party before the Civil War* (1970), shows how events and ideas combined in the formation of a new political party. The pivotal *Dred Scott* case is assessed in Earl M. Maltz's *Dred Scott and the Politics of Slavery* (2007).

On the role of John Brown in the sectional crisis, see Robert E. McGlone's *John Brown's War Against Slavery* (2009). A detailed study of the South's journey to secession is William W. Freehling's *The Road to Disunion*, vol. 1, *Secessionists at Bay, 1776–1854* (1990), and *The Road to Disunion*, vol. 2, *Secessionists Triumphant, 1854–1861* (2007). Robert E. Bonner traces the emergence of southern nationalism in *Mastering America: Southern Slaveholders and the Crisis of American Nationhood* (2009).

On the Buchanan presidency, see Jean H. Baker's *James Buchanan* (2004). Maury Klein's *Days of Defiance: Sumter, Secession, and the Coming of the Civil War* (1997) treats the Fort Sumter controversy. An excellent collection of interpretive essays is *Why the Civil War Came* (1996), edited by Gabor S. Boritt.

## CHAPTER 15

On the start of the Civil War, see Adam Goodheart's *1861: The Civil War Awakening* (2011). The best one-volume overview of the Civil War period is James M. McPherson's *Battle Cry of Freedom: The Civil War Era* (1988). A more recent synthesis of the war and its effects is David Goldfield's *America Aflame: How the Civil War Created a Nation* (2011). The best brief history is Louis Masur's *The Civil War: A Concise History* (2011). A good introduction to the military events is Herman Hattaway's *Shades of Blue and Gray: An Introductory Military History of the Civil War* (1997). The outlook and experiences of the common soldier are explored in James M. McPherson's *For Cause and Comrades: Why Men Fought in the Civil War* (1997. For the global dimensions of the conflict, see Don H. Doyle's *The Cause of All Nations: An International History of the American Civil War* (2015).

The northern war effort is highlighted in Gary W. Gallagher's *The Union War* (2011). For emphasis on the South, see Gallagher's *The Confederate War* (1997). A sparkling account of the birth of the Rebel nation is William C. Davis's *"A Government of Our Own": The Making of the Confederacy* (1994). On the president of the Confederacy, see James M. McPherson's *Embattled Rebel: Jefferson Davis as Commander in Chief* (2014). On two of the leading Confederate commanders, see Michael Korda's *Clouds of Glory: The Life and Legend of Robert E. Lee* (2014) and S. C. Gwynne's *Rebel Yell: Stonewall Jackson* (2014). On the key Union generals, see Lee Kennett's *Sherman: A Soldier's Life* (2001) and Josiah Bunting III's *Ulysses S. Grant* (2004). The controversy over Sherman's March to the Sea is the focus of Matthew Carr's *Sherman's Ghosts: Soldiers, Civilians, and the American Way of War* (2015). For a lively account of the Confederacy's leader, see James M. McPherson's *Embattled Rebel: Jefferson Davis and the Confederate Civil War* (2014).

The history of the North during the war is surveyed in Philip Shaw Paludan's *A People's Contest: The Union and Civil War, 1861–1865,* 2nd ed. (1996), and J. Matthew Gallman's *The North Fights the Civil War: The Home Front* (1994). See also Jennifer L. Weber's *Copperheads: The Rise and Fall of Lincoln's Opponents in the North* (2006). The central northern political figure, Abraham Lincoln, is the subject of many books. See James McPherson's *Abraham Lincoln* (2009) and Ronald C. White Jr., *A. Lincoln: A Biography* (2009).

The experience of the African American soldier is surveyed in Joseph T. Glatthaar's *Forged in Battle: The Civil War Alliance of Black Soldiers and White Officers* (1990) and Ira Berlin, Joseph P. Reidy, and Leslie S. Rowland's *Freedom's Soldiers: The Black Military Experience in the Civil War* (1998). For the

African American woman's experience, see Jacqueline Jones's *Labor of Love, Labor of Sorrow: Black Women, Work and the Family, from Slavery to the Present* (1985). On Lincoln's evolving racial views, see Eric Foner's *The Fiery Trial: Abraham Lincoln and American Slavery* (2010). The war's impact on slavery is the focus of James Oakes's *Freedom National: The Destruction of Slavery in the United States, 1861–1865* (2013) and Bruce Levine's *The Fall of the House of Dixie* (2013). On the emancipation proclamation, see Louis P. Masur's *Lincoln's Hundred Days: The Emancipation Proclamation and the War for the Union* (2012). For a sensory perspective on the fighting, see Mark M. Smith's *The Smell of Battle, the Taste of Siege: A Sensory History of the Civil War* (2014).

Recent gender and ethnic studies include Nina Silber's *Gender and the Sectional Conflict* (2008), Drew Gilpin Faust's *Mothers of Invention: Women of the Slaveholding South in the American Civil War* (1996), Judith Giesberger and Randall Miller's *Women and the American Civil War* (2018), George C. Rable's *Civil Wars: Women and the Crisis of Southern Nationalism* (1989), and William L. Burton's *Melting Pot Soldiers: The Union's Ethnic Regiments*, 2nd ed. (1998). What Civil War veterans experienced after the conflict ended is the subject of Brian Matthew Jordan's *Marching Home* (2015) and Gregory P. Downs's *After Appomattox: Military Occupation and the Ends of War* (2015).

## CHAPTER 16

The most comprehensive treatment of Reconstruction is Eric Foner's *Reconstruction: America's Unfinished Revolution, 1863–1877* (1988). A good brief history is Alan Guelzo's *Reconstruction: A Concise History* (2018). On Andrew Johnson, see Hans L. Trefousse's *Andrew Johnson: A Biography* (1989) and David D. Stewart's *Impeached: The Trial of Andrew Johnson and the Fight for Lincoln's Legacy* (2009).

Scholars have been sympathetic to the aims and motives of the Radical Republicans. See, for instance, Herman Belz's *Reconstructing the Union: Theory and Policy during the Civil War* (1969) and Richard Nelson Current's *Those Terrible Carpetbaggers: A Reinterpretation* (1988). The ideology of the Radicals is explored in Michael Les Benedict's *A Compromise of Principle: Congressional Republicans and Reconstruction, 1863–1869* (1974). On the black political leaders, see Phillip Dray's *Capitol Men: The Epic Story of Reconstruction through the Lives of the First Black Congressmen* (2008).

The intransigence of southern white attitudes is examined in Michael Perman's *Reunion without Compromise: The South and Reconstruction, 1865–1868* (1973) and Dan T. Carter's *When the War Was Over: The Failure of*

*Self-Reconstruction in the South, 1865–1867* (1985). Allen W. Trelease's *White Terror: The Ku Klux Klan Conspiracy and Southern Reconstruction* (1971) covers the various organizations that practiced vigilante tactics. On the massacre of African Americans, see Charles Lane's *The Day Freedom Died: The Colfax Massacre, the Supreme Court, and the Betrayal of Reconstruction* (2008).

The difficulties former slaves had in adjusting to the new labor system are documented in James L. Roark's *Masters without Slaves: Southern Planters in the Civil War and Reconstruction* (1977). Books on southern politics during Reconstruction include Michael Perman's *The Road to Redemption: Southern Politics, 1869–1879* (1984), Terry L. Seip's *The South Returns to Congress: Men, Economic Measures, and Intersectional Relationships, 1868–1879* (1983), and Mark W. Summers's *Railroads, Reconstruction, and the Gospel of Prosperity: Aid under the Radical Republicans, 1865–1877* (1984).

Numerous works study the freed blacks' experience in the South. Start with Leon F. Litwack's *Been in the Storm So Long: The Aftermath of Slavery* (1979). The Freedmen's Bureau is explored in William S. McFeely's *Yankee Stepfather: General O. O. Howard and the Freedmen* (1968). The situation of freed slave women is in the focus of Jacqueline Jones's *Labor of Love, Labor of Sorrow: Black Women, Work and the Family, from Slavery to the Present* (1985).

The politics of corruption outside the South is depicted in William S. McFeely's *Grant: A Biography* (1981). The best recent biography of the 18th president is Ron Chernow's *Grant* (2017). The political maneuvers of the election of 1876 and the resultant crisis and compromise are explained in Michael Holt's *By One Vote: The Disputed Presidential Election of 1876* (2008).

## CHAPTER 17

For masterly syntheses of post–Civil War industrial development, see Walter Licht's *Industrializing America: The Nineteenth Century* (1995) and Maury Klein's *The Genesis of Industrial America, 1870–1920* (2007). On the growth of railroads, see Richard White's *Railroaded: The Transcontinentals and the Making of Modern America* (2011) and Albro Martin's *Railroad Triumphant: The Growth, Rejection, and Rebirth of a Vital American Force* (1992).

On entrepreneurship in the iron and steel sector, and Thomas J. Misa's *A Nation of Steel: The Making of Modern America, 1865–1925* (1995). The best biographies of the leading business tycoons are Ron Chernow's *Titan: The Life of John D. Rockefeller, Sr.* (1998), David Nasaw's *Andrew Carnegie* (2006), and Jean Strouse's *Morgan: American Financier* (1999). Nathan Rosenberg's

*Technology and American Economic Growth* (1972) documents the growth of invention during the period.

For an overview of the struggle of workers to organize unions, see Philip Bray's *There Is Power in a Union: The Epic Story of Labor in America* (2010). On the 1877 railroad strike, see David O. Stowell's *Streets, Railroad, and the Great Strike of 1877* (1999). For the role of women in the changing workplace, see Alice Kessler-Harris's *Out to Work: A History of Wage-Earning Women in the United States* (1982) and Susan E. Kennedy's *If All We Did Was to Weep at Home: A History of White Working-Class Women in American* (1979). On Mother Jones, see Elliott J. Gorn's *Mother Jones: The Most Dangerous Woman in America* (2001). To trace the rise of socialism among organized workers, see Nick Salvatore's *Eugene V. Debs: Citizen and Socialist* (1982) and Patrick Renshaw's *The Wobblies: The Story of the IWW* (1999). The key strikes are discussed in Paul Arvich's *The Haymarket Tragedy* (1984), W. F. Burns's *The Pullman Boycott: A Complete History of the Railroad Strike* (2015), and Paul Krause's *The Battle for Homestead, 1880–1892: Politics, Culture, and Steel* (1992).

## CHAPTER 18

The classic study of the emergence of the New South remains C. Vann Woodward's *Origins of the New South, 1877–1913* (1951). A more recent treatment of southern society after the end of Reconstruction is Edward L. Ayers's *Southern Crossing: A History of the American South, 1877–1906* (1995). A thorough survey of industrialization in the South is James C. Cobb's *Industrialization and Southern Society, 1877–1984* (1984). On southern efforts to rationalize their defeat, see Edward H. Bonekemper's *The Myth of the Lost Cause: Why the South Fought the Civil War and the North Won* (2015).

On race relations, see Howard N. Rabinowitz's *Race Relations in the Urban South, 1865–1890* (1978). Leon F. Litwack's *Trouble in Mind: Black Southerners in the Age of Jim Crow* (1998) treats the rise of legal segregation, while Michael Perman's *Struggle for Mastery: Disfranchisement in the South, 1888–1908* (2001) surveys efforts to keep African Americans from voting. An award-winning study of white women and the race issue is Glenda Elizabeth Gilmore's *Gender and Jim Crow: Women and the Politics of White Supremacy in North Carolina, 1896–1920* (1996). On W. E. B. Du Bois, see David Levering Lewis's *W. E. B. Du Bois: Biography of a Race, 1868–1919* (1993). On Booker T. Washington, see Robert J. Norrell's *Up from History: The Life of Booker T. Washington* (2009).

For stimulating reinterpretations of the frontier and the development of the West, see William Cronon's *Nature's Metropolis: Chicago and the Great West* (1991), Patricia Nelson Limerick's *The Legacy of Conquest: The Unbroken Past of the American West* (1987), Richard White's *"It's Your Misfortune and None of My Own": A New History of the American West* (1991), and Walter Nugent's *Into the West: The Story of Its People* (1999). An excellent overview is James M. McPherson's *Into the West: From Reconstruction to the Final Days of the American Frontier* (2006).

The role of African Americans in western settlement is the focus of William Loren Katz's *The Black West: A Documentary and Pictorial History of the African American Role in the Westward Expansion of the United States*, rev. ed. (2005), and Nell Irvin Painter's *Exodusters: Black Migration to Kansas after Reconstruction* (1977).

The role of women in the West is the focus of Cathy Lucetti and Carol Olwell's *Women of the West* (2017) and Glenda Riley's *Women and Nature: Saving the Wild West* (1999).

The best account of the conflicts between Indians and whites is Robert M. Utley's *The Indian Frontier of the American West, 1846–1890* (1984). For the Sand Creek massacre, see Ari Kellman's *A Misplaced Massacre: Struggling over the Memory of Sand Creek* (2013). On the Battle of the Little Bighorn, see Nathaniel Philbrick's *The Last Stand: Custer, Sitting Bull, and the Battle of the Little Bighorn* (2010). On Crazy Horse, see Thomas Powers's *The Killing of Crazy Horse* (2010).

For a presentation of the Native American side of the story, see Peter Nabokov's *Native American Testimony: A Chronicle of Indian-White Relations from Prophecy to the Present, 1492–2000*, rev. ed. (1999). On the demise of the buffalo herds, see Andrew C. Isenberg's *The Destruction of the Bison: An Environmental History, 1750–1920* (2000).

## CHAPTER 19

For a survey of urbanization, see David R. Goldfield's *Urban America: A History* (1989). Gunther Barth discusses the emergence of a new post-Civil War urban culture in *City People: The Rise of Modern City Culture in Nineteenth-Century America* (1980). John Bodnar offers a synthesis of the urban immigrant experience in *The Transplanted: A History of Immigrants in Urban America* (1985). See also Roger Daniels's *Guarding the Golden Door: American Immigration Policy and Immigrants since 1882* (2004). Walter Nugent's *Crossings: The Great Transatlantic Migrations, 1870–1914* (1992) provides a wealth of demographic information and insight. Efforts to stop

Chinese immigration are detailed in Erika Lee's *At America's Gates: Chinese Immigration during the Exclusion Era* (2003).

On urban environments and sanitary reforms, see Martin V. Melosi's *The Sanitary City: Urban Infrastructure in America from Colonial Times to the Present* (2000), Joel A. Tarr's *The Search for the Ultimate Sink: Urban Pollution in Historical Perspective* (1996), and Suellen Hoy's *Chasing Dirt: The American Pursuit of Cleanliness* (1995).

For the growth of urban leisure and sports, see Roy Rosenzweig's *Eight Hours for What We Will: Workers and Leisure in an Industrial City, 1870–1920* (1983) and Steven A. Riess's *City Games: The Evolution of American Urban Society and the Rise of Sports* (1989). Saloon culture is examined in Madelon Powers's *Faces along the Bar: Lore and Order in the Workingman's Saloon, 1870–1920* (1998).

On the impact of Darwin's theory of evolution, see Barry Werth's *Banquet at Delmonico's: Great Minds, the Gilded Age, and the Triumph of Evolution in America* (2009). On the rise of realism in thought and the arts during the second half of the nineteenth century, see David E. Shi's *Facing Facts: Realism in American Thought and Culture, 1850–1920* (1995). The rise of pragmatism is the focus of Louis Menand's *The Metaphysical Club: A Story of Ideas in America* (2001).

Helpful overviews of the Gilded Age are Alex Axelrod's *The Gilded Age, 1876-1912* (2017), Sean Cashman's *America in the Gilded Age: From the Death of Lincoln to the Rise of Theodore Roosevelt* (1984), and Richard White's *The Republic for Which It Stands: The U.S. during Reconstruction and the Gilded Age* (2017). Nell Irvin Painter's *Standing at Armageddon: The United States, 1877–1919* (1987) focuses on the experience of the working class.

For a stimulating overview of the political, social, and economic trends during the Gilded Age, see Jack Beatty's *Age of Betrayal: The Triumph of Money in America, 1865–1900* (2007). On the development of city rings and bosses, see Kenneth D. Ackerman's *Boss Tweed: The Rise and Fall of the Corrupt Pol Who Conceived the Soul of Modern New York* (2005). Excellent presidential biographies include Hans L. Trefousse's *Rutherford B. Hayes* (2002), Zachary Karabell's *Chester Alan Arthur* (2004), Henry F. Graff's *Grover Cleveland* (2002), and Kevin Phillips's *William McKinley* (2003). On the political culture of the Gilded Age, see Charles Calhoun's *Minority Victory: Gilded Age Politics and the Front Porch Campaign of 1888* (2008).

Balanced accounts of Populism can be found in Charles Postel's *The Populist Vision* (2007) and Michael McGerr's *A Fierce Discontent: The Rise and Fall of the Progressive Movement, 1870–1920* (2005). The election of 1896 is the focus of R. Hal Williams's *Realigning America: McKinley, Bryan, and the Remarkable Election of 1896* (2010). On the role of religion in the agrarian protest movements, see Joe Creech's *Righteous Indignation: Religion and the Populist Revolution* (2006). The best biography of Bryan is Michael Kazin's *A Godly Hero: The Life of William Jennings Bryan* (2006).

## CHAPTER 20

An excellent survey of the diplomacy of the era is Charles S. Campbell's *The Transformation of American Foreign Relations, 1865–1900* (1976). For background on the events of the 1890s, see David Healy's *U.S. Expansionism: The Imperialist Urge in the 1890s* (1970). The dispute over American policy in Hawaii is covered in Thomas J. Osborne's *"Empire Can Wait": American Opposition to Hawaiian Annexation, 1893–1898* (1981).

Ivan Musicant's *Empire by Default: The Spanish-American War and the Dawn of the American Century* (1998) is the most comprehensive volume on the conflict. A colorful treatment of the powerful men promoting war is Evan Thomas's *The War Lovers: Roosevelt, Lodge, Mahan, and the Rush to Empire, 1898* (2010). For the war's aftermath in the Philippines, see Stuart Creighton Miller's *"Benevolent Assimilation": The American Conquest of the Philippines, 1899–1903* (1982). On the Philippine-American War, see David J. Silbey's *A War of Frontier and Empire: The Philippine-American War, 1899–1902* (2007).

A good introduction to American interest in China is Michael H. Hunt's *The Making of a Special Relationship: The United States and China to 1914* (1983). John Taliaferro's *All the Great Prizes: The Life of John Hay* (2013) examines the role of this key secretary of state in forming policy.

For U.S. policy in the Caribbean and Central America, see Walter LaFeber's *Inevitable Revolutions: The United States in Central America*, 2nd ed. (1993). David McCullough's *The Path between the Seas: The Creation of the Panama Canal, 1870–1914* (1977) presents an admiring account of how the United States secured the Panama Canal. A more sober assessment is Julie Greene's *The Canal Builders: Making America's Empire at the Panama Canal* (2009). For a detailed treatment of Theodore Roosevelt's diplomacy as president, see James Bradley's *The Imperial Cruise: A Secret History of Empire and War* (2009).

## CHAPTER 21

Splendid analyses of progressivism can be found in John Whiteclay Chambers II's *The Tyranny of Change: America in the Progressive Era, 1890–1920*, rev. ed. (2000), Steven J. Diner's *A Very Different Age: Americans of the Progressive Era* (1997), Maureen A. Flanagan's *America Reformed: Progressives and Progressivisms,*

*1890–1920* (2006), Michael McGerr's *A Fierce Discontent: The Rise and Fall of the Progressive Movement in America* (2003) and David Traxel's *Crusader Nation: The United States in Peace and the Great War, 1898–1920* (2006). On Ida Tarbell and the muckrakers, see Steve Weinberg's *Taking on the Trust: The Epic Battle of Ida Tarbell and John D. Rockefeller* (2008).

The evolution of government policy toward business is examined in Martin J. Sklar's *The Corporate Reconstruction of American Capitalism, 1890–1916: The Market, the Law, and Politics* (1988). Mina Carson's *Settlement Folk: Social Thought and the American Settlement Movement, 1885–1930* (1990) examines the social problems in the cities. Robert Kanigel's *The One Best Way: Frederick Winslow Taylor and the Enigma of Efficiency* (1997) highlights the role of efficiency and expertise in the Progressive Era.

An excellent study of the role of women in progressivism's emphasis on social justice is Kathryn Kish Sklar's *Florence Kelley and the Nation's Work: The Rise of Women's Political Culture, 1830–1900* (1995). On the tragic fire at the Triangle Shirtwaist Company, see David Von Drehle's *Triangle: The Fire That Changed America* (2003). The best study of the settlement house movement is Jean Bethke Elshtain's *Jane Addams and the Dream of American Democracy: A Life* (2002).

On Theodore Roosevelt and the conservation movement, see Douglas Brinkley's *The Wilderness Warrior: Theodore Roosevelt and the Crusade for America* (2009) For insights into Republicans and Progressivism, see Michael Wolraich's *Unreasonable Men: Theodore Roosevelt and the Republican Rebels Who Created Progressive Politics* (2014). The immensely important election of 1912 is covered in James Chace's *1912: Wilson, Roosevelt, Taft, and Debs— The Election That Changed the Country* (2004) and Sidney M. Milkis's *TR, the Progressive Party, and the Transformation of Democracy* (2009). Excellent biographies include Kathleen Dalton's *Theodore Roosevelt: A Strenuous Life* (2002) and Patricia O'Toole's *The Moralist: Woodrow Wilson and the World He Made* (2019). The racial blind spot of Progressivism is in the focus of David W. Southern's *The Progressive Era and Race: Reform and Reaction, 1900–1917* (2006).

## CHAPTER 22

A lucid overview of international events in the early twentieth century is Robert H. Ferrell's *Woodrow Wilson and World War I, 1917–1921* (1985). For a vivid account of U.S. intervention in Mexico, see Frederick Katz's *The Life and Times of Pancho Villa* (1999). On Wilson's stance toward the European war, see Robert W. Tucker's *Woodrow Wilson and the Great War: Reconsidering*

*America's Neutrality, 1914–1917* (2007). An excellent biography is John Milton Cooper Jr.'s *Woodrow Wilson: A Biography* (2010).

For the European experience in the Great War, see Adam Hochschild's *To End All Wars: A Story of Loyalty and Rebellion, 1914–1918* (2011), Margaret MacMillan's *The War That Ended Peace* (2013), and William Philpott's *Attrition: Fighting the First World War* (2015). Edward M. Coffman's *The War to End All Wars: The American Military Experience in World War I* (1968) is a detailed presentation of America's military involvement. See also Peter Hart's *The Great War: A Combat History of World War I* (2015) and Gary Mead's *The Doughboys: America and the First World War* (2000).

For a survey of the impact of the war on the home front, see Meirion Harries and Susie Harries's *The Last Days of Innocence: America at War, 1917–1918* (1997). Maurine Weiner Greenwald's *Women, War, and Work: The Impact of World War I on Women Workers in the United States* (1980) discusses the role of women in the war effort while Sara Hunter Graham's *Woman Suffrage and the New Democracy* (1996) traces the movement during the war to give women the vote. Ronald Schaffer's *America in the Great War: The Rise of the War Welfare State* (1991) shows the effect of war mobilization on business organization. Richard Polenberg's *Fighting Faiths: The Abrams Case, the Supreme Court, and Free Speech* (1987) examines the prosecution of a case under the 1918 Sedition Act. See also Ernest Freeberg's *Democracy's Prisoner: Eugene V. Debs, the Great War, and the Right to Dissent* (2009).

How American diplomacy fared in the making of peace has received considerable attention. Thomas J. Knock connects domestic affairs and foreign relations in his explanation of Wilson's peacemaking in *To End All Wars: Woodrow Wilson and the Quest for a New World Order* (1992). See also John Milton Cooper Jr.'s *Breaking the Heart of the World: Woodrow Wilson and the Fight for the League of Nations* (2002), Charles L. Mee's *1919 Versailles: The End of the War to End All Wars* (2014), G.J. Meyers's *The World Remade: America in World War I* (2018), and Adam Tooze's *The Deluge: The Great War, America, and the Remaking of the Global Order* (2014).

The problems of the immediate postwar years are chronicled by a number of historians. The best overview is Ann Hagedorn's *Savage Peace: Hope and Fear in America, 1919* (2007). On the Spanish flu, see John M. Barry's *The Great Influenza: The Epic Story of the Deadliest Plague in History* (2004). Labor tensions are examined in David E. Brody's *Labor in Crisis: The Steel Strike of 1919* (1965) and Francis Russell's *A City in Terror: Calvin Coolidge and the 1919 Boston Police Strike* (1975). On racial strife, see Jan Voogd's *Race Riots and Resistance: The Red Summer of 1919* (2008). The fear of Communists is analyzed in Robert K. Murray's *Red Scare: A Study in National Hysteria, 1919–1920* (1955).

# CHAPTER 23

For a lively survey of the social and cultural changes during the interwar period, start with William E. Leuchtenburg's *The Perils of Prosperity, 1914–32*, 2nd ed. (1993). Even more comprehensive is Michael E. Parrish's *Anxious Decades: America in Prosperity and Depression, 1920–1941* (1992). The best introduction to the culture of the 1920s remains Roderick Nash's *The Nervous Generation: American Thought, 1917–1930* (1990). See also Lynn Dumenil's *The Modern Temper: American Culture and Society in the 1920s* (1995).

The impact of woman suffrage is treated in Kristi Anderson's *After Suffrage: Women in Partisan and Electoral Politics before the New Deal* (1996). The best study of the birth-control movement is Ellen Chesler's *Woman of Valor: Margaret Sanger and the Birth Control Movement in America* (1992).

On the African American migration from the South, see James N. Gregory's *The Southern Diaspora: How the Great Migrations of Black and White Southerners Transformed America* (2005). See Charles Flint Kellogg's *NAACP: A History of the National Association for the Advancement of Colored People* (1967) for his analysis of the pioneering court cases against racial discrimination. Nathan Irvin Huggins's *Harlem Renaissance* (1971) assesses the cultural impact of the Great Migration on New York City.

On the radio craze, see Alfred Balk's *The Rise of Radio* (2005). For the automobile culture, see Richard Snow's *I Invented the Modern Age: The Rise of Henry Ford* (2014). On the emergence of airplanes, see Dan Hampton's *The Flight* (2017) and Mike Campbell's *Amelia Earhart* (2016) and Keith O'Brien's *Fly Girls* (2018).

The emergence of jazz is documented in Burton W. Peretti's *The Creation of Jazz: Music, Race, and Culture in Urban America* (1992). Scientific breakthroughs are analyzed in Manjit Kumar's *Quantum: Einstein, Bohr, and the Great Debate about the Nature of Reality* (2010). See also Steven Gimbel's *Einstein: His Space and Times* (2015). The best overviews of cultural modernism in Europe are Ann L. Ardis's *Modernism and Cultural Conflict, 1880-1922* (2008) and Peter Gay's *Modernism: The Lure of Heresy from Baudelaire to Beckett and Beyond* (2009). On southern modernism, see Daniel Joseph Singal's *The War Within: From Victorian to Modernist Thought in the South, 1919–1945* (1982). Stanley Coben's *Rebellion against Victorianism: The Impetus for Cultural Change in 1920s America* (1991) surveys the appeal of modernism among writers, artists, and intellectuals. See also Charles J. Shindo's *1927 and the Rise of Modern America* (2010).

# CHAPTER 24

On Harding, see Robert K. Murray's *The Harding Era: Warren G. Harding and His Administration* (1969) and Charles L. Mee's *The Ohio Gang: The World of Warren G. Harding* (2014). See Nan Britton's account of her affair with Harding, *The President's Daughter* (2008). On Coolidge, see Amith Shlaes's *Coolidge* (2013). On Hoover, see Martin L. Fausold's *The Presidency of Herbert C. Hoover* (1985). The influential secretary of the Treasury during the 1920s is ably analyzed in David Cannadine's *Mellon: An American Life* (2006).

John Higham's *Strangers in the Land: Patterns of American Nativism, 1860–1925,* 2nd ed. (2002) details the story of immigration restriction. The controversial Sacco and Vanzetti case is the focus of Moshik Temkin's *The Sacco-Vanzetti Affair: America on Trial* (2009). For analysis of the revival of Klan activity, see Linda Gordon's *The Second Coming of the KKK* (2017) and Thomas R. Pegram's *One Hundred Percent American: The Rebirth and Decline of the Ku Klux Klan in the 1920s* (2011). The best analysis of the Scopes trial is Edward J. Larson's *Summer for the Gods: The Scopes Trial and America's Continuing Debate over Science and Religion* (1997). On Prohibition, see Daniel Okrent's *Last Call: The Rise and Fall of Prohibition* (2011). For the story of the invention of the airplane, see David McCullough's *The Wright Brothers* (2015).

On the stock market crash in 1929, see Maury Klein's *Rainbow's End: The Crash of 1929* (2000). Overviews of the depressed economy are found in Charles P. Kindleberger's *The World in Depression, 1929–1939,* rev. and enlarged ed. (1986) and Peter Fearon's *War, Prosperity, and Depression: The U.S. Economy, 1917–1945* (1987). On the removal of the Bonus Army, see Paul Dickson and Thomas B. Allen's *The Bonus Army: An American Epic* (2004).

# CHAPTER 25

Two excellent overviews of the New Deal are Ira Katznelson's *Fear Itself: The New Deal and the Origins of Our Time* (2013) and David M. Kennedy's *Freedom from Fear: The American People in Depression and War, 1929–1945* (1999). A lively biography of Roosevelt is H. W. Brands's *Traitor to His Class: The Privileged Life and Radical Presidency of Franklin Delano Roosevelt* (2009). The Roosevelt marriage is well described in Hazel Rowley's *Franklin and Eleanor: An Extraordinary Marriage* (2011).

The busy first year of the New Deal is ably detailed in Anthony J. Badger's *FDR: The First Hundred Days* (2008). Perhaps the most successful of the early

New Deal programs is the focus of Neil M. Maher's *Nature's New Deal: The Civilian Conservation Corps and the Roots of the American Environmental Movement* (2008). On the political opponents of the New Deal, see Alan Brinkley's *Voices of Protest: Huey Long, Father Coughlin, and the Great Depression* (1982). Roosevelt's battle with the Supreme Court is detailed in Jeff Shesol's *Supreme Power: Franklin Roosevelt vs. The Supreme Court* (2010). The actual effects of the New Deal on the economy are detailed in Elliot A. Rosen's *Roosevelt, the Great Depression, and the Economics of Recovery* (2005).

Critical assessments of Roosevelt and the New Deal are Burton Folsom's *New Deal or Raw Deal* (2009) and Amity Schlaes's *The Forgotten Man: A New History of the Great Depression* (2008). James N. Gregory's *American Exodus: The Dust Bowl Migration and Okie Culture in California* (1989) describes the migratory movement. The dramatic Scottsboro court case is the focus of James Goodman's *Stories of Scottsboro* (1995). On the environmental and human causes of the dust bowl, see Donald Worster, *Dust Bowl: The Southern Plains in the 1930s* (1979). On cultural life during the 1930s, see Morris Dickstein's *Dancing in the Dark: A Cultural History of the Great Depression* (2009).

The best overview of diplomacy between the world wars remains Selig Adler's *The Uncertain Giant, 1921–1941: American Foreign Policy between the Wars* (1965). Robert Dallek's *Franklin D. Roosevelt and American Foreign Policy, 1932–1945* (1979) provides a judicious assessment of Roosevelt's foreign policy initiatives during the 1930s.

On Roosevelt's war of words with isolationists, see Lynne Olsen's *Those Angry Days: Roosevelt, Lindbergh, and America's Fight over World War II, 1939–1942* (2013), David Kaiser's *No End Save Victory: How FDR Led the Nation into War* (2014), and Nicholas Wapshott's *The Sphinx: Franklin Roosevelt, the Isolationists, and the Road to World War II* (2015). See also David Reynolds's *From Munich to Pearl Harbor: Roosevelt's America and the Origins of the Second World War* (2001). For the Japanese perspective, see Eri Hotta's *Japan 1941: Countdown to Infamy* (2014). On the surprise attack on Pearl Harbor, see Gordon W. Prange's *Pearl Harbor: The Verdict of History* (1986).

## CHAPTER 26

For a sweeping survey of the Second World War, consult Anthony Roberts's *The Storm of War: A New History of the Second World War* (2011). A detailed treatment of U.S. involvement is Rick Atkinson's multivolume Pulitzer prize–winning series, *An Army at Dawn* (2007), *The Day of Battle* (2008), and *The Guns at Last Light* (2013). Roosevelt's wartime leadership is analyzed in Eric Larrabee's *Commander in Chief: Franklin Delano Roosevelt, His Lieutenants, and Their War* (1987).

Books on specific European campaigns include Anthony Beevor's *D-Day: The Battle for Normandy* (2010) and Charles B. MacDonald's *A Time for Trumpets: The Untold Story of the Battle of the Bulge* (1985). On the Allied commander, see Carlo D'Este's *Eisenhower: A Soldier's Life* (2002). Richard Overy assesses the controversial role of air power in *The Bombing War: Europe, 1939–1945* (2013).

For the war in the Far East, see John Costello's *The Pacific War, 1941–1945* (1981), Ronald H. Spector's *Eagle against the Sun: The American War with Japan* (1985), John W. Dower's award-winning *War without Mercy: Race and Power in the Pacific War* (1986), and Dan van der Vat's *The Pacific Campaign: The U.S.-Japanese Naval War, 1941–1945* (1991).

An excellent overview of the war's effects on the home front is Michael C. C. Adams's *The Best War Ever: America and World War II* (1994). On the transformation to the wartime economy, see Arthur Herman's *Freedom's Forge: How American Business Produced Victory in World War II* (2012) and Maury Klein's *A Call to Arms* (2013). Susan M. Hartmann's *The Home Front and Beyond: American Women in the 1940s* (1982) treats the new working environment for women. Kenneth D. Rose tells the story of problems on the home front in *Myth and the Greatest Generation: A Social History of Americans in World War II* (2008). Neil A. Wynn looks at the participation of blacks in *The Afro-American and the Second World War* (1976). The story of the oppression of Japanese Americans is told in Greg Robinson's *A Tragedy for Democracy: Japanese Confinement in North America* (2009).

On the development of the atomic bomb, see Jim Baggott's *The First War of Physics: The Secret History of the Atomic Bomb* (2010). The devastation caused by the atomic bomb is the focus of Paul Ham's *Hiroshima Nagasaki: The Real Story of the Atomic Bombings* (2015) and Susan Southard's *Nagasaki: Life after Nuclear War* (2015). For the controversy over America's policies towards the Holocaust, see Richard Breitman and Alan J. Lichtman's *FDR and the Jews* (2013).

A detailed introduction to U.S. diplomacy during the conflict can be found in Gaddis Smith's *American Diplomacy during the Second World War, 1941–1945* (1985). To understand the role that Roosevelt played in policy making, consult Warren F. Kimball's *The Juggler: Franklin Roosevelt as Wartime Statesman* (1991). The most important wartime summit meeting is assessed in S. M. Plokhy's *Yalta: The Price of Peace* (2010). The issues and events that led to the deployment of atomic weapons are addressed in

Martin J. Sherwin's *A World Destroyed: The Atomic Bomb and the Grand Alliance* (1975). See also Michael Dobbs's *Six Months in 1945: FDR, Stalin, Churchill, and Truman—From World War to Cold War* (2013).

# CHAPTER 27

The cold war remains a hotly debated topic. The traditional interpretation is best reflected in John Lewis Gaddis's *The Cold War: A New History* (2005). Both superpowers, Gaddis argues, were responsible for causing the cold war, but the Soviet Union was more culpable. The revisionist perspective is represented by Gar Alperovitz's *Atomic Diplomacy: Hiroshima and Potsdam: The Use of the Atomic Bomb and the American Confrontation with Soviet Power*, 2nd ed. (1994). Also see H. W. Brands's *The Devil We Knew: Americans and the Cold War* (1993), Melvyn P. Leffler's *For the Soul of Mankind: The United States, the Soviet Union, and the Cold War* (2007), Ralph Levering's *The Cold War: A Post-Cold War History* (2016), and Odd Arne Westad's *The Cold War: A World History* (2017). On the architect of the containment strategy, see John L. Gaddis, *George F. Kennan: An American Life* (2011). For the Marshall Plan, see Benn Steil's *The Marshall Plan: Dawn of the Cold War* (2018).

Frank Constigliola assesses Franklin Roosevelt's role in the start of the cold war in *Roosevelt's Lost Alliances: How Personal Politics Helped Start the Cold War* (2013). Arnold A. Offner indicts Truman for clumsy statesmanship in *Another Such Victory: President Truman and the Cold War, 1945–1953* (2002). For a positive assessment of Truman's leadership, see Alonzo L. Hamby's *Beyond the New Deal: Harry S. Truman and American Liberalism* (1973) and Robert Dallek's *The Lost Peace: Leadership in a Time of Horror and Hope, 1945–1953* (2010).

The domestic policies of Truman's Fair Deal are treated in William C. Berman's *The Politics of Civil Rights in the Truman Administration* (1970), Richard M. Dalfiume's *Desegregation of the U.S. Armed Forces: Fighting on Two Fronts, 1939–1953* (1969), and Maeva Marcus's *Truman and the Steel Seizure Case: The Limits of Presidential Power* (1977). The most comprehensive biography of Truman is David McCullough's *Truman* (1992).

For an introduction to the tensions in Asia, see Akira Iriye's *The Cold War in Asia: A Historical Introduction* (1974). For the Korean conflict, see Callum A. MacDonald's *Korea: The War before Vietnam* (1986) and Max Hasting's *The Korean War* (1987).

The anti-Communist crusade is surveyed in David Caute's *The Great Fear: The Anti-Communist Purge under Truman and Eisenhower* (1978) and M. Stanton Evans's *Blacklisted by History: The Untold Story of Joseph McCarthy* (2009). Arthur Herman's *Joseph McCarthy: Reexamining the Life and Legacy of America's Most Hated Senator* (2000) covers McCarthy himself. For a well-documented account of how the cold war was sustained by superpatriotism, intolerance, and suspicion, see Stephen J. Whitfield's *The Culture of the Cold War*, 2nd ed. (1996).

## CHAPTER 28

Two excellent overviews of social and cultural trends in the postwar era are William H. Chafe's *The Unfinished Journey: America since World War II*, 6th ed. (2006), William Hitchcock's *The Age of Eisenhower: American and the World in the 1950s* (2018), and William E. Leuchtenburg's *A Troubled Feast: America since 1945,* rev. ed. (1979). For insights into the cultural life of the 1950s, see Jeffrey Hart's *When the Going Was Good! American Life in the Fifties* (1982) and David Halberstam's *The Fifties* (1993).

The baby boom generation and its impact are vividly described in Paul C. Light's *Baby Boomers* (1988). The emergence of the television industry is discussed in Erik Barnouw's *Tube of Plenty: The Evolution of American Television,* 2nd rev. ed. (1990), and Ella Taylor's *Prime-Time Families: Television Culture in Postwar America* (1989).

On the process of suburban development, see Kenneth T. Jackson's *Crabgrass Frontier: The Suburbanization of the United States* (1985). Equally good is Tom Martinson's *American Dreamscape: The Pursuit of Happiness in Postwar Suburbia* (2000).

The middle-class ideal of family life in the 1950s is examined in Elaine Tyler May's *Homeward Bound: American Families in the Cold War Era,* rev. ed. (2008). Thorough accounts of women's issues are found in Wini Breines's *Young, White, and Miserable: Growing Up Female in the Fifties* (1992). For an overview of the resurgence of religion in the 1950s, see George M. Marsden's *Religion and American Culture,* 2nd ed. (2000).

The origins and growth of rock and roll are surveyed in Carl Belz's *The Story of Rock,* 2nd ed. (1972). The colorful Beats are brought to life in Steven Watson's *The Birth of the Beat Generation: Visionaries, Rebels, and Hipsters, 1944–1960* (1995) and Dennis McNally's *Desolate Angel: Jack Kerouac, the Beat Generation, and America* (2003).

Scholarship on the Eisenhower years is extensive. Balanced treatments include Jim Newton's *Eisenhower: The White House Years* (2012) and Jean Edward Smith's *Eisenhower in War and Peace* (2012). For the manner in which Eisenhower conducted foreign policy, see Evan Thomas's *Ike's Bluff: President Eisenhower's Secret Battle to Save the World* (2012).

The best overview of American foreign policy since 1945 is Stephen E. Ambrose and Douglas G. Brinkley's *Rise to Globalism: American Foreign Policy since 1938* 9th ed. (2011). For the buildup of U.S. involvement in Indochina, consult Fredrik Logevall's *Embers of War: The Fall of an Empire and the Making of America's Vietnam* (2012). The Cold War strategy of the Eisenhower administration is the focus of Chris Tudda's *The Truth Is Our Weapon: The Rhetorical Diplomacy of Dwight D. Eisenhower and John Foster Dulles* (2006). To learn about the CIA's secret activities in Iran, see Ervand Abrahamian's *The Coup: 1953, the CIA, and the Roots of Modern U.S.-Iranian Relations* (2013). On the Suez Crisis, see Alex von Tunzelmann's *Blood and Sand: Suez, Hungary, and the Crisis that Shook the World* (2017).

The impact of the Supreme Court during the 1950s is the focus of Archibald Cox's *The Warren Court: Constitutional Decision as an Instrument of Reform* (1968). A masterly study of the important Warren Court decision on school desegregation is James T. Patterson's *Brown v. Board of Education: A Civil Rights Milestone and Its Troubled Legacy* (2001).

For the story of the early years of the civil rights movement, see Taylor Branch's *Parting the Waters: America in the King Years, 1954–1963* (1988), Robert Weisbrot's *Freedom Bound: A History of America's Civil Rights Movement* (1990), and David A. Nicholas's *A Matter of Justice: Eisenhower and the Beginning of the Civil Rights Revolution* (2007). On Rosa Parks, see Jeanne Theoharis's *The Rebellious Life of Mrs. Rosa Parks* (2013). On the testy relationship of Eisenhower and his vice president, Richard Nixon, see Jeffrey Frank's *Ike and Dick: Portrait of a Strange Political Marriage* (2013).

## CHAPTER 29

A superb analysis of John Kennedy's life is Thomas C. Reeves's *A Question of Character: A Life of John F. Kennedy* (1991). The 1960 campaign is detailed in Gary A. Donaldson's *The First Modern Campaign: Kennedy, Nixon, and the Election of 1960* (2007). The best study of the Kennedy administration's domestic policies is Irving Bernstein's *Promises Kept: John F. Kennedy's New Frontier* (1991). See also Robert Dallek's *Camelot's Court: Inside the Kennedy White House* (2013), Thurston Clarke's *JFK's Last Hundred Days* (2013), and Ira Stoll's *JFK, Conservative* (2013). For details on the still swirling conspiracy theories about the assassination, see David W. Belin's *Final Disclosure: The Full Truth about the Assassination of President Kennedy* (1988).

On Barry Goldwater and the rise of modern conservatism, see Rick Perlstein's *Before the Storm: Barry Goldwater and the Unmaking of the American Consensus* (2009). On LBJ, see the magisterial multivolume biography by Robert Caro's titled *The Years of Lyndon Johnson (1990–2013)*. On the Johnson administration, see Vaughn Davis Bornet's *The Presidency of Lyndon B. Johnson* (1984). For an insider's perspective, see Joseph A. Califano's *The Triumph and Tragedy of Lyndon Johnson* (2015). For the inside story of Johnson's White House, see Joshua Zeitz's *Building the Great Society: Inside Lyndon Johnson's White House* (2018). Also insightful is Randall B. Woods's *Prisoners of Hope: Lyndon B. Johnson, the Great Society, and the Limits of Liberalism* (2016).

Among the works that interpret Johnson's social policies during the 1960s, John E. Schwarz's *America's Hidden Success: A Reassessment of Twenty Years of Public Policy* (1983) offers a glowing endorsement of Democratic programs. For a contrasting perspective, see Charles Murray's *Losing Ground: American Social Policy, 1950–1980* (1994). Also see Martha J. Bailey and Sheldon Danziger's *Legacies of the War on Poverty* (2015).

On foreign policy, see *Kennedy's Quest for Victory: American Foreign Policy, 1961–1963* (1989), edited by Thomas G. Paterson, and Patrick J. Sloyan's *The Politics of Deception* (2015). To learn more about Kennedy's problems in Cuba, see Mark J. White's *Missiles in Cuba: Kennedy, Khrushchev, Castro and the 1962 Crisis* (1997). See also Aleksandr Fursenko and Timothy Naftali's *"One Hell of a Gamble": Khrushchev, Castro and Kennedy, 1958–1964* (1997).

American involvement in Vietnam has received voluminous treatment from all political perspectives. For an excellent overview, see Larry Berman's *Planning a Tragedy: The Americanization of the War in Vietnam* (1983) and *Lyndon Johnson's War: The Road to Stalemate in Vietnam* (1989), as well as Stanley Karnow's *Vietnam: A History*, 2nd rev. ed. (1997). An analysis of policy making concerning the Vietnam War is David M. Barrett's *Uncertain Warriors: Lyndon Johnson and His Vietnam Advisors* (1993). A fine account of the military involvement is Robert D. Schulzinger's *A Time for War: The United States and Vietnam, 1941–1975* (1997). On the legacy of the Vietnam War, see Arnold R. Isaacs's *Vietnam Shadows: The War, Its Ghosts, and Its Legacy* (1997).

Many scholars have dealt with various aspects of the civil rights movement and race relations in the 1960s. See especially Carl M. Brauer's *John F. Kennedy and the Second Reconstruction* (1977), David J. Garrow's *Bearing the Cross: Martin Luther King, Jr., and the Southern Christian Leadership Conference* (1986), and Adam Fairclough's *To Redeem the Soul of America: The Southern Christian Leadership Conference and Martin Luther King, Jr.* (1987). William H. Chafe's

*Civilities and Civil Rights: Greensboro, North Carolina, and the Black Struggle for Freedom* (1980) details the original sit-ins. An award-winning study of racial and economic inequality in a representative American city is Thomas J. Sugrue's *The Origins of the Urban Crisis: Race and Inequality in Postwar Detroit* (1996).

## CHAPTER 30

An engaging overview of the cultural trends of the 1960s is Maurice Isserman and Michael Kazin's *America Divided: The Civil War of the 1960s,* 3rd ed. (2007). The New Left is assessed in Irwin Unger's *The Movement: A History of the American New Left, 1959–1972* (1974). On the Students for a Democratic Society, see Kirkpatrick Sale's *SDS* (1973) and Allen J. Matusow's *The Unraveling of America: A History of Liberalism in the 1960s* (1984). Also useful are Todd Gitlin's *The Sixties: Years of Hope, Days of Rage,* rev. ed. (1993) and Bryan Burrough's *Days of Rage* (2015). For a focused study, see James T. Patterson's *The Eve of Destruction: How 1965 Transformed America* (2013). On the popularity of folk music and the role of Greenwich Village, see Stephen Petrus and Ronald D. Cohen's *Folk City* (2015).

For insights into the black power movement, see Peniel E. Joseph's *Stokely: A Life* (2014), and Joshua Bloom and Waldo E. Martin Jr.'s *Black against Empire: The History and Politics of the Black Panther Party* (2013).

Two influential assessments of the counterculture by sympathetic commentators are Theodore Roszak's *The Making of a Counter-Culture: Reflections on the Technocratic Society and Its Youthful Opposition* (1969) and Charles A. Reich's *The Greening of America: How the Youth Revolution Is Trying to Make America Livable* (1970). A good scholarly analysis that takes the hippies seriously is Timothy Miller's *The Hippies and American Values* (1991). A more recent assessment of the "culture wars" since the Sixties is Andrew Hartman's *A War for the Soul of America* (2015).

The best study of the women's liberation movement is Ruth Rosen's *The World Split Open: How the Modern Women's Movement Changed America,* rev. ed. (2006). On Betty Friedan, see Daniel Horowitz's *Betty Friedan and the Making of the Feminine Mystique* (2000). For the point of view of a militant feminist, see Vivian Gornick, *Essays in Feminism* (1978). On the gay liberation movement, see Jim Downs's *Stand by Me: The Forgotten History of Gay Liberation* (2016). The Stonewall riots are featured in Ann Bausum's *Stonewall: Breaking Out in the Fight for Gay Rights* (2016). See also Joanne Meyerowitz's *How Sex Changed: A History of Transexuality in the United States* (2004), Vicki L. Eklors's *Queer America: A People's LGBT History of the*

*United States* (2011), and Julia Seranos's *Outspoken: A Decade of Transgender Activism* (2016).

The union organizing efforts of Cesar Chavez are detailed in Ronald B. Taylor's *Chavez and the Farm Workers* (1975). See also Miriam Pawel's *The Crusades of Cesar Chavez: A Biography* (2014). The struggles of Native Americans for recognition and power are sympathetically described in Stan Steiner's *The New Indians* (1968).

The best overview of the 1970s and 1980s is James T. Patterson's *Restless Giant: The United States from Watergate to Bush v. Gore* (2005). On Nixon, see Melvin Small's thorough analysis in *The Presidency of Richard Nixon* (1999). A good slim biography is Elizabeth Drew's *Richard M. Nixon* (2007). A massive biography is Evan Thomas's *Being Nixon* (2015). An especially critical approach is Tim Weiner's *One Man Against the World: The Tragedy of Richard Nixon* (2015). For an overview of the Watergate scandal, see Stanley I. Kutler's *The Wars of Watergate: The Last Crisis of Richard Nixon* (1990). For the way the Republicans handled foreign affairs, consult Tad Szulc's *The Illusion of Peace: Foreign Policy in the Nixon Years* (1978). The Nixon White House tapes make for fascinating reading. See *The Nixon Tapes* (2014), ed. by Douglas Brinkley and Luke Nichter. Rick Perlstein traces the effects of Nixon's career on the Republican party and the conservative movement in two compelling books: *Nixonland: The Rise of a President and the Fracturing of America* (2007) and *The Invisible Bridge: The Fall of Nixon and the Rise of Reagan* (2014).

The Communist takeover of Vietnam and the end of American involvement there are traced in Larry Berman's *No Peace, No Honor: Nixon, Kissinger, and Betrayal in Vietnam* (2001). William Shawcross's *Sideshow: Kissinger, Nixon and the Destruction of Cambodia,* rev. ed. (2002), deals with the broadening of the war, while Larry Berman's *Planning a Tragedy: The Americanization of the War in Vietnam* (1982) assesses the final impact of U.S. involvement. The most comprehensive treatment of the anti-war movement is Tom Wells's *The War Within: America's Battle over Vietnam* (1994).

A comprehensive treatment of the Ford administration is contained in John Robert Greene's *The Presidency of Gerald R. Ford* (1995). The best overview of the Carter administration is Burton I. Kaufman's *The Presidency of James Earl Carter, Jr.,* 2nd rev. ed. (2006). A work more sympathetic to the Carter administration is John Dumbrell's *The Carter Presidency: A Re-evaluation,* 2nd ed. (1995). Gaddis Smith's *Morality, Reason, and Power: American Diplomacy in the Carter Years* (1986) provides an overview. Background on how the Middle East came to dominate much of American policy is found in William B. Quandt's *Decade of Decisions: American Policy toward the Arab-Israeli Conflict, 1967–1976* (1977). For a biography of Carter, see Randall Balmer, *Redeemer: The Life of Jimmy Carter* (2014).

## CHAPTER 31

The rise of modern political conservatism is well told in Patrick Allitt's *The Conservatives: Ideas and Personalities throughout American History* (2009) and Michael Schaller's *Right Turn: American Life in the Reagan-Bush Era, 1980–1992* (2007).

On Reagan, see John Patrick Diggins's *Ronald Reagan: Fate, Freedom, and the Making of History* (2007), Richard Reeves's *President Reagan: The Triumph of Imagination* (2005), Sean Wilentz's *The Age of Reagan: A History, 1974–2008* (2008), and Thomas C. Reed's *The Reagan Enigma: 1964–1980* (2015). The best political analysis is Robert M. Collins's *Transforming America: Politics and Culture during the Reagan Years* (2007). For insights into the 1980 election, see Andrew E. Busch's *Reagan's Victory: The Presidential Election of 1980 and the Rise of the Right* (2005). On Reaganomics, see David A. Stockman's *The Triumph of Politics: Why the Reagan Revolution Failed* (1986).

For Reagan's foreign policy in Central America, see James Chace's *Endless War: How We Got Involved in Central America—and What Can Be Done* (1984) and Walter LaFeber's *Inevitable Revolutions: The United States in Central America*, 2nd ed. (1993). On Reagan's second term, see Jane Mayer and Doyle McManus's *Landslide: The Unmaking of the President, 1984–1988* (1988). For a masterly work on the Iran-Contra affair, see Theodore Draper's *A Very Thin Line: The Iran Contra Affairs* (1991). Several collections of essays include varying assessments of the Reagan years. Among these are *The Reagan Revolution?* (1988), edited by B. B. Kymlicka and Jean V. Matthews; *The Reagan Presidency: An Incomplete Revolution?* (1990), edited by Dilys M. Hill, Raymond A. Moore, and Phil Williams; and *Looking Back on the Reagan Presidency* (1990), edited by Larry Berman.

The 41st president is the focus of Timothy Naftali's *George H. W. Bush* (2007). The best biography is Jon Meacham's *Destiny and Power: The American Odyssey of George Herbert Walker Bush* (2015). On the 1988 campaign, see Sidney Blumenthal's *Pledging Allegiance: The Last Campaign of the Cold War* (1990). For a social history of the decade, see John Ehrman's *The Eighties: America in the Age of Reagan* (2005). On the Persian Gulf conflict, see Lester H. Brune's *America and the Iraqi Crisis, 1990–1992: Origins and Aftermath* (1993). For the end of the Cold War, see Jeffrey Engel's *When the World Seemed New: George H. W. Bush and the End of the Cold War* (2017).

## CHAPTER 32

Analysis of the Clinton years can be found in Joe Klein's *The Natural: The Misunderstood Presidency of Bill Clinton* (2002). More recent biographies include John F. Harris's *The Survivor: Bill Clinton in the White House* (2006) and Patrick J. Maney's *Bill Clinton: New Gilded Age President* (2016) Clinton's impeachment is assessed in Richard A. Posner's *An Affair of State: The Investigation, Impeachment, and Trial of President Clinton* (1999). The conflict between Clinton and Newt Gingrich is explained in Elizabeth Drew's *The Struggle between Gingrich and the Clinton White House* (1996).

On changing demographic trends, see Sam Roberts's *Who We Are Now: The Changing Face of America in the Twenty-First Century* (2004). For a textured account of the exploding Latino culture, see Roberto Suro's *Strangers among Us: How Latino Immigration Is Transforming America* (1998). On social and cultural life in the 1990s, see Haynes Johnson's *The Best of Times: America in the Clinton Years* (2001). Economic and technological changes are assessed in Daniel T. Rogers's *Age of Fracture* (2011). The onset and growth of the AIDS epidemic are traced in *And the Band Played On: Politics, People, and the AIDS Epidemic,* 20th anniversary ed. (2007), by Randy Shilts.

On the religious right, see George M. Marsden's *Understanding Fundamentalism and Evangelicalism,* new ed. (2006) and Ralph E. Reed's *Politically Incorrect: The Emerging Faith Factor in American Politics* (1994).

On the invention of the computer and the Internet, see Paul E. Ceruzzi's *A History of Modern Computing,* 2nd ed. (2003), Janet Abbate's *Inventing the Internet* (1999), and Michael Lewis, *The New New Thing: A Silicon Valley Story* (1999). The booming economy of the 1990s is well analyzed in Joseph E. Stiglitz's *The Roaring Nineties: A New History of the World's Most Prosperous Decade* (2003).

For further treatment of the end of the cold war, see Michael R. Beschloss and Strobe Talbott's *At the Highest Levels: The Inside Story of the End of the Cold War* (1993) and Richard Crockatt's *The Fifty Years War: The United States and the Soviet Union in World Politics, 1941–1991* (1995).

On the transformation of American foreign policy, see James Mann's *Rise of the Vulcans: The History of Bush's War Cabinet* (2004), Claes G. Ryn's

*America the Virtuous: The Crisis of Democracy and the Quest for Empire* (2003), and Stephen M. Walt's *Taming American Power: The Global Response to U.S. Primacy* (2005).

The disputed 2000 presidential election is the focus of Jeffrey Toobin's *Too Close to Call: The Thirty-Six-Day Battle to Decide the 2000 Election* (2001). On the Bush presidency, see *The Presidency of George W. Bush: A First Historical Assessment*, edited by Julian E. Zelizer (2010) and Jean Edward Smith's *Bush* (2017). See also Fred H. Israel and Jonathan Mann's *The Election of 2000 and the Administration of George W. Bush* (2003). Also see Dick Cheney's illuminating, if self-serving, account of his service as Bush's vice president in *In My Time: A Personal and Political Memoir* (2011). For Bush's memoirs, see *Decision Points* (2010).

On the attacks of September 11, 2001, and their aftermath, see *The Age of Terror: America and the World after September 11,* edited by Strobe Talbott and Nayan Chanda (2001). For a devastating account of the Bush administration by a White House insider, see Scott McClellan's *What Happened: Inside the Bush White House and Washington's Culture of Deception* (2008).

On the historic 2008 election, see Michael Nelson's *The Elections of 2008* (2009). The best biography of Obama is David Maraniss's *Barack Obama: The Story* (2012). See also David Garrow's *Rising Star: The Making of Barack Obama* (2017) and Pete Souza's *Shade: A Tale of Two Presidents* (2018). A conservative critique is provided in Edward Klein's *The Amateur: Barack Obama in the White House* (2012). For insiders' accounts of the Obama administration, see David Axelrod's *Believer: My Forty Years in Politics* (2015) and Ben Rhodes's *The World As It Is: A Memoir of the Obama White House* (2018). The best overviews of the Obama presidency are Peter Baker's *Obama: The Call of History* (2017), and Mark Greenburg and Ken Burns's *Obama: The Historic Presidency of Barack Obama* (2017).

The Great Recession is explained in Alan S. Blinder's *After the Music Stopped: The Financial Crisis, the Response, and the Work Ahead* (2013) and Adam Tooze's *Crashed: How a Decade of Financial Crises Changed the World* (2018). The recession's effects on modern politics are the focus of John B. Judis's *The Populist Explosion: How the Great Recession Transformed American and European Politics* (2016). The Tea Party movement is assessed in Theda Skocpol and Vanessa Williamson's *The Tea Party and the Remaking of Republican Conservatism* (2012) and Elizabeth Price Foley's *The Tea Party: Three Principles* (2012). The polarization of politics is the focus of Russell Muirhead's *The Promise of Party in a Polarized Age* (2015). The partisan gridlock in Congress is analyzed in Thomas E. Mann and Norman J. Ornstein's *The Broken Branch: How Congress Is Failing America and How to Get it Back on Track* (2012). The tension between the conservative majority on the U.S. Supreme Court and the Obama administration is examined in Jeffrey Toobin's *The Oath: The Obama White House and the Supreme Court* (2012). On the growing economic inequality in America, see Joseph Stiglitz's *The Price of Inequality: How Today's Divided Society Endangers Our Future* (2013).

The emergence of Islamist radicalism is explained in Michael Weiss and Hassan Hassan's *ISIS: Inside the Army of Terror* (2015) and Jesssica Stern and J. M. Berger's *ISIS: The State of Terror* (2015). The conflicts in the Middle East are the focus of Dominic Tierney's *The Right Way to Lose a War: America in an Age of Unwinnable Conflicts* (2015).

The dramatic presidential election of 2016 is assessed in James W. Ceaser and Andrew E. Busch's *Defying the Odds: The 2016 Elections and American Politics* (2017), Larry Sabato and Kyle Kondik's *Trumped: The 2016 Election That Broke All the Rules* (2017), and Doug Wead's *Game of Thorns: The Inside Story of Hillary Clinton's Failed Campaign and Donald Trump's Winning Strategy* (2017). Donald Trump explained the purpose of his candidacy in *Great Again: How to Fix Our Crippled America* (2016). Hillary Clinton's assessed her election loss in *What Happened* (2017). For the emergence of populism, see Salena Zito and Brad Todd's *The Great Revolt: Inside the Populist Coalition Reshaping American Politics* (2018).

Inside looks at the chaotic Trump White House include James Comey's *A Higher Loyalty: Truth, Lies, and Leadership* (2018), and Bob Woodward's *Fear: Trump in the White House* (2018).

# PHOTO CREDITS

reserved; **p. 262:** GRANGER — All rights reserved; **p. 264:** GRANGER — All rights reserved; **p. 266:** GRANGER — All rights reserved; **p. 267:** Sarin Images/GRANGER — All rights reserved.

**CHAPTER 7: p. 274:** Photography by Erik Arnesen © Nicholas S. West; **p. 279:** Library of Congress; **p. 282:** Collection of the New-York Historical Society, USA/Bridgeman Images; **p. 287:** Greg Vaughn/ Alamy Stock Photo; **p. 291:** Library of Congress; **p. 295:** Library of Congress; **p. 305:** Sarin Images/ GRANGER — All rights reserved.

**PART III: p. 315:** George Caleb Bingham, American, 1811–1879; The Verdict of the People, 1854–55; oil on canvas; 46 x 55 inches; Saint Louis Art Museum, Gift of Bank of America 45:2001; **p. 316:** Yale University Art Gallery/Wikimedia, pd; **p. 317:** The Walters Art Museum, Baltimore.

**CHAPTER 8: p. 318:** GRANGER — All rights reserved; **p. 325:** © Collection of the New-York Historical Society/Bridgeman Images; **p. 329:** Fenimore Art Museum, Cooperstown, New York, Gift of Stephen C. Clark, N0394.1955. Photograph by Richard Walker; **p. 332:** GRANGER — All rights reserved; **p. 335:** GRANGER — All rights reserved; **p. 340:** Board of Trustees, National Gallery of Art, Washington 1980.62.9.(2794) PA; **p. 341:** Library of Congress; **p. 344:** Library of Congress; **p. 345:** The New York Public Library/Art Resource, NY; **p. 346:** John W. Bennett Labor Collection, Special Collections and University Archives, W.E.B. Du Bois Library, University of Massachusetts Amherst; **p. 347:** GRANGER — All rights reserved.

**CHAPTER 9: p. 352:** Photo © Christie's Images/Bridgeman Images; **p. 357:** The Metropolitan Museum of Art, New York/Rogers Fund, 1942; **p. 359:** GRANGER — All rights reserved; **p. 365:** GRANGER — All rights reserved; **p. 366:** The Metropolitan Museum of Art, New York/Gift of I. N. Phelps Stokes, Edward S. Hawes, Alice Mary Hawes, and Marion Augusta Hawes, 1937; **p. 370:** Courtesy of Historical Society of Pennsylvania Collection,/Bridgeman Images; **p. 373:** Yale University Art Gallery/Wikimedia, pd.

**CHAPTER 10: p. 378:** The Museum of the City of New York/Art Resource, NY; **p. 382:** Library of Congress; **p. 384:** Library of Congress; **p. 387:** National Archives; **p. 390:** GRANGER — All rights reserved; **p. 392:** Library of Congress; **p. 394:** Courtesy Boston Art Commission 2018; **p. 397:** George Caleb Bingham, American, 1811–1879; The Verdict of the People, 1854–55; oil on canvas; 46 x 55 inches; Saint Louis Art Museum, Gift of Bank of America 45:2001; **p. 405:** © CORBIS/Corbis via Getty Images; **p. 406:** Library of Congress.

**CHAPTER 11: p. 414:** Universal History Archive/UIG/Bridgeman Images; **p. 417:** Eron Johnson Antiques; **p. 420:** GRANGER — All rights reserved; **p. 427:** Fotosearch/Getty Images; **p. 431:** © Atwater Kent Museum of Philadelphia/Courtesy of Historical Society of Pennsylvania Collection/ Bridgeman Images; **p. 432:** The New York Historical Society/Getty Images; **p. 437:** Courtesy of the Peabody Museum of Archaeology and Ethnology, Harvard University, PM 35-5-10/53044; **p. 441:** Private Collection/Peter Newark American Pictures/Bridgeman Images; **p. 442:** The Historic New Orleans Collection/Bridgeman Images.

**CHAPTER 12: p. 450:** Munson-Williams-Proctor Arts Institute/Art Resource, NY; **p. 454:** GRANGER — All rights reserved; **p. 457:** The Metropolitan Museum of Art, New York/Rogers Fund, 1942; **p. 461:** Lordprice Collection/Alamy Stock Photo; **p. 464:** FineArt/Alamy Stock Photo; **p. 467:** National Portrait Gallery, Smithsonian Institution; gift of anonymous donor; **p. 469:** GRANGER — All rights reserved; **p. 471:** Library of Congress; **p. 472:** The Walters Art Museum, Baltimore; **p. 477 (left):** Library of Congress; **(right):** Private Collection/J. T. Vintage/Bridgeman Images; **p. 479:** GRANGER — All rights reserved; **p. 484:** GRANGER — All rights reserved; **p. 487:** GRANGER — All rights reserved; **p. 489 (both):** Library of Congress; **p. 492 (left):** GRANGER — All rights reserved; **(right):** Library of Congress.

**PART IV: p. 499:** Private Collection/The Stapleton Collection/Bridgeman Images; **p. 500:** Photo © Civil War Archive/Bridgeman Images.

**CHAPTER 13: p. 502:** Butler Institute of American Art, Youngstown, OH, USA/Gift of Joseph G. Butler III 1946/Bridgeman Images; **p. 506:** Library of Congress; **p. 508:** The Metropolitan Museum of Art, New York/Morris K. Jesup Fund, 1933; **p. 511:** Private Collection/Peter Newark American Pictures/Bridgeman Images; **p. 513:** © North Wind Picture Archives; **p. 517:** MPI/Getty Images; **p. 521:** Sarin Images/GRANGER — All rights reserved; **p. 528:** American Antiquarian Society, Worcester, Massachusetts, USA/Bridgeman Images; **p. 534:** Library of Congress.

**CHAPTER 14: p. 540:** Sarin Images/GRANGER — All rights reserved; **p. 542:** American Antiquarian Society, Worcester, Massachusetts, USA/Bridgeman Images; **p. 544:** Art Resource; **p. 547:** Sarin Images/GRANGER — All rights reserved; **p. 552:** Sarin Images/GRANGER — All rights reserved; **p. 554:** GRANGER — All rights reserved; **p. 557:** ©akg-images/The Image Works; **p. 562:** Pictorial Press Ltd/Alamy Stock Photo; **p. 567:** Hi-Story/Alamy Stock Photo; **p. 569:** Private Collection/Peter Newark American Pictures/Bridgeman Images; **p. 572:** Sarin Images/GRANGER — All rights reserved.

**CHAPTER 15: p. 578:** Chicago History Museum, ICHi-052424; Dennis Malone Carter, artist; **p. 586:** Bettmann/Corbis/Getty Images; **p. 587:** Public Domain; **p. 591:** Private Collection/The Stapleton Collection/Bridgeman Images; **p. 597:** Library of Congress; **p. 599:** Library of Congress; **p. 601:** Library of Congress; **p. 602:** Library of Congress; **p. 607:** Beinecke Rare Book and Manuscript Library, Yale University/Wikimedia Commons; **p. 609:** Library of Congress; **p. 610:** Boston Athenaeum, USA/Bridgeman Images; **p. 613:** Library of Congress; **p. 614:** Library of Congress; **p. 617:** Library of Congress; **p. 621:** Library of Congress; **p. 622:** National Archives.

**CHAPTER 16: p. 638:** Smithsonian American Art Museum, Washington, DC/Art Resource; **p. 641:** GRANGER — All rights reserved; **p. 645:** © Maryann Groves/North Wind Picture Archives; **p. 649:** Library of Congress; **p. 651:** Library of Congress; **p. 656:** Library of Congress; **p. 658:** Bettmann/Corbis/Getty Images; **p. 659:** GRANGER — All rights reserved; **p. 662:** Library of Congress.

**PART V: p. 683:** PhotoQuest/Getty Images; **p. 684:** David J. & Janice L. Frent Collection/Corbis/Getty Images

**CHAPTER 17: p. 686:** GRANGER — All rights reserved; **p. 691:** GRANGER — All rights reserved; **p. 695:** National Archives; **p. 701:** Wikimedia, pd; **p. 703:** Sarin Images/GRANGER — All rights reserved; **p. 704:** Sarin Images/GRANGER — All rights reserved; **p. 707:** Private Collection/Peter Newark American Pictures/Bridgeman Images; **p. 710:** Archives and Special Collections, Vassar College Library, 08.07.05; **p. 716:** T.V. Powderly Photographic Collection, The American Catholic History Research Center and University Archives (ACUA), The Catholic University of America, Washington, D.C.; **p. 717:** Library of Congress; **p. 723:** PhotoQuest/Getty Images.

**CHAPTER 18: p. 730:** GRANGER — All rights reserved; **p. 735:** Library of Congress; **p. 741:** Corbis/Getty Images; **p. 743:** Special Collections, University of Chicago Library; **p. 744:** Library of Congress; **p. 745:** Science Source; **p. 750:** Kansas State Historical Society; **p. 754:** Corbis/Getty Images; **p. 756:** Library of Congress; **p. 763:** Corbis/Getty Images; **p. 769:** Chinese workers who were returned to Rock Springs to work after the 1885 massacre, Wyoming State Archives Photo Collection, #11821, Wyoming State Archives.

**CHAPTER 19: p. 772:** National Gallery of Art, Washington DC, USA/Bridgeman Images; **p. 777:** William Williams Papers, Manuscripts and Archives Division, The New York Public Library, Astor, Lenox and Tilden Foundations, Art Resource, NY; **p. 779:** Library of Congress; **p. 780:** GRANGER — All rights reserved; **p. 781:** Bettmann/Corbis/Getty Images; **p. 782:** © Museum of the City of New York, USA/Bridgeman Images; **p. 783:** Bettmann/Corbis/Getty Images; **p. 786:** Cleveland Museum of Art/Hinman B. Hurlbut Collection/Bridgeman Images; **p. 789:** GRANGER — All rights reserved; **p. 795:** Bettmann/Corbis/Getty Images; **p. 798:** Bettmann/Corbis/Getty Images; **p. 803:** Library of Congress; **p. 805:** Kansas State Historical Society; **p. 807:** GRANGER — All rights reserved; **p. 808:** Bettmann/Corbis/Getty Images; **p. 810 (both):** David J. & Janice L. Frent Collection/Getty Images.

CHAPTER 27: **p. 1110:** Bettmann/Corbis/Getty Images; **p. 1112:** Bettmann/Corbis/Getty Images; **p. 1117:** A 1949 Herblock Cartoon, © The Herb Block Foundation; **p. 1119:** Bettmann/Corbis/Getty Images; **p. 1123:** ClassicStock/Alamy Stock Photo; **p. 1127:** Bettmann/Corbis/Getty Images; **p. 1131:** Francis Miller/The LIFE Picture Collection/Getty Images; **p. 1142:** Private Collection/J. T. Vintage/ Bridgeman Images; **p. 1143:** GRANGER — All rights reserved.

CHAPTER 28: **p. 1148:** GraphicaArtis/Getty Images; **p. 1150:** Corbis/Getty Images; **p. 1154:** Tom Kelley/Getty Images; **p. 1157:** Heritage Image Partnership Ltd/Alamy Stock Photo; **p. 1160:** Hulton Archives/Getty Images; **p. 1161:** Library of Congress; **p. 1162 (left):** Everett Collection Historical/Alamy Stock Photo; **(right):** Mondadori via Getty Images; **p. 1164:** Three Lions/Getty Images; **p. 1166:** Allan Grant/The LIFE Picture Collection/Getty Images; **p. 1169:** Elliott Erwitt/Magnum Photos; **p. 1173:** Charles Moore/Getty Images; **p. 1174:** Bettmann/Corbis/Getty Images.

CHAPTER 29: **p. 1190:** Library of Congress; **p. 1193:** GRANGER — All rights reserved; **p. 1196:** Bettmann/Corbis/Getty Images; **p. 1200:** Bettmann/Corbis/Getty Images; **p. 1205:** GRANGER — All rights reserved; **p. 1206:** GRANGER — All rights reserved; **p. 1209:** AP Photo/Bill Hudson; **p. 1214:** Bettmann/Corbis/Getty Images; **p. 1216:** Bettmann/Corbis/Getty Images; **p. 1218:** National Archives; **p. 1221:** Everett Collection Historical/Alamy Stock Photo; **p. 1226:** PhotoQuest/Getty Images; **p. 1232:** Jack Kightlinger, Lyndon Baines Johnson Library and Museum.

CHAPTER 30: **p. 1240:** Bettmann/Corbis/Getty Images; **p. 1244:** Leif Skoogfors/Corbis Historical/ Getty Images; **p. 1247:** Henry Diltz/Corbis via Getty Images; **p. 1251:** © Globe Photos/ZUMAPRESS. com; **p. 1255:** Eugene Gordon/The New York Historical Society/Getty Images; **p. 1259:** Michael Rougier/ The LIFE Picture Collection/Getty Images; **p. 1262:** Fred W. McDarrah/Getty Images; **p. 1267:** Lee Lockwood/The LIFE Images Collection/Getty Images; **p. 1269:** Bettmann/Corbis/Getty Images; **p. 1272:** Bettmann/Corbis/Getty Images; **p. 1273:** Howard Ruffner/Getty Images; **p. 1276:** Bettmann/Corbis/ Getty Images; **p. 1279:** John Dominis/The LIFE Picture Collection/Getty Images; **p. 1285:** Bettmann/ Corbis/Getty Images; **p. 1286:** Dirck Halstead/The LIFE Images Collection/Getty Images; **p. 1287:** Gerald R. Ford Presidential Museum, Grand Rapids, MI.

CHAPTER 31: **p. 1292:** © Wally McNamee/CORBIS/Corbis via Getty Images; **p. 1295:** © CORBIS/ Corbis via Getty Images; **p. 1300:** Mohsen Shandiz/Sygma via Getty Images; **p. 1301:** Francois LOCHON/ Gamma-Rapho via Getty Images; **p. 1303:** Bettmann/Corbis/Getty Images; **p. 1307:** Bettmann/Corbis/ Getty Images; **p. 1308:** Wally McNamee/Corbis/Getty Images; **p. 1314:** Bettmann/Corbis/Getty Images; **p. 1315:** Peter Turnley/Corbis/VCG via Getty Images; **p. 1319:** AP Photo/Marcy Nighswander; **p. 1322:** Visions of America/UIG via Getty Images; **p. 1324:** STR/Reuters/Newscom; **p. 1327:** MIKE NELSON/ AFP/Getty Images.

CHAPTER 32: **p. 1332:** AP Photo/Alex Brandon; **p. 1337:** AP Photo/James Finley; **p. 1338:** Richard Ellis/AFP/Getty Images; **p. 1342:** AP Photo/Ron Edmonds; **p. 1347:** Robert King/Newsmakers/Getty Images; **p. 1349:** STR/Reuters/Newscom; **p. 1350:** Kevin Lamarque/Reuters/Newscom; **p. 1353:** Ali Jasim/Reuters/Newscom; **p. 1356:** Mario Tama/Getty Images; **p. 1359:** AP Photo/Jae C. Hong, file; **p. 1362:** Jewel Samad/AFP/Getty Images; **p. 1364:** AP Photo/Erich Schlegel, File; **p. 1367:** Darren McCollester/Getty Images; **p. 1368:** AP Photo/Ringo H.W. Chiu; **p. 1372:** Ben Baker/Redux; **p. 1377:** Mladen Antonov/AFP/Getty Images; **p. 1380 (left):** Spencer Platt/Getty Images; **(right):** David McNew/ Getty Images; **p. 1381:** The Photo Access/Alamy Stock Photo; **p. 1384:** Xinhua/Bao Dandan via Getty Images; **p. 1386:** Amy Sussman/Shutterstock; **p. 1387:** MediaPunch/Shutterstock; **p. 1389:** Brian van der Brug/LA Times via Getty Images; **p. 1391:** Jeff Malet Photography/Newscom; **p. 1394:** Yonhap News/ YNA/Newscom; **p. 1395:** U.S. Border Patrol/Handout/Anadolu Agency/Getty Images.

# INDEX

Page numbers in *italics* refer to illustrations.

AAA (Agricultural Adjustment Administration), 1027, 1034
AASS (American Anti-Slavery Society), *405*, 486–88, 490, 494
Abilene, Kansas, 683
abolition movement, 485–91, 496–97
  African Americans in, 491–95, *492*
  African colonization proposed in, 485–86
  early opposition to slavery, 485–86
  Fugitive Slave Act and, 551–52
  gradualism to, 486, *487*
  pamphlets and newspapers mailed by, 404–6, 488
  split in, 488–89
abortion issue, 1252, 1255–56, 1303
Abu Ghraib prison, *1353*, 1354
ACA (Affordable Care Act), *1362*, 1362–63, 1373, 1376–77, 1390, 1396
Acadia, 134, 142
ACHA (American Health Care Act), 1390, *1391*
Acheson, Dean, 1135, 1137
Acoma Pueblos, 35
acquired immunodeficiency syndrome (AIDS), 1319, *1319*, 1320, 1330
ACS (American Colonization Society), 485–86, 496
Act Against Intemperance, Immorality, and Profaneness, 118–19
activist government, 1027
Act of Supremacy, 26
Act to Prevent Frauds and Abuses (1696), 139
Act Up!, *1319*
Adams, Abigail, 159, 167, 168, 217–18, 247, 271
Adams, Charles Francis, 371
Adams, Charles Francis, Jr., 694
Adams, Henry, 677
Adams, John, 155, 159, 168, 169–70, 171, 175, 181, 195, 217, 218, 225, 226, 232, 247, 259, *266*, 275–77, 279, 280, 292, 884
  Alien and Sedition Acts and, 267
  Declaration of Independence and, 171
  description of, 265–66
  domestic discontent and, 266–69
  in election of 1796, 265
  in election of 1800, 269–70, *270*

  French conflict and, 266, *266*
  French Revolution and, 258
  on peace commission, 208
  as vice-president, 246, 247
Adams, John Quincy, 225, 271, 316, 363, 365, *366*, 368, 369, 397, 402, 526
  and Adams-Onís Treaty, 365
  in election of 1828, 373, 374
  on "gag rule," 405–6
  and Treaty of Ghent, 307
  on Lovejoy's murder, 494
  on Mexican-American War, 530
  Monroe Doctrine and, 366, 367
  presidency of, 370–73
  on slavery, 424
  on Tyler, 526
  on Van Buren, 406
Adams, Samuel, 156, 158, 165, 174
  in Committee of Correspondence, 159
  Paul Revere and, 163
  in ratification debate, 242
Adamson Act (1916), 890
Adams-Onís Treaty (1819), 365, 376
*Adarand Constructors v. Peña*, 1339
Addams, Jane, 711, 833–34, 857–58, *858*, 942
Adena-Hopewell culture, *12*, 12–13
Adjusted Compensation Act, 1013
admiralty courts, vice-admiralty courts, 139
adobe, 9
AFDC (Aid to Families with Dependent Children), 1339
affirmative action, 1262, 1290, 1339
*Affluent Society, The* (Galbraith), 1165
Affordable Care Act (ACA), *1362*, 1362–63, 1373, 1376–77, 1390, 1396
Afghanistan
  Soviet Union and, 1298–99
  "surge" in, 1364–65
  Taliban in, 1351
AFL (American Federation of Labor), 720–21, 729, 1047
AFL-CIO (American Federation of Labor-Congress of Industrial Organizations), 1308

Africa
 slaves in, 87–89
 slaves in return to, 485–86
African Americans; *see also* civil rights and liberties;
  civil rights movement; segregation and
  desegregation; slavery; slaves; slave trade
 in abolition movement, 491–95, *492*
 activism in early civil rights movment, *1169*, 1170
 African roots of, 1217
 in American Revolution, 184, 185, *194*, 212, *215*,
  215–16
 in antebellum southern society, 90, *90*, 429–39,
  *434*, *435*
 in baseball, *1127*, 1127–28
 black code restrictions on, *589*, 649–50, 661–62,
  680
 Black Lives Matter, 1371–73, *1372*
 black nationalism, 962–63
 black power and, 1213–17, *1214*, *1216*, 1238
 and CCC, 1025
 as Civil War soldiers, 590, 591, 606–8, *607*
 disfranchising of, 737–38
 education of, 657
 employment for, 1163
 free blacks, *see* free blacks
 GI Bill of Rights for, 1158
 in Great Depression, 1010–11
 Great Migration by, 895–96, 910, 959–60,
  1160–61
 in Jazz Age, 959–63, *961*, *962*
 land policy and, 657–59, *659*
 marriage of, 649–50
 minstrel shows and, 340, *341*
 mulattoes, 431–32
 music and, *952*, 952–53
 and National Recovery Administration, 1026
 New Deal and, 1033–35, *1035*
 in politics, *656*, *658*
 post-war civil rights for, 1125–26
 poverty among, 1165
 in Reconstruction, 639–40, 649, 655–64, *661*
 religion and, 101, *213*, 440–43, *442*, *457*, 457–58,
  656, 657
 segregation and, *see* segregation and desegregation
 in Spanish-American War, 827
 suburban housing for, 1160
 Underground Railroad and, 493–94, 497
 voting rights for, 500, 650, 654–55, *658*, 737–38,
  1225–26
 in West, 747–50, *750*, 750–52
 women's challenges in 1920s, 958
 WWI and, 909–10
 WWII and, 1076–78, *1077*, *1078*, 1078–79, 1103
African Methodist Episcopal (AME) Church, 444–45,
  *457*, 458
Age of Reason, *See* Enlightenment
Agnew, Spiro, 1286
Agricultural Adjustment Act, 1027, 1042, 1052

Agricultural Adjustment Administration (AAA),
  1027, 1034
agriculture
 in colonial period, 52, 72, 102, 109
 corporate, 689–90
 and Dust Bowl, 1027–28
 in early nineteenth century, 333–34
 Farmers' Alliances and, 802–4
 Granger movement and, 801–2, *803*
 of Indians, 7
 in Kentucky, 263
 in New Deal, 1027
 in 1920s, 1000, 1005–7
 in South, 416, 418–21, *422*, *423*, *735*, 735–37, *736*
Aguinaldo, Emilio, 827, 832, 833, *833*
AIDS (acquired immunodeficiency syndrome), 1319,
  *1319*, 1320, 1330
Aid to Families with Dependent Children (AFDC),
  1339
AIM (American Indian Movement), 1260–61
Air Commerce Act (1926), 948
air-conditioning systems, 1158–59
airplanes, 948–49
Air Quality Act, 1223
Akerman, Amos, 673
Alabama, secession of, 572
Alamance, Battle of, 156
Alamo, *517*, 518–19
Alaska, 821–22, *823*, 1187
Albania, 1118
Albany Congress, 142
Albany Plan of Union, 142, 176
Albermarle, 70
Albright, George Washington, 603
alcohol, consumption of, 118–19
Alexander I, Czar, 373
*Alexander v. Holmes County Board of Education,*
  1267
Alexander VI, 20
Algonquian tribes, 13–14, *14*, 83, *86*
Alien and Sedition Acts, 268–69
Alien Enemies Act, 268
Alien Friends Act, 268
*All Creation Going to the White House* (Cruikshank),
  *382*
Allen, Eliza, 520
Allen, Richard, 458
Allende, Salvador, 1277–78
Alliance, Treaty of (1778), 197, 258
Alliance for Progress, 1197
Allied Powers, 897, *899*, 901–2, 938
*All in the Family*, 1263
al-Maliki, Nouri, 1353
almshouses, 1008
al Qaeda, 1109, 1349–51, 1364
alt-right movement, 1387
AMA (American Medical Association), 1223
Amalgamated Clothing Workers of America, 1046

AME (African Methodist Episcopal) Church, 444–45, *457*, 458
American and Foreign Anti-Slavery Society, 490
American Anti-Imperialist League, 833
American Anti-Slavery Society (AASS), *405*, 486–88, 490, 494
American Bible Society, 474
American Birth Control League, 956
American Century, 937
American Colonization Society (ACS), 485–86, 496
American Committee for the Outlawry of War, 993
*American Crisis, The* (Paine), 189
American Enterprise Institute, 1304
American Expeditionary Force (AEF), 914–15, 918
American Federation of Labor (AFL), 720–21, 729, 1047, 1125
American Federation of Labor-Congress of Industrial Organizations (AFL-CIO), 1308
American Health Care Act (ACHA), 1390, *1391*
American Indian Movement (AIM), 1260–61
*American Individualism* (Hoover), 999
American Medical Association (AMA), 1223
American (Know-Nothing) party, *344*, 344–45, 350, 556, *560*
American Protective Association (APA), 780
American Recovery and Reinvestment Act, 1361
American Revenue Act (1764), *see* Sugar Act
American Revolution, 163–75, 180–221, *182*
    African American soldiers in, 184, *194, 215,* 215–16
    American society in, 192–94
    Boston Tea Party and, *132,* 159–60
    British strategies in, 184, 192, 194–95, 201
    British surrender in, 207
    Committees of Correspondence and, 159
    events leading to, 150–56
    finance and supply of, 185
    first battles of, 163–65, *164*
    France and, 180, 183, 197, 206–7
    frontier in, 199–201
    governmental power as driver of, 223–24
    Hessians in, 184, 190, 201
    independence issue in, 168–75, *170*
    Loyalists in, 161, 162, 184, 188, 193–96, 202–4
    militias in, 163–64, 167–68, 184, 194
    nationalism in, 219
    Native Americans and, 183–86, 199–201, 208, 218
    Netherlands and, 180, 183, 197
    New Jersey campaigns, *191*
    New York campaigns, *191, 196*
    Patriot forces in, 165–68, 179–80, 183–87, 193, 194, *194*
    peace efforts in, 167
    Pennsylvania campaigns, *196*
    political participation after, 211–12
    republican ideology and, 209
    slavery and, 172–73, 212–16
    social revolution and, 212–14
    Southern campaigns, *205*
    South in, 201–7
    Spain and, 180, 183, 197
    spreading conflict in, 165–68
    state government and, 210–11
    Treaty of Paris (1783) and, 207–8
    war debt repayment after, 992
    Western campaigns, *200*
    women and, 216–18
American Society for the Promotion of Temperance, 474
American Sunday School Union, 474
American System, 358–59, 369, 376
American Telephone and Telegraph Company (AT&T), 690
American Temperance Union, 474
American Tobacco Company, 770
American Tract Society, 474
American Woman Suffrage Association (AWSA), 855
Americas
    Columbus's exploration of, 17–21, *18*
    diversity in, 2–3
    European biological exchange with, 31–32
    European exploration of, 1–3
    first migrations to, 5–6
    imperial rivalries in, 3
    name of, 20–21
    pre-Columbian, 6–15, *7, 12, 14*
    professional explorers of, 21
    Spanish culture in, 32–33
Ames, Adelbert, 660
Ames, Charles, 834
Ames, Fisher, 285
Amherst, Jeffrey, 148
Anaconda Plan, 584
anarchism, 718–19
Anasazis, 11
Anderson, John, 1304
Anderson, Robert, 572, 574–75, 629
Anderson, William P., 411
André, John, 206
Andrews, Samuel, 701
Andros, Edmund, 138, 139
Anglican Church (Church of England), 25–26, 48–50, 62, 120, 124, 213
Anschluss, 1060–61
*Anschluss,* 1060–61
Anthony, Susan B., *447,* 478, 654, 854
anti-colonial liberation movements, 1111
anti-communism, 1141–42, *1142*
Anti-Debris Association, 751
Antietam (Sharpsburg), Battle of, 600–601, *605,* 636
anti-Federalists, 241, 242, 272
anti-feminism, *1303,* 1303–4
anti-immigrant prejudices, 97–98
anti-lynching bills, 960
Anti-Masonic party, 396–98
Anti-Saloon League, 865

anti-Semitism
    Anschluss and, 1060–61
    Father Coughlin and, 1041
    Hitler and, 1057–58
anti-Semitism in colonial period, 76
anti-slavery movements, *see* abolition movement
anti-trust laws, Wilson and, 885–86
Antrobus, John, 442
Apaches, 35, 507
Apalachees, 15
Appalachian Regional Development Act, 1223
*Appeal to the Colored Citizens of the World* (Walker),
    488
Appomattox, surrender at, 630–32, 636
"Arab Awakening," 1365
*Arabic,* sinking of, 903
Arab League, 1121
Arafat, Yasir, 1341, *1342*
Arapahoes, 38, 759, 761
architecture in New England, 103–4
Ardennes Forest, 1089–91, *1090*
Armory Show (1913), *965,* 966, 970
Armour, Philip, 755
arms control negotiations, 1314–15
Armstrong, John, 304
Armstrong, Louis, 952
Armstrong, Louise V., 1008
Armstrong, Samuel Chapman, 744
Army Air Force
    bombing of Germany, 1085
    women in WWII, 1075
Army-McCarthy hearings, 1155
Arnold, Benedict, 206
art
    modernist, 964–66, *965*
    realism in, 785–87, *786*
    in 1950s, *1166,* 1166–67
Arthur, Chester A., 791, *792*
Articles of Confederation, 142
Articles of Confederation (1781), 180, 196, 211, 224,
    225–26, 272
    calls for revision of, 232, 235
Asbury, Francis, 456
Ashburton, Lord, 524
Asia, 836–37; *see also specific countries*
Asian Americans
    as civil rights activists, 1170
    in Great Depression, 1010
astrolabes, 16
Aswan Dam, 1183
asylums, 474–75
Atahualpa, *4*
Atchison, David, 557
Atlanta Compromise, 646
*Atlanta Constitution,* 732
Atlanta in Civil War, 626–27, *628*
Atlantic, Battle of the, 1083–84
Atlantic Charter, 1069

Atlantic Ocean, Columbus's crossing of, 18–19
atomic bombs, *see* nuclear weapons
atomic spying, 1141
atomic weapons
    in Cold War, 1111–12, 1114, 1134
    in massive retaliation strategy, 1178
Attucks, Crispus, 157
Auburn penitentiary, 475
Auchincloss, Gordon, 924
Augsberg, Treaty of (1555), 23
*Aunt Phillis's Cabin; or, Southern Life As It Is*
    (Eastman), *417,* 418
Austin, Stephen Fuller, 516, 518
Austria
    Anschluss, 1060–61
    Treaty of Versailles and, 926
Austria-Hungary, 897–98, 924, 931
automobiles, 949–50, *950*
AWSA (American Woman Suffrage Association), 855
"Axis" alliance, 1060
Axis powers, 1058–59
Aztecs, 8–9, 28–30, *36,* 44

Babcock, Anson, 582
baby boom generation, 1047–48, 1123
backcountry, 109, 111
Bacon, Nathaniel, 58–59
Bacon's Rebellion, *58,* 58–59, 92
Bad Heart Bull, Amos, *763*
Baez, Joan, 1243, 1250
Bailey, Ann, 217
Baker, Ray Stannard, 855, 873, 929–30
Baldwin, Hanson, 1101
Ballinger, Richard A., 876–77
Ballou, Adin, 485
Ballou, Sullivan, 589–90
Baltimore, first Lord (George Calvert), 59
bands, 9
Bankhead–Jones Farm Tenant Act, 1049
banking regulation in First New Deal, 1022–23
Bank of North America, 226
Bank of the United States, 253–55, 297
    Hamilton's recommendation for, 253–55, 272
    Jackson and, 390–93, *392,* 401, 402–3
    Panic of 1819 and, 360, 361
    second charter of, 354–55, 391–93
Bank of the United States, Second, 376
Banks, Dennis, 1260
Bank War, 390–93, 412
Bannon, Steve, 1387
Baptists, 109, 124, 454, 456
Barbados, 70
Barbary pirates, 281–82, *282,* 312
*Bare Knuckles, 339*
Barnes, George, 900
Barnett, Ross, 1208
Barnett, Sarah, 742
barter, 117

Barton, Clara, 608–9, *609*
Baruch, Bernard, 907–8, 1116
baseball, 950–51, *1127*, 1127–28
Bataan Death March, 1095
Bates, Fanny, 786
bathtub gin, 983
Batista, Fulgencio, 1186
"Battle Hymn of the Republic," 476
Battle of Bull Run, 590
*Battle of Lexington, The* (Doolittle), *164*
Battle of Secessionville, 589
Bay of Pigs invasion, 1198, 1238
beans, 31, 35
Beard, George M., 711
Beats, *1166*, 1166–67, 1188
Beauregard, Pierre G. T., 575, 583, 594
*Beautiful and the Damned, The* (Fitzgerald), 969
Bedford, Gunning, 235
Beecher, Catharine, 460, 475–76, 490
Beecher, Henry Ward, 661
Beecher, Lyman, 473, 474
beefsteak crisis, 1124
Begin, Menachem, 1297
Belgium, 1089
    Bulge, Battle of the, *1090*
    Battle of the Bulge, 1089–91
    and Kellogg-Briand pact, 993
    in WWI, 898
    in WWII, 1063
Bell, Alexander Graham, 690
Bell, John, 568–69, *570*
Bellamy, Madge, 954
Belleau Wood, Battle of, 919
Bellows, George, *786*
Ben-Guion, David, 1121
Benton, Blanche, 987
Benton, Jessie, 514
Benton, Thomas Hart, 359, 514
Bering Strait, 5
Berkeley, John, 77
Berkeley, William, 58–59
Berkman, Alexander, 722
Berlin, Germany, 1089
Berlin airlift, 1118–19, *1119*
Berlin crisis, 1185–86
Berlin Wall, 1199–1200, *1200*, 1238, *1324*, 1324–25
Bernard, Francis, 153
Berrien, John, 395
Berry, Chuck, 1168
Bessemer, Henry, 703
Bessemer converter, 703, 728
Beston, Ann, 742
Bethel African Methodist Church, 458
Bethune, Mary Jane McLeod, 1034
Bethune–Cookman College, 1034
Beveridge, Albert J., 820, 831, 834
BIA (Bureau of Indian Affairs), 1036, 1260
Bibb, Henry, 491

Bible, 22, 23, 495
Biddle, Nicholas, 391–92, 398, 401–2
Biddlecom, Charles, 590
Biden, Joseph, 1359
Bidlack Treaty (1846), 840
Bienville, JeanBaptiste Le Moyne, sieur de, 136
Bierstadt, Albert, *502*
Big Four, Paris Peace Conference, 925
Bill of Rights, English, 139
Bill of Rights, U.S., 244, 247–48, 272; *see also*
    constitutional amendments, U.S.
Bingham, George Caleb, *264, 397*
bin Laden, Osama, 1109, 1349–50, 1365
Birmingham, civil rights demonstrations in, 1208–10,
    *1209*
Birney, James Gillespie, 490
birth control, 955–56, 1297
birthrates in colonial period, 97, 130
birthright citizenship, 119
bison, *see* buffalo
Black, Hugo, 1048
black codes, 115, *589*, 649–50, 661–62, 680
Blackfeet, 765
Black Friday, 669
Black Hawk War, 386–87
Black Kettle, 759
Black Lives Matter, 1371–73, *1372*
*Black Methodists Holding a Prayer Meeting, 457*
black nationalism, 962–63, 970
Black Panther Party for Self Defense (BPP), 1215–17
Black Panthers, 1215–17, *1216*, 1245
    and Gay Liberation, 1216
    and Women's Liberation, 1216
black power, 962, 963, 1213–17, *1214, 1216*, 1238
Black Power, 1256
Black Tuesday, *972*, 1003
Blackwell, Elizabeth, 349
Bladensburg, Battle of, 304, 306
Blaine, James Gillespie, 676, 791, 793–96
Blair, Francis P., Jr., 664
Blake, James, 1172
Bland-Allison Act (1878), 791–92
"Bleeding Kansas," *540, 555, 557*, 557–58, 576
*Blithedale Romance, The* (Hawthorne), 483
blitzkrieg, 1063–65, *1064*, 1065–66, *1066*
blood sports, 339, *339*
*Bloody Massacre, The* (Revere), *158*
*Board of Education of Topeka, Kansas, Brown v.*,
    1170–72, 1188, 1197–98
Board of Indian Commissioners, 667
Bobadilla, Francis, 20
Bok, Edward, 712
Boleyn, Anne, 26
Bolshevik Revolution (1917), 915–16, 937
Bonavita, Rosina, 1076
Bonus Expeditionary Force, 1013–14
*Book of Mormon, The*, 460
boomtowns, mining, 751–52

Boone, Daniel, 201, 263–64, *264*
Booth, John Wilkes, 567, 632, 645–46
bootleg alcohol, 983
border wall, 1391
Bork, Robert, 1283
Bosnia, 1342–43
Boston, in colonial period, *94,* 117–18
*Boston Evening Globe,* 958–59
Boston Massacre, 157–59, *158,* 176
Boston Port Act (1774), 161
Boston Tea Party, *132,* 159–60, 176
*Boston Traveller,* 958
Boulding, G. T. F., 672
Bourke-White, Margaret, *1034*
Bow, Clara, 954
Bowie, James "Jim," 518, 519
Boxer Rebellion (1900), 837
boxing, 339, *339,* 951
boycotts, 161–62
Boy Scouts of America, 908
bracero program, 1079, 1161–62
Braddock, Edward, 143–44, 149
Bradford, William, 47, 64, 83–84
Bradley, Joseph, 674, 739
Bragg, Braxton, 595, 620
Brandeis, Louis D., 881, 890
Braun, Eva, 1093
Breckinridge, John C., 568, 569, *570,* 629
Bremmer, Ian, 1376
Brest-Litovsk, Treaty of (1918), 917
Brezhnev, Leonid, 1280
Briand, Aristide, 993
brinkmanship, 1178
Britain, Battle of, 1065–66, *1066*
British Empire; *see also* American Revolution;
    colonial period; Great Britain
    French Empire compared with, 90–91, 133, 134–36
Broken Mammoth, 5–6
Brooke, Sir Alan, 1085
Brook Farm, 483
Brooks, Preston, 557
Brown, Charles, 662
Brown, John, 558, 566–67, *567*
Brown, Joseph, 613
Brown, William Wells, 491
Brownsville riot, 874
Brown University, 128
*Brown v. Board of Education of Topeka, Kansas,*
    1170–72, 1188, 1197–98
Bruce, Blanche K., 657
Bry, Theodor de, *4*
Bryan, William Jennings, *808,* 808–9, 832, 845–46,
    854, 867, 880
    in presidential elections, 685, 809–11, *811,* 871,
    875
    at Scopes trial, 979–81, *980*
    as secretary of state, 896, 901–3
B-29 Superfortress, 1097, 1099, 1100

Buchanan, James, 568, 629
    *Dred Scott* decision and, 561, 562, 563
    in election of 1856, 559, *560,* 560–61
    in Kansas crisis, 563
    Lecompton Constitution supported by, 563
    Panic of 1857 and, 561
    secession and, 571–72
Buchanan, Patrick, 1319, 1327–28
*Buchanan v. Warley,* 960
Budget and Accounting Act, 988
Buell, Don Carlos, 595
Buena Vista, Battle of, 533
buffalo, 38–39, 764
*Buffalo Hunt, Chasing Back* (Catlin), *506*
*Building the Transcontinental Railroad, 1043*
Bulgaria
    and Marshall Plan, 1118
    in WWI, 897
Bulge, Battle of the, *1090*
    in WWII, 1089–91
"Bull Moose" (Progressive) party, *878,* 878–79
Bull Run (Manassas)
    first Battle of (1861), 583–84
    second Battle of (1861), 598
Bundy, McGeorge, 1198
Bunker Hill, Battle of (1775), *166,* 166–67
Bureau of Aviation, 999
Bureau of Corporations, 870
Bureau of Indian Affairs, 667
Bureau of Indian Affairs (BIA), 1036, 1260
Bureau of the Budget, 988
Burger, Warren, 1267
Burgoyne, John, 194, 195, *197*
burial mounds, 12, *12,* 44
Burke, Edmund, 162, 208
Burn, Harry T., 933
Burn, Phoebe Ensminger, 933
burned-over district, 459
*Burning of the Capitol, The, 305*
Burnside, Ambrose E., 604, 606, 614
Burr, Aaron, 288, 533
    Burr Conspiracy, 289–90
    in election of 1796, 265
    in election of 1800, 269, *270*
    Hamilton's duel with, 288
Burr Conspiracy, 289–90
Burroughs, William, 1166, 1167
Burton, Mary, 116
*Burwell, King v.,* 1376–77
Bush, George H. W., 1320–23
    economy and, 1323
    in election of 1988, 1320, *1321*
    foreign policy of, 1324–28
    Gulf War and, 1326–27
    on Japanese-American internment, 1082
    Panama invasion of, 1325–26
Bush, George W., 1109, 1347–48
    economy and, 1355, 1357–58

in election of 2000, 1345–47, *1346, 1347*
in election of 2004, 1354–55, *1355*
Hurricane Katrina and, *1356,* 1356–57
Second Gulf War and, 1352–54, *1353,* 1357
second term of, 1355–58
September 11, 2001, attacks and, 1348, 1349, *1349*
terrorism and, *1350,* 1350–52
Bush, Jeb, 1387
Bush doctrine, 1352, 1396
business
alliance of politics and, 706–8, *707,* 728
barons of, 700–706, *701, 703, 704*
in late nineteenth century, 699–700
regulation of, 864, 868–69, *869*
Business Roundtable, 1304
Butler, Benjamin F., 595
Butler, Elihu, 388
*Butler, United States v.,* 1042
Byles, Mather, 193
Byrd, Harry F., 1171
Byrd, William, II, 112
Byrnes, James F., 1114

Cabell, William H., 309
cabinet, 247
Cable, George Washington, 738
Cabot, John, 21
Cahokia, 13, 44
Cajuns, 142
Calhoun, Floride, 383
Calhoun, John C., 297, 321, 354, 360, 369, 370, 384, 541
Compromise of 1850 and, 546, 548
death of, 550
Eaton Affair and, 383, 384
First Seminole War, 364–65
internal improvements and, 356
Jackson's rift with, 395–96
on Mexican-American War, 536–37
national bank issue and, 354–55
nullification issue and, 399–401
on slavery, 416, 418, 430, 495
slavery on frontier and, 522, 525
tariffs and, 355, 373, 393–94
on Van Buren, 406
Van Buren's rivalry with, 383
California
affirmative action and, 1339
annexation of, 515, 531–33
Dust Bowl refugees in, 1028
gold rush in, 506, 543–45, *544,* 576
Mexican independence and, 512
settlement of, 510–14
statehood for, 546–56
Compromise of 1850 and, 546–52, *547*
election of 1852, 553–54
Fugitive Slave Act and, 551–52
Kansas-Nebraska crisis, 554–56
*Uncle Tom's Cabin* and, 552–53
Californios, 512
Calley, William L. "Rusty," 1272
Calvert, Cecilius, 59–61
Calvert, George, 59
Calvert, Leonard, 59–61, 112
Calvin, John, 23–25, 62, 68
Calvinism, 24–25, 451
Cambodia, 1179, 1271–72, 1275
Campbell, David, 304
Camp David Accords, 1297–98, 1330
Campell, Alexander, 589
Campell, James, 589
Canada, 40
in American Revolution, 186, 194–95
War of 1812 and, 296, *299,* 299–301
canals, 321, *322–23,* 324–26, *325,* 330
cannibalism, 54
Canning, George, 366–67
Canterbury, archbishop of (Thomas Becket), 26
capitalism, 250
and Cold War, 1113
in Coolidge administration, 997
and Great Depression, 1019
New Deal and, 1050
Capitol Building (Washington), 276, *279*
Capone, Al "Scarface," 984–85
caravels, 16
Carbine, Patricia, 1254
car culture, *1154,* 1154–55
Cardozo, Francis, 667
Caribbean
Columbus in, 19–20
early U.S. trade in, 229–30
slaves in, 113
Spain in, 27
Carleton, Guy, 212
Carmichael, Stokely, 1214, 1215
Carnegie, Andrew, 689, 702–4, *703,* 706, 721, 722, 833
Carnegie Steel Company, *686,* 704, 728
Carolina region (colonial), 47, 70–72
carpetbaggers, 660
Carranza, Venustiano, 847
Carrier, Willis, 1159
cars, 949–50
Carter, James Earl (Jimmy), Jr., 1293, 1294–97, *1295,* 1330
Camp David Accords and, 1297–98, 1330
economy and, 1296
in election of 1976, 1288–89
in election of 1980, 1304, *1305*
foreign policy of, 1297–1300, *1300*
Iran hostage crisis and, 1299–1300, *1300*
Carter, Landon, 174
Carter Doctrine, 1299
Carteret, George, 77
Cartier, Jacques, 40

Cartwright, Peter, 456–57
Casablanca Conference, 1083
Casey, William, 1314
Cass, Lewis, 507, 542, 543, 571–72
Cassady, Carolyn, 1167
Cassady, Neal, 1166
Castro, Fidel, 1186, 1198, 1203
Catawbas, 72, 73
Catherine of Aragon, 25–26
Catholicism/Catholic Church, 44
    in American colonies, 59, 61
    in England, 25, 26, 48–49, 50
    in Ireland, 50
    Irish Americans in, 342, *344*
    and Ku Klux Klan, 977
    missionaries of, 30–31, 34–36, 507, 510–12
    Native Americans and, 30–31, 34–36, 507, 510–12
    prejudice against, 780
    Reformation attacks on, 21–26, *22*
    Smith in 1928 election, 1001
    in Spanish Empire, 30–31, 34–36, 41, 507, 510–12
Catlin, George, *506*
Cato Institute, 1304
Catt, Carrie Chapman, 861, 933
cattle, 753–55, *754*
Cavaliers, 50
CCC (Civilian Conservation Corps), 1025, *1025,* 1034
Ceauşescu, Nicolae, 1324
Celia (slave), 439
censorship of mail, 404–6
Central American Free Trade Act, 1355
Central Intelligence Agency (CIA), 1121, 1144,
        1178–79, 1188
    in Chile, 1277–78
Central Pacific Railroad, *695,* 696, 697
Central Powers (Triple Alliance), 897, *899,* 901, 902,
        938
*Century of Dishonor, A* (Jackson), 767
Cession, Treaty of, 284
chain stores, 945–46
Chamberlain, Joshua, 631
Chamberlain, Neville, 1061
Chambers, Whittaker, 1141
Champlain, Samuel de, 40, 134, *135*
Chancellorsville, Battle of, *614,* 614–15, *619*
Chandler, Zachariah, 584
Chaney, James Earl, 1213
Chaplin, Charlie, 946, *946*
*Charge of the Rough Riders of San Juan Hill, The*
        (Remington), *818*
Charles, Ray, 1168
*Charles Calvert and His Slave, 239*
Charles I, *49,* 49–50, 59, 65
Charles II, 50, 70, 73, 77
    colonial administration under, 137–38
    death of, 138
Charleston, S.C.
    in Civil War, 629

in colonial period, 71, 117
founding of, 71
Thomas Jeremiah execution, 215
in Revolutionary War, 201, 202
slavery in, 72, 115, 172
Charles V, 26
*Charlotte-Mecklenburg Board of Education, Swann
        v.,* 1267
Chase, Salmon P., 242, 551
Chattanooga, Battle of, 620
Chavez, Cesar, 1258–60, *1259*
Cheever, John, 1166
Cheney, Richard "Dick," 1310, 1347, 1351–52, 1389
*Cherokee Nation v. Georgia,* 388
Cherokees, 10, 73, 521
    American Revolution and, 186, 201
    in Civil War, 592
    removal of, 388–90, *390*
Chesapeake colonies, 109
*Chesapeake* incident, 292
Chesnut, Mary, *427,* 427–28, 585, 604, 613, 626, 639
Cheves, Langdon, 361
Cheyennes, 38, 759, 760, 761, 763
Chiang Kai-shek, 1058, 1133, 1278
Chicago, 755–56
    Democratic Convention in (1968), 1235, 1238
    meatpacking industry, 755
    race riot in (1919), 934, *935*
*Chicago Daily News,* 1194
*Chicago Tribune,* 630, 1021, 1112, 1139
Chickasaw, 15, 389, 592
chiefdoms, 13
Child, Lydia Maria, 708
childbirth in colonial period, 97
child labor, 713, 728, 865–67, *866,* 890, 1026
Chile, 30, 1277–78
China, 836–37
    and Kellogg-Briand pact, 993
    before outbreak of WWII, 1055
China, People's Republic of
    in Korean War, 1135, 1137–38
    "loss" of China to, 1111, 1133–34
    Nixon and, 1278–79, *1279*
Chinese Americans, 343, 780, *780*
    in mining camps, *544,* 545
    violence against, 715, 779–80
Chinese Exclusion Act (1882), 780, *780,* 812, 914
Chivington, John M., 759–60
Choctaws, 15, 521, 592
*Christian Century,* 1060
Christianity, conversion of Native Americans to, 83
*Christianity and the Social Crisis* (Rauschenbusch),
        857
Churchill, Winston, 1063, 1067
    Atlantic Charter and, 1069
    and Battle of Britain, 1065–66
    at Casablanca, 1083
    cold war and, 1113, 1114

and Dunkirk, 1064
on FDR, 1032
on global statue of U.S. after WWII, 1102
on Holocaust, 1095
and Lend-Lease Act, 1068, 1069
on Munich Pact, 1061
as national leader in WWII, 1102
and Operation Overlord, 1085–86, 1088
and Pearl Harbor, 1073
on postwar Europe, 937
and race to Berlin, 1089
and second front, 1082
at Tehran Conference, 1084
and U.S. intervention in WWII, 1065
at Yalta, 1091–92, *1093*
Church of England, *see* Anglican Church
Church of Jesus Christ of Latter-day Saints
       (Mormons), 460–63, *461, 462*
CIA, *see* Central Intelligence Agency
CIO (Congress of Industrial Organizations), 1047
cities and towns
    in colonial period, 117–20
    industrialization and, *338,* 338–39
    in late nineteenth century, 773–76, 812
        cultural life and, 780–87, *781, 786*
        immigrants in, 776–80, *777, 779, 780,* 812
        problems of, 774–76
        technology and, 774
Citizen Genet, 259
Citizens' Councils, 1171
citizenship, in colonial era, 119–20
citizen-soldiers, 184, 196
*Citizens United v. Federal Elections Committee,* 1371
"Civil Disobedience" (Thoreau), 468
Civilian Conservation Corps (CCC), 1025, *1025,* 1034
Civil Liberties Act (1988), 1082
Civil Rights Act (1875), 650, 674, 739
Civil Rights Act (1957), 1173–74
Civil Rights Act (1960), 1174
Civil Rights Act (1964), 1219–20, 1238
civil rights and liberties
    in Civil War, 612
    Johnson and, 1219–20, 1238
    Nixon and, 1266–67, *1267*
    Patriot Act and, 1351
    Red Scare (1919) and, 934–36
    in the 1930s, 1033–35, *1035*
    Truman and, 1125–27
    World War I and, 911–13, *912*
    World War II and, 1080–82, *1081*
*Civil Rights Cases* (1883), 674, 739
Civil Rights Commission, 1174
civil rights movement
    African American activism, *1169,* 1170
    black power and, 1213–17, *1214, 1216,* 1238
    *Brown* decision and, 1170–72
    early period of, 1169–76
    expansion of, 1204–17

Little Rock crisis and, *1174,* 1174–76
Montgomery bus boycott and, 1172–73, *1173*
SCLC and, 1176
Civil Service Commisssion, 1140
civil service reform, 791–92, 793–94, 812
Civil War, U.S., 578–637; *see also* Confederate States of
       America; Reconstruction
aftermath of, 640–41, *641*
Anaconda Plan in, 584
Antietam and, 600–601, *605,* 636
Atlanta, 626–27, *628*
Bull Run
    first Battle of, 583–84
    second Battle of, 598
casualties in, 594–95, 601, 633, 636, 639
Chancellorsville and, *614,* 614–15, *619*
Chattanooga and, 620
choosing sides in, 580–83, *581*
civil liberties and, 612
Confederate command structure in, 612–13, *613*
Confederate finances in, 611
emancipation in, 598–608, *601,* 602, *602,* 603–4,
       606–8, *607*
Fort Pillow Massacre, 623
Fredericksburg and, 604, *605,* 606
Gettysburg and, 615–18, *617, 619,* 636
government during, 609–10
Grant's strategy in, 622–23
medicine in, 608
as modern war, 633–34
peninsular campaign in, *596,* 597
regional advantages in, 582–83
secession of South and, 580–83
Sherman's March and, 627–29, *628*
Shiloh and, *593,* 594–95
slavery and, 579, 580, 598–99, *598–99*
soldiers in
    African American, 590, 591, 606–8, *607*
    average life of, 589, *591*
    becoming warriors, 589–90
    recruitment and draft of, 585–87, *586*
strategies in, 583, 585
Union finances in, 610–11
Vicksburg and, 615, 619, 636
West in, 591–95, *593*
women in, 608–9, *609,* 610
Civil Works Administration (CWA), 1024–25
clans, 9
Clark, Francis E., 953
Clark, George Rogers, 199–200
Clark, Mark W., 1084
Clark, Tom, 1140
Clark, William, 285–88
Clay, Henry, 275, 297, 316, 369, 379, 384–85, 401–2,
       404, 408, 426, 541, 543, 553
    African colonization and, 485
    American System of, 358, 369
    Compromise of 1850 and, 546–48, *547,* 549–51

Clay, Henry (*continued*)
  on Eaton Affair, 396
  in election of 1824, 369–70
  in election of 1832, 398
  in election of 1844, 525, 526
  and Treaty of Ghent, 307
  on Jackson, 410
  on Mexican-American War, 530
  Missouri Compromise and, 363
  national bank issue and, 354–55, 391–93
  on Native Americans, 385
  nullification and, 400–401
  Tyler administration and, 523
Clay, Lucius D., 1118
Clayton Anti-Trust Act, 885–86, 893
Clayton-Bulwer Treaty, 840
Clemenceau, Georges, 914–15, 925, 927
Clemens, Samuel (Mark Twain), 697, 708, 833–34
Clemm, Virginia, 470
Clemson, Thomas, 430
*Clermont,* 324
Cleveland, Grover, 724, 780, 790, 806, 834, 913
  on Bryan, 809
  in election of 1884, 794–96, *795*
  in election of 1888, 797–98
  in election of 1892, 805–6
  first term of, 796–98
  Hawaii and, 824
  tariff issue and, 797–98
Clifford, Clark, 1232
Clinton, DeWitt, 324–25, 397
Clinton, George, 242, 288
Clinton, Henry, 167, 201, 202
Clinton, Hillary Rodham, 1328, 1343
  in election of 2008, 1358–59, *1380,* 1396
  in election of 2016, 1379–80, 1383–84, *1385*
Clinton, William Jefferson (Bill)
  assessment of presidency of, 1345
  background of, 1328
  economy and, 1336–37, 1340
  in election of 1992, 1328–29
  in election of 1996, 1340
  first term of, 1335–40
  foreign policy of, 1341–43, *1342*
  impeachment of, 1344–45
  Middle East and, 1341, *1342*
  Republican Congress and, 1338–1339207–1208
  scandals under, 1343–45
clipper ships, 328, *329*
*Clovis* peoples, 6
coal miners, 1123–24
coal strike of 1902, 870
Coast Guard, 1075
Cobb, Howell, 666
Cobb, Thomas Reade, 416, 429
"code talkers," *1080*
Coercive Acts (1774), 160–61
Cohen, Roger, 1354
Cohens v. Virginia, 356
Colbert, Claudette, *1039*
Cold War, 1111
  China and, 1133–34, 1137–38
  containment in, 1115–21, *1117, 1119, 1120,* 1327
    alliances and, 1119–20
    divided Germany and, 1118–19, *1119*
    Israel and, 1121
    Marshall Plan and, 1116–18, *1117*
    NSC-68 on, 1134
    Truman Doctrine and, 1116
  end of, 1327, 1330
  origins of, 1113–14
  Red Scare and, 1144
  and 1950s, 1149
Cole, Thomas, *450*
Coleto, Battle of, 519–20
College of New Jersey (Princeton University), 128
College of Rhode Island (Brown University), 128
College of William and Mary, 128
Collier, John, 1036, *1036*
Colombia, 30
colonial governments
  assemblies' powers in, 140
  charters in, 65, 67, 69, 138
  and Dominion of New England, 138
  English administration and, 136–38
  governors' powers in, 140
  in Maryland, 61, 139, 140
  in Massachusetts, 65, 67–68, 69, 139, 140
  in New Jersey, 140
  in New York, 139
  in North Carolina, 72
  in Pennsylvania, 79
  in Plymouth, 62–64
  in Rhode Island, 68–69
  self-government developed in, 140, 173–75
  in South Carolina, 71–72
  in Virginia, 55, 140
colonial period
  agriculture in, 52, 102, 109
  architecture in, 103–4
  assemblies' powers in, 140
  backcountry in, 109, 111
  birthrates and death rates in, 97
  cities in, 117–20
  colonial wars in, 140–50, *146, 147*
  disease in, 97
  education in, 123
  English Civil War, 69–70
  English Restoration, 70–73
  Enlightenment in, 120–23, 128–29
  ethnic mix in, 109, *110,* 111
  European settlement in, 50–69, *60, 63,* 73–83, *74, 80–81*
  indentured servants in, 55–56, 95, 113
  mercantile system in, 136–37

Native American conflicts in, *58,* 58–59, 73, 83–85, 83–86, 148–49
newspapers in, 119
popular culture in, 339
population growth in, 96–97, 111, 117
postal service in, 119
religion in, 101, 106–8, 123–29
religious conflict and war in, 48–50
slavery in, 47, 71, 72, 87–90, 112–16, *115*
social and political order in, 117–18
society and economy in, 102–12
    middle colonies, 109–11, *110,* 111
    New England, 103–8
    southern colonies, 102–3
taverns in, *118,* 118–19
taxation in, 148, 150–56
trade and commerce in, 72–73, 75, 105–6, *106*
transportation in, 118
ways of life in, 94–131
witchcraft in, 107–8
women in, 96–101, *99*
colonial wars, 140–50, *146, 147*
    French and Indian War, 141–48, *143*
    King William's War, 140
    with Native Americans, 83–85, 148–49
Colson, Charles "Chuck," 1282
*Columbian Centinel,* 285
Columbian Exchange, 31–32, 44
Columbia University, 128
Columbus, Christopher
    background of, 17
    voyages of, 17–21, *18*
Comanches, 38, 507, 761
Comey, James B., 1383–84, *1384,* 1392
Command of the Army Act, 652
commercial agriculture, 321
Commission on Civil Rights, 1126
Committee for Industrial Organization (CIO), 1047
Committee of Correspondence, 159, 161, 176
Committee on Public Information (CPI), 910–11
Committee to Re-elect the President (CREEP), 1282
*Common Sense* (Paine), 168–69, 176, 189
*Commonwealth v. Hunt,* 347
communes, 1249
communication in early nineteenth century, 328–29
communism
    in China, 1133–34
    and Cold War, 1108, 1113
    in Cuba, 1186
    massive retaliation and, 1178
    in Vietnam War, 1179–80
communism, and Red Scare after World War I, 933–36
Communist Party, 1037
communitarianism, 481
Community Action Program, 1221
complex marriage, 483
Compromise of 1850, 541, 546–52, *547,* 553, 576

Compromise of 1877, 677, 680
Compromis of 1790, 253
computer revolution, 1316–17
Comstock Lode, *730, 752,* 770
Concord, Battle of (1775), 163–65
Conestogas, 149, 321, 508–9
Coney Island, *782*
Confederate States of America; *see also* Civil War, U.S.
    Atlanta and, 626–27, *628*
    Chancellorsville and, *614,* 614–15, *619*
    Chattanooga and, 620
    defeat of, 622–32, 634–35, 636, 683
    finances of, 611
    formation of, 573–74, 580–83, *581*
    Gettysburg and, 615–18, *617, 619,* 636
    lost cause of, 629–30
    politics in, 612–13, *613*
    recruitment in, 585–87
    Vicksburg and, 615, 620, 636
confederation, nation vs., 224
Confederation Congress, 211, 225
    diplomacy and, 228–29
    land policies of, 227
    Morris's role in, 226
    Northwest Ordinance, 228
    paper currency issued by, 230
    powers of, 225–26
    trade/economy and, 228–30
Congregationalists, 65, 69, 124–25, *213,* 456
Congress, U.S.
    first meeting of, 246
    in Great Depression, 1005, 1013
    Johnson's conflict with, 652–53
    Johnson's impeachment and, 653–54
    national bank issue in, 253
    in Reconstruction, 643, 648–49
Congressional Reconstruction, 652–53, 675–76, 680
Congressional Union for Woman Suffrage, 889
Congress of Industrial Organizations (CIO), 1047
Congress of Racial Equality (CORE), 1161, 1205
Conkling, Roscoe, 788, 791, 793
Connecticut colony, 69
Connecticut General Court, 69
Connon, Joseph, 868
Connor, Eugene "Bull," 1207, 1208, *1209*
conquistadores, 28–30, 33, 44
*Conscience of a Conservative, The* (Goldwater), 1221
conservation, 872–73
Conspiracy of 1741, 116
Constitution, U.S., 232–41, 279
    drafting of, 233–34
    judicial review principle and, 280
    national bank issue and, 254
    presidency in, 236–37
    ratification of, 241–45, *244, 245*
    separation of powers and, 235–37
    slavery in, 238–40

constitutional amendments, U.S., 247–49
  Eighteenth, 981–83
  Fifteenth, 500, 654–55, *658*, 680
  First, 248–49
  Fourteenth, 500, 651, 652, 680
  Nineteenth, 932–33, 939
  Seventeenth, 862, 892
  Sixteenth, 867
  Tenth, 248, 255
  Thirteenth, 240, 491, 574, 634, 636, 637, 643, 647
  Twelfth, 288
  Twenty-sixth, 1266
Constitutional Convention (1787), 180, *222*, 232–41, *238*
  call for, 232–33
  delegates to, 232–33
  drafting of Constitution at, 233–34
  Madison at, *233*, 233–35, 236, 238, 240
  political rights for women and, 240–41
  presidency issue at, 236–37
  separation of powers issue in, 235–37
  slavery issue in, 238–40
  Virginia and New Jersey Plans at, 235
*Construction of a Dam* (Gropper), *1018*
consumer culture, 970
  in early twentieth century, 944–45, *945*
  in 1950s, *1148*, 1155–65, *1157*
Consumer Financial Protection Bureau, 1363
consumer goods
  after World War II, 1123–24
consumerism, 1156–57
containment policy, 1115–21, *1117, 1119, 1120*, 1146, 1327
  alliances and, 1119–20
  divided Germany and, 1118–19, *1119*
  Israel and, 1121
  Marshall Plan, 1116–18, *1117*
  *NSC-68* on, 1134
  Truman Doctrine, 1116
Continental army, 184–85
Continental Association, 161–62
Continental Congress, First, 161–62
Continental Congress, Second, 165, 197, 204, 211
  independence voted by, *169*, 169–71, 186, 218
  peace efforts and, 167
Continentals, 226
contrabands, 599, *599*
contraception, 955–56, 1297
Contract Labor Act (1864), 715
contract rights, 356
Contract with America, *1338*, 1338–39, 1396
Contras, 1312
Convention of 1800, 269–70
Convention of 1818, 363, *364*, 507
convicts, as indentured servants, 56
Conwell, Russell, 700
Cooke, Jay, 611, 671

Coolidge, Calvin, 933, 944, 963, 975, 994, *996*, 996–1000, 1002, 1306
  and Eisenhower, 1153
  and radio, 947
Coolidge, Grace, 996
Cooper, Alice, 287
Cooper, Anthony Ashley, 72
Copernicus, Nicolaus, 120–21
Copperhead Democrats, 612, 637
Coral Sea, Battle of, 1096
Corbett, William, 474
Corbin, Abel, 668
CORE (Congress of Racial Equality), 1161, 1205
Corey, Giles, 108
corn (maize), 7, 35, 333
Cornbelt Rebellion, 1007
Cornwallis, Charles, 202–4, 206, 207
corporate agriculture, 689–90
corporations
  business, 864, 868–69, *869*
  growth of, 699
Corps of Discovery, 285–88
"corrupt bargain," 370, 377
Cortés, Hernán, 27–30, *28*, 33
cotton, 331–33, 350, 415–16, 419–25, *420, 422*
  population growth and, *423*
  prices in late nineteenth century, 737
  slavery and, 333, 419, 424–25, *441*
Cotton, John, 98
cotton gin, 331, *332*, 350, 421
Cotton Kingdom, 419–25, *420, 422, 423*, 448
Coughlin, Charles E., 1041–42, 1047
counterculture, 1246–47, *1247*, 1290
Counter-Reformation, 25
"Court-packing" scheme, 1048–49, 1052
covenant, 103
Cowpens, Battle of (1781), 204
Cox, Archibald, 1283
Cox, James, 986–87, 1020
Cox, William, 693
Coxey, Jacob S., 806
Coxey's Army, 806, *807*
*Crack in the Picture Window, The* (Keats), 1166
Crawford, Joan, 954
Crawford, William H., 369, 370
Crazy Horse, 763, 764
credit cards, 1157
Creeks, 15, 73, 228, 301–3, 389, 521
Creek War, 301–3
Creel, George, 911
CREEP (Committee to Re-elect the President), 1282
*Creole*, 524
Crevecoeur, J. Hector St. John de, 95
Crimea, Russia's annexation of, 1374–75
crime in colonial period, 117
*Crisis, The* (DuBois), 990
*Crisis, The* (journal), 960
*Criterion, The* (journal), 967

Critical Period, 225, 230
Crittenden, John J., 573
Croatia, 1342
Crockett, David, 301, 360, *517*, 518–19, 520
Croly, Herbert, 886
Cromwell, Oliver, 49–50, 70, 136–37
Cronkite, Walter, 1232
crop-lien system, *735*, 735–37, *736*, 770
Crosby, Bing, 1128
*Crow Quadrilles, The, 341*
Crows, 765
*Crucible, The* (Miller), 1140
C.S.S. *Planter,* 590
Cuba, 27, 835–36
  Bay of Pigs invasion of, 1198, 1238
  Columbus in, 19
  communism in, 1186
  missile crisis in, 1200–1201, 1238
  Obama and, 1366
  Spanish-American War and, 824–25, 826, 827–29, *828*
Cuban missile crisis, 1200–1201, 1238
Cuban War for Independence, 824–25
Cudahy, Michael, 342–43
Cullors, Patrisse, 1371–72
cult of domesticity, 475–76, 496
Cumberland (National) Road, 322–23
currency
  Confederation Congress, 230
  in late nineteenth century, 800
  national bank issue and, 356–57
  shortage of, 230
Currency Act (1764), 151
Custer, George Armstrong, 761–64
CWA (Civil Works Administration), 1024–25
Czechoslovakia, 1117, 1324
  Treaty of Versailles and, 926
  in WWII, 1061–62
Czolgosz, Leon, 838

DACA (Deferred Action for Childhood Arrivals), 1370
DADT (don't ask, don't tell), 1336, 1369
*Daily Dispatch,* 654
*Daily Record,* 741
Daladier, Édouard, 1061
Daley, Richard, 1235
*Daniel Boone Escorting Soldiers through the Cumberland Gap* (Bingham), *264*
Daniels, Jonathan, 1175
Daniels, Josephus, 887
Dare, Elinor, 42
Dare, Virginia, 42
Darrow, Clarence, *980,* 980–81, 987
Dartmouth College, 128
*Dartmouth College v. Woodward,* 356, 376
Darwin, Charles, 783, *783,* 830

Darwinism, 783–85, 812
  banned from public schools, 979–81
  reform, 785, 812
  religious opposition to, 783–84, 979–81
  social, 784, 812
Daugherty, Harry M., 986, 994
Daughters of Liberty, 153, 176
Davenport, James, 127
Davis, Angela, 1216
Davis, Garret, 529
Davis, Hannah, 165
Davis, Isaac, 165
Davis, Jefferson, 579, 678
  Civil War strategy of, 583, 585, 615
  Compromise of 1850 and, 546, 547
  as Confederate president, 573, 575, 611, 612–13, *613,* 626, 629, 632
  end of war and, 629–30
  enlistment efforts and, 585
  Kansas-Nebraska Act and, 554–55
  Pierce and, 554
  on Vicksburg, 615
Davis, John W., 998, 1002
Davis, Rennie, 1242
Davis, Varina, 588
Dawes, Henry L., 767
Dawes, William, 163
Dawes Severalty Act, 767, 771
Day, Henry, 348
Days of Rage, 1245
Dean, John W., III, 1264, 1283
*Death of General Mercer at the Battle of Princeton, The, 182*
death rates in colonial period, 96, 130
Debs, Eugene V.
  opposition to war, 912–13
  Pullman Strike and, 722–24
  as socialist, 723, *723,* 880–83, *882*
debt
  after World War I, 991–92, 1006
  Reagan and, 1317–18
Decatur, Stephen, 282
Decatur, William, 282
Declaration of American Rights, 161
Declaration of Constitutional Principles (Southern Manifesto), 1171–72
Declaration of Independence, *170,* 171–72, 176, 183, 185, 218, 224, 233, 240, 249, 278
Declaration of Rights and Sentiments, 477, 496
Declaratory Act (1766), 154
Deere, John, 333
Defense of Marriage Act (DOMA), 1370
Deferred Action for Childhood Arrivals (DACA), 1370
deism/Deists, 121, 122, 130, 452
Delaney, Martin, 644
Delano, Alonzo, 506

Delaware, 111, 149, 243, *245*
American Revolution and, 201
Delaware colony, 70, 79, 124
Delaware Indians, 111
De La Warr, Lord (Thomas West), 55
DeLay, Tom, 1338
de Lesseps, Ferdinand, 840–41
democracy, direct vs. representative, 209
Democratic National Convention (1968), 1235, 1238
Democratic Party
in Civil War, 612
divisions in late 1930s, 1050
Dixiecrat split in, 1129–31
in elections, *see* elections and campaigns
in Kansas-Nebraska crisis, 556
labor unions and, 1124
late nineteenth-century components of, 789–90
origins of, 371–72
slavery issue in, 563, 568
Democratic People's Republic of Korea (North Korea), 1135
democratic republic, 245
Democratic Republicans, *see* Republicans, Jeffersonian
Democratic Republic of Vietnam, 1179
demographic shifts in population, 1334–35, 1396
Dempsey, William Harrison "Jack," 951
Denmark
and Kellogg-Briand pact, 993
in WWII, 1063
Department of Commerce and Labor, 870
Department of Defense, 1121
Department of Housing and Urban Development, 1224
department stores, 945–46
Depression, Great, 1016, *1018*, 1019; *see also* New Deal
congressional initiatives in, 1013
cultural life during, 1037–39
Dust Bowl migrants in, 1027–28, *1028*
farmers and, 1005–7, 1013–14
hardships of, 1032–36, *1034*
Hoover's efforts at recovery, 1011–12
human toll of, 1006–11
immigration and, 1033
literature during, 1037–38
market crash and, 1003–4, *1004*
onset of, 1002–6
popular culture during, 1038–39, *1039*
and 1937 recession, 1049–50
World War I veterans in, 1013–14
WWII and, 1102
Depression of 1893, *see* Panic of 1893
De Priest, Oscar, 959, 1025
desegregation, *see* segregation and desegregation
Deslondes, Charles, 444
Destroyers for Bases Agreement, 1066

détente, 1278–80, 1290
Detroit, Michigan, 1008
Detroit riots (1943), 1077, *1077*
De Voto, Bernard, 1154
Dewey, George, 827
Dewey, John, 727
Dewey, Thomas E., 1089, 1130, 1132, *1132*
DeWitt, John L., 1080
Díaz, Porfirio, 846
Dickinson, Emily, *469*, 469–70
Dickinson, John, 170, 240
Diem, Ngo Dinh, 1180
Dien Bien Phu, 1180
Dies, Martin, 1033
diplomacy
Confederation Congress and, 228–29
nationalist, 363–67, *364*
shuttle, 1280–81
direct democracy, 209
direct primary, 861
disarmament and arms reduction, 992–93
discovery and exploration, 15–21
biological exchange from, 31–32
by Columbus, 17–21, *18*
Dutch, 40, *41*
English, 21, 40, *41*, 42–43, *43*
French, 40, *41*
by Lewis and Clark, 285–88
Spanish, 17, 20, 27–30, 32–37
disease
American Revolution and, 192, 207
Civil War and, 633
in colonial era, 97, 192
Mexican-American War, 536
Native American susceptibility to, 3, 30, 32, 44
Spanish-American War and, 829
disfranchising of African Americans, 737–38
Dissenters, 48
Distribution Act, 403–4, 412
divine right of kings, 48, 50
Dix, Dorothea Lynde, 475, 608
Dix, John, 529
Dixiecrats, 1130–31, *1131*, 1146
Dodd-Frank bill, 1363
Dodge, Mabel, 966
Dole, Bob, 1340
dollar diplomacy, 845, 849
DOMA (Defense of Marriage Act), 1370
Dominican Republic, 19, 994
Dominion of New England, 138, 139
domino theory, 1116
Donnelly, Ignatius, 769
Donner, George, 513, 514
Donner party, *513*, 513–14
don't ask, don't tell (DADT), 1336, 1369
Doolittle, Amos, *164*
Dorsey, George, 1126

Douglas, Aaron, *961*
Douglas, Stephen A., 237, 330, *554,* 563
  Compromise of 1850 and, 546, 550
  death of, 612
  in election of 1860, 568, 569, *570*
  Kansas-Nebraska Act and, 555–56
  Lincoln's debates with, 563–65
Douglass, Frederick, 428, 430, 440, 491–92, *492,* 552, 553, 603, 607, 654, *656,* 665
Downs, Hugh, 1157
draft
  in Civil War, 585–87
  in Vietnam War, 1243–44, 1272
  in World War II, 1067
Dragging Canoe, Chief, 201
DREAM Act, 1369–70
*Dred Scott v. Sandford,* 562–63, 576
Dreiser, Theodore, 787
drivers on plantations, 428
Duarte, José Napoleón, 1311
Dubinsky, David, 1046
Du Bois, W. E. B., 678, *745,* 745–46, 873, 888, 921, 922, 960, 963, 990
"duck-and-cover" air-raid drills, *1111*
duels, 288, 426
Dukakis, Michael, 1309, 1321, *1321*
Duke, Washington, 732
Dulles, John Foster, 1177–78, 1180
  and Hungary crisis, 1182
  and Suez crisis, 1183
Dunkirk, 1064
Dunmore, Lord, 214
Durand, Asher B., *464*
Durocher, Leo, 1128
Dust Bowl, 1027–28, *1028*
Dutch Americans, 123
Dutch East India Company, 73
Dutch Empire, 73–77, 133
Dutch Reformed Church, 24, 124
Dutch Republic, 40, 75
Dutch West India Company, 75, 76
Dylan, Bob, 1242, 1248, 1250
dynamic conservatism, 1153
*Dynamic Sociology* (Ward), 785

Earhart, Amelia, 948–49
Earle, George, 1140
East Asia, imperialism in, 836–37
Eastern Woodlands peoples, 13–15, 44
East India Company, *132,* 159–60
Eastland, James O., 1171, 1175
Eastman, Mary Henderson, 417, 418
Eaton, John, 383, 384, 395, 396
Eaton, Peggy, 383–84, 396
Eaton Affair, 383–84
*Echoes of the Jazz Age* (Fitzgerald), 1004
Eckford, Elizabeth, *1174,* 1174–75

Economic Opportunity Act, 1221, 1238
Economic Recovery Tax Act (ERTA), 1306, 1307
economies of scale, 690
economy
  after American Revolution, 228–30
  after World War I, 933
  after World War II, 1122–24, *1123*
  Carter and, 1296
  Clinton and, 1336–37, 1340
  in colonial America, 102–12
    middle colonies, 109, *110,* 111
    New England, 103–8
    southern colonies, 102–3
  in early nineteenth century, 320–21, 354–58
  Ford and, *1287,* 1287–88
  George H. W. Bush and, 1323
  George W. Bush and, 1355, 1357–58
  Grant and, 671–72
  Hamilton's views on, 250–57, 281
  Harding and, 988–89
  Jefferson and, 281
  in late nineteenth century, 727
  in late 1930s, 1032, 1049–50
  market-based, 321, 350
  Nixon and, 1268–70, *1269*
  Obama and, 1361
  Occupy Wall Street (OWS) movement and, 1368–69
  Panic of 1819 and, 360–61
  Panic of 1837 and, *378,* 407
  Panic of 1857 and, 561
  Panic of 1873 and, 671–72, 680
  Panic of 1893 and, 806–7
  progressivism and, 853
  Reagan and, 1306, 1307, 1309–10, 1317–18
  in 1920s, 943–45, 1002–6
  in 1950s, 1156
  silver and, 799
  of South, 418–19, 735
  stock market and, 1002–3, *1004,* 1317–18
  in World War II, 1073–82, *1074,* 1074–75
Economy Act (1933), 1024
Eden, Anthony, 1184
Edison, Thomas Alva, 691–92
Edison General Electric Company, 692
education
  of African Americans, 656, 657
  in colonial period, 123
  GI Bill of Rights and, 1158
  higher, *479*
  in nineteenth century, 478–80, *479, 710,* 710–11
  planters' wives and, 427
  religious colleges in colonial period, 128
  segregation and desegregation in, 1170–71, *1174,* 1174–76, 1197–98, 1267
  women and, *479, 710,* 710–11

Edwards, Jonathan, 124–25, *125,* 126
Edward VI, 26
Efficiency Movement, 862–64
Egypt
    "Arab Awakening" and, 1365
    Camp David Accords and, 1297
    Suez War in, 1182–85, *1184*
Ehrlichman, John, 1264, 1281, 1283, 1284
Eighteenth Amendment, 941, 981–83
eight-hour workday, 890
Einstein, Albert, 963–64, 965, 1065
Eisenhower, Dwight D., *1150,* 1192, 1197, 1198, 1202
    assessment of presidency of, 1187
    and atomic bomb decision, 1099
    background of, 1150
    and Berlin crisis, 1186
    and black soldiers in WWII, 1079
    Battle of the Bulge, 1090
    car culture and, *1154,* 1154–55
    civil rights movement and, 1169–70, 1174–76
    communism in Cuba, 1186
    and Cuba, 1186
    dynamic conservatism of, 1153
    election of 1956, 1184–85
    and election of 1948, 1129
    in election of 1952, 1150–51
    in election of 1956, 1182
    on Holocaust, 1094–95
    and Hungary crisis, 1182
    Indochina and, 1179–82
    and Korean War, 1139
    and Loyalty Order, 1140
    McCarthyism and, 1155
    middle way presidency of, 1151–52
    moderate Republicanism and, 1150–55
    and North Africa campaign, 1083
    and Operation Overlord, 1085
    and race to Berlin, 1089
    religion promoted by, 1164–65
    and Sicily, 1084
    *Sputnik* and, 1185
    and Suez crisis, 1183
    Suez War and, 1182–85
    transportation improvements under, 1153–54
    U-2 summit and, 1186
    in World War II, 1085, *1086*
Eisenhower Doctrine, 1185
elections and campaigns
    in 1936, 1047–48
    in 1940, 1041–42
    of 1792, 257
    of 1796, 265
    of 1800, 224, 269–70, *270*
    of 1804, 288–89
    of 1808, 293
    of 1816, 359
    of 1820, 367
    of 1824, 369–70
    of 1828, *372,* 373–75
    of 1832, 398
    of 1836, 406
    of 1840, 408–10, *409*
    of 1844, 525–26
    of 1848, 543
    of 1852, 553
    of 1856, 559, *560*
    of 1860, 567–68
    of 1864, 621–22, 627, 636, 637
    of 1868, 664–65
    of 1872, 670–71
    of 1876, 676–77
    of 1880, 792
    of 1884, 794–96
    of 1888, 797–98
    of 1896, 684–85, 809–11, *811*
    of 1900, 839–40
    of 1904, 871
    of 1908, 875
    of 1912, 880–81, *882,* 895
    of 1916, 904–5
    of 1918, 923
    of 1920, 942, 986
    of 1924, 997–98
    of 1928, 1000–1002
    of 1932, 1014–15
    of 1934, 1029
    of 1936, 1047–48
    of 1940, 1067
    of 1944, 1089
    of 1948, 1130–33, *1131, 1132*
    of 1952, 1150–51, *1152*
    of 1956, 1182, 1184–85
    of 1960, 1192–95, *1193, 1195*
    of 1964, 1221–22
    of 1968, 1233, 1234–35, 1238
    of 1972, 1265–66, 1265–1266 1138–1140, 1281
    of 1976, 1288–89
    of 1980, *1292,* 1301–2, 1304, *1305*
    of 1984, 1309
    of 1988, 1320, 1321, *1321*
    of 1992, 1328–29
    of 1996, 1340
    of 2000, 1345–47, *1346, 1347*
    of 2004, 1354–55, *1355*
    of 2008, 1333, 1358–60, *1359, 1360,* 1396
    of 2012, 1371
    of 2016, 1379–84, *1380, 1385*
electoral college, in Constitution, 237, 288
electricity, 692–93, 1157
Electronic Numerical Integrator and Computer
    (ENIAC), 1316
Eliot, Charles, 833
Eliot, T. S., 963, 966, 967
Elizabeth I, 26, 40–43, 48, 50
Elizabethtown, 77
Elkins Act, 870

Ellington, Duke, 952, *952*
Ellis Island, *777*
Ellison, William, 432
Ellsberg, Daniel, 1274
El Salvador, 1311, 1312
emancipation, 598–608, *601,* 602, *602,* 603, 634, 636
  African American soldiers and, 606–8, *607*
  freedmen's plight after, 639–40
  reactions to, 603–4, 606–8, 639–40
Emancipation Act (British), 487
Emancipation Proclamation, *601,* 602, *602,* 603, 634, 636, 1208
Embargo Act (1807), 292–93, 312
Emergency Banking Act (1933), 1022
Emergency Banking Relief Act, 1022
Emergency Farm Labor Program, 1079
Emergency Immigration Act (1921), 974
Emergency Relief Act (1932), 1013
Emergency Relief Appropriation Act, 1044
Emerson, Ralph Waldo, 451, 465–66, 466–69, 473, 483, 484, 530, 551, 579
*Emigrants Crossing the Plains, or the Oregon Trail* (Bierstadt), *502*
employment, *see* labor
Employment Act (1946), 1122
enclosure movement, 52
*encomenderos,* 30–31
*encomiendas,* 30–31, 44
Endangered Species Act, 1223
Endangered Species Preservation Act, 1268
Enforcement Acts (1870-1871), 672–73, 675
*Engel v. Vitale,* 1211
engineering, 349
England; *see also* Great Britain
  Catholics in, 25, 26, 48–49, 50
  colonial administration under, 90–91, 133, 136–38, 150–56
  colonization by Spain vs., 51
  conquest of Ireland, 50
  explorations by, 21, 40, *41,* 42–43, *43*
  government of, *see* Parliament, British
  immigration restrictions, 120
  monarchy of, 48–50, 136–37, 138–39
  population explosion in, 52
  privateers from, 41
  Reformation in, 25–26
  Spanish Armada defeated by, 40–42
  taxation in, 48, 148, 150–56
English Civil War (1642-1651), 69–70, 77
ENIAC (Electronic Numerical Integrator and Computer), 1316
Enlightenment, 120–23, 128–30, 452
*Enola Gay,* 1100
environment
  conservation and, 872–73
  industrialization and, *338,* 338–39
  Nixon and, 1267–68
Environmental Protection Agency (EPA), 1268, 1290

Episcopalians, 453
Equal Pay Act, 1197, 1251
Equal Protection, 675
Equal Rights Amendment (ERA), 1254, 1255, 1303–4
"Era of Good Feelings," 359–63
Erie Canal, 324–26, *325,* 330, 350, 384
Ervin, Samuel J., Jr., 1283
*Escobedo v. Illinois,* 1212
Espionage Act (1917), 911
Estonia, 926
Ethiopia, 993, 1059
ethnic cleansing, 1343, 1396
Europe; *see also specific countries*
  after World War I, 917
  American biological exchange with, 31–32
  expansion of, 15–17
  Great Depression and economy of, 1006
  religious conflict in, 21–26, *22*
  rise of fascism in, *1056,* 1056–59, *1058*
  World War II battles and campaigns, *1088*
European Recovery Plan, *see* Marshall Plan
evangelism/evangelists, 125–27, 451, 454, 456, 459–60
Evans, Hiram Wesley, 977
Evans, John, 759
Everett, Sarah, 509
Evers, Medgar, 1210
executive branch, 236–37
Exeter Riot, 231
Exner, Judith Campbell, 1196
Exodusters, 750–52, 770
exploration, *see* discovery and exploration
Export Control Act (1940), 1070

Fair Deal, 1129–30, 1133, 1144, 1146
Fairfax, Bryan, 160
Fair Labor Standards Act, 1049–50
fake news, 1393
Fall, Albert B., 995
Fallen Timbers, Battle of (1794), 261
"falling domino" theory, 1180, 1182, 1188
Falwell, Jerry, 1302, 1303, 1338
families, slave, 433, 440, *441*
"fancy trade," 433
*Farewell to Arms, A* (Hemingway), 967
Farmer, James, 1207
Farmers' Alliances, 802–4
Farmers' Holiday Association, 1006–7
Farm Security Administration (FSA), 1049
Farouk (king of Egypt), 1183
Farragut, David G., 595
fascism in Europe, rise of, *1056,* 1056–59, *1058*
Faubus, Orval, 1171, 1174, 1176
Faulkner, William, 732, 1154
FDIC (Federal Deposit Insurance Corporation), 1022–23, 1052
Federal-Aid Highway Act, 1153–54, 1188
Federal Deposit Insurance Corporation (FDIC), 1022–23, 1052

Federal Election Campaign Act, 1266
*Federal Elections Committee, Citizens United v.,* 1371
Federal Emergency Management Agency (FEMA), 1356
Federal Emergency Relief Administration (FERA), 1024, 1031
Federal Farm Loan Act (1916), 890
Federal Farm Loan Board, 890
Federal Highways Act (1916), 890
Federal Housing Administration (FHA), 1027, 1034, 1160
federalism, 225, 235, 272
*Federalist Papers, The* (Hamilton, Madison, and Jay), 242–43, 272
Federalists, 181, 245–46, 245–50, 257
    Alien and Sedition Acts of, 268–69
    in election of 1796, 265
    in election of 1800, 269–70, *270,* 276
    in election of 1808, 293
    in election of 1820, 367
    land policy of, 263
    Louisiana Purchase as seen by, 285, 288
    in ratification debate, 242–43
    War of 1812 and, 298, 308–10
Federal Radio Commission, 999
Federal Republic of Germany (West Germany), 1118–19
Federal Reserve Act (1913), 884–85, 893
Federal Reserve Board, 1005, 1340
Federals, 583
Federal Trade Commission (FTC), 886, 893
Feinstein, Diane, 1375
FEMA (Federal Emergency Management Agency), 1356
*Feminine Mystique, The* (Friedan), 1252
feminism, 1251–57, *1255*
FERA (Federal Emergency Relief Administration), 1024, 1031
Ferdinand II, 17, 19, 25
Ferguson, Patrick, 203
*Ferguson, Plessy v.,* 739–40, 1170
Ferlinghetti, Lawrence, 1167
Ferraro, Geraldine, 1309
feudalism, 15–16
FHA (Federal Housing Administration), 1027, 1034, 1160
Field, Stephen J., 675
field hands, 433, 436, 448
Fifteenth Amendment, 500, 654–55, *658,* 665–66, 679, 680, 854, 860, 960
    backlash to, 666
Fillmore, Millard
    Compromise of 1850 and, 550, 551, 553
    in election of 1856, *560*
Finland
    and Kellogg-Briand pact, 993
    Soviet invasion of, 1063
    Treaty of Versailles and, 926

Finney, Charles Grandison, 459–60, 488
Finnish settlers, 109
"fireside chats," *1021,* 1022
*First, Second, and Last Scene of Mortality, The* (Punderson), 99
First Amendment, 248–49
First Continental Congress, 161–62
First Great Awakening, 123–29, 453
First Peoples, *see* Native Americans
First Reconstruction Act, 652
First Red Scare, 934–36, 939
Fisher, Irving, 1003
fishing in New England, 105
Fisk, James, Jr., 668
Fiske, John, 821
Fitzgerald, F. Scott, 944–45, 951–52, 953, 956, 967, 968, 969, 1004, 1037
Fitzgerald, Zelda Sayre, 944–45, 968
Fitzhugh, George, 381, 427, 430
Five-Power Treaty (1922), 992–93
Flagler, Henry M., 701
*Flaming Youth* (movie), 953
flappers, 956–57, *957,* 970
Florida, 82, 208
    acquisition of, 364–66
    in colonial wars, 147
    in election of 2000, 1346–47, *1347*
    exploration of, 33
    secession of, 572
    Seminoles in, 365, *365*
    Spanish exploration and colonization of, 33
    War of 1812 and, 360
Flucker, Lucy, 193
*Flying Cloud,* 328
Flynn, Michael, 1387, 1392
*Folkways* (Sumner), 784
Food Administration, 908, *908,* 999
Food Stamp Act, 1221
football, 951
Foraker Act, 835
Foran Act (1885), 720
Force Bill (1833), 400–401, 412
Ford, Gerald, 1297, 1310
    in election of 1976, 1288–89
    presidency assumed by, *1286,* 1286–87
Ford, Henry, 949
Ford Motor Company, 949–50
Fordney-McCumber Tariff (1922), 989
foreign policy
    Carter and, 1297–1300, *1300*
    Clinton and, 1341–43, *1342*
    George H. W. Bush and, 1324–28
    Kennedy and, 1198–1204
    Monroe and, 366–67
    Obama and, 1363–66, 1373–76
    Reagan and, 1310–16
    in 1950s, 1177–87
    Trump and, 1391–92, 1394, *1394,* 1395

Foreign Speaking Soldier Subsection, U.S. Army, 907

Forest Reserve Act, 873

Forney, James W., 554

Forrest, Nathan Bedford, 623

Forsyth, James. W., 766

Fort Caroline, 33

Fort Donelson, 592

Fort Duquesne (Pittsburgh, Pa.), 141, 143

Fort Greenville, 260

Fort Henry, 592

Fort Laramie Treaty (1851), 758

Fort Mandan, 286–87

Fort McHenry, 305–6

Fort Mims, 301

Fort Necessity, 141–42

Fort Orange, 75

Fort Pillow Massacre, 623

Fort Sumter, 572, 575, 579, 580, 583, 629, 632

*Fortune,* 1149

forty-niners, 543–44

Fosdick, Harry Emerson, 979

Foster, Stephen, 340

Four-Minute Men, 911

*Four Soldiers,* 194

Fourteen Points, 916–17, 921, 923, 938

Fourteenth Amendment, 500, 651, 652, 675, 679, 680, 854, 960

Fox, George, 77

fractured feminism, 1296–97

France; *see also* French Empire
   American Revolution and, 180, 183, 196, 197, 206–7
   Citizen Genet and, 259
   in colonial wars, 140–50, *146, 147*
   explorations of, 40, *41*
   fall in WWII, 1065
   in Indochina, 1179
   and Kellogg-Briand pact, 993
   late eighteenth-century conflict with, 266, *266,* 269
   liberation of Paris, 1088–89
   Napoleonic Wars (1803–1815), 290–94
   Normandy invasion in, 1086–88, *1087*
   before outbreak of WWII, 1055
   and postwar Germany, 1118
   Revolution in, 257–59
   in World War I, 897, 898, 901, *918,* 925
   World War I debt of, 991–92
   World War II and, 1086–89, *1087*

Franciscans, 511

Franco, Francisco, 1059

Franklin, Battle of, 627, 628

Franklin, Benjamin, *122, 143,* 149, 152, 157, 192–93, 265, 452
   at Albany Congress, 142
   background of, 122
   on Constitution, 241, 242, 244
   at Constitutional Convention, 233–34, 236
   Declaration of Independence and, 171
   and deism, 121, 122
   on German immigrants, 97–98
   on Great Awakening, 124
   on peace commission, 208
   on population growth, 96
   George Whitefield and, 126

Franklin, Sarah "Sally," 152

Franklin, William, 192–93

Franz Ferdinand, 897

Fredericksburg, Battle of, 604, *605,* 606

free blacks, *638*
   freedmen's conventions, 647–48
   land and, 644
   in Old South, 431–32, *432*
   in Reconstruction, 639–40, 649, 655–64, *661*
      black codes and, *589,* 649–50, 661–62, 680
      churches and schools and, 656, 657
      Freedmen's Bureau and, 643–44, 680
      land policy and, 657–59, *659*
      politics and, *656, 658*
      tensions among, 659
      violence against, *589,* 649, 655, 661–62, *662,* 672–73

Freed, Alan, 1168

Freedmen's Bureau, U.S., 643–44, 680

freedmen's conventions, 647–48

freedom of religion, *see* religious freedom

freedom riders, 1205–8, *1206,* 1238

"freedom schools," 1212

Freedom Summer, 1212–13

Free French Resistance, 1089

Freemasons, 396–98

freemen, 61

Free-Soil party, 543, 556, 576

free-speech movement (FSM), 1243

freethinkers, 121

Frémont, John Charles, 514–15, 531–33, 559, *560*

French Americans, 111

French and Indian War, 141–48, *143, 176,* 228

French Empire; *see also* France
   British Empire compared with, 90–91, 133, 134–36
   fur trade in, 75, 83, 134, 135
   in Indian conflicts, 86, 134, *135*
   Native American relations with, 83, 86, 134, *135*

French Indochina, 1070

French Revolution, 257–59, 272–73

Freud, Sigmund, 953–55, 966

Frick, Henry, 871

Frick, Henry Clay, 722

Friedan, Betty, *1251,* 1251–53

frontier, 504–29, 524–25, 527; *see also* West
   American Revolution and, 199–201, *200*
   in colonial period, 155–56
   in early U.S., 260–61
   end of, 767–69
   religious revivals on, *454,* 455–56, 496
   southern, 422–24
   westward expansion and, 504–29, *511,* 524–25, 527

frontier (*continued*)
    annexation of Texas, *521, 522,* 524–25, 527
    Mexico and Spanish West, 506–7
    Oregon fever, 508–9, 538
    Overland Trails, 504–6, *505,* 507–8, *508,* 538
    Plains Indians, 506
    settlement of California, 510–14
    Texas independence from Mexico, 516–22, *517*
    women pioneers, 509–10
  Wilderness Road and, 263–64, *264*
  women and, 757–58
Frum, David, 1371
FSA (Farm Security Administration), 1049
FSM (free-speech movement), 1243
FTC (Federal Trade Commission), 886, 893
Fuchs, Klaus, 1141
Fugitive Slave Act, 551–52, 553, 559, 576
Fulbright, J. William, 1231
Fuller, Margaret, 466
Fuller, Timothy, 362
Fulton, Robert, 324, 357
Fundamental Constitutions of Carolina, 72
fundamentalism, 978–81
Fundamental Orders, 69
fur trade, 109, 507–8, *508*
    Dutch, 74–75, 83
    French, 75, 83, 134, 135
*Fur Traders Descending the Missouri, 508*
Futch, John, 618

Gaddafi, Muammar, 1365–66
Gadsden Purchase, 535–36
Gage, Thomas, 160, 162, 163
"gag rule," 405–6
Galbraith, John Kenneth, 1165
Gallatin, Albert, 278–79, 281, 297, 309
Garcia, Hector Perez, 1129
Garfield, James, 669, 791–93
Garland, Hamlin, 684
Garner, Henry, 430
Garnett, Muscoe, 381
Garrison, William Lloyd, 486–89, *487,* 490, 491, 495, 530
Garvey, Marcus, *962,* 962–63, 990, 1213
Garza, Alicia, 1371–72
*Gaspée,* 159
Gates, Bill, 1317
Gates, Horatio, 195, 202
Gates, Thomas, 55
Gauguin, Paul, 943
Gay Activists' Alliance, 1261
Gay Liberation, 1216
Gay Liberation Front, 1261
gays and lesbians
    marriage and, 1369, 1370–71, 1377
    rights of, 1261–62, *1262*
GDP, *see* gross domestic product
Gehrig, Henry Louis "Lou," 950–51

Geithner, Timothy, 1361
Gelb, Leslie, 1341
General Accounting Office, 988
General Allotment Act, *see* Dawes Severalty Act
General Council of Plymouth Plantation, 64
General Court, Massachusetts, 67–68
General Electric, 869
General Federation of Women's Clubs, 864
General Motors, 1047
General Treaty for Renunciation of War as an
        Instrument of National Policy, 993
Genet, Edmond-Charles, 259
Geneva, Switzerland, 23–24
gentry, 48
George, David Lloyd, 925
George Barrell Emerson School, *479*
George I, 140
George II, 82, 140, 145
George III, *145,* 148, 149, 154, 167, 171, 172, 197, 208,
        212, 223, 229, 249
    accession of, 145–46
    on colonial rebellion, 159, 162–63, 197
    Paine on, 168–69
George V (king of Britain), 948
*George Washington at Princeton* (Peale), *184*
Georgia
    Constitution ratified by, 243, *245*
    secession of, 572
*Georgia, Cherokee Nation v.,* 388
*Georgia, Worcester v.,* 388
Georgia colony
    European settlement of, 82–83
    government of, 82–83
    slaves in, 83, 114
Germain, Lord George, 201–2
German Americans, 82, 97–98, 111
    anti-immigrant prejudices in eighteenth century,
        97–98
    Civil War and, 580, 581
    in colonial period, 150
    in nineteenth century, 341, 343
    World War I and, 911–12
German Democratic Republic (East Germany), 1119
German Reformed Church, 24
Germantown, Pennsylvania, 109
Germany
    Berlin Wall and, 1199–1200, *1200,* 1238, *1324,*
        1324–25
    divided, Cold War and, 1118–19, *1119*
    ethnic cleansing by Soviets, 1114
    and Kellogg-Briand pact, 993
    reparations from, 992, 1006
    in World War I, 897, 898, 911, 917, 918, 921–22,
        *922,* 924–27, 931
Germany, Nazi; *see also* World War II
    Anschluss, 1060–61
    and Axis alliance, 1060
    blitzkrieg tactics of, 1063–65, *1064,* 1065–66, *1066*

collapse of, 1093–94
Hitler's rise and, 1056–57, *1058*
Nazi–Soviet Non-Aggression Pact, 1062
before outbreak of WWII, 1055
and Russian Front, 1082
Soviet Union invaded by, 1068–69
Tripartite Pact, 1070
Geronimo, Chiricahua Apache chief, 766
Gerould, Katharine Fullerton, 936
Gerry, Elbridge, 234, 236, 242
Gestapo, 1057
Gettysburg, Battle of, 615–18, *617, 619,* 636
Gettysburg Address, 620
Ghent, Treaty of (1814), 307–9, 312, 363
Ghost Dance movement, 766
Gibbons, Thomas, 357–58
*Gibbons v. Ogden,* 357–58, 376
GI Bill of Rights, 1123, 1158, 1162, 1188
*Gideon v. Wainwright,* 1211–12
GI Forum, 1129
Gilded Age, 772–813
cities and, 773–76, *775, 776*
cultural life and, 780–87, *781, 786,* 812
immigration during, 776–80, *777, 779, 780,* 812
politics in, 787–811, 812
civil service reform, 791–92, 793–94, 812
Cleveland's reform efforts, 796–98
farmers and, 800–806, *803*
Harrison's administration, *798,* 798–99
local politics and party loyalties, 781–88, *789*
national, 789–90
new third parties, 804–5, *805*
Panic of 1893 and, 806–7
*Gilded Age, The* (Twain and Warner), 708–9
Gilman, Charlotte Perkins, 711
Gingrich, Newt, *1338,* 1338–39, 1344
Ginsberg, Allen, 1166, 1167
Girl Scouts, 908
Gitlin, Todd, 1248
Gladden, Washington, 856, 870
glasnost, 1314–15, 1330–31
Glass, Carter, 886
Glass–Steagall Banking Act (1933), 1022–23
Glennie, Alexander, 441
globalization, 1340–41
Glorious Revolution, 50, 138–39, *140,* 176
Glyn, Elinor, 956
Godkin, E. L., 670, 709
Goetschius, John Henry, 127
Goforth, John Preston, 204
gold, 27, 35
Golden Hill, Battle at, 157
gold rush in California, 506, 543–45, *544*
gold standard, 1022
Goldwater, Barry, 1221–22, 1229, 1281, 1284, 1301
Goliad, 519–20
Gompers, Samuel, 720, 834
*Gone with the Wind* (movie), 414, 1038

Good, Sarah, 108
Goodman, Andrew, 1213
good neighbor policy, 1059
Goodyear, Charles, 331
Gorbachev, Mikhail, 1314–15, *1315,* 1324, 1325
Gordon, John B., 624
Gore, Albert, Jr., 1329, 1336, 1345–47, *1346, 1347,* 1388
Gorges, Ferdinando, 69
Gorsuch, Neil, 1388
"Gospel of Wealth, The" (Carnegie), 705–6
Gould, Jay, 668, 787
government
branches of, 235–37
in Civil War, 609–10
English, *see* Parliament, British
state, American Revolution and, 210–11
transportation and, 330
Gower, Elizabeth, 608
Gower, T. G., 608
Grady, Henry W., 732, 734, 735
Graham, Sylvester, 480–81
Graham cracker, 481
Grahamites, 481
*Graham's Journal of Health and Longevity* (Graham), 480
*Grand Ole Opry, The,* 947
Granger movement, 801–2, *803*
Grant, Madison, 913
Grant, Ulysses S., 530, 585, *621,* 622–23, 649, 651, 652, 653, 676, 678, 763, 790, 793
Civil War strategy of, 622–23
economy and, 671–72, 706
and election of 1872, 670–71
in election of 1868, 664–65
Enforcement Acts and, 672–73
and Harding, 987
Lee pursued by, 623–26, *625*
Lee's surrender to, 631
Liberal Republicans, 669–70
on Mexican-American War, 536
Native Americans and, 667, 761
scandals during administration of, 668–69
at Shiloh, 594–95
at Vicksburg, 615
in the West, 592–93
*Grapes of Wrath, The* (Steinbeck), 1007, 1037
Grasse, François-Joseph-Paul de, 207
Graves, Billy, 514
Gray, L. Patrick, 1283
Great Awakening (First), 123–29, 453
Great Awakening (Second), 453–63, 473, 496
African Americans and, *457,* 457–58
burned-over district and, 459
frontier revivals, *454,* 455–56, 496
Mormons and, 460–63, *461, 462*
women and, 458–59
Great Biological Exchange, *see* Columbian Exchange

Great Britain; *see also* American Revolution; British Empire; England; Parliament, British; War of 1812
   in colonial wars, 140–50, *146, 147*
   Convention of 1818 and, 363, *364*
   and cotton from U.S., 415, 420–21, 425
   early U.S. relations with, 228
   French Revolution and, 258
   impressment, 291–92
   Jay's Treaty with, 259–60, 266
   and Kellogg-Briand pact, 993
   Napoleonic Wars (1803-1815), 290–94
   Northwest Indian War and, 260–61
   Oregon Country and, 528–29
   before outbreak of WWII, 1055
   and postwar Germany, 1118
   and Suez, 1183
   War of 1812 and, *299,* 299–301, 303–8
   in World War I, 897, 900, 901, 925
   World War I debt of, 991–92
   in World War II, 1065–66, *1066*
Great Bull Market, 1002
Great Compromise, 235, 236
Great Depression, *see* Depression, Great
Greater East Asia Co-Prosperity Sphere, 1060
*Great Gatsby, The* (Fitzgerald), 968
Great Law of Peace, 85–86
Great Meadows, Battle of, 142
Great Migration, 970
   after World War I, 895–96, 910, 938, 959–60
   after World War II, *1161,* 1161–63
Great Plains, 37–39, *38,* 731
Great Purge, 1062
Great Railroad Strike (1877), 713–14
Great Recession, 1109, 1333, 1357–58, 1361, 1396
Great Revival, 455
Great Sioux War, 762–63, *763,* 770–71
Greece, 1068
   civil war (1947), 1115–16
   in NATO, 1119
Greece, direct democracy of, 209
Greeley, Horace, 552, 670–71
Green, Israel, 566
Green, William, 1125
greenbacks, 611, 671, 680, 707
Greene, Nathanael, 185, 204–6
Greenland, 21
Greensboro, N.C., sit-in in (1960), 1204, 1205, *1205,* 1242
Greenspan, Alan, 1340
Greenville, Treaty of (1795), 261
*Greer,* USS, 1069
Gregory, Dick, 1204
Grenville, George, 150–52, 154, *155*
Grey, Edward, 898
Grey, Jane, 26
Griffith, D. W., 946
Grimké, Angelina, *489,* 489–90

Grimké, Sarah, *489,* 489–90
Gropper, William, *1018*
Guadalcanal Island, 1096
Guadalupe Hidalgo, Treaty of, 463, 535–36, 538
Guam, 1072
Guatemala, 28, 1179
Guilford Courthouse, Battle of, 204
*Guinn v. United States,* 960
Guiteau, Charles, 793
Gulf War
   First, 1326–27, *1327*
   Second, 1352–54, *1353,* 1357
Guzman, Jacobo Arbenz, 1179
Guzman, Nuño de, 30

Habeas Corpus Act (1863), 612
Haber, Alan, 1242
Habsburg Empire, 897
Haggard, Merle, 1265
Hague, 994
Haida, 11
Haig, Alexander, 1282, 1284
Haiti, 19, 284, 443
Hakluyt, Richard, 52
Haldeman, Bob, 1264, 1282, 1283, 1284
Half-Breeds, 791, 794
Halleck, Henry, 595, 597, 598, 612
Halpin, Maria, 795
Hamilton, Alexander, 181, 224, 232, 246, *250,* 261, 269, 270, 353, 354
   Adams administration and, 265
   background of, 251
   Burr's duel with, 288, 289
   economic vision of, 250–57, 281, 282
   in election of 1800, 269
   *Federalist Papers* and, 242–43
   French Revolution and, 258, 259
   Jefferson compared with, 256–57
   national bank promoted by, 253–55
   in ratification debate, 241–42
   as secretary of the Treasury, 247, 250–57
Hammond, James Henry, 405, 425, 429, 439, 524, 561
Hancock, John, 174
Hancock, Winfield Scott, 792
Hanna, Marcus "Mark," 810, 830–31, 840
Hardenbergh, Isabella "Bell," *see* Truth, Sojourner
Harding, Florence, 986, 987
Harding, Warren G., 931, 942, 984, 986–88
   appointments and policy of, 990–91
   death of, 996
   on disarmament, 992
   racial progressivism and, 989–90
   scandals in administration of, 994–95, *995*
   and World Court, 994
"Hard Times Ain't Gone Nowhere" (song), 1010
Harlan, John Marshall, 739–40
Harlem Renaissance, 960–62, *961,* 970
Harney, William, 535

Harpers Ferry, Va., 566
Harrington, Michael, 1220
Harris, William, 573
Harrison, Benjamin, 171, 834
    in election of 1888, *789*, 797–98
    in election of 1892, 805
    Hawaii and, 824
    reform under, *798*, 798–99
Harrison, Pat, 990
Harrison, William Henry, 359, 406, 797
    death of, 522–23
    in election of 1840, 408–10, *409*
Hart-Celler Act, 1224
Hartford, Treaty of (1638), 84
Hartford Convention (1814), 308–9, 312
Harvard College, 128
"Harvest of Death, A" (O'Sullivan), *617*
Haugen, Gilbert N., 1000
Hawaii, 822–24, 1187
*Hawaii, Trump v.,* 1389
Hawley, Willis C., 1005
Hawthorne, Nathaniel, 328, 466, 469, 476, 483, 579
Hay, John, 829, 837, 840–41
Hayden, Tom, 1242–43, 1246
Hayes, Rutherford B., 676, 692, 714, 739, 767, 791–92
Hay-Herrán Treaty (1903), 841
Haymarket riot, 719, 729
Hayne, Robert Y., *394*, 394–95, 399, 400
Haynes, Lemuel, *213*, 216
Hay-Pauncefote Treaty (1901), 840
Hazzard, Arthur, 958–59
headright system, 57, 92, 109
Head Start, 1221, 1227
health care reform, 1361–63, 1373, 1376–77
Hearst, William Randolph, 824–25, 1112
"Heartbreak Hotel" (song), 1168
Heflin, J. Thomas, 990
Hemingway, Ernest, 967, 968
Hemmings, Sarah "Sally," 278
Henrietta Maria, Queen, 59
Henry, Beulah Louisa, 690
Henry, Patrick, 153, 154, 163, 174, 242
Henry VII, 21
Henry VIII, 25–26
Herbert, Victor, 343
Heritage Foundation, 1304
Hernandez, David Barkley, 910
Herron, George, 856
Hessians, 184, 190, 196, 201
Hickok, Lorena "Hick," 1030–31, *1031*
Hidalgo y Costilla, Miguel, 507
Higginson, Thomas W., 604
higher education, *479*
Higher Education Act of 1965, 1223
highways and roads, 321–24, *322–23*, 355–56, 890
    to frontier regions, 321–24, *322–23*
    Wilderness Road, 263–64, *264*
Hill, John, *325*

Hilles, Florence Bayard, 889
Hillman, Sidney, 1046
hippies, 1246, *1247*
Hirohito (emperor of Japan), 1102
Hiroshima, atomic bombing of (1945), 1099–1101
Hispanic Americans
    demographic shifts in, 1335
    rights of, 1257–60, *1259*
Hispaniola, 27, 31
Hispaniola, Columbus in, 19
Hiss, Alger, 1140–41, 1151
*History of the American People, A* (Wilson), 887
*History of the U.S. Decision Making Process in
    Vietnam, The* (McNamara), 1274
Hitler, Adolf, 926, 930, 1056–57, *1058*, 1059, *1074; see
        also* Germany, Nazi
    annexation of Czechoslovakia, 1061–62
    and Anschluss, 1060–61
    and Axis alliance, 1060
    and Battle of Britain, 1065, 1066
    Battle of the Bulge, 1089–91
    and collapse of Nazi empire, 1093
    Father Coughlin and, 1041
    death of, 1093
    and German morale in WWII, 1102
    goals of, 1056
    and immigration of Jews, 975
    Munich Pact, 1061
    and Operation Overlord, 1086, 1087
    and Poland, 1063
    rise to power, 1057–58
    and Russian Front, 1082
    Sudentenland annexation, 1061
    on U.S. military production capabilities, 1073–74
HIV/AIDS, 1319, *1319*, 1320, 1330
Hoar, Elizabeth, 467
Hoar, George Frisbie, 834
hobos, 1008
Ho Chi Minh, 1179, 1180
*Hodges, Obergefell v.,* 1377
Hoffman, Abbie, 1248
Hoffman, Charles W., 957
Hohokam, 11
*Holder, Shelby County v.,* 1370–71
holding companies, 702, 728
Holland, *see* Netherlands
Holloway, Houston, 639
Hollywood Ten, 1140
Holmes, Oliver Wendell, Jr., 632
*Holmes County Board of Education, Alexander v.,*
        1267
Holocaust, *1094*, 1094–95
Holy People, 10
homelessness during Great Depression, *1008*, 1008–9
Home Owners' Loan Corporation, 1026–27
Homer, Winslow, *638*
Homestead Act (1862), 610, 632–33, 636, 707, *707*,
        756, 757

Homestead Steel strike, 721–22, 729
Hone, Philip, 546
Hong Kong, 1072
Hood, James Walker, 647
Hood, John Bell, 626–28
Hooker, Joseph, 530, 614
Hooker, Thomas, 69
Hooper, William, 185
Hoover, Herbert, 984, 987–88, 998–1002, 1289
    criticism of, 1013–15
    in election of 1928, 1000–1002
    in election of 1932, 1014–15
    recovery efforts of, 1011–12
    and Smoot-Hawley Tariff Act, 1005
    and Social Security, 1046
    in Teapot Dome Affair, 995
    and World Court, 994
    in World War I, 908
Hoover, J. Edgar, 936, 1140, 1141, 1215
Hoover blankets, 1012
Hoovervilles, 1012
Hopedale commune, 485
Hopis, 11, 35
Hopkins, Harry L., 1024, 1043
Hopkins, Mark, 696
*Hopwood v. Texas,* 1339
horizontal integration, 701, 728
horses
    Indians and, 37–39, *38*
    Spanish introduction of, 37–38
Horseshoe Bend, Battle of (1814), 303
House, Edward M., 883–84, 903–5, 921–24, 927, 928,
    930
*House Beautiful,* 1163
House of Burgesses, 140
House of Commons, British, 48
House of Lords, British, 48
*House of Mirth, The* (Wharton), 786
House of Representatives, U.S.; *see also* Congress, U.S.
    in Constitution, 235–36
    violence in (1858), 565
*House of the Seven Gables, The* (Hawthorne), 469
House Un-American Activities Committee (HUAC),
    1140–41, 1146
housing, 1044
    air-conditioning systems for, 1158–59
    in colonial New England, 103–4
    Great Recession (2007-2009) and, 1357–58
    home ownership in 1950s, 1157
    in suburbs, 1158–60, *1160*
Housing Act, 1197
Housing and Urban Development Act of 1965, 1223
Houston, Sam, 301, 519–21, 521–22, 524
Howard, Oliver O., 644
Howe, Elias, 331
Howe, George, 428
Howe, Julia Ward, 476, 854
Howe, Richard, 186, 187

Howe, Samuel Gridley, 476
Howe, William, 167, 186, 188, 189, 192, 195, 198
Howells, William Dean, 786
"Howl" (Ginsberg), 1167
*How the Other Half Lives* (Riis), *854*
HUAC (House Un-American Activities Committee),
    1140–41, 1146
Hudson, Henry, 73
Huerta, Dolores, 1258–59
Huerta, Victoriano, 847
Huggins, Ericka, 1216
Hughes, Charles Evans, 904–5, 987, 992
Hughes, Langston, 960, 961
Hughson, John, 116
Huguenots, 24, 33, 111
Hull, Cordell, 1071
Hull, William, 300
Hull House, 857
human immunodeficiency virus (HIV), 1319, *1319,*
    1320
humanism, 16
human rights, *see* civil rights and liberties
Humphrey, Hubert H., 1130, 1220, 1281
    in election of 1964, 1222
    in election of 1968, 1233, 1235, *1236,* 1237
Hungary, 1182
    ethnic cleansing by Soviets, 1114
    Treaty of Versailles and, 926
hunger during Great Depression, 1007–8
Hunt, E. Howard, 1282
*Hunter's Lessee, Martin v.,* 356
Huntington, Collis, 696, 788
Hurons, 83
Hurston, Zora Neale, 961–62
Hussein, Saddam, 1109, 1326, 1327, 1352
Hutchinson, Anne, 66–67, *67*
Hutchinson, Thomas, 159, 162
hydrogen bomb, 1178

ICC (Interstate Commerce Commission), 797, 812,
    864, 1207
Ice Age, 5
Ignatius de Loyola, 25
illegal immigrants, *see* undocumented immigrants
*Illinois, Munn v.,* 802
*Illinois, Wabash, St. Louis, and Pacific Railroad
    Company v.,* 797
*Illinois, Wabash Railroad v.,* 802
immigrants
    and McCarran Internal Sercurity Act, 1142–43
    in U.S. Army during WWI, 907
immigration
    anti-immigrant prejudices in eighteenth century,
        97–98
    in colonial era, 119–20
    in colonial period, 52, 150
    Constitutional Convention and, 241
    in Federalist era, 249–50

and Great Depression, 1033
in late nineteenth century, 776–80, *777, 779, 780,*
   812
from Muslim countries, 1389, 1390, *1390*
nativism and, *344,* 344–45, 974–76
in nineteenth century, 341–45
   of British, 343
   of Chinese, 343
   of Germans, 341, 343
   of Irish, 341–43
   of Scandinavians, 343
restrictions on, 780, *780*
in 1920s, *974,* 974–75
undocumented, 1334, 1369–70
United States as nation of immigrants, 5
Immigration Act (1917), 913–14
Immigration Act of 1924, *974,* 974–75, 1016, 1143
Immigration Act of 1990, 1322, *1322*
Immigration and Nationality Act (1952), 1143
Immigration and Nationality Services Act (1965),
   1224
impeachment
   of Bill Clinton, 1344–45
   of Andrew Johnson, 653–54, 1241
imperialism, 820–21, 848
   in East Asia, 836–37
   Open Door policy and, 837
   in Pacific, 821–24, *823, 835,* 848
impressment, 291–92, 295
Incas, *4, 8,* 30
income tax
   progressivie, 867
   Revenue Act (1942), 1074
indentured servants, 55–56, 92, 95, 113
Independence Day, 218
Independent Treasury Act, 408, 412, 527
"Indian New Deal," 1036, *1036*
Indian Removal Act (1830), 385, 389, 412
Indian Reorganization Act, 1036
Indians, American, *see* Native Americans
*Indian's Vespers, The* (Durand), *464*
Indian wars, 758–59, *765*
indigo, 100–102, *102,* 113
Indochina, 1179–82, *1181*
   and Eisenhower's legacy, 1187
   and Korean War, 1139
indulgences, 22
industrial democracy, 991
industrial growth in second half of nineteenth century,
   689–90, 728
industrialization, 330–39, 350
   cities and, *338*
   cities and environment, 338–39
   economic success and excess and, 727
   transformation of social life, 708–12, *710*
industrial war, 898–900
Industrial Workers of the World (IWW), 914
infectious diseases, *see* disease

*Influence of Sea Power upon History, 1660-1783, The*
   (Mahan), 820
INF (Intermediate-Range Nuclear Forces) Treaty,
   1315, 1330
Ingersoll, Robert G., 676
Ingham, Samuel, 395, 396
initiative, right of, 861
injunctions, 724
Inness, George, *318*
*Inquiry into the Nature and Causes of the Wealth of
   Nations, An* (Smith), 250–51
Intermediate-Range Nuclear Forces (INF) Treaty,
   1315, 1330
internal improvements, 321, 355–56, 376
Internal Revenue Service, 610–11, 1150
internationalism, 1102
International Ladies Garment Workers' Union, 1046
*Interpretation of Dreams, The* (Freud), 954
interracial marriage, 958–59
interstate commerce, 1050
interstate commerce, regulation of, 357–58
Interstate Commerce Commission (ICC), 797, 812,
   864, 1207
Interstate Highway System, 1153
*Into Bondage* (Douglas), *961*
Intolerable Acts, *see* Coercive Acts
*Intruder in the Dust* (Faulkner), 732
Iowa, Cornbelt Rebellion in, 1007
Iran-Contra affair, 1313–14, *1314,* 1330
Iran hostage crisis, 1299–1300, *1300*
Iraq
   First Gulf War and, 1326–27, *1327*
   rebuilding, *1353,* 1353–54
   Second Gulf War and, 1352–53
   "surge" in, 1357
Ireland, 50
Irish Americans, 111, 150, 341–43, *344*
Irish potato famine, 342
Irish Rebellion, 268
iron curtain, 1114, 1146
Iroquoians, 14–15
Iroquois, *135*
Iroquois League, 85–86, 92
   in American Revolution, 185–86, 200–201
Isabella I, 17, 19, 20, 25
ISIS (Islamic State), 1375
Islamic State (ISIS), 1375
isolationism
   after World War I, 991–94
   to intervention in World War II, 1059–73
      *Anschluss* and Munich Pact and, 1060–62
      Atlantic Charter and, 1069
      "Axis" alliance in, 1060
      Battle of Britain in, 1065–66, *1066*
      conquest of Poland in, 1062–63
      debate on, 1067
      Germany's invasion of Soviet Union in,
         1068–69

isolationism (*continued*)
   Lend-Lease Act and, 1067–68
   Manhattan Project and, 1065
   Pearl Harbor attack in, 1070–73, *1072*
   preparing America for war in, 1065
   Tripartite Pact and, 1070
   U.S. neutrality in, 1060, 1063
   war in Europe and, 1063–65, *1064*
   war in the Atlantic and, 1069–70
Israel, 1121, 1183, 1280–81, 1341, *1342*
Italian Americans, 111, 974
Italy
   and Axis alliance, 1060
   and Kellogg-Briand pact, 993
   Mussolini's rise to power in, 1056, *1056*
   before outbreak of WWII, 1055
   Tripartite Pact, 1070
   in Tripartite Pact, 1070
   in World War I, 925
   in World War II, 1084
itinerants, 124
Iwo Jima, Battle of, *1054*, 1097


J. Pierpont Morgan and Company, 704, 728
Jack (slave), *437*
Jackson, Andrew, 316, 367–75, 379–80, 485, 518, 522,
      541, 884
   annexation of Republic of Texas and, 408
   background of, 368
   Battle of New Orleans, 307, 308
   cabinet of, 396, 406
   Calhoun's rift with, 395–96
   on censoring of mail, 404–6
   in duel, 426
   Eaton Affair and, 383–84
   in election of 1824, 369–70
   in election of 1828, 373–75
   election of 1844 and, 526, 527
   Houston and, 520, 522
   inaugural address of, 329
   inauguration of, 381, *382*
   legacy of, 410–11
   national bank issue and, 390–93, *392*, 401, 402–3
   in Native American conflicts, 365
   Native American policy of, 385–90, *386, 388, 390*
   nullification issue and, 399–400
   in War of 1812, 295, 301–3
Jackson, Elizabeth, 368
Jackson, Helen Hunt, 767
Jackson, Henry, 1281
Jackson, Rachel, 373, 384
Jackson, Thomas "Stonewall," 530, 582, 678
Jacobins, 258
Jamaica, 27, 71
James, Henry, 787
James, William, 834
James I, 48–49, 52, 140

James II, 50, 59
   colonization and, 76
   overthrow of, 138
Jamestown colony, *46*, 52–55, 57, 62
James VI, 23
Japan
   Asian expansion of, *1071*
   atomic bombing of, 1099–1101, *1100*
   and Axis alliance, 1060
   and Kellogg-Briand pact, 993
   Manchuria occupation, 1058
   before outbreak of WWII, 1055
   and Pacific theater (WWII), 1095–1101
   Pearl Harbor attack of, 1070–73, *1072*
   post-war recovery, 1135
   in Russo-Japanese War, 843, 844
   Tripartite Pact, 1070
   in Tripartite Pact, 1070
   in World War II, 1070–73, *1072,* 1097–99
Japanese Americans
   and Ku Klux Klan, 977
   in World War II, discrimination against, 1080–82,
      *1081*
Jaworski, Leon, 1284
Jay, John, 231, 280
   background of, 247
   *Federalist Papers* and, 242–43
   on peace commission, 208
   on Supreme Court, 247
   treaty negotiated by, 259–60
Jayhawkers, 591
Jay's Treaty, 259–60, 266, 272–73
Jazz Age, 951–63, 970, 973, 1003
   African American life in, 959–63, *961, 962*
   F. Scott Fitzgerald and, 968–69
   Freud and, 953–55
   jazz music and, *952,* 952–53
   racism in, 958–59
   radio and, 947
   Sanger and birth control and, 955–56
   sexuality in, 953–59
   women in, 956–58, *957*
JCPA (Joint Comprensive Plan of Action), 1394
Jefferson, Thomas, 165, 180, 181, 214, 218, 219, 226,
      *238,* 249, *254,* 265, 269, 275, 294, 316, 334,
      339, 354, 452
   on acquisition of Canada, 296
   on John Adams, 208
   Alien and Sedition Acts and, 268–69
   Barbary pirates and, 281–82
   on Bill of Rights, 249
   and Burr Conspiracy, 290
   cabinet of, 278–79
   colonial protests and, 161
   on Constitution, 244
   contradictions in character of, 278
   Declaration of Independence and, 171–72, 278
   and deism, 121

as early Republican leader, 246, 257
economic policies of, 281
in election of 1796, 265
in election of 1800, 224, 269–70, *270*
in election of 1804, 288–89
Embargo Act, 292–93
exploration of West promoted by, 285
on *Federalist Papers,* 242
French Revolution and, 257, 258
Hamilton compared with, 256–57
inauguration of, 276–77
on Jackson, 368
on Jay's Treaty, 260
land policy and, 227, 263
Louisiana Purchase and, 283–85
in *Marbury v. Madison,* 279–81
James Monroe and, 359
national bank and, 253, 254–55
Panic of 1819 and, 360
as president, 278–81
as secretary of state, 247, 259, 310
as slaveholder, 278
slavery and, 173, 207, 214, 215, 271, 278, 361, 441
slave trade outlawed by, 290, 432
on women's rights, 218
Jeffersonian Republicans, *see* Republicans,
    Jeffersonian
Jeremiah, Thomas, 215
Jesuits, 25
Jewish Americans, 975
    and Ku Klux Klan, 977
    in Levittown, 1160
Jewish Americans in colonial period, 75, 76, 82, 111
Jews; *See also* anti-Semitism
    Holocaust and, *1094,* 1094–95
Jim Crow laws, 740, *741,* 742, 770, 896, 941, 1010,
    1168
Job Corps, 1221
Johnson, Andrew, 612, 645, *645,* 649
    congressional conflicts with, 650–51, 652–53
    in election of 1864, 621–22
    impeachment and trial of, 653–54, 1241
    Radical Republicans' conflict with, 648–49, 651–52
    Reconstruction plans of, 646–47, 657–58
Johnson, Claudia "Lady Bird," 1218, 1229, 1233
Johnson, Hiram, 1068
Johnson, Hugh S., 1042
Johnson, James Weldon, 934, 960
Johnson, Lyndon B., 1108, 1194, 1217–27, *1226,* 1260
    civil rights and, 1219–20, 1238
    and civil rights movement, 1171–72, 1174
    and Congress, 1197
    in election of 1964, 1221–22
    election of 1968 and, 1244
    Great Society and, *1221,* 1222–27, 1238
    Kennedy assassination and, 1203, 1217, *1218*
    and NYA, 1044
    on Sputnik launch, 1185

Vietnam War and, 1227–33, *1232,* 1232–33
    war on poverty of, 1220–21, *1221,* 1222
Johnson, Matthew, 1215
Johnson, Sally, 439
Johnson, Samuel, 162–63
Johnston, Albert Sidney, 594
Johnston, Joseph E., 597
John Wilkes, 630
Joint Comprensive Plan of Action (JCPA), 1394
joint-stock companies, 51, 92
Jolliet, Louis, 135
Jones, Mother, 717–18
Jones, Philip, 436
Jones, William, 721
Jones Act, 835
Jordan, David Starr, 833
Joseph, Nez Perce chief, 765–66
Joyce, James, 963
Judge, Mychal, 1348
judicial review, 280
judiciary, 237
Judiciary Act (1801), 279
*Jungle, The* (Sinclair), 871, 872

kamikazes, 1097
Kansas-Nebraska Act, 554–56, *555,* 576
    "Bleeding Kansas" and, *540, 555, 557,* 557–58
    proposed by Douglas, 555
    sectional politics and, 559, *560*
    violence in Senate and, 558–59
    Whig party destroyed over, 556
Kansas Territory, 541
    Lecompton Constitution in, 563
    violence in (1856), 558
Kant, Immanuel, 120
Katrina, Hurricane, *1356,* 1356–57
Kaufman, Irving, 1141
*Kearny,* 1070
Kearny, Stephen, 531–33
Keating-Owen Child Labor Act (1916), 890
Keats, John, 1166
Kelley, Abigail, 494–95
Kelley, Florence, 853, 864, 866
Kelley, Oliver H., 801
Kellogg, Frank B., 993
Kellogg-Briand Pact, 993
Kelly Act (1925), 948
Kennan, George F., 1115–17, 1134, 1144, 1178, 1231
Kennedy, Anthony, 1388
Kennedy, Jacqueline, *1218*
Kennedy, John F.
    assassination of, 1203–4, 1228
    background of, 1192, *1196*
    Bay of Pigs invasion and, 1198, 1238
    Berlin Wall and, 1199–1200
    civil rights and, 1197–98, 1207–10
    and Cuba, 1186
    Cuban missile crisis and, 1200–1201, 1238

Kennedy, John F. (*continued*)
    in election of 1960, 1192–95, *1193, 1195*
    foreign policy of, 1198–1204
    New Frontier and, 1192–1204, 1238
    Nixon's debate with, *1193*
    poverty and, 1220
    Vietnam and, 1202–3
Kennedy, Joseph, 1194
Kennedy, Robert, 1196, 1198, 1244, 1259, *1259*
    assassination of, 1234
    as attorney general, 1208
    in election of 1968, 1233, 1234–35
    Johnson and, 1218
Kent State University, murder at, 1272, 1273, *1273*
Kentucky, 263, 592–93, *593*
Kentucky Resolution, 268
Kerensky, Alexander, 915
Kerouac, Jack, 1166, 1167
Kerry, John, 1354, *1355*, 1373, 1374
Key, Francis Scott, 305–6
Keystone Company, 946
Khmer Rouge, 1275
Khomeini, Ayatollah Ruhollah, 1299
Khrushchev, Nikita, 1207
    and Bay of Pigs crisis, 1198
    Berlin crisis and, 1185–86, 1199, *1200*
    Cuban missile crisis and, 1200–1201
    U-2 summit and, 1186
*Kid, The,* 946
Kim Jong-un, 1394, *1394,* 1395
King, Martin Luther, Jr., 468, 857, *1173,* 1194, 1197,
        1208, 1214, *1226,* 1232
    assassination of, 1234, 1235, 1244
    "I Have a Dream" speech of, 1210–11
    Letter from Birmingham City Jail of, 1209
    in March on Washington, 1210–11
    in Montgomery bus boycott, 1172–73
    on school desegregation, 1175
    SCLC and, 1176, 1207
    voting rights and, 1225–26
King, Rufus, 288, 293, 358
King Philip's (Metacom's) War, 84–85, 92
King's College, 128
Kingsley, Bathsheba, 127
King's Mountain, Battle of (1780), 203–4
*King v. Burwell,* 1376–77
King William's War (1689-1697), 140–41
Kinlock, Francis, 202
Kiowas, 38, 761
Kissinger, Henry, 1264, 1277, 1279, 1284, 1298, 1310
    Chile and, 1277, 1278
    Ford and, 1288
    "shuttle diplomacy" of, 1280–81
    Vietnam and, 1270–71, 1274–75
KKK, *see* Ku Klux Klan
Knight, Amelia, 509–10
Knights of Labor, 716, *716,* 717, 719–20, 729
Knights of the White Camelia, 662

Know-Nothing (American) party, *344,* 344–45, 350,
    556
Knox, Henry, 193, 232
Knox, Philander C., 845
Knox, William, 152
Korean War, 1135–39, *1138,* 1177
    economic prosperity after, 1156
    and Eisenhower's legacy, 1187
Kosovo, 1342–43
*Kramer, Shelley v.,* 1160
Krimmel, John Lewis, 352
Kuhn, Walt, 966
Ku Klux Klan (KKK), 623, 1126, 1243
    Freedom Riders and, 1206, 1212–13
    Montgomery bus boycott and, 1173
    in Reconstruction, 662, *662,* 672, 673, 680
    in 1920s, *976,* 976–78, 989
Ku Klux Klan Act (1871), 673
Kwakiutl, 11
Kyner, James H., 752

labor; *see also* slavery; slaves
    child, 713, 728, 865–67, *866,* 890
    in early nineteenth century, *345,* 345–49
    eight-hour workday, 890
    indentured servants, 55–56, 95, 113
    in Lowell system, *335,* 335–38
    New Deal and, 1024–27, *1025*
    organized, *see* organized labor
    rise of professions, 348–49
    of women, 98–101, 349, 545, 713, 908–9, *909,*
        957–58, 1009–10, 1075–76, *1076,* 1163
    in World War I, 908–10, *909*
labor unions, *See* organized labor
Lacey, Edward, 202
*Lackawanna Valley* (Inness), *318*
*Ladies' Home Journal,* 711–12, 953
Lafayette, Gilbert du Motier, Marquis of, 199, *199,* 367
La Follette, Robert M., 863, 998
laissez-faire doctrine, 708, 728
Lake Champlain, Battle of, 306
Land Act of 1796, 263
Land Act of 1800, 263
Landon, Alfred M., 1047
Land Ordinance (1785), 228
Land Ordinance Act (1784), 227
land policy
    African Americans and, 657–59, *659*
    under Articles of Confederation, 227
    in early U.S., 263
    free blacks and, 644
    Reconstruction and, 657–59, *659*
    for surveys and sales, 263
Lansing, Robert, 905, 926, 930
Laos, 1179, *1240*
La Salle, René-Robert Cavelier, sieur de, 135
Las Casas, Bartolomé de, 31, 39
Lathers, Richard, 575

Latin America, 845–46; *see also specific countries*
  and Immigration Act of 1924, 975
  1920s diplomatic relations with, 994
Latinos, 1257–58; *see also* Hispanic Americans
  as civil rights activists, 1170
  in Great Depression, 1010
  post-war civil rights for, 1128–29
  1950s migration of, 1160–61
  women's challenges in 1920s, 958
  in World War II, 1079–80
Latrobe, Benjamin Henry, 279
Latrobe, John H. B., *472*
Latvia, 926
Laurens, Henry, 174, 215
Lawerence, Richard, 402
Lawrence, Kans., *540*, 558
*Lawrence*, USS, 301
lawyers, 348
League of Nations, 923, 925–28, 938, 991, 994, 999,
  1059
League of Spiritual Discovery, 1247
Leahy, William D., 1092
Lear, Norman, 1263
Leary, Timothy, 1247–48
Lease, Mary Elizabeth, 805, *805*
*Leaves of Grass* (Whitman), 469, 472–73
Lecompton Constitution, 563
Lee, Ann (Mother Ann), 481–82
Lee, Billy, 233
Lee, Henry, 261
Lee, Jarena, 458
Lee, Richard Henry, 171, 242
Lee, Robert E., 530, 597, *597*, 614–15, 620, 634, 678,
  874
  at Antietam, 600–601
  at Chancellorsville, 614–15
  end of war and, 629
  at Gettysburg, 615–18, *619*
  Grant's pursuit of, 623–26, *625*
  at Harper's Ferry, 566
  retreat after Gettysburg, 618–20
  surrender of, 631
legal system as profession, 348
Legal Tender Act of 1862, 611, 707
Leibowitz, Samuel, *1035*
leisure for women in the Gilded Age, 782, 783
Lemay, Curtis, 1099
Lemnitzer, Lyman, 1198
Lend-Lease Act, 1067–68, 1069
Lenin, Vladimir Ilyich, 915–17, 935, 1062
Leningrad, German invasion of, 1068–69
Lennon, John, 1248
*Leopard*, HMS, 292
Leo X, 23
Lerner, Max, 1122
lesbians, *see* gays and lesbians
Letter from Birmingham City Jail (King), 1209
Lever Act, 907

Levitt, William, 1159
Levittown, 1159–60, *1160,* 1166
Lewinsky, Monica, 1343–44
Lewis, Isham, 443
Lewis, John L., 1046
Lewis, Lilburn, 443
Lewis, Meriwether, 285–88
Lewis and Clark expedition, 285–88, *286,* 312
Lexington, Battle of (1775), 163–65, *164*
Leyte Gulf, Battle of, 1097
Liberal Republicans, 669–70
*Liberator,* 487
Liberia, 485–86
liberty bonds, 908
Liberty party, 490, 526
Libya, 1068, 1365–66
Liddy, Gordon, 1282
*Lienzo de Tlaxcala, 28*
Lieu, Ted, 1389
*Life* magazine, 1149, 1164, 1242
Liliuokalani, Queen of Hawaii, *822,* 822–23
Lincoln, Abraham, 606, 611, 678, 868
  in abolition movement, 486
  assassination of, 630, 632, 645–46
  Cartwright and, 457
  on Chancellorsville, 614–15
  on Clay, 546
  Douglas's debates with, 563–65, 576
  between election and first inauguration, 569, 574
  in election of 1860, 568–69, *570*
  in election of 1864, 621–22, 627
  emancipation and, 598–608, *601,* 602, *602,* 603,
    634, 636, 1208
  first inauguration of, 574
  Gettysburg Address of, 620
  on Grant, 621, 622
  on Kansas-Nebraska Act, 556
  McClellan's antagonism toward, 597
  Mexican-American War opposed by, 530
  Reconstruction plans of, 642–43
  secession and, 569, 574, 580
  second inauguration of, 630
  Sherman and, 629
  slavery issue and, 541, 579, 598–99
  Union command structure and, 595, 597, 598,
    603–4, 614, 621
  on Vicksburg, 615
  on Webster-Hayne debate, 395
  on women during war, 609
Lincoln, Benjamin, 202
Lincoln, Mary, 588, 624, 645
Lincoln, Willie, 593
Lincoln-Douglas debates, 563–65, 576
*Lincoln's Drive through Richmond, 578*
Lincoln's Loyal League, 666
Lindbergh, Charles A., Jr., 948, 1067
Lingg, Louis, 719
Lippman, Walter, 916, 1021

literature
  during Great Depression, 1037–38
  Harlem Renaissance and, 960–62, *961*
  in mid-twentieth century, 1165–66
  modernist, 963, 966–67
  in nineteenth century, 469–73
  realism in, 785–87
  transcendentalism and, 463–69, *464, 467*
Lithuania, 926
Little, Malcolm, *see* Malcolm X
Little Bighorn, Battle of (1874), 763, *763*
Little Crow, 310
Little Richard, 1168
Little Rock, Ark., desegregation in, *1174,* 1174–76
Livingston, Robert R., 283, 284, 324, 357
*Lochner v. New York* (1905), 867
Locke, John, 121–22, 139
Lodge, Henry Cabot, 820, 903, 923–28, 930, 989
de Lôme letter, 825, 848
Lone Star Republic, 522, 524
Long, Huey Pierce, Jr., 1032, *1040,* 1040–41, 1042,
  1047
Longfellow, Henry Wadsworth, 515
Long Island, Battle of (1776), 187
Longstreet, James, 530, 617
Longview, Tex., race riot in (1919), 934
Longworth, Alice Roosevelt, 997
Lorde, Audre, 1216
Loring, Elizabeth, 189, 198
Lost Cause narrative, 678
Lost Generation, 967–69, 970, 973, 1037
Louis, Joe, 1078
Louisiana
  Hurricane Katrina and, *1356,* 1356–57
  secession of, 572
  slave revolt in, 444
Louisiana Purchase (1803), 283–85, *286,* 288, 312, 707
Louisiana territory, 135–36, 228
  and Adams-Onís treaty, 366
  and Burr Conspiracy, 289–90
  in Treaty of Paris (1763), 147
Louis XIV, 134, 135, 140
Louis XV, 144
Louis XVI, 927
Lovejoy, Elijah P., 494
Low Countries, 1063
Lowell, Francis Cabot, 335
Lowell, James Russell, 569
Lowell girls, *335,* 335–36
Lowell system, *335,* 335–38, *336, 337, 338,* 350
Loyalists
  in American Revolution, 157, 161, 162, 176, 184,
    188, 193–96, 202–4
  exodus after American Revolution, 212–13
loyalty oaths, 1125
Loyalty Order, 1140
Lucas, George, 100
Luce, Henry, 1102

Ludendorff, Erich, 917–18
Luftwaffe, 1066
Luhan, Mabel Dodge, 942
*Lusitania,* 902–3
Luther, Martin, *22,* 22–24
Lutheranism, 23, 33
Luxembourg
  and Kellogg-Briand pact, 993
  in WWII, 1063
luxury goods, 116–17
Lynch, Charles, 202–3
Lynch, James D., 647
lynchings during the 1890s, 470–742, *741,* 742
Lyon, Matthew, 268

MacArthur, Douglas, 1014
  and election of 1948, 1129
  in Korean War, 1135–39
  Pacific strategy, 1096
  in Philippines, 1097
Macdonough, Thomas, 306
Macune, Charles W., 803
Madero, Francisco, 846
Madison, James, 181, 232, 270, 316, 359, 360
  African colonization and, 485
  Bill of Rights and, 247
  at Constitutional Convention, *233,* 233–35, 234,
    236, 238, 240
  debt issue and, 252–53
  as early Republican leader, 246, 257
  in election of 1808, 293
  *Federalist Papers* and, 242–43
  French Revolution and, 259
  government strengthening recommended by, 354
  land policy and, 263
  national bank and, 254, 354
  in ratification debate, 241–42
  as secretary of state, 280, 292
  as slaveholder, 271
  War of 1812 and, 293–95, 297–300, 304–5, 310
*Madison, Marbury v.,* 279–81, 356, 562
Magna Carta (1215), 48
Mahan, Alfred Thayer, 820–21
mail, censoring of, 404–6
Mailer, Norman, 1165
Maine, 69, 362
*Maine,* U.S.S., explosion of (1898), 825, 848
maize (corn), 7, 31, 333
Makohoniuk, Graham, 1367
Malaya, 1072
Malcolm X, 1213–14, *1214,* 1217, 1235
Malick, Abigail, 472
Malick, George, 472
La Malinche (Doña Marina), 27–28
Mamout, Yarrow, *431*
Manassas (Bull Run), first Battle of (1861), 583–84
Manassas (Bull Run), second Battle of (1862), 598

Manchuria
  Japanese occupation of, 1058
  and Kellogg-Briand pact, 993
  Russian troops in, 1101
Mandan Sioux, 286
Manhattan, Dutch settlement of, 75, 76
Manhattan Project, 1065
manifest destiny, 451, 504, 536, 538, 820, 848
Manila Bay, 826–27
Mann, Horace, 348, 478–79
Manson, Charles, 1248
Manucy, Holstead, 1205
manufacturing
  after WWII, 1156
  in early U.S., 255–56
  Lowell system and, *335*, 335–38, *336, 337, 338*
  in WWII, 1073–74
Mao Zedong, 1058, 1133, 1278, 1279
Marbury, William, 280
*Marbury v. Madison*, 279–81, 312, 356, 562
Marcantonio, Vito, 1033
March on Washington, 1210–11, 1238
"March to the Sea," 627–29, *628*, 636
margin loans, 1002–3
Marine Corps, 1075
Marion, Francis, 202, 204
market-based economy, 321, 350
Marquette, Jacques, 135
Marsh, Reginald, *1039*
Marshall, George C., 1115–18, *1117*, 1142
Marshall, John, 280, 381
  African colonization and, 485
  and Burr Conspiracy, 290
  in *Gibbons v. Ogden*, 357, 358
  judicial nationalism of, 356, 363
  in *Marbury v. Madison*, 279–81, 356
  in *McCulloch v. Maryland*, 357
  Native American lands and, 388
Marshall, Thomas, 930
Marshall Plan, 1116–18, *1117*, 1146
Martin, Jefferson, T., 677
Martin, Luther, 242
*Martin v. Hunter's Lessee*, 356
Marx Brothers, 1038–39
Mary I, 25, 26
Mary II, 50, 138, 139, 140
*Maryland, McCulloch v.*, 356–57
Maryland colony, 47, 59–61, *60*
  Anglican Church in, 124
  charter of, 61
  European settlement of, 59–61, *60*
  government of, 61, 139, 140
  indentured servants in, 56
  slavery in, 87, 113, 114
  tobacco in, 55, 102
Mason, George
  at Constitutional Convention, 236
  in ratification debate, 242

Mason, John, 69
Massachusetts
  Constitution ratified by, 243, *245*
  Shays's Rebellion in, *231*, 231–32
Massachusetts Bay Colony
  anti-tavern law in, 118–19
  charter of, 65, 67, 69, 138
  in colonial taxation disputes, 154
  colonial wars and, 125
  European settlement of, *63*, 64–67
  government of, 65, 67–68, 69, 139, 140
  Native Americans and, 83–84
  witch hunts in, 108
Massachusetts Bay Company, 65
Massachusetts Government Act (1774), 160
*Massacre of the Whites by Indians and Blacks in Florida*, 365
massive resistance, 1171, 1176, 1188
massive retaliation, 1177–78, 1188
mass production, 330
materialism, 1155–56
Mather, Cotton, 97, 101
Mather, Increase, 107
Mattis, James, 1395
Mayas, *7*, 8, 27–28
*Mayflower*, 63–64
Mayflower Compact, 64, 92
Maysville Road Bill (1830), *384*, 384–85
McAdoo, William, 905, 998
McAuliffe, Anthony
  Battle of the Bulge, 1091
McCain, John, 1359–60, *1360*, 1366
McCarran, Pat, 1142–43
McCarran Internal Security Act, 1142–43
McCarthy, Eugene, 1233, 1234, 1294–95
McCarthy, Joseph R., 1139, 1141–42, *1142*, 1155, 1202, 1237
McCarthyism, 1141–42, *1142*, 1144, 1146, 1155
McClellan, George B., 530, 596, 597
  at Antietam, 600–601
  in election of 1864, 621–22, 627
  Lincoln's antagonism toward, 597, 601
  peninsular campaign of, *596*, 597
  at second Bull Run, 598
McClure, Samuel S., 855
*McClure's*, 855, 861
McCord, James W., 1282
McCormick, Cyrus Hall, 333–34
McCoy, Joseph G., 753
McCulloch, James, 356
*McCulloch v. Maryland*, 356–57, 376
McFarlane, Robert, 1314
McGovern, George, 1281–82
McGready, James, 455
McGrory, Mary, 1203
McKinley, William, 799, 807–8, *836*
  assassination of, 838
  in election of 1896, 685, 809–10, *811*

McKinley, William (*continued*)
  Hawaii and, 824
  Philippines and, 830–31
  Spanish-American War and, 826, 827
McKinley Tariff (1890), 799
McLane, Louis, 383
McNamara, Robert, 1198, 1229, 1232, 1274
McNary, Charles L., 1000
McNary-Haugen Bill (1927), 1000
Meade, George, 530, 616
Meany, George, 1157
Meat Inspection Act, 872
meat-packing industry, 755, 871, 872, *872*
mechanical reaping machine, 333–34, 350
Medicaid, 1223, 1227, 1238
Medicare, 1223, 1227, 1238
medicine, 348–49, 608
Mellon, Andrew W., 988–89, 997, 1002, 1011, 1013
Melville, Herman, 469, 471
Memminger, Christopher, 426–27
*Memphis Free Speech,* 743
*Memphis Scimitar,* 873
Mencken, H. L., 981, 986, 997
Menendez de Aviles, Pedro, 33
Mennonites, 109
mercantilism, 136–37, 176, 250
Mercer, Hugh, *182*
Mercer, Lucy, 1030, 1093
Meredith, James, 1208
Mesoamerica, 8
mestizos, 34, 36
Metacom (King Philip), 84–85, 92
Methodists, 124, 454, 456
#MeToo movement, 1387, *1387*
Meuse-Argonne offensive, 918, *918*
Mexica, *see* Aztecs
Mexican Americans, 1128–29
  in bracero program, 1161–62
  in Great Depression, 1010–11
  Great Migration of, 1162–63
  and Ku Klux Klan, 977
  in 1920s, 974
  World War I and, 910
  World War II and, 1079–80
  WWII and, 1103
Mexican-American War, 529–37, *532,* 538, 631, 707
  California annexation and, 515, 531–33
  legacies of, 536–37
  opposition to, 530
  outbreak of, 529–30
  peace treaty in, 535–36
  preparations for, 530–31
  Scott and, 533
  Taylor and, 529, 531, 533
Mexico
  Cortés's conquest of, *28,* 28–30
  independence of, 506–7, 512
  Texas independence from, 516–22, *517*
  Wilson's intervention in, 846, *846,* 847
  and Zimmermann telegram, 905–6
Mexico City (Tenochtitlán), 8–9, 28–30
microprocessors, 1316–17
middle class, industrialization and, 709–12, *710*
middle colonies, 73–81, 109–11
Middle East; *see also specific countries*
  "Arab Awakening" and, 1365
  Clinton and, 1341, *1342*
  Ford and, 1288
  Yom Kippur War and, 1280
Middle Passage, 89, 92
Midway, Battle of, 1096
Miles, Nelson A., 766
military-industrial complex, 1144
Military Reconstruction Act (1867), 652–53
Militia Act, 606–7
militias in American Revolution, 163–64, 167–68, 184, 194
Miller, Arthur, 1140
Miller, Stephen, 1387
Milošević, Slobodan, 1342–43
*Milwaukee Sentinel,* 1211
minimum wage, 1049–50
mining, *544,* 545, 730, 751–52, 770
*Mining on the Comstock,* 730
Mininson, Maria, 1149
Mininson, Melvin, 1149
Minnesota, 565
minstrel shows, 340, *341*
Minutemen, 163–64
*Miranda v. Arizona,* 1212
missionaries
  Catholic, 30–31, *34,* 34–36, 507, 510–12
  Spanish, 30–31, *34,* 34–36, 507, 510–12
Mississippi, secession of, 572, 573, 580
Mississippian culture, *12,* 12–13
Mississippi Plan, 737–38, 770
Missouri Compromise (1820), 361–63, *362,* 376, 555–56, 559, 562
Missouri Pacific Railroad, 1008
Mitchell, George, 1260
Mitchell, John, 1264
Mitchell, William D., 1014
Mobile, Ala., 136
mob rule, 741–42
*Moby-Dick* (Melville), 469, 471
Model T, 949
Model T Ford automobile, 949
moderate Republicanism, 1150–55, 1188
modernism, art and literature of, 963–66, *965,* 970
Modocs, 765
Mohawks, 201
Mohegans, 83
Molotov, Vyacheslav, 1114
Monanco, Tony, 907
monarchy, English, 48–50, 136–37, 138–39
Mondale, Walter, 1289, 1309

money, *see* currency
Monongahela, Battle of, 143
monopolies, 701, 728
Monroe, James, 283–84, 309, 316, *359,* 359–60
    African colonization and, 485
    description of, 359–60
    in election of 1816, 359
    in election of 1820, 367
    First Seminole War, 364
    foreign policy under, 366–67
    in ratification debate, 242
    as slaveholder, 271
Monroe, Karl, 1008–9
Monroe, Marilyn, 1196
Monroe, Sarah, 347
Monroe Doctrine, 366–67, 376
Montezuma II, 28–29
Montgomery, Richard, 186
Montgomery bus boycott, 1172–73, *1173,* 1188
Montgomery Ward and Company, 705
Monticello, 278
Moral Majority, 1303, 1330
Moravian Indians, 149
Moravians, 82
Morgan, Daniel, 204
Morgan, J. Pierpont, 689, *704,* 704–5, 869, 901
Morgan, Robin, 1256
Morgan, William, 396–97
Mormons (Church of Jesus Christ of Latter-day
        Saints), 460–63, *461, 462,* 496
Morrill, Justin Smith, 610
Morrill Land Grant College Act (1862), 610, 637, 708
Morrill Tariff, 610, 706
Morris, Gouverneur, 239
Morris, Robert, 226
Morse, Jedidiah, 114
Morse, Samuel F. B., 329
Morton, Ferdinand "Jelly Roll," 952
Moscow, Battle of, 1069
Moses, Robert "Bob," 1212
Mossadegh, Mohammed, 1178–79
Mott, Lucretia, 476, 478
movies
    in early twentieth century, 946, *946*
    during Great Depression, 1038–39, *1039*
Muckogeans, 15
muckrakers, 854–55, 892
Mueller, Robert, III, 1392
Mugwumps, 795, 854
Muhammad, Elijah, 1213–14
Muhlenberg, Peter, 168
mulattoes, 431–32, 448
Mulberry Grove, 331
*Muller v. Oregon* (1908), 867
Munich Pact, 1061–62
municipal reform, 863
*Munn v. Illinois,* 802
Murray, John, 214, 453

Murray, Judith Sargent, 240
Muse, Vance, 1125
Museum of Modern Art, 966
music
    Jazz Age and, *952,* 952–53
    rock 'n' roll, 1167–68
    in 1960s and 1970s, 1250
Mussolini, Benito, 1056, *1056,* 1059, 1065, *1074,* 1084
    and Axis alliance, 1060
    capture and execution of, 1093
    and Italian morale in WWII, 1102
    Munich Pact, 1061
    rise to power, 1056–57
    and Sicily, 1084
My Lai massacre, 1272, *1272*

NAACP (National Association for the Advancement
        of Colored People), 743, 888, 960, 970, 1033
NAFTA (North American Free Trade Agreement),
        1337, 1382, 1396
Nagasaki, atomic bombing of (1945), *1100,* 1101
Nanjing, Japanese capture of, 1059
Napoléon Bonaparte, 269, 283, 284, 290, 291, 294, 507
Napoleonic Wars (1803–1815), 290–94
Napolitano, Janet, 1370
Narragansetts, 68, 83, 85
*Narrative of the Life of Frederick Douglass* (Douglass),
        492
*Narrative of William W. Brown* (Brown), 491
Nash, Diane, 1206
Nashville, Battle of, 628
*Nashville Banner,* 982
Nasser, Gamal Abdel, 1182–83
Nast, Thomas, *662*
Natchez, 15
Nathan, George Jean, 991
*Nation,* 670
Nation, Carrie, 790
nation, confederation vs., 224
National Aeronautics and Space Administration
        (NASA), 1185
National American Woman Suffrage Association
        (NAWSA), 859, 889
National Association for the Advancement of Colored
        People (NAACP), 743, 888, 960, 970, 1033
    and Great Migration, 1161
    and Montgomery bus boycott, 1172
    and 1919 race riots, 933, 934
    separate-but-equal doctrine of, 1170
    and Southern Christian Leadership Conference,
        1176
National Association of Colored Women, 743
National Association of Manufacturers, 1046
national bank, *see* Bank of the United States
National Banking Act, 610, 707
National Consumers League, 864
National Defense Act, 904
National Defense Eduation Act (IDEA), 1185

National Defense Research Committee, 1065
National Environmental Policy Act, 1268
National Guard, 1174–75
National Industrial Recovery Act (NIRA), 1026, 1027, 1042, 1046, 1049
nationalism
  after War of 1812, *274, 352*
  Clay's American System and, 358–59, 369
  development of, 218–19
  in diplomacy, 363–67, *364*
  economic, in early nineteenth century, 354–58
  judicial, 356–58
National Labor Relations Act (NLRA), 1044, 1124
National Labor Relations Board, 1044
National Labor Union (NLU), 715, 729
National Liberation Front (NLF), 1202
National Organization for Women (NOW), 1252
National Prohibition Act, 983
National Recovery Administration (NRA), 1026–27, 1027–28, 1040, 1042, 1052
National Road, *see* Cumberland Road
National Security Act, 1120–21, 1146
National Security Agency (NSA), 1144
National Security Council (NSC), 1121, 1134, 1144, 1200
National Security League, 903
National Socialist German Workers' Party (Nazi Party), 1057
National Teachers Corps., 1223
National Trades' Union, 347, 351
National Urban League, 1161
National Woman Suffrage Association (NWSA), 854
National Women's Political Caucus, 1254
National Youth Administration (NYA), 1034, 1044
Nation of Islam (NOI), 1213–14
Native American conflicts
  Andrew Jackson in, 365
  in colonial period, *58,* 58–59, 73, 83–85, 148–49
Native Americans, 667–68; *see also specific tribes*
  agriculture of, 7
  American Revolution and, 183–86, 199–201, 208, 218
  buffalo and, 38–39, 764
  and California gold rush, 543
  Catholicism and, 30–31, 34–36, 507, 510–12
  and CCC, 1025
  citizenship of, 237–38
  colonial trade with, 2, 72–73
  Columbus and, 20
  culture of Europeans vs., 27–28
  and diseases contracted from Europeans, 3, 30, 32
  Dutch relations with, 76
  English vs. French relations with, 83, 134
  forced labor of, 30, 35, 512
  in French and Indian War, 142, 143–44
  French relations with, 83, 86, 134, *135*
  in fur trade, 74–75, 83, 109, 134, *508*
  Ghost Dance movement and, 766

  Grant's policy toward, 761
  horses and, 37–39, *38*
  Houston and, 521
  Jackson's policy toward, 385–90, *386, 388, 390*
  languages of, 8
  massacres of, 84, 387, 757–58, 766
  in mining camps, 545
  missionaries to, 30–31, 35–36, 507, 510–12
  New Deal and, 1036, *1036*
  in New England, 68, *80–81,* 83–84
  in New York colony, 85–86
  Oregon Trail and, 509
  Peace Policy toward, 667
  pre-Columbian civilizations of, 6–15, *12, 14*
  Puritans and, 83
  Quakers' relations with, 79
  removal of, 385–90, *386, 388, 390,* 760–61
  rights of, 1260–61
  as slaves, 20, 36–37, 72–73
  tribal groups of, 9–10, *80–81*
  Virginia colony and, 52–55, 58–59
  women, 11, 14–15
  in World War II, 1080, *1080*
*Native Son* (Wright), 1035, 1037–38
nativism, *343,* 344–45, 350, 1033
  in eighteenth century, 97–98
  and Know-Nothing party, 556
  in late nineteenth century, 779–80, *780,* 812
  in 1920s, 973–76, 1016
NATO, *see* North Atlantic Treaty Organization
Nat Turner's Rebellion, 445–46, 449
naturalization, 119
Naturalization Act (1740), 120
Naturalization Act (1790), *249,* 249–50
Naturalization Act (1870), 666
natural rights, Locke on, 139, 176
Navajo code talkers, *1080*
Navajos, 10, *1080*
Navigation Act (1651), 137, 176
Navigation Act (1660), 137, 176
Navigation Act (1663), 137, 176
navigation acts, enforcement of, 137–40
Navy, U.S., recruitment poster, *894*
NAWSA (National American Woman Suffrage Association), 859, 889
Nazism; *see also* Germany, Nazi
  Father Coughlin and, 1041–42
  Treaty of Versailles and, 926–27, 930
Nazi–Soviet Non-Aggression Pact, 1062
Negro Act of 1740, 114
Negro nationalism, 962–63
*Negro Village on a Southern Plantation* (drawing), *417*
neoconservatives, torture and, 1351–52
Ness, Eliot, 985
Netherlands, 40, *41*
  American Revolution and, 180, 183, 197
  colonization by, 73–77
  Dutch Republic and, 40

fur trade and, 83
and Kellogg-Briand pact, 993
in rebellion against Spain, 40
in WWII, 1063
neurasthenia, 711
Neutrality Act (1935), 1060
Neutrality Act (1937), 1060
Neutrality Act (1939), 1063, 1070
neutrality laws, 1060
Nevis, 71
New Amsterdam, 75–77, *115*
New Deal, *1018,* 1018–53, *1020–31,* 1108
    African Americans and, 1033–35, *1035*
    agriculture in, 1027
    continuing hardships during, 1032–36, *1034*
    and "Court-packing" plan, 1048–49
    criticism of, 1031–32, 1040–42
    and dynamic conservatism, 1153
    Fair Deal and, 1129–30, 1133
    financial regulation in, 1022–24
    First, 1022, 1052
    industrial recovery program in, 1026–27
    job programs, 1024–26, *1025*
    legacy of, 1050–51
    Native Americans and, 1036, *1036*
    organized labor and, 1046–47
    Second, 1043–51, 1052
    Social Security in, 1044–45, *1045*
    Supreme Court and, 1042, 1048–49
    Tennessee Valley Authority in, 1028–29
    Truman's expansion of, 1122
New Deal liberalism, 1192
New Democrats, 1328
New Echota, Treaty of, 389
new economy, 991, 1340
New England
    architecture in, 103–4
    colonial life in, *94,* 103–8
    colonies of, 47
    fishing in, 105
    Great Awakening in, 123–29
    Native Americans in, 68, *80–81,* 83–84
    religion in, 62, 106–8
    shipbuilding in, 105
    slaves in, 87
    townships, 103
    trade and commerce in, 105–6, *106*
    witchcraft in, 107–8
New England, Dominion of, 138, 139
New France, 40, 51, 134–36, *135*
New Freedom movement, 881, 893, 896
New Frontier, 1192–1204, 1238
New Hampshire, 69, 155, 243, *245*
New Haven colony, 69
New Jersey
    Constitution ratified by, 243, *245*
    Revolutionary War fighting in, 188, 190, *191,* 192,
        195

New Jersey colony, 70, 124
    European settlement of, *74, 77*
    government of, 140
New Jersey Plan, 235
New Lebanon community, 482
New Left, 1242–43, 1246, 1290
*New Method of Assorting the Mail...,* 405
New Mexico, 34–35, 37, 44
New Nationalism, 877
New Netherland, 137
New Netherland colony, 47, 51, 70, 73–77, 123
New Orleans, 595, *1356,* 1356–57
    and Burr Conspiracy, 289–90
    and Louisiana Purchase, 283
    shipping in, 339
    slave markets and "fancy trade," 433
    steamboat traffic in, 324
New Orleans, Battle of (1815), 307–8, 312,
        411
New Orleans, Lou, 136
Newport, R.I., 117
*New Republic,* 886
New Right, 1303–4
Newsom, Robert, 439
New Spain, 27, 30–31, 34–35, 51, 136
newspapers
    in colonial period, 119
    in nineteenth century, *472, 473*
*Newsweek* magazine, 1249
Newton, Huey, 1216
Newton, Isaac, 121
Newton, Sir Isaac, 964
New York
    Constitution ratified by, 243, *245*
    government of, 139
*New York American,* 1033
New York City, *772*
    in colonial period, 117, 118
    homelessness in, 1008–9
    as national capital, 243–44
    poverty in colonial era, 118
    Revolutionary War fighting in, 186–88, 190, *191,*
        192, 194–95, *196*
    slavery in, *115,* 115–16
New York colony, 70
    Dutch origins of, 73–77
    frontier conflicts for, 155
    Native Americans in, 85–86
*New York Herald,* 668, 674
*New York Journal,* 824
New York Stock Exchange, 687
*New York Times,* 632, 670, 799, 828, 934, 966, 1013,
        1126, 1196, 1198, 1235, 1274, 1285,
        1329
*New York Tribune,* 670
*New York World,* 824, 828
New York Yankees, 950–51
Nez Perce bands, 765, 766

Ngo Dinh Diem, 1202
Nicaragua, 994, 1311–12
Nicholas II, 915
Nicodemus, *750*
Nicolson, Harry, 927
Niebuhr, Reinhold, 1019
*Nightclub* (Pene du Bois), *940*
Nimitz, Chester, 1096
*Niña,* 18
Nineteenth Amendment, 932–33, 939, 941
NIRA (National Industrial Recovery Act), 1026, 1027,
        1042, 1046, 1049
Nisei, 1080, 1082
Nitze, Paul, 1134
Nixon, Richard M., 1180, 1263–64, 1277, 1297, 1298,
        1301
    appointments by, 1264
    background of, 1192
    Chile and, 1277–78
    China and, 1278–79, *1279*
    civil rights and, 1266–67, *1267*
    domestic agenda of, 1266
    economy under, 1268–70, *1269*
    in election of 1952, 1151
    in election of 1956, 1182
    in election of 1960, 1192–95, *1193, 1195*
    in election of 1968, 1235, *1236,* 1237,
        1265–12661138–1140
    in election of 1972, 1265–66
    environmental protection and, 1267–68
    Kennedy's debate with, *1193*
    and NYA, 1044
    resignation of, 1285, *1285*
    shuttle diplomacy and, 1280–81
    Soviet Union and, 1279–80
    Truman on, 1108
    Vietnam War and, 1270–77, *1273, 1276*
    Watergate and, 1108, 1241, 1281–87, *1285,* 1290
Nixon Doctrine, 1278
NLU (National Labor Union), 715, 729
NOI (Nation of Islam), 1213–14
No Man's Land, in trench warfare, 900
Nonconformists, 49
Non-Importation Act, 291
nonimportation movement, 153
Non-Intercourse Act (1809), 294
nonviolent civil disobedience, 1172–73, 1176, 1188,
        1209, 1212–13, 1238
Nonviolent Coordinating Committee (SNCC), 1194
Nootka, 11
Noriega, Manuel, 1325–26
Normandy invasion, *See* Operation Overlord
Norris, George, 912
*Norris v. Alabama,* 1035
Norsemen (Vikings), 21
North, Lord Frederick, 157–59, 163, 167, 184, 208
North, Oliver, 1313–14
North Africa, 1068

North Africa campaign (WWII), 1083, *1088*
North American Free Trade Agreement (NAFTA),
        1337, 1382, 1396
North Atlantic Treaty, 1119
North Atlantic Treaty Organization (NATO)
    building of, 1119–20, 1146
    former Yugoslavia and, 1342–43
North Carolina
    colonial conflict in, 156
    mob rule in, 741–42
    Revolutionary War fighting in, 202–5
North Carolina colony
    Anglican Church in, 124
    European settlement of, 70, *71, 72*
    government of, 72
    Native Americans in, 72–73
Northern Securities Company, 869
North Korean People's Army, 1136
*North Star,* 492
Northup, Solomon, 433, 436
Northwest Indian War, 260–61
    War of 1812 and, 295–96, 310
    in West, 758–67, *763, 765,* 770–71
Northwest Ordinance (1787), 228, *229,* 272, 361
Northwest Territory, 227, *229*
Norway
    and Kellogg-Briand pact, 993
    in WWII, 1063
*nouveaux riches,* 709
NOW (National Organization for Women), 1252
Noyes, John Humphrey, 483
NRA (National Recovery Administration), 1026–27,
        1027–28, 1040, 1042, 1052
*NSC-68,* 1134
nuclear weapons
    Soviet Union and, 1134, 1314–15
    in World War II, 1065, 1099–1101, *1100*
nullification and interposition, 393–401, 412
    Calhoun and, 393–94
    Jackson and, 399–400
    South Carolina Ordinance and, 399–401
    Webster-Hayne debate on, *394,* 394–95
NWSA (National Woman Suffrage Association), 854
NYA (National Youth Administration), 1034, 1044
Nye, Gerald P., 1060
Nye Committee, 1060

Obama, Barack
    DREAM Act and, 1369–70
    economy and, 1361
    in election of 2008, 1333, 1358–60, *1359, 1360,*
        1396
    in election of 2012, 1371
    first term of, 1361
    foreign policy of, 1363–66, *1364,* 1373–76
    gay rights and, 1369, 1377
    health care reform and, 1361–63, 1373, 1376–77
    ISIS and, 1375

partisanship and, 1376–78
    Tea Party and, 1366–68
Obamacare, *see* Affordable Care Act (ACA)
Obama Doctrine, 1363–64, *1364*
*Obergefell v. Hodges,* 1377
O'Brien County Court House, 1007
Occupational Safety and Health Act, 1266
Occupy Wall Street (OWS) movement, 1368–69
ocean transportation, 328, *329*
O'Connor, Francis, 535
O'Connor, Sandra Day, *1308,* 1309
OEO (Office of Economic Opportunity), 1221
Office of Economic Opportunity (OEO), 1221
Office of Price Administration, 1075
Ogden, Aaron, 357–58
Ogden, Dunbar, 1175
*Ogden, Gibbons v.,* 357–58
Oglethorpe, James E., 82
Ohio Country, 141–43
Ohio Life Insurance and Trust Company, 561
oil industry, 701–2, *1269,* 1269–70
Okinawa, 1097–98
Old Southwest, cotton production in, 421–22,
    448
Olive Branch Petition, 167
Oliver, James, 757
Oliver, Joe "King," 952
Omaha Beach, 1086–87, *1087*
*Omoo* (Melville), 471
Onate, Juan de, 34, 35, 36
Oneida Community, 483–85, *484*
O'Neill, Bucky, 828
O'Neill, Tip, 1306
"On the Equality of the Sexes" (Murray), 240
*On the Origin of Species* (Darwin), 783, 812
*On the Road* (Kerouac), 1167
OPEC (Organization of Petroleum Exporting
    Countries), 1269, 1326
Open Door policy, 837, 848
open range, 755, 770
open shop, 990–91, 1016
Operation Ajax, 1178–79
Operation Barbarossa, 1068
Operation Desert Storm, 1326, *1327,* 1330
Operation Downfall, 1098–99
Operation Iraqi Freedom, 1109
Operation Just Cause, 1326
Operation Overlord, 1085–88, *1086, 1087*
Operation Rolling Thunder, 1229
Operation Sea Lion, 1065–66
Operation Torch, 1083
Operation Trinidad, 1198
Oppenheimer, J. Robert, 1065
Order of the Star-Spangled Banner, 344
Oregon Country, 528–29
Oregon fever, 508–9, 538
Oregon Trail, *505,* 506, 508–9, 513
Oregon Treaty, 707

Organization of Petroleum Exporting Countries
    (OPEC), 1269, 1326
organized labor
    coal strike of 1902 and, 870
    in early nineteenth century, *345,* 345–49, *346*
    during the Gilded Age, 713, 728–29
        American Federation of Labor (AFL), 720–21,
            729
        backlash against, 719–20, 729
        Haymarket riot and, 719, 729
        Homestead Steel strike and, 721–22, 729
        Knights of Labor, 716, *716,* 717, 719–20, 729
        National Labor Union (NLU), 715, 729
        Pullman strike and, 722–24, 729
        "Sand-Lot" incident and, 715
    Harding and, 990–91
    New Deal and, 1026, 1046–47
Orlando, Vittorio, 925
Orlovsky, Peter, 1167
O'Rourke, P. J., 1248
Orwell, George, 993
Osage, 521
Osborne, Sarah Haggar (Rhode Island schoolteacher),
    108, 127
Osceola, 387–88
O'Sullivan, John L., 504, 536
O'Sullivan, T. H., *617*
Oswald, Lee Harvey, 1203–4
*Other America, The* (Harrington), 1220
Otis, Elwell S., 832
Otis, James, 172
Otis, James, Jr., 156
Ottoman Empire, 897, 898, 924
"Ould Virginia" (Smith), *46*
*Our Country* (Strong), 830
Overland Trails, 504–6, *505,* 507–8, *508,* 538
overproduction, 1004–5
overseers on plantations, 428
Overzee, Syman, 116
Ovington, Mary White, 1033
OWS (Occupy Wall Street) movement, 1368–69

Pach, Walter, 966
Pacific, World War II in, 1095–1101, *1098*
Pacific Railway Act (1862), 610, 696
Page, Margaret, 98
Pahlavi, Mohammad Reza, 1179, 1299
Paine, Thomas, 180, *188,* 188–89
    *The American Crisis,* 189
    *Common Sense,* 168–69, 176, 189
    on representative democracy, 209
*Painter, Sweatt v.,* 1170
Pakenham, Edward, 307
Paleo-Indians, 6
Palestine, Israel and, 1121
Palestine Liberation Organization (PLO), 1312, 1341,
    *1342*
pallisades, 14

Palmer, A. Mitchell, 935–36
Palmer, John M., 809
Palmer, Phoebe Worrall, 458–59
Panama, U.S. invasion of (1989), 1325–26
Panama Canal, 840–42, *841*
Panetta, Leon, 1373–74
Panic of 1819, 360–61, 376
Panic of 1837, *378*, 407, 412
Panic of 1857, 561
Panic of 1873, 671–72, 680
Panic of 1893, 806–7
Pan-Slavic movement, 897
*Parade of the Victuallers* (Krimmel), *352*
Parely, Harry, 1086
Paris, France
    liberation of, 1088–89
Paris, Treaty of (1763), 146–48, 176
Paris, Treaty of (1783), 207–8, 212, 227, 259
Paris Peace Accords, 1275
Paris Peace Conference (1919), 924–26
Parker, Alton B., 871
Parker, Ely, 667
Parker, John, 163–64
Parker, Theodore, 485
Parks, Rosa, 1172, 1173, 1211
Parliament, British, 48
    American Revolution and, 208
    in colonial taxation disputes, 151, 152
    kings' conflicts with, 49–50, 69–70, 136–37
    Naturalization Act (1740), 120
    Restoration and, 50
    taxation and, 48, 151, 152
Parris, Samuel, 108
party bosses, 788, 812
*Passing of the Great Race, The* (Grant), 913
Patent Office, U.S., 331, 690
Paterson, William, 235
Patient Protection and Affordable Care Act, *see* Affordable Care Act (ACA)
Patriot Act, USA, 1109, 1351, 1396
Patriots in American Revolution, 157, 165–68, 176, 179–80, 183–87, 193, 194, *194*
patronage system, 788, 812
patroons, 109
patroonship, 75
Patterson, Haywood, *1035*
Patton, George
    Battle of the Bulge, 1090, 1091
    and Holocaust, 1095
    and North Africa campaign, 1083
Paul, Alice, *888*, 888–89
Paxton Boys, 149
Payne-Aldrich Tariff, 876
Peabody, Elizabeth, 466
Peabody, Sophia, 466
Peace Commission, 767
Peace Corps, 1197
Peale, Charles Willson, 184, 190, 199, *254*, 431

Pearl Harbor, attack on, 1055, 1070–73, *1072*
Pearson, Josephine, 933
"peculiar institution," 416, 448
Pegler, Westbrook, 1112
Pelosi, Nancy, 1356, 1357
Pemberton, John C., 615, 619
*Peña, Adarand Constructors v.,* 1339
Pence, Mike, 1368, 1387
Pendleton, George H., 794
Pendleton Civil Service Reform Act, 794
Pene du Bois, Guy, *940*
Penn, William, 78–79, 109
Pennsylvania
    Revolutionary War fighting in, 195, *196*
    Whiskey Rebellion in, 261–62, *262*
Pennsylvania colony, 70
    anti-immigrant prejudices in eighteenth century, 97–98
    backcountry of, 109, 111
    European settlement of, *74*, 77–79, *78*
    government of, 79
    and Quakers, 77–79, *78*, 123
*Pennsylvania Gazette,* 122, 149
Pennsylvania Society for the Abolition of Slavery, 493
Pentagon Papers, 1274, 1290
People's party (Populists), 769, 771, 805–6, 813, 853
Pequots, 83–84
Pequot War (1637), 83–84
Peres, Shimon, 1341
perestroika, 1314, 1330
performing arts, 340, *341*
    in early nineteenth century, 340
    saloons and, 781–82
    sports and, 950–51
performing arts in early nineteenth century, *341*
Perkins, Frances Coralie, 1044
Permanent Court of International Justice, 994
Perot, H. Ross, 1328, 1329
Perry, Oliver Hazard, 301
Pershing, John J., 847, 902–3, 919
Personal Responsibility and Work Opportunity Act (PRWOA), 1339–40
Perth Amboy, 77
Peru, 30
Petigru, James L., 571
Philadelphia
    in colonial period, 117
    founding of, 79
*Philadelphia* (frigate), 282, *282*, 291
*Philadelphia Public Ledger,* 477–78
Philip II, 26, 41–42
Philippine-American War, 832–34
Philippine Government Act, 834–35
Philippines, 1097
    acquisition of, 830–34
    annexation of, *833*
    first Japanese attack on Allied bases in, 1072

in Spanish-American War, 826–27
in World War II, 1095–96, 1097
Phillips, Sam, 1168
Phillips, Wendell, 668
photons, 964
physicians, 348–49
Pickens, Andrew, 201, 204
Pickering, Timothy, 268, 276
Pickett, George, 617, 618, 634–35
Pickett's Charge, 628
Pickney, Charles, 238–39
Pierce, Benjamin, 554
Pierce, Franklin, 559
  in election of 1852, 553
  in election of 1856, 559
  presidency of, 557
Pierce, Jane, 553, 554
Pike, Zebulon, 300
Pilgrims, 49, 62, 65
Pinchot, Amos, 851
Pinchot, Gifford, 873, 876–77
Pinckney, Charles Cotesworth, 101
  in election of 1800, *270*
  in election of 1804, 288
  in election of 1808, 293
Pinckney, Elizabeth Lucas, 100–101
Pinckney, Thomas, 262–63
Pinckney Treaty (1795), 364
Pinkertons, 721
Pinochet, Augusto, 1278
*Pinta*, 18
Pitcairn, John, 163, 164
Pitt, William, 145, 153, 154, 195–96
Pizarro, Francisco, 30
Plains Indians, 11–12, 37–39, *38,* 506, 764
"plain white folk," 428–29, 448
Planned Parenthood, 956
*Plantation Burial* (Antrobus), *442*
plantation mistresses, 426–28, *427,* 448
plantations, 50, *414,* 425–28
planters, 425–26, 430, 448
Platt Amendment, 836
Plattsburgh, Battle of, 306
Plessy, Homer, 739
*Plessy v. Ferguson*, 739–40, 770, 1170
PLO (Palestine Liberation Organization), 1341
Plunkett, James, 742
Plymouth colony, 62–64, *63*
Plymouth Company, 62
Pocahontas, 56–57
Poe, Edgar Allan, 470–71
*Poetry* magazine, 967
Pogrebin, Letty Cottin, 1254
Poindexter, John, 1314, *1314*
Poinsett, Joel, 401
polio, 1020, 1149
Polish Americans, 111, 974
*Politics in an Oyster House, 472*

Polk, James Knox, 468, 515, 536, 537, 544, 553
  background of, 526–27
  death of, 527
  in election of 1844, 526
  Mexican-American War and, 529, 530, 531
  Oregon Country and, 527
  presidential objectives of, 527–28, *528*
  slavery issue and, 542, 543
Polk, Leonidas, 804
*Pollock v. Farmers' Loan Company,* 867
polygamy, 461
Ponce de León, Juan, 33
Pontiac's Rebellion, 148–49, 176
poorhouses, 1008
*Poor Richard's Almanack* (Franklin), 122
"poor whites" in the Old South, 429
Popé, 37
Pope, John, 598
popular sovereignty, 542–43, 575
population
  in colonial period, 96–97, 111, 117
  cotton production and, *423*
  demographic shifts in, 1334–35, 1396
  density
    in 1820, *336*
    in 1860, *337*
  in 1920s, 943
  slave, 114, *434, 435*
Populists, *see* People's party
Porter, Lavinia, 510
Port Huron Statement, 1242
Portugal, 18, 20, 40
postal service, 119
potatoes, 31
Potsdam Conference, 1099–1100, 1114
Potsdam Declaration, 1100
Pottawatomie Massacre (1856), 558, 566
Potter, John "Bowie Knife," 565
Pound, Ezra, 963, 965, 966, 967
Powderly, Terence V., 717, 720
*Powell v. Alabama,* 1035
Powers, Francis Gary, 1186
Powhatan, Chief, 53, *53,* 54, 56, 57
Powhatan Confederacy, 53–54, 92
praying towns, 83
pre-Columbian Indian civilizations, 6–15, *12, 14*
predestination, 452
prejudice in colonial America, 112–13
Presbyterians, 24, 49, 111, 454, 456
presidency, in Constitution, 236–37
presidios, 510–11
Presley, Elvis, 1168
Preston, Levi, 175
price ceilings, in WWII, 1075
Princeton, Battle of (1777), *182,* 190, *190*
*Princeton*, U.S.S., 525
Princeton University, 128
Princip, Gavrilo, 897

*Principles of Scientific Managment, The* (Taylor), 862
prison reform movements, 474–75
privateers, 41
Proclamation of Amnesty (1865), 646
Proclamation of Amnesty and Reconstruction (1863),
        642
professions, rise of, 348–49, 351
Progressive ("Bull Moose") party, *878*, 878–79,
        880–81, *882*
progressivism, 850–91, 942, 973, 985–86
    assessing, 890–91
    corporate regulation and, 864, 868–69, *869*
    efficiency and, 862–64
    Harding and, 989–90
    income tax and, 867
    muckrakers and, 854–55, 892
    political reforms and, 861–62
    religion and, 856–58, *858*
    settlement house movement and, 857–58,
        *858*
    social justice promoted in, 864–67, *866*
    sources of, 853–55, 892
    Taft and, 875–79, 892
    Theodore Roosevelt and, 852–53, 868–79, *869*,
        *874*, 878–79, 892
    for whites only, 886–88, *887*
    Wilson and, 879–80, 883–86, *887*, 893
    women's suffrage movement and, 858–61, *859*, *860*,
        888, *888*, 889, 892
Prohibition, 981–85, *983*, 1016
    end of, 1024
property and voting rights, 140
proprietary colonies, 59
Prosser, Gabriel, 443–44
Prosser conspiracy, 443–44
prostitution, 100
Protestantism/Protestants, 22–24, 26, 41, 50, 61
Protestant Reformation, 21–26, *22*, 44
Protestant work ethic, 104
Providence, Rhode Island, 68
PRWOA (Personal Responsibility and Work
        Opportunity Act), 1339–40
psychoanalysis, 953–55
Public Credit Act, 671
public domain, 227
public schools in nineteenth century, 478–80, *479*,
        496
Public Works Administration (PWA), 1027
Pueblo Revolt, 37
pueblos, 11, 35, 37
Puerto Ricans, 1161–62
Puerto Rico, 27, 835
Puffer, Mabel, 958–59
Pulitzer, Joseph, 824
Pullman, George, 723, 724
Pullman strike of 1894, 721, 722–24, 729
Punderson, Prudence, 99
Pure Food and Drug Act, 872

Puritans, 92, 101, 105
    Cromwell and, 70
    dissension among, 68
    education and, 123
    in England, 25, 48–49, 50
    in Maryland, 61
    in Massachusetts, 62–64, 64–67, 67–68
    Native Americans and, 83
    in New England, 103
    Quakers and, 78
    Separatists, 48, 62–63
    witchcraft and, 107–8
Purnell, Fred S., 975
Putin, Vladimir, 1374
Putnam, Israel, 166
PWA (Public Works Administration),
        1027

quadrants, 16
Quakers (Society of Friends), 109, 124
    educational efforts of, 123
    and founding of Pennsylvania, 77–79, *78*
    Native Americans and, 79
    women as, *78*
    women members of, 101
quanta, 964
Quantrill, William C., 591
Quartering Act (1765), 152
Quartering Act (1774), 160
Quay, Matthew, 798
Quebec
    founding of, 134
    Revolutionary War attack on, 186
Quebec, Battle of, 145
Queens College (New Jersey), 128
Queenston Heights, Battle of, 300
Quetzalcoatl, 28–29
Quitman, John, 551

Rabin, Yitzhak, 1341, *1342*
race-based slavery, 112–16, *115*, 130, 416, 447, 561; *see
        also* slavery
race riots
    in 1866, 649
    in 1968, 1234
    in Brownsville, Tex. (1906), 874
    in Chicago (1919), 934, *935*
    in Detroit (1943), *1077*
    in Longview, Tex. (1919), 934
    in summer of 1919, 933–34, *935*
    in Washington, D.C. (1919), 934
racial covenants, 1160
racism, 958–59; *see also* segregation and
            desegregation
    African-Americans in WWII, 1076–79
    during Great Depression, 1035
    Japanese-American internment during WWII,
        1080–82

in Jazz Age, 958–59
during the 1890s, 737–46, *741*
radical feminism, *1255,* 1296
Radical Republicans
collapse of, 675
and election of 1872, 670–71
in election of 1864, 621–22
Johnson's relations with, 648–49, 651–52
in Reconstruction, 643, 648–49, 663–64, 680
radio, 945, 947
during Great Depression, 1038
Radio Free Europe, 1182
railroads
building of, 694–99, *695*
in early nineteenth century, 326–28, *327,* 350
Great Strike of 1877, 713–14
ICC and, 797
industrial era and, 694
labor disputes, 1123, 1124
land grants to, 330
laying track for, 697
transcontinental, 694–99, *695, 698*
*Rainbow,* 328
Raleigh, Walter, 42
Randolph, John, 289, 293
Rankin, Jeannette, 906
rationing, 1075
Rauschenbusch, Walter, 857, 870
"Raven, The" (Poe), 470–71
Rawlins, John A., 592
Ray, James Earl, 1234
Reagan, Ronald, 1216, 1222, 1293–94, 1300–1301, *1301*
AIDS epidemic and, *1308,* 1319
anti-feminism and, *1303,* 1303–4
anti-liberalism of, *1308,* 1308–9
arms-reduction agreement and, 1314–15
background of, 1301
budget cuts of, 1307, *1307,* 1308
Central America and, 1311–12
defense buildup under, 1310–11
deficits and, 1317–18
economy and, 1306, 1307, 1309–10, 1317–18
in election of 1980, *1292,* 1300–1304, *1305*
in election of 1984, 1309
first term of, 1305–9
Iran-Contra affair and, 1313–14, *1314,* 1330
legacy of, 1315–16
Moral Majority and, 1303
second term of, 1309–10
Reaganomics, 1306, 1307, *1307,* 1330
Rebels, 583
recession (1937), 1049–50
recessions, 1323, 1357–58, 1361
Reconstruction, 638–82
African Americans in, 639–40, 649, 655–64, *661*
black codes and, *589,* 649–50, 661–62, 680
churches and schools and, 656, 657

Freedmen's Bureau and, 643–44, 680
land policy and, 657–59, *659*
politics and, *656, 658*
tensions among, 659
violence against, *589,* 649, 655, 661–62, *662,* 672–73
carpetbaggers in, 660
Compromise of 1877 and, 677, 680
Congress in, 643, 648–49
end of, 677–78
Johnson's plans for, 646–47, 657–58
Lincoln's plans for, 642–43
Panic of 1873 and, 671–72, 680
political, debates over, 642–43
Radical Republicans and, 643, 648–49, 663–64, 680
scalawags in, 660
significance of, 678–89, 680
white terror in, 660–63, *662,* 672–73
Reconstruction Finance Corporation (RFC), 1013
recreation, urban, in early nineteenth century, 339, *340*
Red army, Russia, 916
Red Cloud, 762
Red Cross, 909, 1012, 1076
redeemers, Southern, 673–75, 680, 734
Red Power activists, 1260–61, 1290
Red River War of 1874-1875, 761
Red Scare, 976
Red Scare (1919), 934–36
Red Scare (second), 1140–45, *1142*
Redstockings, 1253
Red Summer, 934
Reed, Walter, 836
Reedy, George, 1218
referendum, 861
Reformation, 21–26, *22*
reform Darwinism, 785, 812
reform movements, 473–81; *see also* progressivism
anti-slavery, *see* abolition movement
for civil service, 791–92, 793–94, 812
education, 478–80, *479*
food and sex in, 480–81
for prisons and asylums, 474–75
temperance, 474, 496
utopian, 481–85, 496
for women's rights, *447,* 475–78
regulation of corporations, government, 864, 868–69, *869*
Regulators, 156, 231
relativity, general theory of, 964–66
religion
African Americans and, 101, *213,* 440–43, *442, 457,* 457–58, *656, 657*
in colonial period, 101, 106–8, 123–29
deism and, 452
Great Awakening
First, 123–29, 453
Second, 453–63, *454, 457, 462,* 473, 496

religion (*continued*)
in New England, 62, 106–8
progressivism and, 856–58, *858*
rational, 452
religious right and, 1302, 1303
in 1950s, *1164,* 1164–65
in South, 440–43, *442*
Unitarianism and, 452–53, 464, 496
Universalism and, 452–53, 496
women and, 101, 458–59
religious colleges, 128
Religious Education Association, 856
religious freedom, 75
after American Revolution, *213,* 213–14
in Bill of Rights, 248–49
Roger Williams and, 68
and separation of church and state, 68
religious right, 1302–3
Remington, Frederic, *818*
Renaissance, 16
Reparations Commission, 992
*Report on an Exploration of the Country Lying
between the Missouri River and the Rocky
Mountains on the Line of the Kansas and
Great Platte Rivers, A* (Frémont*),* 514
"Report on Manufactures" (Hamilton), 255
"Reports on the Public Credit" (Hamilton), 252
representative democracy, 209
*Representative Men* (Emerson), 469
republican ideology, American Revolution and, 196,
209
Republican National Convention (1980), *1292*
Republican party
Big Business and, 706–8
Contract with America and, *1338,* 1338–39,
1396
in elections, *see* elections and campaigns
emergence of, 556–69
Bleeding Kansas, 557–60
Brown's raid and, 566–67
Buchanan in, 560–61
Democratic party and, 567–68
*Dred Scott v. Sandford* and, 562–63
in 1856 election, 559
Lecompton Composition, 563
Lincoln-Douglas debates, 563–65
Lincoln's 1860 election, 568–69
and South, 565–66
Sumner in, 558–59
late nineteenth-century components of, 790
Republicans, Jeffersonian, 246, 257, 272
Alien and Sedition Acts and, 268–69
divisions in, 289
in election of 1796, 265
in election of 1800, 269–70, *270,* 276
in election of 1820, 367
formation of, 246
land policy of, 263

Louisiana Purchase and, 285
War of 1812 and, 310
republican simplicity, 277, 312
Republic of Korea (South Korea), 1135, 1136
Republic of Texas, 408
reservationists, 928–29
Restoration, English, 50
return to normalcy, 986–88, 1016
*Reuben James,* 1070
Reuther, Walter, 1047
Revels, Hiram, *656,* 657
Revenue Act (1767), 154–55
Revenue Act (1916), 904
Revenue Act (1932), 1012
Revenue Act (1942), 1074
Revenue Act (1964), 1219
Revere, Paul
*The Bloody Massacre, 158*
warning ride of, 163
revivals, religious
First Great Awakening, 123–29, 453
Second Great Awakening, 453–63, *454, 457, 462,*
473, 496
Revolutionary Youth Movement (RYM), 1245
RFC (Reconstruction Finance Corporation), 1013
Rhett, Robert Barnwell, 401
Rhode Island, *245*
Rhode Island colony, 124
European settlement of, 68–69
government of, 68–69
rhythm and blues (R&B) music, 1168
Ricard, Cyprien, 432
rice, 71, 102
Richardson, Elliot, 1283, 1284
Richmond, Va., *641*
*Richmond Times,* 740
Rickey, Branch, 1127, 1128
Ridgway, Matthew B., 1138
Riis, Jacob, 854, *854*
Ripley, George, 483
*Rise of Silas Lapham, The* (Howells), 786
Rivers, Mendel, 1126–27
roads, *see* highways and roads
Roanoke Island, 42–43, *43*
Robards, Rachel Donelson, *see* Jackson, Rachel
Roberts, Ed, 1317
Roberts, John G., 1376–77, 1389
Robertson, Pat, 1338
Robinson, Jackie, *1127,* 1127–28, 1211
rock and roll, 1167–68
Rockefeller, John D., 689, 700–702, *701,* 703, 706, 784,
855
Rockingham, Lord, 154
Roebuck, Alvah, 705
*Roe v. Wade,* 1255–56, 1303
Rogers, Will, 984
Rogers, William, 1264, 1272
Rolfe, John, 57

*Rolling Stone* magazine, 1250
Roman Catholicism/Roman Catholic Church, *see* Catholicism/Catholic Church
Romania, 1118
romanticism, 463–73
   Emerson and, 465–66
   literature and, 469–73
   Thoreau and, 466–68, *467*
   Transcendental Club, 466
   transcendentalism and, 463–65, *464, 496*
Romney, Mitt, 1371
Roosevelt, Eleanor, 935–36, 1020, 1029–31, *1030, 1031,* 1093, 1112
   and African Americans, 1034
   and New Deal, 1019–20
Roosevelt, Elliot, 1020
Roosevelt, Franklin, 935–36, 1107
   death of, 1112
   foreign policy of, 1113
   New Deal of, 1108
Roosevelt, Franklin D., 1020, *1021, 1023,* 1197, 1226; *see also* New Deal
   aid to Great Britain, 1066
   Atlantic Charter and, 1069
   at Casablanca, 1083
   and "Court-packing" plan, 1048–49
   "Court-packing" scheme of, 1048–49
   death of, 1092–93
   early years, 1020
   in election of 1920, 986
   in election of 1932, 1002, 1014–15
   in election of 1936, 1047–48
   in election of 1940, 1067
   and Export Control Act, 1070
   first hundred days of administration, 1021–22
   first inauguration of, 1020–21
   and good neighbor policy, 1059
   growing war involvement and, 1066–67, 1069
   and Hoover, 999, 1014
   and isolationism, 1055, 1060
   and Japanese-American internment, 1081
   and legacy of New Deal, 1050–51
   Lend-Lease Act, 1067–68
   and Manhattan Project, 1065
   military buildup for WWII, 1065
   on Munich Pact, 1061
   as national leader in WWII, 1102
   neutrality laws and, 1060
   on Pacific theater, 1095
   and Pearl Harbor, 1073
   and radio, 947
   and second front, 1082
   second term of, 1047–51
   on Alfred E. Smith, 1000
   at Tehran Conference, 1084
   on Tripartite Pact, 1070
   and U.S. intervention in WWII, 1062, 1063, 1067

   and War Refugee Board, 1095
   at Yalta, 1091–92, *1093*
Roosevelt, James, 1030, 1130
Roosevelt, Sara Delano, 1029
Roosevelt, Theodore, 718, 820, 851, 997, 1020, 1298
   on Armory Show, 966
   big stick diplomacy of, 842–43, *843,* 848–49
   and Chinese Exclusion Act, 914
   coal strike and, 870
   conservation promoted by, 872–73
   death of, 985
   in election of 1900, 839–40
   in election of 1904, 871
   in election of 1912, 880–81, *882*
   Japan relations and, 843, 844
   labor dispute, 1123
   on League of Nations, 925
   Panama Canal and, 840–42, *841*
   progressivism and, 852–53, 868–79, *869, 874,* 878–79, 892
   progressivism of, 973, 985, 988
   race and, 873, 874, *874*
   rise of, 838–42
   Spanish-American War and, 825–26, 827, 828, *828*
   Taft's break with, 877–78
   Taft selected as successor by, 875
   on Wilson, 902, 923
   in World War I, 903, 904
Roosevelt Corollary, 842–43, *843*
Root, Elihu, 844, 875
Root-Takahira Agreement, 844
Rosecrans, William, 620
Rosenberg, Ethel, 1141
Rosenberg, Julius, 1141
Rosenberg, Robert, *1347*
Rosenthal, Joe, *1054*
"Rosie the Riveter," 1076
Ross, Edmund G., 654
Rossiter, Thomas Pritchard, *238*
Roszak, Theodore, 1246
Rough Riders, *818,* 827, 828, *828*
Royal Proclamation of 1763, 149–50, 176
royaneh, 85–86
Rubin, Jerry, 1248
Ruby, Jack, 1203
Ruckelshaus, William, 1283
Rudd, Mark, 1244, 1245
Ruffin, Edmund, 632
Rumsfeld, Donald, 1351–52
Rush, Benjamin, 179, 219
Rush-Bagot Treaty (1817), 363
Rusk, Dean, 1201
Russia; *see also* Soviet Union
   Bolshevik Revolution in, 915–16
   in Russo-Japanese War, 843, 844
   surrender of, World War I, 917–18
   in World War I, 898, 915–16
Russian Americans, 974

*Russian Ballet* (Weber), *965*
Russian Federation, 1327
　Crimea, annexation of, 1374–75
Russian Front, 1082
Russo-Japanese War, 843, 844
Rutgers University, 128
Ruth, George Herman "Babe," 950
Rutledge, David Jamison, 571
Rutledge, Edward, 215, 216
Rutledge, John, 238
Ryan, Paul, 1390, *1391*

Sacagawea, 287, *287*
Sacco, Nicola, 975–76
Sacco and Vanzetti case, 975–76, 1016
Sadat, Anwar el-, 1297
Saenz, J. Luz, 910
St. Augustine, Fla., 33
St. Kitts, 71
St. Lawrence Seaway, 1153
St. Valentine's Day Massacre, 985
Saint Patrick's Battalion, *534*, 534–35
Saipan, 1097
Salem, Mass., 107–8
Salk, Jonas, 1149
saloons, 781–82
SALT I (Strategic Arms Limitation Talks I), 1280
SALT II (Strategic Arms Limitation Talks II), 1298
salutary neglect, 140, 176
Salvation Army, 1012
same-sex marriage, 1369, 1370–71, 1377, 1396
Samoa, 822
Sampson, Deborah, 217
San Antonio, Tex, 136
Sandburg, Carl, 934
Sand Creek Massacre, 759–60
Sanders, Bernie, *1380*
*Sandford, Dred Scott v.*, 562–63, 576
Sandino, César Augusto, 994
"Sand-Lot" incident, 715
Sandwich, Lord, 163
Sandys, Edwin, 57
San Francisco, Cal, 545
Sanger, Margaret, *955*, 955–56
San Jacinto, Battle of, 521–22
San Salvador, 19
Santa Anna, Antonio López de, 517–19, 519–20,
　519–22, 533, 535
Santa Fe, N.Mex., 37
Santa Fe Trail, *505*, 507
*Santa Maria*, 18
Sarah Rosetta Wakeman, 588
Sarajevo, Bosnia, 897–98
Saratoga, Battles of (1777), 195–96, 204
Sassacus, 83
Sassamon, John, 84
Savage, Samuel, 161
Savannah, Ga., 82, *82*

Savio, Mario, 1243
Sawyer, Lorenzo, 751
scalawags, 660
Scandinavia, 21
Scandinavian Americans, 343
Scarborough, Rick, 1377
*Scarlet Letter, The* (Hawthorne), 469
Scenic Rivers Act, 1223
*Schechter Poultry Corporation v. United States*, 1042
Schlafly, Phyllis, 1303–4
school shootings, *1332*
Schrank, John, 880
Schurz, Carl, 665, 669
Schwerner, Michael "Mickey," 1213
SCLC (Southern Christian Leadership Conference),
　1176, 1188
Scopes, John T., 979–81, *980*
Scopes Trial, 979–81, *980*, 1016
Scotland, 23, 48, 49, 51
Scots-Irish Americans, 109, 111
Scott, Dred, 562–63
Scott, Thomas, 703
Scott, Winfield
　in Civil War, 584
　in election of 1852, 553
　on Lee, 597
　in Mexican War, 533–35
Scott-Heron, Gil, 1213
Scottish Americans, 150
Scottsboro case, 1035, *1035*
screwball materialism, 1155–56
SDI (Strategic Defense Initiative), 1311, 1315
SDS (Students for a Democratic Society), 1242,
　1244–46
Sears, Richard, 705
Sears, Roebuck and Company, 705
secession of South, 548–49, 569–75, *572*, 580–83, *581*
　Buchanan's response to, 571–72
　choosing sides in, 580–83, *581*
　efforts at compromise in, 573–74
Second Confiscation Act, 599
Second Continental Congress, 165, 197, 204
　independence voted by, *169*, 169–71, 186, 218
　peace efforts and, 167
Second Great Awakening, 453–63, 473, 496
　African Americans and, *457*, 457–58
　burned-over district and, 459
　frontier revivals, *454*, 455–56, 496
　Mormons and, 460–63, *461*, *462*
　women and, 458–59
second two-party system, emergence of, 410, 412
secularism, 16
Securities Act (1933), 1024
Securities and Exchange Commission, 1024, 1052
Securities Exchange Act (1934), 1024
Sedition Act (1798), 268–69
Sedition Act (1918), 911–12
Seeger, Pete, 1250

segregation and desegregation
in education, 1170–71, *1174*, 1174–76, 1197–98,
1267
in housing, 1160
Montgomery bus boycott and, 1172–73, *1173*
NAACP and, 1161
in nineteenth century, 738–40, *741*
Nixon and, 1267, *1267*
"separate but equal" rubric of, 740, 1170
in World War II, *1078*, 1078–79
seigneuries, 134
Selective Service Act, 907
Selective Training and Service Act, 1067
"Self-Reliance" (Emerson), 465–66
Seligmann, Herbert, 933
Seminoles, 15, 365, *365*, *387*, 387–88
Seminole War, First, 364–65, *365*
Senate, U.S.; *see also* Congress, U.S.
in Constitution, 236
Louisiana Purchase approved by, 285
Treaty of Versailles, 942
violence on floor of (1856), 558–59
Senate Foreign Relations Committee, 1231
Senate Judiciary Committee, 1048–49
Seneca Falls Convention (1848), 476–78, 496
Sennett, Mack, 946
"separate but equal," 740, 1170, 1188
separation of powers, 236, 272
Separatists, 49, 62–63
*Sephardim,* 76
September 11, 2001, terrorist attacks, 1109, 1348,
1349, *1349*
Serbia, in World War I, 897–98
Servicemen's Readjustment Act (1944), 1123
Sessions, Jeff, 1392
settlement house movement, 857–58, *858*
Seven Pines, Battle of, 597
Seventeenth Amendment, 862, 892
Seven Years' War, *see* French and Indian War
Seward, William H., 557, 568, 599
Compromise of 1850 and, 546, 549
Pacific policy and, 821–22, *823*
sewing machines, 331, 691
sex and sexuality, 107
in Jazz Age, 953–59
in movies, 946
in nineteenth century reform movement, 480–81
sexual relations, slavery and, 433, 438, 439
Seymour, Horatio, 664
Seymour, Jane, 26
Shakers, 481–82, 484
shantytowns, *1008*, 1012
sharecropping, 658, *659*, 680, *735*, 770
Share-the-Wealth Society, 1040–41
Sharpsburg (Antietam), Battle of (1862), 600–601, *605*
*Shaw,* USS, 1072
Shawnees, 149, 201, 295–96
Shays, Daniel, *231*, 232

Shays's Rebellion, *231*, 231–32, 272
*Shelby County v. Holder,* 1370–71
*Shelley v. Kramer,* 1160
Sheridan, Philip, 625, 631, 662, 668, 761, 763, 764, 767
Sherman, John, 633, 687, 761–62, 798, 799
Sherman, Roger, 235
Sherman, William Tecumseh, 530, *622*, 633, 644, 668,
678, 687, 761
Atlanta and, 626–27, *628*
on Grant, 665
Grant and, 622
March to the Sea, 627–29, *628*, 636, 637, 640–41
Sherman Anti-Trust Act (1890), 702, 798–99, 864, 869
Sherman Silver Purchase Act (1890), 799, 806
Shevardnadze, Eduard, 1324
Shiloh, Battle of, *593*, 594–95
shipbuilding, 105
shuttle diplomacy, 1280–81
Siberia, 5
Sicily, 1083, 1084
Sickles, Dan, 575
Sidney, Allen, 437
Sierra Leone, 213
*Signing the Constitution* (Rossiter), *238*
Silent Generation, 1165
silver, 27, 35, 799
Sinclair, Upton, 871
Singapore, 1072
Singer, Isaac Merritt, 331
Singleton, Benjamin "Pap," 750
Sino-Japanese War, 1059
Sioux, 10, 38, 761–64, *763*, 1261
Sirhan, Sirhan, 1234
Sirica, John J., 1282
*Sister Carrie* (Dreiser), 787
sit-ins, 1204, 1205, *1205*, 1242
Sitting Bull, 762
Sixteenth Amendment, 867, 884
*Slaughterhouse Cases,* 675
slave codes, 112, 130, 430–31, 449
slavery, 2; *see also* abolition movement; slaves; slave
trade
American Revolution and, 172–73, 212–16
Civil War and, 579, 580, 598–99, *599*
in colonial period, 47, 57, 71, 72, 76, 83, 112–16,
*115*
in Constitution, 238–40
cotton and, 333, 419, 424–25, *437*, *441*
defense of, 417–18, 495
*Dred Scott* case and, 562–63
emancipation and, 598–99, *599*, 602, *602*, 603
indentured servitude vs., 56
in Kansas-Nebraska crisis, 554–56
"Bleeding Kansas" and, *555*, *557*, 557–58
sectional politics and, 559, *560*
violence in Senate and, 558–59
Lincoln-Douglas debates on, 564–65
Missouri Compromise and, 361–63, *362*

slavery (*continued*)
in New York City, *115*, 115–16
origins of, 70, 87–90, *88*
race-based, 112–16, *115*, 416, 447, 561
religion and, 440–43, *442*
southern defense of, 417–18
in territories, 541–45
California and, 543–45, *544*
Free-Soil party and, 543
popular sovereignty and, 542–43
Wilmot Proviso and, 541–42, *542*
urban, 438
violence of, 437–38
and westward expansion, 504
slaves
in Africa, 87–89
African roots of, 87–89, *88*
in colonial period, 47, 57, 71, 76
community of, 439–47
culture of, 89, *90*
family and, 433, 440, *441*
fugitive slave laws and, 551–52
Native Americans as, 20, 36–37, 72–73
population of, 114, *434, 435*
rebellions, 89, 114–16, 284, 443–46, 524
runaway, 89, 114, 212, 446, 493–94
sexual exploitation of, 433, 438, 439
slave trade outlawed, 290
in South, 71, 89, *90*, 112–16, 333, 416–18, 424–25,
428–30, 432–39, *434, 435, 441, 442*
in southern mythology, *414, 417*, 417–18
women, 433, 438–39
slave trade, 2, 72, 87–90, *88*, 105–6, 112–14, 172,
432–33
"Slave Trail," 424
Sloan, John, *772*, 787
Sloat, John D., 531
smallpox
American Revolution and, 192
epidemics, 30, 32, *36*, 47, 64, 86
Smalls, Robert, 590
Smith, Adam, 250–51, 334–35
Smith, Alfred E., 998, 1001
Smith, Bessie, 952
Smith, Edmund Kirby, 595
Smith, Ellison D. "Cotton Ed," 914, 1050
Smith, Emma, 461
Smith, Hyrum, 462
Smith, Jedediah, 508
Smith, Jesse, 994
Smith, John, *46, 53*, 53–54, 56–57
Smith, Joseph, Jr., 460–63
Smith, Red, 1128
Smith College, 958
Smith-Hughes Act (1917), 890
Smith-Lever Act (1914), 890
Smoot, Reed Owen, 1005
Smoot-Hawley Tariff of 1930, 1005

SNCC (Student Nonviolent Coordinating
Committee), 1194, 1212, 1214, 1238, 1243
Snyder, Gary, 1166
soap operas, 945
social Darwinism, 784, 812
social gospel, 856–57
socialism, progressivism and, 854
Socialist Party
Margaret Sanger and, 955
in World War I, 914
social reform, 942
Social Security, 1044–45, *1045*, 1052, 1133, 1266
Social Security Act (1935), 1044–45, *1045*
Society for the Emancipation for Women, 477
Society of Friends, *see* Quakers
Society of Jesus, 25
Sons of Liberty, 153, 157, 172, 176
Sophie, Duchess of Hohenberg, 897
Soto, Hernando de, *4, 33*
Soule, Silas, 759
*Souls of Black Folk* (Du Bois), 745
South, 415–16, 732–34, 770; *see also* Civil War, U.S.;
Confederate States of America;
Reconstruction
African American culture in, 89, *90*, 429–39, *434,
435*
agriculture in, 416, 418–21, *422, 423, 735*, 735–37,
*736*
in American Revolution, 201–5, *205*, 206–7
in colonial period, 102–3
distinctiveness of, 416–18
economy of, 418–19, 735
failings of New South, 734–37
frontier of, 422–24
mythology of, *417*, 417–18, 732–34
"plain white folk" in, 428–29
plantations in, 425–28
poor whites in, 429
poverty in, 735
religion in, 440–43, *442*
secession of, 548–49, 569–75, *572*, 580–83, *581*
slavery in, 504
slaves in, 71, 89, *90*, 112–16, 333, 416–18, 424–25,
428–30, 432–39, *434, 435, 441, 442*; *see also*
slavery; slaves; slave trade
TVA and, 1028–29
violence in, 424, 437–38
white society in, 425–29
women in, 422–24, 426–28, *427*
South Carolina
frontier conflict in, 156
Thomas Jeremiah execution, 215
nullification and, 399–401
Revolutionary War fighting in, 202–5
secession of, 571, *572*, 580
Sherman in, *628*, 629, 640–41
South Carolina colony
agriculture in, 102

Anglican Church in, 124
European settlement of, 70–72, *71*
government of, 71
Native Americans in, 72–73
slaves in, 71, 72–73, 112–14
*South Carolina Exposition and Protest* (Calhoun), 373, 393
South Carolina Ordinance, 399–401
Southern Christian Leadership Conference (SCLC), 1176, 1188
Southern Manifesto (Declaration of Constitutional Principles), 1171–72
Southern Pacifica Railroad, 1008
Southern redeemers, 673–75, 680, 734
Southwest Ordinance, 361
Soviet Union; *see also* Cold War; Russia
Afghanistan and, 1298–99
atomic weapons and, 1134
Berlin crisis and, 1185–86, 1199, *1200*
Cold War-era relations with, 1149
containment policy, 1115–16
Cuban missile crisis and, 1200–1201
dissolution of, 1325, 1327, 1333
Finland invasion, 1063
German offensive (June-August 1944), 1087
Germany's invasion of, 1068–69
and Hungary crisis, 1182
and Kellogg-Briand pact, 993
and Marshall Plan, 1117–18
Nazi–Soviet Non-Aggression Pact, 1062
Nixon and, 1279–80
origins of Cold War, 1113–14
and Pacific theater (WWII), 1101
Poland invaded by, 1063
*Sputnik* launched by, 1185
and Suez crisis, 1183
as superpower after WWII, 1101
in WWI, 1056
space program, 1185
Spain; *see also* Spanish Empire
American Revolution and, 180, 183, 197
colonization by England vs., 51
early U.S. relations with, 228, 262–63
explorations by, 17, 20, 27–30, 32–37
Mexican independence from, 506–7, 512
Mississippi River access and, 228
in NATO, 1119
Spanish Americans, 111
Spanish-American War, 824–30, 848
African Americans in, 827
Cuba and, 824–25, 827–29, *828*
*Maine* incident and, 825, 848
Philippines in, 826–27
pressure for, 825–26
Spanish Armada, 40–42, 44
Spanish Civil War, 1059
Spanish Empire, 27–31
British Empire compared with, 90–91, 133

Catholicism and, 30–31, *34,* 34–35, 34–36, 507, 510–12
challenges to, 40–42
colonization in, 32–39
conquests of, 27–31
culture of, 32–33
decline of, 39
European diseases spread in, 30, 32
Florida as territory of, 33
French Empire and, 136
missionaries in, 30–31, *34,* 34–35, 35–36, 507, 510–12
privateers' attacks against, 41
Spanish flu pandemic, 931–32
specie, 117
Specie Circular, 404, 407
Spencer, Herbert, 784
spirituals, 440, 449
sports
baseball, 950–51, *1127,* 1127–28
boxing, 339, *340,* 951
football, 951
in nineteenth century, 339, *340*
spectator, 950–51
Springfield Armory, 1122
Springs, Elizabeth, 56
*Sputnik,* 1185
Squanto, 64
"Square Deal," 868–69, 871, 877, 892
*Stag at Sharkey's* (Bellows), *786*
stagflation, 1268–70, *1269*
Stalin, Joseph
and Casablanca Conference, 1083
and division of Germany, 1118
and German invasion of Soviet Union, 1069
Nazi–Soviet Non-Aggression Pact, 1062
at Potsdam conference, 1114
Potsdam Conference, 1099–1100
and race to Berlin, 1089
and Russian Front, 1082
at Tehran Conference, 1084
in World War II, 1084
at Yalta, 1091–92, *1093*
Stalin, Yakov, 1069
Stalwarts, 669, 791
Stamp Act (1765), 152, 176
colonial protests against, 153
repeal of, 154, *155*
Standard Oil Company, 701–2, 728, 877
Standard Oil Trust, 855
*Stand Up and Cheer!* (movie), 1038
Stanford, Leland, 697
Stanton, Edwin M., 612, 645, 653
Stanton, Elizabeth Cady, *447,* 476, 478, 654, 854
staple crops, 102, 130
Starr, Ellen Gates, 857–58
Starr, Kenneth, 1343, 1344
"Star-Spangled Banner, The," 306

state constitutions, American Revolution and, 196, 209–11

steamboats, 324–25, 350, 424

*Steamboat Travel on the Hudson River* (Svinin), *357*

Stearns, Junius Brutus, *222*

steel industry, 703–4

Steeplechase Park, Coney Island, *782*

Steer, James, 430

Steffens, Lincoln, 855, 861

Stein, Gertrude, 965, 966–67, 968

Steinbeck, John, 1007, 1037

Steinem, Gloria, 1253–54

Steinway, Heinrich, 343

Stephens, Alexander H., 571, 573, 580, 588, 613, 639

Stephenson, David C., 978

Steuben, Frederick Wilhelm, baron von, 198

Stevens, John L., 823

Stevens, Thaddeus, 612, 648, 653

Stevenson, Adlai
    in election of 1952, 1151, *1152*
    in election of 1956, 1182
    on Suez crisis, 1184

Stewart, Alexander T., 342

Stewart, William, 650

Stiles, Isaac, 127

Still, William, 493

Stimson, Henry L., 1079, 1099

Stockman, David, 1307–8

stock market
    1929 crash of, 1003–4, *1004*
    1987 crash of, 1317–18
    regulation in First New Deal, 1023–24

stock market crash (October 1929), 968, 969

Stockton, Robert F., 531

Stone, Lucy, 495, 854

Stone, William J., *170*

Stonewall riots, 1261, 1262, 1290

Stono Rebellion (1739), 114

Story, Joseph, 381

Stowe, Harriet Beecher, 418, 473, 475, 489, 552–53, 554, 661, 684

Strategic Arms Limitation Talks I (SALT I), 1280

Strategic Arms Limitation Talks II (SALT II), 1298

Strategic Defense Initiative (SDI), 1311, 1315

Strauss, Levi, 343, 545

strikes, 1047

Strong, Josiah, 708, 830

Stuart, J. E. B., 616

Student Nonviolent Coordinating Committee (SNCC), 1212, 1214, 1238, 1243

Students for a Democratic Society (SDS), 1242, 1244–46

Stuyvesant, Peter, 76

submarines
    in World War I, 902–3
    in World War II, 1069–70

subsistence agriculture, 321

suburban sprawl, in 1920s, 950

suburbs, 1158–60, *1160*, 1188

Sudetenland, 1061

Suez War, 1182–85, *1184*, 1188

Suffolk Resolves, 161

*Suffragist,* 889

sugar, 113

Sugar Act (1764), 151

Sullivan, John, 201

Sumner, Charles, 556, 558–59, 612, 643, 648, 649, 650

Sumner, William Graham, 684, 784–85

Sumter, Thomas, 202, 205

*Sun Also Rises, The* (Hemingway), 968

Sunday, Billy, 982

Supreme Court, U.S., 675–76, 1211–12
    on abortion, 1255–56
    on affirmative action, 1339
    appointments to, 247, 270, *1308*, 1309, 1388
    in *Cherokee Nation v. Georgia,* 388–89
    in Constitution, 237
    and "Court-packing" plan, 1048–49
    in *Dartmouth College v. Woodward,* 356
    in *Dred Scott* case, 562–63
    on health care reform, 1376–77
    implied powers broadened by, 254
    in *Marbury v. Madison,* 279–81, 356
    in *McCulloch v. Maryland,* 356–57
    and National Recovery Administration, 1026–27
    New Deal cases, 1042
    *Norris v. Alabama,* 1035
    *Powell v. Alabama,* 1035
    on racial segregation in education, 1171
    on same-sex marriage, 1370–71, 1377
    in *Shelby County v. Holder,* 1370–71

Surratt, Mary, 645

Susquehannock, *46*

*Sussex,* sinking of (1916), 903

Sutter, John A., 512, 543

Svinin, Pavel Petrovich, 357

*Swann v. Charlotte-Mecklenburg Board of Education,* 1267

*Sweatt v. Painter,* 1170

Swedish Americans, 109

Swift, Gustavus, 755

Swiss Americans, 82, 111, 150

Switzerland, Reformation in, 23–24

Symes, Lillian, 957

Syria, 1391–92

Taft, Robert, 1093

Taft, William Howard, 780, 790, 834, 844, 875–79, 913, 982, 988
    Ballinger-Pinchot controversy and, 876–77
    "dollar diplomacy" of, 845, 849
    in election of 1908, 875
    in election of 1912, 880–81, *882*
    progressivism and, 875–79, 892
    Roosevelt's break with, 877–78
    selected as Roosevelt's successor, 875

Taft-Hartley Labor Act, 1124–25, 1133, 1146
Taft-Katsura Agreement, 844
Tainos, 19
Taiwan, 1134
Taliban, 1351
"talkies," 1038
Talleyrand, Charles-Maurice de, 284
Tallmadge, James, Jr., 361
Taney, Roger B., 562, 612
Tappan, Arthur, *405*, 487–88, 489, 490
Tappan, Lewis, 487–88, 489, 490
Tarbell, Ida, 855
Tariff of 1816, 335, 355, 376
Tariff of 1828 ("Tariff of Abominations"), 372–73
Tariff of 1828 (Tariff of Abominations), 393–94, 412
Tariff of 1846, 527, *528*
tariffs and duties
    after War of 1812, 355
    of early U.S., 230
    in late nineteenth century, 706, 728, 797–98, 799
    Taft and, 876
    Trump and, 1393–94
    Wilson and, 884
Tarleton, Banastre, 203, 204
TARP (Troubled Asset Relief Program) (2008), 1358, 1361
taverns, *118*, 118–19
taxation, 105
    British, 48, 148
    in colonial period, 148, 150–56
    during Great Depression, 1012
    Grenville's program of, 150–51
    income, progressivie, 867
    Revenue Act (1942), 1074
    Social Security and, 1045–46
    of whiskey, 281
Tax Cuts and Jobs Act (2017), 1393
Tax Reform Act of 1986, 1309
Tayloe, John, III, 433
Taylor, George, 1087
Taylor, John, 309
Taylor, Susie King, *610*
Taylor, Zachary
    California statehood and, 546
    Compromise of 1850 and, 546, 547, 549–50
    in election of 1848, 543
    on Mexican-American War, 536
    in Mexican War, 529, 531, 533
    Wilmot Proviso and, *542*
Taylorism, 862–64, 892
Tea Act (1773), 159
teaching, 348
Tea Party, 1366–68, 1396
Teapot Dome Affair, 994–95, *995*
technology
    in early nineteenth century, 330–31
    in mid-late nineteenth century, 690–93, *691*
Tecumseh, Shawnee chief, *295*, 295–96, 300

teetotaler, 474
Tehran Conference, 1084
Tejanos, 516, 521
telegraph, 329, 350
telephone, 690
television, 1157–58
Teller, Henry, 767
Teller Amendment (1898), 826
temperance, 474, 496
Temple, Shirley, 1038
temple mounds, 11
tenements, 701, 775, 776, 812
Tennent, Gilbert, 126
Tennent, William, 126
Tennessee
    Civil War and, 592–93, *593*
    women's suffrage in, 932–33
Tennessee Valley Authority (TVA), 1028–29, 1034
Tenochtitlán, 8–9, 28–30
Tenskwatawa, 295–96
Tenth Amendment, 248, 255
Tenure of Office Act (1867), 652, 653
Terrell, Mary Church, 743
territories, 227
terrorism
    September 11, 2001, attacks and, 1109, 1348, 1349, *1349*
    war on, *1350*, 1350–52, 1396
Tesla, Nikola, 693
Tet offensive, 1232–33
Texas
    annexation of, *521*, 522, 524–25, 527
    independence from Mexico, 516–22, *517*
    secession of, 572
    *Texas, Hopwood v.,* 1339
Texas Revolution, *517*, 518–22, 538
Texians, 517, 538
textile industry, 334–35
    Lowell system and, *335*, 335–38, *336*, *337*, *338*
    New South and, 733, 770
Thames, Battle of the, 301
Thieu, Nguyen Van, 1271
Thirteenth Amendment, 240, 491, 574, 634, 636, 637, 643, 647, 679
*This Side of Paradise* (Fitzgerald), 951–52, 953, 967
Thomas, George H., 627
Thomas, Jesse, 362–63
Thoreau, Henry David, 466–68, 466–69, *467*, 503, 530, 1204
Thurmond, Strom, 1130, 1131, 1133
Tibbets, Paul, 1100
Tilden, Samuel J., 676
Till, Emmett, 1171
Tillerman, Benjamin R., 874
Tillman, Benjamin, 738
Timberlake, Henry, 10
Timberlake, John, 383
Timberlake, Peggy O'Neale, *see* Eaton, Peggy

*Time,* 1226, 1234

*Time* magazine, 1165, 1246

Timucua, 15

Tippecanoe, Battle of (1811), 296, 408–9

Title IX of the Educational Amendments Act (1972), 1255

Tituba (slave), 108

tobacco, 733
   in colonial period, 55, 92
   in Maryland colony, 102
   slavery and, 113
   in Virginia colony, 102

Tocqueville, Alexis de, 380, 1103

Todt, Fritz, 1102

Tōjō, Hideki, 1070

Tokyo, firebombing of, 1099

Toleration Act, 139

Toleration Act (1649), 61

Tometi, Opal, 1371–72

Tonkel, Dan, 932

Tonkin Gulf resolution (1964), 1228

Toombs, Robert, 546

Tordesillas, Treaty of (1494), 20

Tories, *see* Loyalists

torture
   neoconservatives and, 1351–52
   U.S. soldiers in Iraq and, *1353*

Totomacs, 28

Toussaint Louverture, 284, 443

Tower, John, 1314

Townsend, Francis E., 1041, 1047

Townsend Recovery Plan, 1041

Townshend, Charles, 154–55

Townshend Acts (1767), 154–55, 176
   colonial protest against, 156
   modification and repeal of, 158–59

township grants, 103

townships, New England, 103

TPP (Trans-Pacific Partnership), 1382

trade and commerce
   after American Revolution, 228–30
   in colonial period, 72–73, 75, 105–6, *106*
   in Confederation period, 228–30
   global, rise of, 16–17
   interstate, regulation of, 357–58
   mercantile system in, 136–37
   with Native Americans, 2, 72–73, 83, 109
   in New England, 105–6, *106*
   with West Indies, 105–6

Trail of Tears, 389–90, *390,* 412

Traister, Rebecca, 1254

Transcendental Club, 466

transcendentalism, 463–65, *464,* 474, 496

transcontinental railroads, 694–99, *695, 698*

Transcontinental (Adams-Onís) Treaty (1819), 365, 376

Trans-Pacific Partnership (TPP), 1382

transportation
   in colonial period, 118
   in early nineteenth century, 321, *322–23*
   government role in, 330
   highways and roads, 321–24, *322–23,* 355–56
   ocean, 328, *329*
   railroads, 326–28, *327,* 350
   water, 321, *322–23,* 324–26, *325*

Travis, William Barret, 518, 519, 520

Treasury, of Confederation, 226

Treasury Department, U.S.
   Hamilton and, 248, 250–57
   Polk and, 527
   under Van Buren, 408

*Treatise on Domestic Economy, A,* 475–76

Treaty of Portsmouth, 843

trench warfare, 898–900, 938

Trenton, Battle of, 190, 196

Triangle Shirtwaist Company fire (1911), 867

triangular trade, 89, 105–6, 130

tribes, 9

Tripartite Pact, 1070

Triple Alliance, *see* Central Powers

Trollope, Anthony, 693

Trollope, Francis, 319

Trotter, William Monroe, 887

Troubled Asset Relief Program (TARP) (2008), 1358, 1361

Truckee Pass, 513

Truman, Harry S., 921, *1112,* 1203, 1301
   assessing, 1144–45
   atomic bomb and, 1099–1101
   atomic weapons development, 1134
   background of, 1112–13
   civil rights and, 1125–27
   on Cold War, 1111, 1114
   containment policy of, 1115–20, 1177
   demobilization under, 1122–23, *1123*
   and election of 1952, 1150, 1151
   in election of 1948, 1130–33, *1131, 1132*
   Fair Deal of, 1129–30, 1133
   foreign policy of, 1113
   Israel recognized by, 1121
   Korean War and, 1135–39
   Potsdam Conference, 1099–1100
   and Red Scare (second), 1140, 1142
   on U.S. after WWII, 1103

Truman Doctrine, 1116, 1146

Trumbo, Dalton, 1140

Trump, Donald, 978, 1109, 1334
   in election of 2016, 1379–84, *1381, 1385*
   foreign policy of, 1391–92, 1394, *1394, 1395*
   immigration and, 1389–91, 1395, *1395*
   "Make America Great Again" campaign of, 1381–83
   as outsider, 1380, 1381
   as populist president, 1385–92

Republican party and, 1382–83
tax reform, 1393
Trump, Fred C., 978
Trump Organization, 1381
*Trump v. Hawaii,* 1389
trusts, 702, 728, 869–70
Truth, Sojourner, *492,* 492–93
Tryon, William, 156
Tubman, Harriet, 493–94
Tucker, Tilghman, 442
Tunney, James Joseph "Gene," 951
Turkey
    civil war (1947), 1116
    in NATO, 1119
    in World War I, 897, 898
Turner, Frederick Jackson, 768
Turner, Nat, 445–46, 449
turnpike, 323–24
Tuscaroras, 73, 186
Tuscarora War, 73
Tuskegee Airmen, *1078,* 1079
TVA (Tennessee Valley Authority), 1028–29, 1034
Twain, Mark (Samuel Clemens), 697, 708, 833–34
Tweed, William, 788
Twelfth Amendment, 288
*Twelve Years a Slave* (Northup), 436
Twenty-first Amendment, 1024
Twenty-sixth Amendment, 1266
*Twice-Told Tales* (Hawthorne), 469
Tyler, John, 408, 523–24, 570, 573
    presidency of, 523–24, 527
*Typee* (Melville), 471
typewriters, 690, 691, *691*

UAW (United Automobile Workers), 1047
U-boats
    in World War I, 902–3, 938
    in World War II, 1069–70, 1082, 1083–84
UFW (United Farm Workers), 1257–60, *1259,* 1290
*Ulysses* (Joyce), 963
UMW (United Mine Workers), 870, 1046
*Uncle Tom's Cabin* (Stowe), 489, *552,* 552–53, 661
underconsumption, 1004–5
Underground Railroad, 493–94, 497
Underwood-Simmons Tariff (1913), 884
undocumented immigrants, 1334, 1369–70
unemployment
    after World War II, 1122, 1123
    Great Depression and, 1007
    New Deal and, 1050–51
    New Deal programs for, 1024–26, *1025*
    in 1950s, 1156
    WWII's effect on, 1074–75
UNIA (Universal Negro Improvement Association),
        962–63
Union Leagues, 666–67
Union of Soviet Socialist Republics (USSR), 937
Union Pacific Railroad, 694, *695,* 696

unions, labor, *see* organized labor
Unitarianism, 452–53, 464, 496
United Automobile Workers (UAW), 1047
United Farm Workers (UFW), 1257–60, *1259,* 1290
United Mine Workers (UMW), 717–18, 870, 1046
United Nations (U.N.), 1107
    Cold War and, 1114
    and Israel, 1121
    Korean War and, 1136, 1138, 1139
United Society of Believers in Christ's Second
        Appearing, 481–82
United States Housing Authority, 1044
*United States v. Butler,* 1042
*United States v. Cruikshank,* 675
*United States v. Windsor,* 1370
*Universal Asylum and Columbian Magazine, The,*
        244
Universalism, 452–53, 496
Universal Negro Improvement Association, 990
Universal Negro Improvement Association (UNIA),
        962–63
UN Security Council, 1107–8, 1136
Upward Bound, 1221
urban recreation in early nineteenth century, 339, *340*
urban slavery, 438
Urey, Harold C., 1134
U.S. Army, World War I-era recruitment by, 907
*U.S. News and World Report,* 1156
U.S. Public Health Service, 1007–8
U.S. Steel, 869
U-2 summit, 1186
Utah Territory, 463, 551
Utes, 765
utopian communities, 481–85, 496

Valdinoci, Carlo, 935–36
Valens, Ritchie, 1168
Valley Forge, winter quarters at (1777-1778), 195–99
Van Buren, Martin, 389, 395–96, *406,* 406–10, 522
    Calhoun's rivalry with, 383
    on censoring of mail, 405
    Eaton Affair and, 383, 384, 395
    in election of 1832, 396
    in election of 1836, 406
    in election of 1840, 408–10, *409*
    in election of 1844, 525–26
    in election of 1848, 543
    Independent Treasury under, 408
    as vice-president, 380
Vance, Cyrus, 1300
Vandenberg, Arthur, 1115–16
Vanderbilt, Cornelius, 689
Vanderbilt, William Henry, 700
van Dyke, Henry, 953
Van Rensselaer, Stephen, 300
Vanzetti, Bartolomeo, 975–76
Vassar College, 957–58
vaudeville, 781, *781*

Vecchio, Mary Ann, *1273*
V-E day, 1093
*Verdict of the People, The* (Bingham), *397*
Verdun, Battle of, 900
Vermont, founding of, 155
Verrazano, Giovanni da, 40
Versailles, Treaty of, 942, 1006
Versailles Treaty (1919), 926–31, *928*, 938, 1057, 1059
vertical integration, 702, 728
Vesey, Denmark, 444–45
Vespucci, Amerigo, 20–21
Vicksburg, Battle of, 615, 619, 636, 637
Viet Cong, 1180, 1188, 1202, 1228–29, 1232
Viet Minh, 1179
Vietnam, 1179–82, *1181*
Vietnam Veterans Against the War (VVAW), *1240*
Vietnam War, 1227–33
    casualties in, 1275, 1276
    collapse of South Vietnam in, 1275–77, *1276*
    context for policy in, 1231
    domestic opposition to, 1108, 1231, 1243–44, *1244,*
        1272–74, *1273*
    draft in, 1243–44, 1272
    escalation of, 1228–29
    gradual withdrawal from, 1271–72
    Kennedy and, 1202–3
    My Lai massacre in, 1272, *1272*1272
    negotiations in, 1274–75
    Nixon and, 1270–77, *1273, 1276*
    Tet offensive in, 1232–33
    Vietnamization of, 1271, 1290
Villa, Francisco Pancho, 847
violence
    against African Americans
        in Reconstruction, *589,* 649, 655, 661–62, *662,*
            672–73
        during the 1890s, *741,* 741–42
    in anti-war movement in late 1960s, 1244–45
    in the House of Representatives (1858), 565
    in the Old South, 424, 437–38
    in the Senate (1856), 558–59
Virginia
    Civil War fighting in, 583–84, 598, 623, *625,*
        630–32
    Constitution ratified by, 243, *245*
    religious freedom in, 213–14
    Revolutionary War fighting in, *205,* 206
    state legislature, 183
*Virginia, Cohens v.,* 356
Virginia colony, *46, 47, 60*
    Anglican Church in, 124, 128
    Bacon's Rebellion in, *58,* 58–59
    first permanent settlement in, 52–55
    government of, 55, 140
    indentured servants in, 56
    John Smith's administration of, 54
    Native Americans and, 52–55, 58–59
    naturalization acts (1680/1705), 119

    Roanoke colony, 42–43, *43*
    as royal colony, 57
    slavery in, 57, 87, 112–14
    Stamp Act and, 154
    "starving time" in, 54–55
    tobacco in, 55, 102
Virginia Company, 52, 54, 57–58
Virginia Plan, 235
Virginia Resolution, 268
Virginia Resolves, 154
Virginia Statue of Religious Freedom (1786), 196,
    214
virtual representation, 153, 176
*Visit from the Old Mistress, A* (Homer), *638*
VISTA (Volunteers in Service to America), 1221
V-J Day, 1101
Voltaire (François-Marie Arouet), 78
Volunteers in Service to America (VISTA), 1221
voting rights
    for African Americans, 500, 650, 654–55, *658,*
        737–38
    property qualifications and, 140
    for women, *850, 858–61, 859, 860,* 888, *888,* 889,
        892, *932,* 932–33, 987
Voting Rights Act (1965), 1225, *1226,* 1266–67,
    1370–71
*Voyage of Life, The* (Cole), *450*
VVAW (Vietnam Veterans Against the War), *1240*

*Wabash, St. Louis, and Pacific Railroad Company v.*
    *Illinois,* 797
*Wabash Railroad v. Illinois,* 802
Waddell, Alfred, 741
Waddill, Joseph, 588
*Wade, Roe v.,* 1255–56, 1303
Wade-Davis Bill, 643
Wade-Davis Manifesto, 643
wage contols, New Deal and, 1026–27
Wagner, Robert F., 1013, 1044, 1049
Wagner Act, *see* National Labor Relations Act
Wagner–Steagall National Housing Act, 1049
Wahunsenacawh, *see* Powhatan, Chief
Waite, Morrison, 675
Wake Islands, 1072
Wakeman, Sarah Rosetta, *587,* 587–88
*Walden* (Thoreau), 468, 469
Walgreen's, 945
Walker, Alice, 1254
Walker, C. J., 709
Walker, David, 488
Walker, Mary Edwards, 609
Walker, Robert J., 527, 563
Walker Tariff of 1846, 527, *528*
Wallace, George, 1208, 1209, 1235–36, *1236,* 1237,
    1263, 1281
Wallace, Henry A., 1129–31, 1133
Wallace, Henry C., 988
Walloons, 111

Wall Street
  Occupy Wall Street (OWS) movement, 1368–69
  regulation in First New Deal, 1023–24
*Wall Street Journal,* 997, 1196–97
Wall Street Reform and Consumer Protection Act, 1363
Walpole, Robert, 140
Wampanoags, 64, 84
Wankan Tanka, 10
Ward, Lester Frank, 785
Warehouse Act (1916), 890
War Industries Board (WIB), 907–8
Warmoth, Henry Clay, 663
Warner, Charles Dudley, 708
War of 1812, *274,* 294–311, *299, 302,* 332, 334
  aftermath of, 307–11
  Battle of New Orleans in, 307–8
  Canada and, 296, *299,* 299–301
  causes of, 295–96
  in Chesapeake, 303–4
  Florida and, 296
  Hartford Convention and, 308–9
  Native American conflicts and, 295–96, 310–11
  northern front of, 298–99, *299*
  preparations for, 297–98
  southern front of, 301–3, *302*
war on terror, 1109
War Powers Act, 1285
War Powers Act (1941), 1073
War Production Board, 1074, *1074*
War Refugee Board, 1095
war relocation camps, 1080–82
Warren, Earl, 1170, 1171, 1211–12
Warren, Joseph, 165
Warren, Mercy Otis, 166, 172–73, 242
Washington, Booker T., *744,* 744–45, 873, *874*
Washington, D.C.
  as national capital, 276
  nonviolent protests in, 1013–14
  race riot in (1919), 934
  in War of 1812, 304–6, *305*
Washington, George, 160, 225, 226, 232, 246–47, 251,
    276, 354
  after American Revolution, 219
  in American Revolution, 165–66, 180, 181, *182,*
    184, *184,* 186–87, 189–90, *190,* 192, 195,
    197–99, 201, 204, 205, 207, 217, 224
  appearance and background of, 165–66
  cabinet of, 247, 256–57
  called from retirement, 246
  on *Common Sense,* 169
  on Constitution, 244
  at Constitutional Convention, *222,* 233, 234, *238*
  death of, 329
  Declaration of Independence and, 173
  farewell address of, 264–65
  and foreign entanglements, 366
  in French and Indian War, 141–42, 143, 144
  French Revolution and, 258, 259

  on immigration and naturalization, 249
  Jay's Treaty and, 260
  on land policy, 227
  letter on future of America, 219
  James Monroe and, 359
  on national bank issue, 253, 254
  in presidential elections, 246–47, 257
  ratification of Constitution by, 241
  retirement of, 209
  on Shays's Rebellion, 232
  slavery and, 212, 214, 216, 441
  Whiskey Rebellion and, 261, *262*
Washington, Martha, 97, 166
*Washington as a Statesman at the Constitutional
    Convention* (Stearns), *222*
*Washington Federalist,* 292
*Washington Globe,* 411
Washington Naval Conference (1921-1922), 992–93
*Waste Land, The* (Eliot), 967
"Waste Land, The" (Eliot), 963
Watergate affair, 1108
Watergate scandal, 1241, 1281–87, *1285,* 1290
water transportation, 321, *322–23,* 324–26, *325*
  canals, 321, *322–23,* 324–26, *325,* 330
Watie, Stand, 592
Watson, Henry, 421
Watson, Thomas E., 804, 809
Watt, James, 334
WAVES (Women Accepted for Volunteer Emergency
    Service), 1080
Wayne, Anthony, 260–61
WCTU (Women's Christian Temperance Union),
    864–65
*Wealth of Nations, The* (Smith), 334–35
wealthy class, industrialization and, 708–9
weapons of mass destruction (WMDs), 1352, 1396
Weather Underground, 1245
Weaver, James B., 805–6
Weaver, Robert C., 1224
Weber, Max, *965*
Webster, Daniel, 330, 381, 402, 404, 406, 524, 553
  African colonization and, 485
  Compromise of 1850 and, 546, 547–49
  Hayne's debate with, *394,* 394–95
  on Mexican-American War, 530
  national bank issue and, 354–55, 391–93
  in Tyler administration, 523
Webster, Noah, 380
Webster-Ashburton Treaty (1842), 524
Weinberger, Caspar, 1311
Welch, Joseph, 1155
Weld, Isaac, 275–76
welfare, 1339–40
welfare capitalism, 991
"welfare state," 1024
Welles, Gideon, 653
Wellington, Duke of, 533–34
Wells, Ida B., 743–44

Welsh Americans, 82, 111
Welty, Eudora, 732
*We Owe Allegiance to No Crown* (Woodside), *274*
West, 504–29, *524–25, 527, 756–52; see also*
      California; frontier
   African Americans in, 747–50, *750,* 750–52
   annexation of Texas, *521,* 522, 524–25, 527
   cattle boom in, 753–55, *754*
   in Civil War, 591–95, *593*
   end of frontier, 767–69
   farmers in, *756,* 756–57, 768, 769, 770, 800–801
West
   Jefferson's promotion of exploration, 285
   migratory stream to, 747, 770
   mining in, *730,* 751–52, 770
   Native American conflicts in, 758–67, *763, 765,*
      770–71
   Overland Trails and, 504–6, *505,* 507–8, *508,* 538
   settlement of California, 510–14
   Spanish, Mexico and, 506–7
   Texas independence from Mexico, 516–22, *517*
   women in, 509–10, 757–58, 770
West, Thomas, 55
West Berlin, 1118–19
West Indies, 105–6
Westinghouse, George, 692–93
Westmoreland, William C., 1229, 1232
*Wet Night on the Bowery* (Sloan), *772*
Weyl, Walter, 851
Wharton, Edith, 786
Wheatley, Phillis, *172,* 173
Whig party
   destruction of, 554
   in election of 1836, 406
   in election of 1840, *409,* 409–10, 543
   in election of 1844, 525–26
   in election of 1848, 543
   in election of 1852, 553
   formation of, 402
   slavery issue in, 546, 556
   Tyler and, 522–23
Whigs, British, 152–53
whiskey, tax on, 281
Whiskey Rebellion, 261–62, *262*
White, Harry, 924
White, Hugh, 157
White, Hugh Lawson, 406
White, John, *14,* 42, 43
White, William, 352
White, William Allen, 986
White army, Russia, 916
White Bear, 767
Whitefield, George, 125–26, *126*
white flight, 1161
White League, 662
White Line, 662
Whitesides, D. B., 662
white society in the Old South, 425–29

white supremacy; *see also* Ku Klux Klan (KKK)
   in Reconstruction, 660–63, *662,* 672–75
   in 1890s, 741–42
Whitman, Walt, 469, *471,* 471–73
Whitney, Eli, 331, *332,* 421
WIB (War Industries Board), 907–8
Wicker, Tom, 1266
wigwams, 14
WikiLeaks, 1384
Wilder, Thornton, 1165
Wilderness, Battle of the, 623
Wilderness Act, 1223
Wilderness Road, 263–64, *264*
Wilhelm II, 897, 905
Wilkins, Roy, 1176
Wilkinson, Eliza Yonge, 240
Wilkinson, James, 289–90
Willard, Frances, 865, 982
Willard, Jess, 951
William III, 50, 138, 139, 140
Williams, Abigail, 108
Williams, Lloyd W., 919
Williams, Roger, 68
Williamson, Hugh, 174
Willich, August, 581
Willkie, Wendell L., 1067
Wills, Garry, 1244
Wilmington Insurrection, 741–42
Wilmot, David, 541–42
Wilmot Proviso, 541–42, *542,* 576
Wilson, Burt, 1081–82, 1093
Wilson, Edith, 903, 930
Wilson, James, 234
Wilson, John S., 419
Wilson, Woodrow, 780, 787, 853, 879–91, *880,* 1020,
      1107, 1177
   anti-trust laws and, 885–86
   and Committee on Public Information, 910–11
   in election of 1912, 880–81, *882,* 895
   in election of 1916, 904–5
   Federal Reserve and, 884–85
   Fourteen Points of, 916–17, 921, 923
   and Hoover, 999
   immigrant prosecution under, 913
   Latin American policy of, 845–46
   League of Nations and, 923, 925–28
   Mexican intervention of, 846, *846,* 847
   at Paris Peace Conference, 924–26
   peacemaking efforts, 923–24
   progressivism and, 879–80, 883–86, *887,* 893, 973,
      985, 988, 989
   race and, 886–88, *887*
   social justice and, 886–88
   stroke suffered by, 929–30
   tariffs and, 884
   Treaty of Versailles, 942
   U.S. neutrality and, 896, 900–904
   Versailles Treaty promoted by, 926–31

women's suffrage and, 888, *888*, 889
  and WWI, 1056
*Windsor, United States v.,* 1370
Winthrop, John, 65, *65*, 67, 68, 69, 104
Wirt, William, 398
"Wisconsin idea," 863
Wise, Henry, 405
witchcraft, 107–8
*Wizard of Oz, The* (movie), 1038
WMDs (weapons of mass destruction), 1352,
  1396
Wobblies, 914
Wofford, Harris, 1197, 1207
*Woman in the Nineteenth Century* (Fuller), 466
*Woman Rebel* magazine, 955
*Woman's Era,* 743
women; *see also* women's rights
  American Revolution and, 216–18
  birth control and, 1297
  and CCC, 1025
  in Civil War, 608–9, *610*
  in colonial period, 96–101, *99*
  Constitutional Convention and, 240–41
  domestic role of, 98–99, *99,* 130, 957–58, *1162,*
    1162–63
  education and, *479, 710,* 710–11
  employment for, 1123
  employment of, 98–101, 349, 545, 713, 908–9, *909,*
    957–58, 1009–10, 1075–76, *1076*
  as frontier pioneers, 509–10
  in Harlem Renaissance, 961
  and leisure in the Gilded Age, 782, 783
  in Lowell system, *335,* 335–36
  middle-class, 710, *710,* 711
  in mining frontier (California), 545
  Native American, 11, 14–15
  in Old Southwest, 422–24
  Quaker, *78,* 101
  religion and, 101, 127, 458–59
  in 1920s, 956–58, *957*
  in 1950s, *1162,* 1162–63
  sexual revolution and, 1297
  slave, 433, 438–39
  on southern plantations, 426–28, *427*
  voting rights and, *850,* 858–61, *859, 860,* 888, *888,*
    889, 892, *932,* 932–33, 987
  in West, 757–58, 770
  White House conference on emergency needs
    (1933), 1031
  witchcraft and, 107–8
  in World War I, 908–9, *909*
  in World War II, 1075–76, *1076*
  in World War II civilian workforce, 1075–76
  WWII and, 1103
Women Accepted for Volunteer Emergency Service
  (WAVES), 1075, 1080
Women's Action Alliance, 1254
Women's Army Corps (WAC), 1075

Women's Christian Temperance Union (WCTU), 790,
  864–65
Women's Liberation
  and Black Panthers, 1216
Women's March on Washington, *1386*
women's rights, 217–18, *447,* 475–78
  abolition movement and, 489–91
  new feminism and, 1251–57, *1255*
  voting and, 655
Women's Strike for Equality, *1255*
women's suffrage movement, 858–61, *859, 860,* 888,
  *888,* 889, 892
Women's Trade Union League, 909
*Woodruff v. North Bloomfield Gravel Mining
  Company,* 751
Woodside, John Archibald, 274
Woodstock Music Festival (1969), 1250
*Woodward, Dartmouth College v.,* 356
Woolworth's, 945
Worcester, Samuel, 388
*Worcester v. Georgia,* 388
workhouses, 1008
working class, 712–13
Working Men's parties, 374
Workingmen's political parties, 348
*Working People and Their Employers* (Gladden),
  856
Works Progress Administration (WPA), *1018, 1043,*
  1043–44, 1052
World Court, 993–94
World Trade Center, 1348, 1349, *1349*
World War I, 895–922
  African Americans and, 909–10
  causes of, 896–97
  civil liberties and, 911–13, *912*
  decisive role of U.S. in, 914–22, *918*
  effects of, 937
  farm sector in, 1005
  financial support for Allied Powers, 901–2
  as industrial war, 898–900
  labor force during, 908–10, *909, 914*
  loyalty and immigration during, 913–14
  managing home front in, 907–8
  maps of, *899, 919*
  Mexican Americans and, 910
  and modernism, 965, 967
  Paris Conference after, 924–26
  propaganda in, *894, 901,* 910–11
  reparations after, 991–92
  submarines and neutral rights in, 902–3
  U.S. Army recruitment, 907
  U.S. entry into, 905–14
  U.S. neutrality in, 896–905, *901*
  U.S. preparedness in, 903–4
  veterans of, 1013–14
  Western Front in, 898, 900, 918–19, *919,*
    938
  women in, 908–9, *909*

World War II, 1054–1105
African Americans and, 1076–78, *1077, 1078*
aftermath of, 1101–3
atomic bombs in, 1065, 1099–1101, *1100*
Battle of Britain in, 1065–66, *1066*
Battle of Iwo Jima in, *1054*
Battle of the Atlantic in, 1083–84
blitzkrieg in, 1063–65, *1064,* 1065–66, *1066*
Battle of the Bulge, 1089–91
and Cold War, 1108
D-day in, 1085–88, *1086, 1087*
demobilization after, 1122–23, *1123*
drive toward Berlin in, 1082–95
economic prosperity after, 1156
economy in, 1073–82, *1074*
effect on U.S. domestic conditions, 1075–82
Europe and North Africa, *1088*
financing of, 1074–75
Holocaust in, *1094,* 1094–95
Japanese Americans and, 1080–82, *1081*
maps of, *1098*
Mexican Americans and, 1079–80
mortality statistics, 1056
Native Americans and, 1080, *1080*
North Africa campaign, 1083
Pacific fighting in, 1095–1101, *1098, 1100*
Pearl Harbor attack in, 1070–73, *1072*
preparing America for, 1065
strategic bombing in, 1085
U.S. deaths in, 1101
U.S. military production for, 1073–75
U.S. neutrality in, 1060
V-E Day in, 1093–94
women in, 1075–76, *1076*
"Worse Than Slavery" (Nast), *662*
Worthington, Amanda, 641
Wounded Knee, S. Dak.
FBI-AIM standoff at (1973), 1261
massacre at (1890), 766, 1261

Wovoka (Jack Wilson), 766
WPA (Works Progress Administration), *1018, 1043,*
1043–44, 1052
Wright, Richard, 959, 1035, 1037–38
Wright, Wilbur and Orville, 948
Wye River Accords, 1341

XYZ affair, 266, *267*

Yale College, 128
Yalta Conference, 1091–92, *1093,* 1113–14
Yalta Declaration of Liberated Europe, 1092
Yamamoto, Isoroku, 1070, 1096
Yamasees, 73
Yancey, William, 568, 573
Yankee Stadium, 951
Yates, Sally, 1389
yellow-dog contracts, 990
yellow journalism, 825, 848
Yeltsin, Boris, 1325
Yippies, 1248–49
YMCA (Young Men's Christian Association),
856
Yom Kippur War, 1280
York, Alvin, 920–21
Yorktown, Battle of (1781), 196, *206,* 206–7
Youmans, E. L., 710, 711
Young, Brigham, *461,* 462–63
Young, Neil, 1273
Young Men's Christian Association (YMCA), 856
Yugoslavia, 897, 1068, 1342–43
and Marshall Plan, 1118
Treaty of Versailles and, 926
Zhou Enlai, 1279, *1279*
Zimmermann, Arthur, 905–6
Zimmermann telegram, 905–6, 938
Zoot Suit Riots, 1080
Zunis, 11, 35
Zwicker, Ralph, 1155